CORINTH

———

VOLUME XVIII, PART IV

THE SANCTUARY OF DEMETER AND KORE

TERRACOTTA FIGURINES OF THE
CLASSICAL, HELLENISTIC, AND ROMAN PERIODS

CORINTH
RESULTS OF EXCAVATIONS CONDUCTED BY
THE AMERICAN SCHOOL OF CLASSICAL STUDIES AT ATHENS

* *Out of print*

CORINTH

RESULTS OF EXCAVATIONS

CONDUCTED BY

THE AMERICAN SCHOOL OF CLASSICAL STUDIES AT ATHENS

VOLUME XVIII, PART IV

THE SANCTUARY OF DEMETER AND KORE

TERRACOTTA FIGURINES OF THE CLASSICAL, HELLENISTIC, AND ROMAN PERIODS

BY

GLORIA S. MERKER

THE AMERICAN SCHOOL OF CLASSICAL STUDIES AT ATHENS

PRINCETON, NEW JERSEY

2000

This book was published with the assistance of a grant from the Rutgers Research Council.

Library of Congress Cataloging-in-Publication Data
Merker, Gloria S. (1936–   )
  The sanctuary of Demeter and Kore : terracotta figurines of the Classical, Hellenistic, and Roman periods / by Gloria Merker.
       p. cm. — (Corinth ; vol. 18, pt. 4)
  Includes bibliographical references and index.
  ISBN 0-87661-184-6 (alk. paper)
  1. Terra-cotta figurines, Greek—Greece—Corinth—Catalogs. 2. Terra-cotta figurines, Classical—Greece—Corinth—Catalogs. 3. Terra-cotta figurines, Hellenistic—Greece—Corinth—Catalogs. 4. Terra-cotta figurines—Greece—Corinth—Catalogs. 5. Sanctuary of Demeter and Persephone (Corinth, Greece)—Catalogs.   I. Title. II. Series.
DF261.C65A6 vol. 18, pt. 4
[NB155]
938'.7 s—dc21
[733'.3'09387]   99-087774

TYPOGRAPHY BY THE AMERICAN SCHOOL OF CLASSICAL STUDIES PUBLICATIONS OFFICE
6–8 CHARLTON STREET, PRINCETON, NEW JERSEY
PRINTED IN THE UNITED STATES OF AMERICA
BY EDWARDS BROTHERS, INCORPORATED, ANN ARBOR, MICHIGAN

This volume is dedicated

to

BRUNILDE S. RIDGWAY

and to

the memory of
SAUL S. WEINBERG

CONTENTS

ACKNOWLEDGMENTS

I would like to thank, most of all, the Directors of the excavations in the Sanctuary of Demeter and Kore, Ronald S. Stroud and Nancy Bookidis, and the Director Emeritus of the Corinth Excavations, Charles K. Williams, II, for the opportunity to study and publish the Classical, Hellenistic, and Roman figurines from the sanctuary. My work on this project has been very much enriched by the information they have provided and by their extremely helpful comments on successive drafts of this manuscript. This study would have been much poorer without their knowledgeable support. I am especially grateful to Dr. Bookidis for her friendship and patient encouragement and for her willing attention to the endless details of an archaeological project of this kind. All errors and omissions, however, are my own. The fine photos are by Ino Ioannides and Lenio Bartzioti. Stella Bouzaki expertly restored the many figurines in need of attention. I owe warm thanks to Dr. Williams for permission to use and illustrate Corinthian comparanda from excavated areas other than the Demeter sanctuary. The photographs on Plates 78 and 79 are courtesy of the National Archaeological Museum, Athens.

Other scholars were most helpful at various stages of this study. Prof. Brunilde S. Ridgway graciously gave her time to read the manuscript, at both earlier and near-final stages, and offered extremely astute and helpful comments. I have also profited greatly from discussions with A. A. Donohue and Jean M. Turfa, and from correspondence with Richard V. Nicholls. Dr. Turfa provided much useful information on the Archaic figurines. Rebecca M. Ammerman was especially helpful with suggestions in the area of West Greek archaeology, and with perceptive comments on the manuscript as a whole. Some of the identifications of imported Argive and Sicilian figurines are owed to Martin Guggisberg and Nunzio Allegro respectively. My husband, Irwin L. Merker, greatly eased the writing process with his computer expertise, vast fund of general knowledge, and good humor at difficult times. This project could never have been brought to a successful conclusion without the expertise and kindly patience of the excellent editorial staff of the ASCSA Publications Office. I also owe a large debt to the work of earlier students of terracotta figurines. Chief among these is Reynold A. Higgins, whose wide understanding of the Greek figurines of many centers provided so much fundamental material for later students. The publication of the figurines from Morgantina by Malcolm Bell, III, was a much-admired model for this volume. The basic work of Agnes N. Stillwell and Gladys D. Weinberg on Corinthian figurines has stood the test of time, requiring only the chronological adjustment made necessary by more recent excavation in Corinth. Finally, the perceptive work of Dorothy Burr Thompson on the figurines of Asia Minor and Athens has shown how much can be learned of Greek society from the work of its coroplasts.

Financial support for this project was provided through a Rutgers University Summer Fellowship and Faculty Research Grant; a Rutgers University Research Council Publication Subvention; a National Endowment for the Humanities Travel to Collections Grant; and a Fellowship Grant from the 1984 Foundation. Membership at the Institute for Advanced Study during the spring of 1989 provided a welcome opportunity for intensive study.

BIBLIOGRAPHY AND ABBREVIATIONS

Agora = *The Athenian Agora: Results of Excavations Conducted by the American School of Classical Studies at Athens,* Princeton.
    III = R. E. Wycherley, *Literary and Epigraphical Testimonia,* 1957.
    VI = C. Grandjouan, *Terracottas and Plastic Lamps of the Roman Period,* 1961.
    XI = E. B. Harrison, *Archaic and Archaistic Sculpture,* 1965.
Albert, W.-D. 1979. *Darstellungen des Eros in Unteritalien,* Amsterdam.
Alroth, B. 1987. "Visiting Gods–Who and Why?," in *Gifts to the Gods,* pp. 9–19.
————. 1988. "The Positioning of Greek Votive Figurines," in *Early Greek Cult Practice,* pp. 195–203.
————. 1989. *Greek Gods and Figurines: Aspects of the Anthropomorphic Dedications,* Uppsala.
Amandry, P. 1981. "L'Exploration archéologique de la grotte," in *L'Antre Corycien* I (*BCH* Suppl. VII), Paris, pp. 75–93.
Ammerman, R. M. 1986. Rev. of Sguaitamatti 1984, in *AJA* 90, pp. 111–113.
————. 1993. "Child Care in the Votive Terracottas from Paestum" (lecture, New Orleans 1992), abstract in *AJA* 97, p. 338.
Amyx, D. A. 1988. *Corinthian Vase-Painting of the Archaic Period,* Berkeley, 3 vols.
Ancient Greek and Related Pottery 1984 = *Ancient Greek and Related Pottery: Proceedings of the International Vase Symposium in Amsterdam, 12–15 April 1984,* H. A. G. Brijder, ed., Amsterdam.
Ancient Greek and Related Pottery 1988 = *Proceedings of the 3rd Symposium on Ancient Greek and Related Pottery, Copenhagen, August 31–September 4, 1987,* J. Christiansen and T. Melander, eds., Copenhagen.
Anderson, W. S. 1986. "Corinth and Comedy," in *Corinthiaca,* pp. 44–49.
Anderson-Stojanović, V. R. 1993. "A Well in the Rachi Settlement at Isthmia," *Hesperia* 62, pp. 257–302.
————. 1996. "The University of Chicago Excavations in the Rachi Settlement, 1989," *Hesperia* 65, pp. 57–98.
Andreiomenou, A. K. 1971. «ʹΕφορεία Ἀρχαιοπωλείων καὶ ʹΙδιωτικῶν Ἀρχαιολογικῶν Συλλογῶν», ἈρχΔελτ 26, 1971 [1975], Χρονικά 2, pp. 561–563.
Andrén, A. 1948. *Classical Antiquities in the Zorn Collection (OpArch* 5), Lund.
ANET = J. B. Pritchard, ed., *Ancient Near Eastern Texts Relating to the Old Testament,* 3rd ed., Princeton 1969.
Arafat, K., and C. Morgan. 1989. "Pots and Potters in Athens and Corinth: A Review," *OJA* 8, pp. 311–346.
Archaische und klassische Plastik = *Archaische und klassische griechische Plastik. Akten des Internationalen Kolloquiums vom 22–25 April 1985 in Athen,* H. Kyrieleis, ed., Mainz 1986.
Arias, P. E., and M. Hirmer. 1962. *A History of Greek Vase Painting,* London.
ARV² = J. D. Beazley, *Attic Red-Figure Vase-Painters,* 2nd ed., Oxford 1963.
Ashmole, B., and N. Yalouris. 1967. *Olympia: The Sculptures of the Temple of Zeus,* London.
Aspects of Ancient Greece = *Aspects of Ancient Greece* (Exhibition catalogue, Allentown Art Museum, September 16 through December 30, 1979), Allentown 1979.
Aupert, P. 1982. "Rapports sur les travaux de l'École française en Grèce en 1981. Argos. 1. Thermes A," *BCH* 106, pp. 637–643.
Avigad, N. 1960. "Excavations at Makmish, 1958: Preliminary Report," *IEJ* 10, pp. 90–96.
Babelon, E., and J.-A. Blanchet. 1895. *Catalogue des bronzes antiques de la Bibliothèque Nationale,* Paris.
Babelon, J. 1929. *Choix de bronzes et de terres cuites des Collections Oppermann et de Janzé,* Paris.
Baines, J. 1985. *Fecundity Figures: Egyptian Personification and the Iconology of a Genre,* Warminster.
Banaka-Dimaki, A. 1997. "La coroplathie d'Argos: Données nouvelles sur les ateliers d'époque hellénistique," in *Moulage,* pp. 315–331.
Barr-Sharrar, B. 1987. *The Hellenistic and Early Imperial Decorative Bust,* Mainz.
————. 1988. "The Hellenistic Home," in E. D. Reeder et al., *Hellenistic Art in the Walters Art Gallery,* Baltimore, pp. 59–67.
Barringer, J. M. 1991. "Europa and the Nereids: Wedding or Funeral?," *AJA* 95, pp. 657–667.
Bartman, E. 1992. *Ancient Sculptural Copies in Miniature,* Leiden.
Baumer, L. E. 1995. "Betrachtungen zur 'Demeter von Eleusis'," *AntK* 38, pp. 11–25.
Beer, C. 1987. "Comparative Votive Religion: The Evidence of Children in Cyprus, Greece, and Etruria," in *Gifts to the Gods,* pp. 21–29.

Before Sexuality = *Before Sexuality: The Construction of Erotic Experience in the Ancient World,* D. M. Halperin, J. J. Winkler, and F. I. Zeitlin, eds., Princeton 1990.

Belov, G. D. et al. 1976. *Antichnaia Koroplastika: Katalog vystavki Gosudarstvennyi Ermitazh,* Leningrad.

Bendinelli, G. 1957. "Un problema inerente al gruppo delle 'Danzatrici' della Colonna in Delfi," in *Hommages à Waldemar Deonna (Coll. Latomus* 28), Brussels, pp. 103–115.

Benedum, C. 1986. "Asklepios und Demeter: Zur Bedeutung weiblicher Gottheiten für den frühen Asklepioskult," *JdI* 101, pp. 137–157.

Benson, J. L. 1984. "Where Were Corinthian Workshops Not Represented in the Kerameikos of Corinth (750–400 B.C.)?," in *Ancient Greek and Related Pottery* 1984, pp. 98–101.

Bérard, C. et al. 1989. *A City of Images: Iconography and Society in Ancient Greece,* trans. D. Lyons, Princeton.

Berger, E. 1967. "Eine Athena aus dem späten 5. Jahrhundert v. Chr.," *AntK* 10, pp. 82–88.

Berve, H., G. Gruben, and M. Hirmer. 1962. *Greek Temples, Theatres and Shrines,* New York.

Besques, S. 1978. "Le Commerce des figurines en terre cuite au IVᵉ siècle av. J. C. entre les ateliers ioniens et l'attique," in *The Proceedings of the Xth International Congress of Classical Archaeology, 1973* II, Ankara, pp. 617–626.

———. 1981. "Deux portraits d'Arsinoé III Philopator?," *RA,* pp. 227–244.

———. 1994. *Figurines et reliefs grecs en terre cuite,* Paris.

Bevan, E. 1986. *Representations of Animals in Sanctuaries of Artemis and Other Olympian Deities (BAR International Series* 315), Oxford, 2 vols.

Bieber, M. 1928. *Griechische Kleidung,* Berlin.

———. 1949. "Eros and Dionysos on Kerch Vases," in *Commemorative Studies in Honor of Theodore Leslie Shear (Hesperia* Suppl. 8), Princeton, pp. 31–38.

———. 1961. *The Sculpture of the Hellenistic Age,* rev. ed., New York.

———. 1961a. *The History of the Greek and Roman Theater,* 2nd ed., Princeton.

———. 1967. *Entwicklungsgeschichte der griechischen Tracht,* 2nd ed., Berlin.

———. 1977. *Ancient Copies: Contributions to the History of Greek and Roman Art,* New York.

Bikai, P. M., and V. Egan. 1996. "Archaeology in Jordan," *AJA* 100, pp. 507–535.

Blech, M. 1982. *Studien zum Kranz bei den Griechen,* Berlin.

Blitzer, H. 1990. "ΚΟΡΩΝΕΪΚΑ: Storage-Jar Production and Trade in the Traditional Aegean," *Hesperia* 59, pp. 675–711.

Blome, P. 1988. "Affen im Antikenmuseum," in *Kanon,* pp. 205–210.

Blum, R., and E. Blum. 1970. *The Dangerous Hour: The Lore of Crisis and Mystery in Rural Greece,* New York.

Boardman, J. 1985. *Greek Sculpture: The Classical Period, A Handbook* London.

Böhm, S. 1990. *Die 'nackte Göttin': Zur Ikonographie und Deutung unbekleideter weiblicher Figuren in der frühgriechischen Kunst,* Mainz.

Bol, P. C. 1983. *Bildwerke aus Stein und aus Stuck von archaischer Zeit bis zur Spätantike* (Liebieghaus-Museum alter Plastik, *Antike Bildwerke* I), Melsungen.

Bol, P. C., and E. Kotera. 1986. *Bildwerke aus Terrakotta aus mykenischer bis römischer Zeit* (Liebieghaus-Museum alter Plastik, *Antike Bildwerke* III), Melsungen.

Bolger, D., and E. J. Peltenburg. 1990. "The Archaeology of Fertility and Birth: Excavations at Kissonerga-Mosphilia, Cyprus, 1987–1989" (lecture, Boston 1989), abstract in *AJA* 94, pp. 328–329.

Bomford Collection = *Ancient Glass, Jewellery, and Terracottas from the Collection of Mr. and Mrs. James Bomford* (Exhibition catalogue, Ashmolean Museum 1971), Oxford.

Bonfante, L. 1984. "Dedicated Mothers," in *Visible Religion* III: *Popular Religion,* Leiden, pp. 1–17.

———, ed. 1986. *Etruscan Life and Afterlife: A Handbook of Etruscan Studies,* Detroit.

———. 1989. "Nudity as a Costume in Classical Art," *AJA* 93, pp. 543–570.

Bookidis, N. 1969. "The Sanctuary of Demeter and Kore on Acrocorinth, Preliminary Report III: 1968," *Hesperia* 38, pp. 297–310.

———. 1982. "A Hellenistic Terracotta Group from Corinth," *Hesperia* 51, pp. 239–247.

———. 1988. "Classicism in Clay," in Πρακτικὰ τοῦ XII Διεθνους Συνεδρίου Κλασικῆς Ἀρχαιολογίας, Ἀθήνα, 4–10 Σεπτεμβρίου 1983 III, Athens, pp. 18–21.

———. 1990. "Ritual Dining in the Sanctuary of Demeter and Kore at Corinth: Some Questions," in *Sympotica: A Symposium on the Symposium,* O. Murray, ed., Oxford, pp. 86–94.

———. 1993. "Ritual Dining at Corinth," in *Greek Sanctuaries: New Approaches,* N. Marinatos and R. Hägg, eds., London, pp. 45–61.

Bookidis, N., and J. E. Fisher. 1972. "The Sanctuary of Demeter and Kore on Acrocorinth, Preliminary Report IV: 1969–1970," *Hesperia* 41, pp. 283–331.

———. 1974. "Sanctuary of Demeter and Kore on Acrocorinth, Preliminary Report V: 1971–1973," *Hesperia* 43, pp. 267–307.

Bookidis, N., J. Hansen, L. Snyder, and P. Goldberg. 1999. "Dining in the Sanctuary of Demeter and Kore at Corinth," *Hesperia* 68, pp. 1–54.

Bookidis, N., and R. S. Stroud. 1987. *Demeter and Persephone in Ancient Corinth,* Princeton.

Bordenache, G. 1960. "Antichità greche e romane nel nuovo Museo di Mangalia," *Dacia* n.s. 4, pp. 489–509.

Borgeaud, P. 1988. *The Cult of Pan in Ancient Greece,* Chicago.

Boulter, P. N. 1953. "An Akroterion from the Temple of Ares in the Athenian Agora," *Hesperia* 22, pp. 141–147.

Boyer, P. 1993. "Cognitive Aspects of Religious Symbolism," in *Cognitive Aspects of Religious Symbolism,* P. Boyer, ed., Cambridge, pp. 4–47.

———. 1994. *The Naturalness of Religious Ideas: A Cognitive Theory of Religion,* Berkeley.

Brelich, A. 1969. *Paides e Parthenoi,* Rome.

Bremmer, J. N. 1984. "Greek Maenadism Reconsidered," *ZPE* 55, pp. 267–286.

———. 1987. "The Old Women of Ancient Greece," in *Sexual Asymmetry: Studies in Ancient Society,* J. Blok and P. Mason, eds., Amsterdam, pp. 191–215.

———. 1994. *Greek Religion,* Oxford.

———. 1995. "The Family and Other Centres of Religious Learning in Antiquity," in *Centres of Learning: Learning and Location in Pre-Modern Europe and the Near East,* J. W. Drijvers and A. A. MacDonald, eds., Leiden, pp. 29–38.

British Museum I = R. A. Higgins, *Catalogue of the Terracottas in the Department of Greek and Roman Antiquities, British Museum* I: *Greek: 730–330 B.C.,* London, 1969.

Brommer, F. 1978. *Hephaistos: Der Schmiedegott in der antiken Kunst,* Mainz.

Broneer, O. 1942. "Hero Cults in the Corinthian Agora," *Hesperia* 11, pp. 128–161.

———. 1947. "Investigations at Corinth, 1946–1947," *Hesperia* 16, pp. 233–247.

———. 1962. "Excavations at Isthmia, 1959–1961," *Hesperia* 31, pp. 1–25.

Brown, B. R. 1973. *Anticlassicism in Greek Sculpture of the Fourth Century B.C.,* New York.

Brümmer, E. 1985. "Griechische Truhenbehälter," *JdI* 100, pp. 1–168.

Brulé, P. 1987. *La fille d'Athènes: La religion des filles à Athènes à l'époque classique. Mythes, cultes et société,* Paris.

Brumfield, A. 1997. "Cakes in the Liknon: Votives from the Sanctuary of Demeter and Kore on Acrocorinth," *Hesperia* 66, pp. 147–172.

Bryson, N. 1991. "Semiology and Visual Interpretation," in *Visual Theory: Painting and Interpretation,* N. Bryson, M. A. Holly, and K. Moxey, eds., Cambridge, pp. 61–73.

Burkert, W. 1983. *Homo Necans: The Anthropology of Ancient Greek Sacrificial Ritual and Myth,* trans. P. Bing, Berkeley.

———. 1985. *Greek Religion,* trans. J. Raffan, Cambridge, Mass.

———. 1996. *The Creation of the Sacred: Tracks of Biology in Early Religions,* Cambridge, Mass.

Calame, C. 1997. *Choruses of Young Women in Ancient Greece: Their Morphology, Religious Role, and Social Function,* trans. D. Collins and T. Orion, Lanham, Md.

Callipolitis-Feytmans, D. 1962. "Évolution du plat corinthien," *BCH* 86, pp. 117–164.

———. 1970. "Déméter, Corè et les Moires sur des vases corinthiens," *BCH* 94, pp. 45–65.

Canarache, V. 1969. *Masks and Tanagra Figurines Made in the Workshops of Callatis-Mangalia,* Constanta.

Canby, J. V. 1986. "The Child in Hittite Iconography," in *Ancient Anatolia: Aspects of Change and Cultural Development. Essays in Honor of Machteld J. Mellink,* J. V. Canby, E. Porada, B. S. Ridgway, and T. Stech, eds., Madison, pp. 54–69.

Carson, A. 1990. "Putting Her in Her Place: Woman, Dirt, and Desire," in *Before Sexuality,* pp. 135–169.

Carter, J. B. 1987. "The Masks of Ortheia," *AJA* 91, pp. 355–383.

———. 1988. "Masks and Poetry in Early Sparta," in *Early Greek Cult Practice,* pp. 89–98.

Carter, J. C. 1975. *The Sculpture of Taras (TAPS* 65, 7), Philadelphia.

———. 1983. *The Sculpture of the Sanctuary of Athena Polias at Priene,* London.

Caskey, J. L. 1960. "Objects from a Well at Isthmia," *Hesperia* 29, pp. 168–176.

Catling, H. W. 1982. "Archaeology in Greece, 1981–82," *AR* 28, pp. 3–62.

Charbonneaux, J., R. Martin, and F. Villard. 1973. *Hellenistic Art, 330–50 B.C.,* London.

Childs, W. A. P., and P. Demargne. 1989. *Le Monument des Néréides: Le décor sculpté (Fouilles de Xanthos* VIII), Paris.

Cipriani, M. 1989. *S. Nicola di Albanella: Scavo di un santuario campestre nel territorio di Poseidonia-Paestum,* Rome.

Clairmont, C. W. 1993. *Classical Attic Tombstones,* Kilchberg, 6 vols.

Clinton, K. 1974. *The Sacred Officials of the Eleusinian Mysteries (TAPS* 64, 3), Philadelphia.

———. 1988. "Sacrifice at the Eleusinian Mysteries," in *Early Greek Cult Practice,* pp. 69–80.

———. 1992. *Myth and Cult: The Iconography of the Eleusinian Mysteries,* Stockholm.

————. 1996. "The Thesmophorion in Central Athens and the Celebration of the Thesmophoria in Attica," in *The Role of Religion in the Early Greek Polis. Proceedings of the Third International Seminar on Ancient Greek Cult, Organized by the Swedish Institute at Athens, 16–18 October 1992,* R. Hägg, ed., Stockholm, pp. 111–125.

Clutton-Brock, J. 1989. *A Natural History of Domesticated Mammals,* Austin.

Cole, S. G. 1984. "The Social Function of Rituals of Maturation," *ZPE* 55, pp. 233–244.

————. 1986. "The Uses of Water in Greek Sanctuaries," in *Early Greek Cult Practice,* pp. 161–165.

————. 1994. "Demeter in the Ancient Greek City and Its Countryside," in *Placing the Gods: Sanctuaries and Sacred Space in Ancient Greece,* S. E. Alcock and R. Osborne, eds., Oxford, pp. 199–216.

Colonna, G. 1977. "Un aspetto oscuro del Lazio antico: Le tombe del VI–V secolo A.C.," *PP* 32, pp. 131–165.

Comella, A. 1978. *Il materiale votivo tardo di Gravisca,* Rome.

Comstock, M. B., and C. C. Vermeule. 1971. *Greek, Etruscan and Roman Bronzes in the Museum of Fine Arts, Boston,* Greenwich.

————. 1976. *Sculpture in Stone: The Greek, Roman and Etruscan Collections of the Museum of Fine Arts, Boston,* Boston.

Connelly, J. B. 1988. *Votive Sculpture of Hellenistic Cyprus,* New York.

Contoléon, N. M. 1947–1948. "Monuments à décoration gravée du Musée de Chios," *BCH* 71–72, pp. 273–301.

Corinth = Corinth: Results of Excavations Conducted by the American School of Classical Studies at Athens.

  VII, iii = G. R. Edwards, *Corinthian Hellenistic Pottery,* Princeton 1975.

  VII, iv = S. Herbert, *The Red-figure Pottery,* Princeton 1977.

  IX = F. P. Johnson, *Sculpture, 1896–1923,* Cambridge, Mass. 1931.

  XII = G. R. Davidson, *The Minor Objects,* Princeton 1952.

  XIII = C. W. Blegen, H. Palmer, and R. S. Young, *The North Cemetery,* Princeton 1964.

  XIV = C. Roebuck, *The Asklepieion and Lerna,* Princeton 1951.

  XV, i = A. N. Stillwell, *The Potters' Quarter,* Princeton 1948.

  XV, ii = A. N. Stillwell, *The Potters' Quarter: The Terracottas,* Princeton 1952.

  XV, iii = A. N. Stillwell and J. L. Benson, *The Potters' Quarter: The Pottery,* Princeton 1984.

  XVIII, i = E. G. Pemberton, *The Sanctuary of Demeter and Kore: The Greek Pottery,* Princeton 1989.

  XVIII, ii = K. W. Slane, *The Sanctuary of Demeter and Kore: The Roman Pottery and Lamps,* Princeton 1990.

  XVIII, iii = N. Bookidis and R. S. Stroud, *The Sanctuary of Demeter and Kore: Topography and Architecture,* Princeton 1997.

Corinthiaca = Corinthiaca: Studies in Honor of Darrell A. Amyx, M. A. Del Chiaro and W. R. Biers, eds., Columbia 1986.

Coroplast's Art = J. P. Uhlenbrock et al., The Coroplast's Art: Greek Terracottas of the Hellenistic World, New Paltz and New Rochelle 1990.

Cory, H. 1956. *African Figurines: Their Ceremonial Use in Puberty Rites in Tanganyika,* London.

Courbin, P. 1980. "Les lyres d'Argos," in *Études Argiennes* (*BCH* Suppl. 6), Paris, pp. 93–114.

Crome, J. F. 1951. *Die Skulpturen des Asklepiostempels von Epidauros,* Berlin.

Culican, W. 1969. "Dea Tyria Gravida," *Australian Journal of Biblical Archaeology* 1, 2, pp. 35–50.

Daffa-Nikonanou, A. 1973. Θεσσαλικὰ ἱερὰ Δήμητρος καὶ κοροπλαστικὰ ἀναθήματα, Volos.

Danish National Museum = N. Breitenstein, Danish National Museum: Catalogue of Terracottas, Cypriote, Greek, Etrusco-Italian and Roman, Copenhagen 1941.

Das Wrack = G. Hellenkemper Salies, H.-H. von Prittwitz und Gaffron, and G. Bauchhenss, eds., Das Wrack: Der antike Schiffsfund von Mahdia, Cologne 1994, 2 vols.

Dasen, V. 1993. *Dwarfs in Ancient Greece and Egypt,* Oxford.

Daux, G. 1967. "Chroniques des fouilles et découvertes archéologiques en Grèce en 1966," *BCH* 91, pp. 623–889.

————. 1968. "Chroniques des fouilles et découvertes archéologiques en Grèce en 1967," *BCH* 92, pp. 711–1136.

————. 1973. "Anth. Pal. VI 280 (Poupeés et chevelure, Artemis Limnatis)," *ZPE* 12, pp. 225–234.

Davidson, G. R. 1942. "A Hellenistic Deposit at Corinth," *Hesperia* 11, pp. 105–127.

Dawkins, R. M. 1953. *Modern Greek Folktales,* Oxford.

de Haan-van de Wiel, W. H. 1971. "Two Apulian Vase-Fragments Reunited," *BABesch* 46, pp. 134–137.

Delivorrias, A. 1969. «Ἀρχαιοτήτες καὶ Μνημεῖα Ἀρκαδίας—Λακωνίας», ἈρχΔελτ 24, 1969 [1970], Χρονικά 1, pp. 130–141.

————. 1974. *Attische Giebelskulpturen und Akrotere des fünften Jahrhunderts,* Tübingen.

————. 1991. "Problèmes de conséquence méthodologique et d'ambiguïté iconographique," *MEFRA* 103, pp. 129–157.

Délos XXIII = A. Laumonier, *Les figurines des terre cuite* (*Exploration archéologique de Délos faite par l'École française d'Athènes* XXIII), Paris 1956.

Dentzer, J.-M. 1982. *Le motif du banquet couché dans le Proche-Orient et le monde grec du VIIe au IVe siècle avant J.-C.,* Rome.

Derrett, J. D. M. 1973. "Religious Hair," *Man* n.s. 8, pp. 100–107.

Despinis, G. 1993. «Ένα σύμπλεγμα εφεδρισμού από την Τεγέα», in *Sculpture from Arcadia and Laconia. Proceedings of an International Conference Held at the American School of Classical Studies at Athens, April 10–14, 1992,* O. Palagia and W. Coulson, eds., Oxford, pp. 87–97.

Detienne, M. 1989. "The Violence of Wellborn Ladies: Women in the Thesmophoria," in *The Cuisine of Sacrifice among the Greeks,* M. Detienne and J.-P. Vernant, eds., trans. P. Wissing, Chicago, pp. 129–147.

———. 1989a. *Dionysos at Large,* trans. A. Goldhammer, Cambridge, Mass.

———. 1994. *The Gardens of Adonis: Spices in Greek Mythology,* trans. J. Lloyd, Princeton.

Deubner, L. 1956. *Attische Feste,* Berlin.

di Cesnola, L. P. 1885. *A Descriptive Atlas of the Cesnola Collection of Cypriote Antiquities in the Metropolitan Museum of Art, New York* I, B, Boston.

Diehl, E. 1964. *Die Hydria: Formgeschichte und Verwendung im Kult des Altertums,* Mainz.

Dörig, J. 1958. "Von griechischen Puppen," *AntK* 1, pp. 41–52.

———. 1987. *The Olympia Master and His Collaborators,* Leiden.

Donohue, A. A. 1997. "The Greek Images of the Gods: Considerations on Terminology and Methodology," *Hephaistos* 15, pp. 31–45.

Douglas, M. 1975. *Implicit Meanings: Essays in Anthropology,* London.

Dowden, K. 1989. *Death and the Maiden: Girls' Initiation Rites in Greek Mythology,* London and New York.

duBois, P. 1988. *Sowing the Body: Psychoanalysis and Ancient Representations of Women,* Chicago.

Dumont, A. and J. Chaplain. 1890. *Les céramiques de la Grèce propre* II, Paris.

Dundes, A. 1981. "Wet and Dry, the Evil Eye: An Essay in Indo-European and Semitic Worldview," in *The Evil Eye: A Folklore Casebook,* A. Dundes, ed., New York, pp. 257–312.

Durand, J.-L., and F. Frontisi-Ducroux. 1982. "Idoles, figures, images: Autour de Dionysos," *RA,* pp. 81–108.

Early Greek Cult Practice = Early Greek Cult Practice: Proceedings of the Fifth International Symposium at the Swedish Institute at Athens, 26–29 June, 1986, R. Hägg, N. Marinatos, and G. C. Nordquist, eds. (Svenska Institutet i Athen, *Skrifter,* ser. 4, 38), Stockholm 1988.

Edwards, C. M. 1981. "Corinth, 1980: Molded Relief Bowls," *Hesperia* 50, pp. 189–210.

———. 1986. "Corinthian Moldmade Bowls: The 1926 Reservoir," *Hesperia* 55, pp. 389–419.

———. 1986a. "Greek Votive Reliefs to Pan and the Nymphs" (diss. New York University 1985).

———. 1990. "Tyche at Corinth," *Hesperia* 59, pp. 529–542.

Eitrem, S. 1915. *Opferritus und Voropfer der Griechen und Römer,* Kristiana.

Elderkin, K. M. 1930. "Jointed Dolls in Antiquity," *AJA* 34, pp. 455–479.

Eliade, M. 1958. *Rites and Symbols of Initiation: The Mysteries of Birth and Rebirth,* trans. W. R. Trask, New York.

Elworthy, F. T. 1895. *The Evil Eye: An Account of This Ancient and Widespread Superstition,* London, repr. New York 1986.

Enea nel Lazio = Enea nel Lazio, archeologia e mito. Bimillenario Virgiliano, Roma 22 Settembre–31 Dicembre 1981, Rome [n.d.].

Eretria = I. R. Metzger, *Das Thesmophorion von Eretria: Funde und Befunde eines Heiligtums (Eretria: Ausgrabungen und Forschungen* VII), Bern 1985.

Eutresis = H. Goldman, *Excavations at Eutresis in Boeotia,* Cambridge, Mass. 1931.

Farnell, *Cults* = L. R. Farnell, *The Cults of the Greek States,* Oxford 1896–1909.

Farnsworth, M. 1951. "Ancient Pigments, Particularly Second Century B.C. Pigments from Corinth," *Journal of Chemical Education* 28, Feb. 1951, pp. 72–76.

———. 1964. "Greek Pottery: A Mineralogical Study," *AJA* 68, pp. 221–228.

———. 1970. "Corinthian Pottery: Technical Studies," *AJA* 74, pp. 9–20.

Farnsworth, M., I. Perlman, and F. Asaro. 1977. "Corinth and Corfu: A Neutron Activation Study of Their Pottery," *AJA* 81, pp. 455–468.

FdD = Fouilles de Delphes, École française d'Athènes, Paris.

    IV, v = F. Chamoux, *Monuments. Figurés: Sculptures: L'Aurige,* 1955.

    IV, vi = M. A. Zagdoun, *Monuments. Figurés: Sculptures: Reliefs,* 1977.

    V, i = P. Perdrizet, *Monuments figurés. Petits bronzes, terres cuites, antiquités diverses,* 1906.

Fillieres, D., G. Harbottle, and E. V. Sayre. 1983. "Neutron-Activation Study of Figurines, Pottery, and Workshop Materials from the Athenian Agora, Greece," *JFA* 10, pp. 55–69.

Firth, R. 1973. *Symbols Public and Private,* Ithaca.

Foley, H. P., ed. 1994. *The Homeric Hymn to Demeter: Translation, Commentary, and Interpretative Essays,* Princeton.

Frenkel, H. E. 1976. "Thermoluminescence Test of a Terracotta Ephedrismos-group in The Allard Pierson Museum in Amsterdam," *BABesch* 51, pp. 96, 108.

Freud, S. 1959. "Medusa's Head," in *Collected Papers* V, J. Strachey, ed., 1st American ed., New York, pp. 105–106.

Fridh-Haneson, B. M. 1988. "Hera's Wedding on Samos: A Change of Paradigms," in *Early Greek Cult Practice*, pp. 205–213.

Friedrich, P. 1978. *The Meaning of Aphrodite*, Chicago.

Frontisi-Ducroux, F. 1989. "In the Mirror of the Mask," in Bérard et al. 1989, pp. 150–165.

———. 1991. *Le dieu-masque: Une figure des Dionysos d'Athènes*, Paris.

Fuchs, W. 1959. *Die Vorbilder der neuattischen Reliefs* (*JdI-EH* 20), Berlin.

———. 1986. "The Chian Element in Chian Art," in *Chios. A Conference at the Homereion in Chios, 1984*, J. Boardman and C. E. Vaphopoulou-Richardson, eds., Oxford, pp. 275–293.

Fullerton, M. D. 1987. "Archaistic Statuary of the Hellenistic Period," *AM* 102, pp. 259–278.

Gabrici, E. 1927. *Il Santuario della Malophoros a Selinunte* (*MonAnt* 32), Milan

Galt, C. M. 1931. "Veiled Ladies," *AJA* 35, pp. 373–393.

Garland, R. 1990. *The Greek Way of Life: From Conception to Old Age*, Ithaca.

Garland, R. S. J. 1984. "Religious Authority in Archaic and Classical Athens," *BSA* 79, pp. 75–123.

Gernet, L. 1981. *The Anthropology of Ancient Greece*, Baltimore.

Ghiron-Bistagne, P. 1985. "Le cheval et la jeune fille ou de la virginité chez les anciens Grecs," *Pallas* 32, pp. 105–121.

Gifts to the Gods = *Gifts to the Gods. Proceedings of the Uppsala Symposium, 1985*, T. Linders and G. Nordquist, eds. (*Boreas* 15), Uppsala 1987.

Gjødesen, M. 1970. "The Artistic Context and Environment of Some Greek Bronzes in the Master Bronzes Exhibition," in *Art and Technology. A Symposium on Classical Bronzes*, S. Doehringer, D. G. Mitten, and A. Steinberg, eds., Cambridge, Mass., pp. 145–165.

Gods Delight = *The Gods Delight: The Human Figure in Classical Bronze*, A. P. Kozloff and D. G. Mitten, eds., Cleveland 1988.

Golden, M. 1988. "Male Chauvinists and Pigs," *EchCl* 32, pp. 1–12.

———. 1992. "The Uses of Cross-Cultural Comparison in Ancient Social History," *EchCl* 36, pp. 309–331.

Goldman, H., and F. Jones. 1942. "Terracottas from the Necropolis of Halae," *Hesperia* 11, pp. 365–421.

Goodenough, E. R. 1956. *Jewish Symbols in the Greco-Roman Period* V and VI: *Fish, Bread, and Wine*, New York.

———. 1958. *Jewish Symbols in the Greco-Roman Period* VII and VIII: *Pagan Symbols in Judaism*, New York.

Graepler, D. 1997. *Tonfiguren im Grab: Fundkontexte hellenisticher Terrakotten aus der Nekropole von Tarente*, Munich

Grandjouan, C. 1989. *Hellenistic Relief Molds from the Athenian Agora* (*Hesperia* Suppl. 23), Princeton.

Greenhalgh, P. A. L. 1973. *Early Greek Warfare: Horsemen and Chariots in the Homeric and Archaic Ages*, Cambridge.

Greenwalt, W. S. 1988. "The Marriageability Age at the Argead Court: 360–317 B.C.," *CW* 82, pp. 93–97.

Griffo, P., and L. von Matt. 1968. *Gela: The Ancient Greeks in Sicily*, Greenwich.

Gualandi, G. 1976. "Sculture di Rodi," *ASAtene* 54, n.s. 38, pp. 7–259.

Guggisberg, M. 1988. "Terrakotten von Argos: Ein Fundcomplex aus dem Theater," *BCH* 112, pp. 167–234; "Nachtrag," pp. 535–543.

Guthrie, W. K. C. 1966. *Orpheus and Greek Religion: A Study of the Orphic Movement*, 2nd ed., New York.

Hadzisteliou-Price, T. 1969. "The Type of the Crouching Child and the 'Temple Boys'," *BSA* 64, pp. 95–111.

———. 1978. *Kourotrophos: Cults and Representations of the Greek Nursing Deities*, Leiden.

Hägg, R. 1987. "Gifts to the Heroes in Geometric and Archaic Greece," in *Gifts to the Gods*, pp. 93–99.

Hafner, G. 1982. "Zwei etruskische Bildnis-Statuen," in *Antike Kunstwerke aus der Sammlung Ludwig, II, Terrakotten und Bronzen*, E. Berger, ed., Basel, pp. 204–228.

Hallpike, C. R. 1969. "Social Hair," *Man* n.s. 4, pp. 256–264.

Hamiaux, M. 1992. *Les Sculptures grecques* I: *Des origines à la fin du IVe siècle avant J.-C.*, Paris.

Hamilton, N., et al. 1996. "Viewpoint: Can We Interpret Figurines?," *Cambridge Archaeological Journal* 6, pp. 281–307.

Hamilton, R. 1989. "Alkman and the Athenian Arkteia," *Hesperia* 58, pp. 449–472.

———. 1992. *Choes and Anthesteria: Athenian Iconography and Ritual*, Ann Arbor.

Hampe, R., and E. Simon. 1959. *Griechisches Leben im Spiegel der Kunst*, Mainz.

Hanfmann, G. M. A. 1962. "An Early Classical Aphrodite," *AJA* 66, pp. 281–284.

Hannestad, L. 1984. "Slaves and the Fountain House Theme," in *Ancient Greek and Related Pottery* 1984, pp. 252–255.

Harrison, E. B. 1977. "Alkamenes' Sculptures for the Hephaisteion, Part I: The Cult Statues," *AJA* 81, pp. 137–178.

———. 1982. "Two Pheidian Heads: Nike and Amazon," in *The Eye of Greece: Studies in the Art of Athens*, D. Kurtz and B. Sparkes, eds., Cambridge, pp. 53–88.

———. 1982a. "A Classical Maiden from the Athenian Agora," in *Studies in Athenian Architecture, Sculpture, and Topography Presented to Homer A. Thompson* (*Hesperia* Suppl. 20), Princeton, pp. 40–53.

———. 1984. "A Pheidian Head of Aphrodite Ourania," *Hesperia* 53, pp. 379–388.

————. 1988. "Greek Sculptured Coiffures and Ritual Haircuts," in *Early Greek Cult Practice,* pp. 247–254.

————. 1996. "The Web of History: A Conservative Reading of the Parthenon Frieze," in *Worshipping Athena: Panathenaia and Parthenon,* J. Neils, ed., Madison, pp. 198–214.

Harward, V. J. 1982. "Greek Domestic Sculpture and the Origins of Private Art Patronage" (diss. Harvard University) [summary in *HSCP* 87, 1982, pp. 321–322].

Haspels, C. H. E. 1949–1951. "Terracotta Figurine," *BABesch* 24–26, pp. 54–56.

Hatzopoulos, M. B. 1994. *Cultes et rites de passage en Macedoine,* Athens.

Hausmann, U. 1960. *Griechische Weihreliefs,* Berlin.

Havelock, C. M. 1995. *The Aphrodite of Knidos and Her Successors: A Historical Review of the Female Nude in Greek Art,* Ann Arbor.

Haynes, D. 1992. *The Technique of Greek Bronze Statuary,* Mainz.

Hedreen, G. 1994. "Silens, Nymphs, and Maenads," *JHS* 114, pp. 47–69.

Helbig⁴ = W. Helbig, *Führer durch die öffentlichen Sammlungen klassischer Altertümer in Rom,* 4th ed., Tübingen, 1963–1972, 4 vols.

Henderson, J. 1991. *The Maculate Muse: Obscene Language in Attic Comedy,* 2nd ed., New York.

Herbert, S. 1986. "The Torch-race at Corinth," in *Corinthiaca,* pp. 29–35.

Herdejürgen, H. 1971. *Die tarentinische Terrakotten des 6. bis 4. Jahrhunderts v. Chr. im Antikenmuseum Basel,* Basel.

————. 1978. *Götter, Menschen und Dämonen: Terrakotten aus Unteritalien (Sonderausstellung im Antikenmuseum Basel 16. April bis 20. August 1978),* Basel.

Herrmann, P. 1891. "Erwerbungen der Antikensammlungen in Deutschland. III. Dresden," *AA (JdI* 6), pp. 164–169.

Hershman, P. 1974. "Hair, Sex and Dirt," *Man* n.s. 9, pp. 274–298.

Higgins, R. A. 1963. *Greek Terracotta Figures,* London.

————. 1967. *Greek Terracottas,* London.

————. 1986. *Tanagra and the Figurines,* Princeton.

Hill, J. N. 1994. "Prehistoric Cognition and the Science of Archaeology," in *The Ancient Mind: Elements of Cognitive Archaeology,* C. Renfrew and E. B. W. Zubrow, eds., Cambridge, pp. 83–92.

Hiller, F. 1971. *Formgeschichtliche Untersuchungen zur griechischen Statue des späten 5. Jahrhunderts v. Chr.,* Mainz.

Himmelmann, N. 1983. *Alexandria und der Realismus in der griechischen Kunst,* Tübingen.

Hinz, V. 1998. *Der Kult von Demeter und Kore auf Sizilien und in der Magna Graecia,* Wiesbaden.

HistNum = B. V. Head, G. F. Hill, G. MacDonald, and W. Wroth, *Historia Numorum: A Manual of Greek Numismatics,* new ed., Oxford 1911.

Hodder, I. 1987. "The Contextual Analysis of Symbolic Meanings," in *The Archaeology of Contextual Meanings,* I. Hodder, ed., Cambridge, pp. 1–10.

Hölscher, T. 1967. *Victoria Romana: Archäologische Untersuchungen zur Geschichte und Wesensart der römischen Siegesgöttin von den Anfängen bis zum Ende des 3. Jhs. n. Chr.,* Mainz.

————. 1974. "Die Nike der Messenier und Naupaktier in Olympia: Kunst und Geschichte im späten 5. Jahrhundert v. Chr.," *JdI* 89, pp. 70–111.

Holloway, R. R. 1975. *Influences and Styles in the Late Archaic and Early Classical Greek Sculpture of Sicily and Magna Graecia,* Louvain.

————. 1986. "The Bulls in the 'Tomb of the Bulls' at Tarquinia," *AJA* 90, pp. 447–452.

Hopkinson, N., ed. 1984. *Callimachus: Hymn to Demeter,* Cambridge.

Horn, R. 1931. *Stehende weibliche Gewandstatuen in der hellenistischen Plastik (RM-EH* 2), Munich.

Hornbostel, W. 1988. "Aphrodite und Eros: Zu einem Weihrelief in Hamburg," in *Kanon,* pp. 171–179.

Houlihan, P. F. 1986. *The Birds of Ancient Egypt,* Warminster.

Hurwit, J. M. 1989. "The Kritios Boy: Discovery, Reconstruction, and Date," *AJA* 93, pp. 41–80.

Hutton, C. A. 1899. «Πήλινα εἰδώλια ἐξ Ἐρετρίας», Ἀρχ Ἐφ, cols. 25–44.

Iacobone, C. 1988. *Le stipi votive di Taranto (Scavi 1885–1934),* Rome.

Işik, F. 1980. *Die Koroplastik von Theangela in Karien und ihre Beziehungen zu Ostionien (IstMitt-BH* 21), Tübingen.

Isthmia = *Isthmia: Results of Excavations Conducted under the Auspices of the American School of Classical Studies at Athens,* Princeton.

   VI = S. Lattimore, *Sculpture II. Marble Sculpture, 1967–1980,* 1996.

   VII = I. K. Raubitschek, *The Metal Objects (1952–1989),* 1998.

Jameson, M. H. 1988. "Sacrifice and Animal Husbandry in Classical Greece," in *Pastoral Economies in Classical Antiquity,* C. R. Whittaker, ed., Cambridge, pp. 87–119.

Johns, C. 1982. *Sex or Symbol: Erotic Images of Greece and Rome,* London.

Johnston, S. I. 1997. "Corinthian Medea and the Cult of Hera Akraia," in *Medea: Essays on Medea in Myth, Literature, Philosophy, and Art,* J. J. Clauss and S. I. Johnston, eds., Princeton, pp. 44–70.

Jones, R. E. 1984. "Greek Potters' Clays: Questions of Selection, Availability and Adaptation," in *Ancient Greek and Related Pottery* 1984, pp. 21–30.

Jones, R. E. et al. 1986. *Greek and Cypriot Pottery: A Review of Scientific Studies* (Fitch Laboratory, *Occasional Paper* 1), Athens.

Jucker, I. 1963. "Frauenfest in Korinth," *AntK* 6, pp. 47–61.

Jung, C. G. 1967. *Symbols of Transformation,* trans. R. F. C. Hull, 2nd ed., Princeton.

Kabirenheiligtum V = B. Schmaltz, *Terrakotten aus dem Kabirenheiligtum: Menschenähnliche Figuren, menschliche Figuren und Gerät* (*Das Kabirenheiligtum bei Theben* V), Berlin 1974.

Kabus-Jahn, R. 1972. *Die Grimanische Figurengruppe in Venedig* (*AntP* 11), Berlin.

Kabus-Preisshofen, R. 1975. "Statuettengruppe aus dem Demeterheiligtum bei Kyparissi auf Kos," *AntP* 15, pp. 31–64.

———. 1989. *Die hellenistische Plastik der Insel Kos* (*AM-BH* 4), Berlin.

Kahil, L. 1983. "Mythological Repertoire of Brauron," in *Ancient Greek Art and Iconography,* W. G. Moon, ed., Madison, pp. 231–244.

Kanon = *Kanon: Festschrift Ernst Berger* (*AntK* Beiheft 15), M. Schmidt, ed., Basel 1988, 2 vols.

Kassab Tezgör, D., and A. Abd al Fattah. 1997. "La diffusion des Tanagréennes à l'époque hellénistique: À propos de quelques moules alexandrins," in *Moulage,* pp. 353–374.

Kauffmann-Samaras, A. 1988. "'Mère' et enfant sur les lébétès nuptiaux à figures rouges attiques du Vᵉ s. av. J. C.," in *Ancient Greek and Related Pottery* 1988, pp. 286–299.

Kearns, E. 1992. "Between God and Man: Status and Function of Heroes and Their Sanctuaries," in *Le Sanctuaire grec* (*Entretiens sur l'antiquité classique* XXXVII), Geneva, pp. 65–107.

Keene Congdon, L. O. 1963. "The Mantua Apollo of the Fogg Art Museum," *AJA* 67, pp. 7–13.

———. 1981. *Caryatid Mirrors of Ancient Greece: Technical, Stylistic and Historical Considerations of an Archaic and Early Classical Bronze Series,* Mainz.

Kekulé, R. 1884. *Die antiken Terracotten. II. Die Terracotten von Sicilien,* Berlin.

Keller, O. 1909. *Die antike Tierwelt,* Vol. I; Vol. II, 1913, Leipzig.

Kerameikos XV = B. Vierneisel-Schlörb, *Die figurlichen Terrakotten. I. Spätmykenisch bis späthellenistisch,* Munich 1997.

Kharayeb = M. Chéhab, *Les Terres cuites de Kharayeb* (*Bulletin du Musée de Beyrouth* 10, 1951–1952 [text]; 11, 1953–1954 [plates]), Paris.

Kingsley, B. M. 1981. "The Cap That Survived Alexander," *AJA* 85, pp. 39–46.

Klein, A. E. 1932. *Child Life in Greek Art,* New York.

Kleiner, G. 1984. *Tanagrafiguren: Untersuchungen zur hellenistischen Kunst und Geschichte,* rev. ed., Berlin.

Knigge, U. 1982. «Ὁ ἀστὴρ τῆς Ἀφροδίτης», *AM* 97, pp. 153–170.

Knoblauch, P. 1939. "Über einige attische Tonfiguren im Archäologischen Seminar der Universität Berlin," *AA* (*JdI* 54), cols. 413–448.

Knossos = J. N. Coldstream et al., *Knossos: The Sanctuary of Demeter* (British School of Archaeology at Athens, Suppl. 8), London 1973.

Königliche Museen = *Ausgewählte griechische Terrakotten im Antiquarium der Königlichen Museen zu Berlin,* Berlin 1903.

Konstantinou, I. 1964. «Ἀρχαιότητες καὶ μνημεῖα Φωκίδος. Δελφοί», ἈρχΔελτ 19, 1964 [1966], Χρονικά 2, pp. 216–222.

Kostoglou-Despini, A. 1988. "Eine Grabstele aus Pydna," in *Kanon,* pp. 180–186.

Kriseleit, I., and G. Zimmer, eds. 1994. *Bürgerwelten: Hellenistische Tonfiguren und Nachschöpfungen im 19. Jh.* (Exhibition catalogue, Staatliche Museen zu Berlin, Antikensammlung, 1994), Berlin.

Kron, U. 1992. "Frauenfeste in Demeterheiligtümern: Das Thesmophorion von Bitalemi," *AA* (*JdI* 107), pp. 611–650.

Krystalli-Votsi, K. 1976. «Αὐστηρορρυθμικὸ κεφάλι κούρου ἀπὸ τὴν Κόρινθο», Ἀρχ Ἐφ 1976 [1977], pp. 182–193.

———. 1976a. «Νομός Κορινθίας», ἈρχΔελτ 31, 1976 [1984], Χρονικά 1, pp. 64–65.

Kunze, E. 1963. "Ausgrabungen in Olympia 1962/3," ἈρχΔελτ 18, 1963 [1965], Χρονικά 1, pp. 107–110.

La Follette, L. 1994. "The Costume of the Roman Bride," in *The World of Roman Costume,* J. L. Sebesta and L. Bonfante, eds., Madison, pp. 54–64.

La Fontaine, J. S. 1986. *Initiation,* Manchester.

Langdon, S. H. 1990. "From Monkey to Man: The Evolution of a Geometric Sculptural Type," *AJA* 94, pp. 407–424.

———. 1990a. "Geometric Votive Figurines and the Rise of Greek Sanctuaries" (lecture, Boston 1989), abstract in *AJA* 94, pp. 316–317.

Langlotz, E. 1927. *Frühgriechische Bildhauerschulen,* Nuremberg, 2 vols.

———. 1946/1947. "Bemerkungen zu einem Basaltkopf in München," *JdI* 61/62, pp. 95–111.

Langlotz, E., and M. Hirmer. 1965. *The Art of Magna Graecia: Greek Art in Southern Italy and Sicily,* trans. A. Hicks, London.

Lattimore, S. 1987. "Skopas and the Pothos," *AJA* 91, pp. 411–420.

Lauter, H. 1976. *Die Koren des Erechtheion (AntP* 16), Berlin.

Lawson, J. C. 1964. *Modern Greek Folklore and Ancient Greek Religion: A Study in Survivals,* repr. New Hyde Park.

Leach, E. R. 1958. "Magical Hair," *JRAI* 88, pp. 147–164.

Leiden = P. G. Leyenaar-Plaisier, *Les terres cuites grecques et romaines: Catalogue de la collection du Musée national des antiquités à Leiden,* Leiden 1979, 3 vols.

Leipen, N., P. Denis, J. R. Guy, and A. D. Trendall. 1984. *Glimpses of Excellence: A Selection of Greek Vases and Bronzes from the Elie Borowski Collection,* Toronto.

Lesky, A. 1963. *A History of Greek Literature,* 2nd ed., New York.

Levi, D. 1967/1968. "Gli scavi di Iasos," *ASAtene* n.s. 29/30, pp. 537–590.

Leyenaar-Plaisier, P. G. 1984. "Smyrne et la culture hellénistique," *Les dossiers: Histoire et archéologie* 81, pp. 69–80.

Liepmann, U. 1975. *Griechische Terrakotten, Bronzen, Skulpturen (Bildkataloge des Kestner-Museums Hannover* XII), Hanover.

Lilibaki-Akamati, M. 1996. Το Θεσμοφόριο της Πέλλας, Athens.

Lincoln, B. 1991. *Emerging from the Chrysalis: Rituals of Women's Initiation,* New York.

Linders, T. 1972. *Studies in the Treasure Records of Artemis Brauronia Found in Athens* (Svenska Institutet i Athen, *Skrifter* 4, 19), Stockholm.

Lindos I = C. Blinkenberg, *Lindos: Fouilles et recherches de l'acropole, 1902–1914,* I, *Les petits objets,* Berlin 1931, 2 vols.

Linfert-Reich, I. 1971. *Musen- und Dichterinnenfiguren des vierten und frühen dritten Jahrhunderts,* Cologne.

Lisle, R. 1955. "Cults of Corinth" (diss. Johns Hopkins University, Baltimore).

Lonsdale, S. H. 1993. *Dance and Ritual Play in Greek Religion,* Baltimore.

Louvre = S. Mollard-Besques, *Musée national du Louvre: Catalogue raisonné des figurines et reliefs en terre-cuite grecs, étrusques et romains,* Paris.

    I = *Époques préhellénique, géométrique, archaïque et classique,* 1954.

    II = *Myrina,* 1963, 2 vols.

    III = *Époques hellénistique et romaine. Grèce et Asie Mineure,* 1972, 2 vols.

    IV, i = *Époques hellénistique et romaine. Italie méridionale-Sicile-Sardaigne,* 1986, 2 vols.

Luce, J.-M. 1992. "Les terres cuites de Kirrha," in *Delphes: Centenaire de la "grande fouille" réaliseé par l'École française d'Athènes, 1892–1903: Actes du colloque Paul Perdrizet, Strasbourg, 6–9 novembre 1991,* J.-F. Bommelaer, ed., Leiden, pp. 263–275.

Lullies, R., and M. Hirmer. 1960. *Greek Sculpture,* 2nd ed., New York.

Lunsingh Scheurleer, C. W. 1930. "Grieksche terracotta's in het Museum Scheurleer, VII," *BABesch* 5, no. 1, pp. 9–12; "Erratum, VIII," *BABesch* 5, no. 2, pp. 13–17.

Lurker, M. 1974. "Zur Symbolbedeutung von Horn und Geweih unter besonderer Berücksichtigung der altorientalisch-mediterranen Überlieferung," *Symbolon* 2, pp. 83–104.

Luschey, H. 1962. *Funde zu dem grossen Fries von Pergamon (BWPr* 116/117), Berlin.

Maas, M., and J. M. Snyder. 1989. *Stringed Instruments of Ancient Greece,* New Haven.

MacDonald, B. R. 1982. "The Import of Attic Pottery to Corinth and the Question of Trade during the Peloponnesian War," *JHS* 102, pp. 113–123.

MacIntosh, J. 1974. "Representations of Furniture on the Frieze Plaques from Poggio Civitate (Murlo)," *RM* 81, pp. 15–40.

Maiuri, A. 1931. *La Villa dei Misteri,* Rome, 2 vols.

Mantes, A. G. 1990. Προβλήματα της Εικονογραφίας των ιερειών και των ιερέων στην Αρχαία Ελληνική τέχνη, Athens.

Marcadé, J. 1969. *Au Musée de Délos: Étude sur la sculpture hellénistique en ronde bosse découverte dans l'île,* Paris.

Mark, I. S. 1984. "The Gods on the East Frieze of the Parthenon," *Hesperia* 53, pp. 289–342.

Master Bronzes = *Master Bronzes of the Classical World,* D. G. Mitten and S. F. Doehringer, eds., [Cambridge, Mass.] 1967.

Mattusch, C. C. 1988. *Greek Bronze Statuary from the Beginnings through the Fifth Century* B.C., Ithaca.

———. 1990. "The Casting of Greek Bronzes: Variation and Repetition," in *Small Bronze Sculpture from the Ancient World. Papers Delivered at a Symposium Organized by the Departments of Antiquities and Antiquities Conservation and Held at the J. Paul Getty Museum, March 16–19, 1989,* M. True and J. Podany, eds., Malibu, pp. 125–144.

———. 1994. "The Production of Bronze Statuary in the Greek World," in *Das Wrack* II, pp. 789–800.

———. 1996. *Classical Bronzes: The Art and Craft of Greek and Roman Statuary,* Ithaca.

Mattusch, C. C., et al. 1996a. *The Fire of Hephaistos: Large Classical Bronzes from North American Collections,* Cambridge, Mass.

McDermott, W. C. 1938. *The Ape in Antiquity,* Baltimore.

McPhee, I. 1987. "Attic Red Figure from the Forum in Ancient Corinth," *Hesperia* 56, pp. 275–302.

Mendel, G. 1908. *Musées Impériaux Ottomans: Catalogue des figurines grecques de terre cuite,* Constantinople.

Merker, G. S. 1970. "The Hellenistic Sculpture of Rhodes" (diss. Bryn Mawr College).

———. 1973. *The Hellenistic Sculpture of Rhodes* (*SIMA* 40), Gothenburg.

———. Forthcoming. "Corinthian Terracotta Figurines: The Development of an Industry," in *Proceedings of the Corinth Centennial Symposium.*

Metzger, H. 1942–1943. "Lébès gamikos à figures rouges du Musée National d'Athènes," *BCH* 66–67, pp. 228–247.

Meyer, M. 1989. *Die griechischen Urkundenreliefs* (*AM-BH* 13), Berlin.

Meyer, M. W. 1987. *The Ancient Mysteries, a Sourcebook: Sacred Texts of the Mystery Religions of the Ancient Mediterranean World,* San Francisco.

Meyers, C. 1987. "A Terracotta at the Harvard Semitic Museum and Disc-Holding Female Figures Reconsidered," *IEJ* 37, pp. 116–122.

Michaud, J.-P. 1970. "Chroniques des fouilles et découvertes archéologiques en Grèce en 1968 et 1969," *BCH* 94, pp. 883–1164.

———. 1972. "Chroniques des fouilles et découvertes archéologiques en Grèce en 1971," *BCH* 96, pp. 593–816.

Milleker, E. J. 1986. "The Statue of Apollo Lykeios in Athens" (diss. New York University).

Miller, R. L. 1983. "The Terracotta Votives from Medma: Cult and Coroplastic Craft in Magna Graecia" (diss. University of Michigan).

Miller, R. L. 1990. "Hogs and Hygiene," *JEA* 76, pp. 125–140.

Miller, S. G. 1974. "Menon's Cistern," *Hesperia* 43, pp. 194–245.

Mills, H. 1984. "Greek Clothing Regulations: Sacred and Profane?," *ZPE* 55, pp. 255–265.

Mitropoulou, E. 1977. *Corpus I: Attic Votive Reliefs of the 6th and 5th Centuries B.C.,* Athens.

Mitten, D. G. 1962. "Terracotta Figurines from the Isthmian Sanctuary of Poseidon" (diss. Harvard University) [summary in *HSCP* 67, 1963, pp. 308–309].

———. 1975. *Classical Bronzes* (*Catalogue of the Classical Collection, Museum of Art, Rhode Island School of Design* II), Providence.

Monloup, T. 1994. *Les terres cuites classiques: Un sanctuaire de la grand déesse* (*Salamine de Chypre* XIV), Paris.

Morgan, C. H. 1953. "Investigations at Corinth, 1953–A Tavern of Aphrodite," *Hesperia* 22, pp. 131–140.

Morgantina = M. Bell III, *The Terracottas* (*Morgantina Studies* I), Princeton 1981.

Moritz, L. A. 1958. *Grain-Mills and Flour in Classical Antiquity,* Oxford.

Morrow, K. D. 1985. *Greek Footwear and the Dating of Sculpture,* Madison.

Moulage = A. Muller, ed., *Le moulage en terre cuite dans l'antiquité: Création et production dérivée, fabrication et diffusion. Actes du XVIIIᵉ Colloque du Centre de Recherches Archéologiques—Lille III (7–8 déc. 1995),* Villeneuve d'Ascq (Nord), 1997.

Müller, V. K. 1915. *Der Polos: Die griechische Götterkrone,* Berlin.

Müller-Wiener, W. et al. 1980. "Milet 1978–1979," *IstMitt* 30, pp. 23–98.

Muller, A. 1997. "Description et analyse des productions moulées: Proposition de lexique multilingue, suggestions de méthode," in *Moulage,* pp. 437–463.

Muthmann, F. 1982. *Der Granatapfel: Symbol des Lebens in der alten Welt,* Bern.

Mylonas, G. E. 1961. *Eleusis and the Eleusinian Mysteries,* Princeton.

Nagele, M. 1984. "Zum Typus des Apollon Lykeios," *ÖJh* 55, pp. 77–105.

Napier, A. D. 1986. *Masks, Transformation, and Paradox,* Berkeley.

Naumann, F. 1983. *Die Ikonographie der Kybele in der phrygischen und der griechischen Kunst,* Tübingen.

Neugebauer, K. A. 1931. *Die minoischen und archaisch griechischen Bronzen* (*Staatliche Museen zu Berlin, Katalog der statuarischen Bronzen im Antiquarium,* I), Berlin.

Neumann, G. 1979. *Probleme des griechischen Weihreliefs,* Tübingen.

Nicgorski, A. M. 1996. "The Chatsworth Apollo and the Magic Knot of Herakles" (lecture, San Diego 1995), abstract in *AJA* 100, p. 368.

Nicholls, R. V. 1952. "Type, Group and Series: A Reconsideration of Some Coroplastic Fundamentals," *BSA* 47, pp. 217–226.

———. 1958. Rev. of *Corinth* XV, ii, in *JHS* 78, pp. 172–174.

———. 1958–1959. "Old Smyrna: The Iron Age Fortifications and Associated Remains on the City Perimeter," *BSA* 53–54, pp. 35–137.

———. 1970. "Architectural Terracotta Sculpture from the Athenian Agora," *Hesperia* 39, pp. 115–138.

———. 1982. "Two Groups of Archaic Attic Terracottas," in *The Eye of Greece: Studies in the Art of Athens,* D. Kurtz, ed., Cambridge, pp. 89–122.

———. 1984. "La fabrication des terres cuites," *Les dossiers: Histoire et archéologie* 81, pp. 24–31.

————. 1995. "The Stele-Goddess Workshop: Terracottas from Well U 13:1 in the Athenian Agora," *Hesperia* 64, pp. 405–492.

Nicholson, F. 1968. *Ancient Life in Miniature. An Exhibition of Classical Terracottas from Private Collections in England, 12th October to 30th November 1968, Birmingham Museum and Art Gallery,* Birmingham.

Nock, A. D. 1972. "Nymphs and Nereids," in *Essays on Religion and the Ancient World* II, Z. Stewart, ed., Cambridge, Mass., pp. 919–927.

Nöth, W. 1990. *Handbook of Semiotics,* Bloomington.

Oakley, J. H. 1982. "The Anakalypteria," *AA* (*JdI* 97), pp. 113–118.

————. 1990. *The Phiale Painter,* Mainz.

Oakley, J. H., and R. H. Sinos. 1993. *The Wedding in Ancient Athens,* Madison.

Obeyesekere, G. 1981. *Medusa's Hair: An Essay on Personal Symbols and Religious Experience,* Chicago.

Olender, M. 1990. "Aspects of Baubo: Ancient Texts and Contexts," in *Before Sexuality,* pp. 83–113.

Olynthus = Excavations at Olynthus Conducted by The Johns Hopkins University Expedition under the Auspices of the American School of Classical Studies at Athens, Greece, Baltimore.

    X = D. M. Robinson, *Metal and Minor Miscellaneous Finds: An Original Contribution to Greek Life,* 1941.

    XIV = D. M. Robinson, *Terracottas, Lamps, and Coins Found in 1934 and 1938,* 1952.

Orlandini, P. 1956. "Gela, 7. Via Fiume 24. Scoperta di un piccolo edificio sacro," *NSc* ser. 8, vol. 10, pp. 252–263.

————. 1966. "Lo scavo del Thesmophorion di Bitalemi e il culto delle divinitá ctonie a Gela," *Kokalos* 12, pp. 8–35.

Orsi, P. 1913. "Rosarno (Medma): Esplorazione di un grande deposito di terrecotte ieratiche," *NSc* Suppl., pp. 55–144.

————. 1917. "Rosarno–Campagna del 1914," *NSc* ser. 5, vol. 14, pp. 37–67.

Osborne, R. 1985. *Demos: The Discovery of Classical Attika,* Cambridge.

Otto, W. F. 1965. *Dionysos: Myth and Cult,* Bloomington.

Palagia, O. 1980. *Euphranor,* Leiden.

————. 1982. "A Colossal Statue of a Personification from the Agora of Athens," *Hesperia* 51, pp. 99–113.

Papaspyridi-Karouzou, S. 1933–1935. «Ἀνασκαφὴ τάφων τοῦ Ἄργους», Ἀρχ Δελτ 15, 1933–1935 [1938], pp. 16–53.

————. 1956. «Ἑλληνιστικὰ ἀντίγραφα καὶ ἐπαναλήψεις ἀρχαίων ἔργων», Ἀρχ Ἐφ 1956 [1959], pp. 154–180.

Paris, P. 1887. "Fouilles au Temple d'Athèna Cranaia: Les ex voto," *BCH* 11, pp. 405–444.

Parke, H. W. 1977. *Festivals of the Athenians,* London.

Parker, R. 1988. "Demeter, Dionysus and the Spartan Pantheon," in *Early Greek Cult Practice,* pp. 99–104.

Parker, R. C. T. 1979. "Dionysos at the Haloa," *Hermes* 107, pp. 256–257.

Pemberton, E. G. 1978. "Vase Painting in Ancient Corinth," *Archaeology* 31, 6, pp. 27–33.

————. 1981. "The Attribution of Corinthian Bronzes," *Hesperia* 50, pp. 101–111.

————. 1985. "Ten Hellenistic Graves in Ancient Corinth," *Hesperia* 54, pp. 271–307.

Peppa-Papaioannou, E. 1985. Πήλινα εἰδώλια ἀπὸ τὸ ἱερὸ τοῦ Ἀπόλλωνα Μαλεάτα Ἐπιδαυρίας, Athens.

Perachora = Perachora: The Sanctuaries of Hera Akraia and Limenia: Excavations of the British School of Archaeology at Athens, 1930–1933, Oxford.

    I = H. Payne et al., *Architecture, Bronzes, Terracottas,* 1940.

    II = T. J. Dunbabin et al., *Pottery, Ivories, Scarabs, and Other Objects from the Votive Deposit of Hera Limenia,* 1962.

Peredolskaja, A. A. 1964. *Attische Tonfiguren aus einem südrussischen Grab* (*AntK* Beiheft 2), Olten.

Pergamon = E. Töpperwein, *Terrakotten von Pergamon* (*Pergamenische Forschungen* 3), Berlin 1976.

Peschlow-Bindokat, A. 1972. "Demeter und Persephone in der attischen Kunst des 6. bis 4. Jahrhunderts," *JdI* 87, 1972, pp. 60–157.

Pfanner, M. 1979. "Bemerkungen zur Komposition und Interpretation des grossen Frieses von Pergamon," *AA* (*JdI* 94), pp. 46–57.

Pfisterer-Haas, S. 1989. *Darstellungen alter Frauen in der griechischen Kunst,* Frankfurt.

————. 1994. "Die bronzenen Zwergentänzer," in *Das Wrack* I, pp. 483–504.

Phaklaris, P. 1977. «ΧΕΛΥΣ», Ἀρχ Δελτ 32, 1977 [1982], pp. 218–233.

Picard, C. 1954. *Manuel d'archéologie grecque: La sculpture* IV, i, Paris.

Pinney, G. F. 1993. "Coming of Age in Ancient Greece," in *Gender, Race, and Identity,* C. Barrow, J. Phillips, and K. Frank, eds., Chattanooga, pp. 99–110.

————. 1995. "Fugitive Nudes: The Woman Athlete" (lecture, Atlanta 1994), abstract in *AJA* 99, pp. 303–304.

Pnyx = G. R. Davidson and D. B. Thompson, *Small Objects from the Pnyx I* (*Hesperia* Suppl. 7), Baltimore 1943.

Pollitt, J. J. 1974. *The Ancient View of Greek Art: Criticism, History, and Terminology,* New Haven.

————. 1986. *Art in the Hellenistic Age,* Cambridge, Mass..

Postgate, J. N. 1994. "Text and Figure in Ancient Mesopotamia: Match and Mismatch," in *The Ancient Mind: Elements of Cognitive Archaeology,* C. Renfrew and E. B. W. Zubrow, eds., Cambridge, pp. 176–184.

Poulsen, V. H. 1937. "Der Strenge Stil: Studien zur Geschichte der griechischen Plastik 480–450," *ActaArch* 8, pp. 1–148.

Priene = T. Wiegand and H. Schrader, *Priene: Ergebnisse der Ausgrabungen und Untersuchungen in den Jahren 1895–1898,* Berlin 1904.

Protonotariou-Deilaki, E. 1971. «Ἀρχαιοτήτες καὶ μνημεῖα Ἀργολιδοκορίνθιας», Ἀρχ Δελτ 26, Χρονικά 1, pp. 68–84.

Prückner, H. 1968. *Die lokrischen Tonreliefs: Beitrag zur Kultgeschichte von Lokroi Epizephyrioi,* Mainz.

Quarles van Ufford, L. 1941. *Les terres-cuites siciliennes: Une étude sur l'art sicilien entre 550 et 450,* Assen.

Quirke, S. 1992. *Ancient Egyptian Religion,* London.

Rank, O. 1990. "The Myth of the Birth of the Hero," in *In Quest of the Hero,* Princeton, pp. 3–86.

Redfield, J. 1982. "Notes on the Greek Wedding," *Arethusa* 15, pp. 181–201.

———. 1991. "Wedding Dolls Dedicated to Persephone and the Nymphs" (lecture, San Francisco 1990), abstract in *AJA* 95, pp. 318–319.

Reeder, E. D. 1987. "The Mother of the Gods and a Hellenistic Bronze Matrix," *AJA* 91, pp. 423–440.

Reeder, E. D. et al. 1995. *Pandora: Women in Classical Greece,* Baltimore.

Rehm, R. 1994. *Marriage to Death: The Conflation of Wedding and Funeral Rituals in Greek Tragedy,* Princeton.

Reho-Bumbalova, M. 1981. "Eros e il gioco dell'ephedrismos su una lekythos di Sofia," *BABesch* 56, pp. 153–156.

Reilly, J. 1989. "Many Brides: 'Mistress and Maid' on Athenian Lekythoi," *Hesperia* 58, pp. 411–444.

———. 1997. "Naked and Limbless: Learning about the Feminine Body in Ancient Athens," in *Naked Truths: Women, Sexuality, and Gender in Classical Art and Archaeology,* A. O. Koloski-Ostrow and C. L. Lyons, eds., London, pp. 154–173.

Renfrew, C. et al. 1985. *The Archaeology of Cult: The Sanctuary at Phylakopi,* London.

Richards, A. I. 1982. *Chisungu: A Girls' Initiation Ceremony among the Bemba of Zambia,* 2nd ed., London.

Richardson, E. 1976. "Moonèd Ashteroth?," in *In Memoriam Otto J. Brendel: Essays in Archaeology and the Humanities,* L. Bonfante and H. von Heintze, eds., Mainz, pp. 21–24.

Richardson, R. B. 1898. "Terra-cotta Figurines from Corinth," *AJA* 2, pp. 206–222.

Richter, G. M. A. 1954. *Metropolitan Museum of Art, New York: Catalogue of Greek Sculptures,* Cambridge, Mass.

———. 1965. *The Portraits of the Greeks,* London, 3 vols.

———. 1966. *The Furniture of the Greeks, Etruscans and Romans,* London.

———. 1968. *Korai: Archaic Greek Maidens,* London.

———. 1970. *Kouroi: Archaic Greek Youths: A Study in the Development of the Kouros Type in Greek Sculpture,* 3rd ed., London.

Ridgway, B. S. 1970. *The Severe Style in Greek Sculpture,* Princeton.

———. 1977. "A Peplophoros in Corinth," *Hesperia* 46, pp. 315–323.

———. 1981. "Sculpture from Corinth," *Hesperia* 50, pp. 422–448.

———. 1981a. *Fifth Century Styles in Greek Sculpture,* Princeton.

———. 1984. "The Fashion of the Elgin Kore," *GettyMusJ* 12, pp. 29–58.

———. 1986. "The Bronzes from the Porticello Wreck," in *Archaische und klassische Plastik,* pp. 59–69.

———. 1988. Rev. of Tölle-Kastenbein 1986, in *Gnomon* 60, pp. 523–527.

———. 1990. *Hellenistic Sculpture* I: *The Styles of ca. 331–200 B.C.,* Madison.

———. 1997. *Fourth-Century Styles in Greek Sculpture,* Madison.

Risser, M. K. 1990. "Corinthian Conventionalizing Painters" (lecture, Boston 1989), abstract in *AJA* 94, p. 327.

Robertson, M., and A. Frantz. 1975. *The Parthenon Frieze,* London.

Robertson, M. R. 1979. "A Muffled Dancer and Others," in *Studies in Honour of Arthur Dale Trendall,* A. Cambitoglou, ed., Sydney, pp. 129–134.

Robertson, N. 1983. "Greek Ritual Begging in Aid of Women's Fertility and Childbirth," *TAPA* 113, pp. 143–169.

[Robinson, E.] 1907. "New Greek and Roman Acquisitions," *BMMA* 2, pp. 5–9.

Robinson, H. R. 1962. "Excavations at Corinth, 1960," *Hesperia* 31, pp. 95–133.

———. 1969. "A Sanctuary and Cemetery in Western Corinth," *Hesperia* 38, pp. 1–35.

Roccos, L. J. 1986. "The Shoulder-Pinned Back Mantle in Greek and Roman Sculpture" (diss. New York University).

———. 1991. "Athena from a House on the Areopagus," *Hesperia* 60, pp. 397–410.

Roebuck, C. 1972. "Some Aspects of Urbanization in Corinth," *Hesperia* 41, pp. 96–127.

Roebuck, M. C., and C. A. Roebuck. 1955. "A Prize Aryballos," *Hesperia* 24, pp. 158–163.

Rohde, E. 1968. *Griechische Terrakotten,* Tübingen.

Rolley, C. 1984. "Autres objets de métal," in *L'Antre Corycien* II (*BCH* Suppl. IX), Paris, pp. 261–280.

———. 1986. *Greek Bronzes,* trans. R. Howell, London.

Romano, I. B. 1988. "Early Greek Cult Images and Cult Practices," in *Early Greek Cult Practice,* pp. 127–134.

———. 1994. "A Hellenistic Deposit from Corinth: Evidence for Interim Period Activity (146–44 B.C.)," *Hesperia* 63, pp. 57–104.

————. 1995. *The Terracotta Figurines and Related Vessels* (*Gordion Special Studies* II), Philadelphia.

Rotroff, S. I., and J. M. Camp. 1996. "The Date of the Third Period of the Pnyx," *Hesperia* 65, pp. 263–294.

Rouse, W. H. D. 1902. *Greek Votive Offerings,* Cambridge.

Rügler, A. 1988. *Die Columnae caelatae des jüngeren Artemisions von Ephesos* (*IstMitt-BH* 34), Tübingen.

Rühfel, H. 1984. *Das Kind in der griechischen Kunst,* Mainz.

————. 1984a. *Kinderleben in klassischen Athen,* Mainz.

Saatsoglou-Paliadeli, C. 1993. "Aspects of Ancient Macedonian Costume," *JHS* 113, pp. 122–147.

Salapata, G. 1997. "Hero Warriors from Corinth and Lakonia," *Hesperia* 66, pp. 245–260.

Sallares, R. 1991. *The Ecology of the Ancient Greek World,* Ithaca.

Salmon, J. B. 1984. *Wealthy Corinth: A History of the City to 338 B.C.,* Oxford.

Samos XII = R. Horn, *Hellenistische Bildwerke auf Samos* (*Samos* XII), Bonn 1972.

Sampson, A. 1980. «Τὸ χοροπλαστικὸ ἐργραστήριο τῆς Χαλκίδας», Ἀρχ Ἐφ 1980 [1982], pp. 136–166.

Scanlon, T. F. 1988. "Virgineum Gymnasium: Spartan Females and Early Greek Athletics," in *The Archaeology of the Olympics: The Olympics and Other Festivals in Antiquity,* W. J. Raschke, ed., Madison.

Schachter, A. 1981. *Cults of Boiotia* (*BICS* Suppl. 38) London, 4 vols.

Schauenburg, K. 1962. "Pan in Unteritalien," *RM* 69, pp. 27–42.

Scheffer, C. 1993. "Girls Playing? Notes on a Fake *Ephedrismos* Group in the Zorn Collections in Mora (Sweden)," *MedMusB* 28, pp. 91–102.

Schefold, K. 1934. *Untersuchungen zu den Kertscher Vasen,* Berlin.

Schmidt, E. 1994. *Martin-von-Wagner-Museum der Universität Würzburg. Katalog der antiken Terrakotten* I: *Die figürlichen Terrakotten,* Mainz.

Schmidt, R. 1977. *Die Darstellung von Kinderspielzeug und Kinderspiel in der griechischen Kunst,* Vienna.

Schmitt, P. 1977. "Athéna Apatouria et la ceinture: Les aspects féminins des Apatouries à Athènes," *AnnEconSocCiv* 32, pp. 1059–1073.

Schneider, L. A. 1972, "Terrakottamaske des Dionysos," *AA* (*JdI* 87), pp. 67–73.

Schneider-Hermann, G. 1946. "Een Terracottafiguur uit Tarente in den Stijl van Scopas," *BABesch* 21, pp. 28–32.

————. 1971. "Der Ball bei den Westgriechen," *BABesch* 46, pp. 123–133.

Schröder, S. F. 1989. *Römische Bacchusbilder in der Tradition des Apollon Lykeios: Studien zur Bildformulierung und Bildbedeutung in späthellenistisch-römischer Zeit,* Rome.

Schuchhardt, W.-H. 1974. "Korinthische Beute in Pergamon," in *Mélanges Mansel,* Ankara, pp. 13–24.

Schürmann, W. 1989. *Katalog der antiken Terrakotten im Badischen Landesmuseum Karlsruhe* (*SIMA* 84), Göteborg.

Schwarz, G. 1987. *Triptolemos: Ikonographie einer Agrar- und Mysteriengottheit* (*Grazer Beiträge* Suppl. 2), Graz.

Seltman, C. 1947. "Two Athenian Marble Thrones," *JHS* 67, pp. 22–30.

Serwint, N. 1993. "The Female Athletic Costume at the Heraia and Prenuptial Initiation Rites," *AJA* 97, pp. 403–422.

Settis, S. 1977. "Bellerophon in Medma," *AA* (*JdI* 92), pp. 183–194.

Sguaitamatti, M. 1984. *L'Offrante de porcelet dans la coroplathie géléenne: Étude typologique,* Mainz.

Shapiro, H. A. 1984. "Notes on Greek Dwarfs," *AJA* 88, pp. 391–392.

————. 1989. *Art and Cult under the Tyrants in Athens,* Mainz.

Shaw, J. W., P. P. Betancourt, and L. V. Watrous. 1978. "Excavations at Kommos (Crete) during 1977," *Hesperia* 47, pp. 111–170.

Shoe, L. T. 1932. "A Box of Antiquities from Corinth," *Hesperia* 1, pp. 56–89.

Simon, E. 1953. *Opfernde Götter,* Berlin.

————. 1972. "Hera und die Nymphen: Ein böotischer Polos in Stockholm," *RA,* pp. 205–220.

————. 1983. *Festivals of Attica: An Archaeological Commentary,* Madison.

————, ed. 1989. *Die Sammlung Kiseleff im Martin-von-Wagner-Museum der Universität Würzburg* I: *Minoische und griechische Antiken,* Mainz

Slater, P. E. 1968. *The Glory of Hera: Greek Mythology and the Greek Family,* Princeton.

Snowden, F. M., Jr. 1976. "Iconographical Evidence on the Black Populations in Greco-Roman Antiquity," in *The Image of the Black in Western Art* I, L. Bugner, ed., Cambridge, Mass., pp. 133–245.

Sourvinou-Inwood, C. 1978. "Persephone and Aphrodite at Locri: A Model for Personality Definitions in Greek Religion," *JHS* 98, pp. 101–121.

————. 1988. *Studies in Girls' Transitions: Aspects of the Arkteia and Age Representation in Attic Iconography,* Athens.

————. 1991. *'Reading' Greek Culture: Texts and Images, Rituals and Myths,* Oxford.

Sperber, D. 1975. *Rethinking Symbolism,* trans. A. L. Morton, Cambridge.

Steiner, A. 1992. "Pottery and Cult in Corinth: Oil and Water at the Sacred Spring," *Hesperia* 61, pp. 385–408.

Steininger, U. 1994. "Zwei Ephedrismosterrakotten im Basler Antikenmuseum," *AntK* 37, pp. 44–50.

Stern, E. 1994. *Dor, Ruler of the Seas: Twelve Years of Excavations at the Israelite-Phoenician Harbor Town on the Carmel Coast,* Jerusalem.

Stewart, A. F. 1977. *Skopas of Paros,* Park Ridge.

————. 1979. *Attika: Studies in Athenian Sculpture of the Hellenistic Age,* London.

————. 1997. *Art, Desire, and the Body in Ancient Greece,* Cambridge.

Stoop, M. W. 1960. *Floral Figurines from South Italy,* Assen.

Strocka, V. M. 1979. "Variante, Wiederholung und Serie in der griechischen Bildhauerei," *JdI* 94, pp. 143–173.

Stroud, R. S. 1965. "The Sanctuary of Demeter and Kore on Acrocorinth, Preliminary Report I: 1961–1962," *Hesperia* 34, pp. 1–24.

————. 1968. "The Sanctuary of Demeter and Kore on Acrocorinth, Preliminary Report II: 1964–1965," *Hesperia* 37, pp. 299–330.

Sturgeon, M. C. 1998. "Hellenistic Sculptures in Ancient Corinth" (lecture, Chicago 1997), abstract in *AJA* 102, p. 408 .

————. 1998a. "Hellenistic Sculpture at Corinth: The State of the Question," in *Regional Schools in Hellenistic Sculpture. Proceedings of an International Conference Held at the American School of Classical Studies at Athens, March 15–17, 1996,* O. Palagia and W. Coulson, eds., Oxford, pp. 1–13.

Szabo, M. 1994. *Archaic Terracottas of Boeotia,* Rome.

Talalay, L. E. 1993. *Deities, Dolls, and Devices: Neolithic Figurines from Franchthi Cave, Greece,* Bloomington.

Tarsus I = H. Goldman, ed., *Excavations at Gözlü Kule, Tarsus,* I, *The Hellenistic and Roman Periods,* Princeton 1950, 2 vols.

Tassinari, S. 1993. *Il vasellame bronzeo di Pompei,* Rome, 2 vols.

Thasos XVII = A. Muller, *Les terres cuites votives du Thesmophorion de l'atelier au sanctuaire* (*Études thasiennes* XVII), Athens 1996, 2 vols.

Thompson, D. B. 1950. "A Bronze Dancer from Alexandria," *AJA* 54, pp. 371–385.

————. 1952. "Three Centuries of Hellenistic Terracottas, IA," *Hesperia* 21, pp. 116–164.

————. 1954. "Three Centuries of Hellenistic Terracottas, IB and C," *Hesperia* 23, pp. 72–107.

————. 1959. *Miniature Sculpture from the Athenian Agora,* Princeton.

————. 1962. "Three Centuries of Hellenistic Terracottas, II C: The Satyr Cistern," *Hesperia* 31, pp. 244–262.

————. 1963. "A Clay Model of an Ephebe," *Hesperia* 32, pp. 88–90.

————. 1963a. "Three Centuries of Hellenistic Terracottas IV: The Early Second Century B.C.," *Hesperia* 32, pp. 301–317.

————. 1965. "Three Centuries of Hellenistic Terracottas V: The Mid-Second Century B.C.; VI: Late Second Century B.C. to 86 B.C.," *Hesperia* 34, pp. 34–71.

————. 1966. "The Origin of Tanagras," *AJA* 70, pp. 51–63.

————. 1973. *Ptolemaic Oinochoai and Portraits in Faience: Aspects of the Ruler-Cult,* Oxford.

————. 1982. "A Dove for Dione," in *Studies in Athenian Architecture, Sculpture, and Topography Presented to Homer A. Thompson* (*Hesperia* Suppl. 20), Princeton, pp. 155–162.

————. 1984. "Les ateliers d'Athènes aux IVᵉ et IIIᵉ siècles," *Les dossiers. Histoire et archéologie* 81, March 1984, pp. 32–38.

Thompson, H. A. 1936. "Pnyx and Thesmophorion," *Hesperia* 5, pp. 151–200.

————. 1947. "The Excavation of the Athenian Agora, 1940–46," *Hesperia* 16, pp. 193–213.

————. 1980. "Stone, Tile and Timber: Commerce in Building Materials in Classical Athens," *Expedition* 22, no. 3, pp. 12–26.

Thönges-Stringaris, R. N. 1965. "Das griechische Totenmahl," *AM* 80, pp. 1–99.

Tiberios, M. A. 1981. "'Saltantes Lacaenae'," Ἀρχ Ἐφ 1981 [1983], pp. 25–37.

Tiryns I = A. Frickenhaus, "I. Die Hera von Tiryns," in *Tiryns: Die Ergebnisse der Ausgrabungen des Instituts* I, Athens 1912, pp. 1–126.

Todisco, L. 1993. *Scultura greca del IV secolo: Maestri e scuole di statuaria tra classicità ed ellenismo,* Milan.

Tölle-Kastenbein, R. 1980. *Frühklassische Peplosfiguren: Originale,* Mainz, 2 vols.

————. 1986. *Frühklassische Peplosfiguren: Typen und Repliken* (*AntP* 20), Berlin.

Töpperwein-Hoffmann, E. 1971. "Terrakotten von Priene," *IstMitt* 21, pp. 125–160.

Török, L. 1995. *Hellenistic and Roman Terracottas from Egypt,* Rome.

Torelli, M. 1984. *Lavinio e Roma: Riti iniziatici e matrimonio tra archeologia e storia,* Rome.

Treasures of the Holy Land = *Treasures of the Holy Land: Ancient Art from the Israel Museum* (Exhibition catalogue, The Metropolitan Museum of Art 1986–1987), New York 1986.

Troy = D. B. Thompson, *Troy: The Terracotta Figurines of the Hellenistic Period* (Suppl. Monograph 3), Princeton 1963.

Trumpf-Lyritzaki, M. 1969. *Griechische Figurenvasen des reichen Stils und der späten Klassik,* Bonn.

Turci, M. 1983. *La culla, il talamo, la tomba: Simboli e ritualità del ciclo della vita. Catalogo della mostra a cura di Mario Turci*, Carpi.

Turner, V. W. 1967. *The Forest of Symbols: Aspects of Ndembu Ritual*, Ithaca.

———. 1969. *The Ritual Process: Structure and Anti-Structure*, New York.

Uhlenbrock, J. P. 1985. "Terracotta Figurines from the Demeter Sanctuary at Cyrene: Models for Trade," in *Cyrenaica in Antiquity* (*BAR* 236), G. Barker, J. Lloyd, and J. Reynolds, eds., pp. 297–304.

———. 1988. *The Terracotta Protomai from Gela: A Discussion of Local Style in Archaic Sicily*, Rome.

Ure, A. D. 1949. "Boeotian Haloa," *JHS* 69, pp. 18–24.

———. 1955. "Threshing-Floor or Vineyard," *CQ* 49, pp. 225–230.

———. 1969. "Demeter and Dionysos on Acrocorinth," *JHS* 89, pp. 120–121.

Vafopoulou-Richardson, C. E. 1981. *University of Oxford, Ashmolean Museum: Greek Terracottas*, Oxford.

———. 1982. "An Unpublished Arula in the Ashmolean Museum: A Minor Contribution to Hellenistic Chronology," *JHS* 102, pp. 229–232.

Van Gennep, A. 1960. *The Rites of Passage*, trans. M. B. Vizedom and G. L. Caffee, Chicago.

Van Straten, F. T. 1981. "Gifts for the Gods," in *Faith, Hope and Worship: Aspects of Religious Mentality in the Ancient World*, H. S. Versnel, ed., Leiden, pp. 65–151.

———. 1993. "Images of Gods and Men in a Changing Society: Self-Identity in Hellenistic Religion," in *Images and Ideologies: Self-Definition in the Hellenistic World*, A. Bulloch, E. S. Gruen, A. A. Long, and A. Stewart, eds., Berkeley, pp. 248–264.

———. 1995. *Hiera Kala: Images of Animal Sacrifice in Archaic and Classical Greece*, Leiden.

Vandenabeele, F. 1971–1972. "À propos de quelques terres cuites grecques à membres mobiles," *BMusBrux* 43–44, pp. 23–52.

Verdelis, N. 1958. "Die Ausgrabung des Diolkos während der Jahre 1957–1959," *AM* 73, pp. 140–145.

———. 1964. «Ἀνασκαφὴ εἰς θέσιν Σπηλιωτάκη», ἈρχΔελτ 19, 1964 [1966], Χρονικά 1, pp. 121–122.

Vermeule, E. 1979. *Aspects of Death in Early Greek Art and Poetry*, Berkeley.

Vernant, J. P. 1991. "Artemis and Rites of Sacrifice, Initiation, and Marriage," in J. P. Vernant, *Mortals and Immortals: Collected Essays*, trans. F. I. Zeitlin, Princeton, pp. 207–219.

Vidal-Naquet, P. 1986. "Recipes for Greek Adolescence," in P. Vidal-Naquet, *The Black Hunter: Forms of Thought and Forms of Society in the Greek World*, trans. A. Szegedy-Maszak, Baltimore, pp. 129–156.

Vollgraff, W., W. van der Pluym, and A. Roes. 1956. *Le sanctuaire d'Apollon Pythéen à Argos* (*Études péloponnésiennes* I), Paris.

von Bothmer, D. 1961. *Ancient Art from New York Private Collections*, New York.

von Gonzenbach, V. 1995. *Die römischen Terracotten in der Schweiz: Untersuchungen zu Zeitstellung, Typologie und Ursprung der mittelgallischen Tonstatuetten*, Tübingen, 2 vols.

von Stackelberg, O. M. 1837. *Die Graeber der Hellenen*, Berlin.

Vorster, C. 1983. "Griechische Kinderstatuen" (Inaugural-Diss. Bonn, 1983), Cologne.

Wallenstein, K. 1971. *Korinthische Plastik des 7. und 6. Jahrhunderts vor Christus*, Bonn.

Walter, O. 1942. "Archäologische Funde in Griechenland von Frühjahr 1940 bis Herbst 1941," *AA* (*JdI* 57), cols. 99–200.

Walters Art Gallery = D. K. Hill, *Catalogue of Classical Bronze Sculpture in the Walters Art Gallery*, Baltimore 1949.

Waywell, G. B. 1978. *The Free-Standing Sculpture of the Mausoleum at Halicarnassus in the British Museum*, London.

Webb, P. A. 1996. *Hellenistic Architectural Sculpture: Figural Motifs in Western Anatolia and the Aegean Islands*, Madison.

Weber, H. 1969/1970. "Coae vestes," *IstMitt* 19/20, pp. 249–253.

Webster, T. B. L. 1978. *Monuments Illustrating Old and Middle Comedy*, 3rd ed. (*BICS* Suppl. 39), London.

Wegner, M. 1982. "Terrakotten einer Frau mit einem Ferkel," in ΑΠΑΡΧΑΙ: *Nuove ricerche e studi sulla Magna Grecia e la Sicilia antica in onore di Paolo Enrico Arias*, M. L. Gualandi, L. Massei, and S. Settis, eds., Pisa, I, pp. 201–219.

Weinberg, S. S. 1948. "A Cross-section of Corinthian Antiquities (Excavations of 1940)," *Hesperia* 17, pp. 197–241.

———. 1954. "Corinthian Relief Ware: Pre-Hellenistic Period," *Hesperia* 23, pp. 109–137.

———. 1957. "Terracotta Sculpture at Corinth," *Hesperia* 26, pp. 289–319.

West, M. L. 1983. *The Orphic Poems*, Oxford.

Westholm, A. 1955. "The Cypriote 'Temple Boys'," *OpAth* 2, pp. 75–77.

Williams, C. K., II. 1977. "Corinth, 1976: Forum Southwest," *Hesperia* 46, pp. 40–81.

———. 1978. "Corinth, 1977: Forum Southwest," *Hesperia* 47, pp. 1–39.

———. 1979. "Corinth, 1978: Forum Southwest," *Hesperia* 48, pp. 105–144.

———. 1979a. "Ancient Corinth," ἈρχΔελτ 34, 1979 [1987] Χρονικά 1, pp. 124–127.

———. 1981. "The City of Corinth and Its Domestic Religion," *Hesperia* 50, pp. 408–421

———. 1982. "The Early Urbanization of Corinth," *ASAtene* n.s. 44, pp. 9–20.

————. 1986. "Corinth and the Cult of Aphrodite," in *Corinthiaca*, pp. 12–24.

————. 1987. "The Refounding of Corinth: Some Roman Religious Attitudes," in *Roman Architecture in the Greek World*, S. Macready and F. H. Thompson, eds., London, pp. 26–37.

Williams, C. K., II, and J. E. Fisher. 1972. "Corinth, 1971: Forum Area," *Hesperia* 41, pp. 143–184.

————. 1973. "Corinth, 1972: The Forum Area," *Hesperia* 42, pp. 1–44.

————. 1976. "Corinth, 1975: Forum Southwest," *Hesperia* 45, pp. 99–162.

Williams, C. K., II, and P. Russell. 1981. "Corinth: Excavations of 1980," *Hesperia* 50, pp. 1–44.

Williams, C. K., II, and O. H. Zervos. 1982. "Corinth, 1981: East of the Theater," *Hesperia* 51, pp. 115–163.

————. 1986. "Corinth, 1985: East of the Theater," *Hesperia* 55, pp. 129–175.

————. 1989. "Corinth, 1988: East of the Theater," *Hesperia* 58, pp. 1–50.

Williams, D. 1983. "Sophilos in the British Museum," in *Greek Vases in the J. Paul Getty Museum* I, Malibu, pp. 9–34.

Williams, D. J. R. 1984. "Close Shaves," in *Ancient Greek and Related Pottery* 1984, pp. 275–281.

Williams, E. R. 1976. "Ancient Clay Impressions from Greek Metalwork," *Hesperia* 45, pp. 41–66.

————. 1978. "Figurine Vases from the Athenian Agora," *Hesperia* 47, pp. 356–401.

————. 1982. "A Terracotta Herakles at The Johns Hopkins University," *Hesperia* 51, pp. 357–364.

Winkler, J. J. 1990. *The Constraints of Desire: The Anthropology of Sex and Gender in Ancient Greece*, New York.

Winter, *Typen* = F. Winter, *Die Typen der figürlichen Terrakotten*, Berlin 1903.

Winter, N. A. 1991. "Terracotta Figurines from Kourion: The Workshops," in *Cypriote Terracottas: Proceedings of the First International Conference of Cypriote Studies, Brussels–Liège–Amsterdam, 29 May–1 June 1989*, F. Vandenabeele and R. Laffineur, eds., Brussels-Liège, pp. 221–224.

Wright, T. 1866. "The Worship of the Generative Powers during the Middle Ages of Western Europe" [1866], repr. in R. P. Knight and T. Wright, *Sexual Symbolism: A History of Phallic Worship*, New York 1957.

Yalouris, N. 1992. *Die Skulpturen des Asklepiostempels in Epidauros* (*AntP* 21), Munich.

Yamauchi, E. M. 1973. "Cultic Prostitution: A Case Study in Cultural Diffusion," in *Orient and Occident: Essays Presented to Cyrus H. Gordon on the Occasion of His Sixty-Fifth Birthday*, H. A. Hoffner, Jr., ed., Neukirchen-Vluyn, pp. 213–222.

Zazoff, P. 1962. "Ephedrismos: Ein altgriechisches Spiel," *AuA* 11, pp. 35–42.

Zeitlin, F. I. 1982. "Cultic Models of the Female: Rites of Dionysus and Demeter," *Arethusa* 15, pp. 129–157.

Zervoudaki, E. 1978. «'Αἰετὸς ὁ Ζεὺς ἦλθεν ἐπ' ἀντίθεον Γανυμήδην'», Ἀρχ∆ελτ 33, 1978 [1984], pp. 24–39.

Züchner, W. 1942. *Griechische Klappspiegel* (*JdI-EH* 14), Berlin.

————. 1950/1951. "Von Toreuten und Töpfern," *JdI* 65/66, pp. 175–205.

Zuntz, G. 1971. *Persephone: Three Essays on Religion and Thought in Magna Graecia*, Oxford.

ABBREVIATIONS OF PERIODICALS AND REFERENCE WORKS

AA = *Archäologischer Anzeiger*

ActaArch = *Acta Archaeologica* [Copenhagen]

AJA = *American Journal of Archaeology*

AM = *Athenische Mitteilungen*

AM-BH = *Athenische Mitteilungen. Beiheft*

AnnEconSocCiv = *Annales: Économies, sociétés, civilizations*

AntK = *Antike Kunst*

AntP = *Antike Plastik*

AR = *Archaeological Reports*

Ἀρχ∆ελτ = *Ἀρχαιολογικὸν ∆ελτίον*

Ἀρχ Ἐφ = *Ἀρχαιολογικὴ Ἐφημερίς*

ASAtene = *Annuario della Scuola archeologica di Atene e delle Missioni italiane in Oriente*

AuA = *Antike und Abendland*

BABesch = *Bulletin antieke beschaving*

BAR = *British Archaeological Reports*

BCH = *Bulletin de correspondance hellénique*

BICS = *Bulletin of the Institute of Classical Studies*

BMMA = *Bulletin of the Metropolitan Museum of Art, New York*

BMusBrux = *Bulletin des Musées royaux d'art et d'histoire, Bruxelles*

BSA = *Annual of the British School at Athens*

BWPr = *Winckelmannsprogramm der Archäologischen Gesellschaft zu Berlin*

CQ = *Classical Quarterly*
CW = *Classical World*
DarSag = C. Daremberg and E. Saglio, *Dictionnaire des antiquités grecques et romaines*
EAA = *Enciclopedia dell'arte antica, classica e orientale*
EchCl = *Echos du monde classique: Classical Views*
GettyMusJ = *The J. Paul Getty Museum Journal*
HSCP = *Harvard Studies in Classical Philology*
IEJ = *Israel Exploration Journal*
IstMitt = *Istanbuler Mitteilungen*
IstMitt-BH = *Istanbuler Mitteilungen. Beiheft*
JdI = *Jahrbuch des Deutschen Archäologischen Instituts*
JdI-EH = *Jahrbuch des Deutschen Archäologischen Instituts. Ergänzungsheft*
JEA = *Journal of Egyptian Archaeology*
JFA = *Journal of Field Archaeology*
JHS = *Journal of Hellenic Studies*
JRAI = *Journal of the Royal Anthropological Institute*
LIMC = *Lexicon Iconographicum Mythologiae Classicae*
LSJ = H. G. Liddell, R. Scott, and H. S. Jones, *A Greek-English Lexicon*, rev. ed.
MedMusB = *Medelhavsmuseet, Bulletin* [Stockholm]
MEFRA = *Mélanges de l'École française de Rome, Antiquité*
MonAnt = *Monumenti antichi*
NSc = *Notizie degli scavi di antichità*
OJA = *Oxford Journal of Archaeology*
ÖJh = *Jahreshefte des Österreichischen archäologischen Instituts in Wien*
OpArch = *Opuscula archaeologica*
OpAth = *Opuscula atheniensia*
PP = *La parola del passato*
Πρακτικά = Πρακτικὰ τῆς ἐν Ἀθήναις Ἀρχαιολογικῆς Ἑταιρείας
RA = *Revue archéologique*
RE = Pauly-Wissowa, *Real-Encyclopädie der klassischen Altertumswissenchaft*
RM = *Römische Mitteilungen*
RM-EH = *Römische Mitteilungen. Ergänzungsheft*
SIMA = *Studies in Mediterranean Archaeology*
TAPA = *Transactions of the American Philological Association*
TAPS = *Transactions of the American Philosophical Society*
ZPE = *Zeitschrift für Papyrologie und Epigraphik*

THE SANCTUARY OF DEMETER AND KORE

TERRACOTTA FIGURINES OF THE
CLASSICAL, HELLENISTIC, AND ROMAN PERIODS

I
INTRODUCTION

The terracotta figurines published in this volume were excavated at the Sanctuary of Demeter and Kore on Acrocorinth between 1961 and 1975, with an additional brief season in 1994.[1] The present collection includes the figurines of the Classical, Hellenistic, and Roman periods, which make up the greater part of the coroplastic finds. Archaic figurines of the later 7th and 6th centuries B.C., together with Archaic survivals of the 5th and 4th centuries B.C., will be published in a later fascicle of this series.

Taking all periods together, the quantity of figurines found in the sanctuary was extremely large, reaching a total of more than 24,000 figurines and fragments. This number encompasses a great range in scale, from miniatures to statuettes originally measuring more than ca. 50 cm in height; a corresponding range of different types; and a surprising differential in technique and concept, from plaques stamped out in large numbers, which are pale reflections of their original models, to pieces that, although moldmade, nevertheless preserve something of the freshness of new creations and probably are close to their archetypes. Such diversity is a key element in the Corinthian coroplastic industry as a whole.[2] An approximate numerical breakdown of the most popular types can be found on pages 2–4. While publications of smaller collections of figurines sometimes include all fragments, it obviously has been impossible to follow that procedure here, and what is published is a representative selection. It may be helpful to describe how the figurines were processed and how the selection was made.

THE COUNTING AND PROCESSING OF THE FIGURINES

Initially, all figurines were inventoried as they were excavated. The large amount of material, however, soon made it necessary to inventory only the best preserved and to store the remainder, after washing, together with the lots of context pottery with which they were found.[3] All the figurine fragments, no matter how small, were retained. After the excavations were completed and the period of study began, the figurines in the approximately 480 lots that contained them were sorted and counted.[4] The initial difficulty was in obtaining an accurate count. It was apparent that few or none of the figurines were in primary deposition, and that a good deal of moving about of earth and of the discarded figurines contained in it, during the various phases of construction in the sanctuary, had resulted in the severe fragmentation and dispersion of many pieces. For example, fragments of the large seated female figurine **C93** were retrieved from four

---

[1] For a description of the excavation, see *Corinth* XVIII, iii. The goddess Kore/Persephone is referred to as "Kore" in this publication, unless the source under discussion uses the name "Persephone."

[2] The history of the Corinthian coroplastic industry, as far as it can be determined from evidence currently available, is discussed by the author in an article, "Corinthian Terracotta Figurines: The Development of an Industry," to be published in the *Proceedings of the Corinth Centennial Symposium.*

[3] The pottery found in the sanctuary was organized into lots, each of which consists of finds from a specific area or

feature of the excavation. The lot number given in the catalogue for each figurine indicates the lot of pottery with which the figurine was found. The lot list on pp. 353–368 provides for each lot the date range of the pottery and a brief description of the archaeological context; if the date of that context is later than the latest date of the pottery, it is so indicated.

[4] The total number of pottery lots recovered was 1,158, and less than half contained figurines. The lot list on pp. 353–368 includes only those lots that contained the figurines catalogued or otherwise mentioned in this volume.

different pottery lots, excavated on both the Lower and Upper Terraces of the sanctuary. Further, since some of the figurines had not been fired very hard, the fragments sometimes were too eroded to show possible joins or crumbled into impossibly small fragments when handled. Even the highly skilled excavation menders had only limited success in restoration. Consequently, it was often impossible to know whether or not a fragment represented the sole remains of a figurine or really belonged with other fragments; the counts therefore should be regarded as approximate. A great deal must really be missing, however, since easily recognizable, thick-walled, large statuettes were represented by only a few fragments. The same is true of much of the terracotta sculpture.[5] If so much loss occurred among the sturdier pieces, it must have been still greater among the more fragile figurines. In fact, the figurines that fared best were those of miniature scale, which were usually solid rather than hollow. Even if one allows for possible duplication in the counting, however, the great variety of types and the many variants of standard types speak for a very large production and a common use of figurines as votives in this sanctuary. Since the very last lot of figurines studied contained several new types and variants, the material that did not survive or that remains in the unexcavated area of the sanctuary must be assumed to contain more that is still unknown. It is clear that even the overwhelming quantity of extant material represents only a portion of what was originally dedicated.

As each lot of contextually associated figurines was studied, the standard types, such as articulated "dolls," easily recognizable even in fragments, were counted and for the most part left with the context pottery. Also left were fragments that could tell little about the original type, such as pieces of plain skirt drapery, limbs, or badly worn heads. It was not unusual for such indeterminate pieces to make up more than half the figurine fragments in a lot. The better-preserved or more informative pieces were withdrawn, marked with the lot number, photographed in groups, and held for further study. The best of these were later inventoried, and a selection showing all identifiable types then was made from the total inventory for the catalogues in this publication. Therefore, the catalogues and discussions of the figurines in this study include both material with formal inventory (MF) numbers and some pieces identified only by the lot number of the pottery with which they were found. Multiple examples are recorded under the appropriate catalogue entries.

The approximate counts of the figurines give some idea of the numbers of such votives offered at the sanctuary in different periods. Of the more than 24,000 figurines or fragments excavated, ca. 1,800 were Archaic or Archaic survivals. Of that number, ca. 510, including both handmade and partially moldmade figurines, demonstrably belong to the 7th and 6th centuries B.C., the larger proportion of the total being Archaic survivals of the 5th and 4th centuries B.C. Archaic survivals include types that were made continuously from the Archaic to the Classical period and others first made in the Classical period in a lingering Archaic style. Since the count for the Roman period was only ca. 30 pieces, most of the figurines, whether Archaic, Classical, or Hellenistic in style, were dedicated between the 5th century and 146 B.C. Within these parameters, allowing for the chronological difficulties discussed below (pp. 5–7), the time of the most prolific production and dedication appears to have been the 4th century B.C., when an increase in wealth after the Peloponnesian War (see p. 115) apparently supported votive activities. At this time, numerous new types were created while concurrently, until the 320s B.C., the workshops of the Potters' Quarter were continuing their conservative production. The largest single concentration of figurines, in the construction fill of the Trapezoidal Building, belongs mostly to the 4th century B.C. The survival of some of the new 4th-century B.C. types into the 3rd century, and the paucity of closely datable contexts, makes impossible an accurate numerical division of figurines between these two centuries, but there was a probable drop in production during the 3rd century B.C. for two reasons:

---

[5] The publication of the terracotta sculpture is forthcoming in a later fascicle of *Corinth* XVIII by Nancy Bookidis.

the prolific Potters' Quarter workshops were no longer active at that time, and fewer new types were introduced by other workshops. There appears to have been a serious numerical and qualitative diminution in production about the middle to third quarter of the 3rd century B.C., followed by a spurt of new types and renewed quality in the last quarter of the 3rd century to 146 B.C.

The numerical proportion of Archaic figurines is low, but figurines do not appear to have been dedicated at the sanctuary until the last quarter of the 7th century B.C., when coroplastic production in Corinth got under way,[6] so that we are comparing only one and one-quarter centuries of Archaic dedications with those of the three and one-half centuries of the post-Archaic sanctuary. Further, the largest proportion of pottery belongs to the 6th and 5th centuries B.C., while the largest proportion of figurines belongs to the 4th. There may have been some change in custom over time, from an emphasis on votive pots to figurines. We cannot know, however, whether the stimulus for this development was an actual change in ritual that required figurines or an industrial change that put on the market fewer or less attractive votive pots but more desirable figurines. There may have been a connection between coroplasts and workshops manufacturing small bronzes, especially in the 4th century B.C. (see p. 343), that resulted in the availability of very fine figurines.

While the repertoire was extremely diverse, especially in the Hellenistic period, when many fine types are known in just a few examples, some popular types or categories discussed in the following chapters can be isolated and counted. Their relative surviving numbers should have some bearing on their cultic importance, as explained in the discussion of the various types in their appropriate chapters. For the reader's convenience, the count of these types is summarized here. The numbers listed below include catalogued figurines, as well as others that received Corinth Museum inventory numbers, but were not selected for cataloguing in this publication, and still more that were only counted and stored with the lots of context pottery. The numbers are approximate. Although the count of 7th- and 6th-century B.C. types and their survivals will be provided in the forthcoming publication of the Archaic figurines, the count of new types of lingering Archaic style that were first produced in the 5th century B.C. is included here[7] to establish them as part of the production of the Classical period. The following list, clearly, does not include all the figurines of each period but only the most popular and clearly recognizable types.

Lingering Archaic types (5th–4th centuries B.C.)
    standing "korai": ca. 230
    seated goddesses: ca. 90
    heads of "korai" or goddesses: ca. 30
    "dolls": ca. 60
    spoon-based protomes: ca. 25
    plaques (Gorgon, sphinx, rooster): ca. 60

Classical types, including survivals (5th–4th centuries B.C., a few 3rd)
    "dolls": nude: ca. 810
           draped: ca. 120
    banqueters: ca. 55
    standing youths: ca. 55
    seated children: ca. 45
    hydriaphoroi: ca. 30
    standing female votaries: ca. 25
    protomes: ca. 25

---

[6] Merker, forthcoming.

[7] I thank Jean M. Turfa for the counts of Archaic and surviving Archaic figurines.

Early Hellenistic types, including survivals (4th–3rd centuries B.C.)
       standing female votaries: ca. 285
       children (all types): ca. 90

Middle Hellenistic type (3rd–2nd centuries B.C.)
       "priestesses": ca. 175

The count of the "dolls" is based on their reliably recognizable torsos, which usually were cast solid, making them much more durable than the more common hollow-cast figurines. Consequently, the count of "dolls" seems overwhelmingly large in relation to the rest of the figurines. The separately made limbs of these "dolls," which, although solid, were much more vulnerable in the unfavorable conditions of preservation in the sanctuary (see p. 8), survived at only about half the rate of the torsos. Even when the count of the "dolls" is adjusted for this factor, however, the type still remains the one most commonly found, and presumably dedicated, at the Sanctuary.

THE ORGANIZATION OF THE MATERIAL

The organization of any collection of material must be determined by both its inherent nature and its context. Some collections of figurines might best be organized on the basis of their manufacture, that is, as products of one or more workshops. Although the material here under study allows some small workshop groupings of figurines to be made on the basis of such criteria as technique, scale, and style, the material as a whole is so diverse that most of the figurines do not have identifiable workshop mates and therefore cannot be so organized. The material is very different in character from that of Archaic Sicily, for example, where large deposits of well-preserved figurines of limited typology have been found, which are very well suited to mechanical study.[8] Further, the workmanship of Classical and Hellenistic Corinthian figurines, with its heavy retouch and creativity in regard to variants, tends to distort and obscure the mold series at the heart of coroplastic technique. The primary purpose of figurines found in a cultic context should be to further the understanding of the cult, particularly when that understanding depends largely on archaeological sources. The best-possible organization of this material is therefore by subject, within the different periods, since the types provide the imagery that conveys the ideas of the cult, and typological development from one period to another may reflect cultic changes. Mechanical relationships are recorded in the catalogues, and a summary of workshops (pp. 344–346) brings together figurines of different types that may have been manufactured together.

A typological organization also emphasizes the wide range of approaches at a given period among different Corinthian artisans. For example, the Classical seated female figurines (pp. 42–47) encompass several updated versions of Archaic coroplastic types, even including the combined handmade/moldmade technique, as well as larger, entirely new creations stylistically dependent upon stone sculpture. Another advantage is that pastiches of various elements can be placed most effectively by subject, as can fragments that reveal only limited mechanical information, of which there are many in this collection of figurines.

As in many archaeological collections of figurines, there are numerous isolated heads that, because they are solid, survived their more fragile torsos. Rather than collect these heads in a sort of extended rogues' gallery, they have been distributed according to their probable original use, among better-preserved figurines to which they are related, if not mechanically, at least typologically or stylistically. It should be kept in mind, however, that a given head type was often used with widely differing torsos.

---

[8] E.g., Sguaitamatti 1984, and rev. by Ammerman 1986.

THE ARCHAEOLOGICAL CONTEXTS AND CHRONOLOGY

A close dating of the figurines has been precluded by the character both of the material and of the site. With regard to the coroplastic medium itself, putting aside archaeological context for the moment, every figurine has two dates, a stylistic date (determined by the style of the archetype from which the mold was taken) and the mechanical date of its actual manufacture in the workshop.[9] The latter date is extremely difficult to determine, since molds theoretically could have been in use over long periods or even brought back into production after a long period of disuse. Further, the pace of production during a given mold series is impossible to determine, regardless of the number of generations documented, since some types could have been produced in large numbers over a relatively short time, while others lingered for a longer period. Therefore, the stylistic date is very important, although it can provide only a *terminus post quem*. The stylistic date is most useful for figurines that are not part of any presently known mold series and show clear mold impressions. In these cases, where there may have been only one generation, the date of manufacture may be close to the stylistic date of the archetype, unless something much older was employed for this purpose. A time lag between figurine and archetype is theoretically possible, since a mold could have been taken from an archetype at any time after the creation of the latter. Because there is no reason to assume a habitually long time lag between archetype and mold in the very large Corinthian coroplastic production, however, archetypal dates can sometimes be very useful. A group that must be dated with particular care is the 4th-century B.C. production of the Potters' Quarter. Here, lingering Archaic or Classical elements were often combined with Early Hellenistic features, the whole pastiche sometimes executed with a kind of folk-art naiveté; in such cases, the latest stylistic elements should provide the *terminus post quem* for the figurines.

With regard to the archaeological contexts in which the figurines were found, there are only a few helpful fixed points, owing to the disturbances of repeated construction in the limited area of the sanctuary.[10] In almost all the lots containing both figurines and pottery, the figurines confirm the dates derived from the pottery, if one uses as chronological criteria archetypal style or contextual evidence available from outside the sanctuary. In a few cases, the date of a figurine seems to be later than the latest pottery in a lot, as indicated in the lot list (pp. 353–368), and there is an occasional lot with only Roman pottery but Greek figurines. Unfortunately, a great many of the lots consist of pottery of mixed date, sometimes ranging from the Archaic to the Roman periods, and the figurines are similarly mixed in date. In the discussion of the figurines in the following chapters, the term "pottery context" refers to the latest date of the pottery with which a figurine was found. The terms "archaeological context" and "architectural context" refer to the overall date of the context, which may be later than the pottery.

The nature of an archaeological context will determine how accurately it can date the period of use of a figurine. In a single undisturbed burial, for example, figurines would have been deposited at the same time as the pottery; if the latter is datable, it fixes the time of use of the figurines, which in most cases should also be close to the time of manufacture, although burials sometimes contain heirlooms. The archaeological contexts of the Acrocorinth sanctuary, however, often include material accumulated over a period of time. The latest datable material in such a lot, whether pottery, coins, lamps, or figurines, is only a *terminus ante quem* and does not necessarily date the period of use of all the figurines in that archaeological context. For example, the construction fill of the Trapezoidal Building, the terminal date of which is the beginning of the 3rd century B.C., contained a few figurines made in the 6th century and discarded long before but introduced in the earth that was gathered for the construction fill. It also contained figurines

---

[9] *Troy*, p. 20.
[10] *Corinth* XVIII, iii, p. xxi.

in a lingering Archaic style, consisting of types known to have been made in the Potters' Quarter during the 5th and 4th centuries, perhaps until the closure of the workshops there in the 320s B.C. This material also was no longer current when the Trapezoidal Building was constructed. For the remaining 4th-century B.C. figurines, the terminal date of the fill serves only as a *terminus ante quem*, and other means must be used to try to date them more closely. The most stylistically advanced figurines are the ones most likely to have been in use near the terminal date; those of somewhat earlier style, given the lingering tendencies of figurines, may or may not have still been in use at the terminal date.[11] A reasonable rule of thumb is that the date of manufacture and use of a figurine falls between its stylistic and contextual dates.

In her study of the Greek pottery from the sanctuary, in the absence of true closed deposits, Pemberton isolated eleven context groups of pottery.[12] Of these, the most useful context for dating the figurines is the above-mentioned construction fill of the Trapezoidal Building on the Middle Terrace of the sanctuary, the pottery from which is mainly later 4th century B.C. in date, the latest dating to the beginning of the 3rd century B.C.[13] This is not a sealed deposit, but there are only two later sherds among the very large quantity of pottery found in the fill. Two heads among the approximately 1,800 figurines should be later; one is of the Middle Hellenistic "priestess" type (a mechanical relative of the head of **H401**) and the other, a "doll's" head (**C159**), shows the surface blistering that indicates the use of a plaster mold. Otherwise the material from this deposit is of 4th-century B.C. style, with a small admixture of earlier material. The deposit exhibits a good range of Early Hellenistic types, but it is as useful for what it excludes. It can be assumed provisionally, until further evidence proves otherwise, that an Early Hellenistic type that is not represented in this large and varied cache was not created until the 3rd century B.C.

Another archaeological context that is of some utility is lot 3217, a mass of discarded pottery found on the Lower Terrace, the latest of which dates to the mid- to later 3rd century B.C., with more than 200 figurines; this material is thought to have been cleared from a pit and discarded in the third quarter of the 3rd century B.C.[14] The latest figurines in this lot are still recognizably Early Hellenistic in type; none of the types that are Middle Hellenistic in style are represented there, which suggests that the new types were not introduced until the last quarter of the 3rd century B.C.

Unfortunately, there is considerably less contextual assistance for dating the figurines of the 5th and earlier 4th centuries B.C. Only lot 887 (Pit A), which contained twelve figurines in the filling of a pit with a deposit of 5th-century B.C. kalathiskoi,[15] provides a dated context for a small number of types. In addition to these three useful context groups, there are occasionally lots in which figurines appear with a small amount of pottery that is not mixed in date. While these lots are not as reliable for dating as those in the context groups, they are mentioned in the discussion whenever they occur.

In the absence of contextual evidence at the sanctuary for some figurine types, well-documented finds of figurines from other sites in Corinth are sometimes helpful. For example, a few figurines similar to those from the Acrocorinth sanctuary, especially of children, were found in undisturbed graves in the North Cemetery, together with datable pottery.[16] The Forum Southwest excavations undertaken in the 1970s uncovered a variety of figurines, a few of them

[11] Similarly, in the Athenian Agora, the Coroplasts' Dump, dated by its pottery to the third quarter of the 4th century, was "composed of three distinct groups: a) Vestigial fragments, dating as early as 470–400 B.C., b) Conservative types of late fifth and early fourth century style, still in production, c) Contemporary figures in contemporary style" (R. V. Nicholls, quoted in D. B. Thompson 1966, p. 54).

[12] *Corinth* XVIII, i, pp. 79–109.

[13] *Corinth* XVIII, i, pp. 91–96 (group 6; of the lots listed there, the following contained figurines discussed in this

volume: lots 1982, 2111, 2249, 2250, 4356, and 4369); *Corinth* XVIII, iii, pp. 242–243.

[14] *Corinth* XVIII, i, pp. 101–103 (group 8); *Corinth* XVIII, iii, p. 211.

[15] *Corinth* XVIII, i, pp. 89–90 (group 5); *Corinth* XVIII, iii, pp. 161–162.

[16] *Corinth* XIII, p. 271, grave 420; p. 282, grave 453; pp. 292–293, grave 496; on the possible unreliability of some of the dates of these graves, see *Corinth* XVIII, i, p. 3.

paralleling types from the sanctuary in datable 4th-century B.C. contexts.[17] A shop deposit in the South Stoa contained figurines, including an archaizing female type known in the Sanctuary, and 3rd-century B.C. coins, which provide a terminal date for the deposit.[18] The deposits of the Potters' Quarter are more difficult to use, since they are mostly concentrations of material, sometimes accumulated over a long period of time, rather than true deposits; further, some are to be redated downward.[19] The date in or near the 320s B.C. at which time the Potters' Quarter workshops ceased operation, however, does provide a *terminus ante quem* for figurines from these workshops excavated in the Acrocorinth sanctuary.[20]

Occasionally, a grave group found elsewhere with imported Corinthian figurines will provide a datable context. For example, a grave group in Argos[21] contains figurines together with a Corinthian unglazed lekanis with stepped lid, a type introduced just before the middle of the 5th century B.C.[22] When these chronological resources fail, stylistic or iconographic relationships can sometimes be established with sculpture, particularly votive reliefs, or occasionally with vase painting, to date approximately the archetype of a figurine. Drawing connections with figurines from other coroplastic centers can be difficult, since local preferences for type and style tended to be strong. Further, other figurines are subject to the same chronological problems inherent in the medium as are Corinthian figurines, making them unreliable as fixed points.

It is apparent that even when archaeological context provides some assistance, the figurines from the Acrocorinth sanctuary can be dated reliably only within rather wide parameters, and any further refinement of this framework must rest on style and comparisons with work in other media. In presenting the figurines in the discussions and catalogues that follow, the nature of coroplastic work has been accommodated by including later repetitions of types within the period of their conception. Hence the chapter entitled "Classical Figurines and Their Survivals" includes figurines of 5th-century B.C. type and style that were still being made well into the 4th, and the chapter "Early Hellenistic Figurines and Their Survivals" includes 4th-century B.C. types that may have lingered into the later 3rd century. The chapter on Middle Hellenistic figurines does not include survivals, since the sanctuary was closed during the Late Hellenistic period, which corresponds with the interim period following the destruction of 146 B.C. The considerably smaller quantity of material for the Middle Hellenistic than for the Classical or Early Hellenistic period is likely to owe something to this circumstance, emphasizing how much of the production habitually centered on earlier, lingering types.

It is important to note that the conventional dating of the Hellenistic period to begin ca. 330 B.C. does not work very well for Corinthian figurines, since departures from Classical practice in both iconography and style are evident by the middle of the 4th century B.C. and probably already in the second quarter. The middle and third quarter of the 4th century B.C. may have been a time of particularly fertile creativity. Hence, apart from figurines of the early 4th century B.C., which artistically still belong to the tradition of the later 5th, and apart from obvious Archaic or 5th-century B.C. survivals into the 4th century, the term "Early Hellenistic" more accurately describes 4th-century B.C. Corinthian figurines than the term "Classical." For the purposes of this study, the third quarter of the 3rd century B.C. is taken as the approximate dividing point between Early and Middle Hellenistic. Questions of terminology and dating are discussed more fully in the appropriate chapters (see pp. 23, 115–116, 249).

[17] E.g., C. K. Williams and Fisher 1972, pp. 162–163.
[18] Davidson 1942, pp. 105–106 for the date.
[19] On the dates, see C. K. Williams 1981, pp. 413–416 (Erosa Shrine, Shrine of the Double Stele, Stele Shrine A, Stele Shrine B); C. K. Williams 1986, p. 22 (Stele Shrine A); Risser 1990 (Stele Shrine A); Nicholls 1958, pp. 172–173 (Stele Shrine A, Aphrodite Deposit, Circular South Shrine).
[20] On the destructive earthquake in Corinth in the third

quarter of the 4th century B.C., see *Corinth* XV, i, p. 49; for a possible alternative date nearer the end of the 4th century, see C. K. Williams and Fisher 1976, pp. 116–117, note 20. For earthquake damage in the Acrocorinth sanctuary, see *Corinth* XVIII, i, p. 91 (third or early fourth quarter of the 4th century B.C.); *Corinth* XVIII, iii, pp. 430–431.
[21] Papaspyridi-Karouzou 1933–1935, pp. 21–44 (grave 5).
[22] *Corinth* XIII, pp. 145–148.

THE DISTRIBUTION AND USE OF THE FIGURINES IN THE SANCTUARY

The building activities within the sanctuary during its long life, with the repeated movement of earth from one place to another, had not only chronological consequences. These activities also inhibit our understanding of precisely where in the sanctuary the figurines originally were deposited as offerings and in what manner.[23] One certain piece of evidence is that most of the figurines were concentrated on the Upper and Middle Terraces, particularly the latter, where ritual activities are thought to have been especially concentrated.[24] Very few figurines, and these fragmentary, were found in and around the dining rooms of the Lower Terrace, from which one may conclude that figurines were not involved in the ritual activities of this area. Figurines from the Upper Terrace were probably incorporated into the earth filling used to level the sloping bedrock, dumped behind the retaining walls at the bottom of the terrace; consequently, the dedication of figurines cannot be connected with any structure there. Generally speaking, the likeliest area for the ritual deposition of figurines is the Middle Terrace, although it is difficult to make specific connections between structures and figurines; after the construction of the Trapezoidal Building ca. 300 B.C., figurines could have been deposited there temporarily before being dumped elsewhere in the sanctuary, but there is no physical evidence to demonstrate this.

Further, the evidence for the ritual deposition of figurines in pits or other votive receptacles is problematic. It is uncertain whether figurines were deposited directly into pits together with or instead of votive vessels, or whether they were placed on or around altars, and perhaps were swept aside or buried in pits later. Pit A (lot 887), the pottery of which dates from the late 6th through the 5th centuries B.C.,[25] contained some figurines, but their fragmentary condition makes ritual deposition questionable, and the lack of a dominant type or at least thematically related types is not encouraging.[26] Probably this pit received pottery ritually, while figurines originally offered elsewhere in the sanctuary, perhaps nearby, were later dumped into the pit with the earth filling. Pit E (lot 4351, late 6th to early second quarter of the 5th century B.C.), which also received pottery ritually, to judge from the predominance of kalathiskoi in the deposit,[27] contained only one figurine fragment of indeterminate type. Visitors to the sanctuary may have placed a pot but apparently not a figurine in this pit before entering the Middle Terrace. Pit B (lot 880) in the Trapezoidal Building received burned animal sacrifices, but the figurines and other objects in it probably belong to the earth dumped into the pit when it went out of use and was filled, near the middle of the 3rd century B.C.[28]

A more convincing possibility of ritual deposition of a figurine is from the pottery pocket in Room E;[29] this pocket of material was gathered in a corner and fenced in with a large tile. The pocket contained the 5th-century B.C. spoon-based protome MF-12057,[30] which is intact and therefore may have been deposited there in the course of a ritual, although it is odd that it is the only figurine among the pottery. A larger quantity of figurines was found in lot 3217,[31] which is thought to represent material cleaned from a votive pit of the 3rd century B.C.[32] While it may be true that at least some of this material comes from a pit, and some of the figurines do match the

[23] Evidence for the ritual placement of figurines in sanctuaries has been collected and discussed by Ammerman in *Coroplast's Art*, pp. 42–43, with bibliography; see also Alroth 1988.

[24] *Corinth* XVIII, iii, pp. 53, 247.

[25] *Corinth* XVIII, i, pp. 89–90; *Corinth* XVIII, iii, pp. 161–162.

[26] The types are as follows: Classical–standing nude male (**C191**), "doll's" head (**C125**), bird (**V9**), hand with alabastron (**V26**), seated female (MF-10942, catalogued with **C82**); Archaic and lingering Archaic–female head (MF-10543), mini-

ature handmade seated female (MF-10539), fragment of a chitoniskos "doll" (MF-10538), worn head of "kore" (MF-10943); uninventoried fragments–standing "kore," protome(?), worn seated female, three of indeterminate type.

[27] *Corinth* XVIII, i, pp. 87–88; *Corinth* XVIII, iii, pp. 163–166.

[28] *Corinth* XVIII, iii, pp. 243–245.

[29] *Corinth* XVIII, i, pp. 84–87; *Corinth* XVIII, iii, p. 159.

[30] Publication forthcoming.

[31] *Corinth* XVIII, i, pp. 101–103.

[32] *Corinth* XVIII, iii, p. 211.

3rd-century B.C. date of the pottery, there are also in this lot types of the 4th century or earlier.[33] This long chronological range makes it likely that material from more than one source contributed to the group, although the latest figurines could have been ritually deposited in the pit.

The difficulty of connecting particular figurine types with areas of the sanctuary, except in the most general way, is well illustrated by the distribution of the easily recognizable Middle Hellenistic "priestess" figurines (pp. 250–255). Among the ca. 175 examples of this type, the largest cluster (28 examples) is from lot 870, which was excavated on the Middle Terrace at grid O–Q:25. It is therefore possible that figurines of this type originally were dedicated in a structure or at an altar near this location, although the finds in this lot come from fill dumped to level the sloping bedrock, unconnected with any structure.[34] A smaller cluster of this type, less than ten figurines from lot 2107, was excavated from the Upper Terrace at Q–S:17–20, a fair distance to the west; as mentioned above, the figurines from the Upper Terrace probably were brought there with the earth filling dumped behind the retaining walls. Still other examples were found scattered widely on the Lower Terrace, singly or in small multiples. The likely explanation for this distribution, that the "priestess" figurines were moved away from their original point of collection (on the Middle Terrace?) during building operations of the Roman period, still does not help to pinpoint their actual place of dedication.

CLASSICAL AND HELLENISTIC COROPLASTIC TECHNIQUES

The fundamental technique common to coroplasts everywhere (the progression from archetype to molds and thence to generations of figurines) has been well described elsewhere[35] and will not be repeated here. The purpose of this discussion is to add to previous publications[36] what can be learned from the Acrocorinth sanctuary material about the technical aspects of Corinthian Classical and Hellenistic figurines. The discussion of technique will include the following: scale; fabric; color; slip and paint; archetypes; molding and modeling; the attachment of parts; plaster molds; tools; backs and venting; the effect of technique on style; and the definition of quality in figurines. A selection of bases has been catalogued and discussed below (pp. 274–276).

SCALE

The scale of the figurines varied greatly, from miniatures of a few centimeters in height to statuettes of more than one-third life size. There does not seem to be any particular correlation of size and chronological period, except that the new types introduced in the Middle Hellenistic period tended to be larger in scale than their forerunners. Factors determining scale must have originated both outside and inside the workshop. Since larger figurines must have been relatively expensive for consumers, general economic conditions must have played some role in the coroplast's choice of scale. The cost and availability of clay, or access to clay beds and kiln space, also would have been pressing matters for the artisan. The primary determining factor, however, may have been the availability of workshop materials at the time a batch of figurines was to be made. That is, the determinants were the molds that were on hand or could be borrowed or purchased; or, in the absence of molds, the archetypes that were available, either in the form of finished products, such as miniature figurines in precious metal or larger bronze statuettes, or in the form of the wax or clay models used by metalsmiths to make such objects.

Since it is difficult for the reader to visualize the size of a complete figure from the measurement in centimeters of a fragment, each catalogued piece has been assigned a numbered size range,

---

[33] E.g., the 4th-century B.C. **C36**, as well as uninventoried "dolls," a horse-rider, and a banqueter.

[34] *Corinth* XVIII, iii, p. 250.

[35] Especially *British Museum* I, pp. 3–7; Nicholls 1952; Nicholls 1982; Nicholls 1984; *Thasos* XVII, pp. 27–47; Muller 1997.

[36] *Corinth* XII, pp. 9–15; *Corinth* XV, i, pp. 82–87.

taken from the list below. In each catalogue entry, after the measurement, a number in parentheses indicates the size range to which the piece belongs, based on an estimation of the size when complete. This can only be approximate, since some fragments are quite small; where there is doubt and a figurine seems to fall between two size ranges, both numbers are given (e.g., 3–4). The original size of each figurine has been calculated without the base, which is seldom preserved, but the size ranges are broad enough that the presence or absence of a base usually will not make any difference. The size ranges are listed below; most of the figurines fall into ranges 2 or 3:

1. Miniatures, from 0.03 to 0.08 in height. Because they are very small and are usually solid, these figurines are often completely preserved. Theoretically, members of this group could be so small because they have lost scale at the end of a mold series, but usually they are well formed and detailed, like the comic dancer **H365**, and are better explained as copies of miniatures in precious metal.[37]

2. Small figurines, up to ca. 0.15 in height.

3. Larger figurines, still held comfortably in the hand, up to ca. 0.25 in height.

4. Small statuettes, up to ca. 0.50 in height. For this category and the one following, the term "statuette" is used to express a difference from the relatively small "figurines." The larger pieces sometimes are all or partly handmade and often approach monumental sculpture in style (see, e.g., the Classical seated peplophoros **C93** and the Hellenistic head **H431**).

5. Larger statuettes, more than 0.50 in height. Because the largest pieces are so fragmentary, the upper end of this size range cannot be determined precisely.

FABRIC

The term "fabric" is used here specifically to describe the material of the figurines after firing; it is not synonymous with the raw material, for which the term "clay" is used.[38] Thus, although five fabrics have been visually distinguished and described below, it is probable that all these derived from a very few clay beds, the visual variants being the result of different handling and firing of the clay by many hands over a period of time. Often, mold siblings are in different fabrics, which emphasizes the essential similarity of the material from one fabric to another; another batch of clay or a different artisan handling it could have been responsible for the resulting fabric. Such fabric distinctions among mold siblings have been noted in the catalogue. Only the very best one, fabric 4, which was used for relatively few figurines, may have been made from a distinctly better clay. In an ancient craft depending largely for its success on the personal judgments and experience of individual artisans, it is natural that there would have been differences in the washing of the clay, the use of various tempering materials, the thickness to which the walls were built, and the surface finishing, all of which would have influenced the outcome. In addition, there must have been differences in kiln construction, the artisans' judgment of heat, and the length of firing allowed. Ideally, every figurine should be analyzed in a laboratory to determine the origin of the clay and the methods of manufacture, but since this is obviously impossible when dealing with thousands of figurines, provisional identification must rest on close visual study and description.

Corinthian fabrics are usually fine in texture, the local clay tending to be very clean in its natural state.[39] The best clay, however, at least after the Archaic period, may have been saved mostly for pottery, where quality of fabric was important functionally, mixtures of good and lesser clays being used for figurines. Sometimes, as in fabric 5, sparse, very small gray, dark red or occasionally white inclusions are visible, suggesting that clays of lesser quality necessitated the use of temper. These inclusions appear to be the same as those employed for Corinthian household pottery and "tile fabric."[40] Sparkling inclusions are rare in Corinthian fabrics, although they do

[37] None has been found in Corinth, but for a gold miniature figurine from Argos, see Daux 1968, pp. 1029, 1036, fig. 28.

[38] On Corinthian clays and fabrics, see Jones 1984, p. 23; Jones et al. 1986, pp. 173–189; Farnsworth 1964, p. 224;

Farnsworth 1970; Farnsworth et al. 1977; Fillieres et al. 1983; *Corinth* XV, ii, pp. 4–7; *Corinth* XII, pp. 9–10; *Perachora* I, p. 192.

[39] Farnsworth 1964, p. 224.

[40] Farnsworth 1964, p. 224.

occasionally appear in small quantities in terracotta sculpture[41] and in figurines, perhaps as a result of a small admixture of sand to the clay. Such inclusions, however, are sparse. When Corinthian and Attic figurines are similar in color, the latter can be distinguished by the appearance in strong light of abundant, very tiny sparkling inclusions throughout the fabric.

Most Corinthian figurines were not fired very hard, with the exception of fabrics 3 and 4, which have the thinnest walls. Many Corinthian figurines, when touched, leave a slight powdery deposit on the hands. This softness may be, in part, the cause of the blurred modeling seen in so many Corinthian figurines; that is, the blurring may have been caused as much by surface wear during the figurines' period of use and burial as by the use of dull molds. Sometimes, when fragments of a figurine have become separated, upon mending one may show more alteration to the fabric than another, depending on the conditions of burial.[42]

To avoid unnecessary repetition in the catalogue, the different fabrics will be referred to there by number, and a full description given only in this chapter. Full descriptions will appear in the catalogue only in the case of imported figurines and for a few figurines whose fabrics do not quite fit within the range of any of the numbered fabrics, but that seem nevertheless to be Corinthian. The five different fabrics that can be distinguished visually are the following:

Fabric 1: This fabric, the most commonly employed, appears in Early Classical figurines and remained in use into Hellenistic times. It was employed for size ranges 2–5 and is usually the fabric of the largest pieces. The walls are up to 0.025 in thickness in the larger examples. The texture is soft and usually fine, but sparse inclusions occasionally are found; they are small and in color are gray, dark red, and less often white. There are sometimes voids as well, indicating burned-out organic temper; the use of temper is to be expected in larger and thicker pieces. The most common colors are orange-buff, shades of buff, and orange, sometimes shading from one to another within the same figurine.

Fabric 2: This fabric is first seen in 5th-century B.C. figurines but is more characteristic of the 4th century. It was employed for figurines in size ranges 2–4, with relatively thick walls, ca. 0.008, for their size. The texture is fine and soft. The distinctive feature of this fabric is a smooth, almost soapy surface, which seems to have been achieved by applying a fine self-slip, which was then polished. Since the white slip applied over the polished surface is better preserved on more of these pieces than is usually the case on Corinthian figurines, it is possible that the polishing was done to enhance the adhesion of the white slip and hence of the colored paints. The polishing may have eliminated minute gaps in the surface that would cause the white slip to flake off. Certainly the smooth surface would have been entirely covered and could not have been appreciated except by the artisans themselves. Figurines in this fabric often show very blurred modeling, which may have been caused in part by the polishing. The color varies from light orange to buff, sometimes shading from one color to another within the same figurine. Figurines in fabric 2 may have been made of the same clay as those in fabric 1, the difference in appearance being the result of the polishing of the surface. In **H137**, the back of the figure is in fabric 1, while the front is fabric 2; apparently only the front was polished.

Fabric 3: This fabric is found in many figurines from the Potters' Quarter, particularly those of the 5th and 4th centuries B.C. It was used mainly for small, thin-walled figurines in size ranges 1–2; the walls are sometimes as little as 0.003 in thickness. The texture is fine and the firing is hard, probably due to the thinness of the walls. When figurines in fabric 3 are lightly struck, a clear, clinking sound is heard. The color ranges from creamy buff to pinkish orange, sometimes shading

---

[41] E.g., in SF-40-6, a thigh fragment from a terracotta metope, the middle semifine layer contains small, sparkling inclusions, Weinberg 1957, pp. 317–318, no. 45b, pl. 73; see *British Museum* I, p. 240, for a few "micaceous" Corinthian figurines. The term "mica" is sometimes used indiscriminately for all sparkling inclusions. Corinthian fabrics usually do not contain real mica; on the nature of micas in non-Corinthian Greek fabrics, see Farnsworth 1964, pp. 222–223.

[42] The same phenomenon has been observed in the pottery from the sanctuary, *Corinth* XVIII, ii, p. 90, note 13.

from one color to another within the same piece. When not fired as hard as usual, it resembles fabric 1, from which it is distinguishable mainly by its thin walls.

Fabric 4: This is one of the best Corinthian figurine fabrics, dating from the late 5th to the 4th centuries B.C., but it is relatively uncommon. The figurines are in size ranges 2–4. They are fairly thin-walled for their size, for example, ca. 0.005 in size range 4. The texture is fine and the firing is hard. The modeling is crisp and clear. The colors are buff, tan, or orange, sometimes shading from one color to another within a single piece. In one well-made piece (**H66**), only the front was made of fabric 4, the back being made of the more common and less fine fabric 1.

Fabric 5: This is a fabric commonly found in 3rd-century B.C. figurines from the sanctuary, in size ranges 2–3.[43] It is coarse, friable, and laminated in fracture. Most examples show voids and inclusions similar to those occasionally found in fabric 1, but the inclusions are more often white. Occasionally there are sparse small, sparkling inclusions as well. The color range is generally similar to that of fabric 1 but with the addition of bright orange and ochre. When ochre or light tan, it somewhat resembles the fabric of some Boeotian figurines. The friability of this fabric is probably owed, at least in part, to poor firing, but the general coarseness of the material reflects the use of inferior clays. The poverty of this fabric suggests that some artisans of the 3rd century B.C. were unable to obtain clay of good quality and perhaps also sufficient fuel for firing. Since we do not know how the local natural resources were controlled and distributed, whether clay beds and stands of wood and brush for fuel were on public land or privately owned, and how the artisan went about obtaining what he needed, we cannot know exactly what this drop in standards meant in economic or social terms. Because some good work was produced at least in the first half of the 3rd century B.C. (e.g., the popular type showing a boy with a goose [**H331**]) and since technical standards rose again in the late 3rd and early 2nd centuries B.C., when a new and quite impressive repertoire of types was introduced, it would be inaccurate to speak of depletion of resources as the cause, although this is inevitable to some extent. There may have been instead some rupture in the established system of artisanship, so that some workers lost the ability either to practice the craft as before or to hand down expertise to the next generation.

COLOR

Color is the factor most often noted in fabric descriptions, yet it may be the least important from the point of view of distinguishing one fabric from another, since it is so dependent upon kiln conditions. Further, Corinthian figurines often shade from one color to another within the same piece. The texture of a fabric, which should be more diagnostic of the original qualities of a clay and should point to the methods used in handling it, was the main criterion used to develop the list of five fabrics given above.

I have attempted to record the colors of the figurines in a manner as useful to the reader as possible. Color description is a notoriously difficult problem, not only because color names are very subjective but also because the customary tool, the *Munsell Soil Color Charts,* is not always accurate for objects of fired clay; unfortunately, this is especially true of Corinthian objects. The C.E.C. charts,[44] which record the colors of fired ceramics, are much more accurate, but not all Corinthian colors are represented on them. The list below provides approximate readings on the Munsell charts for the color names given in the catalogue entries. In most cases, a range of readings is given, within which a particular shade falls; these ranges also allow for variations from one piece to another. The C.E.C. readings, when provided, are very close. It is hoped that the color names will to some degree evoke the variation in color of Corinthian figurines to

---

[43] See also Davidson 1942, p. 106.

[44] Fédération Européenne des Fabricants de Carreaux Céramiques, *C.E.C. Shade Guide,* Basel, n.d.

readers without access to the Munsell or C.E.C. charts. The color described in the catalogue is that of the surface, unless otherwise indicated.

Shades of buff

buff	10YR 8/2–8/4, sometimes grayer, approaching 7/4
creamy buff	10YR 8/3–7/3 (C.E.C. D5)
grayish buff	10YR 7/3
pinkish buff	7.5YR 8/4
yellowish buff	2.5Y 8/2–7/4
greenish buff	5Y 8/2–8/3

Shades of orange

orange-buff	7.5YR 7/4–7/6, often paler (C.E.C. C7 and C8)
light orange	7.5YR 7/6–6/6 (C.E.C. D9)
orange-brown	7.5YR 6/6
pinkish orange	5YR 7/4–7/6 (C.E.C. E7)
orange	5YR 7/6–6/6 (C.E.C. E9)
bright orange	5YR 7/8–6/8
grayish orange	2.5YR 6/6–6/8

Shades of gray (yellowish and greenish gray are often the colors of burned figurines; blue-gray is a core color)

yellowish gray	2.5Y 7/2–6/2
greenish gray	5Y 7/1–7/2
blue-gray	7.5YR 6/0

Other shades

yellow	10YR 8/6
ochre	10YR 7/4–7/6 (C.E.C. C10)
tan	7.5YR 7/4 or 10 YR 7/4

The fabrics of the Roman period will not be listed here, since the few Roman figurines found in the sanctuary have been organized by fabric in the discussion (pp. 311–316). The data are rather scanty, and it is not entirely clear how many of these figurines are imports. Only one of the Roman fabrics, a pale, hard-fired material in use in the 2nd century A.C. (see p. 312), really resembles any of the Corinthian figurine fabrics of the Greek period.

SLIP AND PAINT

The conditions of burial of the figurines did not favor the preservation of paint, but there are sufficient remains of white slip to show that its use was habitual under the paint. The first use of white slip in Corinth can be dated at least to the early 5th century B.C.[45] Occasionally, however, paint was applied directly to the surface, as on the Hellenistic protome **H388**, the mask **C268**, and the male head **C280**. The paint on the mask may have been applied before firing. In the child's head **C238**, paint was applied over slip on the face but directly to the clay on the headdress. In a few carefully painted pieces (e.g., a "doll's" head, **C129**), a thin, bluish white wash was applied to the surface and then a thick white slip over it. Thick slip often must have virtually concealed lightly modeled faces, and in such cases, the colorists essentially must have been painting features from scratch on a blank surface. In good pieces (e.g., **H99**), the slip may be glossy.

Yellow was used as an underpainting for gilding, presumably to make a thin coating of the expensive material seem more brilliant and to hide potential chips or gaps in the gold. It was

---

[45] *Corinth* XV, ii, pp. 5–6, note 10; *Perachora* I, p. 192; for white slip on a Corinthian terracotta sculptured head (SF-1980-1), dated ca. 490–475 B.C., see C. K. Williams and Russell 1981, pp. 31–33, no. 11, pl. 9.

used in this way on drapery (**V27**) and on the hair of female heads (e.g., **H225**). Even when flecks of gilding are not preserved, it is likely that areas of yellow paint, as on the hair of the well-made female head **C142**, originally were gilded.

Female flesh was painted pink (e.g., **H65**) or ivory white (e.g., the "doll's" head **C129**), but pink could also be used for the flesh of youths, as on the banqueter **C213**. There is one example of the use of pink as an underpaint for red on flesh (**V28**). A subtle pale pink shade is found on the faces of children (**H348** and **H349**), and a peach-pink on the pig **V1**. Figurine painting could be a rather garish, slapdash affair, but the use of subtler shades and the almost enamel-like quality of the aforementioned ivory paint point to a greater degree of expertise and sophistication.

Other colors are a bright blue, which Higgins has recognized as characteristically Corin-thian[46] and which appears on drapery from the sanctuary (e.g., **H101**) and a delicate violet on the drapery of a seated nymph (**H282**).[47] It is clear that the better workshops, at least in the 4th century B.C., finished their figurines with care.

ARCHETYPES

I have discussed elsewhere[48] the possibility that at least some of the archetypes used by Corinthian coroplasts were developed from the models made for small bronzes, perhaps by artisans whose specialty was model making. In the indirect casting of bronzes, which has recently been studied in great detail,[49] an original model was created in clay, from which master molds were taken. From these molds wax casts were made to serve as working models. These waxes could be altered and detailed as desired to provide a series of variants of the original model. During the bronze-casting process, only the wax working model was destroyed, leaving both the original model and the master molds intact for further use. This method of altering a basic type to produce variants, sometimes quite distinct from one another, is very like the procedures used by coroplasts. A number of archetypes could be developed from one model by taking a number of casts and altering limb positions, facial features, coiffures, attributes, costume, and even gender. From these slightly or radically varying archetypes evolved distinct but related mold series producing successively smaller generations of figurines. In figurine making, therefore, one may speak of serial production in two ways: the "vertical" or mold series, and the "horizontal" or iconographic series that results from alterations to the original design. This fundamental similarity of method and the references of some figurines to metalwork (noted in the discussion of the figurines and collected in the summary on pp. 342–343) suggest that coroplasts and bronze workers had access to the same body of available models.

MOLDING AND MODELING

On the basis of previous evidence, it has been thought that Corinth was slow to adopt hollow molding.[50] Early Classical hollow-molded figurines from the Acrocorinth sanctuary, however, show clearly that this technique must have been current in Corinth in the early 5th century B.C., the same time as in most other centers. In the stylistically earliest piece that could possibly be called hollow molded, the rider **C186**, the walls are thick, and the interior opening is regularly cylindrical at about a finger's breadth. Perhaps the piece was mounted on a dowel when it was being finished and the legs were added. Owing to the relatively large scale of this rider, as compared to the ordinary run of Corinthian horse-riders, and the thickness of the walls, the rider may have been fired separately from his horse, explaining the temporary mounting. A more

[46] *British Museum* I, p. 265, no. 971.

[47] For lumps of red, yellow, pink, and blue pigment found in the Potters' Quarter, see *Corinth* XV, ii, pp. 6–7. Lumps of pigment found in the South Stoa excavations (Farnsworth 1951) could also have been intended for coroplastic use.

[48] Merker, forthcoming.

[49] Mattusch 1988, pp. 19–22; Mattusch 1990; Mattusch 1994; Mattusch 1996, pp. 10–16; Haynes 1992, pp. 27–29, 57–59 on models.

[50] *British Museum* I, p. 241.

normal hollow-molded figurine is the peplos-figurine **C1**, which has thin walls and an open, smoothly finished interior.

Several different methods of filling the molds with clay were employed. Overlapping horizontal strips of clay were sometimes applied to the mold, and when not smoothed over they can still be seen, as in the interior of the male figurine **H309**. Sometimes the clay was applied in thin, superimposed layers, which can be seen when the outer surface has broken away, as in **H357** and **C126**. This method sometimes was employed to make the best use of a limited quantity of fine clay, which could be used for the outer surface, backing it with coarser material. This method was more commonly employed for larger objects, such as architectural sculpture.

Mold series can be followed most effectively in the abundant and relatively uniform lingering Archaic figurines of the 5th and 4th centuries B.C., especially the standing "korai."[51] Otherwise, as mentioned previously, the customary heavy retouch makes it difficult to identify mold relationships with certainty. Further, after the Archaic period, Corinthian artisans tended not to alter molds with intaglio before firing,[52] preferring instead to create variations on the figurines themselves with retouch and paint. For this reason, parallel molds taken from the same archetype would have been closely similar to one another, and their casts would have been virtually identical. Therefore, the mechanical relationships recorded in the catalogue have been qualified as "probable" or "possible." It was usually not possible to trace a mold series beyond a third generation. A type such as the standing draped female **H88–H98**, which is known in both large and small scale without all the intermediate sizes, probably is not from an incompletely recovered very long mold series but rather originated from archetypes of widely different scale.

In addition to molding, Corinthian coroplasts continued the tradition of modeling figurines by hand after the Archaic period, when handmade horse-riders, standing male and female figures, and grotesques were among the earliest types to be produced. In the 5th and 4th centuries B.C., Archaic handmade types continued in production, in addition to such large handmade pieces as the seated female figure **C93**, which is purely Classical in style. The technique is found even in the Hellenistic period, to which the head of a statuette **H431** belongs. Perhaps the plastic qualities of the local clay encouraged hand modeling; other factors may have been the popularity of terracotta sculpture in Corinth and the use of the same technique in the preparation of models for bronze casting.

THE ATTACHMENT OF PARTS

Apart from the miniatures, Corinthian figurines tended to be cast in several molds and then assembled. The heads were usually solid or nearly so, the long necks terminating in roughly conical tenons that were inserted between the shoulders. Heads of statuette scale, however, such as **H427**, might be hollow to diminish their weight. Sometimes, when the interior was well smoothed, the protruding neck tenon was removed, as in **C95**, but usually it was allowed to remain, as in **H202**, and would have projected into the open space of the torso. In really poor work, for example, the draped "doll" **C184**, a head might be just stuck onto a scored surface, probably with a little slip to aid adhesion. In **H280**, a well-made piece, the hole in the torso to receive the head has a carefully recessed margin, which must have corresponded with cuttings at the base of the neck of the missing head.

Separately made arms were usually attached to a flat joining surface, probably with the addition of slip for adhesion, and then smoothed over with a tool like a spatula. In the seated female figurine **C82**, however, a small hole in the joining surface must have received a tenon at the end of the missing, originally extended forearm. Occasionally, a narrow gap has opened at a joining surface when the drying clay shrank, but often additions were so carefully concealed that

[51] Publication forthcoming; for the type, see *Corinth* XV, ii, pp. 84–94.

[52] On this technique, see Nicholls 1952, pp. 222–223.

they can be seen clearly only in the layers of clay at breaks. The somewhat different molding and assembly of articulated "dolls" is described below (pp. 50–51).

PLASTER MOLDS

Plaster molds came into use in Corinth in the Middle Hellenistic period, to judge from the presence of blisters on the surfaces of some figurines, resulting from air bubbles in the surface of the plaster.[53] One blistered "doll's" head (**C159**) was found in an earlier context, the construction fill of the Trapezoidal Building, the terminal date of which is the beginning of the 3rd century B.C., but since there is no other evidence for such early use of plaster molds in the sanctuary material, and since the fill contains two later sherds and a known Middle Hellenistic figurine type, the blistered head is considered to be a later intrusion in the lot. Blistered surfaces are most commonly found in the "priestess" type, which probably dates to the last quarter of the 3rd century B.C., for example, **H395**. There is reason, however, on the basis of other finds in Corinth, to suggest that plaster molds may have come into use sometime in the first half of the 3rd century B.C. The unpublished contents of grave 1929-23, unfortunately disturbed and not certainly from a single burial, include a semidraped male figurine with a blistered surface,[54] together with figurines of children belonging stylistically to the first half of the 3rd century, as well as an imported Boeotian seated youth of a type found there in tombs with a terminal date of ca. 250 B.C. (see below, pp. 190, 186). If the blistered figurine was consigned to its burial at the same time as the others, it would share their date.

In Corinth, therefore, no matter when in the 3rd century their use began, plaster molds were employed considerably earlier than in Athens, where they are first noted at the end of the 2nd century B.C.[55] It is possible that Corinthian artisans used plaster molds earlier, since there is a tradition of their use by Lysistratos, the brother of Lysippos of Sikyon, as recorded by Pliny (*Naturalis Historia* 35.153).[56] On the other hand, one of the imported figurines from the sanctuary (**I82**) is blistered; since it must date before the destruction of Corinth in 146 B.C., it is evident that another, unidentified center also used plaster molds before Athens. Perhaps the evidence from Athens is as yet incomplete, and plaster molds will ultimately prove to have been used there earlier as well.

Although plaster molds are more fragile and easily worn than those of terracotta, they have several distinct advantages: the material is uniformly fine textured and hence takes a detailed impression quite well; access to a kiln is not needed because plaster does not require firing; plaster shrinks less than clay in drying, and therefore the loss of size in mold series is mitigated.

Unlike most terracotta-molded figurines, Corinthian plaster-molded figurines tended to be cast with all parts, including heads and bases, together in one mold; the backs are usually also molded but without full detail. This technique was not necessarily followed in all plaster-molded figurines; the imported **I82**, for example, shows surface blisters but was constructed in parts and assembled, the usual practice for figurines made from terracotta molds. The Corinthian plaster-molded figurines tend to be thin-walled, although the blistered but thick-walled head of a "priestess" (**H404**) is an exception. Plaster-molded figurines also tend to have somewhat blurred modeling, perhaps because plaster molds became worn more quickly than terracotta. They frequently have little or no retouch, perhaps because their thin walls were too fragile for much handling before firing. That is not to say that every blurred or unretouched figurine was plaster molded, since these conditions are found even in the 5th and 4th centuries B.C., for example, in the standing "korai," for which terracotta molds were found in the Potters' Quarter.[57] A Corinthian figurine with a combination of thin walls, blurring, and little or no retouch, however,

---

[53] On plaster molds, see *Tarsus* I, pp. 298–300; *Agora* VI, p. 3; *Kabirenheiligtum* V, p. 8; Bookidis and Fisher 1972, pp. 316–317, note 37; D. B. Thompson 1965, pp. 35–36; Mattusch 1990, pp. 138–140.

[54] MF-13902.
[55] D. B. Thompson 1965, pp. 35–36; for the date, see p. 44.
[56] Mattusch 1990, pp. 138–139.
[57] KH-49, KH-50, *Corinth* XV, i, p. 104, nos. 51, 52, pl. 37.

even in the absence of blisters, could possibly have been plaster molded, particularly if it was also constructed without piece molding. In such cases, obvious blisters may have been removed from the figurines, or the air bubbles in the molds were patched. If this is true, the number of potentially plaster-molded figurines increases greatly. Since this question must be pursued employing the whole of the Corinthian production, not only the figurines from the sanctuary, in this study only figurines with blistered surfaces are considered plaster molded. One thing is clear: the artisans who made these figurines needed fewer skills, since they did not have to piece the heads and limbs, retouch the surfaces, or model the backs by hand.

TOOLS

Corinthian figurines were often heavily reworked with added elements as well as tooling on both the original surfaces and the added portions of clay. Marks on the surface of the clay sometimes point to the use of particular tools. The principal tool, which appears to have had a small, sharp edge, probably was a metal blade. Its main purpose was to emphasize the molded drapery folds or mark new ones, and most especially to touch up the hair, which often was augmented with added clay. Unfortunately, the tooling was not always done carefully, and some otherwise well made figurines were spoiled by a slashing hand, although some of these deep cuts may have been filled in by the layers of white slip and paint. For examples of such tooling on drapery, see **H102**; on hair, see **C150**. A fine-toothed tool was used for paring; its marks are visible over much of the surface of the standing draped female **H65** and on the nape of the female head **C132**. A small, narrow tool with a flat edge like that of a chisel also may have been used to reduce and smooth the surface, as on the back of **H264**. A pointed tool, probably a very small wooden or metal punch, also was used, especially on facial features and sometimes also on the hair. For example, there are punch marks at the corners of the mouth and on the chin of **H183**; the hair and wreath of the child's head **H347** were delicately punched. There are three examples of C-shaped marks on hair, on **C95**–**C97**, which may have come from a small, broken or open-edged reed used in one workshop as a punch. As mentioned above, a tool like a spatula may have been used for smoothing the surface over joins.

BACKS AND VENTING

The backs of Corinthian figurines were more often handmade than moldmade, the latter being more common in the Hellenistic period. Moldmade backs were often less detailed than the fronts of figurines; therefore, a plain moldmade back distorted by handling could be mistaken for handmade. Similarly, the moldmade back of a head might be obscured by heavy retouch on the hair. Somewhat more detailed moldmade backs including elements of the costume or hair can be found, especially in two popular types, the Early Hellenistic votary carrying a piglet (e.g., **H1**), and the Middle Hellenistic "priestess" (e.g., **H395**). Handmade backs of the Classical and Hellenistic periods usually have some contour, although they are more often somewhat flattened than fully rounded. A few 5th-century B.C. figurines are essentially backless, for example, two peplos-figurines (**C5** and a mold relative of **C3** [see catalogue]) and the banqueter **C215**; these figurines terminate at the back in a narrow rim around the edges. This treatment is rather unusual in Corinth and may have been copied from Tarentine figurines (see p. 26). In nearly all cases, the join between front and back was well smoothed and hidden; some Roman pieces (e.g., **R19**) are exceptions. Occasionally, as in the poorly made articulated "doll" **C184**, the molding margin around the join was not even trimmed away.

Methods of venting are varied, even when figurines seem on other grounds to have been made in the same workshop. For example, the Early Classical peplos-figurines **C1**–**C6** and their mold relatives are very close in style, fabric, and technique and have mold relationships among them; they were probably made in the same workshop (Workshop D, page 345), yet there are three distinctly different arrangements for controlling the flow of heat. **C1** has no vent in back but is open underneath; presumably the base was attached after firing. The two completely backless examples have been mentioned above. Two others (**C2** and **C6**) show the remains of large, rectangular vents, which are the most common form of venting for 5th-century B.C. figurines from other centers.[58] The back of **C33**, which was made in the Potters' Quarter in the 4th century B.C., shows a small rectangular vent (Pl. 4). Round vents appear in the Early Hellenistic period (e.g., in the votary **H2**) or oval vents (e.g., in **H10**), but rectangular vents are cut at the same time (e.g., **H3**), although they are generally smaller than the Classical examples. The vent of the 4th-century B.C. female figurine **C36** is oval at one side, rectangular at the other. When there was no vent at the back, and the base was added before firing, thereby closing off air circulation from below, a vent was sometimes cut into the underside of the base, as in **H118** and **V39**. For solid or very thick-walled figurines, a "pencil-hole" or other opening was sometimes burrowed into the thickest part of the figurine (see **H287** and **H132**). Very small solid figurines, however, were not vented at all, for example, the mantled dancer **H165**.

THE EFFECT OF TECHNIQUE ON STYLE

What is defined as "style" in a figurine is the outcome not only of the selection and modification of the type but also of the artisan's technique, learned from his predecessors and qualified by the competence of his hands, as well as by the plasticity of the material. Thus, the accidental or deliberate manipulation of the figurines when they were removed from the molds, still in the vulnerable leather-hard condition, resulted in some of the features that contributed to coroplastic style. For example, the eyes of some 4th-century B.C. heads tend to slant downward at the outer corners; this could have happened when the coroplast grasped the still pliable clay at the temples to withdraw the head from the mold. Or, when the artisan added the back mold to the front or attached clay for a handmade back, the naturally downward strokes of his tools to smooth the join could have drawn the eyes downward at the outer corners. Subsequent generations derived from such a figurine would have preserved this feature. Such eyes are, in fact, found especially in the much repeated heads made in the Potters' Quarter workshops (e.g., **C163**) and are known also in molds found in the Potters' Quarter.[59]

The degree to which manipulation and additions could change the style of a figurine, and consequently influence our perception of its date, is well illustrated by the two peplos-figurines **C42** and **C43**. A large oval scar on the left hip and thigh marks the mechanical relationship without room for doubt, but the proportions and costume were altered markedly. As a result, the larger of the two, which on mechanical grounds should be earlier, shows more elongated proportions and narrower shoulders, which on purely stylistic grounds might make it seem later. Either manipulation before firing has stretched the figure and caused it to lose width in the shoulders, or the addition of mantle folds around the shoulders of the smaller piece has made them seem wider. Another explanation is that we are dealing with parallel mold series with completely different histories, which both preserve the scar from a flawed archetype.

Another effect of technique on what we perceive as style may have been caused by the common practice of joining heads to torsos by inserting the necks into openings between the shoulders and then smoothing the transition by paring, adding clay if necessary. The result could be a disproportionately wide, spreading neck, as in **C59**. It is also possible that shrinkage during drying, which was greater in the width than in the height of a figurine,[60] resulted in narrower proportions from one generation to the next and hence in an appearance of increasing slenderness.

When new types were developed, earlier features could be inadvertently incorporated into them through the reuse of surviving workshop materials. For example, an Early Hellenistic type

---

[58] E.g., in London, Higgins 1986, p. 102, fig. 117 right.

[59] E.g., KH-36, *Corinth* XV, i, p. 101, no. 38, pl. 35.

[60] D. B. Thompson 1963a, p. 304.

that was new in the later 4th century B.C., the votary **H1**, shows a facial type with a characteristic profile, in which the forehead slopes back from an arched nose and the chin recedes (Pl. 24). While the head type as a whole is convincingly Hellenistic, nevertheless it recalls similar profiles in Archaic heads,[61] suggesting that when the archetype for the new head was constructed, the artisan made use of an earlier archetype, reworking an older design rather than starting completely from scratch.

THE DEFINITION OF QUALITY IN FIGURINES

What constitutes a well-made figurine? Ideally, the components are a well-designed archetype, carefully prepared and well-fired clay, and skillful assembly, retouch, and painting. In reality, however, among the Corinthian figurines there is no particular formula for quality. The industry was large, and apart from the long-lived workshops of the Potters' Quarter, it was not really well controlled. That is, there appear to have been numerous short-lived workshops taking economic advantage of periodic festivals at which they could sell votives.[62] Consequently, although taken as a whole, the general level of quality is high, there is much inconsistency. Larger figurines are likely to have been relatively expensive, but poor workmanship might accompany large size, as in **H196** and **H197**. Excellent fabric might be combined with clumsy retouch, as in the head **H223**. A figurine might be smoothly polished on the surface but at the same time might be thick-walled and carelessly finished inside, as in the dancer **H153**. A well-designed and otherwise decently made figurine might have a back mold belonging to a different type, as in the votary **H1**.

On the whole, the areas of highest quality in the Corinthian industry, from the artisanal point of view, were in archetype design and clay preparation; the poor fabrics of the 3rd century B.C. (see p. 12) stand out as unusual and probably resulted from special circumstances. Retouch was often clumsy and was the weakest aspect of workmanship, although there are a few examples of exceptionally fine retouch. Little paint is preserved, but the use of gilding, enamel-like ivory and subtle pink shades for flesh, and a distinctive bright blue paint (see pp. 13–14) show interest and professionalism in that area of coroplasty. Perhaps panel painters contributed some expertise here. In spite of frequent lapses in one respect or another, Corinthian figurines have earned comparison with the best sculpture in quality;[63] this is true particularly of some of the sanctuary figurines of the Archaic period and the 4th century B.C.

THE CORINTHIAN COROPLASTIC INDUSTRY AS A WHOLE

A thumbnail sketch of the history of the coroplastic industry in Corinth may help to explain the complexities of the local production. The following paragraphs summarize some of the conclusions of an article now in press.[64] The earliest Archaic production documented so far within the city of Corinth dates to the last quarter of the 7th century B.C., when the workshops of the Potters' Quarter added figurines to their output of pottery and terracotta reliefs. There is so far no physical proof in the form of molds or parallel figurine types that the earlier-7th-century Dedalic figurines found at Perachora and elsewhere in the region were actually made in Corinth, although they appear to have been made of Corinthian clay (i.e., clay that is visually identical to that used later in Corinth). The large quantities of widely exported lingering Archaic stock types for which the Potters' Quarter is best known (see p. 23, note 1) were not made before the early 5th century B.C. Although the Potters' Quarter workshops continued to turn out figurines in a generally conservative style until they ceased production in or near the 320s B.C., other workshops, often staffed by better artisans, concurrently manufactured figurines in a more forward-looking

[61] E.g., Wallenstein 1971, p. 130, no. V/A3, pl. 13:3; MF-12016 from the sanctuary, publication forthcoming.

[62] Merker, forthcoming.

[63] Rolley 1986, p. 100; on quality in figurines, see *Thasos* XVII, pp. 42–43.

[64] Merker, forthcoming.

style. The precise locations of these workshops are not known, but the urban organization of Corinth, which consisted of scattered settlements located around water sources and roads with agricultural fields between them (see p. 31), encouraged a dispersed industrial pattern. A lack of physical connection between workshops may have caused, at least in part, the diversity of types and styles within the city.

Relatively few figurines have been found in graves in Corinth. Their principal function apparently was votive, and just as the pattern of production was dispersed, distribution also may have been; figurines may not have been sold at a central market, but instead appropriate types may have been sold at the numerous shrines scattered through the city. The dependence of the industry upon cultic use, and consequently on the calendric rhythm of those festivals that used figurines, may explain why, except for the Potter's Quarter, which was in part supported by its exports, workshops seem to have been short lived. That is, one finds small related groupings of figurines, as if coroplasty were a part-time pursuit, undertaken when an opportunity approached for the sale of figurines. Perhaps there were few or no fully "professional" coroplasts, and potters or other artisans conversant with the handling and firing of clay undertook coroplasty when it was economically feasible. The possibility that the craft depended upon model making for small bronzes to provide archetypes for the figurines is discussed above (p. 14).

USING THE CATALOGUE OF FIGURINES

Because the total of catalogue listings of figurines in this volume approaches 900 items, certain conventions have been adopted to streamline the entries. Catalogue numbers preceded by the letter "C" are Classical or Classical survivals; "H" are Hellenistic or Hellenistic survivals; "V" are Varia; "I" are imports; "R" are Roman. The catalogue entries are confined to technical information and lists of closely related figurines. Discussions of style, iconography, and chronology may be found through the page references at the close of each catalogue entry. Each catalogue entry provides the following information:

Lot numbers: To avoid repetition, the context date of the lot is not given in each catalogue entry but in the cumulative list on pages 353–368.

Size numbers: To help the reader visualize the original size of a fragmentary figurine, a range of five numbered sizes has been provided, as described on pages 9–10. Two numbers separated by a dash indicate that the approximate height of the original figurine overlaps two size ranges. The size range of a seated figurine is determined as if it were standing. Size ranges are not provided for miscellaneous types, such as plaques.

Fabric numbers: Numbered fabrics are described on pages 11–12. Fabrics are fully described in the catalogue only if they do not fall within any of the numbered categories. When mold siblings, earlier or later generations, or similar figurines, are listed in a catalogue entry, a fabric number is given only if the fabric differs from that of the catalogued figurine.

Colors: For descriptions of colors and their Munsell and C.E.C. equivalents, see pages 12–13. When two colors are named, the predominant color is mentioned first; for example, a figurine that is "orange-buff to orange" shows orange-buff over a larger area of the surface than orange. Reference is made to chart numbers only when the color of a figurine does not quite match any of the standard descriptions.

Moldmade and handmade: Figurines are moldmade, unless otherwise stated.

Hollow and solid: Heads and torsos preserved separately are described as hollow or solid. When a figurine preserves both the head and torso, it may be impossible to determine whether the head is solid or hollow, if a solid neck obscures the view of the interior. If the head was molded separately, it is likely that it is solid or nearly so, even if the torso is hollow, since this technique was commonly employed. Isolated heads with solid necks are assumed to be solid if they are heavy.

Thickness of walls: Walls are described as thin or thick only if they depart significantly from the average, as described under fabrics on pages 11–12.

Treatment of backs: Backs of figurines are described as rounded (fully contoured), flat (perfectly flat), or flattened (diminished in depth but with contours indicated). Backs have few or no details, unless otherwise specified. If venting is not mentioned, no information is preserved.

Treatment of undersurfaces: Hollow figurines are open underneath, unless otherwise described.

Additions: Features added to the figurine after it was removed from the mold, such as drapery, jewelry, and hair, are listed. Since heads and extended arms were customarily made separately and attached to the torsos, they are not included among the additions unless the attachment is in some way unusual. When the head and torso were rendered in the same mold, it is so stated. The description "all parts rendered in same mold" means that the mold includes all anatomical features, as well as the base and attributes.

Tooling: When the surfaces of figurines are worn, it is not always clear whether details were molded or were cut into the unfired clay after removal from the mold. For each figurine, the areas are listed in which tooling is fairly obvious.

Figurine descriptions: Figurines are frontal in pose, unless otherwise described. The words right and left refer to the figurine's proper right and left, unless viewer's directions are specifically indicated. When the directions are seen from the viewer's perspective, it is so stated. In descriptions of faces, the predominant shape is given first; for example, a face that is "oval to round" is more oval than round in shape. The description "dull impression" refers to figurines in which the outlines of facial features, drapery, and attributes are blurred. The cause of the blurring is not specified, since such figurines could have been made from later generation molds that were not retouched or from molds that were worn from use, or they could themselves have been worn down during burial. For drapery descriptions, the terminology in Ridgway 1981a, pp. xvii–xix, is employed.

Mold siblings and other related figurines: At the end of each catalogue description, figurines are listed that are either mechanically related or similar in type. Many of these are too poorly preserved to warrant more extensive treatment or illustration. Those from the Demeter sanctuary are referred to by Corinth Archaeological Museum inventory numbers if they were inventoried; if they were not inventoried, the number of the associated pottery lot is provided. If the fabric differs from that of the catalogued figurine, a fabric number is provided. Figurines found elsewhere in Corinth are given their source if they were found in a clearly definable site, such as the South Stoa. The term "Corinth collection" is used for figurines from more scattered locations. Such lists are omitted for the very prevalent articulated "dolls"; in this case, only the total quantity found has been provided (p. 3).

In light of the problems encountered in determining the mold relationships of Corinthian figurines (see pp. 4, 15), some caution has been exercised in listing relatives. "Probable" mold siblings are the most likely candidates, while "possible" siblings are less certain. Similarly, generations may be referred to as "earlier" or "later," rather than numbered (e.g., first generation, second generation). When figurines are listed merely as "mechanically related," the nature of the relationship cannot be determined satisfactorily. Figurines that are "similar in type" are probably not mechanical relatives.

Figurines in museum collections: Apart from Corinthian exports that were found in other excavations and are preserved in museums, a good many of the Corinthian figurines in collections were looted from tombs in the vicinity of Corinth during the 19th century. Such figurines, without archaeological context, are of limited value for the purposes of this study. Therefore, figurines

from museums other than the Corinth Archaeological Museum are recorded only if they complete
or help to clarify the composition of a poorly preserved type, provide chronological information,
or demonstrate noteworthy variations. Otherwise, no attempt has been made to collect parallels
in museums for the sake of collecting them.

Abbreviations used in the catalogue:
    diam. = diameter
    H. = height
    L. = length
    Max.P.Dim. = maximum preserved dimension
    P.H. = preserved height
    P.L. = preserved length

CROSS-REFERENCES

For the convenience of the reader, cross-references are sometimes provided in the text to the
principal discussion of a given subject. For a more complete listing of relevant page references,
the general index should be consulted.

II

CLASSICAL FIGURINES AND THEIR SURVIVALS

The Corinthian coroplastic production of the 5th century B.C. was a mixture of old and new elements. One of the older elements consisted of figurines of lingering Archaic style that were newly created in the early 5th century B.C. but without any concession to new ideas. These types, including standing "korai," seated goddesses, spoon-based protomes, chitoniskos "dolls," and sphinx, rooster, and Gorgon plaques, were made in the Potters' Quarter and were popular locally as well as widely exported.[1] These figurines, which may have continued in production even into the 4th century B.C., were produced beside other types that really were of Archaic origin but continued to be turned out in the workshops as before, retaining their essential form. Handmade animals and horse-riders especially fall into this category.

Beside these two kinds of survivals, entirely new types were created, beginning in the earlier part of the 5th century B.C.; a good example is the peplos-figurine **C1**, which includes new stylistic features also found in Severe-style sculpture. In addition to these altogether new creations, some types inherited from the Archaic period were partially updated in the new, Classical style. For example, the seated goddess type reconstructed from the fragments **C71**–**C73** would be thought Archaic but for the Classical face. Thus the coroplastic workshops of the 5th and early 4th centuries B.C. took three different, although concurrent approaches: maintaining or imitating earlier types or style; introducing entirely new ideas; and adapting old types to fit new conceptions of style.

As time went on, by the second quarter or, at the very latest, the middle of the 4th century B.C., further changes are apparent, but once again, figurines of new types and style do not replace but are produced concurrently with those retaining the Classical forms. This chapter, therefore, deals with part of the complex production of the 5th and 4th centuries B.C. by treating Classical figurines together with their survivals into the Early Hellenistic period. The innovations of the 4th century B.C. form a continuum with what follows and are therefore treated in the next chapter as Early Hellenistic figurines, although some are earlier than the conventional beginning of the Hellenistic period ca. 330 B.C. If it seems strange that Archaic, Classical, and Early Hellenistic styles overlap so thoroughly during the 4th century B.C., the causes of this phenomenon should be sought in the votive character of the material, which tended to prolong the use of types once they were established in the ritual, and also in the character of the Corinthian coroplastic industry as a whole, which was home to workshops varying widely in skills and sources of inspiration.[2]

Although the workshops of the Potters' Quarter were still active through the 5th century B.C. and well into the 4th, other workshops came into existence that infused new life into the Corinthian coroplastic tradition through the greater originality and skill of their artisans.[3] In some cases, technical similarities among figurines point to workshop connections and help to define the

---

[1] Examples of these types found in the Acrocorinth sanctuary will be published in a forthcoming fascicle of *Corinth* XVIII. For previously published examples of the types, see *Corinth* XV, ii, pp. 84–94, pls. 14–17 (standing "korai"); pp. 94–97, pl. 17 (seated goddesses); pp. 97–101, pls. 18, 19 (spoon-based protomes); pp. 154–163, pl. 33 (plaques); *Corinth* XII, p. 33, no. 130, pl. 9 (chitoniskos "doll").

[2] On the industry as a whole, see Merker, forthcoming, and pp. 19–20.

[3] On the existence of sites in Corinth, apart from the Potters' Quarter, in which figurines could have been made, see Davidson 1942, p. 110; *Corinth* XII, pp. 17, 19–22 (on finds of try pieces, wasters, and molds); Stroud 1965, p. 17; Benson 1984.

interests and skills of different groups of artisans. The workshop connections mentioned as the discussion progresses are summarized on pages 344–346.

STANDING DRAPED FEMALE FIGURINES
(C1–C44)

PEPLOS-FIGURINES

As a general type, standing peplos-figurines are notable among the figurines from the Acrocorinth sanctuary for their quantity, longevity, and the numerous variations in the arrangement of the peplos and the style of drapery. Under this heading, figurines with four different peplos arrangements are discussed: (1) with a short overfold; (2) with a long overfold, unbelted; (3) with a long overfold, belted (the so-called peplos of Athena); (4) with a kolpos and overfold. There are variants within all these groups, and each apparently was derived from a different archetype, probably in a different workshop. The history of these groups is very complex and full of gaps, but it would appear that the figurines reflect developments in stone sculpture and small bronzes.

    1. *Peplos-figurines with short overfold* (**C1–C12**).   A break with Archaic tradition is first seen in moldmade peplos-figurines of Early Classical style, which probably represent female votaries (**C1–C6**). Some carry a piglet, a bird, or both, or a ball; all are larger figurines or statuettes (size range 3 or 4). Although these figurines continue in type the long Corinthian Archaic tradition of wholly or partially handmade standing female figurines wearing the peplos, stylistically and technically they stand at the beginning of another long tradition of moldmade figurines lasting into the Early Hellenistic period.

    The departure from tradition is found not only in style but also in subject, since the Corinthian coroplasts of the Archaic period tended to emphasize representations of deities rather than worshipers, while their Classical descendants seem to have turned in part to mortal subjects. The difficulty in distinguishing god from mortal is well known,[4] particularly in the absence of characteristic attributes, costumes, or headdresses. Moreover, it is not always clear whether an object in the hand, such as a bird or piglet, is a divine attribute, a votary's gift about to be offered, or a gift already received by the deity. Similarities of costume and pose among deities, votaries, and cult attendants confuse the issue, suggesting a purposeful blurring of the boundaries between them, perhaps to establish a measure of identity between deities and their worshipers. A mortal may even impersonate a deity in cult ritual.[5] One type new to this period, however, the hydriaphoros, must represent a votary, since the carrying of water was considered a lowly task, unlikely to be assigned to a goddess,[6] and the carrying of water by votaries in religious processions is well documented.[7] Perhaps hydriaphoroi were particularly suitable to this sanctuary because the most copious source of fresh water in the vicinity lies at the fountain of Hadji Mustafa, ca. 200–300 m below the sanctuary.[8] Moreover, there is a notable scarcity among the Classical figurines of heads wearing the polos, which was the typical headdress of the Corinthian Archaic standing and seated goddesses;[9] only the more traditional seated goddesses, such as **C71**, still wear the polos.[10] Without incontrovertible signs of divinity, the Classical standing peplos-figurines

---

[4] On this subject, see Zuntz 1971, pp. 91–97, 272; Connelly 1988, pp. 21–22; *Thasos* XVII, pp. 472–480.

[5] *Troy*, p. 90, citing the worship at Ephesos of a mortal costumed as Artemis.

[6] See Euripides, *Electra*, lines 54–76; Electra's peasant husband takes on the task of carrying water for her because of her royal birth. On the usually low social status of water carriers in vase painting, see Hannestad 1984, with

bibliography; during festivals this social distinction seems to have been dropped.

[7] Diehl 1964, pp. 171–173.

[8] *Corinth* XVIII, iii, pp. 14–15.

[9] On the polos, see *Morgantina*, pp. 81–82, with bibliography.

[10] The head with polos **C104** could have belonged to a standing figurine, but it is a copy of an Attic type rather than a local creation (see p. 48).

are best considered votaries, unless they share distinctive drapery arrangements with sculptures known to represent goddesses.

The drapery style of this small group is generally consistent with Peloponnesian monumental sculpture of the Severe period, but the typical, geometrically constructed peplos with overfold to the waist is worn by figurines in an essentially Archaic pose, with arms pressed closely against the torso and one leg stepping forward rigidly, with stiff knee, as in **C1**. The plastic, rather doughy rendering of the folds and the vertical pleats framing the overfold, dipping in zigzags diagonally to the hips at either side, invite comparison with, for example, the Athena of the Apples of the Hesperides metope from the Temple of Zeus at Olympia.[11] In the overall design of both, the rectangular shapes of the peplos hide the rounded forms of the feminine figure, and plasticity is stressed over detail. In both, the almost vertical skirt folds, accented with vertical grooves especially on the thigh, are comparable, as are the broad shoulders, their outlines softened and rounded by folds appearing from behind. Also similar is the use of bunches of folds to offset the smooth surfaces. The drapery is simpler in the figurines, however, in that the overfold does not have catenaries between the breasts or long omega folds depending from them. The kolpos, which may or may not appear in the sculpture, usually was omitted by the coroplasts. A more Archaic feature is the flat, boat-shaped neckline, which does not show the pleat of loose cloth on the chest that appears in the Olympia sculpture; a better comparison for this feature is the neckline of the so-called Peplos Kore from the Athenian Akropolis, dated ca. 530 B.C.[12] The figurines also may clutch offerings to the chest in the Archaic manner. A similar fusion of Archaic and Classical style can be seen in the rider figurine **C186**; the horizontally grooved hair of this piece is stylistically earlier than its already 5th-century B.C. drapery.

A reasonable stylistic date for the archetypes of this figurine group would be not later than the second quarter of the 5th century B.C. and possibly earlier. Although three of the group (**C1**, **C4**, **C5**) are associated with Archaic to 5th-century B.C. pottery lots, none can be dated more closely through context. Since no members of this group were found in the Potters' Quarter excavations, they were probably made elsewhere in the city. There is enough stylistic and technical coherence among **C1–C6** to suggest that they were made in the same workshop (Workshop D, p. 345). Although other mechanically connected fragments are noted in the catalogue, there is no evidence that any of these figurines gave rise to an extended mold series; in fact, it is not possible to identify even a second generation among the preserved figurines, implying that this workshop either was short-lived or turned to other work. Another possible member of this workshop group is the horse-rider **C186**.

None of the peplos-figurines of this group preserves the head, but the absence of locks of hair on the shoulders of **C1** indicates that the hair was short or bound high on the head. Evidence for the head type may be found in a probably Corinthian figurine from the cave at Pitsa, which wears a similar peplos with plastically rendered folds, although with a kolpos.[13] The mouth and nose were badly distorted in molding, but the head is similar, in its long, narrow shape and large features, to the heads of Early Classical hydriaphoroi discussed below (e.g., **C55**) and to the related heads without clear traces of a hydria or other object, which could have belonged to simple peplos-figurines. The hair of the figurine from Pitsa is arranged in thick strands rolled back from the forehead over a fillet, as in **C61**, which must be somewhat later, however, on the basis of its more developed features. Among the isolated female heads of the period, **C102** also could have belonged to a peplos-figurine.

[11] Conveniently, Ashmole and Yalouris 1967, fig. 188.
[12] Richter 1968, p. 72, no. 113, fig. 351.
[13] *EAA* VI, 1965, p. 205, fig. 227, s.v. *Pitsa* (A. K. Orlandos).

Figurines from the Argolid[14] and Sicily[15] are comparable to this Corinthian group in proportions, pose, and drapery style; the Argive import **I1** is a good example. A similar figurine was found at Lindos.[16] A step further away are the Athenian standing peplos-figurines, which are similar to the Corinthian in the peplos arrangement but seem stylistically later, with more slender proportions, lighter modeling, and a freer leg position.[17] The Athenian type seems to have been exported widely and influenced production elsewhere, for example, Boeotia,[18] but differences in style suggest that the Athenian peplos-figurines and their imitations formed a group separate from the Sicilian and Peloponnesian figurines.[19] It is possible that the distinctive style of the latter was influenced by artisans who had worked at Olympia, perhaps participating in the creation of small-scale clay models for the temple sculptures.[20] A study of the Olympia Master suggests that northeast Peloponnesian artisans took part in the Olympia project.[21]

There are other connections with West Greek figurines apart from style. A probable technical influence can be found in the backless construction of **C5** and a mold relative of **C3** (see catalogue). This technique is found also among the banqueters (**C215**) and is characteristic of Tarentine figurines.[22] In this period, however, Corinthian artisans more commonly made backs with a large rectangular vent, as in **C2**, or without a vent but open underneath, as in **C1**. The piglet carrier provides a typological connection with the West, since the female figurine type holding a piglet, representing either a votary or Persephone, was a Late Archaic Sicilian invention.[23] While most of the Sicilian examples hold the piglet in both hands across the torso, some carry it at the side, grasping the back legs. A peplos-figurine from Syracuse holds the animal diagonally across the thigh, as in **C1**.[24] The earliest Sicilian pig-carrying types, wearing chiton and mantle rather than the peplos, seem not to have affected Corinthian production, the influence first appearing in the Severe period, as is the case also with Tarentine influence on the banqueter type (see p. 66).

In dealing with Early Classical peplos-figurines, the large body of bronze caryatid mirror stands and statuettes should be mentioned;[25] a connection with this class of mirrors may be proposed for the lingering Archaic standing "korai" as well. The preparation of a wax working model, cast from master molds taken from an original "artist's model," probably made of clay, was a necessary preliminary step in the manufacture of bronzes by the indirect casting method.[26] The models for such bronzes could have been made by the same artisans who prepared archetypes for coroplasts, or perhaps metalworkers and coroplasts shared the very same workshop materials. The connection between terracotta and bronze manufacture has long been recognized. For

[14] Cf. *Tiryns* I, pp. 74–75, no. 80, pl. IX:7; p. 81, no. 128, pl. XII:3 (with freer pose); ibid., p. 80, no. 122, pl. XII:4, is similar to **C2** in the rather lumpy zigzag folds and recut skirt folds. Poulsen 1937, pp. 7–34, discusses Argive peplos-figurines in the context of northeast Peloponnesian work.

[15] Gabrici 1927, esp. col. 291, pl. LXXIV:3. More recently, *Morgantina*, pp. 11–12, with bibliography; Sguaitamatti 1984, pp. 94–95, pl. 32, figs. 112, 113.

[16] *Lindos* I, col. 554, no. 2290, pl. 106; photograph in Mendel 1908, p. 33, no. 352, pl. II:12. This figurine is smaller and poorer, with empty hand at the breast and an alabastron or oinochoe in the hand at the side.

[17] E.g., *British Museum* I, pp. 179–180, nos. 669, 673, 674, pl. 88; Poulsen 1937, pp. 52–56.

[18] In London, Higgins 1986, pp. 99–102, esp. figs. 113, 117.

[19] Working before the Demeter sanctuary figurines were available, Bell also used the Olympia sculpture for stylistic comparisons with Sicilian work, *Morgantina*, p. 12.

[20] On the subject of models, see Pliny, *Naturalis Historia* 35.155–156; Ridgway 1970, pp. 19–20, with bibliography on pp. 27–28; Pollitt 1974, pp. 204–215, 272–293; Bookidis 1988; Stewart 1977, p. 82; Stewart 1979, pp. 103–104.

[21] Dörig 1987, p. 16.

[22] E.g., Herdejürgen 1971, p. 40, no. 12, pl. 7 (480/470 B.C.); p. 44, no. 23, pl. 7 (440 B.C.); *British Museum* I, p. 336.

[23] The material has been collected in Sguaitamatti 1984.

[24] *Morgantina*, p. 12, pl. 144, fig. 7; this diagonal position is found among other Sicilian piglet carriers as well, e.g., Sguaitamatti 1984, pp. 94–95, note 3, pl. 32, figs. 112, 113. For a selection of Archaic and Classical Sicilian figurines carrying piglets in different poses, see Griffo and von Matt 1968, p. 136, fig. 98.

[25] On the mirror caryatids, see Keene Congdon 1981; Tölle-Kastenbein 1980.

[26] For descriptions of the indirect casting method, see Mattusch 1988, pp. 19–22; Mattusch 1996, pp. 10–16; Haynes 1992, pp. 27–29, 57–59 on models; for the casting of mirror caryatids, see Keene Congdon 1981, summary on p. 29, fig. 5.

example, Gjødesen points to an interesting correspondence between a South Italian figurine and a caryatid mirror and finds it "natural … that artists employed in terracotta workshops would have been designing for foundries as well."[27] Alternatively, mirror caryatids themselves could have served as the sources for coroplasts' molds, or the foundries could have used terracotta figurines for the same purpose.[28] In whatever way the relationship between the two media was maintained, it is likely to have been very close.

Caryatid mirrors are known to have been made in Corinth, although only a few of the characteristic animal attachments have been found in excavations in Corinth itself.[29] The problems in the attribution of bronzes and the web of conflicting attributions are nearly impenetrable, but a few connections of Early Classical Corinthian figurines with bronzes can be suggested. The mirror caryatids are usually smaller in scale, freer in movement, more slender in proportions, and more elegant in general appearance than the figurines. One may cite, however, a caryatid in Geneva which, although freer in pose and somewhat later in date, has a doughy plasticity in the folds recalling the figurines, as well as a narrow, large-featured face comparable to the common Early Classical Corinthian type discussed below (pp. 39–40).[30] It would not be difficult to imagine a shared inspiration in this case. Alternatively, molds for figurines could have been taken mechanically from bronzes. If any figurine from the Demeter sanctuary was copied from a mirror caryatid or similar bronze figure in this way, the best candidate would be **C9**. This piece is of a suitable scale, pose, and drapery style, and the clumsily added arm and mitten-shaped hand, different in position from the arms of all the other peplos-figurines, could be an attempted copy of a mirror caryatid's bent arm, although the motif of the hand pulling aside the skirt has not been carried through. A similar mitten-shaped hand in this pose, with the pulled skirt folds barely rendered, can be found in a very small bronze figure, thought to be of Peloponnesian origin, in Providence.[31] The thick-walled construction of **C9** is very different from the earliest group of peplos-figurines discussed above, and its freer pose and more fluid drapery are of more advanced stylistic date, perhaps the middle to third quarter of the 5th century B.C. It may be of interest in this regard to mention a fragmentary mold found in the Tile Works in Corinth, showing the lower part of a 5th-century B.C. peplos-figurine; as far as it is preserved, this piece matches mirror caryatids in type and scale and could have been taken from a bronze of this kind.[32]

The fragmentary figurines **C7** and **C8**, taken together, represent the upper and lower parts of a more developed type of peplos-figurine with short overfold. The rigid horizontal line of the hem at the waist remains, but the zigzag folds down the open side of the peplos are more fluid, ending in a characteristic pointed fold at the thigh; clusters of narrow skirt folds frame both legs, and the hem trails somewhat. The same fold pattern is found in a complete figurine of unknown provenience in Paris,[33] which appears to have a mechanical relationship with **C7** and **C8** and may well be Corinthian; it has been adapted to carry fruit or flowers in the lifted overfold. The head of the figurine in Paris also is related in facial type to a Corinthian head from the sanctuary (**C149**). Several other figurines in collections, furnished with different accessories,

---

[27] Gjødesen 1970, pp. 156–157. On connections between terracotta and bronze, see also D. B. Thompson 1963; D. B. Thompson 1966, pp. 54–55; D. B. Thompson 1982, p. 161; *Coroplast's Art*, pp. 15, 31–36; Pemberton 1981.

[28] Keene Congdon 1981, p. 22; p. 69 on comparisons with figurines.

[29] *Corinth* XII, p. 66, nos. 500–502, pl. 48; Morgan 1953, p. 139, pl. 46:d.

[30] Keene Congdon 1981, pp. 182–183, no. 73, pls. 68, 69. The piece is attributed by Keene Congdon to an "Argo-Corinthian" group, pp. 70–72, but to an Attic group by Tölle-Kastenbein 1980, p. 29, no. 3f, pls. 16:b, 17:c. One might also mention a subsequently published bronze statuette of reported

Corinthian provenience: Leipen et al. 1984, p. 40, no. 37; the statuette has a close parallel from Tegea and should be Peloponnesian.

[31] Mitten 1975, pp. 53–55, no. 16.

[32] MF-8733, publication forthcoming by the author. The stance and fold pattern of the mold, as far as it is preserved, recall Keene Congdon 1981, pp. 186–187, no. 77, pl. 73, assigned to an "Argo-Corinthian" group. Another mold from the Tile Works definitely was taken from a bronze, in this case a vessel attachment: Pemberton 1981, p. 106, no. 6.

[33] *Louvre* I, p. 119, no. C228, pl. LXXXVI. Cf. Winter, *Typen* I, p. 78, no. 2, a related Corinthian type.

may also have a workshop connection with **C7** and **C8**.[34] The fragmentary votary with flowers **H28** is similar in scale and workmanship to **C7** and **C8**, and could have been made in the same workshop, but is discussed below (pp. 124–125) with Early Hellenistic votary figurines on account of the offerings it carries; too little of this figurine is preserved to determine its type. Another fragment similar in type to this group, in lot 6508, seems to have raised the right arm high and therefore may have been used as a hydriaphoros. Although the missing right arm of **C7** originally was raised, the angle does not seem to be sharp enough for a hydriaphoros, and the original pose remains uncertain; perhaps the hand touched the shoulder. The molding of the legs as if nude, framed by clusters of folds, suggests that **C8** should be dated stylistically not earlier than the late 5th century B.C., based on developments in sculpture. This manner of revealing both legs is found also in the peplos-figurine type with a long overfold (e.g., **C16**), discussed below. It is likely that **C7** and **C8** actually were made in the 4th century B.C. A fragment mechanically related to **C8** (see catalogue) was found in the construction fill of the Trapezoidal Building, the terminal date of which is the beginning of the 3rd century B.C.

The most debased and smallest (size range 2) versions of the peplos-figurine type with short overfold are **C10–C12**; these figurines probably date to the 4th century B.C. and can be attributed to a Potters' Quarter workshop on the basis of the fabric, concave back, and small plaque base, in which respects they are very like the lingering Archaic standing "korai" made there.[35] **C10** can be connected in pose and costume, and in the use of broken catenaries to show folds across the center of the overfold, with a small bronze figure in Boston of reported Corinthian provenience, showing a girl holding a bowl of cakes and fruit.[36] **C10** also can be compared to terracotta peplos-figurines from Tiryns, which are similar in scale, the form of the base, and the shape of the overfold hem.[37] **C12** is from the construction fill of the Trapezoidal Building, which terminates at the beginning of the 3rd century B.C., as are two mold siblings of **C11** (see catalogue). The elongated proportions and sloping shoulders of **C12** suggest that this figurine stands near the end of the series. The only example with its head preserved (**C11**) shows a face recalling, in its rounded shape, delicate features, and gentle expression, the faces of later 5th-century B.C. Attic sculpture.[38] The narrow chin and relatively broad forehead of **C11**, however, bring one back again to the triangular faces of the lingering Archaic "korai" made at the Potters' Quarter.

Although these latest members of the group are typologically similar to the earlier **C1**, a mechanical relationship between the two cannot be traced. The archaeological record may be incomplete, but it is more likely that a type created by artisans outside the Potters' Quarter was adopted only very slowly, and in a derivative form, by the more conservative workshops within the Potters' Quarter. A similar phenomenon can be seen in the following peplos-figurine group as well. The rather backward nature of this segment of the Corinthian coroplastic industry has already been noted.[39]

---

[34] Two very similar to one another, with fruit in a bowl rather than the lifted overfold, and furnished with wings as Nikai: Bomford Collection, pp. 44–45, no. 117 (= Nicholson 1968, p. 20, no. 52, pl. 36), and Hutton 1899, cols. 31–32, fig. 4 (= Winter, *Typen* II, p. 179, no. 2, in Athens, from Eretria). Another, not winged, with a bowl of fruit: von Stackelberg 1837, pl. LXIII right (= Winter, *Typen* I, p. 78, no. 4). These figurines have been included in the "Maying Group" by Nicholls 1995, p. 425, and assigned to the "Corinthian periphery." The discovery of **C7** and **C8** in Corinth, as well as several fragmentary mold siblings (see catalogue), should make it possible to assign some members of this group to Corinth itself. Only those figurines mentioned here seem to me to be

candidates for Corinthian manufacture. Others on Nicholls' list I would not associate closely, because the head type is not characteristic of Corinth or the drapery arrangement is significantly different. Since in these cases the impressions seem rather dull, the figurines may be adaptations made elsewhere using torso molds derived from the original group.

[35] Cf., e.g., *Corinth* XV, ii, pp. 84–94, pls. 14–17.

[36] Comstock and Vermeule 1971, pp. 54–55, no. 55.

[37] E.g., *Tiryns* I, p. 75, no. 89, pl. IX:3, 4.

[38] Cf. the faces on the relief of Xenokrateia in Athens, Hausmann 1960, pp. 63–64, fig. 33; Mitropoulou 1977, pp. 43–45, no. 65, fig. 103.

[39] Nicholls 1958, p. 173.

In the later 5th and 4th centuries B.C., several distinct peplos-figurine types were being produced at the same time as these survivals of the Early Classical type with short overfold. With their differing drapery arrangements, they must have had entirely different sources, and differences in handling suggest separate workshops as well. The introduction of each new type does not seem to have displaced existing types, since each one was exploited until it virtually wore itself out.

2. *Peplos-figurines with long overfold, unbelted* (**C13–C23**). The stylistically earliest version of this type is **C13**, which still has a distinctly Archaic flavor and seems to be an updated version of lingering Archaic "kore" figurines that carry flowers.[40] Yet in spite of the Archaic reminiscence in pose, the neckline folds of the peplos plunge into sharp V-shape, like the garments of the peplophoroi of the east frieze of the Parthenon.[41] A transition to a more fully Classical treatment can be found in two statuette fragments of excellent quality (**C14** and **C15**), probably dating in style to the middle to third quarter of the 5th century. They are in size range 4–5, and as often happens, the largest and best-made pieces are the most poorly preserved and hence the least comprehensible. The fabric of **C14** shows the addition of the gray, red, and white inclusions characteristic of Corinthian "tile fabric," which also was used for terracotta sculpture.[42] Special care seems to have been taken in the preparation of this piece, as it is also fired harder than usual. The preserved folds suggest that the overfold hem was drawn upward towards the left side; this foreshadows a motif seen later in piglet carriers of the Early Hellenistic period (see **H1**). In another possible reconstruction of the pose, however, the back of the overfold would have been drawn under the bent left elbow and over the head. A marble statuette in Rome takes this pose, with drapery folds similar to the figurine, including the knotted or weighted overfold corner; the statuette is thought to be a copy of a 5th-century B.C. Peloponnesian bronze original.[43]

C14 has no preserved mechanical relatives, as is also true of **C15**, which may come from the same workshop. Presumably there was much less demand for these large, finely made, and undoubtedly expensive pieces. It is also possible that their archetypes were related to models created for use in the manufacture of bronze statuettes, and only secondarily were molds taken for reproduction in terracotta.

The peplos overfold of **C15**, falling to the top of the thighs, is of thin, clinging cloth, almost like a chiton; the folds, as far as they are preserved, are narrow, rather calligraphic ridges. The thigh is visible through the thin cloth as if nude. The arrangement of the dress, although not the drapery style, recalls a Corinthian marble peplophoros of the Severe period, in which the long overfold follows the contours of the front of the figure.[44] While **C15** cannot be followed mechanically into further generations, the peplos-figurine type with a long, clinging overfold, and legs visible through the cloth, reappears in the 4th century B.C. (**C16–C18**); twenty-four fragmentary examples from this period have been counted in the lots. In spite of small variations in pose, the type is easily recognizable, although the extremely dull impressions make it virtually impossible to follow accurately any mold series. On the basis of their similarly thick-walled construction, **C17** and **C18** may have been made in the same workshop. Contributing to the lack of plastic detail may be an archetype characterized stylistically by flat, clinging folds, somewhat like those of an Archaic kore. Of all the Classical peplos-figurine types, this one appears to have been the most popular, suggesting that the image it presented was especially important to visitors

[40] E.g., MF-1580, *Corinth* XII, p. 30, no. 94, pl. 6.

[41] Robertson and Frantz 1975, pl. 12, East VII:53-56.

[42] On this fabric, see Farnsworth 1964, p. 224; *Corinth* XV, iii, p. 347. On its use in sculpture, see Weinberg 1957, pp. 293–294. It appears occasionally in figurines, at Isthmia perhaps more often than in Corinth: Mitten 1962 (1963, p. 309).

[43] Helbig[4] II, p. 320, no. 1504 (Conservatori Museum), with bibliography; a Sikyonian origin has been suggested by

Langlotz 1946/1947, p. 108. Large Roman replicas of similar type are discussed by Tölle-Kastenbein 1986, pp. 67–73, pls. 64–67.

[44] S-1577, found in the Lerna excavations, although perhaps not associated with the water installation: *Corinth* XIV, pp. 143–145, no. 3, pl. 57; Ridgway 1977; Schuchhardt 1974, pl. 14; Tölle-Kastenbein 1980, pp. 259–261, pl. 170; Harrison 1984, pp. 384–385, pl. 75:b–d.

to the sanctuary. Since the long overfold is sometimes associated with younger or unmarried women,[45] these figurines probably represent either Kore or youthful votaries.

The preserved examples vary in the position of the legs, but the stance is always quiet, one leg or the other slightly advanced, with the weight evenly divided and no contrapposto. A pose similar to that of **C21**, with the right leg advanced, is found in a mold of a peplos-figurine from the Potters' Quarter.[46] While no examples are preserved with the feet, it is likely that such lower figurine fragments as **C19** and **C20** belong to this group. These fragments show bare feet, the right foot a little advanced and pointing to the corner of a rectangular base. The ritual participants in Kallimachos' *Hymn to Demeter* line 125 are barefoot,[47] supporting the identification of these figurines as votaries. Perhaps the sandals were divested, along with other ornaments, at the time of ritual, or the bare feet were thought to make more direct contact with the earth as the source of fertility. It should be noted, however, that the seated Demeter or Kore pictured on a Corinthian plate of the Sam Wide group (see p. 43) is also barefoot. The forearms of these figurines were extended, either forward or to the side; one forearm may have been turned slightly inward in some examples. It is not known if anything was held in the hands. The pose belongs altogether to the 5th century B.C., but the proportions, usually slender and sometimes quite elongated, place the figurines in the mid- to later 4th century B.C. The head of **C17** is also of 4th-century B.C. type. The face is distinctive, with a broad forehead, tapering chin, features clustered near the center of the face, and eyes turned down at the outer corners. This face is found also among the articulated "dolls," with an altered coiffure. In fact, the head of **C17** is probably a mold sibling of the "doll's" head **C152**; both heads also share a distinctive retouch. They are members of a workshop group (Workshop B) discussed further below (pp. 56, 344–345).

This mechanical connection with articulated "dolls," which were made in the Potters' Quarter, suggests that this group of peplos-figurines was made there as well. The head of **C17** is of a type known in molds found there.[48] The heavily retouched hair of **C17** contrasts with the torso, which lacks retouch, although the impression is very dull; similarly, all the hand tooling of the "dolls" was lavished on the heads. The walls of the figurines of this group are unusually thick; perhaps they were made this way to ensure uniform firing, if they were baked together with articulated "dolls," the torsos of which are nearly solid. If the connection of these figurines with the Potters' Quarter is correct, their production would have ceased with the closing of the workshops there in the later 4th century B.C.

Since a direct link is lacking in this group with an expected 5th-century B.C. forerunner such as **C15**, we may have another example here, as in the case of **C10** and **C11**, of a sort of delayed reaction in the Potters' Quarter workshops, whereby a type created during the 5th century B.C. elsewhere in Corinth was not reflected in the Potters' Quarter production, which tended to be quite conservative, until some time later.

It is worth considering at this point possible reasons for such discrepancies in the coroplastic production of one city. Some workshops were still producing, in the 4th century B.C., such lingering Archaic figurines as the standing "korai," which were widely exported and have been found in such numbers that they have, unfortunately, almost become synonymous with Corinthian figurines. Although the clay was well prepared and these figurines usually were well fired, they were rarely retouched and were made in a single mold with the least possible attention to the back. It is unclear whether the artisans were motivated by a lucrative demand for the most familiar votive types, had no creative ambitions whatsoever, or were primarily potters who made figurines for festivals as a sideline,[49] but once a successful formula evolved, it appears to have been exploited

---

[45] Bieber 1928, pp. 37–38, pl. V:2; Bieber 1934, p. 33, pl. 18:1.
[46] KH-87, *Corinth* XV, i, p. 96, no. 25, pl. 33.
[47] Hopkinson 1984, pp. 39–41.

[48] E.g., KH-35, *Corinth* XV, i, p. 101, no. 37, pl. 34.
[49] On the identity of potter and coroplast in the Potters' Quarter, see *Corinth* XV, ii, pp. 3–4; on the seasonal nature of the coroplastic industry, see Merker, forthcoming, and p. 20.

in the extensive market, at home and abroad, for small cheap figurines to be used as grave gifts and dedications in cults of different kinds. The accumulation of Corinthian lingering Archaic "stock" types (standing "korai," seated goddesses, sphinx and rooster plaques) excavated in the Corycian cave at Delphi is revealing; more than five hundred examples have been illustrated in group photographs, most probably multiples from a few molds, indicating a substantial trade in these items that was much more than casual.[50] The same point has been made for Corinthian "korai" from Cyrene.[51] More substantial artistic achievements, left to other workshops, were apparently reproduced in smaller quantities and were appreciated and sold chiefly at home. In the terminology of the late-20th-century marketplace, one almost might speak of "mass-market" as opposed to "limited edition" figurines.

While some workshops may have come and gone, the ones producing time-honored types continued to find markets for at least a century. Salmon has suggested that the commercial success of Archaic Corinthian pottery owed much to the strong organization of the Potters' Quarter industry.[52] If this is true, the mechanisms developed for the trade in Archaic pottery may have continued to serve in the 5th century B.C., when the export of pottery declined, for the trade in Potters' Quarter figurines, which are comparable to the pottery in the large number produced, the repetition of types, and the eye-catching design and color. It must be mentioned, however, that the identification of the so-called Long Buildings just inside the city wall as a kind of market area of shops or booths for the sale of pottery, on which Salmon's argument rests, has been questioned.[53] The coroplasts of the Potters' Quarter do seem to have had a monopoly of the trade in Corinthian figurines, and therefore they probably had some control of the mechanisms of trade, but so far only the nature of the product provides an explanation.

A further reason for the stylistic and technical discrepancies among the products of Corinthian workshops may have been the unusual urban organization of ancient Corinth. From the Geometric period onward, areas of habitation developed around different water sources and roads. When the city wall was built, it encompassed these villages, still separated by agricultural fields and cemeteries, within its very spacious boundaries; the Potters' Quarter was one of these areas.[54] While the physical distance certainly would not have prevented contact between the settlements, the distance of custom and psychology could have been sufficient to separate the Potters' Quarter industry from the workshops of other areas,[55] which were more outward-oriented and up-to-date in artistic outlook, and perhaps shared workshop materials with artisans in other crafts. Separation did not mean failure, however, because the Potters' Quarter workshops thrived as long as they were able to sell their products at home and abroad, and only a natural disaster, or perhaps a change in the extent of the city walls, brought their production to an end.

The role of social factors also might be considered. If Salmon's reconstruction of a general Corinthian social stability is correct,[56] conservatism in some workshops could have been encouraged by the peaceful, uninterrupted passing of coroplastic traditions from one generation to the next.

[50] Amandry 1981, pp. 81–82, fig. 4. See also the Corinthian imports from Kirrha: Luce 1992.

[51] Uhlenbrock 1985, p. 301.

[52] Salmon 1984, pp. 101–103, 111–112; Roebuck 1972, pp. 121–122.

[53] C. K. Williams 1982, pp. 17–18. The remains are now believed to belong to blocks of houses; the Quarter, as far as it has been investigated, seems to consist of houses in which potters and coroplasts may have lived and, to some extent, worked. The industrial installations have not yet been found in the relatively narrow area of the plateau so far excavated.

[54] C. K. Williams 1982, p. 12; Roebuck 1972, pp. 122, 125; on the distribution of industrial sites with respect to available resources, see Arafat and Morgan 1989, p. 315. A similar pattern of habitation can still be observed in the modern villages of Corinth.

[55] A similar phenomenon, also based on custom rather than distance, is the existence in large modern cities of neighborhoods with distinctive identities and closely guarded loyalties.

[56] Salmon 1984, pp. 402–405.

The latest versions of the peplos-figurine type with long, unbelted overfold are **C22** and **C23**. Both figurines wear narrow, pointed shoes, which place them in the Early Hellenistic period. The foot-forward pose of **C23**, as well as the triangular fold dropping unbroken from the overfold to the knee, are strikingly similar to a hydriaphoros statue in Syracuse, thought to be a replica of an Early Classical Sicilian type.[57] The significance of this similarity is difficult to explain, particularly since the figurine cannot be Early Classical in date. Perhaps it stands at the end of a series of figurines, which is as yet absent from the archaeological record, originally inspired by Sicilian sculpture. It is typical of the peplos-figurines that an Early Classical type should be reflected so late. A similar tendency has been noted in sculptural production.[58]

As in the case of the peplos-figurine type with short overfold, the chronological information to be gained from the pottery contexts is rather limited, but it confirms what is evident from technique and style. The long-overfold figurines made in the Potters' Quarter must predate the closing of those workshops in the later 4th century B.C. The pottery contexts that are not thoroughly mixed contain pottery ranging from the 6th to the late 4th or first quarter of the 3rd century B.C. **C23**, which is clearly of later style than the others, comes from a pottery context dating from the 5th to the later 3rd century B.C. It is unfortunate that the stylistically earliest and best-made pieces are from mixed contexts.

3. *Peplos-figurines with long overfold, belted* (**C24–C34**). The earliest appearance of this peplos type, the so-called peplos of Athena,[59] may be **C24**, which can be dated to the middle to third quarter of the 5th century B.C. by virtue of a complete example found in an Argive tomb.[60] This figurine, although smaller than **C24**, shows a closely similar fold pattern. Its left leg is slightly advanced and bent, and it stands on a high, rectangular base with splaying sides similar to that of **C19**. Both arms are at the sides; the right hand holds a phiale. The poorly preserved head is small, on a long, thin neck; the hair is bound up. The source, at least for the torso, may be a mid-5th-century B.C. Rhodian type.[61] Most of the Corinthian figurines wearing the belted peplos, however, belong to the later 5th and 4th centuries B.C. Among these figurines a style emerges that is clearly influenced by Attic art of the later 5th century B.C.

Curiously, on the basis of evidence so far available, Attic types and styles seem to have been transferred to Corinthian figurines only to a limited degree directly from Attic coroplastic work. Among the figurines from the Demeter sanctuary, direct mechanical connection with Attic work is likely in the case of an Asiatic dancer (**C281**), which may have been molded from an Attic figurine vase, a female head (**C104**), and a seated Pan (**C277**), the molds for which probably were taken directly from imported Attic figurines. In addition, a draped articulated "doll" (**C181**) is very close to an Athenian type (see pp. 59–60). Influences in the other direction are demonstrated by the presence in the Athenian Agora of imported Corinthian molds and archetypes,[62] as well as Corinthian figurines dating from the late Archaic to the Hellenistic period.[63] Theoretically, the figurines and workshop materials found in Athens that have proven to be Corinthian on the basis of laboratory tests could have been made in Athens of imported Corinthian clay, but they are matched or approximated by pieces in Corinth and seem acceptable as imports.[64] There is some

[57] Tölle-Kastenbein 1986, pp. 57–62, pls. 56–61, with additional replicas and bibliography; the attribution has been questioned by Ridgway's review (1988, pp. 526–527) and the type dated after the Severe period.

[58] Ridgway 1970, pp. 93–105; Ridgway 1997, pp. 11–14, with bibliography on p. 22, note 21.

[59] For a useful collection of sculptured versions, see Berger 1967. For a discussion of one Athena type, see Roccos 1991.

[60] Papaspyridi-Karouzou 1933–1935, pp. 34–35, fig. 17 right (the entire contents of the tomb are described on pp. 21–44). The tomb contents are dated 470–460 B.C. (p. 44) but it

contains a Corinthian unglazed lekanis with stepped lid, a type first introduced just before the middle of the 5th century B.C. (*Corinth* XIII, pp. 145–148).

[61] *British Museum* I, pp. 85–86, no. 223, pl. 38; for a Boeotian version of this type, see *Leiden* I, p. 29, no. 44, pl. 8.

[62] Fillieres et al. 1983, p. 66, nos. 579, 585, 589, 605, 606.

[63] Fillieres et al. 1983, pp. 66–67.

[64] An archetype for a head of Nike from the Athenian Agora (E. R. Williams 1978, pp. 361, 379–380, no. 2, pl. 91) is thought to be of Corinthian clay but Attic manufacture; the clay has not yet been tested. The facial type seems to be Attic.

question regarding the degree to which Corinthian clay may have been brought to Athens as a raw material. Modern ethnographic evidence suggests that clays were not transported very far from their place of origin, and local sources were preferred whenever available.[65] It has been suggested, however, that Corinthian clay was imported to Athens for use as the finer surface layer of architectural terracottas.[66] If this is true, small quantities of the material could have been available to coroplasts. Contrary to the usual practice, Athenian potters were obliged to transport clay a considerable distance even for simple pottery,[67] and consequently they may have had the organization in place for transporting clay from Corinthian beds.

Some Attic figurine imports of the Archaic period are recognizable in the Demeter sanctuary.[68] For the Classical period, there are the early-4th-century B.C. hydriaphoros **I23** and perhaps the seated figurine **C80**, if it is not Corinthian; others are Early Hellenistic in date (**I24–I42**). The Corinth collection contains a few more Attic imports; the Attic "doll" mentioned below (p. 52), from the Forum Southwest excavations, is an import of the Classical period. The trade with Athens in coroplastic workshop materials or finished figurines, never very brisk, apparently was not affected by the intermittent state of war in the later 5th and early 4th centuries B.C., just as Athenian pottery reached Corinth at this time.[69]

In any case, until more imported Athenian coroplastic material of this period is discovered in Corinth, it is best to assume that a significant imprint on the developing Corinthian style was made by Attic sculpture, probably in the course of the general dispersal of Attic-trained sculptors at this time. This movement ultimately created through much of the Greek world and the surrounding lands a welter of local styles more or less derived from Attic sculpture of the second half of the 5th century B.C. As a result, general stylistic resemblances between Attic and Corinthian figurines of this period are more common than exact correlations. The late-5th-century B.C. Attic influence on Sicilian coroplasts also is thought to have come through sources in sculpture and vase painting rather than terracotta figurines.[70] Some of the Attic influence on Corinthian figurines could have come through small marble sculpture, specifically Attic or Attic-type votive reliefs or statuettes, some of which are thought to be reduced copies of well-known monumental sculptures.[71] Both groups would be particularly relevant here, since representations of Demeter and Kore are prominent among them and stylistic connections with the figurines can be cited. This source of inspiration must remain hypothetical, however, because only one rather crude 5th-century B.C. votive relief has been found in Corinth up to now; the rest are not earlier than the 4th century B.C. in date.[72] In truth, it is not encouraging that no votive reliefs were found in the Asklepieion, where they might be expected. There are as yet no 5th-century B.C. statuettes from the excavations.

The new peplos-figurine type treated here wears a long overfold girded at, or somewhat above, the natural waistline, with the cloth puffed lightly over the belt. The style reflected in the figurines is close to the Attic "quiet" style of the later 5th century B.C.[73] No complete example is preserved, but it is conceivable that the lower part is represented by **C26**, which shows the hem

[65] Jones 1984, p. 26; Blitzer 1990, p. 680.

[66] H. A. Thompson 1980, p. 16; Nicholls 1970, p. 116; Nicholls 1995, pp. 408, note 13; 459, note 248.

[67] Arafat and Morgan 1989, p. 316.

[68] Publication forthcoming.

[69] The subject of Attic pottery imports to Corinth in this period is still under discussion. See *Corinth* VII, iv, pp. 3, 15–16; McPhee 1987, p. 277, note 8; MacDonald 1982; Salmon 1984, p. 109, note 55 and p. 176, note 3; Arafat and Morgan 1989, pp. 339–340; *Corinth* XVIII, iii, p. 429. For imported 5th-century B.C. Attic figurines at Argos, see, e.g., Daux 1968, pp. 1028, 1033, fig. 19; p. 1034, fig. 20.

[70] *Morgantina*, p. 23.

[71] Votive reliefs: Peschlow-Bindokat 1972, pp. 109–127; statuettes: pp. 127–139 (including monumental sculpture). Especially relevant to the Corinthian figurines of the 4th century B.C. are Kabus-Jahn 1972 and Kabus-Preisshofen 1975.

[72] Ridgway 1981, pp. 427–428; Krystalli-Votsi 1976, p. 188, pl. 67:γ (early 5th century B.C.); *Corinth* IX, p. 124, no. 255 (S-48, mistakenly called a grave stele).

[73] Ridgway 1981a, pp. 114–117; Harrison 1977, esp. pp. 164–165.

of a long overfold at the upper break and takes the pose of the so-called Demeter from Eleusis.[74] Such a type could have had a long life, but the high, splaying base indicates that **C26** is Classical in date. At a larger scale, and with the pose reversed, is the fragmentary **C27**. Although the curve of the overfold at the hip suggests that the garment was girded at the natural waist like others in this group, the heavier trailing of the hem points to a somewhat later date, certainly not earlier than the 4th century B.C. The original fold pattern of the type is difficult to retrieve, owing to dull impressions and sometimes heavy retouch, but probably the closest to the archetype is the fragmentary **C28**. The mold from which this figurine was made still included the delicately puffed folds over the belt, as well as a realistic detail, the overlap of the back of the peplos where it was pinned at the shoulder.[75] The smaller **C25** is also very finely made, its peplos, almost as thin as a chiton, arranged in a series of shallow catenaries between and below the fully contoured breasts, descending to gently pouched folds over the belt. Its style recalls a marble statuette from the Athenian Akropolis,[76] but the folds are more static and repetitive. In this case, the very regular series of parallel catenaries is more typical of coroplastic work than of sculpture and is also seen in a group of peplos-figurines from the Asklepieion,[77] as well as in Attic figurines wearing this dress.[78]

A group of three figurines (**C29**–**C31**) represents the most common version of the type, its dull impressions and consequent heavy retouch indicating frequent repetition. This group may be derived from the same archetype as **C28**, but if so, the mechanical link has been lost. The upper arms are at the sides, the forearms extended, either forward or slightly to the sides. The diagonal break of **C30**, across the abdomen and up the left side of the torso, suggests that a mantle may have been added, similar to the arrangement of one of the Grimani statuettes.[79] There are no traces of the mantle on the left shoulder, but the ruffling of the hair at that point suggests that something originally was there. Both the figurine and the statuette have long, bound locks of hair down the back.[80] An unusual addition was made to **C31** in the form of a small scarf around the shoulders. In the latest version of the type, the large (size range 4–5), highly sculptural, and unfortunately very fragmentary **C32**, which dates probably to the later 4th century B.C., the belt is high, just below the breasts.

A curious variant can be seen in the nearly complete **C33**. It must have been made in the Potters' Quarter, to judge from its fabric and head type, which is similar to the heads of articulated "dolls," and from its arm with mitten-shaped hand, which is of a type meant to hang loosely from the "doll's" shoulder and is thus attached awkwardly (cf. **C168** for the head and **C122** for the arm). The figurine was made by joining these elements to an unretouched torso and base of such a dull impression that the overfold hem and bodice folds scarcely can be seen. The contrast between this sort of coroplastic pastiche and such sculptural work as **C32** is truly striking. The style and method of this "doll" workshop (Workshop A, p. 344) is so distinctive that two pieces in museum collections may be attributed to it, a standing, draped female figurine in the Louvre, and a seated goddess in Boston; another likely workshop mate is a standing, draped female figurine carrying a rolled fillet and a box (present whereabouts unknown).[81]

[74] Ridgway 1981a, p. 123, with bibliography, fig. 96. For the identification of this statue as Persephone, see Baumer 1995.
[75] For this detail shown very clearly, cf. a fragmentary relief from Eretria, Kabus-Jahn 1972, p. 78 and fig. 3.
[76] Kabus-Jahn 1972, p. 20, figs. 12–15.
[77] T.F.-34, -35, -36, *Corinth* XIV, p. 139, nos. 1–3, pls. 52, 53.
[78] E.g., *British Museum* I, p. 185, no. 697, pl. 91 (late 5th century); p. 195, no. 729 bis, pl. 95 (mid-4th century).

[79] Kabus-Jahn 1972, pp. 75–79, pl. 45. Possible connections with the Grimani statuettes are discussed further below, pp. 132–135.
[80] Kabus-Jahn 1972, pl. 46.
[81] *Louvre* I, p. 99, no. C95, pl. LXXII (originally playing the aulos; for the two holes in the mouth to receive the instrument, see *Corinth* XV, ii, p. 142, no. 4, pl. 29); for the Boston goddess, see *Coroplast's Art*, pp. 126–127, no. 19; for the figurine with fillet and box, see Winter, *Typen* I, p. 80, no. 3. For the head, see also **C158**, a probable mold sibling.

A relatively high girding is to be found in a beautifully made and finished statuette (size range 5), probably of a young girl (**C34**). Her garment is a chiton rather than a peplos, since it is sewn or pinned along the shoulders into brief sleeves, but it is included here because the handling of the drapery is related to the "quiet" style that underlies this group. Its restrained linear style and light touch, however, are more in the spirit of 4th-century B.C. renderings. Most of the representations of young people from the Demeter sanctuary are either large-scale terracotta sculptures[82] or much smaller figurines; this piece stands alone in its size range. These figurines of children probably represented votaries, and **C34** may be a large, fine, and early version of a type such as **H43**. Comparison with the girl votary or priestess type from Brauron, and related statues, comes to mind, but the stylistic differences are considerable.[83]

The peplos-figurines with long, belted overfold could represent either votaries or perhaps one of the goddesses. The long overfold sometimes is thought to have been worn especially by younger or unmarried women,[84] and if this is true, the figurines would represent young female votaries or perhaps Kore. With the addition of a mantle, this peplos type is known for Kore in a statuette from Mycenae representing her with Demeter.[85] The identity of the "Demeter" from Eleusis, who wears a belted peplos with a long overfold, has been questioned, principally because her costume is more often associated with Athena, but the discovery of so many figurines in this costume in the Demeter sanctuary may support the identification of the statue in Eleusis as one of the Eleusinian goddesses (see p. 34, note 74). Attributes, costumes, and coiffures were frequently shared by different deities in the process of artistic cross-fertilization that was normal in Greek art.

The useful pottery contexts containing peplos-figurines with a long, belted overfold include material dating from the 6th or 5th century B.C. to the late 4th or early 3rd. Although the chronology is not specific enough to date the material closely, it does offer some general confirmation of the chronological range suggested by technique and style.

4. Peplos-figurines with kolpos and overfold (**C35–C43**).   The fourth and last peplos-figurine type, ultimately of 5th-century Attic origin but very widespread and lasting into the Early Hellenistic period, shows the overfold to the hips, resting on a thick, richly gathered kolpos. Of the examples in the Demeter sanctuary, the earliest and best is **C35**, unfortunately only a fragment of a large (size range 4–5), well-crafted piece, thin-walled, hard fired, and carefully modeled. Its wide, flat pleats and kolpos decoratively modeled with butterfly folds recall, among votive reliefs, such renderings as the Demeter of a late-5th-century B.C. relief in Copenhagen,[86] thought to be of Peloponnesian workmanship, although of Attic type. It also can be seen, in a more schematic form, among the Grimani statuettes.[87] This type is, of course, one of the most enduring in Greek plastic art. It is associated in different periods with a variety of subjects, especially female divinities, and is known in a seemingly inexhaustible variety of drapery patterns. In the present context, figurines with this peplos arrangement probably represent Demeter or Kore, although they need not be based upon any particular cult image. Small-scale figures of deities often are thought to reflect cult statues, occasionally with specific evidence,[88] based on the generally held assumption that large works of art give rise to smaller copies and adaptations, rather than the reverse. Not only is this assumption rather dubious from the point of view of method, since artists often begin with sketches or models of smaller scale than the intended work, but we cannot know to what extent coroplasts were able to view cult statues, particularly those in other communities.

---

[82] Publication forthcoming by Nancy Bookidis.

[83] Vorster 1983, pp. 330–344, nos. 1–38, with bibliography.

[84] See p. 30, note 45.

[85] Kabus-Jahn 1972, p. 77, fig. 2 opposite p. 78.

[86] Mitropoulou 1977, pp. 45–46, no. 67, fig. 105; Neumann 1979, pp. 43–44, pl. 24:a.

[87] Kabus-Jahn 1972, pp. 51–59, pls. 28–35, veiled Demeter statuette with polos.

[88] E.g., Zuntz 1971, p. 158, note 3; see also Alroth 1989, pp. 106, 108.

The designs for major cult statues could, of course, have been transmitted through models or other workshop materials, but it denigrates the Greek artisan to assume that he could not have constructed a figure of a deity through his own general sense of what the god or goddess ought to look like, in dress, attributes, and physical type. The great variety among peplos-figurines of this type is best explained by such independent creations. See also pages 134–135 on this subject.

Almost certainly a representation of Demeter is **C36**, a 4th-century B.C. peplos-figurine with a swung hip, wearing a shoulder-pinned back mantle, which probably was lifted high in the left hand. This is one of Demeter's typical poses in votive and document reliefs,[89] although figurines in this pose from elsewhere in the Peloponnesos are thought to represent Hera.[90] In Hera's case, the pose refers to the *anakalypteria* of a bride; while Demeter usually is not considered a patroness of marriage,[91] her cult in Corinth appears to have included that function (see pp. 127, 170). A peplos-figurine from Perachora, dated late 5th–early 4th century B.C., also lifts the mantle with one hand while holding in the other a phiale, presumably for libation; in this case, the figurine probably represents Hera, who was worshiped at Perachora.[92] Alternatively, **C36** could have leaned on a long scepter held in the raised left hand, while the right hand held out a phiale; Demeter appears in this pose in a votive relief in Paris.[93] There is a particularly Peloponnesian flavor in the drapery of **C36**, especially in the deeply curved ridge on the overfold, which drops from the left shoulder and encloses and frames the opposite breast. A similar framing mannerism is found, for example, in the akroteria of the Temple of Asklepios at Epidauros.[94] It can also be seen in smaller scale on the above-mentioned relief in Copenhagen.[95] A hip fragment (**C38**) hints at a larger (size range 4–5) and more richly modeled peplos-figurine of this type. A still larger (size range 5) version, preserved only in a tantalizing shoulder fragment (**C37**), could have held a scepter or torch in the upraised hand, since the mantle seems to drop down behind the arm. Its deep modeling is so thoroughly sculptural in concept that it is hard to resist the idea that the archetypes of such terracotta statuettes also served as models for small-scale versions in stone, such as a statuette of Demeter from Kos.[96] A piece of much poorer quality (**C39**) is more typical of figurines of this type found in the sanctuary, however. The skirt fragment of a peplos-figurine of large scale (**C40**) has such deeply cut folds that the inner surface of the right leg has been cut away. The shadows are so deep that one thinks of Hellenistic sculpture, but the stance, with feet fairly close together and one foot drawn to the side, is Classical, the mirror image of **C26**.

Three figurines (**C41**–**C43**) seem to represent the final manifestation of this peplos-figurine type. In these figurines, the overfold hem has disappeared entirely, leaving only the thickened edge of the kolpos. This variant, in which the kolpos forms a definite arch framing the thighs, was used to represent Demeter in a marble statuette from Kos.[97] This statuette, a rather mediocre

[89] E.g., Peschlow-Bindokat 1972, pp. 111–113, figs. 34, 35 (= M. Meyer 1989, p. 266, no. A5, dated 422/421 B.C.); also the relief in Copenhagen, p. 35, note 86 above. On the shoulder-pinned back mantle, see Bieber 1977, pp. 104–117; Roccos 1986, concentrating on its use in Attic representations of Athena and Apollo.

[90] From the Sanctuary of Hera Limenia, *Perachora* I, p. 223, no. 129, pl. 98; *British Museum* I, p. 276, no. 999, pl. 140, with bibliography.

[91] Detienne (1994, pp. 78–82, 116–118), however, stresses that the rituals of the Thesmophoria reinforce the institution of marriage. Plutarch (*Moralia* 138b) mentions the participation of a priestess of Demeter in the preparation of a bride. Demeter was a patroness of marriage and betrothal on Kos: N. Robertson 1983, pp. 164–169. To see Demeter alone in a

dream was considered auspicious for marriage (Artemidoros, *Oneirokritika* 2, no. 39). In the wedding procession of Peleus and Thetis on the François vase, Demeter is grouped with Hestia and the nymph Chariklo at the head of the procession, immediately after Iris and Chiron, approaching the house of Peleus, in which the bride sits (Arias and Hirmer 1962, p. 289, pl. 44 center).

[92] See note 90.

[93] Hamiaux 1992, p. 215, no. 223.

[94] Yalouris 1992, pp. 32–33, no. 27, pls. 30, 31.

[95] See p. 35, note 86; for a detail of this figure, see Hiller 1971, pl. 8, fig. 22.

[96] Kabus-Preisshofen 1975, pp. 46–50, pls. 19–21.

[97] Kabus-Preisshofen 1975, pp. 36–39, pls. 11, 12.

4th-century B.C. rendering, wears a shoulder-pinned back mantle, as in **C42**. The head, which does not join the torso directly and may not belong to it, is a later version of a 5th-century B.C. type, with a straight-sided, heavy-jawed, large-featured face bearing a strong resemblance to **C53**. The figurines of this group are instructive technically, since **C42** and **C43** share a large mold defect on the left thigh. Therefore, the two must be related mechanically, and yet the handmade additions and the tooling are so extensive that the figurines are entirely different in appearance, in both proportions and drapery. As far as the relationship can be reconstructed, **C43**, which is larger, must be the earlier generation; its scar is more pronounced. **C42** and **C41** are equal to one another in size, although the latter seems smaller because it is incomplete at the left side and the shoulder-pinned back mantle was never added; they seem to be from parallel molds. Both show the same revision of the line of the kolpos into an arch, done either to minimize the effect of the scar or to update the drapery style, but in **C41** the mold defect has been completely repaired, while in **C42** only the area above the kolpos has been altered.

In spite of the strong, sculpturally based beginnings of this group, a sharp technical decline can be noted; badly worn molds continued in use, even defective molds, as in **C42** and **C43**. The figurines were roughly touched up with a blade to add detail. The last members of this group may have been made as late as the 3rd century B.C., since **C43** is elongated in proportions and narrow shouldered. While the workshops of the Potters' Quarter may have been conservative and artistically unassuming, there is nothing there to suggest the utter lack of interest in the fundamental standards of workmanship seen in these figurines. Together with other poorly made pieces of 3rd-century B.C. date, they may be part of a general decline in some workshops in Corinth at that time.

The pottery contexts of peplos-figurines with kolpos and overfold are, unfortunately, not very useful, since the contexts either are of completely mixed date or do not show a clear pattern of terminal date. What is clear is that, with the possible exception of **C35**, which could be of later-5th-century B.C. date on technical and stylistic grounds, the figurines of this group belong to the 4th and 3rd centuries B.C. The poorest of all (**C43**) is from a pottery context dating from the 5th to the later 3rd century B.C., and it is likely that it was made well into the 3rd century B.C. Of the four groups of peplos-figurines, this one was the last to be abandoned. There is no evidence that it was made in the Potters' Quarter, and presumably for this reason it was not affected by the closing of the workshops there in the later 4th century B.C. In any case, by the last quarter of the 3rd century B.C., other figurines had taken the place of the last survivors of the Classical tradition of peplos-figurines.

A LOCAL COPY OF A RHODIAN TYPE

A standing female figurine with a mantle draped over the left arm, **C44** is different in type from all the others and is very likely a mechanical copy of a mid-5th-century B.C. imported Rhodian figurine.[98] There are several other instances of Rhodian inspiration in Corinthian figurines in this period. The head **C103** was probably inspired by a Rhodian head type often connected with similar torsos with the mantle over the arm (see p. 48). Another torso (**C24**) also may be of Rhodian inspiration, although in this case the figurine is related to a known local type (see p. 32). For Rhodian influence on protomes, see pages 74 and 76.

---

[98] Cf., e.g., *British Museum* I, p. 83, nos. 210–212, pl. 37; the left hand, however, is more like that of *British Museum* I, p. 85, no. 220, pl. 8; *Lindos* I, col. 549, no. 2269, pl. 105.

HYDRIAPHOROI AND RELATED HEADS
(C45–C69)

The hydriaphoros type first appeared in southwest Asia Minor during the transition from the Archaic to the Severe period.[99] Of the Asiatic examples known up to now, those from Iasos appear to be the earliest, on the basis of style.[100] The type is frequently found in association with the cult of Demeter.[101] Most of the Corinthian hydriaphoroi from the Demeter sanctuary wear the peplos, and for this reason some of the fragmentary peplos-figurines also may have been hydriaphoroi. In addition to the catalogued examples, approximately twenty hydriaphoros fragments have been counted in the lots. Hydriaphoroi are not common in the sanctuary after the 4th century B.C., the only Hellenistic examples being the rather poor types **H48–H51**. Perhaps their place as votives was taken by miniature hydriai, which became an important votive type in the Hellenistic period.[102] The symbolic value of both hydriai and hydriaphoros figurines in a fertility cult is very clear, with references to the ritual bathing of brides and the dead, as well as agriculture.[103] The hydriaphoroi also may reflect the carrying of water jars as a part of cult ritual, perhaps for the purpose of ritual purification.[104] The provision of bathing facilities in many of the dining rooms and the presence of perirrhanteria point to the importance of cleansing in the sanctuary rituals.[105]

The stylistically earliest Corinthian hydriaphoroi are the fragmentary torso **C45** and the heads **C51** and **C52**. They do not seem to be as early as those from Iasos but stylistically should belong to the Severe period. They are similar to a complete hydriaphoros in Copenhagen, of reported Corinthian provenience.[106] On the basis of three similar heads from Tiryns,[107] the type has been considered Argive, but given the Corinthian provenience of the example in Copenhagen and the discovery of this group at the Demeter sanctuary, it is perhaps more likely that the Tirynthian figurines are to be counted among the Corinthian imports at that site.[108] The source of the type is not immediately obvious; probably it developed out of the local peplos-figurines, in imitation of an Asiatic type but in a more Peloponnesian style. It is possible that the hydriaphoros type was known in Corinth in sculptural form in the Severe period. Schuchhardt has suggested that a marble peplophoros found in the excavation of the Lerna fountain could have been a hydriaphoros.[109] Since there is no direct stylistic connection between this sculpture and any of the figurines identifiable as hydriaphoroi, however, it is more likely that the figurines were in this case a separate coroplastic creation.

A cylindrical form on the heads, just below the hydria, resembles a polos but probably was meant to be the head ring used to support the vessel, as seen on red-figured vases[110] and perhaps also on the heads **C58** and **C60**. Other hydriaphoroi, such as Classical and Early Hellenistic examples from Theangela, show such a support very clearly.[111] Perhaps when the type was

---

[99] Işik 1980, p. 77.

[100] Levi 1967/1968, p. 574, fig. 43.

[101] For useful collections of material, see *Knossos*, p. 68; Işik 1980, pp. 181–186; Winter, *Typen* I, pp. 156–159; Diehl 1964, pp. 189–192; Lilibaki-Akamati 1996, pp. 50–51.

[102] *Corinth* XVIII, i, p. 104.

[103] A Subgeometric hydriaphoros figurine from a grave in Crete (Diehl 1964, p. 129, pl. 45:2) is nude, has one hand at her breast, and takes a squatting pose that reveals the pudenda, linking the hydria to fertility symbolism as well as death. Bearing in mind the chthonic nature of the deities honored in the sanctuary, hydriaphoroi could also refer to the Danaids, the eternal water carriers in Hades. I owe this interesting suggestion to Brunilde S. Ridgway.

[104] Cole 1986, pp. 164–165. On the lack of an immediate water source in the Acrocorinth sanctuary, see Bookidis 1990, p. 89; *Corinth* XVIII, iii, pp. 14–15.

[105] *Corinth* XVIII, iii, e.g., pp. 402–405 (bathing rooms); *Corinth* XVIII, i, pp. 75–78 (perirrhanteria).

[106] *Danish National Museum*, p. 40, no. 355, pl. 42 (= Diehl 1964, p. 189, note 137, pl. 45:1). The piece is also discussed by Poulsen 1937, p. 12, fig. 5 on p. 11, with profile view.

[107] *Tiryns* I, p. 81, no. 136, pl. XI:1 (three heads are recorded under this number).

[108] An accurate attribution of Corinthian imports, beyond the well-known standing "korai" and seated goddesses, would be too much to expect of the excavators of Tiryns in 1912.

[109] S-1577, Schuchhardt 1974, p. 22, note 12. For other discussions of this sculpture, see p. 29, note 44.

[110] de Haan-van de Wiel 1971, pp. 135–137, figs. 2, 3.

[111] Işik 1980, e.g., p. 220, no. 88, pl. 13.

created, an existing head type in a polos was incorporated into the archetype.[112] A Corinthian seated female figurine in Paris with a swan, presumably Aphrodite or Leda, has a similar head wearing such a low polos.[113] Clearly, some of the artisans who prepared new archetypes depended in part on available elements, which could be combined into new types. There is also a mixture of styles in this hydriaphoros group, since the coiffure of **C52** combines broad waves framing the forehead, characteristic of heads of the Severe period, with flat, triangular masses of hair framing the neck, a surviving Archaic feature.

A few figurines seem to be later versions of this hydriaphoros type. The fragmentary **C46** has more freely rendered folds, although it still seems to belong to the Classical period. A degenerate survival can be seen in **C47**, which still shows the rectangular outline of its Classical ancestors. The right arm may have been raised to support a hydria, but the detail has been lost in this piece, and the hips are uncharacteristically thrust forward. The woman also carries a piglet in her lowered left hand. The hydriaphoros with piglet is not known in any other examples in Corinth but appears elsewhere in the Peloponnesos.[114] Another late hydriaphoros is the fragmentary **C48**; the swing of the figure's weight to one side suggests a date well into the 4th century B.C. A similar date is indicated for **C49** by the high girding of the peplos. The drawing of the skirt to the side, however, and the horizontally crimped hair are recollections of an earlier style. Only one example (**C50**) is preserved of the Asiatic type of hydriaphoros, in which a mantle is draped across the abdomen and hips.[115]

A quite different hydriaphoros head type, represented by **C53** and **C54**, in which the foot of the hydria is balanced directly on a wide mass of curly hair, is much more vital and plastic in appearance (although the lower face of **C54** is missing) and seems less derivative. Its archetype probably should be dated stylistically ca. 470–460 B.C. It is larger than the previous type, of statuette scale (size range 4). In a technically poorer form, it also is known in Boeotia.[116] In some aspects of their structure, the faces of this group are reminiscent of some faces of Archaic figurines from the sanctuary,[117] and elements of this facial type persist in Corinth even into the Hellenistic period. The shape is distinctly long and narrow, more oblong than oval, with rather straight sides. The forehead is low, the cheeks are flat, and the jaw is rounded and heavy. The level eyes are large, extending nearly to the temples because of the narrowness of the head at this point. The upper and lower lids are equally curved and well defined. The browridge is strongly marked and follows the curve of the upper eyelid. The shape of the nose is often obscured by chipping or abrasion, but it is always large and close to the upper lip. The mouth is wide and the lips very full and unsmiling, even sometimes downturned, though with a strong double arch of the upper lip. Sometimes the outer corners of the lips do not meet, probably because the division between them was continually retouched as the mold series progressed, and the mouth consequently has an almost rectangular outline.

In its general appearance, this head type is the earthy, heavy-jawed, full-lipped, large-nosed, thick-lidded type seen in Severe Style sculpture and well known in the Temple of Zeus at Olympia.[118] In the figurines, however, the head is usually narrower across the cheekbones, in relation to its length, than the Olympia heads; in this respect it finds good parallels in youthful male heads such as that of the Delphi Charioteer[119] and a bronze head from the Athenian

---

[112] To see how this could have happened, one may compare hydriaphoros heads in Copenhagen, *Danish National Museum*, pl. 21, nos. 205, 206, which have supports resembling poloi, with other heads on the same plate wearing the polos alone.

[113] *Louvre* I, p. 99, no. C96, pl. LXXII; *LIMC* II, 1984, p. 92, no. 843, pl. 84, s.v. *Aphrodite* (A. Delivorrias et al.).

[114] Winter, *Typen* I, p. 157, nos. 5, 6, from Tegea.

[115] E.g, *British Museum* I, p. 118, no. 391, pl. 58, from Halikarnassos.

[116] *Eutresis*, pp. 254–257, figs. 314:5, 316:6.

[117] E.g., Stroud 1968, p. 322, pl. 93:c (MF-12146).

[118] Compare, e.g., the head of Figure H (Deidameia?) from the west pediment: Ashmole and Yalouris 1967, pl. 113.

[119] The narrowness of the Charioteer's face is most obvious in photographs in frontal view; see *FdD* IV, v, pl. XVI.

Akropolis thought to be of northeast Peloponnesian origin.[120] A closely similar facial type can be found in the male figurines **C205** and **C206**, which is not surprising, since head molds were often used indiscriminately for male and female figurines, with changes in coiffure. Among non-Corinthian figurines, the closest parallels can be found among heads from Medma, pointing to yet another stylistic connection with West Greek coroplastic art.[121] In a similar stylistic mode is a Sicilian terracotta head from the Demeter sanctuary in Grammichele; this head has been compared to Corinthian heads of ca. 460–450 B.C.[122] The cheeks of this larger head are fuller, but there is a distinct similarity in the distribution of the features over the facial surface and in the mobile, slightly parted, down-curved lips.

These hydriaphoroi also are notable for their bushy, stippled coiffures, which were added to heads with short, wavy hair; in **C55**, for example, wavy locks resembling those of the male head **C206** can still be seen down the left side of the face, beneath the added hair. A double-scalloped wave pattern at the center of the forehead recalls a motif seen repeatedly in the Olympia sculptures[123] and also in a mid-6th-century B.C. limestone head of a sphinx from Corinth.[124] Hair masses that were relatively large and wide in proportion to the face were a prevailing style in terracottas in the 5th century B.C., not exclusive to any one place. Very wide, elaborate coiffures (or wigs) were favored somewhat later in the 5th century B.C. in Boeotian figurines,[125] in the context of bridal iconography, but the arrangements are far more complex and are usually combined with plaits, of which there are no traces in the Corinthian heads. A wide, wavy coiffure is known in later Classical Sicilian protomes in combination with a polos.[126] The all-over stippling of the hair with a small pointed tool is characteristic of the Corinthian figurines of this type and may have been a shorthand suggestion of the ringlets characteristic of some Archaic coiffures.

The long corkscrew curls descending to the shoulders seen in **C53** do not really belong to this bushy coiffure nor to the simply waved, caplike arrangement beneath the bushy mass. They belong to a coiffure in which strands of hair are wrapped over a fillet and tucked behind the ears before falling in front over the shoulders. Replicas of the Mantua Apollo show this arrangement in detail.[127] In **C58** and **C61**, the hair-wrapped fillet appears, probably together with long locks in front. Perhaps the existence of such coiffures on Early Classical figurines may help to clarify questions concerning the Apolline hairstyles of this period found in Roman replicas.[128] Corkscrew curls are also found on an early-5th-century B.C. sculptured terracotta head from the Demeter sanctuary.[129]

Several other heads are included in this group because of their stylistic similarities, although it is not known if they actually were hydriaphoroi. Heads **C55** and **C56**, with oddly flat-topped, bushy hair, originally could have had a hydria or perhaps a tray, basket, or headdress attached with an adhesive to the top, but traces of such objects are lacking. These heads could have

[120] Rolley 1986, pp. 102–103, 238, no. 239; Ridgway 1970, p. 41, no. 11; Hurwit 1989, pp. 51–52, 74–75, fig. 30, with bibliography; the head is variously dated between 480 and 460 B.C.

[121] Cf. Orsi, 1913, pp. 107–113 for female heads. In particular, cf. fig. 127 (top right on plate following p. 108), an early-5th-century B.C. face, with straight sides, a full jaw, and features distributed over the surface of the face in a manner recalling the Corinthian heads; the hair of this head is arranged in a wide mass of ringlets, recalling the wide, stippled hair mass of the Corinthian figurines. A head from Medma is also compared to the Delphi Charioteer by Quarles van Ufford 1941, pp. 131, 133, fig. 71. Cf. also Herdejürgen 1978, p. 80, no. B18, dated ca. 440 B.C. There are no close parallels among the group of Medma figurines in R. L. Miller 1983.

[122] Langlotz and Hirmer 1965, p. 263, pl. 41; Holloway 1975, p. 14, figs. 101, 102.

[123] E.g., Ashmole and Yalouris 1967, fig. 154, the head of Athena in the Stymphalian birds metope.

[124] S-1981-3, C. K. Williams and Zervos 1982, p. 144, no. 85, pl. 46.

[125] Higgins 1986, pp. 102–105, figs. 118–121.

[126] E.g., *Morgantina*, p. 138, no. 96a and b, pl. 23; pp. 141–142, nos. 109, 110, pl. 30. Cf. MF-6365, *Corinth* XII, p. 37, no. 173, pl. 12.

[127] Keene Congdon 1963, pls. 3–6; on Apollo types with this coiffure, see *LIMC* II, pp. 372–374, nos. 35–39, pls. 299, 300, s.v. *Apollon/Apollo* (E. Simon).

[128] Ridgway 1970, pp. 136–138.

[129] SF-65-12: Bookidis and Fisher 1972, p. 317, pl. 63:d.

belonged even to seated types, as in a smaller version of late-5th-century B.C. date in the Corinth collection.[130]

The Early Classical narrow facial type framed by a wide coiffure, sometimes with a particularly long, spreading neck, appears to have continued in use into the 4th century B.C. (**C57**–**C59**, **C65**). The later examples are smaller, but it is not possible to establish a continuous mold series, nor is it clear how many of these heads originally belonged to hydriaphoroi. **C58** and **C60** are pierced at the top of the head, as if they were articulated "dolls," but more likely the added circlets around the holes are the head rings of hydriai, and the holes received dowels, which secured the vessels in place. A similar technique of doweling was used for arms, which were fastened into holes pierced in the elbows of seated figurines, such as **C74** and **C82**. The piercing of the head, however, does suggest a connection with a workshop accustomed to making articulated "dolls." In fact, there is a possible mechanical connection of **C59** with the "doll's" head **C141** (see catalogue); some of the hydriaphoroi have distorted noses, a feature shared by this "doll." Since most of the articulated "dolls" seem to have been made in workshops in the Potters' Quarter, these later Classical variants of the hydriaphoros head type are likely to have been made there as well; **C58** and **C59** somewhat resemble a head mold found in the Potters' Quarter.[131] If this is correct, a pattern of production similar to that of the peplos-figurines is evident. That is, there is no evidence for the production of Early Classical hydriaphoroi in the Potters' Quarter, but artisans in 4th-century B.C. workshops there may have produced variations of models created in the 5th century B.C. elsewhere in Corinth, by craftsmen with better sculptural skills and a wider knowledge of the arts.

C60 and **C61**, also 4th-century B.C. in date by virtue of their high, triangular foreheads, are broken fairly cleanly around the contours of the jaw, suggesting that drapery originally covered the neck and that these figurines therefore were mantled.[132] The same would be true of **C62** and **C63**, two heads probably representing two generations. They are of a large scale similar to that of **C60** and **C61**, but they are much coarser in workmanship and have heavy features that fill the faces. Although these heads are probably of Hellenistic date, their facial structure and coiffure show them to be Classical survivals. The horizontal locks of hair to either side of the central part in **C63** may be all that remains of a more refined and complex coiffure like that of **C61**. The earlier generation of the two heads (**C62**) also is of poor workmanship: the elements of the coiffure are hidden by rough slashes and the earring is separated from the ear. Perhaps we are dealing with parallel mold series.

The carrying of objects other than a hydria on the head, such as a tray or possibly a kanoun, would be consistent with a cult of Demeter,[133] but the evidence for such figurines in Corinth is very slight, the only possibility being **C68**. This head balances what appears to be a tray or the lower part of a kanoun, with a lump at the center, resembling somewhat the kanoun carried by a kanephoros from Tiryns; this vessel holds a round, knoblike cake at the center.[134] If the carrying on the head of any sort of tray or vessel other than a hydria was part of the sanctuary ritual, it has left little mark on the surviving figurines. The large number of model likna from the sanctuary[135] suggests that trays of food offerings were carried, possibly in procession but not necessarily on the head. The partially preserved hollow object on the head of **C66** could be a hydria, but the rather wide base leaves open the possibility that it could be a different type of vessel. The hydria **C69** must have rested on the head of a figurine, to judge from the remains of locks of hair around the

[130] MF-6403, *Corinth* XII, p. 32, no. 123, pl. 8; the hair is waved rather than stippled in this example.
[131] KH-27, *Corinth* XV, i, pp. 98–99, no. 29, pl. 33; a break in the mold has partly obliterated the features. The face of the mold is more oval, but the nose distortion is similar.
[132] The facial structure of the heads is reminiscent of a 4th-century B.C. Tarentine type: Herdejürgen 1978, p. 47, no. A40.

[133] See examples from the Athenian Agora: D. B. Thompson 1954, pp. 94–98.
[134] *Tiryns* I, p. 74, no. 72, fig. 17 (kanoun); pl. X:2 (figurine).
[135] Brumfield 1997; Stroud 1965, pp. 23–24, pl. 11:f (a full-sized cult liknon).

base. Theoretically, it should be possible to date the figurine by comparing the shape of the hydria with the hydriskoi from the sanctuary.[136] Probably because of the smaller scale and indifferent workmanship of **C69**, however, its shape does not quite correspond with any of the votive vessels.

The rounder facial type of Attic inspiration sometimes found among the smaller peplos-figurines (**C11**) and the articulated "dolls" (e.g., **C159**) appears occasionally in this group as well (**C67**). A late-5th-century Attic head type with full cheeks and a triangular forehead also appears (**C64**); it is found in the imported Attic hydriaphoros **I23** but without a demonstrable mechanical connection to the Corinthian figurine. A head archetype from the Athenian Agora,[137] thought to be made of Corinthian clay, is also comparable in facial type.

Pottery contexts are not very helpful in dating the hydriaphoroi and related heads, since most come from mixed fills dating from the Archaic to the Roman periods. However, **C45**, **C56**, **C59**, **C61**, and a mold sibling of **C52** all come from lots with mainly pre-Hellenistic pottery. The latest terminal date, the first quarter of the 3rd century B.C., belongs to **C54**, which, however, is clearly one of the earlier members of the group. It seems fair to say that on the basis of present evidence, this group did not survive the end of the 4th century B.C. If, as seems likely, its later members were made in the Potters' Quarter, the cessation of activity in the workshops there in the later 4th century would account for the loss of the type.

SEATED DRAPED FEMALE FIGURINES AND RELATED HEADS
(C70–C101)

Among the Classical figurines, there are considerably fewer seated than standing females, and their development is not as consistent. Corinthian coroplasts apparently continued to find a market for seated goddess figurines in a lingering Archaic style.[138] Even the stylistically updated 5th-century B.C. versions of Archaic types treated in this chapter show a very strong conservatism, particularly in pose. Their roots in the Archaic period are not surprising, since the frontally seated pose, the polos, and the majestic bearing suggest that these figurines represent goddesses. There may have been some reluctance in the more conservative workshops to develop a new goddess type without a pressing reason to do so; the first appearance of Early Classical style in standing votaries rather than in seated goddesses is consistent with such an attitude. The Classical reworkings of Archaic seated goddesses were developed in the Potters' Quarter, as the discovery there of both molds and figurines demonstrates.

The most direct stylistic descendants of Archaic seated figurines are **C71–C77**. The horizontal projections of the chair and the long locks of hair to the shoulders are familiar elements. The rectangular footstool is also familiar, although now the chair and the footrest are elevated on a rectangular base. The hands may rest flat on the lap, or a bird or flower may be held to the chest.[139] A complete example in the National Museum, Athens, shows both hands at the chest somewhat in the manner of the Early Classical protome type represented by the fragments **C251–C257**.[140] When the heads are preserved, a polos is worn, either high and flaring or low and wide. Newer elements of 5th-century B.C. style are the hair framing the forehead, which waves in rounded masses from a central part, the relatively fluid peplos folds, and, most of all, the face (see **C73**, which is fully Classical). In **C76**, however, the large, protruding eyes recall

[136] *Corinth* XVIII, i, pp. 10–12, 168–169, fig. 1 on p. 11, pl. 50.
[137] E. R. Williams 1978, pp. 361, 379–380, no. 2, pl. 91.
[138] For the type, see *Corinth* XV, ii, pp. 94–97, pl. 17.
[139] In one small fragment in lot 2156, the hand holding the flower rests on the lap.
[140] Poulsen 1937, pp. 14, 56, fig. 34, with Early Classical drapery, but a head still in the Archaic tradition. There is a probable mold sibling of this piece in The Metropolitan Museum, New York, inv. no. 1972.118.128: von Bothmer 1961, p. 46, no. 176, pl. 62. In lot 3222 there is a small fragment of the seat at the right side, showing the characteristic pointed fold that overlaps the seat.

Archaic style. The freely rendered bird of **C77**, with wings outspread, is also worth noting as a new element.[141] The type evolves into the seated figurines of the later 5th and 4th centuries B.C., such as **C78** and **C79**.

The relatively undifferentiated seated figurines of the Archaic tradition probably could have been identified by worshipers with any of several goddesses. In the Classical and Hellenistic periods, the iconography becomes more specific, although sometimes there is still a confusing syncretic overlap of types, probably mirroring the overlap in cultic function. In other arts, when Demeter and Kore are pictured together, they usually are distinguishable from one another by their attributes or characteristic costume, but when they are represented separately, their iconography inevitably overlaps. For example, a Corinthian plate of the Sam Wide group in Athens bears a detailed representation of an enthroned goddess with virtually every attribute imaginable for both Demeter and Kore.[142] Seated outdoors, she holds a torch, ears of grain, and a branch of poppy-seed pods or pomegranates; a fig is set on a rocky altar in front of her; she wears a chiton, peplos, and mantle, is barefoot, and has a kalathos for wool or food on her head; a richly patterned, warp-fringed cloth covers her throne; and a bird flies behind her. She seems to incorporate the chthonic qualities of Kore with the agricultural function of Demeter, as well as the domestic traits implicit in the Corinthian cult title Demeter Epoikidie.[143] The bird is more commonly associated with Aphrodite, but in the cultic iconography of the Lokroi plaques is given also to Kore.[144] When associated with the chthonic goddess, the bird may suggest Aphrodite as well and thus the erotic aspects of a fertile marriage. Although Aphrodite had a well-known sanctuary of her own on Acrocorinth, she is unmistakably represented in a number of 4th-century B.C. figurines from the Sanctuary of Demeter and Kore (pp. 169–176) and may well have been a presence there earlier as well.

Another example of the overlapping attributes of Demeter and Kore can be found in a seated figurine similar in type to the Corinthian, wearing the flaring polos, from the Sanctuary of Demeter Malophoros at Selinus. The figurine holds a pomegranate and a handful of grain, and in the context of that sanctuary ought to represent Demeter.[145] Elsewhere, however, the same attributes are associated with Kore.[146]

The Corinthian seated figurines with attributes preserved hold a flower bud (**C71**), which suggests Kore,[147] or a bird (**C77**), pointing to either Kore or Aphrodite.[148] The shape of the flaring polos could imitate a kalathos, and if this was intentional, the implication of the full basket, namely, abundance, would be most appropriate for Demeter. It is very likely, however, that neither coroplasts nor worshipers intended to distinguish the goddesses from one another as strictly as we would suppose but rather accepted an imagery of abundance and fertility that called all three goddesses to mind.

The latest versions of the old-fashioned seated goddess type (**C78** and **C79**) belong stylistically to the 4th century B.C. Although the hieratic pose and the chair with projections persist, the high girding of **C78**, its softly rounded forms, and the cluster of curls on the head speak of an Early Hellenistic date. Apart from the pose and the chair, the hieratic appearance has melted away from the type. The occupant of the seat, bareheaded, youthful, and holding what appears to

[141] A figurine from Syracuse holds a bird with outspread wings and is also comparable in the chair type and coiffure (Winter, *Typen* I, p. 128, no. 1 = Kekulé 1884, p. 58, pl. II:2).

[142] Callipolitis-Feytmans 1962, pp. 141–143, 163, no. 60, pl. VI; *LIMC* IV, 1988, p. 858, no. 121, pl. 571, s.v. *Demeter* (L. Beschi); *Corinth* XV, iii, p. 368, no. 12; see *Corinth* XVIII, i, pp. 134–136, for examples of this group found in the Sanctuary of Demeter and Kore, showing female figures holding a torch and an ear of grain or a poppy-seed pod; Amyx 1988, I, p. 276, no. 14, pl. 125:6, with bibliography.

[143] "Epoikidie" is the only epithet recorded for Demeter in Corinth: see Hesychios, s.v. On other possible meanings of this epithet, see *Corinth* XVIII, iii, pp. 2, 72, note 23, 411.

[144] Sourvinou-Inwood 1978, pp. 105, 116, 119; *Morgantina*, pp. 84–85.

[145] Gabrici 1927, col. 274, pl. LX:4.

[146] Sourvinou-Inwood 1978, p. 108, a; pp. 108–109, d.

[147] Sourvinou-Inwood 1978, p. 109, h.

[148] Sourvinou-Inwood 1978, p. 116.

be a girl's dedicatory ball, looks more like a young votary than a goddess. Two types seem to have merged in this new creation, the traditional seated goddess, known through repeatedly updated mold series, and a newer type of the Early Hellenistic period, the seated young girl holding an offering (see **H339** and **H340**). In the new type, a cubical, backless seat replaces the goddesses' usual chair, the pose is more relaxed, and the offering is held more naturally on the lap or beside the thigh.[149]

C80 is similarly hieratic in pose, youthful in appearance, and Early Hellenistic in style and is one of the Corintho-Attic puzzles among the figurines. It is the only example of this type yet found in Corinth. It has a long, clinging overfold similar to the standing peplos-figurine **C17**; it has a footstool and slender proportions recalling **C74**; its mixture of old and new elements is familiar in Corinthian coroplastic work. Two examples, however, thought to be Attic, were found in the excavations of the Pnyx in Athens, in a deposit dated to the late 4th century B.C.;[150] they are so similar to the Corinthian figurine as to suggest a mechanical relationship. The fabric of the Athenian examples is burned; the soft, friable fabric of the Corinthian piece does not seem Attic. Either one or the other was an import, or the figurines were made in both places in parallel molds deriving from the same archetype, the origin of which is as yet unknown.

C81, which would seem to represent a seated goddess but for the distorted feet, may be an example of a known Corinthian taste for parodying serious figurine types, perhaps stemming from the coarse humor sometimes associated with fertility cult (see p. 195). A better-preserved example of this genre in Berlin, thought to be from Corinth, shows an enthroned goddess with vessels (for receiving offerings?) at her feet, but she is corpulent and has grotesquely sagging breasts; her right hand rests on the knee in the usual hieratic pose, but the gesture is made humorous by baring the knee and placing an alabastron in her left hand, so that she seems to be rubbing her sore knee with ointment.[151] **C81** may be doing the same thing, and the distorted feet may be part of the humor. Similarly wide, splaying feet, although in a more normal pose, are found in other Early Classical figurines, such as the standing youth **C188**, as well as the parodies **H368** and **H374**.

On a smaller scale, **C82–C85** carry the lingering Archaic seated goddess type into the 4th century B.C. in an updated form. This group is characterized by its small scale (size range 1–2), blocklike, backless seat, and extended forearms. The mantle arrangement in this group falls over the lap and knees to a horizontal edge at mid-calf, covering the left shoulder and arm. **C82** and **C83** are typical representatives of this well-documented Corinthian group; better-preserved examples from elsewhere are bareheaded and hold various objects in their outstretched hands, including birds, small boxes, fruits or cakes (singly or on trays), fillets, and large balls.[152] This array of objects suggests that the figurines represent women or girls offering gifts, rather than goddesses holding attributes. Since this type was popular and is known in a number of variants, it is conceivable that it reflects a point in the ritual when female participants were seated on benches, holding their offerings, before dedicating them to the goddesses. If this is true, **C78**

---

[149] For a Boeotian example in Boston in fully Hellenistic style, see *Coroplast's Art*, p. 117, no. 10, with bibliography.

[150] H. A. Thompson 1936, p. 170, no. 1b, fig. 18. For the date, see D. B. Thompson 1952, p. 119, note 12(3). For the identification of the site, which was once thought to be the Thesmophorion, see *Agora* III, pp. 81–82, no. 224; Clinton 1996, p. 119.

[151] Winter, *Typen* II, p. 465, no. 9, "Reibt sich das Knie mit Salbe" (= Pfisterer-Haas 1989, pp. 62, 136, no. III 48, fig. 109 on p. 215).

[152] E.g., Winter, *Typen* I, p. 86, nos. 1–4; *Königliche Museen*, p. 11, pl. IX top; *Danish National Museum*, p. 41, no. 365, pl. 43; *FdD* V, 1, pp. 163, 201, no. 295, pl. XXII:4, from a grave (incorrectly) dated ca. 400 B.C., with Corinthian pottery of the mid- to later 4th century; see also p. 201, no. 643, pl. XXIII:14; Peredolskaja 1964, p. 10 (the examples from this grave, pls. 7:3–5, 15:6, must be Corinthian, although the author attempts to assign them to Athens as part of her rather unlikely theory that the figurines in the grave illustrate the *Homeric Hymn to Demeter*).

perhaps should be understood in the same way. Corinthian imports of this type were dedicated at the Thesmophorion in Eretria.[153]

Later variants of this group have their skirts spread out to cover the blocklike seats. Their more gently rounded forms, sloping shoulders, and demure appearance place them stylistically in the latter part of the 4th century B.C. **C86**, which may hold an aulos, is a good example from the Demeter sanctuary; other variants are known mainly from museum collections.[154] Although no member of this group was found in the Potters' Quarter, the fabric and workmanship of **C86** suggest that it was made there; in addition, two Potters' Quarter head molds show a similar face and coiffure, although they are larger.[155] A much better made and larger version in the National Museum, Athens, holding a tray of cakes, also looks like a Potters' Quarter product.[156] Perhaps one of the workshops there made a specialty of variations on the theme of seated goddesses and votaries.

Several unusual figurines are seated in wicker chairs. In **C90** and its more clearly detailed mold sibling from the Potters' Quarter,[157] the rounded chair back, the details of the wicker wrapping visible behind the shoulders, and the structural strips in the back clearly belong to such a chair.[158] The seats of **C89** and probably of its mold sibling **C88**, have a conical base and rounded back comparable to Etruscan thrones.[159] These rounded forms probably portray a flexible material such as wicker. It is conceivable that these figurines represent priestesses or other ritual participants, since the Rule of the Andanian Mysteries of Messenia prescribes curved wicker seats for the "sacred women."[160]

C87 is a highly simplified seated figure, in which the projections of the chair back are rendered in one piece with the torso. The combination of a molded head with a flat, handmade body is typically Corinthian. The technique lingers from the Archaic period,[161] but the head is clearly Early Classical in style. These flat, handmade bodies persist even into the 4th century for hieratic types, as is shown by MF-1 in the Corinth collection (Pl. 75), which utilizes an early-4th-century B.C. head type (see p. 46).

The only group of seated female figurines of a clearly borrowed type is composed of **C91**, a closely similar piece in the Corinth collection, MF-8666 (Pl. 75), and the related head **C92**. This type, with the mantle sweeping horizontally across the shoulders from front to back and covering the head, has parallels among Paestan figurines.[162] The face, too, is West Greek in type, with its plump cheeks, strongly marked eyelids, pleasant expression, and large disc earrings.[163]

Possibly also borrowed, this time from Boeotia, is the type represented by **C70**, which wears a peplos of Severe style, comparable to the standing peplos-figurine **C1**. This seated type, characterized by a peplos with a waist-length overfold and a plain central panel flanked by vertical folds to the hips, ending in zigzags, is fairly widespread. Among the major production centers, it is known well in Rhodes[164] and Athens.[165] There are three probable Boeotian imports of this type from the Demeter sanctuary, two torsos (see **I43**) and the head **I44**; there is another,

[153] *Eretria*, pp. 29, 78, nos. 420–426, pl. 22.
[154] E.g., Winter, *Typen* I, p. 86, no. 7, with a head similar to **C158**; *Danish National Museum*, p. 41, no. 363, pl. 43; *British Museum* I, pp. 261–262, no. 962, pl. 135. A fragmentary example is published in *Corinth* XII, p. 33, no. 128, pl. 9 (MF-6395).
[155] KH-31, KH-32, *Corinth* XV, i, p. 100, nos. 33, 34, pl. 34.
[156] Winter, *Typen* I, p. 75, no. 5.
[157] KT-8-3, *Corinth* XV, ii, p. 134, no. 50, pl. 28.
[158] On wicker chairs, see Seltman 1947, p. 24; for similar Roman versions, see Richter 1966, p. 101, figs. 506–508; Macintosh 1974, p. 23.

[159] Richter 1966, pp. 85–86, fig. 434.
[160] M. W. Meyer 1987, p. 53, para. 4.
[161] See, e.g., *Corinth* XV, ii, p. 72, no. 34, pl. 12.
[162] *Danish National Museum*, p. 47, no. 429, pl. 53; Winter, *Typen* I, p. 129, nos. 7, 8; Bol and Kotera 1986, pp. 129–132, no. 67.
[163] Cf. Tarentine heads such as Herdejürgen 1971, p. 55, no. 41, pl. 15; p. 58, no. 46, pl. 15.
[164] E.g., *British Museum* I, p. 86, no. 224, pl. 38, with bibliography.
[165] E.g., *British Museum* I, pp. 180–181, nos. 675 and 677, pls. 88, 89, with bibliography.

fully preserved, in the Corinth collection (MF-2).[166] Since there is not enough evidence to show that the local Corinthian standing peplos-figurines had a corresponding seated series, it seems most likely that in this case Boeotian imports were copied.

Within the category of seated female figurines, the enormous range of Corinthian coroplastic work is demonstrable, from moldmade miniatures with little retouch, such as **C82**, to such statuettes as **C93**. The latter almost belongs to the realm of sculpture and may have been entirely handmade. It must be the work of a craftsman who was familiar with sculpture and who perhaps made models for work in other materials or in larger scale. In photographs, the statuette in its fragmentary state could pass for work in stone, and even in direct examination it has a rough-hewn quality, as if the artisan had stone in mind. A similar quality can be found in the handmade Hellenistic head **H431** and in two probably handmade solid female statuettes in the Corinth collection.[167] In fact, the closest parallels for **C93** are to be found in stone sculpture. The deep, slanted fluting at the sides of the peplos overfold and the deeply pocketed fold looping to the ankle recall the Erechtheion caryatids in style.[168] The deep, U-shaped catenaries on the overfold, however, are found in other Corinthian work (**C94**) and seem to be a local stylistic element. Since the statuette was handmade, a date of manufacture, probably the later 5th century B.C., can be proposed on stylistic grounds. The fragments of the statuette were found scattered, but the pottery of one of the four lots involved has been dated to the 5th–4th centuries B.C. The type appears to have continued well into the 4th century B.C. in a moldmade version (**C94**), also fragmentary, but still recognizable by the deep catenaries on the overfold, the sloping lap, and the fold patterns around the legs. The large size and substance of this group suggests that one of the goddesses was represented, perhaps Demeter.

The final and most tantalizing group, **C95–C99**, is thought to have been seated because its crowned head type is known in better-preserved, although smaller, seated figurines in Corinth and does not appear on any standing types. One such seated figurine is from the Potters' Quarter;[169] another is MF-1 (Pl. 75) in the Corinth collection, an enthroned goddess with a handmade body.[170] The heads of these figurines could represent later generations of the same or related mold series as the group from the Demeter sanctuary. A head mold from the Potters' Quarter also is similar in facial type and coiffure.[171] MF-1 is seated on a separately made throne; **C95**, with no traces of a chair back, may have been similarly composed or placed on a backless seat. The group seems to represent the final stylistic renewal in the 4th century B.C. of the traditional seated goddess type. The first four members of this group, **C95–C98**, must be from the same workshop; the first three of these, which wear a low crown, can be assigned to the same hand, to judge from the retouch, especially the use of a particular tool, perhaps a broken reed (see catalogue). The facial type recognizably descends from the earlier hydriaphoros group, **C53–C56**. In the best mold impression, that of **C98**, the face is more oval than its predecessors, although still long and rather straight sided; the forehead is higher; the temples slope toward the back of the head, so that the face loses the flat, uniplanar look of the 5th-century B.C. hydriaphoroi; and the jaw is more softly rounded. The eyes are still large but now are slightly downturned; the nose remains large and close to the upper lip; the lips are still unsmiling but are more mobile and slightly pursed. There is a general resemblance to heads of the more developed hydriaphoros group (**C60** and **C61**), although these heads retain more of the 5th-century B.C. formal strength. The wide coiffure is still

---

[166] Shoe 1932, p. 59, fig. 3.

[167] MF-3973, MF-5545, *Corinth* XII, p. 41, nos. 222, 223, pl. 18; *Coroplast's Art*, p. 58, figs. 45, 46; also handmade are MF-7395, MF-7393, MF-7394, *Corinth* XII, p. 53, nos. 361–363, pl. 32, a dog, a goat, and a tree.

[168] Lauter 1976, e.g., Kore D, pp. 24–27, pl. 33.

[169] KT-8-8, *Corinth* XV, ii, p. 127, no. 29, pl. 26.

[170] Similar figurines, not all of stated Corinthian provenience but seeming to belong to this group, are Winter, *Typen* I, p. 87, no. 2; *Königliche Museen*, pp. 11–12, pl. IX bottom; also an example from the Corycian cave at Delphi: Szabo 1994, pp. 95, 148, fig. 119.

[171] KH-34, *Corinth* XV, i, pp. 100–101, no. 36, pl. 34.

in evidence, although it is more delicately waved. The goddess has a remote, rather reserved look. A reasonable stylistic date for this head type is the early 4th century B.C.

The fruit, probably a pomegranate, in the lap of MF-1 (Pl. 75) and the fruits in her hands suggest that she represents Kore, although the pomegranate, apart from its obvious mythological link to Kore, can be an attribute of other goddesses, including Aphrodite.[172] On the basis of the connection to MF-1 and others in this group, the heads from the Demeter sanctuary also may represent one of the goddesses, although the heads without the crown (**C98** and **C99**) could have been used for other purposes. The low crown of **C96** is surmounted by a row of oval or round pellets. These call to mind the crown of MF-1, to which three discs were attached; the central disc is now missing, but the others are stamped with a floral pattern.[173] Figurines from Medma wear similar headdresses.[174] In these figurines, the crown takes the form of a very thick, rounded fillet, topped by either discs or what appear to be pointed leaves. If these crowns were floral, the discs may have been intended to be rosettes, with painted details. One figurine from Medma wearing such a crown, a seated goddess accompanied by two erotes, must represent Aphrodite.[175] Since flowers are known as attributes of both Kore and Aphrodite (see p. 125), a floral crown, if that is what it is, would have been a suitable headdress for either goddess. It may be significant that a similar, although still further schematized crown is worn later by Aphrodite, in a Tarentine type of the 3rd century B.C.[176]

A head that bears some relation to this group is **C100**. As far as the head is preserved, it seems to belong stylistically to the later 4th century B.C. Its poor state of preservation is unfortunate, since it is the only head of its period known to have worn a high, crenellated polos. **V14–V15** are larger examples of this type of headdress, broken from their figurines; they are decorated with figured reliefs (see pp. 270–271). In a rather unstable composition, the heavy headdress of **C100** is perched on the tilted head, supported only by the slender neck. It is unclear with which of the preserved torso types, if any, this head is to be associated, although it must represent one of the goddesses. If it belonged to a seated figure, the likeliest candidate in terms of scale would be a late version of **C94**. A standing Persephone from Morgantina, dated within the first half of the 3rd century B.C., has a similar facial type and coiffure, although the headdress is lower and is covered by a veil.[177] **C101** is similar to **C100** in the coiffure, earrings, and to some extent the headdress, which is a high stephane rather than a polos but with a notched border; perhaps the intention was to portray a headdress like that of **C96** or **C100**.

The pottery contexts are, as usual, only partially helpful. The comic figure **C81** is from a pottery context terminating at least in the second quarter of the 5th century B.C. An uncatalogued head wearing a polos (MF-11726) belongs to a pottery lot terminating in the early 4th century B.C.; it is close in type to **C73** (see catalogue), the earliest head type found on the Classical seated figurines, but it is from a different mold series. The usable pottery contexts of the seated figurines terminate at the latest in the early 3rd century B.C. Once again, the demise of the Potters' Quarter workshops in or near the 320s B.C. must have been an important contributing factor, leaving a gap in production to be filled by other workshops with a different repertoire.

---

[172] Muthmann 1982, pp. 39–52 on Aphrodite.
[173] The discs are better preserved on the example from Delphi: Szabo 1994, pp. 95, 148, fig. 119.
[174] Orsi 1913, figs. 126, 135–137, on pls. following p. 108.

[175] Orsi 1917, pp. 60–61, fig. 36.
[176] In San Francisco, *Coroplast's Art*, p. 157, no. 44.
[177] *Morgantina*, p. 133, no. 60, pl. 15.

ISOLATED FEMALE HEADS
(C102–C104)

Among the heads lacking a clear association with any of the groups discussed above, two are of strong outside inspiration: **C103** and **C104** depend upon Rhodian and Attic prototypes respectively. **C103** either could have been copied directly from a Rhodian draped female figurine[178] or could owe its style to Rhodes indirectly, as a descendant of a Rhodian-inspired protome of a type found in the Potters' Quarter.[179] **C104** is of a widespread type known, for example, from Rhodes,[180] Boeotia (see import **I44**), and Athens, where it probably originated. Although no imports of this type have been found in Corinth, it was at least exported to the region, since three fine Attic examples were found in Argos.[181] The modeling of the Corinthian head is so slack that its mold could have been taken directly from an Attic figurine.

C102 has a Sicilian connection in the coiffure, which is bound with a kerchief,[182] but its long, large-featured face falls within the stylistic range of Corinthian Classical types. It may have belonged to a standing peplos-figurine, as do its Sicilian parallels. Of the three heads in this category, only **C102** is from a chronologically useful pottery context, dating to the first half of the 4th century B.C.

ARTICULATED "DOLLS," RELATED HEADS,
AND RELATED FIGURINES OF DANCERS
(C105–C185)

Articulated "dolls" of the Classical period, found in small numbers elsewhere in Corinth, have been published in earlier excavation reports,[183] but the enormous quantity found at the Demeter sanctuary allows a much better understanding of their development. Although only a small, representative sampling can be provided in publication, the observations offered here are based on the whole body of material. These figurines are well known in Greece, where they were made at least as early as the Geometric period. Whether they ever actually functioned as children's toys is uncertain, but the term "doll" is fixed in the scholarly literature and therefore is retained here. They are characterized by freely moving arms and legs or, in the case of seated "dolls" and "dolls" with rigid legs, only moving arms. Some were pegged at the top of the head to allow them to dangle from the hand of the owner.

Since the limbs were attached to the torsos with perishable cords, no complete examples were found in the sanctuary, but a reasonably accurate count can be taken by using the torsos alone. Because most of the torsos are solid or very thick-walled, they often are preserved intact and are easily recognizable among the figurines. Of the approximately 930 torsos counted, the larger proportion, about 810, are nude; the remainder wear a knee-length chiton or peplos.[184]

Although most of the Corinthian "dolls" belong to the later 5th and 4th centuries B.C., they were made from the Late Archaic period onward. The lingering Archaic "dolls" (see p. 23, note 1) are solid, single-molded or handmade plaques; some wear a chitoniskos and polos, while a few are schematically nude. Such "dolls" continued in use through the 5th century B.C., but new double-molded types were created afresh, a nude version by the third quarter of the 5th century B.C. and a draped one perhaps a quarter-century later, to judge from the drapery style.

---

[178] Cf. the heads of such Rhodian figurines as *British Museum* I, pp. 83–84, nos. 210–213, pl. 37.

[179] KT-11-7, *Corinth* XV, ii, p. 101, no. 18, pl. 19.

[180] E.g., *British Museum* I, pp. 85–86, no. 223, pl. 38.

[181] Daux 1968, pp. 1028, 1034, fig. 20.

[182] E.g., Gabrici 1927, col. 290, pl. LXXII:3.

[183] *Corinth* XII, p. 33, nos. 130–138, pl. 9; *Corinth* XV, ii, pp. 145–151, pl. 31; molds: *Corinth* XV, i, pp. 106–107, nos. 66–72, pls. 41–42. The numbered classification suggested in *Corinth* XV, ii, does not work well for the larger repertoire of variants now known, and therefore it is not used here.

[184] "Dolls'" heads were not always pierced for suspension (e.g., **C128**) and therefore cannot be counted as accurately as torsos.

Several uses and meanings have been proposed for the "dolls," most of which represent young women. A summary of published interpretations follows.[185] At the simplest level they are thought to have been toys and sometimes to have been dressed in bits of cloth, although this idea is based on an apparently incorrect emendation of the epigram *Anthologia Palatina* 6.280.[186] They may have been among the toys dedicated at shrines when approaching adulthood and marriage required a symbolic leaving behind of childish pleasures, although the correction of the above-mentioned epigram weakens this interpretation, for which there is no other evidence. When represented in the hands of girls on Attic grave reliefs, they are always nude and have been interpreted convincingly as anatomical votives for a successful puberty.[187] The discovery of "dolls" in the graves of adults points to a chthonic connection or an apotropaic function. The violent movement of which the articulated "dolls" were capable when shaken may have served as a charm. The "dolls'" nudity suggests that sometimes they may have represented hetairai; while there are numerous nude goddess figurines of Geometric and Archaic date,[188] in Classical Greek art, female nudity was generally confined to representations of hetairai, particularly in vase painting.[189] The elaborate coiffures and caps with high, hornlike projections worn by some of the "dolls" have been considered apotropaic. Some "dolls" (although none from the Demeter sanctuary) hold *krotala* and were therefore meant to represent dancers; the knee-length peplos or skirt worn by some also can be associated with dancers.

Given so many choices, all of them appropriate in one way or another to the Sanctuary of Demeter and Kore, it is rather difficult to define specific functions for articulated "dolls" in Corinth. The precise cultic associations of various Greek figurine types are likely to have been a local matter, depending less on any universal significance than on the functions of the shrines in which they were dedicated. Since it is likely that both human and agricultural fertility were celebrated at the Demeter sanctuary, it can be expected that such a large group of votives as the "dolls" served more than one purpose there, the type of "doll" selected for the offering presumably determined by the votary's needs.

Some "dolls" from the Demeter sanctuary hold offerings and therefore may represent votaries. In the hand of **C121** is a long, thin cake, similar to offerings on model likna from the sanctuary.[190] The hand **V21**, which may possibly belong to a "doll," holds a similar long cake together with one shaped like a disc. In the hand of **C122** is a similar disc. On the analogy of the *krotala* held by some "dolls," such discs have been thought to represent tambourines[191] or cymbals,[192] but since they resemble in shape cakes on the model likna,[193] they probably should be so identified, at least at the Acrocorinth sanctuary; here the carrying of cakes may point to the hope of agricultural abundance from Demeter. If the "dolls'" elaborate coiffures were indeed apotropaic and their movement served as a charm, fear of death could have motivated some of the offerings, assuming that they were brought to Kore as the Queen of the Underworld. Since Kore is the quintessential bride in myth, some of the "dolls" could have been offered to her by girls of marriageable age as symbolically relinquished toys of childhood, if such they were, or more likely, since they are nude,

---

[185] On the subject, see Elderkin 1930; Andrén 1948, pp. 61–64 (on both dangling and seated "dolls"); *Pnyx*, pp. 114–118; Dörig 1958; *Troy*, pp. 87–95 (on seated "dolls"); Zuntz 1971, pp. 168–170; Vandenabeele 1971–1972 (Corinthian type, pp. 38–40, incorrectly assigned to Boeotia); R. Schmidt 1977, pp. 115–128 (on "dolls" as toys); *Aspects of Ancient Greece*, p. 244 (on "dolls" as apotropaic objects); *Morgantina*, pp. 94–96 (on seated "dolls"); *Pergamon*, pp. 56–59 (where many seated "dolls" were found in the vicinity of the Demeter sanctuary); Redfield 1991; Nicholls 1995, pp. 435–438.

[186] In the correct reading, according to Daux (1973), Timareta dedicates not her dolls and their dresses but her hair and her own clothing.

[187] Reilly 1997.

[188] Böhm 1990.

[189] Bonfante 1989, p. 559.

[190] Cf. Brumfield 1997, p. 161, no. 29, pl. 47, and p. 163, no. 47, pl. 49, identified as a fruitcake.

[191] *British Museum* I, p. 258, no. 948, pl. 134. For discs as musical instruments, see Meyers 1987.

[192] Elderkin 1930, pp. 461–463, fig. 9.

[193] These cakes seem to be larger than the flat, round *kollyba* (Brumfield 1997, pp. 149–150); they probably correspond with the popana (ibid., p. 150), but without knobs.

as expressions of physical maturity and the fertility of approaching marriage. Because the draped "dolls" represent dancers (see pp. 58–60), the connection with fertility is strengthened, since dancing is frequently associated with fertility cult. The nudity of most of the "dolls," and the elaborately peaked coiffures and caps associated with hetairai worn by some of them, could have had special significance in Corinth, the only city in Greece to have adopted ritual prostitution from the Near East. This factor is considered further in a later chapter discussing the role of Aphrodite at the sanctuary (see pp. 169–172), since it is possible that some of the "dolls" were dedicated to her.

Torsos and Limbs of Articulated "Dolls" (**C105–C123**)

The largest and best made of the nude double-molded "dolls" is **C105**. The completely hollow, thin-walled construction of this figurine gave way gradually, first to a still hollow but thicker-walled construction, as in **C106**, then to a nearly solid form, which became the standard type. Perhaps the greater weight of the solid "dolls" allowed them to dangle and dance better and was considered an advantage. There must have been a reason for the change in technique, since solid "dolls" used much more material and must have been more difficult to fire thoroughly.

In the solid "dolls," the inner surface of each half, after unmolding, was sometimes prepared for joining with a slight indentation or hollowing at the center, so that only the edges joined, in a sort of coroplastic anathyrosis (see **C107**). In smaller and sometimes less carefully made examples, the inner surfaces were left flat but were scored roughly (see **C109**). After joining the two halves, probably with a thin clay solution, a socket was hollowed between the shoulders for insertion of the neck. Sockets also were hollowed in the thighs, and the knees were pierced through from side to side with an awl or pin. After firing, a cord on which the lower legs hung was threaded through the sockets. The shoulders also were pierced, often completely through from side to side, penetrating the neck dowel; after firing, a cord was threaded through to attach the arms, or they were tied to small (wooden?) pegs driven into the holes.

Sometimes the molds were furnished at the bottom with three flanges instead of thigh sockets, as in **C108**; the flanges also were pierced through from side to side. This technique was also used for the lingering Archaic "dolls" (see p. 23, note 1). Front and back molds of flanged "dolls" were found in the Potters' Quarter.[194] This mechanism made unnecessary the hollowing of the thighs and became standard in 4th-century b.c. "dolls." Flanged attachment of the legs is less attractive than the socketed form, which hides the joint, but flanges allow freer movement of the legs. In the latest and poorest examples, the flanges were at least in part made by hand, perhaps because they were lost from the molds as the mold series progressed and degenerated; as a result, the piercing of the side flanges is sometimes higher than the central flange (e.g., **C113**), and at the very end of a mold series, the legs may have been hung from only a central flange (e.g., **C114**).

Limbs of articulated "dolls" are either handmade or moldmade; generally speaking, the smaller limbs are handmade, and while it has not been possible to connect limbs with their original torsos, it is likely that the later, smaller, and poorer "dolls" had handmade limbs. Presumably, molds for the limbs were no longer available. Molds for legs of articulated "dolls," and possibly an arm, were found in the Potters' Quarter; two of the leg molds had offset flanges at the top for piercing, as in **C116** and **C117**.[195] Most legs, however, were simply flattened and thinned at the top before piercing, as in **C118** and **C119**. Both methods simplified insertion of the legs into thigh sockets or between thigh flanges. The offset type may have been intended for socketed rather than flanged torsos, although this cannot be proven. It is, however, very likely that the offset type is earlier, since these legs sometimes have carefully modeled anatomical details (e.g., **C117**), while the flattened type often has a more simply made, undetailed foot or a pointed shoe (e.g., **C118** and

---

[194] KH-65, KH-66, *Corinth* XV, i, p. 106, nos. 66, 67, pl. 41.

[195] KH-68–KH-71, *Corinth* XV, i, pp. 106–107, nos. 69–72, pl. 42; nos. 69 and 70 are legs with offset flanges.

C119). The preserved arms either are bent at the elbow (e.g., **C121** and **C122**) or are short and straight (e.g., **C123**).[196] The mitten-shaped hand is standard, occasionally with painted details preserved representing fingers and jewelry.[197]

"Dolls'" heads and necks usually were doweled into the shoulders, although a few poor and late examples were simply glued onto a scored surface at the top of the torso (e.g., **C184**). The heads were usually strictly frontal in pose, presumably to enable the figurine to dangle properly, but a few are tilted slightly (e.g., **C142**, **C152**). It is remarkable how the seemingly expressionless features of "dolls" come to life when the heads are bent a little. The tops of the heads of dangling "dolls" were pierced for suspension; heads that were not pierced (e.g., **C128**) could have belonged to seated "dolls" or to standing "dolls" with rigid legs, such as **C110**. The holes in the heads are usually larger than those in the shoulders or knees, ca. 0.004–0.007 in diameter, and are sometimes very deep, cutting vertically into the neck tenon and even into the chest in smaller "dolls." Perhaps the holes are deep because sturdy pegging would have been needed to hold the weight of the dangling "dolls."[198] There is no evidence among the "dolls" from the Demeter sanctuary for the use of a metal suspension ring in the head.

The "dolls" range downward in scale from size range 4–5 (e.g., the leg **C116**) to size range 1–2 (e.g., **C113**), that is, from statuettes to miniatures. The smallest torso found, in lot 6638, is only 0.04 in height; **C170** and **C171** are examples of the smallest "dolls'" heads. Some of the smallest may not have come from the end of a mold series but rather may have been independent copies of small "dolls" in other materials, such as bone or ivory.[199] Surprisingly, the pierced head with melon coiffure **C136** shows that large "dolls" were still being made in Hellenistic times, unless the hole served another purpose.

Although it is virtually impossible to follow completely the mold series of the nude torsos or to determine how many series there were, owing to the lack of anatomical detail in most of the "dolls," a few observations can be made. The largest and best-made "doll's" torso (**C105**) is characterized by a subtle anatomical modeling stylistically datable to ca. 440–430 B.C., on the basis of comparison with the sculptured "Stumbling Niobid" in Rome.[200] This figurine may have been followed by only one more generation. The present evidence does not link **C105** with the "dolls" next in size and quality (e.g., **C106** and **C108**), which seem to have had an archetype with a more slender and geometrically organized anatomy. This phenomenon is known in Corinth for other figurine types as well, since the largest, most original, and best-made pieces sometimes were copied at a smaller scale in other workshops; the repetitive mold series evolved from these smaller and presumably cheaper copies, rather than from the original, finer creations. The rather masculine anatomy of the torsos of the smaller "dolls" recalls kouroi of the Ptoön 20 group, but with the bulge of the iliac crest suppressed.[201] It should not necessarily be concluded, however, that the type actually originated in the Archaic period, since the artisans may have made use of workshop materials at hand, adapting an available male torso by adding breasts. For artisans in terracotta who had to create a nude female torso, the nude male torso was an obvious starting point or shortcut.[202] Alternatively, the coroplasts may have been trying to convey the androgynous quality of a very young woman, whose femininity was just emerging.

---

[196] Complete "dolls" in museum collections may have been assembled from parts belonging to different figurines and are not necessarily helpful in assigning limb types to torsos.

[197] E.g., KT-13-28, *Corinth* XV, ii, p. 150, no. 20, pl. 31.

[198] For a representation on a grave relief of a girl holding a doll by its head string, see Dörig 1958, pl. 23:3.

[199] For such "dolls," see *Pnyx*, pp. 110–111, no. 6, fig. 49; Elderkin 1930, pp. 467–468, fig. 18; *Olynthus* X, pp. 15–17, nos. 9, 10, figs. 2, 3; Müller-Wiener et al. 1980, pp. 54–55, pl. 26:5–7, from Miletos.

[200] In the Terme Museum: Boardman 1985, pp. 175, 177, fig. 133:1, with bibliography on p. 245; Ridgway 1981a, pp. 55–57, fig. 25.

[201] Cf. Richter 1970, e.g., a kouros torso in Syracuse, p. 146, no. 183, figs. 550–552; Holloway 1975, pp. 32–33, figs. 187–189; the anatomical detail is clearest in Langlotz 1927, pl. 64.

[202] In an interesting reversal, the male figurine **C199** was constructed from a "doll's" torso by flattening the breasts.

In whatever way it was created, this new archetype ultimately seems to have given rise to both socketed-leg and flanged-leg "dolls," as similarities between **C106** and **C108** suggest. The flanges originally may have been handmade additions to the thighs of a socketed torso, copying the flanges of lingering Archaic articulated "dolls" (see p. 23, note 1). The size difference between **C106** and **C108** is 0.025 (not including neck and flanges), indicating that if these torsos belong to the same or related mold series, **C108** would be a generation later. If the flanges were indeed handmade additions, as suggested, this alteration would have taken place in the earlier of the two generations. Thereafter, socketed-leg "dolls" continued for at least one more generation (there is another 0.02 decrease in size to **C109**), before being replaced altogether by flanged-leg "dolls."

It has been suggested elsewhere that "dolls" with socketed legs are a particularly Attic type, while those with flanged legs are Corinthian.[203] Although undoubtedly there are connections between Attic and Corinthian "dolls," the nature of the relationship is not entirely clear. That the two centers knew each other's "doll" types is certain. An apparently Attic copy of a flat-backed lingering Archaic Corinthian "doll" was found in the Athenian Agora,[204] while an Attic "doll" of limbless type (Pl. 75) was found in a 4th-century B.C. context in Corinth.[205] When the thighs of these Attic limbless figurines terminate in sockets, they are not pierced for the attachment of lower legs,[206] and some, such as the above-mentioned example from Corinth, are not really socketed but are completely open underneath. Published Attic "dolls" with pierced thigh sockets are of later anatomical style than their Corinthian counterparts[207] and therefore on the basis of present evidence cannot be cited as sources. Further finds and studies may clarify the matter, but at present it is probably best not to assign geographical origins to the different methods of attaching limbs.

Shoulders with flat surfaces for the attachment of the arms are the norm in the largest and best "dolls." In others, the torso curves in gently at the waist (e.g., **C109**), and, as a result, the shoulders project slightly. Other examples, which are smaller and later, show angular, projecting shoulders almost like those of a herm (e.g., **C127**). Since a tendency to projecting shoulders is seen even in the flat lingering Archaic "dolls,"[208] it is probably not entirely a chronological development but in part a device to free the arms as much as possible when the "doll" was in movement. Flat shoulders continue to be found in the Hellenistic period among seated "dolls."[209]

A small number of "dolls," both standing and seated, have moveable arms but rigid legs. One such standing "doll" is represented on a grave relief in Athens,[210] and the type may have been more typically Attic than Corinthian. The best-preserved Corinthian example is **C110**, which is later in date, having the attenuated proportions of the Hellenistic period. It may have been made in the same workshop as a seated "doll" with similar rigid legs in the Corinth collection; this "doll," which also resembles **C110** in proportions and workmanship, is from a 3rd- to early-2nd-century B.C. deposit.[211]

[203] *Corinth* XV, ii, pp. 147–148.
[204] Nicholls 1995, p. 483, no. 63, pl. 106, with further imported examples cited on p. 436, note 148.
[205] MF-71-45, from Forum Southwest; for the deposit, Drain 1971-1, see C. K. Williams and Fisher 1972, pp. 154–163 (several figurines noted on pp. 162–163). The context is dated to the third quarter of the 4th century B.C.; since the figurines are otherwise consistently 4th century in date, it is possible that the Attic limbless "dolls" survived well into that period.
[206] For a photograph of the underside of this type, see Vafopoulou-Richardson 1981, fig. 15. On Attic "dolls," see Nicholls 1995, pp. 435–438; on the limbless type, see Reilly 1997.
[207] E.g., *British Museum* I, p. 186, no. 701, pl. 91, dated early Rich Style in Nicholls 1995, p. 438, note 155.
[208] E.g., *British Museum* I, p. 249, no. 913, pl. 132.
[209] E.g., MF-2751, MF-2753, *Corinth* XII, p. 41, nos. 224, 225, pl. 19.
[210] Dörig 1958, pl. 23:3. The construction of this "doll" is not very clear in the relief, but the arms do seem to swing forward, and the legs seem to be pressed together.
[211] MF-2751, *Corinth* XII, p. 41, no. 224, pl. 19. Standing dolls with rigid legs are not very common in Corinth. A late-5th-century B.C. example in London has less elongated proportions: *British Museum* I, p. 259, no. 953, pl. 134.

The rigid lower legs of the fragmentary **C111** could have belonged to a standing "doll," but the clean horizontal break at the knees suggests that the legs may have broken from the flat lap of a seated nude "doll." This type, also of Hellenistic date,[212] is more common in Corinth than standing "dolls" with rigid legs, but in general it is more typical of Central Greece and Asia Minor.[213] A more unusual type of seated "doll," probably of 4th-century B.C. date, is represented by **C112** and the leg **C120**. The legs of these "dolls" were made in two parts, articulated at both the hip and the knee.[214] "Dolls" so constructed could sit or, if the head were pierced, could dangle; the back wall drops to the bottom of the flanges, probably to provide stability on a seat.

In the latest "dolls," distortions in the anatomy appear to be the result of carelessness, as in **C114**, although the corpulence of one example (**C115**) must be deliberate, a parallel to nonarticulated comic figurines parodying serious types (see pp. 196–197). Obese female figurines with articulated arms have been found elsewhere, but they usually have rigid legs and stand on bases; they are thought to represent hetairai.[215]

HEADS OF ARTICULATED "DOLLS" AND RELATED HEADS (**C124–C171**)

Heads of "dolls," even when not attached to a torso, can be recognized in part by their characteristic facial and coiffure types but most reliably by the suspension hole at the top. Sometimes, in fact, it is only the holes that identify them, since the molds were used so often, and the casts consequently were so blurred, that some "dolls'" heads are little more than pierced terracotta lumps. Presumably in these cases the lack of detail was remedied with paint. As mentioned above, however, not every "doll's" head was pierced. The best example of an unpierced "doll's" head is **C128**, which is preserved with the upper part of a flat-shouldered "doll's" torso. This head and torso may have belonged to a fully articulated "doll" that did not dangle, to a "doll" with rigid legs in a seated or standing pose, or perhaps to one with two-part legs, such as **C112**, which could either stand or sit.[216]

While this unpierced head certainly belonged to a "doll" of one sort or another, other heads, now separated from their torsos, originally may have belonged not to "dolls" but to other figurine types, even when they are mechanically related to "dolls'" heads. Heads often were used indiscriminately for different kinds of figurines; in accord with this workshop practice, stylistically or mechanically related pierced and unpierced heads are discussed together in this chapter. The great variety among "dolls'" heads, not only in scale, quality, and workmanship but also in the combinations of facial types, coiffures, and headdresses, precludes a strict division into categories. For this reason, a representative sample has been selected for cataloguing and discussion.

The 5th-century B.C. "dolls'" heads are characterized by a curly, rounded mass of hair wrapped in a sphendone, which is fastened at the top with a soft, flat bowknot, an arrangement that persists and is elaborated upon into the 4th century B.C. The forehead is framed by a row of fat ringlets; the face is usually small, with a narrow, receding chin. Both the ringlets and the receding chin seem to be Archaic survivals. The features are always blurred, perhaps because worn head molds were the basis for new designs. A head of this type (**C125**) was found in Pit A

[212] MF-2751, MF-2753, MF-2754, *Corinth* XII, p. 41, nos. 224–226, pl. 19, from a 3rd- to early-2nd-century B.C. deposit; also, MF-3088, MF-9311 in the Corinth collection. A 3rd- to 2nd-century B.C. tomb in Argos contained a similar "doll": Aupert 1982, pp. 642–643, fig. 9.

[213] Andrén 1948, pp. 61–64; *Troy*, pp. 87–95, both with bibliography.

[214] There is a complete example of this type in Copenhagen (*Danish National Museum*, p. 60, no. 562, pl. 70). The reported provenience is Tanagra, but the "doll" could be Corinthian, since its head is similar to **C132**; the arms and lower legs,

however, do not seem typically Corinthian. In any case, it is not certain that any of the limbs originally belonged to this torso.

[215] Winter, *Typen* II, p. 456, nos. 2, 3; *Lindos* I, col. 578, no. 2387, pl. 112; from the Athenian Agora, D. B. Thompson 1954, pp. 90–91, 106, no. 2, pl. 21, with bibliography.

[216] A parallel for this "doll" type in Copenhagen seems to have an unpierced head, since no hole is mentioned in the description: *Danish National Museum*, p. 60, no. 562, pl. 70; this seems not to be an oversight, since another "doll" in the collection, p. 29, no. 270, is described as pierced.

(lot 887), the terminal date of which is the last quarter of the 5th century B.C. Although this head type was not found in the Potters' Quarter, it may have been made there, since it was used on torsos with projecting shoulders (see **C124**), molds for which were found in the Potters' Quarter. In 4th-century B.C. examples of this head type, a towering, columnar projection of hair sometimes was added to the cranium (**C126**).

A larger and much better made version of a head wearing a bow-tied sphendone, **C130**, could be an example of the type that gave rise to this popular series. The head is not pierced, and there is no observable mechanical link between it and the "doll" type from Pit A, but it could have belonged to a large (size range 3) "doll." It has the long, straight-sided, full-jawed facial shape and large features typical of the Early Classical hydriaphoros group (see pp. 39–40). Another, similar head (**C131**) has a less narrow facial shape. Both heads show more softly rendered features than the hydriaphoros group and a more gently flowing coiffure, suggesting a somewhat later stylistic development. They retain a certain seriousness of expression, however, accentuated by their unsmiling mouths. In both heads, the sphendone bow was not added but was included in the mold, indicating that the archetypes of these heads may have been intended specifically for "dolls," the only type definitely known among the sanctuary finds to utilize this headdress. The pottery context of **C131** dates to the 5th century B.C.; its architectural context is probably of late-4th-century B.C. date. A reasonable stylistic date for the archetype of these heads would be the middle to third quarter of the 5th century B.C. In the facial structure and waving forehead hair, these heads have a parallel in a sculpture from the Athenian Agora, a Pheidian head of Nike, which is a Roman replica related to the Hertz type.[217] The fleshier facial features of the figurines, however, are more Peloponnesian than Attic in style. It is possible that we can see once again a familiar pattern, in which a type developed in Corinth during the 5th century B.C. outside the Potters' Quarter was adapted there in a more modest form and mass produced into the 4th century B.C.

C134–**C136** appear to be later, coarsened versions of this facial type. The coiffures of **C134** and **C135** are detailed, but abstractly, without a real understanding of the hair arrangement. **C136** wears the Hellenistic melon coiffure; its relatively large size demonstrates that late "dolls" are not necessarily small "dolls" at the end of mold series. Two pierced "dolls'" heads, **C140** and **C141**, are descendants, typologically and perhaps also mechanically, of the hydriaphoros type with a long, narrow face. The coroplast of **C141** added a rough sphendone with a slashed bowknot but clearly no longer understood how the sphendone bound up the hair, for he added long locks of hair at the sides as well. In **C140**, the features have lost their definition, and the figurine wears a flat, round hat that resembles a petasos more than the sun hats worn by women, as seen in "Tanagra" figurines; the head therefore may have belonged to a male "doll," although no male articulated torsos of this period have survived. Both heads probably were made during the second half of the 4th century B.C.

The foregoing heads reflect 5th-century B.C. creations, although they were made in the 4th century B.C., but "dolls'" heads of a genuine 4th-century style were made at the same time. In some, the long facial shape is retained, although rounded a little at the sides or tapered somewhat toward the chin. The face loses its uniplanar structure entirely, the forehead becomes higher, the temples slant back more, and the eyes drop down at the outer corners and diminish in size in relation to the face. Sometimes the height of the forehead and the depth of the jaw force the features into a cluster near the center of the face. The serious expression usually persists. Individual heads show these qualities to different degrees, some maintaining a more Classical look, others leaning toward a growing Hellenistic expressiveness. The "anti-Classicism" recognized in 4th-century sculptural style[218] seems to have coexisted peacefully with survivals of Classical

---

[217] Harrison 1982, pp. 53–65.
[218] Brown 1973, pp. 5–24.

style, as a normal feature of figurine production in Corinth, just as in the 5th century B.C. and even into the 4th, Archaic traditions and Classical innovations coexisted.

Among the more Classical heads are **C128**, **C132**, **C133**, and **C137–C139**, one of which (**C138**) is from a pottery context terminating in the mid-4th century B.C. In their faces, a slight downturn of the eyes at the outer corners is coupled with the impassiveness typical of the Classical heads. Only one head (**C132**) is slightly expressive, owing in part to its slight tilt on a powerful neck. The long hair in back and the pellet earrings recall the head of the peplos-figurine **C17**, suggesting that **C132** may have belonged to a figurine of that type. Even if not itself a "doll's" head, **C132** may have a later mechanical relative in the pierced head **C133**, to which a bowknotted sphendone and a towering projection of hair have been added, as in **C126**.

Another group with an early-4th-century B.C. stylistic date is **C142–C144**, all large (size ranges 3–4 or 4) and well made. Of the three heads, only **C142** is pierced. The relationship among them is hard to define, since they are not mechanically related and differ in some ways. In all, the front hair is waved from a central part in the Knidian fashion. **C142** has precisely modeled parallel hair waves, suggesting a metallic source, while the rendering is much freer and more typical of work in clay in the other two heads. The deep, broadly waved locks of **C144** recall a stone sculpture, a female head from the Argive Heraion.[219] **C143** differs in the binding of the hair in back in a sakkos. All share a particular beauty of fabric, which must have been achieved only with considerable effort, even though the surface would have been hidden completely by layers of slip and paint. In fact, the outlines of the features are in part obscured because the slip and paint adhered very well to the carefully prepared surface. There are traces of yellow on the hair of **C142**, probably an underpainting for gilding (see pp. 13–14). These heads represent the very best of the local coroplasts' craft. None of the three is part of a long mold series or even has a clear mechanical relative among the other heads. Just as in the peplos-figurine category, the best work is isolated, and we are probably dealing with a workshop, located outside the Potters' Quarter, that did not mass produce figurines. As before, one must assume in these cases either that the best-made, most sculpturally oriented figurines were prohibitively expensive or that the economic base of their workshops rested on activities other than the production of large quantities of figurines, such as the preparation of models for bronze statuettes.

A few pieces show a fine finish of a different kind. **C129** was painted in three stages. First a thin bluish white wash was applied, then a thick white slip, and over this an enamel-like ivory-colored paint. In addition, the jewelry was gilded. The same piece shows an unusually delicate handling of the hair. The peaked coiffure so carefully detailed in **C129**, however, is given such a summary rendering in **C155** that the hair is rendered with vertical incised strokes, without regard for its natural pattern of growth. Peaked coiffures first appear in Attic art in the 5th century B.C. and were popular ca. 360 B.C., on the basis of their appearance on grave stelai of this time.[220]

A group of heads in a more Attic style (**C145–C148**) shows oval to round faces with triangular foreheads and coiffures that are peaked in front. Similar heads are found on Attic figurine vases, such as a lekythos in Berlin representing Aphrodite and Adonis.[221] A number of Attic figurine vases of the late 5th and 4th centuries B.C. are of reported Corinthian provenience;[222] if this information is accurate, such vases could have been available to Corinthian coroplasts. The Corinthian heads are too large to have been made in molds taken directly from Attic figurine vases, however, and too small to have been taken from Attic head vases, but imported Attic vases could have inspired free copies. Alternatively, Attic molds could have been used. Attic workshop materials were exported to Asia Minor and Egypt,[223] and it is conceivable that

[219] Cf. especially the hair in the profile view in Berve et al. 1962, pl. 84.

[220] *Pnyx*, pp. 120, 143, no. 43, fig. 58.

[221] Trumpf-Lyritzaki 1969, pp. 49–50, no. 137, pl. 20.

[222] Trumpf-Lyritzaki 1969, nos. 25, 34, 47, 48, 49, 104, 137, 161, 167.

[223] Besques 1978; Kassab Tezgör and Abd al Fattah 1997.

Corinth received some as well, although no examples have been recognized as yet among the molds found in Corinth. A head closely similar to **C145** is found on an articulated "doll" with socketed legs in Bowdoin College.[224]

Another facial type with an Attic parallel is **C149**, the style of which compares well with a late-5th- to early-4th-century B.C. head vase from the Athenian Agora.[225] Since these long, narrow faces, now with a somewhat mournful expression because of their tilted pose, parted lips, and downturned eyes, are more typical of earlier Corinthian style than Attic, one might suggest a common Corinthian ancestry. Once again, the relationship is stylistic rather than demonstrably mechanical.

One group of heads (**C149**–**C152**) demonstrates the close workshop relationship between "dolls'" heads and heads used for other figurine types. The rough tooling on the hair of **C149** is so similar to that of the peplos-figurine **C17** as to imply that they were made in the same workshop (Workshop B, pp. 344–345) in the Potters' Quarter; **C149** has long hair bound with a fillet, a coiffure more characteristic of peplos-figurines than "dolls." Also from the same workshop are **C150** and **C151**. **C150** is probably of the generation following **C149**; it shows the same slashing technique for hair retouch but a different coiffure, this time with the locks of hair tied at the top of the head into a flat bowknot with four protruding curls. A trace of a drapery fold at the neck suggests that this head belonged to a mantled figurine, and in fact the head is closely similar in facial type and coiffure to that of a Corinthian mantled figurine in London; this head wears a wreath of leaves.[226] **C151** may be yet another generation, now pierced as a "doll's" head, with very similar hair retouch, but the bowknot altered to a loose cluster of curls. Since coiffures with knotted hair-locks and clusters of curls first appeared in Corinth in the latter part of the 4th century B.C. (see pp. 161–162), these heads would have been among the later products of the workshop, before the destruction of the Potters' Quarter in the 320s B.C. This small group of heads is an interesting illustration of workshop practice. With a similar technique indicating that they were made within a relatively short time, perhaps by the same artisan, they represent three generations of a mold series, probably used for three completely different figurine types, a peplos-figurine, a mantled figurine, and an articulated "doll," all with different coiffures. Still another head in this workshop group is **C152**, probably a mold sibling of the head of the peplos-figurine **C17**, but it is a pierced "doll's" head, with yet another coiffure, this time plaited. Also related is a head from the Potters' Quarter, perhaps from a parallel mold series.[227] One element that remains constant throughout the group is the pair of teardrop-shaped earrings. In the later generations, the forehead increases in height and width and, as a result, the features seem to cluster near the center of the face. Two larger heads also are related in facial type and coiffure. **C154** shows some similarity in workmanship, but its facial features are stronger and the cheeks and jaw are fuller. The tendency to cluster features at the center of the face is exaggerated in **C153**, which has a flowing coiffure like that of **C149**.

Other "dolls'" heads as well have possible workshop relationships outside their types. **C156**, for example, may be a mechanical relative of the head of the mantled figurine **H102** and a head with a bow-knot coiffure (**H234**).

Although a few groups have been described above, most of the "dolls," particularly the more summary, mass-produced examples, do not fall into a coherent pattern. The coroplasts probably possessed head molds descending from a variety of types, which they mixed indiscriminately with different torsos and then added coiffures as the spirit moved them. This freedom to mix types is an important aspect of coroplastic creativity.

---

[224] *Aspects of Ancient Greece*, pp. 252–253, no. 123.
[225] E. R. Williams 1978, p. 397, no. 63, pl. 101.

[226] Higgins 1967, p. 104, pl. 47:c; the 3rd-century B.C. date suggested there seems too late.
[227] KT-10-8, *Corinth* XV, ii, p. 133, no. 42, pl. 28.

The coiffures sometimes have an element of fantasy, perhaps because, after so much repetition, the original designs had lost meaning. The towering projections of **C126** and **C133** are clearly part of the hair; the tooled strokes of better, less exaggerated examples, such as **C139** and **C157**, detail the locks more clearly. But when the strokes become summary and the shape merges with the head into a cone, as in **C159**, the projection begins to resemble a hat. The schematic pattern of horizontal waves across the front of the hair is clearer in its possible mold relative **C158**, which is an unusually crisp mold impression. This head type was used for the peplos-figurine **C33** and is known in a Corinthian seated type as well.[228] **C159** has globular blisters around the forehead, which means that it was formed in a plaster mold (see pp. 16–17) and therefore should not be dated before the later 3rd century B.C. It must be one of the latest of its type.[229]

A head in a conical cap of Scythian type with lappets and a disc finial (**C160**) also would seem to be a fantasy, except that the parallel, horizontal ridges on the cap suggest creases, as on a head in Paris that wears a horizontally creased, pointed headdress.[230] **C161** and **C162** also wear peaked caps; the latter may have lappets and therefore may be a Scythian cap, leaving open the possibility that this figurine originally represented an Amazon.

Some heads have a projecting topknot of hair over the center of the forehead, as in **C127** and **C163**; it is sometimes punched, presumably to suggest curls, as in **C134**. It may have been an exaggerated form of the peak over the forehead into which the front hair was sometimes arranged, as in **C138** and **C155**. Heads with both a high peak in front and a projection in back have a distinctive profile resembling a set of horns, as in **C168**; this coiffure is discussed further below (p. 171). **C169**, which also has a double-peaked coiffure, resembles a mold from the Potters' Quarter in facial type and scale (see catalogue). In other heads, the hair was braided back from the center of the forehead, as in **C164** and **C165**, or the head might be circled by a plait, as in **C128**. The braid pulled back from the center of the forehead is often seen on heads of children[231] as well as young women. The braid sometimes is barely recognizable, as in **C167**; in these cases, one must assume that the coroplast no longer quite understood the arrangement of the coiffure or its original significance. The smiling, full-jawed face of **C167** appears to be a later generation of **C166**, which wears a simpler coiffure, waving away at either side from a central part. Faint waves of this kind can still be seen around the forehead of **C167**, to which the braids in front and around the cranium apparently were added later. **C170** and **C171** are miniatures, corresponding in size with the small torso **C113**.

Relatively little can be learned of the chronology of Corinthian "dolls" from the pottery contexts, as was true also of the peplos-figurines and seated female figurines. Only Pit A (lot 887) is really helpful, yielding the head type **C125**. The "doll" **C124** combines a head closely similar in type and scale to **C125** with a torso with projecting shoulders; through this association, it would appear that relatively small "dolls" with projecting shoulders already were being made by the last quarter of the 5th century B.C., the terminal date of Pit A. While the closing of the Potters' Quarter workshops dates the end of some figurine types, the output of articulated "dolls" seems to have continued, although it may have diminished considerably. Certainly the "dolls'" heads found in the Demeter sanctuary are much more varied in type than the heads and molds preserved in the Potters' Quarter, suggesting other sources. A few heads, such as **C161** and **C162**, stand apart from the others strikingly in their type, workmanship, and relatively large

[228] Winter, *Typen* I, p. 86, no. 7.
[229] **C159** is from lot 878, which is part of the construction fill of the Trapezoidal Building. The architectural context of this lot is therefore early 3rd century B.C. (see lot list, p. 356), but the context does include a very small quantity of later, intrusive material (see p. 6); the use of a plaster mold suggests that this head is later as well.

[230] *Louvre* III, p. 5, no. D18, pl. 5:c. A standing female figurine of reported Corinthian provenience wears a peaked cap with lappets: Winter, *Typen* I, p. 80, no. 3.
[231] E.g., Vorster 1983, p. 349, no. 53, pl. 16:2; p. 387, no. 169, pl. 24:1, 2.

scale. In addition, the head made in a plaster mold (**C159**) could not have come from the Potters' Quarter, where there is no evidence for the use of such molds and which was inactive by the time plaster molds came into use. This head proves that the production of articulated dangling "dolls" continued in some measure well into the 3rd century B.C., even though seated "dolls" begin to appear in Corinth at that time (see p. 52). In the absence of a major producer of dangling "dolls," seated "dolls," introduced from Athens or Asia Minor, may have helped to fill the void. Seated "dolls" never became popular votives in the Demeter sanctuary, however, perhaps because they did not carry the same meaning as the customary dangling "doll."

FIGURINES OF DANCERS RELATED TO ARTICULATED "DOLLS" (**C172**–**C185**)

Torsos of nude "dolls" were used by coroplasts as the basis for a number of other types, not necessarily articulated, such as nude or semidraped Aphrodites (**H266** and **H268**) and even a semidraped male torso (**C199**). The most common adaptation, however, was the bare-breasted dancer in a knee-length, belted skirt (**C172**–**C179**). The coroplasts simply added skirts by hand to the nude hips and thighs, and either hung articulated limbs, as in "dolls," or attached arms and lower legs in various poses, as in ordinary figurines. They might add skirt folds only beside the thighs, as in **C174**, or at the sides and front of the torso, as in **C175** and **C176**, leaving the back nude, paper-doll fashion. When molds were taken from figurines thus transformed, the nude back molds continued to be used together with the draped fronts.

The top of the skirt was either rolled over a narrow belt to hold it up, as in **C172** and **C179**, or attached to a wide, close-fitting belt with borders at the top and bottom, as in **C176** and **C177**. The skirt hem is usually in movement, either swaying slightly or fluttering more actively. One example has crossbands over the chest (**C178**), a common article of clothing on many types of figures in active movement, worn to anchor the cloth. When worn over a nude chest, the bands were intended to help hold up the skirt or were merely decorative. In **C113**, a small, degenerate, completely nude "doll," the crossbands are obviously decorative. Complete figurines in museum collections point to the likelihood that at least some of the figurines in short skirts found in the Demeter sanctuary are of the type commonly called "kalathiskos dancers." **C173** preserves enough of the arms to show that they were posed like those of fully preserved kalathiskos dancers.[232] The head of **C173**, which is the only preserved head in the group, however, does not wear a kalathiskos but has the wavy hair and sphendone commonly found in articulated "dolls."

Representations of such dancers, in different media, were widespread and have been the subject of extensive discussion.[233] The point of interest for the present study is that the figurines probably represent professional dancers whose performances were connected with fertility cult and possibly with marriage.[234] In renderings from various sites, these dancers wear a short chiton, a peplos of knee or hip length, or just a short belted skirt; sometimes there are crossbands over the bare chest. The dancers sometimes wear a kalathiskos or a flaring crown of leaves. They dance on tiptoe, perhaps leaping, with arms moving freely. It is easy to see how a workshop accustomed to making "dolls" would find the subject congenial.

It is not known whether such dance performances actually took place at the Demeter sanctuary or whether images of these dancers, who were known to perform in the context of fertility cult, merely projected the idea of fertility to the votaries who purchased and dedicated the figurines. The sanctuary of the Classical period contained a small theatral area on the Upper Terrace, which apparently was intended for standing spectators watching activities

---

[232] Cf. Winter, *Typen* II, p. 157, nos. 1, 2.

[233] See the following, all with bibliography: Metzger 1942–1943; Contoléon 1947–1948; *Délos* XXIII, pp. 282–283, no. 1364; Bendinelli 1957; *Troy*, p. 100. On their appearance in Neo-Attic sculpture and a possible connection with the sculptor Kallimachos, see Fuchs 1959, pp. 90–96; Fuchs 1986, pp. 284–285; Tiberios 1981; Grandjouan 1989, pp. 5–6.

[234] On the role of dance to mollify the angry Demeter, and to soften the earth so that its fruits (i.e., Kore) may emerge, see Lonsdale 1993, pp. 265–267.

taking place below.[235] It overlooks the central open courtyard of the Middle Terrace, which was the area most suitable for dancing.

Figurines of this type in Berlin, St. Petersburg, Paris, and New York[236] are sometimes assigned to Athens, because the subject appears in Neo-Attic sculpture. As mentioned above, however, the use of this subject was widespread, and several factors suggest that most of the figurines representing these dancers were made in Corinth. The figurine in St. Petersburg is of Corinthian provenience; the clay of the example in Paris is said to be Corinthian; I was able to examine the figurine in New York, and the fabric and workmanship appear to be Corinthian. In addition, the torsos of the Berlin and St. Petersburg figurines look very much like **C179**, in that the method of constructing these figurines is typically Corinthian, using "dolls'" torsos and draping them with added folds; also Corinthian is the slightly awkward, improvised look of the result.[237] In addition, the arm position of the dancers in Berlin is echoed in **C173**. Since the dancers were constructed on the torsos of "dolls," which were not meant to stand upright, and were represented in movement, a curious pillar-and-base arrangement supporting the figure from the back was added in some examples. In this way, the lightly jumping steps characteristic of these dancers could be suggested.

The large, beautifully made, although fragmentary **C172** shows that better Corinthian craftsmen were interested in the subject, but the humbler examples were probably made in the Potters' Quarter, in a workshop that also prepared articulated "dolls." How the subject came into use in the first place can only be a matter of speculation. In Corinth, the type seems to have been put together from local elements in a manner characteristic of local workshops. Perhaps a rendering in terracotta was simply the Corinthian response to a widespread religious custom, which was reflected in Athens in vase painting and sculpture, and elsewhere in various media. All these renderings are sometimes thought to derive from a lost sculpture of Kallimachos; if such a work did indeed exist, however, it need only have been inspired by the same source material.

Hellenistic figurines of dancers wearing similar short skirts and wide belts, and with articulated limbs, have been found in South Italy.[238] They are by this time rather degenerate in style but perhaps could have been derived from Corinthian prototypes. A short skirt with a wide belt is also characteristic of the costume of girl initiates who participated in the races at the Heraia in Argos, but in this case the chiton bares only one breast, and the representations (which are Archaic in date) clearly show a running pose.[239]

Although this group of figurines representing kalathiskos dancers appears to be of local origin, another type of dancer from the Demeter sanctuary (**C180** and **C181**) has very clear Athenian stylistic connections. This type wears a short chiton or peplos that was part of the archetype and was not added to a nude torso, except in the most degenerate examples. The limbs of these dancers are always articulated; the thighs are usually socketed but are occasionally flanged. The drapery is modeled in a simplified form of the "quiet" style of Attic sculpture, which also is seen in the peplos-figurines (see pp. 33–34). The cloth is in movement, as if blown by the wind against the abdomen and around the thighs. The fine folds of **C181** and its very short overfold, revealing the belt beneath, suggest that it is a close, perhaps mechanical copy of an Attic figurine type or was

---

[235] *Corinth* XVIII, iii, p. 429.

[236] Berlin: Winter, *Typen* II, p. 157, nos. 1, 2; *Königliche Museen*, p. 13, pl. XII; Rohde 1968, pp. 18–19, 42, no. 20a, with bibliography (Corinthian fabric seems not to be fully understood in this publication, since the articulated "doll" no. 19b, also called Attic, has a head of Potters' Quarter type and should be Corinthian). St. Petersburg: Winter, *Typen* II, p. 157, no. 2b; Belov et al. 1976, p. 33, no. 101. Paris: Winter, *Typen* II, p. 157, with no. 1; *Louvre* III, p. 68, no. D423

(= CA237), pl. 91:a; Besques 1994, p. 100, no. 94. New York: [E. Robinson] 1907, fig. on p. 7, upper row, second from left.

[237] It should also be noted that Knoblauch (1939, col. 445) records a similarity between the workmanship of the dancer in Berlin and that of a Nike, which happens to have a head of Corinthian type (**H231**).

[238] *Louvre* IV, i, p. 77, nos. D3721, D3722, pl. 69:c, d.

[239] Serwint 1993, esp. p. 407, fig. 1.

made in an imported mold.[240] Both the drapery and a slight forward projection of the upper torso in these figurines are reminiscent of Athenian akroteria. An example from the Temple of Ares in the Athenian Agora shows a similar arrangement of folds between the thighs, as well as a very short overfold lifted by the breeze to reveal the belt.[241] Although the earliest versions of this dancer type included the drapery, much poorer renderings were constructed by adding drapery to nude torsos, as in **C182**, using the technique already seen in the kalathiskos dancers. Probably the latest examples (**C183** and **C184**) have thickened, flaring hems, which are pierced in a sort of compromise between the socketed and flanged forms of attachment. **C184** is the most degenerate; the margin of clay around the joint of the front and back molds was left untrimmed, and the head was merely glued to the scored surface of the shoulders. The sense of movement has been lost in these poor examples, apart from the clumsy, flaring hem, but all must have been intended to represent dancers.

The parodying of nude "doll" types seen in **C115** may be paralleled among the draped "dolls" by **C185**, a corpulent figure with a prominent abdomen, wearing a clinging chiton and crossband. Lacking the hem, one cannot be sure that the figure was portrayed in movement, but the type and costume are otherwise consistent with figurines of dancers.

MALE FIGURINES: NUDE, SEMIDRAPED, AND DRAPED
(C186–C202)

The earliest male figurine in Classical style is the horse-rider **C186**. The figurine is a larger, moldmade version of the usually handmade riders, which date from the Archaic period to the 4th century B.C.[242] In style, this rider retains an Archaic flavor in the horizontally ridged, wiglike hair, but the drapery, with its oval neckline and doughy zigzag folds, links it to the earliest standing peplos-figurines in Classical style (**C1**–**C6**) and suggests that it may have been made in the same workshop (Workshop D, p. 345). Like the peplos-figurines, the rider fuses Archaic and Early Classical stylistic features. **C187** is another but smaller rider, to judge from the straddling pose; the figurine is handmade, but the anatomy of the nude torso and legs is clearly post-Archaic.

Figurines representing horse-riders were frequently dedicated in Corinth in small hero shrines.[243] The large number of such figurines dedicated at the Acrocorinth sanctuary, taken together with other types associated with heroes, such as banqueters, point to the worship of a hero there beside Demeter and Kore (see pp. 332–333). The possible reference of horse-rider figurines to the status and wealth associated in ancient Greece with owning horses[244] would connect well with the worship of a hero. Such figurines might also be emblematic of horse races as part of hero worship.[245] In Greek literature, the taming of horses is a metaphor for bringing girls into readiness for marriage.[246]

Most of the male figurines of the Classical period represent standing youths, usually nude or with a mantle draped down the back and covering only the arms, as in **C190**. They are solid and plaquelike, with flat or concave backs. Sometimes, illogically, the drapery forms a kind of backdrop, without any visible attachment to the figure, as in **C188**, **C189**, and **C191**. There are several possible explanations for this treatment. The most obvious is that the drapery on the arms may have been lost as the mold series progressed, but there may have been a specific

[240] Cf. *British Museum* I, p. 192, no. 721, pl. 94.

[241] Boulter 1953.

[242] *Corinth* XV, ii, pp. 163–176, pl. 35–37. The examples from the Acrocorinth sanctuary will be published in a forthcoming fascicle of *Corinth* XVIII.

[243] E.g., the Heroon of the Crossroads: C. K. Williams and Fisher 1973, pp. 6–12, pl. 3.

[244] Greenhalgh 1973, pp. 42–43.

[245] Broneer 1942, pp. 134–136.

[246] Bremmer 1994, p. 73; Calame 1997, p. 191; Ghiron-Bistagne 1985.

source in a class of Archaic relief figures in the form of miniature stelai. An example of this class is MF-11884,[247] in which a youth with drapery behind him stands on a plinth base like that of the better-preserved Classical youths (**C188** and **C190**). The drapery background is seen also in Archaic terracotta sculpture. A late Archaic draped kouros from Syracuse, for which a Peloponnesian connection has been suggested, wears the mantle over one shoulder, from which it falls behind the back, hips, and thighs like a screen.[248] Although all the standing youths of this group in Corinth were made during the Classical period, the Archaic reflections are clear not only in the drapery but also in the smile of **C188** and the strictly frontal stance of most members of the group. Only **C189** shows a slight contrapposto; in the other figurines, one knee may bend slightly but without a corresponding movement in the hips.

Since the figurines in this group are small (at the lower end of size range 2) and of rather indifferent quality, not much detail is preserved in the heads. The hair is always short, with a few broad waves above a low forehead, in the typical Early Classical style, as in **C188**–**C190**. One example shows a knot at the center of the forehead (**C192**), in a distinctive coiffure that is discussed below (pp. 62–63). A strip of clay was added to most of the heads to form a low, wide headdress, using a technique inherited from the Archaic period. It is not quite clear what kind of headdress was intended; the low form in the shape of a ring suggests a wreath, but in **C190**, in which the headdress is in the mold, the shape looks more like a polos.

The youths, who probably are votaries, carry offerings appropriate to their age and sex: an aryballos (**C188**), a lyre[249] (**C190** and **C193**), and a rooster (**C191**).[250] An oval object in the hand, as in **C191**, could be a vessel longer than an aryballos, such as an alabastron, a lekythos, or perhaps a purse for knucklebones, as seen more clearly in the semidraped youth **C201**. Similar youths with offerings were found at the Asklepieion, where they are thought to have had some connection with the earlier cult of Apollo.[251] There they made up a much larger proportion of the total number of figurines than in the Acrocorinth sanctuary, where the count of standing youths reaches only ca. fifty-five. The nudity of most of the youths, except for a mantle covering the shoulders and arms or used as a backdrop, is worth noting, since the worshipers who approach deities on votive reliefs are usually well wrapped in mantles.[252] The aryballos carried by **C188** could suggest that this figurine represents an athlete; a painted and inscribed Corinthian kotyle offers evidence of a youths' footrace in honor of Persephone,[253] and it may be significant that the one well-preserved figure in this painting is nude but for a mantle draped like a scarf over his shoulders and arms, similar to the garment of the figurines. Boeotian figurines of youths are similarly draped over the shoulders and arms, baring the front of the torso.[254] In the context of coming-of-age rituals, nudity served the purpose not only of revealing sexual maturity but also of symbolically assisting the transformation from one stage of life to the next by removing the outmoded outward trappings.[255] At the Acrocorinth sanctuary, handmade nude male figurines were already offered in the Archaic period (e.g., MF-10374[256]), perhaps pointing to a coming-of-age ritual beginning at that time. At sculptural scale, the terracotta figures of youths from the sanctuary are either wholly nude or semidraped.[257]

---

[247] Publication forthcoming.

[248] Holloway 1975, p. 32, figs. 182–184. A fragmentary late-5th- or 4th-century B.C. terracotta sculpture from the Demeter sanctuary (SF-69-8) shows the legs attached to a roughly modeled background (publication forthcoming by Nancy Bookidis).

[249] The fragment **V13** may be from a model lyre.

[250] On the symbolism of the rooster, which had funerary associations as well as reference to the rising sun or life, see Goodenough 1958, VIII, pp. 59–70.

[251] *Corinth* XIV, pp. 138–140, nos. 9–12, pl. 54.

[252] E.g., a relief in Paris, Hamiaux 1992, p. 216, no. 224.

[253] *Corinth* XVIII, i, pp. 133–134, no. 292, pl. 32; Pemberton 1978, pp. 30–31, 33.

[254] See p. 292, note 42.

[255] The issue of ritual nudity is summarized succinctly in Serwint 1993, pp. 420–421, with bibliography; see also Bonfante 1989, pp. 545–546, note 16, and p. 551, note 45; Scanlon 1988; Lincoln 1991, pp. 103–104; Pinney 1993; Stewart 1997, pp. 27–34, with bibliography on pp. 239–241.

[256] Publication forthcoming.

[257] E.g., SF-65-14, Bookidis 1988, pl. 4 (semidraped).

Insofar as the quality and condition of these figurines will allow comparisons, the slender proportions of **C188** fit in well with Late Archaic bronze statuettes of Peloponnesian provenience, such as the Herakles from Perachora,[258] which is thought to be of Corinthian origin, and farther afield, bronzes from Olympia and Sparta.[259] The latter have crowns of leaves or reeds, which could have inspired the added strip headdresses of the Corinthian figurines. An Early Classical rather than a Late Archaic archetype, however, seems more likely for the still slender but more muscular and developed torso of **C189**. Although the feet are not preserved, the stance has the subtle rhythm of the Oinomaos of the Olympia east pediment, one leg slightly forward, the opposite hip very slightly outthrust.[260] The face of this figurine was poorly molded, but the hair and headdress are of the same type as **C188**. Several different archetypes seem to lurk behind this modest group of figurines, which are similar to one another in type, scale, and workmanship. It would appear that workshop materials of both Late Archaic and Early Classical stylistic date were available concurrently, allowing a version with an Archaic flavor, such as **C188**, to coexist with a more Early Classical rendering such as **C189**. Although only a few standing youths were found in the Potters' Quarter,[261] those from the Demeter sanctuary and the Asklepieion appear to have been made there, perhaps all in the same workshop.

Larger (up to size range 3) and better-made standing nude youths also were produced but have survived only in fragments. **C194** and **C195**, the latter with the left arm swathed in drapery, are without contrapposto, but the anatomical modeling is subtle, showing the iliac crest and abdominal musculature as gentle bulges. The steep groin line and flat zigzag folds of **C195** are still in the Archaic tradition. Both seem slender in proportions, even in their fragmentary state. There is as yet no evidence for continuous mold series from these youths to the smaller figurines.

Although the youths, both large and small, recall in a general way the Boeotian figurines of youths from the Kabeirion at Thebes,[262] and there is one possible Boeotian import of this type from the Demeter sanctuary (**I45**), the archetypes must have been distinctly different in physical type from the stockier Boeotian youths. The influence of Boeotian figurines, however, may be responsible for the coiffure of **C192** and the heads **C203** and **C204**, in which long locks are drawn up to the center of the forehead and knotted. **C204**, together with heads from the Potters' Quarter and Asklepieion related to it and listed in the catalogue, also compare well with Boeotian figurines in facial type.[263] On the other hand, the maker of **C203** combined a Boeotian knotted coiffure with a more typically Peloponnesian narrow, large-featured face (on the facial type, see pp. 39–40).[264]

Knotted hair tends to appear in religious contexts, particularly in association with Demeter or related chthonic deities. The origin of the cult of the Kabeiroi at Thebes is connected in myth with Demeter.[265] Representations of Eleusinian hearth initiates also sometimes show knotted hair,[266] as does the youth, probably Ploutos, of the votive relief to the Eleusinian deities

[258] *Perachora* I, pp. 140–142, pl. 45.
[259] Mattusch 1988, pp. 62–63, figs. 4.13, 4.14, with bibliography. Cf. also a Late Archaic hydria handle in Belgrade, in the form of a youth, attributed to Corinth in Rolley 1986, p. 242, fig. 266.
[260] Ashmole and Yalouris 1967, fig. 18.
[261] *Corinth* XV, ii, pp. 112–114, nos. 1–5, pl. 22.
[262] *Kabirenheiligtum* V, pp. 33–76; cf. esp. pp. 71–72, 164–165, nos. 179–195, pl. 14.
[263] Cf. *Kabirenheiligtum* V, e.g., pp. 46, 155–156, no. 94, pl. 7.
[264] There are a few faces of youths from the Kabeirion, e.g., *Kabirenheiligtum* V, pp. 58, 159–160, no. 135, pl. 10, that look distinctly Peloponnesian and could perhaps have been inspired by Corinthian work.

[265] Farnell, *Cults* III, pp. 207–208; Schachter 1981, II, p. 88.
[266] On the hearth initiates, see Clinton 1974, pp. 98–114; see esp. fig. 7 on p. 103. On p. 106, note 47, uncertainty is expressed whether the coiffure had anything to do with religious custom. Evidence for ritual cutting of hair is strong, however. Perhaps the locks were tied off before cutting and dedicating them; on portrait B from Eleusis, pp. 104, 106, figs. 13, 14, a lock has been cut from the right temple; evidence for setting aside a lock of hair for dedication is recorded by Rouse 1902, p. 242 (his discussion of the dedication of hair at puberty on pp. 240–243). On the offering of hair, see also *RE* VII, 2, 1912, cols. 2105–2109, s.v. *Haaropfer* (Sommer); Gernet 1981, pp. 22–23 (on the dedication of hair to heroes and at the time of marriage); Eitrem 1915, pp. 350–372, 396–397;

in Athens.[267] The much later so-called Antium girl in Rome, perhaps a sacrificial servant of an unknown cult, also wears a rather untidy version of this coiffure.[268] It is not certain whether the presence of knotted hair on the Corinthian figurines indicates that Corinthian youths wore their hair in this way when participating in the rites or whether the hair simply imitates a cultic style known from elsewhere. Since the large-scale sculptured terracotta youths from the sanctuary, which are local creations, do not wear the knot, the latter is probably the case.

Of the remaining fragments of larger nude male figurines, **C196** seems Polykleitan in stance, as far as it is preserved. **C197** is much more three-dimensional than the others and is probably of 4th-century B.C. date; since this youth holds a patera, he may be a later version of a type found in the Asklepieion.[269] The stance of **C197** originally may have been similar to that of the smaller but more fully preserved **C198**. The partially draped **C199** is notable technically because it was constructed from a nude female "doll's" torso, with the breasts smeared away and a mantle added around the hips and arms. Figurines of this type are not very common in Corinth, which may be why this example had to be put together in such a resourceful way. Male figurines draped in this manner are usually found in Asia Minor and Rhodes; generally these types are bearded and wear a polos, and they sometimes hold a patera in the right hand.[270] Here they sometimes are identified as Dionysos or Zeus, by virtue of the polos. The examples from Lindos wear a full beard to the chest, of which there are no traces on **C199**. If it originally had a beard, it would have been shorter, as in the examples from Asia Minor. Similarly draped figurines of youths, which sometimes carry a piglet, are known from Magna Graecia.[271] Perhaps the coroplast who made **C199** had in mind a type known in Corinth through imported figurines, although the precise source is elusive. The mantle of **C200** was included in the mold, not added to a nude torso, but the figurine may depend upon an earlier type, since the stacked folds down the shoulder and arm recall Archaic style.

C201 is a semidraped counterpart of **C188–C193**, although it is of very different style. It is of comparably small scale, also carries offerings, in this case a ball and a knucklebone bag,[272] and shares technical aspects, such as the inclusion of the base in the mold. The strong separation of the legs beneath the mantle suggests that the archetype of **C201** was developed from a nude figure. The peculiarly top-heavy proportions, with oversized arms, are found also in Corinthian seated female figurines.[273] The combination of piled-up hair in front and long locks of hair to the shoulders resembles the coiffure of the large-scale isolated male head **C208**. Like the foregoing figurines of youths, **C201** probably represented a youth dedicating the toys of his childhood; this figurine is likely to have been made in the Potters' Quarter in the 4th century B.C. The last figurine in this group (**C202**) is of uncertain gender, since it is fragmentary, and the drapery is subject to different interpretations (see catalogue). If male, it would have been draped in a mantle similar to that of **C199**.

Burkert 1985, p. 70, with collected ancient sources on pp. 373–374, note 29; Benedum 1986, pp. 140–141, note 18 (on hair offerings to the fertility goddesses Damia and Auxesia, who are thought to parallel Demeter and Kore, together with Hippolytos at Troizen); D. J. R. Williams 1984, pp. 279–280, notes 33–34; on the knotted hair of heads of Apollo to emphasize his ephebic function, see Nicgorski 1996; on the religious and social symbolism of hair, see pp. 117–118, with further bibliography.

[267] Conveniently, Lullies and Hirmer 1960, pl. 172; on the identity of the youth, see Clinton 1992, pp. 39–55.

[268] Ridgway 1990, pp. 228–230, with bibliography on p. 242, note 21, pl. 111:a–c (in the Terme Museum). For other examples of the knotted coiffure in sculpture, see *Corinth* XV, ii, p. 135; Hafner 1982, pp. 221–222; Harrison 1988, pp. 250–251. Other Corinthian figurines with knotted hair: from the Asklepieion, T.-F.-77, *Corinth* XIV, pp. 142–143, no. 43, pl. 56; from the Potters' Quarter, KT-24-7, *Corinth* XV, ii, p. 136, no. 2, pl. 30.

[269] T.F.-13, *Corinth* XIV, p. 140, no. 12, pl. 54.

[270] E.g., from Theangela, Işik 1980, pp. 195–197, 236–237, nos. 169–173, pls. 23, 24; from Halikarnassos, *British Museum* I, p. 141, nos. 520–522, pl. 69 (with different position of left hand); *Lindos* I, cols. 679–680, nos. 2872–2875, pl. 133.

[271] E.g., Poulsen 1937, p. 99, fig. 67.

[272] On the identification of these objects, see Kostoglou-Despini 1988, pp. 181–182.

[273] E.g., *Königliche Museen*, p. 11, pl. IX top.

Pottery contexts support a 5th-century B.C. date for **C188** and **C191**. The latest pottery in the context of the semidraped **C199** dates to the first quarter of the 4th century B.C., although the archaeological context is probably late 4th century. As in the case of the previously discussed figurine types, most of the unmixed pottery contexts associated with the standing male figurines range in date from the Archaic period or the 5th century B.C. to the late 4th or early 3rd century.

ISOLATED MALE HEADS
(C203–C209)

The isolated heads **C203–C209** bear witness to larger male figurines of good quality, even approaching size range 4. Two of the heads (**C203** and **C204**), already mentioned for their knotted coiffures, probably belonged to standing votaries. **C205** and **C206** are related in facial type to the Early Classical hydriaphoros group (see pp. 39–40), but their short, masculine coiffures distinguish them from the female heads. The hair of **C205** is a schematic version of Archaic ringlets around the forehead; that of **C206** is a cap of finger-waves close to the head. Although male and female head types overlap considerably, a distinction usually is made in the coiffures, allowing that some hair arrangements are common to both. In the present examples, the shortness of the hair in back, without any signs of a sphendone or sakkos to bind it, suggests that the heads originally belonged to male figurines, presumably standing votaries. **C205** is unusually deep toward the back of the head and the neck, a peculiarity that is found from time to time among Corinthian heads and could be due to the adaptation of surviving molds or models once used for Archaic vessel protomes, the heads of which are sometimes similarly deep.[274]

Two other heads (**C207** and **C208**), the latter of statuette scale and with remains of the red paint customarily used for male flesh, show the typical Early Classical facial type but in a 4th-century B.C. rendering. **C207** retains the Early Classical double-scalloped wave at the center of the forehead, and **C208** has large ears, recalling Archaic style, but the softer modeling of the features, the rounded browridge, and peaked front hair of **C208**, and the slashed tooling of the hair on both heads point to a later date of execution. A similar coiffure, in which a full, peaked mass of hair frames the forehead and long locks of hair spread over the shoulders, also known in female heads such as **C64**, is found in a smaller 4th-century B.C. figurine of a standing, semidraped youth carrying a ball and knucklebone bag (**C201**), discussed above. It is possible that the two heads originally belonged to a type similar to this one. The fleshiness of the nose and lips of **C208** recalls some Tarentine faces.[275]

C209 is entirely different in facial type, being round in shape, with more delicate features, recalling the round faces of such "dolls" as **C159**. Were it not for a trace of red paint on the flesh, the head could have belonged to a female figurine. The coiffure is too schematic to confirm the gender of the figurine.

Three fragments (**V28–V30**) are known to have belonged to male figurines by virtue of their red paint, which was usually employed for male flesh. They have been catalogued under Varia because they come from figurines of unknown type and uncertain date. Two large isolated feet (**V29** and **V30**) and a hand (**V28**) are of statuette scale and are very well made. In fabric and workmanship they appear to belong to the 4th century B.C., although it is unclear whether they come from figurines of Classical or Early Hellenistic type.

Since the fragments of the larger and better-made male figurines do not find parallels in the Potters' Quarter, and since there are no points of technique to connect them with these

---

[274] Cf., e.g, Wallenstein 1971, p. 130, no. V/A3, pl. 13:3. See also p. 119.

[275] E.g., Herdejürgen 1971, p. 52, no. 37, pl. 9 (a female head dated to the end of the 5th century B.C.).

workshops, one may assume that only the more consistent group of smaller figurines was made in the Potters' Quarter and that the larger figurines, especially the statuettes, were made elsewhere in Corinth.

One further point to be mentioned is the surprising paucity of stylistic and iconographic connections between the male terracotta figurines and the terracotta sculpture from the sanctuary, considering that most of the sculptures also seem to have represented young male votaries. It is, of course, possible that the fragmentary state of the sculpture obscures similarities, but the heads and partial torsos that are preserved seem to belong to a different tradition.[276] The circumstances of manufacture apparently discouraged cross-fertilization between the two crafts. It is very likely that the workshop facilities of coroplasts and sculptors in terracotta were separate. We know that terracotta sculpture was made in the Tile Works,[277] but there is no evidence that figurines were made there. The few figurines dedicated in small shrines in the Tile Works[278] were imported from the Potters' Quarter, where there is no evidence for the manufacture of terracotta sculpture. Hence, the coroplasts who made the figurines of standing youths may have been influenced more by workshop materials such as molds and archetypes available at hand than by direct observation of works outside the familiar technical sphere. Particularly in the conservative atmosphere of the Potters' Quarter, where these figurines were made, there seems to have been little inclination to seek out ideas beyond the traditional ones at hand.

RECLINING MALE FIGURINES (BANQUETERS) AND RELATED HEADS (**C210–C226**)

Figurines representing males reclining on dining couches are first known in Corinth in a few Late Archaic examples. One type is an unusual hand-modeled version, made in the Potters' Quarter in the late 6th century B.C.[279] Also Late Archaic are a large, moldmade, plaquelike torso fragment (MF-13462[280]) and a curious moldmade banqueter, with a head like a satyr's, from the Potters' Quarter.[281] The origin of terracotta banqueters in Archaic bronzes has been suggested;[282] a very fine bronze banqueter in London has been attributed to Corinth,[283] but the most common Corinthian terracotta type is not related to Archaic work in either material. As far as can be determined from the preserved figurines, the banqueter type was entirely redesigned in Corinth during the Early Classical period but without reference to any of the local predecessors. The new version is a semidraped youth holding a phiale (**C210**), a bowl (**C216**), a kantharos (**C213**, **C214**, **C219**), a lyre (**C217**), or an egg (**C212**), and the source is to be found in Early Classical Tarentine terracotta banqueters. The type is well represented in the Potters' Quarter, the Asklepieion, and the Corinth collection as a whole,[284] but, like the standing youths, it does not seem to have been one of the more important votive types in the Demeter sanctuary.

The Corinthian banqueters rarely have the elaborate headdresses of the Tarentine figurines.[285] There are a few exceptions on figurines found elsewhere in Corinth,[286] but presumably the headdresses had a cultic significance inapplicable in the Acrocorinth sanctuary.

[276] Publication of the sculpture by Nancy Bookidis is forthcoming; some examples are illustrated in preliminary reports: Stroud 1965, p. 11, pl. 3:d; Stroud 1968, pp. 324–326, pls. 95:c–e, 97:c, d; Bookidis and Fisher 1972, p. 317, pl. 63:a–d. See also Bookidis 1988.

[277] Weinberg 1957, p. 305, no. 6; p. 310, no. 19; p. 316, nos. 40, 41; pp. 316–317, no. 43; p. 317, no. 44; pp. 317–318, no. 45.

[278] Publication forthcoming by the author. Molds for figurines may have been made in the Tile Works but not the figurines themselves.

[279] *Corinth* XV, ii, pp. 54–55, nos. 1–7, pl. 8.

[280] Publication forthcoming.

[281] KT-19-7, *Corinth* XV, ii, p. 106, no. 1, pl. 19.

[282] *Corinth* XV, ii, p. 106.

[283] Rolley 1986, p. 100, fig. 69.

[284] *Corinth* XV, ii, pp. 104–112, with bibliography.

[285] E.g., Iacobone 1988, pp. 104–107, pls. 98, 99.

[286] KT-26-3, KT-19-97, *Corinth* XV, ii, pp. 111–112, nos. 30, 32, pls. 20, 22; MF-9623 in the Corinth collection.

Only the long fillet ends hanging to the shoulders sometimes survive, as in **C215** and **C216**, but with a simple polos.[287]

Early-5th-century B.C. Tarentine influence is strongly discernible in **C210**, the Corinthian Classical banqueter that is earliest in style, in both pose and facial type;[288] its face in particular retains a strong Archaic flavor. Although there are Tarentine banqueters earlier than **C210** in style, there is no evidence that they were known in Corinth, and Corinthian coroplasts presumably first became aware of this source in the early 5th century B.C. or somewhat later. Both **C210** and the more Classical **C213** have the very full cheeks characteristic of some Tarentine banqueters, and **C213** has the typical fleshy lips as well;[289] the manner in which **C213** holds the kantharos, with the thumb touching the handle, also is known in Tarentine work.[290] A mold sibling of **C213** in the Circular South Shrine of the Potters' Quarter has been dated to the third quarter of the 5th century B.C.[291]

Another figurine with a Tarentine connection is the fragmentary **C224**; little is preserved of the figure, but it reclined on a high-legged couch of Tarentine type.[292] No imported Tarentine banqueters have been recognized among the finds in Corinth, but either molds or figurines may have been brought into the Potters' Quarter workshops. A technical feature probably derived from Tarentum is backless construction, found in the banqueter **C215** as well as in Corinthian standing peplos-figurines (see p. 26).

There are two fragments (**C211** and **C212**) of a banqueter type known in complete form in the Potters' Quarter.[293] It is rather unlike the others in its awkward pose, long narrow face, coiffure with central knot over the forehead, and an egg in the hand. The type seems to be something of a pastiche put together from disparate parts. The head was attached to the torso at an awkward angle, and the right arm, also rather awkward, may have been reworked. The head type is known in Corinth among standing youths, including **C192** from the Demeter sanctuary. The knot in the hair, probably originally borrowed from Boeotian figurines, is now scarcely discernible. The egg in the hand is paralleled in Tarentine reclining figurines.[294] Two very similar banqueters from the Kabeirion are made of a fine, light-colored clay, which to Stillwell seemed Corinthian.[295]

Most of the Classical banqueters from the Demeter sanctuary have mold relationships with figurines from the Potters' Quarter, determining their origin without any doubt. The dates of the useful pottery contexts in the sanctuary, from the 6th to the beginning of the 3rd century B.C., are consistent with this conclusion. **C215** and **C216** have Potters' Quarter parallels from the Circular South Shrine (third quarter of the 5th century B.C. or later) and the Shrine of the Double

[287] For the fillets on an early-4th-century B.C. Tarentine banqueter, see, e.g., *British Museum* I, p. 359, no. 1322, pl. 181.
[288] Cf. *British Museum* I, pp. 337–338, no. 1237, pl. 170, dated early 5th century B.C.
[289] Cf. *British Museum* I, p. 357, no. 1312, pl. 180, dated early 4th century B.C.
[290] Cf. Herdejürgen 1971, p. 7, pl. 29:a.
[291] KT-19-60, *Corinth* XV, ii, pp. 108–109, no. 13, pl. 19; on the date, see ibid., p. 23 (on later material in this deposit, see Nicholls 1958, pp. 172–173).
[292] For such couches in Tarentine figurines, see, e.g., *Louvre* I, p. 61, nos. B401–B404; p. 63, nos. B415, B416, pls. XLII, XLIII.
[293] KT-19-1, *Corinth* XV, ii, pp. 106–107, no. 2, pl. 20, from Stele Shrine A, in a deposit dated first half of the 5th century B.C. (ibid., p. 22). It is possible that this date is too early, although it is not contested in *Corinth* XV, iii, p. 186. The banqueter would fit more comfortably into the second half of the 5th century B.C., and there is an awkward chronological gap between Stele Shrine A and the Shrine of the Double Stele,

which replaced it at the end of the 5th century. On the date of Stele Shrine A, see C. K. Williams 1981, p. 416, note 22; C. K. Williams 1986, p. 22; Risser 1990; Nicholls 1958, p. 172.
[294] Herdejürgen 1971, p. 14, pl. 25:d, with additional examples.
[295] *Kabirenheiligtum* V, pp. 96, 171, nos. 247, 247a, pl. 20; *Corinth* XV, ii, p. 106. The Corinthian origin is doubted by Nicholls 1958, p. 173, and by Schmaltz, *Kabirenheiligtum* V, p. 96, note 464, where a fine, light-colored fabric of Boeotian origin is mentioned. The finer Boeotian fabric, however, is confined to the Archaic period in Higgins 1986, pp. 65, 72, 98, and *British Museum* I, p. 203; it is not included in the discussion of clays in *Kabirenheiligtum* V, p. 4. Corinthian and Boeotian figurines of the Classical period are related only in small points, but certainly casual imports in both directions can be expected. The Potters' Quarter and Kabeirion figurines are probably not mold siblings, as Stillwell thought, but do seem to me to come from the same workshop. The clay of the examples in Corinth appears to be local.

Stele (first half of the 4th century B.C.).[296] **C219** and **C220**, in which the mantle roll around the torso dips below the navel, stylistically should not be earlier than the 4th century B.C.; the pottery context of **C219** terminates in the middle of that century. These two, together with **C218**, are relief plaques. This banqueter type was not found in the Potters' Quarter, but the prevalence there of relief plaques of other types, such as horsemen and sphinxes,[297] is a technical link and suggests that the banqueter plaques were made there as well.

There is no really clear evidence at the sanctuary for the large, usually bearded banqueters, some with seated women at their feet, known to have been made in Corinth in the Hellenistic period.[298] The tiny seated females **H377** and **H378**, which were perched at the ends of couches, may have belonged to parodies of banqueter types (see p. 198). The composition of two large (size ranges 3 and 4), fragmentary, semidraped male torsos (**C221** and **C222**) would be suitable for reclining figurines; the latter is Early Hellenistic in style, but the anatomy and drapery style of **C221** are appropriate to a Classical figurine. Another possible sign of the type is the poorly preserved **C223**, which is bearded but smaller and seems to be Classical in style. Two Classical bearded heads (**C225** and **C226**) are of types suitable for banqueters and could have been inspired by Tarentine figurines.[299] The elegant **C226** is the later of the two in style; its wide face with a delicate jaw is not at all typical of Corinthian figurines, but its source is not readily apparent.

It is difficult to know if there is any specific cultic conclusion to be drawn from the ages of the banqueters, as shown by the presence or absence of beards. Young banqueters unaccompanied by women certainly are more common at the Demeter sanctuary, but they are more numerous than bearded banqueters in Corinth as a whole. The iconographical significance of the reclining figure has been much discussed, but the subject is so complex that even the comprehensive study by Dentzer has not been able to narrow the interpretive possibilities.[300] The very richness of content of these images and the possibility of different interpretations for different purposes must have been the reason for their popularity in so many places for such a long time. Most of the objects held by the youths, vessels of various kinds or a lyre, were normally associated with banquets, but the presence of a snake in one banqueter type (**C219** and **C220**) must have chthonic significance.[301] The egg carried by one type (**C212**) recalls 4th-century B.C. Boeotian protomes representing a young Dionysos holding an egg, sometimes together with a rooster, an attribute more commonly associated with Persephone.[302] It is unlikely that the banqueter with the egg represents Dionysos, since he has a votary's knotted coiffure and does not wear the requisite wreath, but both images suggest a chthonic interpretation.

The likeliest of the many interpretations, in the context of the Demeter sanctuary, seems to be that the reclining figurines represent a young banqueting hero, who either embodied the chthonic powers or could act as an intermediary for the worshiper. Youthful heroes do play a role in the worship of Demeter and Kore elsewhere, as in Boeotia, where the Kabeiroi may be associated with Demeter,[303] or Eleusis, where Triptolemos is the actual bringer of agriculture to humans.[304] It is probably significant that banqueter figurines have been found in hero shrines elsewhere in Corinth.[305] The presence of dining rooms in the sanctuary should be mentioned here,[306] but

---

[296] KT-19-66, KT-19-83, KT-19-87, *Corinth* XV, ii, pp. 110–111, nos. 26–28, pls. 21, 22; for the dates of these deposits, see ibid., p. 23 and *Corinth* XV, iii, pp. 202, 214. See also p. 7, note 19; p. 66, note 293.

[297] *Corinth* XV, ii, pp. 154–163.

[298] *Corinth* XII, pp. 48–49, nos. 302–307, pls. 25, 26.

[299] E.g., Herdejürgen 1971, pp. 41–42, no. 15–17, pl. 6, dated mid-5th century B.C.

[300] Dentzer 1982, pp. 1–20, for a summary of the proposed interpretations. On the Corinthian figurines especially, pp. 168–181; on Corinthian stone reliefs, pp. 371–372. See also Grandjouan 1989, pp. 9–11.

[301] On the meaning of the snake in *Totenmahlreliefs*, see Thönges-Stringaris 1965, pp. 56–57.

[302] *Louvre* I, pp. 97–98, nos. C87, C88, pl. LXX; *British Museum* I, p. 233, nos. 873, 874, pls. 125, 126, with bibliography.

[303] Schachter 1981, II, pp. 88–89.

[304] Schwarz 1987, pp. 249–251.

[305] E.g., C. K. Williams and Fisher 1973, p. 8, pl. 3; C. K. Williams 1978, pp. 11, 35, no. 10, pl. 2.

[306] Bookidis 1990; Bookidis 1993; *Corinth* XVIII, iii, pp. 393–412.

it is uncertain whether the reclining figures were intended to represent actual banqueting as a component of the ritual. While they may indeed have suggested banqueting to the purchaser, the dedication of similar figurines in other shrines and the presence of chthonic attributes in some examples suggest that a symbolic reading probably should be preferred to a literal one, bringing the figurines into connection with the reclining heroes of *Totenmahlreliefs*.[307] This interpretation is still more to be preferred because the actual banqueters occupying the dining rooms at the sanctuary were more likely to have been women than men.[308]

If numbers are a factor, one might conclude that the worship of a hero did not play a very important role in the cult of Demeter and Kore in Corinth, since, apart from the catalogued examples, only ca. thirty-six banqueters have been counted in the lots. It is possible, however, that the numerous handmade horse-riders (see p. 60) also refer to hero cult. If the Demeter of Acrocorinth is indeed the "Epoikidie" mentioned by Hesychios, as the major deity presiding over the home, the domestic cults of each family might have come under her protection. Williams' study of small Corinthian shrines has revealed a devotion to domestic deities and heroes so strong that their worship was pursued in shrines on the sites of destroyed houses.[309] Hence hero worship in the Demeter sanctuary could have been simply a transference of the cult of each family's hero(es) to a more formal venue; it need not necessarily point to the worship by all the Corinthians of specific well-known figures, such as the Kabeiroi or Triptolemos. It may be significant that there was a Mycenaean house on the site before the establishment of the Sanctuary of Demeter and Kore.[310]

SEATED CHILDREN AND RELATED HEADS
(C227–C250)

Children were a favored subject of coroplasts and sculptors in the Classical and Hellenistic periods, and as time went on, they were portrayed with increasing sympathy and naturalism. In this section, the earliest figurines of children preserved in the Acrocorinth sanctuary, the so-called temple boys or crouching children, are discussed. This group consists of small boys seated on the ground in various poses, often with one knee raised. In addition to the catalogued examples and their mold relatives, ca. twenty-four seated boys were counted in the lots. Most of the seated boys lean on the left hand. The left leg rests flat on the base in a folded position, and the right hand rests on the right knee, which usually is raised. Variations occur in the pose of the head, the alignment of the torso, and the angle at which the right leg is bent. **C227–C230** and **C241** take the standard pose; in **C231**, **C232**, and **C242**, the right hand still rests on the knee, but the leg is relaxed on the base; **C233** is similar, but the right lower leg is turned inward; in **C236**, **C237**, **C239**, and **C240**, one or both arms reach up; the head is sometimes thrown back, as in **C236**, **C237**, **C245**, and **C246**. There is only one example from the Demeter sanctuary of a less common type in which both arms are forward, the hands resting on the front of the base (**C234**). Two boys (**C236** and **C237**) wear strings of amulets; since only the cords are rendered, the amulets probably were added in paint.[311] The bases of the seated boys vary from rectangular shapes with vertical sides to low, irregular shapes with rounded edges. The quality of workmanship ranges from excellent (**C241**) to poor (**C235**, **C239**, and **C240**).

The type, which is widely known, is of eastern Mediterranean, probably Cypriote origin, although based on Egyptian prototypes, and may have been introduced to mainland Greece through Rhodes.[312] Because of the solemn, somewhat hieratic appearance of the earliest examples

[307] Thönges-Stringaris 1965, pp. 48–54.
[308] Bookidis 1993, pp. 50–51.
[309] C. K. Williams 1981, p. 418.
[310] *Corinth* XVIII, iii, pp. 13–15.

[311] For detailed amulet cords on seated boys, see, e.g., stone statuettes from Kourion (di Cesnola 1885, pl. CXXXI).
[312] Hadzisteliou-Price 1969, p. 96. More recently on the type, Beer 1987.

and their widespread discovery in sanctuaries, the figurines once were thought to represent divine children or cult attendants. Hadzisteliou-Price, however, has stressed that these figurines are portrayals of real children, either placed in the graves of children or dedicated to patron deities of health, fertility, childbearing, or nurturing, to ensure the growth of families.[313] In Corinth, terracotta figures of seated boys are known in a cultic context not only in the Demeter sanctuary but also in the Asklepieion, where they were dedicated in both small and large scale;[314] they also are known in a funerary context in the North Cemetery.[315]

There is no clear evidence as yet that seated boy figurines were made in Corinth in the Archaic period. The earliest examples from the Demeter sanctuary should date to the 5th century. Stillwell thought that one mold of this type from the Potters' Quarter was late Archaic in style,[316] and it does seem to be the oldest of the preserved molds of seated boys. Since the earliest preserved figurines of this type in Corinth seem to be Classical, however, it is probably best not to isolate this mold from the other molds and the figurines but to regard it as one of the first of its type to appear in the Early Classical period and as somewhat conservative in style.

The earliest seated boys (e.g., **C227**) are not very childlike in appearance or movement, probably because of a tendency in the art of the period, for example, in grave reliefs, to depict children as small adults or with idealized features. Even in well-made figurines in fine fabric, such as **C245**, an adult quality in the face may contrast strangely with the childish torso. In this case, the workshop may have adapted for the child a face mold originally intended for figurines of youths. The result combines a beautifully prepared fabric with a misconceived, rather crudely retouched portrayal of a child, as if the artisan was not equally skilled in all aspects of the craft. Alternatively, more than one artisan, with varying levels of skill, may have contributed to the manufacture of this figurine. The head **C247** is bald, as if to portray an almost hairless infant, and an attempt has been made to show a baby's pursed mouth, but the overall effect is not convincingly babyish. More successful baby's heads can be seen in **C237** and **C238**. Consequently, the ages of the boys represented are somewhat uncertain. The later and more realistic examples are the most informative in this respect. **C236** and **C237**, with pudgy cheeks, wearing amulets and the pilos pulled down over the ears, and reaching up to be carried, are clearly babies who cannot yet walk. The best made of all the seated boys (**C241**) has a similarly babyish anatomy and also wears a baby's pilos, but he seems a little older because of his more mature, subdued pose and more idealized face. As far as one can tell, most of the other figurines in this group also represent baby boys, not beyond the age of toddlers. An exception is the slender **C242**, who is much more grown-up, with a defined waist, long hair, and a mantle over the shoulder; he is probably approaching puberty. This type may be a later survival, created under the influence of Early Hellenistic figurines of older boys who are, however, represented in poses more suited to their age (see pp. 187–191). The head of **C242** is missing, but it could have been similar to the head of **C243**, which has similarly long hair and seems to be about the same age. One of the baby boys (**C230**), however, also has long hair. Children of the intermediate ages between babyhood and puberty cannot be identified among the seated figurines of Classical type but can be found among the Early Hellenistic standing types, such as **H319**. It is uncertain whether some change occurred in cult practice to account for the enlarged repertoire of types or whether we are dealing with a purely artistic phenomenon, the general expansion of Hellenistic subjects to embrace many more aspects of daily life. The question of possible change in the place of children in sanctuary ritual is discussed below (p. 188).

---

[313] Hadzisteliou-Price 1969, pp. 107–110.

[314] *Corinth* XIV, pp. 140–141, nos. 25, 26, pl. 54 (figurines, V 134 and M.F. 9155); p. 140, no. 24, pl. 55, a statuette (V 111), which is thought to be a naturalistic representation of a sick child: Beer 1987, p. 24.

[315] T-2262, T-2260, *Corinth* XIII, p. 282, nos. 453-4, 453-5, pl. 74.

[316] KH-60, *Corinth* XV, i, pp. 105–106, no. 61, pl. 40.

The Classical figurines of children represent boys, with the exception of one girl (**C248**), presumably because of a preference for male offspring.[317]   In a custom recorded by Pollux (*Onomastikon* 3.40) and recently recognized in Attic vase painting, a male child with both parents living (παῖς ἀμφιθαλής) participated in marriage rituals by sleeping with the bride; the child appears to have been regarded as a kind of magical force to ensure successful childbirth, particularly the bearing of male offspring.[318]   Whether or not this custom was followed at Corinth, figurines of baby boys, if dedicated at the time of marriage, could have carried a similar meaning.   The terracotta model likna filled with cakes offered at the Demeter sanctuary[319] recall another ritual task of the παῖς ἀμφιθαλής, who carried an actual cake-filled liknon at the wedding; these cakes are thought to have been symbolic of eagerly awaited children,[320] the parallel perhaps being drawn between the rising and baking of loaves in the oven and the growth of the child in the womb.

As patronesses of agricultural fertility, Demeter and Kore also were invoked to assure human increase; both goddesses sometimes were associated with childbirth,[321] although the evidence suggests a greater emphasis on the nurturing of children.   The association of the Queen of the Underworld with motherhood is somewhat problematic,[322] but the pinakes from Lokroi have been interpreted convincingly to show Persephone as a kourotrophic deity at that sanctuary.[323]   Certainly the rearing of children was an important area of patronage for Demeter.   The quintessential mother in myth, she bore the epithet "kourotrophos" in Athens and plays the role of nurse in the well-known Homeric hymn dedicated to her.[324]   Closer to Corinth, Pausanias (2.5.8) records the story of Plemnaios of Sikyon, whose children all died at birth until Demeter took pity on him, and in disguise she nursed his son Orthopolis safely through childhood.   In addition, the Orphic Hymns, which are understood to be a Roman Imperial compendium of earlier epithets and cult formulas,[325] emphasize the role of Demeter as a protectress of children more insistently than any other goddess, using for her the descriptive terms "kourotrophos," "paidophile," and "polytekne" (*Orphei Hymni* 40, lines 2, 13, 16).   Certainly the epithet "Epoikidie," if understood correctly for the Demeter of Acrocorinth, would encompass child rearing within the concerns of the household.   The images of baby boys found in the Demeter sanctuary, then, would express a wish not only for the birth of children but also for their successful nurturing.   At least five terracotta heads and a number of limbs of small children of sculptural scale found in the Demeter sanctuary[326] fall into the same class of votives.[327]

In connection with this aspect of Demeter's cult, it may be worth mentioning that although a few kourotrophos figurines have been found in Corinth as a whole, a standard type never was created, as was the case in other centers, especially in Italy and Sicily.[328]   The only kourotrophoi from a known cultic context in Corinth are two Archaic examples from the Demeter sanctuary,

[317]   On the evidence for such a preference, see Kauffmann-Samaras 1988, pp. 293–297. Westholm (1955, p. 77) suggests that these figurines were prayers or thank offerings for a male child; some of the Cypriote figures stress the male sex of the child, who lifts his garment as if to reveal it. It has also been suggested that such figurines were offered in Cyprus on the occasion of circumcision: Beer 1987, p. 23.

[318]   Kauffmann-Samaras 1988, pp. 290–292; Reilly 1989, pp. 426–427.

[319]   Brumfield 1997.

[320]   Redfield 1982, p. 193.

[321]   Farnell, *Cults* III, p. 81.

[322]   On this subject, see Zuntz 1971, pp. 80–81.

[323]   Sourvinou-Inwood 1978, p. 117.

[324]   On epigraphic evidence for the epithet, see Farnell, *Cults* III, pp. 81, 333, note 109; as nurse of Demophon, *Homeric Hymn to Demeter*, lines 219–264; also as nurse of Trophonios, Pausanias 9.39.5. See also Hadzisteliou-Price 1978,

pp. 190–191; Clinton 1992, pp. 31–34. Vorster (1983, pp. 76–78) however, denies Demeter any function as kourotrophos, seeing in her the goddess of the Mysteries without interest in the affairs of everyday life. On the connection of Demeter with Asklepios, see Benedum 1986.

[325]   Guthrie (1966, pp. 256–261) discusses evidence connecting the hymns with the precinct of Demeter in Pergamon. For a different view, see West 1983, pp. 28–29, with bibliography.

[326]   Publication forthcoming by Nancy Bookidis.

[327]   A simple modern ritual known in Italy may be a survival of ancient belief in Demeter's protection of children's health. The ritual, described in Turci 1983, pp. 53–56, includes the preparation of bread dough, lumps of which are formed into cakes and applied to the body of a sick child.

[328]   E.g., Bonfante 1984; for kourotrophoi among the figurines from the Thesmophorion at Bitalemi, see Kron 1992, pp. 628–629.

MF-13558 and MF-71-54,[329] one of which is an import.[330] Two kourotrophic Hellenistic actor types (**H363** and **H364**) might be added. Also lacking are figurines of swaddled infants and uterus models, which demonstrate a concern for pregnancy, childbirth, and infant care, as, for example, at Paestum.[331] Unless a large cache with new and different types awaits discovery, Corinthian votives relating to children usually took the form of figurines of children alone, without the nurse or mother, or perhaps of perishable offerings of clothing, sandals, or textiles, which are attested elsewhere.[332]

Further evidence pointing to Demeter as kourotrophos in Corinthian cult may be Corinthian vase paintings in which dancing women appear together with a kourotrophos and a spinner. The cult represented has been assigned by scholars to various deities, including Demeter and Kore.[333]

The presence of Aphrodite in the sanctuary, which could have been connected with the erotic aspects of marriage, might have been linked with children as well, since she was worshiped as a nurturer of children in Cyprus, her original home, where fine stone statuettes of seated boys, very similar in type to the figurines, were dedicated to her.[334]

There is another possible interpretation of figurines of children, particularly when dedicated in a sanctuary of chthonic deities. That is, the figurines could represent children who have died and are being consigned, by way of the images portraying them, to the care of the Queen of the Underworld. Certainly among the most poignant images of ancient art is that of a little boy on an Attic white-ground lekythos in New York, entering the Underworld with his pull-toy.[335] Perhaps the figurines from the sanctuary are to be understood, at least in part, in the same artistic context. When found in graves, similar figurines have been thought to represent the dead child.[336] Certainly the seated boys are represented at the most vulnerable age for children in ancient Greece.[337]

Several different interpretations of figurines of children have been suggested here, without preferring one above the others. We cannot know, of course, precisely what events or thoughts precipitated the offering of figurines, and it is conceivable that a given figurine type was dedicated in the sanctuary for more than one purpose, depending upon the needs and circumstances of each votary.

[329] Publication forthcoming.

[330] Others: MF-1587, MF-3457, *Corinth* XII, p. 34, nos. 140, 141, pl. 10; p. 55, no. 387, pl. 35; a mold from the Tile Works, MF-8634, which is probably based on a Tarentine prototype (publication forthcoming); a Corinthian figurine in Paris, *Louvre* III, p. 54, no. D299, pl. 62:b; an Archaic example in Boston from Selinus, Hadzisteliou-Price 1978, pp. 21–22, no. 58, fig. 9 (on p. 77, no. 813, it is noted that the monkey of KT-30-3, *Corinth* XV, ii, p. 178, no. 3, pl. 39, holds a swaddled baby rather than a loaf of bread, in an apparent parody of a kourotrophos type); a man with a baby in London, *British Museum* I, p. 259, no. 954, pl. 134; several examples of reported Corinthian provenience in Winter, *Typen* I, p. 140, no. 1; p. 141, no. 2b; p. 267, Nachträge to p. 140, nos. 5, 7.

[331] Ammerman 1993.

[332] Rouse 1902, p. 252; Linders 1972, esp. pp. 11–13; Osborne 1985, p. 158, note 9, p. 170; Cole 1984, p. 239; Romano 1988, pp. 129–133. On the survival of the custom into modern times: Lawson 1964, p. 140, on the putting out of chemises from the bridal trousseau to protect childbirth against possibly malevolent Nereids; Blum 1970, p. 324, on the bringing of clothing of sick children to the Church of St. Artemidos on Keos, thought to perpetuate the role of Artemis as kourotrophos. There are also several votives from the Demeter sanctuary in the form of terracotta sandaled feet, to be published with miscellaneous finds.

[333] Jucker 1963, pp. 58–61 (Artemis); Callipolitis-Feytmans 1970; Sourvinou-Inwood 1978, p. 117; Amyx 1988, II, pp. 653–657. Discussions of the "Frauenfest" thus far have not taken into account the material from the Sanctuary of Demeter and Kore; it may be worth noting that the cultic elements represented in the vase paintings, including a connection with Dionysos, would fit the cult of Demeter and Kore as reflected in the figurines (see also pp. 336–337).

[334] Hadzisteliou-Price 1969, p. 106; Beer 1987, p. 22, both with bibliography.

[335] Children in Greek funerary art are discussed in Rühfel 1984, pp. 75–184, with bibliography; the lekythos is illustrated on p. 116, fig. 47:a.

[336] Hadzisteliou-Price 1969, pp. 109–110. Or perhaps figurines of children were offered at the sanctuary in the hope that living children would be spared. An interesting group of modern folktales tells of the granting of a child to a childless couple by a "Lady from the Sea" (perhaps a survival of Aphrodite?), after the eating of a fruit or some other food. Later, when the child reaches maturity, the goddess claims him for herself; see Dawkins 1953, pp. 28–29. Such stories may be metaphors for the untimely death of children.

[337] On childhood mortality, see Sallares 1991, pp. 117–118, and tables on p. 110 and in note 87 on pp. 435–436, with bibliography.

Good parallels for the Demeter sanctuary boys among the figurines and molds from the Potters' Quarter are enumerated in the catalogue, and it is clear that some of the figurines of this type were made there. With so little anatomical detail in the figurines, however, their mechanical relationships are very difficult, if not impossible, to determine accurately. At least six different molds would have been needed to produce the extant figurines, but it is uncertain whether any of the molds found in the Potters' Quarter were involved.

As far as can be determined, the Classical figurines of children from the Demeter sanctuary range in date from the third quarter of the 5th century B.C. to at least the third quarter of the 4th. One boy with both arms forward to rest his hands on the front of the base (**C234**) is likely to be of 5th-century B.C. date; there is a small bronze from Delphi in this pose, with a face of Classical style,[338] and figurines from Sicily and Rhodes in this pose have been dated to the 5th century B.C. (see catalogue). The pottery contexts of the children usually have the same long chronological range as the contexts of the other types from the sanctuary that were made in the Potters' Quarter, that is, the 6th to the early 3rd century B.C. Therefore, one must depend for dates upon the figurines themselves and more closely datable parallels from the Potters' Quarter. **C227**, which seems earliest in style, has a close parallel from the Circular South Shrine, the contents of which are dated to the third quarter of the 5th century B.C. or later.[339] **C230**, which looks much later, has parallels in molds from deposit 3 of the Terracotta Factory, which has been dated to the third quarter of the 4th century B.C.,[340] and in a grave in the North Cemetery of the same date.[341]

The boy reaching up with one or both arms (**C236** and **C237**) is not paralleled in the Potters' Quarter, and the type is so much more naturalistic in concept that it seems a completely separate one, probably developed elsewhere in Corinth in the 4th century B.C. An example of this type was found in a child's grave in the North Cemetery, dated to the third quarter of the 4th century B.C.[342] It is known also in bronze.[343] The tiny (size range 1), very summary, untrimmed **C239** and **C240** seem to be a degenerate version of this type, although without demonstrable mechanical continuity. Nor can the more sophisticated and well-made **C241**, probably of 4th-century B.C. date, be connected with the Potters' Quarter. This figurine is particularly interesting, since the flat, overlapping pleats of the cloth on which he sits, as well as the flattened omega fold on the base, recall the fold pattern of the much earlier seated boy from the east pediment of the Temple of Zeus at Olympia.[344] Although the face of **C241** is somewhat idealized and not as puffy or babyish as the faces of **C237** and **C238**, the pilos is pulled down low over the forehead, with no signs of hair, as in babies' heads. If **C242** was influenced by Early Hellenistic representations of children, as suggested above (p. 69), it is likely to date to the later 4th or early 3rd century B.C., in spite of the almost Archaic appearance of the stacked, curved mantle folds over the arm.

There is only one very small (size range 1) seated girl (**C248**). Her miniature size, uniplanar composition, and fine detail suggest that the mold may have been taken from metal relief. The closest parallels are larger figurines from Ruvo, which are thought to have been made from an imported Attic mold.[345] It is interesting that the very finely modeled folds of the Ruvo figurines also point to a metallic source.

A little boy playing with a Maltese dog (**C249**) has been treated with a preservative, but the original fabric, visible on the underside, seems local. Figurines of children with pets, including

[338] Rolley 1984, pp. 264–265, no. 5.

[339] KT-20-4, *Corinth* XV, ii, p. 115, no. 1, pl. 23; for the date of the deposit, see p. 7, note 19.

[340] KH-61, KH-62, *Corinth* XV, i, p. 106, nos. 62, 63, pl. 41. Deposit 3 is correlated with deposit 1 of the Terracotta Factory (ibid., p. 37), which is dated to the third quarter of the 4th century B.C. in *Corinth* XV, ii, p. 23; *Corinth* XV, iii, pp. 210–211.

[341] T-2262, *Corinth* XIII, p. 282, no. 453–4, pl. 74.

[342] T-2260, *Corinth* XIII, p. 282, no. 453–5, pl. 74.

[343] *Walters Art Gallery*, p. 76, no. 163, pl. 34.

[344] Ashmole and Yalouris 1967, pls. 41–43.

[345] *Louvre* IV, i, p. 63, no. D3642, pl. 54:e; Besques 1994, p. 92, no. 83; Winter, *Typen* II, p. 125, no. 8. For other seated girls, see Hadzisteliou-Price 1969, p. 104, type VII; in sculpture, Vorster 1983, pp. 351–354, pl. 23:1, 3; from Cyprus, Connelly 1988, p. 4, pl. 3, fig. 9.

small dogs of this kind, are known widely and are extremely varied in pose.[346] Nearby, a tomb at Sikyon yielded a figurine of a boy with a Maltese dog, in a different pose but with a head type similar to **C233** and **C235–C238**.[347] The representations of animals in these figurines sometimes are thought to have had chthonic significance.[348]

Since most of the Classical figurines of children are nude, the only item of dress to be discussed is the pointed cap, a pilos with a rolled rim. In two examples (**C233** and **C241**), the upturned rim is stippled, probably indicating that the cap is made of sheepskin, worn fleece inside. Caps of this type were standard headgear worn by both youths and men,[349] but they also are seen in representations of swaddled infants and were used as protective coverings for childrens' heads.[350] Two children (**C236** and **C237**) wear amulet cords diagonally across the chest. A few sit on cloths draped partly over one leg or arm (**C241**, **C242**, **C244**).

One type of boy in a pilos also is wrapped in a mantle (**C250**), a widespread 5th-century B.C. type well represented in the Kabeirion at Thebes; these squatting figures are sometimes thought to represent Hermes but more probably are shepherd boys.[351] Most of the known examples are not from datable contexts, but a similar piece from the Athenian Kerameikos comes from a context dated ca. 420 B.C.[352] The rather degenerate Corinthian example must be later; while there is no reason for seeing in it a particularly Corinthian type, not enough detail is visible to point to the exact source. The pottery context of **C250** dates from the 6th to the mid-4th century B.C.

PROTOMES, THYMIATERIA, AND MASKS
(C251–C273)

The terms "protome," "bust," and "mask" all are used in the literature, sometimes with conflicting definitions, to refer to representations of a head and upper torso. In this discussion, "protome" is used for a head with the neck and all or part of the shoulders, backless but with sides to help it stand upright. "Bust" is used for representations in the round; the busts of this period appear to be thymiateria (**C261** and **C262**). "Mask" is applied here to backless heads, usually somewhat flattened, that terminate at the chin or beard.

Viewed from the perspective of West Greek sites, where they are found in great profusion, protomes seem not to have been particularly important at Corinth. Perhaps the whole story is not yet known, for although only one reasonably well preserved large protome has been found in Corinth,[353] fragments of others have appeared from time to time in the excavations; imported protomes from the Demeter sanctuary are discussed below (p. 293). The most typical Corinthian protomes known up to now are much smaller and were pierced for suspension. They consist of 5th-century B.C. spoon-based protomes of lingering Archaic style (see p. 23, note 1), a backless Late Archaic type (MF-13661),[354] and the Classical types **C251–C257**, which also are backless. There appears to have been a break in the tradition between the Late Archaic and Classical backless protomes, marked by the development of a new archetype. The Archaic type wears a fillet and veil, while the Classical examples wear the polos; the coiffure remains

[346] For a selection of typical compositions, see Winter, *Typen* II, pp. 275–282; the subject is discussed by Klein 1932, pp. 10–13.

[347] Krystalli-Votsi 1976a, p. 65, pl. 58:δ; the tomb is not dated.

[348] On the Maltese dog (the *melitaios*) as a pet, and the question of its interpretation, see Rühfel 1984, pp. 166–168, with bibliography; R. Hamilton 1992, p. 91.

[349] E.g., MF-6362, MF-3339, *Corinth* XII, p. 38, nos. 186, 187, pl. 13; on the pilos: *RE* XX, 2, 1950, cols. 1330–1333,

4, s.v. πῖλος (R. Kreis-von Schaewen); *DarSag* IV, pp. 479–481, s.v. *Pileus* (P. Paris).

[350] Klein 1932, p. 1, pl. I:A.

[351] *Kabirenheiligtum* V, pp. 99–103, 171–172, nos. 251–263, pls. 20, 21.

[352] *Kerameikos* XV, p. 60, no. 179, pl. 33:4.

[353] MF-10083, C. K. Williams 1986, pp. 12, 14, note 6, figs. 2:A, B on p. 16. The protome is from a deposit of the second half of the 5th century B.C.

[354] Publication forthcoming.

similar. From their scanty remains, the Archaic protomes seem closer than the Classical to the East Greek tradition. Both the spoon and the backless types were made in the Potters' Quarter, and a mold closely related to **C251** was found there.[355] This mold shows a female protome in polos and veil; the left hand touches the edge of the veil (as in **C256**), and the right hand seems to display the breast (as in **C257**). These gestures are clearer in examples from Rhodes and Boeotia, in which the veil is actually grasped, as if to lift it (in a gesture of *anakalypteria* or, conversely, to cover the face in modesty), and the other hand clearly surrounds the breast in a displaying gesture or holds a fruit.[356] In other protomes, both hands display the breasts,[357] in a gesture that suggests fertility and is of Near Eastern origin.[358] The type is sometimes interpreted as Persephone as a bride, wearing the marriage veil.[359] This identification also could be valid for the Corinthian protomes, although the suggestion of fertility is appropriate to Demeter or Aphrodite as well. Perhaps the dedicants in this sanctuary offered votives that contained the idea of the bride and fertility rather than a reference to a specific deity.

Although the typical Corinthian Early Classical protome type is preserved in the Demeter sanctuary in only a few fragmentary examples (**C251–C257**), the facial type is reasonably clear in **C251**. In its full-cheeked, oval outline, prominent eyes, and pronounced arch of the brows springing from a flattened nose bridge, this facial type is distinctly different in structure from the long, narrow faces that are so characteristic of Corinthian figurines (see pp. 39–40). **C251** shares stylistic features with the large Corinthian protome mentioned above (see p. 73, note 353); although much of the upper part of the large protome is missing, similarities are evident in the outline of the jaw and the shape of the features.

The small protomes are not entirely consistent among themselves but vary with respect to the mechanism for suspension. In **C251**, the hole for suspension was cut into the hair just above the forehead. In **C252–C255**, the hole was cut vertically into the top of the polos; **C252** and **C253** also show a freer rendering of the hair and facial features, suggesting that they were made in a different workshop or at least that the archetypes were made by a different artisan. **C254** is similar to **C251** in its clearly marked browridge over prominent eyes, but the facial shape is more typical of Early Classical figurines in its narrowness; the polos is low and wide, and the hair frames the forehead in two undetailed masses divided by a central part. A fragmentary example of this type was found at the Potters' Quarter (see catalogue). **C255** appears to be a smaller, degenerate version of this protome type.

In addition to the typical local protomes, at least one type (**C259**) is so similar to Rhodian and Boeotian protomes, and so dull an impression, that it may have been copied mechanically from an import.[360] Two imported protome fragments (**I55** and **I56**) are in fact from heads usually associated with the relevant torso type. The number of imported protomes (**I52–I56**) is relatively large, when compared with the number of local examples. This is a curious phenomenon, in light of the generally abundant production of figurines in Corinth. Perhaps foreign residents, if they participated in the local cults, were the main dedicators of protomes, following a custom more familiar to them than to local residents. Two fragments (**C258** and **C260**) are from types otherwise unknown in Corinth and without clear parallels elsewhere. Perhaps future excavation in Corinth will clarify the matter and bring out more types in regular local production.

---

[355] KH-26, *Corinth* XV, i, pp. 97–98, no. 28, pl. 32.

[356] Cf. *British Museum* I, p. 89, no. 239, pl. 40, from Rhodes; Goldman and Jones 1942, p. 397, no. IV-a-17, pl. XVIII, from Halae.

[357] Cf. *British Museum* I, p. 224, no. 842, pl. 116, from Boeotia.

[358] On the gesture, see Böhm 1990, p. 137.

[359] *Morgantina*, pp. 84–85, with bibliography.   Protomes are also found in association with other deities: see Uhlenbrock 1988, pp. 139–142 (the statement on pp. 141–142 that protomes were absent from the Acrocorinth sanctuary is incorrect).

[360] E.g., *British Museum* I, pp. 89–90, no. 242, pl. 42 (Rhodian); Winter, *Typen* I, p. 249, no. 5 (Boeotian).

Still more unusual in Corinth are two 4th-century B.C. busts (**C261** and **C262**), which are thin-walled and of very fine fabric, and which probably were thymiateria with floral finials, similar to those made in Magna Graecia, elsewhere in mainland Greece, and in Asia Minor from ca. 400 B.C. to the Hellenistic period.[361] The inspiration for such busts in Corinth may have come from South Italian imports. The break at the top of **C261** probably is from a floral finial, but while most of the other known examples include the shoulders, **C261** ends at the collarbones. Another thymiaterion has been found in Corinth, but it includes the shoulders and wears a chiton and veil.[362] Closer in type to **C261** is a shoulderless bust of reported Eleusinian provenience, which also has a break at the top, presumably from a missing finial.[363] It rests on a spool base, which may have been true of **C261** as well. Similar thymiateria found in the Heraion at Foce del Sele are thought to represent Hera,[364] while others, in which Eros appears, must represent Aphrodite.[365] The image probably suggested fertility, in this case supported by the flower, and would have been an appropriate gift for a number of goddesses, including Demeter and Kore. Since the floral cups are missing, we cannot know for certain whether incense actually was burned in them.

The facial type of **C261** and **C262**, oval in shape, with a short nose and narrow, full-lipped mouth, seems more Hellenistic than Classical. **C262**, however, is from a context with pottery dating from the 5th century B.C. to the first half of the 4th. The pottery context of **C261** terminates at the beginning of the 3rd century B.C. The very fine fabric of both thymiateria is known in figurines made in the middle to third quarter of the 4th century B.C. (see p. 136). Apparently at that time one of the better Corinthian workshops adapted the South Italian floral thymiaterion type to local taste, although the production probably was not very large. The face fragment **C263** is of similar scale and is also thin-walled, although of poorer fabric. Its style is Middle rather than Early Hellenistic, resembling the later-3rd-century B.C. heads of "priestesses" (e.g., **H401**); if this head indeed belonged to a thymiaterion, it is evidence that such votives continued to be offered at Corinth well into the 3rd century B.C.

The large, hollow head **C264** could originally have belonged to a bust or perhaps a thymiaterion. The pose of the head is rigidly frontal, the face is rather flat, and the base of the columnar neck could be spreading into a bust. Since the top of the head is missing, it is impossible to know whether it terminated in a finial like that of **C261**. In any case, the facial type of **C264**, with its large, downturned eyes, arched nose, and small chin, is paralleled in such Corinthian heads as that of the Early Hellenistic mantled figurine **H102**. If the idea of making busts with large, hollow, fully three-dimensional heads was borrowed from Italy, it has here been thoroughly adapted to the local taste.

The following protomes are more difficult to discuss because of their fragmentary condition. **C265** is framed by a veil, behind which is an arched flange pierced for suspension. The veil stands away from the head as if windblown, as in the large Corinthian protome mentioned above (see p. 73, note 353), which also has preserved part of the veil. Another fragment from the Demeter sanctuary (MF-13942 [see catalogue under **C265**]), preserves a small part of the flange and veil of a protome of larger scale but probably of similar type. The fragmentary **C266** also could belong to this group. In the cave at Pitsa was found a protome that may be Corinthian and perhaps is related to this group; it has cup-shaped, realistically detailed flowers (probably

[361] See material collected in Stoop 1960, pp. 3–23; later bibliography in *LIMC* IV, 1988, p. 668, d, s.v. *Hera* (A. Kossatz-Deissmann); Romano 1994, pp. 92–93, no. 89; Romano 1995, pp. 17–22; *Coroplast's Art*, pp. 102–103.

[362] MF-1976-50 and MF-1976-51, from the Forum Southwest excavations: C. K. Williams 1977, pp. 57, 72, no. 27,

pl. 25; also the floral cup MF-9252: Romano 1994, pp. 92–93, no. 89, pl. 28.

[363] Winter, *Typen* I, p. 256, no. 2.

[364] *LIMC* IV, 1988, p. 668, nos. 68–74, pl. 407, s.v. *Hera* (A. Kossatz-Deissmann).

[365] Stoop 1960, pls. II:1, 2; III:1.

wild roses) in front of the spreading veil.[366] This entire group very likely was derived from a Rhodian type with a windblown veil sweeping over the head and a pierced, arched flange behind; like the Pitsa example, the Rhodian type is decorated with flowers.[367]

The wreathed headdress of the protome or mask **C267** is appropriate to either a male or female type. A female protome wearing a similar headdress was found among the dedications at the Artemis Altar in Olympia,[368] but thin, stippled wreaths of this kind also appear on Boeotian protomes representing Dionysos.[369]

Certainly representing Dionysos are five masks, generally similar to one another in type but unrelated mechanically or in style (**C268–C272**). The presence of such masks should not be surprising, since the name of Dionysos was inscribed on a terracotta plaque found in the sanctuary,[370] and Demeter and Dionysos were invoked together as the great benefactors of mankind in providing grain and wine (Euripides, *Bacchae*, lines 274–286). Terracotta masks of Dionysos were a specialty of Boeotian workshops,[371] and the impetus to make them could have come to Corinth from that source. **C272** is so similar to one type of Boeotian mask[372] and is such a dull impression that it could have been mechanically copied from an imported piece. Probably the same can be said of **C271**. Both masks probably were made in the Potters' Quarter (see catalogue). As in some female protomes, **C271** has suspension holes driven vertically into the top of the polos.

The remaining Corinthian examples are different in style and detail from Boeotian masks, and presumably the local artisans here followed other sources or their own inclinations. **C268** is a well-formed head from a good mold, but it was splashed with paint, without an underlying slip, in the comic manner usually reserved for handmade grotesques (as in the Archaic MF-11864).[373] **C268** probably was made in the 5th century B.C. in the Potters' Quarter, where this technique is known.[374]

C269 is the most detailed and carefully made of the small masks. Its rather startled expression and parted lips recall a Dionysos protome from the Kabeirion at Thebes, thought to be an Attic import derived from a metallic source.[375] The manner of dressing the hair, with wavy locks at the forehead, and a wreath and a polos or stephane behind, is known in 4th-century B.C. Olynthian figurine vases of Attic type representing Dionysos, although the faces are different.[376] The headband across the forehead is also found in an Attic figurine vase.[377] Since **C269** does

[366] *EAA* VI, 1965, p. 206, fig. 228, s.v. *Pitsa* (A. K. Orlandos).

[367] *British Museum* I, p. 101, no. 295, pl. 50.

[368] Kunze 1963, p. 108, pl. 144:a.

[369] In London, Higgins 1967, pp. 79–80, pl. C; *Louvre* I, pp. 97–98, nos. C87, C88, pl. LXX; the headdress of Louvre C87 is shaped like a stephane similar to **C267** from the Demeter sanctuary.

[370] Stroud 1968, pp. 328–330, pl. 98:h; on Dionysos at the sanctuary, see also Bookidis and Fisher 1974, pp. 290–291; *Corinth* XVIII, iii, pp. 247, 259, 433. For some observations on cultic connections between Demeter or Kore and Dionysos, who like the goddesses was both a chthonic and fertility deity, see Farnell, *Cults* III, pp. 223–224; Ure 1955; Ure 1969; Sourvinou-Inwood 1978, pp. 105–107; R. C. T. Parker 1979; Hopkinson 1984, pp. 138–139, commentary on line 71 of Kallimachos, *Hymn to Demeter*; D. Williams 1983, pp. 29–31; Shapiro 1989, pp. 87–88; Clinton 1992, pp. 123–125; Detienne 1989a, pp. 37–38; on the sacred grove at Lerna, which held statues of Demeter, Dionysos, and Aphrodite, see Pausanias 2.36.7–37.2. Harrison (1996, p. 206) points out that the pose of Demeter and Dionysos on the Parthenon frieze, facing with overlapping legs, is like the pose employed in Egyptian art "to depict the intercourse of the Pharaoh's mother with

a god from whom the king takes his divinity." If the resemblance is not fortuitous, Dionysos would have been understood as Demeter's consort, that is, her partner in the maintenance of fertility; cf. Pindar's reference to Dionysos sitting beside Demeter (*Isthmian Odes* 7.3–5). On the connection of Dionysos with marriage, which appears to have been one of the functions of the Acrocorinth cult, see Bieber 1949. For the opposite point of view, separating Dionysos from Demeter, see Mylonas 1961, pp. 276–278.

[371] Schneider 1972. On Dionysos masks in general, see *LIMC* III, 1986, pp. 424–427, pls. 296–300, s.v. *Dionysos* (C. Gasparri); Frontisi-Ducroux 1991, pp. 207–211; Frontisi-Ducroux 1989, pp. 150–153, on the use of Dionysos masks in rituals.

[372] Cf. a mask in Würzburg, Simon 1989, p. 172, no. 276, pl. 106, with bibliography; dated first half of the 4th century B.C.

[373] Publication forthcoming.

[374] E.g., KT-15-3, *Corinth* XV, ii, p. 50, no. 3, pl. 7.

[375] *Kabirenheiligtum* V, pp. 128–130, 180, no. 347, pl. 27.

[376] Cf. Trumpf-Lyritzaki 1969, p. 67, nos. 203–205, with bibliography.

[377] Trumpf-Lyritzaki 1969, p. 66, no. 200, pl. 26.

not stand near any other Corinthian terracottas, it may have been ultimately derived from an imported vase of this class.

Two masks from the Demeter sanctuary (**C270** and **C273**) resemble superficially a fine, large, bearded mask from the Asklepieion.[378] Although its workmanship is different from that of the Asklepieion mask, **C270** could have been derived from a mask of this type. **C273**, the finest mask from the Demeter sanctuary, is a little smaller than the Asklepieion mask and different in the style of the face and the retouching technique. It is distinctive in facial type and in the presence of small, curving horns above the forehead. The general type, bearded and wearing a wreath of overlapping leaves, suggests Dionysos, particularly in his chthonic aspect,[379] but the goatlike horns are somewhat puzzling. A Corinthian pyxis in Reading shows a beardless figure with goatlike horns springing from the top of his hair; he is identified as Dionysos.[380] The god is seated on a pile of grain and holds a winnowing fan and fork; a pig and a basket of fruit are beside him.

The agricultural theme would appear to link Dionysos (if the identification is correct) with Demeter and could refer to the cult of the Acrocorinth sanctuary. More often, however, representations of a horned Dionysos are understood to show him in the aspect of Dionysos Tauros, and the horns are the thick, incurving ones of a bull.[381] Goat's horns are more appropriate to Pan. Representations of Pan vary considerably in the manner in which his animal nature is shown; the narrow, closely set eyes and rather cruel mouth of the mask do resemble some representations of Pan in a modified way, and the apparently deliberate misshaping of the ears may have been intended to make them look more animal-like.[382] Perhaps the mask was intended to suggest aspects of both deities, whose spheres to a certain degree overlap;[383] the horns may have suggested to the worshiper a particular aspect of Dionysos, his connection with goats, which signify procreation.[384] The sexual symbolism of horns is discussed below (p. 171). If this interpretation is correct, a goat-horned Dionysos mask would be an especially apt image for the Demeter sanctuary, suggesting not only the chthonic and vegetative aspects of Dionysos but also his connection with human increase. In this connection, it is perhaps of interest that in the Orphic Hymns not only Dionysos and Pan are described as horned but also Persephone, in the context of giving fruit (*Orphei Hymni* 29, line 11), and Adonis, invoked as the spirit of growth (*Orphei Hymni* 56, line 6). Perhaps in this case horns are better understood as a symbol of growth and fertility than as an attribute of a particular deity.

The mask has a flange in back for suspension, as do many protomes and masks. It probably was made to hang on a wall. It is conceivable that it was hung on a pillar image of the kind frequently represented in vase painting,[385] although Athenian examples are curved in back to fit a cylindrical pillar,[386] or perhaps it was placed in a liknon.[387] This is so far the only mask of this kind found in Corinth, apart from a fragment with similar hair and wreath (see catalogue). Unfortunately, the original context of the mask is not known. It was found on bedrock on the Upper Terrace, where it appears to have been dumped, incorporated into the earth fill used for

---

[378] V-40, II and IV, *Corinth* XIV, p. 119, no. 1, pl. 29.

[379] Bookidis and Fisher 1974, pp. 290–291.

[380] Ure 1955, p. 228; Ure 1949, pp. 19–21, fig. 3.

[381] Otto 1965, pp. 166–167; *LIMC* III, 1986, pp. 440–441, esp. no. 158a, pl. 313, s.v. *Dionysos* (C. Gasparri). Bronze masks of Acheloös also have taurine rather than goatlike horns: see *LIMC* I, 1981, pp. 31–32, pls. 34, 35, s.v. *Acheloös* (H. P. Isler).

[382] Cf. *Gods Delight*, pp. 142–147, no. 23, with bibliography.

[383] On Dionysos and Pan, see *RE* Suppl. VIII, 1956, col. 1001, s.v. *Pan* (F. Brommer); Borgeaud 1988, pp. 54, 100, 178.

[384] Otto 1965, pp. 167–169. See Napier 1986 on the uses of masks in states of transition; on ancient and modern horned masks, see ibid., pp. 63–71.

[385] *LIMC* III, 1986, pp. 426–427, nos. 33–43, pls. 298–300, s.v. *Dionysos* (C. Gasparri); Durand and Frontisi-Ducroux 1982.

[386] Nicholls 1995, p. 420.

[387] For a Dionysos mask worshiped in a liknon, which implies a connection with Demeter, see a chous by the Eretria Painter, *ARV*² , p. 1249, no. 13; further bibliography in *LIMC* III, 1986, p. 426, no. 29, s.v. *Dionysos* (C. Gasparri).

leveling the area. The mask must already have been broken and discarded by that time, since a few portions, now restored in plaster, are missing.

The pottery contexts of the Dionysos masks terminate at the latest in the late 4th to early 3rd century B.C. There is no evidence that they continued to be made in the Hellenistic period, when the sphere of Dionysos was represented by other types, including figurines of Pan and Silenos (see pp. 199–200).

OTHER TYPES
(C274–C282)

Types of the Classical period outside of the categories discussed above consist of satyrs and Pan, a bearded male type wearing the pilos, and dancers of types other than the kalathiskos dancers discussed above (pp. 58–60).

SATYRS AND PAN (C274–C277)

The satyr figurines are of three sorts. The first (C274) is a widely found piping, squatting type of the 5th century B.C., probably of Rhodian origin; it is known especially in Boeotia and also in Athens.[388] Many of these figurines are indifferently molded and finished, making it difficult to determine sources and mechanical relationships precisely. Unless better evidence is forthcoming, it is probably best to assume that each center copied Rhodian prototypes independently. The Corinthian satyrs were made in the Potters' Quarter (see catalogue). C274 is from a pottery context dating from the 6th to the mid-5th century B.C., but the type probably continued to be made at least into the early 4th century B.C.

The second satyr figurine type (C275) is typically Corinthian. The head is moldmade, but what remains of the body is handmade. The complete figure originally was squatting, propped up by his tail, which acted as a third leg. The use in the Classical period of the Archaic technique of combined molding and hand modeling is typical of Corinthian workshops and is known in other types as well, such as the seated female C87. Also typical of Corinthian work is the three-legged composition, which is known in other grotesques, such as the Archaic MF-11864.[389] While there are no exact parallels for these satyrs in the Potters' Quarter, the interest there in entirely handmade three-legged figurines suggests that the satyrs were made there as well.[390] Similar types in London have been dated to the mid-5th century B.C.,[391] but it is possible that they continued to be made into the 4th century B.C.

The third satyr type is an ithyphallic rider (C276), which probably belongs to a varied 4th-century B.C. Corinthian group showing different grotesque types riding donkeys.[392] C276 is somewhat more sophisticated than other members of this group in that it shows torsion.

In C277, Pan is shown seated and with crossed goat's legs, both elbows resting on the knees and forearms raised, probably to play the syrinx. A closely similar type was found in a grave dating ca. 400 B.C. in the Athenian Kerameikos,[393] together with a piping satyr similar to C274. Since the modeling of C277 is very dull, it could have been mechanically copied from an

[388] Examples collected in *Corinth* XV, ii, p. 143, *sub* no. 7; *Olynthus* XIV, pp. 264–265, no. 364; Schürmann 1989, p. 43, no. 92, pl. 19. On the type, see *Kabirenheiligtum* V, pp. 25–27, 150–151, nos. 39–53, pl. 3. An example from a grave group in the Athenian Kerameikos is datable ca. 400 B.C.: *Kerameikos* XV, pp. 77–79, no. 241, pl. 48:3; an example from the Athenian Agora: S. G. Miller 1974, pp. 225–226, 244, no. 134, pl. 46 (the deposit dates to the 3rd century B.C., but it includes a few pieces of the late 5th and early 4th centuries B.C.[p. 228]).

[389] Publication forthcoming.
[390] Cf. *Corinth* XV, ii, pp. 50–51, nos. 1, 3, 4, 6–8, pl. 7.
[391] *British Museum* I, pp. 253–254, nos. 932–934, pl. 133.
[392] *British Museum* I, pp. 262–263, no. 966, pl. 136, with bibliography.
[393] *Kerameikos* XV, pp. 80–81, no. 246, pl. 49:5.

imported Athenian figurine. Its high, splaying base is a sign of its Classical date. Pan is connected with Demeter and Kore in myth and is a participant in Kore's *anodos* in vase painting.[394] The offering of figurines of satyrs and Pan in the Demeter sanctuary is probably to be understood in the context of fertility imagery[395] and of the worship of Dionysos there (see p. 76).

BEARDED MALE FIGURINES WEARING THE PILOS (**C278**–**C280**)

While the satyr figurines are quite straightforward in form and content, a group of bearded figurines wearing the pilos is more puzzling (**C278**–**C280**). One of them (**C278**) is seated on a chair with horizontal projections in back, like the chairs of seated goddess and female votary types (e.g., **C71** and **C78**); the figurine may portray a deity, but his identity is not easily determined. Hephaistos comes to mind, since he often wears a pilos in Greek art, and an unclear object at the lower break of **C278** could be a tool held in his right hand. Among the relatively few, and usually later, terracotta figurines representing Hephaistos,[396] however, the seated examples are on backless seats and seem to be resting rather than hieratically enthroned. Offerings to Hephaistos might be understandable in a Demeter sanctuary as a request for prosperity in a craftsman's household, but it is worth considering other possible identifications.

There are in Corinth other seated, bearded male figurines wearing the pilos. One from the Potters' Quarter holds an empty tray.[397] In a similar figurine in Berlin,[398] the vessel is better preserved; it seems to have a schematically rendered spool handle at one side and a spout at the other and looks rather like a typical Corinthian mortar. An analogous but beardless seated figurine in Dresden[399] holds what may be a mortar and pestle on his lap and a small rodent as well. Perhaps we are to see in these figurines representations of popular deities or local heroes worshiped in the household, represented wearing the headgear of the ordinary countryman; since the imagery of the figurines may suggest grinding, they may have served as patron deities of the grinding of grain and protectors of the grain supply against rodents. To give examples of deities connected with the grinding of grain, Zeus Myleus is thought to have been a patron deity of millers, and, in addition, Hesychios mentions miller deities in Rhodes.[400] The pilos would be a suitable attribute, since millers, like other Greek workmen, wore these hats.[401] A figurine of such a deity or hero would have been a suitable offering in the Demeter sanctuary.

Hermes also is bearded and wears the pilos, but while representations of him would be very appropriate in a chthonic cult, he usually is not shown enthroned. From Medma come bearded heads in the pilos or a conical cap with earflaps; these figurines are thought to represent Hermes Kriophoros.[402] Their shaggy beards give them a distinctly rustic appearance and may set them apart from the somewhat more urbane **C278**–**C280**, which have shorter, well-trimmed beards.

Hades occasionally wears a pilos,[403] and his representation enthroned would be natural in a sanctuary of Demeter and Kore. There also could be a connection with approximately contemporary Phoenician figurines of an unnamed seated, bearded god in a conical headdress,

[394] Borgeaud 1988, pp. 143–146.
[395] On the similar significance of satyr figurines in the Kabeirion, see *Kabirenheiligtum* V, p. 32.
[396] Brommer 1978, pp. 60–63, pls. 30–32.
[397] KT-23-1, *Corinth* XV, ii, pp. 138–139, no. 8, pl. 26; *Corinth* XV, i, p. 52. Other bearded types wearing a pilos: KT-23-2 from the Potters' Quarter; MF-12592 from the Peribolos of Apollo; MF-3339, *Corinth* XII, p. 38, no. 187, pl. 13.
[398] Winter, *Typen* I, p. 179, no. 1, said to be from Thebes.
[399] Winter, *Typen* I, p. 179, no. 2, said to be from Lokris. The objects in the lap also have been identified as a conical cake in a vessel, Herrmann 1891, pp. 166–167, no. 11. Apollo Smintheus is mentioned here as a protector against rodents,

although the pilos seems to argue against this identification of the figurine.
[400] Hesychios, s.v. μελάντειοι θεοί; μύλας. See Moritz 1958, p. 6.
[401] Millers wear the pilos on a Hellenistic relief bowl showing a milling scene: Moritz 1958, p. 13, fig. 1.
[402] Orsi 1913, pp. 121–124, figs. 164, 165. Robinson 1969, p. 24, no. 49, pl. 5 (a head, perhaps from a kriophoros figurine, MF-11462).
[403] As in a rape of Persephone on an Apulian bell krater: *LIMC* IV, 1988, p. 384, no. 112, pl. 218, s.v. *Hades* (R. Lindner et al.), with bibliography.

found at Kharayeb;[404] similar figurines were found at Makmish, together with figurines of pregnant women, apparently in connection with a fertility cult.[405] Clearly there is a good deal of room for interpretation of the Corinthian bearded male wearing a pilos, who is not necessarily one of the major deities.

DANCERS (**C281**, **C282**)

There are two Classical figurines of dancers from the Demeter sanctuary, apart from the kalathiskos dancers already discussed (pp. 58–59). Both figurines seem to have been made under Attic influence. **C281** is performing the *oklasma*. Dancers in a similar pose and costume are usually female and in Athens are thought to be connected with the worship of Dionysos or perhaps Aphrodite;[406] a few represent youths, who may be Attis.[407] Whatever the correct identification, a number of variants are known, dating from the 5th century B.C. to the Hellenistic period. It is not entirely clear whether **C281** is female or male, since the figure is somewhat shapely, but the chest is quite flat. The pose is close to that of a dancer on an Attic figurine vase dated to the second half of the 4th century B.C.[408] **C281** is such a dull impression and its limbs are so poorly defined that it could have been copied mechanically from such a vase, with no attempt to restore detail by retouch. The drapery style of the figurine is earlier than the vase, however, belonging to the later 5th century B.C., and the high base is normal for figurines of the 5th and earlier 4th centuries B.C. Since the pottery context of the figurine dates from the Archaic period to the late 5th century B.C., if an Attic figurine vase was indeed the source, it must have belonged to an earlier group. If **C281** does represent Attis, in the context of the Demeter sanctuary the reference was presumably to Cybele, who sometimes was equated with Demeter (see p. 254). Otherwise, the recipient of this offering would have been either Dionysos or Aphrodite, both of whom were honored at the sanctuary beside Demeter and Kore.

The second dancer is **C282**; the legs of this figurine are not preserved, but a sense of movement in the torso and drapery suggests that it represents a dancer stepping forward. Dancers in this pose are well known in the Classical period, with varying arm positions and drapery arrangements. The best known are Attic or Attic-inspired,[409] and there are also a few of reported Corinthian provenience.[410] The movement of these dancers tends to be concentrated in the legs and feet, allowing the upper body to remain rather quiet. Perhaps these poses reflect the relatively static nature of this dance, compared with the more active 4th-century B.C. and Hellenistic mantled dancers (see pp. 151–156). **C282** is particularly interesting for its combination of Attic-influenced Rich Style drapery with a face of Peloponnesian style, characterized by large, earthy features. This combination, found also in the sculpture of the Temple of Asklepios at Epidauros, is especially northeast Peloponnesian in spirit. A sense of motion is conveyed in the figurine by the puffed, seemingly air-filled chiton folds over the belt, a device developed by Attic sculptors for active figures, such as Nikai and riders.[411] The figurine's head is related to Epidaurian sculptural style in the wide mouth, downturned, thick-lidded eyes, and the details of the hair.[412] If the connection of the figurine with Epidaurian style has been drawn correctly, the archetype of the figurine should

[404] *Kharayeb*, p. 17, nos. Kh.39–44; p. 20, no. Kh.45; p. 129, pl. VII:4–6.

[405] Avigad 1960, p. 93, pl. 10:A.

[406] The evidence is summarized by Nicholls 1995, pp. 451–453.

[407] *LIMC* III, 1986, pp. 33–34, nos. 240–247, pl. 29; p. 35, no. 281, pl. 33, s.v. *Attis* (M. J. Vermaseren and M. B. De Boer); on the dance represented, the *oklasma*, see *Troy*, pp. 100–102, with bibliography.

[408] Trumpf-Lyritzaki 1969, p. 40, no. 109, pl. 15.

[409] Cf. *British Museum* I, pp. 190–191, no. 717, pl. 94; a

mold from the Athenian Agora (T 1616): Nicholls 1984, p. 30, fig. 13; the right-hand dancer in a two-figure group in Istanbul: Mendel 1908, pp. 176–177, no. 1868, pl. IV:2, and Besques 1978, pl. 183, fig. 2.

[410] Two dancers in Berlin: Winter, *Typen* II, p. 146, nos. 7a and b; another similar dancer from Isthmia: Caskey 1960, pp. 173–174, no. 15, pl. 56.

[411] As in a Nike akroterion of the Temple of Ares in the Athenian Agora, Delivorrias 1974, pp. 124–125, pls. 44, 45.

[412] Cf. Crome 1951, pl. 7, a useful frontal photograph of an Epidaurian head.

be approximately contemporary with the date of the Temple of Asklepios. Taking into account various opinions, that date should be ca. 380–370 B.C.[413] The facial type of this figurine reappears in a possible later generation on figurines of Aphrodite or Leda found in the Potters' Quarter and the cave at Pitsa (see catalogue).

To determine the nature of the source, it is important to note that in several respects the figurine is different from most other Corinthian figurines. The details of the hair and folds have an unusual delicacy and clarity of definition, perhaps due in part to the harder firing of this piece than was usual in Corinth in this period, but also suggesting a metallic source.[414] All the detail was in the mold, not retouched, which is unusual in Corinthian figurines (see p. 17). The head and torso were in the same mold, as was the right arm, even though it was held away from the body. The figurine was not put together from individual parts in the usual way, that is, using a limbless torso archetype and a separate head archetype to prepare partial molds and adding separately made limbs after casts of the head and torso were assembled (see pp. 15–16). Rather, the mold seems to have been lifted in one piece from its archetype. The right arm is attached to the torso with a panel of clay, suggesting that there was a similar attachment in the original. Perhaps the source, then, was metal relief,[415] such as an appliqué on a bronze mirror cover; the size of the figurine is close to that of figures on such covers, and other dancer types are known on mirrors attributed to Corinth.[416] A source in relief is supported by the dancer's back, which is simply a smooth, rounded slab of clay wrapped from side to side, while figurines mechanically copied from metallic originals in the round usually have detailed moldmade backs.[417] To judge from the style, it is likely that the metallic source was northeast Peloponnesian, if not Corinthian.

[413] For discussions of the date, see Delivorrias 1974, pp. 195–196; Brown 1973, pp. 26–28, both with bibliography; Yalouris 1992, pp. 82–83.

[414] E. R. Williams 1976, p. 43, no. 5.

[415] On the relation of terracotta to metal relief, see *Coroplast's Art*, pp. 31–36, with bibliography.

[416] Mirror covers attributed to Corinth range between about 0.15 and 0.20 in diameter. For an example found in Corinth, see Pemberton 1985, pp. 291–294, 301–302, no. 45, pl. 85, with bibliography (MF-11562). For other dancers on mirror covers, see Züchner 1942, pp. 97–98, no. KS 161, fig. 49; p. 98, no. KS 162, fig. 97 on p. 183.

[417] D. B. Thompson 1966, pp. 54–55.

CATALOGUE

For an explanation of the conventions employed in this catalogue, see the Introduction, pages 20–22.

STANDING DRAPED FEMALE FIGURINES

C1 Standing peplos-figurine   Pl. 1

MF-11882. Lot 2141. Preserved: neck to left calf and right knee. Missing part of chest. Mended. P.H. 0.19 (size 3–4). Fabric 1, buff to orange. White slip. Hollow. Fairly thin-walled; interior smooth. Back handmade, rounded. Tooling on neckline fold, hands, animals.

Strides forward in rigid pose on stiff left leg. Right hand holds piglet diagonally across thigh, by back legs, head down. Left hand holds bird by feet and tail at left breast. Peplos overfold falls to slightly below waist; plain rectangular panel at center; vertical folds at either side dip sharply in zigzag folds to top of thighs. Light pleat at center of oval neckline. Folds visible behind rounded shoulders. Skirt folds are wide and nearly vertical, with light grooves down upper left thigh. Figure sturdy, blocklike, broad shouldered. Probable mold sibling in lot 2170. Similar in type: one in lot 3222. For possible workshop mates, see Workshop D, p. 345.

See pp. 15, 17, 18, 23, 24–28, 45, 60, 120, 126, 266, 286.

C2 Standing peplos-figurine   Pl. 1

MF-73-120. Lot 73-144. Preserved: left side, hip and thigh, part of upper arm. P.H. 0.117 (size 3–4). Fabric 1, orange-buff to orange. Hollow. Back handmade, flat, with narrow (0.015) return to finished edge, indicating large rectangular vent. Added: forearm, part of side folds. Tooling on skirt.

Similar in type to **C1**, possibly from same or related mold but heavily retouched, different back. Forearm probably extended forward. Similar in treatment of back to **C7** and hydriaphoros **C46**. For possible workshop mates, see Workshop D, p. 345.

See pp. 17, 18, 24–28, 60.

C3 Standing peplos-figurine   Pl. 1

MF-11700. Lot 2013. Preserved: left front–hip, thigh, wrist, and hand. P.H. 0.077 (size 4). Fabric 1, creamy buff. White slip. Hollow.

Left hand at side, probably empty. Overfold arranged as in **C1** but falls to abdomen. Skirt folds broad, nearly vertical. Fragment from related mold in lot 2044 lacks hand (arm position presumably altered), terminates at side in finished edge as if backless (see also **C5**). Similar fragment of hand and overfold hem in lot 1955, perhaps mechanically related. Similar in type: one in lot 4377. For possible workshop mates, see Workshop D, p. 345.

See pp. 17, 24–28, 60.

C4 Standing peplos-figurine   Pl. 1

MF-13761. Lot 4400. Preserved: left front–rib cage to hip, with elbow, forearm, and hand. P.H. 0.05 (size 3). Fabric 1, orange-buff, with orange core. Hollow. Tooling on fingers.

Left hand holds ball at abdomen. Overfold hem falls to hip, curves upward at side. Folds wide; omega fold below wrist. For possible workshop mates, see Workshop D, p. 345.

See pp. 17, 24–28, 60, 125.

C5 Standing peplos-figurine   Pl. 1

MF-13769. Lots 2230, 2044. Preserved: front–right hip, thighs, to left lower leg. Mended. P.H. 0.113 (size 4). Fabric 1,

harder, orange-buff, with orange core. White slip. Both side edges finished; left edge thickened and squared off, indicating that figurine is backless. Interior smooth.

Left leg slightly bent. Overfold hem dips sharply in zigzag folds at right side. Horizontal projections at upper break may belong to forearm held across waist, with overfold hem just below it. Skirt folds are wide, rather flat, with two light grooves down thigh. For backless construction, see also **C3**. For possible workshop mates, see Workshop D, p. 345.

See pp. 17, 24–28, 60, 294.

C6 Standing draped female   Pl. 1

MF-10622. Lot 896. Preserved: left thigh, hand. P.H. 0.067 (size 3–4). Fabric 1, harder, buff to orange. Hollow. Back handmade, flattened, with narrow (0.012–0.017) return to finished edge, indicating large, rectangular vent. Added: head of bird.

Hand at side, not detailed, holds bird, head up. At side, trace of overfold hem at hip. For possible workshop mates, see Workshop D, p. 345.

See pp. 17, 18, 24–28, 60, 126.

C7 Standing peplos-figurine   Pl. 1

MF-14098. Lot 3226. Preserved: right side–hip and thigh, part of forearm, small part of back. P.H. 0.055 (size 3). Fabric 3, harder, orange to orange-buff. White slip. Hollow. Thin-walled. Back handmade, flattened. Narrow return to finished edge, indicating large, rectangular vent. Added: right forearm. Tooling on folds.

Overfold hem falls to hip at side, shorter at center. Group of narrow, vertical folds falls from missing shoulder. Omega fold at hem probably falls from breast; below it, zigzag folds of open side of peplos, terminating in pointed fold. Forearm extended diagonally to front and side. For lower part of type, see **C8**. Similar in treatment of back to **C2** and **C46**. Probable mold sibling in lot 6508 preserves the thighs, with folds between them; arm lacking, but fully modeled folds down side suggest it was raised high.

See pp. 24–28, 125.

C8 Standing peplos-figurine   Pl. 1

MF-14118. Lot 3230. Preserved: thighs to hem. Missing feet. P.H. 0.087 (size 3). Fabric 3, light orange, pinker at core. White slip. Hollow. Thin-walled. Back handmade.

Lower part of same type as **C7**. Cascade of folds down open side of peplos terminates in comparable pointed fold beside right thigh. Weight on right leg, left knee bent. Legs molded through cloth as if nude, framed by clusters of narrow, vertical folds at center and sides. Probable mold siblings in lots 886, 5613. Probable later generation in lot 2249 (has a small plaque base molded together with skirt).

See pp. 24–28, 125.

C9 Standing peplos-figurine   Pl. 1

MF-10536. Lot 886. Preserved: shoulders to feet. Missing right forearm; bottom chipped. P.H. 0.092 (size 2). Fabric 1, tan, with orange core. White slip. Nearly solid. Back handmade, flattened, but rounded at bottom. Added: left arm and hand.

Overfold to waist, center plain, pleat falls from each breast. Right leg advanced, knee slightly bent. Left hand clumsy, pressed against hip. Upper torso bent back. Possible mold sibling: MF-13803 (lot 3222, with different arm position). A fragmentary mold from the Potters' Quarter, KH-87, is similar in pose and peplos arrangement but does not seem to be mechanically related (*Corinth* XV, i, p. 96, no. 25, pl. 33); for similar type with head, see Winter, *Typen* I, p. 78, no. 2.

See pp. 24–28.

C10   Standing peplos-figurine   Pl. 1

MF-11047. Lot 1953. Preserved: shoulders to base. Missing forearms. Mended. P.H. 0.087 (size 2). Fabric 3, greenish buff. Nearly solid. Back handmade, concave. Added: forearms, base.

Left leg slightly bent, foot forward. Forearms originally extended forward. Peplos has wide V-shaped neck. Overfold hem straight across top of hip, with sharp drop at sides; broken catenary at center. Narrow, vertical grooves down overfold sides and on skirt, but cloth is smooth over legs. Low plaque base. Upper torso slightly bent back. Probable mold siblings: **C11**; MF-10568 (lot 891); for others including head, see **C11**.

See pp. 24–28, 30, 275, 343.

C11   Standing peplos-figurine   Pl. 1

MF-11048. Lot 1953. Preserved: head to waist. Missing right hand, left forearm. P.H. 0.053 (size 2). Fabric 3, greenish buff. Orange paint on hair. Nearly solid. Back handmade, concave; head flattened. Added: forearm. Tooling on hair.

Torso probably from same mold as **C10**. Round face, narrowing at chin. Features small, nose flattened. Hair rounded in front, with light, horizontal waves; long locks of hair to shoulders. Probable mold siblings: two in lot 2249 (one with fillet around head); see also **C10**.

See pp. 24–28, 30, 42.

C12   Standing peplos-figurine   Pl. 1

MF-13871. Lot 2249. Preserved: hips to base in front, thighs to calves in back. Mended. P.H. 0.070 (size 2). Fabric 1, grayish buff. White slip. Nearly solid. Back handmade, rounded. Added: front edge of base.

Similar in type to **C10** but elongated, right foot drawn back. Plaque base.

See pp. 24–28.

C13   Standing peplos-figurine   Pl. 1

MF-13817. Lot 2249. Preserved: neck (with small part of back of head) to right hip, to waist at left; in back to breast level. P.H. 0.052 (size 3). Fabric 3, orange-buff to yellowish buff. Hollow; head solid. Back handmade, flattened. Top of rectangular vent preserved, ca. 0.025 wide.

Right arm at side, left hand holds flower bud(?) at breast. Peplos shows loose V-shaped folds at neck, catenaries down front of overfold, voluminous vertical folds at sides. Zigzag folds down open right side. Folds visible behind shoulders and upper arms. Hem of overfold not preserved but originally fell at least to hips. Long locks of hair along neck.

See pp. 29–32.

C14   Standing peplos-figurine   Pl. 2

MF-13786. Lot 3226. Preserved: front–right hip and thigh. P.H. 0.129 (size 4–5). Fabric similar to 1, harder, slightly coarser, orange-buff to orange, with sparse small gray, red, and white inclusions. Hollow. Added: deep fold at side.

Overall pose uncertain, but right thigh appears to advance rather stiffly. Peplos shows flat fold down side, opening into large, deep omega. At break, trace of folds curving upward across torso, suggesting overfold may have been lifted in left hand, as in later votary with piglet **H119**. Corner of overfold knotted or weighted. Large, well-made piece, similar in scale and quality of workmanship to **C15**.

See pp. 29–32.

C15   Standing peplos-figurine   Pl. 2

MF-13861. Lot 1953. Preserved: front–left hip and thigh, part of side. P.H. 0.101 (size 4–5). Fabric 1, orange-buff to orange, interior grayish buff. Hollow.

Left thigh advanced. Overfold to top of thigh, dipping at side. Thin, clinging cloth. Folds simple, sparse, calligraphic. Flat, vertical pleat down side of torso, narrower ridge curving to inside of thigh; cluster of narrow, vertical folds at center of skirt. Large, well-made piece, similar in scale and quality of workmanship to **C14**.

See pp. 29–32.

C16   Standing peplos-figurine   Pl. 2

MF-11898. Lot 2107. Preserved: shoulders to ankles. Missing forearms, part of lower back. P.H. 0.137 (size 2–3). Fabric 1, orange-buff to orange, with gray core. White slip. Hollow. Fairly thick-walled. Back handmade, flattened. Roughly square vent, ca. 0.023 × 0.02. Added: forearms, locks of hair on shoulders. Tooling on side folds.

Right leg slightly advanced, knee bent. Forearms originally extended forward, probably turned out slightly. Peplos thin, clinging, reveals curving outlines of torso and legs. Overfold to top of thighs, light catenary at center. Narrow folds clustered at sides of figure and between legs. Hem trails slightly. Lock of hair on each shoulder.

See pp. 28, 29–32, 197.

C17   Standing peplos-figurine   Pl. 2

MF-10500. Lot 880. Preserved: head to left thigh and right hip. Missing forearms. P.H. 0.133 (size 2). Fabric 1, buff. White slip. Red paint on hair. Hollow; head solid. Thick-walled. Back handmade, flattened, roughly pared. Rectangular vent, 0.027 wide. Added: forearms, hair, fillet. Tooling on hair.

Similar in type to **C16** but more slender, shoulders sloping; left arm may have been turned inward. Long neck. Small, triangular face. Small features clustered near center of face. Eyes and eyebrows downturned; upper lids defined. Nose close to upper lip. Mouth narrow; lips full. Long, heavily slashed and punched locks of hair cling to neck and spread over shoulders; rounded fillet. Probable mold siblings: one in lot 6215; "doll's" head **C152** (coiffure altered but with similar heavy retouch). Similar in type: one in lot 3215 (preserves both forearms, turned outward). For possible workshop mates, see Workshop B, pp. 344–345.

See pp. 29–32, 44, 55, 56, 118, 254, note 19.

C18   Standing peplos-figurine   Pl. 2

MF-10504. Lot 880. Preserved: shoulders to ankles. Missing forearms, part of back. Mended. Small area at front of left shoulder restored in plaster. P.H. 0.117 (size 2). Probably fabric 1, burned(?), tan. White slip. Red paint on hair. Hollow. Thick-walled. Back handmade, flattened. Added: forearms, locks of hair on shoulders.

Similar in type and slender proportions to **C17**. As in **C17**, left forearm seems to have been turned inward. Cluster of narrow, vertical folds between legs. Dull impression. For possible workshop mates, see Workshop B, pp. 344–345.

See pp. 29–32.

C19   Standing draped female figurine   Pl. 2

MF-11710. Lot 2013. Preserved: thighs to base. Mended. P.H. 0.087 (size 3). Fabric 5, orange-buff to orange. White slip. Hollow. Torso and base probably rendered in same mold. Back handmade, flattened. Rectangular vent, 0.02 wide. Tooling on toes.

Right leg slightly advanced, knee bent; bare foot points to corner of base. Figure as far as preserved is elongated and slender, flat at sides. Hem trails slightly. Base is ca. 0.02 high, rectangular in front, rounded in back, sides slightly splaying.

See pp. 29–32, 275.

C20   Standing draped female figurine   Pl. 2

MF-13811. Lot 4379. Preserved: hem, feet, and front of base. P.H. 0.057 (size 4). Fabric 1, slightly coarser, tan, with sparse small dark inclusions, voids. White slip. Red paint on base. Hollow. Torso and base probably rendered in same mold.

Bare feet on base, 0.022 high, in same position as **C19**, but larger in scale and of better fabric.

See pp. 29–32, 275.

C21   Standing peplos-figurine   Pl. 2

MF-10390. Lot 875. Preserved: shoulders to knees. Missing part of right side, forearms. P.H. 0.066 (size 2). Fabric 1, orange-buff. White slip. Hollow. Back handmade, flattened. Top of large, rectangular vent, 0.02 wide.

Right thigh advanced. Broad shoulders; relatively narrow, flat hips. Overfold arches across hips; wide V-shaped fold at neckline. Forearms originally extended forward. Possible traces of sleeves, perhaps chiton worn beneath peplos.

See pp. 29–32.

C22   Standing peplos-figurine   Pl. 2

MF-13800. Lot 4379. Preserved: hips to feet; large chip in bottom of skirt. Mended. Surface worn. P.H. 0.121 (size 3–4). Fabric 1, interior orange-buff (exterior treated with preservative). Hollow. Back molded, rounded. Possible lower rim of oval vent at break. Added: probably left foot.

Left leg bent; foot in pointed shoe placed to side and slightly back. Peplos open at right side, with traces of zigzag folds ending in a point. Overfold to top of thighs; hem dips at sides, with two pleats probably depending from breasts. Skirt hem trails slightly over left instep. Probable later generation: one in lot 3230 (folds reworked; same pose and pointed fold at open side of peplos).

See pp. 29–32.

C23   Standing peplos-figurine   Pl. 2

MF-13771. Lot 4404. Preserved: shoulders to feet. Missing forearms, fragment of right hip, left ankle and foot. P.H. 0.111 (size 2–3). Fabric 1, orange-buff to orange, with orange core. White slip. Hollow. Back handmade, flattened. Large, oval vent, 0.034 × 0.018. Added: right foot. Tooling on folds.

Steps forward on right leg; foot in pointed shoe projects from hem. Forearms originally extended forward, turned out slightly. Peplos arrangement generally similar to **C22**. Pleats falling from breasts continue into narrowing skirt, where they form a long V-shaped fold to the knee. Trace of long catenary at center of overfold between breasts. Hem trails slightly. Upper torso slightly bent backward.

See pp. 29–32.

C24   Standing peplos-figurine   Pl. 3

MF-13820. Lot 3230. Preserved: chest to top of thighs. Missing right hip, most of back. Mended. P.H. 0.088 (size 4). Fabric 1, buff. Hollow. Back handmade, flat.

Left arm probably at side. Overfold belted at waist, falls to top of thighs. Kolpos is flattened, slightly arched over waist, and is plain at the center, with narrow, vertical folds at either side. Below belt, overfold is pleated across abdomen, with omega fold at hem. Complete type can be reconstructed from a figurine found in a tomb at Argos (Papaspyridi-Karouzou 1933–1935, pp. 34–35, fig. 17 right).

See pp. 32–35, 37.

C25   Standing peplos-figurine   Pl. 3

MF-13832. Lot 2249. Preserved: shoulders to abdomen. Missing forearms. P.H. 0.068 (size 3), Fabric 1, orange-buff, interior orange. White slip. Hollow. Back handmade, flattened. Added: probably forearms (tooling on drapery near elbow).

Garment has fine folds like a chiton but no sleeves; it therefore must be a peplos. Gathered at waist with belt hidden beneath light pouching. Entire top of garment is a series of parallel catenaries falling from shoulders and breasts. Narrow, parallel skirt folds follow curve of abdomen. Forearms originally extended, left one probably slightly turned out. Well-made piece.

See pp. 32–35.

C26   Standing peplos-figurine   Pl. 3

MF-11013. Lot 1953. Preserved: front–left hip and right knee to base. Mended. P.H. 0.133 (size 3). Fabric 2, light orange. Hollow. Added: base. Round hole (diam. 0.006) at break across thigh may be an ancient mend.

Left knee bent, foot drawn back. Hem of long overfold visible at upper break. Deeply folded skirt falls to instep; vertical folds conceal right leg; deep U-shaped fold looped from right thigh to ankle. High, rectangular base with slightly splaying sides.

See pp. 32–35, 36, 275.

C27   Standing peplos-figurine   Pl. 3

MF-13794. Lot 4387. Preserved: front–left hip to foot. Missing sandal sole. Mended. P.H. 0.232 (size 4–5). Fabric 2, orange-buff. Hollow. Added: foot and hem over it. Tooling on folds and feet.

Weight on left leg. Skirt folds are vertical, tubular; trailing hem arches over instep. At broken edge, skirt folds sweep back, indicating that right foot originally was pulled back and to side. Overfold falls to top of thigh in deep folds, follows curve of hip, originally may have been girded at waist. Low-soled sandal; toes incised.

See pp. 32–35.

C28 Standing peplos-figurine Pl. 3

MF-13797. Lot 3230. Preserved: left shoulder to waist, small part of back. P.H. 0.113 (size 4). Fabric 1, tan. White slip. Hollow. Thick-walled. Back handmade, flattened.

Similar in type to **C25** but larger, and with flap of back of garment brought forward on shoulder (flap rendered in mold). Similar in type: one in lot 5613.

See pp. 32–35.

C29 Standing draped female figurine Pl. 3

MF-13833. Lot 2239. Preserved: shoulders to right thigh and left hip. Missing forearms. P.H. 0.094 (size 3). Fabric 1, orange-buff to orange. Hollow. Back handmade, rounded. Irregular, rectangular vent, 0.026 wide at top, narrowing downward. Added: locks of hair on shoulders.

Upper arms at sides; forearms originally extended forward. Finely folded garment, belted at waist, with light kolpos arching over slightly swollen abdomen. Dull impression; neither overfold hem of peplos nor chiton sleeves visible, but wide, deep V-shaped fold of neckline appears just above breasts. Locks of hair outline broad, rounded shoulders.

See pp. 32–35.

C30 Standing peplos-figurine Pl. 4

MF-10455. Lot 878. Preserved: shoulders to hips. Missing right forearm, left arm and side, part of back. Mended. Small area of front near right shoulder restored in plaster. P.H. 0.120 (size 4). Fabric 2, orange. White slip. Hollow. Back handmade, flattened. Vertical edge of rectangular vent preserved. Added: locks of hair on shoulders and back. Tooling on folds, hair.

Similar in type to **C29**, but garment is probably a peplos. Dull impression, all folds slashed; original fold pattern probably similar to **C28**. Long locks of hair lie flat over front of right shoulder, but locks are crimped along edge of left shoulder. Separate mass of hair gathered down back. Probable mold sibling: one in lot 2089, with left upper arm at side. Possible mold siblings: **C31**; one in lot 878.

See pp. 32–35.

C31 Standing peplos-figurine Pl. 4

MF-10477. Lot 878. Preserved: shoulders to left hip in front, to waist in back. Missing forearms. Mended; front chipped. P.H. 0.132 (size 4). Fabric 2, burned(?), back orange, front tan. White slip. Hollow. Back handmade, flattened. Rectangular vent, ca. 0.036 wide. Added: scarf.

Similar in type and scale to **C30**, perhaps a mold sibling. Forearms originally extended forward. V-shaped fold at neckline forms a slight pouch. Scarf around shoulders is rendered by a strip of clay with a row of holes punched along each end to suggest folds. Possible trace of overfold hem just above break at top of thigh.

See pp. 32–35.

C32 Standing peplos-figurine Pl. 3

MF-13850. Lot 4344. Preserved: front–left breast and waist, with bit of upper arm. P.H. 0.077 (size 4–5). Fabric 2, light orange. Hollow.

Similar in type to **C30** but girded higher; folds more sculptural, rendered in mold. One deep, curving fold frames breast, lighter fold slants from nipple to belt; soft pouching at side.

See pp. 32–35.

C33 Standing peplos-figurine Pl. 4

MF-11066. Lot 1962. Preserved: head to base. Missing right arm, part of headdress, right earring, most of base. Mended; nose chipped. Most of base restored in plaster. H. 0.19 (size 3). Fabric 3, orange to buff. White slip. Hollow; head solid. Torso and base rendered in same mold. Back molded, rounded. Small, rectangular vent, ca. 0.025 × 0.015. Added: left arm and hand, headdress, earrings, hair peak at back. Tooling on hair.

Left knee bent, foot to side. Left arm bent, mitten-shaped hand behind thigh. Right arm probably extended to side. Peplos with high, arched belt, overfold to knees, looped fold under each arm. Few folds visible above belt; narrow, vertical folds on skirt, which flares to low, rectangular, splaying base, molded at bottom. Figure tall and slender, with broad shoulders, short upper arm. Long, spreading neck. Small face topped by high, rounded coiffure. Face oval. Eyes large, slightly downturned. Coiffure has high peaks in front (punched) and back (vertically incised). Flaring headdress looks like a kalathiskos in front but is backless. For coiffure with stippled topknot in front, cf. larger head **C134**. Probable mold sibling of head: **C158**, with similar coiffure but different retouch, no headdress. Similar in type: head in the Corinth collection, MF-6075 (*Corinth* XII, p. 34, no. 147, pl. 10). Figurine with similar head in helmet with triangular visor, presumably representing Athena: R. B. Richardson 1898, pp. 220–221, figs. 33, 33a; another head, Paris 1887, pp. 437–438, no. 98, pl. V:8. For possible workshop mates, see Workshop A, p. 344.

See pp. 18, 32–35, 57, 272.

C34 Standing draped girl(?) Pl. 4

MF-11071. Lot 1962. Preserved: shoulders to hips in front, to waist in back. Missing arms below sleeves. P.H. 0.133 (size 5). Fabric 2, buff. Hollow; interior irregular, walls up to 0.02 thick. Back handmade, flattened. Added: arms. Tooling on folds.

Could represent a chitoned youth but, in the context of this sanctuary, is more likely a young girl (see, e.g., Early Hellenistic girl votary **H43**). Chiton girded slightly above natural waistline; belt slightly arched, hidden by lightly pouched folds. Loose, wide V-shaped fold at neckline; looped sleeve folds under each arm. Delicate, linear, ogival folds drop from shoulders to waist; narrow, vertical ridges on skirt. Surface well smoothed and polished in front; left side rougher, perhaps originally covered by arm. Figure broad, stocky, childlike. Large, well-made piece.

See pp. 32–35, 127.

C35 Standing peplos-figurine Pl. 4

MF-69-380. Lot 6214. Preserved: front–part of right hip and abdomen. P.H. 0.077 (size 4–5). Fabric 1, harder, buff. White slip. Hollow. Thin-walled. Tooling on folds.

Wide, slanting, flat fold of overfold is preserved, curving at hem; butterfly folds on kolpos. Narrow skirt folds. It is difficult to place this fragment on the figure, but it probably belongs to the right hip of a quietly standing figure similar to **C38**, with the leg drawn back. Large, well-made piece.

See pp. 35, 37.

C36 Standing peplos-figurine (Demeter?) Pl. 5

MF-12535. Lot 3217. Preserved: Base of neck to thighs; missing right forearm, left arm, upper part of mantle fall at left side, part of skirt front. Mended. P.H. 0.155 (size 4). Fabric 1, orange-buff to orange. White slip. Hollow. Back handmade, flattened. Irregular vent, ca. 0.063 × 0.035, rectangular at left side, oval at right. Added: mantle, arms. Tooling on folds, especially on kolpos, and vertical incisions on mantle fall.

Weight on right leg, hip outthrust; left thigh slightly advanced. Left shoulder higher than right, thus arm originally raised; right arm held away from body, precise position uncertain. Hip-length overfold and kolpos are arched over abdomen. Deep pleat from left breast ends in omega at overfold hem; flatter folds at sides. Right breast framed by curving folds from left shoulder. Triangular folds, turned toward center, shape contour of right hip. Loose V-shaped folds at neck. Bunching of kolpos indicated by slashes and punch marks. Wide, flat skirt folds are indicated by vertical incisions just beneath kolpos. Type modified by addition of shoulder-pinned back mantle, pulled forward into deep loops over shoulders, hanging behind in thin, stiff panel cut off abruptly at hip level. The raised left arm probably lifted the edge of the mantle. Large piece, sculptural in style, although rather flat and schematic in execution.

See pp. 9, note 33, 18, 35–36, 137, 149, 197, 251, 252, 286.

C37 Standing peplos-figurine (Demeter?) Pl. 5

MF-13812. Lot 4349. Preserved: front–left shoulder, breast, part of upper arm and side. Mended. P.H. 0.111 (size 5). Fabric 2, orange, with gray core. White slip. Hollow. Added: arm, part of mantle folds over arm. Tooling on folds.

Similar to **C36** in type but larger, more plastic in execution. Loop of shoulder-pinned back mantle very deeply modeled, mostly rendered in mold. Few folds of mantle on back of arm suggest that originally it fell directly from shoulder; if so, arm may have been raised to hold scepter or other object.

See pp. 35–36.

C38 Standing peplos-figurine Pl. 5

MF-68-366. Lot 5613. Preserved: front–right hip and thigh. Mended. P.H. 0.093 (size 4–5). Fabric 1, orange-buff, interior surface and core orange. Hollow. Tooling on folds.

Peplos similar to **C36**, but figurine is larger, modeling much deeper; more pronounced kolpos, slashed. Triangular folds over hip seen in **C36** are echoed here, but remains of folds at center of overfold suggest a more complex arrangement. Large, well-made, heavily retouched piece in strongly sculptural style.

See pp. 35–36.

C39 Standing peplos-figurine Pl. 5

MF-13874. Lot 3222. Preserved: front–right hip and thigh; small part of back. P.H. 0.078 (size 4–5). Fabric 1, harder, buff. White slip. Hollow. Thin-walled. Back probably handmade, flattened.

Overfold hem and kolpos straight across abdomen, dropping to baggy fold at side. Kolpos not clearly differentiated from overfold; rather mechanical vertical folds on skirt. Large piece, thin-walled and fired hard, but fold patterns summarily executed.

See pp. 35–36.

C40 Standing peplos-figurine Pl. 5

MF-13798. Lot 4387. Preserved: front–right thigh and left knee to feet; back–knees to feet. Missing most of toes; inside of right lower leg chipped. Mended. P.H. 0.121 (size 4). Fabric 1, orange-buff. White slip. Hollow. Thick-walled, solid at bottom. Back molded, flattened. Tooling on folds.

Weight on left leg; right foot drawn to side and slightly back. Vertical folds of skirt are deep, especially fold separating legs; inner part of right leg has been cut away; folds deep also in back. Zigzag folds of open edge of peplos at right side. Curving folds over right ankle originally looped from knee. Hem trails over right instep; folds seem to terminate rather than trail over left instep, but broken surface is unclear. Low-soled sandals; toes of right foot partly preserved.

See pp. 35–36.

C41 Standing peplos-figurine Pl. 6

MF-11018. Lot 1953. Preserved: right shoulder to thighs. Missing left shoulder and arm, right forearm, most of back. P.H. 0.094 (size 3). Fabric 2, orange. Hollow. Back handmade, rounded. Added: forearms, in elbow sockets. Tooling on folds.

Right thigh probably slightly advanced. Upper arms at sides; forearms originally extended forward. Costume generally similar to **C36**. Hip-length, arched overfold is thickened at hem, suggesting that archetype had a kolpos. V-shaped folds at neckline are slashed; two long catenaries pendant from breasts. Vertical, flaring folds at sides of overfold originally may have terminated at hem in omega folds. Probable mold sibling: MF-11709 (lot 2013, fabric 1, with traces of locks of hair on shoulders). Possible earlier generation in lot 3222 (fabric 5). Others of similar type in varying fabrics, so heavily retouched that mechanical relationships are uncertain, in lots 1954, 2239, 3206, 3222, 4381, and 4449. **C42** is similar in type but is scarred due to a mold defect; it may be from a parallel mold series.

See pp. 35–37.

C42 Standing peplos-figurine Pl. 6

MF-11668. Lot 2009. Preserved: shoulders to thighs; front and mantle chipped. Missing forearms. Mended. P.H. 0.106 (size 3). Fabric 2, buff to orange-buff. White slip. Red paint on back at top. Hollow. Back handmade, flattened. Irregular vent at hip level, ca. 0.037 × 0.024, rectangular at top, oval at bottom. Added: mantle, forearms. Tooling on folds. Large, oval scar on left hip and thigh, probably from defect in mold.

Probably mechanically related to **C41**. Forearms originally extended forward, slightly turned out. Nearly all folds of peplos, including wide V-shaped fold at neckline, heavily slashed. Shoulder-pinned back mantle added in thin panel behind left arm and hip, with flap over right shoulder; folds incised. Red paint on back suggests long hair, although no locks of hair are preserved. Perhaps from a mold series parallel to **C41**, which does not show the scar; this defect is similar to that of **C43**, which is larger in scale.

See pp. 18, 35–37, 129.

C43 Standing peplos-figurine Pl. 6

MF-14080. Lot 3231. Preserved: shoulders to right knee, left thigh. Missing arms, most of drapery fall at right side, part of back. Mended. P.H. 0.141 (size 3). Fabric 1, orange-buff to orange, interior orange. Hollow. Back handmade, flattened. Vertical edge of narrow, rectangular vent preserved at hip level. Added: arms, mantle fall at both sides, possibly long locks of hair in back. Tooling on folds. Large, oval scar on left hip and thigh, probably from defect in mold.

Scar on left hip and thigh is similar to that of the smaller **C42**, suggesting a mechanical relationship through a defect in the mold, but proportions of this piece are more elongated, with narrow shoulders, high breasts, long waist. Left arm probably raised to lift mantle; right arm held away from torso. Overfold hem scarcely visible; kolpos hem is horizontal, pouching indicated with gouges. Folds retouched with rough slashes. Coarse workmanship.

See pp. 18, 35–37.

C44 Standing draped female figurine Pl. 6

MF-13646. Lot 2152. Preserved: front–left shoulder to hip, small part of back. P.H. 0.083 (size 3). Fabric 2, light orange. White slip. Hollow. Back rounded.

Mantle covers left shoulder and side; other end draped across waist and over bent left arm. Hand cupped, thumb and forefinger touch. Dull impression.

See pp. 37, 293.

HYDRIAPHOROI AND RELATED HEADS

Torsos of Hydriaphoroi

C45 Pl. 6
Standing peplos-figurine, probably hydriaphoros

MF-13883. Lot 874. Preserved: front–right shoulder to hip; small part of back. Missing right arm. P.H. 0.101 (size 4). Fabric 1, buff. Hollow. Small part of vertical edge of vent preserved. Added: drapery loop under arm. Tooling on folds.

Break at shoulder indicates that arm was raised at sharp angle, as if to hold object on head, probably hydria. Center of overfold plain, falls to just below waist. Two deep, vertical folds at side, flat loop under arm; deep zigzag folds at open side of peplos. Vertical skirt folds. If figurine is a hydriaphoros, it would resemble in type the much smaller and later **C48**; cf. also Winter, *Typen* I, p. 156, no. 4. Similar in scale to the head **C53**; **C45** originally may have had a head of this type. Venting perhaps similar to **C46**.

See pp. 38, 42.

C46 Pl. 6
Standing peplos-figurine, probably hydriaphoros

MF-14065. Lot 3222. Preserved: right side, with part of chest, upper hip, back. P.H. 0.083 (size 3). Fabric 1, orange-buff. White slip. Hollow. Back handmade, flat; narrow (0.015) return to finished edge, indicating large, rectangular vent.

Similar in type to **C45**, with looped underarm fold, arm probably raised very high. In addition, overfold hem seems lifted high above kolpos, as if responding to raised arm. Traces of two catenaries at center of overfold; vertical folds at sides dropping to zigzag hem. Treatment of back as in **C2** and **C7**.

See p. 39.

C47 Pl. 6
Standing peplos-figurine, with piglet (and hydria?)

MF-13863. Lot 1953. Preserved: shoulders to ankles. Missing right arm. Mended; front chipped. P.H. 0.12 (size 2–3). Fabric 5, orange. Hollow. Back handmade, rounded. Tooling on folds.

Weight may be on left leg; hips thrust forward. Left arm at side, holding piglet by back leg, head down. Right arm appears to have been raised high, perhaps to support a hydria. Folds of open peplos down right side; overfold to hips. Degenerate, with few details.

See pp. 39, 120.

C48 Pl. 6
Standing peplos-figurine, probably hydriaphoros

MF-13870. Lot 1953. Preserved: front–right armpit to foot, left thigh to ankle; back–shoulders to ankles. P.H. 0.093 (size 2–3). Fabric 2, friable, orange. Hollow. Back handmade, flattened.

Weight on left leg; right leg bent, drawn to side. Stump of right arm raised at sharp angle, as if to support an object on head, probably a hydria. Drapery folds indistinct, but overfold probably falls to waist, with diagonal zigzag folds to hip at side.

See p. 39.

C49 Pl. 6
Standing peplos-figurine, probably hydriaphoros

MF-13790. Lot 3229. Preserved: shoulders to calves. Missing arms. Mended; front chipped. P.H. 0.092 (size 2–3). Fabric 1, orange-buff to orange. Hollow. Thick-walled. Back molded, rounded. Rectangular vent, 0.017 × 0.024. Added: locks of hair in back and on shoulders, projecting folds at sides. Tooling on hair.

Weight on right leg. Left leg advanced. Break indicates right arm originally raised. Left hand originally held fold of skirt out to side. Peplos girded fairly high; overfold falls to top of thighs. Folds of open right side of peplos summarily rendered, with pointed projections under arm. Skirt has tubular, vertical folds but is smooth over left leg. Long locks of hair are crimped horizontally.

See p. 39.

C50 Pl. 6
Standing draped female figurine, perhaps hydriaphoros

MF-14062. Lot 891. Preserved: front–right side, breast to hip. Missing arm. P.H. 0.059 (size 2). Fabric 1, buff to pinkish orange, interior greenish buff. Hollow. Added: right arm.

Hole in shoulder may be for insertion of arm tenon, similar to seated figurine **C82**, perhaps to strengthen arm in vulnerable position (lifted to balance hydria on head?). Costume a chiton or peplos with mantle around hip. Although the shoulder hole could be a sign of an articulated "doll," Corinthian figurines with articulated arms usually were not mantled (cf., e.g., **C180**).

See p. 39.

Heads of Hydriaphoroi and Related Heads

C51 Head of hydriaphoros Pl. 7

MF-70-236. Lot 6500. Preserved: hydria to neck. Missing right upper arm, panel between arm and head. P.H. 0.063 (size 3). Fabric 1, slightly harder, buff to orange-buff. White slip. Hollow. Head, arm, and hydria rendered in same mold. Back handmade, flattened.

Right hand grasps horizontal handle of hydria. Cylindrical cushion between head and hydria. Face oblong to oval, with low, triangular forehead. Features indistinct. Hair parted in center, not detailed. Similar in type: MF-11667 (lot 2009, with faint waves around forehead); MF-10629 (lot 896); MF-11707 (lot 2013).

See pp. 38, 129.

C52   Head of hydriaphoros   Pl. 7

MF-10559. Lot 890. Preserved: hydria to neck; front of face chipped. P.H. 0.054 (size 3). Fabric 1, buff to orange-buff. White slip. Solid. Head and hydria rendered in same mold. Back handmade, flattened. Vertical handle of hydria pinched up.

Cylindrical form like a polos merges with base of hydria. No traces of hand on hydria. Horizontal handles very small, vertical handle a flat triangle of clay. Remains of face and hair generally resemble **C51**. Wavy forehead hair; flat, triangular masses of hair along neck. Possible mold siblings in lots 4347 (fabric 5), 4379, and 4386 (facial features indistinct but generally similar to **C51**).

See pp. 38, 39, 42.

C53   Head of hydriaphoros   Pl. 7

MF-12553. Lot 3222. Preserved: hydria foot to figurine neck in front, part of back. Missing part of hair at left side; nose chipped. P.H. 0.095 (size 4). Fabric 1, orange-buff to orange. White slip. Red paint on hair and hydria. Solid; torso hollow. Back handmade, rounded. Added: hydria, most of hair. Tooling on hair.

Face narrow, oblong to oval, with low forehead. Eyes large, level; both lids defined. Nose large, close to upper lip. Mouth wide; lips fleshy, slightly parted. Hair arranged in flat-topped, broad mass bulging at sides, with stippled curls. Scalloped waves across forehead and framing face, with double scallop at center. Long corkscrew curls flank long, spreading neck. Rounded form on head is either splaying hydria foot or cushion topped by part of foot. Similar in scale to **C45**; perhaps originally belonged to a torso of this type. Possible mold sibling: **C54**.

See pp. 37, 39–40, 46, 129, 133.

C54   Head of hydriaphoros   Pl. 7

MF-10498. Lot 880. Preserved: hydria to neck; lower face and neck chipped. Missing vertical hydria handle and rim. P.H. 0.087 (size 4). Fabric 1, buff to orange-buff. White slip. Red paint on hair. Solid. Back handmade, rounded. Added: hydria, most of hair. Tooling on hair.

Published: Stroud 1965, p. 10, pl. 2:f.

Perhaps from same mold as **C53**. No locks of hair on neck. Uncertain if hand supported hydria. Vessel has broad base with high, slightly splaying foot. Earlike handles spring from lower body.

See pp. 39, 42, 46.

C55   Head of hydriaphoros(?)   Pl. 7

MF-13770. Lot 4387. Preserved: head and neck, right shoulder and part of back. Missing right shoulder at front. Mended. P.H. 0.097 (size 4). Fabric 1, greenish buff. White

slip. Red paint on hair. Solid; torso hollow. Back handmade, rounded. Added: most of hair. Tooling on hair.

Similar in facial type to **C53** but end of nose distorted, mouth turned down slightly at left. Long, spreading neck. Shoulders probably narrow, sloping. Probable mold sibling: MF-11869 (lot 2156). Possible later generation: heads in lots 3222 and 4433 (the latter has distorted features and originally had an object on the head).

See pp. 25, 40, 46.

C56   Head of hydriaphoros(?)   Pl. 7

MF-12127. Lot 4347. Preserved: head and neck. P.H. 0.062 (size 4). Fabric 1, orange-buff. White slip. Solid. Back handmade, rounded. Added: most of hair, lower part of nose. Tooling on hair.

Similar in facial type to **C53** and **C55**. Eyes in relief, without modeled lids, reminiscent of Archaic technique. Top of head flattened, irregular, as if object originally added.

See pp. 40, 42, 46.

C57   Head of hydriaphoros(?)   Pl. 7

MF-13977. Lot 3222. Preserved: head and neck. P.H. 0.054 (size 3). Fabric 1, greenish buff. Solid. Back handmade, flattened. Added: hair at sides, fillet. Tooling on hair.

Similar in facial type to **C53** but smaller, forehead higher, jaw more oval. Less bouffant hairstyle, but double scallop at center of forehead retained. Probably a later development of type. Thick, tubular fillet. Top of head flattened and smoothed. Possible mold sibling: KT-10-17 from the Potter's Quarter (*Corinth* XV, ii, p. 123, no. 9, pl. 25, from the Circular South Shrine; MF-685 [*Corinth* XII, p. 35, no. 148, pl. 10] is mentioned there as a possible mold sibling, but differences particularly in the treatment of the eyes and the facial shape seem to preclude this possibility). Similar in type: MF-10319 (lot 870, with added fillet and long locks of hair at sides).

See pp. 41, 165.

C58   Head of hydriaphoros(?)   Pl. 7

MF-70-240. Lot 6233. Preserved: head and neck. Missing half of cushion, lock of hair at left side of neck. P.H. 0.059 (size 3–4). Fabric 1, orange-buff. White slip. Solid. Back handmade, rounded. Added: cushion, part of hair. Tooling on hair. Top of head pierced.

Facial type and full coiffure generally similar to **C53** but face narrower, with high, triangular forehead. Nose distorted. Long, spreading neck. Hair parted at center, three thick locks of hair at either side rolled around fillet; below this, a stippled hair mass and long locks of hair to shoulders (at front only, as in **C53**). Head is pierced as in articulated "dolls," but facial type and coiffure are more closely connected with hydriaphoroi. Hydria possibly fired separately and attached with a peg; added strip probably the cushion under hydria.

See pp. 38, 40, 41.

C59   Female head, related to hydriaphoroi   Pl. 8

MF-14045. Lot 4394. Preserved: head and neck. P.H. 0.034 (size 2–3). Fabric 1, orange-buff. White slip. Solid. Back handmade, rounded. Added: part of hair at top, locks of hair along neck. Tooling on hair.

Facial type similar to **C58**, including nose distortion and arrangement of hair in front, but smaller; extremely narrow face contrasts with full coiffure. No fillet; long locks of hair in front only. Long, wide, spreading neck. Similar in facial type and in nose distortion, possibly mechanically related: "doll's" head **C141**.

See pp. 18, 41, 42.

C60   Head of hydriaphoros(?)   Pl. 8

MF-11910. Lot 2066. Preserved: head, with cushion; nose chipped. P.H. 0.05 (size 3–4). Fabric 1, orange. Hollow. Back handmade, rounded. Added: cushion, lower part of hair in front and back. Tooling on hair. Top of head pierced.

Facial type similar to **C53**, but forehead is high, triangular. Eyes slightly downturned, less widely opened. Coiffure rounded, less exaggerated. For explanation of cushion and hole in top of head, see **C58**.

See pp. 38, 41, 46, 163.

C61   Female head, related to hydriaphoroi   Pl. 8

MF-10463. Lot 878. Preserved: head; jaw and hair chipped. P.H. 0.043 (size 3–4). Fabric 2, orange. White slip. Solid. Back handmade, rounded. Added: hair in front, fillet, possibly long locks of hair along neck. Tooling on hair.

Facial type similar to **C60**. Coiffure with locks of hair rolled over fillet; probably long locks of hair originally along neck, similar to **C58**. These three heads are similar to one another in type and scale, although they are not mechanically related.

See pp. 25, 40, 41, 42, 46.

C62   Female head, related to hydriaphoroi   Pl. 8

MF-11867. Lot 2156. Preserved: front–head; missing right earring. P.H. 0.05 (size 4). Fabric 5, orange-buff to orange, slightly burned. Hollow. Added: nose, earring. Tooling on hair.

Face oval, narrowing at jaw, with high, triangular, sloping forehead; receding chin. Features large, seem to fill face. Eyes slightly downturned; lids thick, lower lid lifted. Nose prominent, overhangs upper lip. Mouth wide; lips full, slightly smiling. Coiffure parted at center, close to head, marked with short slashes. Pellet earring too low, does not touch ear. Loss of entire neck suggests figure originally mantled up to chin. Possible later generation: **C63**.

See p. 41.

C63   Female head, related to hydriaphoroi   Pl. 8

MF-14011. Lot 4348. Preserved: head. Missing most of stephane. P.H. 0.044 (size 4). Fabric 1, orange-buff, with grayish buff core. White slip. Pink paint on flesh; red paint on eyes, hair. Hollow. Thick-walled. Back handmade, rounded. Added: stephane. Tooling on hair.

Possibly a later generation of **C62**. May also originally have been mantled up to chin. Face narrower in shape; forehead lower. Coiffure parted at center, with fairly straight, horizontal locks of hair to sides; stephane.

See p. 41.

C64   Female head, related to hydriaphoroi   Pl. 8

MF-14040. Lot 3226. Preserved: head and neck. Missing part of fillet. P.H. 0.032 (size 2). Fabric 1, orange. Solid. Back handmade, rounded. Added: hair, fillet.

Face oval, with full cheeks; high, triangular forehead. Long, spreading neck. Eyes large, downturned. Lips full, almost pursed. Coiffure a large, rounded mass of stippled curls, topped by a fillet, with long locks of hair in front only.

See pp. 42, 64.

C65   Pl. 8

Female head, related to hydriaphoroi, with upper torso

MF-13818. Lot 3222. Preserved: head to chest, with upper part of back. P.H. 0.061 (size 2–3). Fabric 1, yellowish buff to orange-buff. Hollow. Head and torso rendered in same mold. Back handmade, flattened. Possible upper edge of round or oval vent preserved. Tooling on hair.

Upper arms at sides. Traces of drapery folds between and beside breasts. Head tilted slightly forward. Face oval, with high, triangular forehead, narrowing to jaw. Long, spreading neck. Nose wide, flat. Coiffure parted at center, with curving mass of hair at either side, piled high on cranium; long, thick locks of hair spread over shoulders. Dull impression. Rather poor workmanship.

See p. 41.

C66   Female head, related to hydriaphoroi   Pl. 8

MF-13980. Lot 3222. Preserved: head and neck. Missing upper part of object on head. P.H. 0.047 (size 3). Fabric 1, orange. White slip. Solid. Back handmade, flattened. Added: hair at front and right side, object on head. Tooling on hair.

Features distorted, but facial type is similar to **C60** and **C61**; forehead shape changed by addition of hair. Hollow object on head, perhaps originally a vessel, such as a hydria (or kalathiskos?). Similar head, smaller, from the same lot.

See p. 41.

C67   Female head, related to hydriaphoroi   Pl. 8

MF-10626. Lot 896. Preserved: head and neck; top chipped. P.H. 0.022 (size 2). Fabric 1, yellowish buff. Back handmade, flattened. Added: disc on head.

Slightly concave disc at top of head may be a cushion, to which a hydria (or other object?) balanced on head may have been glued. Face oval to round. Nose flattened. Facial type similar to that of peplos-figurine **C11**. Hair flattened at top by disc, arranged in rounded, wavy mass at either side.

See p. 42.

C68   Female head, related to hydriaphoroi   Pl. 8

MF-73-115. Lot 73-144. Preserved: head and part of neck. Missing part of object on head. P.H. 0.034 (size 3). Fabric 1, orange-buff. Solid. Back handmade, rounded. Added: object on head.

Face oblong to oval. Features indistinct. Dull impression; mold seems defective at left side of face. Hair close to sides of head. On head what appears to be a cushion, topped by a wide, slightly concave, round(?), object similar to a tray with a lump at the center, perhaps an offering tray or the lower part of a kanoun.

See p. 41.

C69   Miniature hydria, from a hydriaphoros   Pl. 8

MF-14074. Lot 2013. Preserved: hydria, with locks of hair; front chipped. P.H. 0.053 (probably size 3). Fabric 1, orange-buff. Hollow. Wheelmade. Added: handles, locks of hair.

High foot; squat, globular body; narrow neck; spreading rim. locks of hair, added after hydria was attached to head, adhere to foot and lower body.

See pp. 41–42.

SEATED DRAPED FEMALE FIGURINES AND RELATED HEADS

C70 Seated peplos-figurine (goddess?)	Pl. 8

MF-14057. Lot 2110. Preserved: right shoulder to lap, small part of back, right arm to wrist. P.H. 0.046 (size 3). Fabric 1, orange-buff to orange. Hollow. Back flat.

Upper arm at side. Overfold hem just above waist; plain at center, vertical folds at sides. Shoulders broad and level. Chair back not rendered in mold; either seat was a stool or chair was made separately. No traces of locks of hair on neck or shoulder, thus hair is bound up on the head. Similar in style to the standing peplos-figurine **C1**.

See pp. 45–46, 293.

C71 Seated goddess	Pl. 8

MF-11400. Lot 877. Preserved: head to waist, part of back at right shoulder. Missing most of right arm. Mended; face and top of polos chipped. P.H. 0.079 (size 3). Fabric 2, light orange to buff. White slip. Hollow; head solid. Head and torso rendered in same mold. Back handmade, flat; upper horizontal edge of vent preserved. Added: polos, projections of chair back. Tooling on hair.

Right hand holds flower bud to breast. Peplos arranged as in **C70**. Coiffure as in **C73** but with less detail; hair along neck is horizontally ridged. High, flaring polos. Chair has curved, horizontal projections in back. Bottom probably as in **C72**. Perhaps mechanically related: MF-11217 (lot 1982, has large square or rectangular vent, lacks flower); KT-8-8 and KT-8-9 from the Potters' Quarter (*Corinth* XV, ii, pp. 127–128, nos. 29, 30, pl. 26; no. 29 has a head of 4th-century B.C. type, which must have replaced the original head type when it was no longer usable); T.F.-95 from the Asklepieion (with a large, rectangular vent). Probable later generation of head in lot 878 (fabric 1). Similar in type: smaller head in lot 4379 (fabric 3); MF-10576 (lot 892) is still smaller, has higher, more flaring polos; one from the diolkos excavations (Verdelis 1958, p. 144, pl. 118:2). A mold for this type is in the Corinth collection, MF-3979 (*Corinth* XII, p. 62, no. 467, pl. 43; the mold does not match exactly any of the figurines in Corinth, perhaps because of heavy retouch or distortions resulting from handling before firing; a complete example in Karlsruhe may be related to this mold, Schürmann 1989, p. 35, no. 67, pl. 14).

See pp. 23, 24, 42–43, 79, 132, 157.

C72 Seated goddess	Pl. 8

MF-10630. Lot 896. Preserved: left knee to base. Missing back, right knee, part of left side. Mended. P.H. 0.06 (size 3). Fabric 3, buff. Hollow. Bottom step of base reworked.

Rounded feet, set apart, project from skirt hem and rest on two-stepped base. Side of seat is flat, plain, with one step at bottom. Trace of left hand on knee. Skirt folds are narrow, vertical. Narrowing toward base is characteristic of type; for complete type, see Potters' Quarter examples cited under **C71**. Possible mold siblings: MF-11402 (lot 877, fabric 2); one in lot 875 (fabric 1). Fragment of similar type in lot 878 has large, rectangular vent cut into side of seat.

See pp. 23, 42–43.

C73 Female head, probably from seated goddess	Pl. 8

MF-11065. Lot 1962. Preserved: head and neck. Nose, right eye abraded. P.H. 0.038 (size 3). Fabric 1, buff to orange.

Solid. Back handmade, flat. Added: some of locks of hair along neck. Tooling on hair.

Face oval, with low forehead; jaw narrows, chin recedes slightly. Long, spreading neck. Eyes level, with clearly defined lids. Browridge follows curve of eye closely. Nose wide, close to upper lip. Mouth wide; lips full. Hair loosely waved across forehead from central part; locks of hair along neck crimped horizontally. High, wide polos. Probably from a seated figure similar to **C71**. Probable mold siblings in lots 2107, 3222, 4417, and 6233; MF-1976-72 from Forum Southwest (fabric 2). Similar in type: MF-11726 (lot 2029); MF-11768 (lot 2047).

See pp. 23, 42–43, 47, 132.

C74 Seated goddess	Pl. 8

MF-11041. Lot 1953. Preserved: shoulders to base. Missing forearms, part of lower left side. P.H. 0.081 (size 2). Fabric 2, buff to orange. Hollow; upper part solid. Back handmade, flat at top, flaring at bottom. Irregular, rectangular vent, ca. 0.03 × 0.02. Added: projections of chair back; forearms (hole in left elbow for insertion of forearm).

Forearms originally extended forward. Slender proportions, with narrow shoulders. Peplos overfold falls to lap; vertical folds between legs. Chair as in **C71**, with footstool. Similar in type, larger: one each in lots 2107 (fabric 1) and 4382 (fabric 3).

See pp. 41, 42–43, 44.

C75 Seated goddess	Pl. 9

MF-13825. Lot 4377. Preserved: head to waist; polos chipped. P.H. 0.049 (size 2). Fabric 1, orange-buff. White slip. Red paint on chair back. Solid. Head and torso rendered in same mold. Back: polos concave, shoulders flat, torso concave. Added: projections of chair back. Tooling on hair.

Similar in type to **C74**. Oval face. Eyes large. Nose flattened. Mouth never modeled. Rounded mass of hair frames face; a few light, curving strokes represent waves; one lock of hair on each shoulder. Low, wide polos. **C76** may be a better rendering of head type.

See pp. 42–43.

C76 Female head, probably from seated goddess	Pl. 9

MF-11294. Lot 1993. Preserved: head and neck. Top of polos chipped. P.H. 0.024 (size 2). Fabric 1, yellowish gray, mottled gray. White slip. Solid. Back flat. Tooling on hair.

Face oval, with low, triangular forehead. Eyes large, protruding, with clearly defined upper lids. Nose wide, flattened, close to upper lip. Mouth small, slightly skewed to right. Rounded mass of hair parted at center, frames face; a few light, curving strokes represent waves; locks of hair along neck crimped horizontally. Low, wide polos. Probably from a seated figure similar to **C75**.

See pp. 42–43.

C77 Seated goddess	Pl. 9

MF-13824. Lot 2249. Preserved: neck to lap in front, to waist in back. Missing back of chair at left side. P.H. 0.063 (size 2–3). Fabric 1, orange-buff to orange. White slip. Hollow. Back handmade, flattened. Rectangular vent, 0.025 wide.

Right hand holds bird with spread wings, facing viewer's right, to chest. Left forearm on lap. Long locks of hair along neck. Shoulders fairly broad. Garment a chiton or peplos (lacks sleeves, but horizontal division at waist could be either chiton belt or overfold hem). Chair as in **C71**. Larger, seated peplos-figurine with a spread-winged bird is represented by small lap fragments of two figurines, probably from the same mold, in lots 886 and 3222; the type cannot yet be reconstructed, but the right arm was at the side, and the left hand held the bird.

See pp. 42–43, 126.

C78 Seated draped female figurine   Pl. 9

MF-11091. Lot 1977. Complete. Mended; surface chipped. H. 0.121 (size 2). Fabric similar to 1, slightly coarser, orange-buff, with sparse small white and dark inclusions, voids. White slip. Hollow. Back handmade, flattened at top, rounded at bottom. Large, irregular vent, ca. 0.025 × 0.048. Added: long locks of hair, projections of chair back. Tooling on folds, face, hair.

Seated on a chair as in **C74**, but projections are more angular, back of chair curved forward. Left arm at side; right hand holds spherical object, probably a ball, to breast. Sleeved chiton belted above natural waistline. Skirt smooth over legs, with narrow vertical folds between and beside them. Face oval, with prominent chin. Nose large, close to upper lip. Hair gathered at top of head in cluster of curls, with long locks of hair to shoulders. A torso mold, without forearms, from the Potters' Quarter, KH-85 (*Corinth* XV, i, p. 110, no. 86, pl. 44), is similar in type, scale, and proportions.

See pp. 43–45, 79, 126.

C79 Seated draped female figurine   Pl. 9

MF-13938. Lot 2249. Preserved: shoulders to knees. Missing seat, back from hips down; surface worn. P.H. 0.051 (size 2). Fabric similar to 1, slightly coarser, orange to orange-buff. Nearly solid, lower part more hollow. Back handmade, flat.

Sloping lap. Right arm at side; hand on thigh. Left hand holds unclear object to breast. Chiton(?) girded slightly above natural waistline, with slightly puffed folds over belt.

See pp. 43–44.

C80 Seated peplos-figurine   Pl. 9

MF-11782. Lot 2063. Preserved: front complete. Missing back from hips to base. Mended; surface worn. H. 0.094 (size 2). Fabric 5, tan to orange. White slip. Hollow. All parts rendered in same mold. Back handmade, flattened.

Sits on flat-sided seat, with footstool; sloping lap, hands on knees. Stiff, frontal pose, but with gently rounded forms, slender proportions. Overfold hem forms row of scallops just above knees. Oval face. Long locks of hair to shoulders; head possibly veiled.

See pp. 33, 44, 291.

C81 Seated draped figurine, probably female   Pl. 9

MF-73-113. Lot 73-119. Preserved: waist to feet. Missing left hip, thigh, and knee, upper part of seat at left side, base. Mended; front chipped. P.H. 0.074 (size 3). Fabric slightly coarse orange-buff, interior surface orange, with gray core; sparse small dark inclusions and voids. Solid. Back flattened. Heavily reworked; partly handmade(?).

Sloping lap; right hand on knee. Feet are wide, splaying, turned inward, right foot resting on its side. Curving fold of mantle frames knee. Blocklike seat. Similar in type, perhaps

a later generation: MF-3336 in the Corinth collection (*Corinth* XII, p. 52, no. 345, pl. 31; half the size, left arm position altered).

See pp. 44, 47, 196–197.

C82 Seated draped female figurine   Pl. 9

MF-70-253. Lot 6507. Preserved: shoulders to feet. Missing forearms. P.H. 0.05 (size 1). Fabric 1, grayish buff. Solid. Back handmade, flat. Added: forearms (hole in right elbow for insertion of forearm).

Blocklike figure with flat lap, feet turned outward. Forearms originally extended forward. Vertical folds of chiton are shallow, narrow. Smooth mantle over lap, knees, left upper arm. Plain seat with flat sides. Possible mold sibling: MF-11689 (lot 2011). Earlier generation in lots 878 and 2249 (both fabric 2) and 6503. Later generation: MF-12134 (lot 4352); MF-10942 (lot 887 = Pit A, thus not later than last quarter of the 5th century B.C.). Similar figurine, T-2367, from the North Cemetery is from a grave dated late 5th century B.C. (*Corinth* XIII, p. 271, no. 420-2, pl. 70; the arms of this figurine, which are extended forward, were also set into sockets in the elbows). Similar figurine from Perachora (*Perachora* I, p. 220, no. 106, pl. 96).

See pp. 15, 41, 44, 46.

C83 Seated draped female figurine   Pl. 9

MF-10484. Lot 878. Missing hands and part of forearms. P.H. 0.088 (size 1–2). Fabric 2, orange. White slip. Solid. Head and torso rendered in same mold. Back handmade, flat. Added: forearms, feet, part of hair, including peak. Tooling on skirt folds, hair. Underside irregular, concave.

Similar in type to **C82** but larger; apparently a 4th-century B.C. version of this type, with peaked coiffure. Workmanship less careful, modeling shallower, little detail. Holes behind each elbow show that arms were inserted into sockets, as in **C82**. Upper torso arched backward slightly. Long, wide neck. Face oval to round. Nose large. Hair swept away from face in rounded mass to peak above forehead. Similar in type: MF-10383 (lot 874); MF-8664 in the Corinth collection, with rounded, unpeaked coiffure (Weinberg 1948, p. 235, no. E21, pl. 86).

See p. 44.

C84 Seated draped female figurine   Pl. 9

MF-13869. Lot 3222. Preserved: lap to feet. P.H. 0.039 (size 1–2). Fabric 1, orange-buff to orange. White slip. Hollow. Back handmade, rounded, irregular.

Mantle hem straight across mid-calf, as in **C82** and **C83**, and similar seat with flat, plain sides, but drapery modeled more sculpturally, cloth shaped around legs, with long looped folds to ankles, curving diagonal folds from right knee to left calf. Probable mold sibling in lot 2087.

See p. 44.

C85 Seated draped female figurine   Pl. 9

MF-10562. Lot 890. Preserved: shoulders to hips. Missing lap, forearms. P.H. 0.058 (size 2). Fabric 2, light orange. White slip. Solid. Back handmade, flattened. Added: forearms.

Type of seat uncertain. Right forearm probably extended forward, left perhaps lowered. Chiton girded at natural waistline; catenaries between breasts; mantle folds over left upper arm and across lap. Perhaps similar in type to **C84**; also similar in type but miniature: MF-10666 (lot 1945).

See p. 44.

C86 Seated draped female figurine   Pl. 9

MF-10631. Lot 896. Missing right wrist and hand, fragment of lap. Mended. H. 0.091 (size 2). Fabric 3, orange-buff. White slip. Hollow; head solid. All parts probably rendered in same mold. Back handmade, flattened. Added: part of hair, including peak. Tooling on hair.

Feet parted. Gaze directed down to lap, where mitten-shaped hands hold uncertain object, partly broken, consisting of two rectangular strips with small holes (an aulos?). Upper part of garment not detailed; skirt clings to legs; narrow, parallel folds at sides conceal seat. Wide, spreading neck. Face small, round. Hair drawn up to high, stippled topknot. Seat has splaying sides, no back.

See pp. 45, 152.

C87 Seated draped female figurine (goddess?)   Pl. 9

MF-69-388. Lot 6215. Preserved: head to upper chest. Missing part of nose; surface chipped. P.H. 0.053 (size 3). Fabric 2, orange-buff. White slip. Red paint on hair. Solid. Back flat. Added: fillet. Tooling on hair.

Moldmade head attached to flat, handmade torso. Shoulders raised like wings, probably to indicate projections of chair back. Head tilted slightly to right. Face oval, narrowing at jaw, with low forehead. Eyes large and level; eyebrows and both lids defined. Nose large. Mouth wide, distorted upward toward left side; lips full. Cranium high. Hair parted at center, broad waves over temples. In better-preserved examples, torso and back of chair are rendered as a flat slab, from which both forearms project forward. Similar in type: KT-8-7 from the Potters' Quarter (*Corinth* XV, ii, pp. 123–124, no. 16, pl. 25); MF-75-24 (Pl. 75), from Forum Southwest (both examples have finer, smaller, and stylistically earlier heads than **C87**); MF-2676b in the Corinth collection (*Corinth* XII, p. 24, no. 10, pl. 1, from a deposit dated late 6th–early 5th century B.C.).

See pp. 45, 78.

C88 Seated draped female figurine   Pl. 9

MF-13949. Lot 4377. Preserved: neck to lower legs. Missing lower back, forearms; surface worn. P.H. 0.061 (size 2). Treated with preservative. White slip. Hollow. Back handmade, rounded. Added: forearms.

Seat has a back, which blends into the figure, lacks horizontal projections. Sloping lap. Forearms probably extended forward originally. Only garment detail is upper rolled edge of mantle across lap. Probable mold sibling: **C89**.

See p. 45.

C89 Seated draped female figurine   Pl. 9

MF-13950. Lot 3222. Preserved: abdomen to hem. Mended; lap plastered. P.H. 0.057 (size 2). Fabric 2, light orange. White slip(?). Hollow. Back handmade, rounded. Added: base, skirt folds at sides.

Probably from same mold as **C88**, with lower part of seat preserved. Base of seat is rounded and spreading, almost conical; perhaps a wicker chair (cf. **C90**).

See p. 45.

C90 Seated draped female figurine   Pl. 10

MF-13982. Lot 2159. Preserved: shoulders to hem. Missing left forearm, right arm, feet; right side of lap, chair, and leg chipped. Mended. P.H. 0.076 (size 2). Fabric 2, light orange. Hollow. Thick-walled. Back molded, rounded. Sides of chair open for venting. Added: probably left forearm. Tooling on folds.

Figure of matronly proportions, in sleeved chiton, seated in a very deep chair, thus lap unusually short. Left forearm probably extended forward. Rounded top of chair visible behind left shoulder. Narrow ridging on back probably represents chair construction. For clearer details of chair type, see probable mold sibling KT-8-3 from the Potters' Quarter (*Corinth* XV, ii, p. 134, no. 50, pl. 28; chair seems to be of wicker, its rounded shape probably similar to chair model KT-55-10: ibid., p. 209, no. 11, pl. 45).

See p. 45.

C91 Seated draped female figurine   Pl. 10

MF-11031. Lot 1953. Preserved: head to midriff, slightly less in back. P.H. 0.048 (size 2). Fabric 1, orange. White slip. Nearly solid. Head and torso probably rendered in same mold. Back handmade, flattened.

Mantle draped across shoulders and over head. Nearly horizontal folds across sloping, rounded shoulders; short catenaries between breasts. Face oval to round, with high, narrow, triangular forehead. Eyes large, downturned; both lids defined, lower lid lifted. Nose large, close to upper lip. Lips full, almost pursed. Hair parted in center, swept back from forehead in straight, parallel locks. Round earrings. Rather fine detail, all rendered in mold. Lower part is preserved in probable mold sibling MF-8666 (Pl. 75), from New Museum East, well A (Weinberg 1948, pp. 234–235, no. E20, pl. 86; for this deposit, see *Corinth* VII, iii, p. 208, deposit 36, dated last quarter of the 5th century to ca. 275 B.C.; mantle covers torso to ankles, envelops arms, which are held stiffly at sides, and clenched hands). Another probable mold sibling: MF-10340 (lot 870). Similar head: one from Perachora (*Perachora* I, p. 102, no. 312, pl. 115) is thought to be Attic because of its smooth red fabric, which sounds, however, like Corinthian fabric 2. Similar in type, thought to be Corinthian: one in Paris (*Louvre* III, p. 54, no. D299, pl. 62:b, holding a baby); one in Berlin (Winter, *Typen* I, p. 141, no. 2b).

See pp. 45, 294.

C92 Female head, related to seated figurine   Pl. 10

MF-13763. Lot 878. Preserved: right side of head, upper back. P.H. 0.044 (size 3). Fabric 2, light orange. White slip. Hollow. Back handmade, rounded.

Head similar to that of **C91** but larger; more elaborate coiffure. Eye large, downturned; upper lid defined. Hair in front arranged as in **C91** but with sphendone and topknot, mantle over all. Round earring. Rather fine detail, all rendered in mold.

See pp. 45, 294.

C93 Seated peplos-figurine (Demeter?)   Pl. 10

MF-11830A-C. Lots 2088 (A); 4350, 4378 (B); 6214 (C). Preserved: A–right shoulder to thigh, lower chest, small part of left side, small part of back at right side; B–right lower leg and adjacent throne; C–seat of throne at left side with folds of peplos, part of throne leg and back. Mended. P.H.: A–0.227, B–0.148, C–0.060 (size 5). Corinthian "tile fabric" interior: coarse, orange-buff, with abundant small to large red inclusions; on surface, fine buff layer. Hollow. Thick-walled, 0.025–0.06 (at bottom); interior surface irregular. Back seems fully modeled. Either completely handmade or very heavily retouched.

Overfold falls to lap, is deeply cut at side with parallel folds slanting toward back; rather flat kolpos lies across lap in scalloped folds. Two deep U-shaped folds at center of overfold. Raised fold at edge of neckline, probably a wide V-shaped fold. Mantle over shoulder in parallel, curving folds, with bunched folds below arm. Since mantle covers back, it originally may have fallen over left shoulder as well. A few skirt folds at inside of sloping thigh. Hem trails over instep; deep U-shaped fold frames ankle. Vertical skirt folds between leg and throne. A few skirt folds still visible at inner side of leg suggest that lower legs were separated. Wide, flat throne leg is rectangular, cut into shape of double palmette (cf. Richter 1966, pp. 23–28, figs. 85–122). Back of B is finished with skirt folds, suggesting that bottom of throne was open. Adjacent to seat, lateral face of back rest shows profile in three degrees. Technique more sculptural than coroplastic; high quality obvious despite poor preservation.

See pp. 1–2, 10, 15, 46, 329.

C94 Seated peplos-figurine   Pl. 11

MF-13712. Lot 3206. Preserved: left side and part of front, from near shoulder to ankle. P.H. 0.182 (size 4). Fabric 1, orange-buff; surface treated with preservative. Hollow. Thick-walled, ca. 0.02–0.03; interior irregular. Added: drapery at left side. Tooling on folds.

Sloping lap. Overfold to top of thighs; series of deep catenaries partly preserved in front; kolpos punched to indicate bunching of cloth. Legs seem to have been parted, since folds begin inside left leg. Vertical skirt folds at side conceal seat. Large piece but not as well made as **C93**. One slightly larger, similar in workmanship, in lot 5613.

See pp. 46, 47.

C95 Seated(?) peplos-figurine (goddess?)   Pl. 11

MF-11756. Lot 2044. Preserved: head, left shoulder, part of left breast. Missing most of crown, left earring. P.H. 0.084 (size 3–4). Fabric 3, creamy buff. White slip. Yellow-orange paint on hair. Hollow; head solid(?). Back handmade, flattened. Added: crown, earrings, button. Marks of C-shaped tool (broken reed?) on cranium.

Fairly broad shoulders; long, columnar neck. Peplos fastened at shoulder with large, round button. Face oval, with straight sides; high, triangular forehead; slightly receding chin. Eyes level. Mouth narrow, slightly pursed; lips full. Hair waved horizontally from forehead into full, rounded coiffure. Headdress probably a crown. Earring is a long, rectangular pellet with row of short, horizontal incisions. Impression dull but nicely made, interior even, neck tenon smoothed away. See **C96–C99** for mechanical relatives and similar heads.

See pp. 15, 17, 46–47, 144, 271, 344.

C96 Female head (goddess?)   Pl. 11

MF-11014. Lot 1953. Preserved: head and small part of neck; crown chipped. P.H. 0.049 (size 3–4). Fabric 5, orange-buff to orange. Hollow. Back handmade, flattened. Added:

crown, earrings. Marks of C-shaped tool (broken reed?) on cranium.

Probably made in same mold and by same hand as **C95** and **C97**; similar earrings. Crown is low and flaring, wrapped all around the head, and topped with a row of pellets, some oval, some irregularly round.

See pp. 17, 46–47, 271, 344.

C97 Female head (goddess?)   Pl. 11

MF-10434. Lot 881. Preserved: head and neck. Missing most of crown, part of right side, lower back. P.H. 0.055 (size 3–4). Fabric 3, yellowish buff to orange-buff. Hollow. Back handmade, rounded. Added: crown, earrings. Marks of C-shaped tool (broken reed?) on cranium.

Probably made in same mold and by same hand as **C95** and **C96**; similar earrings. Crown, as far as preserved, shows a pellet between two deep scallops.

See pp. 17, 46–47, 271, 344.

C98 Female(?) head, related to seated figurines   Pl. 11

MF-10473. Lot 878. Preserved: head and neck. Missing most of fillet. P.H. 0.045 (size 3–4). Fabric 1, creamy buff. White slip. Solid. Back handmade, rounded. Added: hair at top and sides, fillet. Tooling on hair.

Head tilted slightly to left; long, spreading neck. Probably from same mold as **C95–C97**, but short, curly locks and fillet added instead of crown, no earrings, C-shaped tool not used. Probably from the same workshop but prepared for a different figurine type by a different hand. Coiffure also suitable for a male figure. Another probable mold sibling: MF-12004 (lot 2239). Probable later generation: KT-10-2 from the Potters' Quarter (*Corinth* XV, ii, p. 123, no. 12, pl. 24). Others similar in scale and facial type: MF-11416 (lot 877); one in lot 3206.

See pp. 46–47, 344.

C99 Female head, related to seated figurines   Pl. 11

MF-11061. Lot 1955. Preserved: head and neck. Missing part of fillet. P.H. 0.034 (size 2–3). Fabric 1, orange-buff. White slip. Red paint on hair. Solid. Back handmade, rounded. Added: most of hair, fillet, earrings. Tooling on hair.

Similar in facial type to **C95**, smaller in scale, perhaps later generation. Hair strands radiating from forehead rendered in mold; above this, mass of curly locks topped by thick, tubular fillet. Long, narrow earrings.

See pp. 46–47.

C100 Female head (goddess?)   Pl. 11

MF-13752. Lot 4379. Preserved: head and neck. Missing upper lip, most of nose, right eye with forehead and hair above, most of crown, hair at nape. Mended. P.H. 0.105 (size 4–5). Fabric 1, slightly coarser, orange, with grayish buff core; sparse small dark red and gray inclusions, voids. Solid. Back handmade, rounded. Added: polos, long locks of hair at nape. Tooling on hair.

Head tilted to left and slightly upward on long neck. Face oval, with fairly high, probably triangular forehead. Eyes downturned, deeply set at inner corners; lower lid lifted and slightly puffy. Browridge rounded, not clearly defined. Lower lip full. Hair swept back from forehead in wavy locks grouped into thick strands, covering tops of ears; deep slash down back of head, as if continuation of central part; long locks of hair originally at nape. Fillet around hair, above which is a high polos, topped by a torus molding and a continuous wavy band resembling crenellations. Pellet earrings; right earring is round, left oval.

See pp. 47, 160, 197, 270.

C101   Female head   Pl. 11

MF-13978. Lot 4377. Preserved: head and neck, with part of tenon. Missing part of hair at nape; stephane chipped. P.H. 0.064 (size 3–4). Fabric 2, light orange. White slip. Solid. Back molded, flattened. Added: hair at nape and over ears, stephane, earrings. Tooling on hair, stephane.

Head tilted to right. Face oblong to oval, with high, ogival forehead. Eyes large, downturned, deeply set, opened wide; upper lids defined. Nose straight, close to upper lip. Mouth narrow; lips full, downturned. Thick locks of hair wave back and downward from central part, cover ears; two long locks of hair spring from nape. Upper edge of stephane notched. Pellet earrings. One crease in neck.

See pp. 47, 160.

ISOLATED FEMALE HEADS

C102   Female head   Pl. 11

MF-72-25. Lot 72-121. Preserved: head and neck. Missing tip of nose, part of hair puff at right; gash down right cheek and neck. P.H. 0.054 (size 3–4). Fabric 2, orange-buff. Solid. Back handmade, rounded. Added: hair in back.

Long, wide, spreading neck. Face oblong to oval. Eyes large, level; both lids well defined. Nose flattened. Mouth turned down at right corner. Kerchief tied across forehead, forming double peak in back. Puff of hair at each temple.

See pp. 25, 48.

C103   Female head   Pl. 11

MF-11849. Lot 2106. Preserved: head and neck. P.H. 0.042 (size 3). Fabric 1, orange-buff. Solid. Back handmade, flattened.

Long, wide, spreading neck. Face oval to oblong, with low, ogival forehead; chin somewhat receding. Eyes large, level, tear ducts defined. Nose large, close to upper lip. Mouth wide; lips full, parted. Cranium and neck deep, perhaps veiled. Hair parted at center, projects over temples in smooth, curving masses. Possible mold sibling: MF-11657 (lot 2009).

See pp. 37, 48, 276, 285, 293.

C104   Female head   Pl. 11

MF-11789. Lot 2048. Preserved: head and neck; surface chipped. P.H. 0.041 (size 3). Fabric 2, light orange. White slip. Solid. Back handmade, rounded.

Face oval to oblong, with low forehead, full cheeks; chin slightly receding. Eyes large. Lips full. Hair in deep waves across forehead from central part, down sides of face to ears; narrow, triangular mass of hair at each side of neck. Low polos forms peak in back, as if veiled. Dull impression. Similar in type: MF-11040 (lot 1953, fabric 5); one in lot 6214; MF-2756 from the Peribolos of Apollo (*Corinth* XII, p. 45, no. 259, pl. 22, from a deposit dated late 4th century BC).

See pp. 24, note 10, 32, 48, 285, 289, 291.

ARTICULATED "DOLLS," RELATED HEADS, AND RELATED FIGURINES OF DANCERS

Torsos and Limbs of Nude Articulated "Dolls"

C105   Torso of nude "doll"   Pl. 12

MF-13987. Lot 4382. Preserved: front–shoulders to abdomen. Missing right hip. Mended. P.H. 0.101 (size 3–4). Fabric 1, orange-buff. White slip. Hollow. Thin-walled. Shoulders pierced for arm attachment.

Nude female torso with youthful proportions: small, high breasts; relatively narrow hips. Joining surfaces of shoulders are flat. Subtle modeling of rib cage, nipples, slightly swelling abdomen. No direct evidence for leg attachment. Large for a "doll"; well made. Possible later generation: MF-11406 (lot 877). Closely related in style and quality to semidraped "doll" **C172**.

See pp. 50, 51.

C106   Torso of nude "doll"   Pl. 12

MF-12552. Lot 3222. Preserved: shoulders to knees; back chipped. P.H. 0.135 (size 3). Fabric 1, orange-buff. White slip. Hollow. Back molded, rounded. Shoulders and knees pierced for limb attachment.

Similar in type to **C105** but smaller, more slender, modeling less detailed. Joining surfaces of shoulders are flat. Thighs are socketed. For clearer impression of anatomy, see **C108**, which may be mechanically related.

See pp. 50, 51–52.

C107   Torso of nude "doll"   Pl. 12

MF-11971 A, B. Lot 2239. Preserved: shoulders to knees. P.H. 0.10 (size 3). Fabric 1, orange-buff. White slip. Nearly solid. Back molded, rounded. Shoulders and knees pierced for limb attachment.

Front and back of "doll" similar in type to **C106**. Not mended, to show treatment of interior: only a margin around edge is smoothed for joining; surface of central area is rough and slightly hollowed.

See p. 50.

C108   Torso of nude "doll"   Pl. 12

MF-10438. Lot 878. Preserved: neck to knees. P.H. 0.136 (size 3). Fabric 1, orange-buff. White slip. Nearly solid. Back molded, rounded. Shoulders and knees pierced for limb attachment. Surface pared.

Published: Stroud 1965, p. 18, pl. 9:a.

Joining surfaces of shoulders are flat; "doll" terminates at knees in three pierced flanges for lower leg attachment. Sloping shoulders; small, high breasts; narrow hips. Modeling shows semicircular lower boundary of thorax, strong median line, one horizontal division of rectus abdominis just above navel. Torso is that of a young woman, but geometric style of anatomy is rather masculine. Perhaps mechanically related to **C106** (a later generation?).

See pp. 50, 51–52.

C109   Torso of nude "doll"   Pl. 12

MF-10409. Lot 877. Preserved: front–shoulders to knees; top chipped. P.H. 0.089 (size 2–3). Fabric 1, orange-buff. White slip. Solid. Added: necklace. Tooling on necklace. Interior flat, scored vertically for attachment to back. Shoulders and knees pierced for limb attachment.

Socketed thighs, as in **C106**, but shoulders are more rounded, joining surfaces project slightly. Curve of torso down to waist is feminine, but subtle modeling of lower torso resembles male figures, e.g., **C194**. Abdomen swells slightly; above navel, median line of torso is flanked by rectus abdominis muscles. Slight swelling of external oblique also indicated. Necklace is a narrow, flat strip with short, vertical slashes.

See pp. 50, 52.

C110 Torso of nude "doll" Pl. 12

MF-12881. Lot 4450. Preserved: shoulders to feet. Missing front of feet, back from shoulders to knees. Mended; left thigh chipped. P.H. 0.160 (size 3). Fabric 1, orange-buff to orange. White slip. Pink paint on right leg. Hollow. Closed underneath. Back molded, rounded. Shoulders pierced for arm attachment.

"Doll" with articulated arms but rigid legs, pressed together. Elongated proportions, with narrow shoulders, relatively wide hips. Little modeling of torso musculature. Large, shallow navel. Torso slightly bent backward at shoulders.

See pp. 51, 52.

C111 Legs of nude "doll" Pl. 12

MF-14043. Lot 4362. Preserved: knees to feet. Missing front of left foot. P.H. 0.072 (size 3–4). Fabric 1, slightly coarser, orange-buff to orange. White slip. Solid. Back molded, rounded. Tooling on toes.

Legs pressed together. From either a seated "doll" or a standing "doll" similar to **C110** but larger in scale. Rather coarse work. Toes marked schematically by deep slashes.

See p. 53.

C112 Torso of nude "doll" Pl. 12

MF-13985. Lot 4452. Preserved: shoulders to hips; surface chipped. P.H. 0.066 (size 3). Fabric 1, yellowish buff to orange-buff. White slip. Probably solid. Back handmade, flattened. Lower part reworked by hand. Shoulders and hips pierced for limb attachment; holes at shoulder are fairly large (as in **C181**).

Youthful female torso similar to **C106–C109**, but legs originally were attached through three pierced flanges at hips, rather than at knees. Rear wall terminates at bottom of flanges.

See p. 53.

C113 Torso of nude "doll" Pl. 12

MF-70-264. Lot 6501. Preserved: neck to knees. P.H. 0.045 (size 1–2). Burned. Solid. Back molded, rounded. Crossbands incised. Shoulders and knees pierced for limb attachment.

Joining surface of left shoulder projects more than right. Slender proportions, with extremely flat hips. Crossbands over chest are unusual for a completely nude "doll" (cf. **C178**). Central hole of knee flanges is lower than lateral holes.

See pp. 50, 51, 57, 58.

C114 Torso of nude "doll" Pl. 12

MF-13986. Lot 4387. Preserved: neck to knees. Missing left knee flange(?). P.H. 0.102 (size 3). Fabric 5, orange. Solid. Back molded, rounded. Added: knee flanges. Surface clumsily pared at sides, probably to conceal mold join. Shoulders and knee flange pierced for limb attachment.

Elongated proportions, with narrow shoulders, relatively wide hips. Upper torso bent to right side. Large, shallow navel. Poor workmanship; knee flanges clumsily applied; left flange either missing or never applied.

See pp. 50, 53.

C115 Torso of nude "doll" Pl. 12

MF-14041. Lot 3233. Preserved: front–waist to knees; part of upper back at right side. P.H. 0.073 (size 2–3). Fabric 5, orange-buff to orange. White slip. Hollow. Thick-walled. Back molded, rounded. Added: knee flanges.

Wide-hipped figure, deep from front to back. Protruding, sagging abdomen, with fold of flesh below; large, shallow navel. Heavy thighs. Sides of figure flattened, perhaps to conceal mold join (cf. paring of **C114**).

See pp. 53, 60, 128, note 78, 197.

C116 Leg of "doll" Pl. 13

MF-10496. Lot 880. Missing toes. P.H. 0.111 (size 4–5). Fabric 1, orange-buff. White slip. Solid.

Pierced, offset flange at top for attachment to large "doll." Leg represented to just above knee; modeling indicates rounded kneecap, shaped calf, shinbone, and ankle bone. Molds for a similar leg type but smaller: KH-68 and KH-69 from the Potters' Quarter (*Corinth* XV, i, pp. 106–107, nos. 69, 70, pl. 42).

See pp. 50, 51.

C117 Leg of "doll" Pl. 13

MF-10332. Lot 870. Toes chipped. P.H. 0.064 (size 3). Fabric 1, buff. White slip. Solid. Surface pared.

Similar in type to **C116** but smaller. Right leg. Modeling of toes indicates joints and nails.

See p. 50.

C118 Leg of "doll" Pl. 13

MF-14067. Lot 877. Complete. H. 0.055 (size 2–3). Fabric 1, buff. Solid.

Simplified leg for a "doll" smaller than **C116** and **C117**. Pierced flange is thinned, not offset. No anatomical modeling. Similar legs: KT-13-96, KT-13-73, and KT-13-85 from the Potters' Quarter (*Corinth* XV, ii, p. 151, nos. 27–29, pl. 31).

See p. 50.

C119 Leg of "doll" Pl. 13

MF-14081. Lot 2249. Complete. H. 0.07 (size 3). Fabric 1, yellowish buff to orange. White slip. Solid. Handmade.

Simplified leg similar to **C118** but wears slipper with up-turned, pointed toe. Pierced flange is thinned, not offset.

See pp. 50–51.

C120 Leg of "doll" Pl. 13

MF-70-263. Lot 6500. One flange chipped. H. 0.046 (size 3). Fabric 1, buff. White slip. Solid. Handmade.

Thigh of "doll" that originally had two-part legs (see torso with arched openings at the hips [**C112**]). Pierced double flange at one end; pierced single, thinned flange at the other.

See p. 53.

C121 Arm of "doll" Pl. 13

MF-69-403. Lot 6185. Missing fingers, part of object in hand. Mended. P.L. 0.11 (size 3–4). Fabric 1, orange-buff. White slip. Solid.

Bent at elbow; pierced and thinned at top for attachment to shoulder of large "doll." Long, thin object, probably a cake, in hand.

See pp. 49, 51.

C122 Arm of "doll"   Pl. 13

MF-10588. Lot 892. Complete. L. 0.059 (size 3). Fabric 1, buff to orange. Solid. Handmade.

From "doll" smaller than **C121**; bent at elbow; pierced at top but not thinned. In mitten-shaped hand, a disc, as in MF-4002 in the Corinth collection (*Corinth* XII, p. 33, no. 137, pl. 9) and KT-13-49 from the Potters' Quarter (*Corinth* XV, ii, p. 150, no. 15, pl. 31).

See pp. 34, 49, 51, 125, 272, 273.

C123 Arm of "doll"   Pl. 13

MF-14066. Lot 877. Complete. L. 0.04 (size 2). Fabric 2, pinkish orange to orange. White slip. Solid.

Pierced at top for attachment to shoulder of "doll." Arm is short, straight, with mitten-shaped hand.

See p. 51.

Heads of Articulated "Dolls" and Related Heads

C124 Head and torso of nude "doll"   Pl. 13

MF-10418. Lot 877. Complete. H. 0.094 (size 2–3). Fabric 1, buff to orange. White slip. Nearly solid. Back molded, rounded. Added: possibly sphendone bow. Top of head pierced for suspension; shoulders and knees pierced for limb attachment.

Joining surfaces of shoulders project and sides are incurved, as in **C109**, but these features are here more pronounced. Small, oval face with receding chin, framed by large, rounded mass of ringlets. Wide neck. Hair bound in sphendone, tied with bow at top. A closely similar head (**C125**) is from a 5th-century B.C. context (Pit A). Molds for this type of "doll" torso: KH-65 and KH-66 from the Potters' Quarter (*Corinth* XV, i, p. 106, nos. 66, 67, pl. 41); KT-13-2 is a similar torso (*Corinth* XV, ii, p. 149, no. 1, pl. 31).

See pp. 54, 57.

C125 Head of "doll"   Pl. 13

MF-10541. Lot 887. Preserved: head and neck, including tenon. P.H. 0.039 (size 2–3). Fabric 1, orange-buff to orange. Solid. Back handmade, rounded. Added: possibly sphendone. Head pierced for suspension, completely through neck.

Head similar in type to that of **C124**, but features indistinct. From Pit A, thus not later than last quarter of the 5th century B.C. Possible mold sibling: MF-10531 (lot 886). Larger head, possibly earlier generation of related mold series: MF-11749 (lot 2038). Variant with large sphendone, like a snood, added: MF-10612 (lot 896); head in lot 2248 has added disc in place of sphendone bow. Similar head from the South Basilica fill, MF-5266 (*Corinth* XII, p. 33, no. 136, pl. 9). Heads of this type are fairly common, but because they are poorly preserved or are dull impressions, their mechanical relationships cannot be determined.

See pp. 8, note 26, 53–54, 57, 163, 296.

C126 Head and torso of nude "doll"   Pl. 13

MF-11920. Lot 2107. Preserved: head to knees. Missing front surface of torso, left knee flange; back, front of hair chipped. P.H. 0.11 (size 2–3). Fabric 1, orange-buff. White slip. Solid.

Back handmade, rounded. Added: hair projection in back, sphendone. Tooling on hair. Shoulders and knees pierced for limb attachment, head for suspension.

Torso similar in type to **C109**, with joining surfaces of shoulders slightly projecting. Long neck. Head similar in type to **C124** and **C125**. Face long, narrow. Coiffure, typical of 5th century B.C., is rounded and wrapped in a sphendone but with 4th-century B.C. high, slashed projection in back. Handmade back unusual for "dolls"; original back mold perhaps no longer usable.

See pp. 15, 54, 55, 57.

C127 Head and torso of nude "doll"   Pl. 13

MF-11024. Lot 1953. Complete. Mended. H. 0.117 (size 2–3). Fabric 1, yellowish buff. Orange-buff slip beneath white slip. Solid. Back molded, rounded, buttocks flattened. Added: hair projection in back. Tooling on hair. Shoulders and knees pierced for limb attachment, head for suspension.

Torso similar in type to **C124**, with joining surfaces of shoulders projecting but with head of 4th-century B.C. type. Wide, spreading neck. Face oval to round, with triangular forehead. Hair arranged in high projections in front and back, giving head a boat-shaped profile. Similar in type: MF-3888 in the Corinth collection (*Corinth* XII, p. 33, no. 133, pl. 9).

See pp. 52, 57, 125.

C128 Head and torso of nude "doll"   Pl. 13

MF-69-394. Lot 6204. Preserved: head to waist. Missing nose, portions of torso in front. Mended; back chipped. P.H. 0.107 (size 3–4). Fabric 1, orange-buff to orange, interior surface gray. White slip. Gilding on left earring, hair at right side. Layer of fine ivory-colored paint over slip on face and back of neck. Hollow; head probably solid. Thick-walled. Back handmade, rounded. Added: earrings, plait, and knot of hair. Tooling on hair, mouth. Shoulders pierced for arm attachment; top of head not pierced.

Torso similar in type to **C106**, with flat joining surfaces of shoulders. Wide, spreading neck; sloping shoulders. Face shows wide, rounded, fairly low forehead narrowing to straight-sided cheeks; prominent chin (cf. similar facial shape of large-scale votive head from the Asklepieion, V-112, V [*Corinth* XIV, p. 119, no. 2, pl. 30]). Eyes slightly downturned; browridge rounded, projecting, follows curve of upper lid closely. Lower lip full, corners lightly punched. Straight locks of hair in front rather roughly slashed and punched (for finer version of this coiffure, see **C129**); plait around top of head; behind it, knot of hair with four radiating ends. Teardrop-shaped pellet earrings.

See pp. 48, note 184, 51, 53, 55, 57.

C129 Head and torso of nude "doll"   Pl. 13

MF-12158. Lot 4369. Preserved: head, shoulders, right breast. Missing left earring; nose chipped. P.H. 0.091 (size 3–4). Fabric 1, orange-buff. Thin, bluish white wash beneath thick, white slip. Fine, ivory-colored paint on flesh; red paint on hair; necklace gilded. Hollow; head probably solid. Thick-walled. Back probably molded, rounded. Added: necklace, part of hair (including knot in back), sphendone. Tooling on hair. Right shoulder pierced for arm attachment (joining surface of left not preserved). Head pierced for suspension.

Torso similar in type to **C106**, with flat joining surfaces of shoulders. Wide, spreading neck; sloping shoulders. Face oval to round, with triangular forehead; small, projecting chin.

Features rather delicate, partly obscured by thick layer of slip and paint. Eyes and browridge downturned. Nose close to upper lip. Mouth narrow; lower lip full. Hair waves up from forehead into central peak; rendered by fine, closely spaced incisions and stippling. For this technique, see large-scale heads from the Asklepieion, V-40, II and IV; V-112, V; and V-99, V (*Corinth* XIV, p. 119, nos. 1–3, pls. 29–31). Sphendone tied at top of head with flat bowknot. At back, wavy locks tied into knot at top of head. Necklace of round beads. Teardrop-shaped pellet earrings. Probable mold sibling of head: MF-11310 (lot 1998, features somewhat clearer, also with bluish underwash).

See pp. 13, 14, 55.

C130 Head of "doll"(?) Pl. 13

MF-1994-31. Lot 1994-78. Preserved: head and neck with tenon. Lower edge of neck chipped. P.H. 0.061 (size 3–4). Fabric 1, grayish buff. Solid. Back handmade, rounded.

Face narrow, oblong to oval, with low forehead. Eyes large, slightly downturned at outer corners; both lids defined. Nose long, narrow, close to upper lip. Mouth wide; lower lip full. Hair parted at center, dividing into two scalloped waves over forehead, then two thick bunches at either side of head; upper bunch shows light, curved incisions to mark locks of hair; lower bunch is plain, covers ears. Hair bound in sphendone tied at top in flat bow; flat ends of bow lie forward over hair. Locks of hair on cranium marked from center outward. Probably mechanically related to **C131** because of similarities in details of hair, but nature of relationship is not clear. **C131** is larger but is a less clean impression, crudely retouched; its facial shape is less narrow. Perhaps **C130** is a later generation in a parallel mold series.

See pp. 54, 163.

C131 Head of "doll"(?) Pl. 13

MF-10603. Lot 894. Preserved: head and neck with part of tenon. Missing nose, hair at lower left. Mended. P.H. 0.058 (size 3–4). Fabric 2, buff. White slip. Solid. Back handmade, rounded. Tooling on hair in back, mouth; ears punched for insertion of earrings. Excess clay at hair parting and above mouth.

Face oblong to oval, with low, rounded, slightly sloping forehead; prominent chin. Eyes large, slightly downturned at outer corners; both lids defined. Nose close to upper lip. Lips fleshy, parted, downturned at corners owing to retouch. Coiffure as in **C130**. Hair on cranium slashed from center outward. Possibly mechanically related to **C130**.

See pp. 54, 163.

C132 Female head, related to "dolls" Pl. 13

MF-12896. Lot 4379. Preserved: head and neck, small part of left shoulder. Missing right earring. P.H. 0.057 (size 3–4). Fabric 2, buff. White slip. Red paint on hair. Solid. Back handmade, rounded. Added: hair, fillet, earrings. Tooling on hair; neck pared; marks of finely toothed tool on back of neck.

Long, wide, spreading neck. Head tilted slightly to right. Facial type similar to "doll" **C128**, but forehead is narrower; eyes more widely set, somewhat more downturned. Nose large, straight, close to upper lip. Dimples at corners of mouth rendered in mold. Coiffure similar to **C128** in front, but long locks of hair are added at sides and back; groove around head for insertion of tubular fillet. Teardrop-shaped pellet earrings.

Coiffure similar to that of peplos-figurine **C17**. Possible later generation: **C133**.

See pp. 17, 53, note 214, 55.

C133 Head of "doll" Pl. 13

MF-72-189. Lot 72-101. Preserved: head and most of neck. P.H. 0.051 (size 2–3). Fabric 1, orange-buff. White slip. Solid. Back handmade, flattened. Added: part of hair (including projection at back), sphendone. Tooling on hair. Head pierced for suspension.

Possibly later generation of **C132**. Coiffure similar to **C132** in front, but sphendone with bowknot and high, slashed projection of hair in back are closer to **C126**.

See pp. 55, 57.

C134 Female head, related to "dolls" Pl. 13

MF-10467. Lot 878. Preserved: head and front of neck. Missing locks of hair along neck. P.H. 0.050 (size 3–4). Fabric 1, tan. White slip. Creamy buff paint on face and part of hair, becoming yellow on cheeks (originally gilded?); red paint on mouth. Solid. Back handmade, rounded. Added: locks of hair along neck, fillet, earrings. Tooling on hair.

Face oval, with high, triangular forehead; projecting chin. Nose large, rather flat, close to upper lip. Mouth wide; lips full. Workmanship of coiffure resembles **C129**, with fine waves swept up from forehead (rendered in mold). Topknot in front is stippled; light stippling also around forehead. Locks of hair originally along sides of neck. Tubular fillet. Inverted teardrop-shaped pellet earrings. Possible later generation: **C135**.

See pp. 54, 57, 166.

C135 Female head, related to "dolls" Pl. 13

MF-10441. Lot 878. Preserved: head and part of neck. P.H. 0.043 (size 3). Fabric 1, grayish buff. White slip. Yellow paint on hair. Solid. Back handmade, rounded. Added: part of hair at top, knot on cranium. Tooling on hair.

Head tilted slightly to right. Similar in facial type to **C134**, but face is somewhat narrower; perhaps a later generation of same or related mold series. Rounded mass of hair waves up from forehead into knot; another knot at top of cranium. Possible mold sibling: MF-10401 (lot 877).

See pp. 54, 166, 177.

C136 Head of "doll" Pl. 14

MF-11828. Lot 2088. Preserved: head and neck. Surface cracked. P.H. 0.04 (size 3). Fabric 2, grayish buff, burned. Red paint on hair. Solid. Back handmade, rounded. Added: plait of hair. Tooling on hair, mouth. Head pierced for suspension.

Face oval, with rounded forehead, narrowing at jaw. Left eye level, right eye downturned; upper lids defined, lower lids raised, puffy. Nose large, close to upper lip. Lips full. Melon coiffure arranged in fourteen sections, diagonally slashed; plait around cranium also slashed.

See pp. 51, 54, 122, note 45, 131, 164, 191.

C137 Head of "doll" Pl. 14

MF-11966. Lot 2234. Preserved: head and neck. P.H. 0.035 (size 3). Fabric 1, orange-buff to orange. White slip. Red paint on hair. Solid. Back handmade, rounded. Tooling on hair. Head pierced for suspension.

Face oval, with rounded forehead, narrowing at jaw. Eyes and browridge slightly downturned. Nose large, close to upper lip. Lips full. Coiffure rounded in front, rising to slight peak; light waves, rendered in mold, radiate from forehead, stippled. Hair in back bound in sphendone, without bowknot.

See p. 55.

C138   Head of "doll"   Pl. 14

MF-10645. Lot 897. Preserved: head and neck; cracked, top of peak of hair chipped. P.H. 0.045 (size 3–4). Fabric 2, light orange. White slip. Solid. Back handmade, rounded. Tooling on hair. Head pierced for suspension.

Wide neck. Face oval, with high, triangular forehead. Eyes and browridge slightly downturned. Nose large, close to upper lip. Lips full, downturned. Coiffure rounded in front, rising to peak. Waves rendered, unusually, by incised wavy lines, parallel to temples. Hair completely wrapped in sakkos in back. Probable later generation: **C139**.

See pp. 55, 57.

C139   Head of "doll"   Pl. 14

MF-10520. Lot 884. Preserved: head and neck. P.H. 0.03 (size 2–3). Fabric 1, buff. White slip. Solid. Back handmade, rounded. Added: knot of hair. Tooling on hair. Head pierced for suspension.

Probably later generation of **C138**. Hair rises to rounded peak in front; waves parallel to temples seem to have been rendered in mold. Hair on top of head rendered by vertical slashes; knot of hair at top of cranium, tied with a cord indicated by a slash.

See pp. 55, 57, 176.

C140   Head of "doll"   Pl. 14

MF-14037. Lot 2152. Preserved: head and neck. Missing hat brim in back. P.H. 0.033 (size 2–3). Fabric 1, orange-buff. White slip. Red paint on hair. Solid. Back handmade, flattened. Added: hat. Tooling on hair. Head pierced for suspension.

Long, slender neck. Face narrow, oblong, with high, triangular forehead. Similar in facial type and wide coiffure to hydriaphoros **C58**; features are smaller, clustered near center of face. Hair is stippled in front, slashed in back. Broad-brimmed hat, similar to a petasos, made of a thin disc of clay, with a smaller disc superimposed at center, then pierced. Hat somewhat similar to petasos worn by Boeotian youths but differently applied (cf. Higgins 1986, pp. 148–149, figs. 179–181, in Athens). A similar hat on a female figurine from the Potters' Quarter, KT-12-10, tips up in back (*Corinth* XV, ii, p. 128, no. 31, pl. 24; cf. also Winter, *Typen* I, p. 78, no. 2).

See p. 54.

C141   Head of "doll"   Pl. 14

MF-68-373. Lot 5613. Preserved: head and neck. P.H. 0.037 (size 2–3). Fabric 5, orange to orange-buff. White slip. Solid. Back handmade, flattened. Added: locks of hair along neck, sphendone bowknot. Tooling on hair. Head pierced for suspension.

Long, wide, spreading neck. Face narrow, oblong to oval, with high, triangular forehead. Similar in facial type and wide coiffure to heads in the hydriaphoros group, **C59** (same scale) and **C58** (larger). Similar nose distortion suggests a mechanical relationship among these heads, but its nature

is unclear. Sphendone marked off by two grooves; bowknot horizontally slashed. Locks of hair along neck are inconsistent with sphendone. Probably a late "doll."

See pp. 41, 54, 172, note 334.

C142   Head of "doll"   Pl. 14

MF-10459. Lot 878. Preserved: head and neck. P.H. 0.048 (size 3–4). Fabric 2, orange-buff to light orange. White slip. Yellow paint on hair, pink and red on eyes and lips. Solid. Back handmade, rounded. Added: hair at nape. Tooling on hair. Head pierced for suspension.

Published: Stroud 1965, p. 18, pl. 8:c, left.

Head tilted slightly to left. Face oval, with ogival forehead. Eyes large, level, deeply set at inner corners; both lids defined, lower lid lifted. Nose large, close to upper lip, upturned. Lips full, parted. Coiffure much more restrained than in most "dolls'" heads. Hair parted at center; unusually regular, parallel strands wave to back of head, covering tops of ears. Long locks of hair down nape. Possible traces of small stephane at top of head. Round earrings(?). Large, well-made piece.

See pp. 14, 51, 55, 343.

C143   Female head, related to "dolls"   Pl. 14

MF-10400. Lot 877. Preserved: head and neck, with most of tenon; nose and mouth chipped. P.H. 0.068 (size 3–4). Fabric 2, orange-buff, with orange core. White slip. Red paint on hair, possibly pink on sakkos. Solid. Back molded, rounded. Added: part of hair. Tooling on hair.

Similar in type, scale, and workmanship to **C142**. Face oval to oblong, with rounded forehead. Eyes large, level, opened wide, deeply set at inner corners; both lids defined, meet at corners. Nose large, wide, upturned, close to upper lip. Lips full and strongly arched, parted. Coiffure somewhat obscured in front, but deep horizontal waves seem to stem from central part. Sakkos covers back of head, with loose, double-pointed fold at rear. Large, well-made piece.

See p. 55.

C144   Female head, related to "dolls"   Pl. 14

MF-12118. Lot 4356. Preserved: head and neck. Missing locks of hair at left side of neck, headdress; nose chipped. P.H. 0.055 (size 4). Fabric 2, light orange to orange-buff. White slip. Red paint on hair. Solid. Back handmade, rounded. Added: locks of hair along neck, headdress. Tooling on hair, ears.

Similar in type and workmanship to **C142** and **C143** but larger. Head tilted slightly to right and back. Face oval to oblong, with ogival forehead. Eyes large, level; upper lids defined; browridge prominent, strongly arched. Nose wide. Lips full, slightly parted, downturned; upper lip rendered by a single arch. Ears punched. Deeply tooled, horizontal locks of hair wave from central part; long locks of hair at sides of neck; nape left bare. Groove around head for insertion of small stephane or fillet. Large piece, good fabric; retouch is broad, not fine, but effect is good.

See p. 55.

C145   Head of "doll"   Pl. 14

MF-10524. Lot 885. Preserved: head and part of neck. P.H. 0.037 (size 3). Fabric 1, orange-buff. White slip. Solid. Back handmade, rounded. Tooling on hair. Head pierced for suspension.

Face round to oval, with high, rounded forehead. Eyes large, slightly downturned; lower lids slightly raised. Nose short, close to upper lip. Lips full. Wavy strands of hair radiate from center of forehead to back of head, mound up slightly into stippled peak at forehead.

See pp. 55–56.

C146   Head of "doll"   Pl. 14

MF-10461. Lot 878. Preserved: head and neck, with tenon. Missing nose. P.H. 0.05 (size 3). Fabric 2, light orange, interior grayish buff. White slip. Yellow paint on hair. Solid. Back handmade, rounded. Added: hair in front. Tooling on mouth, nose, hair. Head pierced for suspension.

Face oval to round, with high, triangular forehead. Eyes and browridge slightly downturned. Nose short, close to upper lip. Lips full, downturned; right corner of mouth and nostril punched. Hair rises to stippled peak in front; back of head wrapped in sakkos, its folds indicated by two incisions, the loose cloth in a small peak at top of head. Similar in type: MF-10643 (lot 896).

See p. 55.

C147   Head of "doll"   Pl. 14

MF-10410. Lot 877. Preserved: head and neck; right eye obscured. P.H. 0.033 (size 2–3). Fabric 1, orange-buff. White slip. Solid. Back handmade, rounded. Added: hair in front, earrings. Tooling on hair. Head pierced for suspension.

Similar in facial type to **C146**. Hair in front rendered by slashed horizontal waves, rising to small knot at top; sphendone without bowknot. Round pellet earrings. Probable mold sibling: MF-10530 (lot 886).

See p. 55.

C148   Head of "doll"   Pl. 14

MF-11081. Lot 1964. Preserved: head and neck. P.H. 0.039 (size 2–3). Fabric 1, orange. Solid. Back handmade, flattened. Added: hair. Tooling on hair. Head pierced for suspension.

Long, spreading neck. Face small, oval to round. Hair a rounded mass of curls, peaked in front, stippled. Possible later generation: MF-10606 (lot 896).

See p. 55.

C149   Female head, related to "dolls"   Pl. 14

MF-12117. Lot 4356. Preserved: head and neck, with part of tenon. Missing lock of hair at left side of neck; top of head chipped. P.H. 0.063 (size 3–4). Fabric 2, orange. Bluish white wash under thick ivory-colored slip. Red paint on hair and lips. Solid. Back handmade, flattened. Added: hair at front and sides, fillet, earrings. Tooling on hair.

Head tilted to right and back. Long, spreading neck. Face oblong to oval, with triangular forehead. Eyes widely set, opened wide, downturned; both lids clearly defined. Nose large, close to upper lip. Lips full, well arched, slightly downturned. Long hair falls to shoulders from central part, closely following contour of head and neck. Hair rendered by rough slashes, horizontal in front, vertical in back; nape is bare. Tubular fillet; oval pellet earrings. For bluish wash, see **C129**, which is otherwise dissimilar. Probable later generation: **C150**. Slashed retouch of hair suggests that head was made in same workshop as peplos-figurine **C17**, as well

as **C150**–**C152**. Similar in type and retouch, smaller: MF-10486 (lot 880, fabric 1). For possible workshop mates, see Workshop B, pp. 344–345.

See pp. 27, 56.

C150   Female head, related to "dolls"   Pl. 14

MF-12136. Lot 4352. Preserved: head and neck. P.H. 0.054 (size 3). Fabric 2, orange-buff to orange. White slip. Red paint on hair. Solid. Back handmade, rounded. Added: hair at front and top, earrings. Tooling on hair.

Long neck. Head tilted to left and back. Face probably later generation of **C149**. Hair parted at center, waved back from forehead with horizontal slashes. Locks of hair tied into bowknot at top of head, with four protruding curls, also slashed. Retouch of hair is similar to **C149**, **C151**, and **C152**, although coiffure is different; possibly made in the same workshop. Teardrop-shaped pellet earrings. Probably trace of mantle fold at left edge and in back. Possible later generation: **C151**; one in lot 6233 (mantle folds at neck). For possible workshop mates, see Workshop B, pp. 344–345.

See pp. 17, 56.

C151   Head of "doll"   Pl. 14

MF-10412. Lot 877. Preserved: head and neck. P.H. 0.044 (size 2–3). Fabric 2, orange. White slip. Red paint on hair. Solid. Back handmade, rounded. Added: hair at top and sides, earrings. Tooling on hair. Top of head pierced for suspension.

Face possibly a later generation of **C150**, but shape is altered. Wide, rounded, high forehead narrows to straight-sided cheeks. Coiffure similar to **C150**, but the four curls are merely clustered, not knotted together; slashed retouch of hair similar to **C149**, **C150**, and **C152**; possibly made in the same workshop. Teardrop-shaped pellet earrings. For possible workshop mates, see Workshop B, pp. 344–345.

See p. 56.

C152   Head of "doll"   Pl. 14

MF-10491. Lot 880. Preserved: head and neck. P.H. 0.041 (size 2–3). Fabric 2, light orange. White slip. Red paint on hair. Solid. Back handmade, rounded. Added: hair at top, earrings. Tooling on hair. Head pierced for suspension.

Head tilted slightly to right. Face probably mold sibling of peplos-figurine **C17**. Hair parted at center, waved back from forehead with horizontal slashes, as in **C150**. Plait around top of head slashed with V-shaped strokes in a herringbone pattern. Retouch of hair is similar to **C149**–**C151**, although coiffure is different; possibly made in the same workshop. Teardrop-shaped pellet earrings. For possible workshop mates, see Workshop B, pp. 344–345.

See pp. 30, 51, 56.

C153   Female head, related to "dolls"   Pl. 15

MF-11322. Lot 1999. Preserved: head and neck, with part of tenon. Missing nose, part of hair at left side of neck, left earring. Mended; chipped at top. P.H. 0.059 (size 3–4). Fabric 2, light orange. White slip. Yellow paint on hair. Solid. Back handmade, rounded. Added: hair at top, sides, and nape; fillet; earrings. Tooling on hair.

Head tilted to right. Face oval, with high, wide, rounded forehead; rather small chin. Features clustered near center of face. Eyes large, downturned; upper lids defined; browridge downturned, close to eyes. Lips full. Long, wide neck, with one crease. Hair roughly slashed; coiffure similar to **C17**; hair parted at center and waved back from temples; long, straight locks of hair at sides of neck and nape. Flat fillet. Oval pellet earrings. A head mold from the Potters' Quarter, KH-29, is similar in facial type and scale (*Corinth* XV, i, pp. 99–100, no. 31, pl. 34).

See pp. 56, 161, 296.

C154   Female head, related to "dolls"   Pl. 15

MF-12148.   Lot 4350.   Preserved: head and neck; nose chipped. P.H. 0.056 (size 4). Fabric 1, orange-buff. White slip. Red paint on hair. Solid. Back handmade, rounded. Added: hair at top, sides, and nape; earrings. Tooling on hair; corners of mouth punched.

Face oval to oblong, with low, triangular forehead; rather full cheeks. Eyes small, widely set, downturned; lids fleshy, eyes nearly closed. Nose short, wide. Mouth wide; lips full. Locks of hair wave down and back from central part, cover ears, wrap around to back; long, straight, heavily slashed locks of hair fall to shoulders from beneath wrapped hair. Pellet earrings.

See pp. 56, 167, 251.

C155   Female head, related to "dolls"   Pl. 15

MF-11964.   Lot 2213.   Preserved: head and neck. Missing back of head; top chipped. P.H. 0.051 (size 4). Fabric 2, orange. Solid. Added: probably sphendone bowknot. Tooling on hair. Head pierced for suspension.

Face oval, with high, triangular forehead. Eyes downturned. Nose close to upper lip. Lips full. Coiffure schematic, rounded, peaked in front, with light, vertical incisions. Hair bound in sphendone with grooved outline, probably tied with bowknot.

See pp. 55, 57.

C156   Head of "doll"   Pl. 15

MF-11301.   Lot 1993.   Preserved: head and part of neck; surface cracked and chipped. P.H. 0.048 (size 3–4). Treated with preservative. Solid. Back handmade, rounded. Added: hair at top. Tooling on hair. Head pierced for suspension.

Face oblong to oval, with high, triangular, sloping forehead; slightly receding chin. Eyes downturned, narrow; fleshy lids almost closed. Nose large, prominent, close to upper lip. Mouth narrow; lips full, slightly pursed. Rounded coiffure shows fine horizontal waves from forehead (rendered in mold), sphendone without bowknot, and mass of curls behind. Possible mechanical relatives: **H234**; head of **H102** (smaller).

See pp. 56, 144.

C157   Head of "doll"   Pl. 15

MF-10512.   Lot 881.   Preserved: head and neck. P.H. 0.042 (size 2–3). Fabric 2, light orange. Solid. Back handmade, rounded. Added: peak of hair in back, sphendone bowknot. Tooling on hair. Head pierced for suspension.

Face narrow, oblong to oval, with high, rounded forehead; receding chin. Features are small and delicate. Eyes almond shaped. Mouth narrow; lips full, slightly pursed. Light stippling around hairline; sphendone outlined with grooves, is tied with bowknot; peak of hair in back lightly slashed.

See p. 57.

C158   Female head, related to "dolls"   Pl. 15

MF-14194.   Lot 4379.   Preserved: head and part of neck.   P.H. 0.039 (size 2–3).   Fabric 1, orange-buff, grayer at core. Solid.

Back handmade, rounded. Added: projection of hair at top. Tooling on hair.

Face round, with triangular forehead. Eyes level. Nose wide. Lips full. Coiffure peaked in front; horizontal lines across front of hair to represent waves are rendered in mold. Sphendone outlined with grooves, lacks bowknot in front. High, cylindrical projection of hair at top of head, lightly slashed; slight horizontal depression at base of cylinder suggests binding. Probable mold sibling: head of **C33**. Possibly mechanically related: **C159**.

See pp. 34, note 81, 57.

C159   Head of "doll"   Pl. 15

MF-10472. Lot 878. Preserved: head and neck; hair chipped. P.H. 0.04 (size 2–3). Fabric 1, greenish buff. White slip. Red paint on hair. Solid. Back handmade, rounded. Added: projection of hair at top, sphendone bowknot. Tooling on hair. Head pierced for suspension. Tiny blisters at hairline indicate use of plaster mold.

Similar in facial type to **C158**, perhaps mechanically related. Wide, spreading neck. Coiffure rounded in front, slightly peaked; horizontal lines across front of hair to represent waves are rendered in mold, barely visible (clearer in **C158**). Sphendone outlined with grooves, tied with large bowknot. Hair projects into a cone atop head, marked with deep vertical slashes; although the rough slashes hardly resemble hair, and the shape of the coiffure is almost like a pilos, the better rendering of **C158** indicates what was intended (for a true conical headdress, rendered with horizontal, not vertical markings to show the creasing of the material, see **C160**). Similar coiffure on a figurine from the Potters' Quarter, KT-10-39 (*Corinth* XV, ii, p. 134, no. 47, pl. 25).

See pp. 6, 16, 42, 57, 58, 64, 125.

C160   Head of "doll"   Pl. 15

MF-14044. Lot 4377. Preserved: head and neck. Missing left lappet of cap; forehead and neck chipped. P.H. 0.052 (size 2–3). Fabric 5, orange. Solid. Back handmade, rounded. Added: cap. Tooling on hair. Head pierced for suspension.

Face oval, with high forehead. Coiffure similar to **C158** in front, with horizontal slashes; stippling along hairline and neck. Cap of Scythian type with long lappets, one of which is preserved along neck at right side. Top of cap drawn into very long conical projection, ending in flat, disc-shaped finial.

See p. 57.

C161   Head of "doll"   Pl. 15

MF-13484. Lot 2152. Preserved: head and small part of neck; top chipped. P.H. 0.045 (size 3–4). Fabric 2, light orange. Solid. Back handmade, rounded. Added: hair in front, headdress. Tooling on hair. Head pierced for suspension.

Head tilted slightly to right. Face oblong to oval, with low, triangular forehead; small, receding chin. Eyes downturned. Nose large, close to upper lip. Mouth distorted. Back of head domed, smooth; headdress uncertain, almost conical but not pointed. Possible remains of lappet beside chin at right side. Coiffure rounded, loosely waved in front, very carelessly tooled; hair at back rendered by hatched incisions. Bottom scored(?) as if a joining surface. Good fabric but poorly molded and retouched. Fabric and workmanship similar to **C162**.

See p. 57.

C162 Head of "doll" Pl. 15

MF-11721. Lot 2026. Preserved: head and neck. Missing front of neck, face at lower left, top of cap. P.H. 0.043 (size 3). Fabric 2, orange-buff. White slip. Blue paint on cap. Solid. Back handmade, rounded. Added: hair in front, cap. Tooling on hair. Head pierced for suspension.

Face oval to oblong, with high, triangular forehead. Eyes and eyebrows slightly downturned. Nose large, close to upper lip. Headdress seems to be a Scythian cap, pointed at the back; possible lappet along neck at left side. Coiffure rounded; curls in front rendered by added, wormlike strips of clay; nape is bare. Fabric and workmanship similar to **C161**; same type may have been intended.

See p. 57.

C163 Head of "doll" Pl. 15

MF-10457. Lot 878. Preserved: head and neck; front of neck, knot of hair chipped. P.H. 0.053 (size 3–4). Fabric 2, light orange. Thin, bluish white wash under ivory-colored paint on flesh; traces of gilding on hair. Solid. Back handmade, rounded. Added: peak of sakkos in back. Tooling on hair, mouth. Head pierced for suspension.

Face oval, with high, rounded forehead; small, pointed chin. Features clustered at center of face. Eyes and eyebrows strongly downturned. Nose thin, arched. Lips full, corners punched. Rounded coiffure with knot of hair in front at top; short, rough strokes to show texture of hair. Hair in back enveloped in sakkos, which has a protruding point in back, rather than a drooping fold, as in **C143**. For bluish wash, see **C129**, which also shows a detailed retouch of hair, although with different tooling. Probable mold sibling: MF-10402 (lot 877, face chipped, but coiffure is the same, and knot of hair is a properly formed lampadion). Probable later generation: MF-10595 (lot 892, fabric 1). A head mold from the Potters' Quarter, KH-28, of similar scale and facial type, includes the knot of hair in front (*Corinth* XV, i, p. 99, no. 30, pl. 33).

See pp. 18, 57.

C164 Female head, related to "dolls" Pl. 15

MF-10381. Lot 874. Preserved: head and neck; back of head chipped. P.H. 0.051 (size 3–4). Fabric 1, orange-buff, orange core. White slip. Solid. Added: probably hair in front. Tooling on hair.

Similar in facial type to **C163**. Face round to oval, with high, triangular forehead; small, receding chin. Features clustered at center of face. Eyes small, closely set, slightly downturned; browridge not defined. Nose straight, upturned. Lips full. Hair arranged in front in three rows of plaits, indicated by gouges; two vertical plaits are pulled up from center of forehead to form a peak. Hair in back enveloped in sakkos. Probable mold sibling: MF-11332 (lot 2003, with plaits barely suggested).

See pp. 57, 137, 144.

C165 Female head, related to "dolls" Pl. 15

MF-11362. Lot 877. Preserved: head and neck; nose chipped. P.H. 0.047 (size 3–4). Fabric 2, harder, light orange. White slip. Red paint on hair. Solid. Back molded, rounded, pinched in at right side. Added: hair at top and back. Tooling on hair.

Head slightly tilted to left. Face oval to oblong. Eyes slightly downturned; both lids defined. Nose large. Mouth wide; lips thin. Coiffure peaked in front; locks of hair plaited

back from center of forehead; plait around cranium. Possible mechanical relative from Epidauros shows facial features more clearly (Peppa-Papaioannou 1985, p. 46, no. A127, pl. 31).

See pp. 57, 144.

C166 Female head, related to "dolls" Pl. 15

MF-12116. Lot 4356. Preserved: head and neck. Missing right eye and temple, hair at right side of neck. P.H. 0.055 (size 3–4). Fabric 1, orange. Red paint on hair. Solid. Back probably handmade, rounded. Added: hair at sides, back, and neck. Tooling on hair, juncture of chin and neck.

Head tilted slightly to right. Face narrow, oblong to oval, with high, ogival forehead; deep jaw. Eye slightly downturned; upper lid defined, lower lid lifted, slightly puffy. Nose large, wide, slightly upturned. Mouth narrow; lips smiling, lower lip full. Locks of hair wave to sides from central part, cover tops of ears; thick roll around back of head; one lock of hair originally along each side of neck. Possible later generation: **C167**.

See p. 57.

C167 Female head, related to "dolls" Pl. 15

MF-10445. Lot 878. Preserved: head and neck; nose chipped. P.H. 0.043 (size 3). Fabric 2, orange-buff. White slip. Red paint on hair. Solid. Back molded, rounded. Added: hair at top and back. Tooling on hair, face.

Head tilted slightly to right. Similar in facial type to **C166**, smaller, possibly a later generation. Eyes more downturned; lids thick, almost closed, tooling behind upper lids. Lips smiling. Sweet expression. Locks of hair wave to sides from central part; piled high at top, with traces of locks of hair plaited back from center of forehead; plait around cranium. Probable mold sibling in lot 2249 (fabric 1).

See p. 57.

C168 Head of "doll" Pl. 15

MF-10641. Lot 896. Preserved: head and neck. P.H. 0.039 (size 2–3). Fabric 1, orange-buff. White slip. Solid. Back handmade, rounded. Added: hair in front, peak of hair in back. Tooling on hair. Head pierced for suspension.

Long, wide, spreading neck. Face small, oval, with high, triangular forehead. Hair roughly slashed; knot of hair in front at top, peak in back. Sphendone outlined with grooves. Probable mold sibling: MF-11384 (lot 877).

See pp. 34, 57.

C169 Female head, related to "dolls" Pl. 15

MF-12020. Lot 2240. Preserved: head and neck. P.H. 0.033 (size 2). Fabric 1, buff. Solid. Back handmade, flattened. Added: hair. Tooling on hair.

Similar in facial type to **C168**, but features are larger and more clearly delineated. Eyes downturned, opened wide; thick lids. Mouth wide; lips full. Coiffure peaked in front, roughly slashed projection of hair in back. Summary work. Probable mold sibling: MF-10511 (lot 881). Similar in facial type and scale to a mold from the Potters' Quarter, KH-39 (*Corinth* XV, i, p. 102, no. 41, pl. 35). For similar tooling of hair, see MF-7411 in the Corinth collection (*Corinth* XII, p. 33, no. 135, pl. 9).

See p. 57.

C170 Female head, related to "dolls" Pl. 15

MF-11843. Lot 2111. Preserved: head and neck. P.H. 0.021 (size 1–2). Fabric 4, light orange. White slip. Paint on face, neck, and hair similar to **C134**, but shade is closer to yellow. Solid. Back handmade, rounded. Added: peak of hair in back. Tooling on hair.

Tiny head, tilted slightly to right. Face oval, with high, wide forehead; pointed chin. Hair not detailed around forehead but stippled at sides, bound in back in sakkos with small peak of hair protruding. Dull impression; summarily retouched, although fabric is good.

See pp. 51, 57.

C171   Head of "doll"   Pl. 15

MF-10611. Lot 896. Preserved: head and neck. P.H. 0.02 (size 1–2). Fabric 1, orange-buff. White slip. Solid. Back handmade, rounded. Head pierced for suspension.

Tiny head with round face. Wide, spreading neck. Coiffure rounded, not detailed, with slight peak at top. This "doll's" head is one of the smallest from the sanctuary.

See pp. 51, 57.

Figurines of Dancers Related to Articulated "Dolls"

C172   Pl. 16
            Torso of semidraped female, related to "dolls"

MF-73-116. Lot 73-108. Preserved: front–shoulders to waist. Missing arms. P.H. 0.07 (size 4). Fabric 4, light orange. White slip. Hollow. Added: belt. Surface shows marks of fine-toothed tool, cross-hatched in places.

Torso similar to "doll" **C105**, but shoulders not pierced for articulated arms. Softness of flesh shown by fat pads at armpits. Upper edge of belt is a thick roll; vertical skirt folds just visible at lower break. Probably a dancer, similar in type to **C176**. Large, well-made piece.

See pp. 58–59.

C173   Pl. 16
            Head and torso of semidraped female, related to "dolls"

MF-11417. Lot 877. Preserved: head to waist. Missing left forearm, most of right arm, sphendone bowknot; nose, top of head chipped. P.H. 0.088 (size 3). Fabric 1, orange-buff to orange. White slip. Red paint on hair. Hollow; head probably solid. Thick-walled. Back molded(?), rounded. Added: arms, hair, sphendone. Tooling on belt, hair, mouth.

Nude upper torso shows small breasts, angular proportions; figurine probably constructed from a "doll's" torso, to which arms were added. Right arm originally raised; left arm at side. Upper and lower borders of tubular belt are incised. Long, wide neck. Head tilted up and turned three-fourths to right. Face small, oblong to oval, with high, triangular forehead. Features indistinct but generally resemble those of "dolls" **C128** and **C132**. Eyes slightly downturned. Mouth wide; lips full. Hair bound in sphendone, waved away from face in coiffure similar to that of **C129** but less carefully rendered; snaky locks along neck; clump of flat curls on cranium.

See pp. 58–59.

C174   Pl. 16
            Torso of semidraped female, related to "dolls"

MF-10322. Lot 870. Preserved: hips to knees. Missing part of drapery at left side. P.H. 0.053 (size 3). Fabric 1, orange, with grayish buff core. White slip. Pink paint on right leg, yellow between legs. Solid. Back molded, rounded. Added: skirt at sides of legs, part of skirt in back (leaving buttocks exposed).

Legs hollowed into cylindrical sockets. Knee-length skirt. Transparency over legs indicated by omitting drapery folds altogether.

See pp. 58–59, 183, 197.

C175   Torso of semidraped "doll"   Pl. 16

MF-13984. Lot 3206. Preserved: back–shoulders to knees. Missing right knee flange. P.H. 0.08 (size 2–3). Fabric 2, light orange to orange-buff, with grayish buff core. White slip. Yellow paint between legs. Solid. Back molded, rounded. Added: drapery, belt. Shoulders and knees pierced for limb attachment.

Torso similar in type to **C109**, with slightly projecting joining surfaces of shoulders, flat hips. Front surface mostly broken away, but thin sheet of clay seems to have been added for drapery; wide, flat belt just above natural waistline. Legs and buttocks of back mold show through, as if nude (cf. **C174**). Skirt flares, suggesting that figure is represented in motion. Similar in type: one in lot 4411 (fabric 1).

See pp. 58–59.

C176   Pl. 16
            Torso of semidraped female, related to "dolls"

MF-10468. Lot 878. Preserved: shoulders to knees. Missing arms. P.H. 0.077 (size 2–3). Fabric 1, orange-buff to orange. White slip. Yellow paint on skirt. Nearly solid. Back molded, rounded. Added: skirt folds at sides, belt in back, probably lower legs. Tooling on folds.

Published: Stroud 1965, p. 18, pl. 7:e.

Figurine was constructed by adding limbs to a "doll's" torso. Right thigh advanced. Arms originally held away from body. Wide belt, with torus border at top and bottom, around rib cage. Finely folded, transparent skirt; rippling hem suggests that figure is represented in motion. Belt and skirt rendered in mold in front; back is nude (cf. **C174** and **C175**). Similar in type: MF-10635 (lot 891, fabric 2, smaller, less well made); one in lot 2249 (fabric 2, larger, well made but lacks belt, which may have been painted); one in lot 3206 (fabric 2, larger).

See pp. 58–59, 184.

C177   Torso of semidraped "doll"   Pl. 16

MF-12055. Lot 2250. Preserved: shoulders to hem. P.H. 0.08 (size 2–3). Fabric 1, orange-buff. White slip. Hollow. Thick-walled. Back handmade, flattened. Added: panel dividing legs. Shoulders and hem pierced for limb attachment.

Wide, bordered belt and knee-length skirt similar to **C176**, but limbs originally were articulated; skirt folds are simpler and wider, showing little movement. Panel divides skirt hem into two sockets for legs; right thigh slightly advanced. Similar "doll" of reported Cypriote provenience (Elderkin 1930, p. 467, fig. 17) looks Corinthian and has a head with hair bound in sakkos, similar to **C143**.

See pp. 58–59.

C178   Torso of semidraped "doll"   Pl. 16

MF-10379. Lot 874. Preserved: neck to thighs, to waist in back. P.H. 0.092 (size 3). Fabric 1, orange. White slip. Blue paint on skirt. Hollow. Back molded, rounded. Shoulders pierced for arm attachment.

Upper edge of garment is rolled down at waist and belted. Crossbands over nude chest are faint at top. Skirt folds swing slightly to left, as if figure is in movement; V-shaped folds on abdomen and between thighs.

See pp. 58–59.

C179 Pl. 16
Torso of semidraped female, related to "dolls"

MF-13988. Lot 4386. Preserved: shoulders to right knee. Missing arms; shoulders chipped. P.H. 0.075 (size 2–3). Fabric 2, light orange. White slip. Hollow. Thick-walled. Back handmade, flattened, pared. Added: skirt at sides and hem. Tooling on folds.

Similar in type to **C176** but workmanship poorer. Figurine constructed from a "doll's" torso, to which arms were added, originally held away from torso. Shoulders bent back; abdomen protrudes. Tubular belt at natural waistline. Skirt folds carelessly grooved. Figurines similar in type, also of poor workmanship, in lots 880, 1993, 2249 (fabric 1).

See pp. 58–59.

C180 Torso of draped "doll" Pl. 16

MF-11052. Lot 1955. Preserved: shoulders to hem. Missing knees, hem in front. P.H. 0.085 (size 2–3). Fabric 1, orange to orange-buff. Hollow. Back handmade, flattened. Added: panel dividing legs. Shoulders and hem pierced for limb attachment.

Short chiton or peplos belted at natural waistline; kolpos puffs over belt, arching over abdomen. Thin cloth, without folds, clings to breasts and abdomen, is thicker at sides, where folds fall from shoulders and hips, and meet between legs. Panel divides skirt hem into two sockets for legs. Similar in type: one in lot 3233 (smaller).

See p. 59.

C181 Torso of draped "doll" Pl. 16

MF-14068. Lot 4379. Preserved: neck to knees. Missing part of hem. Mended. P.H. 0.085 (size 2–3). Fabric 1, orange to orange-buff. White slip. Hollow. Back molded, rounded. Shoulders pierced for arm attachment, holes fairly large, as in **C112**.

Drapery similar to **C180**, but horizontal, scalloped hem of short overfold, just above belt, falls into loops under arms; two catenaries between breasts. Narrow skirt folds follow curves of abdomen and thighs, meet between legs. Probable mold siblings: MF-10754 (lot 869, also has large shoulder hole); one in lot 4352 (hem pierced for leg attachment).

See pp. 32, 59, 291.

C182 Torso of draped "doll" Pl. 16

MF-10450. Lot 878. Preserved: neck to hem. P.H. 0.086 (size 2–3). Fabric 2, orange-buff. White slip. Hollow. Thick-walled. Back handmade, flattened. Added: locks of hair on shoulders, panel dividing legs. Tooling on folds. Shoulders and hem pierced for limb attachment.

Projecting joining surfaces of shoulders as in **C127**. Short chiton has thick belt above natural waistline. Puffed folds under arms. Summary catenaries incised between breasts; vertical grooves between parted legs and at sides; hem flares slightly. Panel divides skirt hem into two sockets for legs. Long locks of hair on shoulders are unusual for "dolls."

See p. 60.

C183 Torso of draped "doll" Pl. 16

MF-10442. Lot 878. Preserved: shoulders to hem. P.H. 0.073 (size 2). Fabric 1, orange-buff. White slip. Bright blue paint on drapery. Solid. Back handmade, slightly concave. Added: skirt hem and central flange. Tooling on folds. Shoulders and hem pierced for limb attachment.

Projecting joining surfaces of shoulders, as in **C182**; similar in dress, but hem is thickened, more flaring. Shoulders bent back. Lateral holes in hem are higher than central hole, as in nude "dolls" **C113** and **C114**.

See p. 60.

C184 Torso of draped "doll" Pl. 16

MF-11969. Lot 2237. Preserved: shoulders to hem; right side of hem chipped. P.H. 0.066 (size 2). Fabric 1, orange. Solid. Back handmade, flattened. Added: skirt hem and central flange, shoulder projections. Hem pierced for leg attachment.

Degenerate version of **C182** and **C183**. Unusually large projections at shoulders are not pierced, thus figure probably armless. Thickened, flaring hem and uneven piercing for leg attachment, as in **C183**. Top scored for joining of head without insertion of neck dowel between shoulders. Molding margin down sides not trimmed. Probable mold sibling: MF-1979-46 in the Corinth collection. Similar torsos in lots 2249 (better trimmed, deep from front to back), 3222.

See pp. 15, 17, 51, 60.

C185 Torso of draped "doll" Pl. 16

MF-72-190. Lot 72-122. Preserved: shoulders to hips; front chipped. P.H. 0.044 (size 2). Fabric 3, orange-buff to creamy buff. Hollow. Back handmade, flattened. Tooling on folds. Shoulders pierced for arm attachment.

Corpulent torso with slightly projecting joining surfaces of shoulders; protruding abdomen. Clinging chiton or peplos belted at natural waistline; narrow, vertical folds; looped fold frames right breast, cloth transparent over breast. Scalloped folds above belt schematically represent either puffed cloth of kolpos, as in **C180**, or hem of short overfold, as in **C181**. Crossband from right shoulder to waist.

See p. 60.

MALE FIGURINES: NUDE, SEMIDRAPED, AND DRAPED

C186 Rider Pl. 17

MF-11699. Lot 2013. Preserved: neck to left hip and right thigh. Missing right forearm; front of neck chipped; scar on chest. P.H. 0.114 (size 3–4). Fabric 1, buff. Red paint on neck, drapery. Hollow. Thick-walled; opening inside is round in section, as if clay wrapped around dowel. Back handmade, rounded. Tooling on folds, hair, hand.

Left arm bent; clenched hand in lap is pierced, probably to hold reins. Right arm perhaps bent, if scar on chest is from hand originally holding an object there. Shoulders broad; biceps well rounded. Hem of short chiton visible on thigh. Chlamys fastened at right shoulder, from which open edge falls to lap in doughy, zigzag folds; oval neckline; widely spaced, curving folds over left arm. Horizontally ridged, wiglike hair at left side of neck. Possible mold sibling: MF-11600 (slightly smaller) from Anaploga (Robinson 1969, p. 22, no. 43, pl. 5). For possible workshop mates, see Workshop D, p. 345.

See pp. 14, 25, 60.

C187 Rider	Pl. 17

MF-14092. Lot 4379. Preserved: shoulders to right thigh and left foot. Missing arms. P.H. 0.049 (size 1–2). Fabric 1, orange. Solid. Handmade.

Nude male figure in rider's straddling pose. Trace of mantle over left shoulder. Figure plump and smooth, anatomy summarily rendered except for genitals; foot scarcely differentiated from ankle.

See p. 60.

C188 Standing youth	Pl. 17

MF-12861. Lot 4395. Preserved: head to base. Missing right forearm. Mended. P.H. 0.093 (size 2). Fabric 2, creamy buff. Red paint on backdrop, pink on flesh, without white slip. Solid. Head and torso rendered in same mold. Back flattened. Added: polos, right forearm, base. Tooling on face, torso.

Nude, with drapery backdrop filling spaces around limbs. Stands on spreading plinth. Left leg slightly bent. Right forearm originally extended forward. Aryballos dangles from left wrist. Proportions slender; head rather large for body. Little anatomical detail on torso. Top of figure bent back slightly. Feet splayed, distorted. Face oval, with low forehead. Features distorted in molding. Eyes level. Nose large, close to upper lip. Lips full, smiling. Hair short, arranged in broad waves around forehead. Low, wide polos. Probable later generation: MF-11691 (lot 2011); MF-9012 in the Corinth collection. Possible earlier generation of face: MF-10522 (lot 885, "doll's" head).

See pp. 44, 60–62, 64, 125, 126, 188, 292.

C189 Standing youth	Pl. 17

MF-12877. Lot 4392. Preserved: head to right ankle and left calf. Missing right forearm. P.H. 0.076 (size 2). Fabric 2, orange-buff. Red paint on backdrop and flesh, without white slip. Solid. Back flattened. Added: polos, right arm.

Similar in type to **C188** but weight on left leg, with slight contrapposto. Top of figure bent back slightly. Head turned slightly to right. Object in left hand unclear. Facial features smeared in molding. Probable mold siblings: MF-13447 (lot 4358) and MF-10623 (lot 896); both hold a large alabastron or lekythos or perhaps a knucklebone bag; MF-1576 in the Corinth collection (*Corinth* XII, p. 38, no. 189, pl. 13). Possible later generation: MF-11333 (lot 2003); KT-21-9 from the Potters' Quarter (*Corinth* XV, ii, p. 114, no. 3, pl. 21).

See pp. 60–62, 125, 188.

C190 Standing youth	Pl. 17

MF-11067. Lot 1962. Intact. P.H. 0.09 (size 2). Fabric 2, buff to orange. White slip. Pink paint on face and neck. Solid. Back flattened. Polos concave at top. Added: base (covering left foot).

Similar in type to **C188**, but both arms are at sides, lyre in left hand. Drapery on upper arms. Probable mold sibling: T.F.-56 from the Asklepieion (*Corinth* XIV, p. 139, no. 10, pl. 54).

See pp. 60–61, 125, 188, 269.

C191 Standing youth	Pl. 17

MF-10540. Lot 887. Preserved: shoulders to ankles. Missing backdrop at lower right. P.H. 0.073 (size 2). Fabric 2, orange. Solid. Back concave.

Similar in type to **C188**, but rooster is held at chest in right arm. Knucklebone bag or perhaps long, narrow vessel (alabastron?) held by the neck in left hand. Possible mold sibling: MF-69-350 (lot 6214, fabric 3, hollow, has handmade back with square or rectangular vent, clearer impression of rooster).

See pp. 8, note 26, 60–61, 64, 188, 269, 274.

C192 Standing youth	Pl. 17

MF-13445. Lot 4466. Preserved: head to waist. Mended. P.H. 0.049 (size 2). Fabric 2, orange-buff to orange. Solid. Head and torso rendered in same mold. Back concave.

Similar in type to **C188**, but both arms are at sides. Hair knotted at center of forehead. Type may be completed by **C193**, which holds a lyre. Dull impression. Probably mechanically related: MF-10945 (lot 1945); MF-13461 (lot 2249); KT-21-1 from the Potters' Quarter (*Corinth* XV, ii, p. 113, no. 1, pl. 22); there are also fifteen to twenty fragmentary unpublished examples from the Potters' Quarter and the Asklepieion. Similar in type, larger: MF-68-51 (lot 5718); MF-13448 (lot 3222). Head type also used for banqueters, such as **C211**.

See pp. 61–62, 66, 188, 293.

C193 Standing youth	Pl. 17

MF-13446. Lot 881. Preserved: waist to thighs, with right forearm, both hands. P.H. 0.043 (size 2). Fabric 2, orange-buff. Solid. Back concave.

Similar in type to **C188**, but lyre is in left hand. See **C192** for possible associated head type.

See pp. 61, 188.

C194 Standing youth	Pl. 17

MF-13439. Lot 2190. Preserved: front–waist to right thigh and left hip. P.H. 0.042 (size 2–3). Fabric 3, orange-buff. Hollow.

Nude; torso without contrapposto. Slender proportions, although not as slender as **C188**, and larger; delicate modeling of external oblique and abdomen.

See pp. 62, 188.

C195 Standing youth	Pl. 17

MF-14058. Lot 4344. Preserved: front–waist to left knee, with adjacent drapery, and right hip. P.H. 0.098 (size 3). Fabric 1, buff to orange. White slip. Red paint on flesh. Hollow. Tooling on folds.

Probably similar in type to **C188** but much larger, with draped shoulder and arm. Torso without contrapposto. Left arm at side but hidden by cascade of zigzag mantle folds; aryballos hangs from wrist. Probable mold sibling: MF-13438 (lot 2249). Similar in scale and style: T.F.-13 from the Asklepieion (*Corinth* XIV, p. 140, no. 12, pl. 54, better preserved).

See pp. 62, 188.

C196 Standing youth	Pl. 17

MF-11049. Lot 1954. Preserved: front–hips to thighs, small part of back. P.H. 0.039 (size 2–3). Fabric 2, orange-buff to orange. White slip. Solid. Added: genitals. Tooling between thighs.

Weight on left leg, left hip somewhat outthrust. Folds along left thigh. External oblique modeled.

See pp. 63, 188.

C197 Standing youth Pl. 17

MF-69-358. Lot 6214. Preserved: right thigh and knee with adjacent support, wrist and hand with drapery. P.H. 0.101 (size 3–4). Fabric 2, orange. Hollow. Back handmade, flattened.

Right knee bent. Hand holds phiale at side. Drapery around wrist; straight fall of mantle down side. More three-dimensional than other youths of this group and heavier in fabric; probably later. Possible later generation: MF-69-359 (lot 6214). Fragments of similar type in lots 2249 and 3222 are less three-dimensional. Similar in scale: T.F.-13 from the Asklepieion (*Corinth* XIV, p. 140, no. 12, pl. 54, with phiale).

See pp. 63, 188.

C198 Standing youth Pl. 17

MF-13444. Lot 4350. Preserved: front–right shoulder to ankle, most of abdomen; surface chipped. P.H. 0.08 (size 2). Fabric 1, orange-buff to orange. White slip. Hollow.

Perhaps similar in type to **C197**. Right leg bent and drawn to side. Right arm at side; hand holds phiale(?) against thigh. Remains of drapery backdrop(?) at sides of leg; drapery over forearm.

See pp. 63, 188.

C199 Pl. 17
Standing semidraped figurine, probably male

MF-10598. Lot 893. Preserved: shoulders to hips. Missing right wrist and hand. P.H. 0.051 (size 2–3). Fabric 1, orange-buff, with orange core. Hollow. Back handmade, flat. Irregular rectangular vent, ca. 0.018 wide. Added: right forearm, drapery around shoulders and hips.

Left arm bent, hand behind hip, covered by drapery. Mantle falls over left shoulder in zigzag folds, covers back, curves behind right shoulder and arm to hip; bunched folds draped loosely across abdomen, secured by hand at left hip. Figurine appears to have been constructed from a nude female "doll's" torso, by pressing down the breasts and adding the mantle.

See pp. 51, note 202, 58, 63, 64, 185, 186.

C200 Standing semidraped male figurine Pl. 17

MF-13459. Lot 4344. Preserved: neck to waist. Missing right arm. P.H. 0.07 (size 3). Fabric 1, orange-buff. Hollow. Back molded, rounded. Added: right arm.

Right arm originally raised. Mantle draped over left shoulder, diagonally across chest to waist. Row of parallel, arched folds down left arm; zigzag folds across chest. Little anatomical definition but drapery well modeled.

See p. 63.

C201 Standing semidraped youth Pl. 17

MF-12131. Lot 4347. Complete; back and base chipped. P.H. 0.096 (size 2). Fabric similar to 3 but slightly sandy, orange-buff to yellowish buff, with sparse small sparkling inclusions. White slip. Blue paint on bag. Hollow. Back molded, flattened. Torso and base rendered in same mold. Added: possibly right hand and ball.

Weight distributed evenly on both legs. Legs are parted, feet slightly turned out; lower legs are too short. Right arm at side; mitten-shaped hand holds ball. Left arm bent; hand holds a knucklebone bag(?), with horizontal lines around its neck possibly indicating cords. Mantle is draped over left shoulder

and arm; upper edge rolled around waist; contours of legs visible through cloth. Little anatomical detail on nude upper torso. Head resembles some female heads (see, e.g., **C11** and **C159**): face is small, on long, wide neck; coiffure is full. Face oblong to oval, with low forehead; prominent chin; flat cheeks. Features perhaps slightly distorted in molding. Hair arranged in high, rounded mass in front, slightly peaked, stippled (in mold); long locks of hair fall to shoulders. Round, flaring base. Probable mold sibling in lot 6214 (fabric 1).

See pp. 61, 63, 64, 125, 188.

C202 Standing draped male(?) figurine Pl. 17

MF-14069. Lot 4387. Preserved: left shoulder to thigh, small part of back. P.H. 0.084 (size 2–3). Fabric 1, orange-buff. Hollow. Back handmade, flattened. Tooling on folds.

Left arm bent; forearm across waist. Mantle falls over shoulder and forearm in zigzag folds. Vertical folds at lower left break could belong either to a mantle draped across the torso and falling to the legs, as in male figurines (e.g., **C199**), or to the peplos skirt of a female figurine.

See p. 63.

ISOLATED MALE HEADS

C203 Head of youth Pl. 18

MF-73-74. Lot 73-138. Preserved: head and neck. P.H. 0.039 (size 3–4). Fabric 1, orange-buff to orange, with orange core. White slip. Red paint on flesh. Solid. Back handmade, rounded. Added: hair at nape.

Face oblong to oval, with low forehead. Eyes large, level; both lids clearly defined; browridge also well defined, follows curve of eye from nose to temples. Nose large, somewhat distorted, close to upper lip. Mouth wide; lips fleshy, slightly downturned. Hair in large knot at center of forehead, waves closely down sides of face to chin level, forms roll at nape. Coiffure similar to that of Boeotian youths (see **I45**), although face is different; probably from a standing figure similar to **I45** but larger.

See pp. 40, 62, 64, 293.

C204 Head of youth Pl. 18

MF-13418. Lot 3222. Preserved: head and small part of neck. P.H. 0.032 (size 3). Fabric 2, light orange. Solid. Back handmade, flat.

Face oval, with low forehead. Features large. Coiffure as in **C203**. Similar heads, larger: KT-24-7 from the Potters' Quarter (*Corinth* XV, ii, pp. 136–137, no. 2, pl. 30); T.F.-77 from the Asklepieion (*Corinth* XIV, pp. 142–143, no. 43, pl. 56).

See pp. 62, 64, 293.

C205 Head of youth Pl. 18

MF-13416. Lot 2240. Preserved: head and front of neck. Missing tip of nose. P.H. 0.04 (size 3–4). Fabric 2, orange-buff to light orange. Hollow in front, cranium solid. Back handmade, rounded. Tooling on hair.

Face oblong to oval, with low forehead. Eyes large, slightly downturned; thick lids meet at corners. Nose large, close to upper lip. Mouth wide; lips full (particularly lower lip), slightly downturned. Coiffure a rounded mass, with two rows of lightly modeled ringlets and a suggestion of tight waves around forehead; probably a schematic version of an Archaic coiffure, as on protome MF-13658 from the sanctuary (publication forthcoming) and T.F.-37 from the Asklepieion (*Corinth* XIV, p. 140, no. 15, pl. 55, probably female). Head is deep (cf. similar construction of KT-24-7 from the Potters' Quarter [*Corinth* XV, ii, pp. 136–137, no. 2, pl. 30]). Facial type similar to female head **C53** and **C206**.

See p. 64.

C206   Head of youth   Pl. 18

MF-13417. Lot 3222. Preserved: head and neck. P.H. 0.05 (size 3–4). Fabric 2, light orange. White slip. Solid. Back handmade, slightly flattened. Tooling on hair.

Facial type similar to **C205**, but hair is arranged in broad waves across forehead and down sides, reaching just below level of ear all around. Neck slender, spreading. Probable mold sibling in lot 6215 (fabric 1, with added fillet). Probable later generation: MF-70-226 (lot 6638).

See pp. 40, 64.

C207   Head of youth   Pl. 18

MF-13946. Lot 3222. Preserved: head and neck. P.H. 0.048 (size 3–4). Fabric 1, orange-buff. Hollow. Back handmade, flattened. Added: part of hair at top and sides. Tooling on hair.

Short, wide, spreading neck. Face oblong to oval, with broad forehead and flat cheeks. Eyes large, level. Nose large, close to upper lip. Lips full, slightly smiling. Hair waves across forehead from central part, with double scallop at center; long locks of hair fan out to shoulders. Probable mold sibling in lot 4377.

See p. 64.

C208   Head of youth   Pl. 18

MF-12157. Lot 4369. Preserved: head and neck. Missing surface of cranium. P.H. 0.08 (size 4–5). Fabric 1, orange-buff, with yellowish buff core. White slip. Red paint on flesh and hair; most of hair painted directly on clay; white slip only in front on hair and face. Solid. Back handmade, rounded. Added: ears; hair. Tooling on hair.

Published: Stroud 1968, p. 323, pl. 94:e.

Face oblong to oval, with low forehead and flat cheeks. Eyes large, level; both lids defined, meet at corners; lower lids slightly lifted; browridge rounded. Nose large, low bridged, close to upper lip, tip reworked. Mouth wide; lips thick. Hair waved loosely across forehead from central part, forms peak at center. Below prominent ears, long locks of hair along neck.

See pp. 63, 64, 137, 292.

C209   Head of youth(?)   Pl. 18

MF-10483. Lot 878. Preserved: head and neck. P.H. 0.021 (size 2). Fabric 2, orange. Red paint on face(?). Solid. Back handmade, flat.

Round face, framed by halo of hair. Slight traces of waves radiating from forehead. Type could be male or female, but possible red paint on face suggests it is male. Similar in type: MF-13471 (lot 881, slightly larger).

See p. 64.

RECLINING MALE FIGURINES (BANQUETERS) AND RELATED HEADS

C210   Banqueter   Pl. 18

MF-10378. Lot 874. Nearly complete. Missing chip from front of couch. H. 0.061, L. 0.066 (size 2). Fabric 3, buff. Hollow. All parts rendered in same mold. Back handmade, flattened, pared.

Youth reclines on left elbow, holding phiale in left hand. Right hand on bent right knee. Mantle draped around waist and over left shoulder, from which it falls in zigzag folds. Face oval, with low forehead. Eyes widely set, prominent. Nose wide. Hair a plain, rounded mass, with long locks of hair at sides. Probable mold siblings: MF-69-355 (lot 6214, fabric 1); KT-19-31 from the Potters' Quarter (*Corinth* XV, ii, p. 108, no. 9, pl. 22, citing additional examples, including figurines from the Asklepieion); MF-1977-61, from Forum Southwest (C. K. Williams 1978, pp. 11, 35, no. 10, pl. 2). Probable later generation: MF-11037 (lot 1953, friable, fabric 5?); MF-11026 (lot 1953, burned). Perhaps still later generation: MF-69-356 (lot 6214, fabric 1).

See pp. 65–66.

C211   Head of banqueter   Pl. 18

MF-11656. Lot 2009. Preserved: head and neck, small part of chest. P.H. 0.033 (size 2). Fabric 1, greenish buff. White slip. Red paint on neck. Solid. Back handmade, flattened.

Face oblong. Cranium high; hair knotted at center of forehead, waves cling to sides of face; coiffure more clearly rendered in **C203**. Profile of chest indicates figure was reclining, although the same head type was used for standing youths, such as **C192**. Probably from a banqueter similar to **C212**. Probable mold sibling: KT-19-1, with torso, from the Potters' Quarter (*Corinth* XV, ii, pp. 106–107, no. 2, pl. 20, citing additional examples; detail of head and upper torso in Krystalli-Votsi 1976, pl. 68:a). Possible later generation: MF-11035 (lot 1953, head of a banqueter or standing figure).

See p. 66.

C212   Banqueter   Pl. 18

MF-13463. Lot 3222. Preserved: front–chest, part of lap, right upper arm, left hand. Surface worn. P.H. 0.04 (size 2). Fabric 3, orange-buff. Hollow.

Mantle folded across waist. Egg in left hand (similar object is called an egg-shaped fruit in *Corinth* XV, ii, p. 106, no. 2). Probably from same figurine type as head **C211**.

See pp. 65, 66, 67.

C213   Banqueter   Pl. 18

MF-11887. Lot 2067. Missing legs, right hand, most of vessel, front of couch. H. 0.113, P.L. 0.106 (size 3). Fabric 2, buff. White slip. Pink paint on torso. Hollow. All parts rendered in same mold. Back handmade, flattened.

Youth reclines on left elbow, holds kantharos in left hand, thumb touching its curved handle. Mantle falls over left arm in six stacked folds; zigzag folds across waist. Biceps and pectorals well rounded. Head slightly raised to left. Face oval to round, with low forehead; cheeks full. Eyes large, level; both lids defined. Nose large, close to upper lip. Lips full. Cranium high; hair rolled over fillet. Probable mold siblings: one in lot 73-138 (burned); one in lot 4458; KT-19-60 from the Potter's Quarter (*Corinth* XV, ii, pp. 108–109, no. 13, pl. 19, preserving kantharos, and another mentioned there, both from later-5th-century B.C. deposits; Stillwell's observation that the surface of KT-19-60 was extensively reworked should be revised, since its surface detail is identical with that of **C213** and therefore must have been rendered in the mold; neither figurine would have been made from the mold of this type from the Potters' Quarter, KH-58 [*Corinth* XV, i, p. 105, no. 59, pl. 39]). Similar in type: KT-19-59 from the Potters' Quarter

(*Corinth* XV, ii, p. 109, no. 14, pl. 18, same coiffure, face more Early Classical in style).

See pp. 14, 65, 66.

C214 Banqueter   Pl. 18

MF-11676. Lot 2010. Preserved: front–part of couch, left leg, lap. P.L. 0.089 (size 2–3). Fabric 3, buff, burned. Hollow.

Similar in type to **C213**, but couch is lower and shows a profile in two degrees. Kantharos rests on couch; handle in banqueter's left hand is just visible at break. End of mantle lies along thigh in zigzag folds. Probable mold sibling: KT-19-62 from the Potters' Quarter (*Corinth* XV, ii, p. 109, no. 15).

See p. 65.

C215 Banqueter   Pl. 18

MF-13441. Lot 2249. Preserved: head to chest, left arm. P.H. 0.056 (size 2). Fabric 3, orange to ochre. Hollow. Backless; flattened edges meet behind neck, apparently to strengthen narrowest part of figurine.

Youth reclines on left elbow; left hand holds bowl(?). Mantle draped over left shoulder and upper arm, possibly also drawn over high, wide polos. Face oval. Rounded coiffure frames face. Long ends of fillet lie on shoulders. Other examples of this type (with different backs) were found in Corinth, mostly in the Potters' Quarter, but owing to the poor preservation of **C215**, its mechanical relationships cannot be determined; see *Corinth* XV, ii, pp. 110–111, nos. 26–28, pls. 21, 22, and other examples cited there. MF-72-30 from the Forum area (C. K. Williams and Fisher 1973, p. 8, pl. 3) is also backless.

See pp. 17, 26, 66–67, 294.

C216 Banqueter   Pl. 18

MF-13440. Lot 3222. Missing head. L. 0.074; P.H. 0.053 (size 2). Fabric 3, yellowish buff to creamy buff. Hollow. Back handmade, flattened at top, flaring at bottom. Added: fillets on shoulders, right forearm and hand. Tooling on folds, arms.

Youth reclines on left side, elbow propped on two cushions; left hand holds bowl. Right forearm rests on thigh; mitten-shaped hand. Mantle covers legs, is folded down over lap; folds over left upper arm. Long ends of fillet lie on shoulders. Probable mold siblings: KT-19-83 and KT-19-87 from the Potters' Quarter (*Corinth* XV, ii, p. 111, nos. 27, 28, pl. 21). See **C215** for references to similar figurines.

See pp. 65, 66–67.

C217 Banqueter   Pl. 18

MF-13443. Lot 3233. Preserved: front–left forearm and hand, part of lap. P.L. 0.04 (size 2–3). Fabric 3, buff, with orange core. Red paint on flesh and drapery. Hollow. Tooling on hand, folds.

Reclines on left elbow; holds lyre in left hand. Mantle draped across lap; folds hang from shoulder, cover upper arm. Other banqueters with lyre: KT-19-80 and KT-19-81 from the Potters' Quarter (*Corinth* XV, ii, p. 110, no. 22, pl. 21; p. 112, no. 34, pl. 20); MF-1023 and MF-4200 in the Corinth collection (*Corinth* XII, pp. 35–36, nos. 158, 159, pl. 11).

See p. 65.

C218 Banqueter   Pl. 18

MF-69-386. Lot 6214. Preserved: head to upper torso. Missing most of couch; cracked. P.H. 0.06 (size 2). Fabric 5, yellowish buff. Hollow; head solid. Probably a plaque; thickened edge at back.

Reclining youth in polos and fillet with long ends, similar to **C215** but proportions elongated. Object in left hand unclear. Little detail visible. Similar in type and proportions: MF-8087 in the Corinth collection (Broneer 1942, p. 148, fig. 7).

See p. 67.

C219 Banqueter   Pl. 18

MF-12853. Lot 4466. Preserved: chest to lower legs. Missing foot of couch and panel between couch legs. P.L. 0.078 (size 2). Fabric 3, creamy buff, with orange core. Probably a plaque; left edge is finished.

Reclines on left side. Left forearm hangs diagonally over edge of couch; right forearm over thigh, hand holds kantharos with stem in two degrees, small loop handles. Mantle roll frames abdomen, revealing navel, and falls over left forearm. For upper torso, see **C220**. Complete type, probably not mechanically related: T-339 in the Corinth collection (from Reservoir 1926-2, filled between 175 and 165 B.C. [Edwards 1986, p. 391, note 12, p. 399 on the date]). In this example, banqueter is a youth wearing a wreath; couch is high, with turned legs (Richter 1966, pp. 55–58); snake held just behind its head in youth's left hand, hangs to floor.

See pp. 65, 67.

C220 Banqueter   Pl. 18

MF-13442. Lot 3222. Preserved: shoulders to hips. Missing most of couch, right forearm. P.L. 0.046 (size 2). Fabric 3, harder, yellowish buff. Probably a plaque.

Similar in type to **C219**. Sinuous curve of torso. Cushion folded double under elbow. Snake in left hand. Similar in type: MF-68-349 (lot 5613, fabric 5, not a plaque, poorer workmanship, on low couch, with empty left hand, possibly phiale in right hand).

See p. 67.

C221 Banqueter(?)   Pl. 19

MF-73-99. Lot 73-144. Preserved: chest, right shoulder and upper arm, small part of back. Mended. P.H. 0.075 (size 4). Fabric 1, rather soft, orange-buff, with orange core. White slip. Hollow. Back handmade, flattened. Added: right forearm. Tooling on folds.

Originally reclined on left side. Right upper arm at side; forearm originally extended forward. Mantle fold, just visible at break, covered left upper arm; bunched folds wrapped closely around waist.

See p. 67.

C222 Banqueter   Pl. 19

MF-11387. Lot 877. Preserved: front–neck, left shoulder, left side of chest. P.H. 0.051 (size 3). Fabric 1, orange-buff, with grayish buff core. White slip. Red paint on chest and neck. Hollow. Tooling on folds.

Torso fragmentary, but conformation of shoulder and chest suggests figure was reclining, leaning on left elbow. Subtle modeling of musculature. Deep, rounded, vertical and diagonal folds of mantle pulled tightly over shoulder.

See p. 67.

C223 Banqueter   Pl. 19

MF-10480. Lot 878. Preserved: head to waist. Missing most of face. P.H. 0.048 (size 2). Fabric 1, orange-buff. White slip. Red paint on hair, beard, and chest. Hollow; head solid.

Thick-walled. Back handmade, flattened. Added: beard. Tooling on beard.

Reclines on left side; both upper arms at sides. Bend in torso begins at lower break. Proportions of torso and neck rather short; beard rests on chest.

See p. 67.

C224 Banqueter   Pl. 19

MF-14079. Lot 2210. Preserved: front–legs and right hand. P.L. 0.071 (size 2). Fabric 1, orange-buff. White slip. Hollow. Tooling on hand.

Reclines on left side; right hand rests on calf of right leg. Looped mantle folds across thighs; bunched folds across lap. Probable mold sibling: MF-9648 in the Corinth collection (figure reclines on separately handmade couch with high, rectangular legs). MF-8056 in the Corinth collection (*Corinth* XII, p. 36, no. 163, pl. 11) shows a similar couch. On the couch type, see Richter 1966, pp. 58–62, figs. 309–333.

See p. 66.

C225 Bearded head, probably of banqueter   Pl. 19

MF-12164. Lot 4388. Preserved: head, neck, small part of right shoulder. P.H. 0.043 (size 3). Fabric 1, orange-buff. Solid. Back handmade, rounded. Added: polos, lower part of beard, hair at sides. Tooling on hair, beard.

Published: Stroud 1968, p. 323, pl. 94:f.

Profile of right shoulder, as far as preserved, suggests figure was reclining on left side. Face oval, features finely modeled. Eyes large, level; both lids defined, upper lids well arched. Nose short. Lower lip full, framed by drooping moustache. Coiffure full at sides; hair and beard stippled to indicate curls. Low polos, concave at top, with uneven edges. Other Corinthian bearded banqueters wearing the polos: MF-1896 from the South Stoa (*Corinth* XII, p. 48, no. 303, pl. 26 [Hellenistic]); KT-19-84 from the Potters' Quarter (*Corinth* XV, ii, p. 112, no. 36, pl. 21, from a 4th-century B.C. deposit, but type thought to have originated in the 5th century B.C.).

See p. 67.

C226 Bearded head, possibly of banqueter   Pl. 19

MF-11714. Lot 2018. Preserved: head and neck. Missing nose; face chipped. P.H. 0.044 (size 3). Fabric 1, orange-buff to orange. White slip. Red paint on beard. Solid. Back handmade, rounded. Added: wreath, probably beard. Tooling on hair, beard, wreath, nostrils.

Head tilted slightly to left. Oval face framed by rounded coiffure; short, elegant beard and well-trimmed moustache. Hair stippled; beard slashed. Eyes downturned. Nose short, wide. Thick, tubular, stippled wreath. Similar head: MF-11012 (lot 1953).

See p. 67.

SEATED CHILDREN AND RELATED HEADS

C227 Seated boy   Pl. 19

MF-10639. Lot 896. Complete. Mended. H. 0.057 (size 2). Fabric 3, greenish buff. White slip. Solid. All parts rendered in same mold. Back flat. Underside concave.

Nude baby boy sits on low, irregular, rectangular base. Boy leans slightly to left side, propped on left hand, which supports weight of figure. Left leg folded flat on base; right foot rests on base, knee drawn up; right hand on knee. Little anatomical detail; left hand and feet merge with base, right hand with knee. Round, bald head on short, wide neck. Eyes prominent. Nose wide. Mouth wide; lips thick. Probable mold siblings: MF-10478 (lot 878); MF-10584 (lot 892); one in lot 2145; one in lot 2249 (fabric 1). Possible mold siblings: MF-2905 in the Corinth collection (*Corinth* XII, p. 38, no. 192, pl. 14); MF-9155 from the Asklepieion (*Corinth* XIV, p. 141, no. 26, pl. 54). KT-20-4 from the Potters' Quarter (*Corinth* XV, ii, p. 115, no. 1, pl. 23) and three others mentioned there are so similar that if they were not mold siblings, they were made in closely related molds. Probable later generation: MF-13424 (lot 2156, nearly featureless). It is possible that some of these figurines were made in a mold found in the Potters' Quarter, KH-60 (*Corinth* XV, i, pp. 105–106, no. 61, pl. 40), since the mold is of suitable pose, facial type, and scale (i.e., slightly larger). The figurines with heads preserved, however, show a different orientation of the head than the mold. Either two different archetypes were involved or perhaps a parallel mold series, in which manipulation of an unfired figurine earlier in the series caused a change in the position of the head. Similar in type: *Perachora* I, p. 254, no. 295, pl. 114 (listed with East Greek figurines on the basis of parallels from Lindos but seems closer to Corinthian examples).

See pp. 68, 69, 72.

C228 Seated boy   Pl. 19

MF-10638. Lot 896. Preserved: front–abdomen to legs; base. Mended. P.H. 0.063 (size 2). Fabric 3, buff. White slip. Pink paint on flesh. Hollow. Torso and base rendered in same mold.

Similar in type to **C227**, but right foot is drawn back. Seated on high base, rounded in back, slightly concave in front. Perhaps a later generation of a mold from the Potters' Quarter, KH-64 (*Corinth* XV, i, p. 106, no. 65, pl. 40); a long ridge indicating the toes of the left foot appears in both, but the base was apparently reshaped.

See p. 68.

C229 Seated boy   Pl. 19

MF-13423. Lot 2249. Preserved: left shoulder to base. Missing right shoulder and upper arm, most of base. Mended. P.H. 0.054 (size 2). Treated with preservative, but fabric seems to be 2, orange. Solid. Torso and base rendered in same mold. Back and underside slightly concave.

Similar in type to **C227**, but torso leans more to left side. Top of base slopes to narrow edge.

See p. 68.

C230 Seated boy   Pl. 19

MF-11305. Lot 1994. Preserved: shoulders to base. P.H. 0.045 (size 2). Fabric 1, orange-buff. Hollow. Torso and base rendered in same mold. Back handmade, rounded. Tooling on torso, hands, hair.

Similar in type to **C229**, but right lower leg is nearly vertical, left arm is further back, shoulders are more sloping and show long locks of hair. Base higher, flat in front, rounded in back. Navel gouged. Similar in type: two parallel molds from the Potters' Quarter, KH-61 and KH-62 (*Corinth* XV, i, p. 106, nos. 62, 63, pl. 41); T-2262 from a North Cemetery grave, dated to the third quarter of the 4th century B.C. (*Corinth* XIII, p. 282, no. 453-4, pl. 74, wearing a pilos). Others of this type, with variations: KT-20-6, KT-20-10, KT-20-12, and

KT-20-13 from the Potters' Quarter (*Corinth* XV, ii, pp. 115–116, nos. 3–6, pl. 23, with additional examples cited there).
See pp. 68, 69, 72.

C231   Seated boy   Pl. 19

MF-10525. Lot 885. Preserved: front–right shoulder to base. Missing left shoulder, most of left arm, part of chest at left side. Mended. P.H. 0.049 (size 2). Fabric 3, orange to orange-buff. Hollow.

Similar in type to **C227**, but right knee rests on base, lower leg stretched diagonally to back, foot flexed (for this leg position, see *Kabirenheiligtum* V, pp. 104, 173, no. 274, pl. 22). Base slightly concave in front. Possible mold sibling: MF-13425 (lot 2048).
See p. 68.

C232   Seated boy   Pl. 19

MF-68-348. Lot 5613. Preserved: shoulders to base. P.H. 0.042 (size 2). Fabric 1, slightly coarser, light orange (grayer), with sparse small black and white inclusions. Solid. Torso and base rendered in same mold. Back handmade, flat. Underside concave. Tooling on hands, genitals.

Similar in type to **C231**, smaller. More relaxed pose; left arm does not support weight. Mitten-shaped hands. Oval base.
See p. 68.

C233   Seated boy   Pl. 19

MF-13422. Lot 3230. Preserved: head to right leg in front, to waist in back. Missing base, left hip, leg, and forearm. P.H. 0.076 (size 2). Fabric 5, ochre to orange. Nearly solid. Back handmade, flattened. Top of irregular, rectangular vent preserved, 0.023 wide. Added: pilos. Tooling on face, pilos.

Similar in type to **C232**, but right lower leg is turned inward. Narrow, sloping shoulders; almost no neck. Head slightly tilted to right, falls forward on chest. Face round, with high, prominent forehead; receding chin. Eyes large, slightly downturned; both lids defined. Nose wide, smeared in molding. Mouth wide; lips slightly smiling. Ears gouged. High, narrow pilos with rolled rim, stippled. Similar in type: MF-13431 (lot 3217).
See pp. 68, 73.

C234   Seated boy   Pl. 19

MF-14073. Lot 2048. Preserved: shoulders to waist. P.H. 0.055 (size 2). Fabric 1, orange-buff, orange core. Solid. Back handmade, flat.

Nude figure, probably a boy, leans forward with weight on both arms; right arm placed in front of torso, probably between legs; left arm probably beside left leg. For this pose see complete mid-5th-century B.C. figurines from Sicily (*British Museum* I, p. 314, nos. 1158, 1159, pl. 158; Hadzisteliou-Price 1969, p. 100, pl. 22:15, 20) and Rhodes (*British Museum* I, p. 93, nos. 258, 259, pl. 45).
See pp. 68, 72.

C235   Seated boy   Pl. 19

MF-10664. Lot 1945. Preserved: head to upper chest. P.H. 0.054 (size 2). Fabric 5, ochre to orange. Hollow. Thick-walled. Back handmade, flattened; upper horizontal edge of vent preserved. Added: pilos. Tooling on hair.

Similar in type to **C233**, but shoulders are less sloping. Face very wide. Long locks of hair. Rough, horizontal grooves on pilos above rolled rim and at juncture with forehead. Gouges on hair. Coarse workmanship. Similar heads with long hair and pilos: MF-13449 (lot 3222, fabric 1); MF-13450 (lot 3206); MF-10579 (lot 892, fabric 2); one in lot 3223 (fabric 1).
See pp. 68, 73.

C236   Seated boy   Pl. 20

MF-13426. Lots 2156 and 2249. Preserved: head to right ankle. Missing left leg, front of base, most of right arm, right foot. Mended; left forearm and hand chipped. P.H. 0.069 (size 2). Fabric 2, orange-buff (back treated with preservative). White slip. Red paint on pilos. Solid; underside concave up to level of hips. Back molded, rounded. Added: arms, round object in back.

Similar in pose to **C227**, but right arm originally was raised. Large, rounded object behind left hand, perhaps a cushion or clump of drapery. A few possible drapery folds at bottom of base in back originally may have reappeared over missing leg and base in front (for the left leg draped in a mantle, see **C241** and **C244**). Faint cord for amulets over left shoulder, looped diagonally over chest (clearer on **C237**). Almost no neck. Head tilted to right and thrown back. Left side of face apparently defective in mold (eye not detailed; left side of mouth and adjacent cheek and jaw are flattened, as if erased; probably made in mold parallel to that of **C237**). Right eye large, downturned; upper lid and browridge well defined. Wears pilos with rolled rim but lower and wider than **C233**.
See pp. 68, 69, 72, 73, 290.

C237   Seated boy   Pl. 20

MF-13427. Lot 4368. Preserved: head to abdomen, left upper arm, part of right arm. P.H. 0.053 (size 2). Fabric 1, orange-buff to orange. White slip. Solid. Back molded, rounded. Added: arms. Tooling on face.

Probably made in mold parallel to that of **C236**; left side of face is fully preserved, but although not flattened, it is distorted, with mouth twisted upward to left. Perhaps the distortion already existed in the archetype and was erased from the mold of **C236** before it was fired. Round face with puffed cheeks, dimpled chin. Nose short, wide. Mouth wide; lips thick; grimace probably due to mold defect. The amulet cord also is clearer here; pendant amulets probably originally painted.
See pp. 68, 69, 72, 73, 192.

C238   Head related to seated boys   Pl. 20

MF-10494. Lot 880. Preserved: head and neck, small part of shoulders; back chipped. P.H. 0.034 (size 2). Fabric 1, orange-buff. White slip. Red paint on pilos and flesh (painted over white slip only on flesh). Solid. Back handmade, rounded. Added: top of pilos. Tooling on pilos.

Similar in type to head of **C233**, but pilos more rounded, rim not rolled but set off with groove. Almost no neck. Head tilted slightly to left, falls forward on chest. Face round, with puffed cheeks. Nose wide. Lips pursed.
See pp. 13, 69, 72, 73.

C239   Seated boy   Pl. 20

MF-13430. Lot 4368. Preserved: shoulders to legs. Missing arms; left knee chipped. P.H. 0.04 (size 1). Fabric 1, orange-buff, with orange core. White slip. Bright pink paint on shoulder. Solid. Back handmade, flattened. Added: arms. Tooling on toes.

Similar to **C230** in position of legs, but arms originally raised. Probably no base. Molding rim around legs and torso not trimmed. Summary work. Probable mold sibling in lot 6214. Possible later generation: **C240**.

See pp. 68, 72.

C240   Seated boy   Pl. 20

MF-13428. Lot 2249. Preserved: head to legs. Missing arms. H. 0.053 (size 1). Fabric 2, orange-buff to orange. Solid. Head and torso rendered in same mold. Back handmade, flattened.

Possibly a later generation of **C239**, with head preserved. Head turned to left. Face oval. High, narrow pilos with rolled rim, as in **C233**. Dull impression. Probably no base. Probable mold sibling: MF-11239 (lot 880, fabric 1).

See pp. 68, 72.

C241   Seated boy   Pl. 20

MF-10493. Lot 880. Complete. Mended. H. 0.089 (size 2). Fabric 2, orange-buff to light orange. White slip. Red paint on pilos, blue-green(?) and yellow on pilos rim. Hollow; head solid. Back molded, rounded. Added: base, right foot, top of pilos(?). Tooling on folds, hands; right leg, back pared.

Published: Stroud 1965, p. 18, pl. 8:e.

Similar in type to **C229** but more gracefully rendered. Right lower leg is diagonal; foot rests on corner of base. Left hand, which supports weight of figure, pulled back behind hip. Boy sits on mantle, one end of which is tucked between right arm and hip. The other end reappears from behind left hip, tumbles over base, is wrapped over left lower leg, and disappears again under right leg. Base is low, roughly oval, following shape of figure. Face round to oval. Eyes level; both lids defined. Nose wide, flattened. Lips full, smiling. Rolled pilos rim is stippled (in mold). Well-made piece.

See pp. 68, 69, 72, 73.

C242   Seated boy   Pl. 20

MF-10413. Lot 877. Preserved: chin to base. P.H. 0.065 (size 2). Fabric 3, orange-buff. White slip. Hollow. Torso and base rendered in same mold, probably head also. Back molded, rounded. Tooling on hair.

Similar in type to **C231**, with both knees resting on base, but slender proportions of torso and lightly modeled pectorals belong to a young boy rather than a baby. Right leg stretched to side; left foot hidden beneath right thigh. Left arm bent, does not support weight of figure; hand rests near front edge of base. Low base is long and narrow, concave in front, rounded in back. Mantle falls over left shoulder and arm in series of parallel, curved folds and is spread smoothly under legs. Long locks of hair on shoulders. Similar in type: MF-73-100 (lot 73-144, fabric 1, fragment of back, showing parallel folds continuing diagonally upward from back of right leg, presumably to shoulder). For possible head type, see **C243**.

See pp. 68, 69, 72, 73.

C243   Head, related to seated boys   Pl. 20

MF-69-352. Lot 6214. Preserved: head. P.H. 0.034 (size 2). Fabric 1, orange-buff. Solid. Back handmade, rounded. Added: pilos.

Face round to oval, with low forehead. Long hair, knotted at center of forehead. High, narrow pilos with thick, rolled rim. Possible head type of **C242**. Similar in type: MF-8667 in the Corinth collection (Weinberg 1948, p. 235, no. E22, pl. LXXXVI, with short hair).

See p. 69.

C244   Seated boy(?)   Pl. 20

MF-14091. Lot 4349. Preserved: left leg, part of front and side of base. P.L. 0.059 (size 2). Fabric 2, orange. Hollow. Tooling on folds.

Bent left leg lies flat on base and is completely wrapped in mantle. Base low, probably rectangular, with flat sides. Possible traces of left hand resting on base.

See p. 73.

C245   Seated boy   Pl. 20

MF-10620. Lot 896. Preserved: head and neck; front–left side of torso from shoulder to hip, left arm. Mended. P.H. 0.094 (size 3). Fabric 2, light orange; interior surface shows some small sparkling inclusions. White slip. Yellow paint on shoulder and arm. Hollow. Back of head handmade, rounded. Tooling on face.

Similar in type to **C246**, with head thrown back, but larger, of better quality. Drapery at lower break. Oval face. Eyes large, slightly downturned; browridge well defined. Nose short, straight, nostrils punched. Lips full, downturned. Ears large. Head bald, as if a baby, but face is adult. Similarly, arm is short as a child's, but biceps are too developed for a child. Good fabric and slip, but retouch is crude. Fragment of similar scale in lot 4350 shows left hand resting near left front corner of a well-made rectangular base. Complete type can be seen in Rhodian and Boeotian figurines (*British Museum* I, p. 93, no. 257, pl. 45 [Rhodian]; *Kabirenheiligtum* V, pp. 104, 173–174, no. 276, pl. 22 [Boeotian]); both show the right foot drawn back and a high, rectangular base similar to **C228**.

See pp. 68, 69.

C246   Head of seated boy   Pl. 20

MF-69-351.   Lot 6214.   Preserved: head to shoulders. Mended. P.H. 0.047 (size 2–3). Fabric 1, orange-buff to orange. Hollow; head solid. Back handmade, rounded.

Right shoulder higher than left, suggesting that pose of complete piece was similar to **C229** and **C230**, leaning to left side. Short, wide neck. Round, bald head tilted to right and thrown back. Features indistinct, but head seems more adult than childlike. Nose flattened.

See p. 68.

C247   Head, probably of seated boy   Pl. 20

MF-73-98. Lot 73-144. Preserved: head and neck. P.H. 0.044 (size 3). Fabric 2, orange-buff. Solid. Back handmade, rounded, deep; join visible well behind ears.

Similar in type to **C245** but slightly larger. Break at right side of neck suggests that head was tilted back and to right. Face oval. Eyes and ears similar to **C245**. Nose wide, close to upper lip. Mouth pursed. Face somewhat more childlike than **C245**, although still not convincing. Similar in type: MF-13415 (lot 2152).

See p. 69.

C248 Seated girl   Pl. 20

MF-11022. Lot 1953. Intact. H. 0.028 (size 1). Fabric 5, orange to orange-buff. Solid. All parts rendered in same mold. Back handmade, rounded, pared. Tooling on folds.

Young girl sits on low base, leaning to right side, propped on right hand, which supports weight of figure. Right leg folded under, but knee does not touch base. Left lower leg stretched to corner of base; hand rests on knee. Details of drapery very clear for such small scale. Chiton slips off right shoulder. Mantle over hips and legs, possibly also over left shoulder; between legs, fan of mantle folds and diagonal cascade of mantle end. Base round in back; front is flat, wedge shaped. Face round. Features indistinct, but face seems childlike. Lips smiling. Plait of hair probably drawn up from center of forehead.

See pp. 70, 72, 343.

C249 Seated boy   Pl. 20

MF-12907. Lot 4430. Preserved: shoulders to base; back chipped at bottom. P.H. 0.063 (size 2–3). Treated with preservative. White slip. Red paint on flesh. Solid; underside concave up to hips. Back handmade, rounded. Added: probably left forearm and hand. Tooling on dog, left hand.

Similar in pose to **C229** but freer; right lower leg stretched out further; arms not attached to torso. Boy holds small dog by tail, upside down, along his right lower leg. Dog is of Maltese type, with long hair, neck ruff, fluffy tail, and small, round ears; its head turns to front. Child's torso similar to **C229** but more slender and supple. Pectorals and fat pad at right armpit lightly modeled. Suggestion of torsion in pose. Low, rectangular base.

See pp. 72, 188.

C250 Seated boy   Pl. 20

MF-10655. Lot 897. Preserved: head, shoulders, part of left upper arm, part of upper back. P.H. 0.045 (size 2). Fabric 2, light orange. Hollow; head solid. Back handmade, flattened. Top of large, rectangular vent preserved, 0.015 wide.

Boy wears pilos and mantle. Little detail; wide folds over left shoulder barely distinguishable. Face oval to round. Similar, perhaps related mechanically: KT-23-12 from the Potters' Quarter (*Corinth* XV, ii, p. 137, no. 6, pl. 29); T.F.-60 from the Asklepieion (*Corinth* XIV, p. 140, no. 19, pl. 54). Complete type squats on round base, with both knees drawn up to chest. Head, perhaps from similar type: MF-13419 (lot 2249, with pilos).

See p. 73.

PROTOMES, THYMIATERIA, AND MASKS

C251 Female protome   Pl. 21

MF-11324. Lot 1999. Preserved: head and neck, right side; polos chipped. P.H. 0.091. Fabric 2, orange-buff. White slip. Hollow. Backless. Pierced for suspension near center of hair.

Head in high, wide polos with projecting lower rim, veil. Face oval, with low, triangular forehead. Eyes large, level, prominent, not detailed; browridge arched. Nose large, attached to upper lip; mouth smeared during molding. Scalloped waves, marked with vertical slashes, frame forehead. Finished edge at right side. Similar in type: mold from the Potters' Quarter, KH-26, although mechanical relationship is unclear (*Corinth* XV, i, pp. 97–98, no. 28, pl. 32, with additional examples; comparison was made with the plaster cast, which

seemed perhaps a generation larger, but plaster shrinks less than clay in drying).

See pp. 42, 73–74, 200, 342.

C252 Female protome   Pl. 21

MF-14097. Lot 2210. Preserved: right side and center of head, from polos to cheek. P.H. 0.078. Fabric 3, orange-buff to orange. White slip. Hollow. Backless. Top of polos pierced for suspension.

Similar in type to **C251**, but polos slightly more flaring, hair more loosely waved, browridge less sharply defined.

See pp. 42, 73–74.

C253 Female protome   Pl. 21

MF-11922. Lot 2152. Preserved: head. Missing upper right side, most of top of polos. P.H. 0.062. Fabric 1, orange-buff, with orange core. Hollow. Backless. Added: ear, top of polos. Tooling on nose, mouth.

Head in low, wide polos with projecting lower rim. Face similar to **C251**, but mouth is reworked, nose sharpened; forehead is higher; hair more loosely waved. Added ear is too high and is Archaic in style, apparently imitating ear at polos rim of such Archaic protomes as MF-11723 from the sanctuary (publication forthcoming).

See pp. 42, 73–74, 132.

C254 Female protome   Pl. 21

MF-1994-30. Lot 1994-68. Preserved: head and part of neck. Missing nose; forehead chipped. P.H. 0.059. Fabric 1, grayish buff, pinker at core. Hollow. Backless. Top of polos pierced for suspension.

Head in low, wide polos. Face oblong to oval, with low, triangular forehead. Eyes large, level, prominent, not detailed; browridge defined. Lips full, parted. Hair parted at center, divided into two rounded, smooth masses framing temples. Round earrings. Similar in type: KT-11-7 from the Potters' Quarter (*Corinth* XV, ii, p. 101, no. 18, pl. 19).

See pp. 42, 73–74.

C255 Female protome   Pl. 21

MF-13660. Lot 4352. Preserved: head and small part of neck. Missing veil. P.H. 0.048. Fabric 1, light orange. Hollow. Backless. Top of polos pierced for suspension.

Similar in type to **C254** but smaller, degenerate. Face narrow. Eyes large. Nose large, close to upper lip. Mouth small. Hair parted at center; waves not detailed. Top of polos slightly concave.

See pp. 42, 73–74.

C256 Female protome   Pl. 21

MF-11346. Lot 878. Preserved: left wrist and hand, part of chest. P.H. 0.068. Fabric 3, pinkish orange to buff. Hollow.

Chest fragment, showing upraised left hand with thumb and forefinger together, probably placed at outer side of left breast. Vertical fold of veil beside hand; fold of neckline of peplos above it. Probably from protome similar in type to **C251**.

See pp. 42, 73–74.

C257 Female protome   Pl. 21

MF-14059. Lot 4385. Preserved: right wrist and most of hand, right breast. P.H. 0.078. Fabric 3, pinkish buff to creamy buff. Hollow.

Chest fragment, showing upraised right hand with thumb and forefinger together, placed at inner side of right breast; drapery fold, perhaps of veil, at outer side of breast. Probably from protome similar in type to **C251**. Fragments of left hand of same scale and smaller right hand in lot 4385.

See pp. 42, 73–74.

C258   Female protome   Pl. 21

MF-13655. Lot 3230. Preserved: left shoulder. P.H. 0.069. Fabric 1, orange-buff. Hollow.

Shoulder fragment, with two rows of zigzag folds. Right edge thickened and tapered, probably finished.

See p. 74.

C259   Female protome   Pl. 21

MF-13564. Lot 3222. Preserved: right forearm and hand, part of chest and waist. P.H. 0.106. Fabric 2, orange-buff to light orange. Hollow.

Torso fragment, showing upraised right hand with thumb and forefinger together, placed over or near right breast. Elbow and waist wrapped in horizontal folds of mantle.

See pp. 74, 293.

C260   Female protome   Pl. 21

MF-69-404. Lot 6215. Preserved: left forearm and part of hand, part of chest, left hip. P.H. 0.077. Fabric 3, orange-buff, slightly burned. Hollow.

Upraised left forearm; looped opening of sleeve drops from forearm, near elbow. Horizontal, slightly curving, flat folds over upper arm and elbow; faint zigzag fold at left break, probably from peplos overfold (for arm position and drapery arrangement, cf. Winter, *Typen* I, p. 247, no. 6). Finished edge at left side.

See p. 74.

C261   Female bust, probably from a thymiaterion   Pl. 21

MF-11844. Lot 2111. Preserved: front and small part of back. Missing part of right side, finial. Mended; nose chipped. P.H. 0.117. Fabric 4, orange, core grayish at finial break. White slip. Red paint on hair. Hollow. Thin-walled. Back handmade, rounded. Added: finial. Marks of fine-toothed tool over surface.

Wide, spreading neck curves down to finished edge at top of chest. Face oval, with high, triangular forehead. Eyes prominent; lower lids slightly lifted; browridge rounded, slightly overhanging. Nose short, slightly upturned. Mouth narrow; lips full; upper lip well arched, overhangs lower lip slightly. Coiffure may have had a small topknot at the front, from which fine, parallel waves (rendered in mold) radiate downward, covering top of ear. Round break at top of head is probably from a floral finial.

See pp. 73, 75, 200.

C262   Female head, probably from a thymiaterion   Pl. 21

MF-10526. Lot 885. Preserved: head and neck. Missing nose, right eye, top of head, parts of left side and back. Mended; front chipped. P.H. 0.078. Fabric 4, orange-buff, with gray core. White slip. Hollow. Thin-walled. Back molded, rounded. Added: hair over ears, earrings. Tooling on hair, neck.

Rigid pose, large scale, and thin walls suggest head is from a thymiaterion similar to **C261**. Wide neck with one crease. Face oval to oblong, with high, ogival forehead. Eyes and eyebrows downturned; eyelids well defined, upper lid arched, lower lid nearly level. Lips full, parted, strongly arched. Hair waves down from central part to cover ears. Teardrop-shaped pellet earrings.

See pp. 73, 75.

C263   Female head, possibly from a thymiaterion   Pl. 21

MF-11104. Lot 1978. Preserved: face and small part of neck. Missing most of forehead, part of right eye and cheek. P.H. 0.048. Fabric 3, orange-buff, interior orange. Hollow. Thin-walled.

Face wide, with rounded cheeks; prominent chin. Eyes prominent, opened wide, slightly downturned; upper lid well defined and arched, lower lid nearly level and blurred. Nose short, broad at base, upturned, close to upper lip. Thin upper lip curves down at corners over lower lip.

See p. 75.

C264   Female head, possibly from a bust   Pl. 22

MF-13888. Lot 4349. Preserved: head and neck, with part of tenon. Missing top of head at right side, most of hair at nape, left earring. Mended. P.H. 0.093. Fabric 2, orange. White slip. Hollow, neck solid. Back handmade, rounded. Added: hair at front and nape, right ear, earring. Tooling on hair.

Face oval to triangular, with wide forehead; narrow jaw, with prominent chin. Eyes large, strongly downturned; both lids defined. Line of large, arched nose continues from sloping forehead; nose is close to upper lip. Mouth relatively narrow; lips full, prominent in profile. Locks of hair wave back from forehead; long locks of hair at nape. Pellet earrings. Face slightly flattened in front. Long, columnar neck. Rigid pose of head, large scale, and hollowness recall busts **C261** and **C262**.

See p. 75.

C265   Female protome   Pl. 22

MF-11925. Lot 2152. Preserved: head and small part of neck. Missing part of veil, part of right side of face, including most of eye. Mended. P.H. 0.127. Fabric 2, orange. Hollow. Backless. Added: headdress; flange in back, pierced for suspension.

Face oval, widening at low forehead. Eye similar to **C267**. Hair seems parted at center, with two curving masses framing forehead; behind, groove for fillet; cluster of curls above each ear. Veil (or mantle) curves forward over head; pierced, horizontal flange behind. MF-13942 (lot 2152) is a fragment of hair, flange, and veil, of similar type but much larger scale.

See pp. 75, 294.

C266   Female head, probably from a protome   Pl. 22

MF-11902. Lot 2107. Preserved: face, part of hair in front. Missing jaw. P.H. 0.072. Fairly coarse orange-buff fabric, with some medium-sized gray and red inclusions, voids. Hollow. Backless.

Rounded cheeks; high, triangular forehead. Eyes large, prominent, opened wide, downturned; both lids well defined. Nose and mouth similar to **C263**. Fabric is coarser than usual, but inclusions seem to be local.

See pp. 75, 294.

C267   Mask or protome   Pl. 22

MF-10474. Lot 878. Preserved: right eye, nose, most of forehead, stephane. Mended. P.H. 0.098. Fabric 2, light orange. White slip. Hollow. Backless. Added: stephane.

Tooling on hair and wreath. Stephane pierced with two holes for suspension.

Face is wide at temples, flattened; forehead is low, wide, triangular. Eye prominent, level, opened wide; upper lid well defined; browridge follows curve of eye. Nose short, straight. Locks of hair swept up from forehead, wrapped over tubular fillet; behind fillet, thin, stippled wreath, then high stephane.

See p. 76.

C268 Dionysos mask Pl. 22

MF-71-49. Lot 6723. Missing chin, part of wreath. P.H. 0.075. Fabric 1, greenish buff. Dark red-brown and black paint (without underlying white slip) splotched on cheeks, mouth, ears, hair; black on wreath; eyebrows and eyelashes lightly outlined. Hollow. Backless; projecting ledge behind forehead. Added: ear ornaments(?).

Face wide, with low, rounded forehead. Eyes level; both lids defined. Hair rolled back from forehead in thick locks, topped with wreath(?). Full beard; drooping moustache. Round ornaments(?) in front of ears.

See pp. 13, 76.

C269 Dionysos mask Pl. 23

MF-11776. Lot 2064. Missing left eye and cheek, part of headdress and beard. Mended. Nonjoining fragments of grape clusters (not photographed). P.H. 0.101. Treated with preservative. Fabric slightly coarse, with some small gray, dark red, and white inclusions. Hollow. Thin-walled. Backless. Added: end of nose, korymbos(?). Tooling on hair, beard.

Published: Bookidis and Fisher 1974, p. 291, pl. 59.

Face wide, short, with low forehead. Eye is level, narrowed; lids thick. Nose short, thin, pointed. Lips parted. Curly beard; drooping moustache. Headband across top of forehead, over which hair(?) seems to puff out at temple. Wreath with korymbos(?) at center, behind which is a low polos or stephane with thickened rim. Nonjoining grape-cluster fragments probably were attached to sides of headdress. Fabric is coarser than usual, but inclusions seem to be local.

See pp. 76–77, 291.

C270 Dionysos mask Pl. 23

MF-10475. Lot 878. Preserved: right eye and cheek, nose, mouth, upper part of beard. Mended. P.H. 0.071. Fabric 2, light orange. Hollow. Backless.

Eye downturned, opened wide, deeply set at inner corners. Lips full, parted. Bearded; drooping moustache.

See pp. 76, 77.

C271 Dionysos mask Pl. 23

MF-12130. Lot 4347. Complete. Mended; surface chipped. H. 0.062. Fabric 5, ochre to orange. Hollow. Backless. Added: top of headdress, edges of beard; three irregular but evenly spaced holes at center and left side of wreath may be for addition of fruit clusters or of other ornaments. Top of polos pierced with two holes for suspension.

Face long and narrow, with high, triangular forehead. Eyes downturned. Nose long, thin, close to upper lip. Lips full, slightly smiling. Hair parted at center; waves swept up from temples. Large, spade-shaped beard, lightly waved, merges with hair at sides of head; triangular lock of hair over chin; drooping moustache. All hair details rendered in mold. Lumpy

wreath; low, wide polos. Similar in type and scale: KT-24-12 from the Potters' Quarter (*Corinth* XV, ii, p. 101, no. 16, pl. 19).

See pp. 76, 293.

C272 Dionysos mask Pl. 23

MF-14120. Lot 4382. Nearly complete; beard chipped at right side. H. 0.068. Fabric 3, orange-buff. Hollow. Backless. Added: top of headdress. Front of polos pierced for suspension.

Similar in type and scale to **C271** but trimmed at sides to narrower shape; beard more pointed, not detailed; polos lower, narrower. Nose wide, flattened. Mouth wide. Dull impression.

See pp. 76, 293.

C273 Dionysos mask Pl. 22

MF-73-3. Not lotted; found on bedrock northeast of the Theater, south of Room G, grid S:26. Missing fragments of stephane, beard, moustache, left temple and cheek (these restored in plaster); right horn, part of left horn, most of leaves of wreath. P.H. 0.182. Treated with preservative; where untreated, the fabric seems to be fabric 1, orange-buff. White slip, also on inner surface. Purplish red paint on hair and beard, bright pink on flesh, possibly green or blue on horns. Hollow. Backless. Added: projecting parts of moustache, leaves, horns. Tooling on eyes, hair, moustache, beard.

Published: Bookidis and Fisher 1974, pp. 290–291, pl. 59.

Straight-sided face with low, triangular forehead. Features clustered near center of face. Eyes small, level, close together, deeply set at inner corners; both lids defined. Nose prominent, almost ski-jump shape. Mouth wide; lips full, downturned. Ears flattened forward. Frowning expression. Hair waves horizontally, probably from central part; possibly two small lobster-claw curls on forehead. Two outward-curving horns and wreath with overlapping leaves in front of stephane. Spade-shaped beard with wavy, vertical incisions; drooping moustache. Horizontal flange for suspension in back at level of wreath, originally must have been pierced. A fragmentary mask from the Southeast Building, MF-2904 (*Corinth* XII, p. 53, no. 358, pl. 32), has similarly arranged hair at the forehead and a wreath with overlapping leaves.

See pp. 77, 332, 338.

OTHER TYPES

C274 Piping satyr Pl. 23

MF-11858. Lot 2171. Missing feet and base. P.H. 0.074 (size 2). Fabric 1, buff. White slip. Red paint on face, hair, flute. Hollow. Back handmade, flattened.

Squatting, nude satyr with knees apart, playing double flute. Elbows propped on knees; each hand grasps one flute. Nose short, wide, flat. Bald head. Full beard; drooping moustache. Possibly mechanically related: one in lot 2211; MF-1034 and MF-1035 in the Corinth collection (*Corinth* XII, p. 38, nos. 194, 195, pl. 14); KT-22-4 from the Potters' Quarter (*Corinth* XV, ii, p. 143, no. 7, pl. 29, with applied polos) and KT-22-6; T.F.-16 from the Asklepieion (*Corinth* XIV, p. 140, no. 20, pl. 54); MF-9453 from the South Stoa. The modeling of these figurines is so dull and their preservation so fragmentary that mold comparisons are very difficult. My observations differ from the listing in *Kabirenheiligtum* V, p. 27, note 132, in which there is an error (*Corinth* XV, ii, p. 143, no. 7 is the same as KT-22-4, but this one piece is placed in two different generations) and also from the still different findings of Stillwell in *Corinth* XV, ii. I have therefore listed them only as possibly mechanically related; there were at least two generations. A small (size 1) and poor example in lot 890 may be a still later generation.

See pp. 78, 152, 199, 294.

C275 Satyr Pl. 23

MF-72-188. Lot 72-122. Preserved: head, upper chest, arms. Missing hands, end of beard. Mended. P.H. 0.043 (size 2). Treated with preservative. Solid. Head moldmade, body handmade.

Arms outstretched to sides. Heavy, arched eyebrows, the left higher than the right. Short, wide nose. Jutting beard; drooping moustache. Probably originally squatting, with legs and tail forming a tripod support. Similar heads: MF-12054 (lot 2250); MF-12160 (lot 4369), both fabric 1.

See pp. 78, 194, 199.

C276 Ithyphallic satyr Pl. 23

MF-11660. Lot 2009. Preserved: shoulders to hips. Missing arms. P.H. 0.033 (size 1). Fabric 1, light orange. Red paint on flesh. Solid. Handmade.

Nude torso; right shoulder pulled back; arms apparently raised. Spreading buttocks and angular left hip suggest that legs originally were parted and figure was a rider.

See pp. 78, 199.

C277 Seated Pan Pl. 23

MF-10502. Lot 880. Preserved: waist to base. P.H. 0.05 (size 1–2). Fabric 1, orange-buff, with orange core. White slip. Red paint on legs. Hollow. All parts rendered in same mold. Back handmade, flattened. Tooling on legs.

Perched atop high, flaring base. A few lumps below feet suggest rocks. Crossed goat's legs are slashed to indicate hair. Elbows rest on knees; forearms originally raised, perhaps playing pipes. Swollen abdomen. Dull impression.

See pp. 32, 78, 152, 200, 289, 291.

C278 Seated male figurine, probably a god Pl. 23

MF-12052. Lot 2250. Preserved: head to waist at right side, to chest at left. P.H. 0.088 (size 3). Fabric 1, buff. Red paint on pilos, lips; dark brown on drapery. Solid. Back handmade, flat. Added: unclear object at lower break.

Bearded figure on a seat with squared, horizontal projections in back (cf. **C78**). Mantle (or exomis?) draped diagonally over left shoulder. Shoulders narrow, distorted; left shoulder, with adjacent chair projection, is lower than the right. Face narrow. Eyes large, level. Nose wide, flattened. Mouth wide. Wears pilos with flat brim. Unclear object at lower break. See also **C279** and **C280**.

See pp. 79, 330, 332.

C279 Bearded head in pilos Pl. 23

MF-10482. Lot 878. Preserved: Head and neck. Missing nose. P.H. 0.03 (size 2). Fabric 2, orange. White slip. Solid. Back handmade, rounded. Added: pilos.

Similar in type to **C278** but smaller; pilos worn further back on head, showing forehead hair.

See p. 79.

C280 Bearded head (in pilos?) Pl. 23

MF-71-26. No context. Preserved: head and neck, with tenon. Missing nose, bottom of locks of hair. Mended. P.H. 0.078 (size 4–5). Fabric 1, yellowish buff, darker (2.5Y 7/4). Black paint on hair and beard (without underlying white slip). Solid. Back handmade, rounded. Added: hair and beard, tooled with rough strokes for locks of hair, as in **C208**.

Face oval to oblong, with low, rounded forehead. Eyes level; browridge clearly defined, following curve of eye. Mouth narrow; lower lip full. Beard pointed, projecting; drooping moustache. Long locks of hair at sides and back. Cranium unfinished, rough circular area probably originally covered by headdress, perhaps a pilos, as in **C278** and **C279**.

See pp. 13, 79.

C281 Asiatic dancer (Attis?) Pl. 23

MF-11772. Lot 2046. Missing right upper arm, left hand, face. P.H. 0.084 (size 1–2). Fabric 3, slightly coarser, orange to buff. White slip. Blue paint on left leg. Hollow from waist down. Probably all parts rendered in same mold. Back handmade, top flattened, bottom spreading. Added: flaring skirt hem.

Oklasma dancer (male or female?) kneels on right knee. Arms over head; left elbow rests on left knee. Short, belted, V-necked chiton; flaring hem shows motion. Paint on leg suggests trousers. Lappet of cap on left upper arm. Base fairly high, rectangular in front, with splaying sides, back rounded. Dull impression.

See pp. 32, 80, 192, 291, 298.

C282 Draped female figurine, probably a dancer Pl. 23

MF-10396. Lot 877. Preserved: head to hips. Missing nose. Mended. P.H. 0.113 (size 3). Fabric similar to 2 but slightly harder, with thinner walls, greenish buff. White slip. Hollow; solid at right hand. All parts rendered in same mold. Back handmade, rounded; part of rectangular vent ca. 0.035 wide.

Published: Stroud 1965, p. 18, pl. 8:d.

Left leg probably advanced. Left hand on hip, elbow slightly pulled back. Right arm at side, attached to hip with panel; hand seems poised to hold a drapery fold but is empty. Chiton falls off right shoulder; flat belt visible at center of waist, with puffed folds dipping at either side. Mantle covers left arm and is wrapped around hips in bunched folds, seemingly gathered up by hidden left hand. Mantle disappears behind right arm, then is draped over head. The end falls in a triangular fold beside the left breast. Although the legs are not preserved, the sense of motion in the chiton folds and the slight forward movement of the left hip suggest that the figure dances forward. Head tilted slightly to the left and forward. Expressive face is oval to round, with triangular forehead. Eyes large, widely set, downturned at outer corners; lids thickened, almost closed. Nose wide, close to upper lip. Mouth wide; lips thick, upper lip has pronounced arch. Hair is parted at center and combed down from cranium into two wavy masses; fine, wavy locks of hair fall to shoulders; all details of hair rendered in mold. Probable mold sibling of head: MF-11016 (lot 1953, fabric 1). Possible later generation of head: **H271**; KT-10-51 from the Potters' Quarter (*Corinth*, XV, ii, p. 130, no. 35, pl. 25; another from Pitsa mentioned there; these heads have different torso types, representing Aphrodite or Leda). Well-made piece.

See pp. 80–81, 120, 147, 167, 168, 296, 343.

III

EARLY HELLENISTIC FIGURINES
AND THEIR SURVIVALS

The discussion of Corinthian Classical figurines revealed that some Classical types survived at least into the 320s B.C., when the Potters' Quarter was destroyed, and a few lingered on even into the early 3rd century B.C. In addition, it will be seen that some new creations of the 4th century B.C. retained a strong 5th-century flavor. By the second quarter of the 4th century B.C., however, figurine types with different sources of inspiration began to appear, linked to Classical types in votive function but created in a different spirit and style. One should perhaps say "styles," since more than one new way of designing figurines emerged, and the creativity continued unabated into the third quarter of the 4th century B.C. The stimuli must have been much the same for Corinthian as for Athenian model makers and coroplasts, that is, the development of new types and styles in 4th-century plastic arts in general and a growing interest during this period in small sculpture for the home, for ritual if not purely decorative purposes.[1] The material prosperity documented for the Greek cities in the middle of the 4th century B.C. must have encouraged the production of attractive votive offerings as well.[2] The coroplasts' solutions in the two centers were quite different from one another, however, conditioned as they were by earlier local experience and interests.

Early Hellenistic coroplastic art is sometimes equated with the so-called Tanagra figurines, which were abundantly produced in Attica and Boeotia and were widely copied elsewhere. Recent research, however, has made it clear that "Tanagras" represent only a part of the history of Hellenistic figurines;[3] in Corinth, an interest in "Tanagra" types was certainly subsidiary to others of more local significance. Although a few imported Athenian and Boeotian "Tanagras" have been found in Corinth (e.g., **I24** and **I48**), there is no evidence for a series of local copies or adaptations of such "Tanagra" types, like those found at Morgantina, for example.[4] Moreover, when similarities can be traced between Corinthian figurines and "Tanagras," they often involve only one aspect of type or style and are probably better attributed to common source material than direct influence. For example, a certain rounding of outlines, a demure quality, and a sweetness of expression reminiscent of early "Tanagra" figurines can be found in some Corinthian figurines, especially in representations of young women (e.g., **H1**), although in pose and drapery arrangement they are not characteristically "Tanagraean." These qualities are in line with the soft, subtle "Praxitelean" sculptural style, which was widely influential in the arts of the time.

When recognizable elements of "Tanagraean" pose and drapery arrangement are employed, as in some of the standing mantled women, a more characteristically Corinthian manner of design is evident, stressing greater plastic volume and broader effects, with less emphasis on delicacy of detail. The entrenched local tradition of broadly styled handmade figurines, which began

---

[1] On the importance in Athens of 4th-century B.C. metal statuettes and stone sculpture for the development of "Tanagra" figurines, see D. B. Thompson 1966, pp. 54–55. On the increased demand for sculpture for the home, see *Gods Delight*, p. 10; Barr-Sharrar 1988, p. 65; on the ritual use of figurines in the home, see Harward 1982, pp. 51–56; *Coroplast's Art*, p. 43.

[2] The principal literary source for this prosperity is Demosthenes 9.40 (Third Philippic, 341 B.C.); also Xenophon,

Constitution of the Spartans 14.3; Plutarch, *Lycurgus* 30.1. On the increase in the production of votive reliefs in the third quarter of the 4th century B.C., see Edwards 1986a, pp. 262–264. See *Morgantina*, p. 23, on the connection between economic conditions and coroplastic activity in Sicily.

[3] See the survey of various coroplastic centers in *Coroplast's Art*.

[4] *Morgantina*, pp. 51–64.

in the Archaic period and never was abandoned entirely, may have been the source of this stylistic tendency. The Corinthian expertise in working clay in sculptural scale, an activity that continued into the Hellenistic period, may also have been a factor in the ability and willingness to design in clay, in a smaller scale, with freedom and panache. Hence, when developing or selecting new types for production, Corinthian workshops often leaned toward drapery arrangements that emphasized plastic form and overall design rather than subtle detail. The play of antithetical tension folds over the surfaces of many "Tanagra" figurines seems to have been foreign to their taste. At times, the Corinthian Hellenistic artisans inclined toward the design solutions of sculptors to such a degree that it is hard to find parallels for their work among the figurines from other places. At the same time, only one actual small-scale copy of a known sculptural type has been identified at Corinth, a copy of Myron's satyr from a 4th-century B.C. context.[5] The local workshops, therefore, do not seem to have habitually imitated well-known sculptural types, as did their counterparts in Myrina and Smyrna (see p. 297). This link with sculptural design without direct dependence upon known sculptural types suggests that the larger and better Corinthian Hellenistic figurines may have had sources in clay models prepared locally for makers of bronze statuettes or perhaps studies for stone sculpture (see pp. 14, 343).[6] Such models could have been obtained by coroplasts for use as archetypes for figurine production.

In determining the chronology of Corinthian Hellenistic figurines, the conventional use of the death of Alexander the Great in 323 B.C. for the beginning of the Hellenistic period is not helpful. The cessation of work in the Potters' Quarter in or near the 320s B.C. merely brought to an end an already outdated production, while new ideas had come into being earlier, in other Corinthian workshops. Dramatic drapery arrangements, the increased representation of female nudity (apart from articulated "dolls"), the successful depiction of people of different ages, the interest in character and atmosphere, and other commonplaces of Hellenistic coroplastic art are part of the branching away from the Classical tradition that began some time in the second quarter of the 4th century B.C. If the beginning of a Hellenistic spirit in Corinthian coroplastic art is to be dated, it happened before the middle of the 4th century B.C. Significantly, the dividing point between Classical and Hellenistic for the forthcoming publication of figurines from the Athenian Agora, which can be dated on objective grounds more closely than the Demeter sanctuary figurines, has been set at ca. 380 B.C.[7]

Although there are no signs of radical typological or stylistic change in the 320s B.C., some economic difficulty may have been experienced in the coroplastic industry in the later 4th and early 3rd centuries B.C. and more serious difficulty in the middle or third quarter of the 3rd century. The seismic activity of the later 4th century B.C. (see p. 7, note 20) could have disrupted other establishments in Corinth besides those of the Potters' Quarter. In some cases, mechanically related figurines are found in both the poorest fabric 5 and the better fabric 1 (e.g., see catalogue under **H1**), as if quality varied from one batch of figurines to another because of decreasing control in the workshop. Perhaps the availability or cost of fuel for firing was a factor. Whether the friability of fabric 5 is due to the use of clay of lesser quality or to poor firing, a reduction in workshop standards must be involved. Apart from the potentially damaging effects of earthquakes on workshop structures and personnel, we do not know what may have been the economic effects of the stationing of a Macedonian garrison on Acrocorinth after 338 B.C. or if any access was lost to the accustomed raw materials, either clay or fuel. Still, some good work was done during the earlier part of the 3rd century B.C., new types were introduced, and a real decline in the quantity and quality of production does not seem to have occurred until the middle or third quarter of the 3rd century B.C.

[5] Mattusch 1996, pp. 195–196, fig. 6:1a, b.
[6] *Coroplast's Art*, p. 58.
[7] I owe this information to Dorothy B. Thompson.

STANDING DRAPED FEMALE FIGURINES:
YOUNG VOTARIES AND RELATED FIGURINES
(H1–H47)

In this section are discussed representations of young women bearing votive offerings and figurines related to them in type and style. Most of the figurines discussed here carry piglets, torches, flowers, balls, or birds; others are without votive gifts. The costume is usually the peplos, but the chiton with a diagonal mantle is found as well. The youngest girls usually wear the chiton alone. A discussion of hydriaphoroi, who are also votaries from the point of view of function, follows this section.

PIGLET CARRIERS

The first of the Early Hellenistic groups to be discussed consists of female votary figurines, which usually wear the peplos and carry a piglet. While they are not the earliest of the new Early Hellenistic types, they will be considered first because they continue the cultic function of Classical votary figurines in a new style and spirit. Two of the elements separating them from their Classical counterparts are a clearer distinction of age through greater anatomical naturalism and manipulation of pose, as well as a stronger impression that these figurines must represent mortals rather than deities. One can see at a glance that **H1** is in the first bloom of womanhood. The figurine projects the ripe, yet innocent quality of a girl in her middle to late teens, with high, full breasts suggesting physical maturity, but also with a demurely bent head, downcast gaze, sweet facial expression, and girlishly lifted overfold. This gesture of grasping the overfold hem is often associated with youth. It is seen in sculptures of children;[8] in a Corinthian figurine in New York, it is reduced to a rolling of the fingers around the overfold hem, suggesting nervous shyness.[9] The gesture also could be a deliberate archaism, referring to the pulling aside of the skirt often found in Archaic sculptured female figures,[10] in Archaic and Classical mirror caryatids,[11] and in lingering Archaic terracotta figurines (e.g., MF-13626).[12] It also functions as a compositional device, breaking the downward flow of drapery lines.[13] In Greek vase painting, a downcast gaze and a closed compositon, with the arms down at the sides, typically convey the modesty of a respectable woman;[14] these features probably should be understood in the same way when found in figurines.

The young woman's hair streams over her shoulders, in the manner documented in the worship of Demeter elsewhere in the Greek world.[15] The manner of dressing the hair is a powerful symbol, the meaning of which varies among different cultures. It can express one's individual personality, stage of life, place in society, and connection with or dissociation from the prevailing culture; it can have erotic associations or signify mourning; the hair itself can have magical properties.[16] The knotted coiffure of boys and young men has already been mentioned (pp. 62–63), but the rarity of representations in the sanctuary suggests that it was not related to the local cult. The unbound, flowing hair of young women, however, is so prevalent in Early Hellenistic votary figurines that it is fair to give this coiffure some ritual significance, although several overlapping meanings are possible. In the context of the Demeter sanctuary, flowing

[8] Vorster 1983, e.g., p. 335, no. 11, pl. 1:1; p. 339, no. 24, pl. 12:1. Both sculptures are dated 330–320 B.C.

[9] The Metropolitan Museum, inv. no. 07.286.21: *Coroplast's Art*, p. 125, no. 18.

[10] Richter 1968, p. 10; e.g., among many, Akropolis Museum, inv. no. 680, pp. 78–79, no. 122, fig. 393.

[11] E.g., Keene Congdon 1981, p. 138, no. 16, pl. 11 (Athens, National Archaeological Museum, inv. no. 11691, Archaic, reported to be from a Corinthian grave).

[12] Publication forthcoming.

[13] As in a statuette of Persephone of the first half of the 3rd century: *Morgantina*, p. 133, no. 60, pl. 15.

[14] Reeder et al. 1995, pp. 124–125.

[15] Kallimachos, *Hymn to Demeter*, line 5; Hopkinson 1984, pp. 39–41, 82–84.

[16] On the symbolism of hair in general, see Leach 1958; Firth 1973, pp. 262–298; Obeyeskere 1981, esp. pp. 13–21; Derrett 1973; Hershman 1974. On the interpretation of Medusa's hair as a symbol of maternal sexuality, see Freud 1959; Slater 1968, pp. 16–18.

hair may have suggested to the worshiper abundant growth, hence the promise of fertility. Girls approaching sexual maturity also loosened their hair in rituals at Brauron.[17] The cutting of long hair sometimes is thought to symbolize the imposition of social control[18] or at least the progression from one social stage to another.[19] Hence the long hair of the figurines might refer to the cutting and offering of the hair before marriage, as a sign of the institutionalizing of sexual instincts. The hair of married women was normally bound up in a variety of bands or cloths.[20] It also has been suggested that the offering of a bride's hair symbolized the death of her previous existence,[21] paralleling the loosening of the hair during mourning and the offering of shorn locks at tombs. For the worship of Demeter, an association with burial customs certainly is appropriate, bringing into play her mourning for the lost Kore and the latter's position as the bride of Hades.

In **H1**, the locks of hair flow over the shoulders much more freely than in such figurines of Classical type as **C17**. The transition from the small head to the narrow shoulders is smoothed by the long hair, and the head thus forms the apex of a narrow pyramid. The overfold sweeps gently into the spreading skirt with scarcely any interruption in outline. Thus, although there is some movement in the tilted head, the hand lifting the overfold, and the bent right leg, the overall impression is essentially static. Even the piglet hangs down heavily. The languid pose is emphasized by the reversed **S**-shaped curve of the figure in profile, with the head and abdomen forward. The atmosphere is muted, conveying something of the sealed, almost enforced serenity of many "Tanagra" figurines, without showing any elements of their drapery, coiffures, or attributes. The entire group of Early Hellenistic young female votaries from the sanctuary shares this quiescence, both girls just reaching maturity (e.g., **H10**) and those somewhat older. One should probably see in these figurines a naturalistic rendering of the shyness and introversion of adolescent girls and young women, who had little contact with the outside world, as well as a cultural statement of the approved demeanor for unmarried females in general.

H1 conveys an image of a person at a particular stage of life and frame of mind; this information gives a specific context to the piglet and defines its meaning. The figurine suggests not simply a woman bringing an offering to a deity but a young, nubile woman asking for a productive marriage through the gift of a piglet, an offering commonly dedicated to Demeter as a symbol of fertility.[22] The term piglet (χοῖρος) also had sexual connotations in colloquial speech. It was employed in Attic comedy to denote the genitalia of immature girls or the depilated parts of mature women.[23] The *Souda* (s.v.) assigns this usage especially to Corinth but seems to be influenced by knowledge of the hetairai of the Aphrodite cult on Acrocorinth. According to Varro (*Res Rustica* 2.4.9–10), Italian and Greek women used the term in the same way as a symbol of marriage; the passage implies that the pig sacrifice stems from this usage. Regardless of the reliability of the *Souda*, the usage is likely to have been widespread, since it was known in both Athens and Italy. The frequent equation of women with pigs in Greek literature has led to the suggestion that the pig should be interpreted more fully as representing the simultaneously beneficial and dangerous sexuality of women, particularly the young.[24] It is therefore legitimate to see another level of meaning, implicitly sexual, in the offering of a piglet by a young woman. If the figurines carrying piglets do indeed represent brides, they set the age of marriage for females

---

[17] Sourvinou-Inwood 1988, pp. 70–71, note 17, on contexts in which the hair was loosened.

[18] Hallpike 1969.

[19] Firth 1973, p. 298. See also pp. 62–63.

[20] On coiffures in Greek art representing status, see Harrison 1988.

[21] R. Garland 1990, p. 219; Redfield 1982, pp. 190–191. On the perception of the transition to womanhood as a death,

see Dowden 1989. On literary and iconographic connections between marriage and death, see Redfield 1982, pp. 188–191; Oakley and Sinos 1993, p. 6, bibliography on p. 131, note 8; Barringer 1991; Rehm 1994.

[22] On the pig, see pp. 265–266; on Demeter as a patroness of marriage, see p. 329.

[23] Golden 1988; Henderson 1991, pp. 131–132.

[24] Golden 1988, pp. 3–10, with bibliography.

in Corinth in the middle to late teens.[25] They also suggest that Corinthian brides may have celebrated a prenuptial ritual like the *proteleia,* known elsewhere in Greece, in which the bride's hair was shorn and dedicated to one or another deity.[26] Perhaps the presence of these figurines at the Demeter sanctuary indicates that such a ritual took place there.

It has been suggested that Sicilian figurines carrying piglets held them head downward to represent women about to hurl the piglets alive into a pit, as at the Athenian Thesmophoria.[27] The lack of a suitable pit at the Acrocorinth sanctuary, however, and the carrying of the piglet horizontally or diagonally across the torso by some of the figurines, will not allow this interpretation in the present instance. Further, the participants in the Thesmophoria rituals appear to have been already married and presumably older women. Pit B in Room 3 of the Trapezoidal Building was fire scarred and full of ash. Although it contained pig bones, its small size and the presence of other, nonsacrificial debris in it make its use as a sacrificial receptacle for live piglets somewhat doubtful.[28] The frequent offering of piglets is documented, in any case, by the numerous bones of young pigs found in the fill associated with the Rock-cut Platform on the Middle Terrace in Area D. Presumably the dedication occurred in this area, which appears to have been in ritual use until ca. 300 B.C.[29] Another documented offering dedicated by brides, the girdle,[30] might be suggested by the unbound peplos of some of the votary figurines (e.g., **H1**), although others are belted (e.g., **H7**).

Another noteworthy quality of **H1** is its distinctive facial profile, with a sloping forehead, arched nose, and receding chin (Pl. 24), which recalls the profiles of Archaic figurine heads and vase protomes (e.g., MF-12016).[31] It is conceivable that a cast was taken from an old mold and reworked before firing to produce a new archetype with updated features but retaining something of the old structure; the unusual depth of the cranium and nape, which is characteristic of some Archaic vase protomes, might be explained in this way.[32] Other Early Hellenistic figurine heads, belonging to different types, show a similar facial profile, although they are normal in depth: for example, the mantled figurine **H102** and a male figurine from the Potters' Quarter.[33]

The small group **H1**–**H4** and the fragments related to it represent three generations of at least two closely related mold series, using at least two different head molds. Although the members of this group are closely similar in both type and stylistic detail, technical differences in retouch and venting suggest that more than one workshop may have been involved in the production. A likely workshop mate for **H1** can be found in a completely different category of figurine, in the nude youth **H299**, which shares its distinctive profile and the unusual depth of the head, as well as the pose of the right arm. While it seems to have been common enough practice to transform a male head to a female by altering the coiffure, and attach it to a female torso (see p. 159), in the present instance the rendering in both **H1** and **H299** of the head and torso in one mold indicates that the transformation occurred when the archetypes were prepared, and they are part of the same iconographic series.[34] Another figurine (**H9**) can be added to this workshop group (Workshop H, p. 346) through an error made in the molding of **H1**; the coroplast apparently was missing the correct back mold and substituted instead a mold very similar to the back of **H9**; since this type is belted, the mold was entirely inappropriate. The level of skill of the coroplasts in this workshop does not seem to match that

[25] On the literary evidence for age at marriage, see R. Garland 1990, pp. 210–213, with bibliography, to which add Greenwalt 1988.

[26] Pollux, *Onomastikon* 3.38; Burkert 1983, pp. 62–63, note 20, with bibliography.

[27] Detienne 1989, p. 134. Further on pig sacrifice, see pp. 265–266.

[28] *Corinth* XVIII, iii, pp. 243–244.

[29] *Corinth* XVIII, iii, pp. 153–154.

[30] Schmitt 1977, pp. 1063–1064.

[31] Publication forthcoming.

[32] Cf., e.g., the profile of an Archaic vase protome in Wallenstein 1971, p. 130, no. V/A3, pl. 13:3 (note depth of crown); the figurine head in *Corinth* XV, ii, pp. 73–75, no. 37, pl. 12 (KT-3-28, less deep).

[33] KT-23-9, *Corinth* XV, ii, p. 140, no. 10, pl. 27.

[34] For the meaning of this term, see pp. 14, 343.

of the creators of the archetypes, which were very well composed and have considerable charm. Apart from the error in **H1**, **H9** is marred by a distortion in the face that occurred during molding, and **H299** has very little retouch. This discrepancy speaks for the production of archetypes as a distinct craft, not necessarily in workshops producing figurines.

The stylistic date of **H1** would be the last quarter of the 4th century. It was found in the construction fill of the Trapezoidal Building, which terminates at the beginning of the 3rd century B.C. Survivals of this and the related types discussed below lasted well into the 3rd century B.C. The group may have come into production when the derivatives of Classical votary types produced in the Potters' Quarter were no longer available. The composition of the peplos, with its lifted overfold hem, recalls a Roman marble statuette in the Vatican thought to copy an original by Euphranor dated ca. 335–325 B.C.[35] Since the torso type of **H1–H4** also is known in another statuette, a bronze in Paris, with attributes of a Muse,[36] it is possible that Corinthian coroplasts were stimulated to develop new molds for votary figurines in connection with new archetypes created by a skilled model maker. A connection with bronze is suggested by the fact that this group is detailed fully in the round, with molded backs, a technique thought to show dependence on metal.[37] While this interpretation is well taken, it is not clear how one could distinguish a well-made figurine descending from a good archetype from which both front and back molds were taken, from one mechanically copied from a metal statuette. Fine "metallic" details are a help,[38] and figures in precious metal would have been delicately detailed, but bronze statuettes do not necessarily share this characteristic and, on the contrary, are often fairly crude. Further, a coroplast could have used a mold taken from the front of a metal figure and added a handmade back, or he could have taken a mold from a metal relief, for which a back would have had to be improvised (see **C282**).

In addition to the catalogued figurines, more than two hundred examples of young female votaries of this and related types were counted in the lots,[39] making them the major new introduction of the Early Hellenistic period. Otherwise votaries carrying piglets are known in Corinth only in the Early Classical **C1** and the degenerate Classical **C47**, although figurines of pigs alone also were dedicated (e.g., the Classical **V1**). Perhaps the continuous production of piglet carriers in Sicily during the Classical period and well into Hellenistic times stimulated a revival of the subject in a new style in Corinth, at a time coeval with Timoleon's period of activity in Sicily.[40] The expedition to Sicily was undertaken with the protection of Demeter and Kore (Diodoros 16.66.3–4; Plutarch, *Timoleon* 8.1), and it is possible that this patronage led to visits to shrines where the use of such votives was observed. Figurines of votaries carrying piglets also were popular in Argos in the Classical period and were exported to Corinth (see pp. 286–287). It is perhaps significant that the Argive workshops appear to have been turning out these votary figurines only in degenerate form, if at all, by the time the Corinthian workshops began their own production, perhaps to compensate for the loss of the Argive product.

[35] Todisco 1993, pl. 216; Palagia 1980, pp. 23–25, fig. 35 (the Uffizi "Hygieia" type). A Hellenistic marble head (S-1820) and a piglet (S-1825) in the Corinth collection are thought to be remnants of a type similar to the figurines, although in the sculpture the head wears a scarf (Sturgeon 1998). A fragment of terracotta sculpture from the sanctuary (SF-65-22) shows a hand holding the hind leg of a piglet, but its date and the sculptural type to which it belonged are still uncertain (publication forthcoming by Nancy Bookidis).

[36] Babelon and Blanchet 1895, p. 56, no. 122. The head of this statuette recalls that of a figurine in Paris (*Louvre* I, p. 119, no. C228, pl. LXXXVI), which is probably Corinthian (see p. 27). For a good photograph of the bronze statuette, showing the similarity of the fold pattern with that of **H1**, see

Babelon 1929, pp. 25–26, no. 13, pl. XII. This bronze has been connected with the "Nemesis" type with lifted overfold: Linfert-Reich 1971, pp. 105–116.

[37] D. B. Thompson 1966, pp. 54–55.

[38] E. R. Williams 1976, p. 43, no. 5.

[39] This number is approximate, since small fragments can be confused with the Middle Hellenistic piglet carriers (e.g., **H395**), which may represent priestesses. Further, some fragments do not preserve the piglet and have been identified with this group on the basis of similarity of head type and drapery.

[40] The Sicilian material is collected in Sguaitamatti 1984. On Timoleon's impact on the worship of Demeter and Kore in Sicily, see Hinz 1998, pp. 229–232.

Some comment regarding the dress of these votaries may be in order, since "Tanagra" figurines, which are thought to reflect the fashion in dress current in the Early Hellenistic period, wear not the peplos but the chiton and mantle.[41] Although there is no evidence for a code of cultic dress regulations at the Acrocorinth sanctuary,[42] the young women may be wearing the peplos as a ritual dress, suitable for the occasion of offering a votive gift, especially one in connection with the traditional business of marriage. Regional, social, or economic considerations, however, probably also influenced the choice of dress. The "Tanagras" probably reflect the fashion of Athens, where they are believed to have originated. The simple peplos could have remained the standard garment elsewhere or perhaps was the dress of ordinary women, the less well-to-do, and servants, contrasting with the more sophisticated attire of the wealthy.[43]

The fragmentary **H5** records a variant in which the overfold hem is not lifted, and the base is different from that of **H1**, being low, rectangular in front, and rounded in back. The clean finish of the hem of the fragment **H6** suggests that it could have been attached to yet another type of base, a flat plaque like **V39**. Related in spirit to **H1–H4**, but different in composition, are **H7–H9**. A technical connection has been established between the two groups through the back molds of **H1** and **H9** (see p. 119). The faces of these two figurines also may be technically related, although distorted in molding in the latter. Also comparable in these two groups are the youthful, demure look, the essentially frontal pose eased by the slight forward movement of the abdomen, and the tilted head. In both, the loose stream of locks of hair over the shoulders contributes to a gradual, pyramidal transition from the small head to narrow shoulders and then to a gently spreading skirt. In both groups, the figures seem to have been set into, rather than on, the round or oval molded bases. In both groups, one also finds a similar compositional device, the breaking of the figure's verticality with a diagonal form, either the line of the lifted overfold hem, as in **H1**, or the arms cradling the piglet, as in **H9**.

The peplos or chiton continues to have a long overfold, but in **H9** it is girded just below the breasts; the curving belt accentuates the forward movement of the abdomen, contributing to the languid look of the pose. The piglet is carried across the torso rather than at the side, its head cradled in the crook of the left arm, the left hand supporting its chest, and the right grasping its left rear leg. The overall proportions of **H9** are more slender, although the pyramidal outline of the figure remains constant in both groups.

H7 and **H8** follow **H9** in composition but use a different head type, more like that of **H2**, although not mechanically related. The sloping profile characteristic of **H1** is absent, the cheeks and jaw are very full, and the forehead is ogival in shape, but in spite of the formal differences, a similar spirit can be discerned in the small mouth, very slightly and sweetly smiling, and in the overall impression of gentle girlishness. The garments worn by these two figurines have short sleeves and technically should be called chitons, but the cloth does not seem to be thinner than a peplos, and the manner of girding is the same as in **H9**; perhaps they wear a chiton beneath the peplos. The one feature of dress that is distinctive here is the long-tailed knot on the belt, also known in better Corinthian renderings (**H144** and **H145**).

H10 shows many of the same qualities of composition and demeanor, but is more rigidly frontal and has a flatter chest and less suggestion of blooming womanhood than **H1**. This version of the votary with piglet seems to have been constructed on a torso type used also for representations of very young girls without offerings, such as **H45**, but utilizes a facial type close to **H8**. The rather childish, slender proportions make the figurine more columnar than pyramidal, but the similarities are sufficient to link it closely to the foregoing votaries.

---

[41] On the basis of sculptural evidence, the peplos is thought to have been old-fashioned by the Hellenistic period: Ridgway 1984, p. 56.

[42] On such codes, see Mills 1984.

[43] The peplos can sometimes be found on 4th-century B.C. red-figured vases in scenes of everyday life. An analysis of who wears it and in what contexts might be instructive.

The piglet carriers discussed above were the most popular types in the sanctuary during the Early Hellenistic period. Their archetypes must have been created at about the same time. Although there is not enough evidence to assign them all to the same workshop, their makers must have shared materials or at least were familiar with one another's work. There are also more degenerate versions, whose pedigrees are difficult to determine, but they are clearly in some way dependent upon the popular types. **H11** may be a degenerate version of **H9**, with an oversized head that spoils the original composition. **H12** and **H13** taken together constitute a very poor version, with an unusually large piglet held horizontally across the chest, and a thick overfold hem with a crudely retouched kolpos. All the preserved examples of this type are equally crude, suggesting either that it was improvised by a poor workshop or that it was the degenerate end of a better mold series, the better, earlier generations of which are missing from the archaeological record. **H14** is a smaller example of this crude type, but it is not demonstrably from the same mold series. The sloping profile of its head links it to **H1**; since it is only marginally smaller than this better piece, it cannot be a later generation but probably was made by a craftsman of limited skill, using a related head mold. The rather poor fragment **H15** holds a large, horizontal piglet over a high-girded chiton; it may have been developed from a torso type similar to **H37**. The poorer workshops appear to have had access to some of the same materials as the better ones, or they copied as best they could. It is even possible that some of the poorest examples of popular types were homemade improvisations based upon commercially available types.

In addition, there are several distinctive larger votary figurines (**H16**, **H17**, **H19**, and **H20**) that bear some relation to the popular types representing votaries with piglets, although the differences seem great enough to preclude the idea that they are mechanically related earlier generations. Of very good quality, they seem to represent a level of creativity akin to some of the larger and better figurines of the Classical period. That is, they are explorations of the variants possible within a limited overall design, out of which more popular types sometimes developed. **H16**, which wears the peplos over a chiton, is related to a quietly standing 3rd-century B.C. female figurine type with both arms at the sides, of which there is a complete example in New York.[44] **H37** may be a considerably later generation of the New York figurine, which is of the same scale as **H16** and shows a similar pose of the right arm and drapery pattern on the overfold. The head type is different,[45] but in both cases the head is larger in proportion to the torso than in **H1**, resulting in a less pyramidal composition. Both seem to have been developed from the same or related archetypes, **H16** being adapted for use as a votary with piglet by altering the position of the left arm and adding long, streaming locks of hair bound with a fillet. Perhaps both **H16** and the New York figurine were ultimately derived from a type related to a mold found in Corinth in the South Stoa (Pl. 77), which shows a long-haired girl in a chiton and peplos, pyramidally composed, with both arms at her sides.[46] The head type of **H16** is different from the other piglet carriers, having a more mature, alert face, generally similar to the isolated heads **H186** and **H187**. These heads, however, have a different coiffure and wear the stephane; they therefore probably did not belong to votary figurines. **H16** recalls in proportions and structure a monumental sculpture, the Apollo Patroos, which dates ca. 330 B.C.; the general resemblance is easiest to see in small-scale copies, such as a marble statuette from the Athenian Agora.[47] The figurine, however, probably was made in the 3rd century B.C., even if derived from a late-4th-century B.C. composition.

[44] The Metropolitan Museum, inv. no. 07.286.21: *Coroplast's Art*, p. 125, no. 18.

[45] The head of the New York figurine is similar in type to **C136**, **H227**, and **H228**.

[46] MF-8993: Broneer 1947, p. 242, pl. LXII:23; *Coroplast's Art*, p. 57, fig. 44.

[47] Palagia 1980, p. 20, no. 10, figs. 20, 21; on the date of the Apollo, see p. 13. See also Ridgway 1997, pp. 335–337, with bibliography on pp. 356–357, pl. 80:a, b.

H17 and two other related figurines (**H21** and possibly **H18**) are linked more closely in pose to popular votary types such as **H9**, particularly in the way the piglet is held. **H17** also shows a pyramidal outline but is considerably more conservative in the greater stiffness of the torso and frontality of the head. The peplos shows a kolpos quite low on the thigh, unlike the other votaries. The folds are broad and flat, resembling in this respect the figurines of young girls (**H43** and **H45**). The most characteristic feature of the drapery is a triangular pleat at the neckline, folded over to the left side. The face does not quite match any of the others, although it is typically Corinthian in its narrow, straight-sided shape. **H21** repeats the torso type but in combination with a head that is a later generation of **H19** and **H20**.

H19 and **H20** with their numerous mold siblings represent another popular votary type but one that followed a different direction. A visual impression of torsion is lent to the composition by the opposing directions of the head, which is turned to the right, and the left arm, which is bent and pulled well back. However, the torso, as far as it is preserved, does not actually twist. There is a clear connection with the smaller **H1–H4** in the relatively narrow-shouldered, high-breasted torso, with the overfold spreading toward the wide hips. The fold pattern of the open side of the peplos is also similar. The knuckles of the left hand rest on the hip, however, and the overfold hem was not lifted at the left side. Although a piglet could have been held head downward in the right hand, none is preserved in the fragmentary figurines. The facial type, with its heavy jaw, full cheeks, and earthy features, is somewhat Magna Graecian, although specific parallels are elusive. The fragmentary **H22** seems to be yet another variant, in which the left arm is relaxed at the side.

In spite of differences in arm position and facial type, it is likely that the archetypes of **H19** and **H20** and of **H1–H4** were in some way related. The similarities in basic composition and proportions are strong; these may have been the fundamental elements in the creation of the archetypes, determining the overall appearance of the torso, while permitting variety through the use of different heads and through the alteration of arm positions and drapery arrangements.

Some imported Argive figurines of votaries carrying piglets also were found in the sanctuary (**I1**, **I6–I8**, see pp. 286–287). One of these (**I1**) is of Classical date, while the others are Early Hellenistic; the latter, which hold the piglet diagonally across the torso, are of rather poor quality and have little observable link with the Corinthian figurines apart from their general type. Following the chronology of Argive figurines (see p. 287), they should date within the 4th century B.C. and seem to be the most degenerate examples yet found. It is possible that they predate the Corinthian Hellenistic piglet carriers and that their demise contributed to the introduction of new local types.

If the foregoing analysis of the mechanical and stylistic relationships among the piglet carriers is somewhat confusing, it illustrates, as did the discussion of articulated "dolls" (pp. 50–53), the complexities of workshop organization and practice and allows some further insight. There seems to have been a common fund of workshop materials, shared in different ways and altered for different purposes. The industrial system reflected here seems to have involved the following elements: (1) the production of archetypes by skilled model makers, in multiple copies and variants; (2) the acquisition of such archetypes, or of molds of complete or partial figures already taken from the archetypes, by craftsmen of differing levels of skill; (3) the consequent sharing of these typologically related materials by craftsmen in different workshops, or their use by different craftsmen in the same workshop; and (4) the free alteration of detail and the creative mixing of different head and torso types within individual workshops. The network of figurine types and styles created thereby is nearly impenetrable, but the result was a vigorous and original coroplastic industry.

A figurine of unknown provenience but probable Corinthian manufacture, in the Liebieghaus Museum,[48] takes this votary type in another direction. A mantle is added around the young woman's hips and legs, and she carries a poppy scepter rather than a piglet. The head is quite like

---

[48] Bol and Kotera 1986, pp. 136–138, no. 70.

that of **H9**, and the narrow, cylindrical base also links this figurine to the piglet carrier group. The good condition of this figurine points to its discovery in a tomb, and the alterations to the type, which may now represent Kore, may have been made for a clearer funerary significance.

TORCH BEARERS

Five figurines (**H23**–**H27**) represent four different versions of a female figure carrying a torch. Since there is so little consistency among the members of this small group, it is a reasonable conclusion that the torch bearer was not an important votive type in the sanctuary but was now and again improvised from existing materials. The best preserved (**H23**) was made from a face mold very similar to **H1**, but frontally composed, and from a mold for a full-breasted torso in a high-girded chiton similar to **H9**. It is remarkable how these elements, composed more hieratically, result in a figurine lacking the sweet, demure air of the piglet carriers. **H24** wears a belt like that of the votary **H7**, with a knot and long ties, but in spite of the similarity of dress, the torso is once again more stiffly frontal. Perhaps the bearing of a torch, suggesting a deity or a cult attendant[49] rather than a votary, explains the difference. Torch bearers in the context of this sanctuary certainly could represent Kore or Demeter.[50] **H23** so closely parallels the votaries that one thinks of a human cult attendant rather than a deity, but the remaining torch bearers are too fragmentary to identify. A fragmentary Sam Wide group plate from the sanctuary shows a woman holding aloft a torch and a stalk of wheat, which must refer to Demeter;[51] perhaps this figure represents a cult attendant. The torch that showed the way to Sicily for Timoleon was said by Plutarch (*Timoleon* 8.3) to resemble the torch used in the mysteries. At any rate, the figurines certainly make reference to the chthonic deities through the attribute of the torch. The "priestess" type of the Middle Hellenistic period (pp. 250–255) also carries a torch. It is possible that an oblique reference to marriage is intended, but the torch-lit processions documented in marriage ceremonies did not take place in sanctuaries but accompanied the bride to her new home.[52] Postholes found beside the monumental stairway in the sanctuary could have been used to hold torches for nocturnal ceremonies.[53]

The torches on the figurines vary in size and shape and in the way they are held. In **H23** the torch is short, thick, and held diagonally across the torso. In **H26** and **H27** it is thinner and is cradled more or less diagonally in the right arm; **H26** may hold a flower as well. **H24** and **H25** may be the upper and lower torso of the same type. Here the torch also is cradled in the right arm but vertically, and it is thick, long, and composed of bundled reeds; the flame burns unrealistically close to the hair and shoulder of **H24**. In this respect, the differently attired Middle Hellenistic "priestess" type with torch, polos, and piglet (e.g., **H395**) is recalled, as are 4th-century B.C. mantled figurines from Nisyros, with polos and long torch, thought to represent Kore.[54] Unfortunately, only one of the torch carriers (**H27**) was found in a chronologically useful context, terminating in the late 4th to early 3rd century B.C.

FLOWER CARRIERS

The two flower carriers (**H28** and **H29**) also differ from one another in type; the former carries a heap of blossoms, perhaps to be identified as wild roses from their scalloped outlines, in the overfold of her garment,[55] and the latter holds a garland across the front of the torso. **H28** probably should be reconstructed with the back of the peplos overfold lifted to shoulder

[49] The *dadouchos* at Eleusis is sometimes considered a torch bearer, but the evidence for the connection of this (male) cult functionary with torches is somewhat vague; see Clinton 1974, pp. 48–49, note 15.

[50] For a useful list of representations of Persephone bearing a torch, see *Morgantina*, pp. 103–104, note 12; for Demeter, p. 104, note 13.

[51] *Corinth* XVIII, i, pp. 135–136, no. 295, fig. 35.

[52] On the use of torches at weddings, see Oakley and Sinos 1993, p. 26.

[53] *Corinth* XVIII, iii, p. 201.

[54] *Louvre* I, p. 105, nos. C126, C127, pl. LXXVI; see also Winter, *Typen* II, p. 167.

[55] In the fragment *British Museum* I, p. 261, no. 961, pl. 137, similar objects are thought to represent cakes.

height in the left hand.[56] It may have been made in the same workshop as the peplos-figurines **C7** and **C8** (see pp. 27–28), which probably date to the first half of the 4th century B.C.

Kore was associated with flowers both in myth, since she was gathering flowers when Hades abducted her, and in votives dedicated to her.[57] The Corinthian figurines, which unfortunately are fragmentary, could represent either Kore or, more likely, votaries offering freshly gathered flowers in commemoration of her marriage to Hades. Flowers are particularly associated with Kore in the Lokroi pinakes representing abductions.[58] Perhaps there also is a connection with the literary use of the flower as a metaphor for virginity.[59] The rose, however, often is the flower of Aphrodite;[60] in Greek art it is applied to Attic figurine vases in great profusion,[61] and the iconography of these vessels emphasizes the circles of Aphrodite and Dionysos. Since the worship of Aphrodite at the sanctuary is suggested by the substantial number of figurines representing her, it is possible that the votary **H28** was carrying rose blossoms in her honor rather than Kore's. A 1st-century B.C. epigram connects roses with a girl's approaching marriage; no deity is named.[62] Earlier flower carriers from the sanctuary include lingering Archaic "korai" (MF-13627, MF-12862, MF-10957); the right hand of the "Spes" type (MF-13626, MF-13628) was pierced to insert a flower.[63] A figurine in Paris, probably Corinthian and mechanically related to the Classical survivals **C7** and **C8** (see p. 27), lifts the peplos overfold to carry fruit or flowers.[64] The overfold-lifting motif, presumably for the same purpose, is also found in a small bronze figure from Temple Hill.[65]

BALL CARRIERS

The Early Classical peplos-figurine **C4** carries a ball; the figurines discussed here, however, are not survivals of that type but new creations. **H30** wears a chiton girded fairly high, in the 4th-century B.C. fashion, and from the flatness of the chest seems to be prepubescent. **H31** and **H32** are Early Hellenistic in their slender proportions and sloping shoulders, but they retain a Classical frontality of pose. Taken together, they preserve a ball carrier whose breasts are small but already developed. The young woman offers the ball in her outstretched right hand. She wears a mantle draped in loose diagonal folds from the left shoulder to the right hip. The chest looks nude in **H31**, but a few faint folds of a chiton sleeve in **H32** and clearer sleeve folds on a better-preserved example in Athens[66] are evidence of a garment beneath the mantle. The clarity with which the legs stand out from the drapery suggests that the archetype may have been constructed from a nude male type similar to **C188–C190**, with skirt folds added around the legs. The semidraped youth **C201** shows similarly defined legs beneath the drapery and also carries a ball. The head of **H31**, with its small, round face and projecting tuft of hair at the top, is like that of Classical articulated "dolls" such as **C127** and **C159**, and the mitten-shaped hand recalls "dolls'" hands such as **C122**. The type is probably best explained as a pastiche put together at the Potters' Quarter in a workshop that made both articulated "dolls" and nude male figurines; in fact, two examples of this type were found at the Potters' Quarter (see catalogue). **H31** and three mold siblings were found in a pottery context terminating at the beginning of the 3rd century B.C., but a better *terminus ante quem* for this type is provided by the destruction of

[56] As in Winter, *Typen* I, p. 78, no. 3.
[57] On the association of Kore with flowers, see Sourvinou-Inwood 1978, p. 109, h; Friedrich 1978, p. 164.
[58] Sourvinou-Inwood 1978, p. 109, h; Prückner 1968, pp. 70–72.
[59] Carson 1990, pp. 146–148.
[60] On the association of Aphrodite with flowers, see Friedrich 1978, pp. 74–75. For the possible association of the rose with Aphrodite at Lokroi, see Sourvinou-Inwood 1978, p. 118, i; Prückner 1968, p. 16. She is associated with roses in Bacchylides 16, line 116. In Mesopotamian art, the rosette is

associated with Aphrodite's Near Eastern counterpart Ishtar: Goodenough 1958, VII, pp. 180–183, with bibliography.
[61] Trumpf-Lyritzaki 1969, *passim*.
[62] *Anthologia Palatina* 6.345; roses are dedicated to the nymphs by men in epigrams 154, 158, and 324, but no. 336 offers roses to the Muses.
[63] Publication forthcoming.
[64] *Louvre* I, p. 119, no. C228, pl. LXXXVI.
[65] MF-77-87, publication forthcoming by Kim Hartswick.
[66] National Archaeological Museum, inv. no. 4410.

the Potters' Quarter in the 320s B.C. **H33** shows a similar costume but is too fragmentary for closer identification. Its flat chest could suggest a prepubescent girl but in this case also could be ascribed to poor workmanship.

The seated female figurine **C78**, of 4th-century B.C. date, is another ball carrier. Although ball games are known in ritual contexts, particularly in the worship of Aphrodite,[67] the small number of ball carriers found in the Acrocorinth sanctuary is not likely to be evidence of such a ritual, even when expanded by the group of figurines representing the ball game called "ephedrismos" (see pp. 200–201). Rather, the balls are probably best understood as examples of the toys customarily dedicated to different deities by girls before marriage and by boys as souvenirs of their adolescence.[68] Balls appear to have been dedicated to Kore at Lokroi in a context that was both nuptial and chthonic.[69]

BIRD CARRIERS

The cultic association of the bird with Kore and Aphrodite has already been mentioned (p. 43), and figurines of birds have been found at the Demeter sanctuary, including the Classical **V9**. Several lingering Archaic "korai" also hold birds (e.g., MF-13642, MF-11219).[70] Classical figurines carrying birds include both standing (**C1** and **C6**) and seated (**C77**) types. It is therefore a little surprising that there is no evidence for a consistent series of Hellenistic votaries carrying birds to parallel the piglet carriers. The bird carriers **H34** and **H35** bear little resemblance to either the Early Classical standing votary **C6** or the seated **C77**. **H34** wears a chiton and diagonal mantle and carries a bird with outspread wings; she has the undeveloped body of a young girl. An earlier generation found in the Potters' Quarter (see catalogue) locates the source of this figurine and provides a terminal date in or near the 320s B.C., when the Potters' Quarter workshops closed.

H35 was probably also a Potters' Quarter product. A strange pastiche, wearing an apparently masculine costume that leaves the legs and chest bare but with feminine breasts, it is probably not a hermaphrodite but a female figurine built upon a male type less successfully than **H31**. The feet rest on a small plinth projecting from a backdrop, as in the nude Classical youth **C188**. A chiton originally may have been added by painting over the chest and legs.

VOTARIES WITHOUT OFFERINGS

H36 is somewhat anomalous in type and is included with the votaries by virtue of its subject, scale, and drapery arrangement. The small figurine represents a young woman in a chiton and diagonal mantle, with the left arm akimbo. To that extent it resembles **H31** and **H32**, but the right hand at the side definitely held no offering. Nevertheless, the general impression of youth and quietude, as well as the long hair, suggests a votary. Although the fabric of this figurine and of its mold siblings is somewhat coarser than usual, it seems to be Corinthian, a product of a workshop separate from the Potters' Quarter and later in date, specializing in small, thick-walled figurines. Other figurines similarly constructed include **H38–H40** and **H42**. The coarse fabric taken together with the slender proportions, sloping shoulders, small head, and the use of a single mold for the entire figurine and its base, all suggest a date in the 3rd century B.C.

Determining the age of a young person represented in a figurine is something of a problem.[71] There are two clear age groups among the female votaries: (1) prepubescent girls under

[67] Kossatz-Deissmann 1978, pp. 38–39; Simon 1983, pp. 40–42, with bibliography; Schneider-Herrmann 1971.

[68] *Anthologia Palatina* 6.280 (a girl dedicates to Artemis before her wedding a ball, a tambourine, a hairband, her hair, and clothing; see p. 49); 6.282 (a boy gives to Hermes as gifts of adolescence a ball, a strigil, clothing, and a bow and arrows); 6.309 (a boy similarly gives a ball, a rattle, knucklebones, and a top).

[69] Sourvinou-Inwood 1978, p. 108, c, with bibliography; Prückner 1968, pp. 47–50.

[70] Publication forthcoming.

[71] On determining the ages of girls in vase painting on the basis of their physical characteristics, see Sourvinou-Inwood 1988, pp. 33–37.

ten–twelve years of age, such as **H43**, characterized by a flat chest and chunky torso without a clearly defined waist; and (2) fully mature young women in their middle to late teens, such as **H1**, characterized by their high, firm breasts, and well-defined waists and hips. Between these two groups there is a gray area of figurines such as **H10**, which have somewhat flat chests but have lost the childlike stockiness and have slender waists. It is possible that these figurines were intended to depict adolescent girls, but unfortunately they are not of the best workmanship, and one must keep in mind that in figurines contour as well as detail can be lost in successive generations or in the clumsy handling of less-skilled artisans. Further, the habit of adapting types for purposes for which they were not originally intended could confuse the issue. **H16** seems a little fuller figured than the other votaries and hence more mature, but the pose, coiffure, and piglet should securely fix the subject as youthful. The figure in the mold from the South Stoa (Pl. 77) from which **H16** may ultimately derive (see pp. 252–253) is heavily built and wide hipped, yet it too must represent a young woman, by virtue of the costume and pose. Clearly the identification of age groups must rest on all the attributes of figurines, not only on physical characteristics.

H43–H45 show the undeveloped figures of girls of prepubescent age. They carry no offerings but press the empty left hand flat against the abdomen. Of the figurines of girls who seem a little older, perhaps already adolescent, without offerings (**H37–H41**), **H40** and perhaps also **H38** have the same hand-to-abdomen gesture.[72] The meaning of the gesture becomes clear in light of three female rim ornaments on an Archaic Corinthian vessel, in which the left hand is placed across the abdomen and the right hand is at the breast; the combination of gestures clearly evokes the bearing and nourishing of children.[73] The hand to abdomen is the "universal gesture of the expectant mother" and is widely known, especially in a large class of Phoenician figurines representing pregnant women.[74] If the similarity in the gesture implies a similarity of meaning, the Corinthian figurines could suggest that girls of prepubescent and pubescent age participated in rituals of the sanctuary intended to orient them toward the next stage of their lives, the physical maturity that would make marriage and motherhood possible.[75] If this interpretation is correct, the cult could have contained an element of social conditioning. Like the rituals and myths of the Sanctuary of Artemis at Brauron, which involved girls of prepubescent age, the control of emerging female sexuality for the sake of familial and social stability could have been an aspect of the Demeter cult in Corinth.[76] One could reasonably expect this function to be absorbed into a cult of Demeter Epoikidie, if the Corinthian household was understood as a microcosm of society. These figurines of children carry a significance quite different from that of the seated children previously discussed (pp. 68–73). The girls have survived the rigors of babyhood and early childhood and are equated in pose and dress with their fully mature elders, perhaps in the hope of a safe arrival at adulthood and a proper discharge of the duties of womanhood. It must be stressed, however, that the number of figurines in this group is small.

The only possible surviving Classical precursor of the standing girl type is the fine statuette **C34**, which probably represents a prepubescent girl. A figurine of excellent quality found in

[72] A female figurine from a Corinthian grave dated to the last quarter of the 4th century B.C. (MF-11558) makes a similar gesture, but she may be holding something in her hand: Pemberton 1985, p. 296, no. 3, pl. 83. An example from the Thesmophorion at Eretria is thought to hold an unidentified object: *Eretria*, pp. 28, 77, no. 376, pl. 21.

[73] Gabrici 1927, cols. 317–319, pls. LXXXV, LXXXVI:10.

[74] *Treasures of the Holy Land*, pp. 174–175, no. 88, with bibliography; Culican 1969, pp. 35–45. The gesture is also known, for example, among Archaic Etruscan bronzes, where it is thought to denote fertility (E. Richardson 1976, p. 24; I thank Jean M. Turfa for this reference).

[75] For small girls portrayed on Corinthian vases participating in rituals together with women, see Jucker 1963, p. 53, pl. 20:2. For ethnographic data on the use of figurines for teaching young people about marriage, social values, and sexual behavior, see Talalay 1993, pp. 40–42. On the importance of symbolic actions in the initiation of girls, to prepare them for adult life, see Lincoln 1991, p. 104. This subject is discussed further below, pp. 336–337.

[76] This aspect of the cult of Artemis Brauronia is discussed by Osborne 1985, pp. 165–170, with bibliography; Cole 1984, pp. 241–242; Kahil 1983, p. 237; Sourvinou-Inwood 1988, pp. 25–30, with bibliography.

the Forum Southwest excavations, MF-71-43 (Pl. 75), from a deposit dated to the third quarter of the 4th century B.C.,[77] depicts a girl of the same age, with an extended left forearm and an overfold reaching the knees.

It is noteworthy that in this sanctuary of fertility goddesses, in which figurines of women were such common dedications, representations of pregnancy are confined to the swollen abdomens of comic types (e.g., **H360** and **H362**).[78] To be sure, representations of pregnancy are rare in Greek art, perhaps because of aesthetic considerations or because the pregnant woman was thought to be very vulnerable[79] and direct representations of the condition might be unlucky. It is conceivable, however, that their absence in the Demeter sanctuary points to the greater concern of the cult with the ability to conceive children and nurture them successfully than with actual childbirth (see pp. 70–71).

Two female figurines (**H37** and **H39**) stand quietly with both arms at the sides, a pose already noted in a Corinthian figurine in The Metropolitan Museum (see p. 117, note 9), with a well-known precedent in the Parthenon frieze procession.[80] Both of these figurines have slender proportions, sloping shoulders, high breasts, and high-girded garments with long overfolds comparable to **H9** and **H10**. It is unclear whether this simple pose has some significance. It is also known in female figurines from the Thesmophorion at Eretria.[81] It does project a passivity perhaps deemed desirable in young women, but its simplicity could have a technical origin, in that the torso mold, with arms so close to the sides, was conveniently complete and required no additions. In one version (**H41**), the arms stop at the biceps and apparently never were added to the torso at all, even in the archetype. This figurine represents the nadir of the group and may date well into the 3rd century B.C. None of the figurines preserves the legs, but it is possible that **H42**, the lower part of a figurine with a long overfold and a round base, originally belonged to a similar type. **H44** shows technical similarities with the hydriaphoros head **H50** and the head in a melon coiffure **H223**; these figurines may have been made in the same workshop (Workshop J, p. 346).

In two figurines (**H46** and **H47**), a mantle is draped over the girl's chiton. In **H46**, the mantle is rolled around the hips and covers the skirt, recalling similarly draped 3rd-century B.C. stone sculptures of girls holding birds in the left hand.[82] The left forearm of **H46** is missing, but the arm must have been bent to clear the mantle roll, and the hand could have held an offering. The little girl from Brauron holding a rabbit also comes to mind.[83] In **H47**, the mantle is worn around the shoulders and arms like a shawl, a "Tanagraean" scheme known in numerous variants.[84] Although it is a rather roughly made piece, **H47** recalls early Attic "Tanagra" figurines in its proportions and rather tubular folds.[85] This comparison could place the archetype of **H47** in the third quarter of the 4th century B.C.

CHRONOLOGY OF VOTARY FIGURINES

The dates of the pottery lots with which the votaries are associated, as well as technical connections with other figurines, suggest that most of the votary types were in use during the second half of the 4th century B.C. and that some continued well into the 3rd. Those made in

---

[77] For several figurines in this deposit, drain 1971-1, see C. K. Williams and Fisher 1972, pp. 162–163.

[78] The only possible pregnant figurine from the Demeter sanctuary, apart from grotesques, is **I59**, a very poorly made piglet carrier perhaps distorted in molding rather than pregnant and probably an import. The articulated "doll" **C115** has a fleshy abdomen, but it sags, and the figurine therefore probably is intended to be obese rather than pregnant. MF-3456 in the Corinth collection (*Corinth* XII, p. 35, no. 153, pl. 10, found at Penteskouphia) is nude, has a swollen abdomen, and seems to be a grotesque. There is also a nude example from

the cave at Pitsa, *EAA* VI, 1965, p. 206, fig. 229 center, s.v. *Pitsa* (A. K. Orlandos), but it is uncertain whether it is Corinthian.

[79] R. Garland 1990, pp. 46–48.

[80] Robertson and Frantz 1975, e.g., pl. 12, East VII:53, 54.

[81] *Eretria*, pp. 28–29, 78, nos. 396, 397, pl. 21.

[82] Vorster 1983, esp. pp. 348–349, nos. 52, 53, pl. 16:2, 3.

[83] Vorster 1983, p. 345, no. 41, pl. 3:1.

[84] Winter, *Typen* II, pp. 70–73; *Morgantina*, Type III, pp. 56–58, 175–176, nos. 361–365, pls. 76, 77, with bibliography.

[85] Cf. D. B. Thompson 1952, pp. 130–132, 159–160, no. 19, pl. 34, with the mantle differently arranged but similar in style.

the Potters' Quarter and therefore dating before the 320s include **H31**, **H32**, **H34**, and **H35**. Those from pottery contexts terminating in the late 4th or early 3rd century B.C. are **H1**, **H7**, a mold sibling of **H9** (see catalogue), **H11**, **H14**, **H20**, **H21**, **H27**, and **H46**. These figurines include all the variants of the votaries with piglet except **H16**. From a pottery context terminating a little later, in the first quarter of the 3rd century B.C., is **H39**, which has both arms pressed to the side of the torso. It is likely that **H16**, which is similarly composed, belongs to this period as well. These types may have first evolved in the early 3rd century B.C. or at the earliest at the end of the 4th. A 3rd-century B.C. date also works well for the related figurine in The Metropolitan Museum (see p. 128). **H44** is the latest, from a pottery context of the middle to second half of the 3rd century B.C.

STANDING DRAPED FEMALE FIGURINES: HYDRIAPHOROI
(H48–H51)

A few hydriaphoroi carry on the earlier tradition (see pp. 38–42). **H49** recalls the Classical **C51** in the solid panel of clay joining the arm and head; the style is updated, however, the narrow, sloping shoulders pointing to an Early Hellenistic date. The elongated proportions of **H48**, which originally may have balanced a hydria on the head with the raised right arm, also suggest a Hellenistic date; the arched overfold recalls the degenerate Classical **C42**. The head **H50** resembles the Classical **C53** in supporting the foot of a hydria without an intervening head ring, but it has the youthful face and long, unbound hair of the votaries discussed above. The hydria of **H49** is somewhat taller than its Classical predecessor, and consequently the arm is raised higher. The base of **H51**, a hydria perhaps broken from the head of a figurine, is very narrow; by comparison with the profiles of miniature hydriai from the sanctuary,[86] it should be Middle Hellenistic in date, indicating the survival of the type.

The only hydriaphoros with a useful chronological context is **H51**, which was found with pottery terminating in the early 3rd century B.C. **H50** can be connected in fabric and workmanship to a head wearing a rough version of the Hellenistic melon coiffure (**H223**) and a figurine of a standing girl (**H44**); they may have been made in the same workshop (Workshop J, see p. 346). The pottery context of **H44** falls into the latter half of the 3rd century B.C.; the hydriaphoros **H50** should date to this time as well, as a product of the same workshop.

This group clearly is not unified typologically or stylistically. Apart from **H49**, which is the most traditional in form and has mold siblings, the figurines seem to have been improvised from other types. The decline in the use of this figurine type already can be seen in the Classical period and probably is to be attributed to the growing popularity of miniature hydriae.[87]

STANDING DRAPED FEMALE FIGURINES: ARCHAIZING
(H52–H54)

At least one workshop developed an archaizing type, **H52–H54**, which resembles some of the figurines of votaries in its slender proportions. The hieratic pose and drapery, however, as well as the retrospective style and the headdress, point to a representation of a goddess. The pose is rigidly frontal, legs together; below the waist is an archaizing arrangement of stiff central pleats and half a swallowtail pattern at the right side; at the left, the swallowtail pattern is eliminated, as if the hand, which lies flat at the side, were drawing the overfold away from the thigh. A flower(?) is held at the chest in the right hand. A polos is worn over long hair streaming over the shoulders, as in a group of Aphrodite and Eros (Pl. 78) of Corinthian provenience

---

[86] *Corinth* XVIII, i, p. 11, fig. 1, pl. 50.
[87] *Corinth* XVIII, i, p. 104.

in Athens.[88] The type is well represented in a 3rd-century B.C. deposit found in the South Stoa, where it is associated with hero cult.[89] A fragmentary example from the Demeter sanctuary was found in Pit B (lot 880, see catalogue *sub* **H52**), the pottery of which terminates in the first quarter of the 3rd century B.C. Given its similarity in proportions to the Early Hellenistic votaries, it is likely that the archetype was created in the later 4th century B.C. The best-preserved face (**H54**), with its strong jaw and earthy features, suggests that the head may be a later generation of the head type of the votaries **H19** and **H20**, with the hair reworked and a polos added.

The popularity of the type, its archaism, the polos, and the offering held to the chest, all suggest that it was a replacement for the lingering Archaic standing "kore" type (p. 23, note 1), itself an archaizing creation of the 5th century B.C., which was probably still in use well into the 4th century. Since no examples of the archaizing type were found in the Potters' Quarter, the occasion for its invention may have been the demise, in or near the 320s B.C., of the workshops where the "korai" were made. Perhaps a demand for traditional figurines with the Archaic flavor of the "korai" led to the creation of a type incorporating an older style within a newer one. The immediate inspiration for the dress may have come from stone *hekataia,* but the archaizing features of the drapery are incorporated into a type close to the Corinthian Early Hellenistic votaries.[90] The goddess represented could be either Kore or Aphrodite. Kore is perhaps to be preferred, if the type took the place of the earlier standing "korai," which probably represented that goddess.

ISOLATED HEAD RELATED TO VOTARIES
(**H55**)

The isolated head **H55** differs in facial type and quality of workmanship from the votaries and is larger in scale, but it is linked to them by its long, streaming locks of hair, fillet, and ogival forehead. Its poor retouch and distorted features may indicate that it is a late attempt, by an artisan of limited skill, to recapture the type and style of a votary figurine. Further, the addition of an earring is untrue to the usually unadorned votary type.

STANDING DRAPED FEMALE FIGURINES: MANTLED
(**H56**–**H138**)

In this section are discussed Early Hellenistic female figurines wearing the chiton or peplos covered by a mantle in various arrangements or wearing the mantle only. A few of the faces are youthful, but the group as a whole consists of fully mature women or goddesses. In the absence of attributes or distinctive headdresses, it is not always easy to distinguish between mortals and deities. In some cases, a particular drapery arrangement known in sculpture will help to identify a goddess. Some figurines of women enveloped in mantles, recalling "Tanagra" figurines in a general way, find their best iconographic parallels among the bystanders in votive reliefs and therefore probably represent mortals. They do not carry specific offerings and perhaps are to be understood as sanctuary visitors in a general sense, not necessarily as the principal participants in rituals, such as the young brides discussed above. In this connection, it is worth recalling the tendency of Hellenistic figurines toward an increasing secularization of type.[91] Whether or not this shift in types signals a changing attitude toward religion is debatable, since more specifically votive types

---

[88] National Archaeological Museum, inv. no. 4160; Papaspyridi-Karouzou 1956, pp. 174–177, figs. 7–10, pl. 6; Lattimore 1987, p. 419, fig. 5, with bibliography.

[89] Davidson 1942, pp. 114–115, fig. 5; Broneer 1942, p. 129. The type was offered at the Thesmophorion in Pella: Lilibaki-Akamati 1996, pp. 51–53, pl. 17.

[90] For archaistic sculpture of generally similar type, see Fullerton 1987, pp. 261–263 on peplophoroi (these are Late Hellenistic, however, and represent Artemis-Hekate); *Agora* XI, pp. 86–107, on *hekataia.* The *hekataia* thus far found in Corinth appear to be of Roman date: Ridgway 1981, p. 431.

[91] Higgins 1986, p. 119.

continued to be offered at the same time. Perhaps it signifies only an increasing attendance at festivals as a by-product of prosperity, a less specifically religious image being considered a suitable offering by those without a specific ritual to perform, vow to make, or favor to ask but wishing nevertheless to demonstrate reverence for the deity.

If one traces the gradual transition of types from the Classical to the Early Hellenistic period, it becomes apparent that there was continuity, either because types were carried into the Hellenistic period as survivals or because new types that conveyed similar meanings replaced them. For example, the articulated "dolls" continued to some extent as survivals, as shown by the pierced head with a melon coiffure (**C136**) but the Classical female votaries were replaced by the Early Hellenistic female piglet carriers, and the seated goddesses were replaced by a much more varied repertoire of standing deities. The mantled women, however, did not replace anything but augmented the existing array of votive types. Therefore, one can speak of secularization of types in the Demeter sanctuary only in the sense of supplementing, not replacing, the votive repertoire. In addition, there is a loss of hieratic style in some types in favor of styles more closely connected with the larger world of the arts. It is perhaps not coincidental that masculine types appear to have declined both in quality and in quantity in proportion to the increasing number of female types. The abundant Archaic handmade horse-riders (see p. 60) that survived into the 4th century B.C. were replaced after the destruction of the Potters' Quarter in the 320s B.C. by moldmade plaques, only one example of which was found in the Demeter sanctuary (**V19**). Similarly, the Classical male banqueter type produced at the Potters' Quarter (see pp. 65–68) was replaced by a new type including a seated female figure, which is identified at the Demeter sanctuary only with some uncertainty (see p. 67). On the basis of this evidence, and if one may assume that the draped feminine types usually were dedicated by women, it may be worth speculating that by Early Hellenistic times the practice of hero cult in the sanctuary suggested by the horse-riders and banqueters had declined; the growing proportion of female figurine types might then signify the increasing participation of women in the rituals.

Before beginning the discussion of the Early Hellenistic draped female types, the question of identifying the headdresses worn by some of these figurines should be addressed. The difficulty in identification stems from the conflation of two types of headdress, the polos and the stephane, in some figurines. In sculpture, for example, in Archaic Attic korai, the two types of headdress are easily distinguishable from one another. The polos of the Lyons kore,[92] for example, is a low, slightly flaring cylinder, flat on top and set on top of the cranium. The stephane worn by the kore Akropolis Museum 674,[93] on the other hand, is a very low crown that partly encircles the head, leaving the cranium, where the locks of hair are clearly rendered, bare.

If one looks at evidence apart from sculpture, terracotta votive poloi, presumably models of real headdresses, are rather different from the sculptured poloi, being tall, open cylinders topped with decorative borders.[94] The stephane, by definition, is nothing more than an encircling headdress,[95] yet it would be wise to narrow this definition somewhat, or the term loses utility by encompassing the many forms of crowns and wreaths found in Greek art. Dorothy Thompson proposed to define the stephane as "a crescent-shaped diadem," usually plain but with variations.[96] This working definition has been adopted for the present study.

Among the Corinthian terracotta figurines, Archaic female types may wear a high, hollow polos[97] or a lower one, formed by an applied strip of clay.[98] On 5th-century B.C. heads, the

[92] Richter 1968, pp. 57–58, no. 89, figs. 275–279.
[93] Richter 1968, pp. 81–82, no. 127, figs. 411–416.
[94] Simon 1972, pp. 206–207, figs. 1–4; *British Museum* I, p. 209, no. 781, pl. 103. See also, from the Demeter Sanctuary, the open poloi **V14** and **V15**, which are broken from figurines.
[95] LSJ, s.v.
[96] *Troy*, p. 49.
[97] E.g., KT-3-6, *Corinth* XV, ii, p. 63, no. 6, pl. 10.
[98] E.g., KT-9-34, *Corinth* XV, ii, p. 79, no. 56, pl. 12.

polos may be high and flaring (e.g., **C71**) or much lower (e.g., the protome **C253**). When the head is solid and the headdress was included in the mold, the polos may also be solid (e.g., **C73**). Thus, the form of the polos depends, in part, upon whether it was a hand-applied strip (and was consequently hollow) or a moldmade, solid cylinder. The coroplastic technique influenced the form, and the applied-strip polos was easily conflated with an encircling stephane. Such confusion sometimes occurs among Early Hellenistic figurines. This confusion is exacerbated by the fact that the backs of moldmade heads, even those of good quality, were often handmade and carelessly finished, with the expectation that the viewer would perceive the headdress and other accessories from the more detailed front. Even when the back was moldmade as well, the headdress was not always finished, as in the half-polos of the "priestess" **H395**. Consequently, the headdresses in this chapter have been identified mainly by their appearance from the front. If the form diminishes at the sides into a rounded or pointed crescent shape, the headdress is called a stephane; if it remains high at the sides, it is assumed that the coroplast had in mind a polos. Sometimes, however, even this simple distinction is hard to draw.

While it is important to the scholar to recognize these headdresses, particularly the polos, which denoted divinity and was worn by brides, the coroplast may not always have concerned himself with such distinctions. For example, the female head **H192** clearly wears a pointed stephane, yet in **H193**, a head of closely related type that was probably made in the same workshop, the headdress is higher at the sides and approaches a polos in appearance. In this case, since the better-made piece clearly shows a stephane, the coroplast may have intended to represent the same headdress in the lesser work. In the case of **H54**, the headdress is clearly a polos in front, although it is abbreviated at the back. On the typologically similar but smaller head of **H53**, however, the headdress approaches a stephane in shape. Since the larger head of this type wears a polos, it is assumed that the coroplasts of the smaller head intended to represent a polos as well, and it is therefore so identified. The only firm statement that can be made about the polos in 4th-century B.C. and Early Hellenistic figurines is that it is low in shape.[99]

FIGURINES IN PEPLOS AND MANTLE (THE GRIMANI TYPE) (**H56–H62**)

Two groups of Classical and Early Hellenistic stone statuettes, most of which represent Demeter and Kore, find parallels among Corinthian figurines. They are the so-called Grimani statuettes, of Cretan origin,[100] already mentioned in connection with Classical peplos-figurines (see p. 35), and a group from the Sanctuary of Demeter at Kyparissi on Kos.[101] The Corinthian figurines connected with them are the large (size range 4) **H56–H60** and the fragmentary variants **H61** and **H62**.

In this type, a small mantle is draped over a peplos, covering only the shoulders and chest. Apart from one of the Grimani statuettes, a generally similar drapery scheme of peplos and small mantle draped across the chest is found in the figure of Demeter on a votive relief from Eleusis, although without the characteristic folds around the breasts,[102] and in a late-4th-century statue from Samos.[103] **H56** preserves the torso in full length, while **H57** supplies the left side missing from **H56**. The two are from different mold series, and still a third series is represented by the fragment **H59**. **H58** probably represents an earlier generation; thin-walled and hard fired, it is evidence of a very large, fine rendition of this type. **H60** may be an earlier generation as well but is obscured by added drapery.

---

[99] For a good example, see the Corinthian Aphrodite and Eros in Athens, National Archaeological Museum, inv. no. 4160 (Pl. 78; see p. 130, note 88).

[100] Kabus-Jahn 1972; Ridgway 1981a, pp. 194–198, with bibliography on p. 219; Strocka 1979, pp. 171–172.

[101] Kabus-Preisshofen 1975.

[102] Peschlow-Bindokat 1972, p. 152, no. R47; *LIMC* IV, 1988, p. 875, no. 379, pl. 589, s.v. *Demeter* (L. Beschi).

[103] *Samos* XII, pp. 1–4, 77–79, no. 1, pls. 1–4.

The mantle draping seems more complex than it really is; the cloth simply hangs over the right shoulder in a brief cape, and is draped across the waist and over the extended left forearm. The characteristic motif is the stretching and pleating of the cloth so that both breasts are framed and accented by curving folds. A similar motif, but with the mantle wrapped like a sheath around the slim figure down to the knees or the hem of a thin chiton, is characteristic of a much repeated sculptural Kore type, sometimes shown in reliefs next to a more matronly, voluminously draped Demeter;[104] it is also seen on the Muse with the aulos on the Mantineia base.[105] It may also be present in the fragmentary **H80**.

The head preserved in **H57** shows a youthful face with the rather oblong shape and full jaw typical of Corinthian heads. The face is framed by a row of corkscrew curls, topped by a low polos that is not fully rounded in back, like the poloi of Middle Hellenistic "priestesses" (e.g., **H395**). The isolated head **H179** also has a youthful face and clusters of corkscrew curls, topped by a flaring, fully rounded polos; it is not known whether **H179** originally belonged to a torso of the same type as **H57**. The polos suggests that the figurines represent a goddess. If so, the goddess is more likely to be Kore than Demeter, to judge from the youthfulness of the face and the corkscrew curls, which may suggest a bridal coiffure.[106]

Curls of this kind are known on terracotta figures of girls from Lavinium, in the context of the Sanctuary of Athena Ilias/Minerva, whose cult was active from the 6th to the 3rd century B.C.; there the curls are connected with the traditional Roman bridal coiffure described in literary sources.[107] An isolated head from the Demeter sanctuary at Knossos also has corkscrew curls,[108] as does its parallel, a standing female figurine in chiton and mantle, of reported Cretan provenience, in London;[109] neither head wears a polos. It should be noted that corkscrew curls also appear at the Acrocorinth sanctuary on a Hellenistic head type wearing a stephane (**H193**), on a Late Archaic figurine (MF-12162[110]), which has red paint on the face and therefore is probably male, and on an early-5th-century B.C. male terracotta sculptured head.[111] In at least one female Archaic head (MF-12034[112]), the long locks of hair on the shoulders are twisted into corkscrew curls, as they are on the Early Classical hydriaphoros **C53** (see p. 40). Outside Corinth, corkscrew curls appear on both male and female types in widely differing contexts; to give just a few examples, they appear on female figures connected with the cult of Isis,[113] on Apollo types from Cyprus,[114] on the bronze "Gabinius" from Herculaneum,[115] and on a statue in Boston identified as Demeter.[116] Unfortunately, the available evidence is not clear enough to explain precisely what, if anything, the wearing of corkscrew curls signified in Corinth.

The head type of **H57** may not have been the only one used with this torso type. The head is rather small in proportion to the torso, and the youthful face is somewhat incongruous with the matronly body, suggesting that the original design called for a larger and more mature head type. The fragmentary **H59** has long, streaming locks of hair on the left shoulder, and a probable mold sibling of **H57** (see catalogue) shows two long, twisted locks of hair on the right shoulder, indicating that heads with different coiffures, at least, were used with this torso type. Long hair would have been suitable for figurines of either Demeter or Kore. It would appear that, as among

---

[104] Palagia 1980, pp. 28–30, figs. 48–50, with bibliography; Kabus-Preisshofen 1975, pp. 50–52, pls. 22–24.

[105] Todisco 1993, pl. 289.

[106] On the polos in representations of Persephone, see *Morgantina*, pp. 81–82.

[107] Torelli 1984, pp. 31–50, esp. pp. 36–41; the interpretation of this coiffure as bridal is not accepted by all (see La Follette 1994, pp. 56–57, esp. note 27 on pp. 62–63). On the possible curling of the hair of brides at the Sanctuary of Hera in Samos, see Fridh-Haneson 1988, p. 213, citing Torelli.

[108] *Knossos*, p. 81, no. 175, pl. 56.

[109] *Knossos*, p. 81, with no. 175, pl. 69:e.

[110] Publication forthcoming.

[111] SF-65-12, Bookidis and Fisher 1972, p. 317, pl. 63:d; the flesh of this head was also painted red.

[112] Publication forthcoming.

[113] Bieber 1961, pp. 89–90, figs. 328–333, with bibliography.

[114] Connelly 1988, pp. 47–48, pl. 18, figs. 66, 67 and pl. 23, figs. 86, 87; p. 79, pl. 29, figs. 110–112.

[115] Ridgway 1986, pp. 64–65, fig. 4, with bibliography.

[116] Comstock and Vermeule 1976, p. 87, no. 135.

the Classical figurines, there is little fixed iconography for the goddesses but rather suggestive images that call one or both to mind.

The comparable Grimani statuette, one of the better-made pieces in its group, is the well-known goddess in a low, lightly crenellated polos, over which the mantle is draped as a veil; she is usually identified as Demeter or Hera.[117] She wears blunt-toed shoes with soles, rather than the soft, narrow, flat-soled slippers of **H56**, her right arm was outstretched, presumably to hold a scepter, the peplos overfold is shorter, and the mantle is drawn over the head as a veil, but the distinctive drapery arrangement over the chest corresponds very closely. In addition, the statuette and the figurine **H56** share an error inherent in the design, the representation of a pouched fold under the right arm, which is incongruous with the folds rendered down the side; these folds indicate that the peplos should be open at the right side. The face of the Grimani statuette is not exactly paralleled by any of the Corinthian figurines, but the oblong shape, full jaw, and strong features with the nose close to the upper lip have a distinctly Peloponnesian flavor.

The essentially rectangular outline of the Grimani statuette and the figurines suggests that the original design should be dated not later than the first half of the 4th century B.C. The very deeply set eyes of the Grimani statuette and the crease marks on the wide central pleat of the overfold, however, put it somewhat later, perhaps in the third quarter of the 4th century B.C. The Corinthian figurines must have been made in the Early Hellenistic period, to judge from the narrow slippers of **H56** and the tooling on the hair of **H57**. The rows of parallel, diagonal slashes on the locks of hair are found on the melon coiffures of Early Hellenistic heads, such as **H224**. Presumably, both the shoes and the head were later alterations to a type of earlier design, of which only the torso remains. Of this group, only **H56** was found in a chronologically useful context, with pottery terminating in the early 3rd century B.C.

The Grimani statuettes, although connected with one another through provenience and technique, actually contain material of diverse type and style. This diversity has been explained by deriving the statuettes from different cult statues, made over a period of more than a half-century in the same Cretan workshop, and representing Demeter and Kore; the statuettes are thought to have been dedicated in the Sanctuary of Demeter at Knossos. If this interpretation is correct, it might support the identification as goddesses of figurines resembling the Grimani statuettes. Ridgway, however, has suggested more sensibly that the workshop drew upon a fund of types generally available to artisans.[118] Certainly some coroplastic workshops made a point of copying well-known statues, as at Myrina and Smyrna (see p. 297), but a blanket derivation of smaller plastic art from particular "important" statues seems to be a distortion of artistic practice as we understand it. Portraying deities in a great variety of ways was fundamental to the imaginative processes of Greek art in general, and there is no evidence that the process had to be linked to the making of images for display and worship in temples. Certainly, the viewing of other artisans' finished works was not the only opportunity for copying. Once designs were created, in the form of either models or drawings, whether specifically commissioned or made for sale to other artisans for different purposes, they would have been available for copying in different media, distributed either in the same place or elsewhere. Some of these designs could have been intended for cult statues but were not necessarily so (see pp. 35–36). When a model maker or sculptor decided how to pose, dress, and coif a statue of a deity, he must have drawn upon general conceptions of the deity's function and appearance, which were common to Greek artisans in all media, since they derived from a shared religion.[119] Votive reliefs,

---

[117] Kabus-Jahn 1972, pp. 51–59, pls. 28–35.

[118] Ridgway 1981a, p. 195: ". . . certain major types probably occurred in more than one version, in more than one place, made by more than one master, and perhaps representing more than one deity."

[119] Alroth (1989, pp. 106–108) concludes that there is no real pattern distinguishable of figurines following cult statues; in some cases, the influence of the cult image is apparent, while in others it clearly is not, and still others are too generic in type and style for certainty. On the whole question of the ancient concept of "cult" statues, see Donohue 1997.

stone statuettes, and figurines may be said to share such conceptions, through the use of similar models in the workshops of stone carvers and coroplasts.

In this view, the intervention of a major statue is not necessary, the smaller plastic arts do not have to derive from the larger, and insofar as the model making or drawing took place at a smaller scale, the position is, in fact, reversed; the availability and exchange of workshop materials become primary factors. The point of this digression is to say that the most likely explanation of the similarity between the Grimani statuette and the figurines is that both derived from the same source, although the statuette was made in Crete and the figurines in Corinth. This prototypical design could have been intended originally as a model for a representation of Demeter, since the goddess also appears in relief sculpture wearing a peplos covered by a small mantle over the upper torso;[120] the model, however, was not necessarily for a cult statue. The intention could have been merely to create a design suitable for votives in different media, and votives need not copy cult images, as is obvious in the vast range of types dedicated at the Demeter sanctuary in Corinth.

OTHER FIGURINE TYPES IN PEPLOS AND MANTLE (**H63**, **H64**)

H63 is a small fragment of another type that may have shown a mantle worn over a peplos, to judge from the wide folds of the skirt, which probably represent heavy cloth. The overlapping open edges of the mantle, which presumably hang from the left shoulder, have been rendered with careful detail. The edge of the mantle front is folded back on itself, while the edge of the mantle back lies over it and in turn is folded back in the opposite direction. The mantle hem undulates in response to the wide skirt folds beneath, which are more like those of a peplos than the thin cloth of a chiton. This large, well-made piece originally must have been very handsome and sculptural in effect.

An entirely different combination of peplos and mantle is found in **H64**, the fairly complex draping of which is described in the catalogue. The closely wrapped breast corresponds with a well-known Kore type,[121] although the mantle arrangement is otherwise different. The originally outstretched right arm suggests that the figurine perhaps held a scepter or torch and could have represented the goddess.

FIGURINES IN MANTLE ONLY (**H65–H79**)

During the 4th century B.C., a number of variants were developed in Corinth of a drapery scheme featuring a heavy, curtainlike fall of mantle folds from the left shoulder to the feet, covering the bent arm and hand, which was placed on the hip. This opaque, enveloping mass of cloth contrasts with the smooth stretching of the mantle over the torso to reveal its contours, recalling the broad, simple, but rather bold effects favored by Corinthian coroplasts in earlier periods. The best-preserved example is **H65**, in which the neck and right shoulder are painted pink, without traces of chiton folds, indicating bare flesh and a costume consisting only of a mantle. Mantle-only drapery arrangements similarly baring the right shoulder are found in 4th-century B.C. Attic red-figure vase painting, for example, in a pelike by the Marsyas Painter, dated to the early third quarter of the 4th century B.C.[122] The painting shows Peleus surprising Thetis at her bath and a seated figure, draped only in a mantle and calmly observing the scene; because Eros is beside her, this figure must be Aphrodite. On the basis of this identification and the presence in the Acrocorinth sanctuary of nude figurines that certainly portray Aphrodite (see pp. 172–174),

[120] See p. 132, note 102.
[121] See p. 133, note 104.
[122] Arias and Hirmer 1962, p. 384, color pl. XLVII. In another vase painting, the mantle reveals the breast as well as the shoulder, *LIMC* II, 1984, p. 33, no. 214, pl. 24, s.v. *Aphrodite* (A. Delivorrias et al.); Eros appears here as well to confirm the identification.

the Corinthian figurines so draped also may represent her. A mantled bronze statuette in the Fogg Art Museum, identified as Aphrodite, bares the right breast as well as the shoulder and holds a dove.[123] Also characteristic of **H65** are stocky proportions and small but prominent breasts; the right breast is slightly lower than the left even though the right arm is raised. Similar proportions are found in small-scale representations, in various media, of the nude Aphrodite with a mirror in her left hand, lifting her right hand to arrange her hair.[124] The archetype of **H65** may have been developed from such a nude figure, adding the heavy drapery fall at the side, the skirt, and a few ridges across the torso to indicate folds of cloth. This procedure would account for the inconsistency between cloth that seems very heavy in the drapery fall but nearly transparent over the torso. While coroplastic technique may account in this instance for the drapery style, Late Classical sculpture, in fact, shows a similar contrast between transparency and weight, as in the Epidauros akroteria.[125]

Since the head of **H65** originally must have been turned to the right, to judge from the tilt of the neck, and the right arm was raised, it is possible that the right hand arranged the hair, as in the nude figures mentioned above. It also may be mentioned in this connection that a bronze Aphrodite pudica statuette in Boston, of reported Corinthian provenience, has similar proportions.[126] The closely and smoothly draped figure with heavy thighs may have been a particular favorite in Corinth in the Early Hellenistic period, since it appears also on a bronze mirror found in a mid-3rd-century B.C. Corinthian tomb; the mirror is thought to be earlier than the tomb, perhaps belonging to the first or early second quarter of the 3rd century B.C.[127]

H65 is made of a hard, fine fabric; the surface was smoothed with a finely toothed instrument, which has left its marks particularly on the thighs. Both fabric and tool marks are very similar to those of a fine Nike figurine (MF-71-42, Pl. 76) from the Forum Southwest excavations.[128] It may be significant that the Nike is even more obviously constructed from a nude torso, to which folds have been added at the sides. The workshop practice noted above (p. 58), in which nude "dolls'" torsos were transformed into dancers through the application of folds, seems to be continued here, but more shapely and feminine torsos were used as the foundation. The Nike is from a deposit dating to the third quarter of the 4th century B.C.[129] **H65** was found in the construction fill of the Trapezoidal Building, which contained pottery dating from the 6th to the beginning of the 3rd centuries B.C. It seems fair to say that Corinthian archetype makers were working with this Aphrodite type in the middle to third quarter of the 4th century B.C. and that it continued in use into the 3rd century B.C.

Two larger figurines (size range 4) of similar type are preserved in the fragments **H66** and **H67**, the latter from the construction fill of the Trapezoidal Building, which terminates at the beginning of the 3rd century B.C. Their original composition can be understood best through the better-preserved MF-3396 in the Corinth collection, a probable mold sibling of **H66**.[130] As in **H65**, the mantle, with no garment beneath, is stretched from the right armpit to the left shoulder, and the close wrapping of the torso contrasts with the heavy fall of drapery at the left side; the right upper arm originally was extended to the side, and the right breast is slightly lower than the left. The fold pattern is different, however, in the arrangement of folds to frame the breasts, as in **H56** and **H57**, and the drapery fall is divided by a horizontal overfold, presumably of surplus

[123] Hanfmann 1962, pls. 73, 74; reportedly from Epidauros.
[124] Cf. variants in *LIMC* II, 1984, pp. 60–61, nos. 490–496, pl. 48, s.v. *Aphrodite* (A. Delivorrias et al.).
[125] E.g., Yalouris 1992, pp. 32–33, no. 27, pls. 30, 31.
[126] Comstock and Vermeule 1971, pp. 62–63, no. 64.
[127] Pemberton 1985, pp. 291–294, 301–302, no. 45, pl. 85 (MF-11562); for the date, see p. 294.

[128] The Nike is preserved only from the waist down, but the overall proportions may have been more slender than **H65**.
[129] Drain 1971-1; on the deposit, see C. K. Williams and Fisher 1972, pp. 154–163.
[130] *Corinth* XII, p. 44, no. 256, pl. 22.

cloth, at hip level.[131] In addition, the two vertical open edges of the mantle meet in zigzag folds down the center of the drapery fall below the overfold. It is not a very felicitous pattern and looks very awkward in a complete example in Paris.[132] This figurine, said to have been found in Tanagra but made of Corinthian fabric, wears an unusual, long-sleeved garment beneath the mantle; it is presumably a later variant of the type, since it is only a little more than half the size of **H66**, has a more rigid fold pattern, and has lost the contrast between the torso and drapery fall. The head, similar in type to **H242**, is wrapped in a sakkos.

A tantalizing fragment of beautiful fabric (**H68**) is evidence of yet another possible variant, in which the zigzag folds marking the open edges of the mantle form a diamond pattern, and the slack cloth down the bent left leg drops into a cuff at the ankle. In another small, but very well made and quite lovely variant (**H69**), the overfold of surplus cloth is carried more gracefully over the bent left arm. This figurine is an instructive example of Corinthian style, when it is compared with the corresponding "Tanagra" version, the so-called Sophocles type.[133] In both versions, the focus of the composition is the same, and the enveloping mantle is visually anchored by the curtain of folds at the left side, divided horizontally at thigh level. While the "Tanagra" composition is developed over the surface through tension folds stretched between anatomical points, however, in the Corinthian rendering, geometric forms and volumes prevail over surface line. Another contrast with the "Tanagra" figurines is technical. The Corinthian figurines in this group, for all the care lavished on finishing the fronts, have handmade backs, flattened and summarily treated, while the "Tanagras" normally have fully molded and fairly detailed backs.

The proportions of **H69** are not stocky, and it is altogether a better-formed figurine than **H65**. Its drapery pattern includes a looped fold around one breast, a mannerism previously noted in the peplos-figurine **C36**. The head is relatively small in proportion to the torso. The facial type, long and straight-sided, with large, earthy features, is entirely Corinthian, recalling the much larger Early Classical youth's head **C208**, although there are no certain mechanical relatives among other Corinthian heads. The coiffure, braided back from the center of the forehead, is usually associated with young women and children and is known in other head types, such as **C164**. Although **H69** is from a mixed pottery context, its proportions, drapery scheme, and good fabric should date it no later than the second half of the 4th century B.C.

H70 is a simplified version that has lost much of the weight of the mantle fall, although the close wrapping of the mantle and the distinctive folds above and below the breasts have been retained. It has gained a knot of drapery in the crook of the arm, which is more clearly outlined beneath the mantle, as well as an attached plaque base. It has more attenuated proportions than those of the preceding figurines, and a strongly outthrust left hip. It was made in the same workshop (Workshop I, p. 346), and possibly by the same hand, as the standing female type in chiton and mantle **H100** and **H101** as well as four other figurines (see catalogue). All share the same shallow, summary modeling, thick walls, and sloppy interior; almost all the members of this workshop group were found in the construction fill of the Trapezoidal Building, the pottery of which terminates at the beginning of the 3rd century B.C. **H65** is from the same archaeological context; it shows a drapery arrangement similar to that of **H70**, although it is very different in proportions and far better in technique. On these grounds, the workshop group probably should be placed at or near the end of its chronological context, at the end of the 4th or beginning of the 3rd century B.C.

---

[131] It is difficult to envision the arrangement of cloth that would produce an overfold only on the drapery fall. The motif may have originated in the capelike overfold of the upper edge of the mantle that stretched across the torso as well as the arm; it appears in sculpture, in the late-4th-century B.C. Dionysos "Sardanapalos" type: *LIMC* III, 1986, p. 545, no. 37, pl. 430,

s.v. *Dionysos/Bacchus* (C. Gasparri); Ridgway 1990, p. 91, with bibliography on pp. 105–106, note 39.

[132] *Louvre* III, p. 14, no. D47, pl. 11:c, there dated ca. 330 B.C.; Besques 1994, no. 49. For a Sicilian figurine with a similar drapery fall, see Winter, *Typen* II, p. 17, no. 6.

[133] Kleiner 1984, pp. 95–105, pl. 5.

The fragmentary **H71** may represent an earlier generation of **H70**, since it is larger and repeats the fold pattern over the abdomen with greater clarity. It was found in a pottery context terminating in the second half of the 5th century B.C., although it is unlikely to be earlier than the 4th century B.C. in date. Female figures closely wrapped in mantles do begin to appear in Attic votive reliefs in the late 5th century B.C.,[134] but I would hesitate to place the origins of **H70** within the 5th century B.C. on the basis of a single fragment that is neither from a closed deposit nor of a type found elsewhere on the site in such an early context. **H72** is between **H70** and **H71** in scale; it is of similar type and shows a looped fold pattern over the abdomen like that of **H71** but is not a clear mechanical relative. This example shows long locks of hair on the shoulder.

In two figurines (**H73** and **H74**), the former also from the construction fill of the Trapezoidal Building, the left arm is not akimbo, but the upper arm is pressed against the side, securing the mantle in place, and the forearm originally was extended forward across the chest; neither piece preserves the right side, but the direction of the folds diagonally upward from the left elbow suggests that the right shoulder may have been covered by the mantle rather than revealed. Both have a knot of drapery in the crook of the arm, as in **H70**; **H73** preserves a stiff zigzag drapery cascade and a cuffed ankle fold, as in **H68**. The drapery motif in which a long cascade hangs from a knot can be found also in a 4th-century B.C. sculptured relief of Aphrodite and Eros, found near Perachora and thought to be Corinthian.[135] In this piece, the knot nestles in the crook of Aphrodite's arm and can be understood as the bunched cloth at the top of the cascade, which is held in place by the forearm.

Mantle folds curving down over the left upper arm appear also in **H75** and **H76**. The former probably has nude shoulders, although a slight ridging on the left shoulder could indicate folds; the mantle originally was wrapped under the right arm, as in **H65**. The right upper torso of **H76** is missing, but from the direction of the folds over the abdomen, the mantle may have been gathered up at the hip in the right hand. In this case, it is likely that the mantle was thrown across both shoulders. This figurine is rather crudely made but echoes **H65** in its stocky proportions and is from the same pottery lot. It is rather reminiscent of the voluminous, heavily mantled figures in red-figure vase paintings of Kerch style, which are often sculpturally based.[136] In two pieces (**H77** and **H78**), the mantle covers both arms but reveals the right shoulder. Two figurines from a grave at Delphi, dated to the end of the 4th century B.C., preserve a similar type; they are mantled nearly to the ankles, the right hand gathering up the cloth at the thigh, with a chiton beneath.[137] A similar mantle arrangement also is found in sculpture, in a Muse from the Altar of Athena at Priene, dated to the later 3rd century B.C.[138] **H78** shows a pattern of tautly stretched flat folds over clearly contoured breasts, which is reminiscent in style of the mantled figurine **H99**. A similar arrangement of the upper mantle edge into horizontal folds across the shoulders is found in MF-8662 in the Corinth collection.[139] In this figurine, chiton folds show at the hem, and the pose is that of a dancer.

At least some of these figurines must represent Aphrodite, since nudity beneath a mantle should probably be understood as suggestive of sexual accessibility. The identification seemed reasonable for **H65** and by extension for **H66**. **H69**, however, has a braided coiffure usually seen on figurines of children and young women. Attempts to identify goddesses can be very subjective, and certainly the fragments are difficult to pin down. Goddesses were often represented without

[134] E.g., on the reverse of the Echelos and Basile relief: Boardman 1985, p. 186, fig. 168:b, nymph at the far right.

[135] Hornbostel 1988, pl. 49; attribution on pp. 178–179.

[136] E.g., Arias and Hirmer 1962, p. 384, pls. 225–228, a nuptial lebes by the Marsyas Painter; on these vases, see Schefold 1934.

[137] Walter 1942, cols. 133–134, fig. 6 in cols. 111, 112.

[138] J. C. Carter 1983, pp. 195–196, 204–207, no. 69, pl. XXXI:a, b; on the problems of dating the Priene sculpture, see Ridgway 1990, pp. 164–167, with bibliography on pp. 202–203, note 16; Webb 1996, pp. 99–100. See also a figurine from Priene: Töpperwein-Hoffmann 1971, p. 142, pl. 47:1, dated to the 2nd century B.C.; *Priene*, p. 332, fig. 370.

[139] Weinberg 1948, p. 234, no. E19, pl. LXXXVI.

specific attributes during the 4th century B.C., in all the arts, and while nude Aphrodite types are easy to identify (see pp. 172–174), the variety of draped goddesses is more confusing. The presence of Eros is the best assurance that a figurine represents Aphrodite, as in a group of Corinthian provenience in Athens (Pl. 78).[140]

A much smaller rendering (**H79**) could have derived from a type similar to those discussed here. A few folds at the upper break probably belong to a chiton worn under the mantle, but the folding down of the upper edge of the mantle to form a doubled cape over the left shoulder recalls the design solutions of this group. This figurine, which leans on an ithyphallic herm, could well represent Aphrodite (see p. 276 on herm supports).

FIGURINES IN CHITON AND MANTLE; THE "POETESS" TYPE (**H80–H98**)

Figurines wearing the mantle over a chiton are the most numerous of the draped types, but unlike the two groups discussed above, they are extremely varied in type. Only one group with a typological development, **H88–H97** (the "poetess" type) is discernible among them.

H80 is only a fragment of the right shoulder, breast, and upper arm of a female figurine, but it is very telling nevertheless. The mantle is wrapped tightly under the arm and across the breast, over a chiton, in a fashion characteristic of Kore in 4th-century B.C. votive and document reliefs and sculpture.[141] Since the upper arm is outstretched to the side, as if to hold a scepter or torch, it is likely that this figurine does indeed represent Kore. Although common in sculpture, including a votive relief from Corinth,[142] the type is relatively rare among the figurines from the Demeter sanctuary and presumably was not produced in any quantity in Corinthian workshops. **H81** may be a much more complicated variant of this type, with the chiton dropping from the right shoulder, and the mantle folded into a capelet over the left shoulder, echoing a motif found in a 3rd-century B.C. stone statuette of Kore from Kos.[143] In the Kos statuette, however, the chiton covers the right shoulder, and the mantle folds that stretch diagonally from the left shoulder are caught under the bent right elbow; this motif probably was not carried through in **H81**. Further, the drapery patterns of **H81** are broken into triangular groups of stretched folds. One group of folds radiates from the left hip across the abdomen to the missing right hip, which was probably outthrust, and another group radiates over the left forearm and hand from inside the elbow. For a Corinthian coroplast, this is an unusually complex arrangement, since the general preference was for broader, simpler effects and less detail. The grouping of tension folds into triangular patterns is more in the tradition of "Tanagra" figurines, and yet this figurine does not follow a known "Tanagra" type. **H81** is perhaps something of a hybrid, the result of imposing "Tanagraean" features on an otherwise local type. The fragment **H82** may be from a figurine of similar type but with the right shoulder covered. In the much less well made **H83**, the coroplast may have been trying to imitate the capelike overfold on the left shoulder, but the more interesting wrapping and pulling of folds is lacking. **H83** also somewhat resembles the larger and better-made **H84** in the looped folds over the abdomen.

H85 is a large and well-made piece that finds its best parallel for pose and drapery arrangement in East Greek male sculptural types. In this figurine type, a mantle is draped over a thin chiton, covering the left shoulder and extended forearm; it is rolled around the waist and covers the skirt. There is a triangular overfold in front, not in the more common pointed form but with a curved edge from the right hip to the left thigh; the surface is broken by arrowhead folds. The matronly figure is broad shouldered, with a rather short waist and low, full breasts; the head is

[140] National Archaeological Museum, inv. no. 4160; see p. 130, note 88.

[141] M. Meyer 1989, p. 298, no. A117, pl. 38:1, dated ca. 330 B.C.; see also p. 133, note 104.

[142] S-48, *Corinth* IX, p. 124, no. 255 (incorrectly called a grave stele).

[143] Kabus-Preisshofen 1975, pp. 50–52, pls. 22–24. The date of the Kore is based on epigraphic evidence.

small in proportion to the torso. There is a faint torsion in the pose, the chest turning slightly to the right while the left leg is frontal. The stance is unexpected, because the weight is carried on the right leg; a 5th-century B.C. sculptor of a figure with an overfold draped toward the left side would have balanced it by bending the right knee.[144] The pose, with its sense of unease and slight torsion, is well paralleled by the mid-4th-century B.C. "Maussollos" from Halikarnassos[145] and less well preserved statues from Rhodes and Kos, believed to depend upon a cult statue of Asklepios of the second half of the 4th century B.C.[146] The drapery style of the "Maussollos" is more impressionistic, but deeply pocketed folds down the straight right leg, seeming to originate from the center of the waist beneath the overfold, and a looped fold from the bent left knee, falling into a cuff around the right ankle, are found in both the figurine and the statue.

Interesting parallels again can be found in Kerch-style vase paintings, particularly in the work of the Marsyas Painter, which is dated to the middle to third quarter of the 4th century B.C. The sculptural quality of his figures has been recognized, and his use of unusual, off-balance poses, and small heads together with massive upper torsos, compares well with our figurine.[147] There is also some resemblance between **H85** and the Demeter of Knidos in the facial type and in the matronly, short-waisted proportions coupled with a relatively small head; a more specific parallel can be found in the coiffure, which shows long locks of hair streaming to the shoulders from beneath waving, horizontal locks of hair wrapped from the temples to the cranium.[148] This coiffure is distinctly different from the long hair of the piglet-carrying votaries, which tumbles over the shoulders completely unbound. Moreover, the votaries usually hold offerings against the body, while the forearms and hands of **H85** originally must have been extended. **H85** may wear a very small stephane but no other headdress indicating divinity. In a votive relief in Paris, worshipers are lined up before a goddess, probably Demeter, who is similarly draped, and pours a libation with her lowered and extended right hand;[149] **H85** could perhaps be completed in this way. While it is certainly possible that this figurine represents a deity, perhaps Demeter sacrificing, it is also conceivable that the arrangement of the mantle, rolled and folded down into an apron in the front, signifies that the figure is a priestess rather than a sacrificing goddess.[150] Other figurines from the Demeter sanctuary wearing mantles that are similarly rolled and folded into aprons (e.g., the Middle Hellenistic **H401**) may be priestesses (see p. 255).

H85 was found with 4th-century B.C. and Early Hellenistic pottery. A chest fragment in very good fabric, probably from the same mold (see catalogue), was found in the construction fill of the Trapezoidal Building, the terminal date of which is the beginning of the 3rd century B.C. Like other fine and large figurines from the sanctuary, **H85** has few mechanical relatives. In addition to the probable mold sibling mentioned above, the head may be mechanically related to **H182** (see p. 159). The only torso with any connection is the fragment **H84**, which is similar in the short-waisted proportions and the fold pattern over the abdomen; the mantle roll is carried up to the left shoulder, however. In two fragments of similarly large scale (**H86** and **H87**), the mantle drops straight down the left side from the shoulder; **H87** also has long hair.

[144] E.g., as in the Velletri Athena: Ridgway 1981a, pp. 176–177, with bibliography on p. 190, fig. 115.
[145] Conveniently, Lullies and Hirmer 1960, pl. 211; Waywell 1978, pp. 97–103, no. 26, pl. 13; Ridgway 1997, pp. 126, 133, with bibliography on p. 150, notes 26 and 27, pl. 28.
[146] Kabus-Preisshofen 1989, pp. 25–51, 228–232, nos. 46–49, pls. 1–3.
[147] See, e.g., his nuptial lebes in St. Petersburg: Arias and Hirmer 1962, p. 384, pls. 225–228.
[148] Conveniently, Lullies and Hirmer 1960, pls. 224–225; Ridgway 1997, pp. 332–333, with bibliography on p. 356, note 21, pl. 79:a–c.

[149] Hamiaux 1992, p. 216, no. 224; Hausmann 1960, p. 69, fig. 36 on p. 67; *LIMC* IV, 1988, p. 850, no. 27, pl. 564, s.v. *Demeter* (L. Beschi).
[150] On the mantle folded into an apron as a priestly attribute, see D. B. Thompson 1973, pp. 29–30; for female figures with mantles similarly folded around the hips, in specifically sacrificial contexts, see the "Antium girl" (Ridgway 1990, pp. 228–230, with bibliography on p. 242, note 21) and the paintings of the Villa of the Mysteries in Pompeii (Maiuri 1931, II, pls. II–IV). Hellenistic grave reliefs of priestesses, however, do not show such a costume (Mantes 1990, pp. 97–103, pl. 45), nor does the statue of Hegeso from Priene, who was a priestess of Demeter (*Priene*, p. 150, fig. 120).

The group of figurines **H88**–**H97** is characterized by a complex drapery arrangement and a rather grand gesture of the right arm, which reaches across the chest to grasp the end of the mantle. The pose seems somewhat forced, at least in the context of figurines representing women, perhaps because the grasping of the mantle across the torso is characteristic of the probable portrait of the orator Hypereides.[151] A certain awkwardness in the too-large hands and stiff-legged, flat-footed pose of **H88**, the best-preserved figurine in the group, contributes to this masculine impression, although some members of the group are more graceful. Perhaps the supposed origin of sculptures with similar drapery arrangements in a poetess type helps to explain the gesture, which might have been suitable for a woman who had achieved public recognition through her literary efforts.[152]

The complicated, logically developed, and detailed drapery arrangement points to a prototype of good quality. The mantle is cleverly arranged to reveal the full length of the chiton skirt at the left side, where the palm of the left hand secures the folds of one mantle end against the hip. At the same time, the right hand reaches across the torso to grasp the other mantle end falling from the left shoulder. Additional features are a sling of cloth for the right arm, a panel of drapery falling behind the left arm, and a zigzag fold cascade down the front. The characteristic chiton of thin cloth with a double hem and very narrow folds indicates that the fragments **H96** and **H97**, which preserve only the lower part, may belong to this type.[153] The skirt drapery scheme, however, also appears with a mantle arrangement and arm position similar to the upper part of **H70**, in a Corinthian figurine in London.[154] A related drapery scheme is found in the fragmentary **H98**, which shares the rather awkward, flat-footed stance with right leg forward and the double-hemmed chiton with narrow folds trailing over pointed slippers.[155] The mantle hem is draped higher, however, across the thighs and is gathered up at the hip. Perhaps all these types were developed at the same time, using the same archetype but reworking the drapery to produce variants. A similar drapery arrangement can be found occasionally among male figurines.[156] It is possible that **H95** in this group is a male figurine or a child; the chest is flat, but since the piece is derivative and not very well made, contours originally present in the figure could have been lost.

The popularity of the type in Corinth is demonstrated by the enormous size range, from statuette scale in the fragments **H89** and **H90** down to the very small (size range 2) **H93** and **H94**. The smallest versions have been simplified, eliminating the zigzag fold cascade in the front and covering the entire chiton skirt with the mantle. Apart from the articulated "dolls," this is the only Corinthian type to show such a range in size. Since there is not enough material to demonstrate mechanical continuity, it is unclear whether the figurines represent many generations of the same or parallel mold series, with details reworked as they lost clarity, or are derived from several archetypes of different sizes. A considerable range is apparent in fabric as well, **H97** being the best; there is no correlation between figurine size and quality of fabric.

This figurine type also was popular elsewhere[157] and is found abundantly at West Greek sites.[158] Its identification is uncertain; it could represent a goddess, although popularity in itself means little (certain types of "Tanagra" figurines also were repeated frequently and represent mortal women). None of the examples from the Demeter sanctuary preserves the head, but there are traces of long hair on the shoulder of **H88**. On the other hand, a figurine of this type in

---

[151] Richter 1965, II, p. 211, fig. 1368.

[152] Linfert-Reich 1971, pp. 68–70.

[153] The double hem may show that two chitons were worn, a shorter one over one of normal length, perhaps to compensate for the transparency of the cloth. There is no attempt, however, to demonstrate transparency by superimposing folds, as in the case of Hellenistic sculptures wearing the delicate mantle thought to be the Koan *vestis*: Weber 1969/1970.

[154] Higgins 1967, p. 104, pl. 47:c.

[155] For this schema in sculptured relief, see Neumann 1979, p. 54, pl. 44:b.

[156] *Kharayeb*, p. 63, nos. Kh. 862–865, pl. LXXII, no. 3; the illustrated example is headless but is thought to represent a boy.

[157] See the collection of figurines, with variants, in Winter, *Typen* II, pp. 8–9.

[158] *Enea nel Lazio*, pp. 215–216, no. D160, with bibliography.

Athens, which may be of Corinthian manufacture, has a coiffure with a cluster of curls at the top of the head similar to **H201**.[159] An example from a tomb at Delphi wears a sakkos;[160] most other heads have some variation of the melon coiffure. The heads, therefore, do not offer any consistent clues to identity. The contexts in which these figurines are found may be more helpful. In Lavinium, a figurine of this type was found in a sanctuary of Athena Ilias/Minerva, who is thought to have been worshiped there not only as a goddess of war but also as a patroness of marriage and childbirth.[161] At Gravisca, the votive deposit in which this type was found included dedications to the Etruscan goddess Turan, who was equated with Venus.[162] At Morgantina, the context is a sanctuary of Persephone.[163] An example also was found in the Sanctuary of Demeter at Knossos.[164] Taking these cultic contexts together with the Demeter sanctuary, there seems to be a repeated connection of the type with fertility cult, although not with the same goddess. In sculpture, this type was used to depict Aphrodite, who can be recognized through the presence of Eros.[165] Its identification as Persephone has also been suggested, with reference to a stone statuette in Boston.[166]

The date is easier to determine than the subject; the group must belong to the 4th century B.C., since **H90** and **H97** were found in the construction fill of the Trapezoidal Building, the terminal date of which is the beginning of the 3rd century B.C., and **H88** is from a 4th-century B.C. pottery context. A fragmentary mold from the Potters' Quarter, preserving the bottom of a draped female from the knees downward, has the characteristic stance with right leg forward, a double-hemmed chiton, and a similarly arranged mantle hem.[167] If this mold was indeed fully of the type, it would date the type before the closing of the Potters' Quarter workshops in the 320s B.C. A fragmentary figurine of large scale from the Potters' Quarter also seems to be of this type.[168] Whether similar figurines continued to be made in other workshops in Corinth into the 3rd century B.C. is uncertain. In other centers, however, similar types continued to be used into the 3rd and 2nd centuries B.C.[169]

Figurines in Chiton and Mantle: "Tanagra" and Other Types (**H99–H138**)

Of the mantled figurines that follow, those that show compositional parallels with "Tanagra" figurines probably represent mortal women rather than goddesses. It is notable that the Demeter sanctuary is not very rich in such mantled figurines, in light of the abundance there of other types and the relative popularity of "Tanagras" elsewhere. Relatively few mantled figurines related to "Tanagra" types have been found in Corinth in excavations outside the Demeter sanctuary, although the plundered tombs that supplied collectors with Corinthian figurines during the 19th century yielded several fine examples.[170] Perhaps such figurines, which probably represented ordinary women in a genre rather than cultic context, were considered more suitable as gifts for women's graves, to represent the deceased as they were in life, than as sanctuary votives.

H99 wears a lightweight mantle over a finely folded chiton. The mantle was wrapped closely around the neck and did not cover the missing head. Since there are no traces of locks of hair on the shoulders, the hair must have been bound with a cloth or arranged on top of the head. The gestures of pulling the edge of the mantle at the neck and lifting the hem are consonant with "Tanagra" iconography, but the style of the figurine is broader. There are tension folds across the

[159] Winter, *Typen* II, p. 8, no. 4.
[160] Konstantinou 1964, p. 218, pl. 259:γ.
[161] *Enea nel Lazio,* p. 189; further on this cult in Torelli 1984.
[162] Comella 1978, p. 33, CI 23a–c, pl. XII:54–56.
[163] *Morgantina*, p. 181, nos. 413, 414, pl. 86, with bibliography.
[164] *Knossos*, p. 72, no. 95, pl. 45.
[165] *LIMC* II, 1984, p. 41, nos. 287–292, pl. 30, s.v. *Aphrodite* (A. Delivorrias et al.), with bibliography.
[166] Comstock and Vermeule 1976, p. 38, no. 52.

[167] KH-92, *Corinth* XV, i, pp. 110–111, no. 92, pl. 44.
[168] KT-5-25, *Corinth* XV, ii, p. 134, no. 52, pl. 28.
[169] The example from Knossos (see note 164) was found in deposit E, dated mid–late 3rd century B.C. (for the date, see *Knossos*, pp. 31–35). For a 2nd-century B.C. example, see *Coroplast's Art*, p. 163, no. 52 (in New York); this figurine carries a fan in the manner of "Tanagra" figurines and therefore probably represents a mortal.
[170] E.g., Winter, *Typen* II, p. 7, nos. 5, 7; p. 108, no. 5.

chest, as in some "Tanagras," but they are wide and flat, not narrow and sharp. The figurine is of relatively large scale, and the quality of the fabric is excellent, yet the back mold belongs to a different figurine type, in which the left hand was lowered at the side to grasp the edge of the mantle in a brief cascade of folds, as in **H105**. Apparently the workshop produced concurrently a variant type of identical scale, of which **H105** could represent a later generation. A similar error occurred in the making of the votary with piglet **H1** (see p. 119). Either the concurrent manufacture of variants led to confusion or the correct back mold was broken or spoiled and could not be replaced; a copy made from an existing figurine would have been too small after shrinkage. This figurine belongs to a pottery context terminating in the first quarter of the 3rd century B.C.

H100 and **H101** taken together make up the headless body of a mantled woman. Her right hand pulls the neckline folds of the mantle down into a triangular pattern from beneath the cloth, in a compositional motif known in sculpture in the so-called Aspasia/Sosandra type, which has been traced to an Early Classical original.[171] Mantled figurines in similar poses were widely made[172] and were perhaps popular for the sake of the interesting pattern of folds and for the opportunity to show the contour of the arm beneath the cloth. Although the polishing of the surface of **H101** has dulled the detail considerably, it is apparent that the cloth of the chiton skirt is crinkly. This figurine type may have been popular in Corinth, since there may be evidence for three generations of **H100** (see catalogue).

The left forearm and clenched hand of **H100** are upright from the elbow and tightly wrapped in the cloth, in a gesture documented also in mantled dancers.[173] This gesture may be the apotropaic "phallic hand," which has survived in Mediterranean lands into modern times to guard against evil; it is also found in the form of amulets.[174] An Attic red-figured pelike in London shows the gesture much more graphically than in our figurines, in the mantled hand of a maenad, who dances while Dionysos sacrifices at an altar.[175] **H101** is one of the few figurines from the Demeter sanctuary preserved with its base, in this case a rather clumsily formed high base with rounded front and flat back, and torus moldings at top and bottom, all set on another base in the form of a plaque. Both **H100** and **H101** were made in the same workshop (Workshop I, see p. 346) as the mantled figurine **H70**, which also stands on a plaque base but without another base intervening. Apparently this rather derivative workshop customarily mounted its figurines on plaque bases and did so even when the type being copied already had a base of its own, as did **H101**.[176] Both **H100** and **H101** were found in the construction fill of the Trapezoidal Building, the terminal date of which is the beginning of the 3rd century B.C. The crinkly folds of the chiton skirt of this type, suggesting the texture of the cloth, are stylistically consonant with a date in the later 4th century B.C. and indicate that the figurine, although derivative, was not far in date from its prototype.[177] A possible mechanical relative in Copenhagen (see catalogue) preserves the head, which shows a peaked coiffure and poorly defined facial features.

H102 is probably a smaller version of this type; although the characteristic upraised left forearm is missing, the surface of the break is consistent with such a restoration. The pose of the right arm differs in that it creates a triangular pattern of tension folds by folding the arm in the mantle cloth as if in a sling. The characteristic diagonal tension fold from the left hip to the right leg was emphasized in **H102** by tooling, but since the proportions have changed considerably towards narrower shoulders and greater slenderness, it is uncertain whether we are dealing with a considerably altered later generation or a figurine with no mechanical relationship.

---

[171] Ridgway 1970, pp. 65–69, with bibliography on p. 75.

[172] E.g., Winter, *Typen* II, p. 32, no. 7, of reported Corinthian provenience.

[173] E.g., Winter, *Typen* II, p. 146, no. 8; probably also **H156**.

[174] Elworthy 1895, pp. 149–155, 255–258; Wright 1866, pp. 65–72. On sexual symbolism as apotropaic, see also p. 171.

[175] Simon 1953, p. 52, pl. 3.

[176] For a similar doubling of bases, see a "Tanagra" figurine in Athens, dated to the late 4th century B.C.: Kleiner 1984, p. 125, pl. 28:a.

[177] On the date range of crinkly drapery, see Palagia 1982, pp. 102–103, with bibliography.

H102 is notable because it includes the head, which is otherwise known in the Demeter sanctuary in a number of isolated examples (see catalogue). The head, too large in proportion to the torso, was not covered by the mantle. The coiffure has been reworked, but there are traces in back of a vertical plait that originally must have been pulled up from the forehead; the plait has been effaced in front, and a modified lampadion knot has been added at the top of the head. The plaited coiffure, generally associated with representations of children (see p. 57), is known in the Demeter sanctuary in **C164** and **C165**, heads related to articulated "dolls." In its later manifestation, the braided coiffure has been reworked for a representation of a mature woman. The profile of the face of **H102** recalls that of **H1** structurally, in its sloping forehead and receding chin, but otherwise the features are dissimilar. More similar features are found in the "doll's" head **C156**, which, however, is different in overall shape. **H102** is from a pottery context terminating in the early 3rd century B.C., as are some of the mold siblings of its head (see catalogue).

Figurines with the right arm wrapped in the mantle as if in a sling, the left hand on the outthrust hip, and the right leg bent or advanced are often called "Sophocleans"[178] because their composition is reminiscent of a sculptured portrait type of Sophocles.[179] **H103** and **H104** are smaller variants of this type. In **H103**, the mantle covers the head and all the hair in front. In spite of the poor state of preservation, one can see that this figurine was originally well conceived and was not heavily reworked, although the fabric is coarser than usual.

H104, in the same pose, is preserved with its plaque base, on which it was mounted to present the three-quarter view. It resembles **H102** in its slender and narrow-shouldered proportions, and the folds of the chiton skirt are crinkly, as in **H101**, but the surface has been so heavily reworked that the original fold pattern is no longer discernible, and it is so heavy for its size that it may even be solid; it is clearly not the work of a very able craftsman. Its pottery context terminates at the beginning of the 3rd century B.C.

The left arm of **H105** is at the side and only slightly bent to allow the hand to grasp the edge of the short and very thin mantle. The pyramidal, frontal composition is static, but the type originally may have been more interesting, emphasizing the transparency of the mantle in a way that is not evident in this dull impression. An earlier generation of this type could have been produced in the good workshop that made **H99**, as suggested above. **H106** is a rather coarse rendering of a similar composition. A better-preserved mold sibling of the head (see catalogue) shows a round, kittenish face more Attic than Corinthian in style, although the frontal pose of the head is not "Tanagraean."

Three small and not very well made mantled figurines are best included here, since in all the left arm was posed as in **H105** and **H106**, down at the side and grasping the edge of the mantle. In **H107** and **H108**, the mantle covered the head; a mold sibling of **H108**, MF-1976-88 in the Corinth collection (Pl. 75), preserves the head, which is somewhat similar in type to **C95**, although much smaller, with the hair bound in a knot on top of the head. The pose of **H109** is somewhat uncertain, since the right arm, which was never completely formed, leans on a pillar, but the figurine is of interest because its two-stepped base is preserved.

From better workshops come two mantled heads and upper torsos, **H110** and **H111**. **H110** has the left arm akimbo, like a "Sophoclean," but the incompletely preserved right arm was at the side, perhaps originally holding something against the leg. The composition recalls a mantled dancer type discussed below (**H153**–**H157**, see pp. 153–154), but the absence of a flying panel of drapery behind the left arm suggests that the figurine is in a quietly standing pose. The face has deep shadows, formed both by the pleated mantle fold overhanging the forehead and by

178 Kleiner 1984, pp. 95–105, pl. 5.
179 Richter 1965, I, p. 129, no. 2, fig. 680, the Lateran type.

the "Skopasian" eyes, deeply set and downturned below prominent brows. The style of the face would date the prototype about the middle of the 4th century B.C.[180]

H111, although similarly draped, is very different in its very narrow, sloping shoulders and its wide-eyed, alert, girlish face, without dramatic shadowing. Beneath the mantle, the hair is piled high and bound across the forehead in a sakkos, a coiffure found also in mantled dancers (e.g., **H170**). Yet despite their differences, both **H110** and **H111** show some similarity to a very fine group of reported Corinthian provenience in the Louvre,[181] representing two standing girls, one a mantled figurine, the other differently draped and holding a ball. The girlish face of **H111** is quite similar to that of the mantled figure of the group, except that her mantle forms an overhanging peak, as in **H110**;[182] the intense, more emotional face of **H110**, however, is more like that of the girl with the ball. Clearly there is no direct mechanical relationship among these figurines, but the similarities point to some connection in the use of workshop materials, combined in different ways. The isolated mantled head **H112** could have belonged to a figurine similar in type to **H111** but with a higher, more pointed coiffure. The poorly defined, expressionless features recall the head of the mantled dancers **H153** and **H154**, but the pose of **H112** seems to be frontal. The very high, pointed sakkos recalls an Attic head type from the Pnyx, dated to the early 4th century B.C.[183]

Given the general preference of Corinthian coroplasts for broad effects, it is not surprising that they successfully produced a mantled type in which the cloth was draped like a tent over the torso, allowing for a pattern of sweeping folds. **H113** and **H114** are fragmentary examples of the type, which is better illustrated by a fully preserved Corinthian example in New York.[184] If, as its fold pattern suggests, **H113** belonged to this type, the mantle would have fallen to the knees in a series of deep catenaries from the hidden right arm to the left wrist, over which the folds of the open edge of the mantle were draped; the chest is preserved, with curving folds across the shoulders and rib cage framing the breasts. The head of the New York figurine, with a Knidian coiffure and long locks of hair at the nape, is not precisely paralleled at the Demeter sanctuary, but heads in the Corinth collection are similar.[185] **H114** differs in several respects: the shoulders are narrower and more sloping; the fold pattern, as far as it is preserved, is different and shows a loose roll of folds around the neck, with an end of the mantle tucked in from the back; and the left hand may have been at the chest, beneath the mantle.

Several fragments of mantled figurines are not sufficiently preserved to accurately reconstruct their original types. **H115** shows the right arm akimbo; its excellent fabric makes the lack of typological information all the more regrettable. It is from a pottery context terminating at the beginning of the 3rd century B.C. The type of **H116**, also beautifully made, is somewhat less mysterious by virtue of a few clues. A deep vertical fold to the left of the missing left foot must have arisen from some movement higher on the figure. It could be the fold dropping from the strongly outthrust left hip of "Sophoclean" figurines.[186] In the pose of the feet, the arrangement of the hemline, and the folds curving up from the right foot there is a resemblance to a popular

[180] On the chronology of the Tegea sculpture and the problems of its attribution, see Ridgway 1997, pp. 48–52, with bibliography.

[181] *Louvre* III, p. 53, no. D298, pl. 63:a.

[182] Another mantled head in the Corinth collection, MF-9261 (Romano 1994, p. 93, no. 90, pl. 28), with an overhanging peak, is also close to the Louvre type; this head may not be an import, as published.

[183] *Pnyx*, p. 143, no. 44, fig. 58.

[184] The Metropolitan Museum of Art, inv. no. 07.286.20, unpublished. On the type, see Kleiner 1984, pp. 124–125, pl. 11:a, d. Two examples of reported Corinthian provenience are published in Winter, *Typen* II, p. 20, nos. 2 and 5; no. 2,

in Würzburg, now published in Schmidt 1994, p. 97, no. 141, pl. 27, does seem to be Corinthian (its rather harshly tooled retouch recalls that of another draped female figurine in the Corinth collection, MF-3396 [*Corinth* XII, p. 44, no. 256, pl. 22]). An example in Boston, with the mantle drawn over the head (*Coroplast's Art*, p. 112, no. 5), is of reported Corinthian provenience, but the clay, although pale, is not really typical of Corinth and the modeling of the folds is rather drier than usual; the fold pattern, however, does recall the New York figurine.

[185] E.g., MF-3875, *Corinth* XII, p. 47, no. 288, pl. 24, there dated to the 3rd century B.C.

[186] E.g., Kleiner 1984, pp. 95–105, pl. 5.

"Tanagra" type with many variants, holding the drapery forward over the hands;[187] in this case, the deep vertical fold would have fallen from the hand rather than the hip. The figurine is wide and relatively shallow and may originally have had a long, rectangular base. It is similar in scale and style to **H88**, and in the somewhat flat-footed look occasioned by the trailing hem over feet set fairly close together, but it is much better in the quality of the fabric; its archetype probably dates to about the same time, probably no later than the third quarter of the 4th century B.C. **H116** is from the construction fill of the Trapezoidal Building, which terminates at the beginning of the 3rd century B.C. Since a possible mold of the type of **H88** was found in the Potters' Quarter (see p. 142), it may be that mantled figurines of good quality were produced there during the third quarter of the 4th century B.C., before the demise of the workshops ca. 320 B.C.

H117 is a smaller mantled figurine of equally good quality that is to some extent a mirror image of **H116**. In this case, the skirt folds are looped from the advanced left foot towards the right hip; at the other side, a group of folds radiates from the top of the thigh. As far as it is preserved, the piece is sufficiently close in size and fold pattern to a group of Boeotian figurines in Boston[188] to suggest collateral molds or perhaps a common archetype. Perhaps significantly, the fragmentary ephedrismos group **H390** (see p. 201), which is of the same fine fabric as **H117**, has a probable mechanical relationship with a Boeotian rendering of the ephedrismos type.[189] Perhaps the parallel between these two cases points to an exchange of workshop materials between certain workshops of Corinth and one of the Boeotian centers. This particular composition is not typical of Athenian "Tanagras." **H118** is a fragment of another figurine in a mantle reaching nearly to the feet, in this case with looped folds over the right ankle; its plaque base has been preserved. It is from a pottery context terminating at the beginning of the 3rd century B.C.

Several fragments show a shorter mantle. In one of these (**H119**), the identification of the costume is not entirely clear. The figurine does not show the differentiation in the weight of the cloth of chiton and mantle usually seen in mantled figurines. The mantle(?) hem is gathered up at the left thigh, with a fold pattern reminiscent of the way the votary **H3** gathers up the hem of her peplos overfold at the hip. The hem of **H119**, however, in its complete form would have fallen at the right side at least to the knees. While a peplos overfold of that length is not impossible, it is longer than those usually seen on Corinthian figurines. Moreover, the cluster of folds gathered at the side looks like the open edges of the garment clumped together, and the peplos is normally open at the right side rather than the left. The composition of **H120**, a smaller and much less well made figurine, is similar in the drapery arrangement, although in this case the coroplast made an attempt to render a mantle of thinner cloth than the skirt. The type is not likely to be identical to the foregoing figurines, since the left knee is bent, and the stance therefore was different. The oval base with torus moldings is preserved.

H121 preserves a similar upward sweep of the hem of a thin mantle, but the figurine is of a completely different type, in which the ankles are crossed and the left side leans against a columnar support. Coroplasts made use of this composition mainly in representations of the seminude Aphrodite,[190] but the upper torso of **H121** must have been entirely draped, since the ends of the mantle hang beside the support as if falling from the left shoulder. Since the figure stands at an angle and seems to have leaned heavily against the support, and there is no sign of the left arm at the side, it is likely that the left elbow originally was propped on top of the column. Such a composition can be seen in a fragmentary figurine in Berlin of reported Corinthian provenience,[191] although the drapery arrangement does not seem to be the same. The cross-legged, leaning pose of **H121** is also found in **H146**, which wears only a chiton; its

---

[187] Kleiner 1984, p. 111, pl. 2:c, d.
[188] *Coroplast's Art*, p. 111, no. 4.
[189] *Coroplast's Art*, p. 128.

[190] E.g., *British Museum* I, pp. 194–195, no. 728, pl. 95 (Attic, mid-4th century B.C.).
[191] Winter, *Typen* II, p. 82, no. 3. See also the imported, draped Argive figurine **I10.**

good workmanship is sufficiently close to that of **H121** to suggest that they were made in the same workshop. In **H122**, the drapery arrangement is reversed; the thin mantle falls to the knee at the left side and is gathered at the right hip, where a cluster of folds suggests that it was originally grasped in the hand;[192] the figurine is preserved with its plaque base.

H123 is much more Classical in style than the more Hellenistic versions of a figurine in chiton and mantle discussed above. The mantle is rolled down over the abdomen into a triangular overfold with a curved edge, similar to that of **H85** but smaller, and drooping below the waist into a graceful curve, in the manner of Classical sculpture of the later 5th century B.C.; also Classical are the transparent chiton folds clinging to the right breast but leaving the shoulder bare,[193] and the sturdy proportions of the torso. For all the Classicism of **H123**, however, there is currently no evidence for a series of Corinthian 5th-century B.C. female figurines in chiton and mantle to which it could have belonged. The closest connection to local 5th-century B.C. work is its resemblance in drapery arrangement and partly in pose to the dancer **C282**, although in a much simplified form. **H123** can best be related in pose, drapery arrangement, and proportions to a fine Corinthian figurine in Athens, depicting Aphrodite and Eros (Pl. 78).[194] The Aphrodite's mantle drops in a heavy fall below the left forearm and is worn as a veil over the head, which in addition shows a polos and the long, streaming locks of hair usually seen in Corinthian votaries. **H123** is cruder and simpler, but a slight rim bordering the left forearm suggests that a mantle fall has been cut away from the left side. In addition, a small projection below the right elbow, without an organic relation to the drapery, could be the remains of the figure of Eros cut away from the right side. If this interpretation is correct, the right arm would have been repositioned across the abdomen when the archetype of **H123** was made. The long locks of hair of the Aphrodite are also preserved on the shoulders of **H123**. Since this figurine is from a pottery context dating to the last quarter of the 4th century B.C., it can help to confirm a 4th-century B.C. date for the Aphrodite figurine, which is sometimes dated too late, in the 3rd century B.C.

Whether **H123** also represents Aphrodite is another question. The long hair could serve for a votary figurine, although the costume is not typical. The hand on the abdomen calls to mind the votaries **H43**–**H45**, although these figurines represent girls rather than mature women and hold the opposite hand to the abdomen; **H123** may simply be grasping the mantle roll. Since the compositional parallel with the Aphrodite in Athens is strong, it seems most likely that **H123** did represent the goddess, although without the accompanying Eros. Whatever the subject of this figurine, it is clear that the 4th-century B.C. coroplastic workshops of Corinth produced not only survivals of 5th-century B.C. types and new compositions with the stylistic features of Early Hellenistic plastic art but also new and highly competent designs in a style that was firmly rooted in the art of the later 5th century B.C. **H124** shows an arrangement of the mantle similar to **H123**, but its essentially Hellenistic style is revealed in the higher girding of the chiton and the tighter wrapping of the mantle around the waist, as in **H85**.

In **H125**, the mantle is draped over the left shoulder and bent arm as in **H123**, but it falls diagonally across the torso from the right shoulder to the left hip; its hem is lifted up at the other side by the raised right forearm. While the composition is built upon triangular forms, as are "Tanagra" types, there is none of the play of tension folds that is one of the defining characteristics of "Tanagras" and therefore no reason to make that connection. In addition to an example in Athens of reported Corinthian provenience,[195] there are others from Italy and Sicily,[196] suggesting that this type could have been developed by the prolific and skilled West Greek coroplasts.[197]

---

[192] Cf. Kleiner 1984, p. 53, pl. 8:a.

[193] The best-known rendering is the garment of the Nike untying her sandal from the balustrade of the Temple of Athena Nike: conveniently, Lullies and Hirmer 1960, pl. 191.

[194] National Archaeological Museum, inv. no. 4160; see p. 130, note 88.

[195] Winter, *Typen* II, p. 14, no. 4b.

[196] E.g., Winter, *Typen* II, p. 14, no. 4d.

[197] On the rich repertoire of draped female types developed in the West, see *Morgantina*, pp. 51–64; *Coroplast's Art*, pp. 64–70, both with bibliography.

The rather poorly made **H125** might then have been a copy of a West Greek type. It was found in a pottery context of the later 4th century B.C. In the crudely reworked and fragmentary **H126**, the torso would have been closely wrapped in the mantle, the upper edge rolled and draped diagonally from the right shoulder. In the well-known version of this mantle arrangement on the Mantineia base,[198] and also on a figurine of reported Corinthian provenience,[199] the rolled edge drops over the left wrist. In **H126**, however, the type was altered and the roll anchored at the hip under the left hand.

H127 preserves only the right hand clutching a fold cascade, but the fragment is sufficiently distinctive to suggest the original type. The complete figurine originally may have resembled a figurine of Corinthian provenience in Athens,[200] which wears a chiton and a small mantle draped over the left shoulder and bent arm; the cloth is draped around the back and reappears at the right thigh, where the hand grasps the end of the mantle in a cascade of folds. A similar cascade, now missing, must originally have been part of the drapery scheme of **H47**, which represents a young girl. A probable mold sibling of **H127** was found in the construction fill of the Trapezoidal Building, which terminates at the beginning of the 3rd century B.C. (see catalogue).

In the draped female figurines that follow, the distinctive element is the mantle roll slung from hip to hip to frame the abdomen, which is revealed almost as if nude beneath the transparent cloth of the chiton. This drapery scheme, which had its origins in late-5th-century B.C. Athenian sculpture, particularly in the Nikai of the parapet of the Temple of Athena Nike,[201] was used in 4th-century B.C. sculpture and reliefs in a variety of subjects.[202] The best-known example of its use is in the 3rd-century B.C. Themis of Rhamnous;[203] by the 2nd century B.C. it is so common as to be almost a cliché.[204] Most of the Corinthian figurines that feature drapery of this kind appear to belong to the 3rd century B.C. The clinging Hellenistic chiton usually worn beneath the mantle can be better observed in the unmantled figurines discussed in the following section.

The overtly sensual pose, which emphasizes the nearly nude abdomen naturally suggests that at least some of these figures, if they are goddesses, represent Aphrodite. This identification makes some sense in the context of the Demeter sanctuary, in which clearly recognizable figurines of Aphrodite were offered (see pp. 172–174). Other identifications, however, are sometimes indicated. A statue draped in this way found in the Sanctuary of Demeter at Knossos has been tentatively identified as Kore, since Aphrodite is not otherwise represented at that shrine.[205] While the finds from the Acrocorinth sanctuary suggest that representations of Aphrodite were appropriate in a shrine of Demeter, a figure so draped definitely does represent Kore on a relief from Eleusis.[206] A figurine from Syracuse in a similar costume also is though to depict Kore.[207] On the other hand, a figurine of reported Corinthian provenience in Berlin is so draped but represents a mortal woman holding a duck.[208]

Among the Acrocorinth figurines, **H128**, leaning languidly against a pillar and wearing a sleeveless, transparent chiton, has two attributes that suggest Artemis, a long torch and a diagonal band across the chest that could be a baldric, although there is no sign of a quiver.[209] The

[198] Todisco 1993, pl. 289.

[199] Winter, *Typen* II, p. 24, no. 1.

[200] Winter, *Typen* II, p. 71, no. 1.

[201] Conveniently, Lullies and Hirmer 1960, pl. 191.

[202] Palagia 1982, p. 100, note 3; M. Meyer 1989, p. 306, no. A142, pl. 42:1, dated 320–310 B.C.

[203] Ridgway 1990, pp. 55–57, with bibliography on p. 70, note 40, pl. 31.

[204] E.g., a 2nd-century B.C. stone "Aphrodite" statuette from Sparta: Delivorrias 1969, p. 134, pl. 127:β.

[205] *Knossos*, pp. 93–95, pls. 71–73.

[206] Mylonas 1961, p. 190, fig. 63.

[207] *Coroplast's Art*, p. 68, fig. 55; *Morgantina*, p. 47, pl. 145, fig. 12.a

[208] Winter, *Typen* II, p. 7, no. 5; Kriseleit and Zimmer 1994, p. 112, no. 31 (the 3rd-century date suggested there is too late; see discussion of head type, p. 162).

[209] For Hellenistic sculptural representations of Artemis in a full-length garment and baldric, see Marcadé 1969, pp. 220–223, pl. XXXVI; Merker 1973, p. 27, no. 18, pl. 8, figs. 16–18; *LIMC* II, 1984, pp. 695–696, no. 974, pl. 518, s.v. *Artemis* (L. Kahil and N. Icard), a votive relief from Brauron dated ca. 330 B.C.; *LIMC* II, 1984, pp. 635–639, nos. 124–168, pls. 454–457.

matronly, short-waisted proportions of this figurine and the flat, round button fastening the garment at the shoulder, which recalls the similar fastenings of the Middle Hellenistic "priestess" type (see p. 250), suggest a later-3rd- or early-2nd-century B.C. date.

In **H128**, the left arm is sharply bent and the hand, covered by mantle folds wrapped around the wrist like a bracelet, lifts the mantle roll to the hip. The fragment **H129**, however, speaks of a different composition in which the bare hand supports the folds of the mantle roll lower down, probably at the top of the thigh. **H130** is yet another version, in statuette scale. In this figurine, the hand is not preserved, but a clump of drapery at the hip suggests that the cloth was secured there. The steep angle of the mantle roll and the broad rendering of the drapery recall a large Corinthian Hellenistic terracotta figure (MF-13017) thought to represent a maenad (Pl. 76). On the basis of style, **H130** could be Middle Hellenistic in date. Its thin-walled, slightly coarse fabric suggests a workshop link with the "Rhodian Aphrodite" **H140** and three other draped female figurines of different types (Workshop K, see p. 346).

Two much smaller, nearly miniature figurines, **H131** and **H132**, preserve more of the composition. In **H132**, the remains of drapery in the back and the raised right arm suggest that the mantle originally was lifted high in the right hand, in a composition usually associated with Leda or Aphrodite (see p. 174). The small size and rather poor quality of this figurine suggest that it may stand at the end of a long mold series. The poorly made and preserved **H133** originally had a raised right arm and seems to have been similar in type to **H132**. In **H131**, the mantle roll is draped over the left forearm. In this more ladylike version, the right arm is at the side and the chiton is not transparent; the narrow-shouldered, high-girded torso is reminiscent of small votary figurines such as **H37**, on which this type may well have been constructed.

H134 is poorly preserved, but the elements that are clear include a high-girded chiton and a mantle dropping steeply from the left upper arm toward the missing right hip. In this case, the drapery scheme includes a heavy mantle fall at the left side, a feature consonant with the date of this figurine, which is from the construction fill of the Trapezoidal Building, which terminates at the beginning of the 3rd century B.C. Another figurine in Corinth (MF-7417) may be of similar type;[210] it shows the steep angle of the mantle roll and preserves the right side, with the shoulder lowered and the arm akimbo. In **H135**, which originally leaned on a support at the left side, the mantle also drops from the upper arm, and in this case from the shoulder as well, but here the upper edge of the mantle is not rolled. Short-waisted proportions similar to **H128** are found in **H136**, in which the only evidence for the mantle roll is a preserved fragment at the right hip. As far as the figurine is preserved, the proportions and composition match a figurine of reported Corinthian provenience in Berlin.[211]

Clearly, there is great variety within this group, as was the case also among figurines more closely wrapped in the mantle, and it is not possible to point to any predominant type that could have had strong cultic significance. Where there is reason to identify a figurine as a deity, the goddesses suggested by attributes or pose are Artemis and Aphrodite. With the exception of **H134**, there is no reason to date any of this group earlier than the 3rd century B.C., and at least one member may actually be Middle Hellenistic.

In two fragmentary figurines (**H137** and **H138**), the mantle, lifted in the left hand, falls like a curtain behind the arm, in a composition recalling the Classical peplos-figurine **C36**. Parallels in sculptured reliefs suggest that **C36** represents Demeter (see p. 36), but **H138** wears a fairly high-girded chiton, a garment less characteristic of Demeter than the peplos. Since possible representations of the nude Aphrodite also lift the mantle in a gesture recalling the *anakalypteria* of a bride (see p. 174), perhaps these two figurines represent Aphrodite rather than Demeter. Both pieces in their original state were large and of good quality. The scale of **H138**, its thin

---

[210] *Corinth* XII, p. 56, no. 390, pl. 35; probably not dancing, as suggested there, and not Roman in date.   [211] Winter, *Typen* II, p. 60, no. 7.

walls, and the high girding of the chiton could bring it into connection with the workshop group (Workshop K, see p. 346) that includes the "Rhodian Aphrodite" **H140**. The pottery context of **H138** terminates in the Hellenistic period, that of **H137** in the early 3rd century B.C.

STANDING DRAPED FEMALE FIGURINES: WITHOUT MANTLE
(H139–H152)

The pieces discussed in this section are clothed in a manner found in both Hellenistic sculpture and figurines, in which the female form is enhanced by a clinging, high girded chiton, usually without an overfold and sometimes sleeveless.[212] While these figurines, in their mostly fragmentary condition, do not preserve mantles, at least two (**H139** and **H140**) may in their complete state have been cloaked. **H139** shows a fold from the right shoulder to the waist that is deeper than the corresponding fold at the left side and therefore could have belonged to a mantle. In **H140**, the arched folds over the originally advanced left thigh suggest that we have a variant, with pose reversed, of the "Rhodian Aphrodite" type.[213] In this type, the mantle does not cover the torso but falls over one shoulder and bent arm, then is draped around the back of the figure, and finally arches over the advanced opposite thigh. In a nice detail of the large and well-made **H140**, the two smallest fingers push aside a fold, perhaps of a mantle, beside the right thigh. It is possible that this figurine represents Aphrodite.

H141 in its complete form is known to have been unmantled, since a mold sibling in the Corinth collection (MF-11457, Pl. 76) preserves the entire type. The slender, shapely figure leans languidly toward the right side against a column, the top of which is draped, presumably with the divested mantle. The sleeved, high-girded, clinging chiton droops from the left shoulder. The coiffure shows a lampadion knot on top of the head and long locks of hair falling loosely over the shoulders. Taking together the pose, the revealing costume, the stately but provocative demeanor, and the long locks of hair, which appear on a Corinthian figurine of Aphrodite and Eros in Athens (Pl. 78),[214] it seems fair to identify MF-11457 and **H141** as Aphrodite. Perhaps the same identification holds for **H142**, which is in mirror image and probably leaned on a support under the left elbow; its drooping chiton sleeve and long hair add to its resemblance to **H141**.

The subjects of the remaining figurines in this group are less clear. **H139** seems slightly off balance, as if leaning toward the left side, yet there are no signs of a support; the arms originally could have been raised toward the head, perhaps to arrange the hair. The right shoulder of **H143** is lifted, as if the figure originally leaned on a support in the manner of **H141**. The proportions, however, are much more matronly. The tantalizing fragment (**H144**) of what must have been a very fine, large figure of sculptural style, shows the belt knotted just beneath the breasts. It reveals little about its subject, unless it is the same as that of **H145**, which has a similarly knotted belt. In **H145**, the diagonal backward sweep of the skirt folds and the corresponding movement of the belt ties indicate that the figure is in motion, perhaps running, as in the ephedrismos type (see p. 201). It could also represent a flying Nike (see pp. 183–184). These two figurines, together with **H130**, **H140**, and possibly **H138**, could constitute a workshop group (Workshop K, see p. 346). They are all large in scale and thin-walled; two of them (**H130** and **H144**) have similar, slightly coarse fabric; and all are of related types.

Two figurines preserving only the lower parts (**H146** and **H147**) show no traces of mantle folds on or around the skirts. **H146** leans to the left side with ankles crossed, in a pose similar to the mantled **H121**. A different, more sensual atmosphere is conveyed, however, by revealing the leg

---

[212] On this garment, see Higgins 1986, pp. 120–121.

[213] This type is known in Corinth in a Roman stone statuette, S-429: see Ridgway 1990, pp. 216–217, with bibliography on pp. 239–240, note 8, pl. 100.

[214] National Archaeological Museum, inv. no. 4160; see p. 130, note 88.

through the clinging cloth and placing the right hand saucily on the hip. **H147** is noteworthy for its particularly fine fabric, which places it in the 4th century; its pottery context terminates at the beginning of the 3rd century B.C. The rather short hem that touches the insteps without trailing is consonant with a relatively early date; the garment could be a peplos rather than a chiton.

The final figurine to be discussed with this group is the skirt fragment **H148**. There are no signs of a mantle in the front, but the bottom of a cascade of folds is preserved beside the left ankle. Mantle folds therefore may have fallen from above, perhaps lifted and carried behind the figure. Instead of the pointed slippers common among standing draped female types, this figurine wears sandals with fairly high, shaped soles, over which the skirt hem collapses.

Two figurines (**H149** and **H150**) are related in the pose of the arms to the popular mantled "pudicitia" type known in both "Tanagra" figurines[215] and sculpture.[216] In this type, one forearm is stretched across the waist to the opposite elbow; the hand of the opposite arm reaches toward the face. The pose makes somewhat more sense in a mantled figure, in which at least one hand holds the drapery in place. In the miniature **H149**, which preserves the composition best, there is a hem across the ankles that could belong to a mantle. Since the forearms are bare, however, the chiton probably has a double hem. In **H150**, which preserves the shoulders better, there clearly are no signs of a mantle. Mantled figures in this pose in both small and large scale usually represent mortal women; in sculpture the pose is a stock type for portraits.[217] The context of the hand-to-elbow, hand-to-face gesture is also sometimes funerary, as in its repeated use in the Mourning Women Sarcophagus.[218] It seems fair, therefore, to identify **H149** and **H150** as mortal women, although nymphs are also known in this pose.[219] The type does not seem to have enjoyed the same popularity in Corinth as in other centers.

H151 lacks the left forearm, but it may be another example of the "pudicitia" type. **H152** is unusual in composition; it recalls the "pudicitia" type in that the right forearm lies across the waist, but in this case the hand may lift a fold of drapery (of a mantle?), and the left arm hangs at the side. The raised right shoulder gives a sense of movement; although there is no torsion, one feels there ought to be and is reminded of the unstable, twisting movement of the Heyl Aphrodite in Berlin,[220] although the pose is not identical. All the figurines of this group are short waisted in proportion and show fairly broad, but rounded shoulders, high breasts, and plump arms; the upper arms are short in consequence of the short waist. Such proportions are reminiscent of 4th-century B.C. Peloponnesian sculpture, as seen, for example, in the Temple of Asklepios at Epidauros.[221] The miniature **H149**, which probably belongs to the end of a mold series, is somewhat elongated in the lower torso and legs. None of this group should be earlier than the 3rd century B.C., and a Middle Hellenistic date is possible, particularly for **H149**.

DANCERS AND RELATED HEADS
(H153–H174)

The ritual use of dance in the worship of certain deities, including Demeter and Kore, has been well established on archaeological and literary grounds.[222] Figurines of mantled dancers presumably represent mortal women dancing to honor the deities in whose sanctuaries they are found, and given the pleasure derived from this activity, it is not surprising that mantled dancer

---

[215] Kleiner 1984, pp. 160–165, pl. 33.

[216] Bieber 1961, pp. 132–133.

[217] E.g., the Cleopatra from Delos: Marcadé 1969, pp. 132–134, pl. LXV.

[218] Conveniently, Lullies and Hirmer 1960, pls. 207–209.

[219] In a votive relief in Athens: Hausmann 1960, pp. 60–61, fig. 30.

[220] Conveniently, Lullies and Hirmer 1960, pl. 272.

[221] E.g., the Nike akroterion: Yalouris 1992, pp. 30–31, no. 25, pl. 26.

[222] The evidence has been collected by Dorothy B. Thompson in *Troy*, pp. 102–105, with bibliography; see also *Morgantina*, pp. 64–65; Clinton 1992, pp. 27–28; Lonsdale 1993.

figurines were generally popular in the Greek world.[223] The best-known mantled dancer is the later-3rd-century B.C. bronze Baker Dancer in New York, the study of which has stimulated a good deal of interest in the terracotta versions as well,[224] but the type appears to have originated much earlier, in the early 4th century B.C. in Athens.[225]

A question previously raised with regard to the Classical kalathiskos dancers is whether or not the votive offering of dancer figurines indicates that ritual dancing actually took place in the Acrocorinth sanctuary (see pp. 58–59). There are few references to music in the material remains from the Acrocorinth sanctuary (the model lyre **V13**, the youths and a banqueter with lyres **C190**, **C193**, **C217**, the piping satyr and Pan **C274** and **C277**, and the aulos held by **C86**). Another problem is the lack of an obviously suitable place for dancing. The Theater on the Upper Terrace, like the theatral area of the Classical period, seems to have been intended for viewers only, not performers, but dancing could have taken place in the Middle Terrace central courtyard, which was expanded after ca. 300 B.C.; from here it could have been seen by spectators gathered in the Theater above.[226] In light of the popularity of mantled dancers and other dancing figurines as votive offerings, it seems perverse not to allow that dances were performed in a sanctuary that housed the worship of two major fertility goddesses, accompanied at least by Dionysos and Aphrodite (see pp. 330–332), who are themselves associated with dancing. In fact, the question may be not whether or not people danced at the sanctuary but to which deities the dances were directed.

Figurines of mantled dancers were dedicated to Demeter in other sanctuaries, including those of Priene, Pergamon, and Kharayeb.[227] It is also possible that Dionysos received such offerings at the Acrocorinth sanctuary. In Athenian red-figured vase painting, mantled dancers are sometimes associated with Dionysos.[228] For example, a bell-krater in Athens shows two mantled dancers in the company of Dionysos, a satyr, and Eros.[229] The association with fertility is in any case unmistakable on an oinochoe in Oxford, where a mantled woman dances in company with an ithyphallic dwarf and a winged phallos.[230] The engraved interior of a bronze mirror cover of reported Corinthian provenience shows a mantled woman holding a thyrsos and dancing before an altar wreathed with ivy and laurel, on which perches a piping Eros, wearing a wreath; the altar is inscribed ΦΙΛΟΠΑΙ, and there is the outline of a mountain in the background.[231] Although Dionysos is not shown, references to him in the thyrsos and ivy are present, and the mirror would then parallel the bell-krater in the combining of dancers with Eros and Dionysos. The thyrsos should identify the woman as a maenad, although maenads are more commonly identified by the fawnskin in combination with loose hair and bare feet;[232] this costume is prevalent in art, although the maenads performed their mountain dances in the winter, when they might be expected to be wrapped well against the cold. Yet another engraved mirror cover of reported Corinthian provenience shows two mantled women dancing on rocky ground; the edges of the mirror are broken, but an alabastron can be seen and a head, probably of a satyr or Pan, watching the dance.[233] Since only a few figurines of mantled dancers, and no kalathiskos dancers, have as yet been found at Corinth outside the Acrocorinth sanctuary,[234] we can surmise that these types were particularly associated with the Acrocorinth cultic area. Do the mirrors,

[223] Generally on these dancers, see Hampe and Simon 1959, p. 34.
[224] D. B. Thompson 1950; *Gods Delight*, pp. 102–106, no. 14, with bibliography; Ridgway 1990, pp. 219–221, with bibliography on p. 240, note 13.
[225] D. B. Thompson 1966, pp. 57, 62.
[226] *Corinth* XVIII, iii, pp. 245–247.
[227] For a list of deities who received figurines of mantled dancers, see *Troy*, p. 104, note 202.
[228] Oakley 1990, pp. 38–39, pls. 52–54, with bibliography.
[229] National Archaeological Museum, inv. no. 1382: Schefold 1934, p. 12, no. 61, pl. 27:2.

[230] Dasen 1993, pp. 236–237, pl. 52; M. R. Robertson 1979, pp. 129–130, pl. 34:2.
[231] Züchner 1942, pp. 97–98, no. KS 161, fig. 49.
[232] On maenadic ritual and costume, see Bremmer 1984.
[233] Züchner 1942, p. 98, no. KS 162, fig. 97 on p. 183.
[234] MF-3937, *Corinth* XII, p. 34, no. 145, pl. 10; pp. 43–44, no. 248, pl. 21; KT-5-21, *Corinth* XV, ii, pp. 125–126, no. 21, pl. 24. The Corinthian dancers in collections outside Corinth, which are completely preserved, were probably taken from graves.

if the Corinthian provenience is correct, then also refer to rituals connected in some way with the Demeter sanctuary? This suggestion may not be so farfetched, since Dionysos appears to have been worshiped there (see p. 332), and both Dionysos and Eros are represented among the figurines. Was the Corinthian maenads' mountain Acrocorinth? Was a winter festival held there parallel to the Athenian Lenaia, which took place in mid-winter and which included the revels of maenads?[235]

The mantled dancers could also refer to marriage. The Classical kalathiskos dancers are thought to represent professional dancers who served fertility cults and may have been cultically related to marriage (see p. 58). While the meaning of mantled dancing may have varied according to the deity for whom it was performed, it is conceivable that in the Acrocorinth sanctuary dancing continued to refer to marriage in the Hellenistic period. If this is correct, do the mantled dancers represent the brides themselves? Literary and visual evidence for Greek weddings does not suggest dancing brides,[236] but brides are known to have been heavily veiled before the *anakalypteria*[237] and are sometimes represented muffled to the eyes, as are some of the dancers. Examples of marital contexts for this costume include a clay impression from a mirror showing Dionysos and Eros with a bride,[238] found in the Athenian Agora, and Attic and South Italian red-figured vases.[239] If the dancers were not actually brides, the costume, in any case, may have been intended to suggest marriage. Both the kalathiskos dancers and some of the mantled dancers from the Acrocorinth sanctuary were produced at the Potters' Quarter, but only the mantled dancers continued to be made into the 3rd century B.C., after the demise of the Potters' Quarter workshops. Whether the replacement of one type by another in the Acrocorinth sanctuary was a function of the marketplace or really represented some change in ritual custom is unclear.

There are several variants among the mantled dancers from the Acrocorinth sanctuary, but they share a few features in common. All dance to the viewer's left and are meant to be seen in three-quarter view; from the movement of the dance, the drapery flies out to the viewer's right; the mantle is all-enveloping, concealing other garments almost completely; the left arm is akimbo or at least partially bent. Variations occur in the position of the right arm, in the pattern of drapery folds, and in the way the cloth is draped around the head. The best-preserved mantled dancer from the sanctuary is **H153**. In pose and drapery arrangement, this figurine closely resembles Attic and Boeotian types of the middle and third quarter of the 4th century B.C.[240] In this version of the dance, the left ankle crosses the right, the mantle hem flares out widely in response to the movement, and the right arm is folded over the chest, with a spray of folds arching from the right hand over the left hip. The thin cloth molds the abdomen and thighs like a second skin but without revealing detail beneath, giving the peculiar impression of being at the same time both transparent and opaque. Although an undergarment hem is visible at the ankles, there are no traces of neckline folds on the upper chest. The lack of detail may in part be due to the polishing of the surface characteristic of Workshop I, in which it was made (see p. 346). For example, the sense in the Boeotian version that the right arm is supported in a sling of mantle cloth, which it pulls down tautly from the neck, is not clearly apparent in **H153**, and the details of the right

[235] Deubner 1956, pp. 123–134; Parke 1977, pp. 104–106; Simon 1983, pp. 100–101. A mantled dancer represents the winter month of Gamelion on the calendar frieze in Athens: Deubner 1956, pp. 251–252, no. 17, pl. 37.
[236] The dances associated with weddings are group line or ring dances, Oakley and Sinos 1993, pp. 24–25.
[237] Oakley 1982, with bibliography.
[238] E. R. Williams 1976, pp. 64–65, no. 22, pl. 11.
[239] *LIMC* II, 1984, p. 150, no. 1569, pl. 153, s.v. *Aphrodite* (A. Delivorrias et al.) (Aphrodite offers an open casket to the

muffled bride); Arias and Hirmer 1962, p. 384, pls. 227, 228 (a nuptial lebes by the Marsyas Painter, showing the bringing of gifts; the bride probably should be identified as the muffled figure being offered a chair, not the seminude enthroned figure, who must be Aphrodite; see Oakley and Sinos 1993, p. 40, where the muffled figure is identified as an entertainer). On the veiling of the bride's face, see Galt 1931, p. 378.
[240] Attic: e.g., *Louvre* III, p. 2, no. D4, pl. 1:f, with discussion of the chronology of the type and further examples. Boeotian: e.g., *British Museum* I, p. 237, no. 886, pl. 128.

hand and the folds around it are not as sharply rendered. The head, also preserved in **H154**, is characterized by an expressionless face with ill-defined features reduced to essentials and by hair piled on top and enveloped in a sakkos; the headdress is pulled low across the forehead, where it is marked by a narrow border. Although superficially attractive, this type seems to be derivative, presumably from an Attic or Boeotian source. The pattern of nearly parallel curving folds marking the flying panel beside the left leg recalls the simplified, repetitive fold systems of such 4th-century B.C. lingering Classical renderings as the Nereid monument from Xanthos.[241] **H153** and **H154** probably were made in the same workshop (Workshop I, see p. 346) as the draped female figurines **H100**, **H101**, and three additional figurines (see catalogue). Both figurines are from the construction fill of the Trapezoidal Building, which terminates at the beginning of the 3rd century B.C.

H156 is a smaller dancer generally similar in type to the above but with a different right arm position. The forearm is missing, but the nature of the break suggests that the right forearm was upright and swathed in the mantle, as in the standing draped figurine **H100** (see p. 143). A fully preserved dancer of reported Corinthian provenience in Boston has a similarly raised and covered hand,[242] as does a mantled dancer on an Apulian red-figured oinochoe.[243] The arm does not pull the mantle down from the neck, as in **H153**, but the cloth is flung over the neck and shoulder like a scarf, covering the chin. The figure in Boston dances on a footstool with lion's feet, kicking one leg out behind her; perhaps **H156** also danced on a footstool. A figurine of reported Corinthian provenience in Athens is another footstool dancer.[244] The particularly smooth, rounded contours of **H156** call to mind the standing figure of a nymph on a 3rd-century B.C. bronze mirror found in a grave in Corinth.[245] Footstool dancers, however, must have been made in Athens much earlier, since an already derivative version was found in the Athenian Agora in a context of the late 5th–first quarter of the 4th century B.C.[246] **H156**, therefore, is likely to be a reworking in Hellenistic style of an Athenian Classical type.

H155 is only a fragment, but, as far as preserved, it follows the composition of **H156**. It is the largest of the dancer figurines from the Acrocorinth sanctuary, approaching statuette scale.[247] Some retouch of the drapery in **H157** altered the type so that the upper edge of the mantle crosses the chest and left forearm in a thick roll. The missing right forearm in this case seems to have been held down and away from the torso, perhaps to hold out a fold of the skirt. The smooth fit of the cloth over the torso has been retained.

H159 resembles **H156** in scale and in the arrangement of the mantle like a scarf over the chin. The fold pattern, however, connects it with **H158**, in which the left arm is not akimbo but only slightly bent and held at the side. Four other mantled dancers also have lowered left arms (**H160–H163**), and in these the left hand grasps the mantle folds beside the hip. In **H160** and **H161**, a long fan of backward-flying folds hangs from the hand nearly to the hem. **H161** is the best preserved of this group, showing that in this type the dancer does not cross her ankles but strides forward with her right leg. The right arm is folded across the chest and pulls down at the neckline folds, somewhat in the manner of **H153**. In **H163**, the left arm is straight and pulls the skirt folds to the side.

Three mantled dancers (**H164–H166**) are of smaller scale, the last two being nearly miniatures. **H164** is of a type known in complete examples, also of small scale, recorded from Athens

[241] Childs and Demargne 1989, e.g., pp. 123–124, no. BM 911, pl. 86; pp. 125–126, no. BM 909, pl. 89.
[242] Galt 1931, p. 376, fig. 3, left.
[243] Charbonneaux et al. 1973, p. 98, fig. 89.
[244] Winter, *Typen* II, p. 145, no. 2b; Dumont and Chaplain 1890, p. 235, pl. XII, right.

[245] Pemberton 1985, pp. 291–294, 301–302, no. 45, pl. 85 (MF-11562).
[246] Nicholls 1995, p. 470, note 303.
[247] Another Corinthian mantled figure of statuette scale, possibly a dancer, is preserved in an unpublished fragment found out of context at the Potters' Quarter (KT 5–29, Pl. 76); the piece is thin-walled and of fine, hard fabric.

and Boeotia.[248] The composition shows torsion; the head and upper torso turn toward the viewer's right, although the dancer moves to the left. The left leg still crosses over the right but now at the knees rather than the ankles, creating a bolder, less mincing movement than in **H153**. The left arm is sharply bent, with a cascade of zigzag folds dropping from the hand to the hem; the right hand pulls some drapery folds around from the back to the abdomen. The mantle covers the lower part of the face. The composition is very well conceived, but the impression of **H164** is dull and the workmanship is indifferent, suggesting that it may have been mechanically copied from an imported figurine.

The mold siblings **H165** and **H166** taken together provide the remains of a lovely mantled dancer type, in which the dancer steps forward on the right leg, while twisting her head and shoulders to the viewer's left. The lower part of the face is covered by the mantle, which once again drops over the left shoulder like a scarf. The torsion is not as great as in **H164**, but the intention to show the turning movement of the dance is similar. Also contributing to the sense of motion is the elaborate drapery pattern. Both hands lift the mantle from beneath the cloth to free the legs for the dance, showing the skirt of the garment beneath, the hem of which is rendered by bent tubular folds opening into omegas; above these, the mantle hem billows into a deep sanguisuga[249] fold. In Attic sculpture, such exaggerated drapery patterns are typical of figures in motion, dating to the end of the 5th or the beginning of the 4th century B.C., such as a Nike akroterion from the Temple of Ares in the Athenian Agora.[250] The torsion of the figurines, however, suggests a later date, not before the second quarter of the 4th century B.C.[251] Since another mold sibling was found in the Potters' Quarter (see catalogue), a *terminus ante quem* of the 320s B.C., when the workshops in that area ceased production, is provided. The miniature scale of these figurines should not in this case point to a late generation, since the detail of **H166** is quite clear. Rather, we are probably dealing with a terracotta adaptation of a small metal figure, possibly Attic, of late Classical style.[252] Although such metal figurines are lacking in the archaeological record, Attic terracotta figurines of forward-stepping dancers are known in several variants (see p. 80). Presumably, the torsion of the Corinthian version was a later addition, effected by twisting back the shoulders. These figurines are probably the earliest of the Corinthian mantled dancers, dating perhaps to the middle or third quarter of the 4th century B.C. They may have been made in the same workshop (Workshop C, see p. 345) as the comic figurines **H365** and **H367**.

A fragment of the lower part of a figurine, showing the garment hems with motion folds (**H167**), may belong to a mantled dancer. If so, the position of the foot suggests that we have here a different type, showing a dancer moving forward with feet apart.[253] A bent, tubular mantle fold opening into an omega is preserved, suggesting that this figurine also is in the later Classical tradition; its drapery style brings to mind the treatment of hem folds in the sculpture of the Temple of Asklepios at Epidauros, which is dated ca. 380–370 B.C.[254]

The two small dancers **H168** and **H169** have a superficial similarity to one another in scale and style but are differently composed. The better-preserved **H168** moves directly forward with

---

[248] Winter, *Typen* II, p. 145, no. 3; no. 4 is similar but larger and with less torsion; *Corinth* XV, ii, pp. 126–127, *sub* no. 26, with bibliography; Schürmann 1989, p. 40, no. 85, pl. 18.

[249] For this term, see Ridgway 1981a, p. xviii (the fold is shaped like a swollen leech).

[250] Delivorrias 1974, pp. 124–125, pls. 44, 45.

[251] Torsion is usually associated with sculpture of the later 4th century B.C. at the earliest, but actually it is found ca. 375 B.C. in the west central akroterion of the Asklepieion at Epidauros: Yalouris 1992, pp. 30–31, no. 25, pl. 26:b. I owe this observation to Brunilde S. Ridgway.

[252] On the derivation of small terracottas from metal figures, see D. B. Thompson 1966, pp. 54–55.

[253] In the composition of the legs, the figurine might have resembled the right-hand dancer of a group of two in Istanbul: Mendel 1908, pp. 176–177, no. 1868, pl. IV:2. A forward-moving dancer of reported Corinthian provenience crosses her feet: Winter, *Typen* II, p. 146, no. 7.

[254] Cf. Yalouris 1992, pp. 31–32, no. 26, pl. 27; on the chronology, see pp. 82–83.

crossed ankles, while **H169** is more like **H164** in design, in that the torso is probably turned away from the legs. Both, however, show very slender proportions and drapery so closely wrapped and unarticulated over the torsos and legs that the figures seem nude. The garment of **H169** thickens at the hem and is probably a mantle, like the very smooth and closely fitted garment of **H153**. These two small figures are likely to be later derivatives of the larger, better-detailed mantled dancers and probably date to the 3rd century B.C.

Five mantled heads probably belonged to dancers. **H170** seems to have leaned backward originally or to the viewer's left. The right hand is brought up to the mouth under the mantle, which covers the face up to the eyes. The headdress is the veiled, high sakkos typical of this group. A dancer of nearly miniature scale (**H171**) preserves the head and a little of the shoulders. **H171** seems originally to have moved to the viewer's left, with the head tilted to the viewer's right. The mantle is drawn across the mouth. This head is unusual in that the facial features are clearly detailed, showing very large eyes. Another of similar type and scale (see catalogue) shows less detail but is noteworthy because the pose seems to be reversed and because it is from a datable context, the construction fill of the Trapezoidal Building, which terminates at the beginning of the 3rd century B.C. **H172** preserves only the head; there is no sign of movement, but since the face is muffled to the eyes, as is **H170**, the head could have belonged to a mantled dancer. There is no discernible reason why in some heads only the chin is covered, in others the chin and mouth, and in others the nose as well.[255]

The last two heads wear a kerchief rather than a sakkos. The kerchief with eye slits was another form of facial covering, although they are usually represented pulled across the forehead, with the loose cloth draped to either side of the head, leaving the face bare.[256] **H173**, in which the kerchief is covered by the mantle, matches the head of a dancer of reported Corinthian provenience.[257] In both, the eye slits of the kerchief are lacking, a triangle of hair shows at each temple, and the mantle is wrapped tightly across the neck to the left shoulder. In the complete figurine, the head would not be seen frontally as illustrated here but glancing down over the right shoulder to the feet. The dancer advances to the viewer's right in a free, almost galloping movement, with swinging skirts. Dancers in such free movement are generally more characteristic of West Greek than mainland Greek renderings,[258] but two fragments of swinging drapery from the Acrocorinth sanctuary could point to such types.[259] In the other head wearing a kerchief (**H174**), the eye slits are rendered correctly. In this figurine, the mantle did not veil the head; the right hand draws the cloth up to the mouth in a manner resembling **H170**, although only the chin is covered. There are no signs of movement in the figurine, as far as it is preserved.[260]

The faces of the mantled dancers, when preserved, do not match closely any of the facial types most characteristic of the Corinthian Hellenistic production (see pp. 157–168). This fact reinforces the conclusion that the mantled dancers were in the main copied from imported types, since there is no evidence that available local workshop materials were employed to construct them. Two additional mantled heads could have belonged to either standing figurines or dancers, but since they are not closely related to any of the figurines discussed here, they are treated among the isolated heads (see **H204** and **H206**).

---

[255] On the veiling of the face, see *Troy*, p. 103.

[256] On the kerchief, see *Troy*, pp. 50–52; it is also worn by one of the Mahdia grotesques: Pfisterer-Haas 1994, pp. 484–486.

[257] Winter, *Typen* II, p. 148, no. 7.

[258] *Morgantina*, pp. 64, 187, nos. 460–462, pl. 91, with bibliography.

[259] In lots 1953 and 6186.

[260] Two other heads in Corinth (MF-4367, MF-185) wear the kerchief with eye slits, without a veil (*Corinth* XII, pp. 46–47, nos. 285, 286, pl. 24, dated to the 3rd century B.C.). Since there are no mantle folds around the neck of either figurine, they probably were not mantled dancers.

SEATED DRAPED FEMALE FIGURINES
(H175–H177)

The seated draped female figurines of the Classical period included types that were easily recognizable as goddesses (e.g., **C71**), but the small group of Hellenistic seated draped figurines does not include any types of hieratic appearance, nor are any known in multiple impressions. Corinthian Hellenistic workshops appear to have emphasized standing types, apart from the representations of the seminude seated Aphrodite or nymphs discussed below (pp. 177–180).

The best of the seated draped figurines in quality is **H175**, a fine Corinthian "Tanagra" type, of which a complete example is preserved in Athens (Pl. 78).[261] In the original type, a woman sits with her right foot propped on a rock, and her elbow rests on her raised knee. Her head, bent strongly to the right, rests on her clenched, mantle-wrapped hand. The pose could represent mourning, but the atmosphere of the figurine is reposeful or reflective rather than sad. The characteristic feature of the drapery is the series of tension folds across the torso from the right forearm to the left upper arm. This figurine is the most accurate rendition of a "Tanagra" type yet found in Corinth. The pottery context of **H175** terminates at the middle of the 3rd century B.C. The head, round faced and youthful, would have been similar to **H220**, which originally could have belonged to a figure leaning on the hand, to judge from the diagonal break across the lower right side of the face and neck. Two fragments in lots 878 and 2249 show a slippered left foot propped on a rock. If these fragments belonged to seated figurines, they suggest that a type may have existed with the pose reversed, the left knee raised and supporting the left arm. These fragments are from the construction fill of the Trapezoidal Building, which terminates at the beginning of the 3rd century B.C.

The two remaining seated figurines (**H176** and **H177**) are more likely to represent mourners. The miniature **H177** preserves a mantled figure seated dejectedly with shoulders hunched and right arm folded across her lap; the left hand grasps the drapery around her head and neck. The arrangement of the arms is like that of the "pudicitia" type (see p. 151). While the details of the face of **H177** are unclear, the hunched shoulders and jutting head suggest an old woman, and it is tempting to see in this figurine a representation of the mourning Demeter, especially since human mourning figurines are generally represented beside a tomb.[262] **H176** could be a larger version of this type but is of poorer quality.

ISOLATED FEMALE HEADS
(H178–H248)

A few of the isolated female heads discussed in this section are preserved with enough of the upper torso to show that they belonged to draped figurines, as in the case of **H178**; even a few folds around the base of the neck are sufficient, as in **H245**. In most cases, however, the original torso type is unknown, since heads were usually molded separately and were used with a variety of torso types, with coiffure or headdress altered as appropriate. Consequently, it must be kept in mind that these heads could have belonged to draped standing or seated figurines of the kind discussed in the foregoing section, representing goddesses or mortals, or to nude or semidraped figurines representing Aphrodite or the nymphs, as discussed below. In some cases, the coiffure or headdress assists in identification. A few heads can be linked with better-preserved figurines either found in excavation in Corinth or of reported Corinthian provenience, but this is no guarantee that the isolated heads from the Acrocorinth sanctuary originally belonged to identical torso types.

---

[261] National Archaeological Museum, inv. no. 4413; Winter, *Typen* II, p. 108, no. 5; Kleiner 1984, p. 170, pl. 36:a–c.

[262] E.g., Winter, *Typen* II, p. 108, nos. 2, 3.

While there are exceptions and variations, in the main the heads of Corinthian figurines of the 4th and 3rd centuries B.C. follow three largely coexisting stylistic trends. One trend, the more characteristically Corinthian, is ultimately derived from the strongly defined Classical head type discussed above (pp. 39–40), although with "modernized" facial features. The face is a long oval with a tendency to flattened sides, resulting in a somewhat oblong shape; the jaw is full and rounded; the forehead is triangular with rounded sides, sometimes tending to a more ogival conformation. The eyes are relatively small, well-opened, fairly widely set, and level or only slightly downturned; at least the upper lid is clearly defined; the browridge is usually rounded in profile. The nose is relatively large and is usually close to the upper lip. The mouth is mobile, with well-arched lips, often parted but unsmiling or only faintly smiling. **H180** is a good example of this trend.

The second trend appears probably in the third quarter of the 4th century, perhaps arising from the same aesthetic movement that produced Attic "Tanagra" figurines. The facial features of these heads still have a good deal of character, but a softer, sweeter impression is conveyed through several means. The outlines of the face are softened, a more oval facial shape and a more delicate jaw being characteristic. The eyes are sometimes heavy lidded, conveying a languid, less alert air. An elaborate coiffure sometimes adds femininity to the head. Good examples of this trend are the votary with piglet **H1** and the head with melon coiffure **H214**.

The third trend shows the greatest dependency on outside sources. These heads are very similar to the heads of 4th- and 3rd-century B.C. "Tanagra" figurines and may have been copied from that source. The heads are characterized by a round shape and delicate features; **H220** is a good example. Others have round or heart-shaped, kittenish faces, often with only sketchily defined features and narrow, slanting eyes. **H244** exemplifies this type. Since there are relatively few Corinthian versions of genuine "Tanagra" types among the draped figurines (see p. 142), it is likely that some of these "Tanagra" heads were attached to torsos of other types. The reader should keep in mind that defining these trends is merely a way of pointing to general stylistic movements. Not every head discussed below can be assigned definitively to one or another trend.

Two heads (**H178** and **H179**) can be connected with **H57**, a draped figurine perhaps representing Kore as a bride (see p. 133). **H179** does not preserve any drapery, but the facial type seems to be similar to that of **H57**, and it is comparable in the arrangement of the hair in corkscrew curls framing the face and topped by a low polos. The workmanship is not comparable, however, suggesting that they were made in different workshops. The dull impression of the face combined with the sharp detailing of the added hair suggests the use of a worn mold or one with poor definition of forms. **H178** wears a mantle, but it is not arranged in the same way as that of **H57**, the few folds above the break showing that it was loosely draped across the shoulders. Although the face is different in conformation from that of **H57**, it too is girlish, the youth of the subject being shown by the short, upturned nose and thin lips. The hair is not arranged in clearly defined corkscrew curls; nevertheless, the coroplast may have intended to represent such curls rather than long, loose hair, since the locks do not flow freely, as in renderings such as **H181**, but cling to the neck as separate strips of clay marked with horizontal slashes. The headdress seems to be a stephane rather than a polos, although it is not clear whether this distinction was deliberate or simply a failure to render the headdress properly at the sides and back. There is some resemblance to the larger and coarser **H197** in the arrangement and retouch of the hair, the headdress, and the facial type, although **H178** is more girlish.

The six heads **H180**–**H185** are sufficiently close to one another in scale, facial type, coiffure, fabric, and workmanship to suggest that they may have been made in the same workshop (Workshop F, see p. 345), although only two of them (**H183** and **H184**) appear to be mechanically related. All members of this group wear the long, flowing hair characteristic of votaries (see pp. 117–118); the preserved shoulder of **H181** shows that the figurine wears a chiton, as do some of the votaries. At size range 3–4, however, they are larger in scale than most of the votaries, being equal in size to **H16**, which also stands outside the common run of votaries in type. They also are less demure than most of the smaller votaries and perhaps for this reason sometimes seem to represent slightly older subjects. There is also a difference in the headdress, since two members of this group (**H180** and **H181**) wear a pointed stephane, while the smaller votaries are bareheaded or wear a fillet. **H182** is bareheaded, but a later generation wears the stephane (see catalogue). Moreover, **H182** may be mechanically related to the head of the fine mantled figurine **H85**, which probably wears a small stephane, and on the basis of pose, costume, and coiffure is more likely a goddess or priestess than a votary.

The wearing of a stephane in itself is not indicative of any particular status. Although originally a mark of divinity, by the Hellenistic period the stephane was also worn by mortal women, perhaps as a connection with the divine during rituals.[263] To complicate the matter further, among Corinthian figurines, the long, flowing hair is not confined to votaries but is also worn by Aphrodite (see pp. 129–130). Probably this workshop prepared figurines of both votaries and goddesses, and while it is fair to say that the bareheaded and filleted heads of this group probably represent votaries, those wearing the stephane may not. It should also be mentioned that **H185** may be mechanically related to **H204**, one of the heads with the curl-cluster coiffure, which seem to have served for a variety of types. Although mechanical relationship is not as good as workmanship as an indicator of workshop identity, since workshop materials appear to have been shared, the possibility should be kept in mind that this workshop may have produced a number of different but interrelated types.

H183 is an interesting example of the mixing of male and female types. Long locks of hair were added at the front of this head but not at the back, revealing a short, masculine coiffure bound with a fillet. Either front and back molds that did not really match were used for convenience or the head type served for both male and female figurines, with coiffures altered as necessary. No examples of this head type have been preserved among the male figurines, but the practice of adapting workshop materials interchangeably regardless of gender can be observed also in the votary with piglet **H1** and the corresponding youth **H299** (see p. 119).

The date of this group is easier to pin down than the subjects represented. Two heads, **H183** and a head similar to **H185** (see catalogue), were found in the construction fill of the Trapezoidal Building, which terminates at the beginning of the 3rd century B.C. The more fully preserved **H85** shows stylistic connections with sculpture of the middle to third quarter of the 4th century B.C. The heads alone, with their long, oval to oblong shape and relatively small eyes with well-defined lids, compare well with the head of Dionysos from the west pediment of the Temple of Apollo at Delphi, which is dated ca. 330 B.C.[264] The coiffure of the Dionysos also matches that of **H85**. It seems fair to date this group of heads to the third quarter of the 4th century B.C.

The particularly long and narrow faces of two heads (**H186** and **H187**) are probably mechanical relatives, although the latter appears to have been distorted when the clay was removed from the mold. Both wear the stephane on long hair, although the locks framing the forehead are swept up and back rather than down. **H187** is remarkable for the traces of bright pink paint on the flesh, gilding on the hair, and blue-green on the stephane, a reminder of just how brightly colored these figurines were in their original state. **H186** was found in the construction fill of the Trapezoidal Building, which provides a *terminus ante quem* of the beginning of the 3rd century B.C.

In several heads with long, full-jawed faces, the locks of hair tumble down in masses of short, tousled, overlapping waves or curls. The best of these heads is **H188**, a voluptuously beautiful

[263] *Troy*, pp. 49–50.

[264] Ridgway 1990, p. 21, with bibliography on p. 62, note 6, pl. 3.

type that may represent a goddess. This identification is suggested first by the earrings the subject wears, which are unsuitable for the typically unadorned votary; in addition, the coiffure, although long, does not have the simple, streaming, uncut style of the votary but is more contrived. The vertical slashes on the upper molding of her high, poloslike stephane suggest the "crenellations" finishing the tall headdress of **C100**, which probably represents a goddess. The notched stephane of **C101** could have been intended to represent the same type of headdress. Whatever the correct identification of **H188**, however, it is clear that the figurine originally was mantled, since there are traces of folds at the neck. The hair was painted yellow, either to signify blondness or perhaps to serve as an underpaint for gilding (see pp. 13–14).

H189 is poorly preserved but appears to have had a coiffure similar to **H188**; in this case, the stephane is decorated with an incised lotus-and-palmette pattern. The facial type clearly belongs in this group but has more deeply set eyes, which are better seen in **H190**. The triangular break at the base of the neck of **H190** suggests that the head was set into a torso wearing a chiton or peplos with a V-shaped neckline. Both heads are of statuette scale. Another, fragmentary but still larger head of a statuette (**H191**) also shows eyes deeply set at the inner corners and a forehead that projects at the center in the manner of the pedimental heads from the Temple of Athena at Tegea.[265] The simple coiffure of **H191**, parted at the center and bound low around the cranium with a fillet, over which the locks of hair are wrapped and then rolled at the nape, has an Early Classical resonance, recalling the hair arrangement of a bronze head of a youth from the Athenian Akropolis.[266] The combination of a 4th-century B.C. facial type with a much earlier hairstyle may indicate that this piece is a Classicizing work of the Hellenistic period. The very large scale would suit a late-3rd- or early-2nd-century B.C. date (see p. 257). The identification of the head is complicated by the use of a coiffure typical of male figures in earlier times, together with pink paint for the flesh, which is normal for female types and children, although it is sometimes found on smaller and less well crafted male figurines, particularly Classical reclining youths (see p. 14). Either the usually masculine coiffure was used for a female figure, as in the sculptured group of Orestes and Electra in Naples,[267] or the head does represent a male and shows that pink paint was also considered appropriate for the flesh of youths in well-made figures at large scale.

A head type that appears to have had some popularity in Corinth is represented by **H192** with its mold siblings (see catalogue) and the smaller **H193**, all probably from the same workshop. There is some recollection in **H192** of "Skopasian" style in the backward tilt of the head and the slight roll of flesh over the outer corner of the eye,[268] but the facial structure is longer and narrower in the Corinthian tradition. This head type was identified in *Corinth* XII as male because of a superficial resemblance to the young Alexander (see catalogue).[269] The strong jaw, lifted chin, and upcast gaze of **H192** do contribute to this impression, but the presence in the Demeter sanctuary of female heads with long hair, stephanai, and similar facial types should fix the type as female.[270] Although none of the heads of this type from Corinth is preserved with any part of the torso, fully preserved standing draped female figurines from Kerch have heads with a similar coiffure and headdress.[271] The overlapping locks of hair of this group form curls rather than waves; in **H193** the curls were rendered by attaching tubes of clay to the sides of the head and slashing them. The intention seems to have been to render corkscrew curls like those of **H57**

[265] Cf. Stewart 1977, pl. 15.
[266] See p. 40, note 120.
[267] Conveniently, Bieber 1961, figs. 784, 785.
[268] For the much more exaggerated heads from Tegea, which are sometimes attributed to Skopas, see Stewart 1977, pls. 13–16; on the problems of this sculpture and its attribution, see Ridgway 1997, pp. 48–52.

[269] The sculptural type in question has been discussed in relation to the Eubouleus from Eleusis: see Ridgway 1990, p. 117, with bibliography on p. 140, note 17.
[270] See also Stroud 1965, p. 10, note 14.
[271] Winter, *Typen* II, p. 50, no. 6.

and **H179**. Moreover, the stephane of **H193** is rather high and shaped like a polos, resembling somewhat the headdress of **H179**. In **H192**, the curls are more irregular, but the hair on the forehead at either side of the central part seems to form residual corkscrew curls.

H194 is generally similar in coiffure and headdress, but the crude tooling of the hair creates some doubt about what was intended. The facial type is also different from the heads just discussed. The chin is smaller; moreover, the closely spaced eyes and the crowding of the features toward the center of the face recall a head type connected with articulated "dolls" (see **C153**). **H194** does not seem to have any workshop connection with other heads wearing the stephane. It has a probable mold sibling in a head with a different coiffure (**H230**). **H195** lacks the stephane, but the overlapping arrangement of rough curls at the sides of the head recalls the coiffure of **H193**.

Two heads (**H196** and **H197**) that are similar to one another in fabric and especially workmanship, and probably were mold siblings, could be by the same hand. The coiffures have been altered, in **H197** to represent a girl in a decorated stephane resembling the headdress of **H178**, and in **H196** to show long hair simply bound with a fillet like that of **H20**. Whether the torso types were correspondingly different is unknown, but the two heads are nevertheless evidence for the alteration of types within a workshop. Although the heads are large in scale, the facial features were crudely retouched, obscuring their mold history. If their size points to an early stage of any of the votary mold series, there must have been other, more carefully prepared materials in use in better workshops. The combination of large scale and crude retouch is known in other Early Hellenistic head types as well (see **H225–H228**). **H198** shows an unadorned coiffure like that of **H184**; it is smaller than **H196** and **H197** but resembles them somewhat in fabric and workmanship, although less crudely retouched.

The heads that will now be discussed have elaborate coiffures, three of which are worn by the Muses on the Mantineia base.[272] In one coiffure, the hair is drawn up loosely from the temples and the nape to be gathered into a cluster of curls at the top of the cranium, in a version of the so-called bowknot coiffure.[273] In the second coiffure, the hair is gathered somewhat further back, leaving room for decorative bands to be wrapped around the head. The third is the aptly named melon coiffure, in which the hair was divided into sections of twisted locks and finished with a surrounding plait, or a bun or cluster of curls at the back. For our purposes, the Mantineia base, a work of more modest quality in its own realm than the figurines are in theirs, is important only for establishing the contemporaneity of these fashions in hair arranging. No longer convincingly connected with Praxiteles, the Mantineia base is now better understood as a pastiche of workshop types rather than an independent creation.[274] A date ca. 330–320 B.C. seems most likely.[275] A better stylistic parallel for the facial type can be found in the head of Eros-Thanatos on the sculptured column drum from the Artemision at Ephesos, dated ca. 320/310 B.C.[276] The Eros, whose facial structure can be compared with that of **H201**, also wears his hair pulled up from the nape to the top of the head.

The heads of this group reflect the second stylistic trend mentioned above (p. 158), conveying a softer, more feminine impression than those previously discussed. The means by which this impression is achieved include a rounder face shape with a more delicate jaw and sometimes dreamy, heavy-lidded eyes, as well as the use of elaborate, upswept coiffures. Heads wearing the cluster of curls (**H199–H206**) show two versions of this coiffure, one in which the locks of hair are pulled up tightly, as in **H199**, and the other in which the arrangement is looser, as in **H201**.

---

[272] See the detailed photos in *Troy*, pl. LIX.
[273] The variants of this coiffure and examples of its use in male and female sculptural and coroplastic types are discussed in *Troy*, pp. 42–44.
[274] Linfert-Reich 1971, pp. 32–42.

[275] Apart from considerations of style and workmanship, the use of a lute by one of the Muses may hold the date of the relief to the period of or after the conquests of Alexander the Great, when this instrument was introduced to Greece: Maas and Snyder 1989, p. 185.
[276] Rügler 1988, pp. 86, 105–107, pl. 27:1, 2.

There is probably no real difference between the two, the original version being the tighter one, and the fuller version arising from the addition of locks of hair when the head was retouched. The curls seem not to have been actually knotted but gathered and tied together and allowed to fall softly to either side. It should be mentioned that these falling locks of hair usually are rendered in the form of corkscrew curls, but it is unclear whether or not this resemblance to the corkscrew-curl coiffure discussed above (p. 133) is fortuitous.

Whatever the interpretation, these heads are lovely. **H199**, the largest of the group, approaches statuette scale and is of a fine, pale, and well-polished fabric.[277] The hair was carefully worked to define the curling locks, and the ears are shown in much greater detail than is usual in the figurines. Perhaps because the polishing process dulled the definition of the features, the face was carefully tooled to open the lips and undercut the upper eyelids. Since most of this detail would have been lost after the slip and paint were applied, one must assume that this figurine was made by a craftsman who took pride in the quality of his work. **H202** is made of the same fine, polished fabric, but the facial features have not been tooled and are consequently less well defined than the hair. The eyes and mouth of **H201** are tooled, although not as carefully, and the fabric is not quite as fine. The tooling of the faces unfortunately obscures mechanical relationships, but the similarities of fabric and workmanship seem great enough to suggest that **H199**, **H201**, and **H202** probably were made in the same workshop (Workshop G, see p. 345), although not by the same hand. To these should probably be added **H203** and **H204**. The smaller, later versions **H200**, **H205**, and **H206** are handled quite differently and probably were made elsewhere in Corinth. Of these, perhaps only **H205** was mechanically related to one of the larger heads.[278] Two other heads (**H214** and **H215**) are also dreamily pretty, but their faces are differently structured, with sloping profiles.

Heads of this type were used with a variety of torsos. **H204** wears the mantle over the head and therefore belonged to either a standing mantled figurine or perhaps a mantled dancer. Since **H203** shows a fold at the base of the neck, it too would have belonged to a mantled figurine but one with a bare head. At the Sanctuary of Demeter at Knossos, a strikingly similar head type appears on a mantled figurine similar to **H104**.[279] A figurine of Corinthian provenience in Berlin, representing a woman holding a duck, has a head very like **H203**, but the mantle is arranged around the hips rather than the neck.[280] A non-Corinthian version of the mantled type **H88** also wears this coiffure.[281] Heads with the curl-cluster coiffure are also found in Corinthian ephedrismos groups, such as one in Boston[282] and another in Berlin.[283] A Corinthian seated Aphrodite with Eros in Paris also has such a head.[284] Clearly, one cannot determine the subjects of these figurines on the basis of the heads alone. In sculpture, a similar head type was used for Hygieia on a votive relief in Paris;[285] at monumental scale, such a coiffure, although more complex, is worn by the Apollo from Halikarnassos.[286]

The chronology of these heads is firmly fixed in the 4th century B.C. Apart from the parallels with the Mantineia base, **H204** and **H206** are from the construction fill of the Trapezoidal Building, the terminal date of which is the beginning of the 3rd century B.C.; in addition, **H202** was found in a context dated by 4th-century B.C. pottery. This head type is so strongly associated with Corinthian figurines that the archetype of a closely similar mold from Smyrna

[277] See the color illustration in *Coroplast's Art*, p. 18, color pl. 1.
[278] A possibly Corinthian head from the Athenian Agora, T-3696, also wears the curl-cluster coiffure.
[279] *Knossos*, p. 70, nos. 73–75, pls. 42–43.
[280] See p. 148, note 208.
[281] Winter, *Typen* II, p. 8, no. 4.
[282] *Coroplast's Art*, pp. 128–129, no. 20.
[283] *Königliche Museen*, p. 16, pls. XVII, XVIII, from Corinth or Megara.
[284] *Louvre* III, p. 54, no. D300, pl. 63:b.
[285] Hamiaux 1992, p. 218, no. 227.
[286] The photograph in Todisco 1993, pl. 169, shows the hair loosely drawn up to the top of the head, and some locks of hair tumbling down.

could well have been a Corinthian figurine, especially since the added locks of hair are included in the mold.[287]

Four heads (**H207–H210**) wear a coiffure featuring, in addition to a cluster of curls, a variety of decorative bands or cloths wrapped around the cranium. Two of these heads, **H209** and **H210**, have faces connected in type to the heads with curl-cluster coiffure discussed above, although there does not appear to be a mechanical or even a workshop relationship. Both heads wear a turban, in which wide, overlapping bands of cloth enclose most of the hair; in **H210** a fringe of curls is allowed to escape around the forehead.[288] These heads probably date to the same time as the heads with curl-cluster coiffure and may have been used in the same ways.

The facial type of **H207**, although partly obscured by the cracking of the surface, resembles that of **H183**, a head with long, streaming hair, probably a votary. The coiffure of **H207**, however, is distinctive. A wide fillet, incised with a running spiral, is wrapped around the hair between the forehead and a cluster of curls on top of the head; the fillet pushes the hair forward into a sort of pompadour around the forehead. This response of the locks of hair to the pressure of the band is nicely observed, and since it has not been obscured by successive generations or retouch, it is likely that the head is close to its archetype. The coiffure of the seated Muse on the Mantineia base is similar but is more schematic.[289] The same coiffure on a smaller head (**H208**) also is more schematic and has lost the naturalistic touch. The face in this case is rather flat, perhaps because of a molding distortion. A similar facial flatness, unusual in Corinthian heads, is also found in a Corinthian standing girl in New York.[290]

The well-made **H211** has a more Classical look, although the rounded browridge and high, ogival forehead are signs of a Hellenistic date. The face is not too far from the hydriaphoros **C60**, although **H211** is softer in expression and more rounded in the outline of the cheeks and jaw. The Classical appearance is largely due to the coiffure, which is arranged in the Knidian fashion in front, swept down to the ears from a central part.[291] The headdress consists of the typical Classical sakkos, which catches the mass of hair above the nape in a snood and is then folded into bands and wrapped over the top of the head. The curls escaping from the snood are arranged in a neat clump rather than a loose cluster. The smaller head **H212** is similar in facial type and also shows full cheeks and a rounded jaw; in this case, all the hair in back is wrapped in a sakkos, the loose cloth allowed to hang in the back in a soft fold over the cranium. A fold at the neck indicates that this figurine originally was mantled. In a possible earlier generation of **H212** from Epidauros (see catalogue), the loose cloth at the cranium is replaced by a loose cluster of curls emerging from a sphendone, which was perhaps the original composition. In scale and treatment of the locks of hair in front, the Epidaurian head corresponds with **H211**. The three heads may have been made in the same workshop.

In two heads (**H213** and **H215**), the coiffure is wrapped in a narrow sphendone tied at the top of the head in a soft bowknot. This, too, is a typically Classical headdress, known especially in the articulated "dolls" and related heads (e.g., **C125**, **C130**, and **C131**). The hair of **H213**, moreover, is arranged in the Knidian manner in front, yet the face is more Hellenistic than Classical. A melting look is conveyed by the thrown-back pose of the head, the narrow, half-closed eyes, and the parted lips. This head is one of the few in which the blurring of the facial features seems to be a deliberate *sfumato* rather than a dull impression from a worn or poorly made mold. The freshness of the mold is indicated by the crisply waved locks of hair in front, which were rendered in the mold and were not retouched. This well-made head bears some resemblance, in the facial shape,

---

[287] *Louvre* III, p. 188, no. D1376, pl. 264:g–i, dated to the 3rd century B.C.

[288] For a similar turban worn by a "Tanagra" figurine, see Higgins 1986, p. 130, fig. 155 (in London).

[289] See the detailed photo in *Troy*, pl. LIX:c. The coiffure here is not entirely consistent, since the hair behind the band is divided into narrow melon sections.

[290] *Coroplast's Art*, p. 125, no. 18.

[291] On the Knidian coiffure, see *Troy*, pp. 37–38.

the well-proportioned and placed features, and the long, narrow eyes, to the late-4th-century B.C. sculptured head from Tegea called the "Hygieia."[292] Since the sculpture also wears a cluster of curls at the back of the head, fastened with narrow bands, it is conceivable that there is some connection through workshop materials between it and the figurine type.

In **H215**, the sphendone and a cluster of curls at the back were superimposed on a head originally designed with a melon coiffure. This manner of dressing the hair, dividing and twisting the locks into sections recalling the rind of a grooved melon, was very popular during the Hellenistic period and is frequently found in representations of young women and children. Among the Acrocorinth figurines, it is also found on a child (**H342**) and an articulated "doll" (**C136**). Variations occur in the number and thickness of sections, in the way the coiffure is finished with plaits, a bun, or curls, and in the overall shape and volume of the design.[293] While the coroplasts of some centers show a preference for specific variations of the melon coiffure, and a chronological pattern emerges from their efforts, Corinthian coroplasts adopted no particularly consistent version of the coiffure. Further, they do not always seem to have understood it very well, sometimes adding the more typically Corinthian cluster of curls to a melon coiffure already augmented with plaits; the bun at the back of the head that is characteristic of the melon coiffure elsewhere does not appear in these Corinthian heads. The facial types of heads with the melon coiffure also vary greatly, some being local, others apparently borrowed from outside sources.

H215 is probably a mold sibling of **H214**, which also shows the curl-cluster finish at the back but has a plait around the cranium instead of a sphendone. Both heads have a heavy-lidded, dreamy look, and while their faces are quite different from that of **H213**, the iconographic intention seems to have been the same. Thick eyelids could result from the use of worn molds, in the absence of the retouch necessary to sharpen details (as in the case of **H234**), but in these faces the heavy lids appear to be intentional. **H216** may have been similar in facial type, but its poor preservation prevents accurate comparison. It is notable for the unusual fullness and volume of the melon coiffure.

Four heads wearing the melon coiffure (**H217–H220**) show faces of rounder shape; the short, rather wide noses and small mouths contribute to the youthful look of these heads. They represent the third trend in the style of Early Hellenistic Corinthian heads. **H217** and **H218** may be mechanically related, but the cluster of curls and earrings added to the latter change its appearance entirely. **H219**, with both a plait and a cluster of curls on the cranium elaborating the melon coiffure, has a possible mechanical relative in Epidauros (see catalogue) with a plait alone. **H220** is broken diagonally across the right side in such a way as to suggest that the head originally leaned on the hand of a seated figurine of "Tanagra" style similar to **H175** (see p. 157). Heads with round, short-nosed faces and wearing the melon coiffure must be of Athenian inspiration and are sometimes found on figurines of "Tanagra" type.[294] It is possible, therefore, that **H217–H220** all originally belonged to "Tanagra" torsos, keeping in mind that separately made heads could have been used with any torso type. The best of these heads in quality, **H220**, was found in the construction fill of the Trapezoidal Building, the terminal date of which is the beginning of the 3rd century B.C. This evidence and the connection with "Tanagra" types should place the origin of this head type within the second half of the 4th century B.C. These heads should be distinguished from another "Tanagra" head type further from Corinthian style, in which the faces

---

[292] Conveniently, Lullies and Hirmer 1960, pl. 205; for side and rear views, see Picard 1954, pp. 201–202, figs. 89, 90; Ridgway 1997, p. 54, with bibliography on pp. 73–74, note 80. The hair of two small marble heads of uncertain date in the Corinth collection (S-2124 and S-2523) is arranged in a cluster of curls on top of the cranium. For another of Hellenistic date, see Sturgeon 1998a, p. 9, fig. 20 (S-2389).

[293] On the variations and their possible chronological implications, see *Troy*, pp. 38–39; *Morgantina*, pp. 66–67; on the coiffure in general, Kleiner 1984, p. 15.

[294] E.g., *Coroplast's Art*, p. 110, no. 3 (in Boston); for a typical head of this type from a dated Athenian context, see S. G. Miller 1974, pp. 218, 242, no. 103, pl. 41. An imported "Tanagra" head from Corinth, MF-1981-38, compares well with **H217**.

are small, rather kittenish, and have poorly defined features. A few such heads (**H243–H245**) have been found at the Acrocorinth sanctuary and are discussed below (pp. 168–169).

Three small heads wearing the melon coiffure are unrelated to other heads or to one another. **H221** has a long, narrow face recalling the hydriaphoroi of Classical type (e.g., **C57**), but the features are more delicate, and the sloping forehead and arched nose evoke such Hellenistic renderings as the head of the votary with piglet **H1**. The coiffure has relatively few, but prominent sections, without an encircling plait; this version is thought to be a relatively early form of the melon style.[295] In this example, the coiffure is finished with a cluster of curls at the nape rather than at the cranium, which is fairly uncommon.

H222 and **H223** show the degeneration of the melon coiffure into a mass of hair roughly marked with slashes. **H223** is noteworthy for the possibility of establishing a workshop link (Workshop J, see p. 346) with two figurines of different types, the standing girl **H44** and the hydriaphoros **H50**. The three pieces are connected by their notably hard, fine, and pale-colored fabric; the hair of both **H50** and **H223** is painted a bright yellow, perhaps indicating that gilding was employed (see pp. 13–14). Yet for all the excellence of the material, the workmanship in all three figurines is indifferent. **H44** and **H223** are very dull impressions, perhaps from worn molds, but the artisans did not have the skill to retouch them properly, leaving the face of **H223** nearly a blank surface and slashing the hair hideously. The pottery context of **H44** falls in the middle to second half of the 3rd century B.C., a date that seems fair for these exhausted figurine types, made in a workshop with access to good material but without the skill to use it to best effect.

The melon sections of hair are tooled so sketchily on **H224** that the coiffure is barely recognizable. The face is unparalleled among the female heads, and since it is less feminine in appearance than the other heads wearing the melon coiffure, it is possible that the hair of a male head was retouched to provide a head for a female figurine. This workshop practice is documented in **H183** (see p. 159).

Four larger heads (**H225–H228**), in size ranges 3–4, are related to one another in facial type and in their crude retouch; three of this group wear the melon coiffure. The largest of these and the best in fabric is **H225**. This head wears a melon coiffure, originally gilded, with deep, well-rounded sections, a variant thought to be relatively early in the use of this hairstyle and to indicate a late-4th-century B.C. date.[296] This head was found with late-4th-century B.C. pottery. **H226** appears to be a later generation in a much poorer fabric, preserving some of the crude facial retouch of **H225** in the mold but wearing a simple coiffure with straight locks of hair combed down from a central part. Such straight hair is generally thought to signal a 3rd-century B.C. date,[297] suggesting that this mold series could have remained in use for some time without significant loss of size or detail. One member of this group (**H227**) has a possible later generation in the construction fill of the Trapezoidal Building (see catalogue), which terminates at the beginning of the 3rd century B.C.; therefore, **H227** should date to the 4th century B.C. It is poorly fired and shows a combination of large size and crude retouch recalling the group **H196–H198** discussed above (p. 161). **H227** has a rudimentary cluster of curls added to the melon coiffure. A head of similar type appears on the running girl of a better-made Corinthian ephedrismos group in Amsterdam.[298] **H228** is also large in scale and crude in retouch. Both a cluster of curls and plaits were added to the melon coiffure, showing a fundamental misunderstanding of this hair arrangement. While the differences in facial features probably preclude a mechanical relationship with this group, the similarities in scale and technical approach could indicate a workshop connection. **H228** also has a mechanical relative in the construction fill of the Trapezoidal Building (see catalogue), which confirms its 4th-century B.C. date. Since this relative preserves a few folds draped closely around the neck, we

---

[295] *Troy*, p. 38, melon coiffure with deep waves.
[296] *Troy*, p. 38.

[297] Cf. Bookidis 1982, p. 246, pl. 67:e.
[298] Frenkel 1976, p. 96, fig. 23 on p. 108.

may assume that these heads sometimes were used for mantled figurines. A head similar to **H228** in type and retouch of the hair appears on a figurine of reported Corinthian provenience in Berlin, portraying a young woman in a chiton and mantle, with her foot propped on a rock.[299]

Two heads (**H229** and **H230**) show a coiffure in which only the hair in front is gathered up into a cluster of curls, the remaining locks falling to the shoulders. This coiffure is known in the Corinth collection in two figurines of a dancing girl wearing a peplos.[300] No fragments of this dancing torso have been recognized among the Acrocorinth sanctuary finds, but it is likely that these heads do represent youthful subjects, since this coiffure is also found in representations of children, such as **H345**. Perhaps this coiffure is connected with the Classical fashion, also associated with youth, in which the hair is pulled back from the forehead in a plait. The face of **H229** was distorted in molding so that the jaw is unusually heavy and prominent, but **H230** is a probable mold sibling of a head type with long hair and a stephane (**H194**). Whatever the original torso types of **H229** and **H230**, they probably represented girls or young women.

The last group of heads with elaborate coiffures to be discussed shows some form of hair knot on top of the cranium. Projecting hair knots of a different sort were very common in Classical figurines, particularly on the heads of articulated "dolls" and heads related to them. In those figurines, the projections may have been apotropaic (see p. 171), but the lack of a shared coiffure type among the Hellenistic heads suggests that here the knots are merely decorative. Each of these heads exhibits a different facial type.

A head very close in both face and coiffure to **H231** is known in a representation of a flying Nike in Berlin[301] and in a semidraped Aphrodite with Eros of reported Corinthian provenience.[302] Two torso fragments from the Acrocorinth sanctuary (**H297** and **H298** [see p. 184]) show an overfold hem flaring with movement like that of the Berlin Nike and may belong to similar types. The good quality of **H231**, and the Classical look imparted by the well-opened eyes with clearly defined lids and the coiffure, which is parted at the center and swept to the sides in the Knidian manner, point to a 4th-century B.C. date. The fresh modeling of the locks of hair in front, which were rendered in the mold, suggests that this figurine is not far from its archetype.

H232, by contrast, has a purely Hellenistic face, with widely set, downturned eyes having puffy lower lids and giving the impression that the gaze is cast upward. The distinctive features of this earthy face are a very large and wide nose, and a particularly wide and fleshy mouth. To judge from the break, the head seems originally to have been turned sharply to the right, and the figure may have been in motion or at least in a restless pose. Since there are remains of folds around the neck, the torso must have been mantled. The locks of hair in front, rendered in the mold, are gathered into a bowknot faintly suggesting volutes, although it is not the elaborate volute knot known in Asiatic figurines.[303] The finishing touch at the back is an added cluster of curls. With two probable mold siblings from the Acrocorinth sanctuary (see catalogue), this head seems to have belonged to a fairly popular type. The earthiness of the facial type is not very different from the more static Classical heads **C134** and **C135**, but better definition of the features, more skillfully rendered hair, and a twisted pose have given this head much greater refinement.

In **H233**, the coroplast added a flaring lampadion knot at the top to the skimpy, caplike waves of the original coiffure. The lampadion knot is unusual in Corinthian figurines, although it appears on a figurine in Berlin that is probably Corinthian,[304] wearing a chiton and mantle

[299] *Königliche Museen*, p. 20, pl. XXV.

[300] MF-1018, MF-1019 (*Corinth* XII, pp. 43–44, no. 248, pl. 21).

[301] Knoblauch 1939, cols. 437–438, 445, figs. 28, 29. This figurine probably is Corinthian; its early attribution to Athens predates significant publication of Corinthian figurines. It is to be noted that the workmanship is compared by Knoblauch

to a kalathiskos dancer in Berlin (see p. 59, note 237), which should also be Corinthian.

[302] Winter, *Typen* II, p. 94, no. 2.

[303] On this form of bowknot, see *Troy*, p. 43; cf. p. 131, no. 214, pl. XLVI.

[304] Winter, *Typen* II, p. 60, no. 7.

arranged somewhat like the costume of **H131**. The triangular shape of the break in front of **H233** probably reflects the V-shaped neckline of a chiton or peplos. This head is from a pottery context terminating in the early 3rd century B.C.

The coiffure of the last member of this disparate group (**H234**) shows the rough outlines of a bowknot at the top and a rough plait around the cranium. The head is poorly made; the eyelids are nearly closed, probably because the mold was badly worn, but the coroplast did not retouch them. The head is dated not later than the beginning of the 3rd century B.C. by its context, the construction fill of the Trapezoidal Building, and a 4th-century B.C. date is confirmed by a connection with the votary with piglet **H1**. Although the facial types are entirely different, the two heads are similar in structure; both are unusually deep in profile and show arched noses, sloping foreheads, and receding chins. It is possible that some shared workshop material underlies both types, although there is nothing to connect them more closely, iconographically, stylistically, or technically. Such a limited connection, but one that can hardly be accidental, confirms the impression that Corinthian workshop connections were very complex, because of the sharing, exchanging, or copying of materials or their purchase from common sources (see p. 123). The face of **H234** is more similar, in the conformation of the features as well as the sloping profile, to the popular head type of the 4th-century B.C. mantled figure **H102**, and, in this case, a mechanical relationship is possible.

Four heads, also with varying facial types, share a style of hairdressing that has Classical roots. The locks of hair are swept away from a central part, in the Knidian fashion, in **H235** and **H236**. In **H237**, the locks spring up directly from the forehead, framing it in an unparted pompadour. In **H238**, the coroplast has taken the trouble to show that this part of the hair is wrapped around to the back of the head. The rest of the locks of hair are either gathered at the nape or fall to the shoulders. The earthy facial features of this head are not unlike those of **H232**. In more fully preserved figurines from the Acrocorinth sanctuary, similar coiffures are found in the Late Classical dancer **C282** and in the fine, standing draped female figurine **H85**. More roughly rendered, this coiffure is found on heads that probably represent votaries, for example, **C154**. In sculpture, it is worn by both male and female deities, particularly Dionysos[305] and Demeter.[306]

H235 has a very slight "Skopasian" flavor, in the short, wide facial shape and rectangular forehead with an ogival point at the hair parting. The same combination can be found in the Dresden maenad, which is sometimes connected with Skopas,[307] although the subject of that sculpture requires an intensity of expression not found in the quieter figurine. The remains of a fold around the neck indicate that **H235** originally belonged to a mantled figurine. The facial features are somewhat more delicate than in most of the heads from the Acrocorinth sanctuary. The very crisp, parallel waves at the front of the coiffure, not retouched, suggest a fresh mold and a nearness to the archetype; they also suggest that the source may have been a bronze statuette. **H236** wears a similar coiffure, rendered with less clarity and freshness, to which a stephane was added. The facial features show a somewhat similar conformation and delicacy, although with less sweetness, and the cheeks are fuller.

The hair of **H237** is rendered as in **H235** in crisp, parallel waves, although the locks of hair are arranged differently. In this case, one must also consider the possibility of a metallic source. In spite of the low-bridged, upturned nose, which is unusual among Corinthian figurines, the long, straight-sided, full-jawed face is of recognizably local type, not too far from **H186**. The clearly marked browridge, well-opened eyes with both lids defined, and serene expression give **H237** a Classical air. Its style belongs to the 4th century B.C., perhaps the second quarter. Since

---

[305] E.g., the head of Dionysos from the Temple of Apollo at Delphi: Ridgway 1990, p. 21, with bibliography on p. 62, note 3, pl. 3.

[306] E.g., the Demeter of Knidos: conveniently, Lullies and Hirmer 1960, pl. 225.

[307] Stewart 1977, pp. 91–93, 140–141, pl. 32:d; on the attribution, see Ridgway 1997, pp. 255–257, with bibliography on p. 278, note 55.

the arrangement of the hair in front is not characteristic of any of the standard feminine coiffures, and the face itself is not particularly feminine, it is conceivable that the head represents Dionysos rather than a woman or goddess.

The remaining head in this group (**H238**) is of lesser technical quality. Although the distorted, flattened nose coarsens its appearance, a certain fleshiness of the lower face seems to be one of its inherent traits. There is some stylistic connection in the earthiness of the face with the head of the Late Classical dancer **C282** and the imported head **I4**, which is probably Argive. In the realm of sculpture, the head of the west akroterion of the Temple of Asklepios at Epidauros affords a parallel.[308] Two possible mold siblings of **H238** from the construction fill of the Trapezoidal Building (see catalogue) provide a *terminus ante quem* for the type at the beginning of the 3rd century B.C.

In four heads (**H239–H242**), the hair is piled into a rounded peak and entirely hidden in a sakkos. In better-preserved figurines from the Acrocorinth sanctuary, headdresses of this kind are found on mantled figurines (e.g., **H111**) and mantled dancers (e.g., **H154**). The import **I10**, which is probably Argive, wears this headdress, is swathed in a mantle, and carries a ball. In an ephedrismos group in Berlin that is probably Corinthian, one of the figures wears a curl-cluster coiffure and the other, a sakkos.[309] A similar headdress, completely covering the hair, also appears on a figurine in Paris,[310] which is costumed in a mantle with a heavy drapery fall at the side like that of **H65** and could represent a goddess. There does not appear to be any pattern of types calling for the concealing of the hair, although when mantled brides are represented in vase painting, their hair is covered in this way beneath the mantle.[311] The ball carried by the Argive **I10** also points to a bridal interpretation. This fashion of dressing the hair originally may have had some specific function on particular figurine types but may have spread to others through the common workshop practice of mixing and exchanging heads and torsos. The facial types connected with this headdress are varied.

H239 resembles **H238** in facial type, repeating its large, earthy features, although no mechanical relationship is discernible. In **H240**, the border of the headdress around the forehead must originally have been painted, but even without this detail, the identification of the headdress is secure because of the loose fold of cloth shown at the back of the head. The face, on the other hand, is detailed and expressive, with deeply set eyes and parted lips. By contrast, **H242** does include the border of the sakkos, but the face is almost as undefined and inexpressive as that of the dancer **H154**. Enough of the strong and broad neck of this figurine is preserved, however, to show that the woman was not closely wrapped in a mantle and is not likely to have been a dancer, at least of the mantled type. In addition, the unusual depth of the neck in back indicates a quiet pose. Heads of this type were made at the Potters' Quarter (see catalogue), providing a *terminus ante quem* in the 320s B.C., when these workshops were destroyed. The headdress of **H241** is distorted but is nevertheless easily identified. Like **H240**, the face is expressive and shadowed.

The last group of heads to be discussed in this section consists of types that are not characteristic of the Corinthian production, although on the basis of fabric and workmanship, they should probably be assigned to local workshops. Four of the six heads in this group were copied from readily identifiable foreign sources. **H243–H245** must be copies of "Tanagra" figurines. The modeling of **H245** is so poorly defined that it may have been made in a mold taken directly from a "Tanagra" figurine and not retouched. **H243** and **H244** show a degree of definition similar to the ordinary run of "Tanagra" figurines and therefore could have been made in imported Attic

[308] Yalouris 1992, pp. 32–33, no. 27, pls. 30, 31.
[309] *Königliche Museen*, p. 16, pls. XVII, XVIII.

[310] *Louvre* III, p. 14, no. D47, pl. 11:c. The piece is classified with Boeotian figurines because of its provenience, but the fabric is thought to be Corinthian.
[311] See p. 153, note 239.

or Boeotian molds. All three show the narrow-eyed, short-nosed, smiling, rather characterless kittenish faces typical of "Tanagra" figurines of the later 3rd century B.C.[312] **H244** and **H245** show variations on the melon coiffure not seen in the more typically Corinthian heads, being finished with a small plaited circlet on the cranium or a small bun. **H245** wears the mantle draped closely around the neck. These heads, together with the less exaggerated **H217–H220**, represent the third stylistic trend in Early Hellenistic Corinthian heads, as described above (p. 158).

H246, with her serious, more Peloponnesian face and long locks of hair clinging close to the head and neck, must be a copy of an Argive type, such as the imported **I9**. Characteristic of the Argive retouch of this coiffure are the diagonal, downward strokes on the locks of hair framing the sides of the face and the neck. Since similar strokes in the hair of **H246** were rendered in the mold rather than by hand, it would appear that this figurine was made in a mold taken directly from an imported Argive figurine.

The two remaining heads are not characteristically Corinthian in facial type, but their sources are not clear. **H247** has deeply set eyes, a thin nose, and pursed lips. The figurine seems to have been burned, obscuring the original appearance of the fabric, but the workmanship is sufficiently like that of Corinthian figurines to include it with the local products. **H248** has asymmetrical features and is flattened at the right side, as if originally attached to something; perhaps it was part of a relief. The deeply shadowed eyes and sense of suppressed emotion suggest a 4th-century B.C. date. Although the detail in the hair is somewhat incoherent, it was probably very fine in the archetype, suggesting a source in metal relief (see p. 81), possibly Attic.

NUDE AND SEMIDRAPED APHRODITE, LEDA, MAENAD(?), NYMPHS, AND RELATED HEADS (H249–H286)

Allusions to Aphrodite in the Classical figurines from the Demeter sanctuary have been mentioned above (p. 43). In addition, the Corinthian Early Hellenistic repertoire of draped female figurines includes some that have been tentatively identified as Aphrodite (pp. 135–136, 138–139, 147, 148). In this section are discussed other figurines, nude or semidraped, some of which are clearly within the iconographical parameters set for Aphrodite in the 4th century B.C. and later. While it is sometimes difficult to distinguish representations of nude mortal women at their toilette from "genuine" representations of Aphrodite, in the context of a sanctuary such distinctions may be unnecessary. Whether a figurine depicted a nude woman, a courtesan, or Aphrodite, the point must have been to evoke a sense of Aphrodite for the worshiper and to allow the mortal to identify with the deity. As mentioned above (p. 24), the very difficulty of distinguishing deity from mortal in these votive gifts is itself the essence of the relationship between the two.

In any case, the presence of Aphrodite in the sanctuary can be felt strongly. The honoring of this goddess in the context of a shrine of Demeter and Kore need not be surprising. If it is true, as suggested above, that some of the figurines found in this shrine were offered for the purpose of ensuring fruitful marriage and protecting children, Aphrodite finds a comfortable niche as a patroness of marriage and a guardian of children, in which roles she is sometimes known.[313] While Aphrodite would seem to be diametrically opposed in meaning to Demeter and Kore, affinities as well as differences among these goddesses have been uncovered through structural analysis.[314] Of all the major goddesses, Aphrodite and Demeter are the only two who are loving mothers in myth, struggling to safeguard their children. Paralleling Demeter's efforts

---

[312] E.g., in London, Higgins 1986, p. 144, fig. 174.
[313] The sources for these roles are collected and discussed in

Farnell, *Cults* II, pp. 655–657; on Aphrodite as kourotrophos, see also p. 71.
[314] Summarized by Friedrich 1978, pp. 206–210.

to reclaim her daughter from the Underworld are the activities of Aphrodite recounted in the *Iliad* (5.311–318) to protect her son Aeneas. Aphrodite also appears in art as an affectionate mother, sometimes fondling the young Eros or pressing him to her side, as in a Corinthian figurine in Athens (Pl. 78).[315]

Aphrodite's place at the Demeter sanctuary could have been strengthened by her position as the protectress of the city of Corinth as a whole;[316] the shrine on the summit of Acrocorinth was dedicated to Aphrodite Ourania; that cult title emphasizes her creation from the genitals of Ouranos and thus her function as a fertility deity. Presumably, it is this dual aspect of protectress of the inhabitants of Corinth and patroness of fertility that assured her role as a "visiting" deity at the shrine of Demeter and Kore.[317] The connection may have been strengthened by Demeter's parallel role elsewhere in Greece as protectress of the state.[318] Another factor contributing to Aphrodite's strong presence at the Demeter sanctuary in the Hellenistic period could have been the Macedonian occupation of Acrocorinth beginning in 338 B.C., which perhaps restricted access to the shrines there,[319] although there are indications of her worship beside Demeter and Kore earlier (see pp. 43, 71, and discussion of "dolls," pp. 50, 171–172). Perhaps it is significant that the most easily identifiable representations of Aphrodite found at the Demeter sanctuary (e.g., **H249**) do belong to the later 4th and 3rd centuries. The most likely conclusion is that necessity increased the worship of Aphrodite at a sanctuary in which she was already honored.

Another link between Aphrodite and the Sanctuary of Demeter and Kore is Aphrodite's worship alongside Persephone at Lokroi; there the two goddesses appear to have been so closely linked that only careful analysis has enabled the separation of their distinctive cultic personalities in the votive offerings.[320] Closer to Corinth, Pausanias (2.36.7–37.2) mentions the presence of a statue of Aphrodite in the sacred grove at Lerna, together with several statues of Demeter and Dionysos, suggesting that all three deities were honored there. Moreover, Aphrodite and Persephone are linked in myth, in their competition for the child Adonis, who finally divided his time between them at the behest of Zeus in a variation of the Demeter-Kore-Hades myth (Apollodoros 3.14.4).

Taking into account the similarities and differences among these goddesses, and some apparent ambivalence in dealing with the different aspects of fertility embodied in their worship, it may be possible to see in the inclusion of Aphrodite in the cult of Demeter and Kore an attempt to mediate between the cults of these deities, to overcome the cultural tendency to separate sexuality from maternity[321] by suggesting that pleasure and the fulfillment of procreative duties are not necessarily mutually exclusive[322] and that girls, first identified with Kore, could ultimately be identified with Demeter through the intervention of Aphrodite. This goddess clearly could have played a role in one of the apparent functions of this cult, the acknowledging and institutionalizing of emerging sexuality, by channeling instinct into marriage and childbearing. Perhaps the inclusion of Aphrodite in this cult of Demeter and Kore also moderated the socially and religiously sanctioned but extrafamilial eroticism in Aphrodite's principal Corinthian cult.

[315] National Archaeological Museum, inv. no. 4160; see p. 130, note 88. The maternal aspect of Aphrodite is also stressed in her depiction on the Parthenon frieze: Mark 1984, pp. 295–301.

[316] On the worship of Aphrodite in Corinth, see C. K. Williams 1986.

[317] On the dedication of votives to deities other than the "official" gods of a sanctuary, see Alroth 1987; Alroth 1989, pp. 65–105.

[318] E.g., Demeter Thesmophoros at Thebes, where her sanctuary was located on the akropolis: Schachter 1981, I, pp. 165–168.

[319] C. K. Williams 1986, pp. 15, 17, note 16.

[320] Sourvinou-Inwood 1978; Prückner 1968; Zuntz 1971, pp. 163–164, 174.

[321] On this widespread tendency, see Friedrich 1978, pp. 181–191. Detienne (1994, pp. 78–82, 116–118) discusses the Athenian Adonia and Thesmophoria in this regard, but in contrast to Detienne's interpretation, see Winkler 1990, pp. 198–206.

[322] On Aphrodite's connection with passion in marriage, see Friedrich 1978, pp. 142–143.

The figurines point to the worship of Aphrodite in this sanctuary not only through the identifiable representations of her discussed below but also indirectly, through figurines representing other subjects, specifically the nude articulated "dolls." This category of figurines is discussed fully above, in terms of technique, typology, and style (pp. 48–53); they are reintroduced here for their possible connection with Aphrodite. The previously published interpretations of "dolls" have been outlined above (pp. 49–50); it is important to keep in mind that the dedication of figurines was largely a local matter, the types taking on the coloration of the place of dedication rather than having a single universal meaning. "Dolls" of the Archaic and Classical periods, which survived into Hellenistic times, are the only examples of full female nudity among the figurines from the sanctuary.[323] Representations of Aphrodite are semidraped, the only fully nude example being **H266**, which appears to have been constructed from a "doll's" torso. The same technique probably was used for the nude maenad(?) **H267**. The "dolls," particularly in the 4th century B.C., sometimes wear elaborate coiffures or headdresses in which the hair is twisted either into a single upright peak or knot from the top or back of the head or into a pair of such peaks, which form a double horn or boatlike crescent in the profile view of the head. Dorothy B. Thompson, who identified the seated "dolls" from Troy as *hierodouloi*,[324] saw single hair peaks as apotropaic, offering protection to the courtesans who wore them.[325] Sexual symbolism can be both apotropaic and, as Zeitlin has suggested, "prostropaic," not turning away evil but gathering up its forces to stimulate fertility.[326] Using either interpretation, the depiction of these coiffures on the Corinthian "dolls" can perhaps be related to the use of *hierodouloi* in the Corinthian cult of Aphrodite, a ritual custom adopted in a modified form from the Phoenician cult of Astarte.[327]

If the single hair peak is protective by virtue of its phallic shape,[328] the double peak may serve the same function by signifying the female genitalia. In a Sumerian poem celebrating the sacred marriage of Inanna and Dumuzi, Inanna compares her vulva to a horn, the Boat of Heaven, and the crescent moon,[329] that is, the shapes embodied in the "dolls' " coiffures. Presumably, in the poem these forms suggested the sexuality of Inanna to the listener and therefore her ability to bring fertility and prosperity, just as the shape of the "dolls' " coiffures might have represented for the Corinthians the sexuality of the *hierodouloi* of Aphrodite and their influence on the prosperity of the city. The connection with Sumerian poetry might seem remote, were it not for the persistence of similar symbols through time.[330] For example, a dancing woman in an Etruscan tomb painting makes the protective double-horn sign with extended little and index fingers, a gesture that has persisted in modern times for the same purpose.[331] A related symbolism is apparent in the so-called Baubo figurines found in the Sanctuary of Demeter at Priene, in which the head and pubes are directly linked, and the coiffure is topped by a roughly crescent-shaped bowknot.[332] It may not be a coincidence that terracotta model vulvas from the Sanctuary of Demeter at Proerna in Thessaly are abstracted into a similar shape.[333]

The Classical and Hellenistic pierced heads from the Demeter sanctuary, which must have belonged to articulated "dolls," do not wear the loosely flowing coiffure associated with

[323] On the question of female nudity in small-scale art before the Classical period, see Scanlon 1988; Böhm 1990; Stewart 1997, pp. 34–42, 231–234, with bibliography on p. 241.

[324] *Troy*, pp. 87–95.

[325] *Troy*, p. 93, with bibliography.

[326] Zeitlin 1982, p. 145.

[327] On Astarte in Corinth, see C. K. Williams 1986, pp. 12–14, 20.

[328] On the transference of the phallos into a horn signifying abundance, see Burkert 1983, p. 72.

[329] *ANET*, p. 643.

[330] On genital symbols as apotropaic devices and reflections of sexual attitudes, see Slater 1968, pp. 320–321; Dundes 1981, pp. 276–293, on the apotropaic use of genital symbolism,

and p. 285, on the crescent as a symbol of female genitalia; Johns 1982, pp. 61–75, on the phallos and the evil eye. On the magical power of nudity and genital representation, see Bonfante 1989, pp. 544–545, with bibliography.

[331] Holloway 1986, pp. 448–449, pl. 32, fig. 3, with bibliography. On crescent and horn amulets and women's horn-shaped headdresses, see Elworthy 1895, pp. 196–220, 258–264. See also *Encyclopedia of Religion* VI, 1987, pp. 462–463, s.v. *horns* (A. Coudert); Lurker 1974, pp. 84–87.

[332] Olender 1990; Török 1995, pp. 132–133; see also the import **I91** (p. 298), a head similar to Baubo's between the horns of a bucranium.

[333] Daffa-Nikonanou 1973, p. 73, no. ΠΡ 190, pl. 11:3.

marriageable girls in this sanctuary (see pp. 117–118),[334] although the nude physiques of the "dolls" are distinctly youthful and virginal in appearance, even rather masculine (see p. 51). Instead, their coiffures are either the elaborations of the *hierodouloi* or the bound-up styles usually associated with married women. Therefore, it is perhaps not too farfetched to suggest that in the Demeter sanctuary at least some of the "dolls" were dedicated by girls of marriageable age to Aphrodite, and rather than symbolizing the toys of childhood dedicated before marriage to the quintessential bride Kore, they symbolized the about-to-be-achieved sexual maturity of the girls.[335] The "dolls" may even have represented the girls themselves as *hierodouloi*, as a sort of substitute for the original form of ritual prostitution known in the Near East and rejected in that form by the Greeks, in which brides had to offer themselves before marriage in the service of the goddess.[336] This form of substitution would have reinforced in a more personal way the Corinthians' provision of slave-*hierodouloi* for Aphrodite. Nudity is also known in the rituals of Brauron, in which girls may have participated in races in the nude,[337] but there the hair was worn loose, not arranged in the fashion of hetairai. If the above interpretation of the Corinthian "dolls" is correct, the large number of "dolls" found at the Demeter sanctuary (see p. 3) could point to Aphrodite's substantial presence there, beginning at least in the Classical period.[338]

A new interest in portraying Aphrodite has been found in Early Hellenistic art as a whole.[339] Although the nude and semidraped figurines of Aphrodite from the Demeter sanctuary confirm this idea, they do not appear to reflect any known large-scale sculptural types. Unless they derived from works that have been lost, it is likely that their archetypes were created entirely within the world of the small-scale arts. The type repeated most often in the Demeter sanctuary is best preserved in **H249** and is fully preserved in a figurine in Berlin, which is published as Corinthian.[340] In this type, Aphrodite's left elbow is propped on top of a high, fluted Ionic column, anchoring there a few folds of one corner of her mantle; the upper edge of the mantle is folded down into a narrow overfold and drops at both front and back in deep, torso-framing curves from the column to her right thigh, where her hand pulls the overfold to the side; the left forearm is raised, the hand lifting an edge of the mantle beside her head. The feet are not detailed, but the soles of the sandals or shoes are high. The complete example in Berlin stands on a two-stepped rectangular base. The design is fundamentally a good one, creating a nice tension between the raised left shoulder and arm, stretching upward to reach the column, the balancing curve of cloth to the opposite side, and the heavy drapery, dropping into deep, weighty folds around the legs. The stretch of the left shoulder toward the column also causes a slight torsion, the chest facing more toward the viewer's right than the bent left knee. The execution of all the extant figurines, however, is rather poor. The figurine in Berlin has an overly large head with a peaked coiffure; the head type is recognizably Corinthian, although not exactly matched in the finds from the site. The left hand has lost its drapery and simply rests against the head in a fist. The result is rather awkward, but there are other examples from Corinthian workshops of the spoiling of good types by artisans without the skill necessary to add heads and limbs properly.[341] The coroplast responsible for **H249** never bothered to provide the figurine with a right arm or a left forearm at all. One might be tempted to call this piece an archetype because it lacks arms,[342] but the addition of a head (now lost) and the liberal application of white slip show that it

[334] The one exception, the pierced head **C141**, has both a sphendone binding up the hair and long locks of hair, showing a misunderstanding of both coiffures.
[335] For a related interpretation of Athenian "dolls," see Reilly 1997. See also p. 339.
[336] Yamauchi 1973.
[337] Kahil 1983, pp. 237–238; against this idea, see Pinney 1995; also discussed in R. Hamilton 1989.

[338] On the connection of "dolls" with Aphrodite cult, see *Troy*, pp. 91–92.
[339] Havelock 1995.
[340] Winter, *Typen* II, p. 93, no. 6; *Königliche Museen*, pp. 15–16, pl. XVI, left.
[341] E.g., an ephedrismos group in Boston, *Coroplast's Art*, pp. 128–129, no. 20.
[342] Cf. an armless torso archetype from Athens: Higgins 1967, p. 2, pl. 1:A–C.

was intended to be a finished figurine. The fabric, scale, thick walls, very rough interior, and venting of **H249** link it with six other figurines probably made in the same, derivative workshop (Workshop I, see p. 346). **H249** is from the construction fill of the Trapezoidal Building, which terminates at the beginning of the 3rd century B.C.; most other members of this workshop group are from the same context. The relatively slender, narrow-shouldered, high-breasted proportions are in line with those of the votary figurines (e.g., **H1**), which are from similarly dated pottery contexts; the slight torsion of the pose also would fit a later-4th-century B.C. date.

H250, from a pottery context terminating in the early 3rd century B.C., repeats some of the squiggles of drapery around the top of the column in **H249**; at a smaller scale, it is probably a later generation, although its technique points to a different workshop. The artisan, apparently similarly unskilled, did not sharpen the dulled impression with tooling. At this point, the right arm was included in the mold to simplify manufacture, and mantle folds were added behind the shoulders to stabilize the arm, thereby changing the composition. The probable mold siblings **H251** and **H252** represent a variant type, with a Doric column and a somewhat different compositional relation of column to torso, without folds separating them; the mantle covers the shoulders in back. The pottery context of **H252** is the same as that of **H249**, terminating at the beginning of the 3rd century B.C.

The fragment **H255** offers a tantalizing hint of the inspiration for these rather poor figurines. Little more than the left thigh and bent knee are preserved, but at statuette scale (size range 5) and with gilding on the drapery, the original piece must have been quite impressive. The drapery seems thin, but the gilded border that falls diagonally across the thigh is best explained as the hem of a mantle arranged like that of **H249**. Apart from the pose of the leg and the mantle arrangement, there is no guarantee that other elements of the composition originally paralleled **H249**, but a thin, fancy mantle with the upper edge draped around the legs does suggest that the figurine represented Aphrodite. A thin fold projecting forward from the mantle fall at the left side may indicate that the garment originally was lifted high in the left hand slightly in front of the figure; in this respect, **H255** would have differed in composition from the figurines discussed here.

Another hint that there may have been larger versions of a leaning Aphrodite is the fragment **H253**, which preserves only the top of a fluted column with drapery. While theoretically the column need not have supported a figure of Aphrodite, there are no other candidates for such a composition, with a mantle laid aside, among the preserved figurines, and the zigzag fold in front of the column rather resembles that on the column supporting **H252**. **H254** is another variant, in which the column is lower, so that the bent elbow rests on it at chest level. **I14** is a better-preserved and better-made example of this type, but it is an import, probably from Argos. The right hand holds the folded edge of the mantle out to the side, as in **H249**, but the drapery is tucked between the thighs and covers only the right leg. Since **H254** is the only preserved example of this type from the sanctuary in Corinthian fabric, it is not likely to have been a popular local type and may have been copied mechanically from an import.

H256 represents yet another variant type, which is fully preserved in an example once in a private collection in Dresden.[343] The fold patterns of the two figurines match very closely. The figurine in Dresden is not identified as Corinthian and is said to have been found at Tanagra; its head, with a peaked coiffure, is of 4th-century B.C. type but is not typically Corinthian. The fabric of **H256** is of a relatively coarse variety (fabric 5) that is recognizable in numerous Corinthian figurines but sometimes can be difficult to distinguish from Boeotian work (see p. 12). Consequently, it is unclear whether **H256** copies a foreign type or is itself an import. There are as well other Boeotian variants of the leaning Aphrodite, which seem to have

---

[343] Winter, *Typen* II, p. 93, no. 5.

been quite popular there.[344] In this type, as fully preserved, the column top is approximately at shoulder height. The mantle is tucked between the legs but from both sides, covering both legs and generating a zigzag fold cascade of the garment edge; the right hand holds the cloth closer to the body. As in **H249**, the sandal sole is high; in this case, the details of the foot are preserved, and the long, narrow toes with heavy folds collapsing over them recall the larger Middle Hellenistic foot fragments **H423** and **H424**. These fragments also show high sandal soles, but they are deeply divided around the toes, indicating a date in the 2nd century B.C. or later (see p. 257). Since there are no other figurine types preserved at the Demeter sanctuary with such footwear, it is possible that these fragments point to the survival of semidraped statuettes of Aphrodite until that time.

A more modestly draped figurine of Aphrodite is known, of reported Corinthian provenience.[345] In this type, the mantle is draped across the waist, leaving only the chest bare, and the hem trails only slightly; Eros is perched on top of the low column. The composition is more Classical than Hellenistic, suggesting a date before the middle of the 4th century B.C. The head, which appears from the published drawing to be very like **H231**, suggests that the reported provenience may well be correct, although the torso type is not represented among the sanctuary finds.

Representations of Leda often resemble those of Aphrodite in the arrangement of the mantle to reveal and frame the nude torso, but among the figurines from the Demeter sanctuary, only one certain representation of Leda (**H261**) can be identified by the presence of a swan. The identification of fragments of suitable composition from which a swan may have broken remains uncertain. Figurines depicting Leda found in the sanctuary could have been appropriate offerings in this cult of fertility goddesses because of the eroticism of the image of Leda's seduction as well as her implied impregnation by Zeus. Throughout the 4th century B.C., Leda was a favorite subject of Boeotian coroplasts, who devised several distinctive designs to portray this subject.[346] As in the case of the Aphrodite types discussed above, there are no clear links with monumental sculpture, although the dramatic gesture of lifting the unfastened mantle high appears in the sculptural Leda type attributed to Timotheos[347] as well as in some of the figurines.[348] In both Leda and Aphrodite types, the raising of the mantle presumably would have suggested to the viewer a very much intensified version of the unveiling of a bride.

In **H257**, the mantle is lifted high at the right side in a composition used for a Leda of reported Corinthian provenience,[349] but the figurine could represent Leda only if the missing left side below the thigh originally included a swan. It is possible that the lower part of the type can be completed by **H260**, which does not have a swan. The slender torso of **H257** with its high, full breasts recalls the proportions of the Aphrodite **H249**, and the pose is similar, although reversed. The fabric, thick walls, and irregular interior surface of **H260** link it technically as well as stylistically with **H249**. Thus it is likely that the two related types representing Aphrodite can be traced to the same workshop (Workshop I, see p. 346), together with five other figurines of different types. The upper torso fragment **H259** could be mechanically related to **H257**, showing the type without added drapery. The very dull modeling of **H259** and its grayish fabric are found also in fragments of right hands lifting drapery in lots 2247 and 2249, which could have belonged to figurines of similar type; the

---

[344] E.g., Liepmann 1975, p. 67, no. T52; Winter, *Typen* II, p. 93, no. 7.

[345] Winter, *Typen* II, p. 94, no. 2.

[346] E.g., *British Museum* I, pp. 231–232, nos. 868, 869, pl. 123; p. 235, no. 880, pl. 128.

[347] *LIMC* VI, 1992, p. 232, no. 6, pl. 108, s.v. *Leda* (L. Kahil

et al.); for figurines of various types representing Leda, see pp. 232–233, nos. 8–14.

[348] E.g., *British Museum* I, p. 235, no. 880, pl. 128.

[349] Winter, *Typen* I, p. 84, no. 4; the mantle is clasped between the thighs, and a small swan sits atop a support beside Leda's left hip.

pottery date of the latter lot, which includes most of the material from the construction fill of the Trapezoidal Building, terminates at the beginning of the 3rd century B.C. The only head that can be associated with this type through the curtain of drapery at the right side is the poorly made and preserved fragment **H263**. It is smaller in scale and if truly related would represent a later generation. The coiffure shows the long locks of hair associated with Corinthian representations of Aphrodite (see pp. 129–130), in this case, without a polos or other headdress. Just as it was possible to suggest from fragments that a version of the Aphrodite **H249** existed at statuette scale, so too the drapery fragment **H258**, which from the direction of the folds should belong to a curtain from the right side of a figure, suggests the existence of a large-scale Aphrodite or Leda generally similar in type to **H257**.

H261 is the only certain Leda in this group, with the body of the swan held against the left hip. The dull impression, without retouch, indicates that an imported figurine may have been mechanically copied to produce this type. **H262** appears to be something of a hybrid. The pillar at the left side points to a composition like that of **H249**, but the added drapery swag at the right side seems to be curving up into a curtain like that of **H257**. The divided toe of the shoe of **H262** probably points to a Middle Hellenistic date; perhaps this figurine is a relatively late survival.

The chiton of **H264** bares the right shoulder and part of the breast. The figure may have been in movement toward the viewer's left, since the mantle, which is raised in the left hand, curves forward as if blown from behind. The design is reminiscent of a Classical figurine in the Corinth collection, representing Leda rushing to the left with her mantle held up behind her.[350] **H264** is from the construction fill of the Trapezoidal Building, the pottery of which terminates at the beginning of the 3rd century B.C., but the delicately modeled drapery could speak for an early-4th-century B.C. date. The scanty remains of the large statuette **H265** are probably best interpreted as a standing Aphrodite leaning on a support at her left side; mantle folds cascade down the front of the support, at the foot of which the baby Eros sits or stands. The gnomelike appearance of Eros may be due to clumsy retouch.

Several nude or nearly nude figurines were constructed from the torsos of articulated "dolls." **H266** originally may have been arranging her hair, the long tresses of which can be seen on the back. The torso has been manipulated to push out the right hip and to advance the left thigh, to achieve a pose similar to that of **H249**. When the lower legs were added, the weight would have rested on the right foot. In this case, it is likely that a coroplast in a workshop that made articulated "dolls" found a simple way to imitate a popular type of bronze statuette[351] without the requisite mold. **H268** even more obviously derives from a "doll's" torso; a mantle was added in an arrangement similar to that of **H249**, but the garment has broken away in back, revealing the nude buttocks.

H267 probably also began as a "doll's" torso, but it has been altered with greater skill, and the fabric is very fine. The pose, in which the right leg moves forward while the shoulders tilt upward to the left, bears a certain resemblance to that of the dancing maenad in Dresden sometimes attributed to Skopas,[352] although the figurine shows less torsion, and the garment is flung completely away from the bare torso. Attic reliefs of the Hellenistic period show maenads dancing so strenuously in a similar pose that they are virtually undressed.[353] Aphrodite is sometimes depicted dancing but fully clothed, as in a figurine of Aphrodite and Eros in

---

[350] MF-6397, *Corinth* XII, p. 34, no. 143, pl. 10, there probably dated a little too early and identified as Aphrodite. On this Leda type and its variants, see *British Museum* I, pp. 231–232, no. 868, pl. 123, with bibliography. The earliest specimens belong to the late 5th century B.C., with later versions being made well into the 4th century B.C.

[351] Cf., e.g., Bieber 1961, figs. 36–39.

[352] Stewart 1977, pp. 91–93, 140–141, pl. 32; on the attribution, see Ridgway 1997, pp. 255–257, with bibliography on p. 278, note 55.

[353] Grandjouan 1989, pp. 4–5, 46–47, pls. 1, 2–4, 25, 27.

London.[354] A votive representing a maenad would not be out of place in the Demeter sanctuary, given that offerings were made to Dionysos there (see p. 76) and that figurines of satyrs also were dedicated. Whatever the correct identification, however, this figurine is of good 4th-century B.C. workmanship and is from the construction fill of the Trapezoidal Building, the pottery of which terminates at the beginning of the 3rd century B.C.

H269 seems to have been developed from a small "doll's" torso. It is not an improvisation, however, but a fully developed type that can be completed with the help of a well-preserved example in Athens (Pl. 79),[355] which has been recognized as Corinthian. The subject is the birth of Aphrodite. She is seated in front of a stylized open shell with scalloped edges, as if emerging from it; a thin garment is spread across her knees and is held out at either side. The head in the complete example wears a coiffure similar to that of the "doll's" head **C139**. **H270** represents a shell that seems originally to have framed a figurine, although its edges, now missing, may not have been scalloped like the shell in the figurine in Athens; other shell fragments in the lots (see catalogue), however, do have scalloped edges but lack the center where signs of attachment to figurines would be found. None of these shell fragments can be associated with certainty with specific figurine types, but of the types found in the Demeter sanctuary, the Aphrodite is the most obvious candidate. Like so many of the more interesting figurine types from the Demeter sanctuary, **H269** is from the construction fill of the Trapezoidal Building, the pottery of which terminates at the beginning of the 3rd century B.C.; the context of **H270** terminates in the second half of the 4th. Although **H269** is an attractive piece, it is actually a simplification of larger and more elaborate renderings of a popular type[356] and also conflates two types. In the best renderings, the marine imagery is very clear, through either a realistically shaped shell[357] or the representation of waves.[358] Aphrodite is kneeling, not seated in the shell, and is not draped; the shell is smooth edged rather than scalloped. One rendering, known in two examples of reported Corinthian provenience,[359] has her kneeling in the shell in front of a mantle held up by Eros; the mantle covers one knee. A related non-Corinthian type has the goddess kneeling on an upright flower rather than a shell;[360] the mantle, held up by Eros or the goddess herself, frames her and covers both knees. The coroplast who designed **H269** has used both types, retaining the mantle over both knees, turning the flower into a skirt, and adding a shell as well. His conflation implies that both types were known in Corinth in their original forms. The shell is believed to have been a symbol of the vulva in ancient Greece, and representations of Aphrodite emerging from shells to have symbolized the phenomenon of birth.[361] Actual shells were frequently dedicated at the sanctuary in Roman times.[362]

The motif of the mantle framing the head and torso is also known in types in which goddesses or nymphs ride on an assortment of animals, with the garment billowing over the head as if windblown. Sometimes the mantle is absent, and the figures are seated on the animals in a variety of poses, often turned to one side or in an only semiseated posture. An Archaic grotesque bird-rider was found at the Demeter sanctuary (MF-11873),[363] but the only later evidence at the

---

[354] *British Museum* I, pp. 263–264, no. 970, pl. 137, identified as Corinthian; in Higgins 1963, p. 19, the woman is identified as Aphrodite. I was able to examine a possible mold sibling of this figurine in The Metropolitan Museum, New York, inv. no. 06.1069 (*LIMC* III, 1986, p. 910, no. 699, pl. 648, s.v. *Eros* [A. Hermary et al.]); the fabric of this piece did not seem to me to be Corinthian. Since an example in local fabric was found in Lindos, the type may be Rhodian, *Lindos* I, cols. 700–701, no. 2985, pl. 138.

[355] National Archaeological Museum, inv. no. 4164; Winter, *Typen* II, p. 202, no. 1.

[356] A number of good examples are collected in Winter, *Typen* II, p. 202.

[357] E.g., Winter, *Typen* II, p. 202, no. 3.

[358] E.g., Winter, *Typen* II, p. 202, no. 2.

[359] Winter, *Typen* II, p. 202, no. 5; the provenience cannot as yet be confirmed by finds in Corinth.

[360] Winter, *Typen* II, p. 202, nos. 6, 7.

[361] On the symbolism of shells, see Goodenough 1958, VIII, pp. 95–105.

[362] *Corinth* XVIII, iii, p. 436.

[363] Publication forthcoming.

sanctuary for such animal mounts is a fragment in lot 2249, perhaps the tail of a bird or sea creature; the rough support below it and the flattened top, as if for a seat, suggest that it could have been part of a rider figurine. MF-10352 in the Corinth collection depicts a woman seated on a bird with a round loaf(?) in her lap. Animal-riders likely to be Corinthian or related to Corinthian types include another female figure on a bird,[364] a Europa in Berlin riding the bull,[365] a semidraped female figure in Copenhagen who rides a hippocamp,[366] and in London Thetis riding a hippocamp and carrying a helmet.[367] These figures do not have billowing mantles.

H271 does have a mantle curved over her head and is in a partly seated pose, as shown by a crease of flesh across her abdomen. While she could represent a mounted goddess, another possible identification is Leda, who in the Timothean sculpture is shown standing but bent at the waist in response to the approach of the swan.[368] The raised right arm of **H271** lifting the garment away from the torso would also be in accord with a representation of Leda. Whatever the correct identification, **H272** may be the head of a comparable figurine. **H271** is from the construction fill of the Trapezoidal Building, the pottery of which terminates at the beginning of the 3rd century B.C.

The very poorly preserved head **H273** is almost certainly from a mounted figure, to judge from the great arc of drapery over it. Although the surface is poorly preserved, earrings are visible, as well as the outlines of a coiffure with a high topknot in front similar to that of **C135**, a head related to articulated "dolls." Good compositional parallels can be found in figurines of Aphrodite Pandemos seated on a goat or other animal.[369] The worship of Aphrodite with this cult title was associated with *hetairai* elsewhere;[370] the coiffure of **H273** points in the same direction (see p. 171), although Aphrodite is not attested at Corinth with this cult title.

Among the semidraped figurines found in the Demeter sanctuary are some that resemble representations of Aphrodite in the baring of the torso, but they are usually perched on rocky outcrops; these seats, suggesting rustic places, usually can be taken to distinguish nymphs from Aphrodite, although representations of the goddess (identified by the presence of Eros or a goose) on a rocky seat are not unknown.[371] Muses also are frequently depicted on rocky seats, but they are usually fully clothed.[372] The very name "nymph," which signifies a young nubile woman, is a connection with marriage; nymphs provide water for the bridal bath in myth and received bridal sacrifices in real life.[373] In myth, nymphs are sometimes amorous and vindictive, as in the story of Daphnis and his nymph lover (Diodoros 4.84), or chaste but irresistible to a god, as in the case of Artemis' nymph Kallisto (Ovid, *Metamorphoses* 2.405–507). Because of their frequent association with lovers in myth, their images in art probably implied sexuality. Nymphs were sometimes the caretakers of children, but nymphs also could be dangerous to them and were sometimes thought to have carried off children who had died.[374] In Euripides' *Electra* (lines 625–627) sacrifice to the nymphs is mentioned for the safety of children and for impending childbirth. Nymphs frequently appear in art with Pan or satyrs, who are also represented at the Demeter sanctuary (see pp. 78–79, 199–200). All these associations work well for this sanctuary, but most importantly, nymphs are known to have been worshiped together with chthonic deities,

[364] Winter, *Typen* I, p. 162, no. 7.
[365] *Königliche Museen*, pp. 24–25, pl. XXXIII, right.
[366] *Danish National Museum*, p. 62, no. 588, pl. 72.
[367] Higgins 1967, p. 104, pl. 47:B.
[368] See p. 174, note 347.
[369] See Knigge 1982, esp. pl. 33. For riding Aphrodite types in general, see *LIMC* II, 1984, pp. 95–101, pls. 89–96, s.v. *Aphrodite* (A. Delivorrias et al.).
[370] For the sources and a discussion of the meaning of Pandemos, see Farnell, *Cults* II, pp. 658–664.

[371] E.g., Winter, *Typen* II, p. 107, nos. 2, 4.
[372] An example of a semidraped Muse (if correctly identified) would be a 4th-century B.C. statuette from the Athenian Agora, attributed to the pediment of the Temple of Apollo Patroos; see Palagia 1980, p. 8, fig. 2.
[373] On the functions of nymphs, see Nock 1972, pp. 924–926; *Morgantina*, pp. 92–93, with bibliography; Hedreen 1994.
[374] Nock 1972, pp. 924–925. The fear that such creatures can harm children has survived in Greece into modern times: Lawson 1964, pp. 140–142.

especially in Sicily.[375] In the cave at Pitsa, the nymphs were worshiped together with Dionysos, Demeter and Kore, and Eileithyia.[376]

H274 is the best-preserved example of the seated nymph type from the Demeter sanctuary. Since the composition shows torsion, which suggests a 4th-century B.C. stylistic date, and two mold siblings (see catalogue) are from the construction fill of the Trapezoidal Building, which terminates at the beginning of the 3rd century B.C., this figurine is probably not too far from its prototype. The proportions of the torso, slender, narrow-shouldered, and high-breasted, are typical of later-4th-century B.C. Corinthian work and resemble those of the Aphrodite **H249**. The rocky seat is high, and the figure half sits, half leans against it. The left knee is raised, and the foot is propped on a shelf at the base of the seat. The torsion arises from the turning of the shoulders toward the right hand, which rests on the seat behind the hip. The left hand and right foot are relaxed. Although not fully seated, the pose is nevertheless natural. In a 2nd-century B.C. sculptural counterpart known in several replicas from Rhodes and Priene, the pose has become contorted and is full of tension, without a natural relation to the seat.[377] This Late Hellenistic sculptural version shows Classicizing elements and may have been developed from a 4th-century B.C. source, to which the prototype of **H274** could have been related.

H275 is probably a later generation of **H274**, in which the mantle arrangement has been altered to cover the whole back; a similar alteration was made to **H250**, which is a later generation of the standing Aphrodite **H249**. **H276** is only a fragment of the lower part, but the distinctive hand, relaxed on the lap with some of the fingers curled under, suggests that the complete type was similar to **H274** but in a reversed pose. Another, rather poor example with pose reversed is in the Corinth collection (MF-7399).[378] **H277** may be derived from the same type, with the pose reversed, but all the interesting elements in the design have been lost. Only the raised left shoulder hints at the original composition; the pose has little torsion, the figure really sits rather than leans, the feet rest on the base at the same level, and the right hand seems originally to have been extended, instead of resting in the lap. An arch of drapery around the shoulders recalls the billowing mantles of animal-riders, but the feet seem to rest on a rocky base. **H278** is similar to **H277** in composition but is of nearly miniature scale, with both forearms originally extended and with the whole rocky seat preserved. The type seems to have been fairly popular, with several distinct mold series. It must have deteriorated already within the 4th century B.C., since one of the fragments from which **H277** is mended is from the construction fill of the Trapezoidal Building, which terminates at the beginning of the 3rd century B.C. The associated head type is unknown, but only MF-7399 has traces of hair on the shoulders; a bound-up coiffure appears to have been more common.

The fragment **H279** wears a chiton beneath a mantle draped around the hips to frame the abdomen. In this respect, the figurine resembles standing draped types such as **H128**, but it could not have been standing because of its greatly reduced depth. The figure originally may have been seated on a separately made base in a languid, half-reclining pose, similar to that of MF-10144 from the Baths of Aphrodite.[379] That figurine, molded together with its rocky seat, is from a deposit dated ca. 375–300 B.C. It is known in complete form in an example in Athens of Corinthian provenience[380] and appears to represent Aphrodite regarding herself in a mirror. **H279** cannot have been identical in type, because the mantle is arranged somewhat differently,

[375] *Morgantina*, p. 93, with bibliography; *RE* IV, 2, 1901, cols. 2755–2756, s.v. *Demeter* (O. Kern).

[376] Daux 1967, p. 644; *EAA* VI, 1965, pp. 200–206, s.v. *Pitsa* (A. K. Orlandos).

[377] The Rhodian type is discussed in Merker 1970, pp. 26–48. See also *Priene*, pp. 372–373, figs. 468, 469; Gualandi 1976, pp. 56–63.

[378] *Corinth* XII, p. 34, no. 144, pl. 10; there dated too early.

[379] H. R. Robinson 1962, p. 124, pl. 47:b.

[380] Winter, *Typen* II, p. 121, no. 7.

but it is similar in scale and fabric to MF-10144; it is possible that the heavy retouch of **H279** conceals a mechanical relationship between the two. Their chronology is in agreement, since the pottery context of **H279** terminates at the beginning of the 3rd century B.C.

Two seated figurines (**H280** and **H281**) wear a chiton slipped from one shoulder and a mantle across the lap, a costume worn by Aphrodite in figurines from other centers.[381] **H280** nevertheless seems to have some typological relation to the nymph **H274** and its variants, although it is of larger scale and better fabric, and its broader shoulders and less slender proportions suggest that the prototype was rooted in the Classical tradition. The relaxed right hand with curled fingers suggests a mirror image of the nymph **H274**, but the hand rests at the side rather than on the lap and seems originally to have held something. The left arm must have been raised, but the position of the hand (perhaps touching the hair?) is unknown. The chiton folds added to the nude torso are clinging and transparent, leaving the right shoulder bare and calling to mind sculptural renderings of the late 5th and early 4th centuries B.C.[382] The combination of bared right shoulder and long locks of hair is found in a Corinthian figurine in Athens, which can be identified as Aphrodite by the presence of Eros (Pl. 78).[383] Whether **H280** represents a nymph, on the basis of its pose, or Aphrodite, on the basis of the costume and coiffure, is uncertain because of the overlapping iconography of the two subjects, but it is clearly another example of a well-crafted piece of excellent fabric that stands alone, apparently outside the general run of more popular figurines (see p. 29). The retouch is extensive even for a Corinthian artisan, and the unusual method of head attachment (see catalogue) further separates **H280** from other Corinthian work. Although the pottery context of **H280** terminates in the early 3rd century B.C., the style and good fabric should place it before the middle of the 4th century B.C.

The original pose of **H281** could have been close to that of the nymph **H274** in reverse, since the pulled-back, raised left shoulder suggests that the hand could have rested on the seat in back; the position of the right shoulder is appropriate to an arm originally resting on the lap. Traces of long locks of hair only on the right shoulder indicate that the head originally may have been turned to the left. Although the pose with its torsion and traces of a mantle across the lap link **H281** with **H274**, the broad-shouldered proportions and the shoulder-baring, transparent chiton connect it with the larger **H280**. The drapery arrangement in the two figurines is reversed, but there are some similarities in the fold patterns of the chitons, particularly in the relatively wide, diagonal double fold that defines the upper edge of the cloth and the looped fold that dips below the navel. The drapery of **H281** is simpler, however, and most importantly, it is rendered in the mold, with little retouch. The maker of its archetype followed the method of the Attic Late Classical Rich Style by adding ridges to a nude torso to indicate transparent cloth, as seen, for example, in the Nike untying her sandal on the Balustrade of the Temple of Athena Nike.[384] At least in the design as preserved, however, the coroplast dispensed with the elaborations and flourishes characteristic of Rich Style drapery, settling on a design more coherent in its emphasis on simplicity and volume.[385] Perhaps the larger **H280** represents an earlier stage in the development of such types, before finished molds were available and the drapery had to be rendered by hand. The fusion in **H281** of compositional torsion with proportions and drapery still based on Late Classical style suggests a date of about the middle of the 4th century B.C. The pottery context of **H281** terminates in the third quarter of the 3rd century B.C., but the figurine must be earlier on stylistic and technical grounds.

---

[381] E.g., Winter, *Typen* II, p. 107, no. 2, with Eros.

[382] On the denuding of the shoulder in representations of Aphrodite, see Delivorrias 1991, pp. 135–150; Harrison 1982, pp. 86–87.

[383] National Archaeological Museum, inv. no. 4160; see p. 130, note 88.

[384] Conveniently, Lullies and Hirmer 1960, pl. 191.

[385] Compare, in this respect, a 4th-century B.C. Tarentine seated female figurine (Herdejürgen 1978, p. 55, no. A55).

Whether the figurines in this group represent nymphs or Aphrodite, a good deal of care was lavished on them, and the subject seems to have engaged the best workshops. The fragmentary **H282**, with its fine fabric and violet mantle, must have been beautiful when complete. A nonjoining fragment shows what appears to be a portion of the rocky seat at the left side of the figure; the mantle folds on it are crumpled in the Rich Style manner, as if crushed by the pressure of the now missing hand, but the collapsing folds between the legs are organized more geometrically. Since the upper broken edge of these folds continues upward, it is likely that the mantle fell from the left shoulder. Whether the upper torso was nude or clothed in a chiton is unknown. The seat originally must have been higher than that of **H274**, since the richly folded mantle collapses onto a shelf well below the level of the feet. The right leg appears to be stretched forward, as if the figure took a languid pose that allowed the mantle to fall between the legs. One of the fragments of this figurine comes from the construction fill of the Trapezoidal Building, which terminates at the beginning of the 3rd century B.C. The high technical quality and the design, as far as preserved, are consonant with a 4th-century B.C. date. **H281** and **H282** are related to one another in their sparing, selective incorporation of Rich Style elements into designs that emphasize structure over surface treatments; a stylistic date for the archetypes in the first half of the 4th century B.C. seems reasonable.

H283 is a still more meager fragment, preserving only the left foot and surrounding drapery, which nevertheless can be identified with some likelihood. The foot does not rest flat on the base but is lifted against an irregular support. The drapery collapses in a thick double fold, suggesting a mantle draped loosely around the legs. Therefore, the figurine may represent a nymph or Aphrodite on a rocky seat. The deeply divided toe of the sandal, however, indicates a Middle Hellenistic date and suggests the survival of this type into the late 3rd or first half of the 2nd century B.C.

The remaining three fragments in this group are less informative. **H284** preserves only the right leg and surrounding drapery. To judge from the angle of the thigh, the figure was either perched on a high seat or bent over in a pose like that of Leda. The diagonal folds at the proper right side of the leg suggest that the drapery was either spread over a seat or lifted in the right hand. Since the folds of the undergarment as well as the mantle are diagonal, the former design is more likely. Because folds envelope the other (inner) side of the leg, the right leg must have been extended forward or the left leg, now missing, was pulled back. The molding of the leg beneath the drapery and the high-soled sandal could suggest that the subject is Aphrodite. The good technical quality and the cuffed fold over the ankle, as in **H85**, point to a 4th-century B.C. date.

In **H285**, the mantle does not collapse but is wrapped neatly around the legs. The pointed slipper, narrowly folded chiton, and the length and fold pattern of the mantle resemble a Corinthian figurine in Paris that probably represents the seated Aphrodite with Eros.[386] **H286** is merely a foot in a sandal with a divided toe, but it belonged to a well-made statuette. Since the mantle is wrapped closely around the ankle on both sides, the foot must have been well advanced. Most likely the figurine originally was seated languidly, with one foot forward.[387] Both fragments are from the construction fill of the Trapezoidal Building, which terminates at the beginning of the 3rd century B.C.

[386] *Louvre* III, p. 54, no. D300, pl. 63:b.

[387] For a typical non-Corinthian example with a similar drapery arrangement, cf. Winter, *Typen* II, p. 107, no. 1.

OTHER DEITIES (EROS, ARTEMIS, ATHENA, NIKE)
(H287–H298)

EROS

Corinthian representations of Eros are not very common, although a few are of very good quality. While Eros was usually depicted as a flying baby in terracotta figurines of the Hellenistic period, in Corinth he appears also as a youth or boy (i.e., as an Eros ephebe). There does not appear to have been a fixed iconographic tradition, however, and there is variety even within this small group. He appears as a young boy standing together with Aphrodite in a Corinthian figurine in Athens (Pl. 78)[388] and another of similar type in the Corinth collection[389] and with a Corinthian seated Aphrodite in Paris.[390] As a youth he accompanies a muffled woman, probably a bride, in a figurine of reported Corinthian provenience in Berlin.[391]

Apart from the fragmentary **H265**, which depicts a baby in front of a drapery panel and is probably all that remains of a statuette of Aphrodite with Eros, four recognizable representations of Eros were found in the Demeter sanctuary. Two of these also depict Eros as a baby; one of the remaining two is an adolescent, and the last is perhaps a slightly younger boy. In addition, there are wing fragments (see **V31**) that could have belonged to a flying figure such as Eros. Several of the isolated heads of children discussed below (pp. 192–193) also could have belonged to representations of Eros. His appearance in the Demeter sanctuary is related either to the shrine's function in furthering human fertility or to the identification of this deity with death, in the form of Eros-Thanatos.[392]

Generally speaking, Eros was depicted as a youth in the Classical period and as a child in Hellenistic times, but this general "rule" is an oversimplification. The transformation of Eros from a youth to a child can be observed better in vase painting than in sculpture or figurines, and it is clear that there was some overlap of types, particularly in the 4th century.[393] Moreover, the ages at which Eros was depicted actually vary greatly, from real babyhood through various stages of prepubescent boyhood and adolescence to fully matured youth. Of the erotes from the Demeter sanctuary, only one is from a datable context, but that one shows that Eros may already have been represented as a baby early in the 4th century B.C. (see discussion of **H290** below).

H287 is a seated Eros of youthful type but with full hips and a childlike softness around the abdomen and thighs. Although there are no traces of locks of hair on the shoulders, the shape of the break suggests that the hair originally fell along the neck. The missing wings were molded separately and inserted into slots at the back, instead of being attached with clay, as in the case of **H291**. Although the right arm is relaxed, the left arm originally was raised very high together with the wing, as is apparent from the break at the shoulder and the raised wing slot. A similarly lifted arm is found in Eros figurines from Myrina, but the figure

---

[388] National Archaeological Museum, inv. no. 4160; see p. 130, note 88.

[389] MF-1060, *Corinth* XII, p. 34, no. 139, pl. 9.

[390] *Louvre* III, p. 54, no. D300, pl. 63:b. The boy is wingless here, but the group seems to represent the two deities.

[391] Rohde 1968, pp. 43–44, no. 23. Although it is not possible to confirm this provenience through finds from Corinth, the broad style, iconography, and fabric seem to be within the parameters for Corinth, to judge from the description and color photo published by Rohde. A somewhat similar type in London from Naukratis has been assigned to Corinth: *British Museum* I, pp. 264–265, no. 971, pl. 137. An Eros with a dancing Aphrodite in the British Museum probably should be dissociated from Corinth (see p. 176, note 354). The provenience of a standing Eros with a small dog, said to be from Corinth (Winter, *Typen* II, p. 246, no. 4B), cannot be confirmed on the

basis of finds from Corinth. MF-9254 in the Corinth collection is a winged boy Eros holding a mirror case (Romano 1994, p. 91, no. 79, pl. 28). MF-8063 is another winged Eros, but several other pieces in the Corinth collection, once thought possibly to represent Eros (MF-3882, MF-39, MF-1423, MF-3863, *Corinth* XII, pp. 52–53, nos. 349, 350, 352, 353, pl. 31), are probably better considered mortals, in the absence of specific attributes and in light of the increased repertoire of Corinthian youths and children now known. A fine, standing youthful Eros from the Forum Southwest excavations (MF-71-38 [Michaud 1972, pp. 638–639, fig. 124]) could be an Attic import.

[392] Vermeule 1979, pp. 161–162, with bibliography.

[393] E.g., a mid-4th-century B.C. nuptial lebes by the Marsyas Painter shows baby and boy erotes in the same painting: Arias and Hirmer 1962, pl. 226.

is flying rather than seated.[394] Although the lower legs of **H287** are missing, to judge from the broken surfaces, the right leg seems to have been stretched forward and the left pulled back. Parallels for such a seated Eros are found in 4th-century B.C. red-figured vases but without the raised arm.[395] The pose is known in sculpture, not for Eros but for a young satyr who is just falling asleep, with his arm resting languidly on his head, still seated upright on a rocky base.[396] When Eros is shown sleeping in sculpture, however, he usually is a small child in a fully recumbent pose or is leaning on a support.[397] Because the base of **H287** is broken away or covered with drapery, it is not clear whether Eros sat on a rock or a backless blocklike seat similar to that of the boys **H335** and **H336** (see p. 191).

H288 represents a nude youth on a rocky seat. Since mortal youths seated outdoors are generally shown mantled, as in **H311**, it is possible that **H288** is another representation of the resting Eros. The pose is different, however, almost leaning against the seat rather than sitting on it, with one hand resting behind on the rock, as in the nymph **H274**. Further, although the left side of the youth is preserved almost up to the shoulder, there is no sign of a wing. It is therefore also possible that the figurine represents the youthful Pan, depicted with human legs, as in **H387**. The compositions of both **H288** and **H387** are flat, almost pictorial, and the figurines have little depth, as if the designs had been taken from reliefs.

Only the head and wings of **H289** are preserved, and it is of rather poor quality, with heavy and clumsy retouch, but the distinctive headdress, a polos, which is unusual for Eros, marks the type and is paralleled by an Attic figurine.[398] The reference of the polos for this deity probably is its use as a bridal crown. Since there is no other evidence for the type in Corinth, perhaps **H289** was mechanically copied from an imported figurine, with the dulled details retouched unskillfully.

The two baby erotes from the Demeter sanctuary are **H290** and **H291**. **H291** preserves more of the torso, although it is smaller and of lesser quality. The remains of one wing are spread, showing that the Eros was in flight; the head is thrown back, and the right arm originally reached forward. The breaks below the arm indicate that the right side originally was attached to something. This Eros is likely to have been hovering in the air, his torso horizontal, above the left shoulder of another figure, probably Aphrodite. If this reconstruction of the composition is correct, the relation of the two figures would have been like that of the Aphrodite and Eros in the "slipper-slapper" sculpture from Delos.[399]

H290 preserves only the head and part of the back but seems originally to have been in a similar pose. The workmanship of this Eros is excellent. The pottery context with which it was found dates to the early 4th century B.C., which may seem early for a flying baby Eros, but there are reasons why this date is likely to be close to the mark. Apart from its context, the fine technique of this figurine suggests that it was made not later than the middle of the 4th century B.C. In addition, it should be kept in mind that Corinthian bronze workers before this time already were designing mirrors surrounded with running and flying figures, including erotes.[400] Consequently, one need not doubt an earlier date for baby erotes in Corinth than the 3rd-century B.C. date usually assigned to their appearance among "Tanagra" and Myrina figurines.[401] **H290** is related in scale, facial type, and workmanship of the hair to the wreathed baby's head **H348** and may have been made in the same workshop (Workshop E, see p. 345). Although wreaths are worn both by Eros and human children, in light of the stylistic and technical relationship between the two pieces, it is possible that **H348** also represents the deity.

[394] E.g., *Louvre* II, p. 37, no. MYR 54, pl. 42:a.

[395] E.g., *LIMC* III, 1986, p. 892, no. 488a, pl. 636, s.v. *Eros* (A. Hermary et al.).

[396] Bieber 1961, p. 140, fig. 576; for bibliography, see Ridgway 1990, pp. 317, 341, note 5.

[397] *LIMC* III, 1986, pp. 916–917, nos. 779–790, pls. 653, 654, s.v. *Eros* (A. Hermary et al.).

[398] Winter, *Typen* II, p. 246, no. 2.

[399] Conveniently, Bieber 1961, pls. 629, 630.

[400] E.g., Keene Congdon 1981, pp. 167–168, no. 55, pl. 51.

[401] In Boston, *Coroplast's Art*, p. 139, no. 26, with bibliography.

Artemis

Representations of Artemis have been recognized among the lingering Archaic figurines (MF-12009, MF-13561).[402] In addition, a Hellenistic standing draped female figurine (**H128**, see p. 148) has been identified tentatively as Artemis because she wears a baldric and holds a torch. Two further female figurines could represent Artemis, **H292**, which is in movement and may be reaching back to a quiver, and **H293**, which wears a baldric and also may have a quiver. The evidence for the presence of Artemis as a "visiting" deity at the Demeter sanctuary is thus not very strong, although some of Artemis' functions, such as her patronage of young people before marriage and her connection with childbirth, would be in keeping with the concerns for human fertility and the safety of children apparent at this shrine.[403] She was worshiped at Corinth as Artemis Eukleia (Xenophon, *Hellenika* 4.4.2); under this epithet at Thebes, Artemis received offerings from brides and bridegrooms, although elsewhere the name defined her as a goddess of war.[404] A small number of figurines of Artemis came to light at Morgantina in association with the worship of Persephone; there these votives are thought to reflect the chthonic worship of Artemis in the West and her function, in the form of Hekate, in the story of Kore's recovery from the Underworld, as told in the *Homeric Hymn to Demeter*.[405]

If the figurines here presented do indeed represent Artemis, **H293** in its complete form may have resembled the sculptured Dresden Artemis type,[406] with the pose reversed. The connection is not unreasonable, since this Artemis type has been connected with a monument in Megara known from both Pausanias and representations on Megarian coins. The more active pose of **H292** echoes another sculptural type known in Roman copies but associated with the 4th century B.C., the Artemis of Versailles-Leptis Magna.[407] Three Artemis types of Roman date (**R15**, **R16**, and **R29**), a much larger proportion of the total, in light of the small quantity of Roman figurines preserved, suggest that the goddess played a more important role in the sanctuary during that period.

Athena

A single representation of Athena (**H294**) has been tentatively identified as such by the Little Owl, the species specifically associated with the goddess, in her hand. In addition, the garment, as far as it is preserved, could be the so-called peplos of Athena (see p. 32). Athena is sometimes represented in various media holding her owl.[408] The relatively high girding of the garment suggests an Early Hellenistic date, with which its archaeological context agrees.

Nike

Nike is probably the subject of **H295**, on the basis of the strong forward movement of the right leg, the flying skirt folds at the sides, and the partially nude (or transparently draped) legs. An example of similar type from the Forum Southwest excavations (MF-71-42 [Pl. 76)[409] is of much better fabric and workmanship and is preserved up to the waist, although the legs are closer together; this figurine, from a context dating to the third quarter of the 4th century B.C., resembles in technique the short-skirted articulated "doll" **C174** and may have been constructed on a "doll's" torso. Another similar Nike figurine from the Athenian Agora is thought to be of

---

[402] Publication forthcoming.

[403] See Farnell, *Cults* II, pp. 444, 566–568. On the worship of Artemis elsewhere in Corinth, see Lisle 1955, pp. 102–103, 116–117; Herbert 1986, pp. 32–35; an inscribed bronze base for a statuette dedicated to Artemis: C. K. Williams and Fisher 1972, pp. 153–154, pl. 23.

[404] Farnell, *Cults* II, pp. 461–462, 471.

[405] *Morgantina*, pp. 91–92.

[406] Conveniently, Bieber 1961, p. 21, fig. 40.

[407] Ridgway 1990, pp. 93–94, with bibliography on p. 106, note 42; *LIMC* II, 1984, p. 645, nos. 250–265, pls. 465–467, s.v. *Artemis* (L. Kahil and N. Icard); *LIMC* II, 1984, pp. 805–806, no. 27, pls. 592, 593, s.v. *Artemis/Diana* (E. Simon).

[408] *LIMC* II, 1984, p. 976, nos. 200–209, pls. 728, 729, s.v. *Athena* (P. Demargne).

[409] From drain 1971-1; on the deposit, see C. K. Williams and Fisher 1972, pp. 154–163.

Corinthian fabric;[410] it is of very good quality and preserves the entire torso but moves forward on the left leg. In spite of variations among Nike figurines of this general type, all probably depend ultimately on late-5th-century B.C. conceptions of Nike, as seen, for example, in the Nike of Paionios in Olympia.[411] Nearer to Corinth, interest in the subject during the 4th century is evident at Epidauros, in the akroteria of the Temples of Asklepios and Artemis.[412] The creation of Corinthian Nike types during the 4th century B.C., such as MF-71-42 and the example in Athens, could have been inspired by the successful activities of Timoleon in Sicily. In fact, there was a connection between Demeter and Nike in Sicily, in a statue at Enna of Demeter holding Nike in her right hand.[413] It is unclear, however, whether **H295** can be explained in this way. The figurine was made unskillfully of poor fabric, with such thick walls that it is nearly solid. While it could have been made during the 4th century B.C. by an unskilled craftsman, its fabric is of a type more common in the 3rd century B.C., and it is more likely to be a later survival of a good 4th-century B.C. type. Perhaps the victory it suggests was agonistic rather than political or military, referring to the races run by youths in honor of Kore (see p. 61). The discovery of a figurine of Nike at Morgantina is explained by her iconographic connection in vase painting with Hades and Persephone, and more generally with wedding scenes.[414]

The three remaining figurines possibly representing Nike are equally poor, suggesting that she was at best a marginal deity at the Demeter sanctuary. **H296** is a miniature with little detail. There are no wings, and the position of the right hand on the hip is not really characteristic of Nike, but the right leg is advanced as if stepping off the base into the air. **H296** is from the construction fill of the Trapezoidal Building, which terminates at the beginning of the 3rd century B.C.

The fragmentary torso **H297** owes its identification as Nike to a flaring, presumably wind-blown overfold like that of a probably Corinthian figurine of Nike in Berlin.[415] On a larger scale, a similar overfold is found on a Nike akroterion from the Artemision at Epidauros[416] and another from Delos.[417] It is, unfortunately, unknown whether **H295** originally had such an overfold because of its poor state of preservation. Although the flaring overfold of **H297** indicates swift movement, the rigidity of the torso suggests that the figurine may have been constructed from a "doll's" torso. If **H297** is correctly identified, **H298** also could represent Nike. In this case, the overfold flares out even more, and the chiton slips down from the left shoulder as well, as it does in the Nike of Paionios. The flaring hem could belong to a dancer's short skirt rather than an overfold, since it is not entirely clear whether or not the thighs were bare, but the skirts of Corinthian dancers are usually longer, reaching the knees, as in **C176**. As in the case of **H297**, the type may have been built on a "doll's" torso. The pottery context of **H298** terminates at the beginning of the 3rd century B.C.

---

[410] Inv. no. T-2309, H. A. Thompson 1947, p. 208, pl. XLV:3. The identification of the fabric was suggested originally by Marie Farnsworth and was conveyed to me by Dorothy B. Thompson, who has also noted that the figurine does not correspond to Attic taste (D. B. Thompson 1984, p. 34, fig. 6); a Pergamene connection is suggested but without supporting evidence. Farnsworth's suggested attribution has merit; the addition by hand of drapery folds around the nude-seeming hips and legs is known in Corinth in the conversion of nude torsos of "dolls" to draped types (see p. 58); the Nike's short-waisted torso proportions and chubby shoulders and arms are also found in Corinthian figurines (e.g., **H281**).

[411] Hölscher 1974.

[412] Yalouris 1992, pp. 19–21, nos. 2–5, pls. 3–8:b; pp. 30–31, no. 25, pls. 24–26; pp. 84–85, fig. 27; Ridgway 1990, pp. 149–150, with bibliography on p. 199, note 1.

[413] Mentioned by Cicero in connection with the crimes of Verres, *Second Verrine* 4.49; for Hellenistic coins of Enna picturing this statue, see *HistNum*, p. 137.

[414] *Morgantina*, p. 94.

[415] Knoblauch 1939, cols. 445, 437–438, figs. 28, 29, published as Attic; on the likelihood that this Nike is Corinthian, see p. 166. Cf. also Schneider-Hermann 1946.

[416] See note 412 above. Figurines of Nike with a fluttering overfold were dedicated at the Thesmophorion in Pella: Lilibaki-Akamati 1996, e.g., p. 34, no. 50, pl. 12στ.

[417] Assigned to the Monument of the Bulls; Ridgway (1990, pp. 174–175) summarizes the widely diverging opinions on the date of the monument and its sculpture; see also Webb 1996, pp. 134–136, with bibliography.

MALE FIGURINES: NUDE, SEMIDRAPED, AND DRAPED
(H299–H313)

The male figurines assignable to the Early Hellenistic period probably represent youths, to judge from the few preserved heads, the generally youthful physiognomy, and the absence of traces of beards. It is possible, however, that poorly made, anatomically undefined examples such as **H305** and **H307** could have represented mature men with short beards, which have left no traces on the torso. The typology of the standing youths is similar to that of the Classical period (see pp. 60–62), although a larger proportion are draped around the lower torso and legs, and the poses are more languid, with outthrust right hips. The general similarity to the earlier youths suggests that these too represent votaries, although only one example (**H302**) preserves an offering in the hand (a bunch of grapes).

H299 appears to be completely nude, although the panel between the legs may indicate a drapery backdrop. The softness of the anatomy and the sinuous pose contribute to the impression of adolescence. The slight effeminacy probably can be attributed not only to the youth of the subject but also to a workshop relationship (Workshop H, see p. 346) with a female figurine, the piglet carrier **H1**. In both figurines, the head and neck are unusually deep; both show long locks of hair over the shoulders and a similar sloping profile; the relaxed position of the right arm is similar, although the youth is empty handed. The youth is somewhat smaller in scale, suggesting that we may be missing an earlier generation. The two figurines are good examples of how a single design could be altered to develop two entirely different mold archetypes, male and female, with a thematic relationship (both represent votaries), forming an iconographic series.

The essentially "Praxitelean" pose of **H299** is shared by two male figurines with nude torsos and partial drapery (**H300** and **H301**). **H300** originally leaned on a support, a composition unusual for votary figurines in Corinth; in this case, the mantle falls over the left shoulder and down the side. This figurine is in a poor fabric and may be relatively late. In **H301**, the youth stretches a mantle behind himself, as if to display the nude torso. This almost plaquelike figurine has a better-preserved parallel in the Corinth collection (MF-3882), which shows a round, smiling face and long locks of hair to the shoulders.[418] Of these three figurines, only **H300** is from a chronologically useful context, which terminates in the third quarter of the 3rd century B.C.

Five standing male figurines wear the mantle draped over the left or both shoulders and around the waist, in a manner comparable to the Classical **C199**. **H302**, the best made of the group, has a softly contoured, childish torso and carries a bunch of grapes as does the boy **H319**, but the hip-thrust pose and drapery are more like those of a youth. The grapes suggest an offering either to Demeter in her function as protector of agricultural fertility or perhaps to Dionysos, who is also represented at the sanctuary (see pp. 76–78).[419] A connection with Dionysos rather than Demeter is suggested by a slightly larger figurine from the South Stoa, similarly draped and with a fleshy torso but carrying a tragic mask rather than grapes.[420] This parallel is from a deposit with a *terminus ante quem* of ca. 250 B.C. It is possible that the slight corpulence of this type points to a representation of Silenos, for whom both the grapes and mask would be suitable attributes,[421] but there are no traces of a beard, and in the absence of a head, a certain identification is difficult. **H304** is similar in type to **H302**, as far as it is preserved, but is of poorer quality. The fragmentary **H303** is a possible rendition of a similar type at statuette scale. The unarticulated torso and protruding abdomen recall **H302**, and the added mantle could have

[418] *Corinth* XII, p. 52, no. 349, pl. 31, identified as Eros.
[419] On the symbolism of grapes and the vine in Greek art, see Goodenough 1956, VI, pp. 46–60. See also p. 194.
[420] MF-1904, *Corinth* XII, p. 51, no. 336, pl. 30, identified

as an actor, but youths and children sometimes carry masks (e.g., Winter, *Typen* II, p. 288, no. 6).
[421] Cf., e.g., a similarly draped Tarentine type with grapes, Winter, *Typen* II, p. 399, no. 11.

been draped in a similar manner, although the poor preservation of the figure precludes certain identification. It is also possible that the statuette represented a mantled boy similar to **H334**.

Three standing male figurines similar to one another in scale are of rather poor quality. **H305** originally may have been of a type similar to **H302** and **H304** but altered by the addition of a draped right arm; the fabric is poor. **H306** is of reasonably good fabric but lacks anatomical definition. An offering may have been held against the torso by the right hand. The composition of **H307** appears to have been distorted, so that the left shoulder is raised very high; perhaps the type originally included a support at the side, like that of **H300**. The fabric and workmanship again are very poor.

Three more standing, semidraped male figures (**H308–H310**) are larger in scale, one of them (**H310**) reaching statuette size, but similarly they are not of the best quality and do not point to an established iconography. All three, in fact, seem to be improvisations in which drapery was added to a nude male type in a stance similar to that of **H299–H301**. The type continues a nude male type known in the Classical period (see p. 63), and it is noteworthy that similarly draped Classical male figures such as **C199** also were ad hoc constructions developed from available materials. Presumably, the demand for this type was limited. **H308** and **H309**, with long locks of hair on the shoulders and no signs of a beard, must represent youths, like the similarly coiffed **H299**. Since terracotta sculptures of youths from the sanctuary are also draped to leave the right side of the torso bare,[422] it is possible that the figurines represent the same subjects offered perhaps by those who could not afford a statue. The technique of **H309** and **H310** is very peculiar, perhaps because they were made by an inexperienced coroplast. Apart from the crudity of the retouch, both figurines are greatly reduced in depth. **H310** was stuffed with lumps of clay, perhaps to add stability to the shallow figure. The unusual technique and flat modeling make these figures appear later in date, but **H309** was found in the construction fill of the Trapezoidal Building, which terminates at the beginning of the 3rd century B.C., and the latest date of the pottery context of **H308** is the early 3rd century B.C.

The lack of mold siblings for any of the Early Hellenistic standing male figurines and their improvisational quality show that they were not very popular votive types. Only **H302** and **H304** are compositionally similar, but these two figurines may have represented children or Silenos rather than youths. The generally indifferent quality of the male figurines supports the impression of marginality. Only **H302** is reasonably well made; the higher quality would be understandable if the figurine represents a boy rather than a youth, since much more attention was lavished on figurines of children.

The three examples of seated male figurines of this period include one of Boeotian inspiration. For the Classical period, a Boeotian figurine type found in the Kabeirion at Thebes may have been the source of one of the standing male types (see p. 62). The source of **H311**, a mantled youth seated on a rocky base, appears to be a class of Boeotian figurines with a number of variants, found in tombs and dated ca. 330–250 B.C.[423] This class represents a youth in his late teens with short, curly hair and wearing a mantle, boots, and a petasos or wreath. The footwear of **H311** is not clearly rendered, and there is no hat or wreath, but the garment is the same, fastened at the right shoulder and leaving the arm bare, and the hair has been retouched to approximate the curly coiffure. That this type was relatively popular in Corinth is suggested by the existence of a later generation (see catalogue). The type also seems to have had funerary significance in Corinth, since a mold sibling of **H311**, MF-13904, was found in a burial in Corinth, together with an imported example (MF-13900) in an orange-brown fabric with sparkling inclusions that is probably Boeotian.[424] The dull modeling of **H311** and MF-13904 suggests that their mold may have been taken from such an imported figurine. MF-13900 cannot itself have been the

---

[422] Bookidis 1988, pl. 4:1, 3 (SF-65-14).

[423] Higgins 1986, pp. 150, 152–154, figs. 186–188.

[424] From grave 1929-23, unpublished.

model, however, since it parallels the arm positions and the fold patterns on the chest but has differently composed legs, with a flatter lap and a more frontal pose. There is evidence for Athenian participation in the development of these ephebic types,[425] but the presence in Corinth of a similar Boeotian version suggests that the immediate source is to be found there.

H312 is a tantalizing fragment of a seated male statuette, probably handmade, wearing a garment that reaches the calf. The thickness of the ankle and the absence of defined toes suggest that he may be wearing soft boots. The similarity of the costume to that of **H311** and the related figurines raises the possibility that **H312** was an attempt to render a similar type at larger scale by hand, in the absence of a suitable mold of the desired size. The lap is flat, like that of the Boeotian MF-13900. The irregularity of the break suggests that the seat could have been a rocky base. The fragmentary and summarily executed **H313**, wearing what appears to be a knee-length tunic, could be yet another youth, this time on a blocklike seat.

ISOLATED MALE HEADS
(H314–H318)

The five isolated heads include three that have short, curly coiffures like the ephebic types discussed above, although the nature of the torsos to which they originally belonged is not known. Most are of size range 3–4, approaching statuette scale and considerably larger than the standing and seated male types discussed above, with the exception of the fragmentary statuette **H312**. With the possible exception of **H317**, these heads were rather poorly made, with distorted or clumsily retouched features. The flat-topped **H315** originally may have worn a hat, perhaps a petasos. It has curved incisions on the cranium, as does **H314**, suggesting that they were made in the same workshop. **H316** wears a wreath, which is also a characteristic ephebic headdress. Its fabric is the poorest of the group; its combination of sharply tooled hair and undefined features speak of a poor mold rather than a worn surface. In spite of the poverty of workmanship, however, the strong turn of the head on the neck points to an interesting design and the possibility that the mold for this figurine also was copied from an imported piece.

H317 has a curly coiffure of chin length similar to the hair of Boeotian figurines of boys,[426] and it originally may have worn a wreath, as do these children. The facial features of **H317**, however, are both more delicate and less childlike. **H318** is somewhat puzzling, since the face, with its pathetic air, is similar in type to the female head **H192**, and the corkscrew curls recall another female head (of **H57**). The female heads wear the polos, however, while **H318** wears a turban. This headdress is found combined with corkscrew curls on the Archaic head MF-12162,[427] which has red paint on the flesh and therefore should be from a male figurine. On the basis of this combination of coiffure and headdress, and since individual head molds could be used for both male and female figurines, **H318** has been included with male figurines, although this identification is not entirely certain.

CHILDREN
(H319–H354)

Representations of children continue to be a significant part of the sanctuary's coroplastic repertoire in the Early Hellenistic period, and the range of figurine types was greatly enriched by a growing interest in portraying children at various stages of physical development and in new poses. The seated baby boys of Classical type (see pp. 68–73) probably continued to be dedicated at least into the third quarter of the 4th century B.C., when the workshops of the Potters' Quarter,

---

[425] D. B. Thompson 1963.
[426] E.g., in London, Higgins 1986, pp. 150, 152, fig. 185.
[427] Publication forthcoming.

which created many of these figurines, ceased production. While the Classical repertoire emphasized babies, with a few older boys, Early Hellenistic workshops reversed the proportion, showing their best and most prolific work in representations of boys perhaps two or three to six years of age.[428] The custom of nudity for boys, as known in the Classical period, continues, revealing the ages of these boys through their sloping shoulders, soft pectorals, fleshy bellies, short, chubby legs, and lack of modeling (presumably to convey the undeveloped musculature of children).

The boys of this group are related to some of the previously discussed Classical and Early Hellenistic youths (**C188–C198** and **H299–H301**) in their standing poses, the offerings in their hands, and the framing of their nude torsos by drapery over the shoulder and down the back. Anatomically, however, the youths are clearly older. The Classical youths (e.g., **C188**) are square shouldered, slender and have flat abdomens, indicating that they are post- rather than prepubescent. The Early Hellenistic youths (e.g., **H299**) are somewhat soft and languid in rendering, but they also have leaner torsos than the younger boys, and their longer-legged proportions are more adult. When part of the anatomy is covered by drapery, it can be difficult to decide whether a figurine was intended to represent a young boy or a youth. **H302** has the soft chest and abdomen of a child, but the figure is draped over the hips and legs like an adult in a mantle with a triangular overfold and on this basis has been grouped with the youths (see p. 185). On the other hand, **H334**, which also is childish anatomically as far as can be observed, is wrapped around the middle with a much-too-large mantle and therefore is probably meant to represent a child.

The ages of figurines representing young males are important because they may illuminate the role of postpubescent youths and prepubescent boys in the sanctuary ritual. It is noteworthy that although there seem to be distinct age groups represented, the offerings they carry overlap in type. Of the Early Hellenistic youths, only one is preserved with anything in his hand, the rather ambiguous **H302**, who carries a bunch of grapes, as does the standing boy **H319** and the seated girl **H339**. Other nude Early Hellenistic boys carry a strigil and pointed aryballos (**H320**), athletic equipment for which a child's body seems too young; a rooster (**H322**); or a bag for knucklebones[429] (**H323**). Similar offerings are carried by the nude Classical youths: **C188** carries an aryballos (albeit of different shape); **C191** holds a rooster and perhaps a knucklebone bag; and the semidraped **C201** carries a knucklebone bag and a ball. The Classical youths' offerings that are not found in this group of boys are the lyre and the phiale, which are not seen again. On the basis of the admittedly limited number of figurines in these groups, it would appear that the offerings once associated with youths have been transferred to younger boys. Perhaps it is not too farfetched to suggest that sometime during the later 4th century B.C. the role of prepubescent boys in the sanctuary ritual was enhanced, paralleling that of prepubescent girls (see pp. 126–127), although speaking in general terms, young children must have participated in rituals earlier.[430] A purely artistic phenomenon, the interest of Hellenistic artists in genre subjects, could have been the impetus for the new types at this time. **H323–H325** (and perhaps **H326** in its complete state) are accompanied by a small dog. This image also continues from work in the Classical tradition, since one of the earlier seated children (**C249**) plays with a small dog.

H319, a boy with grapes, takes a standing pose, but the figure is not static. The lower mantle folds swirl somewhat, and he seems restless, as if about to step forward. This pose is also

[428] On determining the ages of representations of children on the basis of physical chacteristics such as chubbiness, convex profile, and proportions, see Sourvinou-Inwood 1988, pp. 37–39; Canby 1986, pp. 56–57, 63, chart on p. 57, fig. 5-1; Hamilton 1992, pp. 209–219.

[429] On knucklebone bags, see p. 63, note 272.

[430] On children in festivals and cult in Classical Attica, see Rühfel 1984a, pp. 77–174. On the importance of children in

Eleusinian ritual, see Clinton 1992, p. 55. On one of the Pitsa plaques (pinax A) apparently prepubescent boys are musicians and lead the sacrificial sheep to the altar; the scene could represent a bridal sacrifice to the nymphs worshiped at Pitsa, since the young woman bearing the offering tray has shorn hair (*EAA* VI, 1965, pp. 201–202, pl. opp. p. 202, s.v. *Pitsa* [A. K. Orlandos]).

characteristic of a smaller Boeotian figurine in Paris, which is similarly draped; the boy clutches the edge of the mantle in the right hand and carries a fruit in the left.[431] In this case, because of the discrepancy in scale and the apparently better quality of the Corinthian figurine, the Boeotian coroplast may have used workshop materials imported from Corinth. The Boeotian figurine preserves the head, which has long, curly hair and a wreath, but it is not known whether the Corinthian figurine originally had a head of similar type. When Boeotian workshops borrowed the Corinthian ephedrismos type, they used only the torsos, adding their own head types (see p. 201), and the same practice could have been followed here. In another smaller boy figurine, probably Boeotian, formerly in the Bomford collection, the head is bare, and the figure is set at an angle on the base, enhancing the impression of motion.[432] A connection also can be found with other Boeotian figurines, such as a boy from Tanagra,[433] which is similar to **H319** in the upper torso, including the draped, bent left arm, and also in the pose and contours of the left leg; the mantle is differently arranged at the right side, however, and the boy leans on a column and holds a knucklebone bag rather than grapes. The head of **H319** also must have been different, since there are no traces on the shoulders of the long locks of hair of the Boeotian boy. This boy is smaller than **H319** but only by a perhaps insignificant one centimeter, leaving the relationship between the two types unclear. What remains clear is that if the figurines of standing boys were more consistently preserved, one could probably show that a number of variant types were created from related source materials in an iconographic series (see pp. 14, 343), in either a Boeotian center or Corinth, the present evidence favoring the latter. The fragmentary **H321** could be of a type similar to **H319**. Although its workmanship is not out of the ordinary, its fabric is excellent, much better prepared than that of any other figurine of a child.

The torso fragment of a boy with a rooster (**H322**) indicates that figurines of boys of related type were made at a larger scale as well, although there is no evidence for mechanical continuity. There is a considerable drop in scale to the much smaller **H323**, again without demonstrable mechanical continuity. While we may simply be missing the material that would show how the types were altered from generation to generation, on the basis of the evidence at hand, it is probably best to assume that the archetypes were created separately at different scales.

H320, a boy with an aryballos and strigil, shows a connection in pose with the youth **H299**. Although the proportions differ, showing a child on the one hand and a fully matured young man on the other, the poses are in mirror image, with a relaxed arm following the languid curve of the hip and the opposite leg stepping forward. The child figurine is larger in scale, and there is no observable mechanical relationship, but in the process of design of the archetypes, some related workshop materials may have been employed and adapted to represent children. A similar process is more clearly apparent for **H331** (see p. 190). The smaller **H324** and **H325** are very close in pose to the youth **H299**.

Two nude, standing boys (**H326** and **H327**) are preserved with their heads. They are intermediate in scale between the larger and smaller groups just discussed, but in spite of general similarities, they do not provide evidence for mechanical continuity. The facial features are not very clear, but the faces are round and plump, although not as expressive as children's faces sometimes are; the hair is long at the sides, to the chin in **H326**, to the shoulder in **H327**, with the as-yet-uncut hair over the forehead arranged in a topknot or braid.[434] Two additional heads with similar hairstyles (**H328** and **H329**), preserved with part of the nude upper torso, probably belonged to similar types. If the head **H330**, which is quite like that of **H327**, also belonged to a standing nude boy, it would have been similar in scale to the largest of the boys (**H322**).

[431] *Louvre* III, p. 32, no. D173, pl. 39:f. See also Winter, *Typen* II, p. 288, no. 7.
[432] *Bomford Collection*, pp. 46–47, no. 120.

[433] In London, Higgins 1986, pp. 150–151, fig. 183, there dated ca. 330–300 B.C. by the shape of the spool base.
[434] On the keeping of these frontal locks of hair for ritual cutting, see above, pp. 62–63.

The most popular child type in the sanctuary was not nude but semidraped. It represents a standing boy crowned with a stephane and wearing a small mantle over the left shoulder and around the hips (**H331**); he holds a small goose. The type differs distinctly from the other standing boys from the sanctuary not only in the headdress and drapery but also in its more slender proportions and more delicate detail. It cannot be grouped with any of the other figurines of children into an iconographic series (see pp. 14, 343), and it probably stemmed from a completely different source. Since the boy's lean, long-legged proportions are those of an adult rather than a child, the archetype probably was created in conjunction with adult figurine types. There are a few clues to help make the proper connections. The spool base of **H331** also can be found in the votaries with piglet **H1**, **H9**, and **H10**. There is also a similarity of composition and theme with **H9** and **H10**, in that both forearms are pressed to the torso, and an animal is held against the chest; in all three figurines, the stance is similar, with the left leg drawn to the side. All are of similar scale, taking into account that the child naturally would be smaller. The panel between the boy's parted legs is like that of the youth **H299**. Since there is a probable workshop relationship among the figurines of votaries and the youth (see pp. 119–120), it is likely that the boy **H331** also should be brought into this group (Workshop H, see p. 346).

The goose is most likely the *chenalopex aegyptiaca* (χηναλώπηξ), a small goose, rather like a duck, named by the 3rd-century author Herondas (*Mimiamboi* 4.31) as part of a sculptured group of a boy strangling a goose. While this quietly standing figurine can have no connection with the sculpture,[435] such a design, if well known, could have prompted other renderings. Certainly the bird in **H331** seems to be the proper size for a *chenalopex*, for which the modern designation is the *alopochen aegyptiaca*, a bird that had strong religious and erotic associations in Egypt.[436] In Greece and Magna Graecia, the goose was sacred to both Kore and Aphrodite, although probably in its larger wild or domestic form.[437]

The largest assemblage of figurines of boys with ducks and geese is from the Phoenician site of Kharayeb.[438] The types, both standing and seated, nude and draped, vary greatly and include some draped girls as well. None exactly parallels **H331**, which is, in any case, a local Corinthian creation. It is likely that the bird identified as a duck at Kharayeb is actually the *chenalopex*. The figurines are from a *favissa* connected with a fertility cult that invoked both Greek and Egyptian deities.[439] It is perhaps significant that the Greek deities recognized at Kharayeb are Demeter and Kore, Dionysos, Aphrodite, and Eros, partly paralleling the pantheon of the Acrocorinth sanctuary. In both sanctuaries, other figurines of children carry balls or grapes or are accompanied by dogs.

In addition to the thirteen figurines mechanically related to **H331** enumerated in the catalogue, five fragments were counted in the lots. Most belong to the same generation, but probably one more followed. From elsewhere in Corinth, there are two unpublished examples, MF-13901 and MF-13907 from grave 1929-23, including a well-preserved head. Unfortunately the burial was disturbed. There is also an example of the head in an apparently Argive fabric (**I21**), suggesting that molds of this type were exported. A poorly preserved example of slightly larger scale, with the mantle wrapped across the waist (**H332**), indicates another, perhaps earlier use of the type, although a mechanical relationship is not clearly demonstrable.

[435] On the problem of reconciling the sculptural types showing a boy with a goose with the literary sources, see Bieber 1961, pp. 81–82; Pollitt 1986, pp. 140–141; Ridgway 1990, p. 232, with bibliography on p. 243, note 23. The combination of stephane and small goose is found in a sculpture in Athens showing a nude standing boy holding the bird on top of a pillar support: Rühfel 1984, color pl. 95, after p. 240.

[436] Houlihan 1986, pp. 62–65, with bibliography.

[437] Zuntz 1971, p. 172; Sourvinou-Inwood 1978, p. 109, c. On the symbolism of the goose, see Goodenough 1958, VIII, pp. 46–50, with bibliography. See also Keller 1913, pp. 220–227.

[438] *Kharayeb*, pp. 40–44, nos. Kh. 340–496, pls. XLVII–LIII passim (ducks); pp. 47–49, nos. Kh. 539–554, pls. LVII, LVIII (geese).

[439] *Kharayeb*, p. 135. See also p. 328.

One isolated head (**H333**) repeats the head type of **H331** with a different headdress, a sort of flat, angular cap, perhaps an unsuccessful attempt to imitate the beret or kausia worn by Athenian boys, as seen in figurines from Menon's cistern. These mantled boys, some of them wreathed, are quite different in type from the Acrocorinth sanctuary figurines, but it is possible that they also were dedicated to Demeter or Aphrodite.[440]

Yet another type is the seated, nude boy (**H335**–**H338**) unfortunately known in the Acrocorinth sanctuary only in fragments. With variants, the general scheme appears to have included at least some of the following features: a nude torso with plump, separated legs; drapery over one arm and falling over the edge of the seat; an offering, here a knucklebone bag, in one hand; and a blocklike seat, perhaps a chest. An unpublished headless example from grave 1929-23 (MF-13903) has no drapery but holds a bunch of grapes. The general type is not uncommon elsewhere, and better-preserved examples can be cited from Athens, for example.[441]

Paralleling the seated boys are two figurines of seated little girls (**H339** and **H340**). **H339**, which is better in quality, represents a girl of about five years, dressed in a chiton, seated on a blocklike seat, and clutching a bunch of grapes. This type also was found in a Corinthian funerary context, in a North Cemetery grave dated to the first half of the 3rd century B.C. (see catalogue). The type originated in Athens and was widely copied; on the basis of decreasing size, four generations have been identified by Thompson.[442] The Corinthian examples are comparable in size to the third generation, dated by Thompson to the first quarter of the 3rd century B.C. In the original type, the girl did not hold an offering, these additions having been made in the later generations.[443] The head type, as seen in an example from Eleusis,[444] shows a smiling face framed by a crop of curls, but none of the heads preserved in the Demeter sanctuary are really comparable.

The more degenerate and slightly smaller seated girl (**H340**) may have been a local attempt to approximate the original type. It does not seem to be a mechanical relative because of its different anatomy and proportions. It has a head that is too large for the torso, even in a child's figure; since the head and torso were made in the same mold, this error must have been made in an earlier generation. Further, the head and torso are incongruous in type. The round face and coiffure with a braid or knot over the forehead and locks of hair down to chin level, like the hair of the boy **H326**, are those of a child, while the torso shows the small breasts of a maturing girl. The facial type of **H340** is clearer in the similar, but larger head **H341**, which wears a thick, fillet-wrapped wreath.[445] This head could have belonged to a figurine of either a girl or boy, since its hairstyle was unisex.

The torso types of isolated heads of figurines of children are difficult to identify, even when their gender is known. Age is difficult to determine on the basis of the face alone, except in the case of babies or very young children, whose plump cheeks and widely opened eyes are unmistakable. Coiffures are somewhat helpful but cannot alone determine the iconographic context of a figurine of a child. A good example is the coiffure of **H342**, which is summarily rendered but is identifiable as the melon coiffure with an encircling plait, as in the "doll's" head **C136**. Even this apparently feminine coiffure, known, for example, in a statue of a girl from Brauron,[446] was also worn by boys, as in a bronze statuette in Baltimore.[447]

[440] S. G. Miller 1974, pp. 212–217, 240–241, nos. 82–102, pls. 37–40; pp. 216–217 on the deity to whom they were dedicated. On the kausia, see *Troy*, pp. 53–55; Kingsley 1981; Saatsoglou-Paliadeli 1993, pp. 122–142, 146.

[441] From the Pnyx, H. A. Thompson 1936, pp. 172, no. 1g; 174, fig. 20:g. See also Winter, *Typen* II, p. 261.

[442] D. B. Thompson 1966, pp. 58–59.

[443] Figurines of this type were frequently dedicated at the Thesmophorion in Eretria (*Eretria*, pp. 31, 80–83, e.g., nos. 526, 541, 662, pl. 23).

[444] D. B. Thompson 1966, pl. 18, fig. 9.

[445] On such thick wreaths, see *Troy*, pp. 45–48.

[446] Vorster 1983, p. 331, no. 5, pl. 12:2.

[447] *Walters Art Gallery*, p. 3, no. 1, pl. 1; Mattusch et al. 1996a, pp. 247–251, no. 28.

Three more heads with children's faces but coiffures or headdresses known in older types are **H343–H345**. **H343** is a girl, but the arrangement of her long locks of hair is something like that of adult females, such as **H186**, with a narrow wreath instead of a stephane. **H345** has a child's short neck and round, smiling face but wears her hair pulled up into a cluster of curls at the top of the head and long at the sides, a style known also in the Corinth collection in a figurine of a girl dancing[448] and in heads of young women from the Demeter sanctuary (e.g., **H230**). A closely similar head was used for a figurine of Eros,[449] but since there is no trace on **H345** of the mirror Eros holds on his right shoulder, the subject is better identified as a child. **H344** bears some resemblance to **H178**, the head of a draped young woman wearing a stephane, but the short neck, short curls, and more childish face of **H344** suggest a younger girl; her headdress is a curious hybrid, formed like a low polos, but somewhat pointed at the center, like a stephane.

The stephane when worn by children is sometimes placed low on the head, across the forehead, perhaps because a headdress made to encircle an adult's cranium would be too large to fit in the same way on a child's head. A stephane with a scroll pattern is worn in this fashion in one of the best renderings of a child's head from the Demeter sanctuary (**H352**), over the customary child's central braid and side curls. The gender of this child is uncertain, since the stephane, usually associated with goddesses or adult women, on the young is found in representations of both girls and boys.[450] A head similar to this one in facial type and in the heavy-lidded, somewhat dreamy expression, but without the stephane, is found on a mold from the Athenian Agora, representing a nude boy.[451] The Corinthian head, however, is larger than the Athenian mold and consequently cannot be derived from it. There is some flavor of the sculptures of children from Brauron in **H352**, and it is conceivable that there was some Attic connection, but neither its nature nor direction can at present be determined. The mold impression of **H352** is fresh, the stephane was not added but was part of the original composition, and there is no sense that the piece was derivative, unlike the much duller Corinthian figurines that probably were mechanically copied from an Athenian source (e.g., the Asiatic dancer **C281**).

A hint that a related type may have existed in Corinth at statuette scale is given by the head fragment **H354**. Only a portion of the scroll-patterned stephane and forehead are preserved, but the wisps of hair over the forehead are appropriate to a child's head and may approximate a coiffure like that of a terracotta statue of a boy from the Demeter sanctuary.[452] Since the stephane widens slightly towards the viewer's left, and the strokes of the hair should slant towards the ear, the fragment probably belongs to the left temple of the head. In this head, the stephane was worn slightly back from rather than across the forehead. The face of a small head (**H353**), presumably a girl because she wears earrings, may be a later generation of **H352**. The coiffure could have a fringe of wispy bangs as in **H354** but, in this case, the stephane has been replaced by a rather poorly rendered headdress somewhat resembling the feathered wreath found on some Attic figurines.[453]

One would think that the constraints placed upon coroplasts by the physiognomy of a child's face would limit the repertoire of types, but the remaining heads are all quite different from one another. **H346** is similar in its wide nose and thick, wide lips to the Classical seated baby boy **C237**, but the addition of a wreath of leaves and perhaps clusters of berries suggests that the

[448] MF-1018, *Corinth* XII, pp. 43–44, no. 248, pl. 21.

[449] MF-9254, Romano 1994, p. 91, no. 79, pl. 28.

[450] Rühfel 1984, p. 173, fig. 72 (girl); boys on Attic grave reliefs sometimes wear the stephane: Clairmont 1993, e.g., I, pp. 192–193, no. 0.873a.

[451] D. B. Thompson 1982, pp. 160–161, pls. 24:f, 27:c, d.

[452] SF-65-14, Bookidis 1988, pl. 4:2.

[453] From Menon's cistern, S. G. Miller 1974, pp. 212, 240–241, e.g., nos. 88, 97, pls. 37, 40; **H353** is cited on p. 216, note 104, where it is identified as a boy.

figurine could have represented a baby Dionysos.[454] Since the break at the lower right side of the head leaves open the possibility of attachment to another figure, the head could be all that remains of a group depicting a satyr or Silenos carrying the baby Dionysos.[455] Even if the original composition was elaborate, this piece was rather poorly made. The hair, ears, and mouth were crudely retouched, while the eyes were allowed to retain the thick, nearly closed eyelids of a mold that apparently had lost definition of the facial features. The boy or girl **H351** also has an exaggerated mouth but was made much better, with a child's alert, open-eyed expression, and well-modeled cheeks. The unidentifiable broken object on its head was perhaps a vessel.

The earrings of the head **H347** should identify it as a girl. A particularly well made and delicately detailed piece, it may be an earlier generation of the flying Eros **H290**. This workshop (Workshop E, see p. 345) appears to have produced a variety of child types of excellent quality. The head may have had a still earlier use with a curl-cluster coiffure, since the hair is swept up from the temples as in that hairstyle (see, e.g., **H201**). Further, leaf-shaped projections at either side of the head between the ears and the wreath could be the remaining ends of curls tumbling from a cluster of curls, the main part of which was removed when the wreath was applied.

The head of a baby boy or girl **H348** has particular charm, since its too-large wreath has settled at an angle over the typical child's front-plaited coiffure. The composition is particularly nice, the head tilting to the side opposite the slant of the wreath. The details of its good workmanship suggest that this head also may have been made in the same workshop as **H347** and the flying Eros **H290**; because of the technical and stylistic similarities, there is a chance that **H348** represents Eros as well. A mold for a larger wreathed child's head was found in Corinth in the excavations East of the Theater (MF-1988-25, Pl. 76); it too is well designed, although there is no evidence of a mechanical relationship.

H349, the mantled head of an alert, sweetly smiling child, also could represent Eros, who is shown veiled and flying in a 3rd-century B.C. type from Asia Minor.[456] Whether Eros or a mortal child, the face resembles that of a sculpture in the Liebieghaus-Museum.[457] The last head (**H350**) is of still another type. Its very small, smiling mouth, set in puffy cheeks, gives the face a puckish expression. The hair is an unusually (for a child) large mass of punched curls framing the face; the upper layer of curls could originally have been a wreath, misunderstood by the coroplast and retouched like hair. Similarly punched curls are found on the youth's head **H317**. A possible mold sibling has the more common child's central plait (see catalogue).

The attributes associated with figurines of children probably have some reference to the cult. Since the bunches of grapes carried by one boy and one girl probably should be construed as offerings, like a terracotta cluster of grapes from the sanctuary,[458] it is likely that the toys and animals carried by others are also offerings and not merely attributes of childhood. Apart from the bunches of grapes, the items include knucklebone bags, a strigil and aryballos, a small goose, and a rooster, all carried by boys. The dog accompanies boys, but as it is not carried, is not likely to have been an offering. Coiffures and headdresses (the stephane and wreath) appear to be unisex. Wreaths are associated with banqueting and festivals,[459] but when worn by children, only the latter context would apply.

[454] The baby Dionysos is represented on Apulian red-figured pottery wearing a wreath of leaves: *LIMC* III, 1986, pp. 478–479, no. 667, pl. 376, s.v. *Dionysos* (C. Gasparri).
[455] For a group of this type attributed to Corinth, see *Louvre* III, p. 53, no. D295, pl. 61:e, and the less well preserved **H364**.
[456] Bol and Kotera 1986, pp. 162–165, no. 81.
[457] Bol 1983, pp. 204–206, no. 63, with bibliography. The child is surely much younger than the five to eight years suggested in the publication, since the hair has not yet grown long enough for the customary central plait.
[458] MF-11303, publication forthcoming with miscellaneous finds.
[459] *Troy*, p. 46. On the symbolic significance of wreaths, see Goodenough 1958, VII, pp. 154–161.

The grapes immediately suggest a reference to Dionysos[460] and remind one of the Athenian Anthesteria festival, in which small children may have played a role; there, grapes are thought to have had the same symbolic reference for children as wine had for adults.[461] The offering of clusters of grapes to other deities connected with the sanctuary, however, particularly Aphrodite and the nymphs, is also documented (*Anthologia Palatina* 6.190, 191, 299, 300, 324). Eros himself carries a bunch of grapes in an Attic figurine.[462] The offering of knucklebones could parallel the offering of a ball (see p. 126) as a toy of childhood. Hermes receives such gifts from a boy in *Anthologia Palatina* 6.309, but exactly who received them in the Acrocorinth sanctuary is unclear. The strigil and oil bottle could perhaps be similarly construed as an offering, although of youths rather than boys. The goose was associated with both Kore and Aphrodite;[463] the rooster, a symbol of male sexuality, was offered to Kore.[464] The possibly chthonic reference of the pet dog has been mentioned above (p. 73). Although the material is not sufficiently abundant to draw firm conclusions, the themes that emerge are the giving away of objects associated with childhood or youth, growing maturity as seen through the nudity of some of the boys, and references to fertility. What is important is that children are represented participating in ritual, which was not the case with the Classical figurines of children. One thinks of Plato's description of children learning about the gods by observing their parents worshiping at festivals (*Laws* 10.887d).[465] But beyond this, the boys are nude, a state that is taken as a sign of initiation ritual for youths (see p. 61). While the boys are surely too young to be undergoing any ritual preparing them for marriage, their connection with the symbols of sexual maturity and fertility at an early age could parallel the apparent early socialization of girls through cult activity of some kind (see p. 127).

Most of the Early Hellenistic figurines of children are, unfortunately, from mixed contexts. Those with some contextual evidence for date are the following: **H320** and **H339** are from pottery contexts terminating in the late 4th century B.C.; from the construction fill of the Trapezoidal Building, which terminates at the beginning of the 3rd century B.C., are **H347** and a mold sibling of **H326**; **H346** and **H352** are from pottery contexts terminating in the early 3rd century B.C.; **H353** is from a pottery context terminating in the first quarter of the 3rd century B.C.; **H322**, **H350**, and **H354** are from pottery contexts terminating in the third quarter of the 3rd century B.C.; from pottery contexts terminating in the later 3rd century are **H328**, **H329**, and **H349**. Although the numerous fragments of the boy with a goose (**H331**) are from mixed contexts, the absence of the type among the more than 1,800 figurine fragments in the construction fill of the Trapezoidal Building suggests that it was not created before the 3rd century B.C.[466] Indeed, the slender proportions and delicacy of the type are consonant with an early-3rd-century B.C. date.

COMIC ACTORS, PARODIES, AND GROTESQUES
(H355–H384)

Figurines of three separate categories are brought together here for discussion because of their common use of masks or anatomical distortions. Painting or modeling comically misshapen figures was a tradition in Corinth going back to the Archaic period, the best-known examples being the so-called padded dancers of Archaic vase painting.[467] Corinthian figurine types falling into this general category include grotesquely distorted figures of nude women (e.g., **H373**), three-legged satyrs (e.g., **C275**), semihuman monkeys depicted in everyday activities (e.g., **V8**), parodies

---

[460] On the symbolism of the vine, wine, and grapes, see Goodenough 1956, VI, pp. 46–60.

[461] R. Hamilton 1992, pp. 113–117.

[462] Catling 1982, p. 10, fig. 10.

[463] Sourvinou-Inwood 1978, p. 109, c.

[464] Sourvinou-Inwood 1978, p. 108, b.

[465] On religious training within the family, see Bremmer 1995, pp. 30–35.

[466] Two fragments of this type were counted in lot 4474, the pottery of which terminates in the middle of the 4th century B.C., but the figurines must be later.

[467] Amyx 1988, II, 651–652, with bibliography.

of possible cultic activities (e.g., **H367**), and comic actors (e.g., **H355**). Although terracotta models of theatrical masks were dedicated at the sanctuary,[468] it should be noted that the wearing of a mask by a figurine does not necessarily make it a theatrical type, since masking in the theater ultimately derived from that practice in ritual.[469]

COMIC ACTORS AND PARODIES

The comic actor figurines from the Demeter sanctuary are of two sorts: one group follows Athenian comic actors in type and style (e.g., **H355**), and reflects the literary comedy of Athens; a second group may refer instead to local, nonliterary comic performances. While very little is known of the Doric farce of the Peloponnesos, this ancient comic form, apparently consisting of humorous skits rather than full-length plays, is sometimes considered a forerunner of Attic comedy, and the "padded dancers" are cited as visual proof of these performances. Among their varied associations, these dancers appear on Corinthian vases in scenes identified as women's festivals.[470] Whether or not these scenes have anything to do with the rituals of the Sanctuary of Demeter, the connection of comic types in Corinth with women's worship clarifies the appearance of comic figurines in the sanctuary. Certainly buffoonery and coarse humor were associated with the cult of Demeter.[471] Indeed, the very origins of comedy are traced by some to fertility rituals.[472]

Figurines of actors, mainly Attic, have been studied comprehensively, with attempts to connect them to characters in specific plays.[473] One imported Athenian comic actor (**I42**) was found in the Demeter sanctuary; in addition, some of the actors of local manufacture are either copies or adaptations of known Athenian types representing Old and Middle Comedy. **H355** is one of these; the figurine represents an actor, standing or seated, who holds upright beside his head a baby wearing a pilos.[474] Others are **H356**, the masked head of an actor of unknown type; **H357–H359**, comic actors dressed as a pregnant bride unveiling, a type dated 350–325 B.C. by Webster;[475] and **H360** and **H361**, actors portraying a pregnant, mantled woman muffled to the eyes like a bride.[476] One of this group (**H361**) is sufficiently similar to its Attic parallels[477] in its peaked coiffure and fold patterns to suggest a mechanical relationship; indeed, one of the known Attic examples is of reported Corinthian provenience,[478] indicating that an imported figurine could have been available for copying. **H360** is of a type similar to **H361**, but it is slightly larger and is not mechanically related; it is less slender and has a rounded rather than peaked coiffure. The small and summarily worked **H362**, which has lost all its molded detail, could be a derivative of a type similar to **H360**. This group is dated 400–375 B.C. by Webster.

H363 may be a variant of the actor as an old nurse, with one arm pulling the mantle to the chin, the other holding a baby; this type is also dated 400–375 B.C. by Webster.[479] The face, however, is not necessarily a mask, being without the gaping mouth and showing realistically sagging cheeks. Since the impression is very dull, however, and the composition closely resembles the theatrical type, it is probably best to consider this figurine an actor. It may be dull because its mold was taken directly from an imported figurine and was not retouched.

[468] Publication forthcoming with miscellaneous finds.
[469] Burkert 1985, pp. 103–104, with bibliography; see J. B. Carter 1988, on the connection of masks with ritual marriage and girls' initiation ritual; also J. B. Carter 1987, on the connection of Spartan masks with a fertility goddess of Near Eastern origin; on masks and ritual in general, see Napier 1986.
[470] E.g., Jucker 1963, p. 59, pl. 22:4–6.
[471] Olender 1990.
[472] Lesky 1963, pp. 233–236.
[473] Webster 1978.

[474] Perhaps originally similar to Winter, *Typen* II, p. 418, no. 8 (seated). For this type, see also Webster 1978, e.g., p. 83, no. AT 59b–d; p. 84, no. AT 60 (both standing).
[475] Webster 1978, p. 125, no. AT 113c, d (no. 113c is KT-5-20, *Corinth* XV, ii, p. 125, no. 20, pl. 24; no. 113d is *British Museum* I, pp. 401–402, no. 1530, pl. 206: note 4 on p. 401 corrects the identification from Cyrenaic to Corinthian).
[476] Webster 1978, p. 48, no. AT 10p (= **H360**): "local variant without the high hair-dressing."
[477] E.g., Webster 1978, p. 47, no. AT 10a.
[478] Webster 1978, p. 48, no. AT 10k.
[479] Webster 1978, pp. 46–47, no. AT 9.

While Attic comedy was widely performed throughout Greece,[480] it is unclear whether the actual identity of the characters was significant for the dedicators of these figurines. It is perhaps more to the point that the types chosen consist of comic kourotrophoi and pregnant brides,[481] that is, types that refer to the same concerns of visitors to this sanctuary as do other figurines. The actual attributes of these figurines may have been more important to the purchasers than their literary identity.

H364, representing Silenos with the infant Dionysos, is a copy of an Attic type that is thought to refer to Satyric drama; the details of the type are clear in an example in the Corinth collection (MF-1608) and a larger one in London (see catalogue). The impression of **H364** is very dull, perhaps because its mold was taken directly from an imported figurine and not retouched, as may also be true of the old nurse **H363**. The subject is also known in a much larger rendering in Paris, of reported Corinthian provenience.[482]

The remaining figurines in this group, a few of which are masked, cannot be directly connected to the Attic literary tradition but could instead refer to local traditional comic performances, which would not have been out of place in this cult. It is noteworthy that the types, although varied, are all female. The miniature **H365** is a masked actor in the garb and pose of a mantled dancer, similar to **H153**. There is a later generation of **H365** (see below) as well as another miniature dancer type, less well preserved but probably also masked (**H366**), suggesting that these types were fairly popular. If the figurines from the sanctuary representing mantled dancers (**H153–H172**) point to dancing of this kind as part of the ritual, then the masked dancer figurines could suggest that such dances also were parodied, with humorous intention. These masked miniatures may have been made in the same workshop (Workshop C, see p. 345) as the serious miniature dancers **H165** and **H166**. Like them, **H365** shows the swirling drapery typical of the late 5th and early 4th centuries B.C., together with slight torsion, which calls for a date somewhat later in the 4th century B.C. A probable later generation in the Corinth collection was found in the Forum area in a cistern abandoned at the end of the third or beginning of the fourth quarter of the 4th century B.C.[483] Another point of similarity with the serious dancers is the sharp detail in miniature scale, suggesting derivation from a small metal figure (see p. 155). **H367**, a miniature masked hydriaphoros, is another possible workshop mate. It too could represent deliberate parody of a serious sanctuary ritual, if the hydriaphoros figurines found there point to the actual cultic carrying of water jars (see p. 38). Attic comic water carriers do exist[484] but are masked and dressed as actors, while **H367** is garbed as a woman.

The remaining figurines have the anatomical exaggerations appropriate to actors but do not preserve the heads to prove the presence of theatrical masks. The possibility exists that some of these figurines are parodies, if not of rituals, then of the serious iconography found among the other figurines, rather than depictions of actors playing roles. Certainly the nude or virtually nude female types mentioned below cannot be actors. Only the discovery of better-preserved examples of this group can clarify their identification. A liking for parody already can be found in the Classical seated goddess **C81**. Two members of this group (**H368** and **H369**) may parody peplophoros types. **H368** is a corpulent, probably pregnant woman in a vulgar, straddling pose. This figurine actually could be of Classical date. It is from a surface lot with material of all periods, but it has regular, parallel folds on the skirt and overfold, and a wide, splaying, slightly inturned foot recalling the deformed feet of the seated goddess **C81**, which is from a

---

[480] On performances in Corinth, see Anderson 1986, pp. 46–47.

[481] A figurine ascribed to Corinth (Winter, *Typen* II, p. 421, no. 10), also mantled and pregnant, wears the long hair and topknot of a young girl. In this version as well, the joke seems to be the too-late wedding.

[482] *Louvre* III, p. 53, no. D295, pl. 61:e; at present, finds from Corinth cannot confirm the origin of this figurine.

[483] MF-1979-37, C. K. Williams 1979a, p. 125, pl. 30:d.

[484] Webster 1978, pp. 50–51, no. AT 14.

pottery context terminating in the 5th century B.C. With its long, pleated overfold, it could be parodying such a type as the Classical peplos-figurine **C16**. **H369** wears a peplos and probably a shoulder-pinned back mantle, the lappets of which can barely be discerned in front, but the low kolpos is pouched in the front and back in such a way as to give the appearance of a distended abdomen and buttocks. This figurine could parody a goddess type, such as the peplos-figurine with shoulder-pinned back mantle **C36**.

Only the back of **H370** is preserved, but the wide, massive buttocks are sufficient to identify it as a corpulent comic type; the costume is feminine, the mantle just covering the hips, as in **H360**. The full width of **H371** is not preserved, but the figurine appears to have been wide and squat in proportions, although not as exaggerated as **H370**. Its enveloping mantle calls to mind a type such as **H110**. **H372** is the front of a squat, massive figure, with a diagonally rolled mantle like that of **H130**.

H373 is a nude female figure with a swollen abdomen, composed like figurines of Aphrodite (cf. **H266**) but pregnant. A similarly shaped nude articulated "doll" (**C115**), discussed with that group (see p. 53), may also be a parody of a serious type. Grotesquely corpulent, nude female figures signified fertility in Egyptian art,[485] and it is likely that figurines of this kind from the Demeter sanctuary should be similarly interpreted. Obese, nude female figurines sometimes caricatured serious sculptural representations of Aphrodite.[486] A parodied Aphrodite Anadyomene has been found at Corinth,[487] but, as far as **H373** is preserved, the pose, with the right hip outthrust and the left thigh forward, resembles that of the Knidia. A more exaggeratedly obese nude female figurine from the Athenian Agora is an accurate rendering of a pathological condition and has been identified as an old courtesan.[488] There are, however, no parallels to the Athenian woman among the figurines from the Demeter sanctuary, which are best identified as parodies. The Corinthian examples either are vulgarly misshapen, as are **H368** and **H370**, or have swollen abdomens without any other significant anatomical distortion, which should indicate pregnancy.

H374 seems to be a parody of Late Classical transparent drapery, as in **C174**, that here reveals legs like stumps and oversized breasts. Like **H368**, this figurine has wide, splaying feet as well as a drapery style that could point to a Classical date. In the wonderfully comic erotic group **H376**, a sleeping old man is receiving the attentions of an old, nude woman; she seems to be masked, but his open mouth may indicate a snore rather than a comic mask. This figurine must be a parody of serious erotic *symplegma* types. To cite a coroplastic example, a mold from Smyrna in Paris is dated to the Late Hellenistic period but has a couch similar to **H376**.[489] A somewhat similar parodic intention may be seen in an Attic *Totenmahl* with a maenad and Silenos on the couch.[490]

H375 is either a head of such dismal quality that it is virtually a caricature or a parody of the goddess wearing a crenellated polos (see **C100**). If the Corinthian coroplasts were indeed parodying the rituals and deities of the cult, and if the worshipers were offering the figurines in that light, then this irreverence must have been as acceptable to the Corinthian public as Aristophanes' was to the Athenian. The reason for their acceptance was probably the apotropaic sense in which buffoonery, the grotesque, and the obscene were understood.[491]

Only a few of the foregoing actor and parody figurines come from useful pottery contexts. **H364**, the Silenos with the baby Dionysos, **H360**, the muffled bride, and its possible derivative

---

[485] Baines 1985. For Phoenician figurines representing old, nude seated women, see Stern 1994, p. 166.

[486] E.g., a figurine in Athens, Haspels 1949–1951, fig. 1; *Coroplast's Art*, p. 158, no. 45, with bibliography.

[487] From cistern 1979-1, which was abandoned at the end of the third or beginning of the fourth quarter of the 4th century B.C.: C. K. Williams 1979a, p. 125, pl. 30:b (MF-1979-43).

[488] D. B. Thompson 1954, pp. 90–91, 106, no. 2, pl. 21 top; Higgins 1986, pp. 155–157, fig. 193.

[489] *Louvre* III, p. 188, no. D1382, pl. 266:g–i; for a similar figurine from Kerch showing a youth and a woman, see *Louvre* III, p. 59, no. D325, pl. 71:c. Neither the mold nor the figurine is as well made as **H376**.

[490] Trumpf-Lyritzaki 1969, pp. 55–56, no. 152, pl. 21.

[491] Burkert 1985, pp. 103–105.

H362 were found in the construction fill of the Trapezoidal Building, the terminal date of which is the beginning of the 3rd century B.C.; the masked mantled dancer **H365** is from a pottery context of the 4th century B.C.; **H359**, which is probably a bride unveiling, is from a pottery context dating from the 5th century B.C. to the first half of the 4th (although Webster dates the type to the third quarter of the 4th century B.C.[492]); the probable female parody **H372** is from a context of the late 4th century B.C. From contextual evidence, therefore, all the datable figurines of this group date not later than the 4th century B.C. or perhaps the beginning of the 3rd. There is no reason to suggest that any of the others would be later than that. Some probably were made in the Potters' Quarter workshops, where molds of generally similar types were found;[493] for these the *terminus ante quem* would be the destruction of the Potters' Quarter in the 320s B.C. It is notable, however, that while humorous and grotesque types were produced at the Potters' Quarter, there are few really close parallels with the comparable figurines from the Demeter sanctuary.

GROTESQUES

The tiny female figure **H377** appears to perch at the end of a couch, presumably of a banqueter. Legs dangling and wearing a grinning mask, this figure has a somewhat demonic quality. By comparison with the slightly larger although less clearly modeled **H378**, the cylindrical objects in the hands of **H377** resolve themselves into a snake, a not uncommon attribute of banqueters (see p. 67). One might identify these figures as the female companions often seated at the feet of banqueters; such small seated women are found among Tarentine banqueters.[494] The mask of **H377**, however, and the protrusions on the backs of both figures that may be the remains of wings, separate them from the usual banqueter type. A good parallel for a winged female figure in a banqueting scene is an infernal deity who sits at the feet of the reclining man on an Etruscan sarcophagus lid.[495] In Greek art, the figures of Sleep and Death are winged, but they are male.[496] The *eidolon* of the deceased is depicted as a small, often winged replica of the person,[497] but it is hard to connect this concept with banqueters, who themselves are thought to represent the heroized dead and are usually male. In any case, the snakes in the laps of **H377** and **H378** suggest that they do have a funerary connotation.

Three grotesque heads (**H379**–**H381**) wear masks that differ from one another as well as from theatrical types. Since they are short haired or bald, they must represent men (although **H379** has holes in the ears, which may have contained earrings); since the faces are beardless, the heads presumably represent youths. **H380** preserves one bare shoulder and was therefore nude or semidraped. **H379** is a caricature of an almost believable human face with a very low forehead, large nose, and receding chin. Its most striking elements are the large, projecting ears, which call to mind a mask in the Corinth collection with such ears, although a much different facial type.[498] **H380** is more humorous and engaging, and with its uptilted face and open smile, it could almost be a parody of a figurine of a small child, such as the baby Eros **H290**. Its unusually thin neck is not that of a baby, however, and it has prominent ears, almost like those of a mouse, an exaggeratedly snub nose, and a wide mouth resembling a mask. **H381** is the most distinctly animal-like of the three, with ears near the top of the flattened cranium and a prognathous jaw. Both **H379** and **H381** are faintly menacing or at least not really humorous. The precise uses of masks of this kind in Corinth is not known, but an Attic red-figured vase in

---

[492] Webster 1978, p. 125.

[493] *Corinth* XV, i, pp. 102–103, nos. 43–49, pls. 35, 36.

[494] E.g., Iacobone 1988, p. 74, pl. 66:b. The women seated at the feet of Corinthian banqueters are of normal size, e.g., MF-1895, *Corinth* XII, p. 48, no. 302, pl. 25.

[495] Bonfante 1986, p. 116, fig. 29.

[496] Vermeule 1979, pp. 148–153.

[497] Vermeule 1979, pp. 30–31, with bibliography.

[498] MF-2473, *Corinth* XII, p. 50, no. 330, pl. 29.

Tarquinia shows three young men, two of them wearing bald masks with prominent ears, dancing some sort of burlesque with obscene gestures,[499] an activity that would not have been out of place in the context of a cult of Demeter.

H383 probably represents a boy, since the hair is combed forward into a fringe on the forehead, as in a terracotta sculpture of a boy from the sanctuary.[500] The cranium is unusually high and narrow, resulting in a conical shape that is found also in a grotesque head from the Theban Kabeirion.[501] The Boeotian head is similar in the shape of the skull, the high ears, the combed-down hair, the grin, and the squinting eyes, but it is bearded, with a broader face, thicker lips, and shorter, flatter nose. A similar head type is known also at Gela, where it is said to be common, on a mantled type dated to the second half of the 4th century B.C., from a small cult building thought to have belonged to Demeter or a local deity assimilated to her.[502] **H383** is from a pottery context terminating in the early 3rd century B.C.

H382 has a bit of the neck preserved, showing that the head was thrust forward on the chest. The head could have belonged to a figurine of a humpbacked dwarf, similar in type to a figurine of unknown provenience in Boston.[503] The facial features are comparable: the wide, thick-lipped mouth, bulbous nose, and frowning brows. The Boston dwarf carries a bunch of grapes, as do two of the figurines of children from the Demeter sanctuary. A head mold from the Potters' Quarter is comparable in the thick lips, wide nose, and pained expression;[504] while it produced a related dwarf type, it is not mechanically related to **H382**. The dedication of a dwarf figurine at the Demeter sanctuary could be explained by the connection of dwarfs with sexual potency[505] or by their association in Greek art with Dionysos,[506] who also was worshiped at the sanctuary. The representation of medical pathologies in Hellenistic terracotta figurines is well known, but most examples, such as those from Smyrna, are later in date and of a more dramatically grotesque appearance.[507] **H382** is from a pottery context terminating in the early 3rd century B.C.

H384 seems to have been made from a child's head, to judge from the outline of its coiffure. The plait at the top of the head and the locks of hair just reaching chin level at the sides, like those of **H329**, are still visible in spite of the drastic manipulation of the face that has given it an almost birdlike appearance.

SILENOS AND PAN
(H385–H387)

The varied satyr types of the Classical period (**C274–C276**) were replaced in Hellenistic times by representations of Silenos. As in the case of the satyrs, figurines of Silenos can be accounted for in this sanctuary through reference to Dionysos, who appears to have received offerings there (see p. 76). Pan reappears in the sanctuary in the Hellenistic period but is conceived entirely differently from his Classical form, in fully human rather than partly animal shape.

H385 is a nude Silenos, with legs spread on a blocklike seat and wearing a mantle over his arm, in a pose resembling that of the seated boys **H335–H337**. In fact, were it not for the remains of a beard on his chest, the corpulence of this figurine could be taken for the soft physique of a child. **H386**, also seated, is differently composed. The snub-nosed, bearded face and fleshy torso identify the figurine as Silenos, but the pilos on his head and the capelike mantle around his shoulders signify a shepherd. The rocky base on which he sits emphasizes the outdoor location.

---

[499] Bieber 1961a, pp. 42–43, fig. 180, with bibliography; the dance is probably not the kordax of Attic comedy, as identified; see *RE* XI, 2, 1922, col. 1385, s.v. *kordax* (B. Warnecke).

[500] SF-65-14: Bookidis 1988, pl. 4:2.

[501] *Kabirenheiligtum* V, pp. 118, 178, no. 324, pl. 25.

[502] Orlandini 1956, p. 260, no. 3, fig. 5:b on p. 259.

[503] *Coroplast's Art*, p. 162, no. 51.

[504] KH-75, *Corinth* XV, i, pp. 107–108, no. 76, pl. 42.

[505] Shapiro 1984.

[506] Dasen 1993, pp. 236–242.

[507] Leyenaar-Plaisier 1984. On the relation of Hellenistic grotesque figurines to cult, see Török 1995, p. 20.

Silenos is not directly connected with flocks in myth, but his image has here been coopted for this purpose, bringing him into the realm of Pan.[508]

The goat-legged form of Pan appeared earlier in the sanctuary in **C277**, but the god takes his human form in **H387**, where the only signs of a goat are the blurred projections at the center of his hairline, which are presumably his horns.[509] The syrinx is the principal identifier here, the figure being otherwise that of a slender, languid youth, similar in proportions and the softness of the anatomy to **H299**.[510] The rather flat composition and the pictorial quality of the tree-trunk support suggest that the source for this type was a relief. The same stylistic qualities are found in **H288**, which also may represent Pan.

OTHER TYPES
(H388–H394)

PROTOME (H388)

The backless protome **H388** differs markedly from the Classical variety (cf. **C251**), which in its complete form included the shoulders and upper chest. **H388** ends at the collarbones, perhaps through the influence of thymiateria such as **C261**, which terminated just a little below the base of the neck. It is unfortunate that most of the head is missing, since the large eyes and rays of hair waving away from the face must have been striking in effect. Although the dramatic style might suggest a Middle Hellenistic date, the protome was found in a 4th-century B.C. pottery context.

OLD WOMAN (H389)

The small head of an old woman **H389** deserves its own separate discussion because it is a remarkable rendering of its subject at such small scale. This figurine is not in any way a caricature, as the theatrical types representing old people often are, but a highly sympathetic, although truthful, representation of an age-ravaged face. A similar artistic attitude can be found in a mold of an old man's head from the Potters' Quarter.[511] The artist's means were very simple, hollowing the eye sockets and cheeks of a strongly shaped, oblong face, drawing the mouth as a wide slash without lips to show the loss of teeth, and furrowing the forehead. Attention was paid to showing the sinews of the neck as they appear in an older person, straining a little, as if the face were raised.[512] It is possible that the figure was stooped and looking up, like the composition of a late-4th-century B.C. Boeotian figurine of a mantled old woman in Oxford, although the face is different.[513]

The old woman could be identified simply as a genre type, or she may represent Demeter in disguise searching for her daughter, but perhaps the most likely possibility in the context of the sanctuary is that she represents a priestess. Old priestesses played a specific role in the Demeter ritual at Hermione (Pausanias 2.35.6–8).[514] **H389** was associated with pottery of the late 4th century B.C. On the basis of the quality of workmanship, a 4th-century B.C. date is likely.

EPHEDRISMOS GROUPS (H390–H394)

The type here discussed has been linked with a game called "ephedrismos," described by Pollux (*Onomastikon* 9.118–119). The game required the players to throw a ball at a stone to try to

[508] On the connection between Silenos and Pan, see Borgeaud 1988, p. 220, note 4.

[509] Pan is represented in a similar pose, with human legs crossed at the ankles and with horns at the center of his forehead, in Apulian red-figured pottery: Schauenburg 1962, p. 30, no. 49, pl. 14:1; for Pan in his human form in Corinthian sculpture, see Ridgway 1981, p. 428, note 23 (S-2690).

[510] MF-9259 in the Corinth collection (Romano 1994, p. 94, no. 95, pl. 29) is a small fragment showing the syrinx and the

right arm in a higher position, demonstrating that another version of this type was made in Corinth as well; this figurine may not be an import, as suggested in the publication.

[511] KH-24, *Corinth* XV, i, pp. 96–97, no. 26, pl. 33.

[512] In spirit, cf. Pfisterer-Haas 1989, p. 127, no. II 108, fig. 64 on p. 195; p. 153, no. VI 52, fig. 58 on p. 192.

[513] Vafopoulou-Richardson 1981, p. 32, no. 31a.

[514] Detienne 1989, pp. 141–142; on old women in cult, see Bremmer 1987, pp. 197–200.

overturn it; a player who did not succeed was the loser, and as a penalty, he or she had to run to touch the stone, while carrying the winner piggyback, blindfolded by the winner's hands. If properly identified, the game, played by boys, girls, erotes, or satyrs, can be seen in Greek art from the Classical to the Hellenistic periods, in a number of variants (some without blindfolding, some with a ball) and in different media, including sculpture.[515]

The type was popular for terracotta figurines in Boeotia and the West as well as Corinth. The closest similarities are with Boeotian figurines, but since the Corinthian examples are larger and better made, the archetypes may have been developed there, spreading later to Boeotian workshops, which used the torsos but added their own head types.[516] The West Greek variants are mainly Middle Hellenistic in date.[517] Corinthian coroplasts produced two versions, a larger one in which runner and rider moved to the viewer's right, with complete examples in Berlin and Amsterdam,[518] and a smaller one moving to the left, with a complete example in Boston.[519] Both versions show variations in the angle at which the rider is mounted, in the position of her arms, and in the head types employed. Five fragments from the Demeter sanctuary seem to belong to the Boston type. **H390**, preserving the left legs of both runner and rider, is the largest in scale of this group, and is well crafted of excellent fabric, with finely detailed folds. The drapery, transparent over the legs and frothing into omega folds at the hems, approximates Attic Rich Style. The Boston figurine, probably from the same or a related mold series, is later by more than one generation and has lost detail, including the double hem of the rider.

H391 probably preserves the upper torso of the rider, with a little of the back of the runner adhering to the front. It too is larger than the Boston figurine, and the composition must have been somewhat different, since the right shoulder is raised, giving the pose more tension. The plump, short-waisted proportions are comparable to draped female figurines such as **H152**. The head type is unknown, but long locks of hair in back give some hint of the coiffure. **H392** is another torso, less certainly from an ephedrismos group, but it has broken away from something in the front, and the V-shaped fold pattern of the bodice is right for this type. **H393** and **H394** are smaller in scale and are also uncertain. Both preserve the right foot and lower leg of a runner moving to the viewer's left and are suitably shallow in composition as far as preserved; **H394** has the typical frothy drapery with omega folds at the hem.[520]

Two pieces in this group (**H391** and **H394**) were found in the construction fill of the Trapezoidal Building, the pottery of which terminates at the beginning of the 3rd century B.C. A stylistic date for the archetype probably in the first half of the 4th century B.C. is indicated by the drapery style of **H390**. The dedication in the sanctuary of figurines representing ephedrismos may perhaps be explained by the religious associations of ball games, particularly in the cult of Aphrodite.[521] One cannot suppose, on the basis of such limited evidence, that ball games were played at the sanctuary, but figurines of a boy and girls holding balls were offered as votives (see pp. 63, 125–126), and the association of play with a cult that in part focused on young people is plausible.[522]

---

[515] On the game, see Schmidt 1977, pp. 129–138. On the representations, see *Coroplast's Art*, p. 128; Reho-Bumbalova 1981, esp. p. 154, note 11, for renderings in different media; Zazoff 1962; Steininger 1994. On the subject used for a late-4th-century B.C. akroterion at Tegea, see Despinis 1993; for sculpture, see also Ridgway 1997, p. 55, with bibliography on p. 74, note 81, pl. 8.

[516] *Coroplast's Art*, p. 128.

[517] E.g., Schürmann 1989, pp. 220–221, nos. 800–802, pl. 135, Sicilian, dated to the 2nd century B.C., with bibliography.

[518] *Königliche Museen*, p. 16, pls. XVII–XVIII; Frenkel 1976, p. 96, fig. 23 on p. 108. Others: Winter, *Typen* II, p. 136, nos. 4b and c.

[519] *Coroplast's Art*, p. 128, no. 20. Others: from Isthmia, Anderson-Stojanović 1993, pp. 268–269, 288, no. 79, pl. 63; Lunsingh Scheurleer 1930, VII, pp. 11–12; Winter, *Typen* II, p. 136, no. 1b. *Louvre* III, p. 54, no. D301, pl. 62:c, is of reported Corinthian provenience but does not closely resemble other Corinthian examples of the type.

[520] These fragments may belong instead to a runner carrying a ball, a type also known in Corinth: Lunsingh Scheurleer 1930, VIII, pp. 14, 16, pl. I:2.

[521] See p. 126, note 67.

[522] On the role of play in ritual, see Lonsdale 1993; on the possible cultic connection of the ephedrismos type, see Scheffer 1993, pp. 97–98.

CATALOGUE

For an explanation of the conventions employed in this catalogue, see the Introduction, pages 20–22.

STANDING DRAPED FEMALE FIGURINES: YOUNG VOTARIES AND
RELATED FIGURINES

H1   Standing peplos-figurine, with piglet   Pl. 24

MF-10436. Lot 878. Preserved: head to base. Missing hem and base in front, right wrist and hand, most of piglet. Mended. H. 0.16 (size 2–3). Fabric 2, light orange. White slip. Hollow. Thick-walled. All parts probably rendered in same mold. Back molded, rounded. Added: probably lower part of base. Tooling on folds, left hand, hair.

Published: Stroud 1965, p. 18, pl. 8:a; *Coroplast's Art*, p. 55, fig. 40.

Weight on left leg; left hip slightly outthrust. Right leg bent, slightly advanced. Right arm at side; hand holds piglet, head down. Left arm bent. Folds of open side of peplos beside right arm; long, unbelted overfold falls to thigh at right side; left hand daintily lifts hem to hip. Contours of figure are rounded, with narrow, sloping shoulders, high breasts, wide hips. Abdomen forward, S-shaped curve in profile. Garment clings slightly to breasts and sides of torso. V-shaped pouch at neck, deep V-shaped folds between breasts. Long folds dropping from right shoulder and breasts form deep, parallel loops up to left hand. Back is belted; mold belonged to different type, similar to back of **H9**. Head is relatively small, tilted forward, and slightly to left. Head and neck unusually deep in profile. Face oval, with high, sloping forehead; receding chin. Eyes are large blobs, not retouched. Nose high bridged, slightly arched. Mouth narrow, slightly crooked at right side; lips smiling. Sweet expression. Long, unbound hair, parted at center, clings caplike to head, emphasizing its small size; straight locks of hair indicated by incised, roughly parallel lines swept diagonally back from face. Possible oval pellet earring on left ear. Base oval, sides slightly splayed, torus molding at top. Well-composed piece but workmanship careless. Probable mold siblings of head: MF-12032 (lot 2248, fabric 1); others in lots 2210 (fabric 5), 4379 (fabric 1). Possible mold sibling in lot 5613 (fabric 5). Possible later generation: **H14** (head). Probably mechanically related: **H9** (head); others in lots 6233, 6509. Similar in type: **H2–H4**, **H6**. For possible workshop mates, see Workshop H, p. 346.

See pp. 17, 19, 29, 115, 116, 117–121, 122, 123, 124, 127, 129, 143, 144, 158, 159, 165, 167, 173, 190, 203, 251, 252, 342, 343.

H2   Standing peplos-figurine, with piglet   Pl. 24

MF-12875. Lot 4448. Preserved: head to right ankle and left knee. Missing tip of nose, part of fillet. P.H. 0.148 (size 2–3). Treated with preservative, probably fabric 2. White slip. Hollow. Back molded, rounded. Irregular, round vent, diam. ca. 0.023. Added: right forearm, legs of piglet, part of hair in front, fillet. Tooling on folds, hair, piglet.

Similar in type to **H1** but larger; left arm is bent at different angle; depth of head and neck is normal; slope of forehead and chin are less marked; fold patterns are not identical. Sleeve visible on left arm (although not on right), perhaps belongs to chiton under peplos. Piglet is held by its left rear leg. Face oval, with triangular forehead. Eyes deeply set, left eye larger and lower than right; both lids defined. Lips full, slightly smiling. Hair detailed only in front; bound with fillet. Probable mold

siblings: MF-11770 (lot 2045, fabric 1); others in lots 3217 (with small, rectangular vent), 3226, 4349, 6215 (all fabric 1). Others possibly related mechanically in lots 6233, 6509.

See pp. 18, 119–121, 123.

H3   Standing peplos-figurine   Pl. 24

MF-14089. Lot 2102. Preserved: front–shoulders to hips; back–waist to hips. P.H. 0.076 (size 2–3). Fabric 1, pinkish orange. Hollow. Back molded, rounded. Top of rectangular vent preserved, 0.023 wide. Tooling on hands.

Similar in type to **H1** and **H2** but larger, and fold pattern is different; perhaps an earlier generation of a different mold series.

See pp. 18, 119–121, 123, 146.

H4   Standing peplos-figurine   Pl. 24

MF-14088. Lot 869. Preserved: neck and part of back of head to hips. P.H. 0.061 (size 2–3). Fabric 1, grayish buff. White slip. Hollow. Thick-walled. Head and torso probably rendered in same mold. Back molded, flattened. Top of rectangular vent preserved, 0.018 wide.

Similar in type to **H1** and **H2**, but fold pattern is unclear. Others similar in type in lots 2239, 6215 (both fabric 3).

See pp. 119–121, 123.

H5   Standing draped female figurine, with piglet   Pl. 24

MF-13766. Lot 3410. Preserved: left hip and right thigh to base, head and foot of piglet. P.H. 0.083 (size 2–3). Fabric 1, orange-buff, with orange core. Hollow. Thick-walled. Back handmade, flattened, pared. Added: base.

Right foot drawn to side. Both arms at sides. Pig held head down at right side. Overfold, probably of peplos, falls to thighs. Skirt has deep vertical folds; hem is at level of insteps. Feet in pointed slippers. Low base is rectangular in front, rounded at back.

See p. 121.

H6   Standing draped female figurine, with piglet   Pl. 24

MF-13768. Lot 3217. Preserved: right side–hip to hem, including hand holding piglet; lower back. Mended. P.H. 0.092 (size 3). Fabric 3, pinkish orange. White slip. Hollow. Back molded, flattened.

Right arm at side, holding pig by left rear leg, head down. Folds of skirt deeply indented. Perhaps similar in type to **H1** and **H2** but larger. Fragment preserving piglet and right hand in lot 4387 is still larger, perhaps an earlier generation; overfold hem falls to fingertips; folds of open side of peplos are visible behind piglet.

See p. 121.

H7   Standing draped female figurine, with piglet   Pl. 24

MF-70-65. Lot 6503. Preserved: head to hips; surface chipped. P.H. 0.075 (size 2–3). Fabric 1, orange-buff. White slip. Red paint on hair. Hollow. Back probably molded. Added: head and rump of piglet, hair in front. Tooling on face, hair, hands, piglet.

Piglet cradled in left arm, left hand supporting its belly, right hand holding left rear leg. Shoulders narrow, sloping. Sleeved chiton or peplos over chiton belted high; knot at center with loose ends. Head tilted slightly to right. Face oval, with ogival forehead. Features clustered near center of face. Similar in facial type to **H8**. Nose short, wide, close to upper lip. Wavy locks of hair fall to shoulders from central part; bound with fillet. Back lacks detail, perhaps veiled. Probable mold siblings: MF-10573 (lot 892, with handmade back); MF-11731 (lot 2035); others in lots 2210, 3435, 4349 (overfold hem in this example is visible ca. 0.025 below right hand), 4379, 6215, 6503 (fabric 5). Possible mold sibling: **H8** (torso).

See pp. 119, 121, 124, 129.

H8 Standing draped female figurine   Pl. 24

MF-12031. Lot 2248. Preserved: head to chest. P.H. 0.056 (size 2–3). Fabric 1, harder, orange-buff to orange. Hollow. Thick-walled. Back possibly molded, rounded. Tooling on hair; back pared.

Torso possibly from same mold as **H7**. Head tilted to right. Face oval to oblong, with ogival forehead; full cheeks. Eyes level; upper lid arched and well defined, lower lid lifted, fainter; browridge rounded. Nose short, wide, close to upper lip. Mouth narrow; lips smiling, upper lip thin. Sweet expression. Coiffure as in **H7**; paring marks in back give stronger impression of veil.

See p. 121.

H9 Standing peplos-figurine, with piglet   Pl. 24

MF-13709. Lot 3217. Missing top of piglet. H. 0.153 (size 2–3). Fabric 1, orange-buff, with orange core. White slip. Head and torso probably rendered in same mold. Back molded, rounded. Added: base.

Weight on right leg. Left leg slightly bent; foot just visible at side. Abdomen slightly forward. Piglet held as in **H7**, its head and right foreleg resting on girl's forearm. Peplos tied with arching belt, just below breasts; overfold falls to thighs. V-shaped folds between breasts; folds over abdomen emphasize slight swelling; skirt folds are vertical, flattened tubes. Slender figure, with narrow, sloping shoulders, small head; outline is a narrow pyramid. Torso is similar in type to **H7** but no trace of chiton sleeves. Head tilted slightly forward and to right. Face oval, with high, rounded forehead. Eyes downturned. Lips full. Face distorted in molding, lower half pressed to right. Straight locks of hair close to head, caplike, fall to shoulders. Figurine set deeply on oval base with torus molding at top. Probable mold siblings: MF-11913 (lot 2107, with yellow paint on hair, pink on flesh, red on garment); others in lots 2249 (fabric 3), 4349 (two heads). Possible later generation: **H11** (torso). Probably mechanically related: **H1** (head). For possible workshop mates, see Workshop H, p. 346.

See pp. 119–120, 121, 122, 123–124, 128, 129, 190, 276.

H10 Standing draped female figurine, with piglet   Pl. 24

MF-11785. Lot 2063. Missing small fragments of head, right shoulder, left elbow, hip. Mended. H. 0.19 (size 2–3). Fabric 1, orange to orange-buff. White slip. Hollow. Back molded, rounded. Oval vent, ca. 0.022 long. Added: hair at sides, fillet, lower part of base. Tooling on hair.

Weight on right leg. Left leg slightly bent. Piglet held as in **H7**. Sleeved chiton or peplos over chiton belted just beneath girlish, undeveloped breasts; overfold falls to thighs. Vertical, tubular folds drop from belt to slightly trailing hem. Slender figure, less pyramidal in form than **H9**. Torso resembles young

girls with arms at sides (e.g., **H37**) more than other votaries with piglets. Head turned slightly to right. Face oblong to oval, with ogival forehead. Nose close to upper lip. Mouth narrow; lips full. Wavy locks of hair fall to shoulders from central part, fairly close to head; bound with fillet. Base round, with torus molding at top and bottom.

See pp. 18, 118, 121, 127, 128, 190, 276.

H11 Standing draped female figurine, with piglet   Pl. 25

MF-70-265. Lot 6503. Preserved: front–head to left shoulder and right hip; small part of back. P.H. 0.086 (size 2–3). Fabric 5, orange to ochre, burned. White slip. Hollow. Back handmade, rounded. Tooling on hair.

Similar in type to **H9**; torso possibly later generation. Head is large. Face distorted, squarish in shape. Degenerate work.

See pp. 122, 129.

H12 Standing peplos-figurine, with piglet   Pl. 25

MF-14061. Lot 3230. Preserved: front–piglet, wrists and hands, abdomen. P.H. 0.048 (size 3). Fabric 1, yellowish buff, with greenish buff core. Hollow. Tooling on piglet, folds.

Large piglet held horizontally across girl's chest, its head cradled on her left forearm; left hand supports its chest, right hand holds its rear legs. Overfold and kolpos fall to abdomen. Summary work, folds slashed. For lower part of figure, see possible mold sibling **H13**. Probable mold siblings in lots 882, 3222 (both fabric 5), 2107 (fabric 3), 3233.

See pp. 122, 295.

H13 Standing peplos-figurine   Pl. 25

MF-14063. Lot 3223. Preserved: hips to ankles. P.H. 0.09 (size 3). Fabric 1, orange-buff to orange. Hollow. Back handmade, rounded. Bottom of rectangular vent preserved, 0.025 wide. Tooling on folds.

Perhaps from same mold as **H12**, showing lower part of figure. Left leg bent, slightly advanced. Overfold and kolpos fall to hips.

See p. 122.

H14 Standing peplos-figurine, with piglet   Pl. 25

MF-70-266. Lot 6503. Preserved: head to waist. P.H. 0.055 (size 2–3). Fabric 5, orange. Hollow. Back handmade, rounded. Added: fillet, part of piglet. Tooling on hair, face, hands, piglet.

Torso similar in type to **H12** and **H13** but smaller; large piglet held horizontally across chest. Face distorted in molding. Facial profile with sloping forehead, arched nose, and receding chin recalls **H1**; perhaps a later generation. Long locks of hair fall to shoulders; bound with fillet. Heavy-handed retouch over dull impression.

See pp. 122, 129.

H15 Standing draped female figurine, with piglet   Pl. 25

MF-10936. Lot 1945. Preserved: front–piglet, wrists and hands, small part of torso. P.H. 0.044 (size 3). Fabric 1, orange-buff. White slip. Hollow. Added: part of piglet. Tooling on hands.

Head of piglet cradled on left forearm; left hand holds its front legs, right hand holds rear legs. Torso type perhaps similar to **H37**. Garment girded high. Probable mold sibling: MF-10535 (lot 886, fabric 3).

See p. 122.

H16 Standing peplos-figurine, with piglet   Pl. 25

MF-11903. Lot 2107. Preserved: head to thighs. Missing most of back, right shoulder and breast, part of left hip, tip of nose. Mended; rear leg of piglet chipped. P.H. 0.13 (size 3–4). Fabric 2, orange-buff. Hollow. Back probably molded, flattened. Top of rectangular vent partly preserved. Added: hair at sides, fillet. Tooling on folds, hair, hands, piglet; right forearm pared.

Right arm at side; piglet cradled diagonally in bent left arm, hand pressed against its belly. Lively piglet tries to climb away. Peplos worn over chiton, belted high; overfold falls to thighs. Evenly spaced, rather flat, vertical pleats of overfold may have continued into skirt. Full-breasted figure rather matronly in proportions. Head tilted slightly forward. Face oblong to oval, with high, ogival forehead. Eyes level; upper lids arched and well defined, lower lids level and fainter. Nose straight, low bridged. Mouth wide; lips full. Expression pleasant, alert. Straight locks of hair fall to shoulders from central part; bound with fillet. Well-composed piece, although retouch rather crude. Probable mold sibling in lot 4349 preserves more of legs (fabric 5, thick-walled; back handmade; irregular, rectangular vent; weight on right leg, left leg advanced).

See pp. 122, 127, 129, 159, 252.

H17 Standing peplos-figurine, with piglet   Pl. 25

MF-11783. Lot 2063. Missing right side of head, shoulder, upper arm. Surface worn. P.H. 0.205 (size 3). Fabric 5, orange. White slip. Red paint on hair. Hollow. Back molded, rounded. Oval vent, 0.04 long. Added: hair in back, fillet. Tooling on hair, hands.

Weight on right leg. Left leg slightly bent, advanced. Piglet cradled in left arm, hand supporting its belly, with thumb upward; both front legs of piglet visible over forearm; right hand holds its left rear leg. Peplos pouched at neckline; uncertain if belted; overfold and kolpos fall to thighs, slightly higher in front. Folds are wide and flat, incised in back. Hem trails slightly over insteps of rounded, slippered feet. Slender figure, with narrow, sloping shoulders, fairly small head; outline a narrow pyramid. Face oblong to oval, with high, ogival forehead. Eyes deeply set. Nose wide. Lips full, well arched. Wavy locks of hair fall to shoulders from central part; bound with fillet. Probable mold siblings: MF-10510 (lot 881, fabric 1); others in lots 3206 (fabric 3, fragment of back), 5613 (two, both fabric 1, one showing that pouch at neckline is a triangular fold collapsed to left side, as in **H21**), 6500. Probable later generation in lots 4349, 6233, 6503 (fabric 3). Possible later generation: **H21** (torso).

See pp. 122–123, 251.

H18 Standing peplos-figurine, with piglet   Pl. 25

MF-11747. Lot 2038. Preserved: neck to left hip and right elbow in front, to waist in back. P.H. 0.061 (size 2–3). Fabric 1, orange-buff to orange. Hollow. Back molded, rounded.

Piglet held horizontally across waist. Overfold and kolpos fall to hip; overfold shows wide, flat folds similar to **H17**.

See p. 123.

H19 Standing peplos-figurine   Pl. 25

MF-13892. Lot 3217. Preserved: head to hips. Missing forehead, hair in front. Mended. P.H. 0.094 (size 3). Fabric 1, slightly harder and thinner walled, orange-buff. White slip. Red paint on hair. Hollow. Back molded, flattened. Top of

round vent preserved, diam. ca. 0.025. Added: left arm, fillet. Tooling on hair.

Right arm at side. Left arm bent, drawn well back; knuckles rest on hip. Peplos open at right side; pattern of folds there similar to **H1** and **H2**. As far as preserved, proportions are also similar to these figurines, with high, prominent breasts and narrow, sloping shoulders spreading in pyramidal form to hips. Head turned to right, tilted slightly forward. Face better preserved in **H20**. Wavy locks of hair fall to shoulders; trace of fillet in back. Rather well made piece. Probable mold siblings: **H20**; others in lots 6215, 6233, 6503 (fabric 5). Probable mold siblings of head only: MF-10337 (lot 870); others in lots 3217, 3222 (two, one of which is in fabric 5), 3230, 6215 (three). Probable later generation: **H21** (head); others in lots 2107, 4349 (both fabric 5). Possible later generation: **H54** (face).

See pp. 122, 123, 130.

H20 Standing peplos-figurine   Pl. 25

MF-70-254. Lot 6503. Preserved: head, left side to waist, small part of upper arm and back. P.H. 0.087 (size 3). Fabric 1, slightly harder and thinner-walled, orange-buff. White slip. Hollow. Back probably molded. Added: hair at sides and back, fillet. Tooling on hair.

Probably from same mold as **H19**. Head turned to right, tilted slightly forward. Oval face with triangular forehead; prominent chin. Eyes level, deeply set; upper lids well defined. Nose pinched into aquiline shape, close to upper lip. Mouth narrow; lips full, slightly smiling, firmly closed and dimpled at corners. Wavy locks of hair fall to shoulders from central part; bound with fillet. For related figurines, see **H19**.

See pp. 122, 123, 129, 130, 161, 257.

H21 Standing peplos-figurine   Pl. 25

MF-14100. Lot 4379. Preserved: front–head, shoulders, right side of torso to hip, right arm; small part of back. P.H. 0.076 (size 2–3). Fabric 1, orange-buff. White slip. Hollow. Back molded, flattened. Edge of small, round vent preserved.

Triangular fold of drapery at neckline, collapsed to left side, is closely similar to **H17**; perhaps a later generation. Right forearm across waist; hand originally must have held back leg of piglet. Head is probably a later generation of **H19**. Possibly mechanically related: MF-10582 (lot 892).

See pp. 123, 129.

H22 Standing peplos-figurine   Pl. 25

MF-13762. Lot 2107. Preserved: front–left side, neck to hip. P.H. 0.065 (size 2–3). Fabric 3, grayish buff, burned. Hollow. Added: hair. Tooling on hair.

Left arm at side. Overfold probably falls across abdomen, dipping at sides to hip level. Wavy locks of hair fall to shoulder. Probable mold sibling in lot 2170 (fabric 5).

See p. 123.

H23 Standing draped female figurine, with torch   Pl. 25

MF-13788. Lot 4379. Preserved: front–head to hips. Missing left elbow, top of torch; forehead chipped. P.H. 0.087 (size 2–3). Fabric 2, light orange, with grayish buff core. White slip. Hollow. Added: hair, top of torch. Tooling on hands, hair.

Thick torch of uncertain length held diagonally across torso, pointing to right shoulder; right hand supports it near top, left hand lower down. Chiton is girded just beneath breasts. Narrow, sloping shoulders spread to hips; figure has pyramidal outline; breasts full. Face similar in type to **H1**, but pose of head is frontal. Straight locks of hair fall to shoulders, are veil-like in outline, as in **H9**. Probable mold sibling in lot 3226 (fabric 1, overfold hem visible ca. 0.01 below hand).

See pp. 124, 257.

H24   Standing draped female figurine, with torch   Pl. 26

MF-13756. Lot 2107. Preserved: front–neck to hips, left upper arm, top of torch. Mended. P.H. 0.071 (size 2–3). Fabric 3, orange-buff to orange. Hollow. Tooling on torch.

Vertical torch at right side originally must have been supported by right arm; flame blows to right at shoulder level. Chiton(?) girded high, with central knot and loose ends; deep V-shaped folds at neckline. Long locks of hair on shoulders. Torch marked with vertical lines of reeds and horizontal binding. For possible lower part of type, see **H25**. Probable mold sibling in lot 1945.

See p. 124.

H25   Standing draped female figurine, with torch   Pl. 26

MF-14090. Lot 2107. Preserved: front–right hip and thigh, hand, part of torch. P.H. 0.055 (size 2–3). Fabric 3, grayish buff. Hollow. Added: hand. Tooling on hand.

Right hand holds vertical torch at side. Overfold falls to thigh, has wide, vertical folds; narrower folds on skirt. Torch detailed as in **H24**; perhaps lower part of same type.

See p. 124.

H26   Pl. 26

Standing draped female figurine, with torch and flower(?)

MF-13772. Lot 2107. Preserved: front–hips to ankles; skirt chipped. P.H. 0.092 (size 3). Fabric 1, slightly harder and thinner-walled, yellowish buff. White slip. Hollow. Tooling on hands, folds.

Left leg slightly bent, advanced. Right forearm cradles thin, diagonal object, probably a torch. Left hand at hip, holds flower(?) between thumb and forefinger. Overfold falls to thighs. Skirt smooth over left leg; folds are looped around ankle.

See p. 124.

H27   Standing draped female figurine, with torch(?)   Pl. 26

MF-70-241. Lot 6503. Preserved: right hip and left thigh to base, right hand. P.H. 0.075 (size 2–3). Fabric 5, orange-buff, with orange core. White slip. Hollow. Thick-walled. Back handmade, flattened. Added: lower part of base. Tooling on hand.

Right leg slightly advanced; foot points to corner of base. Right hand at side, supports thin object slanting away from body, probably a torch. Overfold falls to thighs; skirt has broad vertical folds. Hem trails heavily over left foot, which wears a fairly high-soled sandal. Base slightly concave in front, irregular in back.

See pp. 124, 129.

H28   Standing draped female figurine, with flowers   Pl. 26

MF-13764. Lot 3222. Preserved: right hip and thigh, arm and hand; very small part of back. P.H. 0.072 (size 3). Fabric 3, tan. White slip. Hollow. Vertical edge of large, rectangular vent preserved. Added: forearm with surrounding drapery, flowers.

Right arm bent; hand lifts hem of long overfold to carry mass of three or more blossoms, clustered beside forearm. Flowers are scalloped, concave discs with pellet centers. Hem of overfold continues upward to cover right upper arm, suggesting that originally the overfold was lifted high in the left hand. Well-made piece.

See pp. 28, 124–125.

H29   Standing draped female figurine, with garland   Pl. 26

MF-13767. Lot 4450. Preserved: front–right hip and thigh, hand, part of garland. P.H. 0.05 (size 3?). Fabric 1, light orange. White slip. Hollow. Tooling on hands; garland stippled (in mold?).

Right hand holds end of garland, which loops across front of figure.

See p. 124.

H30   Standing draped girl, with ball   Pl. 26

MF-13789. Lot 1956. Preserved: front–neck to hips; back–neck to waist. Missing left forearm. P.H. 0.061 (size 2). Fabric 1, orange-buff, with orange core. White slip. Hollow. Back handmade, flat. Top of rectangular vent preserved, 0.025 wide.

Left arm probably at side. Right arm bent; hand holds ball at waist. Chiton girded at natural waistline; wide V-shaped fold at neckline. Shoulders rounded but fairly broad; chest flat; hips narrow; abdomen forward. Clumsy workmanship in back.

See p. 125.

H31   Standing draped female figurine   Pl. 26

MF-13753. Lot 2249. Preserved: head to right foot. Missing right forearm and hand, most of left arm, left foot. Mended. H. 0.125 (size 2). Fabric 1, orange-buff, with orange core. White slip. Hollow. Back handmade, rounded. Rectangular vent, 0.018 × 0.047. Added: hair tuft at top(?). Tooling on hair.

Legs clearly outlined beneath cloth, project from skirt. Right leg bent, slightly advanced. Pose of arms better preserved in **H32**. Mantle is draped diagonally from left shoulder to right hip, covering left arm and falling to feet; left hand grasps cloth at hip; folds cascade down left side. Upper torso appears nude. Face round to oval, with sloping forehead. Features indistinct but similar in facial type to **C159**. Rounded cap of wavy locks of hair drawn up to tuft at top of head, perhaps meant to be a lampadion knot. Bottom of piece thickened and slightly flaring, with suggestion of base on which feet slope downward. Somewhat similar effect of nude legs beneath drapery in **C8**. Probable mold siblings: **H32**; MF-11838 (lot 2111, fabric 2); others in lots 2210, 2249 (three, one of which in fabric 5); KT-23-4 from the Potters' Quarter (*Corinth* XV, ii, p. 126, no. 26, pl. 24; another from the Potters' Quarter and one from Pitsa mentioned there).

See pp. 125–126, 129.

H32   Standing draped female figurine   Pl. 26

MF-11106. Lot 1978. Preserved: neck to feet. Mended. P.H. 0.098 (size 2). Fabric 2, orange. White slip. Hollow. Back handmade, rounded. Rectangular vent, 0.02 × 0.045. Added: right forearm and hand, part of drapery cascade at left side. Tooling on folds.

Probably from same mold as **H31**, but arms are better preserved. Right forearm extended forward; round object, probably a ball, in mitten-shaped hand. Left arm bent; hand on hip. Possible faint folds of right chiton sleeve.

See pp. 125, 126, 129.

H33　Standing draped female(?) figurine　　　　Pl. 26

MF-13872. Lot 2249. Preserved: shoulders to right hip and left thigh. Missing right arm. P.H. 0.047 (size 2). Fabric 1, orange-buff, with orange core. White slip. Hollow. Back handmade, flattened. Top of rectangular vent preserved, 0.018 wide.

Left arm bent. Right upper arm at side. Mantle is draped diagonally from left shoulder to right hip, covering left arm; left hand lifts hem slightly at hip. Thick V-shaped fold at chiton neckline. Chest is flat, although costume suggests a woman rather than a child. Coarse work; molding rim not trimmed around shoulders.

See p. 126.

H34　Standing draped female(?) figurine　　　　Pl. 26

MF-14060. Lot 3230. Preserved: neck to waist. P.H. 0.041 (size 2). Fabric 1, orange-buff. White slip. Hollow. Back handmade, flat. Tooling on folds, bird.

Right arm bent; hand holds bird with spread wings at chest. Left upper arm at side. Mantle is draped diagonally across chest, covers left shoulder and upper arm. A few faint chiton folds visible. Chest is flat, perhaps a girl, although costume is that of a woman. Probable earlier generation: KT-5-6 from the Potters' Quarter (*Corinth* XV, ii, p. 123, no. 11, pl. 25).

See pp. 126, 129.

H35　Standing draped female(?) figurine　　　　Pl. 26

MF-13936. Lot 2249. Preserved: neck to base. P.H. 0.065 (size 1–2). Fabric similar to 1 but slightly sandy, orange-buff, with a few sparkling inclusions. Solid. Back handmade, slightly concave at top, flat at bottom.

Stands with thighs together, feet apart. Right arm bent; hand holds bird at chest. Left arm bent; hand on hip. Mantle covers left shoulder and arm, is draped around waist, with overfold(?) hem diagonally across thighs; slash across knees could be lower edge of mantle. No folds on chest; costume seems masculine, but figurine has breasts. Small plaque base. Probable mold sibling: MF-13491 (no context).

See pp. 126, 129.

H36　Standing draped female figurine　　　　Pl. 26

MF-13747. Lot 3230. Complete. Mended; left shoulder chipped. H. 0.097 (size 2). Fabric 1, slightly coarser, buff, with small dark red inclusions, voids. White slip. Hollow. Thick-walled. All parts rendered in same mold. Back handmade, flattened. Closed underneath. Tooling on hair.

Weight on left leg, left hip outthrust. Right leg bent, foot drawn back. Abdomen forward. Left arm bent; hand on hip. Right arm at side. Slender figure, with narrow, sloping shoulders. Mantle is draped closely around torso, under right arm and over left shoulder, falls to diagonal hem below knees. One diagonal fold from left hip to right knee, catenary across abdomen, in pattern generally similar to **H65** and **H70**. Mantle covers left arm and hand, clump of folds in crook of elbow; light cascade of folds beside left leg. Vertical chiton folds visible at bottom but not where expected on right shoulder.

Small head, deep in profile, tilted slightly to left. Face round, with high forehead. Long locks of hair fall to shoulders. Base roughly rectangular, divided by horizontal incision. Possible mold siblings: MF-13436 (lot 3230); another in lot 5613.

See p. 126.

H37　Standing draped female figurine　　　　Pl. 26

MF-70-238. Lot 6507. Preserved: shoulders to knees; chest chipped. P.H. 0.076 (size 2). Fabric 1, buff to grayish buff. Hollow. Back handmade, rounded. Round vent, diam. ca. 0.019.

Weight on left leg. Right leg slightly advanced. Both arms at sides. Slender figure, with narrow, sloping shoulders. Chiton girded just below full breasts; overfold falls to thighs, has wide, vertical folds; narrower folds on skirt; a few folds visible above belt. Probable mold sibling in lot 2088 (fabric 3); another from same lot, larger, shows arm position as in **H45**. Possible mold sibling: **H39**. Possible earlier generation: **H38**. Possible later generation: **H41**. **I60** is similar; it has been catalogued with imports because of numerous sparkling inclusions in the fabric, but it could be a mechanical relative in Corinthian clay with an admixture of sand.

See pp. 122, 127, 128, 149, 252, 283.

H38　Standing draped female figurine　　　　Pl. 26

MF-14094. Lot 2088. Preserved: front–shoulders to right thigh and left hip; back–neck to chest. P.H. 0.061 (size 2). Fabric 1, orange-buff. Hollow. Thick-walled. Back handmade, flattened. Added: left forearm and hand. Tooling on folds, hands.

Right arm at side. Left forearm held horizontally across torso with hand (empty?) at chest. Similar in drapery arrangement to **H37** but larger, perhaps an earlier generation, with position of one arm altered.

See pp. 126, 127.

H39　Standing draped female figurine　　　　Pl. 26

MF-11342. Lot 880. Preserved: lower part of head to hips; front of head chipped. P.H. 0.045 (size 2). Fabric 1, slightly harder, buff. White slip. Red paint on hair. Hollow. Thick-walled. Back handmade, flattened. Traces of round or oval vent.

Possibly from same mold as **H37**. Wavy locks of hair fall to shoulders in back.

See pp. 126, 127, 129.

H40　Standing draped female figurine　　　　Pl. 26

MF-70-242. Lot 6638. Preserved: head to right thigh and left hip. Missing part of left forearm, right hand, nose. P.H. 0.087 (size 2). Fabric 1, orange-buff. Hollow. Thick-walled. Back molded, flattened. Possible traces of round vent. Added: hair at sides and back. Tooling on hair.

Torso similar in type to **H37**. Left arm bent; palm of hand rests on abdomen. Head bent strongly to left. Face similar to **H2** but somewhat distorted. Fairly straight locks of hair fall to shoulders from central part.

See pp. 126, 127.

H41　Standing draped female figurine　　　　Pl. 26

MF-11748. Lot 2038. Preserved: front–head to abdomen. Missing arms below biceps. P.H. 0.05 (size 1–2). Fabric 1, orange-buff. Hollow.

Torso similar in type to **H37** but smaller; little detail but perhaps a later generation. Head tilted slightly forward and to right. Face oval to oblong, with high forehead; full cheeks. Face distorted in molding. Locks of hair fall to shoulders, possibly bound with fillet. Abrupt termination of arms at biceps suggests arms were not in mold and never were added.

See pp. 127, 128.

H42   Standing draped female figurine   Pl. 26

MF-13801. Lot 2240. Preserved: hips to base. P.H. 0.093 (size 2–3). Fabric 1, orange-buff to orange; sparse small white, dark red, and sparkling inclusions in some areas. White slip. Hollow. All parts rendered in same mold. Thick-walled. Back molded, rounded.

Weight on right leg. Left leg bent and drawn slightly to side. Left arm at side. Hips curve in towards waist, hence garment probably belted. Overfold falls to thighs, slightly higher in front, with wide folds. Skirt smooth over left leg; narrow, vertical folds over right leg. Hem trails over insteps, merges with low, round base.

See pp. 126, 128.

H43   Standing draped girl   Pl. 27

MF-13765. Lot 3228. Preserved: shoulders to thighs. Mended; front chipped. P.H. 0.084 (size 3). Fabric 1, orange-buff, with orange core. White slip. Hollow, upper chest solid. Back molded, flattened. Round vent, diam. ca. 0.022. Tooling on folds, hands.

Right arm at side. Left arm bent; palm of hand rests on abdomen. Chiton girded high with narrow belt; cords hold cloth around shoulders. Overfold falls to thighs, with wide, flat folds; folds over chest incised. Stocky figure, childish in proportions, with thick waist, flat chest, rounded shoulders. Girl probably about eight years old, but pose resembles that of more mature girl **H40**. Probable mold sibling in lot 6214 (fabric 3). Probable later generation in lots 2170, 3222 (fabric 3).

See pp. 35, 123, 127, 147.

H44   Standing draped girl   Pl. 27

MF-69-372. Lot 6184. Preserved: front–shoulders to hips; back–shoulders to waist. Missing one lock of hair. Mended; front chipped. P.H. 0.046 (size 2–3). Fabric 3, greenish buff, with pinkish orange core. Yellow paint on hair. Hollow. Back possibly molded, flattened. Irregular, round vent, diam. ca. 0.018. Added: hair in back. Tooling on hands, hair.

Similar in type to **H43** but slightly more slender; perhaps from a parallel mold series. Long, separate locks of hair fall in back. Dull impression. Similar in pale coloring and hardness of fabric to hydriaphoros **H50** and female head **H223** (also a dull impression), perhaps from the same workshop (Workshop J, p. 346).

See pp. 127, 128, 129, 147, 165.

H45   Standing draped girl   Pl. 27

MF-11719. Lot 2026. Preserved: neck to hem. Mended. P.H. 0.117 (size 2). Fabric 1, orange to orange-buff. White slip. Hollow. Back probably molded, flattened.

Weight on left leg. Right leg slightly drawn to side. Similar in pose to **H43** and **H44** but smaller, proportions more elongated. Overfold a little longer, no binding around shoulders, but folds are similarly wide and flat. Girl seems a little older but

still preadolescent. Probable mold siblings in lots 880, 6214 (fabric 5).

See pp. 121, 123, 127, 147.

H46   Standing draped girl   Pl. 27

MF-12123. Lot 4356. Preserved: front–neck to left hip and right knee; back–neck to waist. Missing arms below biceps (right hand preserved). Mended. P.H. 0.103 (size 2). Fabric 2, light orange with ochre splotches, interior orange-buff. White slip. Hollow. Back probably molded, flattened. Added: arms, parts of mantle roll. Tooling on folds, hand.

Weight probably on left leg. Right leg slightly bent. Right arm originally held away from torso; hand grasps mantle roll. Chiton belted fairly high, cords hold cloth around shoulders; triangular fold at neckline collapsed to left side. Mantle, with heavy roll at top, is draped from right thigh over left forearm to back; hem visible just below right knee. Diagonal folds from knee to left hip. Figure childish, although not as stocky as **H43**; shoulders rounded, fairly narrow and sloping; breasts slightly developed; waist slightly indented. Girl probably a little older, although still preadolescent.

See pp. 128, 129.

H47   Standing draped girl(?)   Pl. 27

MF-70-243. Lot 6640. Preserved: front–shoulders to left hip and right thigh; surface chipped. P.H. 0.06 (size 2). Fabric 5, orange-buff to orange. Hollow. Tooling on folds, hands.

Flat chest is childish, but figure is slender, its outlines rather shapely, and pose is sophisticated for a child. Chiton girded high. Mantle is draped over left shoulder and upper arm, around back, over right forearm to front. Right hand grasps edge of mantle, which must have continued to fall down side. Left arm bent; hand lightly grasps edge of mantle beside waist. Well-composed piece, but workmanship is rather coarse.

See pp. 128, 148.

STANDING DRAPED FEMALE FIGURINES: HYDRIAPHOROI

H48   Pl. 27
Standing peplos-figurine, possibly hydriaphoros

MF-13807. Lot 4409. Preserved: neck to knees. Missing forearms. P.H. 0.067 (size 2). Fabric 1, orange-buff. White slip. Hollow. Back handmade, flat. Rectangular vent with rounded corners, 0.013 × 0.023. Added: forearms.

Right leg slightly advanced. Right upper arm raised, probably to support something on head, perhaps a hydria. Left forearm probably extended to side. Slender, shapely figure in clinging peplos. Overfold hem deeply arched over hips. Folds indistinct but seem clustered at sides of overfold, leaving center plain. Deep loop under right arm. Ends of veil or long locks of hair on shoulders.

See pp. 38, 129.

H49   Hydriaphoros   Pl. 27

MF-70-73. Lot 6233. Preserved: head, right arm, left shoulder, hydria. Mended. P.H. 0.079 (size 2–3). Fabric 1, orange-buff, with orange core. White slip. Solid. All parts rendered in same mold. Back handmade, flat. Tooling on face, hair.

Right arm raised; hand holds one of small, horizontal handles of hydria (vertical handle not shown). Panel of clay between arm and head. Shoulders narrow, sloping. Head turned slightly to right. Face oval to round, with high, triangular forehead. Features indistinct, but face seems youthful. Lips smiling. Hydria has straight sides, relatively tall and narrow proportions, may rest on cushion. Retouch on face is crude. Probable mold siblings in lots 2088, 3231, 4379.

See pp. 38, 129.

H50   Head of hydriaphoros   Pl. 27

MF-70-258. Lot 6507. Preserved: front–head and neck, foot of hydria. P.H. 0.03 (size 2–3). Fabric 3, yellowish buff. Yellow paint on hair, hydria. Hollow. Added: hair, hydria. Tooling on hair.

Head turned slightly to left. Face oval to oblong, with high, triangular forehead. Eyes large, downturned; upper lids heavy. Nose short, slightly upturned. Mouth narrow; lips thin. Straight locks of hair fall to shoulders from central part. Spreading foot of hydria placed directly on hair. Similar in pale coloring and hardness of fabric to standing girl **H44** and female head **H223**, perhaps from the same workshop (Workshop J, p. 346).

See pp. 38, 128, 129, 165.

H51   Hydria, possibly from hydriaphoros   Pl. 27

MF-10506. Lot 877. Preserved: shoulders of vessel to foot. P.H. 0.047 (probably size 3). Fabric 2, light orange. Mold-made(?). Hollow. Added: handles.

Foot of vessel is broken from something, probably head of figurine. Rounded body on narrow foot; traces of handles at shoulder.

See pp. 38, 129.

STANDING DRAPED FEMALE FIGURINES: ARCHAIZING

H52   Standing draped female figurine   Pl. 27

MF-11784. Lot 2063. Intact. H. 0.137 (size 2). Fabric 5, orange-buff to orange. Hollow. Thick-walled. All parts rendered in same mold. Back probably handmade, flattened. Rectangular vent with oval bottom, 0.03 × 0.016. Added: fillet or stephane.

Legs together. Abdomen slightly forward. Left arm at side. Right arm bent; hand holds unclear object (flower?) below right breast. Slender figure, with narrow, sloping shoulders. Chiton (or peplos over chiton) bound with wide, flat belt below small breasts. Below belt, drapery is archaizing. Overfold falls to thighs at center, drops sharply to right knee. Left hand pulls overfold hem to side; cloth was meant to fall from hand in cascade to hem, but hand is relaxed, losing original design. Central omega fold emphasized on overfold; long, fan-shaped fold between legs. Hem merges with low, round base at sides. Base flattened in back, has lightly marked moldings at top and bottom. Head tilted slightly to right. Face oval to oblong, with high forehead. Features indistinct; eyes downturned. Straight locks of hair fall to shoulders from central part, bound with fillet or stephane. Probable later generation: MF-69-371 (lot 6215, with polos and flower?); one in lot 2107 (fabric 1); MF-75-114 from Temple Hill; MF-12569 in the Corinth collection. Similar in type: MF-1866 and MF-4224 in the Corinth collection (*Corinth* XII, p. 43, nos. 239, 240, pl. 20), which wear the polos and hold a flower(?); MF-69-67 from Temple Hill. Similar in type, smaller: one in lot 880 (Pit B, fabric 2); MF-12639 in the Corinth collection.

See pp. 129–130, 276.

H53   Standing draped female figurine   Pl. 27

MF-11033. Lot 1953. Preserved: head to right elbow and left shoulder. P.H. 0.065 (size 2). Fabric 5, ochre. White slip. Red paint on hair. Hollow. Back probably handmade, flattened. Added: hair, headdress.

Right arm at side. Shoulders narrow, sloping. Chiton girded high, with puff of cloth over belt. Face oval to oblong, with high forehead. Nose wide, close to upper lip. Mouth narrow; lips full. Straight locks of hair fall to shoulders from central part. High stephane or polos.

See pp. 129, 132.

H54   Female head   Pl. 27

MF-11112. Lot 1981. Preserved: head and neck. P.H. 0.031 (size 2). Fabric 1, harder, yellowish buff. Red paint on hair. Solid. Back handmade, flattened. Added: hair at right side, nose. Tooling on face.

Face oblong to oval, with high, triangular forehead; prominent chin. Eyes slightly downturned; upper lids defined, lower lids raised. Nose distorted, flattened, close to upper lip. Mouth narrow; lips full. Straight locks of hair fall to shoulders from central part. Headdress probably a polos, although back is flat. Possibly a later generation of face of **H19** and **H20**. Similar in facial type to MF-1866 from the South Stoa (*Corinth* XII, p. 43, no. 239, pl. 20).

See pp. 129–130, 132.

ISOLATED HEAD RELATED TO VOTARIES

H55   Female head   Pl. 27

MF-13979. Lot 4349. Preserved: head and neck, part of left shoulder. Missing one earring. P.H. 0.056 (size 3). Fabric 1, light orange. Red paint on hair. Solid. Back handmade, rounded. Added: hair at sides and temples, fillet, earring. Tooling on hair.

Head tilted to left; chin up. Face oval, with high, ogival forehead. Face distorted in molding. Eyes downturned, right eye lower than left; upper lids well defined, lower lids lifted, puffy. Nose bulbous, close to upper lip. Lips thin. Straight locks of hair fall to shoulders from central part; bound with fillet. Pellet earring preserved on left ear. Seems to be a degenerate version of preceding long-haired votary types but is larger than these figurines and is without close parallels in facial type.

See p. 130.

STANDING DRAPED FEMALE FIGURINES: MANTLED

H56   Pl. 28
          Standing draped female figurine (Demeter or Kore?)

MF-11069. Lot 1962. Preserved: right shoulder to hip, right thigh to foot, left side from hip to hem; about three-fourths of back. Mended; plaster restoration. P.H. 0.275 (size 4). Fabric 1, orange-buff to orange. White slip. Hollow. Back molded, flattened. Added: mantle folds on chest and back. Tooling on folds.

Weight on left leg. Right leg advanced. Right upper arm originally held down and away from torso. Peplos open at right side, with pouching under arm, below which are zigzag folds of open edge (peplos therefore misunderstood, since pouching can occur only at closed side). Overfold hem and kolpos just visible at right hip, fall to mid-thigh in back, probably arched over abdomen originally. Hem trails slightly over instep of narrow, slippered foot. Small mantle is draped over chest, framing right breast and falling in brief cape over right shoulder; in back, mantle is draped from right shoulder to left thigh. Folds deeply modeled; ankle and foot heavily shadowed by deep fold at side. **H57** preserves a head associated with this torso type.

See pp. 132, 134, 136.

H57 Standing draped female figurine (Kore?) Pl. 28

MF-12902. Lot 4388. Preserved: head to waist. Missing arms, part of left shoulder. Mended. P.H. 0.112 (size 3–4). Fabric 1, orange-buff to orange, with orange core. White slip. Red paint on hair. Hollow. Back molded, flattened. Edge of round vent at lower break. Added: part of mantle swag across waist, polos, hair, end of nose. Tooling on folds, hair, face.

Torso similar in type to **H56**, with mantle better preserved. Drapery folds framing right breast continue in a swag across waist, originally must have been draped over extended left forearm. Another group of folds curves from the right shoulder, across the upper chest and down to the left elbow, framing the left breast. A few folds of peplos visible at left shoulder. Back has less detail than **H56**. Proportions of figure seem ample, even matronly, beneath heavy drapery, in contrast to small head and youthful face. Head tilted forward. Face oblong to oval, with high forehead; dimpled chin. Eyes small, downturned; lids fleshy, lower lids puffy; browridge rounded. Nose wide, long, close to upper lip. Corners of mouth punched; lips full. Single row of thick, diagonally slashed corkscrew curls around face and nape. Low polos, not fully rounded in back. Probable mold siblings of torso in lots 4347 (with two long, twisted locks of hair on right shoulder), 4404 (fabric 3). Probable earlier generation: **H58**.

See pp. 132–134, 136, 158, 160, 187.

H58 Standing draped female figurine Pl. 28

MF-14189. Lot 5618. Preserved: front–left side of chest. Max.P.Dim. 0.072 (size 4). Fabric hard, orange-buff, with blue-gray core. White slip. Hollow. Thin-walled. Tooling on folds.

Probably an earlier generation of **H57**, preserving mantle folds framing left breast, part of swag across waist, peplos folds at left shoulder.

See p. 132.

H59 Standing draped female figurine Pl. 28

MF-69-377. Lot 6215. Preserved: front–left shoulder to waist. P.H. 0.081 (size 4). Fabric 2, orange-buff. White slip. Hollow. Added: mantle swag across waist, hair. Tooling on hair.

Similar in type to **H56** and **H57** but with long locks of hair to shoulders.

See p. 132.

H60 Standing draped female figurine Pl. 28

MF-13810. Lot 4357. Preserved: neck to waist. Missing center front of chest, right arm. Mended. P.H. 0.077 (size 4). Fabric 1, orange-buff. White slip. Hollow. Back handmade, flattened. Added: drapery around shoulders. Tooling on folds; joining surface for right arm is scored.

Diagonal folds of peplos or chiton neckline lightly marked above left breast. Mantle is draped heavily over both shoulders and left upper arm, forms a short cape on right upper arm. On

right side, folds lie in two layers, each with a different diagonal orientation. Folds below missing right arm swing out to side, may belong to peplos overfold. Possibly similar in type to **H56** and **H57** but with added drapery. Probable mold siblings in lots 2160 (fabric 4), 3217 (fabric 1, harder).

See p. 132.

H61 Standing draped female figurine Pl. 28

MF-13878. Lot 4357. Preserved: front–left side, waist to top of thigh. P.H. 0.065 (size 3–4?). Fabric 4, tan. White slip. Hollow.

Horizontal overfold and kolpos fall to thigh; narrow, vertical skirt folds below. Mantle is draped across waist in a swag, lower curve of which is preserved. Complete type probably similar to **H56–H59**. Well-made piece.

See p. 132.

H62 Standing draped female figurine Pl. 28

MF-13805. Lot 880. Preserved: left shoulder to thigh, part of right hip. P.H. 0.055 (size 2). Fabric 2, light orange, with ochre splotch. White slip. Solid. Back handmade, flat. Tooling on folds.

Left arm at side. Peplos overfold falls to thigh. Mantle is draped diagonally across chest from missing right shoulder to left upper arm; folds wrapped around forearm; curving folds frame left breast. Long locks of hair on shoulder. Simplified version of a type similar to **H56** and **H57**.

See p. 132.

H63 Standing draped female figurine Pl. 28

MF-11728. Lot 2013. Preserved: front–part of left side, with adjacent drapery; small part of back. P.H. 0.065 (size 4?). Fabric 1, yellowish buff. White slip. Hollow. Added: outermost fold of drapery fall at side, wrapped around to back.

Wavy hem of mantle overfold preserved, probably at thigh level. At left side, overlapping edges of mantle fall from shoulder. Wide, flat, vertical folds of chiton below. Large, well-made piece.

See p. 135.

H64 Standing draped female statuette Pl. 27

MF-13508. Lot 3230. Preserved: shoulders to waist, small part of back. Missing arms. Mended. P.H. 0.087 (size 4). Fabric 1, orange-buff. White slip. Hollow. Back molded, flattened. Added: fold over left shoulder, looped folds at right side. Tooling on folds.

Right arm originally extended to side. Proportions are matronly, with full breasts, short waist. Deep V-shaped folds form peplos neckline; looped folds at right side seem to be excess cloth of peplos bunched up and tucked into mantle roll at waist. One end of mantle is wrapped closely over left breast; remainder of cloth is draped around back, rolled at waist in front, and then draped over left shoulder from back to front.

See p. 135.

H65 Standing draped female figurine (Aphrodite?) Pl. 29

MF-10439. Lot 878. Preserved: neck to hem. Missing right elbow and forearm, part of back. Mended; front chipped. P.H. 0.155 (size 3). Fabric 4, orange-buff to orange. White slip. Pink paint on neck, right shoulder and arm. Hollow. Fairly thick-walled. Back handmade, flattened (treatment rather coarse for well-finished front). Round vent, diam. 0.02. Added: mantle fold behind left arm. Marks of finely toothed tool over surface, especially thighs.

Published: Coroplast's Art, p. 56, fig. 42.

Weight on left leg, left hip slightly outthrust. Right leg bent, foot drawn back slightly. Left arm hidden beneath drapery but probably bent, elbow pulled slightly back, hand on hip. Right upper arm extended to side and lifted. Tilt of neck to right suggests that head originally was turned in that direction. Only garment is a mantle, its upper edge stretched tightly around breasts, under right arm, and over left shoulder, from which it falls to hem in panel of wide, vertical folds, opening into diamond-shaped pleat near bottom. In contrast, cloth clings closely to torso and legs, with only a few curved ridges from right armpit to abdomen, and from left thigh and knee to right ankle. Hem trails slightly over slippered feet. Legs short, thighs heavy. Breasts small, prominent, slightly displaced to left side (perhaps clumsy attempt at torsion); right breast slightly lower than left. Similar in stocky proportions to **H76**. Missing base probably was rectangular in shape to accommodate drapery fall.

See pp. 14, 17, 135–136, 137, 138, 168, 275.

H66 Standing draped female figurine (Aphrodite?) Pl. 29

MF-14071. Lot 2163. Preserved: left shoulder and arm; small part of back. Mended. P.H. 0.100 (size 4). Fabric 4, tan (front); fabric 1, buff (back); interior orange. White slip. Hollow. Thick-walled. Back handmade, flattened.

Left arm bent. Stretched folds of mantle (at upper break) probably originated at right armpit. Single downward-curving fold takes up slack of cloth above elbow. Edge of mantle drops from elbow in three wide, flat, vertical pleats, each one divided by a vertical groove. Mantle continues down side from beneath this overhang of cloth. Probable mold sibling: MF-3396 in the Corinth collection (*Corinth* XII, p. 44, no. 256, pl. 22, more complete but heavily retouched, there dated too late, perhaps because of crude retouch; **H66** is a better impression, folds rendered in mold rather than tooled). Large, well-made piece.

See pp. 12, 136–137, 138.

H67 Standing draped female figurine Pl. 29

MF-14096. Lot 2249. Preserved: front–chest. P.H. 0.064 (size 3–4). Fabric 2, orange-buff, interior orange. White slip. Hollow. Thick-walled; interior very rough, although outer surface is carefully finished. Tooling on folds.

Mantle folds stretched diagonally from right armpit, above breast, toward left shoulder; right breast framed by these folds and two curving folds below it. Perhaps from figurine of type similar to **H66**. For a better-preserved, although simplified version of this drapery arrangement, see **H70**, which may be a later generation or at least a derivative of this type.

See p. 136.

H68 Standing draped female figurine Pl. 29

MF-13856. Lot 2237. Preserved: front–left calf and ankle, with adjacent drapery; small part of back. P.H. 0.091 (size 4). Fabric 4, buff to orange-buff to orange. White slip. Hollow. Thick-walled. Tooling on folds.

Left leg bent, foot drawn back. Curved mantle fold at bend of knee; cuffed folds around ankle. Mantle falls at side in rather stiff, double zigzag cascade, opening into diamond pattern. Type may be generally similar to **H65** and **H66**,

which also are of similar fabric, although weight of **H65** is carried on opposite leg. For similar mantle folds at knee and ankle and stiff zigzags on drapery, see **H73**. Large, well-made piece.

See pp. 137, 138.

H69 Standing draped female figurine Pl. 29

MF-11099. Lot 1978. Preserved: head to left ankle, right calf. P.H. 0.118 (size 2–3). Fabric 2, yellowish buff. Red paint on hair, yellow on back of mantle. Hollow. Back handmade, flattened. Irregular, oval vent, 0.031 long. Added: mantle over head, drapery behind left arm, right hand(?). Tooling on folds, hand.

Published: Coroplast's Art, p. 56, fig. 41.

Weight on right leg, right hip outthrust. Left leg bent, slightly advanced. Both arms bent, elbows pulled back. Right hand rests flat on hip. Left hand also at hip but covered by mantle. Torso wrapped closely in mantle; upper edge folded down and draped from right armpit to left shoulder, from which cloth falls in heavy panel, almost to ankle. Other end of mantle arranged in sling under right arm and draped over head. Arrowhead folds curve diagonally across chest from left shoulder; looped fold frames right breast. Other folds slant from left hip to abdomen or drop in a series of loops to right lower leg. Cloth smooth over thighs. On panel at left side, catenaries drop from forearm; horizontal edge at mid-thigh level, below which zigzag and vertical folds to bottom. Probably no garment beneath mantle. Head is small, tilted forward and to right, set at awkward angle on neck. Face oblong to oval, with triangular forehead. Eyes level; both lids well defined; browridge rounded. Nose wide, close to upper lip. Mouth wide; lips full. Coiffure shows vertical plait pulled up from center of forehead. Small but well-made piece.

See pp. 137, 138, 342.

H70 Standing draped female figurine Pl. 29

MF-10471. Lot 878. Preserved: shoulders to base. Missing right arm, part of left hand, fragments of back, part of drapery at left side. Mended. P.H. 0.190 (size 3). Fabric 2, light orange. White slip. Hollow. Thick-walled, interior surface irregular. Back handmade, flattened. Rectangular vent, ca. 0.105 × 0.025, narrower at top. Added: drapery at left side, base (open underneath, trimmed with a knife all around). Tooling on folds.

Weight on left leg, left hip outthrust. Right leg slightly bent, advanced. Left arm bent; knuckles originally rested on hip. Slender, high-waisted figure, with high, prominent breasts. Only garment is a closely wrapped mantle, as in **H65**, with similar fold pattern from waist to hem. Drapery similar to **H67** in framing right breast above and below with folds. Puff of drapery in crook of left arm, above the wrist. Drapery panel down left side is narrower than in previous examples and falls from behind elbow. Small plaque base. Possible earlier generation: **H71**; MF-3196 (fragment) in the Corinth collection. For possible workshop mates, see Workshop I, p. 346.

See pp. 137–138, 141, 143.

H71 Standing draped female figurine Pl. 29

MF-14099. Lot 4400. Preserved: front–hips and thighs. P.H. 0.076 (size 4). Fabric 2, orange-buff. White slip. Hollow. Tooling on folds.

Fold pattern very similar to **H70**, but figurine is larger, more detailed, perhaps an earlier generation. Diagonal folds from each hip meet at inner thighs; catenaries on abdomen.

See p. 138.

H72   Standing draped female figurine   Pl. 29

MF-72-186. Lot 72-122. Preserved: front–shoulders to hips; back–shoulders to chest. Missing arms; surface chipped. P.H. 0.093 (size 3–4). Fabric 2, orange. Hollow. Back handmade, flat. Added: hair on shoulder. Tooling on folds, hair.

Right arm originally raised. Mantle clings to full-breasted torso. Folds stretched diagonally across breasts from under right arm to left shoulder; looped folds down abdomen.

See p. 138.

H73   Standing draped female figurine   Pl. 30

MF-13791. Lot 2249. Preserved: front–left side, shoulder to ankle. Missing forearm. Mended. P.H. 0.196 (size 3–4). Fabric 2, light orange. White slip. Hollow. Added: forearm (two holes in elbow, probably for attachment of forearm with pegs).

Left leg bent, foot drawn back. Mantle is draped over left shoulder and upper arm; probably covered right shoulder as well. Cloth is gathered up from below elbow and is bunched into knot between chest and upper arm; from here it falls in panel of stiff zigzag folds to mid-calf. Traces of diagonal folds across torso, as in **H69**; arrowhead fold at side of knee to indicate slack cloth; cuffed fold around ankle. Probable mold siblings in lots 878 (with left forearm held diagonally across chest), 2107.

See p. 138.

H74   Standing draped female figurine   Pl. 30

MF-69-378. Lot 6214. Preserved: front–left side, shoulder to hip. Missing forearm. Mended. P.H. 0.08 (size 3–4). Fabric 1, orange-buff, with orange core. White slip. Hollow. Added: forearm.

Similar in type and scale to **H73**, but left hip strongly outthrust.

See p. 138.

H75   Standing draped female figurine   Pl. 30

MF-13792. Lot 2248. Preserved: neck and upper chest. Missing right shoulder. P.H. 0.069 (size 3–4). Fabric 2, orange-buff to light orange, with grayish core. Hollow. Back handmade, flattened, roughly made. Added: hair. Tooling on hair.

Mantle is draped under right arm, across chest, over left upper arm, probably leaving both shoulders bare, although slight ridging on left shoulder could be folds. Long locks of hair fall behind left shoulder but lie along top of right shoulder, suggesting that right arm originally was raised.

See p. 138.

H76   Standing draped female figurine   Pl. 30

MF-11347. Lot 878. Preserved: neck to hem. Missing right half of chest, right shoulder and arm, left hand, feet. P.H. 0.125 (size 2–3). Fabric very heavy, fired hard; grayish buff to orange, with gray core. White slip. Blue paint on drapery. Hollow. Thick-walled. Back molded, rounded. Added: left forearm, drapery panel at left side, folds over shoulder and down back. Tooling on folds.

Weight on left leg. Right leg bent. Left upper arm at side, forearm originally held forward. Only preserved garment is a mantle. Curving horizontal folds across upper chest and left upper arm; other curving folds radiate across abdomen from right hip, as if cloth originally was gathered there in right hand; another group of curving folds from left hip to right ankle. Cloth is looped up under left elbow, is caught between arm and torso, and falls to hem in zigzag cascade. Hem trails over insteps; remains of feet seem high, as if shod in fairly high-soled sandals. Stocky, short-legged proportions and prominent breasts recall **H65**. Retouch rather crude.

See p. 138.

H77   Standing draped female figurine   Pl. 30

MF-70-247. Lot 6638. Preserved: shoulders and upper chest. P.H. 0.064 (size 3–4). Fabric 1, orange-buff. White slip. Hollow. Back handmade, flattened. Top of oval vent preserved. Added: folds around right upper arm and back. Tooling on folds.

Left upper arm pulled back, perhaps originally bent. Upper edge of mantle is rolled down and draped loosely around right upper arm, across chest, and over left shoulder, leaving right shoulder bare.

See p. 138.

H78   Standing draped female figurine   Pl. 30

MF-69-383. Lot 6214. Preserved: front–right shoulder to waist, most of chest. P.H. 0.073 (size 3–4). Fabric 1, orange-buff, interior orange; friable. Hollow.

Right upper arm at side. Mantle is folded down at upper edge and stretched tightly across bare shoulders in flat folds. Other flat folds curve diagonally across chest to right upper arm. Contours of breasts visible through cloth.

See p. 138.

H79   Standing draped female figurine (Aphrodite?)   Pl. 30

MF-13802. Lot 3222. Preserved: left shoulder and right upper arm to base. P.H. 0.07 (size 1–2). Fabric 1, orange-buff to orange. White slip. Nearly solid. Back handmade, flattened. Added: part of base. Tooling on folds.

Weight on left leg, left hip outthrust. Right leg bent, slightly advanced. Right elbow rests on head of ithyphallic herm. Mantle is wrapped closely around body to hem; upper edge is rolled down and draped from under left arm to right shoulder; cloth covers bent right arm and hand, is brought around back, and covers lowered left arm; left hand grasps cloth, which falls to base; two capelike folds appear on left upper arm, perhaps indicating folded-down upper edge of mantle. V-shaped folds of chiton neckline visible just below break. Low base, rectangular in front, rounded in back, slightly splaying. Herm support suggests that figurine may represent Aphrodite.

See pp. 139, 276.

H80   Standing draped female figurine (Kore?)   Pl. 30

MF-70-80a. Lot 6233. Preserved: front–right shoulder, breast, upper arm. P.H. 0.067 (size 3). Fabric 1, creamy buff. White slip. Hollow. Added: arm, with adjacent drapery. Tooling on folds.

Right upper arm extended to side. Short sleeve of thin chiton preserved; heavier mantle wrapped tightly under arm and over right breast, in wide, overlapping folds. Similar type in lot 880 (fabric 2).

See pp. 133, 139.

H81   Standing draped female statuette   Pl. 30

MF-12137. Lot 4352. Preserved: shoulders to left thigh, to waist at right side, small part of back. Missing most of right arm. Mended. P.H. 0.163 (size 4). Fabric 2, orange-buff. White slip. Hollow. Thin-walled. Tooling on folds.

Left arm at side, elbow bent, forearm slightly advanced, hand pressed against thigh. Chiton has slipped from right shoulder, is arranged in horizontal folds over upper arm. Mantle is wrapped under right arm, frames right breast, and is folded diagonally to form short cape over left shoulder; cloth covers arm and hand; pressure of arm against torso pulls diagonal folds from inside elbow to hand; folds radiate from left hip across abdomen. Probable mold sibling: MF-70-78 (lot 6233, fabric 1).

See p. 139.

H82   Standing draped female figurine   Pl. 31

MF-68-378. Lot 5648. Preserved: front–upper part of chest. P.H. 0.055 (size 4). Fabric 1, light orange; sparse small white inclusions, voids. Hollow.

Mantle wrapped over right breast, then draped around back and over left shoulder and diagonally across chest. Mantle folds wide and flat; pleated chiton fold at neckline.

See p. 139.

H83   Standing draped female figurine   Pl. 31

MF-69-379. Lot 6215. Preserved: front–shoulders to left hip and right thigh. Missing most of both arms. P.H. 0.084 (size 3). Fabric 1, orange-buff to pinkish orange. White slip. Pink paint on flesh. Hollow. Tooling on folds.

Right leg advanced. Left arm probably bent originally, with hand behind hip. Looped folds of right chiton sleeve lifted at center to indicate fastening. Upper edge of mantle folded over, draped diagonally from waist at right side to left shoulder; clump of cloth held against torso by left upper arm, from which looped folds radiate across abdomen. Folds heavily slashed, clump of cloth punched.

See p. 139.

H84   Standing draped female figurine   Pl. 31

MF-10415. Lot 877. Preserved: front–right shoulder to hip, part of abdomen. Missing right arm. P.H. 0.075 (size 4). Fabric 4, tan to orange-buff, interior gray. White slip. Hollow. Added: hair, loop of drapery under arm. Tooling on hair, folds.

Rolled upper edge of mantle is draped under right breast and up toward left shoulder or upper arm. Horizontal tension folds across waist; catenaries on abdomen; cloth originally may have been gathered up at left hip. Thinner chiton has loose V-shaped fold at neckline; looped fold under right arm overlaps mantle roll. Ends of three long, wavy locks of hair on right shoulder. Rather stocky, short-waisted figure, similar in proportions and scale to **H85**. Possible mold sibling in lot 2249 (fabric 1, surface heavily retouched, right upper arm extended to side).

See pp. 139, 140.

H85   Standing draped female figurine (Demeter?)   Pl. 31

MF-11786. Lot 2063. Preserved: head to right ankle and left knee. Missing right forearm, left wrist and hand. Mended; drapery panel at left side chipped; surface worn. P.H. 0.275 (size 4). Fabric 2, light orange to orange-buff. White slip. Red paint on hair. Hollow. Back molded, rounded. Round vent, ca. 0.025. Added: right arm, left forearm and surrounding drapery, hair. Tooling on folds, hair.

Published: Stroud 1968, p. 323, pl. 94:d.

Weight on right leg. Left leg bent, advanced. Left arm bent, forearm extended forward. Right arm held away from torso. Abdomen slightly forward. Chiton folds very lightly modeled over chest, deeper on right sleeve. Rolled upper edge of mantle is draped across waist, lower at right side, and diagonally in back to left shoulder, from which it falls in front over left arm to below knee. In front, it forms an overfold with a curved diagonal edge from right hip to left thigh; arrowhead folds across the overfold point from right hip to left hip and from left thigh to right hip. Deep, looped folds down side of right leg; looped fold from left knee ends in wide cuff around right ankle. Most, if not all, of chiton skirt originally covered. Contrast between shallow modeling of chiton and depth of mantle folds. Proportions are matronly, with large, rather low breasts, short waist, wide hips; head is relatively small. Head tilted slightly to right. Face oval, with triangular forehead. Eyes slightly downturned, deeply set; upper lids well defined and arched, lower lids not modeled, slightly lifted; rounded browridge. Nose thin, straight. Lips full, slightly pursed. One crease in neck. Wavy locks of hair from central part were rendered in mold; one thick lock on each side is carried horizontally to back of head; from beneath this, long locks stream down over shoulders, with two thinner locks at back. Possibly low stephane or band at top of head. Probable mold sibling in lot 2249 (fragment of chest, fabric 4). Possible mold sibling of head: **H182**. Similar in proportions and scale to **H84**.

See pp. 139–140, 147, 159, 167, 180, 254, note 19, 256, 329.

H86   Standing draped female figurine   Pl. 31

MF-13860. Lot 2249. Preserved: front–left side, neck to thigh; upper part of back. Missing forearm. Mended. P.H. 0.132 (size 4). Fabric 1, buff to greenish buff. White slip. Hollow. Back handmade, flattened. Part of irregular, round vent, diam. ca. 0.037. Added: forearm. Tooling on folds.

Left forearm originally extended forward. Mantle is draped over left shoulder and arm. Chiton folds on chest.

See p. 140.

H87   Standing draped female figurine   Pl. 31

MF-13793. Lot 2107. Preserved: back–left shoulder and upper arm, upper part of back. P.H. 0.133 (size 4). Fabric 2, light orange. Hollow. Back molded, rounded.

Back only preserved. Mantle is draped over left arm. Lightly modeled catenaries of chiton(?) beneath. Long locks of hair rendered in mold. Possibly from type similar to **H86**.

See p. 140.

H88   Standing draped female figurine   Pl. 32

MF-11079. Lot 1963. Preserved: shoulders to feet; right shoulder chipped. P.H. 0.252 (size 4). Fabric 1, orange-buff. White slip. Red paint on hair, rose or pink on chiton.

Hollow. Back molded, flattened. Added: feet, hair. Tooling on hands, hair.

Weight on left leg, left hip outthrust. Right leg bent, advanced. Both arms bent. Right hand at chest. Left hand lies flat on hip. The mantle is open at the left side. One edge falls in zigzag cascade over left leg; upper corner is crumpled and secured by left hand, ending in brief cascade at hip. The cloth is draped across front and shoulders, forming sling under right arm, and then around the back, where it falls in panel marked by one deep pleat, behind left arm. Upper corner is pulled to front over left shoulder and upper arm, is grasped at chest by right hand, from which it falls in brief cascade. Tension folds over shoulders and arms; looped folds over right hip and thigh and from right calf up towards left hip. Chiton trails over insteps of slippered feet and has double hem; its fine folds are visible at left side up to hip, where mantle lies open. Long locks of hair lie diagonally across left shoulder, suggesting head originally was turned to right. Arms and hands seem too large, pose clumsy. For related figurines, see **H89–H97**.

See pp. 15, 141, 142, 146, 162, 295.

H89 Standing draped female figurine   Pl. 32

MF-13815. Lot 2108. Preserved: front–right shoulder to elbow. Missing right upper arm. Mended. P.H. 0.092 (size 4–5). Fabric 1, orange-buff, with orange and gray core, surface slightly burned. Hollow. Thick-walled. Tooling on folds.

Bent right arm in sling of mantle. Cloth is smooth over elbow and arm, with deep, nearly vertical tension folds from base of neck to arm. Fine chiton folds visible at break. Possibly larger version of **H88**.

See pp. 15, 141.

H90 Standing draped female figurine   Pl. 32

MF-13780. Lot 2249. Preserved: front–left shoulder and most of arm, chest, right hip, right forearm and hand. Mended. P.H. 0.097 (size 4). Fabric 2, light orange, interior grayish buff. White slip. Hollow. Tooling on folds, hand.

Similar in type and scale to **H88** but right forearm is more horizontal, fold pattern not identical. Small puff of drapery above right hand.

See pp. 15, 141, 142.

H91 Standing draped female figurine   Pl. 32

MF-13881. Lot 1953. Preserved: front–left side, shoulder to waist, part of left arm, right hand. P.H. 0.044 (size 2–3). Fabric 2, light orange to orange-buff, interior grayish buff. White slip. Hollow. Tooling on folds, hand.

Possibly later generation of **H88** or **H90**. Little molded detail, folds carelessly incised. Fragment of similar type in lot 6215 falls between **H90** and **H91** in size.

See pp. 15, 141.

H92 Standing draped female figurine   Pl. 32

MF-13879. Lots 892/1953. Preserved: front–left shoulder and part of chest, right forearm and hand, hips and most of thighs; small part of back. Mended. P.H. 0.082 (size 2). Fabric 2, light orange, with grayish buff core. White slip. Hollow. Back rounded. Added: hair.

Similar in type to **H88** but smaller. Cascade from right hand shows zigzag folds. Better made than others in group.

See pp. 15, 141.

H93 Standing draped female figurine   Pl. 32

MF-13781. Lot 4349. Preserved: front–chest to thighs. Missing left arm. Surface worn. P.H. 0.044 (size 1–2). Fabric 1, grayish buff. Hollow.

Similar in type to **H88** but much smaller. Drapery simplified. Perhaps from same mold as **H94**, which preserves the lower part.

See pp. 15, 141.

H94 Standing draped female figurine   Pl. 32

MF-13782. Lot 2107. Preserved: front–hips to left foot and right calf; small part of back. Missing part of drapery panel at left side. P.H. 0.05 (size 2). Fabric 1, grayish buff. Hollow. Back handmade, flattened.

Similar in type to **H88** but much smaller. Drapery simplified, lacking fold cascade on left leg and hip; mantle merely wrapped around chiton skirt. Perhaps from same mold as **H93**, which preserves the upper part.

See pp. 15, 141.

H95 Standing draped female(?) figurine   Pl. 32

MF-13864. Lot 2010. Preserved: shoulders to waist. Mended. P.H. 0.054 (size 3). Fabric 2, light orange. Hollow. Back handmade, flattened. Tooling on hand, hair.

Similar in type to **H88**, but large puff of cloth projects from mantle sling above wrist; left upper arm close to torso. Long locks of hair incised in back. Sex of figurine uncertain; chest seems flat, but all other figurines with this drapery arrangement from the sanctuary are female. Similar in type and scale: MF-13904 in the Corinth collection (definitely female; has puff of cloth above right forearm; left forearm extended forward).

See pp. 15, 141.

H96 Standing draped female figurine   Pl. 32

MF-13862. Lot 1953. Preserved: front–right hip and left thigh to feet; part of back; right knee chipped. P.H. 0.125 (size 3–4). Fabric 1, orange-buff to orange. White slip. Hollow. Back handmade, flattened. Added: feet. Tooling on folds.

Pose of legs, double chiton hem, and slippered feet are similar to **H88**. At upper break, end of fold cascade from right hand is visible. Perhaps similar in type to **H93** and **H94**.

See pp. 15, 141.

H97 Standing draped female figurine   Pl. 32

MF-13829. Lot 2249. Preserved: front–right leg and adjacent drapery. Missing foot. P.H. 0.093 (size 3). Fabric 4, yellowish buff. White slip. Hollow. Tooling on folds.

Pose of leg, double chiton hem, and mantle folds are similar to **H88** but smaller, much better fabric.

See pp. 15, 141, 142.

H98 Standing draped female figurine   Pl. 33

MF-11078. Lot 1963. Preserved: waist to feet, part of left arm. Missing part of right side. P.H. 0.16 (size 3–4). Fabric 1, tan. White slip. Red paint on arm. Hollow. Back molded, rounded. Bottom of oblong vent preserved, 0.033 wide. Added: arm and surrounding drapery, fold cascade at side, feet, and surrounding drapery. Tooling on folds.

Similar to **H88** in pose and double-hemmed chiton with folds trailing over slippered feet. Mantle seems thinner, covers right hip and thigh, and is pulled up to left hip, where it is wrapped around arm and falls at side in brief zigzag cascade.

Diagonal and looped folds over abdomen. Generally similar but relatively coarse figurine in lot 4387.

See pp. 15, 141.

H99 Standing draped female figurine   Pl. 33

MF-11338. Lot 880. Preserved: neck to knees. Mended. P.H. 0.178 (size 4). Fabric 4, orange-buff to orange. White slip, glossy in places. Hollow. Thin-walled. Back molded, flattened at top, rounded below. Irregular, round vent, diam. 0.045. Added: folds around neck, possibly projecting part of left arm. Tooling on folds.

Published: *Coroplast's Art,* p. 18, color pl. 2.

Mantle is draped around shoulders and arms, falls to mid-thigh; hands left free. Right arm bent; hand grasps mantle at hip, from which deep, looped folds radiate across front of torso to opposite hip. Left arm bent; hand grasps edge of mantle at side of neck, from which cloth falls to thigh, terminating in zigzag folds. Flat, linear folds radiate from left breast to right arm. Mantle is fairly thin and stretched across chest, slightly revealing contours of breasts; narrow, vertical folds of chiton are visible at bottom. Folds of back do not match front at left side; mold belonged to different type, similar to **H105**, in which hand grasps edge of mantle, with zigzag fold at side of thigh. One crease in neck. Probable mold siblings: MF-70-72 (lot 6233); another in lot 2051 (both fabric 1).

See pp. 13, 138, 142–143, 144.

H100 Standing draped female figurine   Pl. 33

MF-10447. Lot 878. Preserved: base of neck to right calf and left ankle. Mended; right side, front chipped. P.H. 0.137 (size 3). Fabric 2, light orange. White slip. Possible pink paint on chiton. Hollow. Thick-walled; sloppy overlapping of strips of clay inside. Back molded, flattened. Irregular, rectangular vent, ca. 0.025 × 0.075. Added: left hand.

Weight on left leg, left hip slightly outthrust. Right leg bent, foot originally drawn back. Mantle is draped across front of figure from neck to below knees, covers arms and hands. Right arm bent; hand visible beneath cloth pulling folds down from neck. Left arm bent, forearm up, hand curved into shape of duck's head beneath cloth. Narrow, sloping shoulders. Mantle clings smoothly to torso and originally may have covered head. A few folds curve from left breast to right elbow, drop from left hip to right knee. Faint folds radiate from right hand to shoulder and upper arm. Beside left leg, a few folds show open edge of mantle. Vertical folds of chiton at bottom are slightly crinkled. For probable lower part of type, see **H101**. Probable mold siblings: **H101**; MF-10452 (lot 878, heavily retouched); others in lots 878 (two), 2249 (two, fabric 1), 4362, 6233 (fabric 1). Possible earlier generation in lot 878. Possible later generation in lot 878. Similar left hand in lot 877 (fabric 4). Possibly mechanically related: *Danish National Museum,* pp. 29–30, no. 274, pl. 30 (preserves head). MF-11363 (lot 877) is a skirt fragment with mantle hem, possibly of this type, showing bright blue paint on skirt. For possible workshop mates, see Workshop I, p. 346.

See pp. 137, 143, 154, 315.

H101 Standing draped female figurine   Pl. 33

MF-10449. Lot 878. Preserved: left hip and right thigh to base. P.H. 0.13 (size 3). Fabric 2, light orange to buff, with gray core. White slip. Bright blue paint on chiton. Hollow.

Thick-walled. Back molded, flattened. Bottom of rectangular vent preserved, 0.03 wide. Added: base (open underneath).

Probably from same mold as **H100**, but only bottom preserved, completing type. Crinkled chiton trails slightly over insteps of slippered feet. Base rather sloppily made, 0.03 high, rounded in front, flat in back, with torus moldings top and bottom, and set on plaque base. For possible workshop mates, see Workshop I, p. 346.

See pp. 14, 137, 143, 144, 154, 276, 315.

H102 Standing draped female figurine   Pl. 34

MF-10397. Lot 877. Preserved: front–head to thighs; back–head to hips. Missing most of left arm. Mended. P.H. 0.135 (size 3). Fabric 2, light orange (head and back); slightly coarser in front, with sparse small white and dark red inclusions. White slip. Red paint on hair. Hollow. Back molded, flattened. Added: hair in front, drapery folds at neck. Tooling on folds and hair; earrings are punched, perhaps for insertions.

Similar in pose to **H100** but smaller, more slender, left hip more strongly outthrust. Left upper arm at side, position of forearm uncertain. Fold pattern of mantle also similar, but right arm pulls neckline folds down lower on chest, creating pattern of V-shaped folds. Narrow, sloping shoulders. Head relatively large, turned three-fourths to right and tilted forward. Face oval, with high, sloping forehead; receding chin. Eyes downturned; both lids strongly marked, seem almost closed. Nose large, slightly aquiline, close to upper lip. Lips full. locks of hair wave up and back from forehead to modified bowknot at top; at back, traces of fillet and vertical plait. Original coiffure, now covered by added hair, probably showed plait pulled up from center of forehead, as in **C164** and **C165**. Ring-shaped earrings. Rather coarse retouch. Probable mold siblings of head (all fabric 1): MF-10403 (lot 877); MF-10437 (lot 878); MF-10446 (lot 878); MF-10464 (lot 878); MF-10489 (lot 880); MF-10625 (lot 896); MF-11383 (lot 877); MF-11404 (lot 877); MF-11831 (lot 2088); others in lots 2249 (two), 3222, 4347, 4377, 5613. Possible mold siblings of head, distorted or retouched (both fabric 1): MF-10386 (lot 875); MF-10454 (lot 878). Similar in type and possibly mechanical relatives of head (all are larger but not certainly earlier generations): **H234**; **C156** (head of "doll"); one in lot 2249.

See pp. 17, 56, 75, 119, 143–144, 167, 315.

H103 Standing draped female figurine   Pl. 33

MF-13746. Lot 4387. Preserved: head to right foot and left ankle. Missing left side and top of head, most of face, part of left hip and adjacent drapery; left foot. Mended; face, front of legs, side of right thigh, back of right shoulder chipped. H. 0.137 (size 2–3). Fabric slightly coarse orange-buff, with small dark red and white inclusions, voids, blue-gray core; gray splotches on surface may be signs of burning (fabric not typically Corinthian in appearance, but inclusions seem local). Hollow. All parts probably rendered in same mold. Back molded(?), rounded. Round vent, diam. 0.023. Added: drapery panel at left side. Tooling on folds.

Weight on left leg, left hip outthrust. Right leg bent, slightly advanced. Narrow, sloping shoulders. Mantle is draped across front of figure from head to below knees, covers arms and hands. Right arm bent; hand visible beneath mantle at waist level, pulling folds down from shoulder. Left arm bent; hand at hip. Mantle clings smoothly to torso, seems almost transparent, showing contours of high breasts through cloth; a few folds radiate from right hand to shoulder and across abdomen; zigzag folds of edge of mantle fall from left hand along thigh. Chiton shows fine folds, trails slightly. U-shaped fold frames left ankle. Mantle folded down over forehead.

See pp. 144, 315.

H104 Standing draped female figurine   Pl. 34

MF-12159. Lot 2249. Preserved: base of neck to base. P.H. 0.102 (size 2). Fabric 1, slightly harder, tan. White slip. Red paint on chiton and mantle. Heavy for size, possibly solid or nearly so. Back molded, rounded. Added: foot, plaque base (closed underneath). Tooling on folds.

Figure placed diagonally on base to emphasize three-quarter view. Weight on left leg, left hip slightly outthrust, left foot hidden beneath skirt. Right leg bent, advanced. Mantle arrangement similar to **H100–H103**. Right hand placed as in **H100**; left hand on hip as in **H103**, elbow pulled well back. Drapery cascade behind left arm to hip level. Mantle is closely wrapped around slender, narrow-shouldered torso as in foregoing examples, but surface is heavily tooled with tension folds around arms and across front of torso; diagonal folds from left hip curve around right calf. Crinkled vertical folds of chiton trail over instep of large, rather clumsy foot. Chiton hem pressed down in back to adhere to plaque base.

See pp. 144, 162, 276, 315.

H105 Standing draped female figurine   Pl. 34

MF-10958. Lot 869. Preserved: base of neck to hem. P.H. 0.123 (size 2–3). Fabric 1, orange-buff to buff. Hollow. Back molded, rounded. Added: drapery cascade beside left leg. Tooling on folds.

Similar in type to **H104**, but weight is on right leg; left arm is less bent; wider hips give pyramidal outline. Thin mantle with few folds falls to thighs; cloth of chiton skirt seems heavier than mantle, trails over insteps of nearly hidden feet; long, looped folds from thighs to ankles. Dull impression.

See pp. 143, 144, 315.

H106 Standing draped female figurine   Pl. 34

MF-11064. Lot 1955. Preserved: head to calves; top of head chipped. P.H. 0.095 (size 2). Fabric 5, orange-buff to orange. White slip. Hollow. Thick-walled. All parts probably rendered in same mold. Back handmade, flattened.

Weight probably on left leg, left hip slightly outthrust. Generally similar in type to **H103**, but left arm is not bent; clump of drapery pressed between arm and torso. Mantle hem dips from left thigh to right calf. Surface worn, but better impression of head in lot 6214, probably from same mold, shows round face with delicate features; narrow, slanted eyes; short nose; curly locks of hair piled on top of head.

See p. 144.

H107 Standing draped female figurine   Pl. 34

MF-68-364. Lot 5613. Preserved: neck to ankles. P.H. 0.083 (size 2). Fabric 1, orange, with gray core, slightly burned(?). White slip. Solid. Back handmade, flat.

Mantle is draped across front of figure, covers arms and hands; originally draped over head. Left arm at side; hand lifts fold of drapery in front of thigh. Right forearm incompletely formed but seems to have been held across abdomen, the hand tucked beneath left arm. Looped folds around neck; V-shaped folds on chest; diagonal folds on skirt radiate from right wrist. Probable mold sibling: MF-11020 (lot 1953).

See p. 144.

H108 Standing draped female figurine   Pl. 34

MF-13755. Lot 4349. Preserved: base of neck to hips. P.H. 0.052 (size 2). Fabric 5, buff to orange. White slip. Nearly solid. Back handmade, slightly concave. Added: clump of drapery beside left arm. Tooling on folds.

Mantle is draped across front of figure, covers arms and hands; originally draped over head. Both arms at sides; clump of drapery pressed between left arm and torso. Wrinkled folds across shoulders, catenaries on abdomen. Probable mold sibling: MF-1976-88 in the Corinth collection (Pl. 75), preserving the head.

See p. 144.

H109 Standing draped female figurine   Pl. 34

MF-11046. Lot 1953. Preserved: shoulders to base; back chipped. P.H. 0.09 (size 2). Fabric 1, orange-buff. White slip. Nearly solid. Back handmade, flattened. Added: lower part of base, pillar.

Weight on left leg. Right leg bent. Figure leans slightly back at shoulders and to right. Right arm not formed, merges with rectangular pillar support; in prototype, either elbow rested on pillar, or support was shorter and hand rested on it. Mantle is draped smoothly across front of figure, covers bent left arm; fold cascade drops from left hand. Mantle falls nearly to ankles; a few chiton folds trail over insteps. Figure is rectangular in outline, with fairly broad shoulders. Two-stepped base, rectangular in front.

See pp. 144, 275.

H110 Standing draped female figurine   Pl. 34

MF-10628. Lot 896. Preserved: front–head to hips; back–head to waist; face chipped. P.H. 0.105 (size 3). Fabric 4, buff to orange-buff. White slip. Pink paint on drapery. Hollow. Thick-walled. All parts probably rendered in same mold. Back handmade, flat. Top of rectangular vent preserved. Tooling on folds.

Left hip slightly outthrust, therefore weight probably on left leg. Sloping shoulders. Left arm bent and drawn back slightly; left hand at hip. Right upper arm at side. Mantle is draped over upper torso, covers arms, left hand, head; pleat of cloth overhangs forehead. Folds radiate from left shoulder to right upper arm and abdomen. Head is small, tilted to right in three-quarter view. Face probably oval. Eyes deeply set at inner corners; browridge prominent, slants downward to temples. Lips full. Probable mold sibling in lot 1953 (fabric 5). Head similar in type, smaller: MF-10575 (lot 892, fabric 1).

See pp. 144–145, 197.

H111 Standing draped female figurine   Pl. 34

MF-12024. Lot 2247. Preserved: head, left shoulder, upper arm, part of chest. P.H. 0.057 (size 2–3). Fabric 1, orange-buff to orange. White slip. Hollow. Thick-walled. Back handmade, rounded. Added: drapery around left shoulder. Tooling on folds.

Narrow, sloping shoulders. Mantle is draped over upper torso, covers head. Face oval, narrowing to chin. Eyes large, opened wide, deeply set, wide apart; lower lids puffy. Nose short. Mouth distorted downward at left side; lips full, slightly smiling. Sweet, girlish expression. Concealed hair is piled high and bound in sakkos, lower edge of which is stretched across forehead. Probable mold sibling: MF-11339 (lot 880).

See pp. 144–145, 168.

H112	Female head					Pl. 34

MF-11388. Lot 877. Preserved: head and part of neck; nose, chin, right side chipped. P.H. 0.035 (size 3). Fabric 2, orange-buff to orange. Solid. Back handmade, flattened.

Face oblong, with low, triangular forehead. Eyes down-turned. Lips full. Hair piled into high, pointed mass, enveloped in sakkos, over which mantle is draped, covering neck as well.

See p. 145.

H113	Standing draped female figurine			Pl. 34

MF-13822. Lot 3222. Preserved: shoulders to waist, with drapery at right side. Missing part of left shoulder and arm. Mended; front chipped. P.H. 0.109 (size 3). Fabric 1, orange-buff to orange, with orange core, gray core at neck. Hollow. Back handmade, flattened. Rectangular vent with rounded corners, ca. 0.063 × 0.025. Added: drapery at right side. Tooling on folds.

Mantle is draped diagonally across chest, covers right shoulder and bent arm. A few folds visible at left shoulder probably belong to return of mantle from back. Cloth drops vertically from right elbow, standing away from torso; hand is concealed but probably rested on hip. Folds radiate from elbow diagonally toward skirt; other folds sweep in curves across chest above and below breasts. Others similar in type in lots 6214, 6233 (fabric 3).

See p. 145.

H114	Standing draped female figurine			Pl. 34

MF-13823. Lot 1953. Preserved: neck to right elbow and left breast. P.H. 0.064 (size 3). Fabric 1, orange-buff, interior orange. Hollow. Back molded, flattened. Added: folds around back of neck.

Similar in type to **H113**, but shoulders are narrower, more sloping; mantle is draped across both shoulders, its upper edge twisted and rolled around neck, with one end tucked in from the back. Traces of chiton folds at neckline. Left hand may have been at chest, beneath mantle. Arrowhead fold across breasts.

See p. 145.

H115	Standing draped female figurine			Pl. 35

MF-11292. Lot 1993. Preserved: right arm, part of chest at right side; small part of back. P.H. 0.066 (size 4). Fabric 4, orange-buff to light orange. White slip. Hollow. Back handmade(?), flattened. Tooling on folds.

Right arm bent; hand originally on (or behind?) hip. Wide, flat folds of mantle spread diagonally across chest from upper arm; other folds on arm radiate from wrist. Clump of folds in crook of elbow. Large, well-made piece.

See p. 145.

H116	Standing draped female figurine			Pl. 35

MF-10481. Lot 878. Preserved: knees to feet. Missing most of right lower leg, left foot. Mended. P.H. 0.103 (size 4). Fabric 4, light orange. White slip. Hollow. Back handmade, flattened.

Bottom of rectangular vent preserved, ca. 0.055 wide. Added: right foot.

Weight on left leg. Right leg slightly advanced; slippered foot. Mantle hem falls to right foot, rises to left ankle; at left side, mantle falls in deep, wide folds. Folds curve diagonally upward from right ankle. Fine folds of chiton hem trail over insteps. Large, well-made piece.

See pp. 145–146.

H117	Standing draped female figurine			Pl. 35

MF-13826. Lot 4377. Preserved: front–thighs to feet; back–hips to feet. Missing part of right side. Mended. P.H. 0.115 (size 3). Fabric 4, tan, interior light orange. White slip. Hollow. Back molded, flattened. Added: left foot.

Weight on concealed right leg. Left leg advanced. Mantle hem falls to left foot, rises at right to level of ankle. Folds radiate from top of left thigh, fall in catenaries to right hip and in long loops framing left leg; other loops from right hip to left ankle; cluster of vertical folds at each side. End of mantle hangs in back, presumably from shoulder. Fine folds of chiton hem trail over instep. Well-made piece.

See pp. 146, 291, 293.

H118	Standing draped female figurine			Pl. 35

MF-11218. Lot 1982. Preserved: front–calves to base. H. 0.063 (size 3). Fabric 2, light orange to orange-buff. White slip. Hollow. Added: feet, plaque base (open underneath).

Weight on left leg. Right leg bent. Mantle hem falls nearly to right foot, rises slightly to left ankle. Row of clearly modeled, rather linear, looped folds down right leg. Narrow, vertical folds of chiton trail slightly over slippered feet. Plaque base.

See pp. 18, 146.

H119	Standing draped female figurine			Pl. 35

MF-13505. Lot 3230. Preserved: front–left hip to lower leg. Missing left hand. Mended. P.H. 0.147 (size 4). Fabric 1, orange-buff. Hollow. Added: clump of drapery at left hip. Tooling on folds.

Left hand originally lifted hem of mantle and gathered it up at thigh into clump of overlapping folds; curving folds radiate across torso from this point. Mantle originally fell at least to knee at right side. Deep vertical folds of chiton conceal left leg, on which weight probably rested.

See p. 146.

H120	Standing draped female figurine			Pl. 35

MF-70-251. Lot 6500. Preserved: left hip and right thigh to base. P.H. 0.085 (size 2–3). Fabric 1, yellowish buff to greenish buff. Hollow. Thick-walled. All parts rendered in same mold. Back handmade, rounded. Bottom of irregular, rectangular vent preserved, 0.015 wide.

Weight on right leg. Left leg bent. Mantle is draped over right thigh; hem rises to left hip, where a clump of folds and small cascade suggest it was originally held there by the left hand. Chiton seems heavier than mantle; folds fall heavily over feet. Oval base with torus moldings in front at top and bottom.

See pp. 146, 275.

H121	Standing draped female figurine			Pl. 35

MF-13828. Lot 3230. Preserved: front–left leg to base, right foot; small part of back. Missing right side of base. Mended.

P.H. 0.074 (size 2–3). Fabric 1, orange-buff. White slip. Pink or lavender paint on skirt. Hollow. Back handmade, rounded. Added: pillar. Tooling around feet and hem.

Leans against cylindrical pillar at left side, with left leg crossed over right. Mantle hem falls below left knee, rises toward pillar; mantle ends hang down, presumably from shoulder, partly overlapping pillar. Chiton hem trails over slippered feet. Rectangular base with light torus molding at top. Similar in pose to **H146**.

See pp. 146–147, 150.

H122 Standing draped female figurine Pl. 35

MF-13827. Lot 3217. Preserved: right hip and left thigh to base; back also preserves left hip. Mended. P.H. 0.118 (size 3). Fabric 1, orange-buff, interior orange. White slip. Hollow. Back molded, rounded. Added: folds beside right hip, plaque base (closed underneath).

Weight on right leg. Left leg and foot concealed, probably drawn back. Mantle hem dips from right hip diagonally to left thigh. In back, hem dips to left calf, indicating that back mold belonged to different type; zigzag fold in back, presumably falls from shoulder. Curving folds on right hip, and small cascade of folds at side, suggest that right arm was bent and that hand gathered up mantle there. Vertical chiton folds trail slightly over instep of slippered right foot. Chiton hem pressed down in back to adhere to plaque base; for this technique, see also **H104**.

See pp. 147, 276.

H123 Standing draped female figurine (Aphrodite?) Pl. 35

MF-72-67. Lot 72-134. Preserved: neck to thighs. P.H. 0.062 (size 2–3). Fabric 1, orange-buff. White slip. Hollow. Thick-walled. Back handmade, flattened. Round vent, diam. 0.02. Tooling on hand.

Weight probably on left leg. Right leg advanced. Right arm bent; hand at abdomen. Left arm bent; hand on hip. Mantle covers left shoulder, arm, and hand; cloth is draped around back and across abdomen to left hip; upper edge is rolled and grasped by right hand; hem of overfold curves diagonally across thighs. Thin chiton slips from right shoulder. Figure is plump, somewhat short waisted, wide hipped. Long locks of hair on shoulders. Possible later generation in lot 1953 (fabric 5).

See p. 147.

H124 Standing draped female figurine Pl. 35

MF-70-252. Lot 6507. Preserved: front–left side, shoulder to thigh; small part of back. P.H. 0.079 (size 2–3). Fabric 1, harder, orange-buff, with orange core. White slip. Hollow. Back probably handmade. Tooling on folds.

Left arm bent; hand on hip. Mantle covers left shoulder, arm, and hand, is draped around back and across waist; hem of overfold curves up to left hip, where it is secured under left hand; cascade of folds down left side from hand and wrist. Chiton belted just below breasts. Folds coarsely retouched.

See p. 147.

H125 Standing draped female figurine Pl. 35

MF-69-384. Lot 6189. Preserved: shoulders to left hip and right ankle. Mended. P.H. 0.091 (size 2–3). Fabric 1, exterior orange-buff to orange; interior shows a coarser, thicker layer, orange, with small to large white and dark red inclusions, voids. White slip. Hollow. Thick-walled. Back molded, flattened.

Left arm bent; hand on hip. Small mantle covers left shoulder and arm, is draped around back, over right shoulder and arm, and diagonally across torso to left hip. Right arm bent, forearm lifts hem of mantle; hand pulls down on a fold from shoulder. V-shaped fold at chiton neckline barely visible; irregular, vertical skirt folds.

See pp. 147–148, 294.

H126 Standing draped female figurine Pl. 36

MF-13804. Lot 4349. Preserved: front–left shoulder to hip, left arm and hand. P.H. 0.081 (size 3). Fabric 5, orange. Hollow. Added: drapery across chest. Tooling on folds, hand.

Left arm bent; hand on hip. Shoulder and arm wrapped in mantle, leaving hand free. Roll of drapery across chest may drop from right shoulder. Crude retouch.

See p. 148.

H127 Standing draped female figurine Pl. 36

MF-13787. Lot 4348. Preserved: front–right hand holding drapery. P.H. 0.078 (size 3?). Fabric 1, orange-buff to orange. White slip. Blue paint on drapery. Hollow. Tooling on hand and folds.

Right hand grasps end of mantle, probably at hip level; cloth cascades from hand in zigzag folds, opening into diamond pattern. Probable mold sibling in lot 2249.

See p. 148.

H128 Standing draped female figurine (Artemis?) Pl. 36

MF-11905. Lot 2107. Preserved: shoulders to right ankle and left knee; part of back. Missing right wrist and hand, top of torch, top of pillar support in front. Mended. P.H. 0.125 (size 2–3). Fabric 1, orange-buff. White slip. Hollow. Back handmade, flattened; indented at hip level, flaring below. Added: pillar, torch, button on left shoulder, folds at left wrist. Tooling on folds, torch.

Weight on left leg, left hip outthrust. Right leg bent, advanced. Right elbow rests on pillar support, right shoulder higher than left. Left arm bent; clenched hand on hip. Sleeveless chiton fastened at left shoulder with round button, girded just below breasts; puffed folds over belt; cloth transparent over abdomen. Baldric(?) from right shoulder to belt below left breast. Upper edge of mantle rolled and draped in deep looped fold from hips, framing abdomen. Left hand grasps cloth at hip, folds wrapped around hand and wrist like a bracelet; folds cascade from hand to knee level. Mantle hem falls to calf. Deep U-shaped fold on skirt frames ankle. Full-breasted, short-waisted figure, with plump shoulders and arms. Long torch in front of pillar, tapering toward bottom; reeds and horizontal binding marked by incisions. In back, top of pillar has two horizontal slashes to mark capital.

See pp. 148–149, 178, 183, 256.

H129 Standing draped female figurine Pl. 36

MF-70-250. Lot 6233. Preserved: front–left thigh and hand, with adjacent drapery. P.H. 0.051 (size 3–4?). Fabric 1, orange-buff. Hollow. Thin-walled. Tooling on hand.

Rolled upper edge of mantle is draped diagonally from missing right thigh(?) up to left thigh, where a few folds are grasped in left hand and fall at side. A few chiton folds are visible near upper break.

See p. 149.

H130 Standing draped female figurine   Pl. 36

MF-13840. Lot 2107. Preserved: front–left hip and thigh, adjacent drapery. Mended. P.H. 0.082 (size 4). Fabric slightly coarse, orange-buff, with small white, dark red, and a few sparkling inclusions. White slip. Hollow. Thin-walled.

Rolled upper edge of mantle is draped diagonally from missing right thigh(?) up to left hip; clump of drapery at upper break suggests left hand originally secured cloth there. Skirt folds are vertical at left side of figure, gradually becoming diagonal at right, suggesting that cloth originally was pulled toward advancing right leg. No chiton folds are preserved above mantle roll, but upper torso probably was clothed. Generally similar in type to **H128** and **H134**. Fabric somewhat similar to **H144**. For possible workshop mates, see Workshop K, p. 346.

See pp. 149, 150, 197, 256.

H131 Standing draped female figurine   Pl. 36

MF-13837. Lot 4349. Preserved: base of neck to thighs. Missing left shoulder, upper back, most of right arm. Mended; surface worn. P.H. 0.035 (size 1–2). Fabric 5, ochre to orange. Nearly solid. Back probably handmade, flattened.

Right arm originally at side. Left arm bent. Rolled upper edge of mantle is draped around right hip, below abdomen, and over left forearm. Chiton belted just below breasts.

See pp. 149, 167.

H132   Pl. 36
          Standing draped female figurine (Aphrodite?)

MF-68-369. Lot 5613. Preserved: neck to right hip and left thigh. Missing right forearm. Surface worn. P.H. 0.052 (size 1–2). Fabric 5, orange. Solid. Back handmade, flattened. Round vent hollowed out, diam. 0.013.

Left arm bent; hand probably at hip. Right arm extended to side, forearm originally raised. Mantle is draped over left shoulder and arm, probably over head, and slung low around hips, as in **H131**. Panel of drapery in back visible at right side, probably held up by right hand. Chiton girded just below breasts.

See pp. 18, 149.

H133 Standing draped female figurine   Pl. 36

MF-13460. Lot 2239. Preserved: shoulders to hip at left side, to chest at right side. Missing arms. P.H. 0.045 (size 2–3). Fabric 2, orange. Hollow. Back handmade, flattened. Top of rectangular vent preserved, 0.016 wide. Added: drapery swag in front. Tooling on folds.

Right arm originally raised high. Left arm bent. Mantle covers left shoulder; lump at left side may be hand grasping drapery swag, perhaps rolled upper edge of mantle draped diagonally up to left hip. No chiton folds visible, perhaps due to dull impression.

See p. 149.

H134 Standing draped female figurine   Pl. 36

MF-13866. Lot 2249. Preserved: left side from chest to thigh, left upper arm and adjacent drapery; small part of back. Surface chipped and worn. P.H. 0.104 (size 3–4). Fabric 2, orange to ochre, burned(?). Hollow. Thick-walled. Back handmade, flattened. Added: mantle folds in front, panel in back. Tooling on folds.

Weight on left leg, left hip outthrust. Left arm bent. Mantle is draped diagonally from missing right thigh(?) up to left hip and over upper arm; falls behind in a thin panel. Diagonal skirt folds suggest that cloth originally was pulled toward advancing right leg. Chiton girded just below breasts.

See p. 149.

H135 Standing draped female figurine   Pl. 36

MF-10581. Lot 892. Preserved: shoulders to left hip. Missing part of chest and hip at right side, forearms, drapery adjacent to left hip, part of back. Mended; front chipped. P.H. 0.063 (size 3). Fabric 1, harder, tan. White slip. Hollow. Back molded, flattened. Added: right arm.

Figure leans heavily to left side, originally must have had support for left arm; pose similar to **H109** but reversed. Right shoulder lowered, arm extended to side. Mantle covers left shoulder and upper arm with stacked, curved folds. Flat, looped folds drop to right hip and rise in back diagonally to left shoulder. Faint chiton folds mark short sleeve on right arm; rounded neckline.

See p. 149.

H136 Standing draped female figurine   Pl. 36

MF-13784. Lot 1945. Preserved: front–right side, base of neck to hip. Missing right shoulder and arm. P.H. 0.077 (size 3–4). Fabric 4, yellowish buff. White slip. Hollow. Thin-walled.

Rolled upper edge of mantle is draped around right hip, originally must have dropped below abdomen, as in **H128**. Chiton or peplos folds gathered into narrow belt just below breast; V-shaped fold at center just below belt. Full-breasted, short-waisted figure, with rounded hip. Similar figurine, smaller, in lot 2249 (fabric 1).

See p. 149.

H137   Pl. 36
          Standing draped female figurine (Demeter or Aphrodite?)

MF-13842. Lot 877. Preserved: left upper arm, adjacent drapery. Max.P.Dim. 0.086 (size 4?). Fabric 2, orange-buff to orange (front); fabric 1, orange-buff (back); gray core; surface apparently was polished only in front. White slip. Solid. Back handmade, flattened.

Left upper arm extended to side in front of drapery panel; since vertical edge of drapery at left side is finished, elbow must have been bent and forearm raised to lift cloth. Break at shoulder suggests a sleeve. For possible composition, see **H138**. Large, well-made piece.

See pp. 11, 149–150.

H138   Pl. 36
          Standing draped female figurine (Demeter or Aphrodite?)

MF-13852. Lot 4450. Preserved: front–left side from breast to hip, left upper arm and elbow, adjacent drapery. Mended. P.H. 0.075 (size 3–4). Fabric 1, orange-buff, with orange core. Hollow. Thin-walled. Tooling on folds.

Left arm raised to lift mantle; forearm must have been almost vertical. Chiton girded fairly high; two looped folds of sleeve under arm. Mantle falls in curtain behind figure, seems to have been rendered in mold. For possible workshop mates, see Workshop K, p. 346.

See pp. 149–150, 256.

STANDING DRAPED FEMALE FIGURINES: WITHOUT MANTLE

H139 Standing draped female figurine   Pl. 37

MF-11074. Lot 1962. Preserved: front–shoulders to left hip, to waist at right; back–shoulders to waist. Missing most of arms. P.H. 0.101 (size 4). Fabric 1, coarser, orange-buff, with small dark red and gray inclusions. White slip. Hollow. Back handmade, flattened. Top of rectangular vent preserved, 0.037 wide. Added: arms. Tooling on folds.

Right hip outthrust. Left shoulder slightly higher than right; arm probably raised. Right arm probably extended to side. Slender figure, with high breasts. Peplos or chiton girded fairly high with narrow belt; puffed folds over belt at sides. Clinging drapery; loose V-shaped fold at neckline, catenaries between breasts. Deep fold from right shoulder to waist could belong to a mantle draped over shoulder.

See p. 150.

H140 Standing draped female figurine   Pl. 37

MF-13847. Lot 2248. Preserved: front–abdomen, right hip, right hand. P.H. 0.053 (size 3–4). Fabric 3, orange-buff. White slip. Hollow. Thin-walled. Added: drapery fold at side below fingers. Tooling on hand.

Right hip outthrust. Arched folds at lower break suggest that left thigh originally was strongly advanced, perhaps mantle draped over it. Thumb and first two fingers of right hand rest on hip; the two smallest fingers lift a fold at the side, perhaps belonging to mantle. Chiton clings to rounded hip in narrow, tubular folds; traces of belt at upper break. Large, well-made piece. Probable mold sibling in lot 5613 (fabric 1). For possible workshop mates, see Workshop K, p. 346.

See pp. 149, 150, 256.

H141   Pl. 37
          Standing draped female figurine (Aphrodite?)

MF-69-385. Lot 6214. Preserved: shoulders to abdomen. Missing most of right arm, pillar support. P.H. 0.048 (size 2–3). Fabric 1, orange-buff. White slip. Red paint on hair. Hollow. Thick-walled. Back molded, flattened. Edge of vent of uncertain shape at lower break.

Figure leans to right side. Right upper arm raised. Left arm at side. Chiton girded just below breasts. Slender figure with narrow shoulders, high breasts. Long locks of hair on shoulders. Complete example probably from same mold: MF-11457 in the Corinth collection (Pl. 76).

See p. 150.

H142   Pl. 37
          Standing draped female figurine (Aphrodite?)

MF-13841. Lot 4387. Preserved: head to right breast, to waist at left side. Surface worn. P.H. 0.044 (size 2). Fabric 5, orange to ochre. Hollow. Back handmade, flattened. Tooling on hair, eyes.

Left shoulder is higher than right, suggesting that elbow leaned on a support. Right upper arm at side. Chiton girded high, clings to full breasts; right shoulder bare. Face oblong to oval, with high, triangular forehead. Nose flat. Long locks of hair fall to shoulders from central part. One crease in neck.

See p. 150.

H143 Standing draped female figurine   Pl. 37

MF-70-79. Lot 6233. Preserved: front–right shoulder and left breast to abdomen. P.H. 0.056 (size 3). Fabric 1, orange-buff. White slip. Hollow. Tooling on folds.

Right shoulder raised; perhaps elbow originally leaned on high support, as in **H141**. Chiton girded high; belt merely an indentation, with short, diagonal tension folds from full breasts; figure short-waisted. Catenaries between and above breasts. Similar in type: one in lot 6214, larger.

See p. 150.

H144 Standing(?) draped female figurine   Pl. 37

MF-68-367. Lot 5613. Preserved: front–right breast, center of chest. P.H. 0.072 (size 4–5). Fabric slightly coarse, orange-buff, with small dark and white inclusions, voids. Hollow. Thin-walled.

Narrow belt just below breast, knotted at center, with trailing ends. Deep pleat of cloth at center of neckline, folded to right. A few short tension folds from breast above belt; narrow, vertical folds of skirt below it; a few folds radiate from shoulders. Large, well-made piece. Fabric somewhat similar to **H130**. For possible workshop mates, see Workshop K, p. 346.

See pp. 121, 150, 256.

H145 Draped female figurine (Nike or dancer?)   Pl. 37

MF-13884. Lot 2066. Preserved: front–left shoulder to thigh. Missing arm. P.H. 0.078 (size 3). Fabric 1, orange-buff. Hollow. Thin-walled.

Figure may be moving forward; long ends of belt are in motion and skirt folds at side slant backward. Chiton girded just below full breast with narrow belt, knotted at center. Deep V-shaped folds at neckline, catenary between breasts; puffed folds above belt at side. For possible workshop mates, see Workshop K, p. 346.

See pp. 121, 150, 256.

H146 Standing draped female figurine   Pl. 37

MF-12887. Lot 4418. Preserved: hips to base. Missing fragments of front at left side and center. Mended. P.H. 0.132 (size 3). Fabric 1, harder, orange-buff to orange, with gray core at pillar. White slip. Red paint on pillar. Hollow. Thin-walled. All parts rendered in same mold. Back handmade, rounded. Bottom of rectangular vent preserved, 0.028 wide. Added: right hand. Tooling on hand; back pared.

Figure leans against square pillar at its left side, facing three-quarters to right. Left leg crossed over concealed right leg. Right hand on hip. Narrow folds of thin garment, probably a chiton, cling to rounded hip. Leg appears almost nude beneath cloth. Looped folds from knee to ankle; narrow skirt folds fall vertically to base between leg and pillar. Base rectangular in front, rounded in back. Pillar skewed to left at top. Similar in pose to **H121**.

See pp. 146–147, 150, 275.

H147 Standing draped female figurine   Pl. 37

MF-13799. Lot 2249. Preserved: front–top of thighs to base; back–legs to base. Missing fragments of front at left ankle. P.H. 0.098 (size 3). Fabric 4, yellowish buff. Hollow. Thick-walled. Back handmade, rounded. Added: feet, base.

Weight on right leg. Left leg bent. Rather wide, flat skirt folds fall to slippered feet. Irregular, oval base with torus molding at top.

See pp. 150–151.

H148 Standing draped female figurine   Pl. 37

MF-69-374. Lot 6189. Preserved: front–left leg and foot with adjacent drapery. Mended. P.H. 0.13 (size 4). Fabric 1, orange to orange-buff. White slip. Hollow. Added: foot and adjacent folds, drapery cascade at side. Tooling on folds, foot.

Wide vertical skirt folds conceal leg. Hem collapses over instep of foot. Fairly high-soled sandal indented at toe. Bottom of zigzag drapery cascade preserved at left side.

See pp. 151, 257, note 39.

H149 Standing draped female figurine   Pl. 38

MF-13873. Lot 2156. Preserved: upper chest to base. P.H. 0.047 (size 1). Fabric 1, orange-buff, with orange core. White slip. Red paint. Solid. All parts rendered in same mold. Back handmade, flattened. Tooling on folds, arms; back pared.

Right forearm across waist; right hand touches left elbow; left forearm raised. Chiton sleeve visible on right arm; very long overfold falls to ankles; skirt hem trails over insteps. Slender, elongated figure. Low, round base.

See p. 151.

H150 Seated(?) draped female figurine   Pl. 38

MF-13757. Lot 3230. Preserved: shoulders to waist. Missing left forearm, right hand. P.H. 0.051 (size 3). Fabric 1, orange to grayish buff, burned. White slip. Hollow. Back molded, rounded.

Right forearm across waist. Left upper arm pressed close to torso; forearm may have been raised, as in **H149**. Wall flares out below waist in back, suggesting that figure may have been seated, although wall in front does not form a lap. Short-waisted figure, with high breasts, plump arms. Chiton shows row of V-shaped folds between breasts.

See p. 151.

H151 Standing draped female figurine   Pl. 38

MF-68-365. Lot 5613. Preserved: shoulders to waist. Missing most of left arm, right hand. P.H. 0.061 (size 3–4). Fabric 1, orange-buff. Hollow. Thick-walled. Back molded, rounded. Added: right forearm, drapery below elbow. Tooling on folds.

Right forearm across waist. Left upper arm at side. Chiton sleeve to elbow; thick V-shaped fold at neckline, row of slashed V-shaped folds below; row of catenaries in back.

See p. 151.

H152 Standing draped female figurine   Pl. 38

MF-11306. Lot 1994. Preserved: shoulders to hips. P.H. 0.053 (size 2–3). Fabric 3, grayish buff to orange-buff. White slip. Reddish pink paint on flesh, yellow on drapery. Hollow. Back molded, flattened. Part of round vent preserved, diam. 0.015.

Right shoulder higher than left. Right arm held diagonally across abdomen; clenched right hand seems to lift folds at left hip. Left arm at side; chiton sleeve to elbow. Rather stocky figure with high breasts, plump arms.

See pp. 151, 201, 295.

DANCERS AND RELATED HEADS

H153 Mantled dancer   Pl. 38

MF-10443. Lot 878. Preserved: head to ankles. Mended; back, flying drapery chipped. P.H. 0.188 (size 3). Fabric 2, orange-buff to light orange. White slip. Hollow. Thick-walled; interior surface irregular. Back handmade, flattened. Rectangular vent, narrower at top, ca. 0.075 × 0.02. Added: folds at neck, edge of flying drapery, possibly earrings. Tooling on folds.

Published: Stroud 1965, p. 18, pl. 8:b.

Woman dances with left leg advanced, left ankle crossed over right; probably originally set on base three-quarters to viewer's left, to allow flying drapery at left side to be seen. Right arm bent; hand at chest. Left arm bent, slightly pulled back; hand at hip. Mantle is draped over head, wrapped closely over torso and legs to ankles, covers hands; hem of garment beneath is visible. Curved folds radiating from right hand cover left hip and left hand. Flying panel of looped folds beside left leg; loops radiate from point near top of hip and are probably pulled up by hidden left hand, to free feet for dancing. Since lower edge of panel is finished, figurine originally was attached to base only at feet. Slender figure, with sloping shoulders. Head bent forward, gaze directed down. Face long, oval, expressionless. Eyes deeply set at inner corners. Nose long. Mouth small. Hair piled into high peak in front, enveloped in sakkos, raised border around forehead. Left earring visible. For possible workshop mates, see Workshop I, p. 346.

See pp. 19, 144, 145, 153–154, 155, 156, 196, 288, 291, 296.

H154   Pl. 38
    Mantled head, probably from a dancer figurine

MF-10460. Lot 878. Preserved: head to base of neck, part of shoulder in back. P.H. 0.045 (size 3). Fabric 2, light orange. White slip. Pink paint on face and headdress. Solid. Back handmade, rounded. Added: mantle fold around head.

Similar in facial type and headdress to **H153**, probably from the same workshop and from a similar figurine.

See pp. 144, 145, 154, 168, 288.

H155 Mantled dancer   Pl. 38

MF-72-187. Lot 72-122. Preserved: front–left hip and arm, with adjacent drapery; small part of back. Mended. P.H. 0.11 (size 3–4). Fabric 2, orange-buff, with blue-gray core. White slip. Hollow. Back probably handmade, flattened. Added: flying drapery below forearm. Tooling on folds.

Left arm bent; back of hand rests on hip. Mantle is wrapped closely over hip, covers arm and hand; panel of drapery flies out from forearm. Lightly modeled folds curve from hip to abdomen.

See pp. 144, 154, 288.

H156 Mantled dancer   Pl. 38

MF-13835. Lot 3229. Preserved: head to hips. Missing right forearm. Mended; left side, face chipped. P.H. 0.086 (size 2–3). Fabric 2, light orange. White slip. Hollow. Back handmade, flattened. Added: folds around neck, flying drapery at left side. Tooling on folds.

Somewhat similar in pose to **H153**. Right upper arm at side; break at elbow suggests extended or raised forearm. Mantle is wrapped closely over torso; one end is draped over

head and flung like a scarf across neck and left shoulder, flies out behind left arm; left forearm encircled with folds. Slender figure, with sloping shoulders. Head tilted to right and forward. Face oval to round. Eyes downturned. Mouth wide. Head covering similar to **H153**. Similar head: MF-11684 (lot 2010).
See pp. 143, note 173, 144, 154, 288, 291.

H157   Mantled dancer   Pl. 38

MF-13834. Lot 2249. Preserved: shoulders to right hip and left thigh. Missing right forearm; shoulders, front of torso chipped. P.H. 0.073 (size 3). Fabric 4, grayish buff to light orange. Hollow. Back handmade, flattened. Top of irregular, rectangular vent preserved, 0.022 wide. Added: fold across chest, flying drapery at left side. Tooling on folds.

Similar in type to **H156**. Mantle is wrapped closely over torso, grasped at left hip by covered hand, from which three short folds radiate over hip. Upper edge of mantle is thickly rolled, flung from right shoulder across chest to left arm, below which it terminates in short flying panel of drapery. Panel is marked by short folds radiating from left wrist; curving folds are stacked down right upper arm. Neckline of garment beneath is just visible above mantle roll.
See pp. 144, 154, 288.

H158   Mantled dancer   Pl. 38

MF-69-381. Lot 6214. Preserved: base of neck, shoulders, left breast and arm; upper part of back. P.H. 0.091 (size 3). Fabric 3, orange-buff. Hollow. Back molded, rounded. Round vent, diam. 0.018. Added: folds around left shoulder and back. Tooling on folds.

Left arm slightly bent, shows gently curving outline. Mantle is wrapped high around neck, probably covered head; remains of V-shaped folds on upper chest. Cloth is pulled tightly around left arm, which shows three curved folds radiating from chest. Drapery begins to fly back beside wrist, as in **H160**.
See pp. 154, 288.

H159   Mantled dancer   Pl. 38

MF-69-382. Lot 6214. Preserved: head to waist; small part of back. Missing left shoulder and arm, left side of chest, most of right arm; face chipped. P.H. 0.065 (size 2–3). Fabric 1, slightly sandy, orange-buff to greenish buff, burned(?). Hollow. Back probably handmade, flattened. Tooling on folds.

Similar in type to **H156**, but fold pattern on chest resembles **H158**. Mantle is wrapped closely over torso, and like a scarf around neck, covering chin. Mantle entirely covers high, slightly peaked coiffure; pleat at center of forehead. Head tilted slightly to left. Shape of face obscured by drapery. Eyes widely set, downturned; both lids defined; browridge rounded. Nose wide, flattened.
See pp. 154, 288.

H160   Mantled dancer   Pl. 38

MF-13857. Lot 2249. Preserved: left side from shoulder to hem, almost full width across abdomen and upper thighs; small part of back. Mended. P.H. 0.115 (size 2–3). Fabric 2, light orange, with gray core. White slip. Hollow. Back probably molded. Added: folds around shoulder and back, below hand at side. Tooling on folds.

Right leg advanced. Left arm slightly bent, shows gently curving outline, as in **H158**. Mantle is wrapped closely over torso; remains of V-shaped folds on upper chest; short folds

radiate from crook of arm. Mantle end is draped around back of figure and is grasped beside left thigh in left hand, from which a short fold cascade flies backward; skirt folds also fly back at left side.
See pp. 154, 288, 290.

H161   Mantled dancer   Pl. 38

MF-68-368. Lot 5613. Preserved: base of neck to hem. Mended; surface chipped. P.H. 0.105 (size 2–3). Fabric 1, greenish buff to orange-buff. White slip. Probably solid; closed underneath. Back handmade, rounded. Added: flying drapery in back. Tooling on folds.

Pose rather awkward, with right leg strongly advanced. Right arm bent; hand at chest, as in **H153**. Left arm slightly bent, as in **H160**. Mantle is closely wrapped over torso and legs, covers hands. Right hand pulls down folds of upper edge of mantle, which is draped over left shoulder; flying panel at back. Folds gathered at left thigh by left hand fall into cascade almost to hem. A few crudely cut folds across shoulders and skirt. Probable mold siblings in lots 2239, 3230.
See pp. 154, 288.

H162   Mantled dancer(?)   Pl. 38

MF-13865. Lot 1953. Preserved: left shoulder and arm, left side of torso, with adjacent drapery; small part of back. Mended. P.H. 0.08 (size 3). Fabric 2, orange. White slip. Hollow. Back probably handmade, flattened. Tooling on folds, hand.

Left arm slightly bent. Mantle covers arm to wrist, leaving hand free; hand grasps mantle end, pulling cloth across torso in diagonal folds. No traces of flying drapery, but composition as far as preserved is similar to **H160** and **H161**.
See pp. 154, 288.

H163   Mantled dancer(?)   Pl. 39

MF-13887. Lot 870. Preserved: front–left forearm and part of hand, with adjacent drapery. P.H. 0.068 (size 3–4). Fabric 1, orange-buff. White slip. Hollow. Thin-walled. Tooling on fingers.

Left hand pulls diagonal folds of mantle to side, as in **H162**, but arm probably was not bent. Mantle covers upper part of hand, leaving fingers free; looped folds on arm.
See pp. 154, 288.

H164   Mantled dancer   Pl. 39

MF-11729. Lot 2035. Preserved: base of neck to thighs, part of drapery cascade at left side. Missing left shoulder and upper arm, end of flying drapery. P.H. 0.069 (size 2). Fabric 1, orange-buff to orange, with orange core. White slip. Nearly solid. Back handmade, flattened. Added: flying drapery at side and back. Tooling on folds.

Figure shows torsion; left leg advances to viewer's left, and chest is turned to viewer's right. Mantle is wrapped closely over torso and legs. Right arm slightly bent; hand grasps one end of mantle at hip. Left arm bent; hand on hip, from which a few short, curved folds radiate over hip; cascade of zigzag folds falls beside leg. Flying drapery at left side and back. Catenary between breasts; looped folds from chest to right upper arm. Slender figure, with high, prominent breasts. Well-composed piece, but workmanship is summary.
See pp. 154–155, 156, 288, 291.

H165   Mantled dancer   Pl. 39

MF-11109. Lot 1978. Nearly complete. Mended; back and base chipped; surface worn. P.H. 0.074 (size 1–2). Fabric 5, orange-buff to orange. Nearly solid. All parts rendered in same mold. Back handmade, flat.

Figure shows torsion; right leg advances directly forward, head and chest are turned to right side, leaning downward. Both arms bent; hands lift mantle up and forward, showing hem of garment beneath. Mantle covers head, is wrapped diagonally across lower face, falls behind left shoulder. Oval base. Probable mold siblings: **H166** (better drapery detail); KT-5-21 from the Potters' Quarter (*Corinth* XV, ii, pp. 125–126, no. 21, pl. 24). Probably mechanically related: MF-3937 in the Corinth collection (*Corinth* XII, p. 34, no. 145, pl. 10; there dated too early, to the late 5th century B.C.). Head of similar type: **H171** (larger). For possible workshop mates, see Workshop C, p. 345.

See pp. 18, 154–155, 196, 288, 291, 343.

H166   Mantled dancer   Pl. 39

MF-13759. Lot 3222. Preserved: upper chest to base. P.H. 0.061 (size 1–2). Fabric 2, grayish buff. White slip. Solid. All parts rendered in same mold. Back handmade, flattened. Tooling on folds.

Probably from same mold as **H165**; clearer impression, although lacking head. Looped folds from left shoulder to hand; catenaries across abdomen and thighs from one hand to the other. Two vertical mantle edges, one of them fluttering, meet at flying panel of drapery below left hand. Sanguisuga fold on mantle hem. Omega folds on hem of garment beneath. For possible workshop mates, see Workshop C, p. 345.

See pp. 154–155, 196, 288, 291, 343.

H167   Mantled dancer(?)   Pl. 39

MF-14192. Lot 3206. Preserved: front–left foot, with garment hem. P.H. 0.042 (size 3?). Fabric 1, ochre. White slip. Hollow. Tooling on folds, foot.

Left foot, slightly turned out to left side, in low-soled sandal; long toes. Hem of chiton(?) trails over instep. Mantle hem falls to ankles, shows tubular fold opening into omega; drapery in movement to viewer's left.

See pp. 155, 288.

H168   Mantled(?) dancer   Pl. 39

MF-13930. Lot 4377. Preserved: neck to feet; surface eroded. P.H. 0.092 (size 2). Fabric 5, orange to orange-buff. Nearly solid. Back molded(?), flattened.

Moves forward, with left leg crossed in front of right. Arms at sides; hands grasp skirt folds, which fan out beside legs. Transparent garment (a mantle?) clings to unarticulated torso and legs. Slender figure, with narrow, sloping shoulders. Probable mold sibling in lot 6718 (fabric 1).

See pp. 155–156, 288.

H169   Mantled(?) dancer   Pl. 39

MF-13867. Lot 3222. Preserved: front and sides–hips to hem. Missing front of left foot, part of drapery beside left leg. P.H. 0.078 (size 2). Fabric 1, orange-buff. Hollow. Added: outermost fold at right side.

Moves to right, with left leg crossed in front of right; torso originally may have turned toward the left. Drapery in motion

around feet, sweeps back towards break beside left leg. Garment (a mantle?) clings to torso and legs as if transparent, is thicker around hem.

See pp. 155–156, 288.

H170   Mantled dancer   Pl. 39

MF-11840. Lot 2111. Preserved: head, right shoulder and arm; small part of back. P.H. 0.079 (size 3). Fabric 5, orange. White slip. Hollow. Back handmade, rounded. Tooling on folds.

Right arm bent, elbow pulled back; hand beneath mantle draws cloth over nose and mouth. Looped folds from underside of forearm to chest. Head tilted to right, covered by mantle; hair in front enveloped in sakkos, with raised border stretched low across forehead.

See pp. 156, 296.

H171   Mantled dancer   Pl. 39

MF-13760. Lot 4383. Preserved: head, left shoulder; part of upper back. P.H. 0.035 (size 1–2). Fabric 2, orange-buff. White slip. Solid. Back handmade, flattened.

Head tilted to left; generally similar to **H165** and **H170**, with mantle over head, drawn across mouth. Eyes large, widely set; both lids defined, upper lid well arched, lower lid more level. Nose rather wide. Hair in front enveloped in sakkos, stretched low across forehead. Similar in type: one in lot 2249 (head tilted to right).

See p. 156.

H172   Head, perhaps of mantled dancer   Pl. 39

MF-11412. Lot 877. Preserved: head, small part of neck. P.H. 0.028 (size 3). Fabric 2, orange-buff. White slip. Red paint on drapery. Nearly solid. Back handmade, flattened. Added: mantle fold across face.

Mantle drawn across nose and mouth, as in **H171**. Hair piled into high peak in front, enveloped in sakkos, raised border around forehead. Eyes indistinct. Similar heads in lots 3222, 4387 (both fabric 1).

See p. 156.

H173   Female head   Pl. 39

MF-11896. Lot 2107. Preserved: head to upper chest. P.H. 0.046 (size 3–4). Fabric 2, orange-buff to orange. White slip. Solid. Back handmade, rounded. Added: headdress at top and back. Tooling on folds, hair.

Face round to oval. Eyes slightly downturned; both lids defined. Nose slightly upturned. Mouth narrow, downturned; lips seem compressed, lower lip full. A few wavy locks of hair at temples; bun at back of head visible beneath cloth. Kerchief with grooved border stretched low across forehead; flaps of loose cloth lie on top of head, not completely understood by coroplast (cf. **H174**). Mantle is draped over kerchief and wrapped closely around neck to left shoulder.

See p. 156.

H174   Female head   Pl. 39

MF-13889. Lot 4377. Preserved: head and part of shoulders, draped right hand and wrist. P.H. 0.041 (size 3). Fabric 1, orange-buff. Solid. Back handmade, possibly flattened. Added: kerchief panel in back, hair on shoulders, earrings. Tooling on hair.

Right hand covered by mantle, draws cloth over chin. Face oval. Eyes downturned. Nose broad. Mouth narrow. Hair bound in a kerchief stretched low across forehead, turned down into flat panel at back; eyeholes of kerchief visible just above forehead. Locks of hair at sides wave down over ears; long, wavy locks of hair fall over sloping shoulders. Pellet earrings.
See p. 156.

SEATED DRAPED FEMALE FIGURINES

H175   Seated draped female figurine   Pl. 39
MF-10353. Lot 871. Preserved: shoulders to lap; small part of back. Missing left hand. P.H. 0.08 (size 3). Fabric 2, orange-buff. White slip. Hollow. Back probably handmade. Added: mantle end behind left shoulder. Tooling on folds.
Figure leans slightly forward, wrapped in mantle. Right arm bent; hand beneath mantle held up to chin. Left arm bent; hand originally rested on thigh, grasped one corner of mantle, which is turned to side just below wrist. Tension folds radiate from right forearm to left shoulder and arm. Mantle end hangs behind left shoulder. Folds encircle wrist. Complete type can be seen in figurine of Corinthian provenience in Athens (National Archaeological Museum, inv. no. 4413 [Pl. 78]; Winter, *Typen* II, p. 108, no. 5; Kleiner 1984, p. 170, pl. 36:a–c; similarity of scale and correspondence of folds suggest mechanical relationship).
See pp. 157, 164, 291.

H176   Seated draped female figurine   Pl. 39
MF-11028. Lot 1953. Preserved: Base of neck to lap. Surface worn. P.H. 0.08 (size 2–3). Fabric 5, orange-buff to orange. Hollow. Back probably molded, rounded. Added: fold across neck and down left side. Tooling on folds.
Figurine leans forward, shoulders hunched, wrapped in mantle. Right arm bent, forearm across waist. Left arm hidden beneath thick, flat fold of mantle edge descending vertically from neck. Perhaps original type similar to **H177**.
See p. 157.

H177   Seated draped female figurine   Pl. 39
MF-13758. Lot 3222. Preserved: head to lap. P.H. 0.03 (size 1–2). Fabric 2, orange-buff to orange, with gray core, burned(?). White slip. Dark-colored paint on mantle. Solid. Back handmade, rounded. Tooling on folds.
Figure leans forward, shoulders hunched, wrapped in mantle. Back spreads towards bottom. Right arm bent, forearm rests on lap; hand hidden beneath bent left arm. Head turned to profile right. Mantle covers head, is grasped at neck by left hand, from which short folds radiate across shoulders and arms. Mantle or sakkos wrapped low over forehead.
See p. 157.

ISOLATED FEMALE HEADS

H178   Female head   Pl. 40
MF-12894. Lot 4379. Preserved: head to upper chest. Missing part of stephane at right side. P.H. 0.065 (size 3–4). Fabric 1, orange to orange-buff. White slip. Hollow. Back handmade, rounded. Added: hair at sides and back, stephane. Tooling on face, hair, stephane.
Published: Stroud 1968, p. 323, pl. 94:b.
Head turned slightly to right. Face round to oval, with high forehead. Eyes level; both lids defined, lower lid slightly lifted,

puffy. Nose small, thin, upturned. Mouth slightly downturned; lips thin, parted. Face youthful. Horizontally slashed, wavy locks of hair fall to shoulders and down nape from off-center part, clinging closely to sides of face and neck. Stephane has torus molding at top, row of light punches on surface. Mantle is draped loosely across front from shoulder to shoulder. Well-composed piece, but retouch is coarse.
See pp. 157, 158, 161, 192, 256.

H179   Female head   Pl. 40
MF-68-352. Lot 5613. Preserved: head and neck; face and headdress chipped. P.H. 0.062 (size 3–4). Fabric 1, orange to yellowish buff. White slip. Yellow paint on hair. Solid. Back handmade, flattened. Added: hair, headdress. Tooling on hair.
Face oval to oblong. Features indistinct, but face seems youthful, similar in type to head of **H57**. Eyes slightly downturned; upper lid arched. Two to three overlapping rows of corkscrew curls frame face; no hair in back. Curls are made of cylinders of clay, with rows of diagonal slashes. Flaring headdress, probably a low polos; top uneven, slightly concave.
See pp. 133, 158, 161.

H180   Female head   Pl. 40
MF-13775. Lot 3228. Preserved: head and neck, with tenon. Missing bottom of hair; nose, right cheek, stephane chipped. P.H. 0.087 (size 4). Fabric 1, orange-buff. White slip. Yellow paint on hair. Solid. Back handmade, rounded. Added: hair at sides and back, stephane. Tooling on hair.
Head tilted to right; chin lifted. Face oval to oblong, with triangular forehead. Eyes relatively small, downturned, deeply set; upper lid clearly defined, lower lid slightly lifted, puffy; browridge well defined, follows curve of eyes. Mouth narrow; lips full, parted. Slightly wavy locks of hair fall from central part in heavy masses. Stephane originally may have been pointed at center. One crease in neck. For possible workshop mates, see Workshop F, p. 345.
See pp. 158–159, 258.

H181   Female head   Pl. 40
MF-13893. Lot 4387. Preserved: head, neck, right shoulder, upper arm. Missing upper left part of face, hair in front. Mended; nose chipped. P.H. 0.108 (size 3–4). Fabric 1, buff to gray, burned. Red paint on hair. Hollow. Back possibly molded, head rounded, flattened below. Added: sleeve folds, hair at sides and back. Tooling on hair, folds.
Head tilted slightly to left; chin lifted. Similar in facial type to **H180**, smaller, eyes more level, chin more pointed. Coiffure and headdress also similar; locks of hair stream over shoulder. Stephane rendered in mold, pointed at center. Looped folds of chiton sleeve lifted at center to indicate fastening. Probable mold sibling in lot 6233. For possible workshop mates, see Workshop F, p. 345.
See pp. 158–159.

H182   Female head   Pl. 40
MF-13776. Lot 4344. Preserved: head and neck, with tenon. Missing bottom of hair; surface chipped, cracked. P.H. 0.068 (size 3–4). Fabric 1, orange-buff. White slip. Solid. Back handmade, rounded. Added: hair at sides and back. Tooling on hair.

Head tilted to right; chin lifted. Similar in facial type to **H180**, eyes narrower, browridge less clearly defined; coiffure also similar but without stephane. Possible mold sibling: head of **H85**. Possible later generation in lots 2038 (fabric 5), 2150 (both with stephane). For possible workshop mates, see Workshop F, p. 345.

See pp. 140, 158–159.

H183 Female head   Pl. 40

MF-10476. Lot 878. Preserved: head and neck. Missing hair at right side of neck. P.H. 0.055 (size 3–4). Fabric 2, orange-buff, with orange core. Possible yellow paint on hair. Solid. Back molded, rounded. Added: hair at sides. Tooling on hair, corners of mouth and chin punched.

Chin slightly lifted. Face oblong to oval, with high, triangular forehead. Eyes deeply and widely set, slightly downturned, relatively small, left eye slightly smaller than right; both lids clearly defined, upper lid arched, lower lid nearly level; browridge well marked. Nose straight, rather short. Mouth wide; lips full, slightly smiling. Coiffure in front similar to **H180**; no added locks of hair in back, revealing short, masculine coiffure bound with fillet. Probable mold sibling: MF-12033 (lot 2248). Possible later generation: **H184**. For possible workshop mates, see Workshop F, p. 345.

See pp. 17, 158–159, 163, 165.

H184 Female head   Pl. 40

MF-11096. Lot 1978. Preserved: head to shoulders, with tenon. P.H. 0.051 (size 3). Fabric 2, yellowish buff. White slip. Red paint on hair. Solid. Back handmade, rounded. Added: hair at sides and back. Tooling on hair.

Head tilted to left. Similar in facial type to **H183**, smaller, nose larger. Left eye narrower and more closed than right, similar to deformity in **H183**; perhaps a later generation. Locks of hair wave more freely to shoulders. One crease in neck. For possible workshop mates, see Workshop F, p. 345.

See p. 158.

H185 Female head   Pl. 40

MF-13777. Lot 2107. Preserved: head and neck, with part of tenon. Missing most of hair at sides and back. Mended. P.H. 0.069 (size 3–4). Fabric 1, orange. White slip. Solid. Back probably handmade, rounded. Added: hair at sides and back, fillet. Tooling on hair.

Head tilted slightly to right. Similar in facial type to **H183**, face more oval, features more delicate. Mouth slightly crooked, lower on left side. Locks of hair are straight, added as a sheet of clay, then tooled; bound with fillet. One crease in neck. Similar in type: MF-10458 (lot 878, fabric 2: Stroud 1965, p. 18, pl. 7:f); one in lot 4377 (fabric 5, with stephane). Possibly mechanically related: **H204**. For possible workshop mates, see Workshop F, p. 345.

See pp. 158–159.

H186 Female head   Pl. 40

MF-13778. Lot 2249. Preserved: head and neck. Missing flat slice of right side, from stephane to chin; nose, chin chipped. P.H. 0.063 (size 3–4). Fabric 1, orange to orange-buff. White slip. Solid. Back handmade, rounded. Added: hair at sides and back, stephane. Tooling on hair.

Head tilted to left. Face narrow, oblong to oval, with high, triangular forehead. Eyes fairly small, downturned; upper lids defined, lower lids slightly lifted, puffy. Mouth narrow; lips full, slightly smiling. Upturned locks of hair at either side of central part; long locks of hair at sides of neck. Rounded stephane. Probable mold sibling: **H187**.

See pp. 122, 159, 167, 192.

H187 Female head   Pl. 40

MF-69-392. Lot 6214. Preserved: head and small part of neck. P.H. 0.056 (size 3–4). Fabric 4, creamy buff, with gray core. White slip. Bright pink paint on ear, blue-green on stephane, hair gilded; preservative on painted areas. Solid. Back handmade, rounded. Added: hair at sides and back, stephane. Tooling on hair.

Probably from same mold as **H186** but lower half of face very narrow, distorted to left in molding. Deep, upturned slashes on locks of hair. Stephane slightly pointed.

See pp. 122, 159.

H188 Female head   Pl. 41

MF-69-360. Lot 6214. Preserved: head and neck, with part of tenon. Missing left earring, hair at left side of neck, part of stephane at right side. Mended; nose, right temple chipped. P.H. 0.076 (size 3–4). Fabric 1, creamy buff, slightly greenish. White slip. Yellow paint on hair. Hollow. Back handmade, rounded. Added: hair at front and sides, stephane, earring, mantle fold. Tooling on hair, stephane.

Published: Coroplast's Art, p. 59, fig. 47.

Head tilted to right; chin lifted. Face narrow, oblong to oval, with high, triangular forehead. Eyes large, downturned; both lids defined, fleshy. Nose close to upper lip. Mouth wide; lips full. Coiffure parted at center, arranged in overlapping tiers of short, tousled, wavy locks of hair, deeply engraved. Long locks of hair at sides of neck, nape bare. High stephane with double molding at top, short, vertical slashes along upper edge. Disc earrings. Mantle fold at right side of neck, probably originally draped across front.

See pp. 159–160.

H189 Female head   Pl. 41

MF-13504. Lot 2249. Preserved: head and neck, with tenon. Missing end of nose, most of stephane, part of head in back. Mended; left side of face chipped. P.H. 0.091 (size 4). Fabric overfired, hard, greenish buff. White slip. Yellow paint on hair. Hollow. Thick-walled. Back handmade, rounded. Added: hair at side, neck, and back, stephane. Tooling on hair, stephane.

Head tilted to right; chin lifted. Face oblong to oval, with high, triangular forehead. Eyes large, downturned, deeply set; both lids well defined, upper lid arched, lower lid nearly level. Mouth narrow; lips full, parted, almost pursed. Fairly short, thick, wavy locks of hair tumble down sides of face from central part. Stephane probably low and rounded, incised with lotus-and-palmette pattern. Two creases in neck.

See p. 160.

H190 Female head   Pl. 41

MF-69-395. Lot 6214. Preserved: head and neck, with part of upper chest, tenon. Missing part of top and back of head, left side of forehead, part of left eye, most of nose, locks of hair at right side of neck. Mended. P.H. 0.085 (size 4). Fabric 1, orange-buff to orange. Hollow. Added: hair in front and along neck, stephane. Tooling on hair, face.

Face oblong to oval, with high, triangular forehead. Eyes rather small, widely and deeply set, downturned; both lids well defined, lower lid puffy. Mouth narrow; upper lip thin, lower lip full. Fairly short, thick, wavy locks of hair frame forehead, originally fell along neck. Stephane of uncertain shape. Triangular outline of lower break suggests the V-shaped fold of a chiton or peplos neckline.

See p. 160.

H191 Female head   Pl. 41

MF-12534. Lot 3217. Preserved: back and top of head, with forehead and left eye. P.H. 0.083 (size 5). Fabric 1, orange-buff. White slip. Pink paint on face; dark red on hair, perhaps also on eyebrow and lids. Hollow. Thick-walled. Back handmade, rounded. Added: locks of hair at lower back. Tooling on hair.

Narrow, triangular forehead, strongly projecting forward at center to high-bridged nose. Eye deeply set, slightly downturned; upper lid arched, clearly defined, lower lid lighter, lifted; browridge prominent, fleshy, follows curve of eye from bridge of nose. Hair parted at center; rather straight locks of hair wrapped over fillet worn low on cranium, gathered at nape into roll or bun.

See pp. 160, 258.

H192 Female head   Pl. 41

MF-10959. Lot 869. Preserved: head and neck; nose, chin chipped. P.H. 0.059 (size 3–4). Fabric 1, orange-buff to orange. Hollow. Back probably handmade, rounded. Added: hair at front and sides, stephane. Tooling on hair.

Head tilted to right; chin lifted. Face narrow, oblong, with ogival forehead. Eyes fairly small, downturned; upper lids arched, well defined, lower lids lifted, puffy; browridge follows curve of upper lids, with roll of flesh overhanging outer corners of eyes. Mouth narrow; lips full. Thick, curly locks of hair fall to shoulders from central part; flat locks of hair in back. Pointed stephane. Probably from the same workshop as **H193**. Probable mold siblings in lots 2239, 2247, 6509 (fabric 5); MF-2991 in the Corinth collection (*Corinth* XII, p. 50, no. 326, pl. 29, there called a male head).

See pp. 132, 160–161, 187.

H193 Female head   Pl. 41

MF-10492. Lot 880. Preserved: head and neck. Missing part of upper layers of curls. P.H. 0.051 (size 3). Fabric 2, orange to orange-buff. Hollow. Back probably handmade, rounded. Added: hair at front and sides, stephane. Tooling on hair; corners of mouth punched.

Published: Stroud 1965, p. 10, pl. 2:h.

Similar in facial type and coiffure to **H192**, smaller. Eyes rather flat in modeling, upturned at outer corners. Nose narrow, straight, close to upper lip. Mass of curly hair rendered by two to three overlapping rows of slashed tubes of clay, probably intended to be corkscrew curls. Stephane is higher, more rounded than **H192**; probably from the same workshop. Head of similar type and scale in lot 3231 (fabric 5).

See pp. 132, 133, 160–161.

H194 Female head   Pl. 41

MF-13774. Lot 3228. Preserved: head and neck, with tenon. Missing nose, bottom of hair; stephane chipped. P.H. 0.065

(size 3). Fabric 1, orange-buff. White slip. Solid. Back handmade, rounded. Added: hair at sides and nape, stephane. Tooling on hair.

Head tilted to right. Face oblong to oval, with high, triangular forehead; small chin. Features clustered at center of face. Eyes deeply and closely set, downturned; upper lids defined, lower lids lifted; browridge follows curve of eye closely. Mouth slightly distorted downward to left side; lips full. Locks of hair wave down from central part, cling to sides of face and neck. Rather crude gouging of hair. Stephane probably rounded originally. One crease in neck. Probable mold siblings: **H230** (with different coiffure); MF-10954 (lot 1946, fabric 5).

See pp. 161, 166.

H195 Female head   Pl. 42

MF-73-117. Lot 73-98. Preserved: head. Missing bottom of hair. P.H. 0.034 (size 3). Fabric 5, orange to grayish buff. White slip. Solid. Back handmade, flattened. Added: end of nose, hair. Tooling on hair.

Face oblong to oval, with high, ogival forehead. Eyes small, slightly downturned; upper lids defined, lower lids lifted, puffy; browridge follows curve of upper lids, with roll of flesh overhanging outer corners of eyes. Nose large, overhangs upper lip. Mouth distorted upward to right side; lips full. Coiffure may be a rough version of **H193**, with curls overhanging forehead and arranged in tiers at sides.

See p. 161.

H196 Female head   Pl. 41

MF-13891. Lot 3230. Preserved: head and neck. Hair at top, nose, lower part of face chipped; surface worn. P.H. 0.064 (size 4). Fabric 1, orange-buff to orange. White slip. Nearly solid. Back handmade, rounded. Added: locks of hair at sides, fillet. Tooling on face, locks of hair; corners of mouth, below mouth punched.

Head tilted to left and slightly back. Face oval, with high, triangular forehead. Eyes downturned, outlined with tool; lids thick; left eye distorted in mold. Lips parted; lower lip full. Coiffure originally parted at center, with fairly straight, horizontal locks of hair to either side; bound with fillet; long locks of hair along neck. One crease in neck. Rather crude workmanship. Probable mold sibling: **H197** (nose short).

See pp. 19, 161, 165.

H197 Female head   Pl. 41

MF-13890. Lot 3230. Preserved: head. Missing part of stephane; nose chipped; surface worn. P.H. 0.065 (size 4). Fabric 1, creamy buff. White slip. Nearly solid. Back handmade, rounded. Added: stephane, all of hair. Tooling on face, hair, stephane; corners of mouth, below mouth, nostrils punched.

Probably from same mold as **H196**, same distortion of left eye. Coiffure parted at center, with scalloped waves around forehead, long locks of hair down sides. High stephane with incised palmette pattern. Rather crude workmanship.

See pp. 19, 158, 161, 165.

H198 Female head   Pl. 41

MF-13779. Lot 3230. Preserved: head and small part of neck. Missing locks of hair at left side of neck; cranium chipped. P.H. 0.045 (size 3–4). Fabric 1, orange-buff, with orange core. White slip. Solid. Back handmade, rounded. Added: all of hair. Tooling on face, hair; parting of lips, below mouth, nostrils punched; mouth slightly deformed in tooling.

Facial type similar to **H183**, with relatively small, widely set eyes, but face more oval, nose heavier and closer to upper lip, tooling cruder. Coiffure parted at center, with straight locks of hair down to ears; long, wavy locks of hair along neck; nape bare.

See pp. 161, 165.

H199   Female head   Pl. 42

MF-13748. Lot 3230. Preserved: head and neck. Surface cracked. P.H. 0.065 (size 4). Fabric 2, creamy buff; fine, smooth surface, as in **H202**. White slip. Red paint on hair. Solid. Back handmade, rounded. Added: cluster of curls at top, with surrounding hair. Tooling on hair, face.

Published: Coroplast's Art, p. 18, color pl. 1, left.

Head tilted to right; chin slightly lifted. Face oval, with high, triangular forehead. Eyes deeply and fairly closely set; upper lids undercut, lower lids lifted, puffy; browridge rounded. Nose large, straight, close to upper lip. Lips full, slightly parted. Ears detailed. Straight locks of hair drawn up from temples into cluster of curls at top of head; serpentine curl hangs from cluster in front. One crease in neck. Large, well-made piece. Possible later generation: **H200**. For possible workshop mates, see Workshop G, p. 345.

See pp. 161–162.

H200   Female head   Pl. 42

MF-11107. Lot 1978. Preserved: head and neck; top of head chipped. P.H. 0.031 (size 2–3). Fabric 1, orange. White slip. Solid. Back handmade, flattened. Added: hair at top. Tooling on hair, face.

Head tilted slightly to left. Face seems to be a much smaller, cruder version of **H199**, possibly a later generation. Locks of hair wave down and back from central part; cluster of curls at top of head, lacking any relation to rest of coiffure (original connection between cluster and locks of hair drawn up to it has been lost).

See pp. 161–162.

H201   Female head   Pl. 42

MF-12153. Lot 4362. Preserved: head and neck, with part of tenon. P.H. 0.063 (size 3–4). Fabric 2, ochre. White slip. Yellow paint on hair. Solid. Back handmade, rounded. Added: hair at front, top, and sides. Tooling on hair, face; corners of mouth, below mouth, nostrils, ears punched.

Head tilted to left. Face oval to oblong, with triangular forehead. Eyes small, widely set; undercutting behind upper lid makes them almost round. Nose wide, rather short. Mouth slightly downturned; lips parted. Heavy retouch obscures original facial type, which seems to have been similar to **H202**. Hair arranged at top of head as in **H199**, but locks of hair are more abundant, heavily slashed; long corkscrew curls cascade from cluster at sides. One crease in neck. Probable mold sibling: MF-11841 (lot 2111, fabric 1, without retouch). For possible workshop mates, see Workshop G, p. 345.

See pp. 142, 161–162, 193.

H202   Female head   Pl. 42

MF-11967. Lot 2234. Preserved: head and neck, with part of tenon. P.H. 0.065 (size 3–4). Fabric 2, creamy buff; fine, smooth surface, as in **H199**. White slip. Red paint on hair.

Solid. Back handmade, rounded. Added: hair at top and sides. Tooling on hair; ears punched.

Published: Stroud 1968, p. 323, pl. 94:c.

Head tilted to right. Similar in facial type (without tooling) and coiffure to **H201**. One crease in neck. Probable mold siblings in lots 5613 (fabric 1), 6233 (fabric 4). Probable later generation: MF-11411 (lot 877); two in lot 3230 (all fabric 1). Similar in facial type, slightly smaller: MF-10609 (lot 896), MF-12043 (lot 2249), one in lot 2249 (all fabric 1). For possible workshop mates, see Workshop G, p. 345.

See pp. 15, 161–162.

H203   Female head   Pl. 42

MF-11865. Lot 2156. Preserved: head and neck, with part of tenon. P.H. 0.056 (size 3–4). Fabric 2, orange-buff, with orange core. White slip. Red paint on hair. Solid. Back handmade, rounded. Added: hair at top, probably drapery at neck. Tooling on hair; ears punched.

Head tilted to right and forward. Similar in facial type and coiffure to **H199**. Hair parted at center, with suggestion of two melon sections at top; locks of hair at sides wave horizontally to back of head, not drawn up to top; cluster of cascading curls, as in **H201** and **H202**. Mantle fold at base of neck. Possibly mechanically related: **H205**. For possible workshop mates, see Workshop G, p. 345.

See pp. 161–162.

H204   Female head   Pl. 42

MF-12119. Lot 4356. Preserved: head and neck, with tenon. P.H. 0.063 (size 3–4). Fabric 2, light orange. White slip. Red paint on hair. Solid. Back handmade, rounded. Added: hair at top, mantle. Tooling on hair, folds.

Published: Stroud 1968, p. 323, pl. 94:a.

Head tilted to left. Similar in facial type to **H185**, with mouth slightly crooked, lower at left side. Coiffure as in **H201**. Mantle wrapped closely around head, partly covering jaw, but leaving cluster of curls free. Folds draped toward left shoulder or upper arm. Probable mold sibling in lot 6214 (fabric 1, also mantled). Possibly mechanically related: **H185**, although without elaborate coiffure and added mantle, slightly larger. For possible workshop mates, see Workshop G, p. 345.

See pp. 156, 159, 161–162.

H205   Female head   Pl. 42

MF-13953. Lot 4344. Preserved: head and neck, with tenon. Top of head chipped. P.H. 0.066 (size 3–4). Fabric 1, orange-buff to orange. Solid. Back handmade, rounded; right side of head pinched in molding. Added: hair at top, probably drapery at neck. Tooling on hair.

Head tilted to right and forward. A slightly smaller, more summarily worked version of **H203**, perhaps mechanically related. Mantle fold at base of neck.

See pp. 161–162.

H206   Female head   Pl. 42

MF-14001. Lot 2249. Preserved: head and part of neck. Surface cracked, worn. P.H. 0.028 (size 2–3). Fabric 2, light orange. Solid. Back handmade, rounded.

Face a much smaller, cruder version of **H204**. Outlines of cluster of curls are visible. Mantle similarly wrapped toward left shoulder and seems to have been rendered in mold.

See pp. 156, 161–162.

H207 Female head Pl. 42

MF-11972. Lot 2239. Preserved: head and neck; nose, top of head chipped; surface cracked. P.H. 0.065 (size 3–4). Fabric friable, orange. Solid. Back molded, rounded. Added: hair at top. Tooling on hair, fillet; corners of mouth, ears punched.

Similar in facial type to **H183**; shape more oval, eyes more closely set, coiffure different. Locks of hair gathered up loosely from forehead and nape into cluster of curls at top of head; bound high with wide, flat fillet incised with running spiral. Large, well-composed piece, but retouch of hair is rather rough.

See p. 163.

H208 Female head Pl. 42

MF-14008. Lot 3228. Preserved: head and part of neck. Missing end of nose. P.H. 0.047 (size 3). Fabric 1, orange, burned. Solid. Back handmade, rounded. Added: hair at top, sides, and back. Tooling on hair.

Face oval, rather wide and flat, with high, triangular forehead. Eyes slightly downturned, deeply set; both lids defined. Mouth narrow; upper lip thin. Coiffure similar to **H207** but more schematic, fillet plain; in back, locks of hair are pulled up and over fillet; long curls tumble down from cluster.

See p. 163.

H209 Female head Pl. 42

MF-13932. Lot 4382. Preserved: head and neck, with tenon; left side of neck chipped. P.H. 0.07 (size 3–4). Fabric 1, orange-buff, with orange core. White slip. Solid. Back handmade, rounded. Added: hair at top. Tooling on hair.

Head tilted to right; chin slightly lifted. Face oblong to oval, with high, triangular forehead. Eyes level, deeply set; upper lids defined, lower lids lifted, slightly puffy; browridge rounded. Nose slightly upturned, close to upper lip. Lips full. Turban is wrapped around lower back of head, covers tops of ears; ends of cloth are crossed at center of forehead; cluster of curls spills out over top. One crease in neck. Possible mold sibling: **H210**. Similar in facial type to **H201–H204**.

See p. 163.

H210 Female head Pl. 42

MF-11102. Lot 1978. Preserved: head and neck. Surface cracked. P.H. 0.057 (size 3–4). Fabric 1, orange-buff. White slip. Red paint on hair. Solid. Back handmade, rounded. Added: hair at top, front, and sides. Tooling on hair.

Head tilted to left. Face oblong to oval, with low, ogival forehead. Eyes level. Nose upturned. Lips full. Possibly from same mold as **H209**, with somewhat different coiffure. Head wrapped in wider turban, set higher on head, allowing wavy locks of hair to show around forehead; cluster of curls spills out over top; one long lock of hair at either side of neck; nape bare.

See p. 163.

H211 Female head Pl. 42

MF-10922. Lot 1993. Preserved: head and neck. P.H. 0.041 (size 3–4). Fabric 2, orange-buff. White slip. Red paint on hair. Solid. Back handmade, rounded. Added: hair in front and back, sakkos. Tooling on hair.

Published: Stroud 1965, p. 18, pl. 8:c, right.

Head tilted to right. Face oval, with high, ogival forehead; prominent chin; full cheeks. Eyes large, downturned; upper lids defined, lower lids lifted, puffy; browridge rounded. Nose close to upper lip. Lips full, slightly smiling. Locks of hair wave down over ears from central part. Sakkos wrapped around lower back of head; ends of cloth are wrapped flat over top of head and tucked in below ears; flat curls on cranium. Well-made piece.

See p. 163.

H212 Female head Pl. 42

MF-10759. Lot 869. Preserved: head and small part of neck. P.H. 0.025 (size 2–3). Fabric 2, grayish buff. White slip. Solid. Back handmade, rounded. Added: sakkos folds in back. Tooling on hair, face.

Face oval, with low forehead; full jaw and cheeks. Eyes large, slightly downturned; upper lids undercut, lower lids lifted, puffy. Nose upturned, close to upper lip. Lips full. Similar in facial type to **H211**. Locks of hair slashed, wave back from central part; rest of head covered by sakkos; loose fold on cranium. Mantle fold around back of neck. Well-composed piece, but hair crudely retouched. Possible earlier generation in Epidauros (Peppa-Papaioannou 1985, p. 94, no. B207, pl. 33).

See p. 163.

H213 Female head Pl. 43

MF-69-391. Lot 6214. Preserved: head and neck. Missing part of right side of face. Mended. Small part of forehead and hair in front restored in plaster. P.H. 0.061 (size 4). Fabric 1, pinkish orange to orange-buff, with grayish buff core. Solid. Back probably molded, rounded. Added: hair at top, sphendone bow. Tooling on hair.

Head tilted to right; chin slightly lifted. Face oval, with fairly low forehead. Eyes level, long, narrow; upper lid defined, lower lid lifted, slightly puffy; browridge well defined, follows long curve of eyes. End of nose not fully modeled. Mouth wide; lips parted, upper lip thin. Melting expression. Locks of hair wave to sides from central part, are gathered into clump of curls high on cranium; bound with narrow sphendone knotted at top; flat ends of knot lie forward. Well-made piece; blurring of modeling may be deliberate.

See pp. 163–164.

H214 Female head Pl. 43

MF-12133. Lot 4352. Preserved: head and neck; nose chipped. P.H. 0.047 (size 3–4). Fabric 2, buff. Solid. White slip. Red paint on hair. Solid. Back probably molded, rounded. Added: plait, cluster of curls in back. Tooling on hair; ears punched.

Published: Coroplast's Art, p. 18, color pl. 1, right.

Head tilted to left and slightly forward. Face oval to oblong, with fairly low, sloping forehead; receding chin. Eyes large, downturned; heavy upper lids nearly closed. Lips full, slightly parted. Sweet, dreamy expression. Coiffure divided into about thirteen melon sections, slashed. Plait around cranium; small cluster of curls high in back. One crease in neck. Probable mold sibling: **H215**; MF-12026 (lot 2247, fabric 5, plaited circlet low in back).

See pp. 158, 162, 163, 164.

H215 Female head Pl. 43

MF-70-64. Lot 6503. Preserved: head and neck. Missing one end of sphendone bow; nose chipped. P.H. 0.052 (size 3–4). Fabric 2, orange-buff. White slip. Red paint on hair. Solid.

Back probably molded, rounded. Added: cluster of curls in back, sphendone. Tooling on hair; ears punched.

Head tilted to left and slightly forward. Probably from same mold as **H214**. Similar coiffure, but central part is deeply cut; small cluster of curls high in back; sphendone tied at top with soft bow.

See pp. 162, 163, 164.

H216   Female head   Pl. 43

MF-10556. Lot 890. Preserved: head and neck; nose chipped. P.H. 0.042 (size 3). Fabric 1, grayish buff. White slip. Red paint on hair. Solid. Back molded, rounded. Added: plait. Tooling on hair; ears punched.

Head tilted to left and slightly forward. Face oval to oblong, with high forehead. Nose large, close to upper lip. Mouth narrow; lips full, slightly smiling. Full, rounded coiffure divided into sixteen melon sections. At back of head, locks of hair radiate from center; plait around cranium. Probable mold sibling: MF-11329 (lot 2000).

See p. 164.

H217   Female head   Pl. 43

MF-10336. Lot 870. Preserved: head and neck. Missing back of head, right temple; nose chipped. P.H. 0.039 (size 3). Fabric 5, orange-buff to orange. Solid. Added: plait. Tooling on hair.

Head tilted slightly to right. Face round to oval, with high, wide forehead; small chin. Eyes large, level. Nose short, wide. Mouth narrow; lips full. Sweet, girlish expression. Coiffure divided into at least seven melon sections; locks of hair slashed; plait around cranium. Similar head, with added wreath, in lot 2239 (fabric 1). Perhaps mechanically related: **H218**.

See pp. 164, 169, 291.

H218   Female head   Pl. 43

MF-13952. Lot 3410. Preserved: head and part of neck; back chipped. P.H. 0.036 (size 3). Fabric 1, orange-buff to orange, slightly burned(?). Red paint on hair. Solid. Added: cluster of curls, earrings. Tooling on hair.

Facial type seems close to **H217**; perhaps mechanically related, with different coiffure. Locks of hair drawn up from forehead, perhaps in melon sections, into cluster of curls at top of head, from which long curls tumble forward.

See pp. 164, 169, 291.

H219   Female head   Pl. 43

MF-11861. Lot 2167. Preserved: head and neck, with small part of tenon. Mended; left cheek, front of hair chipped. P.H. 0.054 (size 3–4). Fabric 1, yellowish buff. Hollow. Back molded, rounded. Added: plait, cluster of curls. Tooling on hair.

Head tilted slightly to left; chin lifted. Face oval, with high forehead. Eyes large, slightly downturned; both lids defined, lower lid slightly lifted. Nose wide, rather short, close to upper lip. Lips full, slightly downturned. Hair parted at center, divided into about thirteen melon sections; locks of hair slashed, gathered into small cluster of curls at back; plait around cranium, punched. One crease in neck. Possibly mechanically related: one in Epidauros (Peppa-Papaioannou 1985, p. 94, no. B208, pl. 34).

See pp. 164, 169, 291.

H220   Female head   Pl. 43

MF-14000. Lot 2249. Preserved: front of head, left side of neck. P.H. 0.034 (size 3). Fabric 2, buff to orange-buff. White slip. Red paint on hair. Hollow. Tooling on hair.

Face round, with high, sloping forehead; small chin. Eyes small, level, widely set; upper lids defined, lower lids puffy; browridge rounded. Nose wide, arched, close to upper lip. Mouth narrow; lips full, pursed. Ears well formed. Coiffure divided into at least nine melon sections; locks of hair slashed. Well-made piece.

See pp. 157, 158, 164, 169, 291.

H221   Female head   Pl. 43

MF-14002. Lot 3206. Preserved: head and neck. P.H. 0.031 (size 2–3). Fabric 1, orange to ochre. Solid. Back handmade, rounded. Added: hair at sides, back, and nape. Tooling on hair.

Face narrow, oblong to oval, with high, sloping, triangular forehead. Eyes level, deeply set. Nose arched. Mouth narrow; lips full. Hair parted at center, with eight deeply cut melon sections drawn back to cluster of curls at nape.

See p. 165.

H222   Female head   Pl. 43

MF-70-261. Lot 6233. Preserved: head and neck. P.H. 0.037 (size 2–3). Fabric 1, buff. Solid. Back handmade, rounded. Added: hair at top and back. Tooling on hair.

Head tilted to left; chin lifted. Face oval, with rather wide forehead. Eyes large, downturned; upper lids defined, lower lids lifted, puffy. Nose large, close to upper lip. Mouth narrow; lips full, smiling. Sweet expression. Hair parted at center, roughly divided by slashes into melon sections; small, plaited circlet at back of head.

See p. 165.

H223   Female head   Pl. 43

MF-68-148. Lot 5711. Preserved: head and neck. P.H. 0.029 (size 2–3). Fabric 3, creamy buff to white. Yellow paint on hair. Solid. Back handmade, slightly flattened. Added: plait, earrings. Tooling on hair.

Head tilted slightly to left. Face nearly triangular, with high, rectangular forehead; pointed, receding chin. Dull impression, face distorted in molding. Nose short, upturned. Lips thin, smiling. Coiffure divided into eight flat melon sections, crudely slashed; thick, slashed plait around cranium. Pellet earrings. Good fabric but coarse retouch. Similar in workmanship to MF-1424 in the Corinth collection (*Corinth* XII, p. 45, no. 268, pl. 23, burned). Similar in pale coloring and hardness of fabric to hydriaphoros **H50** and standing girl **H44** (also a dull impression); perhaps from the same workshop (Workshop J, p. 346).

See pp. 19, 128, 129, 165.

H224   Female head   Pl. 43

MF-11309. Lot 1948. Preserved: head and neck. P.H. 0.046 (size 3–4). Fabric 2, orange-buff, with grayish core. White slip. Red paint on hair. Solid. Back probably handmade, rounded. Added: plait. Tooling on hair, face.

Head tilted slightly to left. Face oval to oblong, with high forehead. Eyes slightly downturned; both lids defined, upper lids perhaps undercut. Nose thin, straight. Mouth wide; lower lip full. Face rather masculine. Hair parted at center, roughly divided into eleven melon sections, slashed; summary, slashed plait around cranium.

See pp. 134, 165.

H225 Female head   Pl. 43

MF-12893. Lot 4379. Preserved: head and neck. P.H. 0.067 (size 4). Fabric 1, orange-buff to pinkish orange. White slip. Yellow paint on hair, with flecks of gilding. Probably hollow. Back handmade, flattened. Added: locks of hair all around. Tooling on face, hair.

Head tilted slightly to right. Narrow, oval face, with high, triangular forehead; prominent, pointed chin. Eyes large, slightly downturned; lids fleshy, upper lid undercut. Nose narrow, straight, sharp. Parting of lips tooled; lower lip full. Ears, nostrils punched; slash below mouth. Coiffure divided into about eleven rounded, deeply divided, slashed melon sections. Probable later generation: **H226**.

See pp. 14, 161, 165.

H226 Female head   Pl. 43

MF-13981. Lot 3222. Preserved: head and small part of neck; jaw chipped; surface worn, cracked. P.H. 0.047 (size 4). Fabric 5, orange-buff to ochre. Hollow. Thick-walled. Back handmade, rounded. Tooling on hair.

Probably later generation of **H225**, the facial retouch of which has survived in mold. Coiffure parted at center, with straight locks of hair down to ears, close to head; perhaps cluster of curls originally at nape.

See pp. 161, 165.

H227 Female head   Pl. 43

MF-12874. Lot 4448. Preserved: head and neck. P.H. 0.063 (size 4). Fabric 5, ochre to orange, with orange core. Solid. Back handmade, rounded. Added: fillet. Tooling on face, hair; cranium, ears punched.

Head tilted slightly to left. Face oval to oblong, with high, rounded forehead. Eyes small, slightly downturned; both lids defined. Nose upturned. Lower lip full. Melon coiffure divided into at least twelve sections, slashed; bound with fillet, punched area at top probably represents a small cluster of curls. Possible later generation in lots 2249, 4448 (both fabric 1). Head of similar type and scale in lot 3206.

See pp. 122, note 45, 161, 165, 257.

H228 Female head   Pl. 43

MF-68-372. Lot 5613. Preserved: head and small part of neck. P.H. 0.038 (size 3–4). Fabric 1, orange-buff to pinkish orange. White slip. Red paint on hair. Solid(?). Back probably molded, rounded. Added: plaits, cluster of curls. Tooling on hair.

Face oval to oblong, with high, triangular forehead, slightly sloping; slightly receding chin. Eyes relatively small, level; upper lid defined, lower lid slightly lifted. Nose slightly arched, overhangs upper lip. Mouth wide; lower lip full. Coiffure divided into seven melon sections; double plait (slashed) around cranium; cluster of curls in back at top of cranium. Possible mold sibling in lot 2249 has similar coiffure, mantle folds around neck (face poorly preserved).

See pp. 122, note 45, 161, 165–166.

H229 Female head   Pl. 44

MF-10404. Lot 877. Preserved: head and neck; front of neck chipped. P.H. 0.042 (size 3–4). Fabric 1, slightly sandy, orange-buff. White slip. Red and yellow paint on hair, possible flecks of gilding. Solid. Back handmade, rounded, distorted. Added: hair at top and neck, earrings. Tooling on hair.

Head tilted to left; chin lifted. Face oblong to oval, with triangular forehead; prominent chin, distorted in molding. Eyes level, almond shaped; both lids defined. Ski-jump nose, close to upper lip. Mouth wide; lips full, slightly downturned. Locks of hair gathered up into cluster of curls at top of head; long locks of hair at sides of neck; hair roughly slashed and punched. Disc earrings.

See p. 166.

H230 Female head   Pl. 44

MF-12147. Lot 4350. Preserved: head and neck, with small part of tenon. Missing nose; top of head chipped. P.H. 0.057 (size 4). Fabric 1, creamy buff. White slip. Red paint on hair. Solid. Back handmade, rounded. Added: hair at top, sides, and back. Tooling on hair.

Head tilted slightly to right. Face probably from same mold as **H194**, with different coiffure. Locks of hair drawn up vertically from top of high, squarish forehead into cluster of curls at top of head; long locks of hair wave down sides of face and neck; hair roughly slashed and punched. Another probable mold sibling: MF-10954 (lot 1946, fabric 5). Similar in type: one in lot 5613 (smaller, hair bound with fillet).

See pp. 161, 166, 192.

H231 Female head   Pl. 44

MF-14007. Lot 3226. Preserved: head and neck. P.H. 0.042 (size 2–3). Fabric 1, orange-buff. White slip. Red paint on hair. Solid. Back molded, rounded. Added: topknot. Tooling on hair.

Head tilted to left. Oval face, with high, triangular forehead. Eyes slightly downturned, opened wide; both lids defined. Nose straight. Upper lip thin, lower lip full. Locks of hair rendered in mold, wave to sides from central part, are gathered at back in upright, curly knot; bound with fillet. Probable mold sibling in lot 4377. Similar in facial type and scale: MF-14012 (lot 4349, fabric 2). Well-made piece.

See pp. 59, note 237, 166, 174.

H232 Female head   Pl. 44

MF-11687. Lot 2011. Preserved: head to upper chest. P.H. 0.045 (size 2–3). Fabric 1, orange-buff, with orange core. White slip. Red paint on hair. Solid. Back handmade, rounded. Added: hair in back, earrings. Tooling on hair.

Head probably turned three-fourths to right. Face oval, with triangular forehead. Eyes downturned, widely set; fleshy lids. Nose large, wide, arched, close to upper lip. Mouth wide; lips full, particularly lower lip. Expressive face. Locks of hair wave to sides and down over ears from central part; bowknot at top is rendered in mold; locks of hair at sides are gathered into cluster of curls at back of head. Mantle folds around base of neck. Probable mold siblings: MF-11862 (lot 2164); MF-11889 (lot 2067).

See pp. 166, 167.

H233   Female head   Pl. 44

MF-10424. Lot 877. Preserved: head and neck. P.H. 0.045 (size 2–3). Fabric 2, orange-buff. White slip. Solid. Back handmade, flattened. Added: lampadion knot. Tooling on knot.

Head probably turned slightly to left. Face oval to round, with low, triangular forehead. Eyes slightly downturned. Nose upturned. Mouth wide; lips thin. Locks of hair wave down from central part, close to head, are rendered in mold; large lampadion knot at top of head, roughly gouged.

See pp. 166–167.

H234   Female head   Pl. 44

MF-10685. Lot 878. Preserved: head; top of head, left temple chipped. P.H. 0.047 (size 4). Fabric 1, grayish buff. Solid. Back probably molded (probable traces of molded locks of hair). Added: hair at front, sides, and back. Tooling on hair.

Face oval to oblong, with high, sloping forehead; slightly receding chin. Nose large, arched, close to upper lip. Eyes downturned; lids thick, almost closed. Lips full. Wavy locks of hair at front and sides, rough bowknot at top, flattened roll at nape, rough plait around cranium. Head is unusually deep; this feature and sloping profile recall votary **H1**. Possible mechanical relatives: "doll's" head **C156**; the smaller head of **H102**.

See pp. 56, 164, 167.

H235   Female head   Pl. 44

MF-68-377. Lot 5711. Preserved: head and neck, with tenon. Missing hair at nape; nose chipped. P.H. 0.072 (size 3–4). Fabric 1, orange-buff. Solid. Back probably handmade, rounded. Added: hair at sides of face and nape. Tooling on hair; corners of mouth punched.

Head tilted to right; chin lifted. Face oblong to oval, with wide, ogival forehead. Eyes small, downturned; upper lids well defined, lower lids lifted, slightly puffy. Nose wide at base, possibly upturned. Lips full, well arched but rather delicate. Crisply modeled, smooth locks of hair wave from central part; probably long locks of hair at nape. One crease in neck. Slight projections around base of neck suggest mantle folds. Well-made piece. Possible later generation: MF-10951 (lot 1945).

See pp. 167, 343.

H236   Female head   Pl. 44

MF-13999. Lot 2249. Preserved: head and neck. Missing most of hair at sides and back, headdress; back of head chipped. P.H. 0.037 (size 3). Fabric 2, light orange. White slip. Yellow paint on hair. Solid. Back handmade, rounded. Added: hair at sides and back, headdress. Tooling on hair.

Face oval to oblong, with high, ogival forehead; full cheeks. Eyes small, level; lids thick. Nose arched, distorted, close to upper lip. Mouth narrow; lips full, almost pursed. Locks of hair wave to sides and down from central part; long locks of hair originally fell along neck. Groove around head for stephane, only small part of which is preserved. Probable mold sibling: MF-11414 (lot 877). Similar in facial type: MF-10387 (lot 875).

See p. 167.

H237   Female(?) head   Pl. 44

MF-10570. Lot 891. Preserved: head and neck. Missing hair at left side of neck and back; right cheek chipped. P.H. 0.049

(size 3–4). Fabric 1, orange-buff, with orange core. White slip. Solid. Back handmade, rounded. Added: hair at sides of neck and back. Tooling on hair.

Head tilted to left and slightly forward. Face narrow, oblong to oval, with high forehead; prominent chin. Eyes large, downturned; both lids defined; browridge well defined. Ski-jump nose, close to upper lip. Mouth narrow; lips full, slightly smiling. Carefully modeled parallel locks of hair, rendered in mold, wave up and to sides from forehead, without a part. Long, deeply waved locks of hair fall to shoulders from behind ears. Well-made piece.

See pp. 167, 343.

H238   Female head   Pl. 44

MF-14006. Lot 3222. Preserved: head and neck. Missing hair at nape. P.H. 0.035 (size 3). Fabric 5, orange. Solid. Back handmade, rounded. Added: hair at sides and back. Tooling on hair.

Head tilted to left; chin lifted. Face oval, with low, triangular forehead; receding chin; full cheeks. Eyes large, downturned; both lids defined. Nose wide, flattened, close to upper lip. Lips full. Parallel locks of hair wave up and to sides from forehead, similar to **H237** but with faint central part. Locks of hair wrapped to back of head in a roll above nape. Long, wavy locks of hair fall to shoulders from behind ears. Possible mold siblings: MF-11297 (lot 1993, nose not flattened); another in lot 2249 (both fabric 1).

See pp. 167, 168.

H239   Female head   Pl. 44

MF-14014. Lot 4387. Preserved: head and neck. Missing cranium. P.H. 0.038 (size 3). Fabric slightly sandy, orange-buff, with sparse small sparkling inclusions (probably Corinthian fabric, with admixture of sand). White slip. Hollow.

Head tilted slightly to left. Face oval, with low, rounded forehead. Large, earthy features somewhat obscured by remains of slip. Eyes large, prominent; well-marked browridge follows curve of upper lid. Nose large. Mouth wide; lips full. Hair enveloped in sakkos, tucked behind ears.

See p. 168.

H240   Female head   Pl. 44

MF-13894. Lot 3230. Preserved: head and part of neck; chin, nose, back of head chipped. P.H. 0.045 (size 3–4). Fabric 2, buff. White slip. Solid. Back probably handmade, rounded. Tooling on ears.

Face oval to oblong. Eyes downturned, deeply set; lids thick. Nose close to upper lip. Mouth wide; lips full, parted. Ears tooled with C-shaped instrument. Large, rounded hair mass enveloped in sakkos, with fold of cloth at back of head but only a faint division at forehead; detail presumably painted.

See p. 168.

H241   Female head   Pl. 44

MF-14003. Lot 3217. Preserved: head and neck. P.H. 0.032 (size 2–3). Fabric 1, buff. White slip. Solid. Back probably handmade, rounded.

Head tilted to left. Face oval, with low, wide forehead. Eyes large, deeply set. Nose arched, close to upper lip. Lips rather thin, slightly smiling. Rounded hair mass enveloped in sakkos, lopsided to left.

See p. 168.

H242 Female head   Pl. 44

MF-10755. Lot 869. Preserved: head and neck; top of head, face chipped. P.H. 0.044 (size 3). Fabric 1, grayish buff. White slip. Solid. Back handmade, rounded. Added: point of headdress in back. Tooling on headdress; ears punched.

Head tilted to left; chin lifted. Face oblong to oval. Eyes large, deeply set, downturned. Nose wide, close to upper lip. Lips full, slightly pursed. Unusually large punches in ears, perhaps for inserted earrings. Hair piled into high peak in front, enveloped in sakkos; border around forehead, drooping point in back, slashed folds. Long, spreading neck is deep. Probable mold sibling in lot 6642 (fabric 2). Similar in type and scale: one in lot 2107; KT-10-16 from the Potters' Quarter (*Corinth* XV, ii, p. 133, no. 40, pl. 24); MF-5669 from the South Stoa (*Corinth* XII, p. 44, no. 258, pl. 22, there dated late 4th century B.C.).

See pp. 137, 168, 296.

H243 Female head   Pl. 44

MF-14013. Lot 4379. Preserved: head and neck. P.H. 0.026 (size 2–3). Fabric 1, creamy buff. White slip. Solid. Back handmade, rounded. Added: earrings. Tooling on hair.

Head tilted to right. Face round to oval, with high, sloping forehead; narrow jaw, with small, receding chin. Eyes level, long, narrowed almost to slits. Nose short. Mouth narrow; lips smiling. Locks of hair wave back and down from central part; deep cranium wrapped in sakkos, from which small cluster of curls emerges at back. Small disc earrings.

See pp. 165, 168, 291.

H244 Female head   Pl. 44

MF-70-257. Lot 6500. Preserved: head and neck. P.H. 0.035 (size 2–3). Fabric 1, orange-buff. White slip. Red paint on hair. Solid. Back handmade, flattened. Added: plait. Tooling on hair.

Head tilted to left. Face round, with triangular forehead; narrow jaw, with slightly pointed chin. Features clustered near center of face. Eyes narrow, slightly upturned. Nose short, upturned, close to upper lip. Mouth narrow; lips smiling. Coiffure more or less divided into melon sections; locks of hair drawn up and back from central part; plaited circlet high on cranium. One crease in neck. Probable mold sibling in lot 4349 (fabric 5). Similar in type: one in lot 6502.

See pp. 158, 165, 168–169, 291.

H245 Female head   Pl. 44

MF-13997. Lot 4377. Preserved: head, neck, part of left shoulder. P.H. 0.048 (size 3). Fabric probably 1, slightly sandy, orange-buff. White slip. Red paint on hair. Back probably molded, rounded. Added: folds at neck, bun. Tooling on hair; ears punched.

Head tilted to right; chin lifted. Face oval to round, with fairly low, triangular forehead. Features clustered near center of face. Eyes closely set. Nose short. Mouth very small. Sweet, youthful expression. Coiffure divided by light slashes into ten melon sections; locks of hair gathered into small, cylindrical bun at back. Mantle draped around base of neck. Facial type and rendering of hair are not typically Corinthian, but fabric seems local. Similar in type: two in lot 4379 (both fabric 1).

See pp. 157, 165, 168–169, 291.

H246 Female head   Pl. 44

MF-10624. Lot 896. Preserved: head and neck. P.H. 0.035 (size 3). Fabric 1, orange. White slip. Red paint on hair. Nearly solid. Back handmade, rounded.

Head tilted to left. Oval face with high, triangular forehead. Eyes large, level. Nose close to upper lip. Lips full. Coiffure parted at center. Diagonal locks of hair cling closely to sides of face and neck. Similar in type to to Argive heads such as **I9**. Possibly mechanically related: **I77**.

See pp. 169, 289, 296.

H247 Female head   Pl. 44

MF-14010. Lot 3230. Preserved: head and neck, with small part of tenon. Missing top of head at back; surface slightly chipped. P.H. 0.045 (size 3). Fabric grayish buff, burned(?). White slip. Solid. Back handmade(?). Added: hair at nape. Tooling on hair.

Head tilted to left and slightly forward. Face oblong to oval, with low forehead. Eyes small, level, deeply set. Nose thin, somewhat arched, close to upper lip. Mouth narrow; lips full, almost pursed. locks of hair wave to sides from central part; long, wavy locks of hair at nape; bound with fillet. Pellet earrings.

See pp. 169, 284.

H248 Female head   Pl. 44

MF-11725. Lot 2029. Preserved: front of head. P.H. 0.042 (size 3–4). Fabric 1, orange-buff. Hollow. Added: hair at top. Tooling on hair.

Face oval, with triangular forehead. Eyes downturned, closely set; both lids defined, lower lid lifted. Nose slightly upturned. Mouth wide, distorted downward to left side. Right side of face is flattened, perhaps originally attached to something. Locks of hair wave up and to sides from central part, perhaps originally cluster of curls at top.

See pp. 169, 291.

NUDE AND SEMIDRAPED APHRODITE, LEDA, MAENAD(?), NYMPHS, AND RELATED HEADS

H249 Standing Aphrodite   Pl. 45

MF-12053. Lot 2249. Preserved: shoulders to feet. Missing right arm, left forearm. Mended. P.H. 0.157 (size 3). Fabric 2, orange-buff to orange. White slip. Hollow. Thick-walled; interior surface irregular. Back handmade, flattened. Rectangular vent, 0.085 × 0.028. Added: drapery swag at right side; right arm apparently never added (joining surface for arm at right shoulder seems perfectly flat and finished, no traces of fingers of right hand on lifted drapery swag); left forearm also may have been omitted. Tooling on folds.

Weight on right leg, right hip outthrust. Left leg bent, advanced, foot drawn back. Left upper arm raised; elbow rests on capital of fluted Ionic column. Nude torso is slender and shapely, with high, full breasts. Mantle secured atop capital under elbow; cloth falls in long, vertical folds between figure and column; upper edge is folded over and draped loosely across thighs; swag of cloth originally meant to be pulled away from right thigh by right hand. Deep looped folds from knee to ankle frame left leg; hem trails over feet in high-soled sandals or shoes. For probable position of left forearm, see **H251**. Probable mold sibling in lot 2249 (fabric 1). Possible mold sibling in lot 3230 (fabric 1). Probable later generation: **H250**. For possible workshop mates, see Workshop I, p. 346.

See pp. 170, 172–173, 174, 175, 178, 257, 275, 342, 344.

H250 Standing Aphrodite   Pl. 45

MF-11382. Lot 877. Preserved: shoulders to waist. Missing part of left forearm. Mended. P.H. 0.054 (size 2–3). Fabric 3, pinkish orange to orange-buff. Hollow. Back handmade, flattened. Added: drapery around back.

Probably a later generation of **H249**; fabric harder and thinner, interior neatly smoothed. Left forearm raised, presumably to lift mantle, which frames right shoulder and upper arm. A fragment in lot 3230 shows a left hand, with fingers curving downward, lifting drapery at an angle appropriate to this type. Probable mold sibling in lot 2210.

See pp. 173, 178, 344.

H251 Standing Aphrodite   Pl. 45

MF-13845. Lot 4386. Preserved: shoulders to left hip. Missing right arm, right side below arm. P.H. 0.01 (size 3). Fabric 1, orange-buff. White slip. Blue paint on pillar, mauve on mantle. Hollow. Back possibly molded, rounded. Top of rectangular vent preserved, 0.021 wide. Tooling on folds.

Similar in type to **H249**. Left forearm is raised, and hand lifts mantle, which falls behind figure; fingers not shown; hand may be muffled in cloth. For clearer detail, see probable mold sibling **H252**.

See p. 173.

H252 Standing Aphrodite   Pl. 45

MF-13844. Lot 2249. Preserved: shoulders to hips. Missing right arm, left forearm. P.H. 0.072 (size 3). Fabric 1, orange-buff to yellowish buff. White slip. Hollow. Back handmade, flattened. Round vent, diam. ca. 0.032. Added: mantle around back. Tooling on folds.

Similar in type to **H249**, but column is Doric, torso leans directly against column without intervening vertical folds, thrust of right hip more exaggerated. Torso is not strictly frontal but is turned in toward column. Short zigzag fold falls from top of column; mantle is draped around shoulders in back. Probable mold sibling: **H251**.

See p. 173.

H253 Standing Aphrodite(?)   Pl. 45

MF-13846. Lot 3222. Preserved: front–upper part of column, with drapery. P.H. 0.074 (size 3–4?). Fabric 5, orange-buff to orange. Hollow. Tooling on fluting, folds.

Fluted columnar support with short zigzag drapery fold falling from top; perhaps originally belonged to larger version of Aphrodite type similar to **H251** and **H252**.

See p. 173.

H254 Standing Aphrodite   Pl. 45

MF-10380. Lot 874. Preserved: shoulders to waist. Mended. P.H. 0.044 (size 2–3). Fabric 3, grayish buff to orange-buff. White slip. Blue paint on mantle. Hollow. Fairly thin-walled. Back handmade, flattened. Added: mantle behind right shoulder.

Similar in type to **H249**. Left elbow originally must have rested on support at level of rib cage; hand lifts mantle to just above shoulder level.

See pp. 173, 289.

H255 Standing Aphrodite(?)   Pl. 45

MF-13506. Lot 2247. Preserved: front–left thigh and upper calf, adjacent drapery. Mended. P.H. 0.086 (size 5). Surface treated with preservative; interior fabric 1, orange-buff, with sparse small gray, dark red, and white inclusions. Gilded, with yellow underpaint. Hollow. Added: projecting fold on drapery panel.

Left leg bent, foot probably drawn back. Looped fold at side of knee. Thin garment. Overfold hem lies diagonally across thigh; drapery panel down left side, with long fold projecting in front of it, is perhaps part of mantle originally held up and forward in left hand. Gilding well preserved along overfold hem; traces of it also above hem and on inner face of drapery panel. Large, well-made piece.

See p. 173.

H256 Standing Aphrodite   Pl. 45

MF-13880. Lot 4377. Preserved: front–hips to right foot and left ankle. P.H. 0.058 (size 2). Fabric 5, orange-buff to orange. White slip. Hollow.

Weight on right leg. Left leg bent, advanced. Torso nude; mantle covers both legs, with cascade of folds between legs as in type with one leg bare, **H260**. Row of looped folds down right leg; hem trails over foot with long toes in high-soled sandal; cloth smooth over left leg, looped fold at side of calf.

See pp. 173, 293.

H257 Standing Aphrodite or Leda(?)   Pl. 45

MF-11072. Lot 1962. Preserved: shoulders to right calf and left thigh. Missing forearms. Surface worn. H. 0.142 (size 3). Fabric 1, orange-buff. White slip. Hollow. Back handmade, flattened. Rectangular vent, ca. 0.06 × 0.02. Added: outer edge of drapery cascade at right side, folds over left arm. Tooling on folds.

Weight on left leg, left hip outthrust. Right leg bent, advanced. Nude torso is slender and shapely, with high, full breasts. Right arm raised high to lift mantle, which falls behind like a curtain, arches over the right thigh, and seems to be secured between the thighs, leaving the left leg bare; mantle covers left shoulder and lowered upper arm; left forearm originally held away from body. Pose and drapery are appropriate to either Aphrodite or Leda (if missing lower left side originally included a swan, as in **H261**). Possibly mechanically related: **H259**. Similarly draped raised arm in lot 1954.

See pp. 174, 175, 288, 292.

H258 Standing Aphrodite or Leda(?)   Pl. 46

MF-70-248. Lot 6641. Preserved: fragment of drapery; vertical edges at both sides are broken. Mended. P.H. 0.067 (size 4?). Fabric 2, orange-buff, with orange core. Back handmade, flattened.

Heavy curtain of drapery with curving folds, probably from the right side of a large figure, perhaps similar to **H257**.

See p. 175.

H259 Standing Aphrodite or Leda(?)   Pl. 45

MF-10593. Lot 892. Preserved: shoulders to waist, part of left hip. Missing right arm. P.H. 0.067 (size 3). Fabric fine, hard, grayish buff. Hollow. Back handmade, flattened.

Similar in type to **H257**, perhaps mechanically related. Modeling dull; mantle just visible down side of left upper arm.

See p. 174.

H260 Standing Aphrodite or Leda(?) Pl. 46

MF-13843. Lot 4352. Preserved: front–left hip and right thigh to feet; small part of back at lower right side. Missing front of feet. P.H. 0.112 (size 3). Fabric 2, light orange. Hollow. Thick-walled; interior surface irregular. Added: drapery beside right thigh. Tooling on folds.

Weight on left leg, left hip outthrust. Right leg bent, advanced, foot drawn back. Torso and left leg are nude. Mantle originally fell down right side; upper edge arches over right thigh, is secured between thighs, and falls between lower legs in a triangular cluster of deep folds; cloth clings to leg, seems transparent; U-shaped fold frames ankle. Pose of legs and mantle arrangement similar to **H257**, without any traces of a swan. Similar in type and scale: MF-10398 (lot 877). For possible workshop mates, see Workshop I, p. 346.

See pp. 174, 288.

H261 Standing Leda Pl. 46

MF-13875. Lot 4348. Preserved: hips to left ankle and right calf; small part of back. P.H. 0.063 (size 2–3). Fabric 1, orange-buff. Hollow. Back probably handmade, pared. Corner of vent preserved.

Weight on left leg. Right leg bent, advanced. Left hand just visible, supports body of swan against left hip. Nude torso; mantle cascade beside left leg, presumably from shoulder and arm, shows zigzag fold; at right side, upper edge of mantle is folded down and arches over thigh, covering right leg; mantle originally must have been lifted by right hand, as in **H257**. Modeling dull.

See pp. 174, 175.

H262 Standing Aphrodite(?) Pl. 46

MF-13849. Lot 3222. Preserved: thighs to base. Missing large chip in front, most of left lower leg; bottom of base chipped. Mended. P.H. 0.082 (size 2–3). Fabric 3, pinkish orange to orange-buff. White slip. Hollow. Back handmade, flattened. Bottom of rectangular vent preserved, 0.026 wide. Added: drapery swag across thighs. Tooling on folds.

Figure leans against a smooth-faced pillar, triangular in section. Swag of mantle folds across thighs; narrow cascade of folds down front of pillar; looped folds down bent left leg. Slippers have divided toe. Base is shallow, rectangular in front, rounded in back, with molding at bottom.

See p. 175.

H263 Standing Aphrodite or Leda(?) Pl. 46

MF-13838. Lot 4417. Preserved: head and part of neck, adjacent drapery. Missing nose; surface worn. P.H. 0.023 (size 2–3). Fabric 2, orange-buff to orange, with gray core. White slip. Solid. Back handmade, flattened. Tooling on hair, folds.

Head with drapery behind, as if lifted high by right hand. Face oval to oblong, with triangular forehead. Features indistinct, but eyes are large, prominent. Coiffure parted at center; long locks of hair at sides of neck.

See p. 175.

H264 Running Leda(?) Pl. 46

MF-13851. Lot 2249. Preserved: front–shoulders to right breast and left hip, left upper arm, adjacent drapery; small part of back at left side; front chipped. P.H. 0.064 (size 3). Fabric 2, light orange, with gray core. White slip. Hollow.

Back flat; straight lines on surface may be traces of a flat-edged tool, such as a chisel. Added: part of drapery at left side.

Left upper arm raised to lift mantle. Thin chiton, girded at natural waistline, is unfastened at right shoulder, partly exposing breast. Broken edge of mantle below arm turns inward, suggesting that the mantle was blown forward by the movement of the figure.

See pp. 17, 175.

H265 Standing Aphrodite with Eros(?) Pl. 46

MF-70-66. Lot 2210. Preserved: small part of drapery cascade, head and upper torso of child. Mended; surface chipped. P.H. 0.072 (size 5?). Fabric 4, creamy buff. White slip. Back handmade. Tooling on face.

Child stands(?) in front of a heavy cascade of drapery at the left side of a figure; perhaps represents Eros beside a standing Aphrodite. Child is gnomelike in appearance. Head deeply set between shoulders. Eyes staring. Nose flat. Lips thick, smiling. No remains of wings.

See pp. 175, 181.

H266 Standing Aphrodite(?) Pl. 46

MF-11845. Lot 2106. Preserved: base of neck to knees. Missing left arm, right forearm. P.H. 0.098 (size 3). Fabric 1, orange-buff to orange. White slip. Solid. Back molded, rounded. Added: right arm, hair in back. Tooling on hair, back.

Left leg slightly advanced, right hip outthrust. Right upper arm extended to side; hand originally may have arranged hair. Nude torso is slender, with high breasts. Made from a "doll's" torso, twisted into a less rigid pose. Long locks of hair in back.

See pp. 58, 171, 175, 197.

H267 Aphrodite or maenad(?) Pl. 46

MF-12121. Lot 4356. Preserved: neck to knees. Missing right arm, left elbow and forearm, drapery over left shoulder, bottom of drapery cascade at left side, part of drapery at right side. P.H. 0.073 (size 2). Fabric 4, creamy buff to pinkish orange. White slip. Solid. Back handmade, flattened. Added: arms, mantle. Tooling on folds; paring marks on thighs.

Nude torso leans to right. Right leg advanced. Left upper arm extended to side. Mantle is draped over left arm, drops down left side in wide panel, crosses diagonally in back, reappears swirling beside right thigh. Pose and falling drapery suggest strong movement. Slender torso, with small, high breasts; probably made from a "doll's" torso.

See pp. 171, 175–176.

H268 Standing Aphrodite(?) Pl. 46

MF-13809. Lot 4409. Preserved: shoulders to thighs. Missing right arm, most of left arm, part of drapery in back and at left side. P.H. 0.074 (size 3). Fabric 2, orange-buff to orange. Solid. Back molded, rounded. Added: mantle. Tooling on folds.

Right arm originally may have been raised. Mantle is draped over left shoulder and arm and across left hip to right thigh. Made from a "doll's" torso; mantle originally covered much of back but is now broken away to show "doll's" buttocks beneath. Similar, smaller figurine, with drapery falling from right shoulder, in lot 3411.

See pp. 58, 175.

H269 Seated Aphrodite   Pl. 46

MF-11837. Lot 2111. Preserved: shoulders to feet. Missing arms, part of bottom at right side, most of drapery beside thighs, shell background. P.H. 0.07 (size 1–2). Fabric 1, light orange. Solid. Back handmade, rounded. Added: folds beside right hip. Tooling on folds.

Seated with legs together, feet drawn back. Nude torso; thin mantle lies across thighs and spreads around feet; arms originally lowered, with hands pulling mantle to either side. Rather boyish, "doll"-like torso. Complete type preserved in Athens, National Archaeological Museum, inv. no. 4164 (Winter, *Typen* II, p. 202, no. 1), shows Aphrodite seated in front of a shell (Pl. 79). **H270** is a fragment of such a shell.

See p. 176.

H270 Shell, from figurine of seated Aphrodite(?)   Pl. 47

MF-73-111. Lot 73-108. Preserved: fragment broken all around. Max.P.Dim. 0.061. Fabric 2, orange-buff. White slip. Red paint. Solid. Back handmade.

Curved ribs of shell preserved; clay is smeared at convergence of ribs, as if a figure originally was attached there. Perhaps from right side of figurine such as **H269**. Other shell fragments in lots 3206, 4377 show scalloped edges.

See p. 176.

H271 Seated(?) Aphrodite or Leda(?)   Pl. 47

MF-13751. Lot 2249. Preserved: head to right side of lap. Missing entire left side of torso, most of right arm, adjacent drapery; face and hair chipped; surface cracked. P.H. 0.101 (size 3). Fabric 2, light orange. White slip. Nearly solid. Back handmade, rounded. Added: mantle, hair. Tooling on hair, folds.

Uncertain whether figure is seated or if upper torso just leans forward (crease of flesh across abdomen); perhaps perched on a high seat. Right arm originally extended to side, probably to lift mantle, which covers head and forms an arched background for nude torso; at lower break, mantle lies across lap, presumably covered legs. Breasts widely set, small, prominent. Head relatively small; chipping of hair in front reveals outline of face mold. Face oval, with low forehead; full cheeks. Eyes strongly downturned, widely set; both lids defined, lower lid puffy. Lips full. Hair piled into high, rounded peak at top, single long lock of hair to shoulder. Probable mold sibling of head: KT-10-51 from the Potters' Quarter (*Corinth* XV, ii, p. 130, no. 35, pl. 25; one from Pitsa mentioned there). Possible mold siblings of head: **H272**; one in lot 1964. Possible earlier generation of head: head of **C282**; MF-11016 (lot 1953).

See p. 177.

H272 Head of Aphrodite or Leda(?)   Pl. 47

MF-13943. Lot 2156. Preserved: head, neck, part of left shoulder. P.H. 0.057 (size 3). Fabric 1, orange-buff. Hollow. Back handmade, rounded. Added: hair. Tooling on hair.

Bare shoulder suggests that torso was at least partly nude. Veil or mantle covers head. Face oval, with low forehead; full cheeks. Features indistinct. Hair piled into high peak at top; long lock of hair frames shoulder; curls gouged. Possible mold siblings: **H271**; one in lot 1964.

See p. 177.

H273 Head of mounted Aphrodite(?)   Pl. 47

MF-13853. Lot 4377. Preserved: head and neck, part of right shoulder, arc of drapery behind. Surface worn. Max.P.Dim. 0.065 (size 2–3?). Fabric 1, orange-buff, with grayish core. White slip. Head solid, with thin, handmade panel behind. Tooling on hair.

Head tilted forward slightly. Face round to oval. Features obliterated. Coiffure rounded, with high, punched topknot in front. Possible pendant earrings. Background panel is probably a windblown mantle.

See p. 177.

H274 Seated nymph   Pl. 47

MF-10382. Lots 874, 6215. Preserved: front–shoulders to base; back–shoulders to hips. Missing part of seat at right side, right thigh. Mended. Right thigh and part of lap restored in plaster. P.H. 0.14 (size 3). Fabric 4, buff to greenish buff. White slip. Hollow. Thick-walled. Back handmade, rounded. Top of irregularly shaped vent preserved. Added: seat, feet, base. Tooling on folds, hands.

Perched on a high, rocky seat. Figure shows torsion, with legs toward viewer's right, torso frontal. Left knee and foot higher than right. Right hand leans on seat behind hip. Left hand relaxes on lap. Torso is nude; mantle covers left arm and shoulder, crosses diagonally in back, reappears on seat beside right hip, is draped over legs. End of mantle is bunched between left arm and torso; pointed fold falls into lap; catenaries between thighs; looped folds from right lower leg to left knee. Torso is slender, straight-sided, with narrow shoulders, high, full breasts. Base on which feet rest is part of rocky seat; feet wear pointed slippers. Probable mold siblings: MF-11842 (lot 2111, preserves right thigh); one in lot 2249. Probable later generation: **H275**.

See pp. 178, 179, 180, 182, 294, 296.

H275 Seated nymph   Pl. 47

MF-69-373. Lot 6215. Preserved: shoulders to waist. P.H. 0.041 (size 2). Fabric 1, orange-buff, with blue-gray core, burned(?). White slip. Hollow. Thick-walled. Back handmade, flattened. Tooling on folds.

Probably later generation of **H274**, poorer workmanship. Edge of mantle frames right upper arm, as in **H277**.

See p. 178.

H276 Seated nymph(?)   Pl. 47

MF-13886. Lot 874. Preserved: front–lap to ankles, right hand. P.H. 0.069 (size 3). Fabric 2, orange-buff. White slip. Hollow. Tooling on folds, hand.

Left leg advanced. Right hand is relaxed in lap, reversing pose of **H274**; last three fingers curled under. Two flat, overlapping folds across lap; looped folds from right knee to left lower leg.

See p. 178.

H277 Seated nymph   Pl. 47

MF-11296. Lots 877, 1993. Preserved: front–shoulders to base; back–shoulders to hips. Missing forearms, part of drapery at sides. Mended; right knee chipped. P.H. 0.098 (size 2). Fabric 2, orange-buff. White slip. Hollow. Back handmade, flat, surface irregular. Added: forearms, drapery around back, folds across lap. Tooling on folds.

Similar in type to **H274**, but legs more frontal, slightly parted, both feet at the same level. Left shoulder slightly higher than right. Right hand does not rest in lap; forearm perhaps originally extended forward. Mantle forms an arched, possibly billowing background behind shoulders and right upper arm; overlapping folds across lap.

See p. 178.

H278 Seated nymph   Pl. 47

MF-10636. Lot 896. Preserved: shoulders to base. Missing forearms, lower part of seat in back. P.H. 0.053 (size 1–2). Fabric 3, buff to orange-buff. White slip. Solid to waist, hollow below. Back handmade, flat to waist. Upper part of rectangular vent preserved, 0.013 wide. Added: seat, drapery around back and across lap. Tooling on folds.

Similar to **H277**, smaller. Figure sits more deeply on rock; legs to viewer's left. Both forearms originally extended forward. Drapery spreads over rock beside left thigh; looped folds from left knee to right lower leg.

See p. 178.

H279 Seated(?) Aphrodite or nymph(?)   Pl. 47

MF-13859. Lot 1993. Preserved: waist to hips. P.H. 0.055 (size 4). Fabric 2, light orange. Solid. Back flattened; figure is only 0.015 thick at hips. Tooling on folds.

Perhaps originally half-reclined on separately made rocky seat. Transparent chiton reveals navel; belt visible at upper break, from which deeply tooled, shadowed folds fan out over abdomen. Thick roll of upper edge of mantle draped around hips. Large, well-made piece.

See pp. 178–179.

H280 Seated Aphrodite or nymph(?)   Pl. 47

MF-11407. Lot 877. Preserved: front–shoulders to lap. Missing left arm. P.H. 0.115 (size 4). Fabric 4, creamy buff, interior yellowish buff. Hollow. Thin-walled. Added: hair on shoulders, drapery, right arm and hand. Unusual method of attaching head, with lowered margin around hole in neck, requiring corresponding preparation of tenon. Tooling on folds, hands, hair.

Figure is not deeply seated, perhaps perched on rock. Figure shows torsion; seated with legs toward viewer's right, torso frontal. Right arm at side; hand is lightly clenched and punched through, as if to grasp an object. Left shoulder and breast higher than right, suggesting that left arm originally was raised. Proportions are matronly, with full breasts, wide hips. Drapery was added to nude torso; transparent chiton slips from right shoulder; navel and fold of flesh above it are visible through cloth; sleeve fastenings just visible on arm. Folds rendered by curving diagonal ridges drop from left shoulder to right upper arm; looped fold drops into lap from point of left breast. Heavier mantle is draped across lap. Two long locks of hair on each shoulder, diagonally slashed.

See pp. 15, 179.

H281 Seated Aphrodite or nymph(?)   Pl. 47

MF-13754. Lot 3217. Preserved: front–shoulders to lap; back–shoulders to waist. Missing arms from biceps down. P.H. 0.082 (size 3). Fabric 1, creamy buff to pinkish orange, slightly burned. White slip. Red paint on hair. Hollow. Fairly thick-walled. Back handmade, flattened. Added: hair on right shoulder and back. Tooling on hair.

Figure shows torsion; seated with legs to viewer's left, upper torso frontal and leaning slightly forward. Traces of long locks of hair only on right shoulder, suggesting that head may have turned to viewer's right. Pose may have been that of **H274** reversed. Left shoulder is raised and slightly pulled back, suggesting that left hand originally may have leaned on seat behind hip. Figure has broad shoulders, full breasts. Clinging, transparent chiton drops from left shoulder; navel and fold of flesh above it are visible through cloth. Folds rendered (in mold) by ridges over the nude torso: curving diagonals from right shoulder to left upper arm define upper edge of chiton; catenary between breasts; two looped folds drop from right breast to abdomen; vertical ridge drops from left breast to hip. At lower break, traces of mantle over lap. Well-made piece.

See pp. 179, 180, 184, note 410.

H282 Seated Aphrodite or nymph(?)   Pl. 48

MF-14102A, B. Lots 874, 878. Preserved: (A) front–left leg, thigh to calf, with drapery between legs and perhaps part of right leg; (B) nonjoining fragment, probably of rocky seat, with drapery. Mended. P.H. (A) 0.09; Max.P.Dim. (B) 0.045 (size 3). Fabric 4, greenish buff. White slip. Violet paint on drapery. Hollow. Back of (B) handmade, rounded. Added: drapery on (B). Tooling on folds.

Perched on a high, rocky seat, with legs toward viewer's left. Deeply modeled cascade of zigzag folds (probably a mantle) between parted legs; cloth collapses onto projecting surface ca. 0.02 below feet. Contour of left leg bent at right angle is clear beneath cloth. Right lower leg may have been advanced. Crumpled drapery on rock (B) probably belongs to left of figure (correct orientation of fragment unknown). Well-made piece.

See pp. 14, 180.

H283 Draped figurine, perhaps a seated nymph   Pl. 48

MF-69-375. Lot 6214. Preserved: front–left foot and adjacent drapery. Missing small toe; edges of drapery, sandal sole chipped. P.H. 0.041 (size 4). Fabric 1, orange-buff to orange. Hollow. Added: drapery at viewer's left side. Tooling on folds, toes.

Left foot seems to carry no weight but rests diagonally against a support. Toes long, big toe shorter than middle toes; toenails rendered. Low-soled sandal with divided toe, longer than foot. Drapery, probably a mantle, trails heavily over instep. At viewer's left, wide fall of cloth is folded double, suggesting a heavy collapse from above.

See p. 180.

H284 Seated(?) draped female figurine   Pl. 48

MF-13868. Lot 3230. Preserved: front–right lower thigh to foot, with adjacent drapery. Missing front of foot. Mended; knee chipped. P.H. 0.089 (size 3–4). Fabric 1, orange-buff, with orange core. Hollow.

Right leg well advanced, with drapery rendered on inner side; thigh slanted, as if figure perched on high seat. Mantle falls smoothly over leg to ankle, forms cuffed fold. Folds of mantle and hem of garment beneath are raised diagonally upward at right, suggesting that drapery either was lifted or spread over seat. Foot probably in fairly high-soled sandal. Large, well-made piece.

See p. 180.

H285　Seated draped female figurine　　　　Pl. 48

MF-13830. Lot 2249. Preserved: front–right leg, with adjacent drapery; part of right side. P.H. 0.077 (size 3). Fabric 1, orange-buff. White slip. Hollow. Added: foot. Tooling on folds.

Right leg somewhat advanced. Mantle falls smoothly over leg to ankle; looped folds from inner side of leg probably to left knee. Side is flat; narrow, vertical folds of hem of garment beneath are roughly tooled at front and side. Foot in pointed slipper.

See p. 180.

H286　Seated(?) draped female figurine　　　　Pl. 48

MF-13831. Lot 878. Preserved: front–right ankle and foot, with adjacent drapery. P.H. 0.052 (size 4). Fabric 1, harder, grayish buff. White slip. Hollow. Thick-walled. Tooling on folds and foot.

Right foot must have been well advanced, since ankle is wrapped closely on both sides with drapery; probably belonged to seated figure. Looped fold around ankle. Mantle hem falls to instep; pleated hem of garment beneath is visible. Fairly high-soled sandal shaped around long toes. Large, well-made piece.

See p. 180.

OTHER DEITIES (EROS, ARTEMIS, ATHENA, NIKE)

H287　Seated Eros　　　　Pl. 48

MF-69-349. Lot 6214. Preserved: shoulders to knees, small part of seat between legs. Missing left arm, wings; right elbow chipped. P.H. 0.08 (size 2–3). Fabric 1, orange-buff, with ochre core. White slip. Solid. Back molded, rounded. Added: wings, seat, right arm and hand. Tooling on groin, buttocks, drapery, hand. Slots cut in back for insertion of wings. Pencil hole in left buttock for venting, must have cut through seat as well.

Represented as an adolescent or preadolescent boy; abdomen rather soft, childlike. Right arm at side; hand rests on thigh. Left arm originally raised; left wing probably raised as well, since left slot is higher than right. Seat is backless; cloth draped over it visible between legs.

See pp. 18, 181–182.

H288　Seated youth (Eros or Pan?)　　　　Pl. 48

MF-12886. Lot 4404. Preserved: left shoulder and right side of waist to feet, right hand, rocky seat. Missing right arm; back and front of torso chipped; surface worn. P.H. 0.112 (size 2–3). Fabric 1, orange-buff to orange. White slip. Solid; reduced in depth. Back handmade, flat. Added: drapery, part of seat. Tooling on folds, rocks.

Nude youth perched on high, rocky seat, turned three-fourths to the left; legs dangling. Left knee bent; ankle tucked under right leg. Left hand rests on knee, perhaps holding something against leg; right hand on rock behind hip. Drapery cascades over rocks at right side. Poor workmanship.

See pp. 182, 200.

H289　Eros　　　　Pl. 48

MF-11919. Lot 2107. Preserved: front–head and upper part of wings; back–head to waist; front chipped. P.H. 0.046 (size 2–3). Fabric 3, orange-buff. White slip. Hollow. Back handmade, rounded. Added: wings, polos, hair. Tooling on wings, face, hair.

Original pose uncertain. Face distorted in molding, clumsily retouched. Long, curling locks of hair to neck. High, slightly flaring polos. Diagonal slashes along upper edges of wings in front. Poor workmanship.

See pp. 182, 274.

H290　Flying Eros　　　　Pl. 48

MF-68-347. Lot 5712. Preserved: head and part of back; chin chipped. P.H. 0.046 (size 2–3). Fabric similar to 1, harder, slightly sandy, orange-buff, interior pinkish buff, with small sparkling inclusions. White slip. Red paint on hair. Hollow. Back probably handmade. Added: hair at sides and back. Tooling on hair.

Represented as a baby. Head thrown back; figure probably was flying, as **H291**, but wings are not preserved. Face oval to round, with high, triangular forehead. Eyes large, opened wide; both lids defined. Nose wide, flat. Lips parted, smiling. Hair plaited back from forehead; delicately tooled curls down sides and back. Possible earlier generation: head of girl **H347**. Facial type and workmanship of hair similar to head of baby **H348**, perhaps from the same workshop (Workshop E, p. 345). Well-made piece.

See pp. 181, 182, 193, 198.

H291　Flying Eros　　　　Pl. 48

MF-13989. Lot 2239. Preserved: head, right side of torso, part of right wing and upper arm. P.H. 0.035 (size 1–2). Fabric 1, orange-buff to orange. White slip. Solid. Back handmade. Added: arm, wing, hair at sides. Tooling on hair.

Represented as a baby. Head thrown back and slightly to right. Right arm originally extended forward. Face round. Eyes large. Nose wide, flat. Lips smiling. Curly locks of hair fall to shoulders. Breaks below right arm indicate attachment to another figure or an object. Probably complete type was similar to **H290** but smaller, of poorer workmanship.

See pp. 181, 182.

H292　Standing Artemis(?)　　　　Pl. 48

MF-11895. Lot 2107. Preserved: head to hips; top of head and hand chipped. P.H. 0.045 (size 1–2). Fabric 1, orange-buff, slightly burned(?). White slip. Solid. All parts rendered in same mold. Back handmade, flat. Tooling on folds.

Left arm at side. Right hand raised to head, attached to head with panel of clay. Peplos is belted at natural waistline; overfold falls to hips; fluttering of overfold hem suggests that figure is in movement. Face oblong. Features indistinct. Poor workmanship.

See p. 183.

H293　Standing Artemis(?)　　　　Pl. 48

MF-13885. Lot 2035. Preserved: front–shoulders to rib cage, object behind left shoulder. P.H. 0.042 (size 3). Fabric 5, light orange, with gray core. Hollow. Tooling on folds.

Upper arms at sides. Narrow baldric diagonally across peplos from right shoulder to left side; object behind left shoulder may be a quiver.

See p. 183.

H294　Standing Athena(?)　　　　Pl. 48

MF-11348. Lot 878. Preserved: front–left hip, hand. P.H. 0.034 (size 2–3?). Fabric fine, fired hard, grayish buff, interior gray. White slip. Hollow. Added: hand, owl. Tooling on folds, hand.

Left hand holds small owl at hip; owl turns head to left. Garment has narrow folds; belt visible at upper break.

See p. 183.

H295 Flying Nike   Pl. 48

MF-14056. Lot 2066. Preserved: thighs to hem. Missing feet; drapery chipped. P.H. 0.075 (size 3). Fabric 5, light orange, slightly burned(?). Nearly solid. Back molded, flattened. Added: folds at sides of legs.

Figure in movement; steps forward on right leg. Folds of skirt sweep back in deep curves, revealing contours of legs; hem of skirt flutters around ankles. Similar in type: MF-71-42 from Forum Southwest (Pl. 76).

See pp. 183–184, 274.

H296 Flying Nike(?)   Pl. 48

MF-12122. Lot 2249. Missing head. P.H. 0.035 (size 1). Fabric 2, light orange. White slip. Solid. Back handmade, flat. Bottom slightly concave.

Figure in movement; steps forward on right leg. Right hand on hip, gathers cluster of folds. Left hand lifts mantle above shoulder. Round base. Little detail, but chiton seems to be girded high. Another miniature Nike: MF-70-40 in the Corinth collection.

See p. 184.

H297 Flying Nike(?)   Pl. 48

MF-14039. Lot 3222. Preserved: shoulders to thighs. Missing arms; surface worn. P.H. 0.035 (size 1–2). Fabric 5, orange-buff. Solid. Back handmade, flattened. Added: overfold hem all around.

Left leg advanced(?). Overfold of chiton or peplos flares out around hips, is higher at right side; faint vertical skirt folds below. Figure is probably in movement. Perhaps made from a "doll's" torso.

See pp. 166, 184.

H298 Flying Nike(?)   Pl. 48

MF-14038. Lot 2249. Preserved: front–right shoulder and left breast to thighs. Missing arms; surface worn. P.H. 0.052 (size 2). Fabric 5, orange. White slip. Hollow. Added: overfold hem.

Right leg advanced. Slender torso. Chiton or peplos belted fairly high; fold hangs over belt at left side, suggesting that garment slips down from left shoulder. Overfold falls to top of thighs; hem flares out, suggesting that figure is in movement. There are no folds on the thighs, but an area of clay beside the left thigh seems to be part of a skirt. Perhaps made from a "doll's" torso.

See pp. 166, 184.

MALE FIGURINES: NUDE, SEMIDRAPED, AND DRAPED

H299 Standing nude youth   Pl. 49

MF-11912. Lot 2107. Preserved: head to right calf and left ankle. Missing large fragment of thighs and groin in front. Mended. P.H. 0.11 (size 2–3). Fabric 1, yellowish buff. White slip. Red paint on hair, bright pink on flesh. Hollow. All parts rendered in same mold. Back molded, rounded. Tooling on hand.

Weight on right leg, right hip outthrust. Left leg advanced; legs joinedz with panel of clay. Both arms at sides. Narrow, sloping shoulders. Head and neck unusually deep in profile. Face oval to round, with low, sloping forehead; receding chin. Eyes widely set. Nose wide. Mouth small; lips smiling. Long locks of hair fall to shoulders. General impression of softness, almost femininity. Related to female figurine **H1** in sloping facial profile, depth of head and neck, pose of right arm. For possible workshop mates, see Workshop H, p. 346.

See pp. 119–120, 159, 185, 186, 188, 189, 190, 200, 258.

H300 Standing semidraped youth   Pl. 49

MF-12536. Lot 3217. Preserved: shoulders to right foot, left ankle, part of base at right side. Missing right arm, left forearm and hand with adjacent drapery and part of support. Mended. Surface worn. P.H. 0.131 (size 2–3). Fabric 5, orange to orange-buff, with grayish buff core. Hollow. Back molded(?), rounded, pared. Irregular, rectangular vent, ca. 0.03 × 0.015, at left side. Added: base. Tooling on folds.

Similar to **H299** in pose, proportions, and in panel between legs. Left shoulder higher than right; left elbow originally leaned on support. Mantle is draped over left shoulder and arm, down back, and over support. Base rounded in front with molding at top, flattened and plain in back.

See pp. 185, 186, 188.

H301 Standing nude youth   Pl. 49

MF-10677. Lot 1945. Preserved: base of neck to left calf and right knee. Missing left shoulder and arm, right forearm, part of drapery background. P.H. 0.065 (size 2). Fabric 2, orange. White slip. Nearly solid. Back handmade, slightly concave. Added: right arm, drapery. Tooling on folds.

Weight on right leg; exaggerated outward thrust of right hip. Left leg advanced; pose of legs similar to **H299**. Right forearm originally seems to have been extended to side, holding out mantle, which serves as background for nude torso. Long lock of hair on right shoulder. Piece is relieflike, with little anatomical detail. Similar in type and scale: MF-3882 in the Corinth collection (*Corinth* XII, p. 52, no. 349, pl. 31).

See pp. 185, 186, 188.

H302 Standing semidraped youth or boy   Pl. 49

MF-10671. Lot 6506. Preserved: shoulders to right ankle and left calf. Mended; arms and back chipped. P.H. 0.109 (size 2). Fabric 2, orange-buff to orange. White slip. Pink paint on torso, red on drapery. Hollow. Back molded, rounded. Round vent, diam. ca. 0.015. Added: right arm, grapes. Tooling on folds, grapes, navel.

Weight on left leg, left hip outthrust. Right leg advanced. Right arm at side; hand curves in, holds bunch of grapes against thigh. Left arm bent; hand behind hip. Mantle covers left shoulder and hand; upper edge rolled and draped across abdomen, seems to be anchored at left hip by hand, from which a narrow cascade of folds falls to hem; triangular overfold in front, corner weighted or knotted; hem slopes from right ankle to left calf. Nude upper torso is soft, rather childish; shoulders rounded, sloping; deep navel, somewhat right of center. Similar in type, possibly mechanically related: MF-1904 from the South Stoa (*Corinth* XII, p. 51, no. 336, pl. 30, larger, holding tragic mask).

See pp. 185, 186, 188, 298, 335.

H303 Standing semidraped youth or boy   Pl. 49

MF-12530. Lot 3206. Preserved: shoulders to hips. Missing drapery in front, arms. Mended; surface chipped. Small areas of chest restored in plaster. P.H. 0.192 (size 4–5). Fabric 1, greenish buff; overfired. White slip. Hollow. Thick-walled. Back molded, rounded. Added: mantle, nipple. Tooling on folds in back.

Stands with pelvis forward, shoulders back. Mantle originally draped across hips in front; white slip on left hip suggests hip was nude; folds preserved at back and sides, but arrangement of mantle is uncertain. Abdomen protrudes.

See pp. 185–186.

H304 Standing semidraped youth or boy   Pl. 49

MF-70-227. Lot 6506. Preserved: shoulders to hips. Surface worn. P.H. 0.056 (size 2). Fabric 1, orange-buff. White slip. Hollow. Back handmade, rounded. Top of rectangular vent preserved, 0.023 wide.

Similar to **H302** in pose and drapery arrangement, as far as preserved; workmanship poorer; right hand at side. Roll of drapery over abdomen shows two thick folds; looped fold around left wrist.

See pp. 185, 186.

H305 Standing semidraped male figurine   Pl. 49

MF-12143. Lot 4349. Preserved: shoulders to calves. Surface eroded. P.H. 0.111 (size 2–3). Fabric 5, orange-buff to orange. Hollow. Back handmade, flattened. Irregular, oval vent, 0.025 × 0.019. Added: right arm with drapery, folds beside left hip. Tooling on folds.

Weight on left leg, left hip outthrust. Right leg probably bent. Right arm at side; hand curved in at thigh. Left arm bent; hand behind hip. Mantle is draped over shoulders, arms, hands, and around midriff, leaving only upper chest nude. Cluster of folds between left arm and torso; cloth anchored at left hip by hand, from which falls a short cascade of folds. Diagonal folds from right knee to left thigh. Poor workmanship; folds roughly tooled; no anatomical detail.

See pp. 185, 186.

H306 Standing semidraped male figurine   Pl. 49

MF-13435. Lot 3206. Preserved: shoulders to knees. Missing right forearm; front chipped. P.H. 0.073 (size 2). Fabric 1, orange-buff. White slip. Nearly solid. Back handmade, irregular. Added: right arm, left forearm, drapery. Tooling on folds.

Right leg slightly advanced. Right arm bent, forearm originally may have been held across waist, with hand at abdomen, where there is a scar. Left arm bent; forearm extended forward. Mantle is draped around waist, covers left shoulder, arm, and hand. Cloth drops from hand in flat, triangular fold, which terminates in zigzags at bottom. Diagonal folds from right knee to left hip. Poor workmanship; no anatomical detail.

See p. 186.

H307 Standing semidraped male figurine   Pl. 49

MF-11897. Lot 2107. Preserved: front–shoulders to right thigh and left knee; back–shoulders to waist. Missing arms, sides. Mended. P.H. 0.073 (size 2). Fabric 5, orange to ochre. White slip. Hollow. Back handmade, flattened.

Weight on right leg, right hip outthrust. Left shoulder much higher than right. Mantle is draped around waist, wrapped around left arm below biceps; looped folds around hips. Poor workmanship; no anatomical detail.

See pp. 185, 186.

H308 Standing semidraped male figurine   Pl. 50

MF-11070. Lot 1962. Preserved: shoulders to left hip, to waist at right side, to hips in back. Missing right arm, left forearm. Mended. P.H. 0.115 (size 3). Fabric 1, orange-buff. White slip. Hollow. Back handmade, flattened. Added: folds over and below forearm, locks of hair in back. Hole for attachment of left forearm. Tooling on folds.

Left forearm originally extended forward. Mantle covers left shoulder, is gathered in a roll across waist, and draped over left arm to fall at side. Evenly stacked folds over shoulder; folds otherwise irregular and rather crudely tooled. Modeling of nude torso is broad, rather geometric. Long locks of hair in back.

See p. 186.

H309 Standing semidraped male figurine   Pl. 50

MF-10448. Lot 878. Preserved: shoulders to ankles. Missing right arm, left wrist and hand; left shoulder chipped in back. P.H. 0.21 (size 3–4). Fabric 1, creamy buff. White slip. Hollow. Back probably molded, flattened; back looks handmade, but interior shows overlapping strips of clay, as if pressed into a mold. Added: left forearm, projecting upper edge of mantle at front and back, folds over shoulder, open edges at left. Tooling on folds.

Stands with pelvis forward, shoulders back; figure reduced in depth. Left leg advanced; knee bent. Left arm bent; forearm extended forward. Mantle draped around right hip, across chest to left shoulder and upper arm. Diagonal upper edge of mantle is a projecting ridge; two flat strips represent open edges along left leg. Crudely cut folds radiate from left hip down right leg; looped folds at outer side of left knee, inner side of ankle. Modeling of nude chest is broad. Long locks of hair on shoulders. Similar in technique and workmanship to **H310** but without filling inside.

See pp. 15, 186.

H310 Standing semidraped male statuette   Pl. 50

MF-12899. Lot 2107. Preserved: shoulders to feet. Missing right hip, most of thighs, part of right lower leg, part of chest at upper left side, right arm, part of left forearm. Mended; surface chipped. P.H. 0.34 (size 4). Fabric 1, orange-buff. Hollow; interior stuffed with irregular lumps of clay. Back probably molded, flattened; back looks rough, handmade, but interior shows overlapping strips of clay, as if pressed into a mold. Possible hole cut in plinth for venting. Added: drapery at front, back, and left side; left forearm, feet, base. Tooling on folds; marks of narrow, flat planing instrument and toothed instrument inside.

Figure reduced in depth, strengthened by interior filling and balanced on flat plinth. Weight on left leg. Right foot drawn back slightly; knee originally must have been bent. Left forearm extended forward; elbow rests on pillar support. Upper edge of mantle rolled and draped around right hip to waist at left side; cloth draped from back over left shoulder and upper arm, with narrow folds in front of pillar. Crudely cut folds radiate from left hip to right ankle; looped folds around both ankles. No anatomical detail on nude chest. Plaque base. Similar in technique and workmanship to **H309**.

See p. 186.

H311   Seated draped youth   Pl. 50

MF-70-59. Lot 6503. Preserved: head to base. Missing part of lap, most of back, left foot, right ankle, adjacent areas of base. Mended. Missing portions restored in plaster. P.H. 0.12 (size 2–3). Fabric 3, pinkish buff to buff. White slip. Hollow, including head. All parts rendered in same mold. Back: figure molded, base handmade, rounded. Added: hair, drapery around face and at right side over seat, protruding rocks at left side of base. Tooling on folds, hair.

Published: Bookidis and Fisher 1972, p. 316, pl. 62:c.

Seated frontally, head turned to left. Sloping lap, right knee higher than left. Both arms bent; right hand rests on knee; left hand pulls mantle across chin. Mantle is wrapped around figure and fastened at right shoulder with round button; part of right upper arm in short-sleeved garment is just visible between open edges of mantle; right hand grasps edge of mantle at thigh. Long, looped folds fall from right shoulder, across lap, to left thigh and knee. Oval face. Features indistinct. Coiffure is a cap of curls applied with a spatula. Rocky base. Well-composed piece but impression dull, retouch clumsy. Probable mold sibling: MF-13904 in the Corinth collection. Probable later generation in lot 4349 (fabric 2). Similar in type: MF-13900 in the Corinth collection, imported.

See pp. 182, 186–187, 293.

H312   Seated draped male figurine   Pl. 50

MF-10395. Lot 877. Preserved: right leg and part of lap, with drapery at side. Mended; foot and ankle chipped. P.H. 0.098 (size 4). Fabric 2, light orange. White slip. Hollow; foot and ankle solid. Possibly handmade. Tooling on drapery.

Lap is smooth, flat; figure originally deeply seated. Hem of garment reaches lower calf. Ankle is thick; foot perhaps booted. Folds roughly incised, pulling down towards the break.

See p. 187.

H313   Seated draped youth(?)   Pl. 50

MF-69-387. Lot 6214. Preserved: front–lap to ankles, right hand, part of seat at right side. Surface cracked. P.H. 0.062 (size 2–3). Fabric 1, orange-buff to orange. Hollow. Added: garment hem.

Left ankle crossed over right. Right hand rests on thigh. Garment smooth, reaches knees, probably a youth's tunic. Seat probably block shaped. Summary workmanship.

See p. 187.

ISOLATED MALE HEADS

H314   Head of youth   Pl. 51

MF-73-77. No context. Preserved: head and part of neck. P.H. 0.042 (size 3–4). Fabric 1, orange-buff. White slip. Red paint on hair. Solid. Back probably molded, rounded. Added: hair in front. Tooling on hair.

Face oval to oblong, with high, triangular forehead. Eyes level; upper lids defined; browridge prominent. Nose large, close to upper lip. Mouth distorted in molding. Short curls, close to head; curved incisions over cranium, as on **H315**; perhaps from the same workshop.

See p. 187.

H315   Head of youth   Pl. 51

MF-13944. Lot 2048. Preserved: head and neck; face chipped. P.H. 0.041 (size 3–4). Fabric 1, buff to orange-buff. Solid. Back handmade. Tooling on hair.

Head tilted to left. Apparently distorted in molding or manipulated to support something (a hat?) on top of head; head too deep in back, flattened at top, right side pressed in. Face oval, widening at temples; narrow jaw, with receding chin. Facial type generally similar to **H317**. Mouth narrow; lips full, parted. Hair close to head; curved incisions on surface, as on **H314**, which also is poorly molded; perhaps from the same workshop.

See p. 187.

H316   Head of youth   Pl. 51

MF-13483. Lot 2247. Preserved: head and neck. P.H. 0.035 (size 3). Fabric 5, orange-buff. Nearly solid. Back handmade, rounded. Added: wreath, hair. Tooling on wreath.

Head tilted to left. Face oval. Nose large. Facial features otherwise indistinct. Hair summarily rendered in flat, scalloped waves framing face. Thick, stippled wreath. Probable mold sibling in lot 3206.

See p. 187.

H317   Head of youth(?)   Pl. 51

MF-12895. Lot 4379. Preserved: head and part of neck. Missing part of hair on nape. P.H. 0.046 (size 3–4). Fabric 1, orange-buff. White slip. Red-purple paint on hair. Solid. Back probably handmade, rounded. Added: hair, headdress(?). Tooling on hair.

Head tilted to right. Face oval to round, with fairly low forehead. Eyes large, downturned; upper lid defined; browridge overhangs slightly. Nose short, thin, slightly upturned. Mouth narrow; lips full. Single row of round, punched curls frames face to level of chin; groove behind curls, probably for added fillet or wreath; irregular curls over cranium. Face has soft, feminine appearance, but short, curly coiffure is probably masculine. Probable mold sibling in lot 6215.

See pp. 187, 193.

H318   Head of youth(?)   Pl. 51

MF-70-173. No context. Preserved: head and neck. Missing curls at left side. P.H. 0.052 (size 3–4). Fabric 1, creamy buff to orange-buff. White slip. Dark yellow paint on hair. Solid. Back handmade, rounded. Added: curls, ends of turban at nape. Tooling on hair.

Head tilted to left; chin lifted. Face oblong to oval, with high forehead; deep chin. Eyes downturned; upper lids defined, lower lids faint, lifted. Nose slightly upturned. Mouth narrow; lips full, downturned. Single row of diagonally slashed corkscrew curls frames face; eight curls preserved. Cranium wrapped in a turban; in back, overlapping fold of cloth, with two tied ends of turban at nape. Deep groove immediately behind curls probably for added fillet or wreath.

See p. 187.

CHILDREN

H319   Standing boy   Pl. 51

MF-12144. Lot 4349. Preserved: shoulders to left foot and right calf. P.H. 0.121 (size 2–3). Fabric 5, orange-buff to light orange, with grayish buff core. White slip. Hollow. Back handmade, flattened. Irregular, round vent, diam. ca. 0.02. Added: right arm and hand, drapery around back and sides. Tooling on folds, hands, grapes.

Stands with plump legs apart. Left arm bent; hand holds bunch of grapes at hip. Right arm at side; hand grasps edge of mantle beside thigh. Mantle is draped diagonally in back, covers left shoulder and arm. Hem falls to floor all around, forming background for legs. Shoulders soft, rounded; abdomen protrudes.

See pp. 69, 185, 188–189, 293, 335.

H320 Standing boy   Pl. 51

MF-11908. Lot 2070. Preserved: front–right shoulder to right ankle and left foot; back–right shoulder to waist. Missing left shoulder and most of arm, adjacent part of chest. Mended. P.H. 0.112 (size 2–3). Fabric 2, orange to orange-buff. Hollow. Back handmade, flattened. Tooling on folds, right hand, and objects in hand.

Weight on left leg. Right leg slightly bent, well advanced. Left arm at side. Right arm bent; elbow leans on pillar; hand holds strigil and pointed aryballos. Upper torso leans backward. Mantle is draped over top of pillar, where it cushions right arm, then around back, probably over left shoulder, and down left arm and hand; one fold drops over part of left thigh. Hem falls to floor all around, forming background for legs. Break at top suggests that hair may have been shoulder length. Child's torso rendered as in **H319**. Probable later generation: MF-13433 (lot 3222, fabric 1).

See pp. 188, 189, 194, 290.

H321 Standing boy   Pl. 51

MF-13414. Lot 1945. Preserved: shoulders to chest. Mended. P.H. 0.043 (size 2–3). Fabric 4, buff, with light orange core. White slip. Hollow. Thick-walled. Back handmade, rounded. Top of rectangular vent preserved, 0.028 wide. Added: possibly right arm. Tooling on arm.

Upper arms at sides. Shoulders rounded. Mantle is draped over left shoulder and arm.

See p. 189.

H322 Standing boy   Pl. 51

MF-13408. Lot 3217. Preserved: front–chest, left shoulder and arm. P.H. 0.062 (size 3). Fabric 1, orange-buff to orange. White slip. Red paint on flesh. Hollow.

Left arm bent; hand holds rooster upright against chest; traces of fingers on underside of bird. Mantle is draped over left shoulder. Similar in type to standing youth **C191**, larger, pose reversed; plump torso is that of a child.

See pp. 188, 189, 194, 269.

H323 Standing boy   Pl. 51

MF-69-353. Lot 6214. Preserved: shoulders to base. Surface worn. P.H. 0.058 (size 1). Fabric 5, ochre. White slip. Red paint on flesh. Solid. Back handmade, rounded.

Weight on right leg, right hip outthrust. Left leg slightly bent. Right arm bent; hand on hip. Left arm bent; elbow possibly leaning on a support; hand holds knucklebone bag at hip. Mantle is draped over shoulders and arms, falls down back, forming background for legs. Small dog reaches up beside left leg. Projecting base, rectangular in front, rounded in back. Another type of standing boy with a small dog:

MF-2385 in the Corinth collection (*Corinth* XII, p. 52, no. 348, pl. 31).

See pp. 188, 189.

H324 Standing boy   Pl. 51

MF-13432. Lot 3230. Preserved: shoulders to calves. P.H. 0.05 (size 1–2). Fabric 1, orange-buff. Solid. Back handmade, flattened.

Weight on right leg, right hip outthrust. Left leg advanced. Right arm at side; hand curves in at thigh, as in **H302**. Left arm bent; elbow possibly leaning on a support; hand at hip. Upper torso leans backward. Mantle is draped over left shoulder, arm, and hand. Dull impression. For bottom of type, see probable mold sibling **H325**.

See pp. 188, 189.

H325 Standing boy   Pl. 51

MF-13467. Lot 3233. Preserved: right hip and left thigh to base. P.H. 0.051 (size 1–2). Fabric 1, orange-buff to orange. Solid. Back handmade, flattened. Underside slightly concave.

Probably from same mold as **H324**, preserving feet and irregular, rectangular, splaying base. Drapery at left side falls to feet, with faint outline of dog in front of it, as in **H323**.

See pp. 188, 189.

H326 Standing boy   Pl. 51

MF-13406. Lot 4348. Preserved: head to hips. P.H. 0.051 (size 1–2). Fabric 1, orange-buff, interior surface orange. White slip. Pink paint on torso, red on hair, right hand. Hollow. Back handmade, flat. Added: part of hair. Tooling on hair, right hand.

Weight probably on right leg. Right arm hangs at side. Left arm bent. Mantle is draped over left shoulder, arm, and hand. Trace of red paint at right hand originally may have belonged to mantle beside it. Head tilted slightly forward; short neck. Face round. Eyes level. Nose wide, flat. Lips smiling. Hair piled into peak of stippled curls; perhaps locks of hair originally plaited at the center; curls at sides. Probable mold siblings: MF-13407 (lot 2249); MF-2385 in the Corinth collection (*Corinth* XII, p. 52, no. 348, pl. 31, solid, with pencil hole; mantle draped across to right hip; small dog at left side).

See pp. 188, 189, 191, 194, 298.

H327 Standing boy   Pl. 51

MF-13405. Lot 2239. Preserved: front–head to top of thighs; back–head to chest. Missing right arm, left hand; top of head chipped. P.H. 0.065 (size 2). Fabric 4, orange-buff. White slip. Red paint on hair. Hollow. Back molded, flattened. Corner of vent preserved, seems rectangular, with rounded corners. Added: part of hair. Tooling on folds, hair.

Weight probably on right leg. Right arm probably hung at side. Left arm bent, forearm extended forward. Mantle is draped over left shoulder and arm, leaves wrist and hand free, continues to fall down side. Soft pectorals and abdomen are well modeled; fold of flesh above pubic area. Almost no neck. Face distorted in molding but shape probably round. Eyes level. Nose wide, flat. Lips smiling. Knot of hair or cluster of curls at top of head; long locks of hair fall to shoulders. For better example of head type, see **H330** (larger). Possible later generation of head: MF-10665 (lot 1945, fabric 1).

See p. 189.

H328 Standing boy   Pl. 51

MF-13996. Lot 3228. Preserved: head, neck, right shoulder.
P.H. 0.057 (size 2–3). Fabric 1, ochre. Solid. Back handmade,
rounded. Added: hair. Tooling on hair.

Upper torso nude; shoulder broad, sloping. Face oblong to
oval, with high, triangular forehead. Facial features relatively
small. Eyes level; both lids defined. Nose thin, close to upper
lip. Mouth narrow; lips full, smiling. Coiffure generally similar
to that of **H327**, but locks of hair are gathered further back on
cranium, and long locks of hair to shoulders are more deeply
waved. Similar, smaller head in lot 3206.

See pp. 189, 194.

H329 Standing boy   Pl. 51

MF-13413. Lot 3228. Preserved: head to chest. Missing
lower part of hair at right side. P.H. 0.054 (size 2–3). Fabric 1,
orange-buff. White slip. Red paint on hair. Hollow. Back
handmade, flattened. Added: hair. Tooling on hair.

Upper arms at sides. Chest curves out into plump torso.
Head tilted slightly to left. Face oblong to oval, with high,
triangular forehead. Eyes large. Nose large, close to upper lip.
Lips full. Coiffure shows central part deeply slashed behind
abbreviated knot of hair; locks of hair fall to neck at either side,
flaring out at bottom. Head generally similar in type to **H341**.
Child seems somewhat older than other standing boys. Poor
workmanship. Similar head, wreathed, in lot 4350.

See pp. 189, 194, 199.

H330 Head, probably of standing boy   Pl. 51

MF-10670. Lot 1945. Preserved: head and neck. P.H. 0.033
(size 3). Fabric 1, grayish buff, burned(?). White slip. Red paint
on hair. Solid. Back molded(?), cranium pinched. Added: hair
at top and sides. Tooling on hair.

Face round to oval, with high forehead; full cheeks. Eyes
level. Nose wide, flat. Mouth narrow; lips full, parted. Knot
of hair at top of head; long locks of hair at sides. Similar in
type to head of standing boy **H327**. Probable mold sibling
in lot 3206 (fabric 5).

See p. 189.

H331 Standing boy   Pl. 51

MF-70-27. Lot 6503. Nearly complete. Mended; surface
chipped. H. 0.128 (size 2). Fabric 1, orange-buff. White slip.
Hollow. Head and torso rendered in same mold. Back molded,
rounded. Irregular, round vent, diam. ca. 0.015. Added: base.
Tooling on folds, right arm and hand, bird.

Published: Bookidis and Fisher 1972, p. 316, pl. 62:b.

Weight on right leg, right hip slightly outthrust. Left leg
bent, foot drawn slightly back and to side; legs joined by panel
of clay. Both arms bent; right arm holds bird (probably a small
goose) against torso. Small mantle is draped over left shoulder
and arm, diagonally across back to right hip, and across abdomen, leaving navel exposed; lower edge of mantle dips from
left hip to right knee; left hand, covered by cloth, grasps folds
at chest. Short neck. Face round to oval, with high, triangular
forehead. Eyes level. Nose small, flattened. Lips smiling.
Hair knotted in front of stephane; long locks of hair at sides.
Round base with torus molding at top and bottom. Probable mold siblings: **H333** (head); MF-10662, MF-10669 (both
lot 1945, fabric 2); MF-12010 (lot 2240, head, without stephane); MF-12040 (lot 2239, head, without stephane); others

in lots 3230 (two, fabric 3), 6214 (fabric 3), 6503 (two, including one head), 6507; MF-13901 and MF-13907 in the Corinth
collection. Probable later generation in lot 4387 (fabric 3).
Head with similar hair and headdress: MF-13482 (lot 4350).
Similar in type: **H332**. **I21**, probably of Argive fabric, may
have been made in a parallel mold. For possible workshop
mates, see Workshop H, p. 346.

See pp. 12, 189, 190–191, 194, 276, 286, 288.

H332 Standing boy   Pl. 51

MF-14190. Lot 1945. Preserved: shoulders to abdomen, to
waist in back. P.H. 0.049 (size 2). Fabric 5, ochre to orange.
White slip. Hollow. Back handmade, flattened. Upper edge of
vent preserved.

Similar in type to **H331** but slightly larger; garment is
wrapped around the waist, covering the abdomen. Dull impression.

See p. 190.

H333 Head, probably of standing boy   Pl. 52

MF-11093. Lot 1978. Preserved: head and neck; surface
chipped. P.H. 0.026 (size 2). Fabric 1, orange. White slip.
Traces of red paint. Solid. Back handmade, flattened. Added:
headdress, hair at sides. Tooling on hair.

Dull impression but probably mold sibling of head of **H331**.
Instead of stephane, headdress is flattened and angular, perhaps intended to be a kausia, although it lacks the peak at
the top.

See p. 191.

H334 Standing boy   Pl. 52

MF-13434. Lot 3222. Preserved: shoulders to thighs. Missing
right arm, part of left forearm and adjacent drapery. Mended.
P.H. 0.081 (size 3). Fabric 1, creamy buff, with orange and
gray core. Hollow. Thick-walled. Back molded, rounded.

Shoulders rounded; abdomen protrudes. Left arm bent;
forearm extended forward. Mantle is draped over left forearm;
bulky folds are bunched around abdomen and held in place
by flat, superimposed folds; diagonal, looped folds from right
thigh to left arm. Little anatomical detail on nude upper torso.

See pp. 186, 188.

H335 Seated boy   Pl. 52

MF-13453. Lot 2150. Preserved: right thigh to ankle, right
forearm and hand, right side of seat with drapery; small part
of back; upper surface chipped. P.H. 0.048 (size 2). Fabric 1,
orange-buff. White slip. Seat hollow, figure solid. Back of seat
open. Tooling on folds, hand.

Plump leg of probably nude child seated, with legs apart, on
a plain, rectangular block; nudity suggests that child is a boy.
Rolled cloth of mantle rests on back of seat, is grasped by hand
beside thigh, from which it falls down side of seat in a triangular
zigzag fold; point of fold is knotted or weighted. Similar in type:
MF-13464 (lot 3230, left leg of boy on block seat, with drapery
wrapped around hand); MF-13457 (lot 2087, nude torso of
seated boy).

See pp. 182, 191, 199, 290.

H336 Seated boy   Pl. 52

MF-13454. Lot 4417. Preserved: front–left thigh and knee,
left hand, small part of left side of seat. P.H. 0.027 (size 2). Fabric 1, orange-buff. Seat hollow; figure solid. Tooling on hand.

Similar in type to **H335** but without drapery; part of left side preserved. Hand holds a knucklebone bag, which rests on seat.

See pp. 182, 191, 199, 290.

H337   Seated boy   Pl. 52

MF-69-357. Lot 6214. Preserved: front and part of sides–thighs to base, part of seat with drapery. Missing right foot. P.H. 0.051 (size 2). Fabric 3, light orange, with gray core. White slip. Seat hollow, figure solid. Possible finished edge of seat at right side suggests that back of seat was open. Added: feet and base. Tooling on folds.

Similar in type to **H335**; bottom of seat spreads into plaque base, on which feet rest. End of mantle falls over left thigh and down side of seat in triangular zigzag fold, originally may have been grasped in left hand.

See pp. 191, 199, 290.

H338   Seated boy   Pl. 52

MF-13456. Lot 3230. Preserved: front–base of neck to abdomen; back–base of neck to chest level. Missing right hand, most of left arm. P.H. 0.039 (size 2). Fabric 1, grayish buff. Hollow. Back handmade, flattened. Added: drapery. Tooling on folds.

Seated pose is probably frontal; right shoulder is lower than left; head probably turned to right. Right arm bent; forearm extended forward. Rolled upper edge of mantle is draped around back and over right elbow and forearm. Sloping, rounded shoulders; abdomen soft. Little anatomical detail.

See pp. 191, 290.

H339   Seated girl   Pl. 52

MF-12892. Lot 4379. Preserved: shoulders to feet; left leg, feet chipped. P.H. 0.07 (size 2). Fabric 1, orange-buff to orange. Hollow. Back handmade, flattened. Back of seat open. Added: right arm, grapes, sides of seat. Tooling on folds, hands, grapes.

Seated with legs apart. Left arm bent; hand clenched at hip. Right arm bent; hand holds stem of stippled bunch of grapes, which rests on thigh. Chiton has short sleeves, is belted high on plump, short-waisted torso. Fine folds; deeply looped folds fall into hollow between knees. Possibly mechanically related: T-2717 from the North Cemetery (*Corinth* XIII, p. 292, no. 496-8, pl. 82, from a grave dated first half of the 3rd century B.C.).

See pp. 44, 188, 191, 194, 337.

H340   Seated girl   Pl. 52

MF-13998. Lot 2107. Preserved: head to lap. Missing seat. P.H. 0.062 (size 2). Fabric 1, greenish buff. White slip. Hollow. All parts rendered in same mold. Back handmade, flattened.

Similar in type to **H339**; right hand at abdomen is empty; left hand rests against thigh. Proportions more elongated, with narrow shoulders, more slender torso; outline of breasts suggested. Neck is too thick, perhaps due to failure to trim molding rim in an earlier generation. Head is relatively large, tilts forward. Face round, with high forehead. Features indistinct, but facial type similar to **H341**. Coiffure is peaked in front, with plait or knot at top; locks of hair curve in at sides to chin. Dull impression.

See pp. 44, 191.

H341   Head of child   Pl. 52

MF-13992. Lot 3222. Preserved: head and neck; surface worn. P.H. 0.036 (size 2–3). Fabric 1, light orange to orange-buff. Solid. Wreath probably rendered in mold. Back handmade, flat. Tooling on hair, wreath, mouth.

Face oblong to oval, with high, triangular forehead; full cheeks. Eyes level. Nose wide, flat. Mouth gouged at corners; lips smiling. Hair probably plaited back from forehead; locks of hair curve in at sides to chin. Thick, stippled wreath wrapped with a ribbon. Well-composed piece, but workmanship is poor.

See p. 191.

H342   Head of girl   Pl. 52

MF-13993. Lot 4450. Preserved: head and neck, with small part of back. Surface worn. P.H. 0.039 (size 3). Fabric 1, yellowish buff. White slip. Red paint on hair. Solid. Back molded, rounded. Tooling on hair.

Face oval, with high, rounded forehead; narrow jaw, with slightly receding chin. Eyes large, level. Nose short. Mouth narrow; lips full, slightly pursed. Summary melon coiffure indicated by short slashes (probably rendered in mold; plait around cranium also rendered in mold but retouched). Probable later generation: MF-12140 (lot 4349, fabric slightly coarser than 1).

See pp. 164, 191.

H343   Head of girl   Pl. 52

MF-10678. Lot 1945. Preserved: head and left side of neck. Chin and right cheek chipped. P.H. 0.041 (size 3). Fabric 2, grayish buff. White slip. Hollow. All parts rendered in same mold. Back molded, rounded. Tooling on hair.

Face oval to round, with high, rounded forehead. Eyes level. Nose short, close to upper lip. Mouth narrow; lips full. Coiffure parted at center; locks of hair drawn up from forehead; long locks at sides and back. Narrow wreath. Dull impression.

See p. 192.

H344   Head of girl   Pl. 52

MF-69-396. Lot 6215. Preserved: head and part of shoulders. P.H. 0.033 (size 2–3). Fabric 1, orange-buff, with grayish buff core. Solid. Back handmade, rounded. Added: hair, headdress. Tooling on hair.

Short neck, spreading into shoulders just below chin. Face oval to round, with high, nearly triangular forehead; narrow jaw, with slightly receding chin. Eyes large, level. Nose short. Lips full. Thick, curly locks of hair fall to ears from central part. Headdress is solid, resembling a low polos in shape but is slightly pointed at center, like a stephane. Similar in type to female head **H178**, although **H344** seems to be younger.

See p. 192.

H345   Head of child   Pl. 52

MF-13994. Lot 3233. Preserved: head and neck. P.H. 0.029 (size 2–3). Fabric 1, creamy buff, with orange core. Red paint on hair, pale pink paint on face (without white slip?). Solid. Back handmade, rounded. Added: hair at top, sides, and nape. Tooling on hair.

Head probably turned to right. Face oblong to oval, with high, rounded forehead; full cheeks. Eyes large, downturned. Nose short, wide. Lips full, smiling. Cluster of curls at top of cranium; locks of hair wave down around temples, form curls from ears to chin. Probable mold sibling in lot 5613. Possible earlier generation: MF-3863 in the Corinth collection (*Corinth* XII, pp. 52–53, no. 353, pl. 31). Similar in type (mechanically related?): head of figurine of Eros in the Corinth collection, MF-9254 (Romano 1994, p. 91, no. 79, pl. 28); two additional heads from the same deposit, MF-9263, MF-9265 (Romano 1994, p. 91, nos. 81, 82, pl. 28).

See pp. 166, 192.

H346 Head of child Pl. 52

MF-11401. Lot 877. Preserved: head and small part of neck. P.H. 0.028 (size 2–3). Fabric 2, light orange. White slip. Red paint on hair. Hollow. Back handmade, rounded. Added: hair, wreath. Tooling on face, hair, wreath.

Round face of baby, with high forehead; full cheeks. Eyes large, round, downturned; lids heavy, almost closed. Nose wide, flat. Mouth wide; lips slashed open. Stippled mass at top of head may represent either locks of hair drawn into cluster of curls or cluster of berries belonging to a wreath; blobs added for leaves at sides. Holes punched in ears, perhaps for added ornaments. Head could have been attached to something at right side, perhaps another figure.

See pp. 192–193, 194.

H347 Head of girl Pl. 52

MF-12044. Lot 2249. Preserved: head and neck. Missing left earring; wreath chipped in back. P.H. 0.035 (size 3). Fabric 1, orange-buff to orange. White slip. Red paint on hair. Solid. Back probably molded, rounded. Added: wreath, earring. Tooling on hair, wreath.

Head tilted slightly to right. Round face with high forehead, full cheeks, prominent chin. Eyes large, nearly round, opened wide; both lids defined; browridge not marked. Nose wide, flat, close to upper lip. Lips full, smiling, dimpled at corners. Hair waved loosely up and back from temples to cranium in thick, separated locks. Wreath around cranium is shaped like a thick, tubular fillet, stippled. Leaf-shaped projections between ears and wreath at each side may be remnants of the coiffure or headdress covered by the wreath. Disc earring, punched at center, preserved on right ear. Possible later generation: head of Eros **H290**, perhaps from the same workshop (Workshop E, p. 345). Well-made piece.

See pp. 17, 193, 194.

H348 Head of child Pl. 52

MF-10668. Lot 1945. Preserved: head and neck. P.H. 0.026 (size 2–3). Fabric 1, slightly coarser, orange-buff. White slip. Red paint on hair, pale pink on face. Solid. Back molded, rounded. Added: hair at sides, wreath. Tooling on hair, wreath.

Head of baby, slightly tilted to right. Round face with high forehead; full cheeks. Eyes large, opened wide; both lids defined. Nose wide, flat. Lips full, smiling. Hair plaited back from center of forehead; stippled curls down sides to chin. Stippled wreath, similar to that of **H347**, set across forehead in front of plait; in back, ends of wreath do not join. Facial type and treatment of hair similar to Eros **H290**, perhaps from the same workshop (Workshop E, p. 345). Well-made piece.

See pp. 14, 182, 193.

H349 Head of child Pl. 52

MF-13991. Lot 4404. Preserved: head and neck, with drapery; right edge of drapery chipped. P.H. 0.033 (size 2–3).

Fabric 1, slightly coarser, orange-buff, with grayish buff core, a few small sparkling inclusions. White slip. Pale pink paint on face, blue on drapery. Solid. Back handmade, rounded. Added: drapery.

Head of baby, perhaps tilted to left, since cloth draped around head and across chest falls away from face slightly at left side. Face oval to round, with high forehead; full cheeks. Features clustered near center of face. Alert expression. Eyes large, round, opened wide; both lids defined. Nose short. Lips parted, smiling. Cloth forms a loose pleat at top of head.

See pp. 14, 193, 194.

H350 Head of child Pl. 52

MF-13420. Lot 3217. Preserved: head and neck. P.H. 0.029 (size 2–3). Fabric 1, creamy buff. White slip. Red paint on hair. Hollow. Thick-walled. Back probably molded, rounded. Added: hair. Tooling on hair.

Head tilted to left. Face round, with triangular forehead; full cheeks. Nose wide, flat. Mouth narrow; lips smiling. Coiffure a thick mass of punched curls framing face and neck. Possible mold sibling: MF-10646 (lot 897, hair plaited back from center of forehead, locks of hair at sides curving in to chin, as in **H341**).

See pp. 193, 194, 290.

H351 Head of child Pl. 52

MF-10648. Lot 897. Preserved: head and neck. Missing object broken from top of head. P.H. 0.029 (size 3). Fabric 2, light orange. White slip. Red paint on hair. Solid. Back handmade, rounded. Added: hair at sides and back, object on head. Tooling on hair.

Original position of head uncertain. Face round, with high, sloping forehead; full cheeks; double chin, receding. Eyes large, nearly round, opened wide; both lids defined. Nose prominent. Mouth wide, especially upper lip; lips thick. Short locks of hair wave up and back from forehead. Protrusion like a pad at top of head may have supported a vessel or other object, but pad is off-center and is not level. Pellet earrings. A mold from the Potters' Quarter, KH-38, is similar in facial type and scale but has a more delicate mouth (*Corinth* XV, i, p. 102, no. 40, pl. 35).

See p. 193.

H352 Head of child Pl. 52

MF-10408. Lot 877. Preserved: head and part of neck; chin chipped. P.H. 0.037 (size 3–4). Fabric 2, orange-buff, with orange core. White slip. Red paint on hair. Solid. Back molded, rounded. Added: hair at sides and back, below stephane. Tooling on hair, stephane.

Head tilted slightly forward. Face round to oval, with high forehead; full cheeks. Eyes large, oval, slightly downturned; both lids rather thick, left upper lid is half-closed. Nose up-turned. Mouth tilted slightly up at right side; lips delicately compressed, smiling. Hair plaited back from center of forehead; stephane with incised scroll pattern is set horizontally across forehead, partly concealing plait (stephane is rendered in mold); torus borders on upper and lower edges of stephane; thick curls frame sides of face below stephane. Large, well-made piece. Possible later generation: **H353**.

See pp. 192, 194.

H353   Head of girl   Pl. 52

MF-10497. Lot 880. Preserved: head and small part of neck. Missing left earring. P.H. 0.024 (size 2). Fabric 1, orange-buff. White slip. Red paint on hair. Solid. Back molded, rounded. Added: headdress, earrings. Tooling on hair, stephane.

   Published: Stroud 1965, p. 10, pl. 2:d.

   Face round to oval, with high forehead. Eyes oval, slightly downturned; both lids defined. Nose short. Mouth slightly tilted up to right side, as in **H352**. Hair combed straight up from forehead or perhaps strokes represent fringe of bangs; headdress is decorated with vertical incisions. Disc earring preserved on right ear. Possibly a later generation of **H352**.

   See pp. 192, 194.

H354   Head of child(?)   Pl. 52

MF-14016. Lot 3217. Preserved: fragment of forehead and stephane; surface chipped. Max.P.Dim. 0.062 (size 5). Fabric 5, light orange, with grayish buff core; sparse small dark red and white inclusions, a few small sparkling inclusions. Hollow. Thin-walled. Tooling on forehead, stephane.

   Fringe of hair rendered by light strokes on forehead. Stephane decorated with incised scroll pattern, bordered at top and bottom. Headdress comparable to that of **H352**. Fabric seems local but is slightly coarser than usual, perhaps because piece is large.

   See pp. 192, 194.

COMIC ACTORS, PARODIES, AND GROTESQUES

   Three separate categories of figurines (actors in the comic theater, parodies of serious coroplastic or sculptural types, and grotesques) are catalogued together in this section for convenience, because they are linked in their use of masks or anatomical distortions.

H355   Comic actor   Pl. 53

MF-69-397. Lot 6214. Preserved: head, most of baby(?), hands. P.H. 0.04 (size 3). Fabric 1, orange-buff. Nearly solid. Back handmade, flat.

   Actor in comic mask holds against the left side of his head a baby wearing a pilos; actor's hands are visible one above the other grasping baby. Mask has protruding, arched brows; bulbous eyes; snub nose; wide, gaping mouth; short, pointed beard.

   See pp. 195, 291.

H356   Comic mask, probably from figurine of actor   Pl. 53

MF-11734. Lot 2035. Preserved: mask only. P.H. 0.02 (size 2–3). Fabric 2, light orange to orange-buff. Hollow.

   Mask similar to that of **H355** but mouth deeper, grinning. See pp. 195, 291.

H357   Comic actor in feminine dress   Pl. 53

MF-14019. Lot 3206. Preserved: head to waist. Missing front surface of torso below breasts. P.H. 0.044 (size 1–2). Fabric 5, orange-buff, with orange and gray core. White slip. Solid. All parts rendered in same mold. Back handmade, flat. Tooling on folds.

   Standing female figure. Right arm raised; hand lifts mantle beside head. Left arm bent; hand at hip. Mantle is draped over head and left arm, falls behind figure at right side; rolled upper edge of mantle on midriff. Folds of peplos or chiton

on chest. For possible composition of missing lower part, see **H358** and **H359**. Round, masklike face has wide, flat nose; grinning mouth (mask is clearer in example in London cited below). Long locks of hair fall to shoulders. Poor workmanship. Possible later generation: KT-5-20 from the Potters' Quarter (*Corinth* XV, ii, p. 125, no. 20, pl. 24). Similar in type: **H358** and **H359**. For fully preserved example, see *British Museum* I, pp. 401–402, no. 1530, pl. 206 (possibly mechanically related).

   See pp. 15, 195, 291.

H358   Probably comic actor in feminine dress   Pl. 53

MF-14022. Lot 3223. Preserved: shoulders to knees. Missing right arm. P.H. 0.048 (size 1–2). Fabric 1, orange-buff. Nearly solid. All parts rendered in same mold. Back handmade, flat.

   Similar in type to **H357**, with lower part preserved. Right leg possibly advanced. Left arm bent; hand on hip. Traces of mantle falling behind at right side suggest that right arm lifted cloth. Rolled upper edge of mantle wrapped around midriff. Swollen abdomen. Dull impression; for better detail, see **H359**.

   See pp. 195, 291.

H359   Probably comic actor in feminine dress   Pl. 53

MF-14025. Lot 4492. Preserved: left shoulder and right hip to thighs. P.H. 0.037 (size 1). Fabric 5, light orange. White slip. Hollow. All parts rendered in same mold. Back handmade, flattened. Tooling on folds.

   Similar in type to **H357** and **H358** but smaller, abdomen less exaggerated. Hem of mantle may be preserved at left thigh; cascade of folds drops from left hand; catenary across hips frames bottom of abdomen.

   See pp. 195, 198, 291.

H360   Comic actor in feminine dress   Pl. 53

MF-12046. Lot 2249. Intact. H. 0.096 (size 2). Fabric 2, orange-buff. Hollow. Thick-walled. All parts rendered in same mold. Back molded, flattened. Irregular, oval vent, ca. 0.018 × 0.015.

   Published: Stroud 1968, p. 323, notes 26 and 27, pl. 95:b.

   Standing figure wears mantle over chiton or peplos. Mantle is draped over head, covers arms and torso to thighs. Right arm bent; hand pulls mantle over mouth and nose. Left arm bent; hand grasps mantle edge at hip; short cascade of folds falls from hand. Mantle is stretched taut over swollen abdomen. Skirt falls in narrow, vertical folds to feet in pointed slippers. Low, square base. Head tilted back and to left. Uncertain whether face is masked. Low, triangular forehead. Eyes large, downturned; both lids defined, upper lid arched, lower lid level.

   See pp. 128, 195, 197, 291.

H361   Comic actor in feminine dress   Pl. 53

MF-14193. Lot 2240. Preserved: head to waist. Missing left shoulder and arm, back below head. P.H. 0.046 (size 2). Fabric 1, greenish buff. White slip. Hollow. Head and torso rendered in same mold.

   Similar in type to **H360**, but coiffure is peaked beneath mantle. Parallel curved folds along forearm. Dull impression. See pp. 195, 291.

H362   Probably comic actor in feminine(?) dress   Pl. 53

MF-13488. Lot 2249. Preserved: neck to base. Missing feet, front of base. P.H. 0.079 (size 1–2). Fabric 2, orange-buff to light orange. Nearly solid. Back handmade, flat. Added: base. Tooling on folds.

Standing figure wears mantle covering arms and falling to ankles; open edge of mantle down left side. Upper torso leans backward. Right arm bent; hand at chest. Left arm bent; forearm extended forward. Swollen abdomen. Looped folds broadly incised across front of torso and legs.

See pp. 128, 195, 198, 291.

H363 Comic actor as old nurse holding a child Pl. 53

MF-11027. Lot 1953. Preserved: front–nurse's head to hips. Missing child's head. P.H. 0.068 (size 2–3). Fabric 3, pinkish orange to orange. Hollow.

Nurse is hunched forward, wrapped in mantle, holds child upright in her left arm, against her head and upper torso. Her right arm bent; hand grasps mantle under chin. Domed cranium; sagging flesh over prominent cheekbones. Dull impression. Probable mold sibling: MF-71-30 from Forum Southwest (C. K. Williams and Fisher 1972, p. 163).

See pp. 71, 195, 196, 291.

H364 Actor as Silenos holding baby Dionysos Pl. 53

MF-12120. Lot 2249. Preserved: front–head to knees; back–head to hips. Missing head of baby. Mended. P.H. 0.077 (size 1–2). Fabric 2, light orange, slightly burned(?). Nearly solid. All parts rendered in same mold. Back molded(?), rounded.

Published: Stroud 1968, p. 323, note 24, pl. 94:h.

Silenos has humpback and prominent buttocks, holds legs of baby seated in the crook of his left arm. Right arm bent; hand against hip, holding bunch of grapes. Upper edge of mantle is rolled, wrapped around waist; hem of mantle curves from above right knee to left hip; short cascade of folds beside left hip. Figure originally may have been propped by support under buttocks. Large head, with high, bald cranium; prominent ears. Browridge prominent. Nose short, wide. Full beard, drooping moustache. Dull impression. Slightly larger piece, possibly earlier generation: MF-1608 in the Corinth collection (*Corinth* XII, p. 51, no. 331, pl. 29; clear details of face and drapery; preserves entire swaddled baby). Probably copy of Attic type (cf. *British Museum* I, pp. 197–198, no. 736, pl. 97).

See pp. 71, 193, note 455, 196, 197, 291.

H365 Comic actor as a female dancer Pl. 53

MF-10923. Lot 1963. Complete; front of base chipped. H. 0.067 (size 1). Fabric 2, orange-buff. White slip. Solid. Head and torso probably rendered in same mold. Back probably handmade, rounded. Added: base. Back pared.

Dances with right leg crossed over left. Slight torsion, upper torso turned to left, hips and legs frontal; left shoulder sharply raised; head bent to right. Mantle is wrapped closely around torso from shoulders to hips, covers arms and hands; position of arms similar to dancer **H153**. Clump of mantle folds in crook of left arm; short cascade of zigzag folds beside left hip; skirt swirls around feet. Mask has triangular forehead; large, downturned eyes; bulbous nose; wide, gaping mouth. Hair appears to be arranged in cluster of curls at top of head, similar to **H201**. Low base, roughly rectangular. Probable mold sibling, with higher base, in lot 4421. Probable later generation: MF-1979-37 in the Corinth collection

(C. K. Williams 1979a, p. 125, pl. 30:d). For possible workshop mates, see Workshop C, p. 345.

See pp. 10, 155, 196, 198, 343.

H366 Probably comic actor as a female dancer Pl. 53

MF-13806. Lot 4417. Complete; top of head and base chipped; surface eroded. H. 0.068 (size 1). Fabric similar to 1, slightly sandy, grayish buff, with small sparkling inclusions. Solid. All parts rendered in same mold. Back handmade, flattened.

Dances with left leg crossed over right. Slight torsion, head turned to left, legs to right. Mantle is draped over head, pulled smoothly around torso to ankles, covering both arms. Right arm lifts cloth beside head. Left arm extended to side. Panel of drapery falls from left arm to base in vertical folds; cluster of zigzag folds drops from hand. Face indistinct, seems to be a round, grinning mask. Low base, roughly oval.

See p. 196.

H367 Comic actor as a hydriaphoros Pl. 53

MF-10617. Lot 896. Preserved: head, most of hydria (lacking neck), right forearm and hand, with adjacent drapery. P.H. 0.031 (size 2). Fabric 2, orange-buff. Solid. Back handmade, slightly concave. Added: folds at left side of face, earring. Tooling on face, folds.

Right arm and hand, wrapped in mantle, raised high to hold one of horizontal handles of hydria. Edge of drapery falling beside face at left suggests that mantle covered head. Mask has triangular forehead; large, protruding eyes; prominent cheeks; wide, flat nose; wide, gaping mouth. Locks of hair wave down sides from central part. Large, round earring on right ear. Hydria has low foot, broad base, tall body, and high, flat shoulders. For possible workshop mates, see Workshop C, p. 345.

See pp. 155, 195, 196.

H368 Parody of peplophoros(?) Pl. 53

MF-11032. Lot 1953. Preserved: hips to left foot and right ankle, part of base at left side. Missing front between legs. Mended. P.H. 0.076 (size 2–3). Fabric 3, orange-buff. White slip. Brown paint on left side. Hollow. Torso and base rendered in same mold. Back handmade, flattened. Tooling on folds.

Short-legged, corpulent figure stands with legs apart. Wears thin, clinging chiton or peplos; thickly pleated overfold arches over grossly swollen abdomen; series of lightly grooved, parallel catenaries down abdomen and between legs. Foot is wide, flat, splaying, as in **C81** and **H374**.

See pp. 44, 196–197.

H369 Parody of peplophoros(?) Pl. 54

MF-68-370. Lot 5613. Preserved: shoulders to hips. Missing arms; surface worn. P.H. 0.059 (size 2–3). Fabric 5, orange-buff to orange. Chest treated with preservative. Hollow. Thick-walled. Back molded, distorted. Added: arms and adjacent drapery. Tooling on folds.

Standing(?) figure wears peplos with overfold to waist. Skirt is belted very low; in profile, exaggerated pouching of kolpos gives impression of distended abdomen and buttocks. Arms originally extended to sides. Lappets of shoulder-pinned back mantle visible in front. Piece was much reworked and deliberately distorted manually.

See pp. 196–197.

H370   Parody of female type(?)   Pl. 54

MF-14021. Lot 896. Preserved: back–buttocks, right thigh. Mended. P.H. 0.051 (size 2–3). Fabric 1, orange-buff, interior light orange. White slip. Hollow. Thick-walled. Back molded, rounded. Added: surface of buttocks.

Standing, wide-hipped figure with prominent buttocks. Mantle is wrapped smoothly around back; horizontal tension folds at waist; deep, vertical skirt folds down thigh.

See p. 197.

H371   Parody of female type(?)   Pl. 54

MF-13858. Lot 2107. Preserved: front–right shoulder to thigh. P.H. 0.079 (size 3). Fabric 3, orange-buff. Hollow. All parts rendered in same mold.

Standing, squat figure with right hip outthrust. Right arm bent; hand behind hip. Mantle is wrapped around torso and arm; tension folds across upper arm; mantle hem just visible above lower break, with traces of vertical folds of chiton or peplos skirt.

See p. 197.

H372   Parody of female type(?)   Pl. 54

MF-68-374. Lot 5627. Preserved: front–chest to abdomen. Missing part of left side. Mended. P.H. 0.043 (size 2). Fabric 2, orange. White slip. Hollow. Added: mantle roll. Tooling on folds.

Standing, corpulent female figure. Right breast higher than left, suggesting that right arm originally was raised. Chiton clings to full breasts. Upper edge of mantle is twisted into a thick roll from right hip to waist at left side; looped folds below.

See pp. 197, 198.

H373   Parody of Aphrodite type(?)   Pl. 54

MF-14020. Lot 892. Preserved: waist to knees. P.H. 0.031 (size 1–2). Fabric 1, orange-buff. Solid. Back handmade, rounded.

Nude female figure stands with weight on right leg, right hip outthrust. Left leg slightly advanced. Swollen abdomen.

See pp. 194, 197.

H374   Parody of female type(?)   Pl. 54

MF-71-55. No context. Preserved: shoulders to right foot and left ankle. Missing arms, lower part of drapery at both sides. Mended. P.H. 0.057 (size 1–2). Fabric 2, orange-buff to light orange. White slip. Solid. Back handmade, flat. Added: feet, drapery at sides. Tooling on feet, folds.

Nude female figure stands with very short legs slightly apart. Feet are wide, flat, splaying, as in **C81** and **H368**. Breasts are overly large. Arms probably raised originally. Thin panels of drapery at sides; vertical folds on panels and between legs suggest that mantle fell behind, presumably held up in hands.

See pp. 44, 197.

H375   Parody of crowned goddess type(?)   Pl. 54

MF-14024. Lot 3222. Preserved: head and neck. Missing hair at right side. P.H. 0.037 (size 3). Fabric 1, orange-buff, with orange core. Red paint on hair and flesh. Solid. Back handmade, flattened. Added: hair, crown. Tooling on hair.

Face oblong, with low forehead; protruding jaw. Nose wide, flat, close to upper lip. Mouth wide. Hair rendered by a strip of clay across forehead, roughly stippled, with crimped waves; another strip falls along left side of face to shoulders. Low,

scalloped crown. Either a very badly made piece or a parody of the Classical crowned goddess type (**C95**–**C97**, **C100**).

See p. 197.

H376   Parody of erotic *symplegma*   Pl. 54

MF-10926. Lot 1978. Intact. H. 0.049; W. 0.05 (size 1). Fabric 1, orange-buff. White slip. Red paint on man's hair, yellow on beard. Hollow. Back handmade, flattened. Added: edge of cloth at top. Tooling on torsos, masks, hair.

Nude old man lies asleep on couch adorned with cushion and fringed cloth; his left leg hangs over edge of couch; right foot is tucked under left knee. He lies on his mantle, one corner of which covers his genitals; another corner falls over side of couch below his hanging arm. His masked face has snub nose; mouth opened wide; short, curly beard. Hair wrapped in turban. Nude old woman with pendulous breasts approaches him from rear, gazing intently at his face; her right hand presses his right knee down; her left hand pulls a mantle over her head and shoulders. Her masked face has triangular forehead; large, thick-lidded eyes; prominent cheeks; grinning, gaping mouth. Coiffure is peaked at top; locks of hair wave down from central part. Couch rests on low, rectangular base. Delicate retouch of anatomical details.

See p. 197.

H377   Pl. 54

Seated female figure, masked and winged(?), from group

MF-13948. Lot 4349. Preserved: seated figure. Missing wings(?), remainder of group. P.H. 0.067 (size 1). Fabric 1, creamy buff. White slip. Figure solid; seat hollow, thick-walled. Back handmade; front of figure either handmade or very heavily retouched. Tooling on mask, folds.

Tiny female figure sits at end of what may be a high-legged couch. Legs dangle. Hands rest in lap, each holding a long, narrow object. Narrow, sloping shoulders. Wears mask with open, grinning mouth; punched eyes. Long locks of hair fall to shoulders. Two projections in back may be remains of wings. Probably from a banqueter figurine.

See pp. 67, 198.

H378   Pl. 54

Seated female figurine, masked(?) and winged(?), from group

MF-13947. Lot 3228. Preserved: front of seated figure; small part of back. Missing wings(?), remainder of group. P.H. 0.045 (size 1). Fabric 2, light orange. White slip. Figure solid; seat hollow. Back handmade. Tooling on skirt.

Similar in type to **H377**, slightly larger; front seems mold-made. Figure holds long, narrow, curving object across knees. Projection in back from right shoulder seems to be remains of wing; curved projection at left side, visible in front, may belong to left wing. Face round, possibly masked. Lips smiling. Dull impression.

See pp. 67, 198.

H379   Male head, masked(?)   Pl. 54

MF-69-305. Lot 6215. Preserved: head and small part of neck. P.H. 0.03 (size 3). Fabric 1, orange-buff. Red paint on face. Hollow(?). Back handmade, rounded. Added: ears pinched out. Tooling on mouth, hair; ears punched, perhaps for insertion of ornaments; larger hole below left ear, perhaps for ventilation.

Round face, probably a mask, with low forehead; bulging cheeks; receding chin; long, prominent nose; projecting ears; smiling lips. Hair closely cropped, forms widow's peak close to arching browridge. Not bearded; presumably represents a youth.

See p. 198.

H380 Male head, masked(?) Pl. 54

MF-69-398. Lot 6214. Preserved: head and neck, left shoulder; chin chipped. P.H. 0.041 (size 3). Fabric 1, orange-buff to creamy buff. White slip. Solid. Back handmade, flattened. Added: ears. Tooling on face.

Round face, probably a mask, with low forehead; large, round eyes; snub nose; wide mouth; thick, parted lips; round, projecting ears. Hair closely cropped. Head somewhat pointed in back. Thin neck. Narrow shoulders. Not bearded; presumably represents a youth. Possible earlier generation: MF-3417 in the Corinth collection (*Corinth* XII, p. 35, no. 152, pl. 10, with more hair, there thought to be an old woman and dated too early).

See p. 198.

H381 Male head, masked(?) Pl. 54

MF-14023. Lot 3222. Preserved: head and neck; surface worn. P.H. 0.026 (size 3). Fabric 1, orange-buff. Solid. Back handmade, flattened. Added: ears.

Head has both human and animal characteristics, is probably a mask, with bald, flat cranium, from which rounded animal's ears project; flat cheeks; jutting jaw; deeply set eyes; short, flat nose; thick, pursed lips. Not bearded; presumably represents a youth.

See p. 198.

H382 Head of dwarf Pl. 54

MF-11385. Lot 877. Preserved: front–head and small part of neck. P.H. 0.024 (size 2–3). Fabric 2, light orange. White slip. Red paint on hair. Hollow. Tooling on hair.

Cranium broad and rather flat; frowning brows. Eyes half-closed. Nose wide, bulbous. Mouth wide, grinning; lips thick. Short locks of hair are combed forward into fringe across forehead. Head probably thrust forward on chest.

See p. 199.

H383 Head of boy Pl. 54

MF-11408. Lot 877. Preserved: head, part of neck in front; nose chipped. P.H. 0.022 (size 2–3). Fabric 2, light orange. Solid. Back handmade, flattened.

Cranium a high, oval dome. Small, round ears bent forward. Face wide at cheeks, narrowing to jaw. Eyes are merely slits. Mouth wide, grinning; lips thick. Straight locks of hair combed down from top of head to forehead.

See pp. 199, 298.

H384 Grotesque head Pl. 54

MF-11034. Lot 1953. Preserved: head and neck. P.H. 0.03 (size 2–3). Fabric 1, creamy buff. Red paint on hair. Solid. Probably molded, deliberately distorted. Tooling on mouth, hair in back.

Outline suggests boy's head, with plait at top, locks of hair falling to jaw at sides, as in **H329**. Face pinched into sloping forehead; large, beaked nose; underslung jaw; grinning, slit mouth. No eyes.

See pp. 199, 313.

SILENOS AND PAN

H385 Seated Silenos Pl. 55

MF-11100. Lot 1978. Preserved: front–shoulders to left foot and right thigh; back–shoulders to hips. Missing right hand, most of seat. Mended; surface eroded. P.H. 0.083 (size 2). Fabric 5, orange to orange-buff. Hollow. Thick-walled. Back probably handmade, rounded. Added: drapery. Tooling on torso, folds.

Sits with legs apart on blocklike seat. Arms at sides. Corpulent, nude figure. Narrow shoulders; wide hips; swollen abdomen; unusually deep navel. Clumsily modeled leg with small, pointed foot. Mantle wrapped around left arm and hand; folds on seat under figure. Beard visible at upper break. Poor workmanship.

See p. 199.

H386 Seated Silenos Pl. 55

MF-10323. Lot 870. Intact. H. 0.081 (size 1–2). Fabric 3, creamy buff. White slip. Yellow paint on back. Hollow. Back handmade, flattened. Added: pilos. Tooling on beard.

Perched on a rocky seat. Left leg crossed over right. Both arms bent; right hand rests on thigh, left hand at waist. Narrow shoulders; sagging pectorals; swollen abdomen. In profile, head falls forward, shoulders are hunched; flares slightly at bottom. Mantle covers shoulders, left arm, right upper arm. Snub nose. Stippled beard. High, narrow pilos. Possible mold sibling: MF-13466 (lot 4476, fabric 1; rocky base is higher).

See p. 199.

H387 Pan playing syrinx Pl. 55

MF-12154. Lot 4368. Preserved: front–head to calves; back–head to waist. Mended. P.H. 0.105 (size 2). Probably fabric 2, orange, deteriorated. White slip. Hollow. All parts rendered in same mold. Back handmade, flattened. Tooling on hands, pipes.

Stands with left leg crossed over right. Left elbow leans on tree-trunk support; hand grasps left side of syrinx. Right arm bent; hand grasps lower right corner of syrinx. Mantle falls behind nude torso and over left arm, fills space between figure and support. Slender, graceful figure, with narrow, sloping shoulders. Head tilted forward and to left; pipes conceal lower part of face. Nose wide, flat. Long locks of hair fall to shoulders; possibly two incurving horns above center of forehead; wide, flaring headdress. Fragment of larger figurine with right leg crossed over left, possibly representing Pan, in lot 5613 (fabric 1).

See pp. 182, 199–200.

OTHER TYPES

Protome

H388 Female protome Pl. 55

MF-11775. Lot 2064. Preserved: left side of face and neck, including most of eye, adjacent locks of hair. Nonjoining fragment of hair. Mended. P.H. 0.195. Fabric 1, orange-buff to orange, interior orange. Red paint on necklace, border; black on hair; painting without underlying white slip. Backless. Added: hair. Tooling on hair.

Somewhat flattened face, rather short, with prominent chin. Wide neck spreads into upper chest, which forms base. Backless; edge behind locks of hair along neck is finished. Eye large, downturned; lids thick; browridge prominent, rounded, follows curve of eye. Nose probably short. Wavy, horizontal locks of hair beside eye; long, wavy locks of hair to shoulder. Necklace of two rows of red dots; red border at bottom. Similar in type: MF-69-84 (without context, fragment of neck and hair, ends at base of neck, pink paint on flesh, no necklace).

See pp. 13, 200.

Old Woman

H389   Head of old woman   Pl. 55

MF-13711. Lot 4379. Preserved: head and neck. Missing veil at both sides below cheeks. P.H. 0.03 (size 3). Fabric 1, orange-buff. White slip. Back handmade, rounded. Added: veil, hair at sides. Tooling on veil, hair, face.

Published: Coroplast's Art, p. 60, fig. 49.

Head juts forward, suggesting that shoulders originally were hunched; chin may have been raised somewhat. Face oblong to oval. Forehead has one horizontal furrow and two short, vertical frown marks between eyes; high, prominent cheekbones, sunken cheeks; sagging flesh beneath jaw. Eyes level, almond shaped; lids not defined; browridge prominent. Mouth downturned, sunken, without lips, as if toothless. Veil is probably a mantle carried over the head; pleat at the top center. Well-made piece.

See pp. 200, 340.

Ephedrismos Groups

H390   Ephedrismos group   Pl. 55

MF-11904. Lot 2107. Preserved: front–left legs of both figures, with adjacent drapery. Missing foot of running figure. P.H. 0.116 (size 3–4). Fabric 4, orange-buff. White slip. Hollow. Figures molded separately, joined in back. Added: clump of folds between figures. Tooling on folds.

Group consists of two draped female figures: one figure runs to viewer's left, her left leg bent, hem fluttering around ankles; the other rides on her back, her left foot pressed against the runner's calf. Rider's left leg is separated from the runner's side by a clump of folds hanging from her missing right knee, which originally was supported in the crook of the runner's bent left arm. Fine folds of cloth cling to legs; folds of runner's garment divide at top of thigh to frame the leg. Rider's garment has double hem, terminating in omega folds; foot wears pointed slipper. Large, well-made piece. Probable mold sibling in lot 6215 (fabric 1, foot of rider with slightly more of drapery below). Similar left thigh of runner and left foot with fluttering hem, which may have belonged to this type, in lot 877. Complete ephedrismos group in Boston may be a later generation of this type (*Coroplast's Art*, pp. 128–129, no. 20).

See pp. 146, 200–201, 293.

H391   Ephedrismos group   Pl. 55

MF-13848. Lot 2249. Preserved: shoulders to waist; front chipped. P.H. 0.056 (size 3–4). Fabric 1, orange-buff, with grayish buff core. Hollow. Back handmade, flattened. Added: hair in back. Tooling on folds, hair.

Upper torso of rider, as in **H390**. Right shoulder higher than left. Broken away at bottom from back and left shoulder of runner; right forearm of rider originally leaned against runner's back; left hand rested on runner's left shoulder. Sleeved chiton, girded just below breasts; V-shaped folds at neckline dip down to belt. Full-breasted figure, with plump shoulders and arms. Four long locks of hair in back.

See pp. 200–201, 293.

H392   Ephedrismos group(?)   Pl. 55

MF-13839. Lot 4409. Preserved: front–chest to top of abdomen. Missing arms. P.H. 0.056 (size 3–4). Fabric 1, harder, yellowish buff. White slip. Hollow. Tooling on folds.

Heavily slashed V-shaped folds radiate from fastening of peplos or chiton at shoulders. Garment girded high with narrow belt; raised broken area below belt at right side. Figure short waisted. Thick V-shaped fold at neckline. Possible long locks of hair on left shoulder.

See pp. 200–201, 293.

H393   Ephedrismos group(?)   Pl. 55

MF-13821. Lot 4377. Preserved: right leg, with adjacent drapery, part of base; small part of back. P.H. 0.065 (size 2–3); depth of base 0.027. Fabric 1, creamy buff. Hollow. All parts rendered in same mold.

Female figure runs to viewer's left on shallow, rectangular base; perhaps the runner of an ephedrismos group, or a similarly shallow composition. Curving folds sweep down from knee to hem; foot in pointed slipper.

See pp. 200–201, 293.

H394   Ephedrismos group(?)   Pl. 55

MF-14157. Lot 2249. Preserved: right lower leg, part of foot, part of hem. P.H. 0.042 (size 3?). Fabric 1, light orange, with grayish buff core. Hollow. Tooling on folds.

Female figure runs to viewer's left; perhaps the runner of an ephedrismos group. Garment is double hemmed; upper skirt is blown back into deep curve by swift movement of figure; lower skirt trails over instep, curving folds terminate in omegas at hem. Well-made piece.

See pp. 200–201, 293.

IV

MIDDLE HELLENISTIC FIGURINES

Although the number of figurines discussed in this chapter is much smaller than the total of Early Hellenistic figurines, it would be a mistake to assume that drastically fewer votives of this kind were offered in the sanctuary after the third quarter of the 3rd century B.C. The factor that distinguishes this discussion from the foregoing is the destruction of Corinth in 146 B.C., which means that no Middle Hellenistic types could survive into the Late Hellenistic period, resulting in a diminished total. Although the nature of the site and particularly the lack of chronologically useful stratigraphy make it difficult to determine exactly when many of the figurines were dedicated, it is likely that descendants of some of the Early Hellenistic creations discussed above were still being dedicated after the middle of the 3rd century B.C. For example, in lot 3217, the contents of which appear to have been discarded in the third quarter of the 3rd century B.C.,[1] one finds a small number of good pieces of clear 4th-century B.C. date, but the latest material consists of degenerate survivals of 4th- or early-3rd-century B.C. types. This situation would parallel the continued use of Classical types through the 4th century, beside the newer Early Hellenistic creations (see p. 115). Creativity appears to have revived in the last quarter of the 3rd century B.C., when a major new type was invented, the "priestess" (see **H395–H411**). At that time there is stylistic evidence for the influence of the Greek East, which had had more impact on Corinthian coroplastic work in the Archaic period than in Classical and Early Hellenistic times. Renewal can also be seen in the return of high technical quality, as in the head **H427**, and in the large scale of many pieces.

There is evidence for some habitation of Corinth between 146 B.C. and the establishment of the Roman colony in 44 B.C.,[2] but very little evidence exists for activity at the Sanctuary of Demeter and Kore.[3] There is as yet no evidence for local coroplastic activity during this interim period; indeed, if the larger sanctuaries requiring votives were not active, there would have been little work for coroplasts. There may be some evidence for the importation of figurines at this time, but it is not yet confirmed.[4]

---

[1] *Corinth* XVIII, i, pp. 101–103.

[2] Most recently on this subject, Romano 1994, pp. 62–64, with bibliography.

[3] *Corinth* XVIII, i, pp. 2, 4; *Corinth* XVIII, iii, p. 434.

[4] Romano (1994, pp. 90–94) publishes 21 figurines from deposit 1947-3. This deposit is important because it includes ceramic evidence for activity during the first half of the interim period 146–44 B.C. The question is whether the figurines also provide evidence for such activity, and in this regard, unfortunately, the article must be used with caution. Of the 21 figurines catalogued, only 4 are identified as Corinthian and therefore manufactured before 146 B.C. Of the remainder, 7 are called imports or possible imports, and the Corinthian origin of the remaining 10 figurines is questioned. There is no summarizing discussion of the figurines as evidence apart from the catalogue. No criteria are presented for the determination of origin. The fabric descriptions of some of the pieces sound Corinthian, even while their origin is questioned, sometimes simply because they lack typological parallels in Corinth. The present study, however, should show that this means nothing, since the prolific Corinthian coroplastic industry always produced many different types and variants, some of which are known in only one example or wait a long while before another is found. Probably unintentionally, the impression is created that all but 4 of these figurines are or could be imports, an unusually large proportion for a Corinthian deposit. The identification of imports in this deposit is an important matter, since the importation of figurines (and those of quite good quality) would imply a degree of prosperity, and the existence of the contexts in which figurines were used, i.e., open sanctuaries with enough organization to hold festivals, dwellings nice enough to be decorated, and graves wealthy enough to hold more than the most basic offerings. To make proper use of the coroplastic material in this deposit, the figurines should first be tested for provenience. Then, for those that are definitely not Corinthian, evidence should be sought to determine their origin and whether they really can be dated between 146 and 111 B.C., the date suggested for the closure of this deposit. Since

DRAPED FEMALE FIGURINES AND RELATED HEADS
(H395–H424)

THE "PRIESTESS" TYPE (H395–H411)

This type was quite popular, with a total of about 175 fragmentary figurines surviving, including pieces mentioned in the catalogue and others counted in the lots. The size range is considerable, from size 2–3 up to statuette scale. Whether it represents a priestess or a goddess is not entirely clear; this question will be discussed further, but the name "priestess" is in any case a convenient designation to distinguish this type from others. The type has two variants, both produced in a range of quality from good to poor, in both molding and fabric. The first variant is not fully preserved in any one example, but can be reconstructed from three fragmentary figurines. The first is **H395**, which preserves the type from the head to the hips. It represents a standing female figure, wearing a V-necked peplos on top of a chiton, only the sleeves of which are visible; round buttons[5] fasten the peplos at the shoulders. The coiffure has a central part, a long lock of hair outlining each shoulder and a single thick braid falling down the back; this is a Classicizing motif, recalling the coiffure of the Erechtheion caryatids.[6] On the head is a polos with torus borders at the top and bottom. The pleasant face, with its short nose and crooked smile, does not quite match any of the others, but it is nevertheless within the stylistic parameters of Corinthian Hellenistic facial types. A blister at the right eye indicates the use of a plaster mold. The "priestess" cradles a piglet in her right arm and in her left supports a short, thick, conical torch with a large flame blowing away from her head but still unrealistically close to her hair.[7]

The second fragmentary figurine used to reconstruct this type is **H397**, which can be identified by the torch and piglet, although the torch is slanted closer to the shoulder. It preserves the torso down to the thigh, including the peplos overfold, which hangs, in a rather Classicizing manner, in narrow parallel folds terminating at the center of the hem in an omega (almost butterfly) fold and at the side in eye folds.[8] This pattern also is found on the overfold hem of the third fragmentary figurine used to reconstruct this type (**H396**), which is larger in scale and preserves the type from the hips (including the left hand holding the bottom of the torch) to the base. The skirt hem trails over the insteps of shoes with indented soles and makes a gradual, smooth transition to the edge of the low base.

The state of preservation of these three fragments precludes a determination of mechanical relationship, but they should belong to the same type. **H398** and **H400** appear to be a later generation of **H395**; the torch slants slightly toward the head of **H398** (although not as much as in **H397**) and was never separated from the side of the head after molding. A decline in craftsmanship is evident not only in this shortcut but also in the extremely dull and unretouched impression of **H398** and the poor fabric of **H400**. The smaller **H399**, which is of extremely coarse although probably local fabric, is nearly featureless; it has a torch flame virtually springing from the cheek and represents the nadir of craftsmanship in the first variant of the "priestess" type.

The type, from head to base, was complete in the front mold, with very little retouch; the back was also molded. The polos is flat in back, but its fully rounded contours in other "priestesses" (e.g., **H405**) show that the intended headdress was indeed a polos. The technique of including all elements, including the base, in a single front mold, and molding rather than hand modeling

---

in all periods Corinth imported a small number of figurines, those that could date before 146 B.C. would not be relevant. The figurines in this deposit could tell either a great deal or nothing at all.

[5] On buttons as fasteners, see Richter 1968, pp. 12–13.

[6] Lauter 1976, pl. 11.

[7] On Sicilian figurines carrying both a torch and a piglet, and found especially in sanctuaries of Demeter, see, e.g., Wegner 1982, pl. 58:3; the Sicilian types are quite different from the Corinthian.

[8] Cf., e.g., the Parthenon frieze: Robertson and Frantz 1975, pl. 9, West XII:23, the folds on the tunic hem; photo of cast with better-preserved detail in Ridgway 1981a, fig. 43.

the back, is known in earlier Corinthian figurines, for example, some of the Early Hellenistic votaries (e.g., **H1**), but the combination of this technique with the use of plaster molds is new.

The best-preserved example of the second variant of the "priestess" type is **H401**; it is preserved only to the thighs, but MF-9251 from the Southeast Building (Pl. 77, see catalogue) completes the type to the base. The lower part of the type, including leg positions, skirt arrangement, and base, seems to have been the same in both variants, although the proportions of the second variant are less slender, owing to the bulk of the extra drapery around the hips. In the second variant, a mantle was added to the peplos, covering the left shoulder, arm, and hand, and rolled around the waist to hang straight across the front like an apron; the peplos of this variant has a kolpos as well as an overfold, above which the edge of the mantle forms a second overfold. By the Middle Hellenistic period, the peplos arranged with a kolpos and overfold would have been extremely old-fashioned and must be accounted a Classicizing feature; the kolpos, however, is arranged straight across the top of the thighs, rather lower than the usual Classical arrangement, more like the Early Hellenistic votary **H17** than the Classical **C36**, for example. The torch is longer and thinner than in the first variant, and the flame is so small and pointed that the object resembles a scepter more than a torch; on the analogy of the first variant, however, a torch is probably what is meant. Further, a fragment in lot 6641 shows diagonal incisions along the object, suggesting that it was made of some material tied or twisted together, as a torch would have been.

There are several facial types, all rather similar to one another, associated with this variant. The face of **H401** is rounder and fleshier than the face of **H395**, with a prominent chin. It has level, rather round eyes; a short, wide nose close to the small, smiling mouth; and a thin upper lip. This facial type is known in a beautifully crafted head of statuette scale from the sanctuary (**H427**) and in others of smaller scale in the Corinth collection, none of them wearing the polos (see p. 258). The facial features of **H402** are similar, but the face is wider, and the features are more clustered toward the center. Other heads wearing a polos (**H403** and **H404**) show a generic similarity, but dull impressions or crude retouch conceal possible mechanical relationships. **H404** shows the surface blisters of plaster molding. In fact, many of the surviving heads of this type in the lots are so dull, perhaps in part owing to the use of plaster molds, that they are recognizable only by their general outlines. It is likely that this facial type descends from the type preserved in statuette scale (**H427**).

H405 is puzzling; it is larger than **H401** and was made in a more traditional Corinthian technique in a terracotta mold, suggesting that it could be closer to the original design. There are a few possibly significant differences, however: the polos is narrower and fits differently, set straight across the head; a lock of hair on the right shoulder covers the spot where the round button should be; and the hair in back is gathered into a roll at the nape with long locks of hair falling from it, in a coiffure perhaps similar to that of the Classical **C154**, although in the complete figurine, the long locks of hair in back could have been gathered into the braid associated with the first "priestess" variant. **H406** is another larger head that can be linked to this group, in this case by the preserved lower torus molding of what must be a polos. The facial type, however, is a departure from the norm, with fuller lips and narrowed, downturned eyes. The fabric of this head is also rather peculiar, more like that used for cooking pots than for figurines.

Like these heads, five large-scale torso fragments probably of the "priestess" type are varied in detail and quality of workmanship, suggesting that there was a certain amount of experimentation with this type before it was frozen into the variants reproduced by plaster molds. **H407** preserves only a fragment of the right side and a little of the front, showing an advanced right thigh with folds looped down to the side of the knee, but the characteristic kolpos with two hems above it is preserved. The fabric is excellent. The folds of the kolpos are carefully fashioned, in deep waves, not the random lumps of **H401**; the overfold hem waves more shallowly above the kolpos, and on top of all, the edge of the mantle apron is stretched tautly. A fragment of smaller scale, perhaps mechanically related (see catalogue under **H407**), preserves more of the overfold and shows two widely spaced vertical folds down the right hip, as in **H401**. It is unfortunate that so much is lost, since this must have been a good rendering of the type. Even less is preserved of **H408**, which is only a fragment of the characteristic double hem and kolpos. This piece is either heavily retouched or handmade, and shows that less careful renderings, with the kolpos folds merely indicated by slashes, also existed at statuette scale.

H409 preserves somewhat more of the overfold and skirt. Unfortunately, the surface is chipped, and so it is unclear whether the preserved bit of edge above the overfold hem is the edge of the mantle of a "priestess" type or just the end of an omega fold representing the pleat falling from the breast, as in **C36**. This figure is remarkable both for its size, which borders on sculptural scale, and for the remains of paint in four colors (yellow, bright blue, blue-green, and violet) on the skirt in no discernible pattern. **H410**, another statuette fragment, has the stance of the "priestess" type, a lumpy kolpos at thigh level comparable to that of **H401**, and a raised edge across the upper break that could belong to the right forearm bent to cradle the piglet, but the edge of the mantle is lacking. If the complete figure represented a "priestess," it would be a type combining aspects of **H395**, which lacks the mantle, and **H401**, which has a kolpos. Like **H409**, the skirt folds were deeply recut after modeling to emphasize light and shadow. In this respect, and also in the heavier breaking of the skirt hem over the insteps, **H410** is unlike the plaster-modeled versions. **H411** is a left-shoulder fragment of statuette scale with several elements of the "priestess" type: a long lock of hair framing the shoulder, a round button to fasten the peplos, and a chiton sleeve. This example, however, adds another lock of hair in front of the shoulder. The locks of hair and button were manual additions.

It is apparent from the foregoing discussion that there was great interest in this type in Corinth, and coroplasts found different solutions to its rendering in different workshops. As in other instances among the Corinthian figurines, the larger pieces stand alone, sometimes show a good deal of retouch, and cannot be mechanically connected with the more numerous smaller examples. Mechanical relationships are discernible only for the two plaster-molded series, two generations of which could be traced. It seems likely that the type was first developed at statuette scale and was produced in more than one workshop. Since the plaster-molded variants are identical in technique and have the same conformation of the skirt and base, it is likely that they were made in the same workshop. It is also likely that the plaster-molded versions were developed using workshop materials related to a mold found in Corinth in the South Stoa, well IV (Pl. 77).[9]

How this mold was related to the "priestess" figurines is a fascinating puzzle that shows how freely workshop materials could be reused and adapted to different types, and how difficult it is to reconstruct the workshop process when the evidence is incomplete. The mold, of statuette scale, represents a young woman in a pose and dress typical of votaries, standing quietly with both arms at her sides and wearing an ungirded peplos. Although no exact replica of this type was found at the Demeter sanctuary, its elements are recognizable in related types. The ungirded peplos with overfold to the top of the thighs, in a pyramidal outline and following the contours of the torso, can be found in the votary with piglet **H1**. The position of the arms is paralleled by **H37**. The closest parallel among the votaries is **H16**, which is similar in the wearing of a chiton beneath the peplos, in the fold pattern over the hips, and in the position of the right arm. The mold differs from the votaries in the amplitude of the body, with heavy arms and wide hips; the fastening of the peplos with round buttons; the facial type, which shows a narrow smiling mouth set into full

---

[9] MF-8993: Broneer 1947, p. 242, pl. LXII:23; *Coroplast's Art*, p. 57, fig. 44 (there incorrectly assigned to the Southeast Building).

cheeks and a prominent chin; and the long locks of hair outlining the shoulder. Although the mold must represent a votary, it is immediately apparent that there are elements in common with the "priestess" type: the characteristic shoulder-framing locks of hair, the peplos-over-chiton arrangement fastened with round buttons, the matronly proportions, and the facial type.

Exactly what this means can only be surmised. Of the general run of "priestess" figurines, only **H396** approaches the mold in scale, although it is still smaller. The other figurines are only somewhat more than half the size of the mold. Perhaps, once the "priestess" type was established at statuette scale using conventional techniques, one workshop made a cast from a later generation of a votary mold similar to the example from the South Stoa, remodeling the figure from the chest down and then taking plaster molds from this new archetype. Alternatively, we can assume that we do not have the earliest generations of the "priestess" type, or have them in too fragmentary a state to understand them, and that both the votary type known from the mold and the earliest "priestesses" were developed at the same time from the same archetype, as part of the same iconographic series. What this archetype could have been is another question.

The material from which the design was derived is diverse. Although votaries carrying a piglet were already well known in Corinth in the Early Hellenistic period, the inspiration for a standing female figure cradling a piglet in one arm and also holding a torch in the other is most likely to have come from the long series of Sicilian figurines of this type representing Persephone, which were still being produced in a conservative style through the 3rd century B.C.[10] In this source, the arm positions were reversed, with the piglet carried in the left arm. Apart from the subject, however, the more advanced, purely Hellenistic style of the South Stoa mold and the "priestess" figurines must come from a completely different source. The source for **H401**, with its full-cheeked facial type with a small mouth and prominent chin, coupled with a polos, can perhaps be found in northern Asia Minor and Dacia, where similar heads of figurines are more common; examples from Troy, Callatis, Pergamon, and Gordion can be cited, particularly for figurines of the enthroned Cybele.[11] A similar sculptural iconography for Cybele was brought to Greece, as in double naïskoi of the Mother of the Gods from Delphi, Corinth, and Athens, which show a comparable facial type, round in shape, with a wide, flat nose and thin lips.[12] Pausanias (2.4.7) records a temple and statue of the Mother of the Gods on Acrocorinth, apparently not far from the Sanctuary of Demeter and Kore. While some of the evidence for the worship of the Mother in Corinth must be of Roman or uncertain date, two figurine fragments point to local interest in her iconography during the Hellenistic period[13] and suggest that a representation of her could have been the source for the head of the "priestess" type.

Types other than Cybele, however, also reflect a similar facial type. The head of Nyx (or Persephone) from the Great Altar of Pergamon[14] can be cited as another parallel for the facial type and shows matronly proportions as well, although there are no signs in the "priestess" group of the Pergamene baroque drapery style. The inclusion of Classical, even specifically Atticizing elements, as mentioned above (a coiffure like that of the Erechtheion caryatids, a 5th-century B.C. Attic drapery pattern, the peplos with a kolpos), recall this trend in Pergamene art in the later

[10] *Morgantina*, p. 48.

[11] *Troy*, e.g., p. 82, no. 28, pl. X (there dated later, however, to the early 1st century B.C.); Canarache 1969, pp. 59–61, nos. 26–29, 31 (heads only); Bordenache 1960, p. 501, fig. 14; *Coroplast's Art*, p. 41, fig. 29; pp. 105–106, fig. 100; Romano 1995, esp. pp. 24–25, no. 52, pl. 15. For a collection of Hellenistic terracotta figurines representing Cybele, see Naumann 1983, pp. 269–274.

[12] *FdD* IV, vi, pp. 41–43, no. 11; S-2557 in Corinth is illustrated in fig. 27.

[13] MF-4917 (*Corinth* XII, p. 56, no. 388, pl. 35); MF-2486 (*Corinth* XII, p. 45, no. 260, pl. 22) was associated with Cybele in *Troy*, p. 83, under no. 45. On the Mother of the Gods in Corinth, see Lisle 1955, pp. 31, 118, 166.

[14] A good photograph of the head in nearly frontal view in Pollitt 1986, p. 104, fig. 108. On the identification as Persephone, see Pfanner 1979, pp. 54–55.

3rd and early 2nd centuries B.C.[15] In Egypt, a similar facial type turns up in sculptures of a goddess carrying a torch and wearing a polos, which are identified as Demeter-Isis.[16]

The "priestess" type appears to be based on a remarkable array of sources. If her pose and the attributes of piglet and torch are derived from Sicilian figurines, her facial type is of eastern origin, and her Classicizing elements are Pergamene in flavor, the mantle arrangement of the second variant (**H401**) may be a relatively local affair. Two headless Hellenistic statues from Megara show the mantle draped apron-style around the torso.[17] One statue has the mantle rolled around the waist and over the left shoulder and arm; there are catenaries over the abdomen, as in **H401**, but only the mantle hem shows above the kolpos, the hem of the peplos overfold being hidden. The second statue, a more heavy-set figure, shows both hems, as in **H401**; the mantle is draped over both shoulders and the chest and forms an additional, triangular apron in front. Perhaps the closest in drapery arrangement to **H401**, although the head is unrelated, is a statue from "near Athens" in New York.[18] This figure shows both hems above the kolpos, and the upper torso is similarly draped as well. The subjects of these statues are uncertain. The forearms of all were extended, suggesting an *orans* pose; the examples from Megara could have been portrait statues of priestesses, given the apron motif in one of them.[19] The statue in New York, however, has an idealized rather than a portrait head; she does not wear a polos.

Whatever technique was entailed in the actual creation of the "priestess" type from these disparate elements, it is unlikely to have happened before the later 3rd century B.C. Lot 3217 (Pit 1965-1), which contains pottery dating through the third quarter of the 3rd century B.C. and more than two hundred figurines, has no recognizable fragments of any version of the "priestess" type.[20] While such an *argumentum ex silentio* is certainly not conclusive, the evidence of style in this case also points toward the later 3rd to early 2nd centuries B.C. for the creation of the type.[21]

The final matter to be discussed is the actual identity of the "priestess" type. The polos immediately suggests that we are dealing with a goddess.[22] The closest iconographic parallels for female figurines holding the piglet and torch are from Sicily;[23] they have been convincingly shown to represent Persephone, although the pig and torch are associated with Demeter as well. The Corinthian type already has been published as a representation of Demeter.[24] There is, moreover, a known syncretism between Demeter and Cybele,[25] whose iconography apparently was a factor in the development of this type. The matronly appearance of figure and face might support the identification as Demeter, but the mold from the South Stoa (MF-8993, Pl. 77), which must portray a young votary on the basis of dress, pose, and coiffure, nevertheless has a generously proportioned figure and a not particularly youthful facial type.[26] Although Corinthian coroplasts of the Early Hellenistic period seem to have been adept at rendering persons of differing ages in a

---

[15] Summarized by Pollitt 1986, pp. 83–84.

[16] Besques 1981, pp. 236–239, esp. fig. 20, in Cairo.

[17] Horn 1931, p. 93, pl. 42.

[18] Richter 1954, p. 200, no. 201, pl. CXLII.

[19] On the apron as a priestly attribute, see the discussion of **H85**, p. 140. On the *orans* pose, see *Thasos* XVII, pp. 476–478; a few of the Corinthian peplos-figurines (e.g., **C17**) may have taken this pose, but the forearms are not preserved.

[20] There is one "priestess" head among the more than 1,200 figurines from lot 2249, part of the construction fill of the Trapezoidal Building, the pottery of which terminates at the beginning of the 3rd century B.C. While the material from this lot is almost entirely consistent for the 4th century B.C. and earlier, the fill is not a sealed deposit and contains an occasional stray sherd or figurine fragment. The head must be intrusive in this lot. Similarly, one head in lot 2063 (MF-11781) must be later than the 4th-century B.C. to Early Hellenistic pottery

in the lot. **H401** is from a pottery lot (6502) terminating in the first half of the 3rd century B.C., but the architectural context of the lot is later. On the use of pottery contexts for dating the figurines, see pp. 5–6.

[21] Romano (1994, p. 90, no. 76) has conflated the "priestess" type with the earlier votary with piglet ("pig girl") type and has published a too-long date range that should be disregarded.

[22] On the polos as a sign of godhead, see *Morgantina*, pp. 81–82; Zuntz 1971, p. 92 (not necessarily a sign of a deity); on the polos worn by Cybele: D. B. Thompson 1954, pp. 99–103.

[23] Wegner 1982; *Morgantina*, pp. 81–83, 134–137, nos. 65–84, pls. 17–19.

[24] *LIMC* IV, 1988, p. 856, no. 102, pl. 570 (= **H395**), s.v. *Demeter* (L. Beschi).

[25] Reeder 1987, p. 436, with bibliography.

[26] On the pitfalls of trying to separate Demeter from Kore on the basis of age, see *Morgantina*, p. 82.

naturalistic manner, perhaps in this instance the attempt to distinguish between the two goddesses is ill advised. For one thing, the earlier tradition of votive types appears to have ceased by this time. For another, the coroplast could, consciously or not, have embodied the aspects of both goddesses in one type.[27]

An element that complicates the matter further is the mantle of the second variant, which is wrapped like an apron around the torso in the manner of participants in sacrifices (see p. 140, note 150). There is written evidence for priestesses of Demeter and Persephone in Corinth (Diodoros 16.66.3–4; Plutarch, *Timoleon* 8.1), reporting their dream before Timoleon's expedition to Sicily. On the other hand, deities also are shown in Greek art participating in sacrifice, sometimes wearing a mantle folded into an apron.[28] Certainly the distinction between mortal and deity can be blurred in ritual. At Eleusis, the priestess of Demeter and Kore is thought to have impersonated both goddesses during the celebration of the Mysteries.[29]

Whether goddess or mortal is sacrificing in the figurine type, the ritual context would turn the "attributes" of piglet and torch into, respectively, the sacrificial animal and the means of lighting the altar.[30] A further connection of the torch with this sanctuary is Plutarch's (*Timoleon* 8.3) comparison of the torch that guided Timoleon to Sicily with the torch used in the Mysteries. Perhaps we are dealing here with a type filled with meaning, embodying simultaneously the goddesses themselves, the mortal priestess in the guise of the goddesses, the act of sacrifice, and the sacred symbols of the cult. It is perhaps not insignificant that the "priestess" type was developed at a time when the long series of votaries carrying a piglet appear to have come to an end. If these figurines were dedicated in place of the votary types, does it mean that they, too, represent mortals, or does it show a greater emphasis on the goddesses and their servants, implying some movement in the cult toward greater institutionalization and less personal involvement?[31] Further, if the iconography of Cybele contributed to the creation of a popular votive type, can we assume that worshipers recognized Cybele in the type, and are we to see an expansion in the focus of the cult, at least in the syncretism of Cybele with Demeter, or perhaps with Aphrodite Ourania, with whom Cybele was associated at Isthmia?[32] If the nearby shrine of the Mother of the Gods mentioned by Pausanias (2.4.7) was active in the Hellenistic period, could there have been influence from that source?

OTHER STANDING DRAPED FEMALE TYPES (**H412–H424**)

The possible convergence of priestess and goddess images in the figurine group just discussed has some relevance to **H412**, which also may show some overlap of types. Most of the head of this statuette is missing, but there is enough to show long, thick locks of hair flowing freely over the shoulders. The peplos, more of which is preserved in a later generation (see catalogue), is ungirded and has the pyramidal outline typical of votary figurines (see p. 118); a chiton sleeve is marked on one arm. The later generation has both arms at the sides. Since the unbound coiffure of **H412** is also typical of votaries, it would seem that we have here such a type. The type would be a rougher, less detailed version of a votary resembling the mold from the South Stoa (MF-8993, Pl. 77). In **H412**, however, the right upper arm is extended to the side, in a pose

[27] This may have happened in the case of the seated goddess on the painted Corinthian plate of the Sam Wide Group in Athens (see p. 43).

[28] *Morgantina*, pp. 45–48, with bibliography; for a sacrificing god wearing a triangular apron, see p. 167, no. 295a, pl. 66. See Simon 1953, pp. 67–78, on the Eleusinian deities sacrificing.

[29] Mylonas 1961, pp. 310–311; R. S. J. Garland 1984, p. 100. There is no mention of this aspect of the priestess' function in the material collected by Clinton 1974, pp. 68–76.

[30] Artemis lights the altar with torches in a bronze relief from Delos: *LIMC* II, 1984, pp. 699–700, no. 1027, pl. 525, s.v. *Artemis* (L. Kahil and N. Icard).

[31] Van Straten's study (1993) of the composition of Classical and Hellenistic votive reliefs suggests that the gods seem more distant from humans in the latter period, when they are placed above humans in vertical compositions, implying a relationship of ruler to subject (pp. 263–264).

[32] *Isthmia* VI, pp. 39–43, no. 89, pl. 31:b; Harrison 1982a, pp. 50–51.

expected not of a votary but of a goddess, who might lean on a scepter or long torch. If indeed a votary figure has been so altered, a convergence of mortal and divine types could then be seen in this image. **H414** is similar in scale and technique and could be of the same type; if so, it would show more of the head, but the poor state of preservation reveals only full, parted lips and perhaps a short nose in an oval face.

H415 could belong to this group, although the pose of the head is more rigidly frontal. The broad-cheeked, girlish face, short nose, and long hair call to mind the head wearing a stephane (**H178**), which was found in a pottery context of the late 4th century B.C. The face of **H415** is essentially Classical, but the combination of such a face with deeply shadowed, snaky locks of hair, which are more consonant with a Middle Hellenistic date, suggests that the head was made not earlier than the late 3rd or early 2nd century B.C. The fragmentary **H413** is of similar type, as far as it is preserved, and of still larger scale. All the pieces in this group are of coarse workmanship; in **H413**, the hair in back is merely an added thick, undetailed sheet of clay.

The group that follows is of vastly superior workmanship, but it may be related in type to the preceding group. **H416** is the raised right arm of a statuette with long locks of hair and wearing a sleeved chiton. As such, it calls to mind the type better preserved compositionally in the poorly crafted **H412**; its very large scale and good workmanship, with well-modeled, gilded hair and a violet-painted garment, suggest that it could belong to the type of which **H412** was a poor relation. The piece is not unique, since there are similar statuette fragments in the lots (see catalogue). It is similar in fabric and scale to the possible "priestess" fragment **H411**.

There are also a few pieces of related type in statuette scale made in a pale, thinner-walled and harder-fired fabric, somewhat like one of the better Roman fabrics, as in the Aphrodite figurines **R13** and **R14**. The raised right arm, long locks of hair, and chiton sleeve of **H417** should link it typologically with the group under discussion, particularly since both the sleeve and the hair were manual additions, suggesting that the coroplast was aiming to reproduce a particular type. There are no clear signs of a peplos over the chiton, however. **H418**, which probably belongs to the same statuette on the basis of scale, fabric, and technique, shows a mantle rolled around the hips and a distinctive pattern of arrowhead folds. The only other instance of such folds among the figurines from the Demeter sanctuary are across the mantle overfold of **H85**, where they are more organically coherent. Perhaps the folds of **H418** were pulled into points by the forward movement of the right thigh in the complete figure. The mantle is rolled neither snuggly around the waist, as in **H85**, nor below the navel, framing the abdomen, as in **H128**, but somewhere modestly in between. The outstretched arm certainly suggests that this statuette represents one of the goddesses holding a scepter or perhaps a torch, but there are no clues to her identity.

H419 is another statuette of similar fabric, preserved sufficiently to show the girding of the chiton at the natural waistline. In this case, the rolled mantle falls to just below the knees and is transparent, with very lightly modeled folds, and faint vertical folds of the chiton are visible beneath. The use of gilding and violet paint link it technically with **H416**. Exactly when the rendering of drapery seen through a layer of transparent cloth began is unclear, but it surely was in use by the later 3rd century B.C.[33] A group of large (size range 3 to 4–5), thin-walled, draped female figurines (**H130**, **H138**, **H140**, **H144**, and **H145**) has been discussed in the Early Hellenistic chapter (pp. 149–150) because the drapery arrangements, as far as preserved, could be read as Early Hellenistic. Their fabric and scale, however, which are reminiscent of the group now under discussion, might bring their date of manufacture down into the Middle Hellenistic period.

H420 is a statuette fragment that must represent one of the goddesses, could be a variant of the long-haired type with a raised right arm (e.g., **H417**), and probably should be dated to this

---

[33] The arguments are summarized by Ridgway 1990, pp. 219–220, with reference to the Baker Dancer.

period by virtue of its combination of large scale and coarse rendering. In this case, a mantle originally seems to have been draped behind the figure and over the raised arm from front to back, with the edge folds showing at the extreme right. The hand that emerged from the mantle folds and is now missing grasped a thick, cylindrical object that tapers slightly toward the bottom and is probably a torch. This statuette could represent Kore, although long locks of hair and a torch are attributes of Demeter as well. Another fragment of statuette scale with rough retouch is **H421**, which preserves part of a female type with an advanced left thigh, covered with curving mantle folds, and the mantle end, which must have dropped from the arm, beside it.

Further indications of dramatically draped female types of statuette scale are a number of foot fragments wearing sandals with very high, indented soles and usually showing long toes and heavily collapsing hems over the insteps. Three examples have been catalogued (**H422–H424**), the last of which may have belonged to a seated type. The high soles, deeply indented around the toes, suggest a 2nd-century B.C. date, particularly for **H424** in which the toes slightly overhang the edge of the sole.[34] The thongs or straps are not represented in relief, even at this large scale, and must have been painted.[35] Such high-soled sandals were rendered by coroplasts in Pergamon[36] and Priene[37] during the 2nd century B.C. and are well known in Hellenistic sculptured female figures as well.[38] Among the Corinthian figurines, the only identifiable type from the Demeter sanctuary to wear fairly high-soled sandals is the semidraped standing Aphrodite **H249**.[39] A standing draped female figurine in Munich, which is probably Corinthian, wears very high-soled sandals.[40] The type is otherwise unremarkable, however, wearing a chiton and mantle draped loosely around the hips; the head is similar to **H227**, with a melon coiffure. If the figurine represents a mortal woman, as it seems, the high-soled sandals would simply be a matter of fashion.

The most striking aspect of these Middle Hellenistic figurines is the preponderance of large scale. Doubtless, smaller figurines in the Early Hellenistic tradition were still being made, but there is a noticeable shift away from types that are either also known in bronze or look as if they could have been designed in conjunction with small bronzes, toward types that often call to mind stone sculpture. Perhaps it is not too farfetched to suggest that by the middle or third quarter of the 3rd century B.C. the Corinthian industry that had encouraged the production of terracotta figurines in conjunction with small bronzes was no longer active and that coroplasts had to look elsewhere for models. It is perhaps significant that the influence of stone sculpture on terracotta figurines during the Middle Hellenistic period was felt in other centers as well, such as Priene, where the rich Hellenistic sculptural tradition of Asia Minor was an important factor.[41]

ISOLATED FEMALE HEADS
(H425–H430)

A relatively small number of heads, including some of statuette scale, show facial types and coiffures that were not part of the Early Hellenistic repertoire. **H425** and **H426** have faces that are comparable to the "priestess" **H401**, although they are so degenerate that mechanical relationships are not clear. Both have long, flowing hair and tubular fillets, which are also found in Early Hellenistic votaries such as **H20**. The added veil of **H425** is not paralleled among the earlier figurines, except that their smooth, long locks of hair are sometimes veil-like, as in the torch carrier **H23**.

---

[34] Morrow 1985, pp. 90–97, 162–163, figs. 8, 9.

[35] For sandal details represented in relief on figurines, see, e.g., *Troy*, p. 126, no. 168, pl. XXXVII.

[36] *Pergamon*, pp. 30, 207, no. 101, pl. 15.

[37] Töpperwein-Hoffmann 1971, pp. 142–143, pl. 46:1; *Priene*, p. 351, fig. 416.

[38] E.g., Horn 1931, pl. 18:2 (Tragoidia from Pergamon).

[39] **H148** also wears similar sandals but is too fragmentary to identify.

[40] Züchner 1942, p. 177, fig. 89.

[41] Töpperwein-Hoffmann 1971, pp. 156–160.

A particularly fine head of statuette scale (**H427**) shows a certain structural relation to the head of Nyx (or Persephone) from the Great Altar of Zeus at Pergamon, which was also cited above as a parallel for some of the heads of the "priestess" type.[42] Both heads are wide across the cheekbones and have prominent chins, relatively small eyes with well-defined lids, and fleshy, parted lips; in both, the hair is looped back to the cranium from a central part, all around the head, in thick, separate locks. The heads are not identical—**H427** has a proportionately larger nose and a thinner upper lip, a feature that is found in other Middle Hellenistic Corinthian heads as well (e.g., **H401** and **H428**)—but the similarity is striking enough to suggest a date for **H427** in the second quarter of the 2nd century B.C. The relationship is strengthened by the addition of locks of hair to **H427** to render a coiffure that is found in the Altar in other heads as well, for example, the so-called beautiful head.[43] Like Athens in the second half of the 5th century B.C., Pergamon in the first half of the 2nd century B.C. was the source of a widely disseminated style. Knowledge of that style could have reached Corinth either through craftsmen familiar with it or through imported workshop materials, although not, apparently, through imported figurines.

The same deliberately added coiffure is found on **H428**, another well-made head of statuette scale. It has a longer and more straight-sided face and is in the tradition of such Early Hellenistic heads as **H180**, but the large scale, coiffure, and thin upper lip should make it contemporary with **H427**. This head seems to be a reworking of a local type rather than a new creation based on foreign material. Both these heads show that workshops employing highly skilled craftsmen and interested in the most recent artistic developments were still active in Corinth shortly before the destruction of the city in 146 B.C.

H427 originally wore a stephane, but the subject of the head is unknown, since the stephane could be worn by either goddesses or mortals. The facial type became very popular, reappearing at smaller scale repeatedly, although not clearly in mechanical relationship (see catalogue), in heads wearing different headdresses. For example, **H429**, in which the face has become nearly round, has a coiffure with a bow-knot, which has been nearly concealed by a thick, added wreath wrapped in a fillet. Such wreaths have been dated to the 2nd century B.C.; the wearing of wreaths is associated with festivals, which suggests that **H429** represents a mortal woman.[44] **H430** may be a degenerate version of this facial type, with a veil added; it is the only head from the sanctuary so veiled.

Perhaps the head **H191** should be mentioned here once again. It was discussed with Early Hellenistic heads (p. 160) because of its 4th-century B.C. facial type, but its large scale and classicizing coiffure could point to a 2nd-century B.C. date of manufacture.

ISOLATED MALE HEAD
(H431)

The remaining head (**H431**), of statuette scale, probably represents a male, since the flesh is painted red. The long, centrally parted hair is known for males in the Early Hellenistic standing nude youth **H299**. It is possible, however, that the red paint, which was applied directly to the clay, without the customary underlying white slip, and which covers the eyeballs, was itself an underpainting for the pink paint of female flesh. The head is likely to be entirely handmade and not merely heavily reworked, not only because it has an uneven surface but also because it is solid, and a head of this scale would normally be hollow if it were moldmade. The rendering of the hair suggests that this head must be among the latest Corinthian coroplastic work before 146 B.C., since the snaky, separately modeled, almost Pergamene locks of hair point to the second

---

[42] See p. 253, note 14.

[43] Luschey 1962, pp. 12–19 on the "beautiful head"; for the coiffure, see also p. 4, fig. 3.

[44] On wreaths, see *Troy*, pp. 45–47; Blech 1982.

quarter of the 2nd century B.C. That **H431** is probably handmade is in itself of interest, even though the craftsman was not highly skilled, cutting the nose and mouth crudely and shaping the eyes differently from one another. There is as yet only a little evidence for terracotta sculpture in Corinth in the Hellenistic period,[45] but the existence of a handmade head in size range 5 points to a workshop making what are essentially small sculptures as late as the second quarter of the 2nd century B.C. Another intriguing aspect of this head is that the workshop may have been trying to render a head of the Eubouleus type, a much-copied marble youth based on a 4th-century B.C. work and possibly representing Triptolemos.[46] Taking into account the different material and the rough technique, the sculptor's intention was to create a head of a youth with uncut hair waving in thick locks, with an open pincer of two curved locks of hair on the forehead, and a full-featured face with fleshy lips. This description generally fits the Eubouleus type and points to the possibility that, if this head represents a male, Triptolemos was represented at the sanctuary.

CATALOGUE

For an explanation of the conventions employed in this catalogue, see the Introduction, pages 20–22.

DRAPED FEMALE FIGURINES AND RELATED HEADS

H395 Priestess(?)   Pl. 56

MF-10325. Lot 870. Preserved: head to left hip, to waist at right side. Mended; nose chipped. P.H. 0.109 (size 3). Fabric 3, buff. White slip. Violet paint on polos, orange on torch. Hollow. All parts rendered in same mold. Back molded, rounded. Tooling on torch, hand. Blisters on surface indicate use of plaster mold.

Published: Stroud 1965, p. 22, pl. 11:a.

Right arm bent, cradles across waist piglet with ridged back, fierce expression; front feet of piglet rest in her hand. Left arm at side; conical torch held vertically against torso by missing hand. Vertical reeds of torch and three horizontal bindings are incised; flame is blown to side. Matronly proportions; rounded shoulders. Sleeves of chiton show beneath peplos, which is fastened at shoulders by round buttons; deep V-shaped folds at neck. Face oval to oblong, with high, triangular forehead; prominent chin. Features slightly distorted at right side. Eyes level, deeply set; right eye blistered; lids defined. Nose short, upturned. Lips full, slightly parted, smiling. Creases on neck. Hair parted at center; faint horizontal waves in front; long, twisted locks of hair frame shoulders; outline of thick braid down back. Polos is shallow, flat in back; torus moldings at top and bottom. Round earrings. Probable mold sibling of head: MF-10326 (lot 870, fabric 1); others in lots 3230, 4349, 6214 (fabric 1). Probable later generation: **H400** (head). Similar in type: **H398**. For lower part of type, see **H396** and **H397**.

See pp. 16, 17, 120, note 39, 124, 132, 133, 249, 250, 251, 252, 254, note 24, 314.

H396 Priestess(?)   Pl. 56

MF-10329. Lot 870. Preserved: hips to base. P.H. 0.15 (size 3–4). Fabric 3, orange-buff to orange. White slip. Red paint on feet. Hollow. All parts rendered in same mold. Thin-walled. Back molded, flattened, flaring at bottom. Bottom of rectangular vent preserved, 0.025 wide.

Probably lower part of same type as **H395**, although of larger scale. Weight on left leg. Right leg advanced, knee bent, clearly modeled beneath drapery. Hem trails almost to edge of base, arches over shoes with indented soles. Peplos overfold to top of thighs; omega fold at center; zigzag fold of open edge of peplos at right hip. Left hand holds bottom of narrowing torch against skirt. Base is oval, with torus molding at bottom. Probable later generation in lots 870, 2107 (base lower, without torus molding).

See pp. 249, 250, 253.

H397 Priestess(?)   Pl. 56

MF-14077. Lot 2107. Preserved: front–left side from chest to thigh, left wrist and hand, top of torch; right arm with piglet. Mended. P.H. 0.13 (size 3). Fabric 3, creamy buff to orange-buff. Hollow.

Upper part is similar in type to **H395**; lower part has central omega fold and position of left hand as in **H396**. Upper part of torch leans in towards shoulder, however, and wrist is more flexed; torch probably was short, with hand supporting bottom.

See pp. 249, 250.

H398 Priestess(?)   Pl. 56

MF-14072. Lot 870. Preserved: head to hips. Mended. P.H. 0.113 (size 3). Fabric 3, orange-buff to creamy buff. White slip. Red paint on polos; yellow on peplos. Hollow. All parts rendered in same mold. Back molded, slightly flattened. Top of rectangular vent preserved, 0.021 wide. Tooling on right sleeve. Blisters on surface indicate use of plaster mold.

Similar in type to **H395** but slightly smaller; torch slanted slightly inward toward head. Facial features indistinct. Dull impression.

See pp. 249, 250.

---

[45] Bookidis 1982.

[46] Ridgway 1990, p. 117, with bibliography on p. 140, note 17; Clinton 1992, pp. 57–58, 135–136, nos. 4–14.

H399 Priestess(?)   Pl. 56

MF-69-303. Lot 6215. Preserved: front–center and left side
of head, top of torch; back–head to waist. P.H. 0.072 (size 2–
3). Fabric fairly coarse, orange-brown, with some small to
medium dark red, gray, and white inclusions; sparse small
sparkling inclusions; voids. Hollow. Back molded, rounded;
incised epsilon. Edge of round vent preserved at break.

Polos and top of torch beside head at left side suggest type
originally was similar to **H395**. Dull impression. Fabric not
typically Corinthian, but inclusions seem local.

See pp. 249, 250.

H400 Priestess(?)   Pl. 56

MF-14078. Lot 4350. Preserved: front–head to right shoulder.
P.H. 0.05 (size 3). Fabric 5, orange. White slip. Hollow.

Probably later generation of **H395**; similar distortion shows
on right side of face. Dull impression. Probable mold siblings: MF-10758 (lot 869, fabric 1); others in lots 2107, 4363
(fabric 1).

See pp. 249, 250.

H401 Priestess(?)   Pl. 56

MF-70-26. Lot 6502. Preserved: head to thighs. Missing
fragments of top of chest, left shoulder, right forearm and hip,
back, top of torch. Mended; right side of head chipped. Plaster restorations. P.H. 0.158 (size 3). Fabric 3, pinkish orange
to orange-buff. White slip. Red paint on mantle. Hollow.
All parts rendered in same mold. Back molded, flattened,
flaring towards bottom. Rectangular vent, 0.033 × 0.021.
Possible tooling on skirt folds. Blisters on surface indicate use
of plaster mold.

Published: Bookidis and Fisher 1972, p. 316, pl. 62:d; *Coroplast's Art*, p. 57, fig. 43.

Similar in type to **H395**, but with a long, thin cylindrical
shaft at left side. Peplos shows a kolpos below the overfold hem.
Over peplos is a mantle, rolled around the waist, forming an
apron covering the peplos overfold (hence there are two hems
above the kolpos); row of catenaries down the apron front,
with wide, flat folds at either side. Mantle is draped over left
shoulder, arm, and hand; short cascade of folds below hand.
Piglet has curly tail. Face of priestess is round to oval, with
triangular forehead; prominent chin. Eyes level, rather round;
both lids defined. Nose short, wide, close to thin upper lip.
One long lock of hair at each side, framing shoulders. Bottom
of type completed by probable mold sibling MF-9251 from
the Southeast Building (Pl. 77; Romano 1994, p. 90, no. 76,
pl. 28); skirt and base are similar to **H396**, base slightly lower.
Probable mold siblings of head: MF-11054 (lot 1955, fabric 1);
others in lots 870, 3227, 3230, 6214 (all fabric 1). Possible
earlier generation of head: MF-12022 (lot 2240, fabric 5, polos
fully rounded); others in lots 2249, 6500.

See pp. 6, 75, 140, 249, 251–252, 253, 254, 257, 258.

H402 Priestess(?)   Pl. 56

MF-14075. Lot 2107. Preserved: head to abdomen in front,
to shoulders in back. Missing most of chest, right side of
neck, top of left shoulder. Mended; hand chipped. P.H. 0.116
(size 3). Fabric 3, orange-buff to greenish buff. Hollow. All
parts rendered in same mold. Back molded, flattened. Blisters
on surface indicate use of plaster mold.

Similar in type to **H401**. Cylindrical object at left side

resembles a scepter more than a torch because of small, stiff,
upright "flame," with two rings below it. Creases on neck. Facial type similar to **H401**, but face is wider and shorter, features
more clustered toward center of face. Probable mold siblings:
MF-10328 (lot 870); MF-13147 (lot 4478, fabric 5); MF-11658
(lot 2009); MF-11058 (lot 1955, head, fabric 1); MF-11781
(lot 2063, head); other heads in lots 870, 2107, 3230, 6214
(all fabric 1). Probable later generation in lots 3230 (head,
fabric 1), 6641 (preserves slightly more of skirt).

See pp. 249, 251.

H403 Head of priestess(?)   Pl. 56

MF-11686. Lot 2011. Preserved: head and neck. Missing
outer surface in back; surface worn. P.H. 0.048 (size 3).
Fabric 5, orange. White slip. Hollow. Thick-walled.

Similar in type to head of **H401**. Face quite round, with
puffy cheeks. Neck wide, with creases. Dull impression.

See pp. 249, 251.

H404 Head of priestess(?)   Pl. 57

MF-10948. Lot 1945. Preserved: head. P.H. 0.038 (size 3).
Fabric 5, orange. White slip. Hollow. Thick-walled. Back
probably molded. Tooling on face, hair. Blisters on surface
indicate use of plaster mold.

Similar in type to head of **H401**. Coarse retouch of face
has turned corners of mouth downward. Right eye smaller
than left. Possible later generation: MF-10949 (lot 1945, fabric 1, retains down-curving mouth, but most obvious blisters
removed).

See pp. 16, 249, 251.

H405 Head of priestess(?)   Pl. 57

MF-14076. Lot 2107. Preserved: head to upper chest (front
only). Mended; surface worn. P.H. 0.065 (size 3–4). Fabric 2,
light orange, with sparse small sparkling inclusions. Head
solid, torso hollow. Back molded, rounded. Added: locks of
hair on shoulder.

Similar in type to head of **H401**, but polos is narrower,
with incurving sides, and is fully rounded in back; no earrings.
Hair is rolled in back, with long locks of hair at nape; lock of
hair down front of right shoulder. Probable mold siblings in
lots 2107, 3207. Probable later generation in lots 2107, 3207
(both fabric 1).

See pp. 249, 250, 251.

H406 Head of priestess(?)   Pl. 57

MF-70-260. Lot 6503. Preserved: front–head and neck.
Missing most of right side of face; nose chipped. P.H. 0.059
(size 4). Fabric orange, laminated in fracture, with some small
to medium white, dark red, and gray inclusions; sparse small
sparkling inclusions (somewhat resembles cooking-pot fabric).
Hollow. Added: earring.

Face oblong to oval, with high, triangular forehead; prominent chin. Eyes slightly downturned; lids fleshy, half-closed.
Nose close to upper lip. Lips full. Coiffure parted at center,
with slightly waved horizontal locks of hair to either side; lower
torus border of polos preserved. Large pellet earring.

See pp. 249, 251.

H407 Priestess(?)   Pl. 57

MF-70-249. Lot 6507. Preserved: right side and part of front,
including hip and thigh, adjacent folds. P.H. 0.063 (size 3–4).

Fabric 4, orange to orange-buff, with orange interior, blue-gray core. White slip. Exterior surface polished. Hollow. Tooling on folds, kolpos.

Right leg advanced. Two hems above deeply folded kolpos; lower hem is the overfold, upper hem is probably the apron of the mantle, as in **H401**. Looped folds down outside of thigh to knee (photograph shows side view). Possibly mechanically related: one in lot 6501 (smaller, overfold and kolpos fragment).
See pp. 249, 251–252.

H408 Priestess(?) Pl. 57
MF-68-376. Lot 5613. Preserved: fragment of hip. P.H. 0.036, P.L. 0.073 (size 4–5?). Fabric 1, orange-buff, orange inside. Hollow. Thick-walled. Either surface was very heavily tooled or handmade drapery was added to figure after molding.

Two hems above kolpos, the folds of which are marked by incisions. On basis of costume, type is probably like that of **H401** but in statuette scale.
See pp. 249, 252.

H409 Priestess(?) Pl. 57
MF-13138A, B. Lot 4349. Preserved: A–front-left side, chest to mid-thigh; B–nonjoining, possibly from side (not illustrated). Mended; surface chipped. P.H.: A–0.22; B–0.12 (size 5). Fabric 1, orange-buff, with orange core. White slip. Yellow, bright blue, blue-green, violet paint on skirt. Hollow. Added: possibly kolpos and overfold. Tooling on skirt folds.

Portion of edge preserved above overfold hem could be hem of apron, suggesting that costume is like that of **H401**; this edge, however, also could be the bottom of a pleat dropping from the breast, as in **C36**. Vertical skirt folds are stiff, angular, deeply cut. Fragment B, perhaps from side, shows one clear overfold, no kolpos.
See pp. 249, 252.

H410 Priestess(?) Pl. 57
MF-11073. Lot 1962. Preserved: Right hip and left thigh to hem. Missing feet. Mended. P.H. 0.16 (size 4). Fabric 1, orange-buff, orange inside. White slip. Hollow. Back molded, rounded. Added: vertical folds at both sides. Tooling on folds.

Right leg bent, foot drawn back. Overfold hem and kolpos at mid-thigh. Raised edges at break, perhaps belonging to right forearm folded across torso. Looped folds from right knee to ankle. Skirt folds deeply cut, frame legs at sides; kolpos folds indicated by short, curving strokes. Hem trails over insteps.
See pp. 249, 252.

H411 Priestess(?) Pl. 57
MF-13814. Lot 4362. Preserved: front-left shoulder, with locks of hair. Max.P.Dim. 0.056 (size 5). Fabric slightly coarse, creamy buff to orange-buff, with sparse small gray and white inclusions, voids. Hollow. Added: hair, button. Tooling on hair.

Left shoulder, sloping; upper arm probably originally lowered. Diagonal fold begins V-shaped fold of neckline. Probably wears peplos over chiton: round button fastens peplos at shoulder; two sets of oval grooves from shoulder to upper arm suggest fastening of chiton sleeve. Two long, tubular locks of hair, one framing shoulder, one in front, diagonally slashed.
See pp. 249, 252, 256.

H412 Standing draped female statuette Pl. 58
MF-12142. Lot 4349. Preserved: neck to hips. Missing front of neck, right hip at side, most of arms. P.H. 0.143 (size 4). Fabric 1, orange-buff, with gray core. Hollow. Back handmade, rounded. Added: right arm, locks of hair on shoulders and back. Tooling on drapery, hair.

Left upper arm at side; right upper arm outstretched diagonally to side. Peplos is worn over chiton; incision marks sleeve edge on right upper arm. Deep V-shaped folds at neckline and abdomen, curving folds from left breast. Head originally turned slightly to left. Long, thick locks of hair, gouged, fan over shoulders and down back, some in back indicated only by zigzag incisions. Poor workmanship. Probable later generations in lots 4387 (fabric 5, missing right arm), 6507 (smallest example, right arm is at side, more of overfold preserved at left). For possible head type, see **H414**.
See pp. 255–256.

H413 Draped female statuette, probably standing Pl. 58
MF-69-363. No context. Preserved: lower part of face to left side of chest in front, small part of back. Mended. P.H. 0.15 (size 5). Fabric 1, orange-buff. Hollow. Added: hair. Tooling on folds, hair.

Neckline folds indicated with diagonal incisions; vertical folds below breast. Thick sheet of clay, without detail, added in back for hair; long lock of hair marked with curved slashes falls in front, pointed end visible below break. Creases on neck. Poor workmanship.
See p. 256.

H414 Female head Pl. 58
MF-14101. Lot 3223. Preserved: cheeks to neck. Missing locks of hair at left side; nose, upper lip chipped. P.H. 0.056 (size 4). Fabric 5, orange. Hollow. Thick-walled. Back handmade, flattened. Added: hair. Tooling on face, hair.

Head tilted to left; chin raised. Face oval. Lips probably slightly parted; lower lip full, indented below. Long locks of hair at sides of neck, marked with diagonal slashes; roughly vertical slashes on back of hair. Poor workmanship. Perhaps from a figurine similar to **H412**.
See p. 256.

H415 Female head Pl. 58
MF-10748. Lot 869. Preserved: front-left eye and right cheek to base of neck. Missing chin, hair at right side; nose chipped. P.H. 0.08 (size 5). Fabric 1, creamy buff. White slip. Red paint on hair. Hollow. Added: locks of hair at side. Tooling on face, hair.

Face probably oblong to oval, with full cheeks. Eye is low, downturned, opened wide; both lids defined, pupil in relief, iris incised. Nose wide, short, upturned. Lips full, parted. Face seems youthful. Long, tubular, wavy locks of hair along neck, deeply shadowed. Similar in type and scale: MF-71-82 (no context, fragment of lower face); one in lot 2064.
See p. 256.

H416 Draped female statuette, probably a goddess Pl. 58
MF-70-169. Lot 6638. Preserved: part of right upper arm, with lock of hair. P.L. 0.068 (size 5). Fabric slightly coarse, creamy buff to orange-buff, with gray core, sparse small to large red and gray inclusions. White slip. Violet paint on

sleeve, yellow on lock of hair, with traces of gilding. Solid. Added: lock of hair.

Arm outstretched to side. Chiton sleeve of thin cloth, edge stretched diagonally due to position of arm. Long, twisted lock of hair lies along upper edge of arm. Other outstretched arm fragments of statuette scale with long locks of hair in lots 2239, 3223, 6215, 6638 (with gilding on hair).

See p. 256.

H417   Draped female statuette, probably a goddess   Pl. 59

MF-13813. Lots 1945, 2107 (forearm). Preserved: neck, upper part of chest, with small part of back, right shoulder and arm to wrist. Mended. Max.P.Dim. 0.182 (size 4–5). Fabric slightly coarse, fired hard, somewhat brittle, yellowish buff, with sparse small dark inclusions. Hollow (including upper arm). Torso thin-walled. Added: arm, chiton sleeve, locks of hair. Tenon for insertion of head is short, pointed, scored.

Right arm extended to side; forearm raised, perhaps to hold scepter or long torch. Head originally turned to right. Lightly modeled pleats at diagonal neckline suggest thin cloth of chiton rather than peplos; sleeve has ridge along top of arm, suggesting fastenings of chiton. Long locks of hair down sides of neck, along top of left shoulder, slashed. **H418** is so close in fabric and technique that it may belong to same piece.

See p. 256.

H418   Pl. 58

Standing draped female figurine, probably a goddess

MF-13783. Lot 1945. Preserved: front–hips and upper thighs. Missing part of center. Mended. P.H. 0.079 (size 4–5). Fabric as **H417**. Hollow. Thin-walled. Added: upper part of mantle roll. Tooling on folds.

Upper edge of mantle is rolled and loosely draped across hips; roll is slashed. Folds across thighs are tubular ridges, dominated by large arrowhead fold pointing from left hip to right thigh; at left side, traces of overlapping folds of drapery fall following curve of thigh. Lightly modeled vertical folds of chiton are preserved at break just above roll. **H417** is so close in fabric and technique that it may belong to same piece.

See p. 256.

H419   Standing draped female figurine   Pl. 59

MF-12011. Lot 2240. Preserved: front–left side and part of center, waist to left lower leg. P.H. 0.148 (size 4). Fabric fine, fired hard, orange-buff. White slip. Yellow and violet paint on both garments, flecks of gilding over yellow, violet over yellow in places (yellow perhaps an underpainting). Hollow. Thin-walled.

Left thigh slightly advanced. Transparent mantle is rolled at upper edge and stretched across hips in a slight upward diagonal toward left hip; lightly modeled, slightly curved folds radiate from left hip to right leg. Narrow belt of chiton preserved at upper break, seems to be at natural waist; faint vertical chiton folds visible underneath mantle just below roll; chiton folds also at lower break, below mantle hem. Well-made piece.

See p. 256.

H420   Standing Kore(?)   Pl. 59

MF-11675. Lot 2010. Preserved: neck, right shoulder, drapery fall over right upper arm to hip level, small part of back. Mended. P.H. 0.138 (size 4–5). Fabric 1, buff. Hollow.

Thick-walled. Added: hair, probably entire drapery fall, with torch. Tooling on folds, hair.

Right arm raised high, apparently to hold long, cylindrical object represented in front of folds; object narrows slightly toward bottom, probably a torch. Mantle draped over upper arm, behind torch; forearm and hand originally would have supported torch from behind. To judge from break at right shoulder, torso would have projected in front of mantle, which originally may have been draped around back, to reappear at left side of figure. Diagonal mantle folds from upper arm to torso; long, flat, triangular fold to right of torch. Chiton or peplos folds on right shoulder. Head originally turned slightly to right. Two long, wavy locks of hair on each shoulder.

See pp. 256–257.

H421   Standing draped female statuette   Pl. 59

MF-13808. Lot 3230. Preserved: front–left hip and thigh, with side, small part of back. P.H. 0.117 (size 4–5). Fabric 1, orange-buff to orange, with gray core. Hollow. Added: all drapery at side. Tooling on folds.

Left leg advanced, knee bent. Diagonal folds of mantle curve from hip to inner side of leg. Heavy cascade of folds at side, with pointed mantle end.

See p. 257.

H422   Foot of draped female statuette   Pl. 59

MF-69-376. Lot 6214. Preserved: front–right foot, toes and front of sandal sole; big toe chipped. P.H. 0.056 (size 5). Fabric 1, yellowish buff, with sparse small dark inclusions. Solid. Handmade(?). Tooling on toes.

Sandal has high (0.03), indented sole. Toenails indicated; divisions of toes deeply incised. Bit of drapery beside smallest toe. Break at top and along inside of foot presumably where hem arched over foot. Similar sandal type: **H423** and **H424**; MF-70-245 (lot 6500); other high-soled sandals in lots 882, 2107.

See p. 257.

H423   Foot of draped female statuette   Pl. 59

MF-13796. Lot 4349. Preserved: front–right foot and surrounding drapery; lower surface of sole, drapery chipped. P.H. 0.057 (size 4–5). Fabric 2, light orange. Hollow. Added: foot and sandal sole, with adjacent folds. Tooling on toes, folds.

Sandal has high, indented sole. Skirt folds collapse onto foot; hem arches over instep but does not trail on ground. Divisions of toes deeply incised. Big toe is short; only two other toes uncovered. Possible later generation in lot 4380 (fabric 1). Similar sandal type: **H422** and **H424**.

See pp. 174, 257.

H424   Foot of draped female statuette   Pl. 59

MF-13795. Lot 2107. Preserved: left foot and surrounding drapery. P.H. 0.042 (size 4–5). Fabric hard, slightly coarse, creamy buff, with sparse small dark inclusions. Solid. Rear surface is finished. Tooling on toes.

Sandal has high, indented sole. Skirt folds collapse onto foot; hem trails on ground. Toenails indicated. Divisions of toes deeply incised. Slope of lower surface of sole and finish of back suggest that figure was seated, as in **H283**. Fabric resembles that of some Roman figurines (especially an Aphrodite in the Corinth collection, MF-1981-1 [Pl. 77]), but this type so far seems to be Hellenistic in Corinth. Similar sandal type: **H422** and **H423**.

See pp. 174, 257.

ISOLATED FEMALE HEADS

H425   Draped female figurine, probably standing   Pl. 60

MF-11314. Lot 1998. Preserved: head to chest. P.H. 0.055 (size 3). Fabric 1, orange-buff. White slip. Hollow. All parts rendered in same mold. Back probably moldmade, flattened. Added: veil.

Shoulders narrow, rounded. Prominent V-shaped fold at neckline of garment. Face small in proportion to long neck. Face round, with high, triangular forehead; small, receding chin. Eyes level. Nose short, wide, close to upper lip. Hair parted at center, bound with thick fillet; long locks of hair to shoulders. Clumsily added veil gives impression of cap. Probable mold sibling: MF-11311 (lot 1998). Possible mold sibling in lot 6500.

See p. 257.

H426   Draped female figurine, probably standing   Pl. 60

MF-11312. Lot 1998. Preserved: front–head and neck; back–head to chest level. Mended. P.H. 0.07 (size 3). Fabric 5, pinkish orange. Hollow. Back probably molded, flattened. Tooling on face.

Face round, with high, triangular forehead; prominent chin. Eyes small, level, closely set. Nose flattened over upper lip. Hair parted at center, bound with tubular fillet; long locks of hair to shoulders. Probable mold siblings: MF-10516 (lot 882, head); another in lot 2088. Possible mold sibling in lot 2107 (fabric 1).

See p. 257.

H427   Female head   Pl. 60

MF-13507. Lot 3230. Preserved: head and part of neck. Missing locks of hair at top and left side, part of stephane. Mended. P.H. 0.068 (size 4–5). Treated with preservative. White slip. Yellow paint on hair. Hollow. Back probably molded, rounded. Added: hair, stephane, earrings. Tooling on hair.

Published: Coroplast's Art, p. 60, fig. 48.

Head tilted slightly to left. Face oblong to oval, with high forehead, full cheeks; prominent, nearly pointed chin. Eyes slightly downturned; upper lid arched, lower lid slightly lifted; browridge well defined, follows curve of eye from bridge of nose. Nose slightly aquiline. Lips parted, smiling; thin upper lip, full lower lip; corner of mouth punched. One end preserved of stephane around cranium. Locks of hair looped in clumps from all around face and nape up and back to stephane; top of head, within stephane, roughly modeled. Locks of hair incised with roughly parallel lines. Similar in type: smaller heads in the Corinth collection, with different headdresses; in order of decreasing size, they are MF-8994; MF-9212; MF-3465 (*Corinth* XII, p. 47, no. 289, pl. 24; Romano 1994, pl. 29); MF-11459 (Robinson 1969, p. 19, no. 36, pl. 5); MF-3875 (*Corinth* XII, p. 47, no. 288, pl. 24); see also **H429** and **H430**.

See pp. 15, 249, 251, 258.

H428   Female head   Pl. 60

MF-11914. Lot 2107. Preserved: head and neck. Missing locks of hair at top, left side and back of head; nose chipped. P.H. 0.099 (size 5). Fabric 1, slightly coarser, orange-buff to orange, with sparse small to medium white and reddish brown inclusions. Nearly solid. Back probably handmade. Added:

hair, earrings. Tooling on face, hair. Corners of mouth, ears, nostrils punched.

Head tilted slightly to right. Face oblong to oval, with wide, low forehead; dimpled chin. Eyes level; upper lid strongly arched, lower lid lifted. Lips parted, upper lip thin. Locks of hair looped loosely from forehead to cranium (for arrangement, see the better-preserved **H427**). Shape of earrings unclear. Creases on neck. Similar in type: smaller head in lot 6501 (burned, more exaggerated, head thrown back on neck, lips fuller and more parted).

See p. 258.

H429   Female head   Pl. 60

MF-72-68. Without context. Preserved: head and neck, part of tenon; nose chipped. P.H. 0.079 (size 3–4). Fabric 1, orange-buff. Red paint on hair. Hollow. Back molded, rounded. Added: locks of hair at nape, wreath, earrings. Tooling on hair, wreath.

Head tilted slightly to left. Face round, with high, triangular forehead; small, prominent chin. Eyes small, slightly downturned; lids fleshy, half-closed. Nose wide, close to upper lip. Lips smiling; lower lip full. Coiffure parted at center, bound with fillet with round knot at center, arranged at top in bowknot; over this, thick wreath wrapped with a fillet and punched; two long, wavy locks of hair spring from nape. Pellet earrings. Creases on neck. Similar in type: one each in lots 6215 (fabric 5) and 6233 (badly worn, tilted to right). See also **H427**.

See p. 258.

H430   Female head   Pl. 60

MF-12015. Lot 2240. Preserved: head and neck, part of tenon. Missing part of top of head; nose chipped; surface worn. P.H. 0.061 (size 3). Fabric 2, orange-buff. Hollow. Back molded, rounded. Possible tooling on face, hair.

Head tilted to left. Face round to oval, with high, triangular forehead. Eyes slightly downturned; lids fleshy, left eye half-closed. Corners of mouth possibly punched. Coiffure parted at center, hair piled high. Veil, like a curtain behind head, originally fell to shoulders. Earrings probably round. Creases on neck. See also **H427**.

See p. 258.

ISOLATED MALE HEAD

H431   Male head   Pl. 60

MF-68-291. Lot 5624. Preserved: head and neck. Nose, lower lip, locks of hair chipped. P.H. 0.086 (size 5). Fabric 1, orange-buff. Dark red paint overall, without white slip. Solid. Handmade(?).

Published: Bookidis 1969, p. 309, pl. 78:c.

Head turned to left, tilted. Face oval to round, with low, triangular forehead. Eyes almond shaped; left eye larger than right, slightly downturned; lids rendered more sharply on right eye, are thicker on left. Nose short, wide, close to upper lip. Lips full, especially upper lip, which is strongly arched. Hair constructed of overlapping strips of clay, beginning close to nape, and becoming thicker towards cranium; locks of hair then defined with a knife. Coiffure parted at center, with wavy locks of hair clinging to head and neck, covering ears; two thin, incurved locks of hair on forehead form an open "pincer."

See pp. 10, 15, 46, 258–259.

V

CLASSICAL AND HELLENISTIC VARIA

In this chapter of miscellany, six unrelated categories, belonging to either or both the Classical and Hellenistic periods, will be discussed. These categories are (1) figurines of animals; (2) reliefs: headdresses, a votive shield, and a rider plaque; (3) votive offerings in isolated hands, separated from figurines of unknown type; (4) miscellaneous figurine fragments of uncertain date and unknown original type, of interest technically or iconographically; (5) bases and supports; and (6) molds.

ANIMALS
(V1–V13)

In this section are discussed the Classical and Hellenistic animals, which, with one exception, are moldmade. The finds of Archaic animal figurines in the Demeter sanctuary are more numerous and are more varied in the kinds of animals represented.[1] It is likely that some of these handmade types continued to be produced into the Classical and perhaps even the Hellenistic period. New creations after the Archaic period include moldmade pigs, a bull, a ram, a sheep or goat, a monkey, birds, roosters, and a tortoise.

Presumably, those of the animal figurines that are appropriate refer to the practice of animal sacrifice, perhaps providing a substitute when the dedicator could not afford to provide the real thing (see p. 322). At another level, the animal figurines could have been symbolic, referring to specific deities or to the concerns of the dedicators.

PIGS

The symbolic connection of pigs and their young to fertility cults is too well known to need more than a brief explication here.[2] The very nature of the pig, its large litters and its highly efficient conversion of almost any food into an edible product for humans, must be at the basis of its ancient link to abundance. In addition, the ability of the pig to dispose of a large variety of wastes contributed to the hygiene of the community.[3] If Demeter at this sanctuary was considered a guardian of the health of children, as has been suggested above (p. 70), then the connotation of the pig here perhaps could be extended from fertility to health.

Another extension of the symbolic link between the pig and fertility is found in the colloquial use of the word "piglet" to refer to the genitals of maidens (see p. 118). Ritually, this usage is significant, because the piglet has been taken as a symbol for Kore herself descending into the Underworld, particularly when the animals were cast into pits, as in the preliminary rituals of the Eleusinian Mysteries and at the Athenian Thesmophoria.[4] The late *aition* for this practice is the swallowing up of the swineherd Eubouleus and his animals together with Kore.[5] While it is unclear whether or not piglets were cast into pits in the Demeter sanctuary (see p. 119), bones of

---

[1] Publication forthcoming.
[2] Bevan 1986, I, pp. 67–73.
[3] R. L. Miller 1990.

[4] Burkert 1983, pp. 256–264; Clinton 1988, pp. 72–80; Detienne 1989, pp. 133–135.
[5] On this myth, see Clinton 1992, pp. 56, 60.

young pigs have come to light,[6] and the discovery of substantial numbers of figurines show-ing votaries and possibly also priestesses carrying piglets (see pp. 117–124, 250–255) should be evidence enough that piglets were sacrificed at this sanctuary, at least by those who could afford them.[7]

V1–V4 are four fragmentary moldmade adult pigs.[8] The first three are similar to one another in their fabric and construction. All are thin-walled and made in two symmetrical molds, one for each side of the animal; all parts, including the base, were included in the molds, and only **V3** and **V4** show any retouch, in spite of the generally dull impressions. Other fragments in the lots (see catalogue under **V1**) are generally similar in technique. This straightforward approach to figurine making is typical of some of the workshops of the Potters' Quarter; although no pig figurines were found in the Potters' Quarter, it is likely to have been the source of these pieces. **V3** is the largest of the three but seems to be of a different mold series. Instead of the typically flattened, upturned pig's snout, it has a pointed, almost canine face. In this respect it resembles a fully preserved figurine in the Corinth collection (MF-10293), which is a nicely observed depiction of a nervous or playful, almost crouching young animal.[9] **V4** is of a coarser fabric but is probably also Corinthian. There is also a fragmentary imported pig (**I90**) of uncertain provenience. None of the pigs was found in a datable context, but the high, splaying, rectangular base of **V2** is of a Classical type (see p. 275), and the probable connection with the Potters' Quarter provides a *terminus ante quem* of the 320s B.C.

The two pigs with preserved bodies (**V1** and **V2**) have the short legs and fat bodies of sty pigs rather than herded animals, which are leaner and longer-legged.[10] Their bellies touch the base, apparently either to show animals fattened and ready for slaughter or to suggest that they are pregnant.[11] The type of pig domesticated in ancient Corinth appears to have had a pronounced dorsal ridge of bristles, marked with light strokes in the figurines.

In spite of signs that the Corinthian moldmade pigs were produced in some quantity without much regard for the rendering of detail, they are more naturalistically designed and better made than pig figurines from other places. These are sometimes misshapen and usually rest on pointed stumps for feet, without bases.[12] Only one of the pigs from the Demeter sanctuary (MF-13739)[13] can be dated to the Archaic period by its technique (it is handmade and solid, with a pinhole vent). In the Classical period, at least two new, moldmade versions of the subject were created, represented by **V1** and MF-10293; **V3** and **V4** are too fragmentary to determine whether they represent different creations or are merely variants. **V1** shows delicate parallel incisions to represent the bristles; since the incisions were in the mold, the mold could have been taken from a bronze (see p. 81). The increased interest in pig votives after the Archaic period could perhaps be explained by the creation of new types in bronze that stimulated coroplasts. There may also be some connection with the absence of figurines representing votaries carrying piglets at the Demeter sanctuary before the Early Classical period; **C1** is the earliest, although they were already popular in Sicily in the 6th century B.C. (see p. 26). It is surprising, however, that the total number of pig figurines actually preserved at the sanctuary for all periods, including fragments counted and left in the lots, is only about twelve. Among the terracotta sculptures, there is a fragment showing a hand holding the rear leg of a piglet down at the side.[14]

[6] *Corinth* XVIII, iii, e.g., p. 153.

[7] On the economics of pig sacrifice, see Jameson 1988, pp. 98–99. A piglet cost three drachmas, a substantial price, in Classical Athens. See also Keller 1909, pp. 388–405, esp. pp. 400–403, on the pig in cult; Van Straten 1995, pp. 170–186.

[8] A piglet published in Stroud 1965, p. 10, pl. 2:g, has been omitted because it appears to have been broken from a larger figurine, probably a votary.

[9] Bookidis and Stroud 1987, fig. on title page.

[10] Clutton-Brock 1989, pp. 74–75.

[11] On the sacrifice of pregnant pigs to Demeter, see Golden 1988, p. 5, note 21; M. W. Meyer 1987, p. 54, para. 6 (The Rule of the Andanian Mysteries of Messenia).

[12] For useful collections of material from other sites, all with bibliography, see *Olynthus* XIV, pp. 244–247, pls. 100, 101; *Aspects of Ancient Greece*, pp. 238–239, no. 116; *Thasos* XVII, pp. 448–451, nos. 1138–1156, pl. 138.

[13] Publication forthcoming.

[14] SF-65-22: publication forthcoming by Nancy Bookidis.

BULL

A figurine of a bull could have been offered at the Demeter sanctuary as a substitute for an actual bull sacrifice, although no bones of bulls have been recovered. At Eleusis, a bull was sacrificed by the ephebes at the conclusion of the Mysteries.[15] The figurine also could have been offered as a request for success in animal husbandry. The bull was closely associated with Dionysos, who appears to have been worshiped at this sanctuary as well, because it was known for both generative power and potential destructiveness, symbolizing the dual nature of the god.[16] While there is only a single post-Archaic, locally made bull figurine from the sanctuary (**V5**), there are several earlier, handmade renderings (MF-10392, MF-11906, MF-71-270[17]), two imported pieces (one a bucranium [**I91**] and one a cow or bull [**I92**]), and three small bronze bulls.[18]

Although **V5** is only a fragment and is a rather dull impression, roughly tooled, the nicely detailed original design survives in the folds of skin on the forehead and the tongue in the open, bellowing mouth. The source of this figurine probably was a bronze, since in addition to the bronzes found in the sanctuary, others, dated to the 5th century B.C., have been found in Corinth,[19] and it is not difficult to find good examples from nearby centers, for example, in the Argolid[20] and Isthmia.[21] Some of these bronze bulls are shown with their heads down, and it is possible that **V5** should be reconstructed similarly.

RAM

V6 is a head fragment of a curly-horned, moldmade ram. Although its fabric is a little coarser than usual, it does seem to be Corinthian. All the ram figurines from the sanctuary are curly horned, but most are smaller, handmade, and probably earlier (e.g., MF-11753[22]). As in the case of other domesticated animals, the presence of such figurines at the sanctuary could be interpreted either as a request for the success of flocks or as a substitute for an actual animal sacrifice. The sacrificial ram could have had a specific meaning at this sanctuary, since rams are known to have been sacrificed to Kore at Eleusis and elsewhere.[23] Although the complete design of **V6** may have been quite good, little detail remains in this dull mold impression, and nothing can be determined about the origin of the type. A small bronze ram dated to the 5th century B.C. has been found in Corinth,[24] but it cannot be connected to representations in terracotta. A fine, naturalistically detailed, moldmade terracotta figurine of a curly-horned ram in London is of Boeotian manufacture.[25] It is slightly smaller than **V6**, but the dull impression of the Corinthian figurine could indicate that its mold was taken directly from a good imported piece similar to the Boeotian version.

SHEEP OR GOAT

The fragmentary **V7** represents a caprine with straight, shaggy fleece; there is no indication of its sex. This figure is technically much different from the animals discussed above, since it is thick-walled and fired very hard, is of statuette scale, and was probably handmade, with the fleece rendered by means of slashes. It shows a contradiction in the quality of its workmanship that is seen elsewhere in Corinthian coroplastic work (see p. 19), when rough tooling is combined with well-prepared and well-fired fabric. The right rear leg is bent backward, showing that the

[15] Burkert 1983, pp. 292–293; Clinton 1988, p. 71; *Corinth* XVIII, iii, p. 233, note 1.
[16] Otto 1965, pp. 165–167; Goodenough 1958, VII, pp. 14–20.
[17] Publication forthcoming.
[18] Stroud 1965, pp. 18–19, pl. 9:b (MF-10785); Bookidis and Stroud 1987, p. 17, fig. 15 (MF-12170); MF-10653.
[19] MF-3429, MF-523, *Corinth* XII, pp. 65–66, nos. 497, 498, pl. 47.

[20] Protonotariou-Deilaki 1971, p. 84, pl. 70:β.
[21] *Isthmia* VII, pp. 1, 4–5, nos. 1–7, pls. 1, 2.
[22] Publication forthcoming.
[23] Burkert 1983, pp. 145, 282–283; on the symbolism of sheep, including the association of the ram with generative power, see Goodenough 1958, VIII, pp. 71–85.
[24] MF-115, *Corinth* XII, p. 65, no. 496, pl. 47.
[25] *British Museum* I, p. 233, no. 872, pl. 125.

animal was in movement. The direction of the locks of the fleece on the remaining stump of the right front leg suggests that the leg originally was advancing, and the animal would in this case be leaping rather than walking. If this statuette represented a sheep, it presumably would have been offered in lieu of a sacrificial animal; if a goat, its tie to this sanctuary also might have been the goat's symbolic connection with sexuality and with the god Dionysos.[26] This piece belongs to a context terminating in the early 3rd century B.C., but similar large terracotta animal figures were made elsewhere into Roman times.[27]

MONKEY

The head of a monkey **V8** belongs to a well-known class of Corinthian comic types, consisting of monkeys in a variety of human activities (see p. 194). Such monkeys were made in Rhodes as well,[28] but it was the Corinthian coroplasts who fully realized the comic potential of this subject. In some of these types, the monkeys are pictured with mortars and pestles, either turning a somersault in the mortar[29] or grinding grain while wearing a veil or a crown of pointed leaves and eating a cake.[30] The veil and crown probably are a reference to bridal headdresses. Monkeys are thought to have been fertility symbols and apotropaic devices,[31] and in these figurines the impish monkeys both help in women's work and spoil it by rolling in the grain or consuming the prepared cake. The mouth of **V8** is opened wide and twisted to the right side; something has been broken away from it, suggesting that it originally belonged to a type similar to one in London, mentioned above, in which the monkey stands before a mortar, grinding with a pestle while eating a round, flat cake.[32] **V8** was probably made in the Potters' Quarter, where molds for monkey figurines were found.[33] If this is correct, its *terminus ante quem* would be the 320s B.C., the date of the demise of the Potters' Quarter workshops.

BIRDS

Terracotta figurines of birds, both flying and at rest, were an important votive type in Corinth. Most of those found in the Demeter sanctuary are handmade and are either Archaic in date or Archaic survivals.[34] **V9** is a moldmade type with a delicate feather pattern along the top of the tail, rendered in the mold. Since it is both moldmade and concave underneath, it falls between two classes of birds recognized by Stillwell among the Potters' Quarter finds, class XXVII, which is concave underneath but handmade, and XXVIII, which is moldmade but solid.[35] The schematic feather pattern, similar on all the moldmade examples, shows a plain panel down the center flanked by curved feathers. A source in bronze is likely, not only because the engraving is so delicate but also because an Archaic example in bronze was found in Perachora.[36] Since **V9** is not fully rounded underneath, the pattern was necessarily flattened and part of the effect lost, but the intention is clear nevertheless. **V9**, which must have been made in the Potters' Quarter, was found in Pit A, the terminal date of which is the last quarter of the 5th century B.C. The bird represented is probably a dove, which could suggest some connection with Aphrodite,[37] but birds were commonly offered in Corinth at hero shrines.[38] There are doves among the terracotta sculpture from the sanctuary as well.[39]

[26] Otto 1965, pp. 167–169. On sheep or goat bones found in the sanctuary, see *Corinth* XVIII, iii, pp. 78, 243.

[27] E.g., from Chalkis, Sampson 1980, p. 164, no. 119, pl. 60 (sheep with shaggy fleece).

[28] *British Museum* I, pp. 60–61, nos. 105, 106, pl. 20 (riding a pig, playing a lyre). For a collection of monkey figurines, see McDermott 1938, pp. 161–214.

[29] An example in Basel, Blome 1988, p. 206, pl. 56:4.

[30] *British Museum* I, p. 260, nos. 957, 958, pl. 135.

[31] Langdon 1990, pp. 419–420, with bibliography; see also Keller 1909, pp. 3–11.

[32] *British Museum* I, p. 260, no. 958, pl. 135.

[33] KH-76, KH-77, *Corinth* XV, i, p. 108, nos. 77, 78, pl. 43.

[34] Publication forthcoming.

[35] *Corinth* XV, ii, pp. 184–188.

[36] *Perachora* I, pp. 133–134, pls. 40:3, 4, 41.

[37] On the symbolism of the dove, which was generally associated with fertility goddesses in the Near East, see Goodenough 1958, VIII, pp. 27–46.

[38] E.g., at the Heroon of the Crossroads: C. K. Williams and Fisher 1973, p. 8, pl. 3.

[39] SF-61-17 and SF-62-10, publication forthcoming by Nancy Bookidis.

V10 is a wing that appears to belong to a bird or birdlike creature, probably composed in an upright position. Since neither the pose nor the incised pattern of overlapping feathers matches any of the common Corinthian votive bird types, the figurine could have represented a birdlike creature usually shown in an upright pose. A siren comes to mind for its chthonic associations. A stone siren with a somewhat similar feather pattern was found at the Potters' Quarter.[40]

ROOSTERS

The best-known Corinthian terracotta roosters are the lingering Archaic plaques made at the Potters' Quarter,[41] a few of which were found at the Acrocorinth sanctuary.[42] Figurines of a youth and a boy carrying roosters were found, however (**C191** and **H322**), as well as an Archaic handmade rooster (MF-71-276[43]) and later handmade (**V11**) and moldmade (**V12**) examples. Both of the later figurines are fairly dismal creations of uncertain date, following neither the Corinthian plaques in type nor three-dimensional rooster figurines from elsewhere, such as those found in Rhodes.[44] **V12** could be of Roman date because of its very large eye, which is often found in Roman rooster figurines.[45] The rooster is an attribute of Persephone on the Lokroi plaques[46] and is an appropriate dedication to the chthonic deities.

TORTOISE

The fragment of a tortoise shell **V13** is unlike figurines of tortoises, which usually represent the entire body. This fragment seems not to represent the living animal but to be part of a model chelys-lyre.[47] In the construction of this instrument, the patterned side of the shell of *testudo marginata*, which is native to Greece, was utilized for the back; a piece of hide was drawn tightly across the front to form the sound box and was wrapped to the back over the edge, forming a border, as seen in **V13**. In the Archaic period, the sound box took the natural oval or round shape of the animal's carapace, but the more sophisticated construction technique of the 5th and 4th centuries B.C. altered the shape to that seen in **V13**.

This is the only piece of its kind yet found in Corinth, although there is a figurine of a youth carrying a lyre from the sanctuary (**C190**), a type also known in the Asklepieion (see catalogue). Actual lyres or model lyres made from small tortoise shells have been found at Argos and elsewhere,[48] dedicated to Apollo or placed in graves. Either the dedication of a model lyre at the Demeter sanctuary makes a connection with Asklepios and Apollo, through the interest of the cult in the health of children and the coming-of-age of youths, or the use of model lyres as grave gifts suggests that they are appropriate dedications to chthonic deities. **V13** belongs to a pottery context terminating in the later 3rd century B.C. There is also a tortoise among the terracotta sculptures.[49]

RELIEFS
(**V14–V19**)

In this section are discussed types characterized by figures in relief, either made separately and added to the surface, as in the headdresses **V14–V17**, or formed in the mold together with the background, as in the votive shield **V18** and the rider plaque **V19**.

---

[40] S-1473, *Corinth* XV, i, pp. 70–71, 80–81, no. XX, pls. 26, 27.

[41] On the type, see *Corinth* XV, ii, pp. 155–156, 160–161, nos. 3–13, pl. 33.

[42] Publication forthcoming.

[43] Publication forthcoming.

[44] E.g., *British Museum* I, p. 79, no. 188, pl. 35.

[45] E.g., MF-3393, *Corinth* XII, p. 59, no. 433, pl. 39; *Agora* VI, p. 68, no. 822, pl. 20; von Gonzenbach 1995, Vol. A, pp. 257–262; Vol. B, pls. 114–116.

[46] Sourvinou-Inwood 1978, p. 108, b.

[47] On the chelys-lyre, see Maas and Snyder 1989, pp. 36–112 (Archaic and Classical), 178–180 (4th century B.C.).

[48] Phaklaris 1977; Courbin 1980.

[49] SF-71-1: publication forthcoming by Nancy Bookidis.

HEADDRESSES

V14 consists of two nonjoining fragments of a polos decorated with figures in relief and topped with a torus molding finished with crenellations. While model poloi are known to have been dedicated as votives in themselves,[50] the surface of this polos is pinched up at the back of both fragments, suggesting that originally it was joined to something, presumably a head. The female head **C100** wears a polos of similar type, although being a good deal smaller, the polos is plain, without added figures in relief. In addition, the headdress **V17** is contoured at the bottom as if to accommodate the curves of a coiffure, and there are remains of what is probably the top of the head at both the front and back of **V16**.

It is tempting to try to extract from the relief figures on the surface of the polos **V14** references to the cult followed at this sanctuary, but this would be a mistake, since the figures are known to be stock types also used to decorate miniature altars and relief pottery. The most fully preserved groupings are found on "Tarentine" arulae and consist of Apollo and Leto, Dionysos with a satyr and maenad, Poseidon and Amymone (identified by the hydria she carries), and a female figure (Nike?) decking a trophy.[51] The arulae are thought to be of Athenian origin and are dated before the middle of the 3rd century B.C.[52] There are examples of these relief figures on Corinthian pottery and workshop material as well as arulae.[53] The scene on the polos, which does not have narrative continuity, has been described in detail in the catalogue.

Beginning at the viewer's left of fragment A (Pl. 62), a female figure is shown carrying a vessel in the lowered right hand. The chiton or peplos is girded high, and the left hand is raised to the chest. This figure is identified as Amymone on the arulae. The two remaining figures on fragment A are physically connected, a female figure nearly in profile, possibly veiled, with a scepter, followed by a semidraped, frontal male figure who reaches out toward her shoulder; both wear mantles with a triangular overfold. The male figure would be Poseidon, who normally is shown next to Amymone; the female figure usually appears with a seated Apollo (as on fragment B) and should be Leto. Of the three figures on fragment B, the central one clearly represents the seated, nude Apollo holding a kithara or lyre on his lap. At the viewer's left of Apollo is a draped female figure reaching out to deck a trophy; at his right is a poorly preserved enthroned female figure, presumably a goddess. This array of figures seems to be a pastiche of what was available to the coroplast. **V15** is another, cruder polos fragment, showing the female figure decking a trophy.

V16 could belong to a headdress more like a tiara than a polos, since its finished edge at the viewer's right indicates that it was open at the back. The fragment must belong to the left side of the head, showing three figures. The two figures at the viewer's left are a maenad and Dionysos, recognizable from better impressions,[54] but instead of the expected accompanying satyr, Leto appears at the other side of Dionysos. The crenellations of this poor piece have degenerated into scallops.

The last of the headdresses (**V17**) also has a finished edge and apparently an open back, like **V16**, but would belong to the right side of the head. Although the quality is poor, the figures of gods in relief are easily recognizable, in a different array than before. From the viewer's left are Apollo with a kithara, this time standing, draped, and looking over his shoulder; Artemis in a short chiton; and Poseidon holding a trident, with his right foot on a rock. The technique of

[50] D. B. Thompson 1954, pp. 99–103, pl. 23, with bibliography; Simon 1972; *British Museum* I, p. 209, no. 781, pl. 103; Naumann 1983, pp. 275–276.

[51] For bibliography on the arulae, see Schürmann 1989, p. 188, no. 692, pl. 112; for good photographs, see Vafopoulou-Richardson 1982, pls. XI, XII; on the uses of arulae, see C. K. Williams 1979, pp. 136–140.

[52] D. B. Thompson 1962, pp. 259–260.

[53] MF-2465, *Corinth* XII, p. 131, no. 889, pl. 65; Züchner

1950/1951, p. 193, fig. 29; Weinberg 1954, pp. 135–136, pl. 33:a, b; Edwards 1981, p. 196, pls. 43, 44; Edwards 1986, p. 396, pl. 90; MF-9270, Romano 1994, p. 94, no. 98, pl. 30 (figure not recognized as Apollo); a mold from the excavations East of the Theater (MF-1985-72), similar in scale to the polos.

[54] MF-2465, *Corinth* XII, p. 131, no. 889, pl. 65; Weinberg 1954, p. 136, pl. 33:a, b; a similar grouping appears on an arula from Athens: D. B. Thompson 1962, pp. 259–260; *LIMC* III, 1986, p. 484, nos. 724, 725, pl. 383, s.v. *Dionysos* (C. Gasparri).

this headdress is different, with the figures molded together in a strip in a plaster mold (the surface of **V17** is blistered) and then attached all together to the surface of the headdress.

The Greek crenellated polos is thought to be based upon the mural headdress of Hittite city goddesses; it is worn by various goddesses, particularly Cybele, and sometimes also by brides.[55] In **V15**, the surfaces of the wall are plain, the crenellations marked with simple knife cuts. In the better-made **V14**, vertical slashes were added, perhaps to represent narrow windows for archers.[56] The form of this crown is different from the more elaborate mural crowns that try to render a wall fully, sometimes with towers, as in sculptural representations of Tyche,[57] but there are variants in this type of headdress, and the intention to represent a kind of mural crown seems clear enough. At Corinth, the deity wearing such a crown must have been strongly identified with the fortifications of Acrocorinth and the safety of the city. The most likely candidate among the deities associated with this sanctuary would be Aphrodite (see p. 170). Although the relief figures of deities surrounding the headdresses do not make obvious reference either to Aphrodite or to Demeter and Kore, they could have had a general apotropaic purpose. The selection of Apollo and Poseidon in particular is appropriate to Corinth. This high, crenellated crown should not be confused with the low crown worn by the seated goddess type (**C95–C97**), who could be either Kore or Aphrodite. The low crown, when fully rendered, is topped by a border of rosettes, although they sometimes degenerate into simple discs, which rather resemble lumpy crenellations (see p. 47).

VOTIVE SHIELD

V18 is a small fragment of a votive shield. A nearly complete terracotta shield of the same type from the Potters' Quarter[58] shows that the subject is an *apobates*, an armed rider dismounting from his moving horse; the rider carries a small round shield of the same shape as the votive shield. All the preserved shields found in Corinth appear to have been made in the Potters' Quarter, where most were found. A fragmentary example found in the Tile Works, apparently brought there for dedication in a small shrine,[59] has a better-preserved surface with fine linear detail for the horse's mane, a sign of metallic origin (see p. 81).

Since both the *apobates* as a subject and votive shields in general have already been discussed in the literature in some detail, only a few points need be emphasized here. The connection with West Greece is quite strong, both in the selection of this subject and in style. To the already published citations now may be added a warrior's burial in Lanuvium, dating to the beginning of the second quarter of the 5th century B.C. This grave contained athletic equipment and a bronze disc incised with a similar "desultor."[60] Discussion of another votive shield type from Medma[61] indicates that the published dating of the Potters' Quarter shield to the end of the 6th century B.C. probably should be lowered at least to the first quarter of the 5th. A later date also would bring the Potters' Quarter shield into line with the other finds in the deposit in which it was found, Stele Shrine A. A shield brought to the Demeter sanctuary probably should be associated with hero cult, as already suggested for the banqueters (see pp. 67–68). There also may be some votive association with horse-rider figurines (see p. 60).

RIDER PLAQUE

V19 is a fragmentary rider plaque. This common Corinthian votive type, connected with hero cult, took the place of the handmade horse-rider figurines, which were made in the Potters'

---

[55] Müller 1915, pp. 46–51, 87–88; D. B. Thompson 1954, pp. 99–103; Simon 1972, pp. 213–214; Monloup 1994, esp. p. 32.

[56] On crenellations, see Nicholls 1958–1959, pp. 108–113.

[57] For a Roman example from Corinth, see Edwards 1990, p. 531, pl. 83:a (S-802).

[58] KN-1, *Corinth* XV, ii, pp. 227–228, no. 5, pls. 48, 49.

[59] MF-8636: publication forthcoming by the author.

[60] Colonna 1977, pp. 154–157, fig. 10, with bibliography; for the date, see p. 151. The horseman carries a spear rather than a shield and the pose is reversed.

[61] Settis 1977, p. 186.

Quarter, after the demise of the coroplastic workshops there in the 320s B.C.[62] Since a number of handmade horse-rider figurines were found in the Acrocorinth sanctuary,[63] it is surprising that there is only one rider plaque, given the long history of the sanctuary after the Potters' Quarter products were no longer available. Perhaps there is some connection with the scarcity at the sanctuary of later banqueter figurines (see p. 67), as if some change took place in the Early Hellenistic period with regard to the following of hero cult.

VOTIVE OFFERINGS BROKEN FROM FIGURINES
(V20–V26)

The seven fragments **V20–V26** are offerings broken from figurines of votaries of unknown types, all but one with the hands attached to the object; most of the hands are mitten shaped, like the hands of articulated "dolls" and some female figurines made at the Potters' Quarter (see, e.g., **C122** and **C33**). In three cases (**V20**, **V22**, and **V23**), the mitten-shaped hand supports the offering, a cake or a dish of cakes, from beneath, indicating that the forearm must have been outstretched, and the figurine therefore could not have been an articulated "doll." In **V21** two cakes are held at the edge by the thumb; the arm of an articulated "doll" (**C122**) holds a cake similarly. **V24** holds a box in the flat of the hand but with the fingers curled around one edge. **V26** is the only hand with fingers indicated, wrapped around an alabastron, apparently held at the side against the thigh. It is unclear whether the smooth surface represents the nude thigh of a male, since the smoothness could be attributed to a lack of folds at the side of a female figurine. **V25**, a rolled, narrow piece of cloth, perhaps a fillet, lacks a hand but is likely to have been attached to a figurine originally.

Seven types of cakes are represented; only one of them, cake no. 5 below, corresponds closely to cakes shown on the model likna from the sanctuary,[64] suggesting that the types of cakes offered in different rituals in the sanctuary may have varied. Only a few of the many sorts of cakes described in the ancient literature can be accurately identified in art, and there is a certain degree of confusion and overlap.[65] The cakes held by the figurines are as follows:

1. A round, fat cake with a single flattened knob at the top (**V20**), perhaps a simple bun like a brioche. It may be the *popanon monomphalon* of the likna,[66] but it is not as flat. Could this be similar to the *kribanai*, the Spartan breast-shaped cakes mentioned by Athenaios (14.646a [54]), eaten at women's banquets when the hymn in praise of a bride was sung?

2. A squarish, fat cake, divided into three segments and topped with two superimposed discs (**V22**). The most similar cake in the likna is the *plakous*, a fat cake filled with cheese and honey, but the examples there have either a single central knob and multiple segments or four segments and no knob at all.[67]

3. A round, flat disc covered with punch marks (**V21**). Irregular, stippled, flat masses in the likna have been identified as maza[68] or porridge, but this cake is clearly stiff enough to be held upright in the hand; the punch marks may indicate seeds sprinkled over the surface. A similar flat cake was found at Perachora.[69]

4. A long, thin cake with tapered ends, appearing together with the punched disc in **V21**. Oblong cakes on the likna have been identified as fruit cakes, but there they are flattened; other long shapes are thought to represent wool, which would not be sufficiently stiff to be held as it is in the figurine.[70]

[62] *Corinth* XII, pp. 49–50, nos. 308–319, pls. 27, 28; Broneer 1942, pp. 145, 148, fig. 7, upper right; Davidson 1942, pp. 110–113, fig. 3:11–22.

[63] Publication forthcoming.

[64] For the cakes in the likna, see Brumfield 1997.

[65] Grandjouan 1989, pp. 57–67, with bibliography.

[66] Brumfield 1997, p. 150.

[67] Brumfield 1997, pp. 151–152.

[68] Brumfield 1997, pp. 152–154.

[69] *Perachora* II, p. 328, no. 3445, pl. 130.

[70] Brumfield 1997, p. 156.

5. A plain, flat disc, placed in a bowl (**V23**) together with nos. 6 and 7. This cake closely resembles a type in the likna, the small discs called *kollyba*,[71] although it seems to be larger. It also resembles the type of cake eaten by a Corinthian monkey in London[72] and held in the hand of the articulated "doll" **C122**.

6. A conical cake, in the same bowl as nos. 5 and 7 and not represented on the likna. Conical or pyramidal cakes are frequently arranged with fruits or round cakes on the tables in funerary banquet reliefs and in this context would be sacred to chthonic deities.[73] They could have been offered in the Acrocorinth sanctuary with a similar purpose.

7. A flat, oval cake, slashed down the top, in the same bowl as nos. 5 and 6. This is probably the most interesting of the cakes, since its resemblance to terracotta model vulvas from the Demeter sanctuary in Proerna[74] suggests that it is an example of the *aidoia*, the genital-shaped cakes baked for fertility rituals elsewhere.[75] If this cake has been correctly identified, could the cylindrical cake no. 4 represent the phallos?

That three different sorts of cakes, nos. 5, 6, and 7, are placed together in one bowl may not be fortuitous and could have symbolic reference to different aspects of the cult. One can only attempt an interpretation, but the *aidoion* and the conical cake could refer to birth and death respectively; if the flat disc represents the sun[76] and refers to life, the bowl could contain symbols of the entire life cycle. Generally speaking, in the context of a fertility cult, cakes may refer to children, if reproduction is taken as an analogue of baking (the "father's loaves").[77]

The offering in the hand of **V24** is a box with a thin lid. It is perhaps parallel to the small chest that was associated with Persephone at Lokroi,[78] although it is flatter and simpler than the chests usually represented with women in household and nuptial contexts.[79] The box also has been recognized as a womb symbol.[80]

V25 probably represents a rolled, narrow cloth, such as a fillet. It is unknown how this fragment should be reconstructed on a figurine, but a Corinthian seated figurine in Athens unrolls on her lap what appears to be a narrow cloth,[81] and a fragmentary draped, standing female figurine from Eutresis, thought to be a Corinthian import, holds a rolled fillet in the outstretched hand.[82] One standing female figurine of reported Corinthian provenience holds both a rolled cloth and a small chest.[83] There is epigraphic evidence that pieces of weaving were dedicated by women in other sanctuaries.[84] Certainly such offerings would have been appropriate also in the Acrocorinth sanctuary, since the cult appears to have dealt with women's concerns.[85]

[71] Brumfield 1997, pp. 149–150.

[72] *British Museum* I, p. 260, no. 958, pl. 135.

[73] For cakes represented in *Totenmahlreliefs*, see Thönges-Stringaris 1965, e.g., pls. 11:2, 20:2. For a Corinthian example, see *Corinth* IX, pp. 126–127, no. 263 (S-322); restored drawing in Broneer 1942, p. 131, fig. 1. On pyramidal cakes, see *Pnyx*, pp. 109–111, no. 3, figs. 49, 50.

[74] Daffa-Nikonanou 1973, p. 73, no. ΑΕ 190, pl. 11:3. Similarly shaped objects, also thought to represent vulvas, are the "eggs" on which a phallos-bird sits, on a Gallo-Roman relief (Wright 1866, pp. 14–17, pl. III); see also anatomical votives, e.g., Comella 1978, p. 81, type DVI, pl. XXXVI:213.

[75] Brumfield 1997, p. 157; KT-51-4, a similar cake from the Potters' Quarter, apparently broken from a dish, was identified by Stillwell (*Corinth* XV, ii, pp. 234, 238, no. 19, pl. 52) as a "fruit of doubtful identity," probably under the influence of other terracottas that clearly do represent fruits; there are no other cakes from the Potters' Quarter. On the survival in Europe into modern times of cakes baked in the form of

male and female genitals, particularly for the Easter season, see Wright 1866, pp. 87–90.

[76] Jung 1967, pp. 79–117. On round objects simultaneously symbolizing bread and the solar disc, see Goodenough 1956, V, p. 66.

[77] duBois 1988, pp. 120–121.

[78] Sourvinou-Inwood 1978, p. 110.

[79] For a plain, flat box type small enough to rest in the palm of the hand, see Brümmer 1985, p. 96, fig. 27:c.

[80] Jung 1967, p. 209; Rank 1990, pp. 63, 79–80, note 8; on containers as metaphors for women, see Reeder et al. 1995, pp. 195–199.

[81] National Archaeological Museum, inv. no. 5963.

[82] *Eutresis*, p. 261, fig. 308:6 on p. 248.

[83] Winter, *Typen* I, p. 80, no. 3.

[84] E.g., Brauron, see Linders 1972, esp. pp. 11–13.

[85] Approximately one hundred thirty loomweights also were found in the sanctuary: publication forthcoming with miscellaneous finds.

An alabastron is held in the hand of **V26**, which could possibly have been a standing youth; a more fully preserved standing youth from the same lot (**C191**) may hold an alabastron in one hand, while carrying a rooster in the other. If so, he would have been bringing an offering appropriate to the chthonic deities (the rooster; see p. 269) together with a gift more appropriate to Aphrodite, as an object of beautification. In the Lokroi plaques, it is Aphrodite who is associated with the alabastron.[86] Actual alabastra, however, are rare at the sanctuary.[87] The pottery context of these two pieces is Classical, terminating in the last quarter of the 5th century B.C.

MISCELLANEOUS FRAGMENTS
(V27–V32)

Included here are pieces of technical or typological interest that are too fragmentary to be assigned to specific sections of the discussion. **V27** is a portion of the skirt folds of a large statuette, probably female. Its interest lies in the remains of paint, pink, red, and yellow over white slip, as well as gilding. The pattern made by the different colors can no longer be recovered, if indeed there was a pattern and not an impressionistic splashing of colors. Where the gilding has worn away, an underlying layer of yellow paint can be seen, probably employed to intensify the color of the gilding and to make any chipping of the gold paint less obvious (see pp. 13–14). The pottery context of this piece, from the construction fill of the Trapezoidal Building, terminates at the beginning of the 3rd century B.C. Whatever the type originally represented, this fragment shows that very large, gilded, and presumably expensive statuettes were being made in Corinth, probably in the later 4th century B.C.

V28 and **V29** are merely a hand and a foot fragment respectively, but they are of statuette scale and of good quality. The slight remains of red paint show that the fragments originally belonged to male figurines. The shape of the break and the hollowing at the top of the foot suggest that it was added to the hem of a long garment, presumably the mantle of a semidraped type. Underpainting was used on the hand, this time pink under red. Both fragments are from the same pottery context as **V27** and demonstrate that large male statuettes of good quality were being dedicated during the 4th century B.C. The smaller foot **V30** does not show any red paint but must belong to a nude male type, since the leg is bare above the ankle. This foot, from the same pottery context as the three foregoing fragments, is of excellent fabric and is well detailed anatomically, showing that the molds of 4th-century B.C. male figurines were sometimes taken from archetypes made by highly skilled artisans.

V31 is the outspread wing of a creature, perhaps Eros or Nike, in flight. The wing is different in form, however, from those of the Eros **H289**, the only one with the wings well preserved. The wings of the fragmentary Nike **H295** are not preserved. **V32**, a sleeved arm with a clenched, pierced hand that originally held something, is all that remains of a type of which nothing else is preserved in the sanctuary. The sleeve suggests an Oriental costume, perhaps worn by a rider holding the reins of his horse. Another possibility is that the arm belonged to an actor wearing a sleeved costume.

BASES AND SUPPORTS
(V33–V43)

In this section are discussed Classical and Hellenistic figurine bases of different shapes, preserved either alone or with only slight remains of the bottom of the figure, as well as supports of various types preserved without the figures that leaned on them. The bases discussed here were made separately and attached to the figurines, but similarly shaped bases could also be molded together

---

[86] Sourvinou-Inwood 1978, p. 105.   [87] *Corinth* XVIII, i, p. 53.

with the torso, particularly in derivative production (e.g., **H120**). Sometimes only the upper part of the base was molded, while the bottom was added by hand (e.g., **H109**).

CLASSICAL BASES

The bases of Classical figurines and their survivals from the Acrocorinth sanctuary are rectangular. They are found in several variants: low and straight sided, as in **C20**; low and slightly splaying, as in **C19**; or high and splaying, as in **C26**. When the back of the figurine is handmade, the back of the base may be rounded off, presumably to simplify construction, as in **C19** and **H146**. All these bases are plain, without any moldings. The highest of the rectangular bases is **V36**, which splays into a flat, spreading foot. This well-made variant is likely to be of 4th-century B.C. date; it is from the construction fill of the Trapezoidal Building, which terminates at the beginning of the 3rd century B.C.

A two-stepped rectangular base type is preserved only in isolation in the sanctuary; **V33** is a complete base of this type, and there are fragmentary examples as well, from pottery contexts containing both Classical and later material. The type may have been copied from small bronzes, since two-stepped rectangular bases were used for bronzes in the Archaic and Early Classical periods.[88] This base type, however, may not have been used for terracotta figurines until later; a 4th-century B.C. Corinthian terracotta Aphrodite in Berlin of the type of **H249**[89] has a base of this type. Sometimes the lower step is quite low, as in a Corinthian figurine of a woman with a duck in Berlin,[90] recalling the use of a rectangular base set on a low plaque to support small bronzes.[91] **V33** is handmade, and the two steps are clearly differentiated, but when figurines with two-stepped bases were reproduced in subsequent generations, the clear definition of the two steps appears to have been lost, and the lower step survives merely as a flat molding at the bottom of the base, as in **V34**. The top of this base was closed up from inside with a strip of clay, as if to imitate the solid top of a separately made base, and was then punched with holes for venting.

The more elaborate **V35** is a high, rectangular base with moldings at the top and bottom. Since only one side is preserved, it is not certain whether it originally was a large base for a statuette or a long, narrow base suitable for a figurine with a strongly horizontal composition, such as **H65**, with its wide drapery fall at the side. A high base such as this one would go far toward correcting the rather stocky proportions and flat-footed look of **H65** and others like it. The excellent fabric of **V35** should date it to the 4th century B.C.; it is from a pottery context terminating in the early 3rd century B.C. The simplest form of base is the abbreviated plaque on which some 5th-century B.C. figurines stand, for example, **C10**. These bases usually were molded together with the torso. They can be compared with, and probably were modeled after, similar small plinths on Archaic bronze statuettes,[92] but while the bronzes were probably meant to be attached to something else, a plinth of this kind on a figurine appears to have been the entire base.

HELLENISTIC BASES

While the base types discussed above sometimes continued to be used into the Hellenistic period for figurines of surviving Classical types, two new base types are typically Hellenistic, the spool and the plaque. The spool base is well known elsewhere in terracotta figurines of the 3rd and 2nd centuries B.C.[93] and must be derived from bases employed for small bronzes, as in an Aphrodite in Boston.[94] The best examples of spool bases are wheelmade and of good fabric, with

---

[88] E.g., Neugebauer 1931, pp. 79–80, no. 180, pl. 28; Mattusch 1988, p. 114, fig. 5.12.

[89] Winter, *Typen* II, p. 93, no. 6.

[90] Kriseleit and Zimmer 1994, p. 112, no. 31; the drawing in Winter, *Typen* II, p. 7, no. 5, omits the bottom step.

[91] E.g., Rolley 1986, pp. 100–101, fig. 70; p. 137, fig. 118.

[92] E.g., Rolley 1986, p. 106, figs. 76, 77.

[93] E.g., Langlotz and Hirmer 1965, pp. 298–299, pls. 149, 151, dated Late Hellenistic; pp. 248–249, color pls. XVII, XVIII, dated to the 2nd century B.C.

[94] Comstock and Vermeule 1971, pp. 64–65, no. 65.

sharply defined edges; the bases are either straight sided, as in **V37**, or concave sided and wider at the bottom, as in **V38**. More often, the spool base appears in its narrower form, not wheelmade but handmade, or moldmade together with its figurine, and with thicker, less clearly defined flat or torus moldings at the top and bottom. Several examples of such bases have been preserved in the sanctuary complete with their figurines (e.g., the votaries **H9** and **H10** and the boy **H331**). These fully formed spool bases should not be confused with the early-4th-century semicircular type that looks like a spool in front but is flat in back.[95] The relationship between the two types is unclear. The base of **H101** is a hybrid; it has the semicircular form, but it is also set on a plaque base.

The thin plaque base is known elsewhere mainly in "Tanagra" figurines[96] and appears in the sanctuary in the isolated base **V39** and in such small, "Tanagra"-like pieces as **H104** and **H122**. These bases were made separately; the figurine was attached by pressing down a part of the garment hem toward the back. A ridge on the surface of **V39** near one corner is all that remains of the hem of the missing figurine. This base has a hole cut at the center for venting, but the complete figurines are uncut at the bottom. The small **H104** apparently was not vented at all and may have been solid; **H122** could have been vented in the missing upper part of the torso.

The last base (**V40**) is rather puzzling. It appears to represent a kind of shelf like a console, on which the figurine stands, as a larger piece might be displayed on a real shelf fastened to a wall.[97] An animal relief decorates the front of the shelf, between the two projections of the console.

SUPPORTS

V41 and **V42** are herm supports broken from the left sides of figurines of unknown type. The one complete figurine leaning on a herm support (**H79**) is a standing female, draped in a voluminous mantle. Since the herm support is placed at the right side rather than the left, the isolated herms cannot belong to this figurine type. **V41** has lost detail and preserves only the main outlines; **V42** preserves only the head, but it can be identified through complete parallels.[98] The style of **V42** is Early Classical, the two smooth shocks of hair framing the forehead resembling the coiffure of **C103**. The style of the herm support, however, does not necessarily date the figurine, which probably belonged to the 4th century B.C. or later, when such supports were popular. Another old-fashioned type to serve as a support is the archaizing female figure, of which **V43** is an example. While the fragment is not well preserved, the peplos arrangement is roughly similar to that of the archaizing figurine from the sanctuary **H52**.

MOLDS
(**V44–V46**)

Five fragments of molds were found in the sanctuary, three of which (**V44–V46**) are sufficiently well preserved to be identifiable in type. **V44** represents a female figure holding a piglet across her chest. The lower part of the piglet and the forearm that originally supported it from below apparently were rendered in a separate mold, since the lower edge of **V44** is finished. The complete type probably was similar to one of the votaries carrying a piglet, such as **H9**, but in larger scale. Its pottery context, which terminates in the early 3rd century B.C., is too early for the later-3rd-century "priestess" type (p. 254). The fragment **V45** shows only a draped left breast

[95] As in Boeotian figurines, *British Museum* I, pp. 229–230, nos. 862–864, pl. 123.

[96] Kleiner 1984, e.g., pls. 1–5; on the introduction of this base type for "Tanagras" in Athens, based on metallic sources, see D. B. Thompson 1966, p. 54.

[97] The available evidence for shelves, however, suggests that they were very simply constructed and used mainly for utilitarian objects: Richter 1966, pp. 78–79.

[98] E.g., *Lindos* I, col. 567, no. 2340, pl. 110.

and a few adjacent folds, which may belong to a mantle draped over the shoulder and upper arm.
V46 is part of a wing mold, from near the attachment to the body, presumably of such a figure
as Eros or Nike; it is from a pottery context terminating in the first quarter of the 3rd century B.C.

While these types are suitable for dedication in the sanctuary, it is curious that they appear
in the form of molds. Figurines and other votives may well have been sold from booths within
the sanctuary,[99] but there is no evidence for a workshop there. Indeed, the scarcity of water
and probably wood in the immediate vicinity would have made the location impractical for
a workshop. Perhaps coroplasts or their families offered molds, just as herdsmen or farmers
dedicated figurines of animals, to ensure the success of their labors.

CATALOGUE

In this section are catalogued figurines of animals; reliefs; votive offerings broken from figurines; miscellaneous
fragments; bases and supports; molds. For an explanation of the conventions employed in this catalogue, see the
Introduction, pages 20–22.

ANIMALS

V1 Pig   Pl. 61

MF-10676. Lot 1945. Preserved: front and back of animal,
part of left side. Missing bottom of feet, base. L. 0.117.
Fabric 3, orange-buff. White slip. Peach-pink paint on flesh.
Hollow. Two molds; all parts rendered in molds.
Published: Stroud 1965, p. 22, pl. 11:b.
Space between legs and belly filled with clay, perhaps origi-
nally attached to base, as in **V2**. Ridge along back with light
vertical strokes, in mold (on reverse, not visible in photograph).
Long, upturned snout. Well-made piece. Possible later gen-
eration: **V2**. Fragments of similar moldmade pigs in lots 2170,
3230, 3233.
See pp. 14, 120, 266, 343.

V2 Pig   Pl. 61

MF-10660. Lot 1945. Preserved: rump, rear legs, part of belly,
part of base. Mended. P.H. 0.065. Fabric 3, greenish buff,
overfired. Hollow. Two molds; all parts rendered in molds.
Possibly later generation of **V1**. Curly tail. Base originally
rectangular, spreading, slight indication of torus molding at
bottom. Belly touches top of base; space between back legs
and belly filled with clay.
See p. 266.

V3 Pig   Pl. 61

MF-14174. Lot 2239. Preserved: head and part of neck. P.L.
0.07. Fabric 3, orange-buff. Hollow. Two molds. Tooling
on face.
Pointed snout; nostrils punched. Long eye. Mouth slashed,
downturned. Long ear flat against head. Largest of the
moldmade pigs.
See p. 266.

V4 Pig   Pl. 61

MF-10667. Lot 1945. Preserved: front and top of head.
P.L. 0.057. Fabric slightly coarse, orange to orange-buff, with
gray interior, some small to medium white, gray, and dark red
inclusions; sparse small sparkling inclusions; voids. Hollow.
Tooling on face.

Narrow, upturned snout; nostrils punched. Eye large,
slanted. Flaring ridge on head. Fabric coarser than usual,
but inclusions seem local.
See p. 266.

V5 Bull   Pl. 61

MF-11834. Lot 2104. Preserved: one side of head. Missing
horn. Mended. P.L. 0.067. Fabric 1, orange-buff, with
orange core. Solid. Tooling on mouth, nostrils, ear, top of
head, neck.
Mouth open, as if bellowing; tongue visible inside. Nostril
marked with curved slash. Oval eye. Hair at top of head
punched. Diagonal slashes show folds of skin on neck.
See pp. 267, 343.

V6 Ram   Pl. 61

MF-11878. Lot 2153. Preserved: top of head; surface
chipped. P.H. 0.024. Fabric slightly coarse, orange-buff, with
orange core, some small white and dark gray inclusions, voids.
Hollow. Thin-walled. Two molds. Dull impression.
Spiral horns, flat against head. Forehead slopes down to
oval, slanted eyes.
See p. 267.

V7 Sheep or goat   Pl. 61

MF-10422. Lot 877. Preserved: chest to rump. Missing front
legs, rear lower legs, part of back. Mended; surface chipped.
P.L. 0.18. Fabric similar to 1, fired harder, buff. White slip.
Possibly red paint on fleece. Hollow. Thick-walled. Round
vent in belly, diam. ca. 0.007. Probably handmade. Tooling
on fleece.
Walking or leaping to viewer's right. Fleece rendered by
deep, closely spaced, irregular vertical and diagonal slashes.
Edge of fleece hangs under belly. Similar in type: MF-12551
(lot 3222, midsection only, nearly solid, tooling summary).
See pp. 267–268.

V8 Monkey   Pl. 61

MF-69-399. Lot 6215. Preserved: head, including tenon; face
chipped. P.H. 0.019. Fabric 1, grayish buff. Back probably
handmade, rounded. Tooling on face.

[99] *Corinth* XVIII, iii, p. 201.

Round head, with projecting browridge and jaw. Nostrils punched. Mouth cut open; something apparently broken from mouth at right side. Short pointed tenon for insertion into body. Another monkey head, larger, from Forum Southwest: MF-75-31.

See pp. 194, 268.

V9 Bird   Pl. 61

MF-10542. Lot 887. Preserved: neck to tail; edge of tail chipped. P.L. 0.077. Fabric orange-buff, with sparse small dark inclusions. White slip. Red paint on legs. Body molded; legs handmade. Concave underneath. Added: legs.

Slender body, with curving back and breast. Pointed legs, without feet. Long tail touches ground, acts as third "leg." Delicate pattern of feathers on wings is in mold. Possible earlier generation: MF-7579 in the Corinth collection, with clearer feather details.

See pp. 8, note 26, 126, 268.

V10 Bird(?)   Pl. 61

MF-10681. Lot 869. Preserved: right wing. P.L. 0.056. Fabric 1, orange-buff. Hollow. Tooling on feathers.

Composition apparently more upright than usual Corinthian bird type (cf. **V9**). Three rows of overlapping feathers outlined.

See p. 269.

V11 Rooster   Pl. 61

MF-14093. Lot 4381. Preserved: head to chest. Missing top and front of head. P.H. 0.059. Fabric 2, light orange. White slip. Hollow. Probably handmade. Back flattened; only one side modeled. Tooling on ruff.

Faces left. Pellet eye. Traces of wattles and crest. Flaring ruff; feathers shown with vertical incisions.

See p. 269.

V12 Rooster   Pl. 61

MF-13945. Lot 2088. Preserved: head, part of neck at left side. P.H. 0.057. Fabric 3, greenish buff. Hollow. Two molds; back summarily modeled.

Faces right. Domed head, probably meant to include crest. Eye large, almond shaped, placed low and close to beak. Wattles rendered.

See pp. 269, 312.

V13 Tortoise shell   Pl. 61

MF-14064. Lot 4404. Preserved: one-third of shell, at left side. Max.P.Dim. 0.077. Fabric 1, orange-buff. Probably handmade.

Thickened edge; divisions of shell are grooved. Only the shell represented, not the entire body. Probably a model lyre.

See pp. 152, 269.

RELIEFS

V14 Polos   Pl. 62

MF-11927A, B. Lot 2107. Preserved: A–one fragment, with most of three figures, broken diagonally at upper right side; B–two joining fragments, with parts of three figures, broken diagonally along bottom and at upper left side. P.H.: A–0.06; B–0.049. Fabric 1, orange-buff to orange. White slip. Hollow. Background handmade, crenellations cut with a knife

and punched, torus border added; figures molded separately, then applied and tooled.

Published: Stroud 1968, p. 324, pl. 97:a, b.

Probably not a separate votive polos but worn by a head similar in type to **C100**, only much larger; clay pinched up at back on both A and B may indicate attachment to head. Finished at top with crenellations on a torus border. Figures on fragment A, beginning at viewer's left: (1) Standing female, slender, with weight on left leg, left hip slightly outthrust; right arm at side, holding vessel beside leg; left arm bent, object held at chest; peplos girded fairly high, overfold to top of thighs, dropping a little at sides. (2) Standing female, turned to viewer's left, with weight on right leg, left leg bent and pulled back; right arm raised, holds scepter(?) with flaring top; wears peplos and mantle with roll at waist, triangular apron across abdomen; left arm at side, hand may hold edge of apron; mantle may cover head and left shoulder and arm. (3) Standing semidraped male, turned to viewer's left, with head in profile, weight on left leg, right leg bent; right arm outstretched to touch left shoulder of figure 2, seems to follow her; nude chest; mantle draped around waist, folded down into triangular apron in front; left arm at side, hand may hold edge of apron; looped folds from right lower leg up to left leg. Figures on fragment B, beginning at viewer's left: (4) Standing female, smaller than other figures on polos, missing part of head; hips and legs turned three-fourths to viewer's right, head and upper torso in profile; weight on left leg, right leg bent and pulled back; arms outstretched, apparently reaching toward adjacent figure, unclear object(s) in hands; closely wrapped in smooth mantle to ankles, draped under right arm, presumably over left shoulder, with end falling down back; pillar (or herm?) in front of figure. (5) Seated nude male preserved from head to hips, probably Apollo, in profile to viewer's right; kithara on lap, right arm raised and bent to touch strings. (6) Poorly preserved seated female figure, head and upper torso, in profile to viewer's left; back of throne visible and armrest with left arm. Similar in type: **V15** and **V16**; MF-70-98 (no context, small fragment with crenellations and trace of figure).

See pp. 47, 269–271, 291.

V15 Polos   Pl. 62

MF-68-301. Lot 5614. Preserved: one fragment, with part of one figure. Missing part of border. P.H. 0.033. Fabric 1, orange to orange-buff, with gray core. Hollow. Background handmade, crenellations cut with a knife, border added; figure molded separately and applied.

Published: Bookidis 1969, p. 309.

Similar in type to **V14** but of poorer workmanship. Figure preserved from head to waist, same as figure 4 of **V14** but cruder.

See pp. 47, 269–271.

V16 Headdress   Pl. 62

MF-70-162. No context. Preserved: one fragment, with three figures. P.H. 0.053. Fabric 1, orange-buff to orange. Hollow. Background handmade, crenellations and border added; figures molded separately and applied.

Similar in type to **V14** but of poorer workmanship; crenellations merely scalloped, border is flat rather than torus, impressions of figures are dull and not detailed with tooling. Traces of top of head at front and back. Fragment must come from left side of head. Originally must have been open in back:

vertical edge at viewer's right is finished, shape becomes flatter, and border narrows at this end; surface is broken behind. Figures beginning at viewer's left: (1) Draped female figure in profile to viewer's right, leaning backward as if dancing, with fluttering drapery, perhaps a maenad. (2) Nude male leaning toward viewer's left, probably Dionysos; head abuts border. (3) Same as figure 2 of **V14** but 0.01 smaller. For identification of figures, see a miniature altar in the Corinth collection, with a Dionysiac scene in relief: MF-2465 (*Corinth* XII, p. 131, no. 889, pl. 65).

See pp. 269–270.

V17 Headdress Pl. 62

MF-10956. Lot 1945. Preserved: one fragment, with most of three figures. Missing part of surface at viewer's right, most of upper border. P.H. 0.028. Fabric 2, orange-buff to orange. White slip. Yellow paint. Hollow. Background handmade; figures molded all together in a strip and applied to cover entire background. Blisters on surface suggest use of plaster mold.

Probably a headdress similar to **V14** but of poorer workmanship. Figures crude, not detailed. Narrow torus border at top. Traces of top of head at front and back. Fragment must come from right side of head. Originally must have been open in back: vertical edge at viewer's left is finished, and piece is quite flat (for headdress type, see **V16**). Figures beginning at viewer's left: (1) Standing draped Apollo in profile to viewer's left, head turned to look back over left shoulder; holds kithara, left arm raised and bent to touch strings. (2) Artemis stands three-fourths to viewer's right, with weight on right leg, left leg bent; arms down in front of torso; knee-length garment with overfold. (3) Poseidon stands frontally with right foot on rock; right arm leans on knee, with trident in crook of elbow; left side missing.

See pp. 269–271.

V18 Votive shield Pl. 62

MF-12880. Lot 4461. Preserved: fragment of lower part of shield. P.H. 0.035; thickness ca. 0.005. Probably fabric 1, slightly burned. White slip. Red paint. Moldmade; wheelmarks inside.

Similar to shield with *apobates* relief from the Potters' Quarter, KN-1 (*Corinth* XV, ii, pp. 227–228, no. 5, pls. 48, 49). Right foot and ankle of rider and horse's left front leg from elbow to knee are preserved. Other shield fragments: MF-11880 (lot 2151); from the Tile Works, MF-8636, MF-8636 bis, MF-8784, MF-8785.

See pp. 269, 271, 343.

V19 Rider plaque Pl. 62

MF-13412. Lot 2210. Preserved: rider from shoulders to feet, part of neck and flank of horse. Surface worn. P.H. 0.041. Fabric ochre to orange, with some small white and dark gray inclusions, voids. Solid. Back flat, surface irregular.

Rider's nude torso turned to front; chlamys wrapped around right arm. Dull impression. Possible mold sibling: MF-4036 from a votive deposit, probably of a hero shrine (*Corinth* XII, p. 49, no. 309, pl. 27, there dated late 4th or early 3rd century B.C.). Perhaps mechanically related: MF-1886 from the South Stoa (Davidson 1942, p. 112, no. 18, fig. 3 on p. 111; poorly preserved, wears a polos).

See pp. 131, 269, 271–272.

Votive Offerings Broken from Figurines

V20 Hand with offering Pl. 62

MF-13926. Lot 4398. Preserved: right hand and forearm, with offering. P.L. 0.043 (size 3). Fabric 1, greenish buff. Solid. Handmade.

Forearm originally extended horizontally, with offering set on flat palm of mitten-shaped hand. Offering probably a cake shaped like a brioche, spherical, with smaller sphere on top.

See pp. 272, 298.

V21 Hand with offering Pl. 62

MF-13924. Lot 4385. Preserved: left hand and part of forearm, with offering. Missing fingers, except thumb; edge of disc chipped. P.L. 0.036 (size 3). Fabric 1, orange-buff to orange. Solid. Handmade. Tooling on disc.

Original position of arm uncertain. Thumb grasps long object with tapered ends, in front of a large disc with punched surface; both objects probably cakes. Similar in type: one in lot 4377 (same offerings, fingers rendered).

See pp. 49, 272, 298.

V22 Hand with offering Pl. 62

MF-14042. Lot 3230. Preserved: right hand and part of forearm, with offering. P.L. 0.032 (size 3). Fabric 1, yellowish buff. Solid. Handmade. Tooling on offering.

Forearm originally extended horizontally, with cake set on flat palm of mitten-shaped hand. Cake is thick and squarish, divided vertically into three segments, topped with two small superimposed discs.

See pp. 272, 298.

V23 Hand with offering Pl. 62

MF-13922. Lot 2152. Preserved: left(?) hand with offering. P.H. 0.028 (size 3). Fabric 1, orange-buff. Solid. Handmade. Tooling on offering.

Forearm originally extended horizontally, hand grasping bottom of small shallow bowl. In center of bowl, a conical cake, beside which is a flat, round cake (probably a *kollybos*) and an oval cake with one deep slash down the center.

See pp. 272, 273, 298.

V24 Hand with offering Pl. 62

MF-13925. Lot 3228. Preserved: left hand and part of forearm, with offering. P.L. 0.023 (size 3). Fabric 1, orange-buff to creamy buff. Solid. Handmade. Tooling on offering.

Original position of arm uncertain. Mitten-shaped hand grasps rectangular box; fingers curled around one side. Thin lid indicated by incised line around edge of box.

See pp. 272, 273, 298.

V25 Offering(?) Pl. 62

MF-14036. Lot 1953. Broken at one end. Diam. 0.012. Fabric 5, orange. Solid. Handmade. Tooled.

Tightly rolled, narrow band of cloth, probably originally attached to a figurine. Broken end suggests that band was partly unrolled.

See pp. 272, 273.

V26 Hand with offering Pl. 62

MF-10544. Lot 887. Preserved: front and side–right hand, adjacent thigh. Max.P.Dim. 0.04 (size 2–3). Fabric 3, light orange. White slip. Hollow. Added: rim of vessel. Tooling on hand, vessel.

Gender of figurine uncertain. Alabastron held mouth downward, against thigh; mouth opening punched.

See pp. 8, note 26, 272, 274.

MISCELLANEOUS FRAGMENTS

V27 Drapery — Pl. 63

MF-12045. Lot 2249. Preserved: front–part of skirt. Mended; chipped. P.H. 0.116 (size 5?). Fabric slightly burned; treated with preservative. White slip. Pink, red, and yellow paint; gilding. Hollow. Possibly handmade. Tooling on folds.

Vertical tubular folds. Yellow paint on surface where gilding has worn away, perhaps an underpaint.

See pp. 14, 274.

V28 Hand of male figurine — Pl. 63

MF-13476. Lot 2249. Preserved: left hand and wrist. Missing part of index finger. P.L. 0.06 (size 4). Fabric 2, orange-buff. White slip. Pink paint, and red over pink. Solid. Handmade.

Tapering fingers; thumb too large. Fingers curled, as if cradling object in hand; since palm is rough but painted, object must have been added after firing. Red paint on flesh, over pink, indicates figure must have been male.

See pp. 14, 64, 274.

V29 Foot of male figurine — Pl. 63

MF-13473. Lot 2249. Preserved: right foot, including most of sole, part of instep. Missing small toe; cracked. P.L. 0.070 (size 4–5). Fabric treated with preservative. White slip. Red paint. Nearly solid. Probably handmade. Tooling on toes.

Foot is bare. Break across instep and slight hollowing at top suggest foot was added to a draped figure. Toes well modeled; toenails rendered. Red paint on flesh indicates figure must have been male.

See pp. 64, 274.

V30 Foot of male figurine — Pl. 63

MF-13475. Lot 2249. Preserved: right foot and ankle. P.H. 0.035 (size 2–3). Fabric 4, buff. White slip. Solid.

Foot is bare. Anatomy well rendered; details probably in mold. Unless this is an unusually well rendered leg of an articulated "doll," the figurine probably was male. Absence of drapery on leg suggests either full nudity, more common among male figurines from the sanctuary, or male costume.

See pp. 64, 274.

V31 Wing — Pl. 63

MF-13404. Lot 4349. Preserved: left wing. Missing tip of one feather. P.L. 0.045. Fabric 1, orange-buff. Solid. Back not detailed. Tooling on feathers.

From a winged figure, probably in flight, such as Eros or Nike. Originally attached directly to shoulders, not slotted as in the Eros **H287**. Underwing is slightly concave. Two rows of blunt feathers, each slashed down the center: five secondaries and four longer primaries, with row of eight shorter feathers overlapping them. Similar in type: one in lot 4344 (open wing, one row of feathers).

See pp. 181, 274.

V32 Rider(?) — Pl. 63

MF-13940. Lot 878. Preserved: right forearm and hand; fingers chipped. P.L. 0.034 (size 2–3). Fabric 4, creamy buff. White slip. Solid. Probably handmade. Tooling on fingers; hole punched through hand.

Arm in long sleeve. Clenched hand originally held a long, narrow object, perhaps the reins of a rider, in Oriental costume. Similar in type: arm in long sleeve in lot 2249 (missing hand).

See p. 274.

BASES AND SUPPORTS

V33 Base — Pl. 63

MF-11398. Lot 877. Base intact. L. 0.073, W. 0.057. Fabric 1, orange-buff, interior orange. Hollow. Thick-walled. Handmade.

Irregular, rectangular, two-stepped base. Marks of attachment of figurine on upper surface.

See pp. 274–275.

V34 Base — Pl. 63

MF-14084. Lot 2107. Preserved: base with small part of figurine. Missing one short side. Mended. L. 0.069, W. 0.046 (at bottom). Fabric 3, orange-buff. Hollow. Tooling on foot and hem of figurine.

Rectangular base, with slightly splaying sides, flat molding at bottom. Right foot and adjacent trailing hem of female figurine preserved, pointing toward corner of base. Figurine probably rendered in same mold as base; top of base within hem closed with clay strip, punched with two vent holes, 0.006 in diam.; surface of clay strip shows impression of coarse cloth or mat.

See pp. 274–275.

V35 Base — Pl. 63

MF-14082. Lot 877. Preserved: part of one long side and top. P.L. 0.085. Fabric 4, orange-buff. White slip. Hollow.

Long, rectangular base; ovolo molding at top, splaying molding in two degrees at bottom. Upper surface rough where figurine was attached.

See pp. 274–275.

V36 Base — Pl. 63

MF-14085. Lot 4369. Preserved: one corner, with parts of two sides and top. H. 0.05. Fabric 2, orange-buff, with gray core, interior orange. Hollow.

High, probably rectangular base, with slightly splaying sides; flat, spreading foot. Simple in form, but smoothness and regularity suggest it was moldmade.

See pp. 274–275.

V37 Base — Pl. 63

MF-13715. Lot 3227. Base nearly intact; lower edge chipped, surface cracked. Diam. top 0.115. Fabric 3, greenish buff. White slip. Red paint. Hollow. Wheelmade.

Spool base, with fairly straight sides, flaring top and resting surface. Upper surface painted before attachment of figurine. Similar in type: MF-13745 (lot 3217); MF-13714 (lot 2249).

See pp. 274, 276.

V38 Base Pl. 63

MF-13713. Lot 1962. Base intact; top cracked. Diam. top 0.075. Fabric 3, orange-buff. White slip. Hollow. Wheelmade.

Spool base, with concave sides, flat edge around resting surface, which is greater in diameter than top. Two incised grooves around upper edge.

See pp. 274, 276.

V39 Base Pl. 63

MF-14086. Lot 4377. Base intact. L. 0.059 (front), 0.045 (back); W. 0.037. Fabric 1, orange-buff, with orange core.

Trapezoidal plaque, with irregular oval cutting at center for venting. Trace of oval hem of figurine at back of upper surface.

See pp. 18, 121, 274, 276.

V40 Base Pl. 63

MF-13933. Lot 2249. Preserved: base with feet and hem of figurine. Missing projection on left side. L. 0.042, W. 0.026 (at top of base). Fabric 1, orange-buff. White slip. Hollow.

Female figurine stands on a kind of shelf or console, which has two short legs in back and two projections in front; relief panel between projections shows perhaps griffin chasing two animals. Figurine has weight on right foot, pointing to corner of base, left foot drawn to side; pointed slippers. Mantle falls nearly to feet; narrow folds of chiton or peplos visible above left foot and between feet.

See pp. 274, 276.

V41 Herm support Pl. 64

MF-13937. Lot 2249. Preserved: head to just below phallus, left arm. P.H. 0.063. Fabric grayish buff to orange, slightly sandy, voids. White slip. Hollow. Back flattened. Vertical edge of rectangular vent.

Herm support. Pillar(?) visible at right side of head and drapery of figurine(?) on top. Dull impression. Face lacks detail, but shape of head and beard suggests similarity to **V42**. Flat, rectangular arm. Faint outline of phallus. Diagonal slash across chest probably accidental. For figurine leaning on a herm support, see **H79**.

See pp. 274, 276.

V42 Herm support Pl. 64

MF-13411. Lot 2249. Preserved: front–head and part of left shoulder. P.H. 0.033. Fabric 1, pinkish orange to orange-buff. Hollow.

Head probably from herm support similar to **V41**; traces of attachment to figurine at right side of head. Eyes prominent, almond shaped. Nose bulbous. Moustache droops over slightly smiling lips. Full beard. Hair parted at center into two shocks framing triangular forehead. Early Classical in style.

See pp. 274, 276.

V43 Support Pl. 64

MF-73-119. Lot 73-144. Preserved: top of pillar with drapery to knees of figure. P.H. 0.083. Fabric 1, orange-buff to greenish buff. Hollow. Back handmade, flattened. Part of round vent preserved, diam. ca. 0.025.

Pillar support with archaistic female figure in front. Figure in rigidly frontal pose, with left arm at side; peplos girded high, with overfold hem lifted at center; long lock of hair to left shoulder. On top of pillar, left elbow of figurine (Aphrodite?) resting on drapery folds, which fall over right side of face and torso of support figure.

See pp. 274, 276, 298.

MOLDS

V44 Mold Pl. 64

MF-11396. Lot 877. Preserved: upper arm of figure, part of chest, part of piglet. Max.P.Dim. 0.061, thickness ca. 0.02. Fabric hard, orange-buff, with sparse small dark inclusions, grayish core. Surfaces smooth; back curved.

Cast shows back of piglet across chest of figure, drapery folds above. Horizontal lower edge of mold seems to be finished; remainder of piglet, forearm cradling it, and skirt of figure probably rendered in another mold. Type probably similar to **H401**.

See p. 276.

V45 Mold Pl. 64

MF-69-289. Lot 6214. Preserved: one breast, surrounding drapery. Max.P.Dim. 0.057, thickness 0.012. Exterior fabric orange-buff, with abundant small to large gray inclusions ("tile fabric"); interior fabric 2, orange-buff. Back curved.

Cast shows left breast of draped female figurine; diagonal folds along left side may belong to mantle draped over left shoulder. Other mold fragments possibly showing drapery folds: MF-11395; MF-11397 (both lot 877).

See pp. 276–277.

V46 Mold Pl. 64

MF-11261. Lot 880. Preserved: part of wing, all edges broken. Max.P.Dim. 0.052, thickness 0.008. Fabric 2, light orange. Back curved.

Cast shows wing with row of diagonal feathers along upper and lower edges; lighter feathers probably belong to upper part of wing, which narrows towards viewer's right; must be left wing of flying figure such as Eros or Nike.

See pp. 276–277.

VI

CLASSICAL AND HELLENISTIC IMPORTED FIGURINES; EXTERNAL RELATIONS

DEFINING IMPORTS

This chapter is devoted to the figurines of non-Corinthian fabrics. Sometimes the fabrics and iconography of these figurines are sufficient to reveal the sources without much doubt. Most of the Argive and Attic figurines, for example, can be attributed with some confidence. The sources of a few figurines have been identified definitively by scholars visiting Corinth and have served as guides to identify others. Ideally, the sources of imported figurines should be pinpointed on the basis of both fabric and type. Sometimes, however, published typological parallels are lacking for figurines that seem to be of identifiable fabric. In these cases, the figurines are included provisionally under their likely sources. When the sources of figurines of non-Corinthian fabric are not clearly recognizable, they have been grouped together at the end of this chapter, to avoid possibly misleading attributions. It is hoped that they will eventually be identified by students of other coroplastic centers.

The most troublesome figurines are those that might be called "anomalous Corinthian"; their fabric may resemble Corinthian to a certain degree, yet they are not convincingly local and have therefore been included under the category of figurines of uncertain provenience. The problem of identifying such figurines is exacerbated by the large number of workshops that appear to have been active in Corinth, some perhaps only for a short time and varying greatly in the quality of their output (see p. 19). Are marginal fabrics just poor local work not up to standard for some reason? Corinth was such a prolific center of all sorts of terracotta products that one might expect a certain amount of marginal or opportunistic activity, outside the main workshops, by people with sufficient expertise to produce some figurines to sell at a festival, without having access to the best materials or facilities. Or perhaps such figurines were made in other northern Peloponnesian communities with access to similar clays, in imitation of Corinthian work.

For example, three figurines (**I60**, **I65**, and **I86**) are thick-walled and heavy for their relatively small size. Their fabric is of convincingly Corinthian color but is sandy in texture, which is not normal for most Corinthian work. On the basis of their technical similarities to one another, it seems possible to assign them to a common workshop. **I60** is of a distinctly Corinthian type, a youthful peplophoros with her arms at her sides, and may be mechanically related to **H37**, which is of Corinthian fabric. One might be tempted to say that sand was added to the clay by a local craftsman, perhaps in response to a temporary shortage of better material. Yet **I65** has a probable mold sibling (**I66**) in a fabric that does not look at all Corinthian. Further, its type, as well as that of **I86**, is not convincingly Corinthian.

Two other "anomalous" figurines, the dancer **I72** and the female head **I74**, are of fabric that could be Corinthian but is coarser than normal because of the use of organic temper, which has burned out, leaving voids. Since this practice is unusual for Corinthian coroplasts, such figurines may have been made in neighboring workshops, if they were not simply marginal local work.

The female head **I79** presents a different scenario; its fabric is very like the Corinthian fabric 1 (see p. 11), and its facial type could be local, but the tooling of the hair differs from local work in its stiffness and dryness and in the tendency to pattern the hair geometrically. Such tooling is more typical, perhaps, of Megarian work (see p. 297). Seen beside Corinthian heads, **I79** stands apart. Perhaps such figurines were not made in workshops in Corinth itself, but were made sufficiently nearby to obtain clay with physical properties similar to the Corinthian clay and perhaps Corinthian workshop materials; the workshop practices might well have differed enough, however, to produce figurines that were not entirely Corinthian in appearance, even when Corinthian molds were employed. Still other "anomalous" pieces discussed below, under the category of figurines of uncertain provenience, show other departures from the expected local techniques, so that the total number of imported figurines with little or no connection to Corinthian workshops is somewhat reduced.

Looking to the nearby larger sites, figurines appear to have been manufactured at Isthmia, where molds of Corinthian fabric have been found.[1] Some of the figurines found at Isthmia seem to be Corinthian imports,[2] but others may have been made locally of clay similar in appearance to Corinthian. For example, an ephedrismos figurine[3] is of a type closely paralleled in the Demeter sanctuary (see pp. 200–201), but it apparently was constructed by pressing a thin layer of fine clay into the mold and backing this layer with slightly coarser material, so that the surface layer has in part flaked away. This method of construction is unusual in Corinth itself for Hellenistic figurines of this relatively small scale, being more characteristic of terracotta sculpture. Its use may suggest a scarcity of the finest grade of clay in some places outside the main center.[4]

It is unfortunate that we know little of the coroplastic industries of Megara and Sikyon, since one might expect imports from those cities. Two pieces from the Acrocorinth sanctuary, the above-mentioned female head I79 and the male figurine I84, resemble figurines of reported Megarian provenience in retouch or construction (see pp. 297, 298), but they do not resemble one another in fabric. The Classical and Early Hellenistic figurines from the Sanctuary of Apollo Maleatas at Epidauros include many Argive and Corinthian, some of good quality, and other more modest pieces that could be of local manufacture.[5] The inhabitants of any small village in the Corinthia, however, assuming they possessed the necessary skills, materials, and firing facilities, conceivably could have produced figurines for festivals, even in the absence of major coroplastic activity. In such cases, we may never know the precise sources.[6]

Finally, because of the difficulty in some cases in drawing a distinction between Corinthian and non-Corinthian, or in identifying fabrics that have been burned, there are a few figurines that have been catalogued and discussed among the main body of Corinthian figurines, although there is a slight doubt about their origin (e.g., **H247**).

NUMBERS OF IMPORTS AND THE TRADE IN FIGURINES

An effort was made to take note, on the basis of fabric, of all figurines of identifiable types that could have been imported. The total number of imports of the Classical and Hellenistic periods is 115, including catalogued figurines and duplicates in the lots accounted for under the catalogued entries; there are probably a few imports of the Roman period as well, although in the present state of knowledge they cannot be identified (see p. 313). Adding the approximately 50 imports recorded for the Archaic period,[7] it is apparent that imported figurines constitute only a tiny fraction of the total number found in the sanctuary (see pp. 2–4). This is hardly surprising,

[1] Anderson-Stojanović 1993, p. 269.

[2] Anderson-Stojanović 1993, pp. 268–269; Anderson-Stojanović 1996, p. 89; Mitten 1962.

[3] Anderson-Stojanović 1993, p. 288, no. 79, pl. 63.

[4] Other, coarser fabrics are represented at Isthmia as well, including one similar to the Corinthian "tile fabric" (Mitten 1962 [1963, p. 309]), which was not used for figurines in Corinth.

[5] Peppa-Papaioannou 1985.

[6] The "Corinthian periphery" described in Nicholls 1995, p. 425, note 84, includes work that can now be assigned to Corinth itself, as well as figurines thought to have been made by itinerant Corinthian craftsmen elsewhere, even as far away as Athens. This concept, which is not employed in the present study, should not be confused with the problem at hand, which is largely a matter of geographical propinquity.

[7] Publication forthcoming.

given the very large local production. There are fewer imports datable to the 5th and early 4th centuries B.C. than to the Archaic and Early Hellenistic periods, but local copies of Rhodian and Attic Classical female types (**C103** and **C104**), and the strong influence of Tarentine banqueter figurines (see p. 66), show that Corinthian coroplasts must have had either imported figurines or molds.

Under what circumstances did these figurines reach Corinth? With regard to actual commerce, one should probably think in terms of small-scale, opportunistic trade (see below), by vendors taking advantage of festivals to sell a few baskets of figurines of appropriate types in the market or at the sanctuary itself. Another factor would have been the casual importation of figurines by individuals, without the intention of trading them, just as modern pilgrims collect small souvenirs of a religious nature at the holy sites they visit.

For the Classical and Hellenistic periods (including both catalogued figurines and duplicates in the lots), the Argive imports are the most numerous, at 38 figurines; there are 21 identified Attic imports, 10 Boeotian, 5 Rhodian, and 2 West Greek. The remaining imported figurines are from a variety of unknown sources; including the "anomalous Corinthian" figurines, this category numbers 39. Some of these are likely to be East Greek, the uncertainty stemming from the lack of available comparative material to help identify fabrics. Compared to the imports of the Archaic period, there is more Boeotian and less Rhodian.[8]

The trade with Argos was probably the best organized, since there are mold multiples or later generations of several head types (e.g., **I9**, see catalogue) among the figurines from the sanctuary. This is not true of any of the other imported fabrics, although the Rhodian protome **I52** has a possible mold sibling in the Corinth collection. It should be possible to apply to the Corinthian imports the model for the trade in Archaic figurines developed by Uhlenbrock for the very large number of imports at the Sanctuary of Demeter at Cyrene;[9] here, three forms of commerce appear to have been operative: the bulk trade, in which a cargo of substantial size would be delivered by commission directly to a site; the basket trade, in which a relatively small number of figurines would have accompanied a more important cargo, perhaps to take advantage of potential sales at a specific festival; and an indirect form of trade called the "bazaar" trade, in which small transactions along the route would have resulted in the gradual dispersal of the original inventory and the acquisition of new figurines for sale further on. These three forms of trade are reflected in the numbers of figurines from individual workshops arriving at the destination, most especially the number of duplicates from the same molds. The bulk trade would result in a substantial number of mold duplicates, and the basket trade in fewer; the bazaar trade would bring figurines technically unrelated to one another, from a variety of sources. While the numbers of imports at Corinth are much smaller than at Cyrene, owing to the large local production, it seems fair to describe the figurine trade with Argos as basket trade, since there are a few Argive mold duplicates. The relatively short trip from Argos to Corinth with a donkey-load of figurines is not hard to imagine, particularly with a sure market at a festival at the end of the journey.

Understandably, there are no signs of bulk trade in figurines to Corinth, although Corinthian figurines traveled elsewhere in that manner. The assortment of fabrics and types among the group of unknown provenience, however, suggests either the operation of the bazaar trade or the casual carrying of figurines by individuals, as suggested above. The same is likely to be true of the small group of West Greek figurines. Although there is one mold connection of a Boeotian figurine from the sanctuary with one in the Corinth collection, there is otherwise a great disparity

[8] Archaic imports: 18 Argive, 12 Rhodian, 8 other East Greek, 7 Attic, 3 West Greek, 1 Boeotian, and 3 of uncertain provenience; this information was kindly provided by Jean M. Turfa.

[9] Uhlenbrock 1985.

within this group and no sense of coherent workshops. Similarly, among the Attic imports there is a considerable range of types, no mold duplicates, and no close parallels among the few Attic imports found elsewhere in Corinth. Once again, either the bazaar trade was operative or at least part of this diverse material consists of casual imports by individuals.

THE IMPORTED FIGURINES

The imported figurines are discussed below by place of origin, in order of their abundance at the sanctuary, beginning with the Argive. Within each group, the organization follows that used for the Corinthian figurines. The relatively small number of Classical imports are discussed first, then the more abundant Early Hellenistic and survivals in the following order: female votaries, other female types, female heads, deities, males, children, other types (actors, protomes, animals, etc.). All but a few of the imported figurines find general typological parallels among the Corinthian figurines from the sanctuary, indicating a degree of selection to conform to local custom.

ARGIVE FIGURINES (I1–I22)

Some members of this group, as indicated in the catalogue, have been identified as Argive by Martin Guggisberg. The fabric of these figurines, particularly **I7**, has been used as a basis of comparison to suggest an Argive origin for the remaining figurines, including a few for which no exact typological parallels have been published. The typical fabric is orange (5YR 6/6) in color and rather coarse in texture, with some small dark and sparkling inclusions and some voids. The fabric of the better-made and less-worn figurines, such as **I10** and **I11**, is slightly finer in texture.

The above-mentioned likelihood of a basket trade in Argive figurines at Corinth is strengthened by the observation that Argive imports include three types specific to this sanctuary: female votaries carrying piglets (**I1**, **I6–I8**); the "priestess" type (**I22**); and the head of a boy (**I21**), which is mechanically related to the Corinthian boy with a goose (**H331**). The presence of these types, among the most popular at the sanctuary, points to a deliberate selection of figurines known to be saleable.

Five of the Argive figurines (**I1–I5**) are datable stylistically to the Classical period. **I1** preserves only part of the right side of a female figurine, showing the overlapping folds of the open side of the peplos and the hand holding what could be the rear leg of a piglet. Since there is no sign of the peplos overfold on the preserved part of the torso, it must have been short, the type perhaps resembling the Corinthian Classical votary with a piglet **C1**. **I2** is the upper part of a peplos-figurine, which can be completed by examples from Argos and Tiryns.[10] In the original design, the left arm is extended to carry a plate with a votive cake.[11] The head type is similar to **I4**; it has the large, earthy features familiar among some Corinthian faces. Two further heads of this type were noted in the lots (see catalogue). A Classical rather than Hellenistic date for **I2** is suggested by the broad shoulders, the nearly plain overfold with very light catenaries, and the framing of the upper arms with drapery. The parallel from Argos is dated to the third quarter of the 5th century B.C., but the peaked coiffure should bring the date down to the early 4th century B.C.

I3 is the lower part of a different peplophoros type, dated to the Classical period by virtue of the omega folds at the hem of the overfold, probably dropping from the breasts, as in the Corinthian **C36**, and the very straight skirt folds. The overfold hem lifts at the left side, and the open side of the peplos is parted, as if in response to a raised left arm. The isolated head

---

[10] Guggisberg 1988, pp. 197–198, 230, no. 55, fig. 11; *Tiryns* I, p. 80, no. 120, pl. XII:7.   [11] *Tiryns* I, pp. 79–80 on the cake.

I5 has a Classical look in its large features that seem to fill the face, its level, widely opened eyes, and the smoothly rounded coiffure.

I6–I8 are variations of a votary type wearing the peplos and carrying a piglet diagonally across the torso; there are six additional examples of similar type in the lots, making the votary type with a piglet the most popular of the Argive imports. Its meaning at the Acrocorinth sanctuary must have been the same as that of the Corinthian votaries carrying piglets (see pp. 117–124). These figurines belong to a traditional Argive type dating back to the 5th century B.C. and are thought to have concluded by the early 4th.[12] The poor quality, dull impressions, and narrow-shouldered proportions of **I7** and **I8**, however, suggest that degenerate renderings of the type persisted at least until the later 4th century B.C. **I7** is a poorer version of a variant found at Speliotaki.[13]

I6 is the best in quality of the examples of this group from the Demeter sanctuary, and on stylistic grounds it should be the earliest. An example of this variant from Tiryns, in which the left elbow pulls the mantle down like a sling, has a head similar to **I9**.[14] The good quality of this head indicates that better renderings of these votaries were exported to Corinth as well. There are three additional examples of this head type (see catalogue). The coiffure of **I9** clings closely to the head and neck, as if veiled.[15] The features are delicate, the eyes are small, and the mouth is narrow and thin lipped.

I10, which is muffled in a mantle and carries a ball or fruit, could, in the context of the Demeter sanctuary, represent a bride; this figurine has a close parallel from Argos.[16] The subject of another draped female figurine (**I12**) is known from a better-preserved example in Argos;[17] the mantle is wrapped closely around the shoulders, covering the bent right arm and hand; the left elbow is propped on the support, and the hand, as in **I10**, holds a ball or fruit. **I11**, with the hand on the hip and the mantle lifted behind the left shoulder in a gesture of unveiling (see pp. 36, 149, 174) and tucked between the thighs, probably represents Aphrodite; the type is known in other examples from Argos,[18] with a head similar to **I4**, which is also known on a peplophoros type (see **I2**). While the clinging drapery and fine folds of these draped female types are survivals of Attic Rich Style, the figurines are unlikely to date earlier than the later 4th century B.C., because of their narrow, sloping shoulders.

I10 and **I11** could have been made in the same workshop. Although they are different from one another in type, they share compositions in which the figure leans on a pillar at the left side. They both have finely folded, closely clinging garments, narrow, sloping shoulders, and high, cuplike breasts. They have trailing hems over pointed shoes, and the bases are rendered in the mold together with the torso. **I12**, which is somewhat smaller, shares these characteristics as far as it is preserved and may belong to the same workshop group. The head **I4** shows tool marks similar to those on **I11** and could perhaps be brought into the group as well.

The fragment **I13**, which shows the mantle curving over the thigh and probably tucked between the thighs, could be an Aphrodite type similar in part to **I11**. In this case, the composition includes a cluster of folds of uncertain purpose beside the right hip. Its good quality should place it in the 4th century B.C., and indeed it was found in the construction fill of the Trapezoidal Building, the terminal date of which is the beginning of the 3rd century B.C.

---

[12] Guggisberg 1988, pp. 222–225, for a summary of the development of Argive figurines. None of the types published in Banaka-Dimaki 1997 was found at the sanctuary.

[13] Verdelis 1964, pp. 121–122, pl. 122:α, right.

[14] *Tiryns* I, p. 79, no. 113, pl. IX:12.

[15] Cf. Guggisberg 1988, pp. 204–205, 231, no. 73, fig. 14, on a peplos-figurine dated to the third quarter of the 5th century B.C., but as in the case of **I4**, the peaked coiffure of **I9** should lower the date.

[16] On muffled brides, see p. 153. For the parallel from Argos, but lacking the head, see Guggisberg 1988, pp. 202–203, 231, no. 61, fig. 13, there dated too early, to the first quarter of the 4th century B.C.

[17] Guggisberg 1988, pp. 202–203, 231, no. 63, fig. 13, there dated to the third quarter of the 4th century B.C.

[18] Vollgraff et al. 1956, p. 20, fig. 18.

Two Argive figurines may be similar to Corinthian types found in the sanctuary: the nearly nude Aphrodite **I14**, also with the mantle tucked between the thighs (cf. **H260**), and the Aphrodite or Leda **I16**, lifting the mantle with the right arm (cf. **H257**). A 4th-century B.C. date is likely for both; **I14** was found with 4th-century B.C. pottery, and **I16** is from the construction fill of the Trapezoidal Building, which terminates at the beginning of the 3rd century B.C. The fragmentary **I15** could be another such Aphrodite or Leda, since the right side of the torso is framed with folds, perhaps of a mantle lifted at that side. The sturdy proportions of the torso point to a 4th-century B.C. date. The nearly nude **I14** shares a distinctive motif with the fragmentary **I17**, although the latter wears a chiton beneath the mantle; in both, the mantle is folded down at the hip, and this short overfold is held out in the right hand. Although the two figurines are not mechanically related, they may have been developed from related archetypes. **I17** is from a pottery context terminating in the early 3rd century B.C. The mantled dancer **I18** is from the construction fill of the Trapezoidal Building, which terminates at the beginning of the 3rd century B.C. The general type is known in the Demeter sanctuary in a number of Corinthian examples (**H153–H169**).

Two isolated Argive female heads cannot be connected with any of the torso types preserved at the sanctuary. The hair of **I20** is simply parted in the front in the Classical manner and clings closely to the neck. The coiffure of **I19**, which is peaked in a braid above the forehead and has a cluster of curls on the cranium, has familiar Corinthian elements but in a combination unusual in Corinth.[19] The head, which is of 4th-century B.C. style, is from the construction fill of the Trapezoidal Building, which terminates at the beginning of the 3rd century B.C. Three poor, worn female heads of possible Argive fabric in lots 2239, 3217, and 6214 are of uncertain type. The head in lot 2239 seems to have drapery lifted behind the left shoulder. The head in lot 3217 may be a distorted version of **I4**; it is only half the size and, if Argive, would demonstrate that at least one type continued to be made very late in a degenerate form. The head in lot 6214 is larger, but it may also be a degenerate example of the same type. The first two heads have peaked coiffures.

I21 is one of the most interesting of the Argive figurines, since it appears to be of Argive fabric but nevertheless looks like a mold sibling of a 3rd-century B.C. Corinthian type popular at the sanctuary, the boy with a goose (**H331**). Since it is unlikely that the Corinthians would have imported the rather coarse Argive clay for figurines, when their own clay was much finer and paler, the best explanation is that an Argive workshop acquired a Corinthian mold collateral to the one used for **H331** and with it produced a type known to be saleable in Corinth. A lingering Archaic spoon-based protome (MF-12891)[20] is an earlier example of a popular Corinthian type in Argive fabric, probably made in an imported mold. The import of Corinthian molds is documented for Athens (see p. 32), Isthmia (see p. 284), and Lakonia,[21] but the return to Corinth of the resulting products is so far not known for other sites. The exchange of coroplastic workshop materials between Corinth and Argos is paralleled by their brisk trade in Hellenistic molded relief bowls and the consequent sharing of designs.[22]

I22 is another 3rd-century B.C. Corinthian type specifically associated with the Demeter sanctuary, the "priestess" type (pp. 250–255). Only the upper part is preserved, but the type, with its thick torch, polos, and chubby face, is unmistakable. In this case, however, there are no mechanical relatives in Corinthian fabric. Probably the corresponding Corinthian mold relatives have not been found, since the piece bears too many resemblances in details to the Corinthian versions to be an entirely free copy created at another site. One of the imported figurines included with those of uncertain provenience, the archaizing support **I95**, could possibly be of Argive fabric.

[19] Cf. Guggisberg 1988, pp. 206–207, 231, no. 79, fig. 15, there dated to the mid-4th century B.C.
[20] Publication forthcoming.
[21] Salapata 1997.
[22] Edwards 1981, pp. 201–202.

In addition to the imported figurines, connections with Argos can be adduced by other means. The Corinthian head **H246** (see p. 169) could have been mechanically copied from an Argive figurine similar to **I9**. Another possible copy of an Argive type is the Aphrodite **H254** (see p. 173), which, as far as it is preserved, closely parallels **I14**. Further, Argive workshops may have provided the sanctuary worshipers with figurines of votaries carrying piglets during the later 5th and much of the 4th century B.C., until new Corinthian types were developed in the Early Hellenistic period (see pp. 117–124).

ATTIC FIGURINES (**I23**–**I42**)

The fabric of figurines made in Athens is quite distinctive. Its shade of orange can be closely matched on the Munsell charts as 5YR 6/6. At its best (as in **I24**) it is a fine fabric, with a polished surface; when examined closely in bright sunlight, it reveals an abundance of extremely small sparkling inclusions. A few examples (e.g., **I28**) are paler on the outer surface, sometimes through the application of a slip. In a number of examples the texture is slightly coarser. A few figurines (e.g., **I40**) are orange-buff rather than orange in color, but since they have the abundant small sparkling inclusions typical of the orange figurines, they have been assigned to Athens. The attributions include types that have not previously been recorded for Athens, but they have been catalogued here nevertheless on the basis of their fabric.

Unlike the Argive figurines, there are no mold duplicates and no clear workshop groupings among the twenty-one imports attributed to Athens. It was suggested above (p. 286) that the diversity among the Attic figurines points to casual imports by individuals or perhaps to the bazaar trade rather than an organized trade in figurines directly from Athens. The types generally correspond with the local offerings; however, fully one-third of the Attic figurines represent children, a significant proportion suggesting that, to the extent that these figurines may have been carried to Corinth by Athenian visitors to the sanctuary, rituals concerning children may have been the focus of interest.

After the Archaic period, for which seven Attic imports are recorded from the sanctuary,[23] the earliest would be the fragmentary hydriaphoros **I23**, which has a well-known Attic facial type.[24] The absence of earlier Classical Attic imports is probably an accident of discovery, since two Corinthian figurines (**C104** and **C277**) seem to be local copies taken mechanically from Attic figurines of that period, presupposing the presence of imports. All the remaining Attic imports are probably Early Hellenistic in date.

Three figurines (**I24**–**I26**) should be classified as early "Tanagras." While they are not identical in composition, as far as they are preserved, to published examples of known Athenian provenience, they are of convincing style and workmanship for this group.[25] The fabric of **I25** is slightly coarser than the other two, but it still seems to be Attic. On the basis of the Athenian evidence, they should date to the last quarter of the 4th century B.C.; **I25** is from a pottery context of the 4th to early 3rd century B.C. **I27**, with the mantle wrapped shawl-like around the shoulders, is a member of a group of figurines of heavily draped young girls that prefigures the "Tanagra" types, although without their elegance.[26] Figurines of this group are recognizable by their thick, meaty folds, blunt modeling, and rather slapdash retouch. **I27** has parallels from the Athenian Agora.[27] **I28** is another, of ambiguous gender but identifiable as a girl through a parallel from the Pnyx.[28] This figurine shows in an exaggerated form a motif of some early

[23] Publication forthcoming.
[24] Kindly attributed by Richard V. Nicholls to the CD Group, early Rich Style, corr. Feb. 23, 1995. Cf., e.g., heads from the Pnyx, dated early 4th century B.C.: *Pnyx*, pp. 142–143, nos. 41, 42, fig. 57, but wearing a stephane.
[25] Cf. D. B. Thompson 1966, pls. 17:8 (for **I26**), 20 (for **I24** and **I25**); from Menon's cistern, S. G. Miller 1974, pp. 219,

242, no. 105, pl. 41 (for **I25**); D. B. Thompson 1952, pp. 130–131, 159–160, no. 19, pl. 34 (for **I26**).
[26] D. B. Thompson 1952, pp. 130–137, 159–160, nos. 19–23, pls. 33–35.
[27] Cf. D. B. Thompson 1952, pp. 132–133, 160, nos. 20a, 20b, pl. 34.
[28] H. A. Thompson 1936, pp. 172–173, nos. 2h, 2i, fig. 19:h, i.

"Tanagras," the rendering of the pouched corners of the mantle, which seem to have been used as pockets.[29] These figurines also should be datable within the latter part of the 4th century B.C.; **I27** is from the construction fill of the Trapezoidal Building, which terminates at the beginning of the 3rd century B.C.

I29 originally held something across her waist; the break suggests the outline of a small animal; it could have been a piglet, but such a type is not otherwise recorded for Athens. Although the breasts of this figure are developed, the short-waisted proportions contribute a girlish look; perhaps this figurine represented a young votary. The mantled figurine **I30** is probably standing, although the slight flare of the drapery fall at the left side leaves open the possibility that it represents a mantled dancer; Corinthian dancers are sometimes identifiable by the flaring drapery (cf. **H160**). The strongly sloping shoulders of **I30** speak for a 3rd-century B.C. date; the pottery context of this figurine terminates in the third quarter of the 3rd century B.C. **I31** is a puzzling fragment of the front of a mantled figurine, presumably a woman, but it is not entirely clear which part of the figure is preserved. Perhaps the looped folds are drawn across the abdomen and originally were held at the hip in the right hand; in this case, the left thigh is strongly advanced, perhaps in a dance. Alternatively, we have the narrow, sloping shoulders of the figure swathed in the mantle, with the left forearm extended. In either case, the delicacy of the folds is noteworthy.

Two isolated female heads (**I32** and **I33**) wear the melon coiffure. **I33** has a childlike quality because of the round face and widely opened eyes. The faces of young girls with this coiffure, however, are usually smiling.[30] The break just beneath the chin suggests either that the neck was as short as a child's or, more likely, that a mantle was wrapped closely under the chin.

Two of the imported Attic figurines (**I34** and **I35**) represent youths. **I34** is just a fragment of the right side, but the drapery arrangement and pattern of folds correspond well with a better-made figurine of a mantled youth from Tanagra, of similar scale, dated ca. 330–300 B.C.[31] The folds are slightly diagonal to reflect the youth's movement to his left side. **I34** may have been made from a mold related to the youth from Tanagra, but it has been awkwardly retouched, and a diagonal fold has been added over the hand. The other figurine of a youth (**I35**) preserves only the booted bare right leg crossed over the left. Since the thigh is completely bare, he probably wore only a chlamys. He seems to be leaning against a rocky support.

Several of the figurines discussed above may represent young girls, but the seven pieces following are definitely children. **I36** is a baby reaching up, generally corresponding in type to the Corinthian Classical **C236**. **I36**, however, which reaches up with both arms, is more advanced in style. The figurines of children include types that are paralleled among the finds from the Assembly Place filling III of the Pnyx; the lower chronological limit of this material is 326 B.C., but it is thought to contain figurines of the first half of the 4th century B.C.[32] Two figurines with parallels from the Pnyx are the seated nude boy **I37**[33] and the wreathed head **I38**.[34] In the example from the Pnyx, the wreathed head type belongs to a mantled figurine thought to represent a girl. Such heads are also known from Menon's cistern, where they belong to figurines of cloaked boys.[35] The seated boy corresponds with the Corinthian boys **H335–H338** (see p. 191), and the wreathed head to **H350** (see p. 193). Of the remaining children, the fragmentary **I39** probably represents a semidraped child, to judge from the chubby, childlike arm and hand, but Corinthian versions such as **H320** use the mantle as a side

---

[29] Cf. D. B. Thompson 1966, pl. 17:8.
[30] E.g., in London, Higgins 1986, p. 142, figs. 171A, 172.
[31] In Athens, Higgins 1986, p. 148, no. 179.
[32] For the revised dating of the Pnyx figurines, see D. B. Thompson 1952, pp. 118–119, note 12; Nicholls 1995, p. 424, note 78; Rotroff and Camp 1996.

[33] H. A. Thompson 1936, pp. 172, no. 1g; 174, fig. 20:g.
[34] H. A. Thompson 1936, p. 173, no. 2m, fig. 19:m.
[35] S. G. Miller 1974, pp. 214, 241, e.g., no. 98, pl. 40; pp. 213–214, 240, no. 84, pl. 37, for the associated torso.

drape, leaving the torso bare. **I40** is a delicately detailed head that stands apart from most representations of children in its large, overhanging nose; perhaps a repair to the nose at some point in the history of the mold series distorted the original form. It is from the construction fill of the Trapezoidal Building, which terminates at the beginning of the 3rd century B.C. The remaining head (**I41**) is poorly preserved, but the round face is that of a child, wearing a small, flat headdress of uncertain type and drawing the mantle over the chin.[36] The head is from a pottery context of the late 4th century B.C.

The remaining Attic import is a figurine of an actor (**I42**), identifiable by the padded costume, although exact parallels are hard to pinpoint because of the loss of the head and attributes. With the left arm akimbo, and the himation caught in the belt at the right side, the type, as far as preserved, resembles one in which the actor lifts the himation at the right side,[37] in an apparent parody of a woman's unveiling gesture. This type is placed in the second quarter of the 4th century B.C.

On the general question of coroplastic give-and-take between Corinth and Athens, see pages 32–33. The situation is somewhat clouded by the pervasive nature of Attic stylistic influence, particularly in the representation of drapery, in the arts of the Classical period. This influence need not have reached Corinthian workshops through coroplastic channels. Apart from the imported figurines, connections with Attic coroplastic work of the Classical period can be seen in two Corinthian figurines that may have been mechanically copied from Attic imports, the female head **C104** (see p. 48) and the Pan **C277** (see pp. 78–79). The same may be true of the draped articulated dancer **C181** (see pp. 59–60); since the detail of the drapery is quite clear, however, the "doll" may have been made in an imported mold. Derivation from Attic figurine vases is possible for the Asiatic dancer **C281** (see p. 80) and the Dionysos mask **C269** (see pp. 76–77). The seated female figurine **C80** (see p. 44) could have been made in a mold collateral to that of a figurine from the Pnyx; unfortunately, the latter is burned, and therefore the fabric cannot be identified as Attic with certainty.

For the Hellenistic period, one might expect a local series of copies of female "Tanagra" types, but instead there are only a few scattered examples. Rather, one finds a general reflection of the "Praxitelean" stylistic underpinning of "Tanagra" figurines in types of a different nature (see p. 115). The most convincing female "Tanagras" are the seated woman **H175** (see p. 157) and the heads **H217–H220** (see pp. 164–165) and **H243–H245** (see pp. 168–169). It is not possible, however, to isolate the specific sources, and it is not always clear whether one should look toward Attic or Boeotian workshops; perhaps the latter, since one fragmentary standing "Tanagra" (**H117**) can almost certainly be connected with a Boeotian workshop, and exchange of workshop materials between Corinthian and Boeotian workshops is demonstrable for other Hellenistic types as well (see p. 201). In the case of dancer figurines, the sources of two derivative Corinthian types could be either Attic or Boeotian workshops: see the discussion of **H153** (pp. 153–154) and **H164** (pp. 154–155). Two other dancer types (**H156** [see p. 154], and **H165** and **H166** [see p. 155]) are likely to have been of Attic inspiration, the latter perhaps through metalwork. Another piece possibly from Attic metalwork is the female head **H248** (see p. 169).

While the above connections are sometimes speculative, the use of Attic figurines of actors is clear. **H355–H364** (see pp. 195–196) are copies or adaptations of Attic figurines. One final area in which Athenian influence, although less direct, can be pointed out is in the relief figures on the polos **V14** (see p. 270). These figures are closely connected with reliefs on arulae that are thought to have originated in Athens.

---

[36] Cf. a fully preserved figurine of a boy in a kausia and chlamys drawn over his chin: Rühfel 1984, p. 205, pl. 83.

[37] Webster 1978, p. 73, no. AT 35a; *British Museum* I, p. 198, no. 737, pl. 97.

Boeotian Figurines (I43–I51)

The designation "Boeotian" for figurines is sometimes employed for much of Central Greece.[38] Unfortunately, illicit excavation and the delayed publication of some important material have made it difficult to sort out the points of origin of some of these figurines. Ten Classical and Hellenistic figurines from the Acrocorinth sanctuary can be attributed to Boeotia with some confidence on the basis of fabric and, in most cases, type as well; there is one Archaic Boeotian import.[39] The fabric is somewhat coarse, with dark and/or white and sometimes sparkling inclusions. The color varies; using the terminology adopted here for the Corinthian figurines (see pp. 12–13), it ranges through orange-buff, light orange, orange, orange-brown, and ochre. On the basis of published descriptions, this fabric seems to correspond with that of figurines produced in workshops in Thebes and Tanagra.[40] Sometimes it can be difficult to distinguish this fabric from the relatively coarse Corinthian fabric 5 (see p. 12).

I43 and I44 are respectively the torso and head of an Early Classical seated goddess type, which is completely preserved in MF-2 in the Corinth collection.[41] The goddess, who wears a low polos and a peplos with a short overfold, sits with her hands on her knees. This votive type corresponds in general with the long series of Corinthian seated goddesses in Archaic and lingering Archaic style and their local Classical counterparts (see pp. 42–43).

I45 is poorly preserved, but it can be clearly identified as a semidraped standing youth of a type well known in the Kabeirion at Thebes, wearing a mantle draped over the shoulders.[42] The head I46 probably also belonged to a figurine of a youth, since the coiffure, with a roll of hair above the nape, is masculine. Although the fabric closely resembles that of other figurines in this group, the face, which somewhat resembles the Corinthian Classical C208, has larger, earthier features than more typically Boeotian faces, and the hair lacks the knot over the forehead characteristic of the Kabeirion youths (see p. 62). As votive types, the youths correspond to such Corinthian figurines as C188.

The remaining five figurines belong to the 4th or 3rd century B.C. I51 probably represents Leda, although the left side of the figure, against which the swan should appear, is not well preserved. The figurine is similar in composition and proportions to the Corinthian H257, which could represent Aphrodite rather than Leda (see p. 174). There is also a possible Argive rendering of the same subject (I16). I51 has been assigned here to a Boeotian workshop on the basis of fabric; published Boeotian representations of Leda are not the same in composition,[43] although the existence of several versions quite different from one another suggests a particular interest in the subject and the possibility of still more types. I51 is from the construction fill of the Trapezoidal Building, which terminates at the beginning of the 3rd century B.C.

The fabric of the fragmentary draped female figurine I50 is close to that of I51. It includes a rather clumsy version of a motif found in some 4th-century B.C. Boeotian figurines, in which the right hand pulls the mantle overfold slightly to the side.[44] I47 is a variant of a type found at Tanagra, dating to the first half of the 4th century B.C. and thought to represent Demeter.[45] Characteristic of this type is the mantle with an overfold, which was lifted in the right hand and draped over the head.

I48 is a well-known "Tanagra" type.[46] On stylistic grounds it should date to about the middle of the 3rd century B.C.; its pottery context, which terminates in the third quarter of

---

[38] *British Museum* I, p. 203.

[39] Publication forthcoming.

[40] Higgins 1986, p. 65.

[41] Shoe 1932, p. 59, fig. 3.

[42] *Kabirenheiligtum* V, e.g., pp. 46, 156, no. 104, pl. 7.

[43] E.g., *British Museum* I, pp. 230–232, nos. 863, 868, 869, pl. 123; p. 234, no. 877, pl. 127; p. 235, no. 880, pl. 128.

[44] Cf. *British Museum* I, p. 234, nos. 876 (woman), 877 (Leda), pl. 127.

[45] In Paris, Higgins 1986, pp. 107–109, fig. 127.

[46] In London, Higgins 1986, pp. 132–134, figs. 159, 160.

the 3rd century B.C., helps to confirm this date. The better-made **I49** is unfortunately only a fragment of a standing draped female figurine, but its plaque base and the arrangement of folds with one pointed shoe drawing the hem to the side support its identification as another "Tanagra" type.

I71, which may represent a seated nurse and could perhaps be of Boeotian fabric, is discussed below with figurines of uncertain provenience. The draped female figurine **I62**, also discussed below, may possibly be of Boeotian fabric and technique. One of the protomes (**I56**), discussed below with the Rhodian protomes, could perhaps be of Boeotian fabric as well, but too little of the head is preserved to identify the type precisely.

In addition to the imported figurines, connections with Boeotian workshops during the Classical period can be found in the seated peplos-figurine **C70** (see pp. 45–46), which is likely to have been copied from a Boeotian type like **I43** and **I44**. There is also Boeotian influence on the knotted coiffures of the Corinthian figurines of youths **C192**, **C203**, and **C204** (see p. 62) presumably through imports similar to **I45**. The Dionysos masks **C271** and **C272** (see p. 76) may have been mechanically copied from imported Boeotian masks. The protome **C259** (see p. 74) could have been mechanically copied from an imported protome, although it is uncertain whether the source was Rhodian or Boeotian.

For the Hellenistic period, the possible Boeotian contribution to Corinthian "Tanagras" has already been mentioned in the discussion of Attic imports (p. 291). The mantled figurine **H117** could be mechanically related to certain Boeotian "Tanagras" (see p. 146); since the Corinthian piece seems too fresh to be a copy, and is very close in scale to the Boeotian examples, it may have been made in a collateral mold or stem from the same archetype. There seems to have been a certain amount of exchange of workshop materials between Corinthian and Boeotian workshops. The ephedrismos type **H390–H394** (see p. 201) demonstrates a contribution from Corinth to Boeotia, and the same can be said of the standing boy type **H319** (see p. 189). The Aphrodite **H256** has a parallel from Tanagra of which it could be a copy, but there is a chance that it could itself be a Boeotian import (see p. 173). The seated youth **H311** (see pp. 186–187) was almost certainly copied from a Boeotian type, although perhaps directly from an imported figurine rather than an imported mold. A final possible connection with a Boeotian workshop may be found in the ram **V6** (see p. 267), which may have been copied from an imported figurine.

RHODIAN FIGURINES (**I52–I56**)

The five pieces attributed to Rhodes (**I52–I56**) are all fragments of protomes of 5th-century B.C. date.[47] They have been attributed by type, since their coarse fabrics are not absolutely identical to one another in visual examination, but there seems to have been a certain degree of variation within Rhodian fabric that might explain this.[48] The group, however, could also contain copies of Rhodian protomes made elsewhere (especially **I56**), which perhaps were made in Boeotia, where this type is known to have been copied.[49] The type shows the right hand curved around the breast and a spray of curved folds radiating from the left hand. The long, serious face with a mobile mouth, characteristic of these Rhodian protomes, is known elsewhere in Corinth in a probable mold sibling of **I52**.[50]

Other evidence for 5th-century B.C. imports from Rhodes can be found in Corinthian copies of Rhodian head and torso types (**C103** and **C44**). The protome **C259** (see p. 74) may have been copied mechanically from an imported Rhodian (or perhaps Boeotian) protome.

[47] For a complete example, see *British Museum* I, p. 89, no. 239, pl. 40.

[48] *British Museum* I, p. 19.

[49] *British Museum* I, pp. 223–224, no. 841, pl. 115.

[50] C. K. Williams 1986, p. 14, note 6, fig. 2:A, B on p. 16.

Another protome type, with a windblown veil (**C265** and **C266** [see pp. 75–76]), is very likely derived from a Rhodian source, as is probably the piping satyr **C274** (see p. 78). There is no evidence for connection during the Hellenistic period.

West Greek Figurines (**I57, I58**)

Two imported figurines can be identified as West Greek with some confidence. **I57** was identified as Geloan by Nunzio Allegro. **I58** should be Tarentine on the basis of both type and fabric. **I57**, a head from a small female bust wearing a polos decorated with rosettes, belongs to a popular Sicilian type.[51] These busts represent Persephone and were dedicated to her in their homeland; **I57**, therefore, should be seen as a dedication to Kore in the Acrocorinth sanctuary. The inability to assign other Classical and Hellenistic imports to the same source suggests that **I57** was a casual import by an individual rather than an item of organized trade.

The Tarentine female figurine **I58** also appears to stand alone, but here the case is more complex, since the influence of Tarentine banqueter types on Corinthian figurines (see p. 66) suggests that there were Tarentine imports not represented in the archaeological record. Seated semidraped female figurines from Tarentum similar to **I58** sometimes hold masks, identifying them as Muses.[52] In **I58**, however, neither hand is free to hold an attribute; the right hand originally was raised to the hair, and the left must have been propped on the seat. Unless a mask rested against the base, the figurine was not specifically a Muse, and in the context of the Acrocorinth sanctuary it could have represented a nymph, similar to the Corinthian **H274**, or perhaps Aphrodite.[53] The slightly friable orange-buff fabric, with a creamy buff slip and small sparkling inclusions, is typically Tarentine. Two other seated figurines (**I69** and **I70**) are included below among the figurines of uncertain provenience, but the chair type of **I70** points to a possible West Greek origin.

With regard to demonstrable relations apart from the preserved imports, a Tarentine connection can be found in the backless construction of two Early Classical Corinthian figurines, the peplos-figurine **C5** (see p. 26) and the banqueter **C215** (see p. 66). This technical feature points perhaps to a local artisan who had worked in Tarentum, although local workshops could simply have copied the feature from imported figurines that have not survived. One of the Corinthian Classical seated types (**C91** and **C92** [see p. 45]) was known in Paestum; since it has a facial type paralleled in Tarentum, a Western source is likely, although the precise route is unclear. Typological influence from the West includes the introduction of the piglet carrier (see p. 26), a well-known type particularly in Sicily, although in the West the type seems to have represented Persephone rather than a votary, as in Corinth. The typical Corinthian Classical face, best exemplified in the hydriaphoroi, has West Greek parallels (see p. 40), although perhaps the influence in this case traveled from the Peloponnesos to the West.

Fewer connections can be demonstrated for the Hellenistic period. A rather poor mantled female figurine (**H125** [see pp. 147–148]) may have copied a West Greek type. A few skirt fragments may indicate the presence of a Western dancer type (see p. 156). Finally, some Sicilian material could have been involved in the development of the Middle Hellenistic "priestess" type (see p. 253).

Imported Figurines of Uncertain Provenience (**I59–I96**)

The figurines in this group, of various fabrics, appear to be of 4th-century B.C. or Hellenistic date. They are arranged by type, regardless of fabric, to show their connection with the local figurine groups and their place in the rituals of the sanctuary. Provenances are suggested provisionally whenever possible. Fabric descriptions are provided in the catalogue.

---

[51] E.g., *Morgantina,* p. 138, nos. 96a, 96b, pl. 23; *British Museum* I, p. 320, no. 1182, pl. 161.

[52] In London, Higgins 1967, p. 126, pl. 60:D.

[53] Cf., in San Francisco, *Coroplast's Art,* p. 157, no. 44, a Tarentine nude seated female figure wearing a low crown and identified as Aphrodite.

Votaries

The standing draped female figurines **I59–I61** probably represent young votaries corresponding to Corinthian types. The crudely made **I59**, with a large piglet held horizontally across the abdomen, is generally similar to the Corinthian **H12**. It is unclear whether the swollen abdomen visible in the profile view intentionally represented pregnancy or is the result of poor workmanship. **I60**, a quietly standing girl in a peplos with her arms at her sides, is mechanically related to a Corinthian mold series, but the fabric is sandier than typical Corinthian fabrics; this figurine may have been made in a marginal or neighboring workshop (see p. 283). **I61** is degenerate in the disfigured facial features, which were neither repaired in the mold nor corrected on the figurine itself. The fold pattern of the peplos, as far as it can be discerned, and the coiffure that clings closely to the head suggest that this figurine could represent the last gasp of an Argive mold series, wherever it was actually made. Its pottery context is late 4th century B.C.

Standing Draped Female Figurines

I62–I67 are draped figurines of widely varying types. **I62** wears a mantle that originally was arranged in a heavy fall down the left side. Neither the fabric nor the method of venting by punching a small round hole in the back is typically Corinthian. The venting is similar to Boeotian practice,[54] and indeed, the fabric might possibly be Boeotian, but in scale and style, this figurine is close to the Corinthian **H88**.

I63 and **I64** are similar to one another in their small size, thick-walled construction, and fabric; they were probably made in the same workshop. The pose of **I63**, with the left arm at the side, the right across the waist, recalls the larger Corinthian figurine **H152**; **I63** could be a derivative of the Corinthian type, which has a more complex pose with torsion.

I65 and **I66** are probably mold siblings, which together reconstruct the type almost completely. The type is known in a mid-3rd-century B.C. figurine from Tanagra, which holds a pomegranate in the extended right hand and is thought to represent Persephone.[55] The two smaller figurines from the sanctuary are likely to be derivatives of this type. One of them (**I65**) is of a sandy, marginal Corinthian fabric (see p. 283). This "Tanagra" type is not represented at the sanctuary among the preserved Corinthian figurines.

Some of the standing draped female figurines discussed thus far could have been made in marginal or neighboring workshops (see pp. 283–284), but the last figurine in this group bears no resemblance to the Corinthian figurines from the sanctuary and must have been imported from a distance. **I67** is characterized by heavy masses of drapery collapsing over the feet in broken folds. The style is not earlier than Middle Hellenistic; it calls to mind sculpture more than figurines and an origin in Asia Minor.[56] The heavy collapse of folds suggests that a mantle is falling from the body and that the figurine might therefore represent either Aphrodite or Leda. Other possible connections with Asia Minor consist of the head of the Corinthian "priestess" type (see p. 253) and the bucranium **I91** (see p. 298), which could perhaps be from Priene.

Seated Draped Female Figurines

All four seated female figurines are clearly non-Corinthian in both fabric and type. In **I68**, the foot overhangs the footstool considerably, and the hem drops at the left side, as if draped over part of the seat. The curved legs of the footstool terminate in hooves. Footstools often have animals' feet but more commonly terminate in lions' paws[57] than hooves, which are more common in folding stools.[58] Further, the footstool in **I68** is a good deal higher than other examples; in height,

[54] Cf., in London, Higgins 1986, pp. 68, 138–139, fig. 166:B.
[55] In London, Higgins 1986, p. 136, fig. 163.
[56] Cf., e.g., *Pergamon*, pp. 30, 207, no. 101, pl. 15; Töpperwein-Hoffmann 1971, p. 158, pl. 48:2, a seated figure with broken, collapsing drapery folds, from Magnesia on the Maeander, dated Late Hellenistic on the basis of style.
[57] Richter 1966, pp. 50–51, type 2.
[58] Richter 1966, pp. 43–45, type 1, e.g., fig. 247.

it resembles rather a folding stool, but it does not have the crossed, hinged legs. Perhaps the form of the stool has been confused by the coroplast; bronze mirror supports are known consisting of draped female figures standing on hooved folding stools,[59] suggesting that **I68** may be standing on a misunderstood folding stool, rather than seated.

I69 and **I70** are closely similar to one another in their rather coarse, orange-brown fabric and were probably imported from the same source. **I70** is part of a seat and preserves only a few drapery folds of the figure on it. The seat, which has turned legs and a frieze of lions with curving tails, is paralleled by a chair in an Early Hellenistic Tarentine relief;[60] chairs with turned legs and figured friezes below the seat rails are pictured in 4th-century B.C. Apulian vase painting as well,[61] suggesting a South Italian origin for these two figurines. **I69** would not have been seated on such a chair, since the left thigh slopes, and the right leg was a little higher; the figure must have been perched, half-sitting, half-leaning, on an irregular support, such as a rock. The figurine may have represented a nymph, her mantle draped around her legs, generally similar to such Corinthian nymphs as **H274**. **I69** and **I70** are from the construction fill of the Trapezoidal Building, the terminal date of which is the beginning of the 3rd century B.C.

I71 is a very dull impression, but the knees and lower legs of a draped figure can be discerned, possibly with a child perched on the lap. This figurine could be an old nurse holding a child, a well-known Attic and Boeotian type;[62] the rather coarse brownish fabric of **I71** could perhaps be Boeotian.

Dancers

I72 appears to be a degenerate version of the Late Classical Corinthian dancer **C282**. Since the fabric looks Corinthian apart from the abundant voids, which indicate a use of organic temper that is not normal for Corinthian workshops, **I72** may have been made in a marginal or neighboring workshop (see p. 283). The mantled dancer **I73** is of the same general type as the Corinthian dancer **H153**, but since the head is bent strongly towards the right shoulder, the composition probably was closer to that of the fragmentary **H170**. It is from the construction fill of the Trapezoidal Building, the terminal date of which is the beginning of the 3rd century B.C.

Isolated Female Heads

I74 is a head of a distinctly Corinthian type, but the coarse fabric should place it in a marginal or neighboring workshop (see p. 283). The rounded coiffure tied with a sphendone is typical of Corinthian articulated "dolls" (cf. **C125**), and the clustering of the features near the center of the face is also a local trait, as in the head **C153**. A similar source may be supposed for **I75**, which appears to be a degenerate form of a Corinthian head type similar to **H242**. In the original type, the sakkos covered all the hair; in **I75**, however, the band bordering the forehead has been retouched as hair, so that the sakkos looks like a hat perched on the head.

The much more elegant and better-made **I76** is foreign in both type and material. It is known in the Demeter sanctuary in two generations (see catalogue), which might suggest more or less regular trade with its place of origin, but the distinctive orange fabric does not appear in any other figurines. A closely similar type with upswept curls is known at Delos,[63] but it is unclear whether it was actually made there, since many figurines were imported to the island, as were clays, in the absence of suitable local material.[64]

I77 probably is mechanically related to **H246**, a head in Corinthian fabric apparently copying an Argive type, although the workmanship is so different that one cannot easily associate the two

[59] Richter 1966, figs. 252, 253.
[60] J. C. Carter 1975, p. 48, no. 54, pl. 12:c.
[61] Richter 1966, p. 22, figs. 76, 78.
[62] D. B. Thompson 1966, pp. 56–57, with bibliography;

in London, Higgins 1967, p. 103, pl. 44:B; in San Francisco, *Coroplast's Art*, p. 122, no. 15, with bibliography.
[63] *Délos* XXIII, p. 247, no. 1129, pl. 86.
[64] Higgins 1967, p. 107.

heads with the same workshop. In **I77**, the coroplast added accessories unusual in Corinth, a very small stephane and large earrings that project at an angle. The fabric is very fine, like Corinthian in texture, but it has been fired hard and is gray in color; if it is Corinthian clay, a further departure from the normal practice is the application of a thick slip, which has fired to the common Corinthian colors of greenish buff and orange-buff. **I77** could be the product of a good neighboring workshop.

I78 seems to imitate a Boeotian head type used for figurines of Leda,[65] with two lumps of clay added in place of the lampadion knot of the original; the fabric is not Boeotian, however, but resembles Corinthian fabric 1 (see p. 11). **I79** is also of a fabric resembling Corinthian, but the firm, geometrically organized retouch of the hair is not a local trait. This style of retouch is rather like that on a head of a figurine in Berlin of reported Megarian provenience.[66] Both heads could be from neighboring workshops.

Figurines of Deities

Among the figurines of uncertain provenience, there are several likely representations of deities, apart from **I69**, which could represent a nymph. Only the lower half of **I80** is preserved, but the skirt clings so closely to the slim, elegant, and nude-seeming legs as to suggest a representation of Aphrodite. Both fabric and type, as far as preserved, are non-Corinthian.

I81 is a mirror image of a Boeotian Leda type,[67] but the style and workmanship (except for the shape of the vent) are rather closer to the Aphrodite **I14**, which has been assigned to Argos. The fabric of **I81**, however, is finer than the Boeotian and Argive fabrics available for comparison. **I81** is from the construction fill of the Trapezoidal Building, the terminal date of which is the beginning of the 3rd century B.C.

The only other figurine of uncertain provenience that could represent a deity is the fine nude male **I82**, which has a parallel in sculpture. As far as the pose is preserved, the sharply raised right upper arm, extended left forearm, and outthrust right hip recall the Apollo Lykeios, an Athenian sculpture thought to be connected with the reorganization of the Athenian *ephebeia* in the 330s B.C.[68] In the context of the Demeter sanctuary, a representation of Apollo is unexpected, since this deity otherwise appears only in miniature relief among the deities on the polos **V14**. Perhaps the ephebic connection in Athens drew the type into the orbit of coming-of-age, which appears to have been part of the function of the Acrocorinth sanctuary. The rendering in small-scale terracotta of well-known statues was a specialty of workshops in Asia Minor, particularly Myrina and Smyrna.[69] The latter center especially produced copies of male sculptural types, but the fabric of **I82** is not the distinctive Smyrnaean fabric, and, in any case, the coroplastic output of Smyrna is dated mainly to the 1st century B.C. and 1st century A.C., through most of which period the Demeter sanctuary was not open.[70] Under the circumstances, it is probably best to identify this figurine not as Apollo but as Dionysos, who is otherwise known at the Acrocorinth sanctuary (see p. 76). A similar composition was used to represent Dionysos in Hellenistic terracottas, although apart from the pose, **I82** does not resemble any of the extant figurines.[71] The pottery context of **I82** unfortunately does not help to date it, but the figurine shows the surface blisters that result from the use of a plaster mold. The use of this technique should date **I82** not earlier than the 3rd century B.C. (see p. 16).

[65] *British Museum* I, p. 235, no. 880, pl. 128.

[66] *Königliche Museen*, pp. 16–17, pl. XIX.

[67] *British Museum* I, p. 235, no. 880, pl. 128.

[68] On the type, its replicas, and its chronology, see Milleker 1986; on the cultic associations, see esp. pp. 52–58; Nagele 1984; *LIMC* II, 1984, pp. 193–194, no. 39, pls. 184, 185, s.v. *Apollon* (W. Lambrinudakis et al.); *LIMC* II, 1984, pp. 379–380, no. 54, pl. 302, s.v. *Apollon/Apollo* (E. Simon and G. Bauchhenss); Ridgway 1990, p. 91, with bibliography on p. 105,

note 36; Ridgway 1997, p. 265, with bibliography on p. 284, note 77.

[69] Bartman 1992, pp. 20–22; Higgins 1967, pp. 111–112; E. R. Williams 1982; *Coroplast's Art*, p. 77. One Corinthian small-scale copy is known, Myron's Satyr, from a 4th-century B.C. context: Mattusch 1996, pp. 195–196, fig. 6.1:a, b.

[70] *Corinth* XVIII, ii, pp. 4–5; *Corinth* XVIII, iii, p. 434.

[71] Schröder 1989, pp. 13–15.

I83 has the short, curly hair around the forehead of a youth, and a closely fitting cap with lappets, indicating that it may represent Attis; since the head is thrown back, the figurine may have represented Attis dancing.[72] A similar subject from the sanctuary is the probably female Asiatic dancer **C281**.

Male Figurines

As is the case among the Corinthian figurines, the male figurines of uncertain provenience are relatively few. The three preserved torsos are small in scale and are from standing mantled figures. **I84** is a compact figure of slender proportions on a high, cylindrical base. The provenience of similarly constructed figurines in Berlin is reported to be Megara.[73] **I85** is slightly fleshy and, like the Corinthian **H302**, could perhaps represent a boy. **I86** is made of a sandy fabric similar to that of **I60** and **I65** and may be from a marginal Corinthian workshop.

Children

Two of the three figurines of children may be grotesques. The mantled boy **I87** is distinctly dolichocephalic and perhaps represents a pathological condition. It is of a general type known also in Hellenistic small bronzes,[74] and in subject it approximates the Corinthian **H383**. The fabric of **I87** is close to that of the nude male figure **I82**, and it also has surface blisters indicating the use of a plaster mold. The two figurines are probably from the same non-Corinthian source. **I88** is also mantled and has an overly large head; the wide, flat nose gives the face a somewhat negroid cast, but the coiffure is like that of other figurines of children (e.g., **H326**) and is not the very short, curly hair of African heads. **I89** is a very dull impression of a child's head in a stephane. Although the fabric is rather similar in appearance to Attic, the blunt modeling and absence of retouched detail are not typical of Attic workmanship.

Varia

The animals of uncertain provenience (**I90–I93**) consist of one pig and three bovines, a different proportion from the Corinthian figurines, among which pigs predominate. The bucranium **I91** could perhaps be attributed to Priene, although no comparative material is available for identification of the fabric. No comparable bucrania have been excavated in Priene, but the tiny female head over the forehead between the horns has an exaggerated bowknot coiffure, and with its puffy cheeks and triangular forehead resembles the heads of Baubo figurines from Priene.[75] One of the cow's heads, **I93**, is from the construction fill of the Trapezoidal Building, the terminal date of which is the beginning of the 3rd century B.C.

The remaining imports consist of a hand offering what may be a buttoned purse (**I94**), presumably belonging to a figurine of a votary and comparable to the Corinthian hands with offerings **V20–V24**; a support for a standing figurine in the form of an archaizing female figure (**I95**), the fabric of which could perhaps be Argive; and another support (for a figurine of Aphrodite?) at the base of which a winged figure, probably Eros, sits (**I96**). The remains of a fairly large rectangular vent at the back of **I95** point to a date within the Classical period. The Corinthian support **V43** also takes the form of an archaizing female figure but wears a different costume.

---

[72] On dancing Attis types, see *LIMC* III, 1986, pp. 33–35, nos. 240–278, pls. 29–32, s.v. *Attis* (M. J. Vermaseren and M. B. De Boer).

[73] *Königliche Museen*, p. 18, pls. XXII, left and right, XXIII.

[74] In Boston, Comstock and Vermeule 1971, p. 78, no. 81; Andreiomenou 1971, p. 563, no. 5, pl. 570:ε.

[75] Olender 1990, pp. 110–113, figs. 3.1–3.5; see also p. 171 on the symbolism of horns and Baubo figurines.

CATALOGUE

For an explanation of the conventions employed in this catalogue, see the Introduction, pages 20–22.

ARGIVE FIGURINES

I1 Standing peplos-figurine   Pl. 65

MF-14087. Lot 3231. Preserved: front and part of side–right hand and wrist, adjacent area of hip and thigh. P.H. 0.057 (size 3–4). Fabric as **I7** but thick-walled, gray at core. Tooling on folds, hand.

Clenched hand holds left rear leg of small animal, probably a piglet held head downward, as in **C1**. Folds of open side of peplos beside wrist.

See pp. 26, 123, 286.

I2 Standing peplos-figurine   Pl. 65

MF-14055. Lot 2237. Preserved: shoulders to abdomen, to shoulder blades in back. Missing most of right arm, left forearm. P.H. 0.045 (size 2–3). Fabric slightly coarse, probably burned or overfired, grayish buff with orange core, laminating fracture; inclusions as in **I7**. White slip. Hollow. Back probably molded, flattened.

Left arm bent; forearm originally extended forward. Shoulders broad; chest flat. Peplos overfold falls to abdomen; wide V-shaped neckline, with faint catenaries below. Identified as Argive by Martin Guggisberg.

See pp. 286, 287.

I3 Standing peplos-figurine   Pl. 65

MF-11390. Lot 877. Preserved: hips to hem. Missing feet. P.H. 0.11 (size 3). Fabric similar to **I7**, slightly finer, with gray interior. White slip. Hollow. Back molded, flattened.

Weight on left leg, left hip outthrust. Right leg bent, foot drawn to side. Peplos overfold falls to top of thighs at center, lower at left side; at right side, zigzag folds of open edge of peplos, which parts over thigh; two pleats in overfold hem terminating in omega folds may fall from breasts. Skirt folds are vertical, tubular at left side; looped folds from right ankle to left leg; hem originally trailed over feet. Figurine rather square in section.

See p. 286.

I4 Female head   Pl. 65

MF-13972. Lot 3222. Preserved: head and neck; hair chipped in front. P.H. 0.042 (size 3). Fabric as **I7**, with gray core. Solid. Back handmade, flattened. Added: panel of clay in back for hair, tooled with spatulate instrument, leaving shallow channels with rounded ends; similar tool marks on drapery of **I11**.

Face oval, narrowing to triangular forehead; full cheeks. Eyes large, downturned; lids defined. Nose wide, flat, smeared, close to upper lip. Mouth wide; lips full. Coiffure similar to **I9**, but waves are broader. Possible later generation: one in lot 4377. Similar in type: one in lot 6214 (smaller).

See pp. 168, 286, 287, 288.

I5 Female head   Pl. 65

MF-14191. Lot 4377. Preserved: head and neck. Neck chipped; surface worn at left side. P.H. 0.036 (size 2–3). Fabric similar to **I7**, slightly finer, yellower. Solid. Back handmade, rounded. Added: topknot.

Face oval, narrowing at chin, with low, triangular forehead. Eyes large, level, opened wide; lids defined. Nose large, wide

at base. Mouth wide; lips full. Neck slender. Coiffure parted at center, arranged in a rounded, slightly wavy mass, with little detail, covering ears; small topknot on cranium.

See pp. 286–287.

I6 Standing draped female figurine   Pl. 65

MF-14054. Lot 2160. Preserved: front–left side from upper chest to thigh; small part of back. P.H. 0.072 (size 3). Fabric as **I7**. White slip. Pink paint on drapery. Hollow. Vertical edge of large rectangular vent in back. Tooling on hand.

Similar in type to **I7** but piglet supported only by left hand, which rests on piglet's right shoulder. Left elbow caught in sling of mantle, as in **I8**. Peplos overfold falls to abdomen in front, to hip at side; one pleat, probably from breast. Vertical skirt folds. Similar in type: one each in lots 2249, 3223, 5613. Identified as Argive by Martin Guggisberg.

See pp. 123, 286, 287.

I7 Standing peplos-figurine   Pl. 65

MF-68-375. Lot 5613. Preserved: shoulders to knees in front, to shoulder blades in back. Missing fragment of torso at right side. P.H. 0.096 (size 2–3). Fabric rather coarse orange (5YR 6/6), with some small dark and sparkling inclusions, voids. Hollow. Back probably molded, flattened. Added: lock of hair on shoulder.

Right arm at side; hand supports rump and back legs of piglet, which is held diagonally across torso from right hip, pointing to left shoulder. Left arm bent; hand supports piglet's chest. Proportions of figure elongated, with narrow, sloping shoulders. Overfold of peplos to top of thighs. Vertical, tubular skirt folds. Long lock of hair to right shoulder. Dull impression. Similar in type: MF-10952 (lot 1945, left hand and head of piglet, with round eye; fabric similar to **I2**); one in lot 2088. Identified as Argive by Martin Guggisberg.

See pp. 123, 286, 287.

I8 Standing draped female figurine   Pl. 65

MF-14053. Lot 4404. Preserved: head to left hip and right shoulder. Mended; surface worn. P.H. 0.07 (size 2–3). Fabric as **I7**, shading to ochre in back. Hollow. Back probably molded, flattened.

Similar in type to **I7** but piglet in less sharply diagonal position. Peplos or chiton has wide V-shaped neckline. Mantle draped over left shoulder, forming a sling under elbow, possibly veiling head. Possible long locks of hair to narrow, sloping shoulders. Similar in type: one in lot 3206. Identified as Argive by Martin Guggisberg.

See pp. 123, 286, 287.

I9 Female head   Pl. 65

MF-14052. Lot 2145. Preserved: head and neck. P.H. 0.038 (size 3). Fabric as **I7**. White slip. Red paint on hair, lips. Solid. Back handmade, flattened, pared.

Face oblong to oval, with high, rounded forehead; slightly pointed chin. Eyes slightly downturned; lids fleshy. Nose large, close to upper lip. Mouth small; lips thin. Coiffure peaked at top; nearly horizontal, lightly modeled waves at top, falling close to head, covering ears and ending in long locks of hair to shoulders. Possibly veiled. Probable mold siblings: MF-11968 (lot 2237); MF-12128 (lot 4347). Possible later generation in lot 4379. Identified as Argive by Martin Guggisberg.

See pp. 169, 285, 287, 289.

I10 Standing draped female figurine Pl. 65

MF-10485. Lot 878. Preserved: head to base. Missing most of back, fragments of skirt and base in front. Mended. Plaster restorations. P.H. 0.151 (size 2–3). Fabric similar to **I7** but slightly finer. White slip. Hollow. All parts rendered in same mold. Back probably molded, rounded, pared. Edge of oval vent preserved.

Left foot crossed in front of right, foot pointed. Left arm bent; elbow leans on fluted column with echinus capital and square base; hand holds ball or fruit below left breast. Right arm at side, slightly bent. Slender figure, with narrow, sloping shoulders. Head and entire body, except fingers of left hand, draped in mantle to ankles; cloth wrapped closely around neck but reveals contours of breasts, abdomen, and thighs. Catenaries between breasts; looped folds from right hand, which lifts cloth from beneath, to left leg; zigzag fold of mantle edge from left hand to hem. Narrow, crinkly folds of chiton hem trail over feet in pointed slippers. Eyes large, downturned. Hair and forehead wrapped in pointed sakkos beneath mantle. Base rectangular in front, with slightly rounded sides, originally rounded in back.

See pp. 168, 286, 287.

I11 Standing Aphrodite Pl. 65

MF-10444. Lot 878. Preserved: shoulders to base. Missing top of pillar, fragment of base, part of drapery at left side. Mended. P.H. 0.159 (size 2–3). Fabric similar to **I7** but slightly finer. White slip. Possible yellow paint. Hollow. Torso and base rendered in same mold. Back molded, rounded. Rectangular vent, 0.07 × 0.031. Added: strip of drapery behind shoulders. Tooling on left hand, adjacent drapery (for tool marks, see **I4**).

Published: Stroud 1965, p. 18, pl. 7:d (with head **I19** incorrectly restored).

Weight on right leg, right hip outthrust. Left knee bent. Right arm akimbo; back of hand against hip. Left upper arm rests on top of square pillar; forearm raised; hand holds up edge of mantle behind shoulder. Narrow, sloping shoulders; small, high, prominent breasts; wide hips. Thin, clinging chiton leaves right shoulder bare; looped folds from right shoulder to breast, V-shaped folds below breasts and radiating from pubic area over abdomen. Mantle is draped from raised left hand behind right shoulder and arm; cloth is brought to front at hip to cover entire right leg with looped folds; cloth is held in place between thighs with a clump of folds at pubic area from which zigzag folds fall to base; shorter zigzag cascade in front of pillar. Base oblong.

See pp. 286, 287.

I12 Standing draped female figurine Pl. 65

MF-10456. Lot 878. Preserved: waist at left side and right hip to base, small part of back. Missing lower left corner. P.H. 0.09 (size 2–3). Fabric similar to **I14**. White slip. Red paint. Hollow. Torso and base rendered in same mold. Back probably molded, rounded, pared.

Weight on right leg; left leg slightly bent. Leans against pillar at left side. Hem of mantle falls to mid-thigh, slightly lower at left side. Looped folds from right thigh to left hip suggest gathering of cloth there; flat vertical folds of narrow mantle fall in front of pillar. Skirt folds narrow, vertical; hem trails over feet in pointed slippers. Low rectangular base. Similar in technique and style to **I10** and **I11**. Identified as Argive by Martin Guggisberg.

See p. 287.

I13 Standing Aphrodite(?) Pl. 65

MF-13968. Lot 878. Preserved: front–right hip and upper thigh, with adjacent drapery. P.H. 0.045 (size 3). Fabric similar to **I7** but slightly finer, thinner-walled. White slip. Pink paint. Hollow. Added: probably outer edge of mantle.

Chiton folds radiate from pubic area; mantle looped to front over thigh and probably originally held in place between thighs. Ends of vertical folds are preserved beside hip. Well-made piece.

See p. 287.

I14 Standing Aphrodite Pl. 66

MF-11077. Lot 1963. Preserved: neck to base. Missing part of back, fragment of drapery at left side. Mended. P.H. 0.178 (size 3). Fabric fairly fine, light orange (7.5YR 6/6), with some small sparkling inclusions, voids; coarser in fracture but similar to fabric of **I7**. White slip. Hollow. All parts rendered in same mold. Back molded, flattened, pared; edge of rear mold visible at right shoulder and arm. Corner of rectangular vent preserved.

Weight on right leg; right hip outthrust. Left knee bent; foot drawn back. Left arm bent; elbow leans on pillar with square capital and base. Right arm at side, slightly bent. Slender figure with small, high breasts; flat hips. Torso and left leg are nude. Mantle is lifted behind left shoulder and carried around back; upper edge of cloth is folded down and brought to front at hip to cover entire right leg with looped folds; right hand pulls overfold slightly to side; cloth is held in place between thighs and falls to base in pleats; on pillar, pointed fold at top, vertical folds with zigzag edge in front. Base is plain and rounded in back; two steps at front and sides diminish in width towards front, which is slightly concave.

See pp. 173, 288, 289, 297.

I15 Standing Aphrodite(?) Pl. 66

MF-13965. Lot 1953. Preserved: front–right breast to hips. Mended. P.H. 0.048 (size 2–3). Fabric similar to **I7** inside, surface smoother; slightly burned. White slip. Hollow.

Right hip outthrust. Nude torso with drapery visible down right side. Right breast somewhat displaced to side, suggesting that arm was raised high and to side. Broad, small-breasted torso.

See p. 288.

I16 Standing Aphrodite or Leda(?) Pl. 66

MF-13967. Lot 878. Preserved: right wrist to shoulder, with adjacent drapery, small part of back. P.H. 0.059 (size 3). Fabric similar to **I7**, with gray core. White slip. Pink paint on drapery. Nearly solid. Back flattened.

Arm raised and bent, pulling mantle high above shoulder; cloth covers forearm and most of upper arm. Fan of folds radiates from wrist.

See pp. 288, 292.

I17   Standing Aphrodite(?)   Pl. 66

MF-13964. Lot 1962. Preserved: right side from waist to knee, small part of back. P.H. 0.09 (size 3). Fabric as **I7**. White slip. Hollow. Back flattened. Vertical edge of rectangular vent preserved. Tooling on hand.

Arrangement of mantle and pose of right hand as in Aphrodite **I14**, but chiton folds on abdomen show that torso was not nude.

See p. 288.

I18   Mantled dancer   Pl. 66

MF-13960. Lot 2249. Preserved: shoulders to ankles, to knees in back. Mended. P.H. 0.084 (size 2). Fabric slightly coarse, orange to grayish buff, with some small to medium white, gray, and sparkling inclusions. Hollow. Thick-walled. Back handmade, flattened, pared. Tooling on folds.

Steps forward on right leg; left hip slightly outthrust. Left arm akimbo; right arm at side. Figure covered entirely with mantle, but contours of torso and legs revealed beneath. Slender figure, with rounded shoulders; high, prominent breasts. Most of torso and legs smooth. Folds lightly modeled: catenaries between shoulders, radiating folds from inside of left elbow, curved folds down right arm and between legs, vertical folds at sides of skirt.

See p. 288.

I19   Female head   Pl. 66

MF-13514. Lot 878. Preserved: head and neck. P.H. 0.038 (size 2–3). Fabric similar to **I7**, finer. White slip. Red paint on hair, sakkos. Solid. Back handmade, rounded. Added: cluster of curls. Tooling on hair.

Published: Stroud 1965, p. 18, pl. 7:d (incorrectly restored with torso **I11**).

Head tilted slightly to left. Face oblong to oval, narrowing to high, rounded forehead. Eyes downturned; lids defined. Nose large, arched, overhangs upper lip. Lips full. Coiffure peaked at top, with central braid in front; lightly modeled waves cover ears; sakkos covers hair in back, with cluster of curls emerging from cloth at top of cranium. Probable mold sibling: MF-13975 (lot 4379). Probable later generation: MF-10465 (lot 878).

See p. 288.

I20   Female head   Pl. 66

MF-14051. Lot 4349. Preserved: head and neck. P.H. 0.03 (size 2–3). Fabric as **I7**. White slip. Solid. Back handmade, flattened.

Face oval to oblong, with high, triangular forehead. Eyes level, opened wide; lids defined. Nose large, arched, close to upper lip. Lips full, parted. Coiffure parted at center; nearly horizontal waves from forehead; long locks of hair to shoulders. Possibly veiled. Identified as Argive by Martin Guggisberg.

See p. 288.

I21   Head, probably of boy   Pl. 66

MF-10950. Lot 1945. Preserved: head and neck. P.H. 0.023 (size 2). Fabric similar to **I7** but finer. White slip. Red paint on hair. Hollow. Back handmade, rounded. Tooling on hair.

Probably a mold sibling of Corinthian standing boy with goose **H331**.

See pp. 286, 288.

I22   Priestess(?)   Pl. 66

MF-10327. Lot 870. Preserved: head to chest. Mended; polos chipped. P.H. 0.085 (size 3). Fabric similar to **I7** but finer, shading to orange-buff. Hollow. All parts rendered in same mold. Back molded, distorted. Upper edge of rectangular vent preserved.

Similar to Corinthian "priestess" type **H398**. Torch more slanted toward head, the flame at eye level, touching hair. Similar in facial type to **H401** and **H402** but wears higher polos; creases on neck clearly marked.

See pp. 286, 288.

ATTIC FIGURINES

I23   Head of hydriaphoros   Pl. 66

MF-13941. Lot 1953. Preserved: hydria, missing most of neck and fragments of front; head and part of neck of figure, right hand. Mended. P.H. 0.067 (size 3). Fabric fine, orange, with orange-buff slip, blue-gray core, sparse small sparkling inclusions. Solid. Back handmade, flattened, pared. Tooling on hair.

Hydria high shouldered, broad at base, balanced by right hand. Face oblong, with narrow, triangular, sloping forehead; cheeks full. Eyes level. Nose wide, flat, close to upper lip. Mouth wide; lips full. Coiffure parted at center, with rounded mass of curls down each side to neck.

See pp. 33, 289.

I24   Standing draped female figurine   Pl. 66

MF-13927. Lot 3228. Preserved: front–hips to hem; back–hips and part of left side. Missing right foot. Mended. P.H. 0.098 (size 3). Fabric fine, orange, with polished surface, abundant small sparkling inclusions. Hollow. Back molded, flattened.

Weight on right leg, right hip slightly outthrust; left leg slightly bent. Mantle is wrapped closely around right hip and upper thigh, and is pulled up to left hip in narrow, shallow, looped folds; end of mantle falls in clump of vertical folds at left hip. Skirt folds are broader, deeper; hem arched over right instep.

See pp. 33, 115, 289.

I25   Standing draped female figurine   Pl. 66

MF-68-371. Lot 5715. Preserved: right hip and left knee to hem. Surface chipped. Missing right foot. P.H. 0.075 (size 2–3). Fabric slightly sandy, interior orange, exterior orange-brown, with abundant small sparkling inclusions. Nearly solid; closed underneath. Back molded, flattened. Tooling on folds.

Weight on left leg; right leg bent, foot drawn back. Mantle is wrapped closely around right hip and thigh; its hem rises toward left side; incised folds radiate down over hip from waist. Skirt folds are deeper, tubular; looped fold from right ankle to knee.

See pp. 33, 289.

I26   Standing draped female figurine   Pl. 66

MF-70-256. Lot 6507. Preserved: front–right shoulder and left breast to knees. Missing left arm, part of right forearm and hand. P.H. 0.076 (size 2–3). Fabric as **I24**. Hollow. Tooling on folds.

Weight probably on left leg, left hip outthrust. Languid pose, with hips forward. Right shoulder slightly higher than left. Left arm probably akimbo; right arm at side, slightly bent. Slender, shapely figure. Chiton girded just below full breasts; knot of belt is not rendered, but diagonal ends of ties are visible. Mantle draped over left shoulder, originally around back; folds reappear at right thigh, must have been held in place by hand.

See pp. 33, 289.

I27   Standing draped female figurine   Pl. 66

MF-13961. Lot 2249. Preserved: left side from shoulder to hip, small part of back. P.H. 0.055 (size 2–3). Fabric similar to **I24**, shading to orange-buff, with sparse small sparkling inclusions. White slip. Hollow. Back flattened. Added: folds over arm. Tooling on folds.

Left arm bent; hand at chest. Mantle draped around shoulders; heavy folds fall diagonally across chest and over wrist and hand. Plump hand; fingers not rendered.

See pp. 33, 289–290.

I28   Standing draped female figurine   Pl. 67

MF-13479. Lot 3217. Preserved: shoulders to ankles. P.H. 0.076 (size 2). Fabric similar to **I24** but slightly coarser, with orange-buff slip. White slip. Nearly solid. Back handmade, flattened, flaring at bottom. Added: drapery fall at left side. Tooling on folds.

Weight on left leg; right leg bent, drawn to side. Mantle envelops figure, baring only upper chest; cloth draped over shoulders; upper edge rolled, falls diagonally across chest and left forearm; left hand lifts cloth from beneath, flaring drapery fall descends from hand to hem; right arm folded over chest, hand pulls down edge of mantle; looped fold from right ankle to left hip. Folds are thick when rendered, but cloth is smooth over lower torso and right leg.

See pp. 33, 289–290.

I29   Standing draped female figurine   Pl. 67

MF-13966. Lot 4466. Preserved: neck to thighs, to chest in back. Missing object in front. Mended; surface worn. P.H. 0.063 (size 2). Fabric as **I24**. White slip. Hollow. Back molded, flattened. Added: object in front. Tooling on hands.

Both arms bent, with hands at abdomen; fingers curled, appear originally to have held an object across the waist (perhaps a small animal, such as a piglet, the back legs held in the right hand, the front legs in the left, the animal's head cradled on the left forearm). Shoulders narrow, rounded; figure stocky, short waisted. V-shaped folds of chiton neckline over chest; group of skirt folds pulled diagonally to center from right side, perhaps right leg advanced.

See pp. 33, 290.

I30   Standing draped female figurine   Pl. 67

MF-13963. Lot 3217. Preserved: shoulders to right hip and left thigh. Surface slightly worn. P.H. 0.075 (size 2–3). Fabric as **I24**. Hollow. Back probably handmade, flattened. Top of rectangular vent preserved.

Weight probably on left leg; left hip slightly outthrust. Left arm akimbo, hand behind hip. Mantle covers entire figure. Right arm folded over chest beneath cloth; hand pulls down folds from neck. Taut folds from right forearm to waist at left side; folds radiate from waist over left arm; cascade of folds flares out from hip at left side. Figure rather stocky, with sloping shoulders.

See pp. 33, 290.

I31   Standing draped female figurine   Pl. 67

MF-13882. Lot 2240. Preserved: front–waist to thighs(?). P.H. 0.043 (size 2–3). Fabric slightly coarse, orange, with orange-buff surface, gray core, abundant small sparkling inclusions. Hollow.

If this is the lower torso of the figurine, the left thigh is strongly advanced. Garment, probably a mantle, gathered across abdomen in looped folds; stretched folds between thighs. If this piece represents the shoulders to hips of the figurine, the folds are across the chest, and the left forearm is extended.

See pp. 33, 290.

I32   Female head   Pl. 67

MF-12021. Lot 2240. Preserved: head and neck, with tenon. Surface worn. P.H. 0.041 (size 3). Fabric similar to **I24**, slightly softer. Solid. Back molded, rounded. Tooling on hair.

Head tilted slightly to left. Face oval, with high, triangular, slightly sloping forehead; slightly receding chin. Eyes slightly downturned; upper lid defined, lower lid slightly lifted. Nose large, wide, close to upper lip. Lips full. Coiffure divided into eight melon sections, tooled with diagonal strokes.

See pp. 33, 290.

I33   Female head   Pl. 67

MF-11827. Lot 2088. Preserved: head and small part of neck. Surface worn. P.H. 0.028 (size 3). Fabric similar to **I24**, slightly coarser. Solid. Back handmade, rounded. Added: plait of hair, earrings. Tooling on hair.

Face round, with high forehead. Eyes large, opened wide. Nose short, wide. Lips full. Coiffure divided into seven melon sections, tooled with diagonal strokes; plait around cranium. Perhaps a young girl.

See pp. 33, 290.

I34   Standing draped youth   Pl. 67

MF-13969. Lot 2239. Preserved: front–right side from chest to thigh, forearm and hand. P.H. 0.069 (size 2–3). Fabric as **I24**. Hollow. Added: edges of mantle down chest and over wrist. Tooling on folds, hand.

Right arm bent; hand at hip. Heavy folds of mantle draped down left side and over arm; clump of triangular folds falls from clenched hand; protruding edge of cloth down chest; flaring diagonal edge over wrist gives impression of movement.

See pp. 33, 290.

I35   Standing youth   Pl. 67

MF-13939. Lot 4349. Preserved: front–right leg, left ankle and foot, part of support at right side, part of base. P.H. 0.066 (size 2–3). Fabric similar to **I24**, paler (5YR 7/6). Hollow. Added: boot cuff.

Right leg crossed over left. Right side of figure leans against an irregular support, probably a rocky outcrop. Bare legged; wears boots with cuff at mid-calf. Oval base.

See pp. 33, 290.

I36   Seated baby   Pl. 67

MF-68-147. Lot 5714. Preserved: head to thighs. Missing arms, genitals. Mended; face and cranium chipped. P.H. 0.059 (size 2). Fabric similar to **I24**, with some small sparkling inclusions, slightly burned. Nearly solid. Back molded, rounded. Tooling on hair.

Nude baby, probably a boy, sits with legs apart; arms originally outstretched, left shoulder higher than right; head thrown back. Face round, with high forehead, plump cheeks. Eyes large, opened wide; both lids defined. Hair stippled; possible wreath on cranium.

See pp. 33, 290.

I37 Seated boy Pl. 67

MF-13455. Lot 3206. Preserved: shoulders to ankles. Missing fragment of lower back. Mended. P.H. 0.066 (size 2). Fabric as **I24**, surface smooth. White slip. Hollow. All parts rendered in same mold. Back molded, slightly flattened.

Rectangular, blocklike seat is a stool, with legs faintly marked in mold and area between filled with clay. Child's legs slightly apart. Left arm at side, hand on seat; right arm folded over chest; hand clenched. Swollen abdomen. Traces of drapery on seat beneath thighs. Similar in type: MF-13452 (lot 2152, seat without legs, drapery over left arm and under hand).

See pp. 33, 290.

I38 Head of child Pl. 67

MF-14017. Lot 3229. Preserved: head and neck. Missing wreath at left side. P.H. 0.03 (size 2–3). Fabric as **I24**. White slip. Red paint on hair. Solid. Back handmade, flat. Added: hair in front, wreath. Tooling on hair, wreath.

Face round to oval, with high forehead. Features slightly deformed at left side. Eyes level, opened wide; lids defined. Nose wide, flat, close to upper lip. Lips smiling. Curls rendered by a row of punched lumps of clay framing face down to jaw. Stippled wreath.

See pp. 33, 290.

I39 Standing semidraped child(?) Pl. 67

MF-71-140. No context. Preserved: right hip and thigh, with forearm and hand, small part of back. P.H. 0.046 (size 2–3). Fabric as **I24**, surface smoother in front than rear. White slip. Hollow. Back probably molded, flattened. Vertical edge of rectangular vent preserved. Added: possibly upper edge of drapery and part of hand. Tooling on hand.

Right arm at side; hand touching upper edge of drapery. Mantle draped horizontally around thigh; upper folds protrude; no drapery visible on torso. Plumpness of abdomen and arm suggests figure is a child.

See pp. 33, 290.

I40 Head of child Pl. 67

MF-13421. Lot 2249. Preserved: head and neck. Missing front of headdress. P.H. 0.024 (size 2–3). Fabric fine, orange-buff, with light orange core, abundant small sparkling inclusions. White slip. Red paint on hair. Solid. Back molded, rounded. Added: Hair at sides, headdress. Tooling on hair.

Face round, with high forehead, full cheeks. Eyes large, level, opened wide; lids defined, upper lid thick. Nose wide, pointed, overhangs upper lip. Smile pronounced; "laughter lines" deeply marked on cheeks. Locks of hair above forehead marked by light strokes, drawn into small cluster of curls in front; flat masses of punched curls at sides of head; nape bare. Untooled wreath or rolled fillet.

See pp. 33, 289, 291.

I41 Head of draped child Pl. 67

MF-13974. Lot 4379. Preserved: head, with part of upper chest. Surface chipped, worn. P.H. 0.041 (size 3). Fabric as **I24**. White slip. Head solid, torso hollow. Back handmade, rounded. Added: hair at sides and back, headdress. Tooling on hair.

Head slightly forward. Mantle wrapped across chest, covering chin. Face round, with high forehead. Eyes level. Nose wide. Lips smiling. Long, curly locks of hair down sides and back, stippled. Flat, irregularly shaped headdress on top of head.

See pp. 33, 291.

I42 Comic actor Pl. 67

MF-14018. Lot 3217. Preserved: left shoulder and right side of chest to thighs. Surface worn. P.H. 0.043 (size 2). Fabric slightly coarse, orange, laminated in fracture, with paler slip. Solid. Back handmade, flat.

Stands with legs together. Left arm akimbo, hand on hip. Padded tunic to top of thighs; flat belt. Mantle over left shoulder, folds secured at waist by left hand; folds looped over belt at right side.

See pp. 33, 195, 291.

BOEOTIAN FIGURINES

I43 Seated peplos-figurine Pl. 68

MF-13959. Lot 2249. Preserved: front–shoulders to ankles. Missing left side, including most of left arm; right side below arm. P.H. 0.114 (size 2–3). Fabric similar to **I44**. White slip. Hollow.

Seated in rigid pose, with hands resting on knees; thumb and forefinger of each hand come together, but nothing is held. Broad-shouldered, blocklike figure, with sloping lap. Peplos overfold to lap, smooth in front, a few vertical folds at sides; rear overfold covers part of upper arm. Dull impression. Similar in type: MF-2 in the Corinth collection (Shoe 1932, p. 59, fig. 3, larger). Original head type probably similar to MF-2 and **I44**.

See pp. 45, 292, 293.

I44 Head, probably of seated female figurine Pl. 68

MF-11677. Lot 2010. Preserved: head and neck, with part of left shoulder. Missing peak of headdress in back. P.H. 0.055 (size 3). Fabric fairly coarse, light orange to orange-brown, with some small brown and white inclusions, sparse small sparkling inclusions, voids. White slip. Solid. Back handmade, flattened.

Face oval to oblong, with low forehead; cheeks full. Eyes large. Nose small, straight. Mouth distorted to left side; lips full. Hair arranged in scalloped waves around forehead to ears; long, crimped locks of hair fall from behind ears down sides of neck. Low polos covered with veil, originally forming peak in back. Probable mold sibling: head of MF-2 in the Corinth collection (see **I43**). Similar in type: one in lot 6214.

See pp. 45, 48, 292, 293.

I45 Standing semidraped youth Pl. 68

MF-13458. Lot 1953. Preserved: head to waist. Missing most of right arm, part of back at right side; surface worn. P.H. 0.07 (size 2–3). Fabric fairly coarse, orange to ochre, with sparse small dark inclusions, voids; friable, possibly burned. Hollow. Back handmade, flattened.

Upper arms at sides, left arm perhaps originally bent. Mantle arranged symmetrically over shoulders, leaving chest bare; rounded stacked folds down arms. Face oval. Features indistinct. Hair short, knotted at center of forehead.

See pp. 62, 292, 293.

I46 Head of youth   Pl. 68

MF-14005. Lot 3222. Preserved: head and neck; surface worn. P.H. 0.039 (size 3). Fabric fairly coarse, orange to ochre, with some small dark inclusions, sparse small sparkling inclusions, voids. White slip. Red paint on hair. Solid. Back handmade, rounded. Added: roll of hair in back.

Head tilted slightly to left. Face oval, with rounded forehead, rather pointed chin. Eyes large, slightly downturned, deeply set at inner corners; lids defined. Nose large, overhangs upper lip. Mouth wide; lower lip full. Coiffure parted at center; thick, undetailed roll of hair at each side in front and around nape; cranium smooth.

See p. 292.

I47 Standing draped female figurine   Pl. 68

MF-68-290. Lot 5711. Preserved: chest to base. Missing arms, upper part of back, most of base and hem, left foot. Mended; surface worn. P.H. 0.183 (size 3–4). Fabric slightly coarse, ochre, with some small white inclusions, voids. Nearly solid. Back handmade, flattened. Added: projecting ridge of drapery at right thigh.

Weight on left left; right leg bent, foot drawn to side. Hips forward. Arms originally held away from torso. Chiton or peplos belted at natural waistline, with folds of kolpos shown at right side; catenaries over chest. Upper edge of mantle is folded down into triangular apron and slung from right hip to waist at left side; lower edge falls to knees; diagonal edge of apron over right thigh projects, suggesting that right hand originally pulled cloth to side; folds along left side suggest mantle originally covered shoulder. On skirt, looped folds over right leg, tubular vertical folds over left.

See p. 292.

I48 Standing draped female figurine   Pl. 68

MF-13710. Lot 3217. Preserved: shoulders to hem. Missing part of upper back. Mended. P.H. 0.145 (size 2–3). Fabric fairly coarse, orange-buff to orange, with some small gray, white, and sparkling inclusions, voids. Hollow. Back molded, flattened. Round vent, diam. ca. 0.025. Added: locks of hair in back. Tooling on folds.

Weight on right leg; left leg bent, foot drawn back and to side. Right arm akimbo; elbow pulled back. Left arm at side. Mantle covers shoulders, arms, and hands, and skirt from right knee diagonally to left thigh; looped folds over right hip; stretched diagonal folds from left shoulder to right elbow and from right elbow to left hand; short cascade of folds below left hand. Mantle did not cover head; long locks of hair visible in back.

See pp. 115, 292–293.

I49 Standing draped female figurine   Pl. 68

MF-11777. Lot 2064. Preserved: knees to base. P.H. 0.082 (size 3–4). Fabric sandy, orange-buff, with abundant small to medium white and gray inclusions, some small sparkling

inclusions, voids. White slip. Hollow. Thin-walled. Back molded, flattened. Added: base, open underneath. Tooling on folds.

Weight on left leg; right leg bent, foot drawn back and to side. Looped folds from right ankle to knee; hem trails over instep; pointed slipper.

See p. 293.

I50 Standing draped female figurine   Pl. 68

MF-69-390. Lot 6214. Preserved: right side from waist to knee, with forearm and hand, small part of back. P.H. 0.061 (size 3). Fabric similar to **I51**. White slip. Hollow. Back flattened. Added: probably object in hand. Tooling on folds.

Weight probably on right leg, since right hip seems outthrust. Incised crinkly folds of chiton visible on hip. Mantle folded down at top, upper edge rolled and draped loosely around hip, probably to waist at left side. Right arm at side; hand holding baglike bundle of folds.

See p. 292.

I51 Standing Leda(?)   Pl. 68

MF-13773. Lot 2249. Preserved: shoulders to ankles, to chest in back. Missing right hand, upper left side of torso and arm. Mended. P.H. 0.14 (size 3). Fabric fairly coarse, ochre to orange, with some small to medium gray and white inclusions, abundant small sparkling inclusions. White slip. Solid at top, hollow from chest down. Back handmade, flattened at top. Upper part of rectangular vent preserved, narrowing downward. Added: possibly edge of drapery loop at right side.

Pose and drapery arrangement similar to **H257**, but knees are deeply bent; drapery at left side falls in narrow folds over an irregularly shaped support, such as a rock, against which figure leans at the hips. Mantle covers both legs; bare torso is framed by mantle, which is lifted high at right side; edge of mantle is folded over right elbow and forearm like an envelope flap. Slender, small-breasted figure. Lump beside left hip may be remains of swan.

See p. 292.

RHODIAN FIGURINES

I52 Protome   Pl. 69

MF-13656. Lot 2107. Preserved: left hand, with adjacent drapery. Mended. Max.P.Dim. 0.09. Fabric grayish buff, with gray core, some small to medium gray, white, and brown inclusions, sparse small sparkling inclusions, voids. White slip. Hollow. Thin-walled.

Raised, cupped left hand, with long fingers. Curved folds radiate from thumb, originally to left shoulder and arm. Possible mold sibling: MF-10083 in the Corinth collection (Robinson 1962, p. 113, pl. 41; C. K. Williams 1986, p. 14, note 6, fig. 2:A, B on p. 16; fabric similar in texture but color less pale).

See pp. 74, 285, 293.

I53 Protome   Pl. 69

MF-13659. Lot 4349. Preserved: part of chest, including right breast and hand. P.H. 0.056. Fabric slightly coarse, orange, with some small gray and brown inclusions, abundant sparkling inclusions, voids. White slip. Hollow. Thin-walled. Tooling on hand.

Right hand raised, cupped, below right breast; hand is small. Thick V-shaped fold indicates garment neckline.

See pp. 74, 293.

I54 Protome   Pl. 69

MF-13559. Lot 3206. Preserved: right breast and hand. Surface worn. Max.P.Dim. 0.068. Fabric orange-buff, interior orange, with sparse small dark and sparkling inclusions. Hollow. Thick-walled.

Right hand raised, cupped, beside right breast, perhaps holding object (flower?) between thumb and fingers.

See pp. 74, 293.

I55 Protome   Pl. 69

MF-70-230. Lot 6233. Preserved: fragment of right upper side of head, including part of eye. Max.P.Dim. 0.061. Fabric brownish yellow (C.E.C. C9), with sparse small sparkling inclusions, voids. Hollow. Tooling on eye.

Eye well opened; upper lid clearly defined; browridge prominent. Hair wrapped in sakkos, with horizontal band across forehead; wave of hair emerges from under it.

See pp. 74, 293.

I56 Protome   Pl. 69

MF-13569. Lot 4387. Preserved: part of top of head, most of right eye. Mended. Max.P.Dim. 0.072. Fabric coarse, bright orange, with grayish core, some small to large white and gray pebbly inclusions. Hollow. Thick-walled.

Thick, well-defined eyelids meet at outer corner; rounded browridge. Hair bound in sakkos, with horizontal band across forehead.

See pp. 74, 293.

WEST GREEK FIGURINES

I57 Female head   Pl. 69

MF-11918. Lot 2107. Preserved: head and neck, part of crown. Missing upper right side of head; center, right side, and top of crown; most of back. P.H. 0.072 (size 3–4). Fabric fairly coarse, orange (darker, 5YR 6/6–5/6), with abundant small sparkling inclusions, voids. Hollow. Back handmade, flat. Added: rosette on crown.

Imported from Gela. Probably from a small bust; base of neck projects slightly at left side; part of bottom flat, may be original resting surface. Face oval to oblong, with high, triangular, slightly sloping forehead; slightly receding chin. Face expressionless. Nose large, as wide as mouth, arched, overhangs upper lip. Lips full. Wide coiffure similar to Corinthian Classical **C55**, but punched curls are in mold. Tall crown covered with rosettes, some in mold. Irregularly shaped earrings. Identified as Geloan by Nunzio Allegro.

See p. 294.

I58 Seated nymph or Muse(?)   Pl. 69

MF-13749. Lot 3228. Preserved: head to hips. Missing front of left hip, right arm, left hand, most of wreath, part of nose; surface chipped. P.H. 0.117 (size 3). Fabric fairly fine, orange-buff, with creamy buff slip, some small sparkling inclusions. Hollow, head probably solid. Back molded, slightly flattened. Added: wreath, hair at back. Tooling on folds, hair.

Imported from Tarentum. Seated in languid pose on backless, probably irregular seat, such as a rocky outcrop; originally perched on left hip, leaning on left hand, which rested on top of seat. Torso is nude; shoulders are broad; breasts are round but rather flat. Mantle covers left shoulder and arm, is draped diagonally across back to right hip; slashes for folds. Long neck with creases. Head relatively small, tilted to left. Face oval to round, with fairly low, rounded forehead; small chin. Eyes downturned; lids defined. Lips full, downturned. Coiffure parted at center; locks of hair not defined in front but divided at cranium into five melon sections with diagonal slashes, gathered at nape into punched cluster of curls. Wreath of overlapping ivy(?) leaves.

See p. 294.

IMPORTED FIGURINES OF UNCERTAIN PROVENIENCE

I59 Standing peplos-figurine, with piglet   Pl. 69

MF-70-244. Lot 6500. Preserved: neck to right knee and left thigh. Missing left shoulder. P.H. 0.116 (size 3). Fabric slightly coarse, bright orange to yellowish buff, with some small dark and sparkling inclusions. White slip. Hollow. Thick-walled. Back handmade, flattened. Irregular, rectangular vent, ca. 0.02 × 0.025. Added: forearms, head of piglet, lock of hair in back; globs of clay daubed on left side.

Both arms bent; hands grasping legs of large piglet, facing viewer's right, held horizontally across abdomen. Peplos girded just below breasts; kolpos and overfold fall to top of thighs. Narrow, sloping shoulders; protruding abdomen. Long lock of hair to shoulder. Squarish in section. Poor workmanship.

See pp. 128, note 78, 295.

I60 Standing peplos-figurine   Pl. 69

MF-70-239. Lot 6505. Preserved: neck to base. Missing fragments of bottom of base. P.H. 0.096 (size 2). Fabric sandy, orange-buff to orange, grayish buff in back, with some small sparkling inclusions. White slip. Nearly solid but open underneath. All parts rendered in same mold. Back handmade, flattened. Tooling on hands, locks of hair.

Probably mechanically related to Corinthian **H37** but preserved to bottom. Weight on left leg; right knee bent. Locks of hair along neck marked with horizontal incisions. Base oval in front, flat in back, slightly splaying, with faint torus moldings at top and bottom. Dull impression. Similar to **I86** in sandiness and thickness of fabric.

See pp. 283, 295, 298.

I61 Standing peplos-figurine   Pl. 69

MF-13951. Lot 4379. Preserved: head; front–left shoulder to waist at right side, upper arm. Surface chipped and worn. P.H. 0.048 (size 1–2). Fabric slightly coarse, orange, with sparse small white and dark inclusions, some sparkling inclusions. Head solid, torso hollow.

Right upper arm at side. Slender figure, with narrow, sloping shoulders, relatively large head. Folds from right shoulder to waist. Features nearly obliterated. Coiffure close to head.

See p. 295.

I62 Standing draped female figurine   Pl. 69

MF-13785. Lot 4377. Preserved: front–shoulders to rib cage, left forearm; back–shoulders to hip. Missing right arm. P.H. 0.092 (size 3–4). Fabric slightly coarse, buff to orange-buff, with gray core, small white, brown, gray, and a few sparkling inclusions. White slip. Hollow. Back handmade, flattened. Edge of small, round, punched vent at lower break. Added: mantle folds around neck. Tooling on folds.

Left arm bent. Right upper arm originally extended to side. Mantle falls over left shoulder and arm in vertical folds, is draped diagonally across back. V-shaped fold at chiton neckline; curving folds below full breasts, where fairly high belt originally gathered cloth together.

See pp. 293, 295.

I63   Standing draped female figurine   Pl. 70

MF-13816. Lot 3206. Preserved: neck to thighs. P.H. 0.062 (size 2). Fabric slightly coarse, orange-buff to orange, with some small dark and sparkling inclusions. Hollow. Thick-walled. Back probably handmade, flattened. Tooling on hands, folds.

Weight on left leg; right thigh advanced. Left arm at side; right forearm folded across waist. Chiton falls from left shoulder; looped fold from waist to left hand, which probably draws skirt aside. Perhaps dancing? Dull impression. Probably from same workshop as **I64**.

See p. 295.

I64   Standing draped female figurine   Pl. 70

MF-13876. Lot 2240. Preserved: front and left side from chest to ankle, part of right leg. P.H. 0.072 (size 2). Fabric slightly coarse, orange to ochre, with some small dark and sparkling inclusions. Hollow. Thick-walled. Added: hand. Tooling on hand.

Weight on left leg; right leg advanced. Left arm at side. Garment of thin, clinging cloth, probably a chiton, girded high. Probably from same workshop as **I63**.

See p. 295.

I65   Standing draped female figurine   Pl. 70

MF-70-259. Lot 6638. Preserved: waist at right side and left hip to base, left hand. P.H. 0.096 (size 2–3). Fabric slightly sandy, orange-buff to orange, with some small sparkling inclusions. White slip. Hollow. Thick-walled. Back handmade, flattened. Bottom of rectangular vent preserved, 0.012 wide. Added: base.

Weight on right leg; left knee bent; foot drawn back and to side. Left arm at side. Upper part of type preserved in **I66**. Small part of mantle roll across chest is preserved at upper break. Left hand at hip pulls diagonal stretched folds from waist at right side; mantle covers right hip and thigh with looped folds; hem curves upward to left hip; ends of cloth hang at both sides in flaring folds. Skirt folds are vertical, tubular. Low base, roughly oval in shape. Probable mold sibling: **I66**.

See pp. 283, 295, 298.

I66   Standing draped female figurine   Pl. 70

MF-13836. Lot 4384. Preserved: shoulders to hips. Missing right arm. Surface worn. P.H. 0.052 (size 2–3). Fabric slightly coarse, grayish buff, with abundant small dark and sparkling inclusions. White slip. Hollow. Back handmade, flattened. Top of irregular, rectangular vent preserved, 0.016 wide.

Probable mold sibling of **I65**, preserving upper part of type. Mantle is draped under right arm, which originally was held away from torso, and over left shoulder, covering left arm and hand; diagonal upper edge across chest is rolled.

See pp. 283, 295.

I67   Pl. 70

Standing draped female figurine (Aphrodite or Leda?)

MF-70-81. Lot 6233. Preserved: thighs to base, break lower at sides and back. Mended; surface worn. P.H. 0.096 (size 3). Fabric slightly coarse, friable, orange, with some small sparkling inclusions. White slip. Hollow. Back handmade.

Right knee bent, perhaps left knee also. Heavy drapery, presumably a mantle, collapses around feet as if loosened above. Barefoot; toes long, toenail rendered on right big toe. Base deep, oval from front to back; torus molding at top and bottom.

See p. 295.

I68   Seated(?) draped female figurine   Pl. 70

MF-13934. Lot 4348. Preserved: front–hem, left foot, footstool. P.H. 0.049. Fabric slightly coarse, yellowish gray to orange-buff, with sparse small white, dark, and sparkling inclusions, voids. Painted without underlying white slip: red on footstool, blue on folds, purple under hem. Hollow. Added: foot and projecting hem folds.

Left foot in pointed slipper advances, projects over edge of footstool, which is detailed only in front, showing curving animal legs and hooved feet; space between legs of footstool filled with clay panel. Folds of skirt hem flare, drop below top of footstool at left side onto traces of another support; hem projects beyond foot in front.

See pp. 295–296.

I69   Seated nymph(?)   Pl. 70

MF-13928. Lot 2249. Preserved: front–left arm, hip, and most of leg; right knee and part of calf. P.H. 0.083 (size 3). Fabric rather coarse, orange-brown, with gray core, some small to medium gray inclusions, small sparkling inclusions, voids. White slip. Hollow. Thick-walled. Tooling on folds, hand.

Perched with right leg higher than left, probably on an irregularly shaped seat, such as a rocky outcrop. Legs heavily draped, probably with mantle; left forearm rests on thigh, hand grasping drapery. Deep folds between legs; zigzag folds down side of thigh. Fragment in lot 2249 could belong to the bottom of this figurine; it shows the left foot, collapsing pointed drapery folds with knotted ends, and a low, curved base.

See pp. 294, 296, 297.

I70   Chair of seated draped figurine   Pl. 70

MF-13708. Lot 2249. Preserved: left side of chair, front half, with adjacent drapery. Mended. P.H. 0.09. Fabric similar to **I69** but thinner-walled, hence uniform at core. White slip. Yellow paint. Hollow. Added: finial. Tooling on relief.

One leg preserved, showing three lathe turns. Seat rail terminates in front in flat, round finial decorated with rosette. Narrow relief panel along side of chair below seat rail shows, from viewer's left, lion walking left with tail curved down under legs, rear part of lion walking right with tail curved up over back. Panel of clay fills space between legs of chair. Drapery folds at upper break. Nonjoining fragment of another leg, possibly from this figurine, in lot 2249.

See pp. 294, 296.

I71   Seated draped female figurine   Pl. 70

MF-69-401. Lot 6214. Preserved: front–lap to base. Missing left lower leg, most of base; surface worn. P.H. 0.086 (size 3). Fabric coarse, yellowish brown (near 10YR 6/6), with abundant small to medium brown, gray, and white pebbly inclusions, voids. Hollow. All parts rendered in same mold.

Relieflike composition. Figure seated three-fourths to right, with legs somewhat parted, left knee lower than right. Object, possibly a child, on left side of lap. Unintelligible object beside right lower leg. Catenaries between lower legs. Low base has torus moldings at top and bottom. Dull impression.

See pp. 293, 296.

I72 Dancer Pl. 70

MF-13970. Lot 3215. Preserved: neck to hips, to chest in back. Missing most of right arm. P.H. 0.068 (size 2–3). Fabric creamy buff to orange-buff, with some small to medium white, gray, and reddish brown inclusions, abundant voids. White slip. Hollow. Back handmade, flattened. Top of rectangular vent preserved, 0.022 wide.

Right thigh possibly advanced. Left arm bent; hand at front of hip. Lightly modeled chiton falls from right shoulder, revealing breast. Mantle draped over left shoulder and arm; upper edge rolled across waist; looped folds over abdomen. Slender figure, with sloping, rounded shoulders, high breasts. Color and inclusions of fabric similar to Corinthian, but large amount of burned-out organic temper indicated by abundant voids is unusual in Corinthian figurines.

See pp. 283, 296.

I73 Mantled dancer Pl. 70

MF-14095. Lot 2249. Preserved: head; to waist in back. P.H. 0.041 (size 2). Fabric fairly coarse, tan, with gray interior, sparse small dark and sparkling inclusions, voids. White slip. Hollow. All parts rendered in same mold. Back molded, flattened.

Head thrown back and tilted to right. Sakkos covers hair and forehead; mantle drawn across mouth and chin. Similar in type to Corinthian **H171**, but pose is reversed, and headdress is more pointed.

See p. 296.

I74 Female head Pl. 70

MF-10534. Lot 886. Preserved: head and neck. Mended; left side, back, nose chipped. P.H. 0.053 (size 3–4). Fabric fairly coarse, tan, with some small to medium white, red, and dark gray inclusions, voids. White slip. Solid. Back handmade, flattened. Added: probably hair at sides and cranium. Tooling on hair.

Small face with relatively large cranium, wide neck. Face oval, with high, rounded forehead. Features clustered at center of face. Eyes small, closely spaced. Lips full. Curly locks of hair framing face are punched; sphendone behind, with bowknot at top; hair on cranium slashed. Coiffure similar to that of Corinthian articulated "dolls" (see **C125**).

See pp. 283, 296.

I75 Female head Pl. 71

MF-13929. Lot 4377. Preserved: head and neck. Surface chipped, worn. P.H. 0.056 (size 3–4). Fabric slightly coarse, tan to orange, with some small white and brown inclusions, voids. White slip. Solid. Back handmade, rounded. Added: folds of headdress in back. Tooling on neck, hair, headdress.

Face oval, with high, rounded forehead, narrowing to jaw. Eyes small, closely set, slightly downturned; lids thick. Nose

large, arched, close to upper lip. Lips full, distorted to right side. Coiffure parted at center, with row of curls framing forehead; remainder of hair enveloped in sakkos, peaked at top, with loose, pointed fold hanging in back. Creases on neck.

See p. 296.

I76 Female head Pl. 71

MF-13976. Lot 4386. Preserved: head and neck. Forehead, nose, back of hair chipped. P.H. 0.054 (size 4). Fabric slightly coarse orange shading to grayer tone, with gray core, some small sparkling inclusions. Solid. Back handmade, rounded. Added: knot and ends of hair in back. Tooling on hair.

Head tilted to right. Long, rather narrow oval face with high, rounded forehead, narrowing to jaw. Eyes downturned; upper lid well defined, lower lid slightly lifted and blurred. Lips full. Coiffure parted at center; thick locks of hair drawn up from forehead to top of high cranium, forming modified lampadion knot; at back, below knot, two lumps of clay indicate curling ends of locks of hair. Probable later generation: MF-13973 (lot 3222, fabric brighter orange, with some small white, gray, and sparkling inclusions; white slip).

See p. 296.

I77 Female head Pl. 71

MF-11060. Lot 1955. Preserved: head and neck. P.H. 0.039 (size 2–3). Fabric fine, hard gray. Greenish buff to orange-buff slip, mottled. Solid. Back probably handmade, rounded. Added: stephane, earrings, locks of hair in back. Tooling on hair.

Face oval, with high, triangular forehead. Eyes slightly downturned. Nose close to upper lip. Lips full. Coiffure parted at center; diagonal locks of hair cling closely to sides of head; long locks of hair at nape, slashed; hair on cranium stippled. High, narrow stephane. Long pellet earrings project diagonally. Wide, spreading neck. Possibly mechanically related: **H246**.

See pp. 296–297.

I78 Female head Pl. 71

MF-11095. Lot 1978. Preserved: head and neck. P.H. 0.040 (size 2–3). Fabric similar to Corinthian 1, orange-buff to greenish buff. White slip. Yellow paint on hair. Solid. Back handmade, rounded. Added: hair at top, sides, and back, earrings. Tooling on hair.

Head tilted slightly to left. Face narrow, oblong, with wide, rather low forehead. Eyes large, level. Nose upturned. Lips full, smiling. Locks of hair wave up and to sides from forehead; two lumps at top may be a rough lampadion knot; long locks of hair fall to shoulders from behind ears. Disc earrings.

See p. 297.

I79 Female head Pl. 71

MF-14009. Lot 3230. Preserved: head and part of neck. P.H. 0.033 (size 2–3). Fabric similar to Corinthian 1, orange-buff to orange. White slip. Red paint on hair. Solid. Back handmade, rounded. Added: plait, cluster of curls. Tooling on hair.

Head tilted to left. Face oval, rather wide, with high forehead; narrow jaw, with small chin. Eyes large, downturned; upper lids defined, lower lids lifted, puffy. Nose large, close to upper lip. Mouth wide; lips full. Coiffure divided into fourteen melon sections; locks of hair slashed, gathered into small, stippled cluster of curls at back; slashed plait around cranium. Small disc earrings.

See pp. 283–284, 297.

I80 Standing Aphrodite(?)   Pl. 71

MF-69-393. Lot 6214. Preserved: thighs to base, small part of back. Missing left lower leg, bottom and left side of base; surface chipped. P.H. 0.099 (size 3). Fabric coarse, bright orange, with gray core, abundant small to medium gray, white, and yellow inclusions, voids. Hollow. Torso and base rendered in same mold. Finished edge behind right ankle may belong to vent. Tooling on base.

Weight on left leg; right leg bent, foot drawn back. Drapery falls heavily between legs and around feet. Support or drapery fall at right side. Long, slender proportions as far as preserved. Oval base with molding in three degrees at top.

See p. 297.

I81 Standing Leda   Pl. 71

MF-10440. Lot 878. Preserved: shoulders and part of right upper arm to base. Missing upper part of drapery fall at right side, fragment of abdomen and swan's chest, part of base in back. Mended. P.H. 0.24 (size 3–4). Fabric fairly fine, orange-buff to light orange, with sparse small to medium gray, brown, white, and sparkling inclusions, voids. Hollow. All parts rendered in same mold; base reworked. Back probably molded, flattened. Oval vent, ca. 0.03 × 0.027.

Weight on left leg; right knee bent. Right shoulder and arm raised to lift mantle, which leaves torso nude but covers right leg with looped folds from mid-thigh to ankle; cloth secured between thighs, from which zigzag folds fall to base; mantle covers left shoulder and arm and falls down left side to base in vertical folds. Swan held against Leda's left hip, its head reaching up between her breasts. Base splaying, round in front, oval in back; face slightly concave, except at left side where it has been reworked by hand; clay added to bottom for stability.

See p. 297.

I82 Standing nude male figurine, probably a deity   Pl. 71

MF-73-6. Lot 73-99. Preserved: shoulders to right knee and left foot. Missing right arm, left hand, left side and center of chest, toes of left foot, phallus. Mended. P.H. 0.235 (size 3–4). Slightly coarse orange-buff, with some small white, brown, and sparkling inclusions; layer of finer clay over surface; some areas splotched (not gradually shaded) yellowish buff, mottled with blue-gray. White slip. Torso and upper thighs hollow, lower leg and arm solid. Back molded, rounded. Added: arms, probably lower legs; pinhole in broken surface of left wrist perhaps for strut to support added hand. Tooling on back; legs are pared, show marks of finely toothed instrument. Blisters on left side of groin and on left thigh beside testicle indicate use of plaster mold.

Weight on right leg; right hip outthrust; left leg slightly bent, foot drawn to side. Right arm originally raised high; left arm bent, forearm extended forward. Pose languid, seems unstable in present condition. Slender figure; rather shallow modeling of anatomical details.

See pp. 16, 297, 298.

I83 Probably male head in Scythian cap   Pl. 72

MF-12025. Lot 2247. Preserved: head and neck. Missing back and cap at right side; surface chipped. P.H. 0.039 (size 3–4). Fabric sandy, ochre, with orange core, sparse small dark and sparkling inclusions, voids. White slip. Red paint on hair. Solid. Back probably handmade, rounded. Added: lappets of cap. Tooling on face, hair.

Head thrown back and tilted to left. Face oval, with high, wide, slightly sloping, furrowed forehead; slightly receding chin. Eyes large, downturned; upper lid defined, lower lid slightly lifted. Nose short, upturned. Lips thin, parted, downturned. Somewhat pained expression. Short, lightly punched curls frame forehead. Closely fitting cap with lappet preserved at left side.

See p. 298.

I84 Standing semidraped male figurine   Pl. 72

MF-69-354. Lot 6214. Preserved: shoulders to base. Front chipped; surface worn. P.H. 0.082 (size 2). Fabric coarse, bright orange, with ochre slip, some small to medium dark red and gray inclusions, voids. Solid. All parts rendered in same mold. Back handmade, flat.

Left arm slightly bent, hand behind hip. Right arm at side, holds object (mask?) against thigh. Slender figure, with narrow, sloping shoulders; bent backward at shoulders. Upper torso bare. Mantle covers left shoulder and arm, hips, and legs; diagonal folds from left hip to right leg. Pointed feet. Base round in front, high and narrow in proportion to figure, with torus moldings at top and bottom. Dull impression.

See pp. 284, 298.

I85 Standing semidraped male figurine   Pl. 72

MF-13480. Lot 2240. Preserved: shoulders to right hip and left thigh, small part of back. P.H. 0.062 (size 2). Fabric fairly fine, orange-brown, with some dark and sparkling inclusions, voids. Hollow. Thin-walled. Tooling on folds.

Right arm at side; left arm slightly bent, hand in front of hip, perhaps grasping drapery folds. Mantle draped from left shoulder to waist at right side, upper edge folded down, leaving right side of chest and arm bare; left arm covered, perhaps hand as well. Cloth smooth over torso, with diagonal fold from left hip to right thigh.

See p. 298.

I86 Standing draped male figurine   Pl. 72

MF-13962. Lot 2247. Preserved: waist to ankles. Missing left hip in back. P.H. 0.082 (size 2–3). Fabric slightly sandy, grayish buff, with some small sparkling inclusions. White slip. Hollow. Thick-walled. Back molded, rounded. Closed underneath. Tooling on folds.

Weight on right leg; left leg slightly bent, advanced. Mantle pulled closely around hips and legs; closure at bottom indicates that drapery stopped here and that bare ankles and feet of male figure originally were added; diagonal folds from left hip to right thigh and from right ankle to left calf; at left side, end of mantle falls in two wide, flat, overlapping folds to hem. Similar to **I60** in sandiness and thickness of fabric.

See pp. 283, 298.

I87 Standing draped boy   Pl. 72

MF-10674. Lot 1945. Almost complete. Mended; face chipped. P.H. 0.087 (size 1–2). Fabric close to **I82**. Red paint on face. Solid. Head and torso rendered in same mold. Back molded, rounded; mold join not concealed. Added: feet. Tooling on feet, face. Blisters on right side of face and between drapery folds at left side indicate use of plaster mold.

Weight on right leg, right hip outthrust; left leg advanced. Right arm folded over chest, with hand at chin; left arm bent, forearm held diagonally against hip. Mantle wrapped closely around body from neck to feet, leaving only left hand free; right hand beneath cloth pulls at neckline fold; rounded folds over left forearm; wide, flat, overlapping zigzag folds down left side to hem; front smooth except for line of groin, horizontal tension folds from left armpit to chest. Fairly high-soled sandals. Narrow, sloping shoulders, hunched; slightly swollen abdomen. Large head, with high cranium, tilted forward. Face oval, with high, wide forehead; full cheeks; narrow chin. Eyes large, level. Nose wide, flat. Lips full. Ears set far back on head. Lightly incised locks of hair combed forward over forehead; head otherwise smooth.

See p. 298.

I88   Standing draped child   Pl. 72

MF-12141. Lot 4349. Preserved: head to chest. Surface worn, chipped; friable. P.H. 0.057 (size 2). Fabric coarse, orange to ochre, with some small to medium gray inclusions, small sparkling inclusions; probably slightly burned. White slip. Head solid, torso hollow. Head and torso probably rendered in same mold. Back molded, flattened.

Relatively large head; short neck sloping directly to elbows, without articulation of shoulders. Mantle wrapped closely around neck. Right arm bent, grasps mantle at neck from beneath cloth. Left arm bent; position of forearm unknown. Round face with full cheeks, narrowing at forehead. Nose wide, flat. Lips smiling. Coiffure peaked at top; waves down to neck at sides. Dull impression.

See p. 298.

I89   Head of child   Pl. 72

MF-13990. Lot 3230. Preserved: head, with neck in back. Stephane chipped. P.H. 0.041 (size 3). Fabric similar to Attic but slightly sandy, interior orange, exterior paler. White slip. Red paint on hair and stephane. Solid. Back probably molded, flattened. Added: possibly hair in front.

Head tilted to right. Face oval to oblong, with high forehead; full cheeks. Lips smiling. Curly hair rendered summarily by lumps of clay framing face down to jaw. Flaring stephane. Dull impression.

See p. 298.

I90   Pig   Pl. 72

MF-10661. Lot 1945. Preserved: front—head and small part of neck. P.L. 0.041. Fabric slightly coarse, orange, with sparse small white, gray, and sparkling inclusions. Tooling on mouth.

Faces viewer's left. Long, upturned snout. Large, slanting, almond-shaped eye.

See pp. 266, 298.

I91   Bucranium   Pl. 72

MF-10607. Lot 897. Missing part of rim in back, ends of horns and ears. H. 0.046. Fabric possibly Argive but much finer than **I7**, with fewer and smaller inclusions. White slip. Hollow. Added: ears, horns, rim in back, head and bowknot between horns. Tooling on head and bowknot.

Large, slanting, eyes; creases on brows and muzzle. Horns and ears project to sides. At center between horns, a head in relief, with full cheeks, triangular forehead, thick shock of hair at each side; bowknot above. Backless, with 0.006-wide flange forming rim around opening.

See pp. 171, note 332, 267, 295, 298.

I92   Cow or bull   Pl. 72

MF-11835. Lot 2104. Preserved: rear half of body, right rear leg. Missing hoof. Mended. P.L. 0.066. Fabric coarse, orange to bright orange, with abundant small to medium white inclusions, sparse small sparkling inclusions, voids. Hollow. Back molded, flattened.

Bovid walking toward viewer's right. Space between legs filled with clay panel. Long tail curved at top, hangs down below elbow.

See pp. 267, 298.

I93   Cow   Pl. 72

MF-11344. Lot 878. Preserved: front and top of head; surface worn. P.L. 0.048. Fabric fairly coarse, brown (5YR 5/6), with abundant sparkling inclusions, voids. White slip. Nearly solid. Probably two molds. Tooling on mouth.

Faces viewer's right. Eye distorted in back. Mouth open.

See p. 298.

I94   Hand with offering   Pl. 72

MF-13923. Lot 2239. Preserved: left hand and wrist. P.L. 0.025 (size 3). Fabric fairly fine orange, with some small sparkling inclusions. White slip. Solid. Handmade. Tooling on fingers.

Forearm probably outstretched originally. Wrist well articulated; fingers deeply slashed. Rectangular object, probably a purse, rests on palm, with fingers curled around edge; two horizontal slashes on short sides create three layers, suggesting folded cloth or leather; fastened with two buttons on top.

See p. 298.

I95   Support of standing figurine   Pl. 72

MF-11080. Lot 1964. Preserved: left hand and part of forearm of figurine, support from head to thighs, adjacent drapery, small part of back. P.H. 0.091 (figurine probably size 3). Fabric similar to **I7**, finer. Hollow. Back flattened. Vertical edge of rectangular vent preserved. Tooling on fingers.

Support is an archaizing female figure in rigid stance, with left arm pressed against side; right arm concealed by drapery of figurine. Garment clings to body without folds, except deep V-shaped fold at neckline; wide, flat belt. Face shows "Archaic smile"; prominent eyes. Hand of figurine rests languidly on drapery piled on head of support; hand covers forehead of support; zigzag fold down left side covers left shoulder of support.

See pp. 288, 298.

I96   Support   Pl. 72

MF-69-389. Lot 6215. Preserved: front—lower part of support, with base. P.H. 0.059. Fabric slightly coarse, orange, with some small sparkling inclusions. White slip. Hollow.

Pillar support and low base of standing draped figurine. Small, winged figure, probably Eros, sits in frontal pose on base, arms at sides. Drapery folds at viewer's left side of support. Dull impression.

See p. 298.

VII

ROMAN FIGURINES

Although the harvest of Roman figurines at Corinth as a whole has been smaller than that of the earlier periods, a fair number of interesting pieces await comprehensive study.[1] In particular, the different Roman fabrics need to be sorted out, and criteria have to be developed to distinguish imports from the local production. The absence of such an overall study has somewhat handicapped the following discussion of the small number of Roman figurines from the sanctuary. Further, the sanctuary finds do not include material from the first 50–75 years of the Roman colony's existence, making possible links with pre-Roman Corinth hard to forge. Consequently, any conclusions reached here should be considered provisional.

Although some people continued to live at Corinth between its destruction by the Romans in 146 and its refounding as a Roman colony in 44 B.C.,[2] there is no clear evidence for activity at the Sanctuary of Demeter and Kore until the first or second quarter of the 1st century A.C.[3] Thus, unless the cult was pursued elsewhere in Corinth or in the neighborhood by the survivors of the disaster and, later, the earliest colonists, there was a break in its continuity lasting at least a century and a half. The rebuilding of the sanctuary after such a long interval, however, shows that in some way the cult was remembered. Perhaps it was helpful that the buildings apparently remained visible, since the sanctuary was never actually destroyed but only abandoned. The Roman colonists showed a tendency to revive some of the abandoned Greek sanctuaries of Corinth but not necessarily to recreate the original rituals.[4] New realities and the influx of new people must have stimulated changes in the way the functions of the Demeter sanctuary were perceived, but the figurines of Roman times do show some iconographic similarity with those of the earlier periods. Although the interval of cult inactivity was long, perhaps recollection of what was done in the old days, handed down by descendants of the surviving Corinthian population, inspired a renewal of offerings of figurines paralleling the older types. Alternatively, the renewed patterns of worship could have been inspired by uninterrupted cultic practices followed elsewhere in honor of the goddesses. It is certainly hard to imagine a complete lacuna of at least a century and a half, with no attention paid in Corinth to these important fertility and chthonic deities.

In whatever way votive practice was renewed, it is at once apparent that the quantity of figurines dedicated at the sanctuary is much smaller than in the preceding periods, both in absolute numbers and relative to the quantity of other finds. The catalogue of 29 Roman figurines contains all the material found for the approximately three-century duration of the Roman sanctuary. This small number is not merely a sampling, as in the case of the much more abundant earlier figurines, but the total harvest, apart from a few lumps of apparently Roman fabric but unidentifiable shape. Further, among this number are several pieces that may, in fact, be Hellenistic (see below). Given that more than 24,000 figurines or fragments were found at the sanctuary, the number assignable to the Roman period is minuscule, and one must infer that the dedication of figurines did not play an important role in the conduct of the cult.

---

[1] The largest group published so far is in *Corinth* XII, pp. 55–62, pls. 34–43.

[2] On habitation during the interim period, see p. 249.

[3] *Corinth* XVIII, ii, pp. 4–5; *Corinth* XVIII, iii, p. 434.

[4] C. K. Williams 1987, esp. pp. 31–32.

While it is hard to draw conclusions from such a small statistical base, a degree of continuity can be found in the overall pattern of types dedicated. The Roman figurines, excluding drapery and limb fragments belonging to unknown types, include two or possibly three representations of Aphrodite; three of Artemis; possibly one of Nike; possibly one of Athena; six draped females; one nude male; one draped boy; four or possibly five children; three grotesques; and one representation of Pan. Unless some of the fragmentary draped females represent Demeter or Kore, or **R12**, which may represent Matrona, refers to Demeter, the goddesses do not appear among the figurines. Aphrodite makes a good showing, as she did earlier (see pp. 169–177), but Artemis is more prominent than before (see p. 183), perhaps absorbing some of the function relating to coming-of-age, for which she was responsible elsewhere. Nike was known in the Hellenistic sanctuary, although only marginally (see pp. 183–184). The only male deity is Pan, who also was known earlier (see p. 200). As before, there are more female than male figurines, and a number of figurines of children and grotesques. A rooster figurine included with Varia (**V12**) could perhaps be of Roman date (see p. 269).

There is more cultic than technical continuity with earlier figurines, presumably because the destruction of Corinth in 146 B.C. caused the closure of its coroplastic workshops (see p. 249). One could not expect technical expertise to be handed down with the same persistence as religious tradition, particularly in the absence of opportunities to practice it. Among the Roman figurines from the sanctuary, two groups are recognizable by their fabrics. For one, the coroplasts appear to have employed the well-known fine, pale Corinthian clay (see p. 10). The Roman figurines in this fabric, however, usually are slightly coarse, owing to the presence of small dark inclusions, which are only occasionally found in the earlier figurines. Most of the figurines in this fabric are relatively small, in size range 2 or 2–3. They are usually fired harder than before. On the basis of style, they probably belong to the 2nd century A.C. The figurines in this fabric include two Aphrodites (**R13** and **R14**); two figurines of Artemis (**R15** and **R16**); two children (**R17** and **R18**); one base (**R19**); and a mantled boy (**R20**).

The second fabric is unlike any used previously for figurines in Corinth, and there is some question of its origin. It is a coarse reddish brown, with a moderate amount of inclusions and voids. The inclusions are sometimes gray, red, and white, resembling the material typically added to the pre-Roman Corinthian "tile fabric" (see p. 10). When the figurine is thin-walled, as in **R8** and **R9**, the fabric to some degree resembles that of Corinthian cooking pots. It is possible that the Roman figurines in this fabric were made in Corinth. Presumably because of the coarseness of the fabric, the scale of these figurines, which are usually in size range 3–4, is somewhat larger than that of the group in the paler, finer fabric. They are also much more closely linked to Hellenistic style, so much so that if one could prove that this fabric was in use before the destruction of Corinth, there would be little difficulty in assigning them to the Hellenistic period. Nevertheless, since one figurine of coarse fabric, the child's head **R7**, was found in a pottery context that was 97 percent Roman, dating to the late 1st to possibly the mid-2nd century A.C.,[5] and since the influence of Hellenistic forms might still be expected at this time, figurines in the coarse fabric are here tentatively assigned to the Roman period. The coarse figurines must be earlier than the fine on stylistic grounds; since the rebuilding of the sanctuary in the first or second quarter of the 1st century A.C. gives a *terminus post quem,* a date in the second half of the 1st century A.C. is suggested here for the figurines, taking into account the date of the associated pottery. It is not yet clear exactly how soon after the founding of the Roman colony of Corinth in 44 B.C. its coroplastic industry revived, but these figurines are unlikely to represent the very first efforts. The figurines in this fabric include a possible Aphrodite (**R1**); a possible Nike (**R2**); a nude male (**R6**); a child's head (**R7**); and four draped females (**R8**–**R11**).

---

[5] Lot 73–143; see *Corinth* XVIII, ii, p. 142.

The remaining Roman figurines are distinct in fabric from both groups of figurines discussed above. In a few examples, although the fabric as a whole looks quite similar to the coarse fabric described above, the inclusions are pebbly and do not resemble anything used before in Corinth. The fragmentary head **R12** has pebbly inclusions and probably represents Matrona, a type created in Athens in the early 3rd century A.C.;[6] it could be an import. The long plaits are typical of these heads, as is a high crown, the lower part of which is preserved here. If this head is an import, the grotesque heads **R3–R5**, which also have pebbly inclusions, could be Athenian as well, although there are no published parallels. In any case, pending a more comprehensive study of the Roman figurines in Corinth as a whole, the possibility that at least some of the figurines of coarse fabric are imports should be kept in mind.[7]

For the sake of convenience, the Roman figurines will be discussed by fabric rather than in typological order, as in the case of the earlier figurines. The figurines of coarse fabric, which are earlier, will be considered first. **R1** is a rather blocklike female torso fragment, with little anatomical detail. Enough of the right shoulder is preserved to show that the arm originally was raised, suggesting a pose in which one hand, at least, arranged the hair. If this reconstruction is correct, the type recalls popular Hellenistic renderings in various media of Aphrodite or a woman arranging her hair.[8] The bent right leg of **R2** seems to be dangling rather than standing, and the drapery behind her, originally perhaps spread out to the right, is windblown. Perhaps she originally represented a flying Nike.[9] For such a coarse fabric, the drapery shows a fair amount of skillful detail. The fabric of these two figurines is closely similar, with gray and brown inclusions.

The following three figurines, all grotesque heads, have gray and white pebbly inclusions. **R3** is a type of head with a deliberately misshapen face and slit mouth, known in the Demeter sanctuary also in Hellenistic fabric (see **H384**). The very wide nose and thick lips of **R4** are a caricature of an African's features; the lower part of the face of **R5** is not preserved, but the short, curly hair could indicate that the subject is similar. African children and young men were very popular subjects for Hellenistic small bronzes and terracotta figurines,[10] and a few such figurines are published from elsewhere in Corinth.[11] Whether or not the heads from the sanctuary are imports, the ultimate source of inspiration for these types is thought to be Alexandria.[12]

The nude male upper torso **R6** is a rather puzzling piece in that it apparently has a finished margin all around the shoulders, chest, and waist. Only the head appears to have been broken off; it was never intended to have arms or a lower torso. One thinks of an archetype, but in that case a head would not have been added, and the figure seems to have broken away from a background of some sort. Perhaps the intention was to make a bust, but the lower margins were never properly finished. In fact, busts on bronze roundels used to decorate chests and the fulcra of couches are of similar shape and size, and it seems likely that the mold of **R6** was taken from such a bust.[13] The fabric of this figurine shows red, white, and gray inclusions similar to those of earlier Corinthian fabrics (see p. 10). The same inclusions appear in the head **R7**, which is from a pottery context dated late 1st to possibly mid-2nd century A.C. The upper part of the face is not preserved, but the round shape, plump cheeks, and short nose suggest a child's head.

---

[6] *Agora* VI, pp. 9–11, cf. esp. pl. 5.

[7] On Roman coroplastic imports in Corinth, see *Corinth* XII, p. 21.

[8] E.g., *LIMC* II, 1984, pp. 55–56, nos. 424–454, pls. 40–43, s.v. *Aphrodite* (A. Delivorrias et al.); Winter, *Typen* II, pp. 208–213.

[9] Cf., e.g., a type found in small Roman bronzes: Hölscher 1967, pp. 37, 47, pl. 4:3.

[10] E.g., *Gods Delight*, pp. 124–131, nos. 19, 20, with bibli-

ography on p. 127. In general on Africans in Roman art, see Snowden 1976, esp. pp. 212–245.

[11] *Corinth* XII, p. 59, no. 429, pl. 39 (MF-5454); pp. 60–61, no. 449, pl. 41 (MF-1524, both are heads); a crouching African child, C. K. Williams and Zervos 1989, p. 20, no. 19, pl. 7 (MF-1988-14).

[12] Himmelmann 1983, pp. 64–67; Rolley 1986, pp. 218–220.

[13] E.g., Barr-Sharrar 1987, p. 78, no. C178, pl. 53, dated first half of the 1st century A.C.

The two draped fragments **R8** and **R9** could belong to the same large, thin-walled female figurine, although they do not join. **R8** shows a full-breasted figure wearing a peplos over a chiton. The double garment and the thick, deep V-shaped fold of the neckline recall Hellenistic drapery as, for example, in the "priestess" **H395**. If **R9** belongs to the same figurine, a mantle was draped around the hips and knotted at the left side. One thinks of the knots on Isiac costume, but they are usually at the breast. **R10** is merely an arm at statuette scale, but its short sleeve indicates that this figurine also could have been wearing a similar costume. **R11** is another arm of a statuette, but extended forward and draped in a mantle.

The figurines of fine fabric, almost certainly of local origin, are somewhat more coherent in terms of typology and style. Although not enough material has been recovered to identify workshops, the qualitative difference between the barely articulated Artemis **R16** and the nicely modeled, carefully retouched children **R17** and **R18** indicates either that more than one workshop was active or that figurines in this fabric and small scale were made over a span of time. There is also some difference in the degree of fineness of the fabric, **R15** being slightly finer than the others, **R14** a little coarser. The backs of these figurines usually were molded, and the mold join sometimes is visible when it was not trimmed smoothly. In the Corinthian Hellenistic workshops, when backs were molded, the joining techniques were usually much better. **R14** shows surface blisters, indicating the use of a plaster mold. In Athens also, plaster was used as an alternative material for molds during the Roman period.[14] As in the case of the Corinthian Middle Hellenistic figurines, surface polishing may have removed the blisters from some plaster-molded figurines (see pp. 16–17), but terracotta molds certainly continued to be employed in Roman times.[15]

Two different but related Aphrodite types were produced. **R13** is a fragment of a type with the left arm raised to the hair, while the right hand grasps the mantle around the thighs. Better-preserved examples have been found in Corinth: the possible mold sibling MF-1981-1 (Pl. 77) and an example from the excavations East of the Theater, in a context of the second half of the 2nd century A.C.[16] In another fragment (**R14**), the drapery appears to have been held in place only by a knot over the pubes, and both missing arms probably were raised to the hair. This "Anadyomene" pose of the arms is found in other Roman Aphrodite figurines from Corinth but in variant types, completely nude and with dolphin or herm supports.[17] Both types, with one hand to the hair or both, are known in renderings in other media.[18] The Corinthian coroplasts were therefore drawing ideas from the common artistic pool of the period.

Among the figurines of fine fabric are also two different Artemis types, both fragmentary. The original form of **R15** can be restored through a complete example in Corinth (MF-1156 [Pl. 77]). The fragment preserves a torch blazing just beside her hair at the left side, as in the Middle Hellenistic "priestess" **H395**; the top of her quiver is visible above the right shoulder. From the complete example one can add a knee-length chiton with an overfold to the hips, a patera in the lowered right hand, and a dog standing at the right. Despite the long artistic gap of the interim period, the typically Corinthian long, straight-sided, full-jawed, large-featured facial type reappears once again. A similar type from the excavations East of the Theater is from a context dated to the second half of the 2nd century A.C.[19] A similar type also was known at Myrina.[20] **R16** preserves the lower part of the second Artemis type, showing a dog seated at her right and a high, rectangular base molded at the top and bottom. **R16** and the

---

[14] *Agora* VI, p. 3.

[15] E.g., *Corinth* XII, p. 63, nos. 477–481, pls. 45, 46.

[16] C. K. Williams and Zervos 1986, p. 154, no. 15, pl. 33 (MF-1985-48); also MF-1985-49.

[17] *Corinth* XII, p. 55, nos. 378, 379, pl. 34 (MF-4406, MF-5099).

[18] Both hands to the hair, e.g., *LIMC* II, 1984, pp. 76–77, nos. 667–687, pls. 66–68, s.v. *Aphrodite* (A. Delivorrias et al.); one hand to the hair, *LIMC* II, 1984, p. 79, no. 705, pl. 71.

[19] C. K. Williams and Zervos 1986, p. 157, no. 23, pl. 34 (MF-1985-14).

[20] *Louvre* II, p. 83, no. MYR 198(190), pl. 101:f; there dated perhaps too early, to the end of the 1st century B.C.

Aphrodite **R13**, which are similar in fabric and in the dull impression, could have been made in the same workshop.

The two children (**R17** and **R18**) are the best-made figurines among those of fine fabric. They are probably mold siblings; from the two, the type from the thighs downward can be reconstructed. The chubby legs seem to belong to a child of less than five years, probably a boy, since little girls usually were not represented nude. The child leans on a low pillar support, and the whole is raised on a typically Roman high, rectangular base, molded at the top and bottom. The base **R19** is included here, in spite of the loss of the figurine it supported, for the sake of the possible relief decoration on the front panel and the animal feet.

The following three figurines are discussed here by virtue of their hard-fired, pale fabric, although differences in subject or scale separate them from the other figurines of fine fabric. **R20** represents a child older than **R17** and **R18**. The figurine is of a type known in small bronzes and sometimes called the "child orator"; this name arises from the combination of a boy's narrow-shouldered, plump-bellied anatomy, with a pose and mantle arrangement best known in portraits of the great intellectual figures of the Greeks. A good example is a fine Late Hellenistic or Roman bronze in Boston, thought to represent a schoolboy presenting an exercise in rhetoric;[21] although the pose of the arms is reversed, the bronze shows attenuated proportions like those of **R20**. Another figurine of this type but of different fabric (MF-10767) is from a tomb in Corinth.[22]

Two heads (the helmeted **R21** and the Pan **R22**) are larger in scale. Only the upper part of the helmeted head **R21** is preserved, and the coiffure is so poorly detailed that it is uncertain whether the head is male or female. The Athenian helmet would be appropriate for a representation of Athena or Roma,[23] but the subject also could be a warrior. The head of Pan (**R22**), like the Aphrodite **R14**, retains the surface blisters left by a plaster mold. The facial features of the Pan are well articulated and detailed, suggesting that the mold was taken from something like the handle mask of a bronze vessel[24] or perhaps an ivory relief.[25]

The remaining figurines are different from the above two groupings of figurines made of coarse and fine fabrics and also are different from one another in their individual combinations of subject, fabric, and scale. **R23** is from a pottery context terminating in the Early Roman period; if it is properly placed after the interim period, it should belong to the 1st century A.C. In spite of the flat chest, it is likely to represent a woman, since both the androgynous shape of the body and the long, drooping folds are paralleled in Early Roman portrait statues of women.[26]

R24 is, unfortunately, only a fragment of a head of large scale and probably good quality. In spite of the sensuousness of the mouth, the round jaw, small chin, and almost pursed lips suggest that the head is that of a small child. Of similar statuette scale is the hand **R25**; the short, plump fingers look like those of a child. Something has broken from the palm, either an object held in the hand or the top of the support on which the hand rested. The former is probably the case, since a bracelet was incised only on the inner side of the wrist, suggesting that it was visible and hence held upward.

The two fragmentary mantled female figurines (**R26** and **R27**) are assigned to the Roman period with some hesitation. They are of a fabric resembling the earlier fabric 1 (see p. 11), and the subject, in which one arm pulls down on the mantle as if in a sling, is certainly at home in the Hellenistic period. Nevertheless, when viewed beside the Corinthian Hellenistic figurines with similar mantle arrangements (**H100–H105** [see pp. 143–144]), certain differences become

[21] *Master Bronzes*, p. 136, no. 137; see also Comstock and Vermeule 1971, p. 77, no. 80; *Walters Art Gallery*, p. 74, no. 158, pl. 34.
[22] Grave 1962-23; the lower chronological limit is the 1st century A.C., but the figurine is from disturbed fill.
[23] For Roma, e.g., *Gods Delight*, pp. 333–336, no. 64. A

similar, better-preserved head, MF-71-219, was found in the Gymnasium excavations, in a context dated 4th century A.C. but with earlier material: Michaud 1970, pp. 953, 955, fig. 139.
[24] Cf. Tassinari 1993, I, e.g., pl. CVII:4, 6.
[25] E.g., D. B. Thompson 1959, no. 43 (2nd century A.C.).
[26] E.g., Horn 1931, pp. 75, 81, pl. 41:3.

apparent. The Hellenistic figurines are draped with the mantle close around the neck, while in **R26** and **R27** the sling arm pulls the top of the mantle down to reveal the V-shaped folds of the chiton neckline. In addition, the folds are rather thick and fit awkwardly over the contours of the figure, unlike the more organically coherent Hellenistic renderings.

    R28 is another fragment that could be misplaced in this chapter. It represents a standing female figure, her hand propped on a short support at the left side, with a mantle draped around her hips. Unfortunately, the fabric cannot be identified owing to the use of preservative to protect the colored paints. The rendering is crude and could be late, but the coroplast used a very bright blue paint known in Hellenistic figurines (see p. 14). Unless the technique of using this paint was revived in Roman times, this figurine could be Hellenistic. The final figurine fragment is an Artemis (**R29**), which is similar to **R15** in its complete form (Pl. 77) in the torch at the left side, the high boots, and the long overfold, but it is larger in scale, coarser in fabric, and more static in drapery style.

CATALOGUE

For an explanation of the conventions employed in this catalogue, see the Introduction, pages 20–22.

R1   Standing Aphrodite(?)   Pl. 73

MF-10331. Lot 870. Preserved: front–right shoulder and left breast to waist. P.H. 0.041 (size 2–3). Fabric coarse, reddish brown, with abundant small to medium gray and brown inclusions, voids. Nearly solid. Sides of torso trimmed flat.

    Nude torso. Right arm probably raised. Little anatomical detail; breasts high, rather flat.

    See pp. 312, 313.

R2   Nike(?)   Pl. 73

MF-10947. Lot 1945. Preserved: right leg to ankle, drapery at right side. P.H. 0.068 (size 3). Fabric as **R1**. Nearly solid. Back handmade, flattened, rough. Added: drapery.

    Nude right leg is bent loosely, as if no weight is placed on it; figure perhaps flying. Panel of drapery at right side shows looped folds, as if originally held out in right hand; curving motion folds at bottom of panel, as if windblown.

    See pp. 312, 313.

R3   Grotesque head   Pl. 73

MF-69-306. Lot 6214. Preserved: head and neck. Beard chipped. P.H. 0.038 (size 3–4). Fabric coarse, reddish brown, with some small to medium gray and white pebbly inclusions, voids. Solid. Back probably handmade, rounded. Added: strips of hair at top, beard. Tooling on hair.

    Projecting ears. Nose bulbous. Mouth open, twisted to side. Bumpy forehead; head bald, with a few slashed locks of hair on top of cranium.

    See p. 313.

R4   Grotesque head   Pl. 73

MF-14031. Lot 2107. Preserved: front–cheeks to chin. P.H. 0.04 (size 4). Fabric as **R3**. Hollow. Thick-walled.

    Caricature of African face. Chin small; features fill face. Nose wide, flat, with flaring nostrils. Mouth wide, with thick, parted lips.

    See p. 313.

R5   Grotesque head   Pl. 73

MF-69-400. Lot 6215. Preserved: top of head, forehead, right eye. Max.P.Dim. 0.048 (size 4?). Fabric as **R3**. Hollow. Thick-walled.

    Mass of short, curly locks of hair, bound with horizontal fillet across top of bumpy forehead. Eye large, heavily rimmed.

    See p. 313.

R6   Nude male bust(?)   Pl. 73

MF-11900. Lot 2107. Preserved: front–shoulders to waist, arms to biceps. P.H. 0.051 (size 3). Fabric coarse, reddish brown, with some small to medium white, red, and gray inclusions, voids. Hollow. Thick-walled. Added: protrusion on left shoulder.

    Molding rim preserved around shoulders, arm stumps, sides of chest, and bottom of waist, indicating that figure originally had neither arms nor a lower torso. Protrusion on left shoulder may be either a long lock of hair or the end of a fillet.

    See pp. 312, 313.

R7   Head of child   Pl. 73

MF-73-122. Lot 73-143. Preserved: front–face from cheeks to chin, most of neck. P.H. 0.031 (size 3–4). Fabric coarse, reddish brown, with sparse small white, red, and gray inclusions, voids. Hollow. Thick-walled.

    Full cheeks; jaw rounded. Nose wide, possibly upturned. Lips full.

    See pp. 312, 313.

R8   Draped female figurine   Pl. 73

MF-14029. Lot 2107. Preserved: front–part of chest, including left breast. P.H. 0.039 (size 3–4). Fabric coarse, reddish brown, with sparse small white and dark inclusions, voids. Hollow. Thin-walled. Tooling on folds.

    Thick V-shaped fold at neckline, with lighter slashed folds above, probably peplos worn over chiton. Figure full breasted. Perhaps from same figurine as **R9**.

    See pp. 312, 314.

R9 Standing draped female figurine(?) Pl. 73

MF-14030. Lot 2107. Preserved: front–drapery fragment. Max.P.Dim. 0.03. Fabric as **R8**. Hollow. Thin-walled.

Knot of drapery with curving folds, perhaps from mantle draped across hips and knotted at left side, with vertical folds of mantle end falling from knot. Perhaps from same figurine as **R8**.

See pp. 312, 314.

R10 Standing draped female(?) statuette Pl. 73

MF-14028. Lot 2107. Preserved: right arm, to wrist. P.H. 0.113 (size 4). Fabric fairly coarse, reddish brown, with sparse small dark inclusions, voids. Upper arm hollow.

Angle of break suggests that upper arm was held down at side of figure; forearm slightly extended forward. Smooth short sleeve.

See pp. 312, 314.

R11 Standing draped female(?) statuette Pl. 73

MF-14033. Lot 1945. Preserved: front–left forearm and elbow, with drapery fall. Missing hand. P.H. 0.076 (size 4?). Fabric coarse, reddish brown, with some small to medium white and gray inclusions. Hollow. Thick-walled.

Left forearm extended forward. Mass of folds, presumably of mantle, originally carried across waist, draped over arm into vertical fall at side of figure. Folds flat, summarily rendered.

See pp. 312, 314.

R12 Head of Matrona(?) Pl. 73

MF-14035. Lot 4344. Preserved: back of head. Missing top of crown. P.H. 0.041. Fabric coarse, orange (5YR 6/6, grayer), with gray core, some small white and gray pebbly inclusions, voids. Hollow. Tooling on plaits.

Squarish in section; cranium flat. Long plaits marked with diagonal slashes. Lower part of crown preserved towards front.

See pp. 312, 313.

R13 Standing Aphrodite Pl. 73

MF-14032. Lot 869. Preserved: head, with shoulders and left arm; to waist in back. Surface worn. P.H. 0.074 (size 2–3). Fabric slightly coarse, fired hard, creamy buff, interior surface orange-buff, with some small gray and sparse small sparkling inclusions, voids. Hollow. All parts rendered in same mold. Back molded, flattened. Molding rim not trimmed.

Left arm bent; hand raised to shoulder, lifts long lock of hair. Right upper arm at side. Sloping shoulders. Face oval. Features obliterated. Round earring. Complete type preserved in possible mold sibling MF-1981-1 in the Corinth collection (Pl. 77, torso nude, right hand grasps mantle around thighs). Dull impression.

See pp. 256, 312, 314, 315.

R14 Standing Aphrodite Pl. 73

MF-73-118. Lot 73-144. Preserved: hips to feet. Missing front of feet and hem. P.H. 0.062 (size 2). Fabric fairly coarse, fired hard, creamy buff, with some small white and gray inclusions, voids. Nearly solid. Back molded, flattened. Mold joins pared. Blisters on surface indicate use of plaster mold.

Weight on left leg; right knee slightly bent. Mantle gathered around hips into large knot at center, from which cascade of zigzag folds falls to hem. Folds radiate from knot down legs. Since mantle is not held up by hands, both arms probably were raised.

See pp. 256, 312, 314, 315.

R15 Standing Artemis Pl. 73

MF-11863. Lot 2164. Preserved: head to shoulders, with top of torch and quiver; to waist in back. P.H. 0.051 (size 2–3). Fabric fairly fine, creamy buff, with sparse small white and dark inclusions. Hollow. Thick-walled. All parts rendered in same mold. Back molded, flattened. Molding rim not trimmed.

Torch at left side, with flame beside head; two horizontal ridges on torch below flame. Quiver behind right shoulder. Face oblong, wider at temples, with low, triangular forehead. Features smeared. Coiffure parted at center; long locks of hair to shoulders in front. Headdress unusual, consists of wide band with vertical divisions resembling crenellations but topped by low stephane. Fabric finer than **R13**, but technique is similar. Possible later generation: MF-1156 (Pl. 77) and MF-2193 in the Corinth collection (*Corinth* XII, p. 55, nos. 384, 385, pls. 34, 35; no. 384 preserves entire figure, holding patera in right hand, "fawn" [more likely a dog] at right side; probably from a parallel mold series, since facial features are better defined).

See pp. 183, 312, 314, 316.

R16 Standing Artemis Pl. 73

MF-13983. Lot 2087. Preserved: front–thighs to base, with lower part of dog at right side. P.H. 0.087 (size 2). Fabric as **R13**. Hollow. Thin-walled. Front mold ends at left side with a short return, thus very flat; mold seems deeper at right side.

Weight on right leg; left leg bent, slightly advanced. Wears short garment to knees and boots. Dog seated on base at right side. Base high, slightly splaying, with faint, flat molding at top and bottom. Dull impression.

See pp. 183, 312, 314–315.

R17 Standing child Pl. 74

MF-70-262. Lot 6507. Preserved: knees to base. Missing front of left leg, most of support. Mended. P.H. 0.073 (size 2–3). Fabric slightly coarse, orange-buff, with some small white and gray inclusions, voids. Nearly solid, base hollow. Back molded, rounded. Tooling on toes.

Chubby, babyish nude legs; right knee bent; left foot advanced. Pillar support at left side has base in two degrees. Child stands on high rectangular base, with moldings in two degrees at top and bottom. Probable mold sibling: **R18**.

See pp. 312, 314, 315.

R18 Standing child Pl. 74

MF-14027. Lot 2107. Preserved: thighs to ankles. P.H. 0.053 (size 2–3). Fabric slightly coarse, fired hard, greenish buff, with sparse red inclusions, voids. Nearly solid. Back molded, rounded.

Probable from same mold as **R17**. Left leg advanced; both knees slightly bent. Top of pillar support has molding in two degrees. Drapery folds(?) atop pillar.

See pp. 312, 314, 315.

R19 Base Pl. 73

MF-14026. Lot 2088. Preserved: base, with bottom of figurine. P.H. 0.054. Fabric fairly fine, fired hard, gray, with orange core. Hollow. Thin-walled. Figurine and base originally rendered in same mold. Back molded, rounded; mold join visible at right side. Closed underneath.

High, splaying base, flat in front, rounded in back. Design in relief on front panel unclear, may include two frontal animal paws at bottom.

See pp. 17, 312, 315.

R20 Standing draped male figurine (a boy?)   Pl. 74

MF-13819. Lot 3230. Preserved: shoulders to ankles, to bottom in back. P.H. 0.116 (size 2–3). Fabric fairly fine, fired hard, grayish buff to orange-buff, with sparse small dark inclusions, voids; surface probably polished. Hollow. Thick-walled. Back handmade; upper back flat, more rounded below. Mold defect or distortion of surface at right hand.

Weight on left leg; right knee slightly bent. Right arm folded over chest; hand at neck. Left arm bent, forearm extended forward. Elongated figure, with narrow, sloping shoulders, slightly protruding abdomen; shoulders bent backward. Figure closely wrapped in mantle, which falls to ankles. Right hand pulls at fold around neck from beneath cloth; lightly modeled looped folds from right elbow across abdomen; diagonal folds radiate from left hip to right knee and lower leg; left hand lifts cloth from beneath into narrow drapery fall to hem, with zigzag folds at bottom. Similar in type: MF-10767 in the Corinth collection (more exaggerated proportions and pose, probably later in date).

See pp. 312, 315.

R21 Helmeted head   Pl. 74

MF-72-66. No context. Preserved: front–head and neck. Missing top of helmet. P.H. 0.051 (size 3–4). Fabric fine, fired hard, gray (10YR 5/2, burned?). Hollow. Thin-walled.

Face squarish, with very low forehead. Features indistinct. Flat, squarish curls frame forehead; possible long locks of hair at sides. Helmet of Athenian type, with pointed visor. Dull impression. Similar in type: MF-71-219 in the Corinth collection.

See p. 315.

R22 Head of Pan   Pl. 74

MF-11860. Lot 2168. Preserved: front–forehead to beard. P.H. 0.039 (size 3–4). Fabric fairly fine, fired hard, buff. White slip. Hollow. Blisters on surface indicate use of plaster mold.

Prominent cheekbones. Beetling brows overhang eyes. Nose wide, flat. Drooping moustache over parted lips; lower lip full. Curly hair and beard. Horn at right side of head.

See p. 315.

R23 Standing draped female(?) figurine   Pl. 74

MF-13750. Lot 3410. Preserved: shoulders to thighs, with upper part of back. Missing left hand, part of drapery over left side of chest, fragments of front at waist level. Mended. P.H. 0.119 (size 3–4). Fabric slightly coarse, orange-buff to orange, with sparse small dark inclusions, voids. White slip. Hollow. Back probably molded, flattened. Round vent, diam. 0.033. Added: drapery over left side of chest and over left wrist. Tooling on folds.

Left arm at side; forearm slightly raised. Right forearm folded over chest. Elongated figure, with narrow, sloping shoulders. Heavily draped in mantle; cloth draped from right

hip to left shoulder and arm, around back over right shoulder and arm; end of mantle draped in curving diagonal folds from right forearm to left wrist, leaving left hand free. V-shaped neckline of undergarment visible; right hand holds edge of cloth from beneath; catenaries over abdomen; diagonal folds over right hip and radiating downward from left hip. Folds heavily slashed.

See p. 315.

R24 Head of child   Pl. 74

MF-73-121. Lot 73-144. Preserved: front–mouth to chin, part of neck. P.H. 0.04 (size 4–5). Fabric fairly coarse, laminated in fracture, orange, with gray core, sparse small dark inclusions, voids. Hollow. Thick-walled.

Jaw rounded, with small chin. Full, well-shaped lips, parted, almost pursed.

See p. 315.

R25 Hand, probably of child   Pl. 74

MF-11832. Lot 2088. Preserved: left hand. Missing part of wrist, thumb. P.L. 0.058 (size 4–5). Fabric slightly coarse, orange-brown, core and surface of palm orange, with some small white and gray inclusions, sparse small sparkling inclusions, voids. Hollow. Thick-walled. Two molds, back of hand and palm. Added: object in hand. Tooling on fingers, bracelet.

Plump, short hand, with fingers held flat, thumb extended. Fingernails, first joints, and dimpled knuckles rendered. Underside of fingers tooled before object of unknown type placed in hand. Narrow bracelet in incised ladder pattern on inner side of wrist.

See p. 315.

R26 Standing draped female figurine   Pl. 74

MF-13854. Lot 1953. Preserved: shoulders to waist. Missing part of right hand. P.H. 0.065 (size 3–4). Fabric fine, orange-buff (similar to fabric 1). Hollow. Back handmade, flat. Round vent, diam. 0.029. Added: right hand.

Left upper arm at side. Right arm folded across waist. Figure short waisted, broad shouldered. Mantle draped over shoulders; right arm caught in sling; hands pulls down taut diagonal folds from both shoulders, revealing V-shaped fold of chiton neckline; bunched folds under left arm. See also **R27**.

See pp. 315–316.

R27 Standing draped female figurine   Pl. 74

MF-13855. Lot 3230. Preserved: shoulders to left breast and waist at right side, with upper part of back. Missing right hand. P.H. 0.057 (size 3). Fabric fine, grayish buff, with gray core, slightly burned (similar to fabric 1). Hollow. Thick-walled. Back handmade, flattened. Top of round vent preserved, diam. ca. 0.023. Added: hand. Tooling on folds.

Type, proportions, venting, and fabric similar to **R26** but smaller, thicker-walled.

See pp. 315–316.

R28 Standing draped female figurine   Pl. 74

MF-69-85. No context. Preserved: front–left hip, with hand, upper part of support. P.H. 0.054 (size 4). Fabric treated with preservative. White slip. Bright blue paint on drapery, pink on hand, red on support. Hollow. Thick-walled. Added: side of pillar. Tooling on folds, hand.

Left hand rests on top of pillar support. Thick roll of mantle folds draped probably from right hip; folds around hand. Vertical folds of chiton above roll. Folds deeply cut, angular.

See p. 316.

R29 Standing Artemis Pl. 74

MF-14034. Lot 2104. Preserved: front–left side from hip to calf, part of torch. P.H. 0.064 (size 3). Fabric sandy, light orange. Hollow. Thin-walled. Tooling on folds.

Left leg bent. Short garment falls to knee, with overfold to top of thigh; widely spaced vertical incisions for folds. Boot reaches mid-calf; horizontal band at top of boot, with semicircular tab projecting from center of upper edge, vertical incisions below. Torch at left side; reeds shown by vertical, binding by horizontal incisions.

See pp. 183, 316.

VIII

SUMMARIES

THE FIGURINES AND THE CULT

Throughout the preceding chapters, in discussions of different aspects of the figurine types represented at the sanctuary, interpretations of meaning in relation to the cult were proposed when evidence seemed sufficient to allow them. Since the organization of this study by iconographic types has resulted in the physical separation of these interpretive attempts, they are here gathered together in an overall synthesis, to determine how the figurines illuminate the rituals and underlying ideas of the cult. Page references in parentheses refer to more detailed discussions in the above chapters, although for complete information the reader should refer to the general index. Keeping in mind that the figurines cannot explicate all aspects of the cult, since they did not necessarily play a role in all rituals, in this chapter I will try to determine, on the basis of the coroplastic and associated evidence, when in the course of the year and for what purposes figurines were offered at the sanctuary. The definitive statement regarding the nature of the cult as a whole must await the final volume of the sanctuary excavation report,[1] which will gather together all of the evidence: the rather slim literary and epigraphic data, the architecture, the use of space, the different categories of images and votive gifts, and the analyses of organic materials.

Since the conclusions reached in this summary are based mainly upon the figurines, although supported when possible by other evidence, they are subject to revision when the sanctuary with its rich finds is studied as an entity. Nevertheless, given that the very large quantity of figurines found in the sanctuary demonstrates the importance of this class of votives in its rituals, that the offering of votives was a central ritual act for worshipers at Greek sanctuaries,[2] and that figurines were important carriers of spiritual expression, their evidence inevitably will play a significant role in the final interpretation. It is more difficult to derive evidence for the cult from the Archaic figurines, since there are fewer types and these tend to be generic, but whenever they are useful, Archaic types are included in this discussion.[3] It is important to emphasize at the start that ancient written evidence for the function and significance of figurines is very scarce. Hence all discussions like the present one must depend upon inferences drawn from the figurines themselves, supplemented by comparative evidence.

The discussion will begin with a definition of the functions of figurines in the ancient Mediterranean and Near East and then will move on to methodological questions regarding interpretation and the use of supporting evidence; a consideration of figurine types; and an evaluation of the information the figurines provide about the nature and conduct of the cult.

FUNCTIONS OF FIGURINES

It may help to consider first the functions terracotta figurines historically served and the limitations of their evidence. Prehistoric figurine types consist mainly of animals and human females, often with more or less exaggerated sexual characteristics and occasionally shown in the act of giving birth. There are relatively few clearly male figurines; some are without defineable gender. These early figurines are sometimes found in concentrations and circumstances that can

---

[1] Forthcoming in a later fascicle of *Corinth* XVIII, by Ronald S. Stroud and Nancy Bookidis.

[2] Burkert 1985, pp. 68–70, 92–94.

[3] Publication of the Archaic figurines is forthcoming.

be identified as cultic, but scattered finds in settlements could have had other uses (e.g., as toys),[4] although perhaps still with underlying spiritual and cultural import. When traceable at a single site for a long period of time, the pace of development and change appears to have been very slow and the pull of tradition very strong.[5] For subsequent periods, the possibility remains of some everyday use, but the bulk of excavated material comes from graves or the often large votive deposits of sanctuaries; intact figurines in museum collections are likely to have been robbed from graves. When found in homes, figurines and other small sculptures are thought to have had a votive as well as a decorative purpose.[6] Although the repertoire of types increased greatly, particularly in the 4th century B.C. and later, the traditional repertoire remained strong, with types persisting virtually unchanged, sometimes for more than a century after they were stylistically outdated or with old-fashioned elements clinging to new creations.

Although the vast amount of material dating to the periods following the Bronze Age and the incomplete record of publication have so far precluded definitive statistical analysis, the general assumption is probably correct that figurine types remained predominantly female throughout the history of production. The assemblages of some cult places, however, such as those of the Kabeirion at Thebes[7] and to a lesser extent the Asklepieion at Corinth,[8] have produced mainly male types. On the basis of its gender, pose, costume, and attributes, a figurine often can be associated with the worship of a particular deity or at least with a type of deity serving a particular function. Whatever the name of the deity, that function often is connected in one way or another with fertility, as illustrated by the cycle of birth, reproduction, and death.

The view that terracotta figurines found in sanctuaries were merely cheap substitutes available to everyone in place of more valuable offerings,[9] such as live sacrificial animals or statues, is probably an oversimplification. Animal figurines certainly could be interpreted in this way, given the costs of animal sacrifice;[10] that they were indeed dedicated as substitutes has been proven by inscriptions on Mesopotamian dog figurines of the Bronze Age.[11] Small terracottas, however, were made long before large-scale dedications at sanctuaries became status symbols. In the historical periods, we do not know that the rich who paid for large-scale dedications did not also offer figurines. Further, some terracotta figurines are large, elaborately designed, highly detailed, painted, and even gilded creations that could not have been cheap. Others, such as articulated "dolls," have no known monumental or precious counterparts. The point is that figurines, which were probably the oldest continuously produced art form in the ancient world, were from their first use in cult meaningful images in their own right and not merely small substitutes for other images.

In spite of a general similarity of purpose, patterns of dedication of figurines were not uniform over the entire Greek world but show considerable variation from place to place in the quantity of figurines offered and, when the recipient deity is known, in the specific figurine types deemed appropriate. Therefore, parallels from other sites may provide clues for interpretation but do not necessarily determine definitively what that interpretation should be. In the present study, we are fortunate to have an assemblage from a sanctuary whose principal resident deities are

[4] For the current state of study of prehistoric figurines, see N. Hamilton et al. 1996; Talalay 1993, especially pp. 37–44 on the question of use. For examples of early figurines in religious contexts, see Renfrew et al. 1985, pp. 209–280; Bolger and Peltenburg 1990; Postgate 1994.

[5] E.g., Bikai and Egan 1996, pp. 516–517 (Neolithic animal figurines from 'Ain Gazal).

[6] *Coroplast's Art,* p. 43, with bibliography; Harward 1982, pp. 121–149 on the religious rather than purely decorative function of small sculpture in domestic contexts, and pp. 51–56 on figurines specifically; the evidence for figurines is less conclusive than for sculpture.

[7] *Kabirenheiligtum* V.

[8] *Corinth* XIV, pp. 138–143.

[9] Burkert 1985, p. 93 (the substitute object is "a sign of the sign").

[10] On the economics of sacrifice, see Jameson 1988; Van Straten 1995, pp. 170–186.

[11] Postgate 1994, pp. 176–180. For a terracotta bull placed on an altar at Kommos in the Late Hellenistic period, see Shaw et al. 1978, p. 143, pl. 40:f.

identifiable on literary and epigraphic grounds, so that the interpretation of its votive figurines rests on a firm basis.

INTERPRETATION OF THE FIGURINES[12]

In light of recent work on the "reading" of images in ancient art as cultural signs,[13] few would now accept the view that the iconography of votive figurines is arbitrary and carries no particular cultic significance, that figurines are essentially interchangeable in the gift-giving process.[14] This view probably was encouraged by the often seemingly unrelated iconography of the rich variety of types, which seemed to point in no particular direction. When studied with attention, however, the images do fall into interrelated groups with apparently clearly directed meanings. Most semiological study so far has centered on Attic vase painting, because networks of images, that is, interacting figures in different combinations, are thought to give up their meanings more readily than isolated images.[15] Figurines presumably count as isolated images, but when they are discovered in the course of archaeological excavation, an interpretive context is provided by where and how they were found and with what other artifacts.

In place of the narrative that a vase painting supplies within its frame is the narrative that the dedicator of a figurine in effect devises when the gift is offered. The figurine is, in a sense, an extension of the worshiper and is deposited along with personal hopes, not only in a prescribed cultic act. The dedicator may construct the narrative according to a cultural formula or may have in mind a personal narrative composed from the needs of the self and close associates. Thus the offering of a figurine becomes a private as well as a public ritual.[16] The private aspects of dedication remain unknown, except insofar as they intersect the public, but it is important to see dedicators as individuals interpreting the cult for themselves and not as prisoners of ritual.[17] This personal element may in part explain the diversity of figurine types offered apparently for the same purpose. A given figurine type did not necessarily carry exactly the same symbolic force for everyone, and more than one type could express, with different emphases, the same idea.

The interpretation of figurines in a cultic context falls into two parts, functional (i.e., expressive of a specific ritual act) and symbolic[18] (i.e., expressive of underlying concepts inherent in the cult). The figurines represent only a portion of the symbolic content of the cult, however, which would include as well the conformation and use of the ritual space, the speech and actions of the participants, and the other categories of votive offerings. The symbols taken together form a code, which is recognized by the participants and passed on to the young.

---

[12] The following works have been particularly useful and inspiring for this project: Firth 1973 on social symbols; Bryson 1991 on the relation of pictorial images to society; Turner 1967 and Turner 1969 on the use of symbols in ritual; Douglas 1975 on the cross-cultural analysis of symbols; Jung 1967 on symbolism as a projection of the human psyche; and Sperber 1975, Boyer 1993, and Boyer 1994, pp. 47–60, on cognition and religious symbolism. Boyer, building on Sperber's work, has argued that some aspects of religious learning are genetically rather than culturally determined; see now also Burkert 1996. Although a theoretical model applicable to material such as ours has not yet appeared in the literature, a biological underpinning could be germane to fertility cults because of their antiquity and fundamental concern with survival. On the interpretation of figurines in funerary contexts, see Graepler 1997, pp. 149–159.

[13] E.g., Bérard et al. 1989; Sourvinou-Inwood 1991.

[14] Rouse 1902, pp. 391–393; *Corinth* XV, ii, pp. 7–9; *Corinth* XII, p. 17; against this idea, C. K. Williams 1986, p. 23, note 48.

[15] Bérard et al. 1989, p. 25.

[16] On the convergence of the public and private elements of worship in Corinth at the Sacred Spring, see Steiner 1992, pp. 405–406.

[17] For ethnographic evidence of differences in interpretation among participants in the same ritual, see, e.g., Richards 1982, pp. 165–166.

[18] In this study, the term "symbol" is synonymous with "sign"; for a summary of the various usages of the term "symbol," see Nöth 1990, pp. 115–120. It is also possible to define a symbol as only one kind of sign. For a clear explanation of the distinction among different kinds of signs (signals, icons, and symbols), see Hodder 1987, pp. 2–3; this usage is not followed here. The utility of symbols is succinctly described by Turner (1969, p. 25) as follows: "What is made sensorily perceptible, in the form of a symbol. . ., is thereby made accessible to the purposive action of society, operating through its religious specialists."

The code is socially accepted but is subject to change over time; new meanings may be given to old symbols, new symbols may be introduced to express existing ideas, or new symbols may express entirely new ideas.

To give an example of function and symbol in figurines, the presence of hydriaphoros types may be functional, representing a ritual procession of female water carriers (see p. 38). On the other hand, the type may be only symbolic, the hydria symbolizing the abundance of water needed for agricultural fertility/for the bridal bath/for the rituals surrounding death. The type also may be functional and symbolic simultaneously. The hydriaphoros is a good example of the multivocality of symbols, which can have more than one meaning even within a single ritual situation;[19] in this case, the symbol functions simultaneously as a reminder of agriculture, marriage, and death.

THE USE OF SUPPORTING EVIDENCE: MATERIAL EVIDENCE

Of the supporting evidence available for the interpretation of the figurines, the strongest is from Corinth itself. It consists of other finds from the Acrocorinth sanctuary; finds from other cultic sites in the city, such as hero shrines and the Asklepieion; and Corinthian vase paintings showing cultic scenes. Less strong are objects of reported Corinthian provenience in museum collections, especially bronze caryatid mirrors and the later folding mirrors with relief covers. I have made use of these, with caution, when they portray subjects related to the figurines. Winter's 1903 compendium of figurines housed in European collections or on the market at that time includes a substantial number of figurines of reported Corinthian provenience or attributed to Corinth. On the basis of comparisons with figurines later excavated at Corinth, most of the dispersed figurines do indeed appear to be Corinthian. For this reason, it may not be necessary to be completely skeptical of the reported Corinthian provenience of bronzes, particularly when there are links with figurines in subject and style.

Caution is also in order for iconographic comparisons with non-Corinthian material, since there is no guarantee that the meaning of a figurine type remained constant from place to place.[20] On the other hand, it would be perverse to deny, for example, that figurines of pigs from Corinth symbolize fertility, because there is no direct evidence for this interpretation stemming from Corinth itself, when the meaning seems to be pervasive elsewhere in the Greek world.

THE USE OF SUPPORTING EVIDENCE: LITERARY EVIDENCE

Regrettably, the iconography of the figurines from the Acrocorinth sanctuary must be studied, for the most part, without the enrichment of a large body of literature.[21] All the written material cited in the chapters above is non-Corinthian in origin, and sometimes it is late in date as well. Although literary references to figurines are rare, there are nevertheless some useful intersections with literary sources.[22] For example, Kallimachos' description of votaries in the *Hymn to Demeter* (see p. 30) helps to identify some of the figurines as such. The accounts of votives in the *Anthologia Palatina* (see pp. 125, 194) point to possible divine recipients for the objects held by some of the figurines. On the other hand, it is difficult to recognize specific myths of Demeter and Kore in the figurines, which have, in any case, little capacity for narrative presentation. For example, is it valid to connect the Corinthian figurines of votaries carrying piglets with the late *aition* that links the ritual of throwing piglets into a chasm at the Athenian Thesmophoria with the swallowing up of the swineherd Eubouleus and his animals (p. 265)? Probably not, because of the lateness of the source.

---

[19] Turner 1969, pp. 41–42.
[20] On the uses and pitfalls of cross-cultural comparison, see Golden 1992.

[21] For the written sources relating to the worship of Demeter and Kore on Acrocorinth, see *Corinth* XVIII, iii, pp. 1–8.
[22] See the index of literary sources cited on p. 369.

THE USE OF SUPPORTING EVIDENCE: ETHNOGRAPHIC EVIDENCE

Although evidence of cult practice in modern times offers no proof of ancient rituals or the thought behind them, ethnography nevertheless is a rich source of analogous material, which enables the researcher to offer plausible if not provable explanations.[23] At the disposal of the ethnographer are spatial data, indicating how objects actually were placed and manipulated, as well as the interpretations of their acts by the participants themselves. Such information can offer very useful insights. Also useful are the apparent survivals into modern times of pagan customs and symbols, transferred from the original context into the orbit of Christian ritual or popular superstition. In the absence of documentation of historical links, the value of such analogies can be denied, however, no matter how striking they may be.[24] In the present study, references are given to analogous material when it may prove useful, for example, with regard to apotropaic symbols and gestures (p. 143), the preparation of special cakes for festivals (p. 273), or the use of figurines in rituals (p. 337, note 97).

FIGURINE TYPES: CHOICE OF TYPES AND THE QUESTION OF CHANGE

When Socrates visited a country shrine near Athens (Plato, *Phaedrus* 230b), he recognized that it was sacred to Acheloös and the nymphs by the nature of its figurines and statues. Figurine types, then, during this period, were expected to be characteristic in some way of the cults in which they were offered. Unlike votives with intrinsic value, which could have been offered at any shrine for the sake of the material, regardless of iconography, terracotta figurines have value mainly in the subjects they represent. Not all deities received terracottas as a matter of course, but in cults related to fertility, figurines were customary dedications. We know from archaeological evidence that a single type could be offered at shrines sacred to different recipients. For example, horse-riders were a common dedication at the Sanctuary of Poseidon at Isthmia, where they are accompanied by bulls and model boats.[25] Horses and bulls are closely associated with Poseidon in myth, and the reference of boats to the sea god is obvious. Horse-riders, however, also were frequently dedicated to heroes in Corinthian shrines, where they are part of a very different assemblage, including banqueters, goddesses, and snake-and-helmet stelai (p. 60). The horse-rider figurines are identical in both cases, but their contexts determined their different meanings. The cult is defined, therefore, not by one type but by the assemblage of different types offered, which represents the collection of pertinent symbols. In shrines of Demeter in different places, the figurine assemblage varies but generally with overlapping types.[26] For example, the figurines from the Thesmophorion in Eretria[27] are predominantly female, like those of the Acrocorinth sanctuary, and include the familiar hydriaphoroi, protomes, seated females, and children; proportionately, however, there are many more children and young women than at Corinth. The Eretrian assemblage lacks a series like the Corinthian piglet carriers, but it has a group of female musicians, a type not found in the Acrocorinth sanctuary. The assemblage from the Thesmophorion at Bitalemi,[28] on the other hand, includes many piglet carriers, as well as protomes and seated goddesses, and also kourotrophoi, which are not an Acrocorinth type (pp. 70–71).

The fundamental question must be, how did the Greeks decide which types to offer in a shrine? Were the design parameters set solely by the artisans? How much were the worshipers involved? Individuals could not easily commission the firing of a few figurines, owing to the process of repetitive molding and the large number needed to fill a kiln sufficiently to make the firing economically worthwhile, but they were the purchasers and presumably could reject a type

[23] On the use of ethnography in the study of Neolithic figurines, see Talalay 1993, p. 40.
[24] On the use of later analogies and the limitations of such information, see Hill 1994, pp. 87–89.
[25] Mitten 1962 (1963, p. 309).

[26] Cole 1994, pp. 203–204, with bibliography. On types from Demeter sanctuaries in Asia Minor, see Töpperwein-Hoffmann 1971, pp. 131–132.
[27] *Eretria*, pp. 23–53, 69–93, pls. 16–31.
[28] Kron 1992, pp. 624–629.

they thought unsuitable. If we accept figurines as symbols, and allow that these symbols were culturally determined, by what mechanism were they created? Did the priestesses deliberate on what types were suitable and then commission them in quantity from the workshops?[29] An otherwise empty area beside the central staircase in the Acrocorinth sanctuary is thought to have held booths for selling votives.[30] The notion that the sanctuary may have profited from the sale of votives opens the possibility that its officials had some control over the wares. On-site purchase of at least some of the types is favored by the presence only at the Acrocorinth sanctuary of one of the most popular types dedicated there, the young female votary carrying a piglet; it has as yet been found nowhere else in Corinth. On the other hand, without input from the cult authority, the artisan, working within the confines of his skills and available workshop materials, and knowing what had been done before and what would and would not express the code, could have created a suitable type and tried to market it at the site during festivals, directly from his workshop, or at a shop in the marketplace. The close association of certain types with particular shrines in Corinth suggests that figurines tended to be sold at or near the site.[31] Even a possible shop deposit in the South Stoa, with figurines of the 3rd century B.C.,[32] is matched by the closely similar figurines of a nearby votive deposit.[33]

After the Archaic period, the pace of change of figurine types quickened; more specifically descriptive types were created, often with variants. A similar phenomenon has been noted among Geometric small bronzes, which show a development from generic, multipurpose types to others more specifically referring to the cult.[34] New types need not necessarily show change or discontinuity in the cult, although they may, but they may also reflect some impetus for intensifying worship in one way or another. For example, by the second quarter of the 5th century B.C., new types were introduced to the sanctuary that were also offered elsewhere in Corinth in hero shrines. These types were the banqueters (see p. 65) and the lingering Archaic standing "korai," which probably represent Aphrodite or Kore (see p. 23). During the Archaic period, the handmade horse-rider figurine had been the typical dedication to heroes, both in their own shrines and at the Acrocorinth sanctuary (p. 60). The new types appeared at a time of rebuilding and expansion in the sanctuary;[35] they did not replace but supplemented the horse-riders. The use of banqueters and "korai" elsewhere in Corinth as dedications for heroes suggests that in the early 5th century B.C. this aspect of ritual at the sanctuary may have been enhanced. For the banqueters, Tarentine types were the source (see p. 66); the molds for the "korai" appear to have been developed in connection with bronze mirror caryatids (see pp. 26–27). It is not clear why hero cult may have become more prominent at the sanctuary at this time, but if it is true, the local artisans responded to the need for figurines by adapting available materials with some connection to the new purpose, to create acceptable types.[36]

If it is accepted that changes in figurine types could reflect changes in cult practice, certain developments can be seen over time. The introduction of new rituals or the intensification of some activities did not necessarily last forever. For example, by the later 4th century B.C. there is almost no evidence for hero cult among the figurines. Similarly, there is coroplastic evidence for the initiation of youths (see p. 61) and bridal rituals (see pp. 337–338) beginning in the 5th century B.C., and for the initiation of younger boys in the 4th century B.C. (p. 188), but by the later 3rd century B.C.

[29] This idea was suggested to me by Jean M. Turfa.
[30] *Corinth* XVIII, iii, p. 201.
[31] Merker, forthcoming.
[32] Davidson 1942, pp. 126–127.
[33] Broneer 1942, pp. 145, 148, fig. 7. The relationship of cultic requirements to the production and distribution of figurines in Corinth is discussed in Merker, forthcoming.
[34] Langdon 1990a.
[35] *Corinth* XVIII, iii, pp. 427–428.

[36] For the role of the painter in a similar process in more recent times, see Bryson 1991, p. 70: "The painter assumes the society's codes of recognition, and performs his or her activity within their constraints, but the codes permit the elaboration of new combinations of the sign, further evolution in the discursive formation. The results of painting's signifying work, these are then recirculated into society as fresh and renewing currents of discourse."

all this has disappeared. Since the local coroplastic industry was reinvigorated with new types, including some pieces of high quality, in the later 3rd century B.C. (see p. 249), workshop inactivity was not the reason for these changes. Either the conduct of some rituals changed so as to exclude the dedication of figurines or perhaps the ceremonies were discontinued at this location, in favor of other shrines. In any case, the major new Middle Hellenistic type does not represent a votary like those so popular in Classical and Early Hellenistic times, but either a priestess or the goddess Demeter herself or perhaps a combination of the two (pp. 254–255).

There were three major periods of rebuilding and expansion of the sanctuary: the late 6th–early 5th century B.C.; the second half of the 5th century B.C.; and the late 4th–early 3rd century B.C.[37] It is difficult to connect coroplastic changes directly with these building periods, since we do not know whether the new structures housed cultic activities that employed figurines; further, other explanations could account for coroplastic change. Nevertheless, new types appeared in the sanctuary by the second quarter of the 5th century B.C., which could have arisen from increased participation in rituals following the opening of new facilities. In addition to the banqueters and "korai" mentioned above, other lingering Archaic types were introduced, as well as the earliest in a long series of peplos-figurines (see p. 23). To some extent, the growth in the number of figurine dedications in the 4th century B.C. could have resulted from late-5th-century B.C. building activities, although this increase may be related to the wealth of the period (p. 115). Similarly, new figurine types introduced in the later 4th or early 3rd century B.C., such as the votaries carrying piglets (see pp. 117–124), could have been related to building at that time but also could have been stimulated by the closing of the Potters' Quarter workshops in the 320s B.C. and the consequently increased coroplastic activity elsewhere in Corinth. The Macedonian presence on Acrocorinth in this period might also have been a factor in the appearance of new Aphrodite types at the sanctuary in the Early Hellenistic period (p. 170).[38]

THE NATURE AND CONDUCT OF THE CULT, AS SEEN IN THE FIGURINES

The principal difficulty in the use of figurines to illuminate cultic activities at the sanctuary is the very long period during which figurines were dedicated, from the late 7th to the mid-2nd century B.C., with some slight revival of the custom in the Roman period. Since no single type survived the entire life of the sanctuary, we are dealing with a patchwork of types, all with a rather loose chronology (see pp. 5–7), and so it is difficult to gain a clear picture of cultic activities during any one period. Further, figurines speak to us only of rituals in which they were offered, leaving aside other activities in which they played no part. With that caveat, the discussion of this subject will first consider deities: how representations of deities can be recognized; which deities are represented in different periods, and their iconographic forms; and what roles they may have played in the cult. A discussion of the participants in the cult will follow: their gender and age, their possible reasons for visiting the sanctuary, which deities they honored, and any evidence for specific rituals and festivals.

The Deities

One of the most difficult tasks in studying this group of figurines is identifying the deities among them. To begin with, there is sometimes a blurring of identity between the deity and the worshiper, and it is not always clear whether an object carried is a votary's gift or a deity's attribute (p. 24). A few cases are more certain: the Classical hydriaphoroi who carry water must be worshipers (p. 24); the Classical enthroned female figures wearing the polos must be goddesses (p. 24), although this type is generic and can only be assigned a goddess' name by

---

[37] *Corinth* XVIII, iii, pp. 427–433.

[38] For apparent changes in cult practice in the Forum area after the Macedonians came to Corinth, see C. K. Williams 1978, p. 12.

the context in which it is found, if at all. The wearer of a polos is probably a goddess, although not necessarily (p. 254, note 22), and not every goddess wears this headdress, but the combination of polos and dignified enthronement should be a sign of divinity. At the Acrocorinth sanctuary, this type presumably was intended to represent either Demeter or Kore, the flower or bird sometimes held favoring the latter; the flaring polos, shaped like a kalathos, could suggest either goddess, depending upon whether it is thought of as a symbolic container for grain (Demeter) or fruit and flowers (Kore, pp. 47, 125). A similar ambiguity can be found in another type wearing the polos, the standing "kore" (p. 23, note 1), which was created early in the 5th century B.C. in a lingering Archaic style and was among the most popular types dedicated at the sanctuary. Most members of this group hold attributes (fruit, flowers, birds) that would serve for either Kore or Aphrodite, but the rooster held by a few ought to signify Kore. Does this mean that all figurines of this group were intended to represent Kore or only those with roosters? Were the goddesses even intended to be distinguished from one another at all?[39] Perhaps the very ambiguity of identifiers in most of the likely goddess figurines shows that the worshipers did not need or want them, that the generic symbols fixed the meaning sufficiently and the participants completed the cultic narrative with their own thoughts.

In the absence of attributes, because the type lacks them or the figurine is fragmentary, it is necessary to fall back on pose and costume alone. These elements can be helpful if the type is found in a recognizable cultic or mythological scene in votive or document reliefs, in vase painting, or occasionally in monumental sculpture. Although most of this evidence is non-Corinthian, and can be ambiguous when different deities share iconography, it is used of necessity. Such evidence is quite helpful when one seeks representations of Demeter, even though her iconography sometimes overlaps that of Hera in drapery arrangement and pose.

The deities recognizable among the figurines from the sanctuary are the following: Demeter, Kore, Aphrodite, the nymphs, Artemis, Nike, Athena(?), Cybele(?), Eros, and Dionysos and his circle (Silenos, satyrs, Pan). Of these, the most important in terms of frequency of representation and occasional supporting evidence are Demeter, Kore, Aphrodite, the nymphs, Eros, and Dionysos. To give a few examples of similar pantheons, near and far, a partly overlapping array is found at the cave at Pitsa; primarily sacred to the nymphs, there is evidence also for Dionysos, Demeter and Kore, and Eileithiya (p. 178). In the West, a similar, though not identical, range of deities was represented at Morgantina: Persephone (but not Demeter), Hades(?), Artemis, the nymphs, Eros, Nike, Athena, and Herakles.[40] An example of an eastern shrine is the *favissa* at Kharayeb in Phoenicia, which is thought to have belonged to a fertility cult honoring both Egyptian and Greek deities (p. 190). The deposit includes figurines of Demeter (but not Kore), Dionysos, Aphrodite, and Eros, forming a smaller group than the Acrocorinth pantheon, but one that includes most of its important deities. The assemblage from Kharayeb also resembles the Acrocorinthian in the dedication of figurines of children and grotesques. A literary source for an array of deities invoked together with Demeter and Kore may be found in Aristophanes' *Thesmophoriazusae* (lines 969–994), in which the chorus calls on Hera, Artemis, Hermes,[41] Dionysos, Pan, and the nymphs, as well as Demeter and Kore. Clearly, dedications representing an assortment of deities are to be expected in a Sanctuary of Demeter and Kore,[42] but not all were necessarily formally worshiped beside the nominal owners of the shrine. Dionysos and Aphrodite, perhaps, have the strongest claims to actual rituals there.

---

[39] On the difficult identification of this type, see Zuntz 1971, p. 177.

[40] *Morgantina*, pp. 81–94.

[41] A bearded sculptured head from the sanctuary (SF-64-5, Stroud 1968, p. 326, pl. 97:c) is thought to be from a herm (personal communication, Nancy Bookidis).

[42] Alroth 1987; for "visiting" deities in four shrines of Demeter, see p. 17, table 6.

Demeter

The cult title Epoikidie mentioned by Hesychios for Demeter at Corinth has been linked by Stroud and Bookidis to her worship on the Middle Terrace in a small cult building (hence the diminutive form), as well as the taking of communal meals in the houselike setting of the dining rooms on the Lower Terrace.[43] This interpretation need not contradict the one suggested by the figurines, of Demeter as the patroness of the household and its concerns (p. 70), since religious symbols are polysemous (p. 324). Perhaps the epithet, originally assigned to the goddess of agriculture as a description of the place in which she was worshiped locally, gradually took on another meaning associated with the household, as is implied by the name itself.[44] The local custom of setting up shrines over destroyed houses[45] suggests that a certain sanctity was attached to the household, which may have been extended to this cult. In any case, there are two functions relating to the household that are illustrated by the figurines, fertile marriage (pp. 127, 170) and the nurturing of children (p. 70). The figurine types involved are young female votaries carrying piglets and probably representing brides (pp. 117–124); a possible representation of Demeter in the unveiling pose usually associated with Hera as a bride (p. 36); kalathiskos dancers referring to weddings (pp. 58–59); and baby boys, the hoped-for result of marriage and a source of anxiety for parents (pp. 68–73). These functions would have been analogous to the successful planting and raising of crops and the husbandry of animals, which were sought with other types of dedications, including miniature hydriai, hydriaphoroi (pp. 38–42), and handmade quadrupeds,[46] the last mentioned probably referring to the increase of herds.[47] The narrative that the dedicator brought to the ritual, however, is likely to have been deeper than the seeking of Demeter's patronage for a successful (i.e., fertile) marriage and through the identification of the young human bride and her mother with Kore and Demeter, to have embodied aspects of the feminine social and psychological experience.[48]

There are no certain representations of Demeter among the figurines. The most likely candidates are standing peplophoroi and mantled figures with drapery arrangements and poses characteristic of Demeter on votive and document reliefs, including the above-mentioned type in the act of unveiling or perhaps leaning on a scepter and pouring a libation. The fine, large **H85**, if correctly identified as Demeter, probably also represented the goddess pouring a libation (pp. 139–140). A large but fragmentary seated peplophoros (**C93**) could have been Demeter by virtue of its size, pose, and costume, and because it was handmade and of high quality, as if a rather special piece of work (p. 46). Another way in which Demeter might possibly have been portrayed is as a seated, mourning figure (p. 157). The pig figurines (pp. 265–266) probably were dedicated to Demeter, although Dionysos also received pig sacrifice.

Kore

The difficulty of distinguishing one goddess from another has already been discussed (p. 43); the goddess most affected is Kore, whose attributes overlap both Demeter's and Aphrodite's. The lingering Archaic standing "korai" and the seated goddess wearing the polos (p. 23, note 1) could represent Kore.[49] Another candidate is the seated goddess wearing a low crown decorated with rosettes; a complete example in the Corinth collection (MF-1, Pl. 75) has a fruit, probably a pomegranate, on her lap (pp. 46–47). Even here, however, the same attributes could also speak for Aphrodite. The low crown is found on a fragmentary 5th-century B.C. kotyle from the

[43] *Corinth* XVIII, iii, pp. 2, 72, note 23, p. 411.
[44] On the worship of Demeter unconnected with agriculture in Sparta, see Parker 1988, p. 103: "The cycle of crops was, in a sense, a metaphor, through which the cult of Demeter dealt with other concerns and satisfied other needs."
[45] C. K. Williams 1981, p. 418.
[46] Publication forthcoming.
[47] Talalay 1993, pp. 43, 46–48.
[48] For this experience as reflected in the *Homeric Hymn to Demeter*, see Foley 1994, pp. 103–137.
[49] On the probable association of the "korai" with Demeter and Kore, whether or not they represent either of the goddesses, see *British Museum* I, p. 246, under no. 904.

sanctuary, inscribed with the name of Persephone; here the crown is surmounted by a row of short vertical lines (for leaves?).[50] Another type that could represent either Kore or Aphrodite wears a chiton and a distinctively arranged mantle known in sculpture for both goddesses (p. 148). At Lokroi the personalities of Aphrodite and Kore can be distinguished from one another,[51] but at Corinth the iconography of the two goddesses is inextricably combined, perhaps because the figurines do not provide the evidence of narrative representation available on the Lokroi votive plaques. There is at least one rendering at the sanctuary of a Kore type known in reliefs, wearing a closely fitting mantle wrapped under one arm (p. 139); this is probably the only certain representation of Kore. Heads with a combination of polos and corkscrew curls are likely to represent Kore, since the polos usually signifies divinity, and the curls may be known elsewhere as a bridal coiffure (p. 133).

If the seated goddesses represent Kore, she would have been portrayed as Queen of the Underworld, and her chthonic, fearful aspect would have been emphasized. It is curious that there is no sign of Hades, who is enthroned beside her on the Lokroi plaques, unless **C278**, an enthroned bearded male wearing a pilos, represents him (pp. 79–80, 332). There are a few figurines of roosters, however, and rooster plaques (p. 269), showing that some people dedicated one of the typical attributes of the chthonic deities and therefore probably had the Underworld in mind.[52] Otherwise, Kore would have functioned in a very different role, as the prototype of the girlish, unwilling bride. The protomes may have been dedicated to Kore, in light of their frequent use in her worship in the West, where they are believed to represent Persephone as a bride (p. 74). Evidence for a race run by youths in honor of Kore (p. 61) suggests that at least some of the Classical and Hellenistic figurines of youths could have been dedicated to her, either before or after the race.

Cult Statues(?)

Unfortunately, there is no type that can reasonably be considered a copy of a cult statue of either Demeter or Kore. We are not even certain exactly where such an image might have been housed in the Greek sanctuary.[53] For Roman times, the head of a probable cult statue has been recovered,[54] but we do not have the benefit of information from Pausanias, since he records that the statues were not on view during his visit.[55] Only the standing "korai" and the seated goddesses show any consistency of representation among numerous renderings, as if they might be imitating important works. The "korai," however, probably were developed from bronze mirror caryatids (pp. 26–27), and although the seated goddesses could imitate a cult statue, the type is generic, and the stylistic and formal changes in the heads from the 5th to the 4th centuries B.C. speak of a type more capable of development than one fixed to a cult statue.

Aphrodite

Although Aphrodite's functions and iconography sometimes overlap those of Demeter and Kore, she is unquestionably portrayed in Hellenistic figurines, almost nude, leaning on a column, her torso framed by the folds of a mantle (pp. 172–173). That figurines of Aphrodite should have been dedicated at the Acrocorinth sanctuary is not unexpected, given her close relationship with Persephone at Lokroi (p. 170), but the quantity of figurines referring to Aphrodite in one way or another is surprising. In addition to the nude renderings, there are others draped in a mantle with no garment beneath, which have been assigned to Aphrodite on the basis of a similar type identifiable in a mythological context in vase painting (pp. 135–136). Still other draped female

[50] *Corinth* XVIII, i, pp. 133–134, no. 292, fig. 34.
[51] Sourvinou-Inwood 1978.
[52] For Hades beside Kore at Lokroi, together with a rooster, see Prückner 1968, e.g., pp. 75–76, type 86, fig. 14, pl. 22.

[53] *Corinth* XVIII, iii, pp. 70–72.
[54] *Corinth* XVIII, iii, p. 333.
[55] For the text and commentary, see *Corinth* XVIII, iii, pp. 3–4.

figurines also could represent Aphrodite, on the basis of drapery arrangement, type of support, or the presence of Eros (p. 174). Heads wearing a crown or polos with crenellations are likely to be Aphrodite because she was the city goddess (p. 271). It was also suggested above (pp. 171–172) that some of the articulated "dolls" were dedicated to Aphrodite rather than to Kore.

The possible cultic role of Aphrodite at the sanctuary has been discussed in detail above (pp. 169–170). Very briefly, in sum, while Aphrodite's persona in myth and art projects a sophisticated, freewheeling sexuality, which is directly opposed to the innocence of Kore and the responsible motherhood of Demeter, nevertheless, as protectress of the city and kourotrophos in her own right (p. 71), her role must have been to reinforce, not diminish, the social functions of Demeter as patroness of marriage and nurturer of children. Indeed, her presence may have enhanced the acceptability of marriage by emphasizing its erotic as well as its social aspect. Further, her worship had a chthonic aspect,[56] and her images, viewed in the context of Kore's sanctuary, would have expressed for the worshiper the unity of erotic and chthonic that is fundamental in Greek religion.[57]

Nymphs

The association of nymphs in myth and art with love, marriage, and the protection of children could account for the dedication of figurines representing them at the sanctuary; they also received bridal(?) sacrifice at the nearby Pitsa cave (p. 188, note 430). The nymphs are recognized here in seminude figures perched on rocky seats (pp. 178–180).

Artemis

Among the earlier figurines, the only goddess identifiable with certainty, by the uniqueness of her hunting attributes, is Artemis, although in only a few 5th-century B.C. lingering Archaic examples (MF-12009, MF-13561).[58] In addition, there are a few possible representations of the Hellenistic period (p. 183). It is certainly not uncommon to find "visiting" deities represented in the sanctuaries of other gods,[59] and the association of Artemis with children and coming-of-age, overlapping one of the apparent concerns of this cult, probably is the reason for her representation among the figurines. The chthonic association of Artemis with Hekate could also have been a factor. She may have been more prominent after the rebuilding of the sanctuary in Roman times, since there are three clearly identifiable Roman Artemis figurines, a substantial showing among the proportionately very small number of figurines preserved for that period (pp. 314, 316).

Nike, Athena(?), and Cybele(?)

The ties of the remaining three goddesses to this cult are rather weak, to judge from the figurines. The few images of Nike are small and of poor quality (pp. 183–184); the two possible figurines of Athena are a fragment of a female figure holding an owl, and a Roman helmeted head (pp. 183, 315); Cybele is accounted for only in reminiscences of her iconography in the Middle Hellenistic "priestess" type, but if worshipers recognized her because they were familiar with images of the Mother of the Gods at her nearby shrine, a mental link might have been made with Demeter (pp. 254–255). The thymiaterion type with a female bust and a floral cup is known in the worship of Cybele in Asia Minor (p. 75, note 361), although the type could have been dedicated in the Acrocorinth sanctuary to Demeter or Kore as well. Of these three goddesses, Cybele is the one most "at home" in the sanctuary.

---

[56] C. K. Williams 1986, p. 12, note 5, with bibliography.
[57] Zuntz 1971, pp. 174–175.

[58] Publication forthcoming.
[59] Alroth 1987.

Eros

Among the small number of figurines representing Eros, no single predominant type emerges but rather an array of seated and flying types, including both youths and babies (pp. 181–182). In addition, at least one of the heads discussed under the category of children may represent Eros, although no attributes are preserved (p. 193). The potential association of Eros with this sanctuary is most obviously through Aphrodite, but he is also connected iconographically with Dionysos.[60] He may have been viewed here as Eros-Thanatos, and his chthonic as well as fertility functions emphasized.

Dionysos and His Circle (Silenos, Satyrs, Pan)

The worship of Dionysos at the Acrocorinth sanctuary is attested epigraphically (p. 76). Dionysos himself, however, is represented only in the form of masks (pp. 76–78) and perhaps as a baby, originally carried by Silenos (p. 196). Of his followers, there are a few figurines of Silenoi and satyrs from the Classical and Hellenistic periods (pp. 78, 199–200); Classical and Hellenistic figurines of Pan are also found (pp. 78–79, 199–200). The ties of Dionysos to the sanctuary are likely to have been strong through the association of his name and images with fertility and the Underworld. He paralleled Demeter in the provision of wine to her grain and was referred to as her companion (p. 76, note 370). He appears before the enthroned Persephone on the Lokroi plaques.[61] Evidence from Sparta and Olympia that Dionysos was a patron of prenuptial rituals for girls,[62] and from elsewhere that he may also have been concerned with rites of passage for youths and boys,[63] suggests that some of the cult activities of this nature at the sanctuary, evidenced by the numerous figurines of children and young people, may have been directed toward him. Two figurines of boys and one of a girl carry grapes, a symbol specifically associated with Dionysos (pp. 185, 188, 191, 194).

The large mask **C273** may have been affixed to a pillar image of Dionysos or perhaps was placed in a liknon during the ritual (pp. 77–78). If it was so used, it would have been a cult image rather than a dedication, unless it served both functions. None of the masks, large or small, can be dated later than the 4th century B.C., or perhaps the early 3rd, but the significance of this is uncertain, since references to Dionysos continue into the Hellenistic period through figurines of his circle or of actors and through offerings carried by votaries. In the Roman sanctuary, Dionysos must be the referent of a group of theatrical masks.[64]

Unknown Male Deity(?)

The enthroned bearded male figure wearing a pilos **C278** could perhaps represent Hades. Because similar figurines hold mortars, however, he may be instead a minor local deity whose name is not recorded but who functioned as a protector of the storage and processing of grain and as such could be honored under the wing of Demeter, the provider of grain (pp. 79–80).

The Hero(es)

The assemblage of figurines from the Acrocorinth sanctuary includes numerous examples of types associated elsewhere in Corinth with hero cult:[65] horse-riders (p. 60), Archaic goddesses with moldmade heads and applied necklaces on handmade bodies,[66] banqueters (pp. 65–68), lingering Archaic standing "korai" (p. 23, note 1), birds (pp. 268–269), a votive

[60] On the Eros-Dionysos link as seen in vase painting, see Albert 1979, pp. 49–189.
[61] Prückner 1968, p. 78, type 107, pl. 25:5.
[62] Serwint 1993, pp. 418–419.
[63] E.g., possibly in the Kabeirion at Thebes, Burkert 1985, p. 281; the subject is currently being researched by G. Ham, "Male Initiation Ritual in Dionysiac Cult," *American School of Classical Studies at Athens Newsletter* No. 36, Fall 1995, p. 5.

[64] Publication forthcoming with miscellaneous finds.
[65] C. K. Williams and Fisher 1973, p. 8, pl. 3 (the Heroon of the Crossroads); the typical vessel dedicated there is the mesomphalic phiale, which is also known in the Acrocorinth sanctuary: *Corinth* XVIII, i, pp. 31–34. On heroic assemblages in general, see Hägg 1987, pp. 95–96 on figurines.
[66] Publication forthcoming.

shield (p. 271), a few helmets, and a snake-and-helmet stele.[67] Although the goddesses and "korai" are generic types that could have been dedicated for other reasons, their presence in hero shrines together with more specifically "heroic" types suggests that at least some of these figurines from the Acrocorinth sanctuary also were dedicated to heroes. On the basis of the above types, it seems likely that at least one hero was honored there. Most of the horse-riders are Archaic (or surviving Archaic) handmade figurines, a type that was made at Corinth from the later 7th century B.C. onward. Until the Archaic figurines from the sanctuary are fully studied, their precise date of introduction will be uncertain, but if the horse-riders began to be dedicated in the sanctuary in the later 7th century B.C., together with another early type, the goddesses with moldmade heads and necklaces, the introduction of hero cult there could perhaps be approximately coeval with the beginning of the Heroon of the Crossroads in the Forum area, which shows similar figurines,[68] in the Early Corinthian period.

The presence of a heroon within or very close to a sanctuary of a major deity is by no means unusual.[69] To use an example from a Peloponnesian sanctuary, Pausanias (2.35.9) records that a temple of the hero Klymenos stood opposite that of Demeter Chthonia at Hermione and that he received sacrifices. Pausanias' further comment, that Klymenos is a cult title of Hades, suggests that a hero at the Acrocorinth sanctuary could have been similarly understood to signify Hades, who is not otherwise represented there, or to serve as an intermediary to the fearsome god of the Underworld. At Morgantina, Hades is thought possibly to have been represented as a youth.[70] On the other hand, the hero might be similar to the Eleusinian Triptolemos, emphasizing the agricultural rather than the chthonic aspects of the cult and serving as an intermediary to Demeter. In still another possible interpretation, the figurines might have been offered not to one specific cultic hero but to each family's ancestral hero, by way of placing the cult of the household under the protection of Demeter Epoikidie (p. 68).

It is worth noting that while the horse-riders, the goddesses, and many of the birds are Archaic productions, the banqueters, standing "korai," and the votive shield were not produced until the first or second quarter of the 5th century B.C. It may be concluded either that a change in the hero cult took place or perhaps that worship intensified at this time. The honoring of a hero or heroes may not have been part of the functions of the sanctuary to the end of its history, but it is not quite clear when the custom actually stopped. The handmade horse-riders may have been dedicated even into the 4th century B.C., as part of the conservative production of the Potters' Quarter workshops. After the demise of the Potters' Quarter in the 320s B.C., these handmade horse-riders were replaced by moldmade rider plaques produced elsewhere in Corinth; however, only one example of this new type was found in the sanctuary (pp. 271–272). Similarly, there is no clear evidence that the banqueter types, which also were made in the Potters' Quarter, were replaced by the larger, bearded banqueters with seated women at their feet, which are typical of the 3rd century B.C. (p. 67). It is therefore possible that in the later 4th century B.C. either the custom of dedicating figurines to a hero or heroes changed, perhaps becoming the offering of other, perishable votives of which we have no traces, or more likely, since the dedication of figurines was characteristic of hero cult elsewhere in Corinth both before and after this date, the cult was discontinued or moved to another, perhaps more easily accessible location. In the 3rd century B.C., deposits of the new "heroic" figurine types appear in the Forum area, suggesting new foundations there, especially in and near the South Stoa.[71] Conceivably, the political realities of the later 4th century B.C. influenced some changes in local hero cult, which we see reflected in the changing patterns of coroplastic offerings.

---

[67] Publication of the helmets and stele is forthcoming with the miscellaneous finds.

[68] C. K. Williams and Fisher 1973, pp. 6–12.

[69] Kearns 1992, pp. 77–93.

[70] *Morgantina*, pp. 88–91.

[71] Broneer 1942.

THE PARTICIPANTS, THE RITUALS, AND THE FESTIVALS

When figurines provide plausible information about the participants in a cult, they may do so indirectly. The presentation of votives was a highly personal affair, even though enacted in a public arena, often for publicly sanctioned purposes, since it was a direct communication from the votary to the deity, either requesting assistance or giving thanks for perceived help.[72] Because the transaction so closely involved the votary, one might assume that when a figurine represents a mortal, it must be the votary. A figurine need not represent a cult activity, however, but may only be symbolic of an idea embodied in the cult (p. 324). Further, in some cases, the subject clearly cannot be the votary; for example, when the subject is a baby, the dedicator is likely to be a parent or would-be parent. But whoever actually carried the figurine to the offering place, and whether the narrative is direct or symbolic, some information emerges about who participated in the rituals and for what reasons. Another related and also misleading assumption is that if the figurines from a sanctuary are predominantly female in type, the cult must have been celebrated mainly by women. To be sure, certain rituals celebrated in honor of Demeter in Athens and elsewhere were, on the basis of written evidence, restricted to women,[73] but votive reliefs show Demeter approached by whole families[74] or by groups of men,[75] not to mention the large number of male Eleusinian *mystai*. In addition, other deities appear to have been honored at the sanctuary besides Demeter and Kore, and masculine names of worshipers are recorded among the finds. Therefore, the relative paucity of male figurine types at the sanctuary could cause us to undervalue the participation of men in the cult.[76] In any case, that youths and boys participated in rituals at the sanctuary is fairly certain.

On the evidence of the terracotta sculpture, young (i.e., beardless) males and boys played a role in the cult, bringing offerings of small animals and other gifts.[77] This evidence is supported by the male figurine types, most of which are, indeed, youths and boys, although they do not correspond to the sculpture in style or detail. A fragmentary kotyle from the sanctuary, dated to the second quarter of the 5th century B.C. or slightly earlier, is painted with a scene of youths running to the right; another fragment of the same vessel shows the head of Persephone, identified by an inscription.[78] Since she faces left, the youths must have been running toward her, but since the vessel is so fragmentary, it is uncertain whether Demeter or another deity was also represented on it. This painting is thought to represent a cult activity of the sanctuary, although it is not clear how races could have been accommodated within its boundaries; the actual running may have been done outside the premises, perhaps on the way to the sanctuary in advance of the processions.[79] The youthful male figurines of the early 5th century B.C., which are nude but for a scarflike mantle over the shoulders, help to confirm the connection of the painting, in which the youths are similarly clad, with a cult activity at the sanctuary. Since nudity is consonant with initiation rituals (p. 61), it seems fair to suggest that this figurine type was dedicated to Kore at a festival incorporating social initiation rituals for youths.[80] The figurines

[72] For a useful collection of epigraphic evidence for the intent behind gift-giving, see Van Straten 1981, pp. 90–104.

[73] See examples in Bookidis 1993, pp. 50, 57, 60, note 5.

[74] E.g., a relief in Athens, Van Straten 1995, p. 291, no. R68, fig. 82.

[75] E.g., a relief from Eleusis, Van Straten 1995, p. 290, no. R64, fig. 84; in Paris, Hamiaux 1992, p. 216, no. 224. On male worshipers of Demeter, see Cole 1994, p. 204, note 21. Nearly 20 percent of the figurines from the Sanctuary of Demeter at S. Nicola di Albanella are male types: Cipriani 1989, especially pp. 140–141.

[76] The male figurine types from the Acrocorinth sanctuary, taken as a whole, would include not only votaries, but also deities, banqueters, isolated male heads, actors and grotesques,

and Archaic handmade horse-riders, which are not included in this volume. Evidence for participation in the cult, however, should be sought only among the votaries. Including both standing youths and boys, these number less than fifty figurines for the Classical and Hellenistic periods. For the Archaic period, there are only a few recognizable males, apart from the horse-riders; some of the handmade figurines are of uncertain gender.

[77] Publication forthcoming by Nancy Bookidis.

[78] *Corinth* XVIII, i, pp. 133–134, no. 292, fig. 34: Pemberton 1978, pp. 30–31, 33.

[79] On the processions, see *Corinth* XVIII, iii, p. 429.

[80] The bibliography of works on male and female initiation is considerable; for basic works and newer works with

presumably show the youths bringing offerings to Kore, either before or after the race; the simple headdress made of a strip of clay may have been intended as a wreath, perhaps of victory. The identifiable offerings are a rooster, which is an attribute of the chthonic deities, a lyre, an athlete's aryballos, and a knucklebone bag. The last three could perhaps be objects associated with the pastimes of youth, which were symbolically relinquished at the transition to adulthood (pp. 126, 194). An inscribed Corinthian aryballos from the Temple of Apollo showing a dancing chorus of nude youths[81] could perhaps be associated with initiations because of the nudity. Since the figures are slender and only slightly shorter than the adult flutist, they would be postpubescent, and comparable in age to the figurines of youths from the sanctuary. There is no evidence, however, to connect this event to the Acrocorinth rituals.

A few handmade Archaic nude male figurines may possibly be the forerunners of this type;[82] one member of this group is beardless and has long hair (MF-10374), and others have a strip headdress (e.g., MF-11053) like that of the Classical youths. If these figurines are indeed forerunners, initiations could already have existed in the Archaic period. Intermediate between these handmade figurines and the Early Classical type are two Late Archaic heads of youths (MF-73-97, MF-11856) and a fragmentary plaque (MF-11884), although only the plaque, which preserves nude legs and mantle folds at the side, has any real claim to be of a suitable type.

The 5th-century B.C. figurines of youths appear to be in their early teens. The dedication of similar figurines probably continued into the 4th century B.C., since they were made in the Potters' Quarter, which conservatively produced 5th-century B.C. types long after they were first designed. After the demise of the Potters' Quarter in the 320s B.C., a small number of figurines of nude youths takes the place of the Classical type, suggesting that the rituals for youths continued. Another group of semidraped youths is introduced, however, which does not fit into the athletic activities. What is interesting is that the Early Hellenistic nude youths are empty handed, while offerings very similar to those of the Classical youths are found in the hands of contemporary figurines of younger boys, not more than about six years of age, even when offerings such as athletic equipment are not really suitable. These boys are also nude, sometimes with a mantle over the shoulder. If these figurines can be trusted to describe the ritual, the youths may have continued to participate in races into the Early Hellenistic period, while the responsibility of carrying offerings to Kore was handed over to small boys, perhaps by way of marking the point in their lives at which they were separated from the *gynaikeion* and began their formal education.[83] Speaking generally of Greek religion, there is ample evidence in literary and artistic sources that children were included in ritual and were educated by observing the religious conduct of adults (p. 194).

On the basis of the slim evidence available, we can try to place these activities within the calendar year. One of the nude boy figurines (**H319**) and another semidraped figurine representing either a chubby youth or a boy (**H302**) carry grapes. Floral remains recovered from a limited area through flotation include grape, pomegranate, and fig, suggesting that one festival may have taken place in the late summer or early autumn,[84] although the physical evidence is very slight and such fruits could have been preserved into another season by drying or other means. The offering of grapes by the boys, taken together with nudity of most of the youths and the boys (which suggests reasonably warm weather) and the running of races (which would have been better accomplished on dry ground), suggests that initiation rites for young males may have taken place at this time. The grapes also make symbolic reference to Dionysos, who may

bibliography, see Brelich 1969, esp. pp. 14–44; Van Gennep 1960 (1909); Eliade 1958; La Fontaine 1986; Dowden 1989; Lincoln 1991; Richards 1982; Cole 1984; Serwint 1993; Vidal-Naquet 1986; Sourvinou-Inwood 1988; Vernant 1991; Brulé 1987; R. Garland 1990, pp. 163–198; Pinney 1993; Hatzopoulos 1994, esp. pp. 41–53.

[81] Roebuck and Roebuck 1955.
[82] Publication forthcoming.
[83] On the age of six as the desirable one for these changes, see Plato, *Laws* 7.794c; R. Garland 1990, p. 134.
[84] Bookidis et al. 1999, pp. 29–30.

have been honored at this festival as well as Kore, for the sake of the grape harvest; he is known to have been involved elsewhere in rites of passage (p. 332).

The only remaining substantial group of male figurines consists of the baby boys, who probably should be understood symbolically as wished-for, healthy children and could have been participants only insofar as babies may have been brought to the sanctuary for blessing. The custom of presenting babies to a goddess is documented in Corinthian vase painting in the late 6th to early 5th century B.C. (see below); it is also documented elsewhere, for example, figurines of women carrying small children on their shoulders were found at the Thesmophorion at Bitalemi, and there is an apparent survival of this custom at that site into modern times.[85] If the foregoing interpretation is correct, three ceremonies at the Acrocorinth sanctuary are indicated for a Corinthian boy, although the evidence belongs to different periods: he would have been brought as a baby by his mother, probably to Demeter or Kore, to increase his chances of survival (Late Archaic and Classical periods); at the age of about six he would have brought offerings, probably to Kore or Dionysos, to mark the beginning of the socialization process (Early Hellenistic period); and on reaching puberty, he would have participated in races in honor of Kore (Late Archaic period) and brought offerings to her (Classical period).

The Corinthian painted vases mentioned in the preceding paragraph are useful pieces of evidence; taken together, they are thought to depict a "Frauenfest."[86] Various theories have been put forward to identify the deity or deities being honored; the theory most cogently argued to date gives the festival to Artemis, but in light of the finds from the Acrocorinth sanctuary, this identification should be reconsidered. The question of how far vase painting is to be taken as literal representation of ritual is a difficult one,[87] but it seems best to take each painting or group of paintings as a separate case, depending upon other evidence. The Corinthian "Frauenfest" vases cannot be discussed in detail here, but briefly they appear to combine functional and signifying elements, nearly all of which can be accounted for at the Demeter sanctuary among the figurines or other finds: the predominance of women, the kourotrophic goddesses, the presence of little girls, the references to Dionysos, and dancing; the male banqueters could be associated with the hero(es) of the sanctuary; and the spinners[88] and the women carrying a robe could signify the work of women honoring Demeter of the Household (the Demeter or Kore on a Sam Wide group plate in Athens sits on a throne covered with a very elaborate cloth [p. 43]). Further, an example of the unusual bottle shape typical of some of the "Frauenfest" vases, unfortunately fragmentary but recognizable in shape, was found in the sanctuary.[89] If the connection between the "Frauenfest" vases and the sanctuary is correct, the paintings may help to explain the figurines of girls, although it must be kept in mind that the figurines are Early Hellenistic, much later in date than the vase paintings.

The girls on the "Frauenfest" vases are distinctly shorter than the women, reaching to the chests of the women on bottles in Béziers and Montpellier[90] and only to the waist on an example in London.[91] While the schematic drawing does not reveal their ages precisely, their relatively small size should indicate that they are intended to be very young, probably prepubescent.[92] The inclusion of prepubescent girls in rituals of Demeter and Kore is known elsewhere. For example, at the Thesmophorion at Eretria, where the figurine assemblage consists largely of children and young women, there are two female age groups, four–five and fourteen–sixteen years.[93] Three age groups are accounted for in the girls' races at the Heraia at Olympia, on the basis of literary

[85] Orlandini 1966, pp. 32–33, pl. IX.

[86] Amyx 1988, I, pp. 228–230; II, pp. 653–657, with bibliography; R. Hamilton 1989, p. 471.

[87] On this question, see R. Hamilton 1989; R. Hamilton 1992, esp. pp. 123–146; Pinney 1995.

[88] The spinners are identified as Moirai by Callipolitis-Feytmans (1970).

[89] *Corinth* XVIII, i, pp. 63, 114, no. 215, fig. 27, pl. 23.

[90] Jucker 1963, pl. 17.

[91] Jucker 1963, pl. 20:2.

[92] On determining the ages of girls in vase painting, see Sourvinou-Inwood 1988, pp. 33–37.

[93] *Eretria*, p. 23.

evidence (Pausanias 5.16.2–4), and have been proposed also for the girls' rituals for Artemis at Brauron.[94]   As analyzed by Sourvinou-Inwood, the groups consist of children below the age of ten, girls approaching menarche, and postpubescent girls. The figurines of young female votaries from the Acrocorinth sanctuary form two clear groups, one consisting of children of less than ten years, the other of young women in their mid- to late teens (pp. 126–127). Between these two groups are a number of less easily defined figures, with neither the stocky forms of children nor the shapely ones of young women; perhaps they are intended to show approaching adolescence, and if so, they could correspond with the middle group at Brauron. Unfortunately, these intermediate figurines are also of poorer workmanship than the others, which could account for the apparent differences. In the absence of clear evidence for three age groups, it is here assumed that there were only two, as at Eretria, pre- and postpubescent, until further evidence should prove differently.

In any case, there is no evidence at Corinth for a single ritual encompassing both groups, like the girls' races at Olympia and Brauron. Nevertheless, the crowning of the girls with wreaths on the "Frauenfest" vases is suggestive of agonistic victory and the possible running of races by at least prepubescent Corinthian girls. Wreaths could have been associated more generally with participation in a festival,[95] but the portrayal of the girls in the act of being crowned suggests that a more specific interpretation is permissible. It should be remembered, however, that the extant "Frauenfest" vases do not show running girls. Given that these scenes of crowning incorporate kourotrophic figures, the ritual for the younger, prepubescent girls could be construed as a form of social initiation, paralleling that suggested above for the boys of about six years, and preparing them at an early age for their future role in society. The myth of the rape of Kore has been interpreted to reflect initiation,[96] but this evidence does not help to explain the figurines, which represent girls younger than Kore at the time of her abduction. Nevertheless, the likely association of Demeter and Kore with female initiation on literary grounds is helpful. Some of the figurines of little girls, in spite of their youth, press one hand to the abdomen, in a gesture usually associated with pregnancy (p. 127). The inclusion in the "Frauenfest" paintings of prepubescent girls in a ceremony in which a goddess functioned as kourotrophos could clarify the gesture of the figurines. That is, in the joyful context of physical activity and celebration, the girls were shown, and they accepted, what their lives as adults would entail.[97] If little girls received their cultic and social lessons at the same time of year as little boys, the festival on the vase would also have taken place in the late summer or early autumn. One figurine of a seated little girl (**H339**) carries grapes, like the above-mentioned figurines of boys.

The figurines of the older group are very different, in that they show fully matured young women, who wear their hair unbound and carry piglets (pp. 117–124). If these figurines are not only symbolic and a specific ritual is being described, it is likely to have been bridal, parallel to the *proteleia* recorded for Greek marriage elsewhere (p. 119). That is, the figurines show that a sacrifice is about to be made, in this case a piglet, and the hair is about to be shorn. Although the customs of one polis cannot automatically be transferred to another, one may mention that the customary month for weddings elsewhere in Greece was Gamelion (January–February), the time of the sacred marriage of Zeus and Hera.[98]   Whether there was a specific festival in Corinth at which all prospective brides appeared,[99] or families came separately with their new brides,

---

[94] Sourvinou-Inwood 1988, pp. 25–30.

[95] On the use of wreaths in the cults of Demeter and Kore, see Blech 1982, pp. 252–257.

[96] Lincoln 1991, pp. 77–90.

[97] On ethnographic evidence for the aim of girls' social initiation rites being to emphasize the responsibilities of marriage

and adult life, and to reinforce the prevailing moral order, see Richards 1982; La Fontaine 1986, pp. 169–179. On the use of figurines to reinforce the lessons, see Cory 1956, pp. 52–65, 82–96, 114–125, 144–151; see also Talalay 1993, pp. 40–42.

[98] Deubner 1956, p. 117.

[99] On the Cretan custom of confining marriages to a specific

it is possible that the Corinthians also married at this time of year, and if this is true, this group of figurines may reflect rituals at the sanctuary during the winter. The bridal ritual is likely to have been addressed to Demeter, whose patronage of marriage is known elsewhere (p. 36) and in whose honor piglets were often sacrificed. As for the chronology of this ritual, figurines of young women with piglets are uncommon at the sanctuary before the later 4th century B.C. There is one Early Classical example (**C1**), but the gap between this one and the large Early Hellenistic group must be filled in mainly with a small number of Argive imports (pp. 286–287). Perhaps before the Early Hellenistic period, a different figurine type was offered by brides. Two possible candidates are the Classical figurines of young women similarly garbed in the unbelted peplos (pp. 29–30), but without offerings, and the articulated "dolls" (pp. 48–53). The series of votaries carrying piglets gradually diminished during the 3rd century B.C. Another piglet-carrying type, the Middle Hellenistic "priestess," followed, but it appears to have had a different meaning, which is discussed below (p. 340).

Another related, winter cult activity at the sanctuary might possibly be illustrated by the female figurines muffled in their mantles, especially the mantled dancers. When seen in context in vase painting or on mirror covers, muffled figures represent brides or Dionysiac revelers (pp. 152–153). The winter was the time of the Athenian Lenaia, which included the mountain revels of maenads and probably the erection of mask idols of Dionysos.[100] On the calendar relief in Athens, the emblem for the winter month of Gamelion is a mantled dancer (p. 153, note 235). If the Corinthians celebrated a winter festival, the mantled dancers from the sanctuary could perhaps represent the local Dionysiac revelers (pp. 152–153). The large mask of Dionysos **C273**, which is suitable for hanging on a pillar or placing in a liknon, could have been a ritual object in such a festival, at which the small masks of Dionysos (pp. 76–78) might also have been dedicated.

The visits of a Corinthian woman to the Acrocorinth sanctuary during her lifetime thus can be partially outlined by the finds. As in the case of the males (see above), the evidence is not chronologically consistent. Whether she was presented to the goddesses as a baby, as her brothers probably were, is unknown. Whether or not she was given formal education to parallel that of the boys, her education in her future duties as a wife and mother may have begun before the age of ten years (Early Hellenistic period). At that time, she may have been introduced, in the company of adult women, to the place in the sanctuary where kourotrophic rituals were held; it is possible that she participated in a race and was crowned if she won (Late Archaic period). We cannot know whether all girls of suitable age participated in such rituals, the wreathed girl on the vases then being symbolic of all the girls, or only one or a few. Neither do we yet know whether there were further rituals at or near puberty (see below), but at the time of her marriage in the middle to late teens, she returned to the sanctuary to sacrifice a piglet (Classical and Early Hellenistic periods) and to have her hair ritually cut (Early Hellenistic period). Thereafter, she would return as a mother to present her babies and later, to bring her children for initiation, to ask for children if necessary, and perhaps to participate in the dances or simply to honor the protecting deity of her household.

While the principal deities have been suggested, to whom the above-postulated rituals might have been addressed, such distinctions could not have been absolute. For example, as mentioned already, Aphrodite had a kourotrophic function elsewhere; Dionysos was associated elsewhere with girls' initiations, and the pig was also his sacrificial animal; Aphrodite and the nymphs also were associated with marriage, the latter at the nearby Pitsa cave. One has to assume that while the most popular types of figurines are likely to point to some consistent ritual use, the deities

---

time, see R. Garland 1990, p. 219; for the suggestion that bridal rituals at festivals point to group marriage, see Dowden 1989, pp. 200–201.

[100] Deubner 1956, pp. 123–134; Parke 1977, pp. 104–106; Simon 1983, pp. 100–101.

to whom they were addressed represented to the dedicators power over some facet of life also controlled by other deities.

The likelihood that these votives could have been applied to more than one deity, with an altered sense, is suggested by the case of the articulated "dolls," most of them nude, which were dedicated at the sanctuary in very large numbers. After years of study, there is still a question about this class of figurines that has not been satisfactorily answered, although it should be the clue to their meaning: that is, why are the limbs articulated? The human body is disjointed in other types, specifically in anatomical votives and also in Neolithic figurines that consist only of a partial body.[101] The fragmentation of the body in anatomical votives was meant to call attention to the part of the body that needed to be cured. The use and meaning of Neolithic partial figurines are still under discussion, but ethnographic evidence points to the widespread symbolic use of the human body and its parts.[102] At a superficial level, the movement of the limbs of an articulated "doll" may well have been entertaining, but this can hardly have been the reason why so many of this class of votives were dedicated. With more than eight hundred nude "dolls" surviving, thousands must have been brought to the sanctuary over the years. A clue to a deeper level of meaning may be found in the interpretation of the nude, Attic limbless "torso dolls" as girls' votives for a successful puberty.[103] In the articulated "dolls," a similar attention is drawn to the naked torso not by eliminating limbs altogether but by making them adjuncts to the centrally important torso. Just as figurines in modern African initiation rituals help to teach girls what will be expected of them as wives,[104] the ancient Corinthian "dolls" could have taught the powerful lesson that a girl's primary value resided in her nude torso, the vehicle for child-bearing and nourishment.[105] While the "dolls" may have conveyed these ideas to girls through their distinctive form, they still functioned as votive gifts. The receiving deities could have been Kore, through identification of the girls with her (pp. 49–50), or Aphrodite, who may have received the "dolls" that wear the elaborate coiffures of *hierodouloi*; if the "dolls" are to be identified with the young votaries, these coiffures transform them into *hierodouloi*, and the "dolls" might then be viewed as substitute dedications to Aphrodite in place of the girls themselves (pp. 171–172). However they are interpreted, it is clear that, although the term "doll" is a convenient appellation, these figurines were not toys in anything but a symbolic sense; in the context of the sanctuary, they were cult objects, whose special significance is shown by the large numbers in which they were dedicated.

Who dedicated these figurines? The girls who hold "dolls" on Attic grave reliefs are either adolescent or clearly prepubescent.[106] If a similar association obtained at Corinth, the articulated "dolls" may have been dedicated by girls at or approaching the time of puberty. After the demise of the Potters' Quarter, at which most of the "dolls" were made, in the 320s B.C., the type was replaced by seated "dolls," for which there is little evidence at the sanctuary; a few late, usually poor versions of the customary dangling type probably belong to the 3rd century B.C. Therefore, it is likely that the custom of dedicating "dolls" was rare after the later 4th century B.C.

The above discussion accounts for the major figurine types dedicated at the Acrocorinth sanctuary. Other, smaller groups point to activities generally associated with worship, such as water carrying, perhaps in procession (p. 38), which could have belonged to any set ritual,

[101] Talalay 1993, pp. 31, 49–50.
[102] Talalay 1993, p. 50, with bibliography.
[103] Reilly 1997.
[104] Cory 1956, pp. 52–65, 82–96, 114–125, 144–151.
[105] As Reilly (1997, pp. 164–165), working independently of the present study, has stated with regard to the Attic limbless "dolls": "These figures were icons or emblems of the desired qualities of femininity. In dedicating her votive she

probably learned the appropriate attitudes towards her body and sexuality. These figures taught her to desire the body that would enable her to fulfill the roles of bride, wife, and mother. The anatomical votive in particular, an image of the important parts, taught her the parts that really mattered." Ancient Egyptian "dolls" are similarly now understood as fertility figures: Quirke 1992, pp. 124–125, figs. 72–74.
[106] Reilly 1997, p. 159.

or torch bearing (p. 124), which suggests either chthonic deities or marriage. That there is an example of parody of the hydriaphoros (p. 196) suggests that a water-carrying element actually existed in the ritual. Were such parodies actually performed in the sanctuary in the tradition of buffoonery for Demeter? Although there are quite a few figurines of dancers, there is surprisingly little reference to musical instruments, unlike the Thesmophorion at Eretria, which yielded many figurines of female musicians. Does this mean that the dancers are symbolic of bridals or Dionysiac revels but do not illustrate actual cultic activities? But there are parodies of mantled dancers (p. 196), which support the existence of the activity. There are female figures and children on simple seats, holding offerings. Why are they seated? They are not enthroned, and there is no other sign of divinity, such as the polos. Perhaps they are waiting their turn to dedicate offerings.

One female type sits in a curved wicker chair, a type of seat specified for the "sacred women" of the Andanian Mysteries (p. 45). Perhaps these figurines represent cult officials or priestesses of the Acrocorinth sanctuary. The old woman **H389** could be a priestess, since old priestesses are documented elsewhere in Demeter's cults (p. 200), but the only other consistent type that could possibly represent a priestess is the Middle Hellenistic type carrying a piglet and torch and sometimes wearing a sacrificial apron (pp. 250–255). In this case, there are attributes recalling a goddess as well (the polos, the dignified, hieratic bearing, and a resemblance to the iconography of Cybele) that speak for a representation of Demeter about to sacrifice a piglet. The overlap of types, however, is what is significant about this group, bringing us back to the initial thesis that some types incorporate qualities of both mortals and deities, probably to reinforce the efficacy of ritual through identification. This type came into being after the series of votaries carrying piglets came to an end. Was it a replacement in bridal rituals? If so, there was a shift away from representing the mortal bride toward a rendering more like a goddess or priestess. Although the votary herself presumably still offered the figurine, the functional figure in the transaction between offerant and deity was no longer the mortal votary represented as herself, but either the votary in the guise of the goddess or an official of the cult. This imagery, I believe, suggests some change in the perception of this transaction, in which the mortal votary in her own shape was no longer considered sufficiently effective (p. 255).

The Early Hellenistic figurines of children are not replaced in the later 3rd and early 2nd centuries B.C., nor are the youths, although there are handsome new female types belonging to this period. Did the old customs die out with time, or were they moved to the patronage of other deities? Was there some deterioration of the existing age-class system by the 3rd century B.C.? Pausanias (2.3.6) mentions a ritual in which Corinthian children cut their hair and wore black in honor of Medea's children; this ritual is now thought to have been a form of initiation, in which seven boys and seven girls withdrew to the temenos of Hera Akraia.[107] Pausanias says that the ritual was discontinued when the city was destroyed, which implies that it was in existence immediately before 146 B.C. Was the function of initiating children transferred in the 3rd century B.C. from Demeter to Hera?

There still remain many figurines that do not form consistent groups and therefore are hard to connect to rites so established in custom as to become referents for figurine types. There are many draped female figurines without the offerings expected of votary types, which may simply represent visitors to the shrine. Just as not everyone who attends church takes communion, it need not have been necessary to approach the deities for any particular purpose. Women who already had gone through the rituals of childhood and marriage, and who no longer sought children, might nevertheless have wished to offer something to ensure divine protection for their families

---

[107] Brelich 1969, pp. 355–365, including further sources for
this ritual; Brulé 1987, pp. 218–221; Johnston 1997.

and households. Draped female figurines might then simply have represented such women, to remind the goddesses of their continuing faithfulness to the cult.

The final pieces of evidence for ritual are the offerings carried by some of the figurines, although none of these can be firmly tied to specific festivals. Balls (pp. 125–126) are likely to fall into the category of the toys of childhood relinquished symbolically upon their owner's arrival at marriageable age. A small box also may have been a bridal offering (p. 273). The cakes are for the most part different from those on the model likna, and two types might possibly parallel the *aidoia* of the Athenian Thesmophoria (pp. 272–273). The differences suggest that some types of cakes may have been offered at a different ritual than the model likna; such a custom need not be surprising in light of the widespread modern customs of baking for various religious holidays special breads and cakes, which are not prepared at any other time. There are a few representations of floral offerings, one of them perhaps showing the gathering of wild roses (pp. 124–125), which might suggest an early summer festival, that is, at the time of the harvesting and threshing of grain, but the evidence of the figurines is very scanty, and the flowers probably just refer to Kore's myth. There is one piece of coroplastic evidence for the dedication of cloth, perhaps a woven fillet or hairband (p. 273). It is also possible that incense was burned in the thymiateria (p. 75), but the receptacles that would show traces of burning are missing; further, there is no clear supporting evidence for thymiateria among the Greek pottery from the sanctuary.[108]

For the Roman period, too few figurines were found to derive significant information from this class of votives. There appears, however, to have been a continuing interest in children[109] and continued reference to Aphrodite and to Dionysos (in the form of theatrical masks[110]). The one surprise is the strong showing, in this small group of figurines, of Artemis, who perhaps took over the role of protectress of the young, as she was honored elsewhere in Greece.

It will be apparent to the reader that the interpretations of cultic activity in the Acrocorinth sanctuary provided above are speculative to a greater or lesser degree. Whenever possible, they have been supported by external evidence, but because of the nature of the evidence, they are at best not more than reasonable inferences based upon available material. In the main, they are intended to show how coroplastic evidence may be used to illuminate cult practice and to encourage further study and discussion.

THE FIGURINES AND OTHER ARTS

The following discussion brings together the observations made in the course of this study regarding the relationship of the figurines to other arts. The purpose of this summary is to clarify the workings of the Corinthian coroplastic industry.

An important key to the nature of the industry is to understand how the archetypes were created from which the molds were made. Although the manufacture of figurines required knowledge of the preparation and firing of clay, it did not necessarily presuppose artistic ability and training, nor was the preparation of archetypes always the responsibility of the coroplast. In a paper on the nature of the Corinthian coroplastic industry as a whole,[111] I examined the uses to which the very large production of figurines was put in Corinth in different periods and came to the conclusion that their major function was as votives in shrines. Relatively few figurines were deposited in graves, and there is little evidence for purely decorative use. A mainly votive function would tie the production to the seasonal pattern of festivals, when the bulk of figurines would have been offered, even allowing for sporadic visits to shrines at other times of the year.

[108] *Corinth* XVIII, i, p. 61. For the Roman thymiateria, see *Corinth* XVIII, ii, pp. 66–71.
[109] This interest is supported by the Roman marble portraits of girls, S-2666 and S-2667 (Stroud 1965, p. 21, pl. 10:b, c).
[110] Publication forthcoming with the miscellaneous finds.
[111] Merker, forthcoming.

Taking into account that figurines were not customarily offered to all the deities worshiped in Corinth, the coroplasts probably were seasonal workers with other sources of livelihood. Although Corinthian figurines were widely exported, most of the exports were limited to a small range of lingering Archaic types produced in the Potters' Quarter (see p. 23, note 1). Consequently, few craftsmen were able to supplement their work through exports. The seasonal nature of the industry would explain why workshop groupings of technically related figurines are very small and diverge widely from one another (see the summary of workshops on pp. 344–346). It also would explain why, apart from the Potters' Quarter, there is little sense of continuity. One concludes that artisans who had access to the necessary materials and facilities and had the expertise to prepare and fire clay were able to take the opportunities for making and selling figurines as they arose, without being what we would consider fully competent, full-time "professionals."

Indeed, the first figurines from the Potters' Quarter show by their technique and materials that they were made by potters.[112] In addition to pottery, however, Corinthian artisans manufactured terracotta sculpture, architectural revetments, and household items such as mortars, miniature altars, and loomweights. Molds were employed for much of this work, and the coarser clay used for such products usually was covered with finely textured clay like that used for figurines. Artisans accustomed to work of this nature would have had the expertise to prepare the clay for figurines and to mold and fire them, but they would not have had the necessary artistic skills, at least at miniature scale. There are abundant examples among the figurines from the Acrocorinth sanctuary of well-designed figurines spoiled by clumsy handling, such as harsh retouch (e.g., the draped female figurine **H69**); the use of back molds that belong to types different from the front (e.g., the votary **H1**); the omission of limbs (e.g, the Aphrodite **H249**); or the use of unnecessarily thick walls that make one think the artisan was more accustomed to making larger-scaled terracottas (see the figurines of Workshop I, p. 346). Therefore, when we consider relations with other arts, we should think not necessarily of the craft of the coroplast but of the separate craft of the well-trained model maker, who provided the archetypes that coroplasts could use either well or poorly, depending upon their level of skill. The work of model makers, who appear to have provided workshop materials for other craftsmen as well, brought the coroplastic industry into contact with the wider world of the arts. When coroplasts were largely separate from such influence, as in the case of the Potters' Quarter workshops, their work took on a highly conservative, rather naive, folk-art quality, as in the case of Workshop A (see p. 344).

Although it might naturally be assumed that the Corinthian coroplastic industry was connected closely with the active local terracotta sculpture workshops, in fact there is little sign of such a link. Among the figurines from the sanctuary, only the small female protome **C251** shows a facial type that recalls terracotta sculpture and perhaps could have been transmitted through large-scale protomes (see p. 74). Part of the reason for the lack of connection may be that much terracotta sculpture served a public, architectural purpose, using mythological subjects that were not popular for votives. Even when subjects overlap, however, as in the case of the standing nude or seminude youths dedicated at the sanctuary in the form of both terracotta sculpture and figurines (see p. 65), there are clear differences in type and style. The reason for this must be that the coroplasts, whether or not they admired and wished to emulate the sculptures, needed actual workshop materials in the form of archetypes or molds already made from the archetypes, in order to produce the figurines. The craft of the terracotta sculptor did not produce such materials, but that of the worker in small bronzes did.[113]

A few figurines preserve the crisp detail usually thought to reflect metalwork; their molds may have been taken from completed bronzes or their models. Examples of the Classical and

---

[112] *Corinth* XV, ii, pp. 3–4.

[113] On the range of workshop materials in a metalworker's atelier, see Reeder 1987, pp. 439–440. Such materials must have been the main source of inspiration for small-scale works of art in general.

Hellenistic periods[114] are the dancer **C282** (see p. 81), the mold for which may have been taken from the relief on a mirror cover; the female heads **C142** (see p. 55), **H235**, and **H237** (see p. 167); the pig **V1** (see p. 266); and the votive shield **V18** (see p. 271), which is merely a small fragment but shows fine detail in more complete examples. Four finely detailed miniatures might also have had metallic sources: the seated girl **C248** (see p. 72); the mantled dancers **H165** and **H166** (see p. 155); and the comic dancer **H365** (see p. 196). Sometimes typological parallels for the figurines can be found among small bronzes. Both lingering Archaic standing "korai" and Early Classical peplos-figurines may have been developed either from or together with bronze mirror caryatids (see pp. 26–27); the peplos-figurine **C10** (see p. 28) has features in common with a bronze of reported Corinthian provenience; small bronze bulls are so common in the archaeological record that a well-detailed terracotta example such as **V5** (see p. 267) could be dependent on one; the piglet carrier **H1** (see p. 120) has a close parallel for its drapery arrangement in a small bronze. Some of the base types are directly copied from those used to support small bronzes (see pp. 275–276).

Recent studies of the manufacture of ancient bronzes, particularly of small scale, have shown how close some of the techniques are to the preparation of terracotta figurines (see p. 14). The artisans prepared a clay model, from which master molds were taken to cast any number of secondary wax models that were used (and destroyed) in the casting process. The secondary models could be revised to produce many variants of the original model, which was preserved for reuse as needed. The bronze-worker's original model served the same function as the coroplast's archetype; the coroplast also habitually rang changes on a basic type to produce innumerable variants, what is called in this study an "iconographic series." Given the present state of the evidence, it is not difficult to propose a close relationship between workers in bronze and terracotta, but it is not clear just how the workshops were organized. A possible clue may be that the larger and better-made figurines are often known in only one or two examples. Even though the archaeological record is far from complete, multiple examples of some types are known, and one must therefore assume that some types were indeed made in more abundance than others and that relatively few copies of these better figurines were produced. Figurines that are well designed but clumsily handled could well be the work of potters or other workers in terracotta who purchased a few molds or archetypes from a model maker, but who were the skilled workers who made small numbers of large, fine figurines? Were these pieces expensive enough to make this activity worthwhile? We tend to think of terracottas as being cheap, but perhaps good quality was valued even in this medium, although the material was not precious. Or perhaps the economics of this practice can be explained by linking the production of large, well-made figurines to the same workshops in which fine models were prepared for the manufacture of bronzes; the sale of the models might have provided enough income to allow the production of a few good terracotta figurines as a secondary activity.

While the making of models is technically essential to the production of bronzes, it is not to the carving of stone sculpture, and there has been much discussion of the nature of the stone sculptor's preparatory work (see p. 26). Whether the sculptors relied on drawings or small three-dimensional models, some method of recording the repertoire is presupposed by the pastiches of types reappearing in different combinations on such monuments as votive and record reliefs. When Corinthian figurines reflect knowledge of the types and styles of stone sculpture, it is more likely that the model makers knew these trends through workshop materials than by direct observation of sometimes far-flung monuments (see pp. 134–135).[115] When the figurines reflect

---

[114] The publication of Archaic figurines with this feature is forthcoming.

[115] The existence of closely similar 3rd-century B.C. Rho-dian Ganymede statuettes in both terracotta and marble (Zervoudaki 1978) points to the use of matching workshop materials by coroplasts and sculptors in stone.

the architectural sculpture of Olympia (see p. 26), Athens (see p. 33), Epidauros (see, e.g., pp. 80–81), or Pergamon (see pp. 253–254), it is conceivable that artisans who participated in these projects later worked in Corinth, but the knowledge gained of these monuments still had to be recorded in some way for other artisans to use. Whatever the means of transmission, stylistic and iconographic connections, apart from the architectural sculpture mentioned above, have been noted with a number of specific works, including the Mantineia base (see p. 161), the Apollo Patroos (see p. 122), the Grimani statuettes (see pp. 132–135), the "Hygieia" from Tegea (see p. 164), the "Maussollos" from Halikarnassos (see p. 140), the portrait of Hypereides (see p. 141), and the head of Eubouleus (see p. 259). Lesser-known works include votive reliefs (see, e.g., p. 35) and female statues from Megara (see p. 254). There is no demonstrable derivation of any of the Corinthian types from a major cult statue (see pp. 134–135). Clearly the range of knowledge of sculptural iconography and styles was wide, and there was no area of particular emphasis. One should assume that workshop materials were readily available in Corinth from a wide range of sources, as one would expect in a major Greek city, and that local artisans readily made use of ideas that came to their attention, contributing to the diversity that is a hallmark of the Corinthian coroplastic industry.

WORKSHOPS

In the preceding chapters, it was occasionally possible to link figurines into workshop groups, using technical and stylistic idiosyncracies as criteria, keeping in mind that the nature of the coroplastic industry in Corinth encouraged workshops of short duration (see pp. 19–20). While many more figurines could be linked by mold relationships, the use of common molds, without other confirming similarities, is not in itself proof of common workshops, since collateral molds could have been used in different locations. Subsequent generations in a mold series may show variations in fabric and technique strong enough to place them in different workshops (e.g., **H249** and **H250**).[116] In this chapter, the principal workshop groupings are summarized, emphasizing those for which more than one type has been preserved, in order to reveal the interests of the artisans and their procedures. Workshops that can be recognized in only one type, for example, the heads of seated goddesses **C95–C98**, are not included here but can be retrieved through the index (*s.v.* Workshops). The Potters' Quarter workshops are listed first.

Potters' Quarter Workshops

Workshop A (see pp. 34, 342):   standing peplos-figurine **C33**; standing draped female aulos-player in Paris; seated goddess in Boston; standing draped female figurine with fillet and box (present whereabouts unknown).

The figurines in this group are characterized by heads that are typical of articulated "dolls" and are small in relation to the torso. The small faces are topped by tall coiffures, and large headdresses not typical of "dolls" were added. The mitten-shaped hands are like those of "dolls," and the arms actually may be adapted "dolls'" arms. The narrow drapery folds are shallowly modeled. The result is rather awkward and unsophisticated. The workshop may have made primarily articulated "dolls," adapting figurines of peplophoros type from their available materials. The size range is 3. The workshop probably was active in the third quarter of the 4th century B.C., to judge from the high girding of **C33**.

Workshop B (see pp. 30, 56):   standing peplos-figurines **C17** and **C18**; head of "doll" **C152**; head of female mantled figurine **C150**; other female heads **C149** and **C151**.

---

[116] On the identification of hands in workshops through idiosyncrasies of technique, see N. A. Winter 1991.

This workshop (possibly one hand?) can be identified mainly by the characteristic slashed tooling of the hair, which is constant even when the coiffure changes. The faces of **C17** and **C149**–**C152**, which are all mechanically related, are triangular in shape, with downturned eyes and features clustered near the center of the face. This facial type is characteristic of some figurines and molds found in the Potters' Quarter. The head of the peplos-figurine, the mantled figurine, and the "doll" are of successive generations, suggesting that this artisan made a new mold from an existing figurine when he wanted to change the type; that is, he did not have access to the archetype, which would have allowed the scale to remain constant. Therefore, the three generations do not necessarily imply a long span of time. This workshop, like Workshop A, made "dolls" as well as standard figurines. The walls of the peplos-figurines are unusually thick for their size, perhaps to compensate for firing them together with the solid "dolls." The size range is 2 or 3. To judge from the coiffures, this workshop was probably active in the third quarter of the 4th century B.C.

Workshop C (see pp. 155, 196):   mantled dancers **H165** and **H166**; comic actors as a dancer and a hydriaphoros **H365** and **H367**.

This workshop produced delicately detailed miniatures of both serious and comic types. The molds may have been derived from metallic sources. The location of the workshop is confirmed by the discovery of a miniature dancer at the Potters' Quarter. This workshop probably was active in the middle to third quarter of the 4th century B.C.

WORKSHOPS OUTSIDE THE POTTERS' QUARTER

Workshop D (see pp. 17–18, 25, 60):   standing peplos-figurines **C1**–**C6**; horse-rider **C186**.

The figurines from this workshop are held together by their generally good craftsmanship, their doughy vertical and zigzag folds, and their combination of Early Classical and Archaic features. The female subjects, when identifiable, are votaries carrying offerings. The thickened oval necklines of both **C1** and **C186** suggest the use of common workshop material in the development of both female and male types. The size range is 3 or 4, two members of the group approaching statuette scale. This workshop was active not later than the second quarter of the 5th century B.C. and possibly earlier.

Workshop E (see pp. 182, 193):   head of baby Eros **H290**; head of a girl **H347**; head of a child, possibly Eros **H348**.

This workshop produced beautifully crafted and delicately detailed child and Eros figurines in size ranges 2 and 3. The output appears to have been small, and no other types can convincingly be assigned to this group. On contextual evidence and the quality of the workmanship, the workshop may have been active in the first half of the 4th century B.C.

Workshop F (see pp. 158–159):   female heads **H180**–**H185**.

This workshop produced mostly relatively large heads (size range 3–4), rather crudely retouched, wearing the long hairstyle usually associated with votaries. Since some members of the group wear a stephane, however, the subjects perhaps included goddesses as well as votaries. One head of this group (**H183**) was constructed on a head with a masculine coiffure, showing that male figurines were produced by this workshop as well. **H184** is smaller than the other heads and may represent a later generation. On stylistic grounds, this workshop probably was active during the third quarter of the 4th century B.C.

Workshop G (see p. 162):   female heads **H199**, **H201**–**H204**.

This workshop produced lovely heads, large in scale (size range 3–4 or 4), wearing the curl-cluster coiffure. The two heads that have drapery attached originally belonged to mantled figurines of different types, suggesting that the workshop had some iconographical range. Although the fabric is sometimes very good, the retouch can be clumsy. On contextual evidence, this workshop was active in the 4th century B.C.; stylistic parallels point to a date in the last quarter.

Workshop H(?) (see pp. 119–120, 185, 190):   votaries with piglet **H1** and **H9**; standing nude youth **H299**; boy with a goose **H331**.

Because the output of votary figurines was large and their technical interrelations very complex (see p. 123), it has not been possible to divide them accurately into workshop groupings. There are, however, striking connections in workshop materials between one of the votaries and two entirely different types, a youth and a boy. Because of similarities in the head and overall pose, the youth **H299** may have been constructed from workshop material related to that of the votary **H1**, although one is a nude male and the other, a draped female. The boy **H331** may also have been developed, somewhat later, from an archetype related to the youth; it also has a spool base similar to that of the votaries. The second votary (**H9**) is brought into the group by virtue of its back mold, which is close to that incorrectly used for **H1**. The scale of the group is relatively small, at size range 2 or 2–3; the workmanship is careless, although the designs are very good. These figurines are grouped together with some hesitation, because this workshop appears to have lasted longer than most outside the Potters' Quarter. The evidence for the length of time is the discrepancy between the dates of the votary **H1** and the boy **H331**. The votary belongs on stylistic and contextual grounds not later than the last quarter of the 4th century B.C., but on similar grounds, the boy cannot be earlier than the early 3rd century B.C.

Workshop I (see pp. 137, 143, 153, 154, 173, 174, 342):   standing draped females **H70**, **H100**, and **H101**; mantled dancers **H153** and **H154**; Aphrodites **H249** and **H260**.

The products of this workshop are so distinctive that they may belong to a very short period of production. The figurines, at size range 3, are thick-walled, with an unusually rough interior surface. The outer surface, at least of the front, is smoothly polished, but there is little retouch, and the base, when preserved, can be sloppy. The arms of **H249** were never added. The types are mostly derivative, the impressions are dull, and detail is lacking. Contextual and stylistic evidence places the group at the end of the 4th or the beginning of the 3rd century B.C.

Workshop J (see pp. 128, 129, 165):   standing girl **H44**; head of hydriaphoros **H50**; female head **H223**.

This group is characterized by its excellent hard, fine, pale fabric, used in figurines of very poor workmanship, with dull impressions and coarse retouch. The two heads have yellow paint on the hair, suggesting that they could have been gilded, even though they were not well formed. The scale range of these exhausted types is 2 or 2–3. Contextual evidence suggests a date in the second half of the 3rd century B.C.

Workshop K (see pp. 149, 150):   standing goddess(?) **H138**; Nike or dancer(?) **H145**; standing draped females **H130**, **H140** (Aphrodite?), and **H144**.

This group is characterized by its hard, occasionally slightly coarse fabric, thin walls, and the large size of most of its members (size range 3 up to 4–5). The style is sculptural, and the types probably include goddesses. **H138** is from a pottery context terminating in the Hellenistic period. The possible "Rhodian Aphrodite" type **H140** is unlikely to be earlier than the later 3rd century B.C., as may also be true of **H130**, with its steeply arched mantle roll. If a Middle Hellenistic date is assigned to this workshop, its products would fit very well with the sculpturally based renewal of the Corinthian coroplastic industry in the last quarter of the 3rd century B.C., when large figurines of good quality were once again made.

CONCORDANCE OF INVENTORY
AND CATALOGUE NUMBERS

Inventory no.		Catalogue no.
MF-10319	sub	C57
MF-10322		C174
MF-10323		H386
MF-10325		H395
MF-10326	sub	H395
MF-10327		I22
MF-10328	sub	H402
MF-10329		H396
MF-10331		R1
MF-10332		C117
MF-10336		H217
MF-10337	sub	H19
MF-10340	sub	C91
MF-10353		H175
MF-10378		C210
MF-10379		C178
MF-10380		H254
MF-10381		C164
MF-10382		H274
MF-10383	sub	C83
MF-10386	sub	H102
MF-10387	sub	H236
MF-10390		C21
MF-10395		H312
MF-10396		C282
MF-10397		H102
MF-10398	sub	H260
MF-10400		C143
MF-10401	sub	C135
MF-10402	sub	C163
MF-10403	sub	H102
MF-10404		H229
MF-10408		H352
MF-10409		C109
MF-10410		C147
MF-10412		C151
MF-10413		C242
MF-10415		H84
MF-10418		C124
MF-10422		V7
MF-10424		H233
MF-10434		C97
MF-10436		H1
MF-10437	sub	H102
MF-10438		C108
MF-10439		H65
MF-10440		I81
MF-10441		C135
MF-10442		C183
MF-10443		H153

MF-10444		I11
MF-10445		C167
MF-10446	sub	H102
MF-10447		H100
MF-10448		H309
MF-10449		H101
MF-10450		C182
MF-10452	sub	H100
MF-10454	sub	H102
MF-10455		C30
MF-10456		I12
MF-10457		C163
MF-10458	sub	H185
MF-10459		C142
MF-10460		H154
MF-10461		C146
MF-10463		C61
MF-10464	sub	H102
MF-10465	sub	I19
MF-10467		C134
MF-10468		C176
MF-10471		H70
MF-10472		C159
MF-10473		C98
MF-10474		C267
MF-10475		C270
MF-10476		H183
MF-10477		C31
MF-10478	sub	C227
MF-10480		C223
MF-10481		H116
MF-10482		C279
MF-10483		C209
MF-10484		C83
MF-10485		I10
MF-10486	sub	C149
MF-10489	sub	H102
MF-10491		C152
MF-10492		H193
MF-10493		C241
MF-10494		C238
MF-10496		C116
MF-10497		H353
MF-10498		C54
MF-10500		C17
MF-10502		C277
MF-10504		C18
MF-10506		H51
MF-10510	sub	H17
MF-10511	sub	C169
MF-10512		C157

MF-10516	sub	H426
MF-10520		C139
MF-10522	sub	C188
MF-10524		C145
MF-10525		C231
MF-10526		C262
MF-10530	sub	C147
MF-10531	sub	C125
MF-10534		I74
MF-10535	sub	H15
MF-10536		C9
MF-10540		C191
MF-10541		C125
MF-10542		V9
MF-10544		V26
MF-10556		H216
MF-10559		C52
MF-10562		C85
MF-10568	sub	C10
MF-10570		H237
MF-10573	sub	H7
MF-10575	sub	H110
MF-10576	sub	C71
MF-10579	sub	C235
MF-10581		H135
MF-10582	sub	H21
MF-10584	sub	C227
MF-10588		C122
MF-10593		H259
MF-10595	sub	C163
MF-10598		C199
MF-10603		C131
MF-10606	sub	C148
MF-10607		I91
MF-10609	sub	H202
MF-10611		C171
MF-10612	sub	C125
MF-10617		H367
MF-10620		C245
MF-10622		C6
MF-10623	sub	C189
MF-10624		H246
MF-10625	sub	H102
MF-10626		C67
MF-10628		H110
MF-10629	sub	C51
MF-10630		C72
MF-10631		C86
MF-10635	sub	C176
MF-10636		H278
MF-10638		C228

MF-10639		**C227**	MF-11040	*sub*	**C104**	MF-11344	**I93**
MF-10641		**C168**	MF-11041		**C74**	MF-11346	**C256**
MF-10643	*sub*	**C146**	MF-11046		**H109**	MF-11347	**H76**
MF-10645		**C138**	MF-11047		**C10**	MF-11348	**H294**
MF-10646	*sub*	**H350**	MF-11048		**C11**	MF-11362	**C165**
MF-10648		**H351**	MF-11049		**C196**	MF-11363	*sub* **H100**
MF-10655		**C250**	MF-11052		**C180**	MF-11382	**H250**
MF-10660		**V2**	MF-11054	*sub*	**H401**	MF-11383	*sub* **H102**
MF-10661		**I90**	MF-11058	*sub*	**H402**	MF-11384	*sub* **C168**
MF-10662	*sub*	**H331**	MF-11060		**I77**	MF-11385	**H382**
MF-10664		**C235**	MF-11061		**C99**	MF-11387	**C222**
MF-10665	*sub*	**H327**	MF-11064		**H106**	MF-11388	**H112**
MF-10666	*sub*	**C85**	MF-11065		**C73**	MF-11390	**I3**
MF-10667		**V4**	MF-11066		**C33**	MF-11395	*sub* **V45**
MF-10668		**H348**	MF-11067		**C190**	MF-11396	**V44**
MF-10669	*sub*	**H331**	MF-11069		**H56**	MF-11397	*sub* **V45**
MF-10670		**H330**	MF-11070		**H308**	MF-11398	**V33**
MF-10671		**H302**	MF-11071		**C34**	MF-11400	**C71**
MF-10674		**I87**	MF-11072		**H257**	MF-11401	**H346**
MF-10676		**V1**	MF-11073		**H410**	MF-11402	*sub* **C72**
MF-10677		**H301**	MF-11074		**H139**	MF-11404	*sub* **H102**
MF-10678		**H343**	MF-11077		**I14**	MF-11406	*sub* **C105**
MF-10681		**V10**	MF-11078		**H98**	MF-11407	**H280**
MF-10685		**H234**	MF-11079		**H88**	MF-11408	**H383**
MF-10748		**H415**	MF-11080		**I95**	MF-11411	*sub* **H202**
MF-10754	*sub*	**C181**	MF-11081		**C148**	MF-11412	**H172**
MF-10755		**H242**	MF-11091		**C78**	MF-11414	*sub* **H236**
MF-10758	*sub*	**H400**	MF-11093		**H333**	MF-11416	*sub* **C98**
MF-10759		**H212**	MF-11095		**I78**	MF-11417	**C173**
MF-10922		**H211**	MF-11096		**H184**	MF-11656	**C211**
MF-10923		**H365**	MF-11099		**H69**	MF-11657	*sub* **C103**
MF-10926		**H376**	MF-11100		**H385**	MF-11658	*sub* **H402**
MF-10936		**H15**	MF-11102		**H210**	MF-11660	**C276**
MF-10942	*sub*	**C82**	MF-11104		**C263**	MF-11667	*sub* **C51**
MF-10945	*sub*	**C192**	MF-11106		**H32**	MF-11668	**C42**
MF-10947		**R2**	MF-11107		**H200**	MF-11675	**H420**
MF-10948		**H404**	MF-11109		**H165**	MF-11676	**C214**
MF-10949	*sub*	**H404**	MF-11112		**H54**	MF-11677	**I44**
MF-10950		**I21**	MF-11217	*sub*	**C71**	MF-11684	*sub* **H156**
MF-10951	*sub*	**H235**	MF-11218		**H118**	MF-11686	**H403**
MF-10952	*sub*	**I7**	MF-11239	*sub*	**C240**	MF-11687	**H232**
MF-10954	*sub*	**H194, H230**	MF-11261		**V46**	MF-11689	*sub* **C82**
MF-10956		**V17**	MF-11292		**H115**	MF-11691	*sub* **C188**
MF-10958		**H105**	MF-11294		**C76**	MF-11699	**C186**
MF-10959		**H192**	MF-11296		**H277**	MF-11700	**C3**
MF-11012	*sub*	**C226**	MF-11297	*sub*	**H238**	MF-11707	*sub* **C51**
MF-11013		**C26**	MF-11301		**C156**	MF-11709	*sub* **C41**
MF-11014		**C96**	MF-11305		**C230**	MF-11710	**C19**
MF-11016	*sub*	**C282, H271**	MF-11306		**H152**	MF-11714	**C226**
MF-11018		**C41**	MF-11309		**H224**	MF-11719	**H45**
MF-11020	*sub*	**H107**	MF-11310	*sub*	**C129**	MF-11721	**C162**
MF-11022		**C248**	MF-11311	*sub*	**H425**	MF-11723	*sub* **C253**
MF-11024		**C127**	MF-11312		**H426**	MF-11725	**H248**
MF-11026	*sub*	**C210**	MF-11314		**H425**	MF-11726	*sub* **C73**
MF-11027		**H363**	MF-11322		**C153**	MF-11728	**H63**
MF-11028		**H176**	MF-11324		**C251**	MF-11729	**H164**
MF-11031		**C91**	MF-11329	*sub*	**H216**	MF-11731	*sub* **H7**
MF-11032		**H368**	MF-11332	*sub*	**C164**	MF-11734	**H356**
MF-11033		**H53**	MF-11333	*sub*	**C189**	MF-11747	**H18**
MF-11034		**H384**	MF-11338		**H99**	MF-11748	**H41**
MF-11035	*sub*	**C211**	MF-11339	*sub*	**H111**	MF-11749	*sub* **C125**
MF-11037	*sub*	**C210**	MF-11342		**H39**	MF-11756	**C95**

MF-11768	*sub*	**C73**		MF-11964		**C155**		MF-12536		**H300**
MF-11770	*sub*	**H2**		MF-11966		**C137**		MF-12551	*sub*	**V7**
MF-11772		**C281**		MF-11967		**H202**		MF-12552		**C106**
MF-11775		**H388**		MF-11968	*sub*	**I9**		MF-12553		**C53**
MF-11776		**C269**		MF-11969		**C184**		MF-12853		**C219**
MF-11777		**I49**		MF-11971		**C107**		MF-12861		**C188**
MF-11781	*sub*	**H402**, 254[20]		MF-11972		**H207**		MF-12874		**H227**
MF-11782		**C80**		MF-12004	*sub*	**C98**		MF-12875		**H2**
MF-11783		**H17**		MF-12010	*sub*	**H331**		MF-12877		**C189**
MF-11784		**H52**		MF-12011		**H419**		MF-12880		**V18**
MF-11785		**H10**		MF-12015		**H430**		MF-12881		**C110**
MF-11786		**H85**		MF-12020		**C169**		MF-12886		**H288**
MF-11789		**C104**		MF-12021		**I32**		MF-12887		**H146**
MF-11827		**I33**		MF-12022	*sub*	**H401**		MF-12892		**H339**
MF-11828		**C136**		MF-12024		**H111**		MF-12893		**H225**
MF-11830		**C93**		MF-12025		**I83**		MF-12894		**H178**
MF-11831	*sub*	**H102**		MF-12026	*sub*	**H214**		MF-12895		**H317**
MF-11832		**R25**		MF-12031		**H8**		MF-12896		**C132**
MF-11834		**V5**		MF-12032	*sub*	**H1**		MF-12899		**H310**
MF-11835		**I92**		MF-12033	*sub*	**H183**		MF-12902		**H57**
MF-11837		**H269**		MF-12040	*sub*	**H331**		MF-12907		**C249**
MF-11838	*sub*	**H31**		MF-12043	*sub*	**H202**		MF-13138		**H409**
MF-11840		**H170**		MF-12044		**H347**		MF-13147	*sub*	**H402**
MF-11841	*sub*	**H201**		MF-12045		**V27**		MF-13404		**V31**
MF-11842	*sub*	**H274**		MF-12046		**H360**		MF-13405		**H327**
MF-11843		**C170**		MF-12052		**C278**		MF-13406		**H326**
MF-11844		**C261**		MF-12053		**H249**		MF-13407	*sub*	**H326**
MF-11845		**H266**		MF-12054	*sub*	**C275**		MF-13408		**H322**
MF-11849		**C103**		MF-12055		**C177**		MF-13411		**V42**
MF-11858		**C274**		MF-12116		**C166**		MF-13412		**V19**
MF-11860		**R22**		MF-12117		**C149**		MF-13413		**H329**
MF-11861		**H219**		MF-12118		**C144**		MF-13414		**H321**
MF-11862	*sub*	**H232**		MF-12119		**H204**		MF-13415	*sub*	**C247**
MF-11863		**R15**		MF-12120		**H364**		MF-13416		**C205**
MF-11865		**H203**		MF-12121		**H267**		MF-13417		**C206**
MF-11867		**C62**		MF-12122		**H296**		MF-13418		**C204**
MF-11869	*sub*	**C55**		MF-12123		**H46**		MF-13419	*sub*	**C250**
MF-11878		**V6**		MF-12127		**C56**		MF-13420		**H350**
MF-11880	*sub*	**V18**		MF-12128	*sub*	**I9**		MF-13421		**I40**
MF-11882		**C1**		MF-12130		**C271**		MF-13422		**C233**
MF-11887		**C213**		MF-12131		**C201**		MF-13423		**C229**
MF-11889	*sub*	**H232**		MF-12133		**H214**		MF-13424	*sub*	**C227**
MF-11895		**H292**		MF-12134	*sub*	**C82**		MF-13425	*sub*	**C231**
MF-11896		**H173**		MF-12136		**C150**		MF-13426		**C236**
MF-11897		**H307**		MF-12137		**H81**		MF-13427		**C237**
MF-11898		**C16**		MF-12140	*sub*	**H342**		MF-13428		**C240**
MF-11900		**R6**		MF-12141		**I88**		MF-13430		**C239**
MF-11902		**C266**		MF-12142		**H412**		MF-13431	*sub*	**C233**
MF-11903		**H16**		MF-12143		**H305**		MF-13432		**H324**
MF-11904		**H390**		MF-12144		**H319**		MF-13433	*sub*	**H320**
MF-11905		**H128**		MF-12147		**H230**		MF-13434		**H334**
MF-11908		**H320**		MF-12148		**C154**		MF-13435		**H306**
MF-11910		**C60**		MF-12153		**H201**		MF-13436	*sub*	**H36**
MF-11912		**H299**		MF-12154		**H387**		MF-13438	*sub*	**C195**
MF-11913	*sub*	**H9**		MF-12157		**C208**		MF-13439		**C194**
MF-11914		**H428**		MF-12158		**C129**		MF-13440		**C216**
MF-11918		**I57**		MF-12159		**H104**		MF-13441		**C215**
MF-11919		**H289**		MF-12160	*sub*	**C275**		MF-13442		**C220**
MF-11920		**C126**		MF-12164		**C225**		MF-13443		**C217**
MF-11922		**C253**		MF-12530		**H303**		MF-13444		**C198**
MF-11925		**C265**		MF-12534		**H191**		MF-13445		**C192**
MF-11927		**V14**		MF-12535		**C36**		MF-13446		**C193**

MF-13447	*sub*	**C189**	MF-13755	**H108**	MF-13817		**C13**
MF-13448	*sub*	**C192**	MF-13756	**H24**	MF-13818		**C65**
MF-13449	*sub*	**C235**	MF-13757	**H150**	MF-13819		**R20**
MF-13450	*sub*	**C235**	MF-13758	**H177**	MF-13820		**C24**
MF-13452	*sub*	**I37**	MF-13759	**H166**	MF-13821		**H393**
MF-13453		**H335**	MF-13760	**H171**	MF-13822		**H113**
MF-13454		**H336**	MF-13761	**C4**	MF-13823		**H114**
MF-13455		**I37**	MF-13762	**H22**	MF-13824		**C77**
MF-13456		**H338**	MF-13763	**C92**	MF-13825		**C75**
MF-13457	*sub*	**H335**	MF-13764	**H28**	MF-13826		**H117**
MF-13458		**I45**	MF-13765	**H43**	MF-13827		**H122**
MF-13459		**C200**	MF-13766	**H5**	MF-13828		**H121**
MF-13460		**H133**	MF-13767	**H29**	MF-13829		**H97**
MF-13461	*sub*	**C192**	MF-13768	**H6**	MF-13830		**H285**
MF-13463		**C212**	MF-13769	**C5**	MF-13831		**H286**
MF-13464	*sub*	**H335**	MF-13770	**C55**	MF-13832		**C25**
MF-13466	*sub*	**H386**	MF-13771	**C23**	MF-13833		**C29**
MF-13467		**H325**	MF-13772	**H26**	MF-13834		**H157**
MF-13471	*sub*	**C209**	MF-13773	**I51**	MF-13835		**H156**
MF-13473		**V29**	MF-13774	**H194**	MF-13836		**I66**
MF-13475		**V30**	MF-13775	**H180**	MF-13837		**H131**
MF-13476		**V28**	MF-13776	**H182**	MF-13838		**H263**
MF-13479		**I28**	MF-13777	**H185**	MF-13839		**H392**
MF-13480		**I85**	MF-13778	**H186**	MF-13840		**H130**
MF-13482	*sub*	**H331**	MF-13779	**H198**	MF-13841		**H142**
MF-13483		**H316**	MF-13780	**H90**	MF-13842		**H137**
MF-13484		**C161**	MF-13781	**H93**	MF-13843		**H260**
MF-13488		**H362**	MF-13782	**H94**	MF-13844		**H252**
MF-13491	*sub*	**H35**	MF-13783	**H418**	MF-13845		**H251**
MF-13504		**H189**	MF-13784	**H136**	MF-13846		**H253**
MF-13505		**H119**	MF-13785	**I62**	MF-13847		**H140**
MF-13506		**H255**	MF-13786	**C14**	MF-13848		**H391**
MF-13507		**H427**	MF-13787	**H127**	MF-13849		**H262**
MF-13508		**H64**	MF-13788	**H23**	MF-13850		**C32**
MF-13514		**I19**	MF-13789	**H30**	MF-13851		**H264**
MF-13559		**I54**	MF-13790	**C49**	MF-13852		**H138**
MF-13564		**C259**	MF-13791	**H73**	MF-13853		**H273**
MF-13569		**I56**	MF-13792	**H75**	MF-13854		**R26**
MF-13646		**C44**	MF-13793	**H87**	MF-13855		**R27**
MF-13655		**C258**	MF-13794	**C27**	MF-13856		**H68**
MF-13656		**I52**	MF-13795	**H424**	MF-13857		**H160**
MF-13658	*sub*	**C205**	MF-13796	**H423**	MF-13858		**H371**
MF-13659		**I53**	MF-13797	**C28**	MF-13859		**H279**
MF-13660		**C255**	MF-13798	**C40**	MF-13860		**H86**
MF-13708		**I70**	MF-13799	**H147**	MF-13861		**C15**
MF-13709		**H9**	MF-13800	**C22**	MF-13862		**H96**
MF-13710		**I48**	MF-13801	**H42**	MF-13863		**C47**
MF-13711		**H389**	MF-13802	**H79**	MF-13864		**H95**
MF-13712		**C94**	MF-13803	*sub* **C9**	MF-13865		**H162**
MF-13713		**V38**	MF-13804	**H126**	MF-13866		**H134**
MF-13714	*sub*	**V37**	MF-13805	**H62**	MF-13867		**H169**
MF-13715		**V37**	MF-13806	**H366**	MF-13868		**H284**
MF-13745	*sub*	**V37**	MF-13807	**H48**	MF-13869		**C84**
MF-13746		**H103**	MF-13808	**H421**	MF-13870		**C48**
MF-13747		**H36**	MF-13809	**H268**	MF-13871		**C12**
MF-13748		**H199**	MF-13810	**H60**	MF-13872		**H33**
MF-13749		**I58**	MF-13811	**C20**	MF-13873		**H149**
MF-13750		**R23**	MF-13812	**C37**	MF-13874		**C39**
MF-13751		**H271**	MF-13813	**H417**	MF-13875		**H261**
MF-13752		**C100**	MF-13814	**H411**	MF-13876		**I64**
MF-13753		**H31**	MF-13815	**H89**	MF-13878		**H61**
MF-13754		**H281**	MF-13816	**I63**	MF-13879		**H92**

MF-13880	**H256**	MF-13977	**C57**	MF-14042	**V22**
MF-13881	**H91**	MF-13978	**C101**	MF-14043	**C111**
MF-13882	**I31**	MF-13979	**H55**	MF-14044	**C160**
MF-13883	**C45**	MF-13980	**C66**	MF-14045	**C59**
MF-13884	**H145**	MF-13981	**H226**	MF-14051	**I20**
MF-13885	**H293**	MF-13982	**C90**	MF-14052	**I9**
MF-13886	**H276**	MF-13983	**R16**	MF-14053	**I8**
MF-13887	**H163**	MF-13984	**C175**	MF-14054	**I6**
MF-13888	**C264**	MF-13985	**C112**	MF-14055	**I2**
MF-13889	**H174**	MF-13986	**C114**	MF-14056	**H295**
MF-13890	**H197**	MF-13987	**C105**	MF-14057	**C70**
MF-13891	**H196**	MF-13988	**C179**	MF-14058	**C195**
MF-13892	**H19**	MF-13989	**H291**	MF-14059	**C257**
MF-13893	**H181**	MF-13990	**I89**	MF-14060	**H34**
MF-13894	**H240**	MF-13991	**H349**	MF-14061	**H12**
MF-13922	**V23**	MF-13992	**H341**	MF-14062	**C50**
MF-13923	**I94**	MF-13993	**H342**	MF-14063	**H13**
MF-13924	**V21**	MF-13994	**H345**	MF-14064	**V13**
MF-13925	**V24**	MF-13996	**H328**	MF-14065	**C46**
MF-13926	**V20**	MF-13997	**H245**	MF-14066	**C123**
MF-13927	**I24**	MF-13998	**H340**	MF-14067	**C118**
MF-13928	**I69**	MF-13999	**H236**	MF-14068	**C181**
MF-13929	**I75**	MF-14000	**H220**	MF-14069	**C202**
MF-13930	**H168**	MF-14001	**H206**	MF-14071	**H66**
MF-13932	**H209**	MF-14002	**H221**	MF-14072	**H398**
MF-13933	**V40**	MF-14003	**H241**	MF-14073	**C234**
MF-13934	**I68**	MF-14005	**I46**	MF-14074	**C69**
MF-13936	**H35**	MF-14006	**H238**	MF-14075	**H402**
MF-13937	**V41**	MF-14007	**H231**	MF-14076	**H405**
MF-13938	**C79**	MF-14008	**H208**	MF-14077	**H397**
MF-13939	**I35**	MF-14009	**I79**	MF-14078	**H400**
MF-13940	**V32**	MF-14010	**H247**	MF-14079	**C224**
MF-13941	**I23**	MF-14011	**C63**	MF-14080	**C43**
MF-13942	*sub* **C265**	MF-14012	*sub* **H231**	MF-14081	**C119**
MF-13943	**H272**	MF-14013	**H243**	MF-14082	**V35**
MF-13944	**H315**	MF-14014	**H239**	MF-14084	**V34**
MF-13945	**V12**	MF-14016	**H354**	MF-14085	**V36**
MF-13946	**C207**	MF-14017	**I38**	MF-14086	**V39**
MF-13947	**H378**	MF-14018	**I42**	MF-14087	**I1**
MF-13948	**H377**	MF-14019	**H357**	MF-14088	**H4**
MF-13949	**C88**	MF-14020	**H373**	MF-14089	**H3**
MF-13950	**C89**	MF-14021	**H370**	MF-14090	**H25**
MF-13951	**I61**	MF-14022	**H358**	MF-14091	**C244**
MF-13952	**H218**	MF-14023	**H381**	MF-14092	**C187**
MF-13953	**H205**	MF-14024	**H375**	MF-14093	**V11**
MF-13959	**I43**	MF-14025	**H359**	MF-14094	**H38**
MF-13960	**I18**	MF-14026	**R19**	MF-14095	**I73**
MF-13961	**I27**	MF-14027	**R18**	MF-14096	**H67**
MF-13962	**I86**	MF-14028	**R10**	MF-14097	**C252**
MF-13963	**I30**	MF-14029	**R8**	MF-14098	**C7**
MF-13964	**I17**	MF-14030	**R9**	MF-14099	**H71**
MF-13965	**I15**	MF-14031	**R4**	MF-14100	**H21**
MF-13966	**I29**	MF-14032	**R13**	MF-14101	**H414**
MF-13967	**I16**	MF-14033	**R11**	MF-14102	**H282**
MF-13968	**I13**	MF-14034	**R29**	MF-14118	**C8**
MF-13969	**I34**	MF-14035	**R12**	MF-14120	**C272**
MF-13970	**I72**	MF-14036	**V25**	MF-14157	**H394**
MF-13972	**I4**	MF-14037	**C140**	MF-14174	**V3**
MF-13973	*sub* **I76**	MF-14038	**H298**	MF-14189	**H58**
MF-13974	**I41**	MF-14039	**H297**	MF-14190	**H332**
MF-13975	*sub* **I19**	MF-14040	**C64**	MF-14191	**I5**
MF-13976	**I76**	MF-14041	**C115**	MF-14192	**H167**

MF-14193		**H361**	MF-69-378		**H74**	MF-70-245	*sub*	**H422**
MF-14194		**C158**	MF-69-379		**H83**	MF-70-247		**H77**
MF-68-51	*sub*	**C192**	MF-69-380		**C35**	MF-70-248		**H258**
MF-68-147		**I36**	MF-69-381		**H158**	MF-70-249		**H407**
MF-68-148		**H223**	MF-69-382		**H159**	MF-70-250		**H129**
MF-68-290		**I47**	MF-69-383		**H78**	MF-70-251		**H120**
MF-68-291		**H431**	MF-69-384		**H125**	MF-70-252		**H124**
MF-68-301		**V15**	MF-69-385		**H141**	MF-70-253		**C82**
MF-68-347		**H290**	MF-69-386		**C218**	MF-70-254		**H20**
MF-68-348		**C232**	MF-69-387		**H313**	MF-70-256		**I26**
MF-68-349	*sub*	**C220**	MF-69-388		**C87**	MF-70-257		**H244**
MF-68-352		**H179**	MF-69-389		**I96**	MF-70-258		**H50**
MF-68-364		**H107**	MF-69-390		**I50**	MF-70-259		**I65**
MF-68-365		**H151**	MF-69-391		**H213**	MF-70-260		**H406**
MF-68-366		**C38**	MF-69-392		**H187**	MF-70-261		**H222**
MF-68-367		**H144**	MF-69-393		**I80**	MF-70-262		**R17**
MF-68-368		**H161**	MF-69-394		**C128**	MF-70-263		**C120**
MF-68-369		**H132**	MF-69-395		**H190**	MF-70-264		**C113**
MF-68-370		**H369**	MF-69-396		**H344**	MF-70-265		**H11**
MF-68-371		**I25**	MF-69-397		**H355**	MF-70-266		**H14**
MF-68-372		**H228**	MF-69-398		**H380**	MF-71-26		**C280**
MF-68-373		**C141**	MF-69-399		**V8**	MF-71-49		**C268**
MF-68-374		**H372**	MF-69-400		**R5**	MF-71-55		**H374**
MF-68-375		**I7**	MF-69-401		**I71**	MF-71-82	*sub*	**H415**
MF-68-376		**H408**	MF-69-403		**C121**	MF-71-140		**I39**
MF-68-377		**H235**	MF-69-404		**C260**	MF-72-25		**C102**
MF-68-378		**H82**	MF-70-26		**H401**	MF-72-66		**R21**
MF-69-84	*sub*	**H388**	MF-70-27		**H331**	MF-72-67		**H123**
MF-69-85		**R28**	MF-70-59		**H311**	MF-72-68		**H429**
MF-69-289		**V45**	MF-70-64		**H215**	MF-72-186		**H72**
MF-69-303		**H399**	MF-70-65		**H7**	MF-72-187		**H155**
MF-69-305		**H379**	MF-70-66		**H265**	MF-72-188		**C275**
MF-69-306		**R3**	MF-70-72	*sub*	**H99**	MF-72-189		**C133**
MF-69-349		**H287**	MF-70-73		**H49**	MF-72-190		**C185**
MF-69-350	*sub*	**C191**	MF-70-78	*sub*	**H81**	MF-73-3		**C273**
MF-69-351		**C246**	MF-70-79		**H143**	MF-73-6		**I82**
MF-69-352		**C243**	MF-70-80A		**H80**	MF-73-74		**C203**
MF-69-353		**H323**	MF-70-81		**I67**	MF-73-77		**H314**
MF-69-354		**I84**	MF-70-98	*sub*	**V14**	MF-73-98		**C247**
MF-69-355	*sub*	**C210**	MF-70-162		**V16**	MF-73-99		**C221**
MF-69-356	*sub*	**C210**	MF-70-169		**H416**	MF-73-100	*sub*	**C242**
MF-69-357		**H337**	MF-70-173		**H318**	MF-73-111		**H270**
MF-69-358		**C197**	MF-70-226	*sub*	**C206**	MF-73-113		**C81**
MF-69-359	*sub*	**C197**	MF-70-227		**H304**	MF-73-115		**C68**
MF-69-360		**H188**	MF-70-230		**I55**	MF-73-116		**C172**
MF-69-363		**H413**	MF-70-236		**C51**	MF-73-117		**H195**
MF-69-371	*sub*	**H52**	MF-70-238		**H37**	MF-73-118		**R14**
MF-69-372		**H44**	MF-70-239		**I60**	MF-73-119		**V43**
MF-69-373		**H275**	MF-70-240		**C58**	MF-73-120		**C2**
MF-69-374		**H148**	MF-70-241		**H27**	MF-73-121		**R24**
MF-69-375		**H283**	MF-70-242		**H40**	MF-73-122		**R7**
MF-69-376		**H422**	MF-70-243		**H47**	MF-1994-30		**C254**
MF-69-377		**H59**	MF-70-244		**I59**	MF-1994-31		**C130**

LOT LIST
LOT CONTEXTS AND POTTERY DATES,
WITH PUBLISHED FIGURINES

In this list, arranged by pottery lot number, are the dates of the pottery with which the figurines are associated and brief descriptions of the archaeological contexts in which the figurines and pottery were found. Full discussions of the buildings and other contexts can be found in *Corinth* XVIII, iii. The entire date range of the pottery in each lot is provided; when the archaeological context is later than the date of the latest pottery, that date is provided as well. Dates are B.C. unless otherwise indicated. LT = Lower Terrace; MT = Middle Terrace; UT = Upper Terrace.

Lot 869   mixed, to Roman; no grid reference, surface

H4	**H242**	MF-10754
H105	**H415**	MF-10758
H192	**V10**	
H212	**R13**	

Lot 870   Archaic–Roman; MT, O–Q:25, surface

C117	**H395**	MF-10319
C174	**H396**	MF-10326
H163	**H398**	MF-10328
H217	**I22**	MF-10337
H386	**R1**	MF-10340

Lot 871   Archaic–250 B.C., Byzantine coin; MT, P–Q:25, general fill

H175

Lot 874   6th–4th, Roman; MT, O–P:24–25, surface

C45	**C210**	**H276**
C164	**H254**	**H282**
C178	**H274**	MF-10383

Lot 875   6th–4th, Roman; MT, P:24–25, general fill over Trapezoidal Building

C21
MF-10386
MF-10387

Lot 877   6th–early 3rd; MT, P:24, deposit west of Pit B in Trapezoidal Building

C71	**H137**	MF-10398
C109	**H172**	MF-10401
C118	**H229**	MF-10402
C123	**H233**	MF-10403
C124	**H250**	MF-11363
C143	**H277**	MF-11383
C147	**H280**	MF-11384
C151	**H312**	MF-11395
C165	**H346**	MF-11397
C173	**H352**	MF-11402
C222	**H382**	MF-11404
C242	**H383**	MF-11406
C282	**V7**	MF-11411
H51	**V33**	MF-11414
H84	**V35**	MF-11416
H102	**V44**	
H112	**I3**	

Lot 878 6th–late 4th (later figurine), Hellenistic sherd, context early 3rd; MT,
P:24–25, construction fill, Trapezoidal Building

C30	**C256**	**V32**
C31	**C267**	**I10**
C61	**C270**	**I11**
C83	**C279**	**I12**
C92	**H1**	**I13**
C98	**H65**	**I16**
C108	**H70**	**I19**
C134	**H76**	**I81**
C135	**H100**	**I93**
C142	**H101**	MF-10437
C146	**H116**	MF-10446
C159	**H153**	MF-10452
C163	**H154**	MF-10454
C167	**H183**	MF-10458
C176	**H234**	MF-10464
C182	**H282**	MF-10465
C183	**H286**	MF-10478
C209	**H294**	
C223	**H309**	

Lot 880 5th–first quarter 3rd; MT, P:24–25, filling of Pit B

C17	**C241**	**H353**
C18	**C277**	**V46**
C54	**H39**	MF-10486
C116	**H62**	MF-10489
C152	**H99**	MF-11239
C238	**H193**	MF-11339

Lot 881 late 5th–third quarter 4th (later figurine), context not later than end of 4th but
possible Roman contamination; MT, Q:25, foundation trench, south wall,
Room A

C97	MF-10510
C157	MF-10511
C193	MF-13471

Lot 882 mixed, to Roman; MT, Q:24-25, surface
MF-10516

Lot 884 mixed, to Roman; MT, Q:24, Roman fill
C139

Lot 885 (with 881) late 5th–first half 4th; MT, Q:24-25
C145
C231
C262
MF-10522

Lot 886 Archaic–Roman; MT, Q:25, fill over Pit A

C9	MF-10531
I74	MF-10535
MF-10530	

Lot 887 6th or 5th, into last quarter; MT, Q:25, Pit A

C125	**V26**
C191	MF-10942
V9	

Lot 890 mixed, to Roman; MT, O:24–25, surface
C52
C85
H216

Lot 891   Archaic–Roman; MT, P–Q:24–25, surface
C50   MF-10568
H237   MF-10635

Lot 892   Archaic–Roman; MT, P–Q:24–25, Roman fill in Room A
C122   **H373**   MF-10579
H92   MF-10573   MF-10582
H135   MF-10575   MF-10584
H259   MF-10576   MF-10595

Lot 893   Archaic–first quarter 4th, context probably late 4th; MT, P:24–25, Room A,
          fill over bedrock
C199

Lot 894   5th, to at least middle (later figurine), context probably late 4th; MT, Q:25,
          same as 893
C131

Lot 896   Archaic–Roman; MT, P–Q:24, surface
C6   **C228**   MF-10606
C67   **C245**   MF-10609
C72   **H110**   MF-10612
C86   **H246**   MF-10623
C168   **H278**   MF-10625
C171   **H367**   MF-10629
C227   **H370**   MF-10643

Lot 897   6th–mid 4th (later figurines); MT, P–Q:24, general fill
C138   **I91**
C250   MF-10646
H351

Lot 1945   Archaic–Roman (late 4th A.C.); MT, Q:19, Well 1961-11, upper fill
C235   **H417**   **R11**
H15   **H418**   MF-10662
H136   **V1**   MF-10665
H301   **V2**   MF-10666
H321   **V4**   MF-10669
H330   **V17**   MF-10945
H332   **I21**   MF-10949
H343   **I87**   MF-10951
H348   **I90**   MF-10952
H404   **R2**

Lot 1946   Classical–Roman (late 4th A.C.); MT, Q:19, Well 1961-11, lower fill
MF-10954

Lot 1948   mixed, to Roman; MT, Q:24, under tile layer (see 1947)
H224

Lot 1953   Archaic–Roman; MT, R–S:25, surface
C10   **H53**   **I15**
C11   **H91**   **I23**
C15   **H92**   **I45**
C26   **H96**   **R26**
C41   **H109**   MF-11012
C47   **H114**   MF-11016
C48   **H162**   MF-11020
C74   **H176**   MF-11026
C91   **H363**   MF-11035
C96   **H368**   MF-11037
C127   **H384**   MF-11040
C248   **V25**

Lot 1954   Late Archaic–late 4th; MT, O–P:23, general fill
C196

Lot 1955   Archaic–Roman; MT, O–R:23–24, surface

C99	**I77**
C180	MF-11054
H106	MF-11058

Lot 1956   mid–second half 5th (later figurines); MT, R:25, Room G, floor
H30

Lot 1962   Archaic–early 3rd; MT, R:23–24, Area D, general fill south of Grave 1962-1

C33	**H56**	**H410**
C34	**H139**	**V38**
C73	**H257**	**I17**
C190	**H308**	

Lot 1963   4th; MT, R:23–24, fill on bedrock south of Area D
H88
H98
H365
I14

Lot 1964   Archaic–Classical, Roman coin, context at least second half 4th A.C.; MT,
O:23–24, general fill over Roman Stoa
C148
I95

Lot 1977   6th–5th (later figurine), context Late Roman; MT, R:23–24, surface
C78

Lot 1978   Archaic–Roman; MT, R:23–24, surface

C263	**H184**	**H376**
H32	**H200**	**H385**
H69	**H210**	**I78**
H165	**H333**	

Lot 1981   mixed, to Roman; MT, Q:23–24, disturbance
H54

Lot 1982   (= 2249) Archaic–later 4th/beginning 3rd; MT, P:24
H118
MF-11217

Lot 1993   (= 2249) Archaic–late 4th; MT, P:23–24

C76	**H277**
C156	**H279**
H115	MF-11297
H211	

Lot 1994   Archaic–early 4th? (later figurine), Late Roman coin; MT, O–P:23, general fill
C230
H152

Lot 1998   mixed, to Roman; MT, Q:24, surface
H425
H426
MF-11310
MF-11311

Lot 1999   mixed, to Roman; MT, Q:24, fill over tile layer
C153
C251

Lot 2000   Archaic (later figurines), context at least late 4th, possibly to Roman; MT,
             R:24, accumulation over Area D
             MF-11329

Lot 2003   Archaic–mid-5th (later figurine), context late 4th; MT, P–Q:24, general fill
             MF-11332
             MF-11333

Lot 2009   Archaic–Roman; MT, P–Q:26–27, surface
             C42   MF-11657
             C211   MF-11658
             C276   MF-11667

Lot 2010   Archaic–early 4th A.C.; MT, P–Q:27, quarry, general fill to bedrock
             C214   **I44**
             H95   MF-11684
             H420

Lot 2011   Archaic–late 5th (later figurine); MT, P:26, Room E, collapse of north wall
             H232
             H403
             MF-11689
             MF-11691

Lot 2013   Archaic–Roman; MT, R:26, surface
             C3   **H63**
             C19   MF-11707
             C69   MF-11709
             C186

Lot 2018   Archaic–Roman; LT, M–N:26–27, surface
             C226

Lot 2026   6th–mid-5th (later figurine) context no later than late 5th, figurine is
             contamination; LT, Building N–O:25–26, packing behind south wall.
             C162
             H45

Lot 2029   5th–early 4th; LT, Building M–N:25–26, Room 2, general fill
             H248
             MF-11726

Lot 2035   6th–4th A.C.; MT, R:26, fill over bedrock
             H164
             H293
             H356
             MF-11731

Lot 2038   Archaic–Roman; MT, Q–R:26–29, surface to bedrock
             H18
             H41
             MF-11749

Lot 2044   Archaic–Roman; MT, Q:25–26, general fill east of Pit A
             C5
             C95

Lot 2045   Classical–Roman; MT, P:27–30, surface
             MF-11770

Lot 2046   Archaic–late 5th; MT, P:26, fill over terrace floor north of Wall 2
             C281

Lot 2047 Classical–Roman; LT, O:28–30, surface
MF-11768
MF-13425

Lot 2048 Archaic–Roman; MT, Q:25–26, surface
C104
C234
H315

Lot 2063 chiefly 4th–early Hellenistic (later figurine); UT, R:20, fill overlying
lower steps of Theatral Area

C80	**H17**	**H85**
H10	**H52**	MF-11781

Lot 2064 4th; UT, R:20, Theatral Area, burnt deposit
C269
H388
I49

Lot 2066 Archaic–Roman; LT, O:26, surface
C60
H145
H295

Lot 2067 5th–third quarter 4th (later figurine); LT, general fill overlying
Building N–O:25–26
C213
MF-11889

Lot 2070 5th–late 4th; LT, N:27, general fill
H320

Lot 2087 7th–Roman; MT, Q:20–22, surface
R16
MF-13457

Lot 2088 Archaic–Roman; MT, Q:20–22, tile layer

C93	**V12**	**R25**
C136	**I33**	MF-11831
H38	**R19**	

Lot 2102 Roman; MT, P:22–23, tile patch B
H3

Lot 2104 6th–Roman; MT, Q:22–23, tile patch D
V5
I92
R29

Lot 2106 7th–Roman; MT, P–Q:22–23, fill under tile layer
C103
H266

Lot 2107 Archaic–Roman, Byzantine; UT, Q–S:17–20, surface to bedrock

C16	**H185**	**H424**
C126	**H289**	**H428**
C266	**H292**	**V14**
H16	**H299**	**V34**
H22	**H307**	**I52**
H24	**H310**	**I57**
H25	**H340**	**R4**
H26	**H371**	**R6**
H87	**H390**	**R8**
H94	**H397**	**R9**
H128	**H402**	**R10**
H130	**H405**	**R18**
H173	**H417**	MF-11913

Lot 2108   Classical–Roman; MT, P:20–21, Cistern 1964-1, tunnel
           H89

Lot 2110   5th–first half 4th, context ca. third quarter 4th; LT, N–O:24–25,
           pottery dump over Building N–O:24–25
           C70

Lot 2111   (= 2249) 4th–beginning 3rd; MT, O–P:23
           C170   MF-11838
           C261   MF-11841
           H170   MF-11842
           H269

Lot 2141   Archaic–end 5th, Roman; LT, general fill over Building N–O:24–25
           C1

Lot 2145   chiefly 4th, Roman, Byzantine; MT, O–P:23, Trapezoidal Building,
           intrusive fill
           I9

Lot 2150   Early Archaic–Roman; MT, O–P:18–20, surface
           H335

Lot 2151   6th–second half 4th A.C.; MT, P:19–20, fill against south wall,
           Building O–P:19–20 (Propylon)
           MF-11880

Lot 2152   5th–4th, context at least late 4th; LT, N–O:23, dumped pottery fill over
           Building N–O:22–23
           C44   **C253**   MF-13415
           C140   **C265**   MF-13452
           C161   **V23**   MF-13942

Lot 2153   Roman, few Classical; MT, P–Q:20–22, surface
           V6

Lot 2156   Archaic–Roman; MT, P–Q:20–22, surface and general fill
           C62   **H272**
           C236   MF-11869
           H149   MF-13424
           H203

Lot 2159   Archaic–Roman; LT, near J:23, general fill
           C90

Lot 2160   5th–early 4th (later figurines); MT, O–P:21, test in west end of
           Trapezoidal Building, layer 1
           I6

Lot 2163   Archaic–Classical, Roman contamination; MT, O:22–23, fill north
           of Roman Stoa
           H66

Lot 2164   Archaic–Late Roman; MT, Q:23, dark deposit at base of Theatral Area
           R15
           MF-11862

Lot 2167   Archaic–4th, coin of 4th A.C.; MT, P:23, general fill in Trapezoidal Building
           H219

Lot 2168   Classical–Late Roman, context 5th–6th A.C.; MT, Q:22, fill over
           Late Roman Grave 1964-4 (no. 26).
           R22

Lot 2171   6th–mid 5th; LT, dumped pottery fill west of Building N–O:22–23
           C274

Lot 2190   6th–Roman; LT, N:24, general fill
C194

Lot 2210   Archaic–Roman; LT, M–O:27–29, quarry
C224
C252
H265
V19

Lot 2213   5th–4th; LT, O:27, general fill in quarry
C155

Lot 2230   6th–late 5th; MT, P–Q:26, Room E, removal of floor 2
C5

Lot 2234   first half 4th, later?; MT, O–P:23, early floor under Trapezoidal Building
C137
H202

Lot 2237 Archaic–Roman; MT, P:23, Roman fill over Archaic oikos wall
C184
H68
I2
MF-11968

Lot 2239   Archaic–Roman; MT, robbing trench, west wall of Building O–P:19–20
(Propylon)

C29	**H291**	**I94**
C107	**H327**	MF-12004
H133	**V3**	MF-12040
H207	**I34**	

Lot 2240   Archaic–Roman; MT, fill on floor of Building O–P:19–20 (Propylon)

C169	**H419**	**I64**
C205	**H430**	**I85**
H42	**I31**	MF-12010
H361	**I32**	MF-12022

Lot 2247   Archaic–Roman; LT, N–O:19–20, surface

H111	**I83**
H255	**I86**
H316	MF-12026

Lot 2248   Archaic–Roman; MT, robbing trench, north wall, Building O–P:19–20
(Propylon)
H8
H75
H140
MF-12032
MF-12033

Lot 2249   few 6th, chiefly 5th–4th, beginning 3rd, MT, O:22–23, construction fill,
Trapezoidal Building

C12	**H33**	**H160**
C13	**H35**	**H186**
C25	**H67**	**H189**
C77	**H73**	**H206**
C79	**H86**	**H220**
C119	**H90**	**H236**
C215	**H97**	**H249**
C229	**H104**	**H252**
C236	**H134**	**H264**
C240	**H147**	**H271**
H31	**H157**	**H285**

Lot 2249 (cont.)

H296	**V29**	**I69**
H298	**V30**	**I70**
H347	**V40**	**I73**
H360	**V41**	MF-12043
H362	**V42**	MF-13407
H364	**I18**	MF-13419
H391	**I27**	MF-13438
H394	**I40**	MF-13461
V27	**I43**	MF-13714
V28	**I51**	

Lot 2250 (= 2249) MT, O:22–23

C177
C278
MF-12054

Lot 3206 mixed, to Roman; LT, M–O:17–20, surface and discarded baskets

C94	**H303**	**I54**
C175	**H306**	**I63**
H167	**H357**	MF-13450
H221	**I37**	

Lot 3215 Archaic–Hellenistic, possibly Early Roman; MT, same as 3208

I72

Lot 3217 5th–third quarter 3rd; LT, N–O:17–18, Pit 1965-1

C36	**H241**	**I28**
H6	**H281**	**I30**
H9	**H300**	**I42**
H19	**H322**	**I48**
H122	**H350**	MF-13431
H191	**H354**	MF-13745

Lot 3222 Archaic–3rd A.C.; LT, votive pottery dump over Building M:16–17

C39	**C216**	**H297**
C46	**C220**	**H334**
C53	**C259**	**H341**
C57	**H28**	**H375**
C65	**H79**	**H381**
C66	**H113**	**I4**
C84	**H166**	**I46**
C89	**H169**	MF-12551
C106	**H177**	MF-13433
C204	**H226**	MF-13448
C206	**H238**	MF-13449
C207	**H253**	MF-13803
C212	**H262**	MF-13973

Lot 3223 5th–Roman; LT, M:18–19, general fill

H13
H358
H414

Lot 3226 Archaic–Roman; LT, Building M:16–17, dumped fill over Room 1

C7
C14
C64
H231

Lot 3227 5th–Hellenistic; LT, Building M:16–17, general fill in Room 2

V37

Lot 3228   4th–later 3rd, context to 146 B.C.?; LT, Building M:16–17, filling in
of Room 2

H43	**H328**	**I24**
H180	**H329**	**I58**
H194	**H378**	
H208	**V24**	

Lot 3229   6th–Hellenistic; LT, Building M:16–17, Room 1, fill over collapsed south wall

C49
H156
I38

Lot 3230   Archaic–Early Roman; LT, Building M:16–17, Room 1, collapse of south wall

C8	**H121**	**H338**
C24	**H150**	**H421**
C28	**H196**	**H427**
C233	**H197**	**V22**
C258	**H198**	**I79**
H12	**H199**	**I89**
H34	**H240**	**R20**
H36	**H247**	**R27**
H64	**H284**	MF-13436
H119	**H324**	MF-13464

Lot 3231   5th–later 3rd?; LT, Building M:16–17, Room 2, phase 2, raising of floor level,
removal of bench

C43
I1

Lot 3233   6th probably to 146 B.C., Early Roman; LT, Building M:16–17, Room 1,
stratum under collapsed wall, over floor

C115
C217
H325
H345

Lot 3410   Hellenistic to 146 B.C., Early Roman; LT, Building M:16–17, Room 1,
stratum immediately over floor and west couch

H5
H218
R23

Lot 4344   Archaic–Roman; LT, M–N:25–26, surface

C32	**H182**
C195	**H205**
C200	**R12**

Lot 4347   5th–end 4th; LT, general fill overlying Building N–O:22–23

C56
C201
C271
MF-12128

Lot 4348   Archaic–Roman; LT, O:20–21, surface

C63
H127
H261
H326
I68

Lot 4349   7th–Roman; LT, O:18, surface

C37	**H131**	**V31**
C244	**H305**	**I20**
C264	**H319**	**I35**
H55	**H377**	**I53**
H93	**H409**	**I88**
H108	**H412**	MF-12140
H126	**H423**	MF-14012

Lot 4350   7th–Roman; LT/MT, O:18, robbing trench for Roman terrace wall 11

C93	**H230**
C154	**H400**
C198	MF-13482

Lot 4352   late 8th/early 7th–Roman; MT, O–P:22–23, general fill over north side of
Archaic oikos

C150	**H214**
C255	**H260**
H81	MF-12134

Lot 4356   (= 2249) MT, O–P:22-23

C144	**H46**
C149	**H204**
C166	**H267**

Lot 4357   mixed, to Roman; MT, P:21–22, Roman fill in wall trench of dismantled
north wall of oikos
H60
H61

Lot 4358   mid–third quarter 5th; MT, O–P:22, fill in Pit 1965-3 (Pit E)
MF-13447

Lot 4362   Archaic–Roman; MT, O:20, robbing trench of east wall of
Building O–P:19–20 (Propylon)
C111
H201
H411

Lot 4368   mixed, to Roman; MT, O:21–22, surface
C237
C239
H387

Lot 4369   (= 2249) MT, O:22
C129
C208
V36
MF-12160

Lot 4377   Classical–Late Roman; UT, Q–R:16–17, S–T:20, surface fill

C75	**H168**	**H393**
C88	**H174**	**V39**
C101	**H245**	**I5**
C160	**H256**	**I62**
H117	**H273**	**I75**

Lot 4378   5th–4th; UT, R:17, Theatral Area, deposit on bedrock
C93

Lot 4379   late 4th (later figurine), context could be late 4th/beginning 3rd or Roman;
           UT, R:17, Theatral Area, north deposit over bedrock

C20	**C187**	**H317**
C22	**H21**	**H339**
C100	**H23**	**H389**
C132	**H178**	**I41**
C158	**H225**	**I61**
C181	**H243**	MF-13975

Lot 4381   Archaic–Roman; MT, O:20–21, pillaging trench over Roman terrace wall 11
           V11

Lot 4382   Archaic–4th; MT, O:21, fill in entrance court above Pit F
           C105
           C272
           H209

Lot 4383   Classical, Roman coin; MT, O:21, contents of Pit F in entrance court
           H171

Lot 4384   mixed, to Roman, MT, O–P:15–17, surface to bedrock
           I66

Lot 4385   Archaic–Roman; MT, O–P:13–15, same as 4384
           C257
           V21

Lot 4386   Archaic–Roman; MT, N–O:15–17, same as 4384
           C179
           H251
           I76

Lot 4387   Archaic–Roman; MT, N–O:13–15, same as 4384

C27	**C202**	**H239**
C40	**H103**	**I56**
C55	**H142**	
C114	**H181**	

Lot 4388   Classical–4th (later figurine), context could be as late as Roman; MT, N:20,
           general fill in entrance court
           C225
           H57

Lot 4392   5th–late 4th; LT, fill north of Building N–O:22–23
           C189

Lot 4394   5th–later 4th; LT, Building N–O:23–24, foundation trench for north wall
           C59

Lot 4395   5th; LT, Building N–O:22–23, fill in northeast corner of room
           C188

Lot 4398   late 6th–5th (later figurines), context third quarter 4th or slightly later;
           LT, Building N:21, Room 2, general fill in north end
           V20

Lot 4400   6th–second half 5th (later figurine, must be contamination); LT,
           Building N–O:22–23, packing behind south wall
           C4
           H71

Lot 4404   5th–later 3rd; LT, Building N–O:17–18, clay layer overwe st end

C23	**V13**
H288	**I8**
H349	

Lot 4409 6th–Roman; LT, M–N:12, surface
    H48
    H268
    H392

Lot 4417 Archaic–Roman; MT, N–O:13–17, robbing trench for Roman terrace wall 11
    H263
    H336
    H366

Lot 4418 Classical (later figurine), context to end 4th; MT, Building O–P:19–20
    (Propylon), foundation trench for south wall
    H146

Lot 4430 5th–4th; MT, same as 4429, fill above oval cutting
    C249

Lot 4448 4th–Hellenistic, few Roman; LT, Building N:21, Room 1, phase 2,
    abandonment
    H2
    H227

Lot 4450 (= 4448) 4th; LT, N:21
    C110
    H29
    H138
    H342

Lot 4452 5th–late 4th, Roman contamination; LT, Building N:21, Room 1,
    phase 1, fill over floor
    C112

Lot 4461 5th–late 4th; LT, same as 4458
    V18

Lot 4466 late 6th–mid-4th; LT, Building N:21, Room 1, phase 3, fill covering
    earlier south couch
    C192
    C219
    I29

Lot 4476 5th–4th; LT, Building N:21, Room 2, fill over floor
    MF-13466

Lot 4478 4th–146 B.C.; LT, Building M–N:25–26, Room 3, top fill in cistern
    MF-13147

Lot 4492 5th–first half 4th; LT, Building N:22–23, fill covering west wall and
    west side of building
    H359

Lot 5613 mixed, to Roman, Byzantine; LT, L–N:15–20, miscellaneous finds

C38	**H144**	**H369**
C141	**H151**	**H408**
C232	**H161**	**I7**
H107	**H179**	MF-68-349
H132	**H228**	

Lot 5614 late 5th–2nd; MT, Hellenistic fill against south face of north foundation,
    Roman Propylon
    V15

Lot 5618 Classical–Roman; LT, Roman fill over Building M–N:19
    H58

Lot 5624   Classical–2nd; LT, fill covering Building M–N:19
H431

Lot 5627   late 4th; LT, Building M–N:19, stratum over floor
H372

Lot 5648   6th–3rd quarter 3rd; LT, Building M:16–17, Room 1, top layer on
east couch
H82

Lot 5711   Classical–late 4th, later?; LT, Building M:16–17, Room 4, debris
over west wall
H223
H235
I47

Lot 5712   early 4th, context late 4th or early 3rd; LT, Building M:16–17,
Room 4, floor 5
H290

Lot 5714   6th–5th, at least last quarter; LT, Building M:16–17, general fill
under Room 4
I36

Lot 5715   late 4th–early 3rd; LT, M:15, general fill west of Building M:16–17
I25

Lot 5718   mixed, to Roman; LT, L:15–16, general fill
MF-68-51

Lot 6184   mid–second half 3rd; LT, Building M–N:19, stratum covering
south couch, phase 2
H44

Lot 6185   late 4th/early 3rd; LT, Building M–N:19, stratum covering south couch,
phase 1
C121

Lot 6189   later 4th; LT, Building M–N:19, fill in south closet
H125
H148

Lot 6204   end 4th, context at least 146 B.C.; MT, O:20–21, debris over entrance court
C128

Lot 6214   mixed, to Roman; LT, J–M:19–22, miscellaneous finds from surface layers

C35	**H187**	**H422**
C93	**H188**	**V45**
C197	**H190**	**I50**
C218	**H213**	**I71**
C243	**H283**	**I80**
C246	**H287**	**I84**
H74	**H313**	**R3**
H78	**H323**	MF-69-350
H141	**H337**	MF-69-355
H158	**H355**	MF-69-356
H159	**H380**	MF-69-359

Lot 6215   mixed, to Roman; LT, J–N:20, miscellaneous finds from stairway

C87	**H275**	**I96**
C260	**H344**	**R5**
H59	**H379**	MF-69-371
H83	**H399**	
H274	**V8**	

Lot 6233   mixed, to Roman; UT, Q–R:15–16, Theatral Area, fill over bedrock

C58	**H143**	MF-70-72
H49	**H222**	MF-70-78
H80	**I55**	
H129	**I67**	

Lot 6500   mixed, to Roman; UT, S–T:21, Late Roman fill over Theater
C51
C120
H120
H244
I59
MF-70-245

Lot 6501   mixed, to Roman; UT, S–T:21, same as 6500
C113

Lot 6502   5th–first half 3rd (later figurine), context probably later, Early Roman?;
UT, S–T:21, fill over lowest step of Theater
H401

Lot 6503   late 4th–early 3rd (later figurines), few Roman, context probably Roman;
UT, S–T:21, miniature hydria dump over Theater

H7	**H20**	**H311**
H11	**H27**	**H331**
H14	**H215**	**H406**

Lot 6505   Classical–Late Roman; UT, Building T–U:22 (East Temple), fill in trenches
of dismantled walls
I60

Lot 6506   Classical–Early Roman; UT, Building T–U:22 (East Temple), working chip
construction fill behind south wall
H302
H304

Lot 6507   Archaic–Roman; UT, R–U:21–23. Miscellaneous finds, Upper Terrace

C82	**H407**
H37	**I26**
H50	**R17**
H124	

Lot 6638   Classical, Late Roman; UT, Building T:16–17 (West Temple),
destruction debris
H40
H77
H416
I65
MF-70-226

Lot 6640   Late Classical–Early Roman; UT, Building T:16–17 (West Temple),
construction packing behind south wall
H47

Lot 6641   Classical, Late Roman; UT, Building S–T:16–17 (Hellenistic Temple?),
debris over south wall bedding
H258

Lot 6723   late 6th–late 4th/early 3rd; LT, same as 6722, lower fill
C268

Lot 72-101   second half 5th–second half 4th, three Geometric sherds; LT,
Building N:12–13, phase 1, filling in of west room
C133

Lot 72-121   first half 4th; MT, O–P:27–28, quarry, fill over bedrock
  C102

Lot 72-122   Mycenaean–Classical; LT, J–K:12–18, miscellaneous finds
  C185
  C275
  H72
  H155

Lot 72-134   last quarter 4th; LT, Building K–L:25–26, debris covering Room 2
  H123

Lot 73-98   Classical–Roman; UT, same as 73-96, destruction debris on floor
  H195

Lot 73-99   Roman, 1st to later 4th A.C.(figurines are Greek); UT, same as 73-96,
  robbing trenches
  I82

Lot 73-108   5th–second half 4th; MT, P:24–25, foundation trenches for south wall, Pit B
  C172
  H270

Lot 73-119   6th–at least second quarter 5th; LT, Building K:23, packing beneath
  earliest floor
  C81

Lot 73-138   mid–end 5th; MT, P–Q:25, fill against east wall, Room A
  C203

Lot 73-143   mostly Roman, late 1st–possibly mid-2nd A.C.; MT, Q:22, baulk under
  Late Roman grave 1964-4
  R7

Lot 73-144   mixed, to Roman; LT/MT, L–M:23–24, P–Q:25–26, miscellaneous finds

C2	**C247**	**R24**
C68	**V43**	MF-73-100
C221	**R14**	

Lot 1994-68   late 5th–first half 4th (?); LT, Building N:21, Room 1, removal of phase 2,
  floor 2
  C254

Lot 1994-78   last quarter 5th, early (?); LT, Building N:21, Room 1, construction fill
  for phase 2, overlying floor 4
  C130

INDEX OF ANCIENT TEXTS CITED

INDEX OF CORINTH COMPARANDA

COMPARANDA FROM THE SANCTUARY OF DEMETER AND KORE CITED IN THE DISCUSSION

SCULPTURE AND MISCELLANEOUS FINDS, INCLUDING SMALL BRONZES

S-2666	341^{109}	SF-64-5	328^{41}	SF-71-1	269^{49}
S-2667	341^{109}	SF-65-12	40^{129}, 133^{111}	MF-10653	267^{18}
SF-40-6	11^{41}	SF-65-14	61^{257}, 186^{422}, 192^{452}, 199^{500}	MF-10785	267^{18}
SF-61-17	268^{39}	SF-65-22	120^{35}, 266^{14}	MF-11303	193^{458}
SF-62-10	268^{39}	SF-69-8	61^{248}	MF-12170	267^{18}

ARCHAIC AND LINGERING ARCHAIC FIGURINES

MF-10374	61, 335	MF-11884	61, 335	MF-13561	183, 331
MF-10392	267	MF-11906	267	MF-13626	117
MF-10538	8^{26}	MF-12009	183, 331	MF-13661	73
MF-10539	8^{26}	MF-12016	19^{61}	MF-13626	125
MF-10543	8^{26}	MF-12034	133	MF-13627	125
MF-10943	8^{26}	MF-12057	8	MF-13628	125
MF-10957	125	MF-12162	133, 187	MF-13739	266
MF-11053	335	MF-12862	125	MF-71-54	71
MF-11753	267	MF-12891	288	MF-71-270	267
MF-11856	335	MF-13462	65	MF-71-276	269
MF-11864	76, 78	MF-13558	71	MF-73-97	335
MF-11873	176				

COMPARANDA FROM ELSEWHERE IN CORINTH CITED IN THE CATALOGUE AND DISCUSSION

This list includes only single pieces cited in the discussion. References to groups of figurines can be found in the general index by reference to type, e.g., banqueters.

FIGURINES AND MOLDS CITED IN THE CATALOGUE

MF-2	*sub* **I43, I44**	MF-2991	*sub* **H192**	MF-8056	*sub* **C224**
MF-685	*sub* **C57**	MF-3196	*sub* **H70**	MF-8087	*sub* **C218**
MF-1023	*sub* **C217**	MF-3396	*sub* **H66**	MF-8636	*sub* **V18**
MF-1034	*sub* **C274**	MF-3417	*sub* **H380**	MF-8636bis	*sub* **V18**
MF-1035	*sub* **C274**	MF-3465	*sub* **H427**	MF-8664	*sub* **C83**
MF-1156	*sub* **R15**	MF-3863	*sub* **H345**	MF-8666	*sub* **C91**
MF-1424	*sub* **H223**	MF-3875	*sub* **H427**	MF-8667	*sub* **C243**
MF-1576	*sub* **C189**	MF-3882	*sub* **H301**	MF-8784	*sub* **V18**
MF-1608	*sub* **H364**	MF-3888	*sub* **C127**	MF-8785	*sub* **V18**
MF-1866	*sub* **H52, H54**	MF-3937	*sub* **H165**	MF-8994	*sub* **H427**
MF-1886	*sub* **V19**	MF-3979	*sub* **C71**	MF-9012	*sub* **C188**
MF-1896	*sub* **C225**	MF-4002	*sub* **C122**	MF-9155	*sub* **C227**
MF-1904	*sub* **H302**	MF-4036	*sub* **V19**	MF-9212	*sub* **H427**
MF-2193	*sub* **R15**	MF-4200	*sub* **C217**	MF-9251	*sub* **H401**
MF-2385	*sub* **H323, H326**	MF-4224	*sub* **H52**	MF-9254	*sub* **H345**
MF-2465	*sub* **V16**	MF-5266	*sub* **C125**	MF-9263	*sub* **H345**
MF-2676b	*sub* **C87**	MF-5669	*sub* **H242**	MF-9265	*sub* **H345**
MF-2756	*sub* **C104**	Mf-6075	*sub* **C33**	MF-9453	*sub* **C274**
MF-2904	*sub* **C273**	MF-7411	*sub* **C169**	MF-9648	*sub* **C224**
MF-2905	*sub* **C227**	MF-7579	*sub* **V9**	MF-10083	*sub* **I52**

FIGURINES AND MISCELLANEOUS FINDS, INCLUDING MOLDS, CITED IN THE DISCUSSION

SCULPTURE AND SMALL BRONZES CITED IN THE DISCUSSION

INDEX OF COMPARANDA
IN MUSEUMS AND COLLECTIONS

GENERAL INDEX

This index is based mainly upon the discussions of the figurines on pp. 1–81, 115–201, 249–259, 265–277, 283–298, 311–316, and 321–346. The catalogues on the intervening pages have received only a limited indexing, since such subjects as attributes and costume, when significant, are also covered in the discussions, where references to specific catalogue numbers can be found. Consequently, the catalogues have been indexed only for figurine types (e.g., animals; children: Hellenistic), for names of deities, and for specific references to excavation sites in Corinth and elsewhere. The catalogue of imported figurines has been indexed only for provenience and names of deities. References to comparanda in both the discussions and the catalogues can be found in the *Index of Corinth Comparanda* (pp. 370–372) and the *Index of Comparanda in Museums and Collections* (p. 373). Alternate terms employed in the text are indicated in parentheses, e.g., "document (record) reliefs."

ACHELOÖS 77[381], 325

Acrocorinth. *See* Corinth

actors 71, 185[420], 194–196, 197–198, 244–245, 274, 332, 334[76], 345; Attic 195, 291

adaptation of types. *See* workshop organization and practice

adolescence: adolescent votaries 127, 336–337; representation of 118, 185, 337

Adonis 77, 170; Adonia, at Athens 170[321]

Aeneas 170

Africa: modern rituals using figurines 337[97], 339

Africans: bronzes 313; figurines 298, 313 (Roman); in Roman art 313[10]

age: age groups 126–127, 188, 336–337, 340; at marriage 118–119, 338; naturalistic representation of 117, 254–255. *See also* old age

   Age of: banqueters 67; children 69, 126–127, 188, 191, 315 (Roman), 335, 336–337; Eros 181; female votaries 117, 126–127, 337; youths 188, 335

aidoia. See cakes

'Ain Gazal: Neolithic figurines 322[5]

alabastron: associated with Aphrodite 274; figurines carrying 272, 274

Alexander 160, 161[275]

Alexandria: source of African types 313

altar: of Eros 152; at Kommos 322[11]. *See also* arulae

Amazon: figurine of(?) 57

amulets 68, 69, 73, 143, 171[331]

Amymone: on arulae and polos 270

anakalypteria (unveiling) 36, 74, 149, 153, 174, 195, 198, 287, 291, 329

anatomical votives 49, 71, 273[74], 339

anatomy: distortions or exaggerations 44, 53, 194, 196, 197, 198, 199, 291, 295, 313 (Roman), 321 (prehistoric)

Andanian Mysteries of Messenia 45, 266[11], 340

animals: animal-riders 78, 176–177, 178; figurines 265–269, 277–278, 322[5] (Neolithic); imports 266, 267, 298; as symbols 265. *See also* handmade figurines or parts: animals; sacrifice; *individual animals by name*

anomalous Corinthian figurines 283–284, 285, 295, 296, 297, 298

Anthesteria 194

Anthologia Palatina 324. *See also* Index of Ancient Texts Cited, p. 369

Aphrodite:

   Attributes and dedications: alabastron 274; attributes shared with Kore 43, 47, 126, 190, 194, 328, 329, 330; birds 43, 126; "dolls" 50, 171–172, 331, 339; dove 136, 268; flowers 125, 176; goose 190, 194; grapes 194; headband 273; pomegranate 47; swan 39

   Functions: chthonic aspect 331; maternal aspect 169–170; nurturer of children (kourotrophos) 71, 169, 331, 338; overlap with Demeter 330, 331; patroness of fertility 74, 170; patroness of marriage 71, 169, 170, 331, 338; protectress of city 170, 271, 331

   Cult titles: Ourania 170, 255 (equated with Cybele); Pandemos 177

   Worship: on Acrocorinth 43, 118, 170, 171; at Athens 191; ball games 126, 201; in Cyprus 71; dance 80, 152; at Demeter sanctuary 43, 71, 125, 148, 169–171, 328, 331; *hierodouloi* (hetairai) 118, 171, 172, 339; at Kharayeb 190, 328; at Lokroi 125[60], 170, 274, 330

   Myths: birth 176; linked with Persephone 170

   Iconography: Anadyomene 197, 314; coiffure 159, 175, 179; dancing 175–176; distinguishing from mortals 169; distinguishing from nymphs 177, 179; nude 135–136, 139, 149; pudica 136; represented with brides 153[239]; seated 47, 157, 162, 178, 180, 181, 235, 294

   Figurines:

   CORINTHIAN 43, 47, 58, 81, 129, 130, 135, 136, 138–139, 146, 147, 148, 149, 150, 157, 162, 166, 169–177, 178, 179, 180, 181, 182, 231–234, 257, 271, 275, 289, 292, 326, 327, 329, 330–331, 342, 346; parodies 197; Roman 256, 312, 313, 314, 315, 316, 317, 341

188, 190; Maltese 72–73; Mesopotamian figurines of 322

"dolls" 2, 48–53, 94–96, 141, 322, 339, 345; adapted for other types 58, 63, 136, 171, 175, 176, 183, 184; and Aphrodite 50, 58, 170, 171–172, 331, 339; Attic 32, 33, 52, 58, 172[335], 339; cakes carried by 49, 273; chitoniskos (lingering Archaic) 23, 48, 50, 52; coiffures of 171–172, 296; construction 50–52; dedication 50, 172, 331, 338 (by brides), 339; draped 32, 50, 59–60; educative purpose 339; grotesque 128[78]; handmade 50; heads of "dolls" and related heads 30, 34, 41, 42, 48[184], 51, 53–58, 96–101, 125, 144, 161, 163, 164, 166, 176, 177, 191, 344, 345; nudity 49, 50, 171, 172, 339; parodies 53, 60, 197; quantity found 3–4, 48, 172; scale 51; seated 48, 49[185], 52, 53, 58, 171, 339; survivals 131; symbolism 49, 339; torsos and limbs 50–53, 125, 272; uses and meanings 49, 339; with rigid legs 48, 52, 53. *See also* archetypes: of "dolls"; molds: mold types: "dolls"; dancers: related to "dolls"

donkey-riders 78

dove. *See* birds

drapery: added or reworked, to adapt types 58, 60, 125, 136, 141, 175, 178, 184[410], 186.

Drapery motifs: arrowhead folds 139, 256; baring of shoulder 147, 175, 179, 184; butterfly folds 250; cape over shoulder 133, 139; collapsing (trailing) hem folds 151, 174, 180, 250, 252, 257, 287, 295; crease marks 134; crinkly skirt folds 143, 144; cuffed fold around ankle 137, 138, 140, 180; eye folds 250; knot in crook of arm 137, 138; knot in Isiac dress 314; looped (curved) folds around breasts 36, 133, 137; mantle billowing over head 176, 177, 178; mantle curtain behind or beside figure 60–61, 135, 149, 175, 185; mantle roll framing abdomen 148–150, 178; omega folds 155, 201, 250, 252, 286; sanguisuga folds 155; tension folds in triangular pattern 139, 142, 143, 147, 157; transparent chiton 147, 148, 179, 197, 201; transparent mantle over chiton 141[153], 256; triangular pleat at neckline 123

Drapery style: Archaic 63, 72; Attic "quiet" style 33, 59; Attic Rich Style 80, 179, 180, 201, 287, 289[24]; Classical 25, 28, 147, 179; Classicizing 250; 4th-century B.C. 134, 136, 155; Hellenistic 142–143

dress: codes, cultic 121. *See also* costume

duck. *See* birds

dwarfs: associated with Dionysos 199; head 199; ithyphallic 152

EARS: projecting, in grotesques 198

earrings 45, 47, 160, 177, 192, 193, 198, 297

earthquake 7[20], 116

East Greek: imported figurines 285; influence on figurines 249; protomes 74; sculpture 139. *See also* Asia Minor; *individual sites by name*

economics:

Of coroplastic industry: 325, 343; decline in 3rd century B.C. 116; effects of prosperity on 115, 131; sale of figurines and workshop materials 20, 123, 277, 285, 326; in Sicily 115[2]; trade in figurines, model for 285–286

Of sacrifice: 266[7], 322

education 194, 335, 338, 339. *See also* marriage: preparation of girls for; social aspects of figurines

egg: carried by banqueters 65, 66, 67

Egypt: Alexandria as source of African types 313; Demeter-Isis 254; Egyptian deities at Kharayeb 190, 328; fertility figures 197, 339[105]; meaning of *chenalopex* in 190; Pharaonic iconography 76[370]; seated children 68. *See also* Naukratis

Eileithyia 178, 328

Eleusis 67, 333; bull and ram sacrifice 267; children in ritual 188[430]; *dadouchos* 124[49]; Eleusinian deities sacrificing 255[28]; Eubouleus 160[269], 259, 344; figurines 191; hearth initiates 62; impersonation of goddesses by priestess 255; male *mystai* 334; Mysteries 255, 265, 267; statue of Demeter 34, 35; thymiaterion 75; votive reliefs 62–63, 132, 148, 334[75]

Enna: statue of Demeter 184

ephedrismos 126, 146, 150, 162, 165, 168, 172[341], 189, 200–201, 248, 284, 293

Ephesos: Artemision, sculpture 161

Epidauros: Argive figurines 284; bronze 136[123]; Corinthian figurines 101, 163, 164, 227, 228, 284; Sanctuary of Apollo Maleatas, figurines 284; Temple of Artemis, sculpture 184; Temple of Asklepios, sculpture 36, 80–81, 136, 151, 155, 168, 184, 344

epigraphic evidence: for gift-giving 334[72]; name of Persephone on kotyle 61, 329, 330; for worship of Dionysos 76, 332

Epoikidie. *See* Demeter: functions and cult titles

Eretria: Corinthian figurines 28[34], 45; Thesmophorion, figurines 45, 127[72], 128, 191[443], 325, 336, 337, 340; votive relief 34[75]

Eros, erotes: age of 181; associated with Dionysos 153, 332; with brides 181; in cult of Demeter and Kore 181; Eros-Thanatos 161, 181, 332; on mirrors 152; piping 152; in sculpture 138, 142, 161, 182; on a thymiaterion 75; in vase painting 135, 152, 181, 182; worshiped at Kharayeb 190, 328

Figurines: 153, 192, 236, 328; with Aphrodite 47, 129, 135, 139, 142, 147, 150, 162, 166, 170, 174, 175, 176, 179, 180, 181, 182, 298, 331, 332; as a baby 181, 182, 193, 332, 345; with a dog 181[391]; in ephedrismos groups 201; flying 181–182, 193, 274, 277, 332; heads 193, 345; holding a mirror 181[391], 192; seated 181–182, 332; as a youth (Eros ephebe) 181, 182, 332

erotic *symplegma:* parody 197

ethnographic evidence: for interpretation of figurines 323[17], 325, 339; for use of figurines 127[75], 337[97], 339

mortals: dancers 151; distinguishing from deities 24, 117, 130, 169, 255, 256, 327; images converging with deities' 250, 255, 256, 327, 340; impersonating deities 255; mantled figurines represent 151; relation to deities on reliefs 255[31]; ritual connection with deities 159, 255; "Tanagra" figurines represent 142. *See also* votaries; worshipers

mortars 79, 268, 342

Mother of the Gods: naïskos of, from Delphi 253; worship in Corinth 253, 255, 331

mourning: figures 157; Demeter 157, 329; loosening and offering of hair 118

Mourning Women sarcophagus 151

Muses 120, 133, 138, 161, 163, 177, 294, 305

museums and collections: figurines in 21–22, 322. *For references to individual museums, see* Index of Comparanda in Museums and Collections, p. 373

music, musical instruments 340; figurines of musicians (Eretrian) 325, 340; kithara 270; lute 161[275]; lyre 269; lyre, figurines carrying 61, 65, 67, 188, 269, 270, 335; model chelys-lyre 152, 269; monkey playing lyre 268[28]; musicians on Pitsa plaque 188[430]; piping Eros 152; syrinx 200; tambourines, cymbals 49, 126[68]. *See also* satyrs: piping

Mycenae: statuette 35

Myrina 181, 182, 314; small-scale copies of sculpture 116, 134, 297

Myron: satyr, small-scale copy 116, 297[69]

myths: Sumerian 171. *See also Homeric Hymn to Demeter; individual deities and mythological characters by name*

NATURALISM: of animals 266; of children and young people 117, 118, 158, 185, 188, 254–255; Hellenistic 117; of old age 200

Naukratis: figurine 181[391]

Near Eastern fertility goddesses 74, 195[469], 268[37]

"Nemesis" type 120[36]

Neolithic figurines 322[5], 325[23], 339

Nereid monument, Xanthos 154

Nike: associated with Demeter 184; on arulae and polos 270; and marriage 184; Roman bronzes 313[9]; sculpture 54, 80, 147[193], 148, 151[221], 155, 179, 184
  Figurines: 28[34], 59[237], 136, 150, 166, 183–184, 237, 274, 277, 328, 331, 346; Roman 312, 313, 316

Nisyros: figurines 124

nudity: apotropaic 171[330]; of boys 70[317] (babies), 188, 194; of "dolls" 49, 50, 171, 172, 339; in parodies 197; in ritual 61, 172, 194; symbolism 61; of youths 61, 185, 334, 335

nurse: old 195, 196; seated 293 (Boeotian), 296 (Athenian and Boeotian)

nymphs 151, 157, 176, 325, 328; and marriage 177, 188[430], 331, 338; and childbearing and nurturing 177, 331; and Dionysos 178; and Pan 177; and satyrs 177; distinguishing from Aphrodite 177, 179;

grapes offered to 194; in cult of Demeter and Kore 177–178; in myth 177; sacrifice to 177, 331; sculpture 178; worship 177–178
  Figurines:
    CORINTHIAN: seated 177–180, 234–235, 294, 296, 331
    NON-CORINTHIAN: Tarentine 294, 305; uncertain provenience 296, 297, 306

Nyx: on Pergamon Altar 253, 258

OBESITY (corpulence): representations 53, 128[78], 196, 197, 199

obscenity: apotropaic use 197, 199

oklasma 80

old age: old courtesan 197; old nurse 195, 196; old woman 157, 200, 248; old women in cult 200, 340

Olympia: Artemis Altar, protome from 76; bronzes from 62; Heraia, girls' races at 336–337; Nike of Paionios 184; ritual at 332; Temple of Zeus, sculpture 25, 26, 39, 40, 62, 72, 344

Olynthus: figurine vases 76
  Figurines: "dolls" 51[199]; pigs 266[12]; satyrs 78[388]

orans pose 254

Orestes and Electra 160

Orphic Hymns 70, 77

Ouranos 170

owl. *See* birds

PAESTUM: figurines 45, 71, 294

painting of figurines 13–14, 19, 53, 55, 64, 133, 159, 160, 252, 256, 274; without underlying slip 76, 258; use of bright blue 14, 316; use of pink and red paint for flesh 14, 64, 133, 159, 160, 258, 274. *See also* gilding

παῖς ἀμφιθαλής 70

Pan 77, 152; and Demeter 79; and Dionysos 77, 79; and Kore 79; and nymphs 177
  Figurines: 32, 78–79, 114, 182, 199–200, 247, 291, 328, 332; Roman 312, 315, 318

parodies 44, 53, 60, 67, 71[330], 194–195, 196–198, 245–246, 291, 340, 343, 345

patera 63, 314

Pausanias 330. *See also* Index of Ancient Texts Cited, p. 369

Peleus and Thetis 36[91], 135

Pella: Thesmophorion: figurines 130[89], 184[416]

Peloponnesian War 2, 33

Penteskouphia: figurine 128[78]

peplos. *See* costume

peplos-figurines (peplophoroi) 283, 327, 329; molds 27, 30; parodies 196, 197
  CORINTHIAN: Classical seated 44, 46, 89, 90, 92–93, 293, 329; Classical standing 23–37, 38, 48, 56, 82–87, 149, 343, 344, 345; with short overfold 24–29, 294; with long overfold, unbelted 29–32; with long overfold, belted 32–35; with kolpos and overfold 35–37

vents 17–18, 266, 295

Venus 142

vine. *See* grapes

"visiting" deities 170, 183, 328[42], 331

votaries 272, 324, 334, 339; age of 117, 126–127, 337; convergence of images with deities or priestesses 255, 256, 327, 340; quantity found 3–4, 120

Figurines of female votaries:

CORINTHIAN: adolescent (postpubescent) 127, 336–337; chronology 128–129; prepubescent 35, 125–128, 336–337; representing brides 329; seated 44–45

Periods: Classical 24, 28, 30, 35, 44, 49, 131, 167, 294, 345; Hellenistic 17, 117–130, 131, 147, 202–208, 251, 252–253, 254, 255

Types: with ball 24, 44, 117, 125–126; with bird 24, 44, 117, 126; with box 44; with fillet 44; with flowers, fruit, or cakes 28, 44, 117, 124–125, 341; heads 158–159, 163; with piglet 17, 24, 26, 29, 117–123, 129, 131, 140, 143, 158, 159, 165, 167, 185, 190, 252, 253, 254[21], 255, 266, 276, 287, 294, 324, 325, 326, 327, 329, 337, 338, 340, 342, 343, 346; without offerings 126–128

NON-CORINTHIAN: Argive 120, 123, 286–287, 289; Attic 290; uncertain provenience 295, 298, 305

Figurines of male votaries: youths 61, 63, 64, 65, 67, 125, 185, 334[76], 335

See also children: in ritual; worshipers; youths: in ritual

votive polos 131, 270

votive reliefs. *See* reliefs

votive shields 269, 271, 279, 332–333, 343

votives: in *Anthologia Palatina* 125, 194, 324; sale of votives in sanctuary 326

vulva: apotropaic 171; coiffure symbolizing 171; shell symbolizing 176; terracotta models 171, 273

WATER: carrying in procession 24, 38, 324, 339, 340; in the sanctuary 24, 38; symbolized by hydria 324. *See also* hydriaphoroi

West Greek: votive shields 271

Figurines: 141, 147–148; dancers 156, 294; exported to Corinth 285 (quantity found), 294, 305; facial types 45, 64, 66, 123, 294; protomes 40, 73, 330; source for Corinthian figurines 148, 294; trade in figurines 294

See also Sicily; South Italy

wicker chair. *See* seats

wings 274, 280; attachment 181; mold 277; winged figures 198, 269. *See also* Eros; Nike

winter cult activities 153, 338

womb: box symbolizing 273

women in cult: cult and female experience 329; festivals of women 195; Hellenistic increase in

female types 131; humor and women's worship 195, 340; identification of women with Demeter 170, 329; participation of women in rituals 131, 334, 336, 338, 340–341; women equated with pigs 118; women's dedications 273. *See also* initiation: of girls; pottery: Corinthian: "Frauenfest" vases; votaries: figurines of female votaries

workmanship: decline in 3rd century B.C. 37, 116, 250; quality of workmanship and design 19, 116, 186, 249; technical standards 12, 19, 37. *See also* techniques, coroplastic

workshop materials. *See* workshop organization and practice

workshop organization and practice: adaptation or alteration of figurines or workshop materials to create other types 18–19, 40, 51, 58, 60, 63, 64, 119, 122, 123, 125, 126, 127, 134, 136, 141, 147, 149, 159, 161, 171, 173, 175, 176, 178, 183, 184, 185, 186, 189, 199, 252, 270, 294, 326, 344, 345, 346; availability of workshop materials 62, 65, 135, 344; complexity of workshop practice 123, 167; differences in 284; effect of economic conditions on 115, 116, 131; illustrated by votaries 123; male and female heads interchangeable 40, 64, 119, 159, 165, 185, 187, 345; male and female types from common workshop materials 51, 119, 125, 126, 159, 185, 190, 345, 346; mixing of head and torso types 53, 56, 123, 124, 133, 145, 157, 162, 168, 191; production of archetypes separate from coroplasty 120, 123, 341; sharing and exchange of workshop materials 55–56, 123, 134–135, 146, 159, 167, 189, 190, 284, 288, 291, 293, 342, 343; substituting back molds 119, 143, 159, 342, 346; use of metalworkers' and sculptors' workshop materials 3, 20, 26–27, 29, 55, 116, 164, 258, 342, 343–344

workshops:

CORINTHIAN: 19–20, 23–24, 28, 29, 31, 46, 55, 62, 65, 119, 125, 126, 132, 134, 143, 147, 157, 158, 159, 160, 161, 163, 165, 173, 187, 193, 252, 253, 258, 283, 295, 326, 342; closure 312; locations 23[3]; neighboring 283–284; number 19, 283; Roman 314, 315; Workshops A–K 344–346; Workshop A 34, 342, 344, 345; Workshop B 30, 56, 344–345; Workshop C 155, 196, 345; Workshop D 17–18, 25, 60, 345; Workshop E 182, 193, 345; Workshop F 158–159, 345; Workshop G 162, 345; Workshop H 119–120, 185, 190, 346; Workshop I 137, 143, 153, 154, 173, 174, 342, 346; Workshop J 128, 129, 165, 346; Workshop K 149, 150, 346

NON-CORINTHIAN: Argive 287; Boeotian 291, 292

See also Corinth: Potters' Quarter: workshops; industry, coroplastic, Corinthian

worshipers 327, 334–341; representations of 24, 140. *See also* mortals; votaries

wreath: symbolism 193[459]. *See also* headdresses

XANTHOS: Nereid monument   154

YOUTH: naturalistic representation   117, 118, 158, 188
youths: age of   188, 335; bronzes   62; costume   334;
    Hades represented as a youth   333; in ritual   188,
    334; terracotta sculpture compared to figurines   65,
    334, 342
    Figurines:
    CORINTHIAN: dedicated to Kore   330, 334–335; Eros
        ephebe   181, 182, 332. *Archaic:* 335. *Classical:*
        heads   62, 64, 105–106; quantity found   3, 61;
        standing   60–65, 103–105, 185, 186, 188, 269,

274, 334–335. *Hellenistic:* 340; grotesques   198–
199; heads   187, 193, 258–259; seated   186–
187, 239, 293; standing   159, 185–186, 188,
237–238, 346
    NON-CORINTHIAN: Attic   187, 290; Boeotian   61,
    62, 186–187, 292, 293
See also initiation;   nudity: of youths;   races;   votaries:
    figurines of male votaries

ZEUS: figurines   63; and Hera, marriage of   337; and
    Leda   174; Zeus Myleus   79. *See also* Olympia:
    Temple of Zeus;   Pergamon: Altar of Zeus

PLATE 1

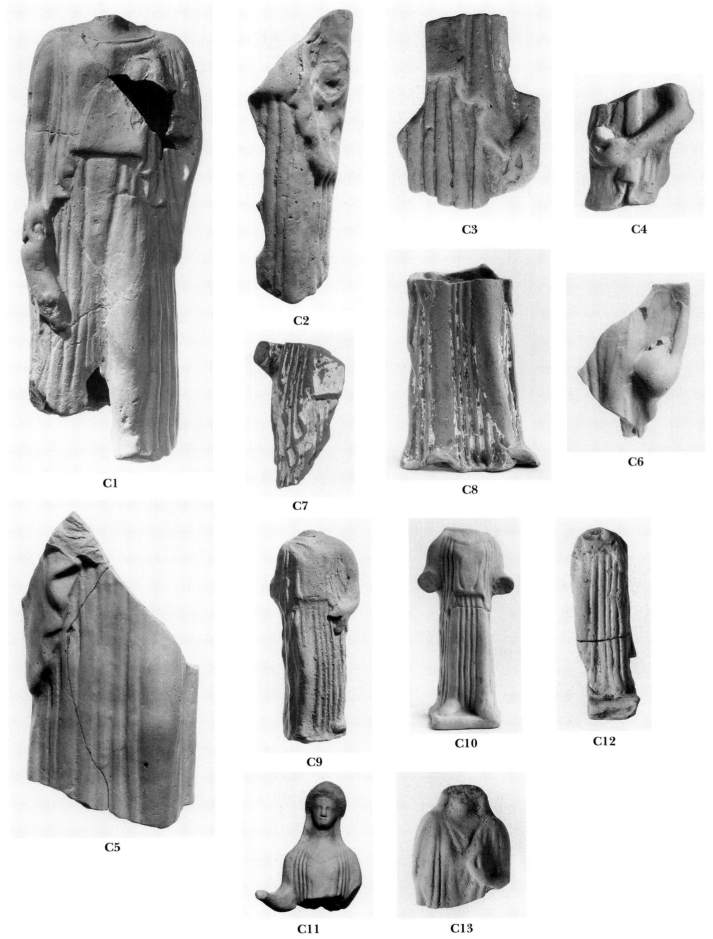

C1

C2

C3

C4

C5

C6

C7

C8

C9

C10

C11

C12

C13

Scale 2:3

PLATE 2

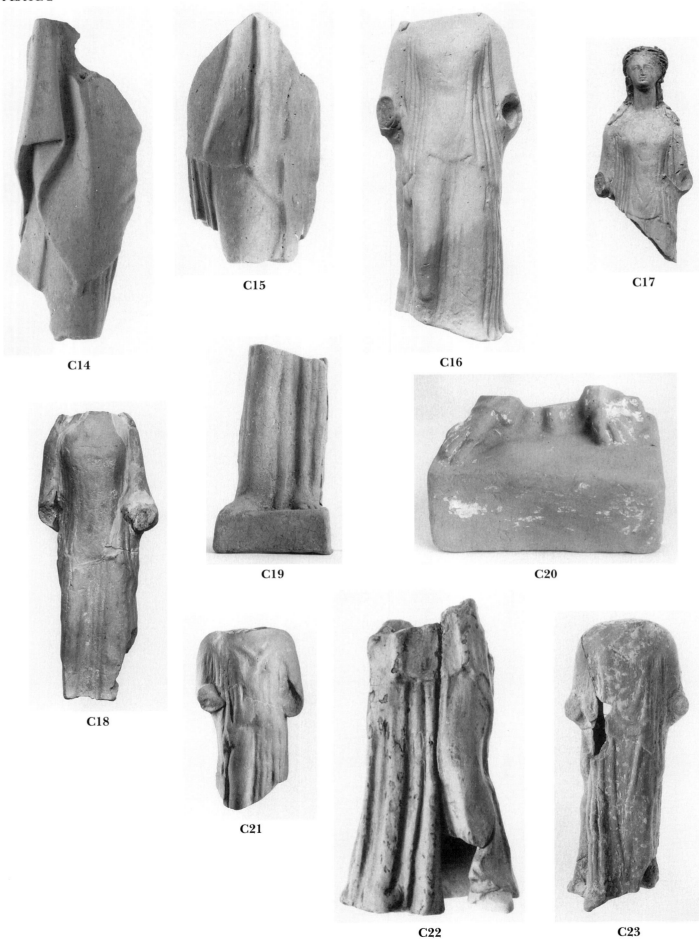

C14

C15

C16

C17

C18

C19

C20

C21

C22

C23

Scale 2:3

PLATE 3

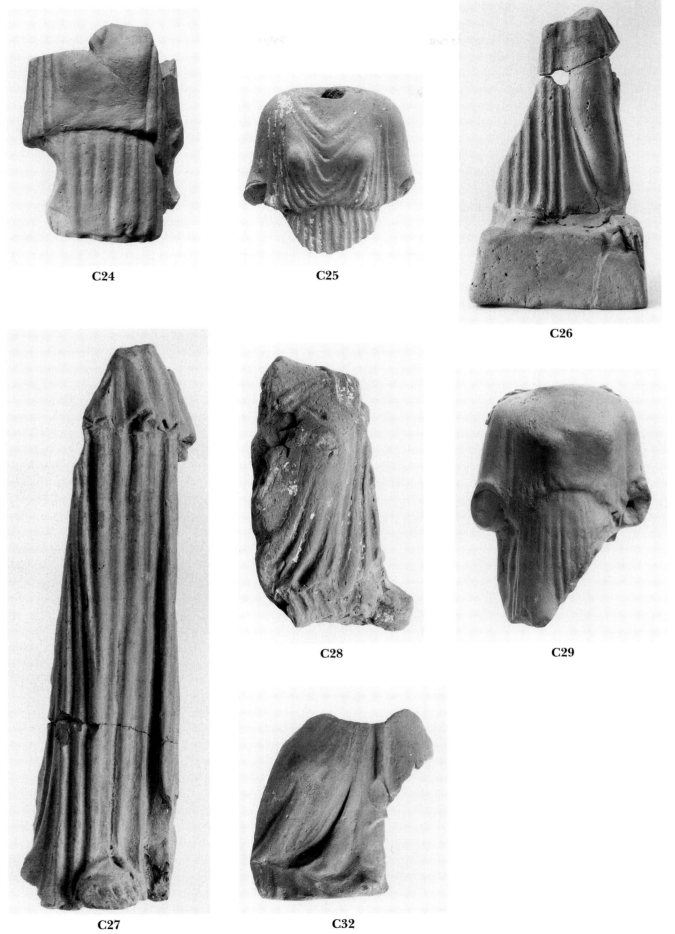

C24

C25

C26

C27

C28

C29

C32

Scale 2:3

PLATE 4

C30

C31

C32: *see* Plate 3

C35

C33

C34

Scale 2:3

PLATE 5

C36

C37

C38

C40

C39

Scale 2:3

PLATE 6

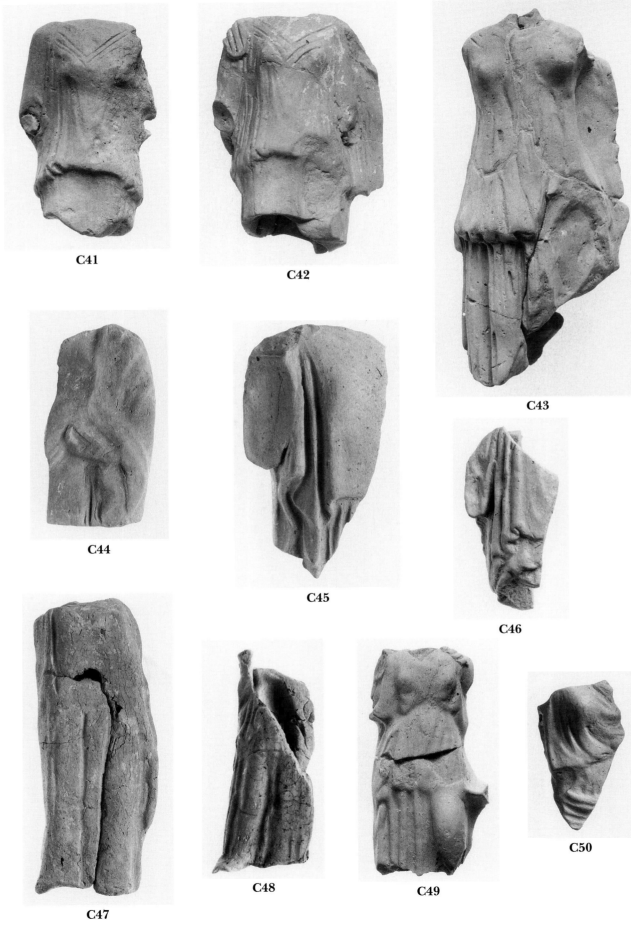

C41

C42

C43

C44

C45

C46

C47

C48

C49

C50

PLATE 7

C51

C53

C54

C57

C56

C55

C58

C52

Scale 1:1

PLATE 8

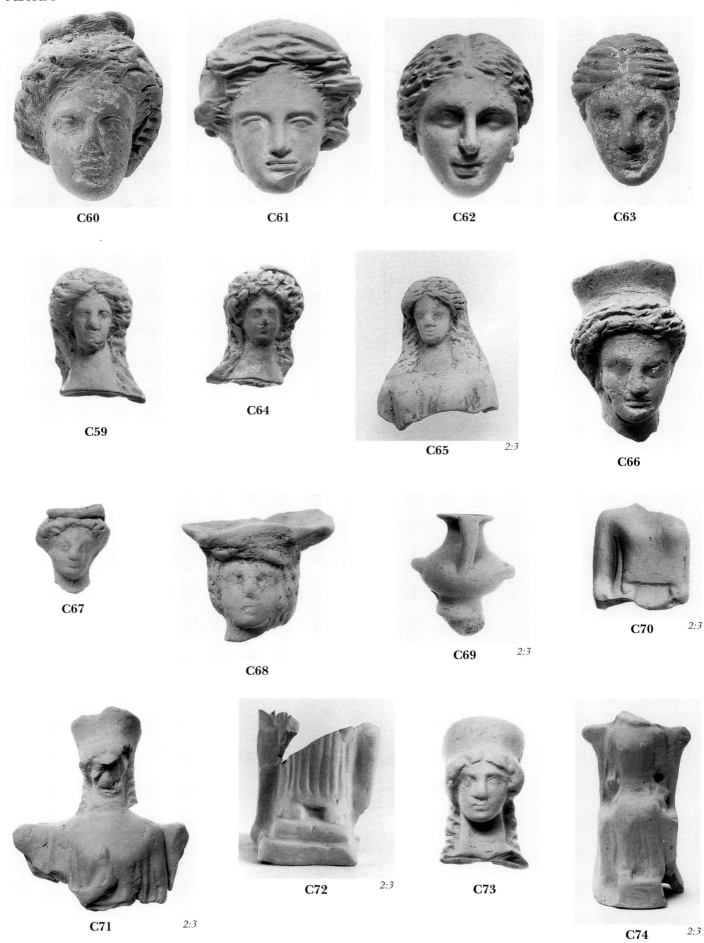

C60

C61

C62

C63

C59

C64

C65 *2:3*

C66

C67

C68

C69 *2:3*

C70 *2:3*

C71 *2:3*

C72 *2:3*

C73

C74 *2:3*

Scale 1:1 except as noted

PLATE 9

C75

C76 *1:1*

C77

C78

C79

C80

C81

C85

C83

C82 *1:1*

C84

C86

C87

C88

C89

Scale 2:3 except as noted

PLATE 10

C90

C91 *1:1*

C92 *1:1*

C93A

C93B

C93C

Scale 2:3 except as noted

PLATE 11

C94   *2:3*

C95   *2:3*

C96

C97

C98

C99

C101

C100

C102

C103

C104

Scale 1:1 except as noted

PLATE 12

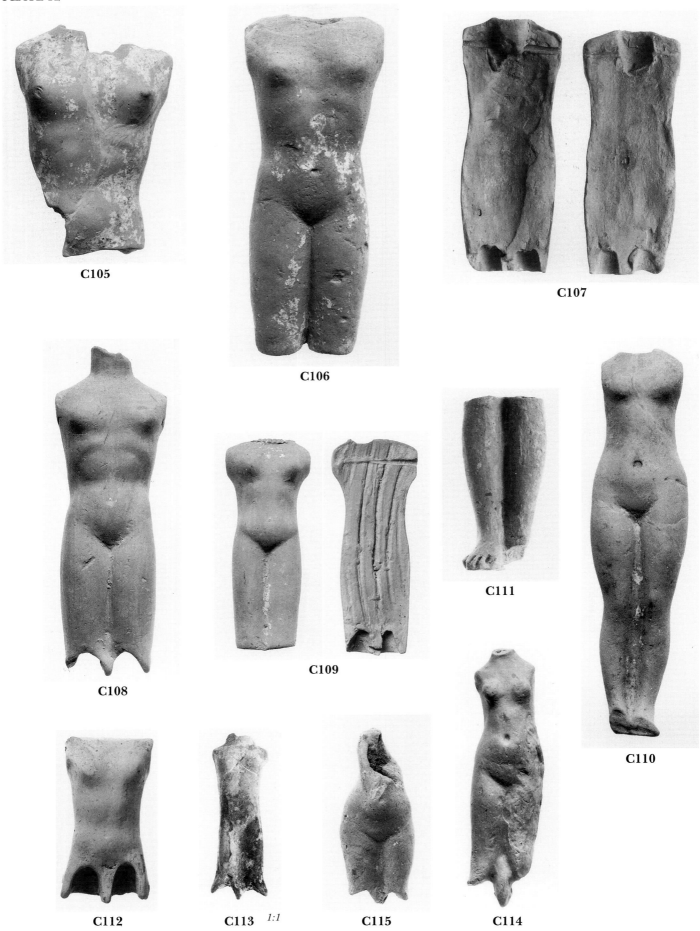

C105

C106

C107

C108

C109

C111

C110

C112

C113 *1:1*

C115

C114

Scale 2:3 except as noted

PLATE 13

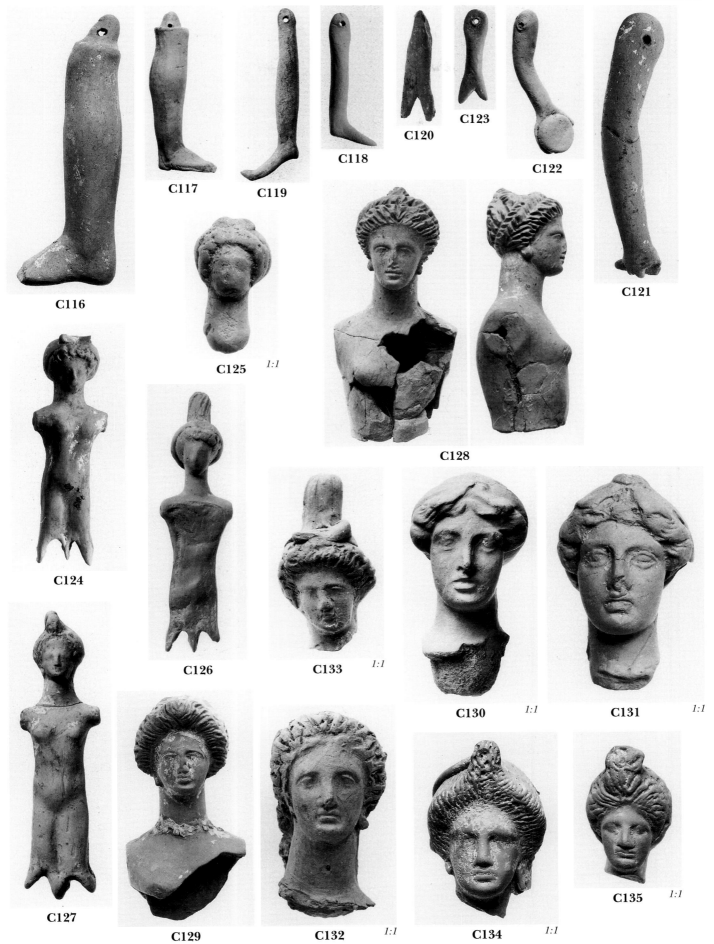

C116

C117

C119

C118

C120

C123

C122

C121

C125 *1:1*

C128

C124

C126

C133 *1:1*

C130 *1:1*

C131 *1:1*

C127

C129

C132 *1:1*

C134 *1:1*

C135 *1:1*

Scale 2:3 except as noted

PLATE 14

C136

C137

C138

C139

C140

C141

C142

C145

C143

C144

C149

C146

C147

C150

C151

C152

C148

Scale 1:1

PLATE 15

C153

C154

C155

C157

C156

C158

C159

C160

C161

C162

C163

C167

C169

C164

C165

C166

C168

C170

C171

PLATE 16

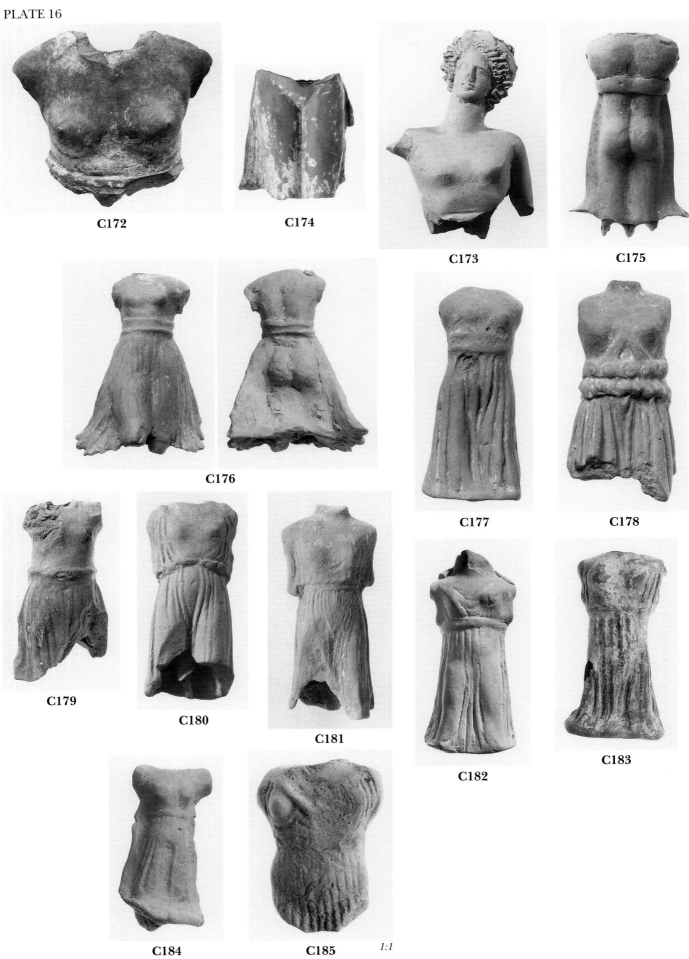

C172

C174

C173

C175

C176

C177

C178

C179

C180

C181

C182

C183

C184

C185

1:1

Scale 2:3 except as noted

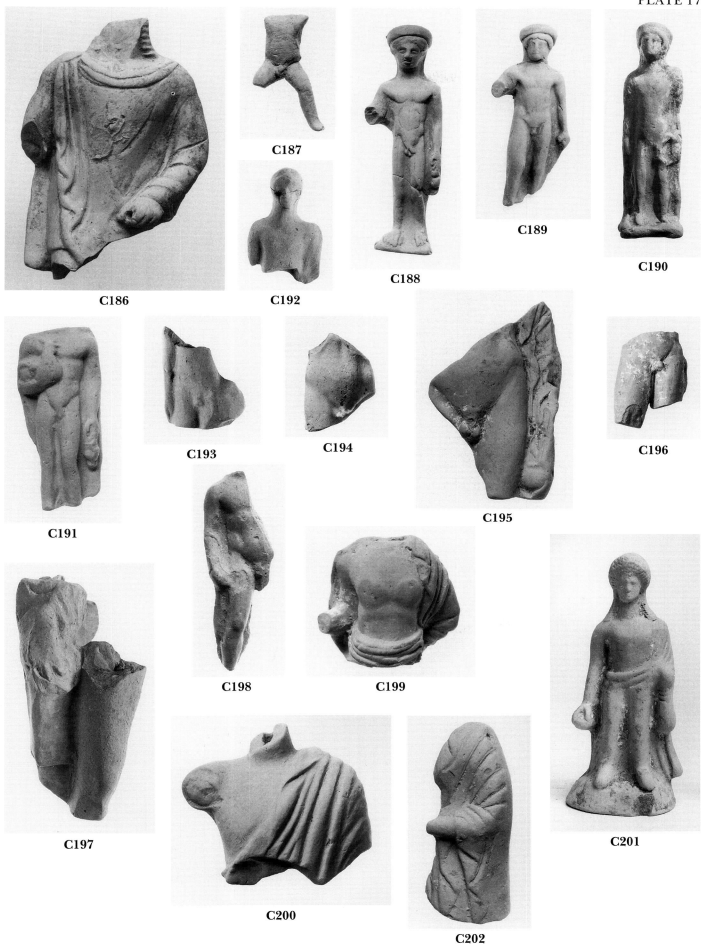

PLATE 17

C186

C187

C192

C188

C189

C190

C191

C193

C194

C195

C196

C197

C198

C199

C200

C201

C202

PLATE 18

C203   *1:1*

C204   *1:1*

C205   *1:1*

C206   *1:1*

C207   *1:1*

C209   *1:1*

C208   *1:1*

C210   *2:3*

C217   *2:3*

C211   *1:1*

C212   *2:3*

C215   *2:3*

C216   *2:3*

C218   *2:3*

C214   *2:3*

C219   *2:3*

C220   *2:3*

C213   *2:3*

PLATE 19

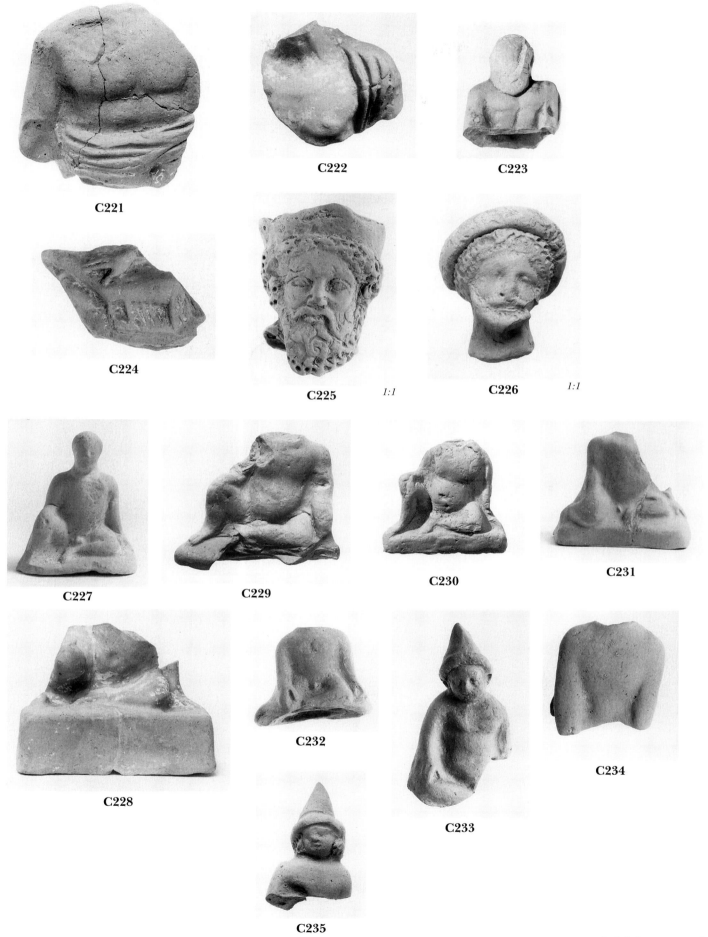

C221

C222

C223

C224

C225   *1:1*

C226   *1:1*

C227

C229

C230

C231

C228

C232

C233

C234

C235

Scale 2:3 except as noted

PLATE 20

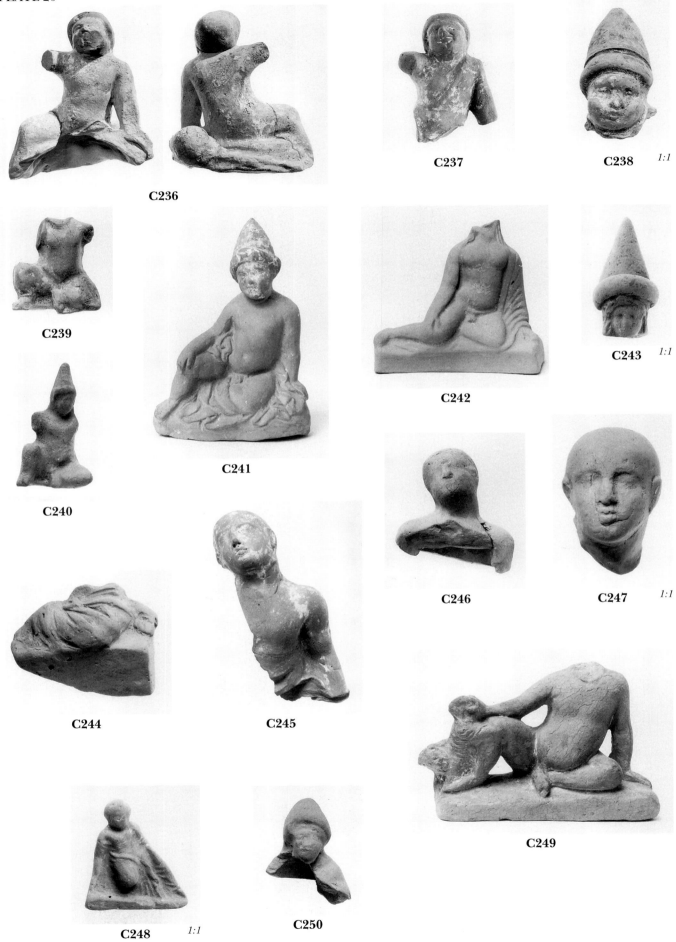

C236

C237

C238   *1:1*

C239

C240

C241

C242

C243   *1:1*

C244

C245

C246

C247   *1:1*

C249

C248   *1:1*

C250

Scale 2:3 except as noted

PLATE 21

C251

C252

C253

C254   *1:1*

C255   *1:1*

C256

C257

C258

C259

C260

C261

C262

C263

Scale 2:3 except as noted

PLATE 22

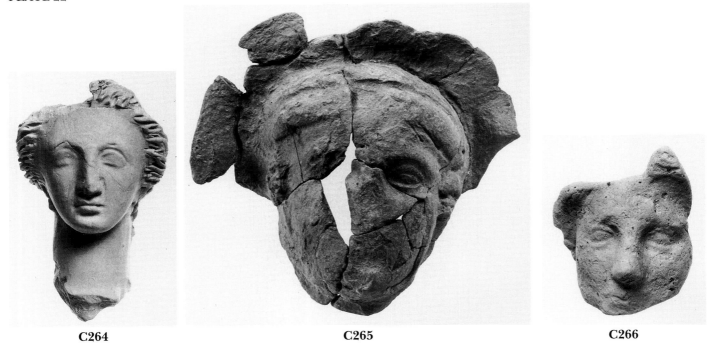

C264

C265

C266

C267

C268

C273

PLATE 23

C269

C270

C271

C272

C274

C275

C276   *1:1*

C277

C279   *1:1*

C278

C280   *1:1*

C281

C282

Scale 2:3 except as noted

PLATE 24

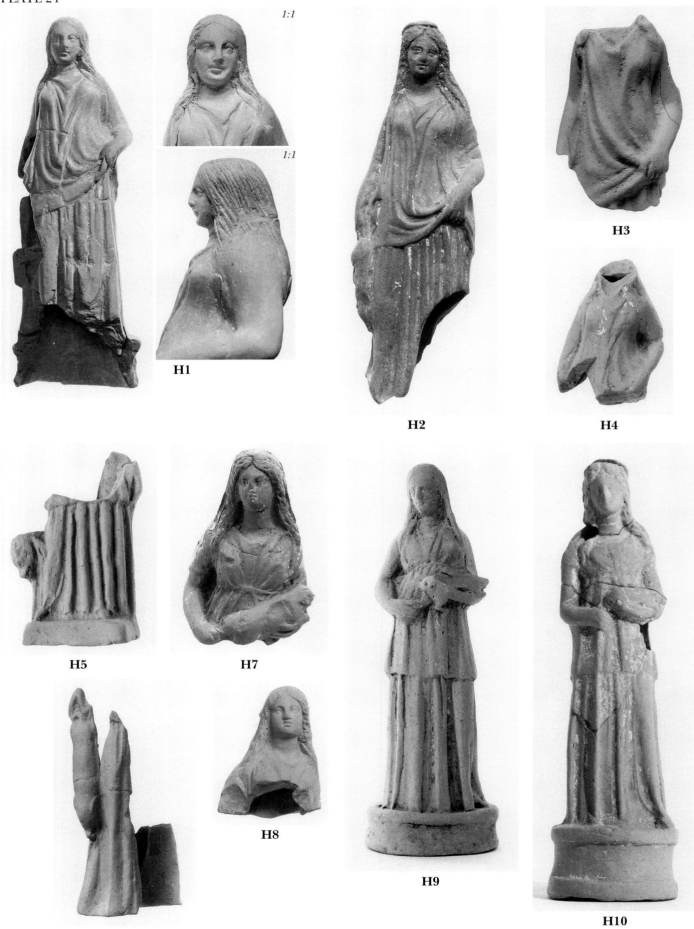

1:1

1:1

H1

H2

H3

H4

H5

H6

H7

H8

H9

H10

Scale 2:3 except as noted

PLATE 25

H11

H12

H14

H13

H18

H15

H16

H17

H19

H21

H22

H20

1:1

H23

Scale 2:3 except as noted

PLATE 26

H24

H25

H26

H27

H28

H29

H30

H33

H34

H31

H32

H35

H41

H36

H37

H38

H39

H40

H42

Scale 2:3

PLATE 27

H43

H45

H46

H47

H44

H48

H50 *1:1*

H49

H51

H52

H53

H54 *1:1*

H55 *1:1*

H64

PLATE 28

H58

H59

H61

H62

H57

H56

H60

H63

Scale 2:3

H64: *See* Plate 27

PLATE 29

H65

H66

H67

H68

H69

H70

H71

H72

Scale 2:3

PLATE 30

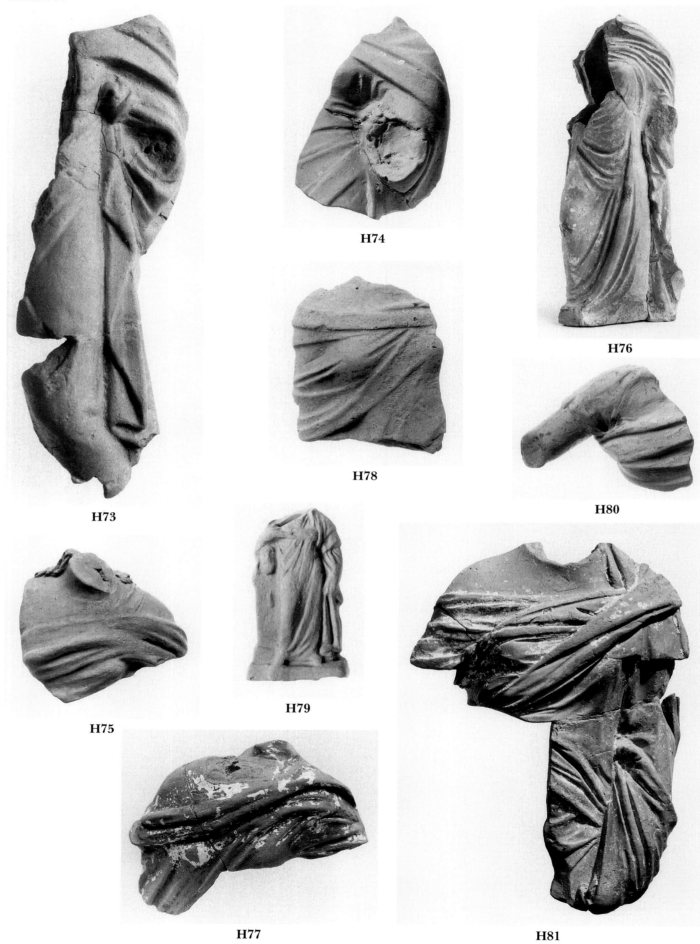

H73

H74

H76

H78

H80

H75

H79

H77

H81

Scale 2:3

PLATE 31

H87

H86

H85

H82

H83

H84

Scale 2:3

PLATE 32

H89

H92

H90

H91

H88

H96

H93

H94

H95

H97

Scale 2:3

PLATE 33

H98

H99

H100

H101

H103

H102: *See* Plate 34

Scale 2:3

PLATE 34

1:1

H102

H105

H106

H104

H108

H107

H109

H111

H112

1:1

H110

H114

H113

Scale 2:3 except as noted

PLATE 35

H116

H117

H119

H115

H118

H124

H120

H121

H122

H125

H123

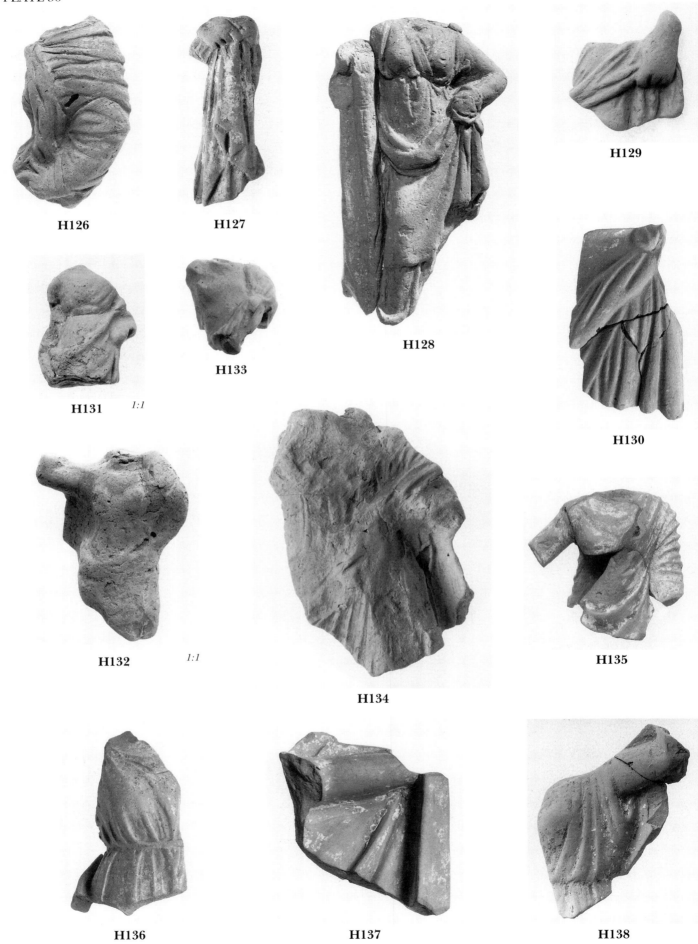

PLATE 36

H126

H127

H129

H128

H131   *1:1*

H133

H130

H132   *1:1*

H134

H135

H136

H137

H138

Scale 2:3 except as noted

PLATE 37

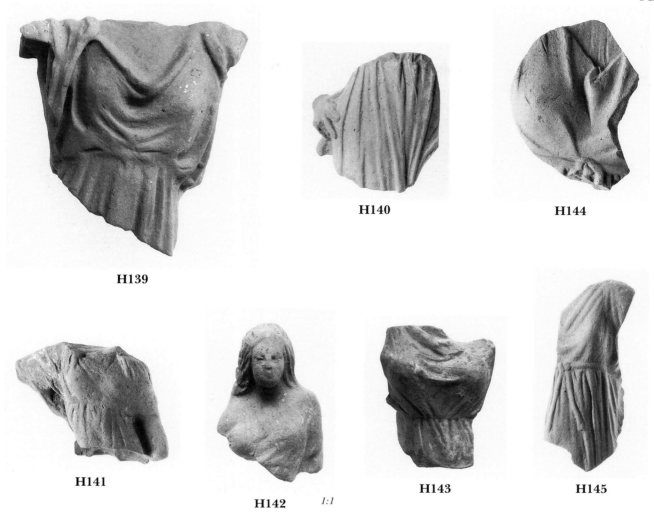

H139

H140

H144

H141

H142 *1:1*

H143

H145

H146

H147

H148

Scale 2:3 except as noted

PLATE 38

H149 *1:1*

H150

H151

H152

H154 *1:1*

H156

H153

H155

H157

H159

H158

H161

H160

H162

Scale 2:3 except as noted

PLATE 39

H163 *2:3*

H164 *1:1*

H165 *1:1*

H166 *1:1*

H167 *1:1*

H168 *2:3*

H169 *2:3*

H170 *2:3*

H171 *1:1*

H172 *1:1*

H173 *1:1*

H174 *1:1*

H175 *2:3*

H176 *2:3*

H177 *1:1*

PLATE 40

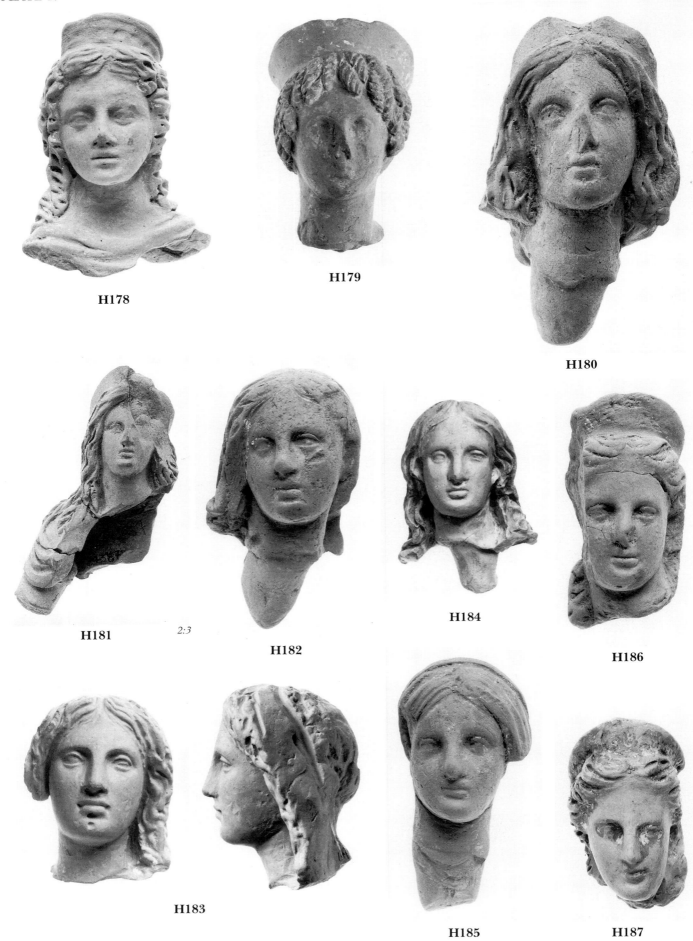

H178

H179

H180

H181

2:3

H182

H184

H186

H183

H185

H187

Scale 1:1 except as noted

PLATE 41

H191

H188

H189

H190

H192

H193

H194

H195: *see* Plate 42

H198

H196

H197

PLATE 42

H199

H201

H202

H203

H205

H200

H195

H206

H204

H209

H207

H208

H210

H211

H212

PLATE 43

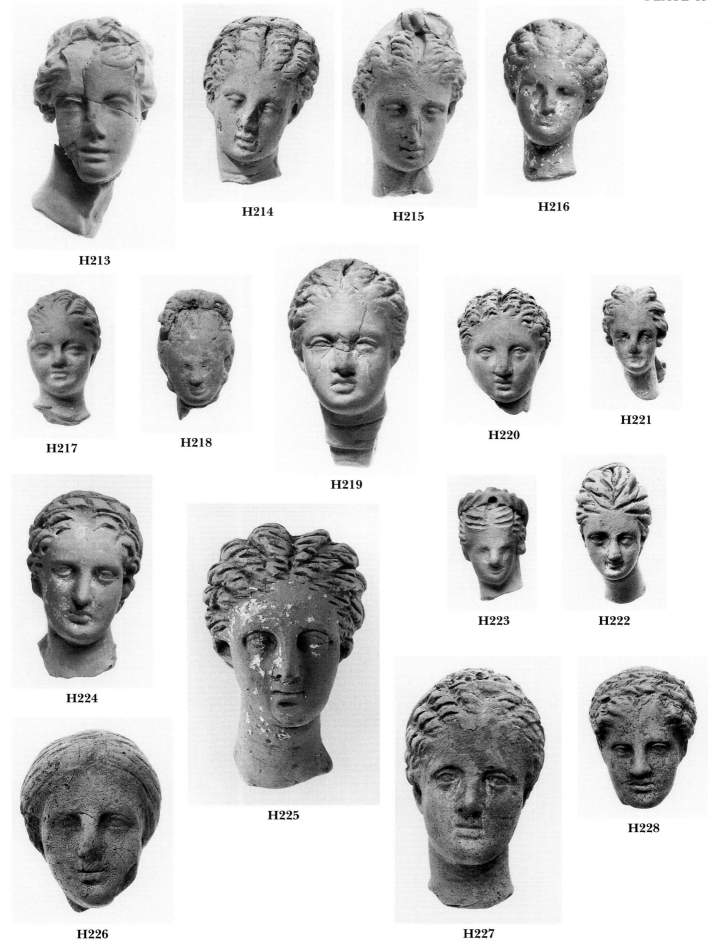

H213

H214

H215

H216

H217

H218

H219

H220

H221

H224

H223

H222

H225

H226

H227

H228

Scale 1:1

PLATE 44

H229

H230

H231

H232

H233

H234

H236

H237

H235

H238

H239

H240

H241

H242

H243

H244

H245

H246

H247

H248

Scale 1:1

PLATE 45

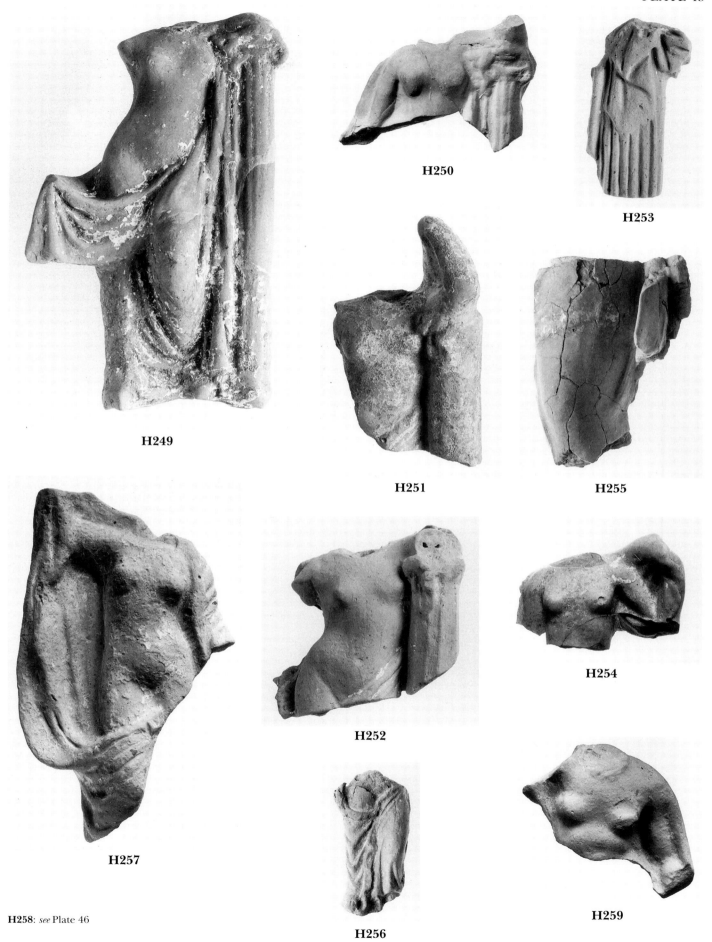

H249

H250

H253

H251

H255

H252

H254

H257

H258: *see* Plate 46

H256

H259

PLATE 46

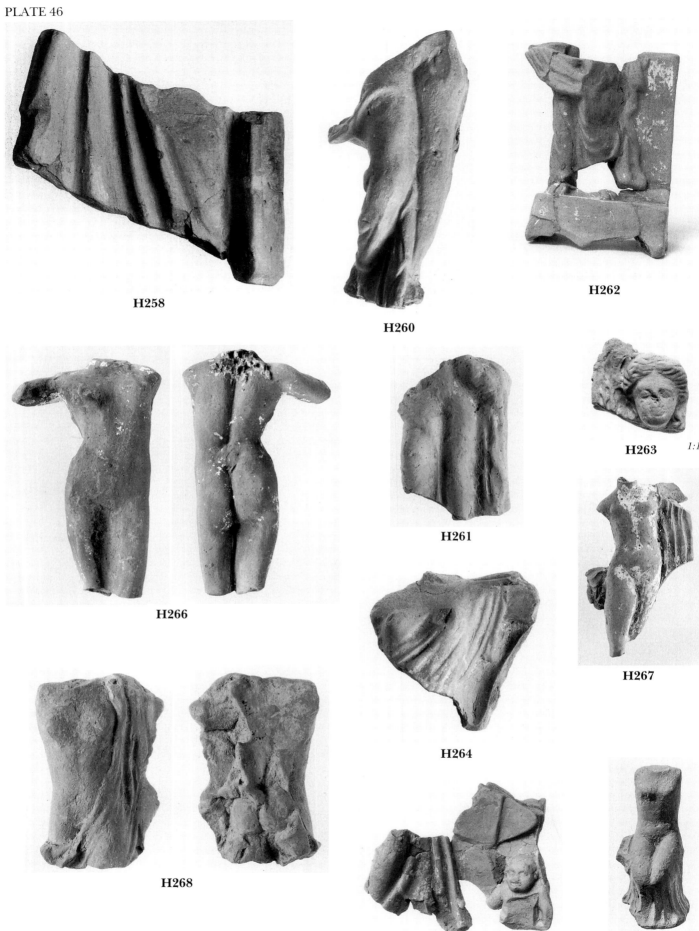

H258

H260

H262

H266

H261

H263   *1:1*

H267

H264

H268

H265

H269

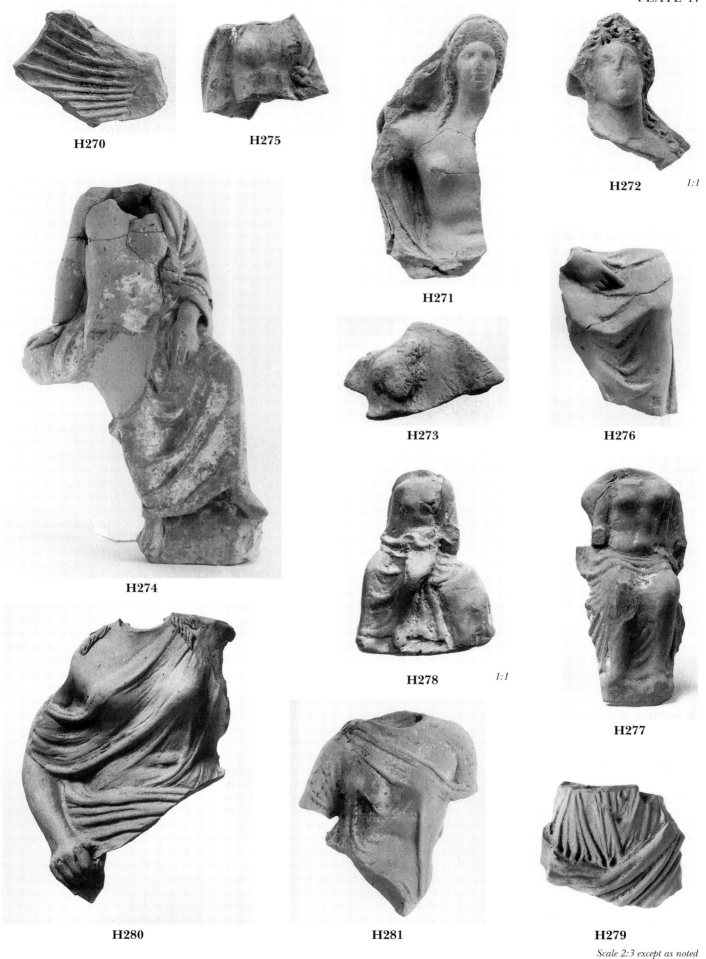

PLATE 47

H270

H275

H271

H272 *1:1*

H273

H276

H274

H278 *1:1*

H277

H280

H281

H279

Scale 2:3 except as noted

PLATE 48

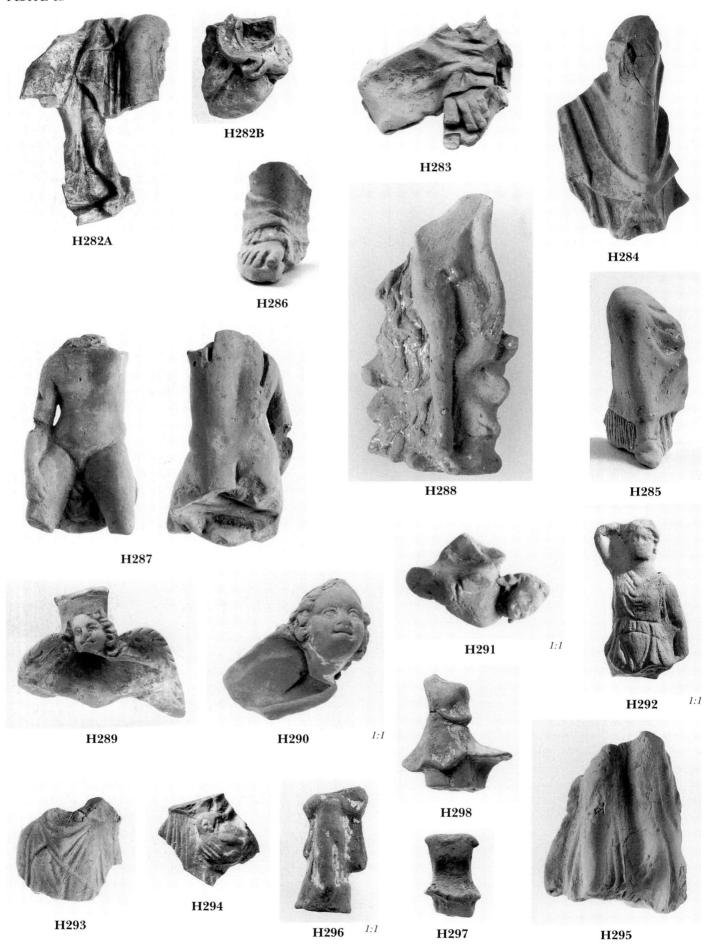

H282B

H282A

H283

H284

H286

H288

H285

H287

H289

H290   1:1

H291   1:1

H292   1:1

H298

H293

H294

H296   1:1

H297

H295

PLATE 49

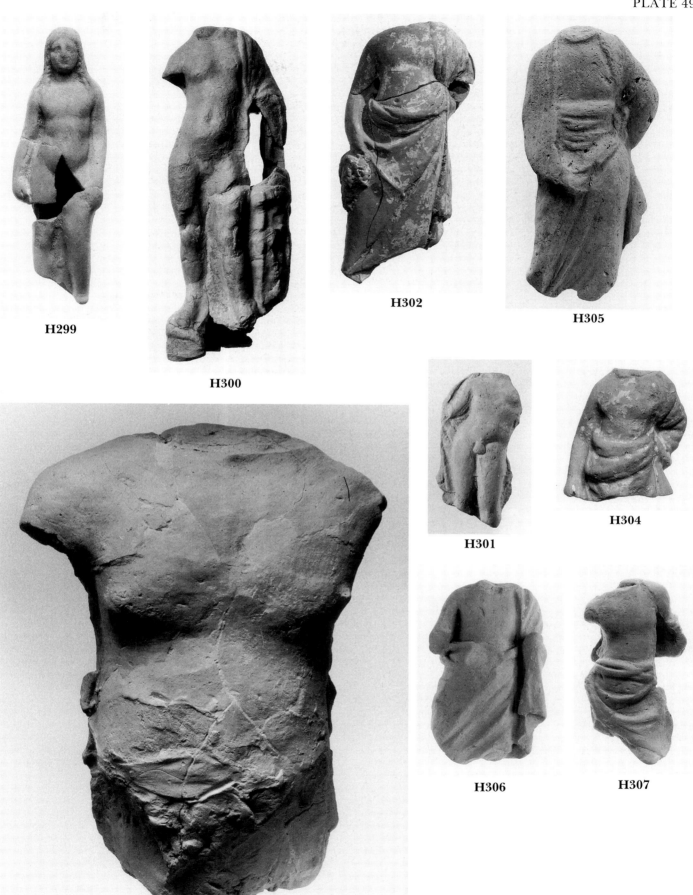

H299

H300

H302

H305

H301

H304

H303

H306

H307

Scale 2:3

PLATE 50

H310

1:3

H309

H312

H308

H311

H313

PLATE 51

H314 *1:1* **H315** *1:1* **H316** *1:1*

H317 *1:1*

H318 *1:1*

H319

H320

H321

H322

H323

H324

H325

H326

H327

H328

H329

H330 *1:1*

H331

H332 *1:1*

Scale 2:3 except as noted

PLATE 52

H334   *2:3*

H335   *2:3*   **H337**   *2:3*   **H338**   *2:3*

H336   *2:3*

H339   *2:3*   **H340**   *2:3*

H333

H341

H342

H343

H344   **H345**

H346

H347

H348

H349   **H350**

H351

H352   **H353**

H354

Scale 1:1 except as noted

PLATE 53

H355

H356

H357

H358

H359

H360

H361

H362

H363   *2:3*

H364   *2:3*

H365

H366

H367

H368

Scale 1:1 except as noted

PLATE 54

H369

H370

H371

H372

H373

H374

H375

H379

H380

H377

H378

H376

H381

H382

H383

H384

Scale 1:1

PLATE 55

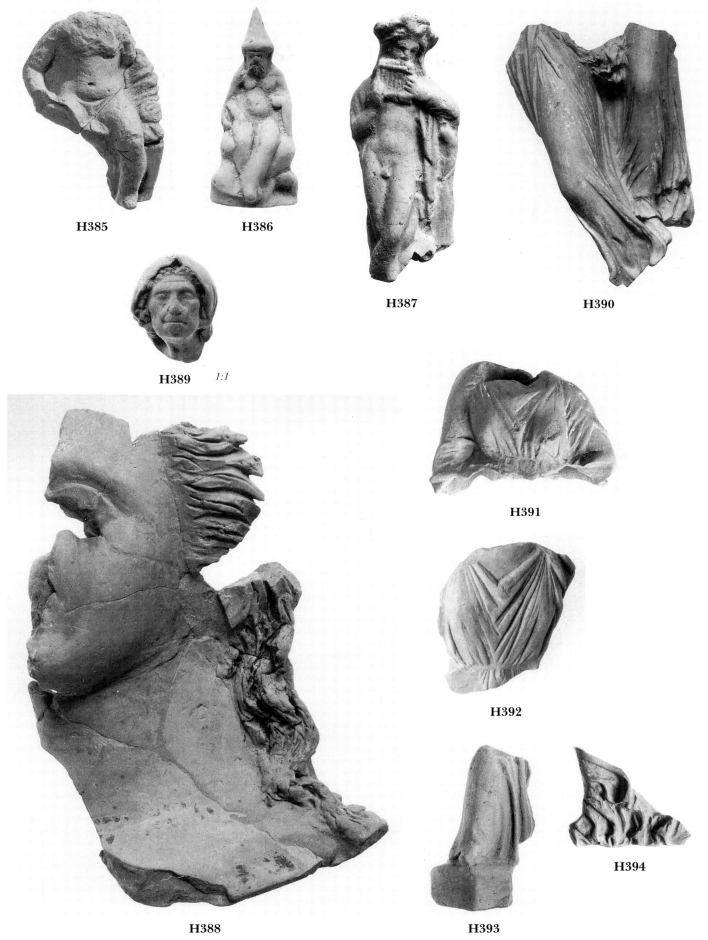

H385

H386

H387

H390

H389   *1:1*

H391

H392

H388

H393

H394

Scale 2:3 except as noted

PLATE 56

H395

H396

H397

H398

H399

H401

H402

H400 *1:1*

H403 *1:1*

Scale 2:3 except as noted

PLATE 57

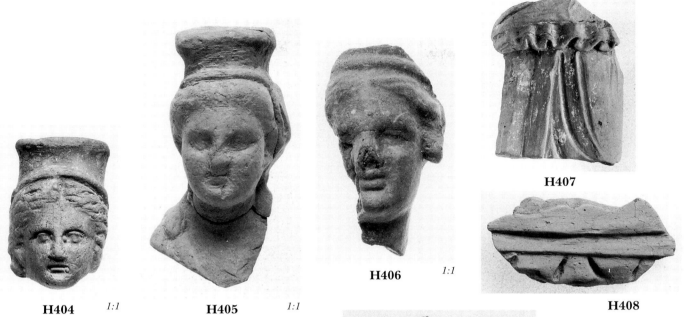

H404 *1:1*

H405 *1:1*

H406 *1:1*

H407

H408

H409

H411

H410

Scale 2:3 except as noted

PLATE 58

H412

H413

H414 *1:1* **H416**

H415 *1:1*

Scale 2:3 except as noted

H418

PLATE 59

H417

H419

H420

H423   *1:1*

H421

H422   *1:1*

H424   *1:1*

Scale 2:3 except as noted

PLATE 60

H425

H427

H426

H429

H428

H431

H430

Scale 1:1

PLATE 61

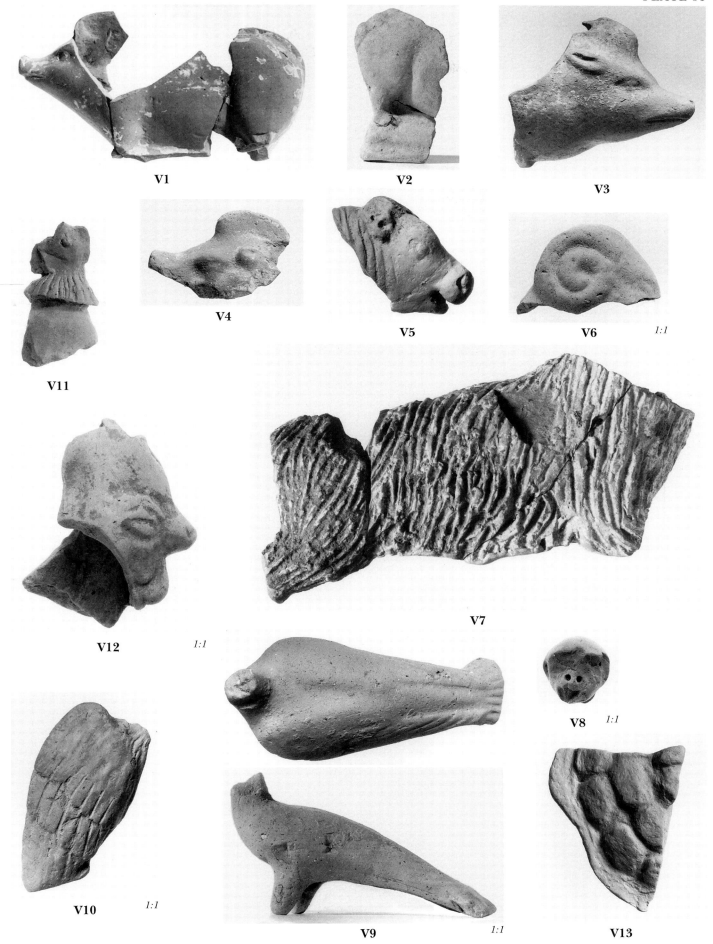

V1

V2

V3

V4

V5

V6   *1:1*

V11

V12   *1:1*

V7

V10   *1:1*

V9   *1:1*

V8   *1:1*

V13

Scale 2:3 except as noted

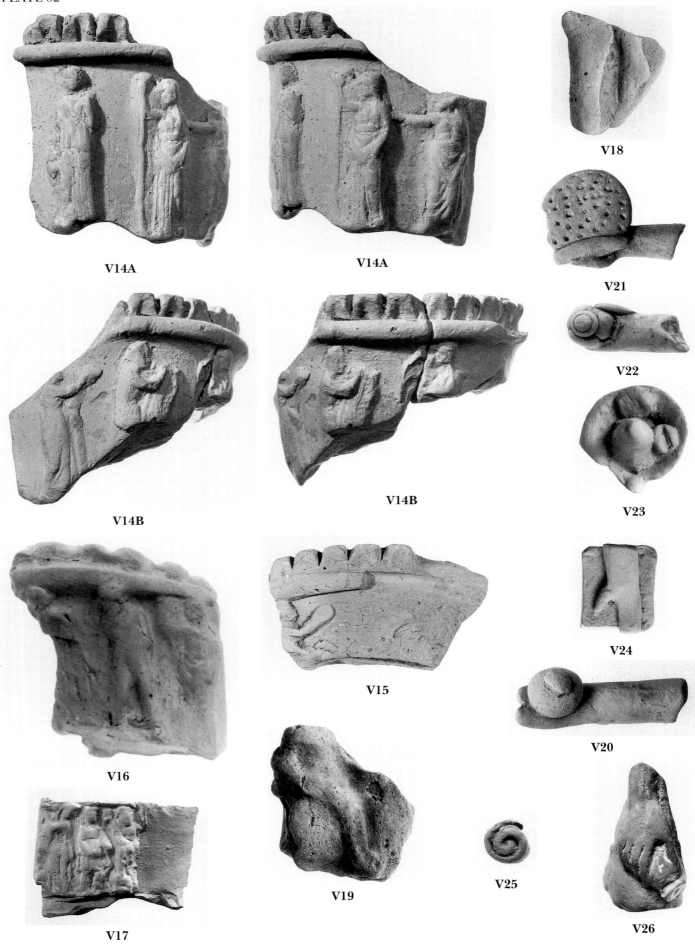

PLATE 62

V14A

V14A

V18

V21

V14B

V14B

V22

V23

V16

V15

V24

V20

V17

V19

V25

V26

Scale 1:1

PLATE 63

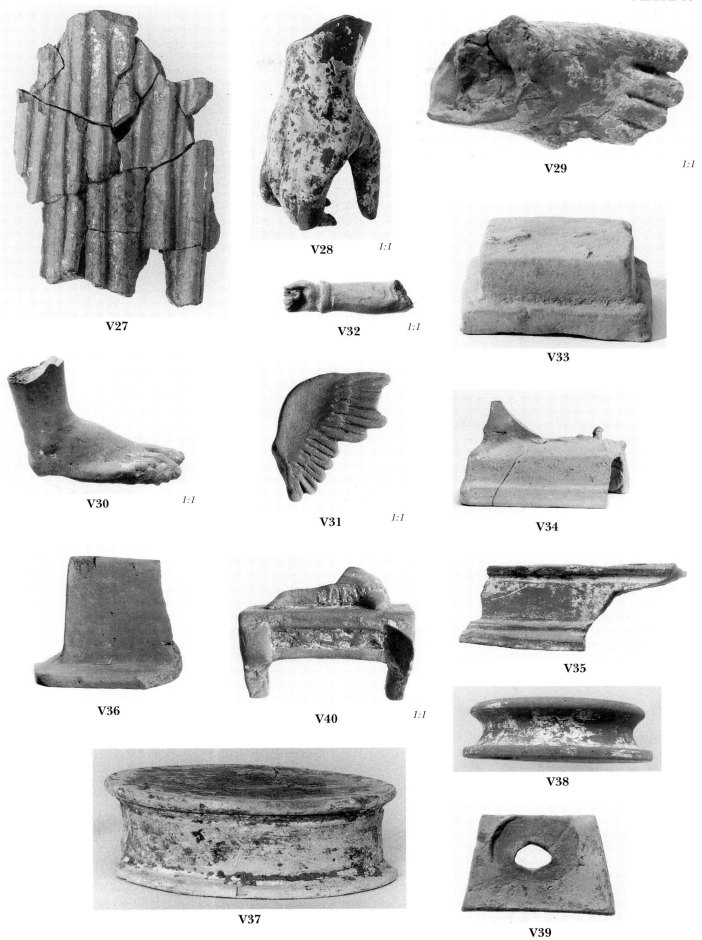

V27

V28 *1:1*

V29 *1:1*

V32 *1:1*

V33

V30 *1:1*

V31 *1:1*

V34

V36

V40 *1:1*

V35

V38

V37

V39

Scale 2:3 except as noted

PLATE 64

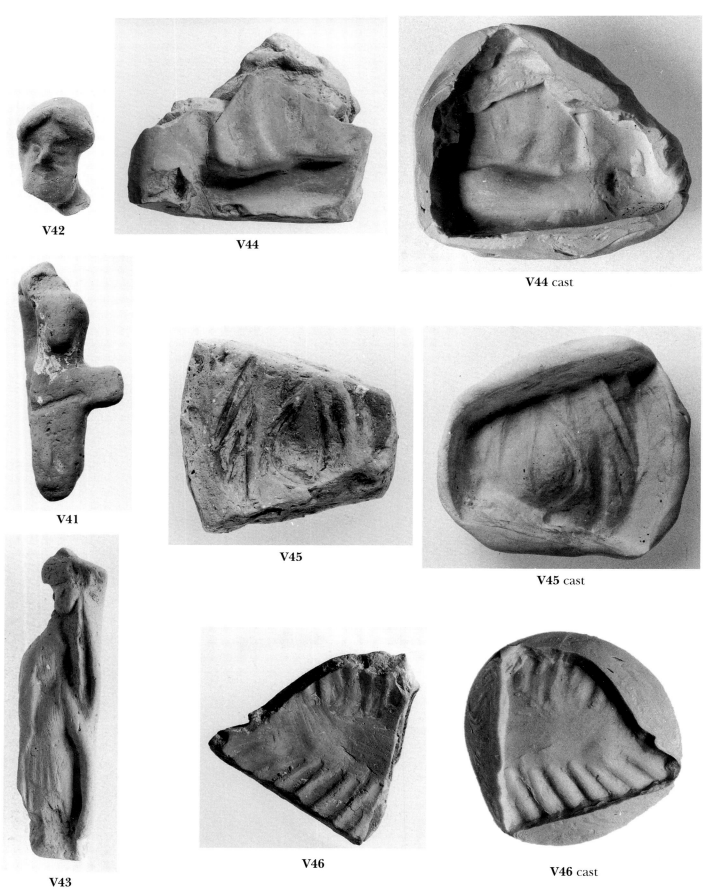

V42

V44

V44 cast

V41

V45

V45 cast

V43

V46

V46 cast

Scale 1:1

PLATE 65

I1

I2

I3

I4   *1:1*

I5   *1:1*

I6

I7

I8

I9   *1:1*

I10

I11

I12

I13   *1:1*

Scale 2:3 except as noted

CLASSICAL AND HELLENISTIC IMPORTED FIGURINES:
ARGIVE

PLATE 66

I16

I17

I18

I14

I15 *1:1*

I22

I19 *1:1*

I20 *1:1*

I21 *1:1*

I23 *1:1*

I24

I25

I26

I27

Scale 2:3 except as noted

CLASSICAL AND HELLENISTIC IMPORTED FIGURINES:
ARGIVE; ATTIC (**I23–I27**)

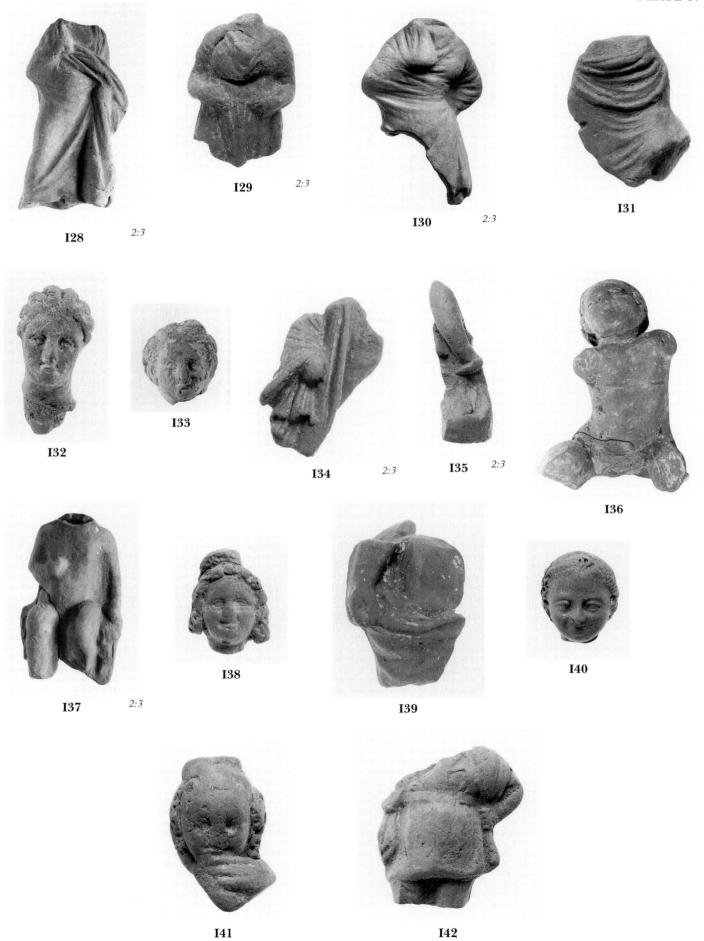

PLATE 67

I28   *2:3*

I29   *2:3*

I30   *2:3*

I31

I32

I33

I34   *2:3*

I35   *2:3*

I36

I37   *2:3*

I38

I39

I40

I41

I42

Scale 1:1 except as noted

CLASSICAL AND HELLENISTIC IMPORTED FIGURINES:
ATTIC

PLATE 68

I43

I44

I45

I46   *1:1*

I47

I48

I51

I49

I50

CLASSICAL AND HELLENISTIC IMPORTED FIGURINES:
BOEOTIAN

PLATE 69

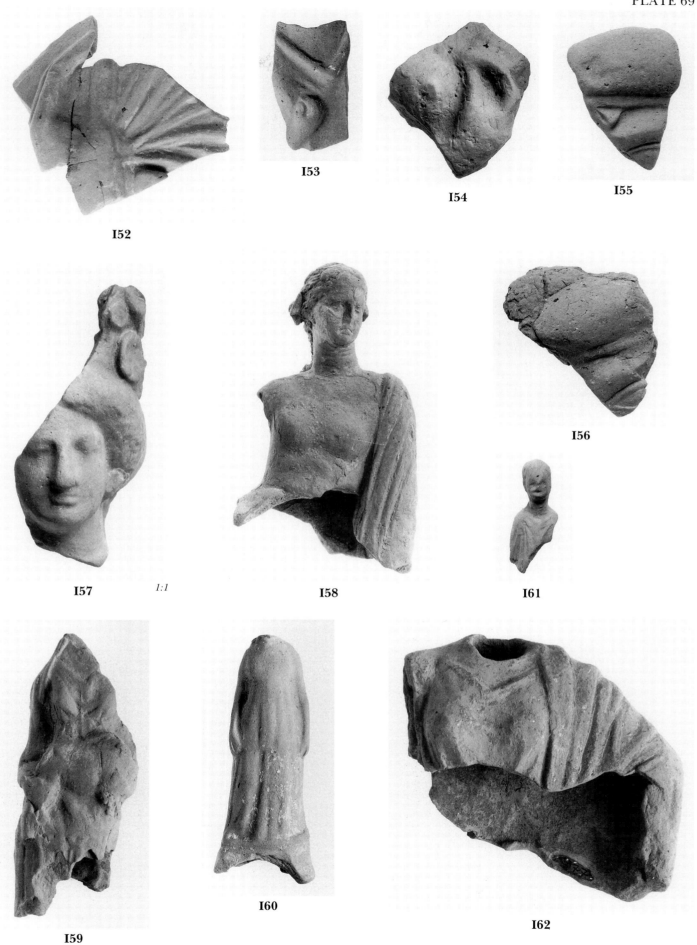

I53

I54

I55

I52

I56

I57   *1:1*

I58

I61

I59

I60

I62

Scale 2:3 except as noted

CLASSICAL AND HELLENISTIC IMPORTED FIGURINES:
BOEOTIAN (I52–I56); WEST GREEK (I57, I58); UNCERTAIN PROVENIENCE (I59–I62)

PLATE 70

I63

I64

I65

I66

I67

I68   *1:1*

I69

I70

I71

I72

I73   *1:1*

I74   *1:1*

Scale 2:3 except as noted

CLASSICAL AND HELLENISTIC IMPORTED FIGURINES:
UNCERTAIN PROVENIENCE

PLATE 71

I75

I76

I77

I78

I79

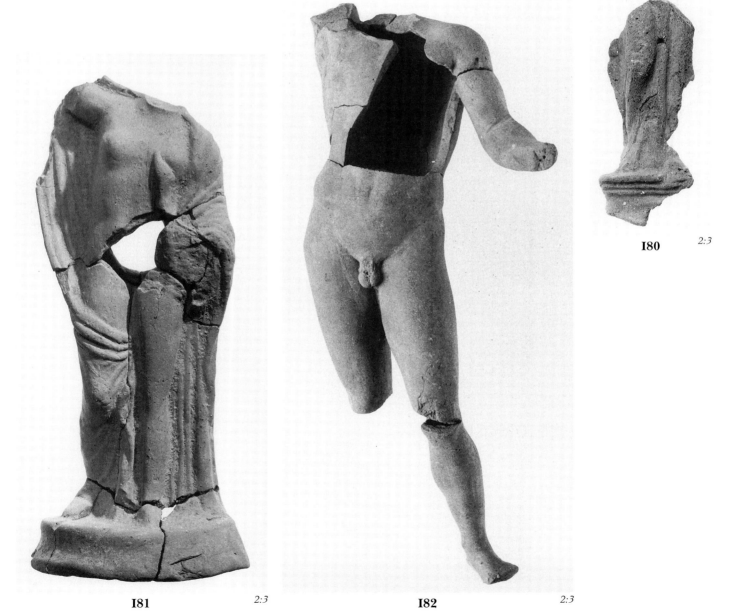

I81   2:3

I82   2:3

I80   2:3

Scale 1:1 except as noted

CLASSICAL AND HELLENISTIC IMPORTED FIGURINES:
UNCERTAIN PROVENIENCE

PLATE 72

I83 *1:1*

I84

I85

I86

I87

I88

I89 *1:1*

I90

I91 *1:1*

I93 *1:1*

I94 *1:1*

I92

I95

I96

Scale 2:3 except as noted

CLASSICAL AND HELLENISTIC IMPORTED FIGURINES:
UNCERTAIN PROVENIENCE

PLATE 73

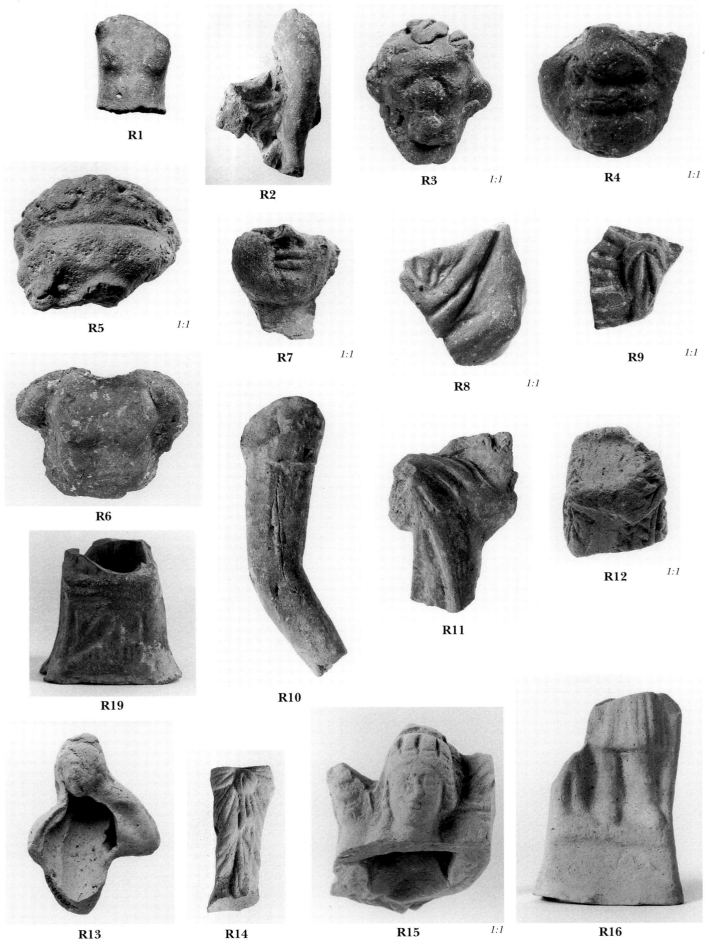

R1

R2

R3 *1:1*

R4 *1:1*

R5 *1:1*

R7 *1:1*

R8 *1:1*

R9 *1:1*

R6

R19

R10

R11

R12 *1:1*

R13

R14

R15 *1:1*

R16

Scale 2:3 except as noted

ROMAN FIGURINES

PLATE 74

R17

R18

R21   *1:1*

R20

R19: *see* Plate 73

R22   *1:1*

R24   *1:1*

R23

R26

R27

R25   *1:1*

R28   *1:1*

R29   *1:1*

Scale 2:3 except as noted

PLATE 75

MF-75-24

MF-1976-88

MF-1

MF-8666

MF-71-45

MF-71-43

Scale 2:3

CORINTH COMPARANDA

PLATE 76

MF-71-42

MF-11457

MF-13017 *1:3*

KT-5-29

MF-1988-25 cast

Scale 2:3 except as noted

CORINTH COMPARANDA

PLATE 77

MF-8993 mold and cast

1:2

MF-1156

MF-9251

MF-1981-1

CORINTH COMPARANDA

Scale 2:3 except as noted

PLATE 78

Athens, National Archaeological Museum, inv. no. 4160

Athens, National Archaeological Museum, inv. no. 4413

COMPARANDA IN ATHENS

PLATE 79

Athens, National Archaeological Museum, inv. no. 4164

COMPARANDA IN ATHENS